▶ Ultrasound Physics
and Instrumentation 6th Edition

The author and publisher of this book have used their best efforts in preparing this book. Their efforts include the development, research, and testing of the theories and problems to determine their effectiveness. The author and publisher shall not be liable in any event for incidental or consequential damages in connection with, or arising out of, the furnishing, performance or use of these programs.

This work is protected by United States copyright laws. Dissemination or sale of any part of this work (including on the World Wide Web) destroys the integrity of the work and is not permitted.

A Cataloging In Publication Record is available from the Library of Congress

Printed in the United States of America

Last Digit is the print number: 9 8 7 6 5 4 3 2 1

ISBN-13: 978-1-933250-12-0

Copyright 2022 by Miele Enterprises, LLC

All rights reserved. No part of this book may be reproduced in any form or by any means, electronic or mechanical, including photocopy, recording, or any information storage and retrieval system, without permission in writing from Miele Enterprises, LLC and Pegasus Lectures, Inc.

Dedication

As always, I dedicate this book to my family, the people who give meaning to my existence. As I write this dedication I am reminded of the dedications for each of the past editions, when the children were still little – alas, not so much anymore.

First, to my wife Carol who has tirelessly contributed so much to the writing and editing of this 6th edition. Next, to our oldest son Paul who is now in medical school, and our oldest daughter, Gina, a sophomore in college at my alma mater. To our twins, Cristiana and Franco, who are a year from college, and to our youngest, Pietro, entering high school. I am so very proud of the adults they are becoming, and I cherish every minute with them, knowing that they are only on loan to us for an all too brief period of life. What better motivation for writing this book than wanting to make sure that my family's medical care, when they need it, keeps them safe for me.

Finally, I want to thank my parents, Frank and Graziella, whose sacrifices provided me with the education needed for working in this field. They are truly selfless people – people who deserve tremendous gratitude.

Author
Frank R. Miele, MSEE

Coordination
Carol Gannon, RN, RVT, RDCS, FSVU
Cindy Davis
Vicki Moore

Cover and Graphic Design
Kathryn Tyler, MFA

Editorial
Carol Gannon, RN, RVT, RDCS, FSVU
Eric Brandler
Debbie Abbott

Illustrations & Motion Graphics
Halan Le
Kathryn Tyler, MFA

Information Technology
Halan Le
Bart van de Rotsheide
Erik de Bruin

CONTRIBUTING AUTHORS

Chapter 10 | *Contrast and Harmonics*
Patrick Rafter, MS
Clinical Scientist
Philips Healthcare
Andover, MA

Chapter 14 | *Patient Care and Sonographer Safety*
Carolyn Coffin, RDMS, MPH, RDMS, RDCS, RVT
Co-founder & CEO, Sound Ergonomics, LLC
Kenmore, WA

Chapter 16 | *Elastography*
Brian S. Garra, MD
Medical Officer
Division of Imaging, Diagnostics & Software Reliability
CDRH, FDA
Silver Spring, MD

Chapter 18 | *Focused Ultrasound*
Arik Hananel, MD, MBA
CEO, FUSMobile
Alpharetta, GA

Suzanne LeBlang, MD
Neuroradiologist, Director of Clinical Relationships
Focused Ultrasound Foundation
Charlottesville, VA

Neal Kassell, MD
Founder and Chairman
Focused Ultrasound Foundation
Former Co-Chair of Neurosurgery, University of Virginia
Charlottesville, VA

Jean-François Aubry, PhD
Director of Research
Institution Physics for Medicine Paris, INSERM, CNRS, ESPCI
Paris, PSL Research University
Paris, France

Chapter 19 | *Musculoskeletal Ultrasound*
Jamie Bie, RDMS, RVT, RMSKS
Founder, Learn MSK Sono
Senior Musculoskeletal Ultrasound Specialist
Columbia University
New York, NY

Chapter 20 | *Physics-Based Image Optimization*
M. Robert De Jong, RDMS, RDCS, RVT, FAIUM, FSDMS
Owner, Bob DeJong, LLC
An ultrasound educational company
Baltimore, MD

Steven B. Feinstein, MD, FACC, FESC
Professor of Medicine, Division of Cardiology
Rush University Medical Center
Chicago, IL

Brian S. Garra, MD
Medical Officer
Division of Imaging, Diagnostics & Software Reliability
CDRH, FDA
Silver Spring, MD

A special thank you to my friends and colleagues who took the time and made the effort as contributors, section reviewers, and who provided quality images. Your time, suggestions, and expertise are much appreciated.

REVIEWERS

Jamie Bie, RDMS, RVT, RMSKS
Founder, Learn MSK Sono
Senior Musculoskeletal Ultrasound Specialist
Columbia University
New York, NY

M. Robert De Jong, RDMS, RDCS, RVT, FAIUM, FSDMS
Owner, Bob DeJong, LLC
An ultrasound educational company
Baltimore, MD

Abraham Ettaher, MD, RVT
Jobst Vascular Institute
Toledo, OH

Brian S. Garra, MD
Medical Officer
Division of Imaging, Diagnostics & Software Reliability
CDRH, FDA
Silver Spring, MD

Jeffrey C. Hill, BS, ACS, FASE
Echocardiography Educator
Worcester, MA

Marge Hutchinsson, BS, RVT, RDCS, RPhS
Vascular Testing, Director of Accreditation
Intersocietal Accreditation Commission
Ellicott City, MD

Anne Jones, RN, RVT, RDMS, FSVU, FSDMS
Consultant
Winston-Salem, NC

Nancy Leahy, MA RDMS, RVT
RAD-AID Ultrasound
RAD-AID International
Austin, TX

David Prater, MS
Design Engineer
Philips Medical Systems
Andover, MA

Patrick Rafter, MS
Development Engineer
Philips Healthcare
Andover, MA

Cheryl Vance, MA, RT, RDMS, RVT
CEO, C&D Advance Consultants
San Antonio, TX

IMAGE CONTRIBUTORS

Individuals

Michelle Carter, MBA, RDMS, RVT, RDCS
Ultrasound Clinical Marketing Manager
Mindray North America
Dallas, TX

M. Robert De Jong, RDMS, RDCS, RVT, FAIUM, FSDMS
Owner, Bob DeJong, LLC
An ultrasound educational company
Baltimore, MD

Jeffrey C. Hill, BS, ACS, FASE
Echocardiography Educator
Worcester, MA

Chih Chung Huang, PhD
Associate Professor of Biomedical Engineering
National Cheng Kung University
Tainan, Taiwan

Thomas Marini, MD
University of Rochester Medical Center
Rochester, NY

Rafaella Righetti, PhD
Texas A&M Engineering
Texas A&M University
College Station, TX

Jill Sommerset, RVT
Technical Director
PeaceHealth Southwest Washington Medical Center
Vancouver, WA

Lissa Sugeng, MD, MPH, FACC, FASE
Associate Professor, Yale University School of Medicine
Medical Director of Echolab Quality
Yale New Haven Hospital System
New Haven, CT

Mengxing Tang, PhD
Biomedical Imaging Chair
Department of Bioengineering
Imperial College London

Arun Thitaikumar, PhD
Indian Institute of Technology Madras
Department of Applied Mechanics
IIT Madras, Chennai

(continued)

David Tomberlin, ARRT, RDCS, RVT
Ultrasound Clinical Specialist
Dallas, TX

Cheryl Vance, MA, RT, RDMS, RVT
CEO, C&D Advance Consultants
San Antonio, TX

Steven Walling, BS, RCS, RDCS, FASE
Program Director and Clinical Coordinator
Hoffman Heart and Vascular Institute
School of Cardiovascular Technology
Saint Francis Hospital and Medical Center
Hartford, CT

Patrick A. Washko, BSRT, RDMS, RVT, FSVU
Supervisor/Technical Director
UNC Rex Healthcare
North Carolina Heart and Vascular Hospital Peripheral Vascular Laboratory
Raleigh, NC

Susan Koon Whitelaw, RT, RVT, RDMS
Vascular Supervisor
Cleveland Clinic
Cleveland, OH

Special Acknowledgement
Jonathan Ophir, PhD (deceased)
Professor Emeritus, Diagnostic and Interventional Imaging
Department of the University of Texas Medical School
Houston, TX

Corporations

AIP Publishing | Melville, NY
AIUM | Laurel, MD
ATS Laboratories | Bridgeport, CT
BC Group International, Inc. | St. Charles, MO
Butterfly Network, Inc. | Guilford, CT
Canon Medical Systems USA, Inc. | Tustin, CA
Caption Health | Brisbane, CA
CIRS, Inc. | Norfolk, VA
Clarius Mobile Health | BC, Canada
Diasonixs | Ra'anana, HaMerkaz, Israel
Flometrics, Inc. | Solana Beach, CA
Focused Ultrasound Corporation | Charlottesville, VA
FUJIFILM VisualSonics Inc. | Toronto, ON, Canada
GE Healthcare | Milwaukee, WI
Health Best International, LLC | Miami, FL
Hologic Supersonic | Marlborough, MA
Insightec | Tirat Carmel, Israel

Intechopen.com | London, England
Kolo Medical Inc. | San Jose, CA
MDPI Journal of Applied Sciences | Basel, Switzerland
Mindray | Nanshan, Shenzhen, P. R. China
Olympus America | Webster, TX
Onda Corporation | Sunnyvale, CA
Philips Innovation Services | Cambridge, MA
Philips Medical Systems | Bothell, WA
Precision Acoustics, Inc. | United Kingdom
Recor Medical | Palo Alto, CA
Royal Society Publishing | London, England
Samsung Medison | Pangyyo, Republic of Korea
Shelley Medical Imaging Technologies | North York, ON, Canada
Siemens Ultrasound | Mountain View, CA
Sun Nuclear Corporation | Middleton, WI
True Phantom Solutions | Windsor, ON, Canada
Verasonics, Inc. | Kirkland, WA

Preface

Since authoring the 1st edition of this book in 2005, a great deal has changed in the healthcare industry and the world at large. Technological advancements for ultrasound usage in diagnostic care have been substantial. An emphasis on the economic necessity for preventive care over corrective care has thrust ultrasound into the foreground for procedural utility. Increasingly, through emerging technologies, ultrasound related techniques are being developed which supplant more invasive or more expensive technologies.

In the past, ultrasound was viewed primarily as a diagnostic tool. Whereas diagnosis is still the primary application, the use of ultrasound for treatment is growing rapidly and likely to continue for many years to come. Additionally, the portability and usability of diagnostic equipment has improved to the point where it will benefit a worldwide population rather than a select few. I have witnessed this change firsthand, initially in visits to the African nation of Uganda in 2009-2012 and more recently in my work in the Andes and the Amazon of Peru. While the world around us changes, the principle cryptically described by Thomas Edison does not: "good fortune often happens when opportunity meets with preparation." As my career has placed me before thousands of students and professionals, I know this to be true.

For this reason, I continue to emphasize understanding foundational and underlying principles in mastering any individual field. Specific to the subject matter throughout this book, and as I have stated in previous editions, every reader possesses a different level of knowledge, experience, and ambition. For many, this book represents their first exposure to ultrasound, and this book will serve as a foundation on which to build. Others bring twenty or more years of experience and will use this book as a way to reinforce the principles by which they perform their daily scans, or as a means to better understand new ultrasound techniques. Some are using this book in an ultrasound educational program, and others hope to prepare for a credentialing exam.

The Importance of Understanding the Structure of this Book

There are three reasons why understanding the structure of this book is so important:
1. So that you can customize usage of this book to your experience level and goals.
2. In order to have a systematic approach to increase your knowledge and clinical abilities.
3. To have a clear indication of when you are knowledgeable and ready to take a credentialing exam.

Complementing the printed content within this textbook is a web-based resource, 6e Online Extras, designed to reinforce your comprehension of the subject matter. An extensive collection within 6e Online Extras features animations, flow models, video clips, and supplemental exercises intended to strengthen your aptitude and familiarity with this textbook's content.

Author's Note: 6e Online Extras

It cannot be stressed enough that your exposure to a full battery of exercises and illustrations is key to absorbing these concepts. Although the temptation exists to focus solely on the printed material, this will ultimately short-change your learning experience.

A Final Word about this Book's Structure

By writing this book in three different levels, I hope to reach out to a wider audience, increasing knowledge for both the experienced and the neophyte in ultrasound. I have chosen to create a book that takes students through an introductory level into fluency and beyond with clear direction toward the knowledge necessary to demonstrate competency at the credentialing exam level. I have tried to write this book so that each level becomes appropriate as the reader's knowledge grows.

I believe the first step to knowledge is a true assessment of where you are, where you want to be, and what path you are willing to take to get there.

And so starts the journey.

Preface **vii**

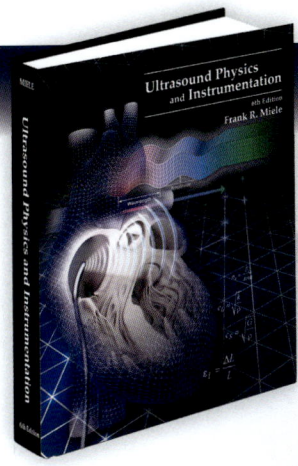

WHAT'S NEW IN THIS EDITION

Enhanced Features

- Chapter introductions which detail the clinical significance of the physics concepts and provide critical learning objectives
- New images and animations
- 'Exam Tip' CheckPoints reinforce concepts commonly tested on board exams
- Author's Notes provide additional conceptual perspectives based on Frank Miele's years of experience
- Access to additional chapters in the digital eBook with advanced concepts

- New 6e Online Extras, including:
  – Library of additional images and original animations
  – Clarifying Clips offer verbal explanations of challenging concepts
  – Interactive Exercises and Conceptual Questions with immediate feedback and scoring
  – Additional chapters regularly updated with new content
  – Instructor Dashboard allows college instructors to monitor the progress of each student, quickly identifying areas of content weakness

New and Updated Content

- CMUT transducer technology
- New beamformer and image generation techniques
- Advanced ultrasound system operation
- Artificial intelligence (AI) and its applications in ultrasound and medicine
- Effects of new monitor technology on ultrasound viewing
- Ultrafast Doppler, spatiotemporal filtering, and other Doppler techniques
- Color Doppler and surface rendering
- Artifacts related to new medical devices
- New, approved applications of ultrasound

- Bioeffects and quality assurance
- Physics of stress and strain
- New elastography techniques
- Image optimization based on physics

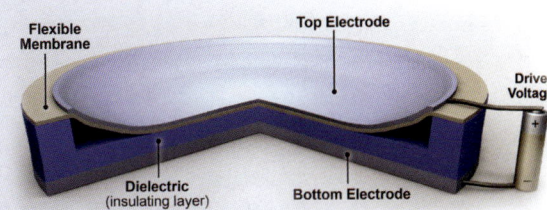

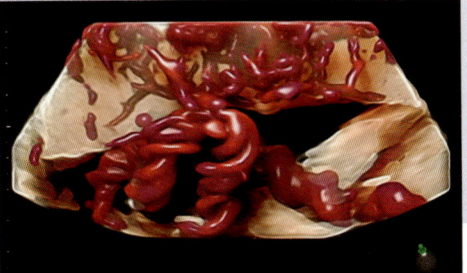
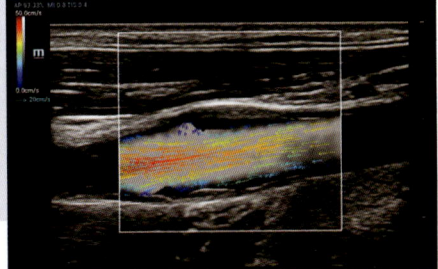

viii   Ultrasound Physics & Instrumentation

Book Structure

Levels
Topics are divided into levels, allowing readers to progress at a pace appropriate to their background.

Learning Objectives
Each chapter begins with a quick glance at the content with an outline of learning milestones.

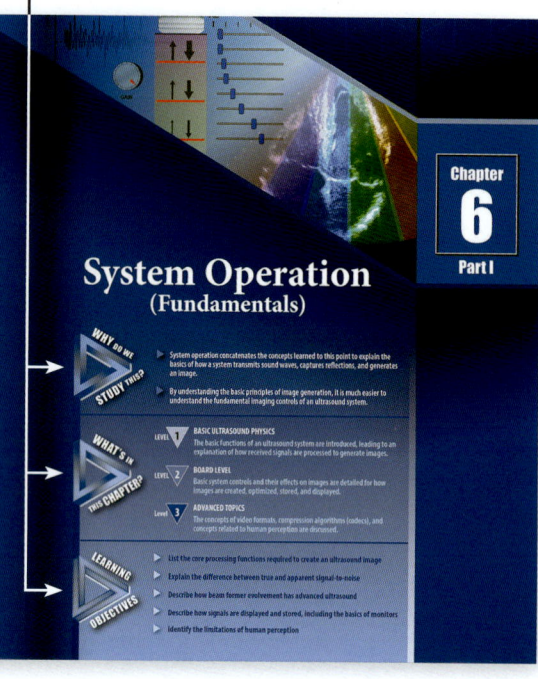

Checkpoints
Exam tip checkpoints are provided throughout the book to highlight important concepts often seen on board exams.

Author's Notes
Notes from the author provide additional conceptual perspectives based on Frank Miele's years of ultrasound experience.

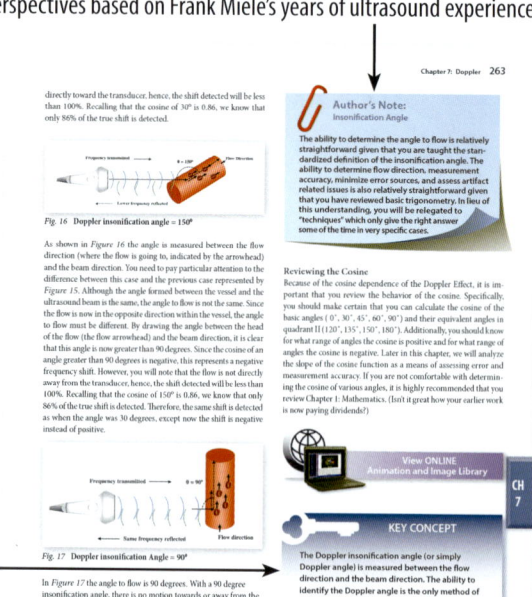

BASIC ULTRASOUND PHYSICS
Level 1 material focuses on the underlying physics and basic concepts critical for developing skill in the use of diagnostic ultrasound. Level 1 presumes no knowledge other than the basic abilities that come from general schooling. This level also serves as a good refresher for people who have ultrasound experience but weaker backgrounds in physics and basic mathematics.

BOARD LEVEL
Level 2 material covers basic topics often outlined on the credentialing exams and is intended to generate a more profound understanding of the concepts. The relationship of the physics fundamentals to the quality of the diagnostic ultrasound should be understood. In other words, understanding Level 2 should not only prepare you for your board exams, but also result in better patient care.

ADVANCED TOPICS
Level 3 material contains advanced topics, newer ultrasound techniques, and higher level material for those who want to be challenged. At times, Level 3 will also contain specific applications of the physics to a specialty area such as cardiac, vascular, or general ultrasound.

Key Concepts
Critical concepts are summarized to improve comprehension and enhance retention of material.

Book Features

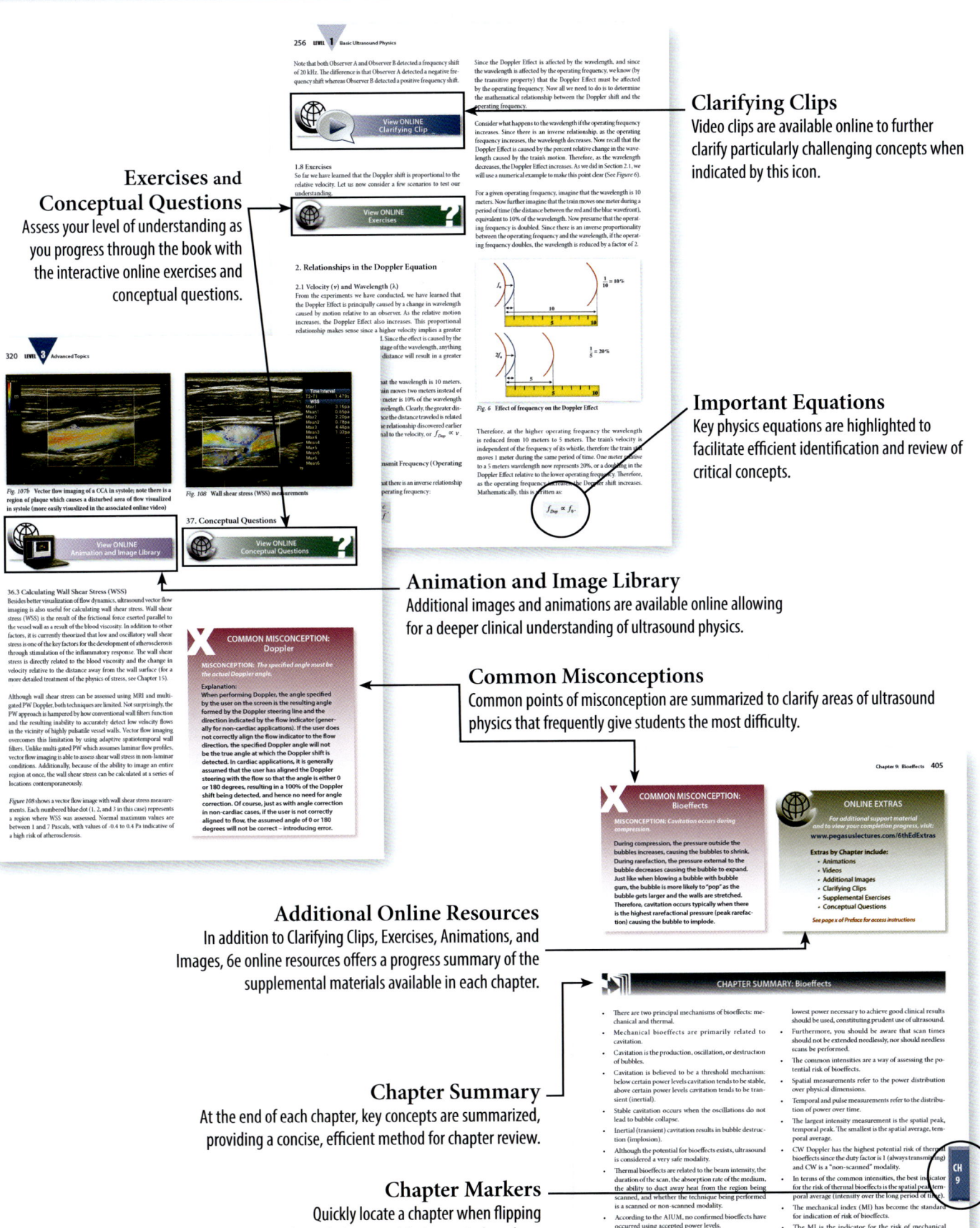

Clarifying Clips
Video clips are available online to further clarify particularly challenging concepts when indicated by this icon.

Exercises and Conceptual Questions
Assess your level of understanding as you progress through the book with the interactive online exercises and conceptual questions.

Important Equations
Key physics equations are highlighted to facilitate efficient identification and review of critical concepts.

Animation and Image Library
Additional images and animations are available online allowing for a deeper clinical understanding of ultrasound physics.

Common Misconceptions
Common points of misconception are summarized to clarify areas of ultrasound physics that frequently give students the most difficulty.

Additional Online Resources
In addition to Clarifying Clips, Exercises, Animations, and Images, 6e online resources offers a progress summary of the supplemental materials available in each chapter.

Chapter Summary
At the end of each chapter, key concepts are summarized, providing a concise, efficient method for chapter review.

Chapter Markers
Quickly locate a chapter when flipping through the text with the vertical markers.

Online Extras

Accessing Online Content

Supplemental online materials can be accessed through Pegasus Lectures using your unique My Pegasus account.

Note: In order to maximize functionality of the interactive online material, it is advised to view on a computer or tablet.

① Upon purchase, a **My Pegasus** account will be created for you (or updated to include this book if you already have one).

② There are <u>two</u> ways to access 6e Online Extras:

Go to **pegasuslectures.kotobee.com** and log in with your My Pegasus credentials to view your Digital Books Library. Online Extras are linked throughout the eBook.

OR

Log into your My Pegasus account at **www.pegasuslectures.com** (top right corner of the home page).

Open the **Textbooks and Online Extras** section to access the 6th Edition Extras and digital chapters. *(Note that the 6e Digital Version icon will redirect you to pegasuslectures.kotobee.com)*

③ From the My Pegasus main page, open the **CME Center** section to access continuing education credit exams and certificates.

If you have any questions or technical issues, please email Pegasus Lectures, Inc. at: **info@pegasuslectures.com**

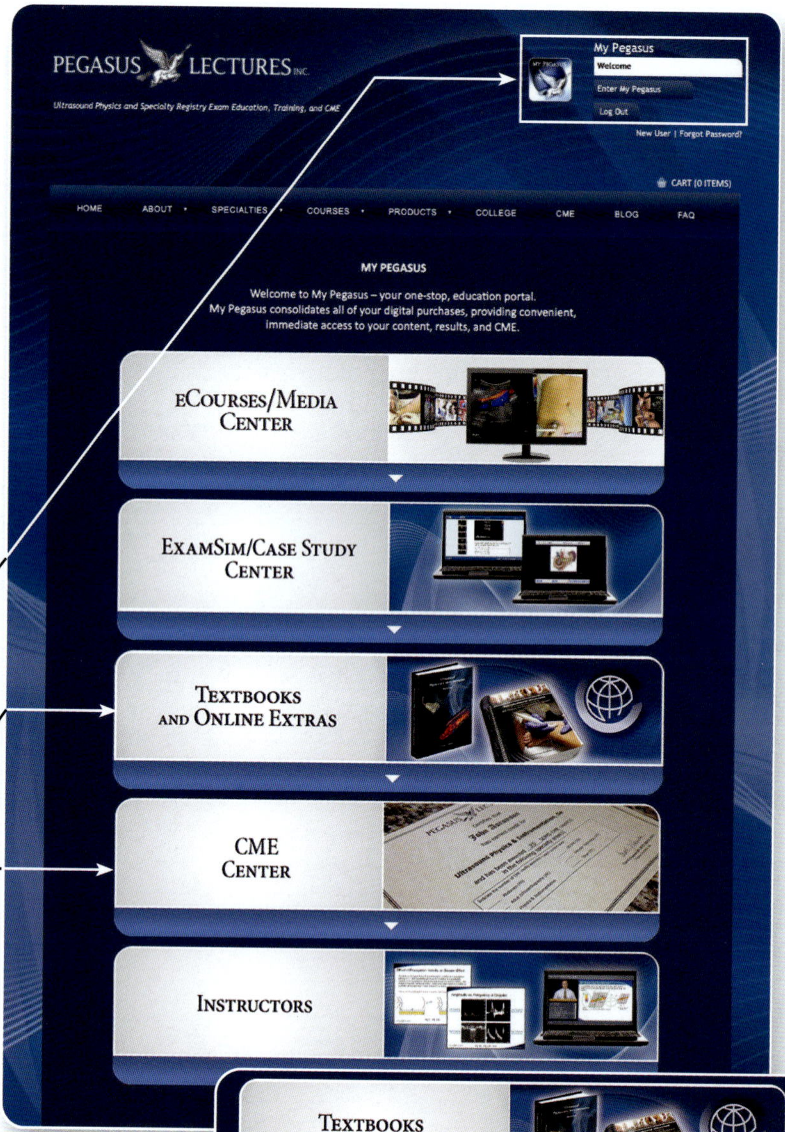

Access your supplemental online materials now!

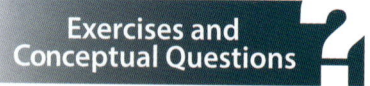

CME Credits

Continuing Medical Education (CME) Credits
In addition to this text and supplemental online material, Pegasus Lectures, Inc. offers many activities to prepare for ultrasound physics credentialing exams and/or accreditation. These programs, which include eCourses, exam simulations, and case studies, allow sonographers to earn CME credits.

The **CME Center** section located in **My Pegasus** provides convenient, immediate access to continuing education credit exams and certificates.

To receive CME credit for this text:

① Visit **www.pegasuslectures.com**

② Log into **My Pegasus**

③ Open the **CME Center** panel

④ Click on **Access CME Quizzes**

⑤ Select **Ultrasound Physics & Instrumentation, 6e** to complete the post-test

⑥ Upon successful post-test and evaluation completion, your certificate will be issued immediately

For more information about CME offerings, including several Free CME courses, please visit **pegasuslectures.com/cme.php**

Table of Contents

▶ **CHAPTER 1: Mathematics** 1
   Introduction 2
   How Much Math Will You Need? 2
   How to Learn Mathematics 3
   A Structured Approach, Time, Work, and Patience 3
   1. Mathematics Basics 3
      1.1 Numbers 3
      1.2 Basic Mathematical Notation (symbols used in basic mathematics) 4
      1.3 Basic Mathematical Definitions 4
      1.4 The Value of Estimating 4
      1.5 Exercises: Estimating 4
   2. Fractions, Decimal Form, and Percentages 4
      2.1 Exercises: Fractions and Percentages 6
   3. Reciprocals 6
      3.1 Exercises: Reciprocals 6
   4. Units 6
   5. Variables 6
   6. Applying Reciprocals 7
      6.1 Exercises: Applying Reciprocals 7
   7. Numbers Raised to a Power 7
      7.1 Positive Powers 7
      7.2 Exercises: Numbers to a Positive Power 8
      7.3 Numbers to a Negative Power 8
      7.4 Exercises: Numbers to a Negative and Positive Power 9
      7.5 Numbers to the Zero Power and Exponent Rules 9
      7.6 Exercises: Numbers to the Zero Power and Exponent Rules 10
   8. Exponential Form (Notation) 10
      8.1 Exercises: Exponential Notations 11
      8.2 Deciding How to Write a Number 11
      8.3 Exercises: Deciding How to Write a Number 11
   9. The Metric System and Metric Abbreviations 11
      9.1 Conversions for Metric and Non-metric Systems 11
      9.2 Metric Abbreviations 11
      9.3 Exercises: Metric Abbreviations 12
      9.4 Abbreviations: Physical Units 12
      9.5 Combining Abbreviations 13
      9.6 Exercises: Combining Abbreviations 13
      9.7 Reciprocals of Metric Units 13
      9.8 Exercises: Reciprocals of Metric Units 14
      9.9 Converting Between Metric Units 14
      9.10 Conversions (a more intuitive approach) 14
      9.11 Exercises: Conversions 16
      9.12 Exercises: Using Exponents 16

10. Proportionality and Inverse Proportionality 16
　　10.1　Direct Proportionality 16
　　10.2　Direct Linear (Simple) Proportionality 16
　　10.3　Inverse (Simple) Proportionality 17
　　10.4　Exercises: Proportionality and Inverse Proportionality 18
11. Distance Equation 18
　　11.1　Exercises: Distance Equation 18
12. Math Terminology 19
　　12.1　The Language of Mathematics: Translating English into Mathematics 19
　　12.2　Mathematical Definition 19
　　12.3　Exercises: Math Terminology 20
13. Distance Equation Revisited 20
　　13.1　The Roundtrip Effect 20
　　13.2　When the Propagation Velocity of 1540 m/sec is Incorrect 21
　　13.3　Exercises: Distance Equation Revisited 22
14. Non-Linear Relationships 22
　　14.1　Direct Non-Linear Proportionality 22
　　14.2　Complex - Inverse Proportionality 23
15. Interpreting Relationships Within Linear and Non-Linear Equations 23
　　15.1　Assessing an Equation and Expressing the Relative Relationship 23
　　15.2　Exercises: Assessing an Equation 24
　　15.3　Exercises: Proportionality 24
16. Dealing with Percentage Change 24
　　16.1　Simple Calculations with Proportional Variables 24
　　16.2　Calculations with Non-linearly Related Variables 24
　　16.3　Rules for Dealing with Percentage Change 25
　　16.4　Examples 25
17. Logarithms 26
　　17.1　Properties of Logarithms 27
　　17.2　Exercises: Logarithms 27
18. Trigonometry 27
　　18.1　Angles, Quadrants and Signs 30
　　18.2　The Value of Knowing Basic Trigonometry in Ultrasound (and Medicine) 31
　　18.3　Exercises: Trigonometry 31
19. The Decimal System and the Binary System 31
　　19.1　Decimal (Base 10) and Binary (Base 2) 31
　　19.2　Exercises: Decimal Conversions 32
　　19.3　Binary 32
　　19.4　Converting from Binary to Base 10 32
　　19.5　Converting from Decimal to Binary 33
　　19.6　Exercises: Binary 33

▶ **CHAPTER 2: Waves** 37
Introduction 38
1. The Motivation for Studying Waves 38
2. Waves 38
　　2.1　Definition of a Wave 38
　　2.2　Examples of Waves 38
3. Classification of Waves 39
　　3.1　Benefit to Classifications 39
　　3.2　Electromagnetic (EM) Waves 39
　　3.3　Mechanical Waves 39
4. Conceptual Questions 39

- 5. Propagation of Mechanical Waves...........39
  - 5.1 Transverse Waves...........40
  - 5.2 Longitudinal Waves...........40
  - 5.3 Problems with Static Drawings of Waves...........41
- 6. Variations in the Medium with Propagation (Acoustic Variables)...........42
  - 6.1 Pressure...........42
  - 6.2 Density...........42
  - 6.3 Temperature...........43
  - 6.4 Particle Motion...........43
- 7. Conceptual Questions...........43
- 8. Wave Characteristics and Parameters...........44
  - 8.1 General...........44
  - 8.2 Four Basic Parameters and the Many Associated Parameters...........44
  - 8.3 Frequency (f) and Period (P)...........44
  - 8.4 Propagation Velocity...........46
  - 8.5 Wavelength...........47
  - 8.6 Amplitude...........50
- 9. Addition of Waves...........51
  - 9.1 Constructive Interference (In Phase Waves)...........51
  - 9.2 Destructive Interference (Out of Phase Waves)...........52
  - 9.3 Partial Constructive (or Partially Destructive) Interference...........52
- 10. Exercises and Conceptual Questions...........53
- 11. Relating Wave Characteristics to Application and Relevance in Diagnostic Ultrasound...........53
- 12. Wave Characteristics and Parameters...........53
  - 12.1 Frequency and Period...........53
  - 12.2 The General Term Frequency...........53
  - 12.3 Propagation Velocity...........55
  - 12.4 Wavelength...........60
  - 12.5 Amplitude...........61
- 13. Decibels (dB)...........64
  - 13.1 The Need for Decibels...........64
  - 13.2 The Definition of Decibels...........64
  - 13.3 The Equation for Decibels...........64
  - 13.4 Applying the Equation for Decibels...........65
  - 13.5 The Amplitude Form of the Decibel Equation...........65
  - 13.6 Why Two Forms and When to Use Which Form...........66
  - 13.7 Exercises and Conceptual Questions...........66
- 14. Comparing Frequency with Amplitude...........66
  - 14.1 Frequency and Amplitude are Disjoint...........66
  - 14.2 Graphical Representation...........67
  - 14.3 Exercises and Conceptual Questions...........67

▶ **CHAPTER 3: Attenuation**...........71
- 1. Attenuation...........72
- 2. Absorption...........72
  - 2.1 Absorption and Viscosity...........72
  - 2.2 Absorption and Frequency Dependence...........72
- 3. Reflection...........72
  - 3.1 Geometric Aspects of Reflection...........73
  - 3.2 Acoustic Aspects of Reflection...........76
- 4. Refraction...........78
  - 4.1 Refraction Defined...........78
  - 4.2 Visualizing Refraction...........78

- 4.3 Oblique Incidence but No Change in Propagation Velocities ... 79
- 4.4 Normal Incidence (Incident angle = 0°) ... 79
- 4.5 Snell's Law ... 80
- 4.6 The Critical Angle ... 81
5. Conceptual Questions ... 82
6. Ultrasound Terminology ... 82
   - 6.1 Echogenicity ... 82
   - 6.2 Uniformity ... 83
   - 6.3 Plaque Surface Characteristics ... 83
7. Attenuation Rates ... 83
   - 7.1 Table of Attenuation Rates ... 83
   - 7.2 Calculating Approximate Attenuation ... 84
   - 7.3 Interpreting Calculated Attenuation ... 84
8. Absorption in the Body ... 84
   - 8.1 In Soft Tissue, Absorption is the Dominant Factor Creating Attenuation ... 84
   - 8.2 Absorption Increases Exponentially with Increasing Frequency ... 84
   - 8.3 Fluids and Absorption ... 85
9. Reflection in the Body Based on Geometric Conditions ... 85
   - 9.1 Specular Reflection ... 85
   - 9.2 Scattering in the Body ... 87
   - 9.3 Rayleigh Scattering ... 88
   - 9.4 Reflection in the Body Based on Acoustic Aspects ... 88
10. Refraction in the Body ... 92
    - 10.1 Effects of Refraction ... 92
    - 10.2 The Critical Angle and Refractive Shadowing ... 93
    - 10.3 Applying Snell's Law ... 94
    - 10.4 Important Points about Refraction ... 95
11. Exercises and Conceptual Questions ... 95
12. Review of Attenuation ... 96
13. Table of Acoustic Values ... 96
14. Reflection and Transmission Percentage for Non-normal Incidence ... 97
15. Matching Layer ... 97
16. Two Matching Layers ... 98
17. Determining the Maximum Imaging Depth from the Dynamic Range ... 99

▶ CHAPTER 4: Pulsed Wave Operation ... 103

1. Motivation for Using Pulsed Wave (PW) ... 104
   - 1.1 Range Ambiguity and Continuous Wave (CW) ... 104
   - 1.2 Range Specificity and Very Short Pulse ... 104
   - 1.3 Range Specificity and Longer Pulse Pulsed Wave (PW) ... 105
   - 1.4 Range Ambiguity and a Longer Pulse ... 105
2. Pulsed Wave Definitions ... 105
   - 2.1 Time-Related Pulsed Wave Definitions ... 105
   - 2.2 Distance-Related Pulsed Wave Definitions ... 107
3. Relating Wave Parameters and Pulsed Wave (PW) Parameters ... 108
   - 3.1 The Difference Between a Wave Parameter and a PW Parameter ... 108
   - 3.2 Time-Related Wave Parameters and PW Parameters ... 108
   - 3.3 Distance-Related Pulsed Wave Definitions ... 109
4. The Foundational Drawing for Pulsed Wave ... 110
5. Pulsed Wave and the Need to Understand Timing ... 110
6. Definitions for Pulse Wave Related Imaging Parameters ... 111
7. PW and Image Generation ... 111
   - 7.1 Non-Scanned Modalities ... 111
   - 7.2 Scanned Modalities ... 112

8. Relating PW Parameters to Ultrasound 113
   8.1 The Pulse Duration 113
   8.2 The Pulse Repetition Period and the PRF 114
   8.3 The Spatial Pulse Length 115
   8.4 Using the PRP (Line Time) to Calculate the Frame Time (and Frame Rate) 116
   8.5 Comparing Temporal Resolution for Scanned and Non-Scanned Modalities 118
9. Color Doppler, Frame Rate, and Temporal Resolution 118
   9.1 General 118
   9.2 Creating a Color Scan 118
   9.3 Calculating the Color and Overall Frame Rate 119
   9.4 Color and Poor Temporal Resolution 119
   9.5 Choosing a Packet Size, the Trade-Off 120
10. Optimizing Frame Rate and Temporal Resolution 120
11. Typical Values and Ranges for Wave and PW Parameters 121
12. The Foundational Drawing for Pulse Wave Revisited 122
13. Bandwidth 122
   13.1 Bandwidth Defined 122
   13.2 Pictorial Representation of Bandwidth 123
   13.3 Bandwidth Calculation 123
   13.4 Fractional Bandwidth 123
   13.5 Quality Factor 123
   13.6 The Value of Greater Bandwidth 123
14. Pulse Duration (Width) vs. Bandwidth 125
   14.1 The Reciprocal Relationship 125
   14.2 The Meaning of the Operating Frequency and Bandwidth Relationship 126
   14.3 Bandwidth Required for Doppler 126
15. Exercises and Conceptual Questions 126

▶ **CHAPTER 5 | Part I: Transducers (Piezoelectric)** 131
Introduction 132
1. Transducer Basics 132
   1.1 Transducers Defined 132
   1.2 Examples of Transducers 132
   1.3 Ultrasound Transducers and Bi-directionality 133
2. Ultrasound Transducers Mechanisms of Operation 133
   2.1 The Piezoelectric Effect 133
   2.2 The Piezoelectric Mechanism 133
   2.3 Natural Piezoelectric Materials 135
   2.4 Manufactured Piezoelectric Materials 135
   2.5 Poling 135
   2.6 Curie Point 135
3. Frequency of Operation and Crystal Dimension 136
   3.1 Pulse Wave 136
   3.2 Continuous Wave 136
4. Impulse Response of a Transducer 137
5. Beam Characteristics with a Simple, Single Disc Transducer 138
   5.1 Simple, Single, Disc Transducers 138
   5.2 The Beam Parameters 139
   5.3 The Natural Focus 139
   5.4 Varying the depth of the Natural Focus 140
   5.5 Depth of Focus (Focal Depth) and Equation 140
   5.6 Depth of Field (Focal Region) 142
   5.7 True Beam Shapes 142
   5.8 Changing Intensity from Beam Convergence and Divergence 143

6. Limitations of the Simple Crystal 144
7. Minimizing the Acoustic Impedance Mismatch 144
    7.1 High Impedance Piezoceramics 144
    7.2 Matching Layer 145
    7.3 Quarter Wavelength Thickness 145
    7.4 Composites with Lower Acoustic Impedances 145
8. 2D Image Planes 146
9. Detail Resolution 146
    9.1 General 146
    9.2 Axial Resolution 146
    9.3 Lateral Resolution 147
    9.4 Elevation Resolution 149
    9.5 Detail Resolution Summary 149
10. Transducer Block Diagrams 150
11. Exercises 150
12. Transducer Evolution Overview 151
13. The Pedof (Blind, Doppler Only Transducer) 151
14. Creating a 2-Dimensional Scan Sequentially 152
15. Static B-Scan 153
16. Mechanical Steering 153
17. Mechanical Annular Array 155
18. Sequencing 156
19. Linear Switched Array 157
20. Electronic Steering 158
    20.1 Creating an Array 158
    20.2 Understanding the Term Phase 158
    20.3 Electronic Steering for Transmit 159
    20.4 Electronic Steering for Receive 159
    20.5 Electronic Focusing for Transmit 160
    20.6 Electronic Focusing for Receive 161
    20.7 Focusing and Steering Together 161
21. 1-D Phased Array Sector 161
22. 1-D Linear Phased Array 163
23. 1-D Curved Linear Phased Array 167
24. Plano Concave (Hanafy Lens) 168
    24.1 1-D Arrays and Sub-optimal Elevation Control 168
    24.2 Hanafy Lens 168
25. Multi-dimensional Arrays 169
    25.1 1.5-D Arrays 169
    25.2 2D Arrays 169
26. Piezocomposite Materials 170
27. PMN-PT (Single) Crystals 171
28. Wireless Transducers 171
29. Important Concepts for Transducers 172
30. Exercises and Conceptual Questions 172
31. The Piezoelectric Effect 173
    31.1 Use of Piezoelectric Materials 173
    31.2 Crystal Structures 173
    31.3 Intermolecular Bonds 173
    31.4 Polarization 173
32. Newer Technologies 174
    32.1 New Crystal Growth Technology 174

CHAPTER 5 | Part II: Transducers (CMUT) 179
Introduction 180
1. Capacitive Micromachined Ultrasonic Transducer (CMUT) 180
   1.1 Capacitance and Capacitors 180
   1.2 Fundamentals of Capacitance 181
   1.3 Basic CMUT Theory (Non-Collapse Mode) 181
   1.4 Collapse Mode 182
2. CMUT Acoustic Impedance Matching 183
3. Acoustic Window and Bandwidth 184
4. Backing Material 184
5. Focusing 184
6. CMUT Transducer Model 184
7. CMUT Transducers 185
   7.1 CMUT Arrays (1-D) 185
   7.2 CMUT Matrix Arrays (2D) 187
   7.3 CMUT Advantages 187
   7.4 Application of Increased Bandwidth 188
8. Conceptual Questions 190

CHAPTER 6 | Part I: System Operation (Fundamentals) 193
Introduction 194
1. The Basic Processes of Real-Time Imaging 194
2. Important System Definitions 194
   2.1 Transmit Power 195
   2.2 Dynamic Range 195
   2.3 Signals, Noise, and Signal-to-Noise Ratio (SNR) Definitions 195
   2.4 Pre-processing and Post-processing 199
3. Analog to Digital (A/D) Conversion 199
   3.1 Nyquist Criteria 202
4. Basic Functions of a System (Simplified) 204
   4.1 Putting the Pieces Together 204
5. Transmit Beamformer 205
   5.1 Function 205
   5.2 The System Control for Transmit Power 206
   5.3 Practical Concerns 206
6. Receiver 206
   6.1 Amplification (Receiver Gain) 206
   6.2 Compensation (Time Gain Compensation) 208
   6.3 Compression 210
   6.4 Demodulation 212
   6.5 Reject 213
7. A-mode (Amplitude mode) 213
   7.1 A-mode Display 213
   7.2 Interpreting an A-mode 213
   7.3 The Use of A-mode 214
8. Exercises 214
9. System Block Diagram 214
10. Transmit Beamformer 215
    10.1 Transmit Beamformer Function 215
    10.2 Transmit Aperture and Apodization 215
11. Controls that Affect Transmit and Power Distribution 216
    11.1 Transducer Frequency and Transmit Power 216
    11.2 Imaging Modalities, Image Generation, Image Size, and Transmit Power 216

- 11.3 Imaging Depth and Transmit Power ... 216
- 11.4 Focus and Transmit Power ... 217
- 12. TGC and Gain Revisited ... 217
  - 12.1 Internal TGC Profiles ... 217
  - 12.2 Internal Color TGC Profiles ... 218
  - 12.3 "Pre-compensated" TGC Profiles ... 218
  - 12.4 TGC Controls and Imaging Scenarios ... 219
  - 12.5 Appropriate Use of Receiver Gain with TGCs ... 220
- 13. Analog to Digital Conversion ... 220
  - 13.1 Analog Received Signal and Digital Conversion ... 220
  - 13.2 The Motivation for Converting from Analog to Digital ... 220
- 14. Scan Conversion ... 221
  - 14.1 Paradigm Shift: From A-Mode to B-Mode ... 221
  - 14.2 Creating a Sequential B-mode From Multiple A-modes ... 221
  - 14.3 The Role of the Scan Converter ... 222
  - 14.4 Polar Scan Conversion and Lateral Distortion ... 222
- 15. The History of Beamformers ... 223
- 16. Pre-processing and Post-processing Revisited ... 225
- 17. Compression ... 225
  - 17.1 Compression: A Multi-Stage Process ... 225
  - 17.2 Dynamic Range of 2D Echoes ... 225
  - 17.3 Dynamic Range of the Human Eye ... 225
  - 17.4 Why the System Allows for Compression in the Back End of the System ... 226
  - 17.5 Compression Controls on the System ... 227
  - 17.6 Using Compression Controls Correctly ... 229
- 18. Tissue Colorization ... 230
- 19. Measurements ... 230
  - 19.1 Area Measurements ... 230
- 20. Video Display and Monitors ... 231
  - 20.1 Cathode Ray Tube (The Olden Days) ... 231
  - 20.2 Liquid Crystal Displays (LCD) ... 232
  - 20.3 Monitor Frame Rates and Why They Matter ... 233
  - 20.4 LED and LCD ... 233
  - 20.5 LCD Advantages and Disadvantages: ... 234
  - 20.6 Subdividing Horizontal Lines into Pixels ... 234
  - 20.7 Relating Brightness Levels to Binary ... 235
  - 20.8 Brightness Levels and Ambient Light ... 235
- 21. Data Storage ... 236
  - 21.1 Data Storage Devices ... 236
  - 21.2 DICOM ... 236
- 22. Data Storage (Internal) ... 236
  - 22.1 Cine (Cine Loop) Review ... 236
  - 22.2 Purposes for Cine Review ... 236
  - 22.3 The Recording Length of a Cine Memory ... 237
- 23. Zoom (Res Mode, Magnification) ... 237
  - 23.1 Acoustic Versus Non-acoustic ... 237
  - 23.2 Non-acoustic Zoom (Read Zoom) ... 237
  - 23.3 Acoustic Zoom (Write Zoom) ... 238
- 24. Ultrasound Modes ... 239
  - 24.1 C-mode (Constant Depth Mode) ... 240
  - 24.2 M–Mode (Motion Mode) ... 240
  - 24.3 Real-Time Imaging ... 241
- 25. Exercises and Conceptual Questions ... 241

26. Digital Formats and Compression 241
    26.1 Data Compression and Decompression (CODEC) 241
    26.2 Video Formats Versus Codec 241
    26.3 Comparison of Video Formats 242
    26.4 A Partial List of Codecs 243
27. Compression Algorithms and Techniques 243
    27.1 Truncation 243
    27.2 Run Length Encoding (RLE) 243
    27.3 Indexing (Lookup Table) 243
    27.4 Spatial Interpolation 244
    27.5 Temporal Interpolation 244
    27.6 Mathematical Transforms 244
    27.7 Statistical Approaches 244
    27.8 Motion Detection 244
    27.9 Combining Algorithms 245
28. Digital to Digital Format Conversion 245
29. More About Monitors 245
    29.1 OLED and QLED Monitors 245
    29.2 Frame Rates and Human Perception 246
    29.3 Flicker Fusion and Perception 246
    29.4 Flicker Fusion as an Advantage 246
    29.5 Unconscious and Conscious Sensing of Flicker 246
    29.6 When 60 Hz is Not Enough 246

▶ **CHAPTER 6 | Part II: System Operation (Advanced)** 251
Introduction 252
1. Resolution and Trade-Offs 252
    1.1 FOV, Line Density, and Temporal Resolution 252
    1.2 Transmit Focal Depth, Transmit Aperture, Sensitivity, and Lateral Resolution 254
    1.3 SNR and Contrast Resolution vs. Temporal Resolution 254
2. Averaging Techniques 254
    2.1 Theory of Averaging 254
    2.2 Line Averaging 256
    2.3 Frame Averaging 256
    2.4 Spatial Compound Imaging 257
    2.5 Frequency Compounding (Fusion) 260
    2.6 Image Persistence 262
    2.7 Spatial Averaging 262
3. Receive Focusing Techniques 263
    3.1 Continuous Dynamic Receive Focusing 263
4. Effective (Composite) Beam 263
5. Transmit Focusing Techniques 264
    5.1 Active Single Focus 264
    5.2 Multiple Transmit Foci 264
    5.3 Dynamic Transmit Focusing Retrospective Gating and Synthetic Aperture 267
6. Image Generation Techniques and Trade-Offs 270
    6.1 Sequential (Single Line Transmit and Single Line Receive) 270
    6.2 Ultrafast Imaging: General 271
    6.3 Multi-Line Acquisition (MLA) 271
    6.4 Multi-Line Transmit (MLT) 274
    6.5 Plane Wave and Diverging Wave 274
    6.6 Comparison of Image Generation Approaches 277
7. Extended Field of View/Panoramic Imaging 278

- 8. Adaptive Processing / Auto Optimize ... 279
- 9. Sound Speed Compensation ... 281
- 10. 3D Imaging ... 281
- 11. Fusion (Modalities) ... 285
- 12. Resolution Summary ... 287
- 13. Artificial Intelligence (AI) ... 287
  - 13.1 What is AI? ... 287
  - 13.2 A Brief History of Artificial Intelligence and Its Rapid Growth ... 288
  - 13.3 Categorizations of AI ... 289
  - 13.4 Methods Utilized in Artificial Intelligence ... 289
  - 13.5 AI in Ultrasound ... 290
  - 13.6 The Future of AI ... 292
- 14. Conceptual Questions ... 292

▶ CHAPTER 7: Doppler ... 299
- Introduction ... 300
- 1. The Doppler Effect ... 301
  - 1.1 Change in Frequency ... 301
  - 1.2 The Doppler Thought Experiment ... 301
  - 1.3 The Relationship Between Velocity (v) and the Doppler Shift ... 302
  - 1.4 Wavelength (λ) and the Doppler Effect ... 303
  - 1.5 Relative Motion ... 303
  - 1.6 The Relative Shift ... 303
  - 1.7 Determining the Relative Doppler Shift Numerically ... 303
  - 1.8 Exercises ... 304
- 2. Relationships in the Doppler Equation ... 304
  - 2.1 Velocity (v) and Wavelength (λ) ... 304
  - 2.2 Wavelength (λ) and the Transmit Frequency (Operating Frequency f_0) ... 304
  - 2.3 Wavelength (λ) and the Propagation Velocity (c) ... 305
  - 2.4 Roundtrip Effect ... 305
- 3. A Simplified Doppler Equation ... 305
  - 3.1 Equation with No Angle Effects ... 305
  - 3.2 Simplified Numeric Form ... 306
  - 3.3 Examples of Doppler Relations Applied ... 306
- 4. Solving the Doppler Equation for Velocity ... 307
- 5. Conceptual Questions ... 307
- 6. Completing the Doppler Equation ... 307
  - 6.1 Removing the "Directly Toward or Directly Away" Assumption ... 307
  - 6.2 Relative Motion and Angle ... 307
- 7. Doppler Shifts from Red Blood Cells ... 308
  - 7.1 The Rayleigh Scattering/Frequency Paradox ... 308
  - 7.2 The Optimal Frequency for Doppler ... 308
  - 7.3 Red Blood Cell Aggregation and Reflectivity ... 309
  - 7.4 Rouleaux and Spontaneous Contrast ... 309
- 8. Identifying the Doppler Angle (Insonification or Insonation Angle) ... 310
  - 8.1 Standardized Angle Determination ... 310
  - 8.2 Examples of Insonification Angles ... 310
  - 8.3 The Effects of Angles Greater and Less Than 90° ... 311
- 9. Exercises ... 312
- 10. Spectral Doppler System Operation ... 312
  - 10.1 The Value of a Block Diagram ... 312
  - 10.2 Why You Need to Also Know About Analog Waveform and Unidirectional Doppler ... 312
  - 10.3 The Doppler Block Diagram ... 313

11. The Processes Involved in Spectral Doppler..313
    11.1 Transmit Ultrasound Into the Body: (Pulser)..313
    11.2 Frequency Shift from Moving Blood 314
    11.3 Amplification: (Amplifier) 314
    11.4 Doppler Shift Detection: (Mixers)...314
    11.5 Wall Filtering 315
    11.6 Variable Gain: (Gain) 318
    11.7 Audio: (Speakers)..319
    11.8 Analog to Digital Conversion (A/D) 319
    11.9 Fast Fourier Transform (FFT) 319
    11.10 Post-processing (Compression and Reject or Grayscale) 320
    11.11 Display 320
12. Frequency vs. Amplitude...320
13. PW vs. CW Comparison 321
    13.1 Trade-Offs..321
    13.2 Timing and Basics of CW Doppler 321
    13.3 Timing and Basics of PW Doppler 321
    13.4 Range Specificity: Advantage PW 322
    13.5 Aliasing: Advantage CW 322
    13.6 The Maximum Detectable Frequency Shift in PW 323
    13.7 Parameters Affecting Aliasing in PW Doppler..323
    13.8 Appearance of Aliasing in a Doppler Spectrum 323
    13.9 Practical Limit in CW Doppler and Aliasing 324
    13.10 Changing the Scale in PW Doppler 324
14. The Maximum Detectable Velocity 325
15. Spectral Windows and Modal Flow...326
    15.1 The Presence of a Spectral Window 326
    15.2 Spectral Doppler Modal Flow 327
16. PW Versus CW Comparison..328
17. PW Range Ambiguity 328
    17.1 Dispelling the Myth 328
    17.2 The Mechanism that Causes Range Ambiguity 328
    17.3 Range Ambiguity and Mitigating Factors 328
    17.4 Risk Factors 329
    17.5 Determining if Range Ambiguity is Present 329
18. HPRF Doppler...329
    18.1 Using the Trade-Offs...329
    18.2 Using Range Ambiguity to Create HPRF Doppler 329
19. Doppler Insonification Angle and Error Sources 330
    19.1 Cardiac and Alignment with Flow 330
    19.2 Vascular Doppler and the Need to Angle Correct..330
    19.3 Angle Correction and the Doppler Angle 331
    19.4 Peak Velocity and Pressure Gradient 332
    19.5 Angle Correction Error (5 Degree Table)...332
    19.6 Exercises 333
20. Color Flow 334
    20.1 The Blessing and the Curse 334
21. Color Doppler Versus Spectral Doppler 334
    21.1 Differences in Gating Techniques for Doppler Modalities 334
22. Overview of How Sequential Color Doppler is Performed 335
    22.1 Multiple Approaches...335
    22.2 Similarities of Color to Spectral Doppler and 2D Imaging 335
    22.3 Color Overview 335

- 22.4 Creating a Sequential Color Scan ... 336
- 22.5 Temporal Resolution and Sequential Color ... 336
- 22.6 Color Display and Velocity Interpretation ... 336
23. Time-Correlated Color ... 337
- 23.1 Overview ... 337
- 23.2 Ultrafast Doppler ... 337
- 23.3 Ultrafast Color Doppler Compound Imaging ... 337
- 23.4 Beamforming and Processing Requirements of Ultrafast Doppler ... 338
- 23.5 Optimizing Ultrafast Color Doppler Compound Imaging ... 339
- 23.6 Ultrafast PW Doppler ... 339
24. Color Gain ... 340
- 24.1 Setting the Appropriate Color Gain ... 340
25. Interpreting the Color Bar Relative to Spectral Doppler ... 342
26. Color Invert and Aliasing ... 342
27. Color Wall Filters ... 342
- 27.1 Wall Filter and Color Scale Integration ... 342
- 27.2 The Absence of Color ... 342
- 27.3 Interpreting the Color Bar Relative to Nyquist and the Wall Filters ... 343
28. Determining Flow Direction in Color Doppler ... 344
- 28.1 Why Colors Change Even When Velocity Doesn't ... 344
- 28.2 Defining the Doppler Insonification Angle ... 344
- 28.3 Cosine Revisited ... 345
- 28.4 Determining Flow direction: Step-by-Step Approach ... 345
- 28.5 Direction of Flow in the Body ... 352
29. Color Persistence ... 355
- 29.1 The Purpose and Effects of Color Persistence ... 355
- 29.2 Persistence and Temporal Distortion ... 355
- 29.3 Important Points about Persistence ... 355
30. Color Priority ... 355
- 30.1 How Color Priority Works ... 355
- 30.2 Important Points about Color Priority ... 355
31. Color Power Doppler ... 356
- 31.1 Color Power Doppler Encoding ... 356
- 31.2 Disadvantages ... 356
- 31.3 Advantages ... 357
- 31.4 Directional Power Doppler ... 358
32. Surface Rendered Color Doppler ... 358
- 32.1 Concept and Theory ... 358
- 32.2 2D Color Doppler Surface Rendering ... 359
- 32.3 3D Color Renderings ... 360
33. Slow Flow (Microvascular) Detection ... 360
- 33.1 Conventional Color Doppler and Wall Filters ... 360
- 33.2 Adaptive Spatiotemporal Wall Filtering ... 361
34. Angle Correction Error (10 degree error) ... 364
35. Understanding the Behavior of Color Wall Filters ... 364
- 35.1 Digital Filtering ... 364
- 35.2 Comparing Spectral Doppler Wall Filters with the Color Wall Filter ... 364
- 35.3 Color Wall Filters and Nyquist ... 365
- 35.4 Effect of Signal Strength on Color Wall Filtering ... 365
36. B-Flow ... 366
- 36.1 Increasing Blood Signal Strength ... 366
- 36.2 B-Flow Display ... 367
37. Vector Flow (V Flow) Imaging ... 368

	37.1 Representing Flow as Vectors	368
	37.2 Image Interpretation	369
	37.3 Calculating Wall Shear Stress (WSS)	370
38.	Comparing Flow Detection Techniques	370
39.	Conceptual Questions	370

▶ CHAPTER 8: Artifacts 377

Introduction 378
1. The Source of Artifacts 378
   1.1 Assumptions for Imaging 378
2. Categorizing Artifacts 382
   2.1 Image Detail Resolution Related 382
   2.2 Locational Artifacts 382
   2.3 Attenuation Artifacts 382
   2.4 Phase-Related 382
   2.5 Doppler Artifacts 382
3. Detail Resolution 383
   3.1 Lateral and Axial Resolution 383
   3.2 Elevation Resolution 384
4. "Locational" Artifacts 385
   4.1 Refraction 385
   4.2 Reverberation 386
   4.3 Multi-Path Artifact 393
   4.4 Side Lobe (Single Element) and Grating Lobe (Arrays) Artifacts 393
   4.5 Speed Error Artifact 394
   4.6 Range Ambiguity Artifact 396
   4.7 Mirror Artifact 396
5. Attenuation Artifacts 399
   5.1 Shadowing 399
   5.2 Figure-of-Eight Artifact 402
   5.3 Enhancement Artifact 402
6. Phase-Related Artifacts 403
   6.1 Speckle Basics 403
   6.2 Beam Aberration 408
7. Doppler and Color Doppler Artifacts 410
   7.1 Aliasing 410
   7.2 Range Ambiguity 411
   7.3 Spectral Mirroring 411
   7.4 Harmonic Double Spectral Artifact 412
   7.5 Spectral Spread (Broadening) Artifact 413
   7.6 Blossoming 414
   7.7 Color Blossoming (Bleeding) 414
   7.8 Circuit Saturation 415
   7.9 Wall Filter Saturation 415
   7.10 Color and Power Doppler Flash Artifact 416
   7.11 Doppler Spectral Dropout 417
8. Color Doppler Dropout 417
   8.1 Color Dropout 417
   8.2 Flow Dropout Related to Occlusion 418
   8.3 Doppler Angle 418
   8.4 Inadequate Sensitivity 418
   8.5 Color Dropout Related to Scales and Wall Filtering 419
   8.6 Color Dropout and Speckle Noise Related to Gain 420

        8.7   Color Dropout Related to Color Priority 421
        8.8   Color Dropout from Acoustic Shadowing 422
   9. Conceptual Questions 422

▶ **CHAPTER 9: Bioeffects** 427
   Overview 428
   1. Mechanisms of Bioeffects 428
        1.1   Thermal Bioeffects 428
        1.2   Mechanical Bioeffects 429
        1.3   The Concept of a Threshold Effect 430
   2. Safeguarding the Patient 430
        2.1   Confirming Safe Levels 430
   3. Research and Standards 431
   4. Power Measurements as a Basis for Gauging the Risk of Bioeffects 432
   5. Common Intensities 432
        5.1   Pulsed Wave Timing Revisited 432
        5.2   The Common Intensities 432
        5.3   Deciphering the Common Intensities by Concepts 433
        5.4   Putting the Concepts Together 434
   6. The Significance of the Common Intensities 434
        6.1   Common Intensity Analogy 434
        6.2   Mechanical Bioeffects and the I_{SPPA} 435
        6.3   Thermal Bioeffects and the I_{SPTA} 435
        6.4   Conversion Between a PA and a TA Intensity: (Duty Factor) 435
        6.5   Conversion Between SP and SA Intensity: (BUF) 436
   7. Exercises 436
   8. Relating Risks of Bioeffects to Ultrasound Modes 436
        8.1   Scanned Versus Non-scanned Modalities 436
        8.2   Ultrasound Modalities in Order of Thermal Risks 437
        8.3   Transmit Voltages for Various Modalities 437
        8.4   Ultrasound Modalities in Terms of Cavitation 438
        8.5   Theory of FDA Limits 438
   9. Acoustic Power Measurements 438
        9.1   Overview of Acoustic Power Measurements 438
        9.2   The Hydrophone 439
        9.3   Six Degrees of Freedom 440
        9.4   Beamplots 440
   10. Output Display Standards 441
   11. Mechanical Index (MI) 441
   12. Thermal Indices 442
        12.1 Absorption Rates of Various Mediums 442
        12.2 Thermal Indices Defined 442
        12.3 The Three Thermal Indices 442
        12.4 Underestimation of Worst Case 442
   13. AIUM Statements Regarding Ultrasound and Bioeffects 443
        13.1 Acknowledging the AIUM 443
        13.2 How Best to Use the Following Pages 443
        13.3 Conclusions Regarding the Safety of Ultrasound 443
        13.4 ALARA Principle 443
        13.5 Safety Concerns Regarding the Use of Ultrasound in Training and Research 444
        13.6 Mammalian In Vivo Biological Effects 445
        13.7 The Mechanical Index and Gas Bodies 446
        13.8 Conclusion Regarding Heat and the Thermal Indices (TIS, TIB, TIC) 446

- 13.9 Fetal Safety..448
- 13.10 "In Vitro" Biological Effects 450
- 13.11 AIUM Conclusions Regarding Epidemiology for Obstetric Ultrasound 450
- 14. Conceptual Questions 451
- 15. Review Sheet for Converting Intensities 451
  - 15.1 Conversion Between Spatial Peak and Spatial Average 451
  - 15.2 Converting Between the Pulse Average and the Temporal Average 451
  - 15.3 Steps for Converting Between Intensities 451
- 16. Hydrophones..452
  - 16.1 Hydrophone Performance Comparison 452
  - 16.2 Membrane Hydrophones 452
  - 16.3 Capsule "Golden Lipstick" Hydrophones..452
  - 16.4 Needle Hydrophones..452
  - 16.5 Needle Reflecting Hydrophones 453
  - 16.6 Fiber Optic Hydrophones 453

▶ **CHAPTER 10: Contrast and Harmonics**..459
- 1. Motivation for Contrast Imaging..460
  - 1.1 Overcoming Too Much Attenuation 460
  - 1.2 Conventional Approaches 460
  - 1.3 Increasing the Acoustic Impedance Mismatch...460
  - 1.4 Increase in Signal Amplitude with Contrast 460
- 2. Fundamentals of Harmonics 461
  - 2.1 Motivation for Harmonic Imaging 461
  - 2.2 Mechanisms that Produce Harmonic Signals 462
- 3. Technology Advances 462
- 4. Relative Amplitudes...462
- 5. Generation of Harmonics 463
  - 5.1 Non-linear Wave Propagation 463
  - 5.2 Harmonics and Depth Dependence 464
  - 5.3 Effective Harmonic Beam Shape 464
- 6. Advantages and Disadvantages of Conventional Harmonics 464
  - 6.1 Improved Lateral Resolution 464
  - 6.2 Reduction in Grating Lobes 465
  - 6.3 Reduction in Reverberation and Clutter Artifacts 465
  - 6.4 Reduction in Phase Aberration 466
  - 6.5 Degradation in Axial Resolution..467
- 7. Pulse or Phase Inversion 467
- 8. Current Uses of Contrast Imaging..468
- 9. Properties of Contrast 469
  - 9.1 Composition of Bubbles 469
  - 9.2 Microbubble Interaction with Ultrasound and Resonance............................469
- 10. The Mechanical Index (MI) 470
  - 10.1 Understanding the MI 470
  - 10.2 Non-uniformity of the MI 470
  - 10.3 Effect of MI on Microbubbles 471
  - 10.4 Bubble Disruption..472
- 11. Transmit Focus..473
  - 11.1 Bubble Concentration and Signal Amplitude 474
- 12. Contrast Specific Detection Techniques 474
  - 12.1 Contrast Harmonic Imaging 474
  - 12.2 High MI Techniques 475
- 13. Challenges at High MI: Triggered Acquisition..477

14. Very Low MI Techniques..477
    14.1 Fundamentals of Low MI Imaging..477
    14.2 Pulse or Phase Inversion...477
    14.3 Amplitude or Power Modulation..478
    14.4 Importance of Low Frequencies..479
15. Challenges at Very Low MIs: Signal-to-Noise..479
    15.1 Coded Pulses (Coded excitation)..479
    15.2 New Indication for the US: Liver Contrast...480
16. The Future...482
    16.1 3D Contrast...482
    16.2 Development of Fast Frame Rates for 3D Contrast..483
    16.3 Direction...484
    16.4 Molecular Imaging Field..484
    16.5 Sonothrombolysis and Other Therapeutic Applications...484
17. Conceptual Questions...485

▶ **CHAPTER 11: Quality Assurance** **489**
Introduction..490
1. Laboratory Accreditation..490
    1.1 Accreditation Providers...490
    1.2 Commitment to Quality...490
    1.3 Individual Personnel Credentialing / Certification 491
    1.4 Personnel Qualifications...491
    1.5 Document Storage and Record Keeping...492
2. Transducer Care..492
    2.1 Inspection and General Care...492
    2.2 Current Leakage Tests...492
    2.3 Disinfection and Sterilization..493
    2.4 General Cleaning...493
    2.5 Low-Level Disinfection...493
    2.6 High-Level Disinfecting..493
    2.7 Sterilization..493
    2.8 Potential Risks of Not Following Sterilization/Disinfection Guidelines......................................494
    2.9 Precautions to Take When Performing High-level Disinfection or Sterilization.........................494
    2.10 Instrumentation and Quality Assurance..495
3. Equipment Testing..495
    3.1 The Need for Tight Testing Controls...495
    3.2 Purpose of Testing...495
4. 2D and Doppler Testing..495
    4.1 Tested Parameters..495
5. Doppler Testing and Phantoms...496
    5.1 Types of Doppler Phantoms..496
    5.2 Flow Phantoms..496
    5.3 Doppler String Phantoms..502
6. Imaging Phantoms and Test Objects..503
    6.1 Detecting Performance Degradation...503
    6.2 Test Repeatability..503
    6.3 Varying Pin Separation and Testing Detail Resolution..503
    6.4 Uniformly Spaced Pins and Testing Depth Accuracy and Sensitivity...504
    6.5 Area and Volume Measurement Accuracy...504
    6.6 Contrast Resolution Testing..505
7. Commercially Available Imaging Phantoms..505
8. Commercially Available Specialty Phantoms..509

- 9. Conceptual Questions ... 516
- 10. Quality Assurance Statistics ... 516
  - 10.1 As Part of the Quality Program ... 516
- 11. Q&A Statistics ... 516
  - 11.1 The Value of Statistics ... 516
  - 11.2 What is Statistical Testing? ... 516
- 12. Making Statistical Indices More Intuitive ... 517
  - 12.1 Presume that the Gold Standard is Perfect, Adhering to the "Golden" Rule ... 517
  - 12.2 Pay Particular Attention to the English of the Statistical Terminology ... 518
  - 12.3 Pay Close Attention to the Labels and Layout of any Table of Data ... 518
- 13. Building the Table of Data ... 518
- 14. Exercises: Interpreting the Statistical Table ... 520
- 15. Statistical Parameters ... 520
  - 15.1 Sensitivity ... 520
  - 15.2 Specificity ... 520
  - 15.3 Accuracy ... 520
  - 15.4 Positive Predictive Value ... 520
  - 15.5 Negative Predictive Value ... 520
- 16. Numerical Example ... 521
- 17. Real World Understanding ... 521
- 18. Exercises: Statistical Indices ... 522

CHAPTER 12: Fluid Dynamics ... 527

- 1. Flow Analogy ... 528
  - 1.1 Foreword on Flow ... 528
  - 1.2 Flow Analogy ... 528
  - 1.3 Flow Analogy Exercises ... 528
- 2. Fluid Dynamics ... 528
  - 2.1 Fluid Dynamics: Flow and Related Terms ... 528
  - 2.2 Fluid Dynamics: Definitions ... 529
  - 2.3 Power, Work and Energy in Practical Terms ... 530
  - 2.4 Energy ... 530
  - 2.5 Potential and Kinetic Energy ... 531
  - 2.6 Hydrostatic Pressure ... 532
  - 2.7 Volumetric Flow (Q) ... 532
  - 2.8 Velocity (v) ... 533
  - 2.9 Capacitance ... 533
  - 2.10 Compliance ... 534
  - 2.11 Fluid Viscosity ... 534
  - 2.12 Exercises: Flow and Related Definitions ... 534
- 3. Derivation of Equations ... 534
  - 3.1 Introduction ... 534
  - 3.2 The Resistance Equation ... 535
  - 3.3 Volumetric Flow (Continuity Equation) ... 536
  - 3.4 Simplified Law of Hemodynamics ... 537
  - 3.5 Poiseuille's Law ... 538
  - 3.6 Simplifications Made for the Equation ... 539
- 4. Bernoulli's Equation and Energy ... 539
  - 4.1 Conservation of Energy and an Apparent Contradiction ... 539
  - 4.2 Bernoulli's Equation (Simplified) ... 539
  - 4.3 Simplified Bernoulli and Modified Simplified Bernoulli Equation ... 540
  - 4.4 Bernoulli's Equation with Hydrostatic Pressure Term ... 541
  - 4.5 Bernoulli's Equation Heat Term ... 541

- 4.6 Understanding Bernoulli's Equation (An Airfoil and Lift) ... 541
5. Basics of Flow and Flow Diagrams ... 542
    - 5.1 Simplifications and Assumptions for These Equations to be Employed ... 542
    - 5.2 Flow Definitions ... 543
    - 5.3 Steady Flow in a Rigid Tube ... 543
    - 5.4 Steady-State Flow in a Curved Vessel ... 544
    - 5.5 Flow Examples ... 544
6. Reynolds Number and Turbulence ... 546
    - 6.1 Reynolds Number ... 546
7. Exercises ... 547

CHAPTER 13: Hemodynamics ... 551
Introduction ... 552
1. Removing Some of the Simplifications ... 552
    - 1.1 The Assumption: Steady State Flow ... 552
2. The Assumption: Rigid Flow Conduits ... 553
    - 2.1 Elastic Arteries ... 553
    - 2.2 The Impact on Poiseuille's Law ... 553
    - 2.3 The Assumption: Single Flow Conduit ... 554
    - 2.4 The Assumption: Conservation of Energy and No Energy Loss to Heat ... 557
3. Pressure, Flow, and Resistance in the Cardiovascular System (The Simplified Law) ... 560
    - 3.1 Overview ... 560
    - 3.2 Left Heart ... 560
    - 3.3 The Arterial System ... 561
    - 3.4 The Venous System ... 563
    - 3.5 Right Heart ... 563
    - 3.6 The Lungs ... 564
    - 3.7 Return to the Left-Sided Heart ... 564
4. The Healthy Cardiovascular System as a Whole ... 564
    - 4.1 Velocity Versus Cross-Sectional Area ... 564
    - 4.2 Pressure Changes Across the Arterial System ... 565
    - 4.3 The Venous System ... 566
5. The Subcritical Diseased Cardiovascular System at Rest ... 571
    - 5.1 Asymptomatic Patients ... 571
    - 5.2 Asymptomatic Patients with Exercise (Unmasking a Subcritical Stenosis) ... 573
    - 5.3 Symptomatic Patients and Critical Stenoses ... 574
6. Spectral Doppler as a Means of Assessing Hemodynamics ... 574
    - 6.1 What Doppler Tells Us ... 574
    - 6.2 Returning to the Hemodynamic Equations ... 575
    - 6.3 Characteristics of the Arterial Spectrum ... 575
    - 6.4 Velocity Criteria ... 579
    - 6.5 Calculating Pressure Gradients ... 579
    - 6.6 VTI and TAMV ... 580
    - 6.7 Doppler Indices and Ratios ... 583
    - 6.8 Characteristics of the Venous Spectrum ... 584
    - 6.9 Murmurs and Bruits ... 585
7. Flow Visualization ... 586
8. Conceptual Questions ... 588

CHAPTER 14: Patient Care and Safety ... 593
1. Introduction to Good Practices of Patient Care ... 594
2. Safety Aspects of Patient Care ... 594
    - 2.1 Equipment Performance ... 594

2.2	Patient Safety	594
2.3	Technical Proficiency	594
2.4	Patient Identification and Exam Verification	595
2.5	Standard Precautions (previously known as Universal Precautions)	595
2.6	Informed Consent	595
2.7	Students and Preliminary Reports	596
2.8	Emergency Situations	596

3. Personal Aspects of Patient Care ... 596
   3.1 Staffing Issues ... 596
   3.2 Patient Communication ... 596
   3.3 Managing Patient Expectations ... 596
   3.4 Right to Refuse ... 597
   3.5 Patient Comfort ... 597
   3.6 Values ... 597

4. Sonographer Safety ... 597
   4.1 Work-related Musculoskeletal Disorders ... 597
   4.2 Factors Contributing to WRMSD ... 597
   4.3 Patient Engagement and Sonographer-Neutral Postures ... 602
   4.4 Sonographer Safety Summary ... 604

5. Conceptual Questions ... 604

CHAPTER 15: Physics of Stress and Strain ... 607

Introduction ... 608

1. Theory of Stress and Strain ... 608
   1.1 The Concept of Stress (σ) ... 608
   1.2 The Concept of Strain (ε) ... 609
   1.3 Strain and the Elastic Limit ... 609
   1.4 Hooke's Law: The Relationship Between Strain and Stress ... 609
   1.5 Elastic Modulus (*EM*) ... 610
   1.6 Wave Propagation Speed ... 612
   1.7 Poisson's Ratio (υ) ... 613
   1.8 Isotropic and Anisotropic Materials ... 615

2. Relationships Between Elastic Moduli ... 616
   2.1 Equations ... 616
   2.2 Applying the Relationship Between E, G, and υ ... 616

3. Producing Strain with Ultrasound ... 617
   3.1 Movement and Manual Compression ... 617
   3.2 Acoustic Radiation Force Impulse (ARFI) ... 617

4. Shear Wave Elastography ... 619
   4.1 Mechanisms for Generating Shear Waves ... 619
   4.2 Shear Wave Production from Longitudinal Wave Propagation ... 620
   4.3 Acoustic Radiation Force to Create a Mach Cone ... 621
   4.4 Shear Wave Speed Changes with Stiffness ... 624

5. Relating the Elastic Moduli ... 625
   5.1 Relating Young's (E) Modulus and Poisson's Ratio (υ) ... 626
   5.2 Relationship Between Young's (E), Shear (G), and Poisson's (υ) ... 626
   5.3 Relating Young's Modulus (E) with Bulk Modulus (K) ... 627
   5.4 Deriving the Relationship Between K, G, and E ... 628

6. Why an Incompressible Isotropic Material has a Poisson's Ratio of 0.5 ... 628

7. Conceptual Questions ... 629

CHAPTER 16: Elastography 633
Introduction 634
- 1. Types of Elastography 634
  - 1.1 Static or Strain Elastography 634
  - 1.2 Shear Wave Elastography 635
- 2. Clinical Applications of Strain Elastography 636
  - 2.1 Breast Cancer 636
  - 2.2 Strain Elastography of Other Organs 639
- 3. Clinical Applications of Shear Wave Elastography 639
  - 3.1 Diffuse Hepatic Disease 639
- 4. Clinical Acceptance of Elastography 640
- 5. Progress in Improving Quantitative Elastographic Reliability 642
- 6. The Future 644
- 7. Conceptual Questions 646

CHAPTER 17: Speckle Tracking and Strain Imaging 651
- 1. Introduction to Myocardial Mechanics and Strain Imaging 652
  - 1.1 The Need for Cardiac Deformation Imaging 652
  - 1.2 Cardiac Mechanics: Translation, Rotation, and Torsion 652
  - 1.3 Rotation, Twist, and Torsion of the Left Ventricle 652
  - 1.4 The Strain Equation 653
  - 1.5 Strain Application 653
  - 1.6 Strain Applied to Ventricular Function 654
  - 1.7 The Strain Rate Equation 654
- 2. Speckle Tracking Concepts 654
  - 2.1 Speckle and Reflection 654
  - 2.2 How Speckle Tracking Works 655
  - 2.3 The Effects of Frame Rate on Speckle Tracking 655
  - 2.4 Causes of Error in Speckle Tracking and 2D Imaging 655
  - 2.5 Effects of Image Quality on Speckle Tracking 655
- 3. Clinical Application of Strain 656
  - 3.1 Strain Waveforms 656
  - 3.2 Global Longitudinal Strain 656
  - 3.3 Automation of Strain Measurements 657
  - 3.4 Additional Application of Strain Imaging 658
  - 3.5 Future Applications of Strain Imaging 658
- 4. Conclusion 658
- 5. Conceptual Questions 659

CHAPTER 18: Focused Ultrasound 661
- 1. Focused Ultrasound (FUS) Overview 662
  - 1.1 Definitions 662
  - 1.2 History of Focused Ultrasound 663
  - 1.3 Development in MR Imaging and Thermometry 663
- 2. Physical Principles of Operation 664
  - 2.1 Focusing Ultrasound Beams 664
  - 2.2 Tissue Heating with Ultrasound 664
  - 2.3 Cavitation 665
  - 2.4 Defocusing 665
  - 2.5 Biological Effects 666
- 3. Guidance Systems 667
  - 3.1 MRI Guided 667
  - 3.2 Ultrasound Guided 667

	3.3	Other Guidance Systems ... 667
4.	Clinical Indications ... 667
	4.1	Currently Approved Indications ... 668
	4.2	Other Indications for Focused Ultrasound Therapy ... 668
5.	Future Landscape for Focused Ultrasound ... 668
6.	Conceptual Questions ... 670

CHAPTER 19: Musculoskeletal Ultrasound ... 675

Introduction ... 676

1. Ultrasound Transducers Used in MSK ... 676
   - 1.1 Transducer Types and Image Formats ... 676
   - 1.2 Operating Frequency in the MSK Ultrasound System ... 676
   - 1.3 Linear Array Transducers ... 677
   - 1.4 Curved Linear Array Transducers ... 678
   - 1.5 Transducer Orientation ... 678
   - 1.6 Transducer Notch ... 678
   - 1.7 Ultrasound Coupling Gel ... 679
2. Physical Principles of Ultrasound and Image Optimization ... 681
   - 2.1 Field of View ... 681
   - 2.2 Harmonics ... 681
   - 2.3 Extended Field of View: Panoramic ... 683
   - 2.4 Dual Screen ... 683
   - 2.5 Tissue Colorization: Orange Tint Setting ... 684
   - 2.6 Power Doppler ... 685
   - 2.7 Beam Steering ... 685
   - 2.8 Cine Loops ... 686
3. Tissue Imaging Characteristics ... 687
   - 3.1 Speed of Sound ... 687
   - 3.2 Acoustic Impedance ... 687
   - 3.3 Absorption and Reflection ... 687
   - 3.4 Reflecting Surface ... 687
4. Normal and Pathologic Tissue Signatures ... 687
   - 4.1 Ultrasound Terminology ... 687
   - 4.2 Normal Tissue Signatures ... 688
   - 4.3 Pathologic Tissue Signatures ... 690
5. Artifacts ... 692
   - 5.1 Anisotropy ... 692
   - 5.2 Shadowing ... 694
   - 5.3 Enhancement ... 695
   - 5.4 Reverberation ... 696
6. Conceptual Questions ... 697

CHAPTER 20: Physics-Based Image Optimization ... 701

Introduction ... 702

Part I: 2D Imaging and Optimization ... 702

1. Imaging High Body Mass Index (BMI) Patients ... 702
   - 1.1 Using the Correct Frequency ... 702
   - 1.2 Using the Correct Transducer ... 702
   - 1.3 Transmit Power ... 704
   - 1.4 Correct Preset ... 704
   - 1.5 Focus ... 704
   - 1.6 2D Only ... 705
   - 1.7 Fundamental, Not Harmonic Imaging ... 705

- 1.8 Sliding Receive Filters (Dynamic Frequency Tuning) ... 705
- 1.9 Tissue Aberration Correction ... 705
- 1.10 Improve SNR by Increasing Averaging ... 705
- 1.11 Coded Excitation and Special Techniques ... 705
- 1.12 Imaging High BMI Patients Summary ... 705
2. Improving Superficial/Near Field Imaging ... 705
   - 2.1 Transducer Frequency ... 705
   - 2.2 Correct Transducer ... 706
   - 2.3 Elevation Focus ... 706
   - 2.4 Appropriate Coupling ... 706
   - 2.5 Appropriate Transmit Power ... 706
   - 2.6 Appropriate Receiver Gain ... 706
   - 2.7 Focus-Related ... 706
   - 2.8 Harmonics ... 707
   - 2.9 Angulation for Artifact Reduction ... 707
   - 2.10 Spatial Compound Imaging ... 707
   - 2.11 Eliminating Range Ambiguity Artifact ... 707
   - 2.12 Field of View (Trapezoidal/Panoramic) ... 707
   - 2.13 Color / Power Doppler and Spatiotemporal Filtering ... 707
   - 2.14 Superficial Imaging Summary ... 707
3. Improving Imaging of Patients with Dry Skin ... 708
   - 3.1 Background ... 708
   - 3.2 Dry Skin and Impedance Mismatch ... 708
   - 3.3 The Solution ... 708
4. Improving Elastography Imaging ... 708
   - 4.1 Strain Elastography ... 708
   - 4.2 Shear Wave Elastography ... 710
5. Improving Contrast-Enhanced Ultrasound (CEUS) ... 711
   - 5.1 Basics of Bubbles ... 711
   - 5.2 The Mechanical Index (MI) ... 711
   - 5.3 Contrast Concentration ... 711
   - 5.4 Cardiac-Specific ... 711
   - 5.5 Liver-Specific ... 713

Part II: Spectral Doppler Optimization ... 713

6. Improving Spectral Doppler Sensitivity ... 713
   - 6.1 The Correct Transducer and Frequency ... 713
   - 6.2 Transmit Power ... 714
   - 6.3 The Modality ... 714
   - 6.4 PW: The Correct Sample Volume (Gate) Size ... 715
   - 6.5 CW: Beam Overlap ... 716
   - 6.6 The Correct Doppler Angle ... 716
   - 6.7 The Correct Acoustic Window ... 716
   - 6.8 Improving Doppler Sensitivity Summary ... 717
7. Improving Spectral Doppler Velocity Measurement Accuracy ... 717
   - 7.1 Adequate Doppler Sensitivity ... 717
   - 7.2 Minimizing Doppler Angular Error ... 717
   - 7.3 Appropriate Receiver Gain ... 720
   - 7.4 Appropriate Scales ... 721
   - 7.5 Improving Doppler Measurement Accuracy Summary ... 722
8. Optimizing Spectral Doppler Wall Filters ... 722
   - 8.1 Wall Filter Function ... 722
   - 8.2 Wall Filters and Operating Frequency ... 723
   - 8.3 Wall Filter Settings ... 723

	8.4 Detecting Low-Velocity Flow	723
	8.5 Optimizing Wall Filters Summary	724
9.	Reducing Aliasing	724
	9.1 Aliasing and Nyquist	724
	9.2 Doppler Scales	724
	9.3 Aliasing Situations	724
	9.4 Reducing Aliasing Summary	727
Part III: Color Doppler Optimization		727
10. Improving Color Image Sensitivity		727
	10.1 The Correct Transducer and Frequency	727
	10.2 Transmit Power	728
	10.3 The Modality	728
	10.4 The Correct Doppler Angle	731
	10.5 The Correct Acoustic Window	731
	10.6 Improving Color Doppler Sensitivity Summary	731
11. Optimizing Color Doppler Low-Velocity Detection		731
	11.1 Color Doppler Wall Filter Function	731
	11.2 Color Box Size	732
	11.3 Color Priority	732
	11.4 Color Power (Angio) Doppler	733
	11.5 Ultrafast Color Power	733
	11.6 Spatiotemporal Filtering	734
	11.7 Contrast Enhanced Ultrasound (CEUS)	734
	11.8 Optimizing Color Low-Velocity Detection Summary	734
12. Optimizing Color Temporal Resolution		734
	12.1 Minimizing Color Box Size	735
	12.2 Decreasing Color Packet Size	735
	12.3 Decreasing Color Line Density	735
	12.4 Decreasing Reference 2D Image Size	735
	12.5 Use Parallel Processing	735
	12.6 Use Ultrafast Color Doppler	736
	12.7 Optimizing Color Temporal Resolution Summary	736
13. Conceptual Questions		736

Appendix A: Glossary	739
Appendix B: Index	761
Appendix C: Abbreviations	785
Appendix D: Equations	787
Appendix E: Listing of Figures and Tables	793

Chapter 1

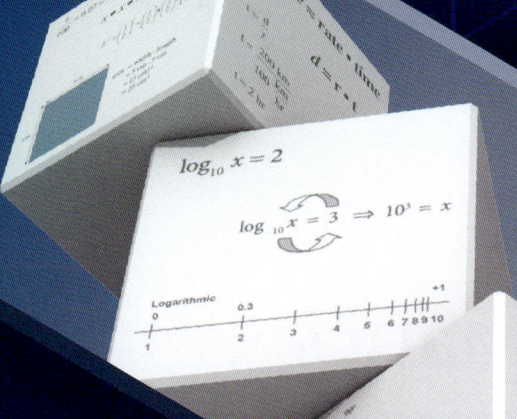

Mathematics

WHY DO WE STUDY THIS?

▷ To understand physics, and not just memorize facts, you must have a rudimentary understanding of mathematics

▷ Ultrasound registry exam physics questions require an understanding of the mathematical relationships of the variables in an equation

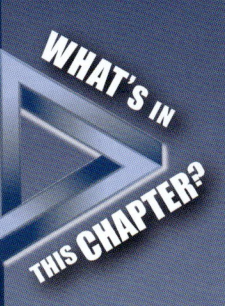

WHAT'S IN THIS CHAPTER?

LEVEL 1 — BASIC ULTRASOUND PHYSICS
Basic mathematical functions and relationships of variables within equations are introduced.

LEVEL 2 — BOARD LEVEL
Higher level math skills are presented including logarithms, the binary system, and concepts needed to understand Doppler hemodynamics.

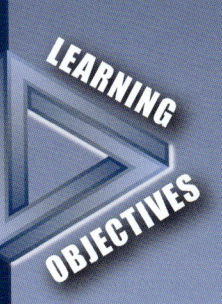

LEARNING OBJECTIVES

▷ Describe the value of mathematics in ultrasound

▷ Determine the basic relationship of variables within an equation

▷ Apply the concept of fractions, percentages, decimal notations, reciprocals, exponents, the basic trigonometric functions of sine and cosine, and logarithms

▷ Explain the difference between absolute and relative information and linear and non-linear relationships

Chapter 1
Mathematics

Introduction

Most people think of mathematics in terms of basic arithmetic and numerical manipulation. While this is certainly true, it represents a very narrow view of mathematics. Mathematics is really an enormous field that includes many different topics. The field of mathematics includes many disciplines such as algebra, number theory, geometry, calculus, trigonometry, topology, and even logic and reasoning. Although you will not need to become an expert in any of these, the more you learn in mathematics, the easier it will be to understand physics.

> **KEY CONCEPT**
>
> Without math, it is not possible to learn physics. Math is to physics what a paintbrush is to a painter, or physical conditioning is to an athlete. The foundation of physics is mathematics. Therefore, to understand physics, and not just memorize facts, you must have a rudimentary understanding of mathematics.

How Much Math Will You Need?

Some people in the field of ultrasound will state that there is very little mathematics on the board exams. I do not agree. I think this disparity in opinions stems from the very narrow definition of mathematics as numerical calculations. Admittedly, there are very few numerical calculations on most credentialing exams, and certainly not intensive computations that would require a calculator. However, depending on the specific credentialing test and the test version, there are approximately twenty-five to forty percent of the questions that involve some form of mathematics.

As you will discover throughout this book, the mathematics included on the credentialing exams generally does not include performing many calculations, but rather asks relative relationships and logical conclusions from the mathematical relationships between variables. In other words, instead of asking you to calculate the resistance to flow for a fluid flowing through a vessel, you may be asked how the resistance to flow will change with changes in parameters that define the vessel. Instead of asking you to calculate a Doppler shift for a given transducer frequency, given a specific angle to flow and a blood flow velocity, you may be asked how the Doppler shift would change if a different transducer operating frequency were used given the same angle to flow and blood flow velocity. Answering this type of "relative" question involves math skills, which many students have not used for a long period of time, or may have never developed. This last point is precisely why it is so critical for you to learn the basic mathematics, as outlined below.

To learn the basics of ultrasound (Level 1) you will need a proficiency in the basic mathematical functions. Specifically, you will need to:

- Be comfortable with the language of mathematics and translating English into mathematical functions
- Add, subtract, multiply, and divide
- Deal with fractions, percentages, and decimal notation
- Understand exponential form and become fluent with the metric system
- Understand the concept of reciprocals
- Understand basic relationships of variables within an equation (proportionality and inverse)
- Perform algebraic manipulation of equations

To master Level 2, you will need some higher-level math skills. Specifically you will need to:

- Understand the difference between absolute and relative information
- Understand the difference between linear and non-linear relationships
- Recall or determine the equations commonly used in ultrasound physics and in hemodynamics
- Understand the basic trigonometric functions of sine and cosine
- Understand and apply the concepts of logarithms and decibels
- Understand the basics of the binary system (relative to base 10)

Author's Note:
Online Math Assessment and Perspective

Many students panic when they see a math quiz. Don't worry – just take your time and be diligent and you will be successful. The purpose of this quiz is to identify your strengths and weaknesses so you know which concepts you need to focus on most. You do not need to become a mathematician, but every skill you learn or polish will make learning the physics easier. Think of the math as a tool kit that you can use whenever there is an equation you are required to know, or a complex concept you must learn to apply. Investing time in building your math skills is like upgrading your tools so that you always have the right tool needed for the job. Just realize, you will not get everything correct, and that is OK! After the quiz, the exercises in this chapter are designed to build understanding – and getting things wrong is part of that process.

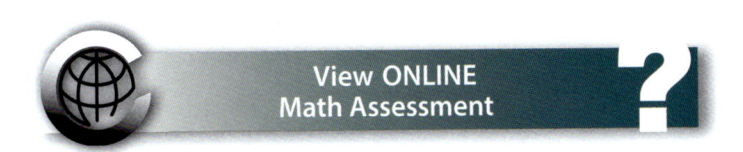

View ONLINE Math Assessment

How to Learn Mathematics

The good news is I have never encountered a student unable to master the mathematics necessary to pass the examination. The bad news is that learning this mathematics requires a structured approach, time, work, and patience.

A Structured Approach, Time, Work, and Patience

Adults don't learn the same way children learn. Children tend not to be afraid of making a mistake in front of their peers. Adults, in comparison, live in dread that someone will recognize that they are ignorant of even the slightest detail. I believe this approach of learning in fear puts an extraordinarily heavy and unfair burden upon adults in the position of student.

There is no way that anyone will understand everything just by reading the material once. Expecting to understand immediately is not only unreasonable, but puts a tremendous stress on the student. If you realize that learning is a process that only comes slowly over time through work and patience, you will not panic when something isn't clear the first time. I often use the analogy that learning is like building a house. Before you can get to the fun part of decorating the interior with intricate art and furniture, you have to go through the backbreaking work of digging a hole in the ground, setting up forms, and building a foundation. Without a solid foundation, the house will never stand.

It is time to dig the hole and do the work necessary so that you can build the foundation.

CHECKPOINT: Exam Tip

Credentialing and board exams are all about percentages. If you take 10% longer to complete the exam because relational math concepts are not second nature to you, or you miss 10% of the questions because of simple math comprehension errors, that 10% may be the critical difference between passing and failing. In fact, we have heard from students that most who do not pass, fail by one, two, or three questions.

1. Mathematics Basics

1.1 Numbers
In mathematics, there are many categorizations which group numbers together based on their similar properties. For example, there are counting numbers (the natural numbers), negative counting numbers (the negative natural numbers), the set of all the natural numbers, negative numbers and 0 (called the integers), numbers which can be expressed as the ratio of two integers (rational numbers), and numbers which cannot be expressed as the ratio of two integers (irrational numbers), etc.

Natural Numbers: 1, 2, 3, 4, …
Negative Natural Numbers: -1, -2, -3, -4, …
Integers: -5, -4, -3, -1, 0, 1, 2, 3, 4, 5, …
Rational Numbers: (all numbers which can be expressed as p/q where p and q are integers)
Irrational Numbers: (all numbers which cannot be expressed as p/q where p and q are integers)

For ultrasound physics, you will not need to know precise definitions of all of the various classifications of numbers. What you will need is a general ability to work with numbers including the basic mathematical operations of addition, subtraction, division, and multiplication.

1.2 Basic Mathematical Notation (symbols used in basic mathematics)

Addition	+	
Subtraction	−	
Multiplication	x	Example: m x f implies the variable m multiplied by the variable f
	*	Example: t * v implies the variable t multiplied by the variable v
	•	Example: c • v implies the variable c multiplied by the variable v
	( )	Example: 3(7) implies the number 3 times the number 7
No symbol		Example: 3z implies the number 3 multiplied by the variable z
Division	/	Example: m / f implies the variable m divided by the variable f
	÷	Example: j ÷ k implies the variable j divided by the variable k
Equality	=	

Inequalities:
Greater than	>	Example: g > 3 is read as g is greater than the number 3
Less than	<	Example: h < 6 is read as h is less than the number 6
Greater than or equal to	≥	Example: k ≥ r is read as k is greater than or equal to r
Less than or equal to	≤	Example: h ≤ 6 is read as h is less than or equal to 6

*Note: Children generally learn to use the letter "x" to stand for multiplication. Once students reach algebra, there is a notational shift that occurs such that symbols other than "x" are often used to denote multiplication. This shift occurs since the letter x is used to stand for the unknown quantity in an algebraic expression. Since it is easy to confuse the "x" that stands for multiplication with the "x" that stands for a variable, other symbols become more commonly used. Therefore, there are many symbols used to indicate multiplication, such as: x, •, *, and sometimes ( ). All of these symbols will be used throughout this text and interchanged freely so as to accustom you to each of these notations.*

1.3 Basic Mathematical Definitions

Constant: A number which cannot change (Example: 3, 7, -14, 6 are all constants)

Natural constant: A number which reoccurs naturally in the universe in relation to a specific parameter (Example: pi (π) for circles)

Coefficient: A constant term used as a multiplier of a variable (Example: in the expression $7z^2$, the number 7 is the coefficient for the variable term z^2)

Variables: A physical quantity which can vary or change (Example: in the expression $3x^2$, the variable is represented by the letter x)

1.4 The Value of Estimating

The ability to estimate quickly is very handy in every day life. Learning to make good estimates comes from practice and a little bit of thinking. For example, if you were asked to solve the problem what is 19 times 20, and you were not allowed to use a calculator or paper and pencil, what would you do?

Approach 1: (rounding off: estimation)
Find a way of rounding off the numbers into two numbers you can easily multiply in your head. For example, 19 x 20 is a little less than 20 x 20. Since 20 x 20 is 400, your first answer would be just a little less than 400.

Approach 2: (actual answer using estimation to simplify the math)
Start with Approach 1 and add one more step. Since 19 x 20 can be written as (20-1) x 20 which is the same as (20 x 20) – (1 x 20), you can actually solve this problem in your head. As you solved in Approach 1, 20 x 20 is 400. Since the correct answer is actually 20 less than 400, the answer is 380.

In terms of ultrasound physics and hemodynamics, there are times when you should estimate the answer to a problem to make certain that you have not made a simple math calculation error. The best way to develop this ability is to put away the calculator and start practicing calculating and estimating in your head.

1.5 Exercises: Estimating

View ONLINE Exercises: Estimating

2. Fractions, Decimal Form, and Percentages

One of the earliest learned skills in mathematics is how to deal with fractions and percentages. Unfortunately, the use of calculators has, for most people, caused this skill to deteriorate. Being able to deal with fractions and percentages is critical in physics and medicine.

A fraction consists of two parts: a number on top called the numerator, and a number on the bottom called the denominator. An increase in the numerator with no change to the denominator results in an increase in the fraction (see proportionality in Section 10.1).

For the fraction defined as: $Fraction = \frac{p}{q}$.

*An increase in p implies an increase in $\frac{p}{q}$: $\left(\text{if } p \uparrow \Rightarrow \frac{p}{q} \uparrow\right)$.

Conversely, an increase in the denominator with no change to the numerator results in a decrease in the fraction (see inverse proportionality in Section 10.3).

For the same fraction defined as: $Fraction = \frac{p}{q}$.

An increase in q implies a decrease in $\frac{p}{q}$: $\left(\text{if } q \uparrow \Rightarrow \frac{p}{q} \downarrow\right)$.

Look at the simple table of fractions below. Look for the obvious patterns. First, we see that as n increases, 1/n decreases. Second, notice that each factor of 10 increase in the denominator results in a decimal shift in the decimal form of the fraction. Third, notice that by knowing the values of 1/n, you can easily solve for any multiple such as 1/n multiplied by 2 (2/n).

n	$\frac{1}{n}$	$\frac{1}{10*n}$	$\frac{1}{1{,}000*n}$	$\frac{2}{n}$
1	1.000000	0.100000	0.001000	2.000000
2	0.500000	0.050000	0.000500	1.000000
3	0.333333	0.033333	0.000333	0.666666
4	0.250000	0.025000	0.000250	0.500000
5	0.200000	0.020000	0.000200	0.400000
6	0.16667	0.016667	0.000167	0.333333
7	0.142857	0.014286	0.000143	0.285714
8	0.125000	0.012500	0.000125	0.250000
9	0.111111	0.011111	0.000111	0.222222
10	0.100000	0.010000	0.000100	0.200000
11	0.090909	0.009090	0.000091	0.181818

Table 1 **Fractions and Patterns**

Often, a fraction is not written in its simplest form, implying that there is a multiplying factor which is common between the numerator and the denominator. In these cases, the fraction can be "simplified", or reduced to "simplest form" by dividing both the numerator and denominator by the common multiple.

◊ *Examples:*

$$\frac{4}{8} = \frac{4*1}{4*2} = \frac{4}{4}*\frac{1}{2} = 1*\frac{1}{2} = \frac{1}{2}$$

$$\frac{14}{200} = \frac{2*7}{2*100} = \frac{2}{2}*\frac{7}{100} = 1*\frac{7}{100} = \frac{7}{100}$$

$$\frac{120}{1200} = \frac{120*1}{120*10} = \frac{120}{120}*\frac{1}{10} = 1*\frac{1}{10} = \frac{1}{10}$$

*Note: the symbol ($\Rightarrow$) stands for the word "implies."

Additionally, all fractions can be written in decimal form and as percentages. Converting from fractions to decimal form is simply the process of division. Converting from decimal form to percentages is just multiplication by 100%.

◊ *Examples:*

$\frac{1}{1} = 1 = 100\%$ $\frac{1}{2} = 0.5 = 50\%$

$\frac{1}{3} = 0.333 = 33.3\%$ $\frac{1}{4} = 0.25 = 25\%$

$\frac{2}{1} = 2 = 200\%$ $\frac{5}{2} = 2.5 = 250\%$

Another way of thinking of percentages is how many times something occurs per hundred events. As such, it is easy to convert fractions to percentages when the denominator is a factor of 10. (You should notice that this process is equivalent to counting the number of decimal point shifts.)

◊ *Examples:*

$\frac{7}{100} = 0.07 = 7\%$ $\frac{2}{10} = \frac{20}{100} = 0.2 = 20\%$

$\frac{43}{1000} = \frac{4.3}{100} = 0.043 = 4.3\%$ $\frac{16}{10} = \frac{160}{100} = 1.6 = 160\%$

CHECKPOINT: Exam Tip

You must become fluent in writing fractions in decimal form. Frequently, answer choices are written in decimal form instead of as fractions since decimal form is much easier to write in software.

2.1 Exercises: Fractions and Percentages

View ONLINE Exercises: Fractions & Percentages

3. Reciprocals

In mathematics the reciprocal or inverse of any number is the number which, when the two numbers are multiplied, gives unity (1).

◊ *Example:*
What is the reciprocal or inverse of the number two?

Because 2 * 1/2 = 1, the reciprocal or inverse of 2 is 1/2.

◊ *Example:*
What is the reciprocal of 8?

Because 8 * 1/8 = 1, 1/8 is the reciprocal of 8.

The property of reciprocals, although quite simple, is extremely powerful. The starting point is learning how to take the reciprocal of a number. Later in this chapter we will learn how to take the reciprocal of a variable, and the reciprocal of physical units. With this knowledge, as you will learn in Chapter 2, you will be able to convert easily between frequency and time. Once the basic understanding of reciprocals is in place, we will extrapolate the concept to include reciprocals within a question. This skill will prove very important since recognizing reciprocals cuts the number of ways of asking a question in half. For now, it is important that you master the basic concept of reciprocals. Once this skill is mastered, we will learn to extrapolate this technique to logic and reasoning skills for answering test questions.

> **CHECKPOINT: Exam Tip**
>
> The concept of reciprocals will be applied in many topics. Although a seemingly simple concept, understanding reciprocal relations will help you not only with physics questions, but also sharpen your skills in answering test questions in general.

3.1 Exercises: Reciprocals

View ONLINE Exercises: Reciprocals

4. Units

In mathematics, a unit is the reference for how a measurement of a physical quantity is made. Consider how distance is measured. There are many ways by which a distance could be measured. For example, distance could be measured in inches, feet, yards, miles, meters, kilometers, knots (nautical distance), light years (based on how long it takes light to travel), etc. Each measurement system has its own unit (standard of measurement). Of course, the same distance measured by different measuring systems results in a different number of units. For example, if someone's height in inches is 60, their height in feet is 5, and their height in centimeters is approximately 152, which is equivalent to 1.52 meters. The person's height does not change, but depending on the unit (reference) the measurement result sure does change. Also notice that if you give someone's height without expressing the measurement unit, the answer is ambiguous. Clearly it does not make sense to say someone is 152 tall. You must express the units to make a measurement unambiguous.

Invariably, at one point in your life as a student, you had a math or science teacher who would give you no credit if you did not express the units when answering a question which involved a calculation. Although you probably saw this as harsh and unfair punishment, there was a good reason. Learning to use units not only makes your answer unambiguous, but it also helps you determine what equation to use and if you have solved the problem correctly.

For example, if you are asked to determine the wavelength of ultrasound in a particular medium, you know that the answer must have units of distance such as meters. The word "length" within the word wavelength makes this fact explicit. Therefore, if you write and solve an equation and the resulting unit comes out to be anything other than a unit of distance, you know you either remembered the equation incorrectly, or you made a mathematical error during your calculations.

Throughout the book, you will be learning the units used for the various measurements made in ultrasound.

5. Variables

Note that many times in mathematics, a physical quantity can change. The letter used to represent the physical quantity that can change is called a variable. In an equation, when you use a letter like: n, x, y, f, l, c, etc., you are using a shorthand so as not to have to write out the entire word(s) for which each symbol stands. Also, since the variable ultimately represents a number, you can treat these symbols like numbers in mathematical expressions.

◊ *Examples:*

Let's say you have $4.00 to spend on apples and each apple

costs $1.00. How many apples can you buy?

Mathematically:

$$(\$1.00) \bullet (\text{number of apples bought}) = \$4.00$$

For simplicity, instead of writing "number of apples bought" we will replace it with any letter we want, remembering that this letter really stands for the physical quantity: "number of apples bought". Let's assume that we let the letter "n" stand for the number of apples bought, the above expression is now shortened as follows:

$$(\$1.00) \bullet (n) = \$4.00$$

If we want to solve the equation to determine the value of n, we now follow the basic rules of manipulating an equation from algebra. In essence the basic rule for manipulating an equation is that whatever you do to one side of the equation, you must do to the other side of the equation for it to still hold true.

dividing both sides by $1.00

$$\left(\frac{\$1.00}{\$1.00}\right) \bullet (n) = \left(\frac{\$4.00}{\$1.00}\right)$$

$$(n) = 4/1 = 4$$

So you can buy 4 apples.

You should now make a distinction in your mind between variables and constants. As already defined, a variable is a letter which stands for a physical quantity which can change, or vary. A constant, is a fixed number which cannot change. Let's look at the following basic equation and identify the various components of the equation.

$$y = 3x + 2$$

In this equation there are two variables, specifically x and y. The number 2 is a constant. The number three is called a coefficient. Since a coefficient is fixed within an equation, you can also think of a coefficient as a constant term. In other words, the 3 and the 2 within the equation cannot change, but the values for x and y can change.

6. Applying Reciprocals

In Section 3 of this chapter we learned the general concept of reciprocals and how to take the reciprocal of a number (a constant). We can now learn how to take more complex reciprocals as fractions, units, and variables have been introduced.

Reciprocal of a fraction:

◊ *Example:*

The reciprocal of 2/7 is 7/2

because: $\dfrac{2}{7} \bullet \dfrac{7}{2} = \dfrac{2 \bullet 7}{7 \bullet 2} = \dfrac{14}{14} = 1$

Reciprocal of a variable:

◊ *Examples:*

Just as the reciprocal of 3 is 1/3

because: $\dfrac{3}{1} \bullet \dfrac{1}{3} = \dfrac{3 \bullet 1}{1 \bullet 3} = \dfrac{3}{3} = 1$

the reciprocal of x is $1/x$

because: $\dfrac{x}{1} \bullet \dfrac{1}{x} = \dfrac{x \bullet 1}{1 \bullet x} = \dfrac{x}{x} = 1$

In some cases, the expressions will contain both variables and constants.

◊ *Example:*

The reciprocal of $14z^3$ is $1/14z^3$

because: $\left(\dfrac{14z^3}{1}\right) \bullet \left(\dfrac{1}{14z^3}\right) = \dfrac{14z^3 \bullet 1}{1 \bullet 14z^3} = \dfrac{14z^3}{14z^3} = 1$

6.1 Exercises: Applying Reciprocals

View ONLINE
Exercises: Applying Reciprocals

7. Numbers Raised to a Power

7.1 Positive Powers

In the expression x^y, x is called the base and y is called the exponent or the power. For the moment, we will consider only cases where y is an integer greater than zero. When the exponent is a positive integer, the exponent tells how many times the base is used as a factor (multiplication) with itself.

◊ *Example:*

2^3
the base is 2
the exponent is 3
(so 2 is used as a factor 3 times)
or $2^3 = 2 \cdot 2 \cdot 2 = 8$

◊ *Example:*

$4^3 = 4 \cdot 4 \cdot 4 = 64$

◊ *Example:*

$x^2 = x \cdot x$

There is a special name for the case where an exponent is 2 or 3.
If the exponent is 2, it is called a square.
If the exponent is 3, it is called a cube.
You can see why if you consider the following examples:

◊ *Example:*

Find the area of the square.

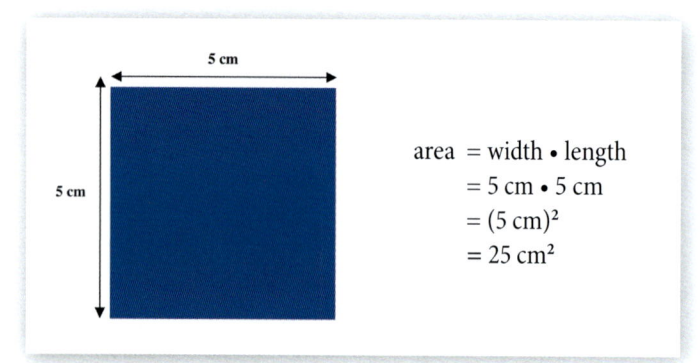

area = width • length
= 5 cm • 5 cm
= $(5 \text{ cm})^2$
= 25 cm²

Fig. 1 **Area = 25 cm²**

◊ *Example:*
Find the volume of the cube
(recall for a cube the length = width = height).

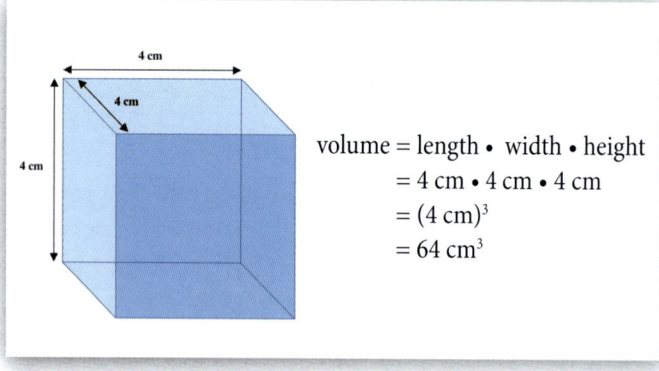

volume = length • width • height
= 4 cm • 4 cm • 4 cm
= $(4 \text{ cm})^3$
= 64 cm³

Fig. 2 **Volume = 64 cm³**

Any number raised to the 1st power (which means that the exponent = 1) is itself.

◊ *Example:* $5^1 = 5$

◊ *Example:* $26^1 = 26$

We have just seen how powers can be used to calculate the area of a square and volume of a cube. The following table illustrates the method of calculating the dimensional measurements associated with a square and circular object.

Important Calculations:

Dimensional Measurement	Square	Circle	Units
Perimeter (Circumference)	$x + x + x + x = 4x$	$2\pi r$	m^1
Area	$x \cdot x = x^2$	πr^2	m^2
Volume	$x \cdot x \cdot x = x^3$	$\frac{4}{3}\pi r^3$	m^3

Table 2 Dimensional Measurement of Squares and Circles

Note that any time you see the variable "r" for radius, you should expect to see the natural constant π as a multiplier, where π is approximately equal to 22/7 or:

$$\pi \text{ is a natural constant} \approx \frac{22}{7} \approx 3.14$$

7.2 Exercises: Numbers to a Positive Power

View ONLINE
Exercises: Numbers to a Power

7.3 Numbers to a Negative Power

Although most people are pretty comfortable with positive integer exponents, negative exponents (and fractional exponents) are generally perceived as much more problematic. To understand what a negative exponent implies, it is first important to analyze the notational significance of a positive exponent. In essence, a positive exponent is shorthand for expressing multiplication using the base. So if the exponent is a positive 3, then the base is used as a factor three times. Similarly, if the exponent is a positive 7, then the base is multiplied together (used as a factor) seven times. Therefore, if a positive exponent is shorthand for multiplication, it should make sense that a negative exponent would serve as shorthand for division. As we learned earlier, another way of expressing division is to multiply by a reciprocal. Therefore, a negative exponent (or power) tells how many times the reciprocal of the base is used as a multiplier.

◊ *Example:*

$5^{-3} = ?$
Base = 5
Exponent = -3 ⇒ the reciprocal of the base of 5 is $\frac{1}{5}$

Therefore:

$$5^{-3} = \left(\frac{1}{5}\right)^3 = \left(\frac{1}{5}\right) \bullet \left(\frac{1}{5}\right) \bullet \left(\frac{1}{5}\right) = \frac{1}{125}$$

◊ *Example:*

$$3^{-2} = \left(\frac{1}{3}\right)^2 = \left(\frac{1}{3}\right) \bullet \left(\frac{1}{3}\right) = \frac{1}{9}$$

◊ *Example:*

$$4^{-2} = \left(\frac{1}{4}\right)^2 = \left(\frac{1}{4}\right) \bullet \left(\frac{1}{4}\right) = \frac{1}{16}$$

◊ *Example:*

$$\left(\frac{1}{2}\right)^{-3} = \left(\frac{2}{1}\right)^3 = \left(\frac{2}{1}\right) \bullet \left(\frac{2}{1}\right) \bullet \left(\frac{2}{1}\right) = 8$$

◊ *Example:*

$$2^{-3} = \left(\frac{1}{2}\right)^3 = \left(\frac{1}{2}\right) \bullet \left(\frac{1}{2}\right) \bullet \left(\frac{1}{2}\right) = \frac{1}{8}$$

Understanding the notational meaning of a negative exponent, it should now become clear that x^{-y} is another way to write the expression:

$$\frac{1}{x^y}$$

In other words, x^y and x^{-y} are reciprocals.

We will multiply x^y and x^{-y} together to show that these terms are reciprocals $x^y \bullet x^{-y} = x^y \bullet \frac{1}{x^y} = \frac{x^y}{x^y} = 1$.

7.4 Exercises: Numbers to a Negative and Positive Power

View ONLINE
Exercises: Numbers to a Power

7.5 Numbers to the Zero Power and Exponent Rules

With respect to integer powers, we now know how to solve an expression to a positive power and to a negative power. This leaves only the case where the exponent equals zero. Any number raised to the zero power, or the exponent = 0, is defined as 1.

◊ *Example:* $263^0 = 1$

◊ *Example:* $(1/10)^0 = 1$

◊ *Example:* $x^0 = 1$

The relationship of any number to the zero power equalling one is true because of the property of reciprocals. To demonstrate this point we will consider what happens when you multiply together two exponential expressions with the same base. In the process, we will also learn a very valuable rule on simplification when dealing with multiple exponential terms.

Consider the problem $10^3 \bullet 10^2 = ?$ The first term, 10^3, means that 10 will be used as a factor 3 times. The second term, 10^2, means that 10 will be used as a factor 2 more times. Clearly, in this problem 10 will be used as a factor a total of 5 times. Therefore, $10^3 \bullet 10^2$ is really the same as 10^{3+2}, or 10^5. In most algebra books you see this rule written formally in terms of abstract variables such as:

$$x^a \bullet x^b = x^{a+b}$$

All this equation really says is that if x is used as a factor "a" times, and then used as a factor "b" more times, x would be used as a factor a total of "a + b" times.

So how does this expression relate to the fact that any number to the zero power equals one and the property of reciprocals? Consider the following problem:

What does $4^2 \times 4^{-2} = ?$

Solving the problem the long way:

$$4^2 \bullet 4^{-2} = (4 \bullet 4) \bullet \left(\frac{1}{4} \bullet \frac{1}{4}\right) = \frac{4 \bullet 4 \bullet 1 \bullet 1}{1 \bullet 1 \bullet 4 \bullet 4} = \frac{16}{16} = 1.$$

But if we use the rule: $4^2 \bullet 4^{-2} = 4^{2-2} = 4^0$.

And since these are two different approaches to solving the same problem, the answer from the long approach must be the same as the answer to the shortcut approach, or: $4^0 = 1$.

In other words, when you multiply two reciprocals together the power becomes 0. Since the product of reciprocals is always 1, any number raised to the zero power must equal 1 (in essence the property of reciprocals).

The following are some examples which demonstrate how the above rule can be used to simplify problems.

◊ **Example:** $10^3 \cdot 10^2 = 10^{3+2} = 10^5$
proof:
$1{,}000 \cdot 100 = 100{,}000 = 10^5$

◊ **Example:** $10^{-2} \cdot 10^2 = 10^{-2+2} = 10^0 = 1$

◊ **Example:** $10^2/10^2 = 10^2 \cdot 10^{-2} = 10^{2-2} = 10^0 = 1$

◊ **Example:** $(1.2 \cdot 10^{-3}) \cdot (2 \cdot 10^9) = (1.2) \cdot (2) \cdot 10^{9-3} = 2.4 \cdot 10^6$

KEY CONCEPT

The rules for exponents really represent common sense. In essence, they state that if you use x as a factor "a" times and then x as a factor "b" more times, you have used x as a factor a total of "a+b" times.

7.6 Exercises: Numbers to the Zero Power and Exponent Rules

View ONLINE Exercises: Exponent Rules

CHECKPOINT: Exam Tip

You should expect to see dimensional measurement related questions on physics exams. Note that the exponent (power) indicates the number of dimensions in a measurement. For example, circumference is 1 dimensional, area is 2 dimensional and volume is 3 dimensional.

8. Exponential Form (Notation)

Exponential form, or notation, takes advantage of how easy it is to work with multiples of 10 when using the base 10 counting system. With a base of 10, the exponent tells you how many times to move the decimal point, the + or − sign, as related to the exponent, tells you the direction to move the decimal point. A positive (+) exponent says move the decimal point to the right to make the number larger, while a negative (−) exponent indicates that the decimal point should be moved to the left, making the number smaller. In light of the last section dealing with the meaning of negative and positive exponents, these directions should make sense. A negative exponent implies division by multiples of 10 (multiplying by the reciprocal of the base) and hence leads to a smaller number. A positive exponent implies multiplication, by factors of 10, obviously resulting in larger numbers.

◊ **Example:** $1 \cdot 10^2 = 1 \cdot 10 \cdot 10 = 1 \cdot (100) = 100$
$1 . 0\ 0 = 100$
(right 2)

◊ **Example:** $3 \cdot 10^3 = 3 \cdot 10 \cdot 10 \cdot 10 = 3{,}000$
$3 . 0\ 0\ 0 = 3{,}000$
(right 3)

◊ **Example:**

$$2 \cdot 10^{-2} = 2 \cdot \left(\frac{1}{10}\right)^2 = 2 \cdot \frac{1}{10} \cdot \frac{1}{10} = 2 \cdot \left(\frac{1}{100}\right) = \frac{2}{100}$$

$$= \frac{2}{100} = 0.02$$

$0\ 2 . 0 = 0.02$
(left 2)

◊ **Example:**

$$1.6 \cdot 10^{-6} = 1.6 \cdot \left(\frac{1}{10}\right)^6 = 0\ 0\ 0\ 0\ 0\ 0\ 1\ .\ 6 = 0.0000016$$

(left 6)

◊ **Example:**
$3 \cdot 10^4 = 3 . 0\ 0\ 0\ 0 = 30{,}000$
(right 4)

There are a few significant benefits to dealing with numbers in exponential form. First, when dealing with very large or very small numbers, it is quite common to lose track of the number of zeroes in the number and hence misinterpret the number. In exponential form, the number of zeroes is contained within the exponent. Second, when you have to multiply large or small numbers, exponential form makes the mathematics less cumbersome. In other words, with exponential form, you are much less likely to make a mistake representing where the decimal point should be.

Note: Exponential notation is an efficient way of writing large numbers, which takes advantage of how easy it is to work with the number 10 raised to a power.

◊ **Example:** $6,320,000,000,000,000 = 6.32 \cdot 10^{15}$

This form is much easier to both read and write.

You should also note that there is not necessarily a right way or a wrong way of writing a number. Every number can be written in many ways as indicated in the following example.

◊ **Example:**
$6.32 \cdot 10^{15} = 63.2 \cdot 10^{14} = 632 \cdot 10^{13} = 0.632 \cdot 10^{16}$

8.1 Exercises: Exponential Notations

View ONLINE Exercises: Exponential Notations

8.2 Deciding How to Write a Number

In general, we choose to write numbers minimizing the number of digits before or after the decimal point. Furthermore, since our comma notation separates numbers by groupings of 3, we generally try to write the exponent in powers of 3 (+3, +6, +9, or -3, -6, -9, etc.). For example, instead of writing the number 0.0000047, we would more likely write 4.7×10^{-6}. Of course, 47×10^{-7}, and 0.47×10^{-5} are both correct and perfectly reasonable ways of writing this number. Similarly, instead of writing 6,000,000, we would more likely write 6×10^6. Again, this number is the same as 0.6×10^7 or 60×10^5, and both forms are perfectly acceptable ways to write the same number.

8.3 Exercises: Deciding How to Write a Number

View ONLINE Exercises: Writing Numbers

9. The Metric System and Metric Abbreviations

9.1 Conversions for Metric and Non-metric Systems

As we have just discussed, there are some major advantages to using exponential form, especially when using a base of 10. The metric system is based on measuring physical quantities by taking advantage of these benefits. Since the metric system is based on powers of ten, converting between measurement units is a simple process of sliding the decimal point.

In comparison, converting between measurements in non-metric measuring systems, such as the English system used in general practice in the United States, is a much more cumbersome and unwieldy process. Consider how the liquid measure of cups is converted to gallons. To convert, you must first know the conversion from cups to pints, then pints to quarts, and then quarts to gallons. In marked contrast, in the metric system, converting between milliliters and liters is a simple process of sliding the decimal point. Later in this chapter we discuss how to perform the conversion. Before learning to perform conversions, it is imperative that you first learn the definitions used in the metric system.

9.2 Metric Abbreviations

The metric abbreviations are based on exponential form using a base of 10. Instead of having to carry the entire mathematical expression with the power of ten written out, these powers of ten are abbreviated into a prefix. As shown in the table below, the ninth power of ten, (10^9), is abbreviated as giga. As suggested by the use of the word prefix, these abbreviations for powers of ten are then affixed to a unit such as Hz for frequency, liters for liquid measure, or meters for distance. So 1 GHz implies 1×10^9 Hz, or 1 billion Hertz.

Table 3 displays the most commonly used metric abbreviations for ultrasound physics and ultrasound in general. There are certainly many more metric abbreviations which are not routinely used in ultrasound and hence not included in this table.

Prefixes (metric)	Number		Numerically	Mnemonic
G (**G**iga)	$= 10^9$	= billion	1,000,000,000	**g**ood
M (**M**ega)	$= 10^6$	= million	1,000,000	**m**others
k (**k**ilo)	$= 10^3$	= thousand	1,000	**k**indly
h (**h**ecto)	$= 10^2$	= hundred	100	**h**elp
da (**d**e**ca**)	$= 10^1$	= ten	10	**d**ads
d (**d**eci)	$= 10^{-1}$	= tenth = 1/10	0.1	**d**evelop
c (**c**enti)	$= 10^{-2}$	= hundredth = 1/100	0.01	**c**aring
m (**m**illi)	$= 10^{-3}$	= thousandth = 1/1000	0.001	**m**others
μ (**m**icro)	$= 10^{-6}$	= millionth = 1/1,000,000	0.000001	**u**nderstand
n (**n**ano)	$= 10^{-9}$	= billionth = 1/1,000,000,000	0.000000001	**n**eed

Table 3 **Common Metric Abbreviations Used in Ultrasound**

Note:

$G = 10^9 \Rightarrow$ reciprocal $= 1/10^9 = 10^{-9} = n$
$k = 10^3 \Rightarrow$ reciprocal $= 1/10^3 = 10^{-3} = m$
(The symbol $\Rightarrow$ means "implies")

> **KEY CONCEPT**
>
> Note that the metric table is based on reciprocals such that the reciprocal of giga is nano, the reciprocal of mega is micro, etc. Learning the table in terms of reciprocals makes conversions between frequencies and periods significantly easier.

You should note that some of the letters in this table come from the Greek alphabet. The use of Greek letters is common in physics and mathematics, perhaps because there are many more parameters that we need to measure than can be represented by 26 letters in the English alphabet. You should also note that these prefixes are "case sensitive." Being case sensitive means that a capital letter does not necessarily mean the same thing as a small (uncapitalized) letter. Note the difference between M which stands for mega and m which stands for milli. You must pay attention to the letter case, or your mathematics can be off by many factors of 10.

As already mentioned, these abbreviations are used to simplify writing numbers. Look at the following examples:

◊ *Example:*

3.2 M	represents	3,200,000
2.8 G	represents	2,800,000,000
1.9 m	represents	0.0019
23 m	represents	0.023

Note: Recall from the earlier section on exponential form that the exponent tells you how many places, and in which direction to move the decimal point.

The following two examples show how we can write out the abbreviated expressions in an unabbreviated form.

◊ *Example 1:*

$3.2\,M = 3.2 \times 10^6 \Rightarrow$ move decimal point 6 times to the right.

Step 1: *add decimal point if not already displayed*

Step 2: *add zeros as place holders*

$3.2\,M = 0003.200000000000....M$

Step 3: *replace prefix with meaning*

$3.20000000....M = 3.20000000 \times 10^6$

Step 4: *move decimal point*

$3.20000000....M = 3\,2\,0\,0\,0\,0\,0\,.0$
$1\,2\,3\,4\,5\,6$

(The +6 exponent indicates that the decimal point moves to the right 6 places)

Step 5: *add commas to make number readable*

Answer: *3,200,000.00*

◊ *Example 2:*

$27\,\mu = 27 \times 10^{-6}$

Step 1: *add decimal point if not already displayed*

$27.0\,\mu$

Step 2: *add zeros as place holders*

$27\,\mu = ...00000027.0000...\mu$

Step 3: *replace prefix with meaning*

$...00000027.0000..\mu = ...00000027.0000... \times 10^{-6}$

Step 4: *move decimal point*:

$0\,0\,0\,0\,0\,0\,2\,7.0000...$
$1\,2\,3\,4\,5\,6$

Answer: *0.000027*

9.3 Exercises: Metric Abbreviations

View ONLINE Exercises: Metric Abbreviations

9.4 Abbreviations: Physical Units

As with any field, it is cumbersome to have to deal with long names. Hence, a series of abbreviations have been developed to make communication easier. Of course, the communication only becomes easier when there is a fluent understanding of the abbreviations and their physical meanings. This understanding will be developed in the chapters within this book. For now, you need to begin the familiarization process.

Related to time:

P or T	Period (seconds)
PD	Pulse Duration (the time for which the transmit pulse lasts)
PRP	Pulse Repetition Period (the time to transmit and receive an acoustic line of data)
Frame time	The time required to build up a frame = the time per acoustic line multiplied by the total number of lines in the frame

Related to frequency:

f	Frequency (Hz)
f_o	Operating or transmit frequency of a transducer (for diagnostic ultrasound 2-20 MHz common)
PRF	Pulse Repetition Frequency = 1/PRP (typically less than 10 kHz)
Frame rate	The reciprocal of the frame time (typically less than 100 Hz)
Hz	Hertz = 1 cycle/second

Various parameters that have units of amplitude:

V	Volts: unit of electromotive force
m	Meters: unit of distance (metric system)
Z	Rayls: unit of acoustic impedance
R	Resistance, either electrical or to fluid flow
P	Pressure: mmHg, atm, dynes/cm², kg/m², etc.: unit of pressure (*not to be confused with P for period or P for power)

Related to power:

P	Power: units of Watts (*not to be confused with P for period or P for pressure)
W	Watts
I	Intensity = power/area = W/m² or W/cm²
dB	Decibels: a logarithmic power ratio

Related to distance:

d	distance (*not to be confused with D or d for diameter)
λ	Lambda: wavelength which has units of distance
SPL	Spatial Pulse Length
NZL	Near Zone Length, the distance from transducer face to the natural focus

Related to measure and circular dimensions:

ρ	Density = mass/volume : units of kg/m³
r	Radius of a circle: units of distance
d	Diameter of a circle = 2*radius: units of distance
A	Area: units of m²
Vol	Volume: units of m³
Q	Volumetric flow: units of volume per time, or m³/sec

Related to motion:

r	Rate: the general term usually used in the distance equation for the velocity. (*not to be confused with r for radius)
v	velocity of blood: units of m/sec
c	propagation speed of sound: units of m/sec

Related to hemodynamics:

P	Pressure: mmHg, atm, dynes/cm², kg/m², etc.,: units of pressure (*not to be confused with P for period or P for power)
ΔP	Pressure gradient (change in pressure = P1 – P2 where P2 is the distal pressure and P1 is the proximal pressure): units as above
Q	Volumetric flow: units of volume per time, or m³/sec
R	Resistance, either electrical or to fluid flow

Note: Caution must be used since many letters can stand for more than one physical quantity. Also, pay attention since in some cases a capitalized letter indicates a different parameter than a lower case letter.

9.5 Combining Abbreviations

In an effort to further simplify writing measurable quantities, abbreviations can be combined. Note that the metric prefix always come first, followed by the physical unit.

◊ **Example:** 27.3 mW = 27.3 milliWatts
= 27.3 x 10^{-3} Watts
= 0.0273 Watts

◊ **Example:** 4.3 cm = 4.3 centimeters
= 4.3 x 10^{-2} meters
= 0.043 meters

9.6 Exercises: Combining Abbreviations

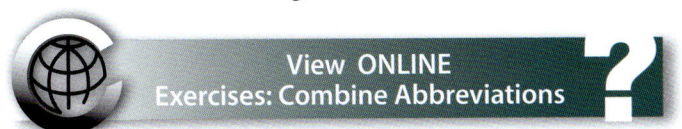

View ONLINE
Exercises: Combine Abbreviations

9.7 Reciprocals of Metric Units

As already mentioned, the metric table is developed using reciprocals, which facilitates performing mathematical calculations in your head. Consider the following problem:

What is the reciprocal of 10 MHz?

The reciprocal of 10 MHz is $\dfrac{1}{10 \text{ MHz}}$.

However, this is certainly not in the "simplest" form you would expect. Therefore, we would rewrite the answer as follows:

$$\frac{1}{10 \text{ MHz}} = \frac{1}{10} \cdot \frac{1}{M} \cdot \frac{1}{Hz} = 0.1 \cdot \mu \cdot \sec \quad (\text{or simply: } 0.1 \text{ μsec})$$

Note: By using the reciprocal relation of mega and micro, we were able to answer the question without expanding the mega into 10^6, performing division by 10^6, and then converting the answer back into units of microseconds, all the while running a very high probability of missing a decimal place somewhere in the process.

9.8 Exercises: Reciprocals of Metric Units

View ONLINE — Exercises: Reciprocals of Units

9.9 Converting Between Metric Units

Quite frequently, when you measure or calculate a physical quantity, the resulting number will be either very large or very small. In Section 8.1 and 8.2, we discussed the idea that although there is not necessarily a right or a wrong way of expressing numbers, in general, we prefer to write numbers in a way that makes them appear as simple as possible. For example, using the English system for distance, presume you calculated that the distance between your house and your work to be 10,560 feet. Although this may be the correct distance, the numeric part of the expression is so large, that it is difficult to imagine how far this really is. If you convert this distance in feet to miles (by knowing that there are 5,280 feet per mile), you arrive at the equivalent expression of the distance being 2 miles. Now although these two answers are equivalent, 2 miles certainly appears to be a more readily comprehendible form. Luckily, since in medicine and physics we use the metric system, your conversions will not be as complicated as dividing by numbers such as 5,280 as was needed in the above example.

Another reason why you frequently need to convert between units is that when you solve an equation, you must make sure that the units are consistent. Once the mathematical expression is written in terms of consistent units, the expression can usually be greatly simplified.

◊ **Example 1:** How many days will it take to run 1 Gm if you run 10 km per day?

$$\#\text{days} = \frac{\text{total distance}}{\text{distance per day}}$$

so

$$\#\text{days} = \frac{1 \text{ Gm}}{10 \text{ km/day}}$$

Converting Gm into km

$$1 \text{ Gm} = 1 \times 10^9 \text{ meters} = 1{,}000{,}000{,}000 \text{ meters}$$
$$= 1{,}000{,}000 \cdot \underline{10^3} \text{ meters}$$
$$= 1{,}000{,}000 \underline{\text{ k}} \text{ meters}$$

so # days $= \dfrac{1{,}000{,}000 \text{ km}}{10 \text{ km/day}}$

Answer: 100,000 days
or **100 · 10³ days**
or **100 k days**

◊ **Example 2:** 12 nsec = how many μsec?

$$12 \text{ nsec} = 12 \cdot 10^{-9} \text{ sec}$$
$$= 0.000000012 \text{ sec}$$
$$= 0.012 \cdot 10^{-6} \text{ sec}$$

Answer: 0.012 μsec

9.10 Conversions (a more intuitive approach)

Although the previous approach is mathematically clear, it is frequently a little bit daunting for many people. We can accomplish the same conversions by using the rules about mathematical relationships of proportionality and inverse proportionality that we have already learned.

Think of each measure of a physical quantity as consisting of two parts, a "numeric" part and the "units" part. (For example, 3 MHz has 3 as its numeric part and MHz as its units part.) If the goal is to convert an expression to having a different units part, then the numeric part must also change. Consider the following example:

Example: 12 donuts = ?? dozen

Let's start by comparing the units part. On the left side of the equation, the unit is a single donut. On the right side of the equation, the unit is a dozen. Since the unit (dozen) on the right side of the equation is larger than the corresponding unit (donuts) on the left side, the numeric (or quantity) on the left side must be larger than that on the right in order to balance the equation. This is graphically presented below using arrows:

12 donuts = ?? dozen

Because this is a non-metric example, we have to know that the conversion between dozens and donuts is 12 to 1, or that 12 donuts = 1 dozen.

With the metric system, this process is actually easier, as long as you know the metric table. Consider the following example:

◊ **Example 1:** How many meters are in 5.2 km?

Rewriting this mathematically we have: x m = 5.2 km

Comparing the units leads us to the following graphical representation:

$$x \,\uparrow \quad m \downarrow = 5.2 \quad km \uparrow$$

So we know that the number of meters in 5.2 km must be greater than 5.2 (which should make intuitive sense since a meter, m, is a shorter distance than a km). Now, assessing the prefix of the units, an m represents no decimal shifts (there is no prefix in front of the unit of meters) and a km represent 3 decimal shifts to the right. Therefore, there is a total of 3 decimal shifts between m and km. So the numerical part of the expression in front of m must be greater than 5.2 by 3 decimal point shifts or 5,200 m. This is shown graphically below:

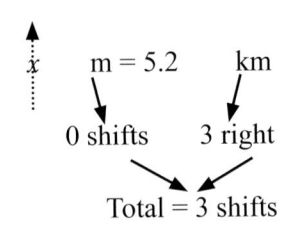

$$x \quad m = 5.2 \quad km$$
$$0 \text{ shifts} \quad 3 \text{ right}$$
$$\text{Total} = 3 \text{ shifts}$$

So starting with 5.2, you must move the decimal point 3 times making the number bigger or, 5,200.

Therefore, 5,200 m = 5.2 km.

◊ **Example 2:** How many centimeters are in 3.2 km?

Rewriting this mathematically we have: x cm = 3.2 km

Comparing the units leads us to the following graphical representation

$$x \,\uparrow \quad cm \downarrow = 3.2 \quad km \uparrow$$

So we know that the number of cm in 3.2 km must be greater than 3.2 (which should make intuitive sense since a cm is a short distance and a km is a long distance relatively speaking). Now, assessing the prefix of the units, a cm represents 2 decimal shifts to the left and a km represents 3 decimal shifts to the right. Since these decimal shifts are in opposite directions, there are a total of 5 decimal shifts between cm and km. Therefore, the numerical part of the expression in front of cm must be greater than 3.2 by 5 decimal point shifts or 320,000 cm. This is shown graphically as:

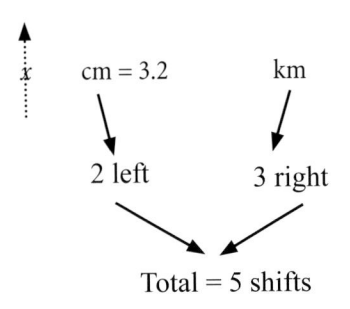

$$x \quad cm = 3.2 \quad km$$
$$2 \text{ left} \quad 3 \text{ right}$$
$$\text{Total} = 5 \text{ shifts}$$

So starting with 3.2, you must move the decimal point 5 times making the number bigger or, 320,000.

Therefore, 320,000 cm = 3.2 km.

◊ **Example 3:** How many MHz equal 600 kHz?

Rewriting this mathematically we have: x MHz = 600 kHz

Comparing the units leads us to the following graphical representation

$$x \,\uparrow \quad MHz \downarrow = 600 \quad kHz \uparrow$$

So we know that the number of MHz that is equivalent to 600 Hz must be less than 600 (which should make intuitive sense since a MHz is a bigger unit than a kHz). Now, assessing the prefix of the units, a MHz represents 6 decimal shifts to the right and a kHz represents 3 decimal shifts to the right. Since these decimal shifts are in the same direction, there are only 3 decimal shifts between MHz and kHz. Therefore, the numerical part of the expression in front of MHz must be smaller than 600 by 3 decimal point shifts or 0.600 MHz. This is shown graphically below:

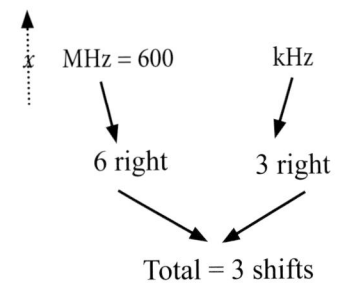

$$x \quad MHz = 600 \quad kHz$$
$$6 \text{ right} \quad 3 \text{ right}$$
$$\text{Total} = 3 \text{ shifts}$$

So starting with 600, you must move the decimal point 3 times making the number smaller or, 0.600.

Therefore 0.600 MHz = 600 kHz.

Note: Whenever you complete a conversion, you should always apply the "common sense" test; "does the answer calculated make physical sense?" For example, if you were measuring the length of a table, the number of centimeters in the length should be greater than the number of meters in the length.

View ONLINE Clarifying Clip

KEY CONCEPT

We grow up learning to perform conversions early in grade school where we first learn to convert inches to feet, feet to yards, etc. Conversion within the metric system is much easier (if you know your metric prefixes) as all conversions are performed by factors of 10 (unlike the English system in which you must memorize every conversion factor). If you apply common sense, conversions become much easier. For example there are many microseconds in a second, just as there is only a very small fraction of a kilometer in a centimeter.

9.11 Exercises: Conversions

View ONLINE Exercises: Conversions

9.12 Exercises: Using Exponents

View ONLINE Exercises: Using Exponents

10. Proportionality and Inverse Proportionality

10.1 Direct Proportionality

Proportionality is one of the most important concepts in learning to interpret equations and for applying mathematics. Proportionality is a general term which describes a relative relationship between two variables. There are two different types of proportional relationships described by mathematical equations: direct proportionality and inverse proportionality. When two variables are directly proportional, an increase in one variable results in an increase in the related variable. When two variables are inversely proportional, an increase in one variable results in a decrease in the related variable.

As with all languages (and mathematics clearly uses its own language) there are abbreviations and symbols used to shorten how we write frequently used terms. Just as the "=" sign stands for the concept of equivalence, the $\propto$ symbol is mathematical shorthand for the concept of proportionality.

> The symbol for proportionality is: $\propto$

In addition to the two types of proportionality (direct and inverse) there are different rates at which both of these types of relationships can change. The concept of how fast one variable changes with respect to a related changing variable is perhaps the most important mathematical concept you will learn. This concept is critical since it relates directly to understanding not only ultrasound physics, but also sound interactions within the human body, vision and hearing, disease processes, the compensatory mechanisms of the body in response to disease and other stresses, and much more. In this first section, we will deal with the simpler cases of when the power of the two related variables are equal, leading to a simple way of expressing the rate of change between the two related variables. In Level 2, the concept of unequal powers and the more complicated relationships will be introduced. As you will learn throughout ultrasound, understanding these relative relationships (especially the more complex, non-linear relationships) will be critical to providing high quality patient care and to passing your credentialing exams.

10.2 Direct Linear (Simple) Proportionality

This first example demonstrates direct linear proportionality. It is called a "linear" relationship because when you graph the two dependent variables against each other, the resulting plot is a straight line. When two variables have a linear relationship, a change of some percentage in one variable results in the exact same percentage change in the related variable.

For the purposes of this book, we will adopt the term simple proportionality to signify that the power of the two related variables are equal.

◊ *Example:* $y = 3 \cdot x \Rightarrow y$ is proportional to x.

Consider if: $x = 1 \Rightarrow y = 3 \cdot 1 = 3$

$x = 2 \Rightarrow y = 3 \cdot 2 = 6$

$x = 5 \Rightarrow y = 3 \cdot 5 = 15$

So as **x** increases, **y** increases.
Similarly as **x** decreases, **y** decreases.
Symbolically we write: $y \propto x$.

Also note that both x and y increase or decrease at the same rate.

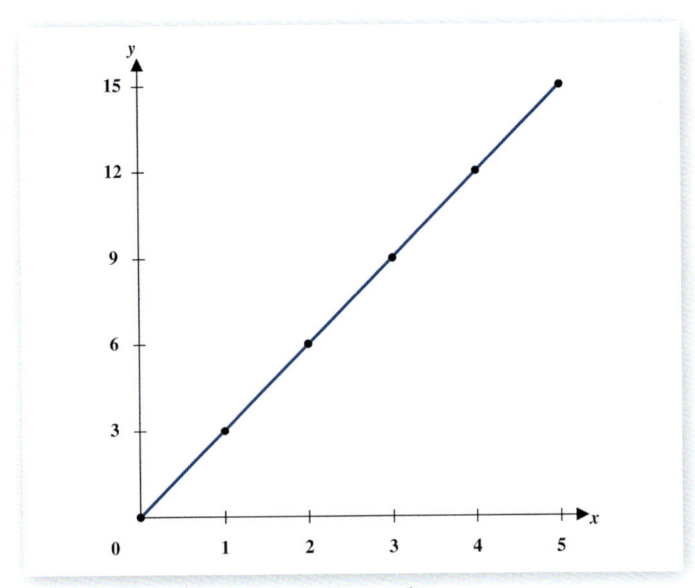

Fig. 3 **Linear proportional relationship**

In the real world, there are many examples of direct linear proportional relationships. For example, let's say that you work at a job where you are paid straight hourly rates (excluding overtime rates). If you double the number of hours you work, your pay will also double. If you decrease the number of hours you work by a factor of 13, your pay will also decrease by a factor of 13.

Another example of direct linear relationships is the relationship between time and distance traveled (assuming a fixed rate). For example, if you drive at a constant rate of 60 mph and you drive for triple the time, you will have traveled triple the distance.

10.3 Inverse (Simple) Proportionality

As the name suggests, inverse proportionality implies an "opposite" relationship between the two variables. In other words, when two variables are inversely related, an increase in one variable results in a decrease in the related variable. All inverse relationships are non-linear, implying that when you graph the relationship, the graph is not a straight line.

Again we will adopt the term simple inverse relationship to refer to any case where the powers of the two related variables are equal, and reserve discussion of the more complex cases when the powers are not equal for Level 2. Note that in the following example, the power for x and y is 1, and hence qualifies as a "simple" inverse relationship.

◊ **Example:** $y = 3/x \Rightarrow y$ is inversely proportional to x.

Consider if: $x = 1 \Rightarrow y = 3/1 = 3$
$x = 2 \Rightarrow y = 3/2 = 1.5$
$x = 5 \Rightarrow y = 3/5 = 0.6$

So an increase in x results in a decrease in y.
Similarly, a decrease in x results in an increase in y.

Note that stating "y is proportional to the inverse of x" is equivalent to stating "y is inversely proportional to x". Instead of creating a new symbol for inverse proportionality, we use the same proportional symbol and then we invert the variable.

$$x \propto \frac{1}{y} \quad \text{or} \quad y \propto \frac{1}{x}$$

With simple relationships, you can easily express the rate of change. For simple proportional relationships, an increase in one variable by a factor of x produces an increase in the related variable by a factor of x. For simple inverse relationships, an increase in one variable by a factor of x produces a corresponding decrease in the related variable by the same factor of x.

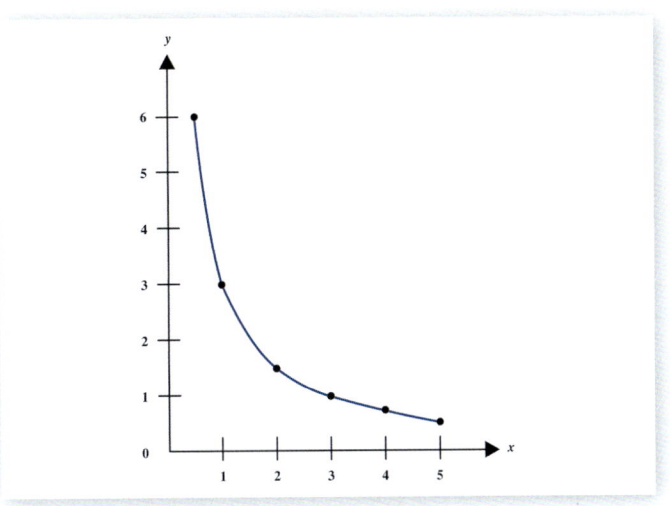

Fig. 4 **Inverse proportional relationship**

Note: The inverse operation of multiplication is division, just as the inverse of addition is subtraction. Therefore, multiplying by a reciprocal is exactly the same as division.

✓ **CHECKPOINT: Exam Tip**

Proportionality is a method of describing relationships in a relative way instead of an absolute way (as results within equations using the equal sign). When we specify how two variables are related, we do not necessarily know the values of the variables, but rather how the variables change with respect to each other. In medicine, many of the measurements made are relative and not absolute. For example we often will describe a specific measurement relative to the measurement from that patient from an earlier date, or relative to what is considered "normal." Many exam questions require the ability to describe and understand relative relationships.

10.4 Exercises: Proportionality and Inverse Proportionality

View ONLINE Exercises: Proportionality

11. Distance Equation

The distance equation is generally well understood, since we use it virtually every day to calculate driving times. The equation is:

$$\text{Distance} = \text{rate} \cdot \text{time}.$$

◊ **Example:**
How far can you drive in two hours at 60 mph?

$$60 \cdot \frac{\text{miles}}{\text{hr}} \cdot 2\ \text{hr} = 120\ \text{miles}$$

◊ **Example:**
How far can you drive in two hours at 60 km/h?

$$60 \cdot \frac{\text{km}}{\text{hr}} \cdot 2\ \text{hr} = 120\ \text{km}$$

◊ **Example:**
How long will it take to drive 200 km if the speed limit is 100 km/h?

$$d = r * t$$

rewriting the equation for time yields:

$$t = \frac{d}{r}$$

$$t = \frac{200\ \text{km}}{100\ \frac{\text{km}}{\text{hr}}}$$

$$t = 2\ \text{hr}$$

The same distance equation we use to calculate driving times is equally applicable to traveling ultrasound waves. Let's presume that ultrasound travels at a rate of 1540 m/sec in the body. Knowing that rate, we can easily calculate the time it will take sound to travel whatever distance required in the body. Consider the following problem:

How long would it take sound to travel 1 cm in the body?

Start by writing out the information given to solve the problem.

$$d = 1\ \text{cm}$$
$$r = 1540\ \frac{\text{m}}{\text{sec}}$$
$$t = ?$$

Next, write out the equation needed to solve the problem.

$$d = r \times t$$

Then, rewrite the equation so that it is written in the form required.

$$\frac{d}{r} = t \quad \text{(result from dividing both sides by "r" to get "t" alone)}$$

Now plug in the numbers to solve the equation.

$$\frac{1\ \text{cm}}{1540\ \frac{\text{m}}{\text{sec}}} = \frac{0.01\ \text{m}}{1540\ \frac{\text{m}}{\text{sec}}} \quad \text{(convert to consistent units and cancel out)}$$

$$= \frac{0.01\ \text{sec}}{1540} = .00000649\ \text{sec} \approx 6.5 \times 10^{-6}\ \text{sec} = 6.5\ \mu\text{sec}$$

Note: The unit of seconds is "under" two reciprocal bars and hence is equivalent to the unit of seconds being on the top of the expression.

How long would it take sound to travel 2 cm in the body?

From the equation, we know that the relationship between time and distance is direct proportionality. Therefore, if the distance traveled is doubled, the time is doubled, equal to 13 μsec.

It is very useful to remember the results of this calculation. As we will discuss in Chapter 2, we generally presume that the propagation speed of sound in the body is approximately 1540 m/sec. Since we know that the relationship between distance and time is linearly proportional, and if we remember the 6.5 μsec travel time per cm, we can always just scale this number to any distance required.

In Level 2 (Section 13.1), we will also stress a very important fact about how ultrasound imaging is performed. With ultrasound, sound is transmitted into the body and then the reflected signal is received. This means that if we want to image (view) a structure at a depth of 10 cm, the total travel for the ultrasound beam is not 10 cm, but rather 20 cm. This factor of 2, often referred to as the "roundtrip effect" must be taken into account when calculating real world ultrasound problems.

11.1 Exercises: Distance Equation

View ONLINE Exercises: Distance Equation

12. Math Terminology

12.1 The Language of Mathematics: Translating English into Mathematics

Perhaps the greatest difficulty is not mastering the mathematical concepts, but rather learning how to interpret the math from language used to express the question. There are many terms commonly used which always, or nearly always, indicate the same mathematical function. If you are unfamiliar with the translation of these terms, it will always be difficult to answer a mathematically based question.

Below are some examples used to illustrate the English form of what are really mathematical expressions.

◊ *Example 1:* By what factor does the distance you travel increase, if your speed of traveling doubles?

◊ *Example 2:* What is ten percent of the number 354?

◊ *Example 3:* What is ten percent less than the number 354?

◊ *Example 4:* Assuming you are paid hourly, what happens to your pay if your working hours are reduced by a factor of four?

◊ *Example 5:* If you are paid $200 a week, and the tax is 25% of your pay, how much spending money do you have per week?

12.2 Mathematical Definition

So as to learn how to translate the English words into mathematical form, we will start with a simple list of definitions.

Factor:	implies multiplication (and division)
Increase:	to become larger
Decrease:	to become smaller
Reduce:	decreased, to become smaller
Less:	subtraction
More:	addition
Percent:	a fraction written relative to 100 representing the whole, or 1
Of:	multiplication (and division)
Reciprocal:	inverted, the opposite
Doubles:	increased by a factor of 2 (multiply by 2)
Halves:	decreased by a factor of 2 (divide by 2)
Quadruples:	increase by a factor of 4 (multiply by 4)
Quarters:	decrease by a factor of 4 (divide by 4)

This above list generally seems quite simple until multiple terms are used together. The following table puts some of the definitions together in the ways in which they are commonly combined.

Common Combined Term	Meaning
increased by a factor of x	multiplied by x
decreased by a factor of x	divided by x
reduced by a factor of x	divided by x
x percent of y	multiply y by $x/100$
x percent less than y	multiply y by $x/100$ and then subtract the resulting value from y
x percent more than y	multiply y by $x/100$ and then add the resulting value to y
reciprocal of x	$1/x$

Table 4 **Common Combinations of Mathematical Definitions**

Using these definitions, let's review the previous examples.

◊ *Example 1:* By what factor does the distance you travel increase if your speed of traveling doubles?

Since the distance traveled is directly related to the speed at which you travel, doubling the speed doubles the distance traveled. From our definitions, we know that doubling the distance is the same as saying that the distance increased by a factor of 2. Since the question asks for the factor of increase, the answer is 2.

◊ *Example 2:* What is ten percent of the number 354?

Recall that the term "percent of" implies multiplication. Since percent represents a fraction written relative to the number 100, ten percent = 10/100 = 1/10. So multiplying 354 by 1/10 yields 354/10 = 35.4.

◊ *Example 3:* What is ten percent less than the number 354?

In Example 2 we calculated ten percent of 354. Notice that this question includes one more step. This question asks for ten percent less than 354. Since less implies subtraction, we need to subtract the ten percent of 354 from the number 354, or 354 − 35.4 = 318.6.

You should note that this question is really the same as asking what is ninety percent of the number 354. In other words, if you take away 10% of a number, what you have left is 90% of that number. To show this fact, let's perform the calculation.

Ninety percent = $\frac{90}{100} = \frac{9}{10} = 0.9$. So multiplying 354 by 0.9 = 318.6.

Hence the same answer is achieved either way the problem is solved.

Note: We have just seen how the same question can be asked in a reciprocal manner. Ten percent reduction is the same as asking for ninety percent. The ability to recognize reciprocals in a question is critical to passing the credentialing exams.

◊ **Example 4:** Assuming you are paid hourly, what happens to your pay if your working hours are reduced by a factor of four?

From the definitions, being "reduced by a factor of four" means divided by four. Since your pay is directly related to your working hours if you are paid hourly, reducing your hours by a factor of four means that your pay is also reduced by a factor of four, which is the same as saying that your pay is quartered, or that you receive only one fourth, or 25% of your original pay.

◊ **Example 5:** If you are paid $200 a week, and the tax is 25% of your pay, how much spending money do you have per week?

To answer the question you must understand that a tax implies that the money is taken away, or subtracted. In other words, you have to subtract 25% of the $200 you earn. First we must calculate 25% of 200. Since 25% = 25/100 = ¼ = 0.25, 25% of 200 = 200 multiplied by 0.25 = 50. So the tax is $50, and you get to spend $200 - $50 = $150.

You should also note that taking away 25% of the $200 is the same as leaving 75% of the $200. (These are reciprocal ways of stating the same information.) So this problem can also be solved by multiplying $200 by 0.75 = $150. Hopefully you are starting to realize that recognizing reciprocals can often simplify your life.

KEY CONCEPT

The ability to understand physics in general, and many of the test questions specifically, is related to your ability to understand math terminology. You should be able to convert back and forth between the terminology used and the mathematical equivalence.

12.3 Exercises: Math Terminology

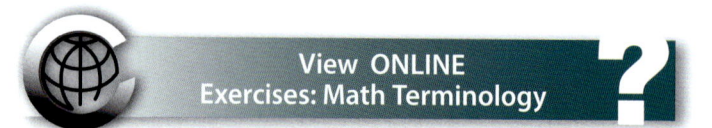

View ONLINE Exercises: Math Terminology

LEVEL 2: Board Level

13. Distance Equation Revisited

In Level 1, the general equation for distance was given and discussed both in terms of a traveling car and sound traveling in the body. For sound propagating in the body, we calculated that sound would require 6.5 μsec to travel 1 cm, presuming the propagation velocity of 1540 m/sec. With respect to diagnostic ultrasound, we must now consider two other points.

1) For imaging, the sound must travel into and back out of the body (roundtrip effect).
2) The propagation velocity might not always be the presumed 1540 m/sec.

13.1 The Roundtrip Effect

For medical imaging there are two fundamental modes which can be used, transmission mode, or reflection mode. A transmission modality is like x-ray, where the x-rays are transmitted through a patient and the change in transmission properties are recorded on film. In comparison, diagnostic ultrasound is a reflected modality, where sound is transmitted into the patient, and changes to the reflected beam are received and processed. The fact that ultrasound is a reflective mode dictates that the sound must travel twice as far as the distance to the structures we desire to image. This factor of 2 in flight (travel) time and flight path is referred to as the roundtrip effect. This effect is pictured below.

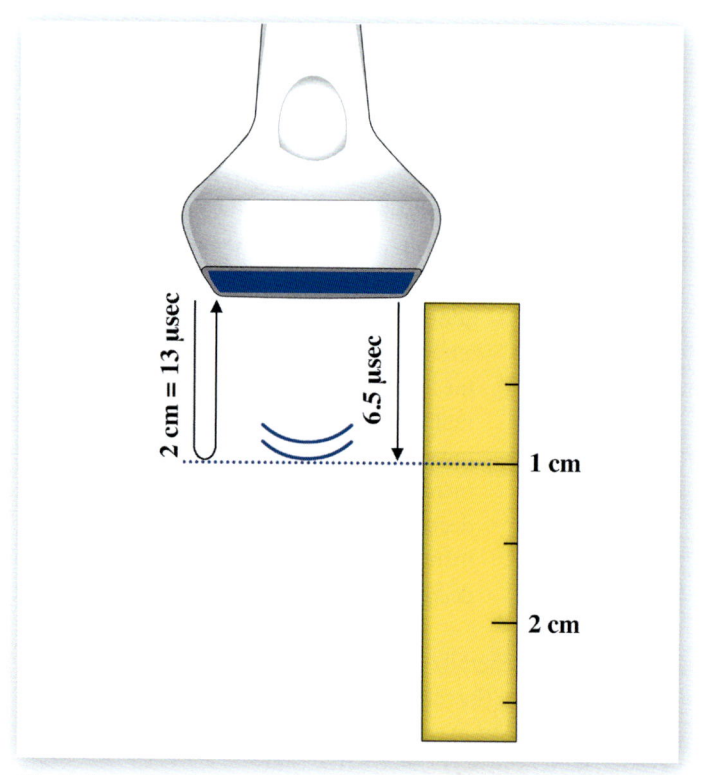

Fig. 5 **Imaging 1 cm requires 13 μsec**

When we refer to imaging depth in ultrasound, we are speaking about the actual depth within the patient, not the total distance the sound beam must travel. Therefore, if the imaging depth is 2 cm, the total distance traveled by the ultrasound beam will be 4 cm. Similarly, if the imaging depth is 12 cm, then the total distance traveled by the ultrasound beam will be 24 cm. The calculation of 6.5 µsec per cm of travel still holds true assuming the propagation speed of 1540 m/sec. However, when the transit time for a sound beam is calculated, you must always pay attention to the wording of the question, paying particular attention as to whether or not you need to include the roundtrip effect. The table below illustrates this principle:

Imaging depth	Total distance	Time
0.5 cm	1 cm	6.5 µsec
1 cm	2 cm	13 µsec
2 cm	4 cm	26 µsec
3 cm	6 cm	39 µsec
4 cm	8 cm	52 µsec
5 cm	10 cm	65 µsec
8 cm	16 cm	104 µsec
10 cm	20 cm	130 µsec
15 cm	30 cm	195 µsec

Table 5 **Propagation Times in the Body Assuming 1540 m/sec**

From this table, it should be clear that you have two choices. You can choose to remember the 6.5 µsec per cm of travel and then multiply by the total travel distance, or you can choose to remember the 13 µsec per cm of imaging depth and then multiply by the imaging depth instead. Obviously, these two methods are equivalent, but you must always make certain that you are interpreting the wording correctly so as not to be incorrect by a factor of two in your calculations:

The following examples should clarify this point for you.

◊ **Example 1:** How long does it take ultrasound to travel a distance of 3 cm in the body?

Since the question says "travel a distance of", the total travel distance is 3 cm. Since it takes 6.5 µsec per cm of travel, the total time would be 3 times 6.5 µsec, or 19.5 µsec.

◊ **Example 2:** How long does it take ultrasound to image to a depth of 3 cm in the body?

Since the question says "image to a depth of 3 cm", the total distance traveled is 6 cm. Since it takes 6.5 µsec per cm of travel, the total time would be 6 times 6.5 µsec, or 39 µsec. Note that the same answer can be achieved by using 13 µsec per cm of imaging depth and multiplying by 3 cm, yielding the same answer of 39 µsec.

◊ **Example 3:** How long does it take ultrasound to travel down and back to a structure of 10 cm deep in the body?

Since the question says down and back to a structure 10 cm, the total distance traveled is 20 cm. Since it takes 6.5 µsec per cm of travel, the total time would be 20 times 6.5 µsec, or 130 µsec. Equivalently, using the imaging depth of 10 cm multiplied by 13 µsec, the same answer of 130 µsec is achieved.

13.2 When the Propagation Velocity of 1540 m/sec is Incorrect

As you will learn in Chapter 2, the speed of sound is not always 1540 m/sec. How fast sound travels is a function of various properties of the medium. If the speed of sound is not 1540 m/sec, you cannot use the pre-calculated rate of 6.5 µsec per cm of distance or 13 µsec per cm of imaging depth. Instead, you will need to use the distance equation and perform the calculation using the actual speed of sound for the medium in question.

◊ **Example 1:** If the speed of sound in air is 331 m/sec, how long will it take sound to travel 331 m?

$$c = 331 \, \frac{m}{sec}$$

$$d = 331 \, m$$

$$t = ?$$

Rewrite the distance equation in terms of time,

or: $t = \dfrac{d}{r}$.

Plug the values given into the equation:

$$t = \frac{331 \, m}{331 \, \frac{m}{sec}} = 1 \, sec.$$

◊ **Example 2:** If the speed of sound in a medium is 1,000 m/sec, how long will it take sound to travel 420 m?

$$c = 1,000$$

$$d = 420 \, m$$

$$t = ?$$

Rewrite the distance equation in terms of time,

or: $t = \dfrac{d}{r}$.

Plug the values given into the equation:

$$t = \dfrac{420 \text{ m}}{1{,}000 \dfrac{\text{m}}{\text{sec}}} = 0.42 \text{ sec.}$$

If you assume a propagation speed that is incorrect, obviously, the calculated time will also be incorrect. This error occurs quite frequently in diagnostic ultrasound. The ultrasound system is designed to always presume a propagation velocity of 1540 m/sec. However, the propagation velocity can certainly vary within the body. As a result of this incorrect time estimate, the system will sometimes portray structures in a deeper or shallower location than reality. This error is referred to as speed error. Differences in propagation velocity from the assumed 1540 m/sec will be discussed in Chapter 2 and speed error will be discussed in more detail in Chapter 8. For now, it is important that you make sure you can calculate the distance equation correctly for various propagation velocities and various imaging depths.

KEY CONCEPT

The distance equation is the foundation of ultrasound imaging. By applying the distance equation with an assumed speed of sound in the body, we can determine the origin of echoes, and hence present depth information in our ultrasound images. When the speed of sound is 1540 m/sec, sound requires 6.5 microseconds to travel 1 cm, or 13 microseconds to travel 2 cm (which is equivalent to imaging 1 cm).

13.3 Exercises: Distance Equation Revisited

View ONLINE
Exercises: Distance Revisited

14. Non-Linear Relationships

In Level 1 (Section 10.1) we discussed simple relative relationships between variables. In these cases, the powers of the related variables were always the same and always equal to 1. You will also note that only the operations of multiplication and division were expressed in the equations, never addition and subtraction. As a result, we were able to simply express that a change in one variable by a factor of x produced a corresponding change in the related variable by the same factor of x. When the relationship was proportional, then both variables increased and decreased together. When the relationship was inversely related, the variables changed in inverse directions.

We now must discuss more complex relationships where the powers of the related variables are not always equal and not always equal to 1. As mentioned in Level 1, understanding and interpreting these more complex relationships will be the most important mathematical tool you will develop both for taking the exam and for truly understanding how ultrasound behaves in predicting the body's response to disease. As you progress through this book, you will learn that many of the equations which dictate the behavior of ultrasound and the behavior of the body with respect to disease will behave in these complex non-linear fashions.

14.1 Direct Non-Linear Proportionality

As discussed in Section 10.1, the word 'direct' implies that both related variables change in the same direction, or an increase in one variable produces an increase in the related variable, and a decrease in one variable produces a decrease in the related variable. Quite frequently, the word direct is dropped and just assumed, so that the word direct is implied in the expression non-linear proportionality. In these complex cases where the powers of the two related variables are not equal, a change in one variable will produce a more significant change in the related variable. Unlike the simple case discussed in Section 10.2, a change in one variable by a factor of x produces a bigger change in the related variable than a factor of x. The following example demonstrates a non-linear proportionality.

◊ *Example:*
$y = 3 \cdot x^2 \Rightarrow y$ is proportional to x^2
(Recall that the symbol ($\Rightarrow$) means "implies")
If $\quad x = 1 \quad \Rightarrow \quad y = 3 \cdot (1)^2 = 3$
$\quad\quad x = 2 \quad \Rightarrow \quad y = 3 \cdot (2)^2 = 12$
$\quad\quad x = 5 \quad \Rightarrow \quad y = 3 \cdot (5)^2 = 75$

So an increase in x, results in a greater increase in y. Similarly, a decrease in x results in a greater decrease in y, or $y \,\alpha\, x^2$.

Note that for this example, a change in x by a factor of 2 results in a change in y by a factor of 2^2, or 4, clearly a non-linear relationship.

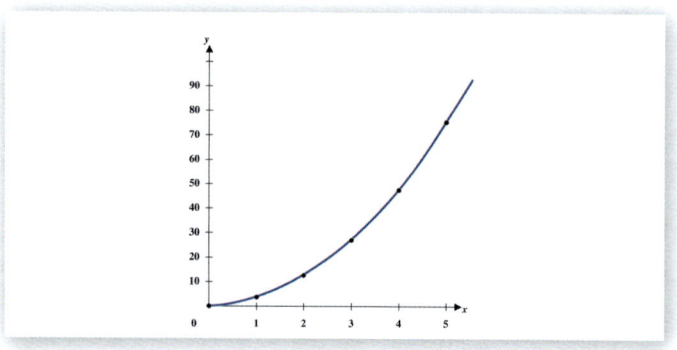

Fig. 6 $\;\mathbf{y = 3x^2}$

14.2 Complex - Inverse Proportionality

As mentioned in Section 10.3, all inverse relationships are non-linear. However, when the powers of the two variables are not equal and are not equal to one, then a much more complex non-linear relationship results. In the simple case when the powers are equal and equal to 1, an increase in one variable by a factor of x produces a corresponding decrease in the related variable by the same factor of x (and vice versa). For more complex inverse relationships, a change in one variable by a factor of x will produce a corresponding change in the opposite direction not by the same factor of x, but by a power of that factor x. In other words, small changes in one variable produce significantly greater changes in the related variable.

◊ **Example:** $y = 3/x^2 \Rightarrow y$ is inversely proportional to x^2.
If $\quad x = 1 \quad \Rightarrow \quad y = 3/1^2 = 3$
$\quad\quad x = 2 \quad \Rightarrow \quad y = 3/2^2 = 3/4$
$\quad\quad x = 5 \quad \Rightarrow \quad y = 3/5^2 = 3/25$

So if x increases a small amount, y decreases a much larger amount or $y \propto 1/x^2$

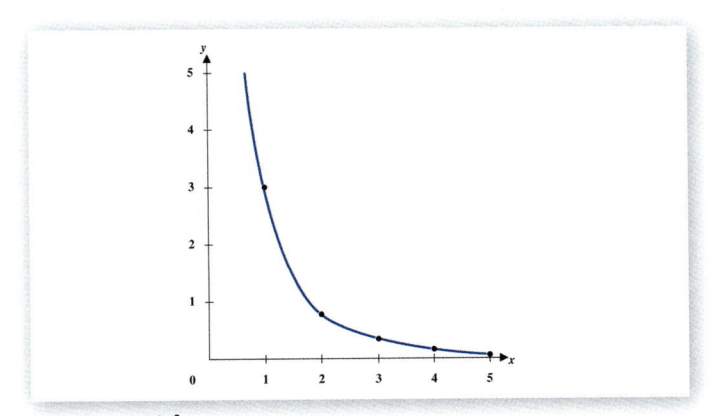

Fig. 7 **y = 3/x²**

15. Interpreting Relationships Within Linear and Non-Linear Equations

Remember that these mathematical concepts are powerful tools when understood well enough to be applied. In this section, we will develop the skills necessary to apply these concepts to general equations. We will start off with simple equations and work our way toward seemingly more complex equations. However, since the concepts to be applied are always the same, once you have adequate exposure and experience in these concepts, even more complex appearing equations will not present any greater challenge than apparently simple equations.

15.1 Assessing an Equation and Expressing the Relative Relationship

We have already seen that within an equation if two variables are in the numerator on opposite sides of the equal sign, that the variables are directly related. We have also seen that when two variables are on opposite sides of the equal sign, but one is in the numerator and the other is in the denominator, that the variables are inversely related. When the power is not equal to 1, all we have to do is keep the power with the variable to express the relative relation. Take for example the following equation:

$$g = \frac{h^2 d^3}{z}$$

From this equation we know that:

$$g \propto h^2$$
$$g \propto d^3$$
$$g \propto \frac{1}{z}$$

Determining the Dominance of the Variables

Although this sounds complicated, it is nothing more than looking at the powers of each of the variables and ranking them from largest to smallest. Higher powers imply greater dominance. Again consider the previous equation. In that equation the variable "d" has the highest power, followed by "h", and then by "z".

The value of knowing the dominance of variables is that you now have a way of assessing which variable has the greatest impact on the related variable (in this case the variable g).

Consider what would happen to the variable g, if h were doubled.

since $g \propto h^2 \Rightarrow$ a factor of 2 change in h results in a 2^2 change in g, or a factor of 4.

Consider what would happen to the variable g, if d were doubled.

since $g \propto d^3 \Rightarrow$ a factor of 2 change in d results in a 2^3 change in g, or a factor of 8.

Consider what would happen to the variable g, if z were doubled.

since $g \propto \frac{1}{z} \Rightarrow$ a factor of 2 change in z results in an inverse change in g by a factor of 2, or a factor of 0.5.

Clearly, very small changes in d result in very large changes in the related variable g, for this equation. Hence, d is the dominant variable.

> **KEY CONCEPT**
>
> Many of the relationships related to ultrasound physics, imaging, and interpretation are non-linear. Non-linear relationships imply that small changes in one variable can result in much more dramatic changes in the related variable. Whenever you are assessing a parameter that has a non-linear relationship, you should exercise increased caution.

Discussing Relative Changes

We have now arrived at the point in our mathematical review which is the crux of whether an individual passes the physics exam or does not. Not surprisingly, we are also at the point in our mathematical understanding of determining if an individual will be able to relate the physics equations with what is experienced in the world. Given an equation, and assessing the equation for relationships, it is now possible to determine how changes in one variable will influence a related variable. In case this point doesn't sound too important to you, consider that the value of an equation is its ability to predict how physical parameters will behave in the world. Quite frequently, we cannot directly measure the physical parameter that has the greatest importance to the well being of the patient. But we may be able to measure a parameter that is mathematically related to the parameter we really need to know and quantify. For example, let's say that you really want to determine how much blood flow occurs, but all you can measure is the size and shape of the vessel or blood flow path. If you have an equation that predicts how blood flow will change with changes in the vessel flow path, by measuring the vessel flow path, you can now predict what will happen hemodynamically to your patient.

Of course, this last step requires that you actually understand what the equation means, how the parameter that you measured relates to the parameter you really want to assess, and if there are any other parameters that have not been accounted for in your equation.

Perhaps the best way to determine if you understand how to assess relative changes between related variables is to try some practice questions.

15.2 Exercises: Assessing an Equation

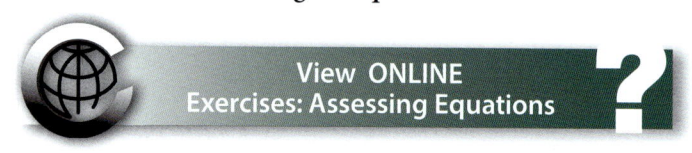

View ONLINE Exercises: Assessing Equations

15.3 Exercises: Proportionality

View ONLINE Exercises: Proportionality (Level 2)

CHECKPOINT: Exam Tip

The concepts taught in this section will be tested very heavily on the exam. In the introduction to this chapter, it was stressed that although you would not have to perform intensive math calculations, you would be expected to determine and express the mathematical relationships between variables. Of course, on your boards they will not be worded "What is the mathematical relationship between the wavelength of an ultrasound wave and the frequency of the ultrasound wave?" Instead, you will be asked hypotheticals such as "How would the wavelength change if you changed your imaging transducer from a 3 MHz to a 6 MHz operating frequency?"

16. Dealing with Percentage Change

16.1 Simple Calculations with Proportional Variables

For a variable that has changed, calculating a percentage change is performed by subtracting the old value of the variable (before the change) from the new value of the variable (after the change) and then dividing by the old value, or:

$$\% \text{ Change} = \frac{(\text{new value} - \text{old value})}{\text{old value}} \times 100\%.$$

◊ **Example 1:** By what percentage has the price of gas increased if the price changed from $2 per gallon to $2.50 per gallon?

$$\% \text{ Change gas price} = \frac{(\$2.50 - \$2.00)}{\$2.00} \times 100\% = \frac{0.50}{2.00} = \frac{0.25}{1.00} = .25 \text{ or } 25\%.$$

◊ **Example 2:** By what percentage has the cross-sectional area of a vessel changed if originally it was 1.0 cm^2 and with disease it became 0.8 cm^2?

$$\% \text{ Change vessel area} = \frac{(0.8 \text{ cm}^2 - 1.0 \text{ cm}^2)}{1.0 \text{ cm}^2} \times 100\% = \frac{-0.2}{1} = -.2 \text{ or } -20\%.$$

16.2 Calculations with Non-linearly Related Variables

Quite frequently, we are required to measure the change in a parameter over time and then express the percentage change in a non-linearly related variable. For example, you might measure the radius of a vessel at a first and follow up visit, and then express the percentage change in cross-sectional area or volume. Since the area and the volume are non-linearly related to the radius, the rate of change in the area term and volume term will be greater than the rate of change in the measured radius.

The following general rules will work for all problems in which a percentage change must be calculated from a measured parameter. As such, this approach is much better than trying to memorize certain relationships.

16.3 Rules for Dealing with Percentage Change

1. Express the percentage change in the measured variable as a fraction (always new value in terms of old value).
2. Write the mathematical relationship between the related variables.
3. Apply the mathematical relationship to the fraction from step 1.
4. Convert the fraction back into a percentage.
5. Most importantly, watch out for reciprocals in the question.

16.4 Examples

The best way to solidify this percentage change concept is to see these steps applied in a few examples:

◊ **Example 1:** If the radius of a vessel is reduced by 10%, what is the percentage residual cross-sectional area?

We will solve this problem by following the steps as listed above.

Step 1: $r_{new} = \frac{9}{10} r_{old}$ (always write new in terms of old)

Note: A 10% reduction in radius implies a 90% residual radius. Since we always write the new parameter in terms of the old parameter, we convert 90% to a fraction, not the 10%.

Step 2: area $\propto r^2$

Step 3: $area_{new} \propto r_{new}^2 = \left(\frac{9}{10} r_{old}\right)^2 = \frac{81}{100}(r_{old})^2$

Step 4: $\frac{81}{100}(r_{old})^2 = 81\%$ of original (old area).

Therefore, the residual area with a 10% reduction in radius is 81%. As you can see, the non-linear relationship between radius and area results in a faster change in area than in radius.

Note: Since the calculation results in the new area as a percentage of the old (residual area) there is no step 5 to perform. Compare this example carefully with the next example.

◊ **Example 2:** If the radius of a vessel is reduced by 10%, what is the percentage decrease in area?

Step 1: $r_{new} = \frac{9}{10} r_{old}$ (always write new in terms of old)

Step 2: area $\propto r^2$

Step 3: $area_{new} \propto r_{new}^2 = \left(\frac{9}{10} r_{old}\right)^2 = \frac{81}{100}(r_{old})^2$

Step 4: $\frac{81}{100}(r_{old})^2 = 81\%$ of original (old area).

Step 5: 100% - 81% = 19%.

Notice that this problem is really just the reciprocal of the first example. The most common mistake students make performing these calculations is ignoring the terminology which indicates a reciprocal calculation. In Example 2, the first clause of the problem did not change, but the second clause was the reciprocal of the second clause of Example 1.

◊ **Example 3:** If the residual vessel radius is 10%, what is the percentage residual area?

Step 1: $r_{new} = \frac{1}{10} r_{old}$ (always write new in terms of old)

Note: This problem gives the residual radius as 10%. Since the residual is an expression of the new in terms of the old already, no reciprocal is necessary in this step as was necessary in Example 1 and Example 2.

Step 2: area $\propto r^2$

Step 3: $area_{new} \propto r_{new}^2 = \left(\frac{1}{10} r_{old}\right)^2 = \frac{1}{100}(r_{old})^2$

Step 4: $\frac{1}{100}(r_{old})^2 = 1\%$ of original (old) area.

Note: Since the calculation results in the new area as a percentage of the old (residual area) there is no step 5 to perform. Compare this example with Example 4.

◊ **Example 4:** If the residual vessel radius is 10%, what is the percentage decrease in area?

Now that we can recognize reciprocals in questions, it should be clear that this question is just the reciprocal of the previous example. Therefore, the first four steps are as just performed in Example 3, and all that is necessary is to calculate the change in area as the reciprocal of the residual area, or:

Step 5: 100% - 1% = 99%

KEY CONCEPT

When dealing with percentage change there are two important points to recall:

- the percentage change always uses the prior state, or "old," as the reference (what the patient is like today relative to a previous measurement)
- always convert percentages into fractions before performing calculations (to minimize the chance of error in your calculation)

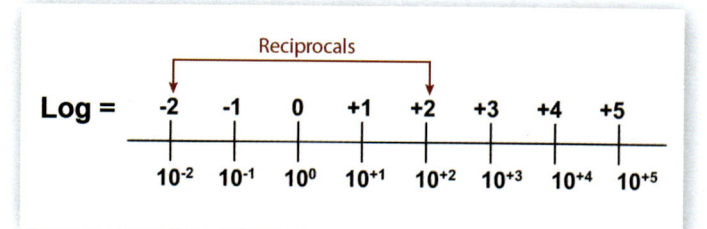

Fig. 8 **Visualizing and understanding logarithms**

From the graphic representation of base 10 logarithms in *Figure 8*, it should become clear that solving the logarithm of any power of 10 is the same as expressing the power to which 10 is raised. For example, the log of 100 is 2 since 10 raised to the second power is 100. The log of one tenth is -1 since 10 raised to the -1 power is one tenth. The log of 10,000 is 4 since $10^4 = 10,000$.

17. Logarithms

Logarithms are an extremely powerful non-linear mathematical tool. Logarithms are particularly useful as a mathematical method to deal with relatively large numbers and relatively small numbers simultaneously.

Effectively, logarithms provide a mechanism to compress a large range of numbers into a smaller range. This functionality is critical in ultrasound since the range of signal amplitudes which are reflected from the body (the signal dynamic range) is enormous, especially relative to the range which can be displayed by a monitor and the range which can be interpreted by the human eye.

Logarithms are defined as the power to which a base must be raised to get the desired number. The following examples demonstrate how to mathematically solve a logarithm.

◊ *Example:*
$\log_{10}(x) = 3 \Rightarrow 10^3 = x \Rightarrow x = 10 \cdot 10 \cdot 10 = 1{,}000$
Note: think circle when solving logarithms

$\log_{10} x = 3 \Rightarrow 10^3 = x$

◊ *Example:*
$\log_{10}(100) = x \Rightarrow 10^x = 100$, since $100 = 10^2$

$10^x = 10^2$
or $x = 2$

Note: If no base is given, the base of 10 is assumed $\Rightarrow (\log x = 2) = \log_{10}(x) = 2$.

As expressed in the first paragraph of this section, logarithms are really a non-linear compression scheme to help us deal with large ranges of numbers or data. When we graph data logarithmically, the logarithm of the data point is an indication of how much the data has been compressed to be displayed on that particular graph. For example, on a logarithmic graph, the number 100 has been compressed by 2 factors of 10 to be displayed. Similarly, the number 1,000 represents 3 "orders" of compression. Having studied reciprocals, we can now simply state that since a positive logarithm represents a compression of data, a negative logarithm must represent a decompression of data. Therefore, if a factor of 100 is 2 orders of compression, a factor of 1/100 represents 2 orders of decompression.

There is one logarithm you must memorize: the log (2) = 0.3. Knowing the logarithm of 2, as well as being able to solve for the log of any power of ten, will allow you to solve virtually any logarithm. This concept will become clear in the next section as we learn some nice properties associated with logarithms.

$$\log_{10}(2) = 0.3$$

Although you have to memorize the fact that the log of 2 is 0.3, we can show graphically why this logarithm should make sense.

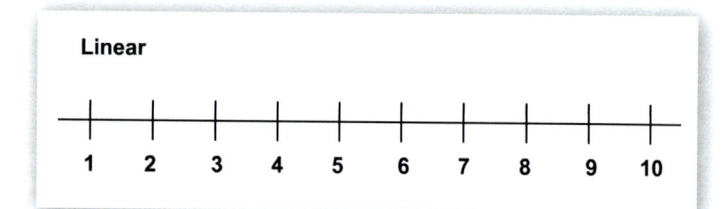

Fig. 9 **Linear scale**

Compare the graph from 1 to 10 above (*Figure 9*) with the graph of the same range (from 1 to 10) below (*Figure 10*). The graph above is a linear graph. Notice how the spacing between numbers remains fixed, so that a number twice as big will be twice as far up on the graph. In comparison, the logarithmic graph presents each successive number closer to the previous number, indicating increasing compression with greater numbers. Clearly, if you double the number, you do not double the distance on the graph (a non-linear mapping).

You should also notice that the number 2 is a little less than a third of the way from the number 1 toward the number 10. This shows graphically why the log of 2 is 0.3.

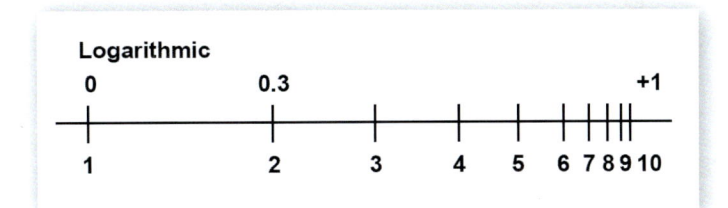

Fig. 10 **Log scale and the log of 2**

17.1 Properties of Logarithms

One of the reasons why logarithms are a very powerful tool in mathematics is that logarithms convert multiplication into addition and division into subtraction.

$$\log(x*y) = \log(x) + \log(y)$$

and

$$\log\left(\frac{x}{y}\right) = \log(x) - \log(y)$$

This mathematical relationship should make sense to you. Since a logarithm is a compression scheme, compressing data by a factor of "x" times "y" is the same as compressing the data by a factor of x and then by a factor of "y." Again, recall that multiplication and division are inverse operations, so if logarithms convert multiplication into addition, it should be intuitive that logarithms convert division into subtraction. Note that the first example below is given to demonstrate why this mathematical relationship "makes sense." The next three examples demonstrate how this information can be used to calculate many logarithms that are not powers of 10. This is one of the reasons you memorized that the $\log(2) = 0.3$.

◊ *Example 1:*

$$\log_{10}(1000) = \log_{10}(10 * 100) = \log_{10}(10) + \log_{10}(100) = 1 + 2 = 3$$

◊ *Example 2:*

$$\log_{10}(20) = \log_{10}(2 * 10) = \log_{10}(2) + \log_{10}(10) = 0.3 + 1 = 1.3$$

◊ *Example 3:*

$$\log_{10}(4) = \log_{10}(2 * 2) = \log_{10}(2) + \log_{10}(2) = 0.3 + 0.3 = 0.6$$

◊ *Example 4:*

$$\log_{10}(5) = \log_{10}(10/2) = \log_{10}(10) - \log_{10}(2) = 1 - 0.3 = 0.7$$

Notice that Examples 2, 3, and 4 all demonstrate how knowing the log of 2, in addition to knowing some properties of logarithms can help you solve many other logarithms.

17.2 Exercises: Logarithms

View ONLINE Exercises: Logarithms

KEY CONCEPT

Logarithms are a non-linear compression technique. When data spans too large a range (dynamic range) to be visualized adequately, compression is required to reduce the dynamic range. Logarithms are very important in ultrasound since the dynamic range of echoes (sound wave amplitudes) reflecting from the body are tens of thousands of times greater than the range of signals visible at one time to the human eye. Therefore, ultrasound data is compressed using logarithms so that images can be displayed in real time.

18. Trigonometry

Trigonometry is a mathematical discipline that deals with the physical relationship between angles and dimensions of triangles. Many physical situations can be modeled using triangles and hence, by using trigonometry. For example, the height of an object can be calculated by measuring the length of its shadow, given that you know the angle of the light to the object. One of the easiest ways of learning trigonometry is to start with what is called the unit circle. A circle is actually a collection of all the various proportioned triangles which exist. When you look at the examples, this concept of a circle including all of the triangles should become clearer.

We will start with a unit circle. It is called a unit circle because the radius has a length of one, or one unit.

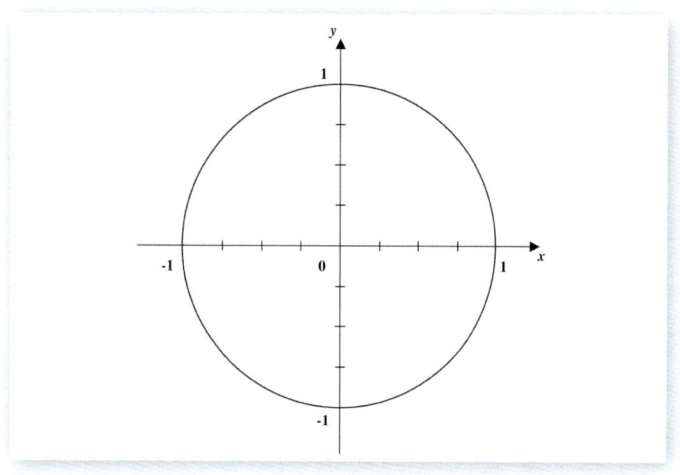

Fig. 11 **Unit circle**

To determine the cosine (or cos) of an angle (θ), draw the angle onto the circle, and then project the intersection with the circle onto the *x*-axis.

◊ ***Example:*** What is the cosine at $\theta = 60°$?

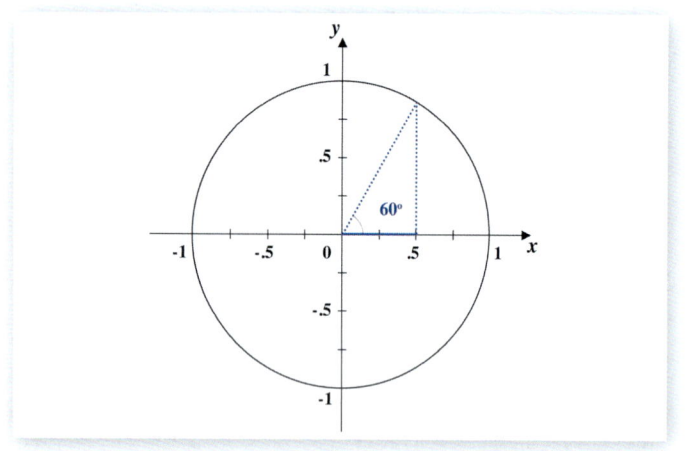

Fig. 12 **Cosine (60°) = 0.5**

To determine the sine (or sin) of an angle (θ) - draw the angle onto the unit circle and project the intersection onto the y-axis.

◊ ***Example:*** What is the sine (60°)?

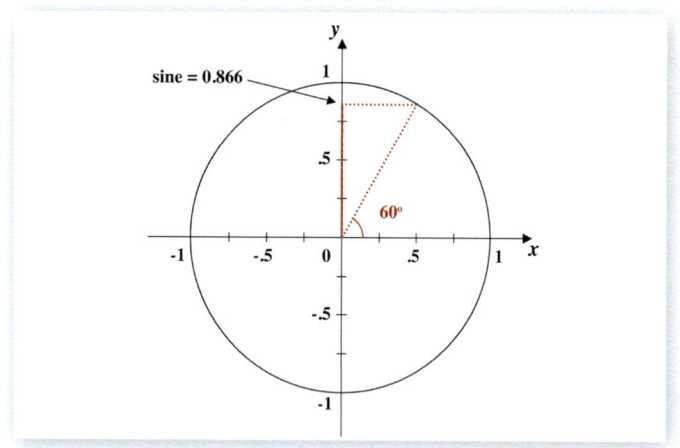

Fig. 13 **Sine (60°) = 0.866**

◊ ***Example:*** What is the cosine (0°)?

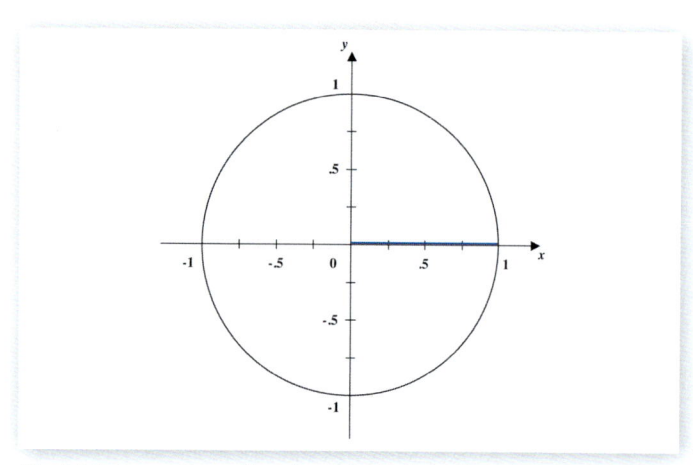

Fig. 14 **Intersection of angle with circle is already on axis, where x = 1, so cosine (0°) = 1**

◊ ***Example:*** What is the cosine (90°)?

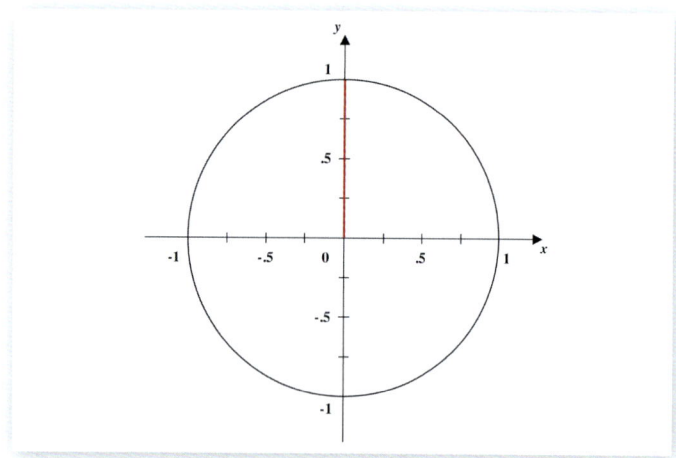

Fig. 15 **Projection of the intersection of the angle and the circle is at x = 0, so cosine (90°) = 0**

View ONLINE Animation and Image Library

The following table lists the sines and cosines of the "basic" angles in each of the four quadrants. The basic angles are just the angles which we easily recognized on a unit circle that can serve as reference points for other angles.

Angle (θ)	Cos (θ)	Sin (θ)
0°	1	0
30°	0.866	0.5
45°	0.707	0.707
60°	0.5	0.866
90°	0	1
120°	-0.50	0.866
135°	-0.707	0.707
150°	-0.866	0.50
180°	-1	0
210°	-0.866	-0.50
225°	-0.707	-0.707
240°	-0.50	-0.866
270°	0	-1

Table 6 **Cosine and Sine**

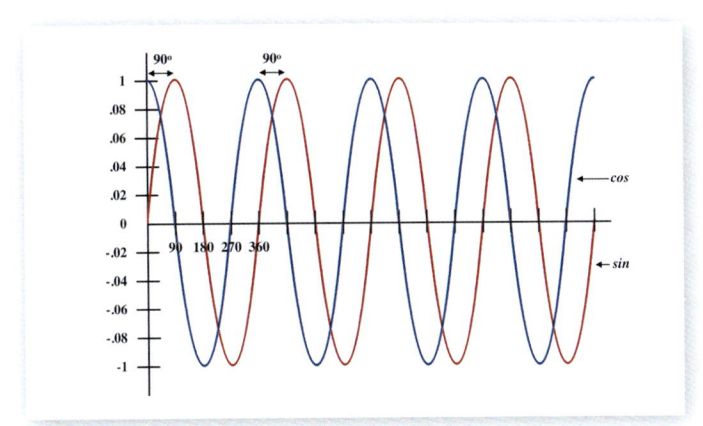

Fig. 16 **Graphical representation of the sine and cosine versus angle**

Notice that the sine and cosine look the same on the graph except for a "phase" difference. The cosine leads the sine by 90°.

Reconciling this approach with the classic explanation of trigonometry is relatively easy. Below are the definitions most people associate with trigonometry:

$$\cos(\theta) = \frac{\text{adjacent}}{\text{hypotenuse}}$$

$$\sin(\theta) = \frac{\text{opposite}}{\text{hypotenuse}}$$

$$\tan(\theta) = \frac{\sin(\theta)}{\cos(\theta)} = \frac{\text{opposite}}{\text{adjacent}}$$

$$\cos(30°) = \frac{\text{adjacent}}{\text{hypotenuse}} = \frac{0.866}{1} = 0.866$$

$$\sin(30°) = \frac{\text{opposite}}{\text{hypotenuse}} = \frac{0.5}{1} = 0.5$$

$$\tan(30°) = \frac{\sin(\theta)}{\cos(\theta)} = \frac{\text{opposite}}{\text{adjacent}} = \frac{0.5}{0.866} = 0.58$$

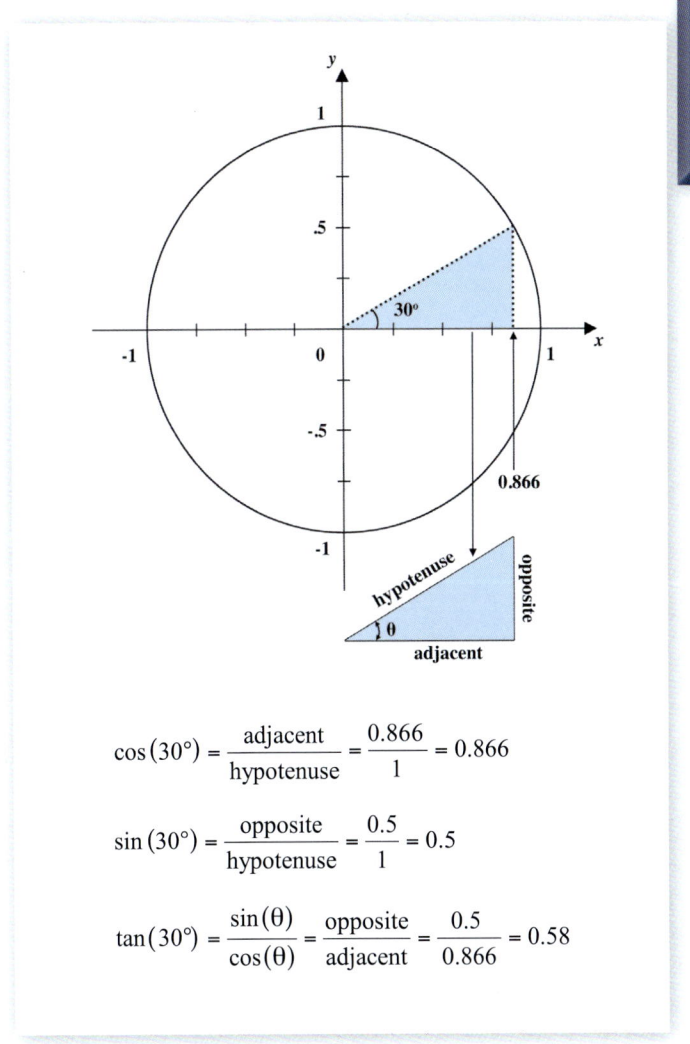

Fig. 17 **Trigonometric relationships**

For completeness:

The **secant** is the reciprocal of the cosine.

The **cosecant** is the reciprocal of the sine.

The **cotangent** is the reciprocal of the tangent.

By placing the triangle onto a unit circle, the hypotenuse = 1, which makes calculating the trigonometric functions easy. If you were given a right triangle for which the hypotenuse is not 1, you can calculate the cosine as the adjacent side divided by the hypotenuse. Similarly, you can calculate the sine as the opposite divided by the hypotenuse.

18.1 Angles, Quadrants and Signs

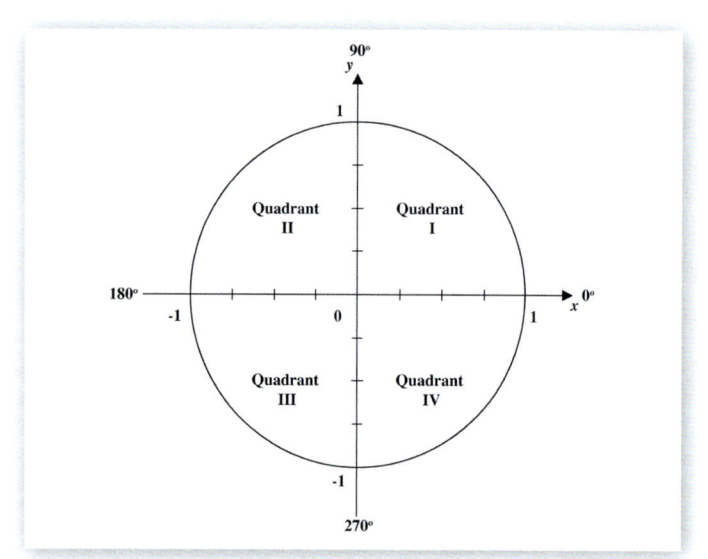

Fig. 18 **Quadrants of a circle**

One fourth of a circle is called a quadrant. The first quadrant of a circle is from 0° to 90°. The second quadrant is from 90° to 180°. The third quadrant is from 180° to 270°, and the fourth quadrant is from 270° to 360°. The quadrants of the unit circle are displayed in the above graph. You should know in which quadrants the cosine is negative and in which quadrants the cosine is positive. Similarly, you should know in which quadrants the sine is positive and in which quadrants the sine is negative. This is really quite simple to remember if you draw your unit circle and recall how the sine and cosine are determined. Since the cosine is the projection onto the *x*-axis, the cosine is positive in quadrant I and quadrant IV, and negative in quadrants II and III. In contrast, the sine is the projection onto the *y*-axis and hence is positive in quadrant I and II, and negative in quadrants III and IV.

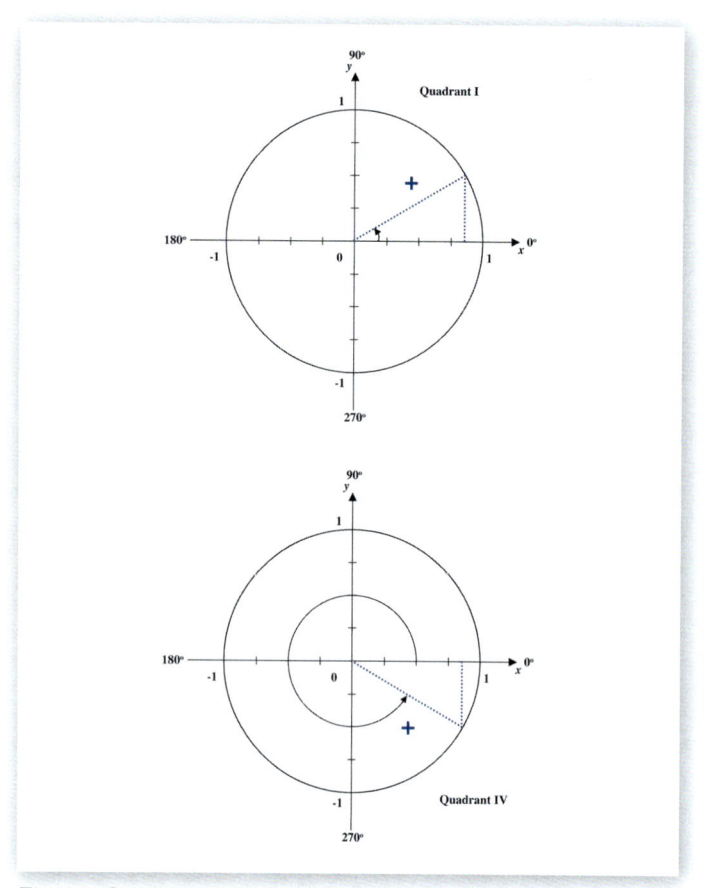

Fig. 19 **Cosine is positive in quadrant I and quadrant IV**

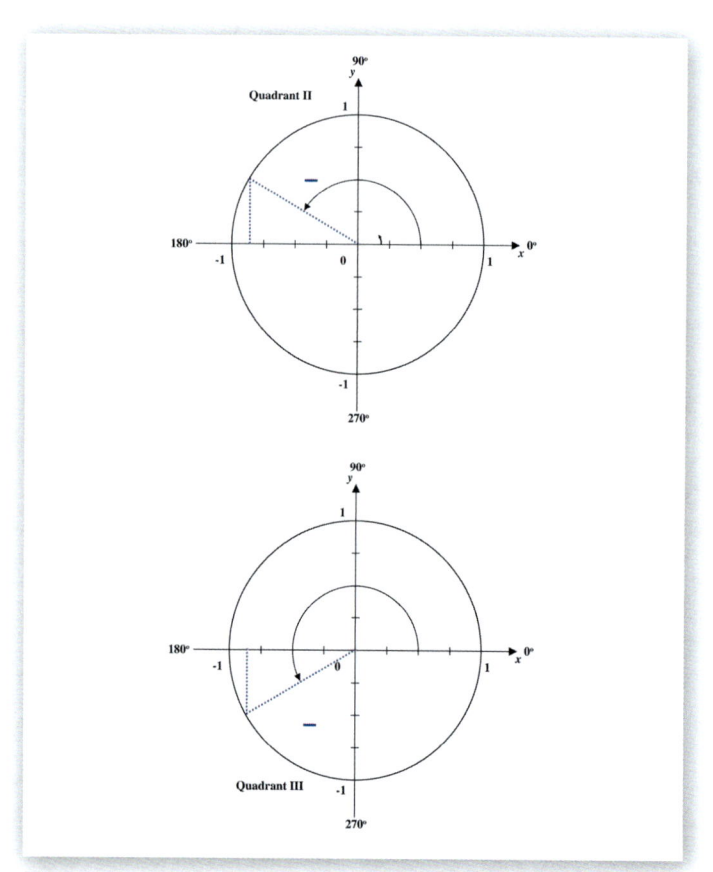

Fig. 20 **Cosine is negative in quadrant II and quadrant III**

18.2 The Value of Knowing Basic Trigonometry in Ultrasound (and Medicine)

As was mentioned, one aspect of trigonometry is a mathematical approach to dealing with the ratios of sides of various triangles. Why should you care about triangles and angles? The answer is that many parameters we would like to know, we cannot measure directly. Instead, we are forced to measure what is commonly referred to as a projection or "shadow" of the actual object. However, the length of the "shadow" can be affected by changing angles.

Consider how the length of a long bone would change on an x-ray as the angle to the bone changes with respect to its long axis. Although the bone does not vary in length over the time it takes to perform this test, the length of the projection of the bone will certainly vary. In other words, there are angle effects which impact your measurement accuracy.

The same phenomenon certainly occurs in ultrasound. As the angle between the ultrasound beam and a structure varies, the dimensions of the structure will vary in the image. Also, discussed in Chapter 7, when we measure blood velocity using Doppler, changes in Doppler angle (insonification angle) will produce changes in our measurement. Clearly, we would like to have some approach to eliminate, or at least minimize, the errors associated with these angle effects.

Trigonometry provides us with the mathematical tool to somewhat correct the "distortion" caused by angle effects, as well as a means by which to model how significant the error will be, and at what angles the error will be greatest.

It is expected that you will be able to solve the sine and the cosine of all of the basic angles (0°, 30°, 45°, 60°, 90°, 120°, 135°, 150°, 180°, 270°, 360°). By knowing the sines and cosines of the basic angles you will be able to use these known values (fiducial points) to help you make relatively accurate estimates for the sines and cosines of every angle. As noted earlier, it is not critical to know every sine and cosine value by memory. What is important is that you understand how these values vary by angle dependency.

You will notice from the graph of the sine and cosine that these two functions are extremely non-linear in their behavior. As a result, you should expect that any measurement you make that depends on the sine or cosine of the angle will have very non-linear associated errors. This point is critical, since that information can then be used to help determine how measurements can be best made so as to minimize error and maximize clinical accuracy. For now, it is important that you learn the basics of trigonometry. In Chapter 7, when discussing Doppler, the concepts of angular effects and trigonometry will be revisited and applied. Chapter 7 also presents a mathematical treatment of how to quantify the error associated with angular effects.

> **KEY CONCEPT**
>
> Trigonometry is a mathematical tool which accounts for angular effects. The cosine of an angle represents the projection towards the "ground" or the x-axis. The sine of an angle represents the projection toward the "wall" or the y-axis. The basic angles are the angles which can be easily visualized in the first quadrant of the unit circle (0°, 30°, 45°, 60°, 90°) and the corresponding angles in quadrant II (180°, 150°, 135°, 120°). Knowing the sines and cosines of the basic angles allows for relatively good estimation of the sines and cosines at all other angles.

18.3 Exercises: Trigonometry

View ONLINE Exercises: Trigonometry

19. The Decimal System and the Binary System

19.1 Decimal (Base 10) and Binary (Base 2)

For daily use, our number system is base 10, or decimal. Base 10 means that there are ten digits (0 - 9) which are used to represent all numbers. Base 10 is very convenient, given the fact that we have ten fingers and ten toes, which essentially served as our first calculators. To facilitate learning how to use other base counting systems, it is usually easiest to review how the already familiar base 10 system works.

◊ **Example 1:** Look at the number $732_{10} \Rightarrow 732$

* *Note: we normally do not write the subscripted 10; it is assumed.*

Another way of writing 732_{10} is:

$$732 = 700 + 30 + 2$$
$$= 7(100) + 3(10) + 2$$
$$= 7(10)^2 + 3(10)^1 + 2(10)^0$$
(note powers of ten)

In table form 732 =

·····	10^4	10^3	10^2	10^1	10^0	10^{-1}	10^{-2}	10^{-3}	·····
	0	0	7	3	2	0	0	0	

Decimal point

◊ **Example 2:** Look at the number 6,327.64

$$6{,}327.64 = 6(10)^3 + 3(10)^2 + 2(10)^1 + 7(10)^0 + 6(10)^{-1} + 4(10)^{-2}$$

.....	10^4	10^3	10^2	10^1	10^0	10^{-1}	10^{-2}	10^{-3}	10^{-4}
	0	6	3	2	7	6	4	0	0

Decimal point

◊ **Example 3:** Look at the number 372_8

Do you think we would use decimal (base 10) if we had been born with 8 fingers? Base 8 works just like base 10 except you now can only use the eight digits (0 -7).

$$372_8 =$$
$$3(8)^2 + 7(8)^1 + 2(8)^0$$
$$3(64) + 7(8) + 2(1) = 250 \text{ base 10}$$

.....	8^4	8^3	8^2	8^1	8^0	8^{-1}	8^{-2}	8^{-3}	8^{-4}
	0	0	3	7	2	0	0	0	0

Octal point

In other words, there is absolutely nothing unique or special about the counting system of base 10. There are an infinite number of counting systems which could have been chosen; we chose base 10 because of convenience relative to our anatomy. Understanding how to use another base is really the same as understanding how to count in the base 10 system.

19.2 Exercises: Decimal Conversions

View ONLINE
Exercises: Decimal Conversions

19.3 Binary

In our daily life, we are most familiar with the counting system using base 10, utilizing ten digits: 0, 1, 2, …, 9. With electronics, a distinct voltage must be used for each digit. Imagine how difficult it would be to represent numbers electronically using base 10; there would have to be ten distinct voltage levels.

A commonly used base for electronics and computers is called binary, or base 2. The binary system functions exactly as all other base systems, except it only uses the digits 0 and 1. For binary, only two voltage levels are necessary to represent the digits. The digit 0 is represented by 0 Volts, and the digit 1 is usually represented by +5 Volts. As electronic devices become smaller with a desire to use less power, a lower voltage (3.5 Volts or less) is more often being used to represent the digit 1.

Memory, like your computer memory or RAM, is really the storage or encoding of voltage levels representing numbers in binary.

19.4 Converting from Binary to Base 10

We will start by considering how a binary number can be converted to base 10. Note that the binary system is based on powers (groupings) of twos just as the decimal system is based on powers or groupings of tens. Just as we wrote the base 10 number in a grid form, we will take the same approach with binary. Notice that instead of the 1's column, the 10's column, the 100's column, etc., we have the 1's column, the 2's column, the 4's column etc.

◊ **Example:** 1011_2 (binary)

2^3	2^2	2^1	2^0
1	0	1	1

= $1(2)^3$ + $0(2)^2$ + $1(2)^1$ + $1(2)^0$
= $1(8)$ + $0(4)$ + $1(2)$ + $1(1)$
= 8 + 0 + 2 + 1

so $1011_2 = 11_{10}$

◊ **Example:** 1100_2 (binary)

2^3	2^2	2^1	2^0
1	1	0	0

= $1(2)^3$ + $1(2)^2$ + $0(2)^1$ + $0(2)^0$
= $1(8)$ + $1(4)$ + $0(2)$ + $0(1)$
= 8 + 4 + 0 + 0

so $1100_2 = 12_{10}$

◊ **Example:** 1111_2 (binary)

2^3	2^2	2^1	2^0
1	1	1	1

= $1(2)^3$ + $1(2)^2$ + $1(2)^1$ + $1(2)^0$
= $1(8)$ + $1(4)$ + $1(2)$ + $1(1)$
= 8 + 4 + 2 + 1

so $1111_2 = 15_{10}$

Note that in binary form, all even numbers end in a zero and all odd numbers end in a 1. This fact can be helpful to eliminate at least a few choices on an exam. For example, if you were asked:

Which of the following is the decimal equivalent of the binary number 10001?

    a)   18
    b)   17
    c)   16
    d)   15
    e)   14

You should know that the answer has to be an odd number since the binary number ends in the digit 1. Therefore, you can automatically eliminate the three even choices (A, C, and E), leaving you only two choices. The correct answer is choice B since:

◊ *Example:* 10001_2 (binary)

2^4	2^3	2^2	2^1	2^0
1	0	0	0	1

$$= 1(2)^4 + 1(2)^3 + 0(2)^2 + 1(2)^1 + 1(2)^0$$
$$= 1(16) + 1(8) + 0(4) + 1(2) + 1(1)$$
$$= 16 + 0 + 0 + 0 + 1$$

so $10001_2 = 17_{10}$

Author's Note: Converting from Decimal to Binary Form

For the exam, it is much more common to have you convert a number from binary form to decimal form than from decimal form to binary form. I have included converting in the reverse direction only for completeness sake. Make certain to know the voltage representation of binary numbers: 0 Volts for 0 and +5 Volts for a 1.

KEY CONCEPT

For general mathematics, we usually use a base 10 system to count (10 digits (0 though 9)). Base 10 is convenient primarily because we are born with simple calculators for base 10 – 10 fingers and 10 toes. For electronics, we generally use a binary system to count (2 digits (0 and 1)) as the system is much simpler to produce in electronics. With binary, only two voltage levels are required, whereas if we used a base 10 system, 10 voltage levels would be required.

19.5 Converting from Decimal to Binary

To convert from decimal to binary, you must successively remove the highest powers of 2 contained within the number you are converting. As an example, in the number 19, the highest power of 2 is the fourth power, or 16. This results in a 1 in the 16's column (2^4), with a three left over. The highest power in the remaining value of three is the first power, putting a 1 in the (2^1) column, and leaving a remainder of 1. The highest power of 2 in the remaining 1 is the zero power, putting a 1 in the (2^0) column. This process is shown graphically below.

19.6 Exercises: Binary

View ONLINE Exercises: Binary

◊ *Example:*   Write the number 19 in binary

$$19 = 16 + 2 + 1 \;\; = 1(2)^4 + 0(2)^3 + 0(2)^2 + 1(2)^1 + 1(2)^0$$
$$= \;\;\;\;\; 1 \;\;\;\;\;\;\; 0 \;\;\;\;\;\;\; 0 \;\;\;\;\;\;\; 1 \;\;\;\;\;\;\; 1$$

$19_{10} = 10011_2$

COMMON MISCONCEPTION: Mathematics

MISCONCEPTION: *Math is not important to pass the exam*

Explanation:
Although there are usually not many absolute calculations on the credentialing exams, math is critical to exam success. Generally, at least 40% of the physics-based credentialing exams require application of relative mathematics principles. For example:

- How does the wavelength change if the transmit frequency is increased from 2 MHz to 6 MHz?
- How does the cross-sectional area change if the radius of the vessel is reduced by 50%?
- How is the Doppler shift affected if the transmit frequency is reduced from 4 MHz to 2 MHz?

COMMON MISCONCEPTION: Mathematics

MISCONCEPTION: *Knowing the equations is not important in the clinical world since the system performs all of the calculations*

Explanation:
Whereas it is true that the system performs the calculations for you, there are at least three good reasons why you should know the equations (besides the need to know the equations for the exams).

1) On multiple occasions I have seen either the wrong button clicked or the wrong analysis selected on an ultrasound system, resulting in the wrong calculation (or the calculation performed on incorrect caliper placements). By knowing the equations, you can estimate the answer independent of the system calculation so that you have a way of determining if the system calculation makes sense.

2) By knowing the equations used in the calculations you can determine the potential magnitude of the error in the calculation relative to any potential error within your measurement. For example, a 10% error in the measurement of a radius would result in a 10% error in the calculated circumference (a linear relationship). However, a 10% error in the measurement of a radius would results in a 27% error in the calculated volume (a cubed (nonlinear) relationship).

3) Understanding the equations that govern structure measurements and functions of the body such as the volume of a mass, blood flow, resistance to flow, etc. gives insight into the severity of disease and how the body will try to compensate for that disease. Acquiring that insight allows you to be proactive, instead of reactive, in looking for related problems within the patient.

CHAPTER SUMMARY: Mathematics

- Most of the mathematics you will need for the exam involves relative expressions, not absolute calculations.
- You must be familiar with the concept of relationships between variables (proportionality and inverse proportionality).
- Understanding the difference between linear and non-linear relationships is critical.
- Linear relationships express the fact that two related variables change at the same rate.
- Non-linear relationships express the fact that small changes in one variable result in larger changes in the related variable.
- Understanding math terminology is another area which greatly affects scoring. You must be able to translate terms such as increase, decrease, factor, etc. into mathematical expressions.
- The property of reciprocals is used repeatedly throughout ultrasound physics.
- Knowing the metric table (and the reciprocal relationships within the table) greatly simplifies many calculations.
- The distance equation expresses a linear relationship between time and distance.

$$d = r \times t$$

- If you presume a propagation velocity of 1540 m/sec, it takes 6.5 microseconds for sound to travel 1 cm. To image 1 centimeter requires that the sound travel 2 cm (roundtrip effect) thereby requiring 13 microseconds.

$$ID\,(imaging\,depth) = 1\,cm \Rightarrow travel = 2\,cm \Rightarrow 13\,\mu sec$$

- You should remember the 13 microsecond per cm of imaging depth calculation. Because of the linear relationship, you can easily calculate the imaging time for any other depth by scaling. For example: to image 5 cm requires $5 \times 13\,\mu sec = 65\,\mu sec$.
- Logarithms provide a powerful tool to compress data non-linearly.
- You should know the log of any power of 10 and the log of 2. The log of any power of 10 is simply the power (exponent).

$$log(2) = 0.3$$

- You should know how to calculate the sine and the cosine of the basic angles including (0°, 30°, 45°, 60°, 90°, 120°, 135°, 150°, 180°, 270°, 360°).
- The cosine is the projection to the x-axis and hence, is positive in quadrants 1 and 4 and negative in quadrants 2 and 3.
- The sine is the projection to the y-axis and hence, is positive in quadrants 1 and 2 and negative in quadrants 3 and 4.
- The sine and the cosine are separated by a 90 degree phase shift.
- Any variable which is dependent on the sine or the cosine of an angle behaves non-linearly since the cosine and the sine are non-linear.

ONLINE EXTRAS

For additional support material and to view your completion progress, visit:

www.pegasuslectures.com/6thEdExtras

Extras by Chapter include:
- Animations
- Videos
- Additional Images
- Clarifying Clips
- Supplemental Exercises
- Conceptual Questions

See page x of Preface for access instructions

Chapter 2
Waves

Introduction

Understanding a topic is easier when you first understand the motivation for learning the material instead of just memorizing a series of facts and figures. As a result, in Level 1 we will begin by discussing the reasons this material is important to anyone performing ultrasound related tests followed by the principles of waves in general, developing the foundation for Level 2. In Level 2, many of the same topics will be reviewed, but this time with specific references to ultrasound, application, and relation to topics to be discussed in later chapters. In this way, you will be exposed to the topic multiple times, reviewing and building a more solid foundation.

1. The Motivation for Studying Waves

So why do we need to study waves? The simple answer is diagnostic ultrasound is based on how sound waves interact with various structures in the body. Since changing parameters of the sound wave can lead to changes in the diagnostic quality of the clinical study performed, and since changing some of the parameters can also increase the potential risk of bioeffects (biological changes that potentially cause harm to the patient), it is useful to discuss the various parameters of the ultrasound wave. Specifically, we will need to know what can be changed by you the sonographer, what cannot be changed, and how these parameters relate to the quality of the clinical study and the risk of bioeffects.

Note: Although the risk of bioeffects with ultrasound is very low, the potential does exist. Bioeffects will be discussed in Chapter 9, and also throughout the entire text as related topics are covered.

KEY CONCEPT

We study waves because:

- controlling the waves can improve clinical data acquired
- controlling the waves can reduce the risk of bioeffects (tissue damage)

2. Waves

2.1 Definition of a Wave

A wave is a mechanism which transfers energy from one location to another. If a wave is the result of a sudden impact or impulse of energy, it is generally referred to as a "shock wave." When a wave has a somewhat repetitious source, the wave is referred to as cyclical. Therefore, a wave with a repetitious source can be defined as a cyclical transfer of energy from one location to another location. The use of the term "cyclical" is useful since there is a clear indication that the energy of the wave results in changes that are repetitious. The term "cycle" refers to a single event or phase, while "cyclical" refers to the cycle repeating multiple times, relatively uniformly. For ultrasound, we will be concerned primarily with cyclical waves.

Since there are many different forms of energy that can be transported, there are many types of waves. For the purpose of ultrasound, we are primarily concerned with acoustic (sound) energy. Therefore, we can reduce the wave topics to cover only to those topics most directly related to sound waves as apply to diagnostic ultrasound.

2.2 Examples of Waves

We will not need to go into depth about wave types other than sound waves. However, so as to get across basic principles, it is instructive to consider other types of waves beside sound waves. Think about what all of these different types of waves have in common:

- water in the ocean
- sound
- television signals
- light
- oscillation of a guitar string
- a bunch of people doing the "wave" at Fenway Park

All of these waves clearly transport energy from one location to another. Also, interpreting the characteristics of these waves will yield information about the source. For example, is the wave strong or weak, does it vary quickly, can it travel a long distance, can it penetrate through an object in its path, what effect does it have on the medium (material) through which it propagates?

3. Classification of Waves

3.1 Benefit to Classifications

Classification schemes are useful as a technique to subdivide large groups into smaller groups. The benefit of subdividing a topic according to similar characteristics is a simplification in the amount of information that must be retained.

Consider how colleges subdivide students according to the year of graduation and then subdivide each year into specific majors. By dividing the entire student body into years of graduation, the classification of freshman, sophomore, junior, or senior alone tells how much more time there is until the individual student will graduate. By further dividing the class into majors, the specific curriculum is somewhat defined, limiting the number of elective classes an individual student can take.

For waves, one useful classification is based on how the wave propagates (travels). The first classification distinction we will discuss is the concept of an electromagnetic wave versus a mechanical wave.

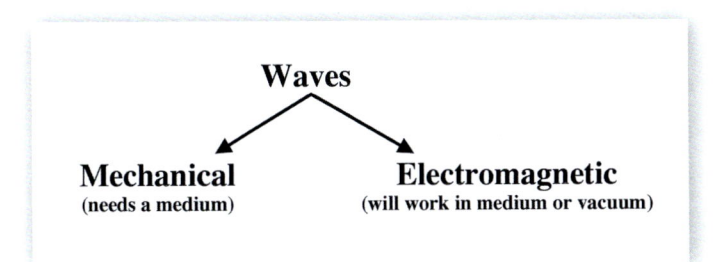

Fig. 1 **Classification of waves**

3.2 Electromagnetic (EM) Waves

An electromagnetic wave is a transfer of energy through a varying electrical and magnetic field. Some examples of EM waves are:

- light
- heat
- X-rays
- gamma rays
- television signals

The equations that define and describe electromagnetic wave theory and propagation are very complex and are generally confined to higher order mathematics. Fortunately, sound is not an electromagnetic wave, so you will not be required to know much more than the absolute basics about electromagnetic waves.

One of the defining characteristics of an electromagnetic wave is that it can travel both through a medium (a material such as air, water, tissue, metal, etc.) as well as through a vacuum (the absence of a medium, or space). You are not required to know much more about electromagnetic waves than this one defining characteristic. However, you should be very appreciative of the importance of this one characteristic. If electromagnetic waves could not travel through a vacuum like space, sunlight would not reach the earth and you would not exist to read this textbook which, without an author, would also not exist.

3.3 Mechanical Waves

A mechanical wave requires a physical interaction. For mechanical waves, the medium affects the wave, and the wave affects the medium. In other words, mechanical waves must have a medium, or the wave cannot exist. From the first list of waves, described in Section 2.2, ocean waves, sound, the vibration of a guitar string, and people at a ball park are all examples of mechanical waves.

The term mechanical as a classification is very useful since the word itself invokes some relationships critical for ultrasound. For example, the fact that the wave is mechanical indicates that the wave will interact with the tissue of the patient (the medium), and that the tissue of the patient will interact with the wave. As a result, we should expect potential changes in the patient as the wave propagates. Furthermore, we should also anticipate changes to the characteristics of the wave with propagation through the patient. In fact, each of these "interactions" is so important that they will spawn entire chapters: one chapter entitled bioeffects, and the other chapter entitled attenuation.

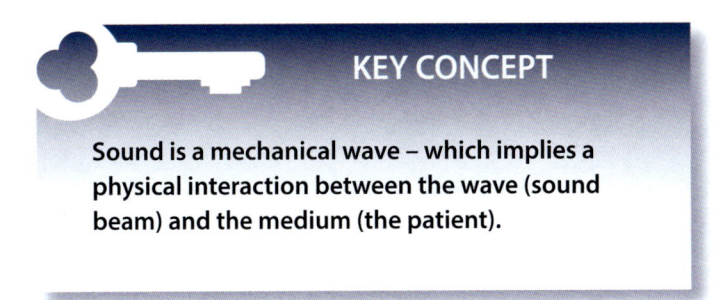

KEY CONCEPT

Sound is a mechanical wave – which implies a physical interaction between the wave (sound beam) and the medium (the patient).

4. Conceptual Questions

View ONLINE Conceptual Questions

5. Propagation of Mechanical Waves

As indicated in *Figure 2*, there are two distinct mechanisms by which a mechanical wave can propagate: in transverse mode or longitudinal mode. The word propagate implies that the wave "travels" from one location to another. However, the word travel does not adequately describe the concept of wave (energy) propagation. Wave propagation really implies that there is a change in the location of energy concentration per time. When the wave is being created, the highest energy associated with the wave is close to the source. With time, the energy interacts with the neighboring molecules of the medium, imparting momentum. With momentum, the higher energy molecules then interact with neighboring molecules, imparting energy, hence giving up some of their original energy. In this manner, the wave "propagates" or "travels" away from the source.

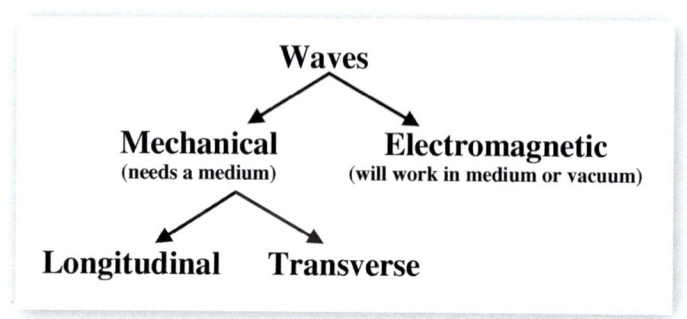

Fig. 2 **Further classifying waves**

5.1 Transverse Waves

As the prefix "trans" suggests, a transverse wave is a wave whose particles move "across" or perpendicular to the wave propagation direction. The term movement may be more accurately described as an oscillation, since the particles actually vibrate back and forth about the center position, as the wave propagates along its path. The following diagram illustrates how the particles of a transverse wave "oscillate" with the wave propagation.

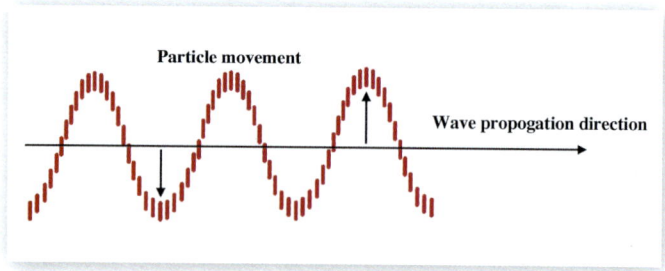

Fig. 3 **Transverse waves**

In *Figure 3*, the wave is traveling from left to right (left side of the page toward the right side of the page), while the particles of the medium are oscillating back and forth about the mean or center position. For this drawing, each short line segment represents a particle of the medium, and the distance away from the center line of the image represents the distance the particles traveled.

As you are about to learn, sound is **NOT** a transverse wave. In previous versions of this book, the further development of transverse wave concepts was therefore halted at this point, with continuing emphasis throughout the book only on longitudinal waves. In recent years, ultrasound has begun utilizing transverse waves for shear wave imaging in elastography. As a result, transverse waves will be further discussed in Chapter 15.

Note: You may have already noticed a theme developing. Quite frequently, the terminology used in physics is very descriptive of the associated physical parameter. In other words, if you pay close attention to the meaning of the root words and prefixes, it becomes significantly easier to recall the definition of each term.

5.2 Longitudinal Waves

Definition and Depiction

For a longitudinal wave the particle motion is "along" the direction of the wave propagation.

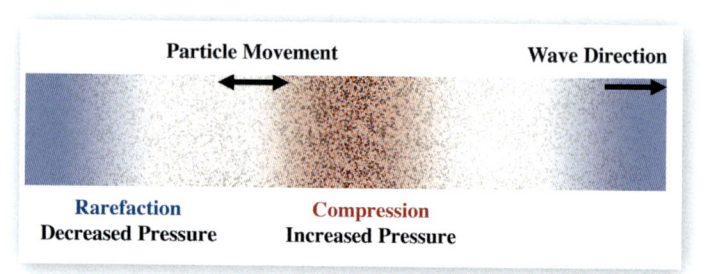

Fig. 4 **Longitudinal waves**

In *Figure 4*, the small dots represent particles or molecules of the medium. When the dots are drawn close together, it represents a high particle density. Conversely, when the dots are far apart, it represents a lower particle density.

Sound is a longitudinal wave, which implies that sound travels through compressions and rarefactions of the medium. The following diagram shows the classification of sound within the broad category of waves.

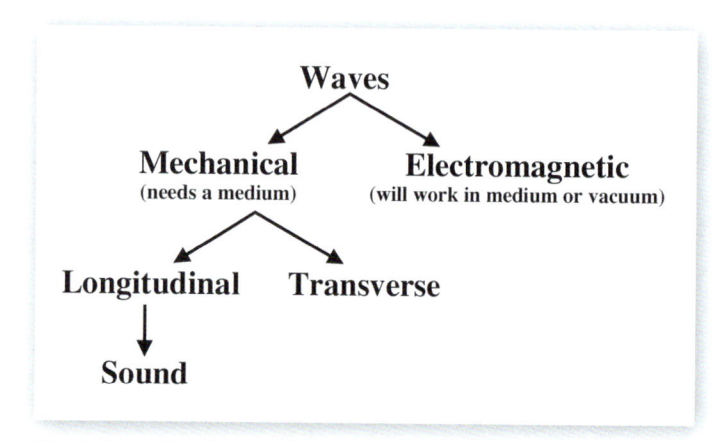

Fig. 5 **Sound is a longitudinal, mechanical wave**

Developing a More Thorough Understanding of Longitudinal Waves

The description of a longitudinal wave is usually "a series of compressions and rarefactions which cause particles within the medium to vibrate back and forth, along, or in the same direction as the wave propagation direction." Instead of starting from this definition of sound as a longitudinal wave, we will take a more intuitive step-by-step approach to understanding the physical interactions which give rise to this definition and this terminology. More importantly, this intuitive approach should yield a much more thorough understanding of how sound interacts with the medium.

Recall that all waves transfer energy. For a longitudinal wave, the source of the wave imparts energy to the particles (molecules) of the medium in contact with the source. When this energy is imparted to the nearest particles, these particles begin to move. Since these particles have neighbors that have not yet been affected by the wave, the higher energy particles encroach on the space of the lower energy neighbors. This collision results in two responses. First, some of the energy of the higher energy molecules is now transferred to the neighboring lower energy particles. Second, from the collision, the higher energy molecules reflect back towards the wave source. This process of colliding and imparting energy with neighbors continues until all of the energy of the wave is eventually dissipated.

Now consider the moment when the higher energy molecules traveled and collided with their neighbors. During that collision period, in that neighborhood, there was a higher concentration of molecules than normal, referred to as a state of compression. After the collision occurred and the compressed molecules traveled away from each other, there was a decrease in molecular density relative to normal, referred to as rarefaction. Since this process continues repeatedly, we now have the definition of a longitudinal wave as a series of compressions and rarefactions. Since the particle motion is in the direction of the wave propagation, we now have the second part of the definition, "along", or in the same direction as the wave propagation.

KEY CONCEPT

Sound is a longitudinal wave, which means it propagates (travels) through a series of compressions and rarefactions of the molecules of the medium.

5.3 Problems with Static Drawings of Waves

There are two major difficulties with static drawings of waves:

1) Motion must be inferred by the person interpreting the picture.

Understanding the motion of a wave with respect to time is critical. On a static picture, distance and time appear along the same dimension of the graph (along the horizontal axis). As a result, it is easy to confuse the concept of distance measures with time measures for a wave. To rectify this problem, it is usually instructive to show physical waves in a dynamic (changing) state.

2) Drawing a longitudinal wave is challenging and time consuming.

Although a sound wave propagates longitudinally, virtually every picture depicting a sound wave uses a transverse diagram. This depiction is particularly confusing for students when such painstaking efforts are made in every physics book to point out differences between longitudinal and transverse wave propagation.

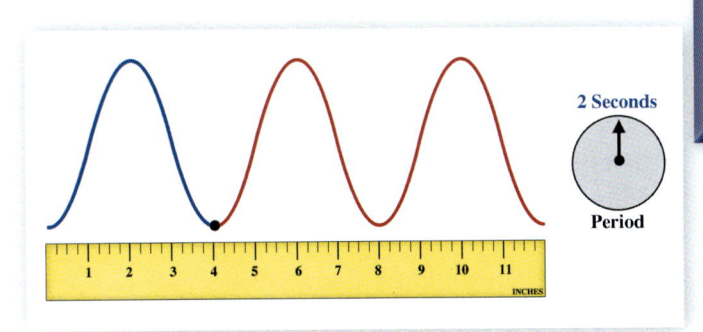

Fig. 6 **Case 1: period = 2 seconds, wavelength = 4 inches**

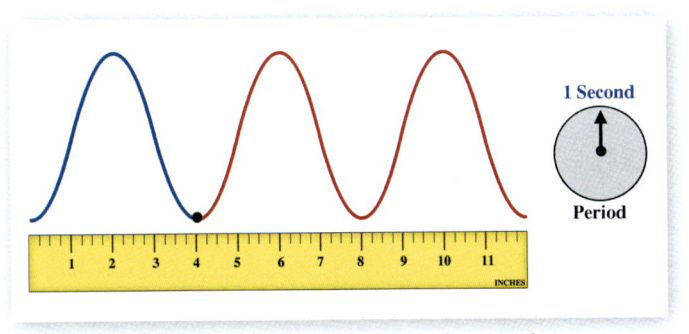

Fig. 7 **Case 2: period = 1 second, wavelength = 4 inches**

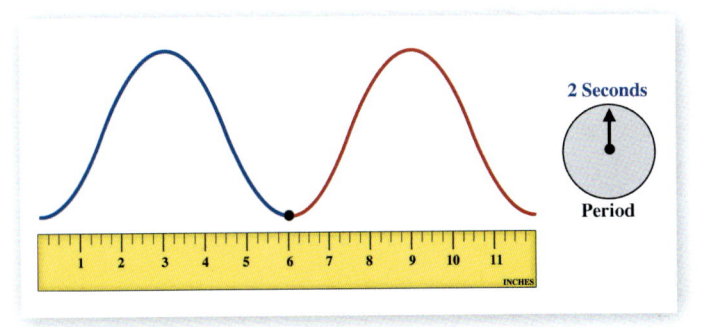

Fig. 8 **Case 3: period = 2 seconds, wavelength = 6 inches**

So why use a transverse depiction of a longitudinal sound wave? The reason is quite simple: transverse waves are easy to draw and longitudinal waves are not. Therefore, with only a few exceptions from this point on, sound waves, although longitudinal in nature, will be depicted using transverse drawings.

To fully appreciate a static drawing of a wave, you must pay close attention to the parameters being displayed. Between *Figure 6* and *Figure 7*, both waves travel the same distance but in different time periods. In contrast, *Figure 6* and *Figure 8* display waves that travel different distances in the same time period. An animation is included to help clarify the differences between time and distance.

View ONLINE Animation and Image Library

6. Variations in the Medium with Propagation (Acoustic Variables)

The fact that sound is a mechanical wave indicates a physical interaction with the medium. Therefore, it should not be surprising that the cyclical interaction of the wave with the medium can cause cyclical changes to certain parameters in the medium itself. In fact, careful reading of the description of how a longitudinal wave propagates indicates how some of these interactions occur, and even what these changes might be. The changes that occur to the medium are referred to as acoustic variables. Since the word variable refers to a changing quantity, and acoustic refers to sound, this nomenclature should be relatively easy to remember.

As displayed in the diagram, there are four quantities that vary with the propagation of sound. Specifically, these four variables are pressure, density, temperature, and particle motion.

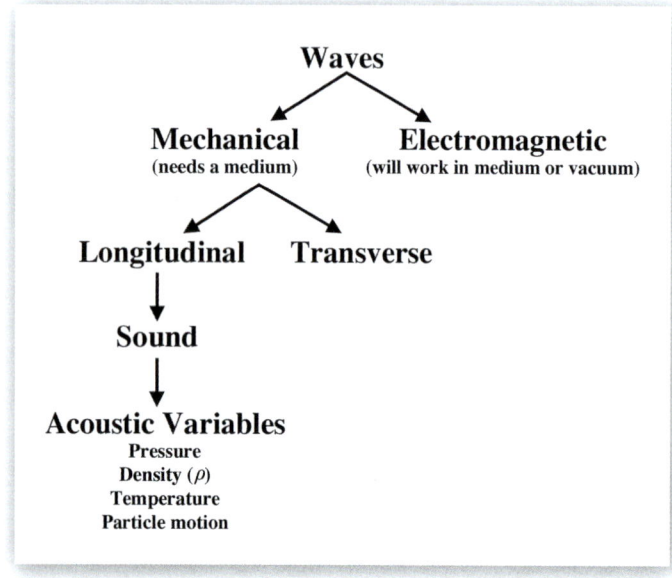

Fig. 9 The acoustic variables

CHECKPOINT: Exam Tip

The acoustic variables represent characteristic measures of amplitude that vary as the sound wave propagates through the medium including pressure (the change in concentration of force from compression through rarefaction), density (molecules are compressed and decompressed), temperature (heating as a result of frictions between molecules), and particle motion (the movement of molecules back and forth in response to transfer of energy).

6.1 Pressure

Pressure is defined as a concentration of force, or force per area. In the compression phase of the sound wave, the pressure increases. During the rarefaction phase, the pressure decreases. Clearly, the pressure varies cyclically as the wave propagates through the medium.

There are many different units commonly used to measure pressure. Some of the most common units are:

- Atmosphere (atm)
- Millimeters of mercury (mmHg)
- Pascals
- kg/m^2, (metric system)
- lbs/in^2 (English system)
- $Dynes/cm^2$

6.2 Density

The Equation for Density

The concept of density is quite familiar to most people. There are two parameters that combine to form the concept of density, specifically, the mass and the volume. Let's consider the following comparative situations:

Situation 1:

If there are two blocks of material identical in volume, but block A weighs more than block B, then block A has a higher density than block B.

This fact implies that: $density\ (\rho) \propto mass$

Situation 2:

If there are two blocks of material identical in mass, but block A is much larger than block B, then block B has a higher density than block A.

This fact implies that: $density\ (\rho) \propto \dfrac{1}{volume}$

Combining these two relationships together yields the equation:

$$density\ (\rho) = \dfrac{mass}{volume}$$

Now note that if we happen to be using kilograms of the unit of measure for mass, and cubic meters as the unit for volume, we can specify that density can be expressed as kilograms per cubic meters, or:

$$density\ (\rho) = \dfrac{mass}{volume}\ \left(\dfrac{kg}{m^3}\right)$$

Density as an Acoustic Variable
From our description of how a longitudinal wave propagates, we know that there are periods of higher particle concentrations (higher density) and lower particle concentrations (lower density). Therefore, as the wave propagates through the medium, there are cyclical variations in the density of the medium. During compression, the density is increased, whereas during rarefaction, the density is decreased. Although the change in density may not be that great, as you will learn in later sections, this change in density can have dramatic effects, and will lead to a non-linear imaging technique called harmonic imaging.

6.3 Temperature

Generation of Heat
Not surprisingly, any mechanical system produces heat. As the wave vibrates the particles in the medium, some of wave energy is lost to heat within the medium. Locally, as the particles go from higher to lower concentrations the temperature will also fluctuate cyclically.

Measuring Temperature
There are three relatively well known temperature scales: Kelvin, Celsius, and Fahrenheit. Degrees Kelvin is the scale of choice for many physics applications including cryogenics and superconductors. Fortunately, this safely eliminates the need for further description in a physics book intended for application of ultrasound. The two remaining scales are both based on the freezing and boiling point of water molecules under standard conditions.

The conversion from Celsius to Fahrenheit can be easily derived by comparing the two known state transition points as follows:

	Celsius	Fahrenheit
Freezing	0 degrees	32 degrees
Boiling	100 degrees	212 degrees

Table 1 **Boiling and Freezing Points for Water**

In the Celsius scale, there is a difference of 100 degrees from freezing to boiling. For the Fahrenheit scale, the same transition occurs over a difference of 180 degrees. Therefore, a ratio is easily determined between Celsius and Fahrenheit:

$$\dfrac{Fahrenheit}{Celsius} = \dfrac{180°}{100°} = \dfrac{18}{10} = \dfrac{9}{5}\ or\ 1.8$$

Now we must also take into account the fact that the Fahrenheit scale references freezing to 32 degrees whereas the Celsius scale references freezing to 0 degrees. Therefore, the conversion can be written as:

$$Temperature\ in\ Fahrenheit = 1.8 * (temperature\ in\ Celsius) + 32°$$

6.4 Particle Motion
Again referring to our description of wave propagation, we discussed particles of the medium being imparted with momentum and traveling into the locale of the nearest neighbors. In essence, the particles move (or more precisely, oscillate) back and forth about their original location, allowing the concentration of energy to propagate along the wave path. It is very important to note that the particles vibrate in their position and do not actually "travel" with the wave. The wave may travel a great distance, but ultimately, the particles should ultimately exist at or very close to their original starting location, depending on the elastic properties of the medium.

> **KEY CONCEPT**
>
> The physical interaction with the medium produces changes within the medium referred to as acoustic variables — an important concept as this creates the foundation for understanding bioeffects.

7. Conceptual Questions

View ONLINE Conceptual Questions

8. Wave Characteristics and Parameters

8.1 General
There are many parameters of a wave which can be used to specify the wave characteristics. As we will learn in Level 2 and in later chapters, understanding these parameters is important since changing any of these ultimately may change the quality of a clinical ultrasound study, or potentially change the risks to the patient associated with bioeffects. For now, it is enough to learn the parameters and their physical meanings.

8.2 Four Basic Parameters and the Many Associated Parameters
There are four basic wave parameters which we will need to either be able to calculate or measure:

Frequency/Period	$\Rightarrow$	Determined by the wave source
Wavelength	$\Rightarrow$	Determined by both the wave source and the properties of the medium
Propagation Velocity	$\Rightarrow$	Determined by the properties of the medium
Amplitude	$\Rightarrow$	Determined by the wave source initially, changes as wave propagates

> **CHECKPOINT: Exam Tip**
> You should have noticed that frequency and period are grouped together as one parameter. The reason is that time and frequency are reciprocals. Therefore, the frequency and the period specify the same information, just in reciprocal form.

Related to these four parameters is a group of related parameters, as listed below. It is imperative to develop a thorough understanding of the four basic parameters since they serve as the foundation for understanding the entire list of associated parameters.

Related parameters:
- power
- attenuation and attenuation rate
- reflection
- penetration
- speed of sound
- intensity (and intensity limits)
- absorption
- refraction
- sound vs. ultrasound (definition)
- acoustic impedance

Note: These related parameters will be discussed in Level 2 and in later chapters. They are introduced here as a motivation for learning the fundamental parameters.

8.3 Frequency (f) and Period (P)

General
Frequency is a measure of how often an event occurs per time. The unit for frequency is cycles/second, commonly referred to as Hertz, abbreviated as (Hz). You should realize that to be a measure of frequency, there must be a time reference. For example, all of the following are acceptable measures of a frequency:

- once per day
- occurrences per year (# of events implied)
- once per century (# of events implied)
- 3 times per minute

However, "17 times" is NOT an acceptable measure of frequency. Frequency is a rate, so without the time reference, 17 times is just a number of occurrences. From the number 17 times, it is unclear if what is implied is 17 times per second, or 17 times per minute, or 17 times per lifetime.

Frequency of a Sound Wave
The frequency of a sound wave refers to the number of compression or rarefaction cycles that occur per time. If there were only one compression cycle in a second, then the frequency of the wave would be 1 Hz. If there are 20,000 compression cycles per second, then the frequency is 20,000 Hz or equivalently, 20 kHz.

> **CHECKPOINT: Exam Tip**
> The transmit frequency is determined by the transducer and ultrasound system, not by the characteristics of the medium. This fact does not imply that the frequency chosen for imaging is independent of the patient, as deeper imaging requires a lower transmit frequency.

Graphical Depiction of Frequency
As we mentioned earlier in this chapter, although sound is a longitudinal wave, it is significantly easier to depict the wave in terms of transverse characteristics. Therefore, although we have accurately described the frequency of a sound wave as the number of compression cycles per second, we will depict a cycle using a transverse drawing as in the following diagram. In order to relate the transverse depiction with the actual characteristics of the sound wave, we will imagine that a peak corresponds to a compression and that the minimum corresponds to rarefaction.

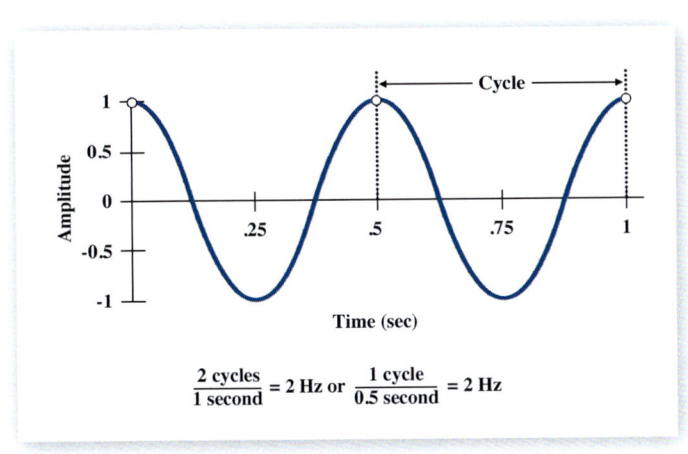

Fig. 10 **Transverse depiction of a 2 Hz wave**

$$\frac{2 \text{ cycles}}{1 \text{ second}} = 2 \text{ Hz or } \frac{1 \text{ cycle}}{0.5 \text{ second}} = 2 \text{ Hz}$$

When there are more compressions per time, the frequency increases, as depicted in *Figure 11*.

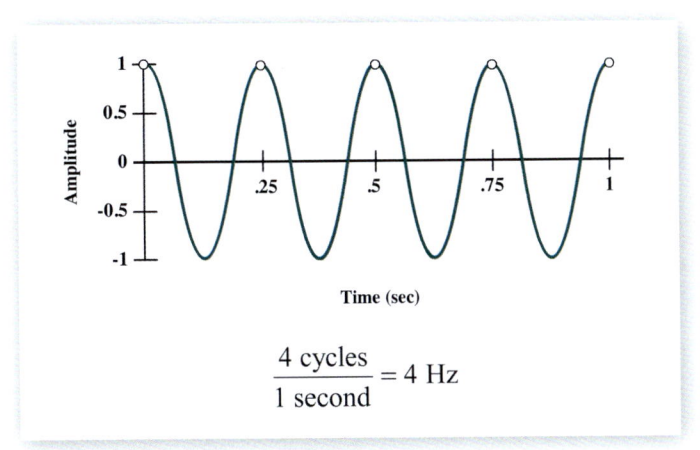

Fig. 11 **Transverse depiction of a 4 Hz wave**

$$\frac{4 \text{ cycles}}{1 \text{ second}} = 4 \text{ Hz}$$

KEY CONCEPT

The frequency of a wave is determined by the source. For sound waves, the frequency corresponds to the number of compressions (or rarefactions) per time.

Determining the Frequency

The frequency of a wave is determined by the source of the wave. If the source creates many compressions per second, then the wave will have a high frequency. If the source produces fewer cycles per second, then the wave will have a lower frequency. The medium does not determine the frequency of the wave. For ultrasound, the source is considered to be a combination of the transducer, the ultrasound system, and the user.

◊ *Example:*
If a 10 MHz wave traverses a tissue-blood boundary, is it still a 10 MHz wave?

Answer:
A 10 MHz transducer produces a 10 MHz wave in both water and soft tissue.

The Relationship Between Time (Period) and Frequency

The word period refers to time, so the period refers to the time between repeating events, or equivalently, the time per cycle. Notice that this definition is the reciprocal of the definition for frequency. Therefore, if you are given the frequency, no other information is required to calculate a period. Conversely, if you are given the period, no additional information is required to calculate the frequency.

$$Period = \frac{1}{Frequency}$$

The following examples demonstrate how to convert a frequency to a period, serving as a review of the exercises you performed in Chapter 1: Mathematics. Notice that knowledge of the metric table makes the process significantly simpler.

◊ *Example:*

Frequency/Period

10 Hz ⇒ 1/(10 Hz) = 0.1 seconds

5 Hz ⇒ 1/(5 Hz) = 0.2 seconds

12 kHz ⇒ 1/(12 kHz) ≈ 0.083 msec

2 MHz ⇒ 1/(2 MHz) = 0.5 μsec = 500 nsec

$$\left[units = \frac{1}{Hz} = \frac{1}{\left(\frac{1}{seconds}\right)} = \frac{seconds}{1} = seconds \right]$$

This reciprocal relationship between time and frequency always holds true. Therefore, whenever you are asked to convert a measurement from a time-based measurement to a frequency-based measurement (or vice versa) you will simply calculate the reciprocal. As you will notice from the following examples, it does not matter what the modifying term is before the basic measurement of time or frequency, the reciprocal nature never changes.

◊ **Examples:**

$$\text{Payment period} = \frac{1}{\text{payment frequency}}$$

$$\text{Transmit period} = \frac{1}{\text{transmit frequency}}$$

$$\text{Pulse repetition frequency} = \frac{1}{\text{pulse repetiton period}}$$

$$\text{Work frequency} = \frac{1}{\text{work period}}$$

$$\text{Frame time} = \frac{1}{\text{frame (rate) frequency}}$$

Interpreting the Period

For a sound wave, the period represents the time that transpires between the occurrence of one compression and the occurrence of the next compression. The period can be equivalently expressed as the time between the occurrence of one rarefaction and the occurrence of the next rarefaction.

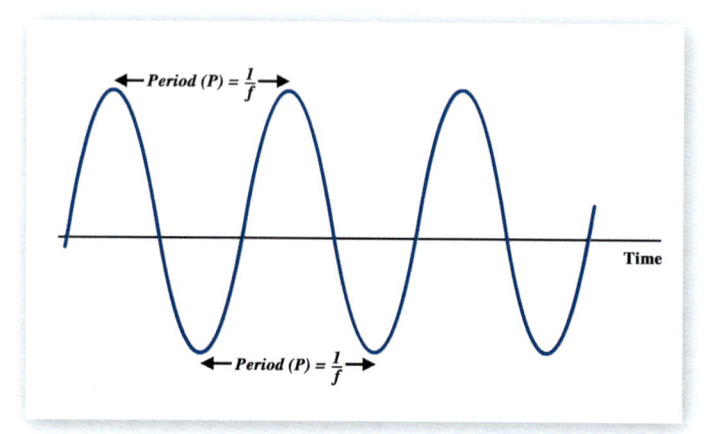

Fig. 12 Depiction of the period as the reciprocal of the frequency

Note that the horizontal axis in *Figure 12* represents time, not distance. Although an imperfect depiction, as already discussed, it is not possible to demonstrate motion in a static picture.

KEY CONCEPT

One of the most important relations to learn is that frequency and time are reciprocals. You will use this fact repeatedly within ultrasound physics.

8.4 Propagation Velocity

Defining Speed and Velocity

The rate at which the wave propagates through the medium is termed the propagation velocity. In general physics, the term velocity is used distinctly from the term "speed." Specifically, speed is a "scalar" quantity, referring only to the rate of travel. In contrast, the velocity is a "vector" quantity, referring to both the speed and a direction of travel. For sound in the body, the assumption is generally made that all sound propagates in a relatively straight path, hence making the distinction between these terms less significant. Therefore, you will hear the propagation velocity also referred to as the propagation speed or the speed of sound in the medium. Whereas the term velocity is more precise, there is little information lost in using the terminology of speed in this case. Therefore, to get you accustomed and comfortable with either terminology, both terms will be randomly intermixed throughout the book.

Units and Graphical Representation

Since the "propagation velocity" is a "velocity" term, the units are distance per time. In the metric system, a velocity is specified as meters/sec, or m/sec. *Figures 13* and *14* graphically demonstrate how a velocity can be measured by comparing physical location with respect to time. If there is a long distance in a short time between the first and second measured locations, the velocity is very high. Conversely if there is a short distance in a long time between the first and second measured locations, the velocity is very low.

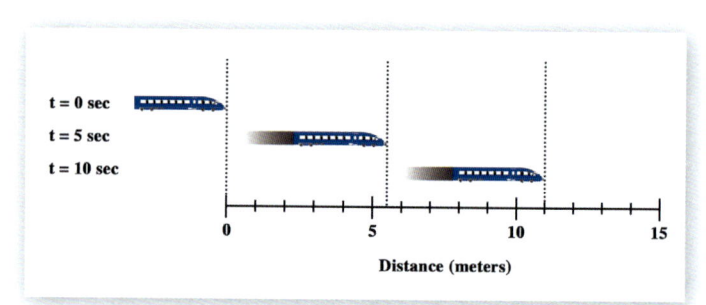

Fig. 13 **The train has traveled 11 meters in 10 seconds, so its velocity is 1.1 m/sec**

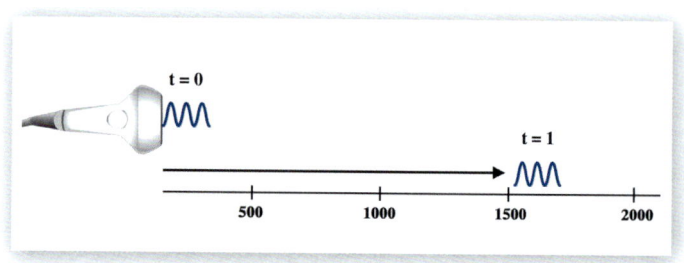

Fig. 14 **Sound has traveled 1500 meters in 1 second, so it has a propagation velocity of 1500 m/sec**

Note: In both Figures 13 and 14, the horizontal axis represents a measure of distance, not time.

What Determines the Speed of Sound

The propagation velocity is determined by the properties of the medium and is virtually unrelated to the frequency of the wave. Whereas the frequency can have slight effects on the propagation velocity, the effects are so small that we will consider them negligible. In other words, the propagation velocity for a 10 MHz wave and a 2 kHz wave will be virtually the same traveling through the same medium.

Since the speed of sound is dependent on the medium, different mediums have different propagation speeds. In Level 2, the precise properties which affect the propagation speed and a table of propagation speeds will be given. For now, it is important to become accustomed with the variables used, the units, and the physical meaning of each of these parameters.

Graphical Depiction of Propagation Speed for Sound Waves

When many cycles are drawn in a wave, it is quite easy to confuse the frequency of the wave with the concept of propagation velocity. Study the following scenarios carefully to avoid making these mistakes. As you will see, understanding the propagation velocity will simplify other related concepts such as the wavelength, an artifact called speed error, and the Doppler effect.

Scenario 1:
In *Figure 15*, both wave A and wave B start at the same location and travel the same distance in 1 second. Therefore both waves are traveling at the same speed. However, wave A has 3 cycles in one second (3 Hz) whereas wave B has 6 cycles in one second (6 Hz). Therefore these two waves are of different frequencies.

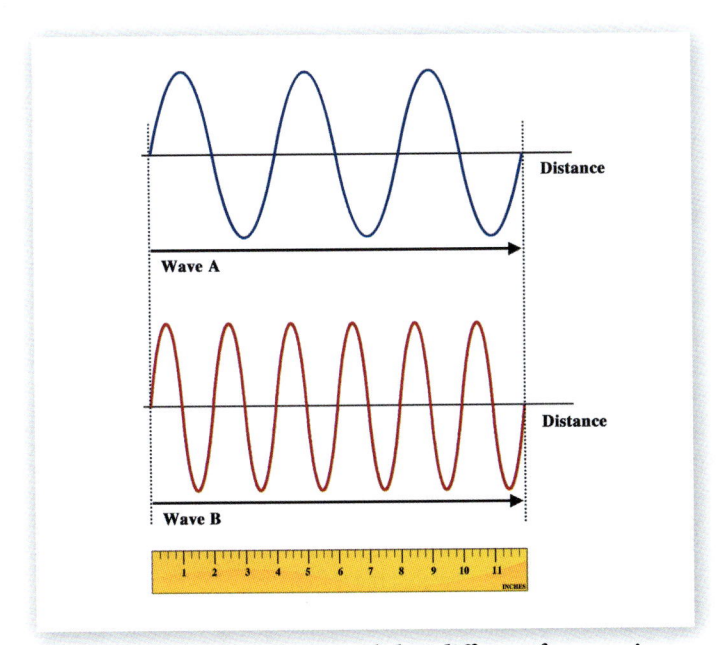

Fig. 15 **Same propagation speeds but different frequencies**

Scenario 2:
In *Figure 16*, both wave A and wave B have 3 cycles per second (3 Hz) and both waves start at the same location. However, although both waves start at the same location, wave B travels a shorter distance than wave A during the same 1 second time period.

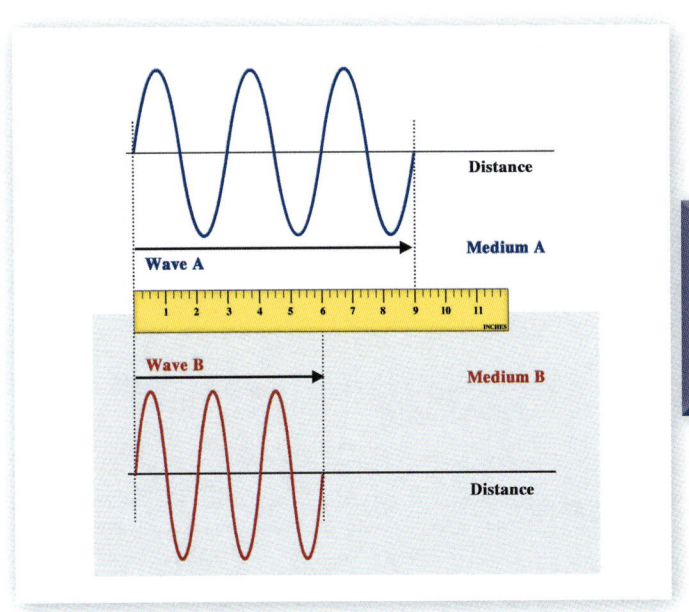

Fig. 16 **Same frequencies but different propagation speeds**

In this case, both wave A and B are the same frequency. However, since wave B traveled a shorter distance per time than wave A, wave B is in a lower propagation velocity medium than wave A.

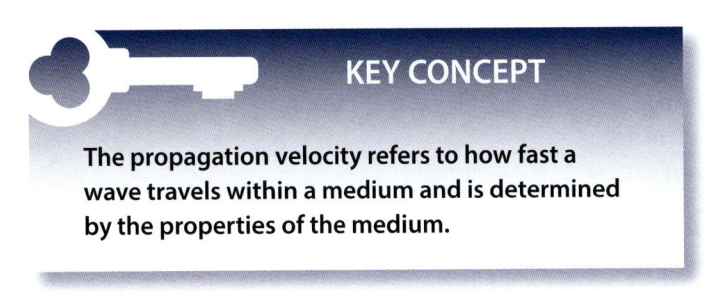

View ONLINE Animation and Image Library

KEY CONCEPT

The propagation velocity refers to how fast a wave travels within a medium and is determined by the properties of the medium.

8.5 Wavelength

Definition
The letter used to represent the variable of wavelength is the Greek letter lamda (λ). As the name suggests, a wavelength refers to a physical distance. Specifically, the wavelength is the physical distance from one peak compression to the next peak compression. Similarly, the wavelength can be measured as the distance from one rarefaction to the next rarefaction, or, from any point on the cyclical wave to the next point where the cycle repeats. This definition of wavelength is depicted in *Figure 17*.

Graphical Representation

◊ *Example 1:*

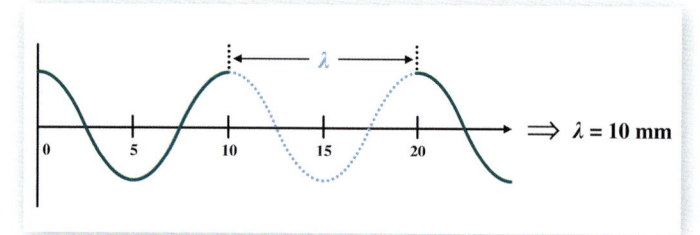

Fig. 17 **Longer wavelength**

◊ *Example 2:*

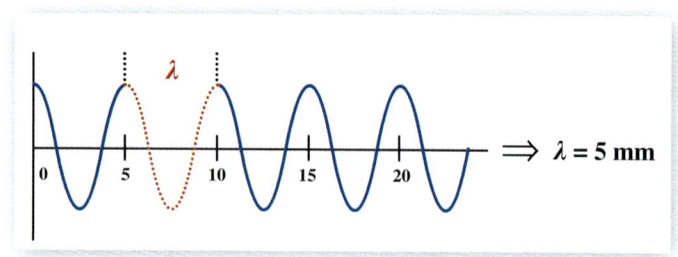

Fig. 18 **Shorter wavelength**

Distinguishing the Wavelength from the Period

Again we must stress how important it is for you to pay attention to the labels on the axes of any graph of data. For a still image, the depiction of the period and the depiction of the wavelength appear identical. For static images, the only way of distinguishing between the two very different parameters is to label the data indicating whether the physical unit is time or distance. *Figure 19* demonstrates the difference between the depiction of the period and the depiction of the wavelength. Although Wave A and Wave B look identical, Wave A is a depiction of the period and Wave B is a depiction of the wavelength.

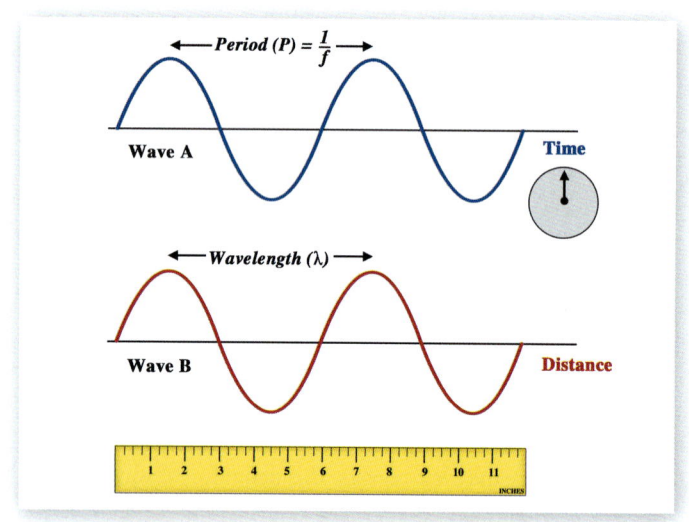

Fig. 19 **Understanding the difference between the period and the wavelength**

What Determines the Wavelength

The wavelength changes with changes in the frequency of the wave and with changes in the propagation velocity of the wave. In other words, the wavelength depends on characteristics of both the source and the medium. The illustrations of *Figure 20* and *Figure 21* demonstrate how the wavelength varies with change in the frequency of the wave, and with change to the propagation velocity of the wave.

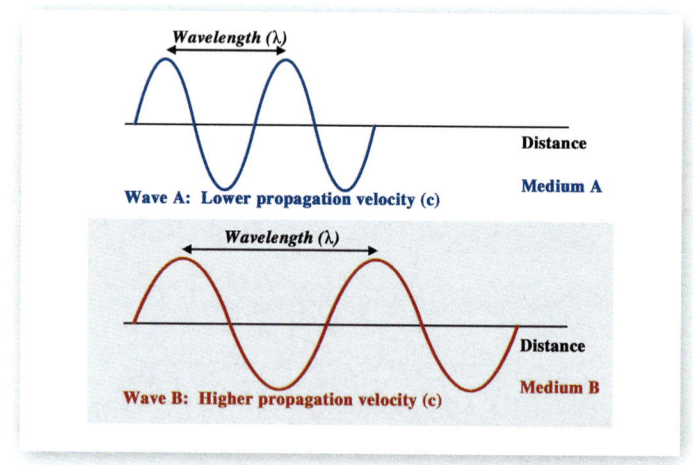

Fig. 20 **Wavelength dependence on propagation velocity**

Scenario 1:

Referring to *Figure 20*, waves A and B are both the same frequency since both waves have 2 cycles per second (2 Hz). However, wave B travels a greater distance than wave A during 1 second, so medium B has a higher propagation velocity than medium A. From *Figure 20*, it is clear that wave B also has a longer wavelength. Therefore, as the propagation velocity increases, the wavelength also increases, or mathematically we can say that the wavelength and the propagation velocity are proportional:

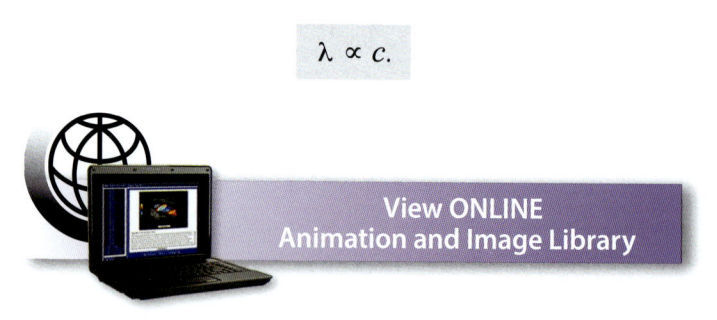

$$\lambda \propto c.$$

Scenario 2:

Referring to *Figure 21*, waves A and B are in the same medium and hence, have the same propagation velocity. However, wave A has three cycles per second, whereas wave B has only two cycles per second. Wave A represents a higher frequency wave than wave B. From *Figure 21*, it is clear that wave B has a longer wavelength. Therefore, as the frequency decreases, the wavelength increases, or mathematically we can say that the wavelength and the frequency are inversely proportional:

$$\lambda \propto \frac{1}{f}.$$

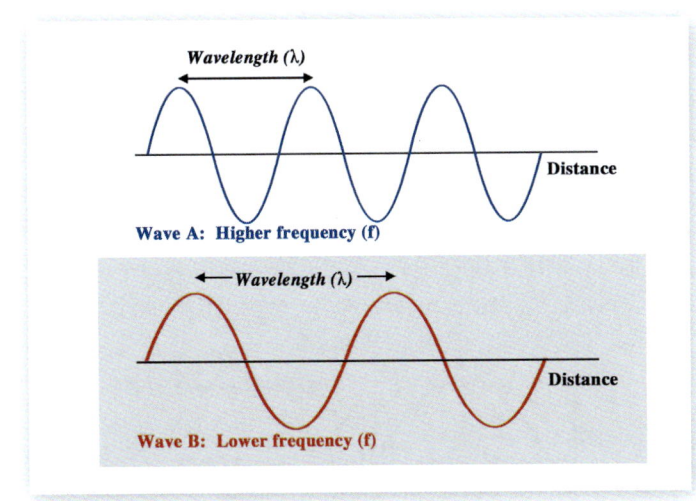

Fig. 21 **Wavelength dependence on frequency**

> **KEY CONCEPT**
>
> The wavelength is the physical distance between compressions (or rarefactions) within a medium.

The Wavelength Equation

The two relative expressions just derived can be combined into one equation, or:

$$\lambda = \frac{c}{f}.$$

This equation is referred to, not surprisingly, as the wavelength equation. Because of its importance in diagnostic ultrasound, we will be reviewing the wavelength equation in more depth in Level 2 and then persistently throughout the rest of this text. You must commit this equation to memory.

Different Ways of Remembering the Wavelength Equation

Beside brute force memorization, there are at least two other means by which you can recall the all important wavelength equation. The first of these two approaches is to go through the mental thought experiments just discussed. This approach is very useful since it forces you to think about the physical relationships between the wavelength and the frequency and between the wavelength and the propagation velocity.

The other approach is to use the units to help you recall the equation. Consider the units for frequency, propagation velocity, and wavelength:

Frequency (f) • *Wavelength (λ) = Propagation Velocity (c)*

f	λ	c
$\left(\frac{1}{sec}\right)$	m	$\frac{m}{sec}$

Visually, it should be obvious that multiplying $\left(\frac{1}{sec}\right) * m = \frac{m}{sec}$, or, $f * \lambda = c$.

This is the same equation we derived, just written in terms of c instead of lambda.

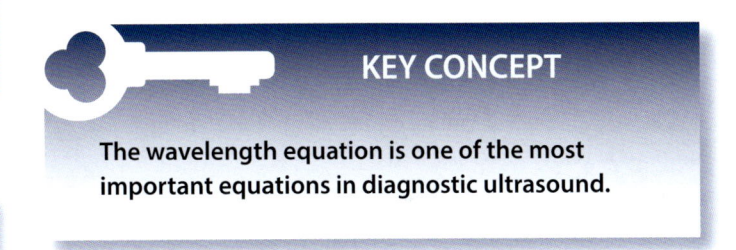

> **KEY CONCEPT**
>
> The wavelength equation is one of the most important equations in diagnostic ultrasound.

Longitudinal Wave Depiction

Now that we have learned the wave parameters of frequency, period, and wavelength, it is useful to relate these parameters shown on a transverse wave depiction with the parameters as displayed on a longitudinal wave depiction (*Figure 22*).

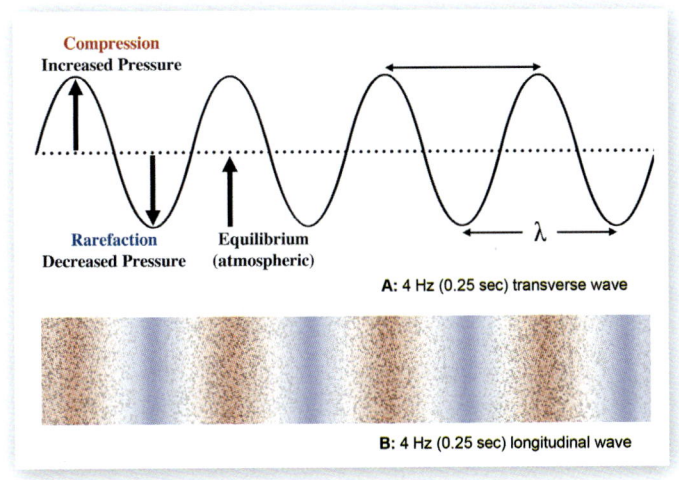

Fig. 22 **Relating transverse depiction with longitudinal wave characteristics**

8.6 Amplitude

Definition
In simplest terms, the amplitude of a physical quantity is defined as the strength, volume, or size of that physical quantity. For example, when listening to music, the amplitude of the music is determined by the volume knob. If you increase the volume on the stereo, the music becomes louder, meaning the amplitude becomes higher. In more formal terms, the amplitude is defined as the maximum variation of a variable from its mean value.

Units
The measure of amplitude can be applied to many different physical quantities such as pressure, density, temperature, distance, electropotential energy, etc. As a result, the unit associated with an amplitude measurement is dependent on the parameter that is being measured. Earlier in this chapter, we were exposed to many different units for amplitude when we discussed the acoustic variables.

Just as there are parameters which change when a sound wave propagates through a medium (the acoustic variables), there is an electrical variable which varies with the propagation of an electrical wave, more commonly referred to as the voltage. Not surprisingly, the unit for voltage is Volts.

Graphical Representation
Since Volts is a unit for amplitude, we can use *Figure 23* of a varying electrical signal as an illustration of amplitude. In this case, the amplitude is measured as 2 Volts.

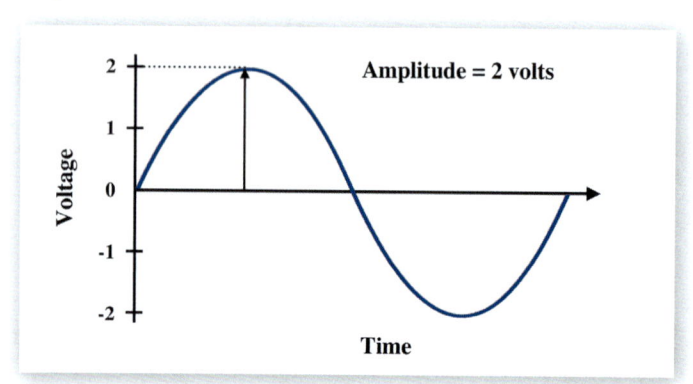

Fig. 23 **Measuring the amplitude**

Calculating the Amplitude
Using the formal definition of amplitude, it is relatively intuitive how to measure or calculate the amplitude of a cyclically varying signal. Since the definition of the amplitude is the maximum variation of a variable from its mean, the following steps can be employed to determine the equation for the amplitude:

1) Start by identifying the mean.
2) Graphically display the "maximum variation" or farthest point of the signal from the mean (the arrow in the following figure).
3) Label the maximum.
4) The difference between these two values is the amplitude. Mathematically, a difference implies subtraction.

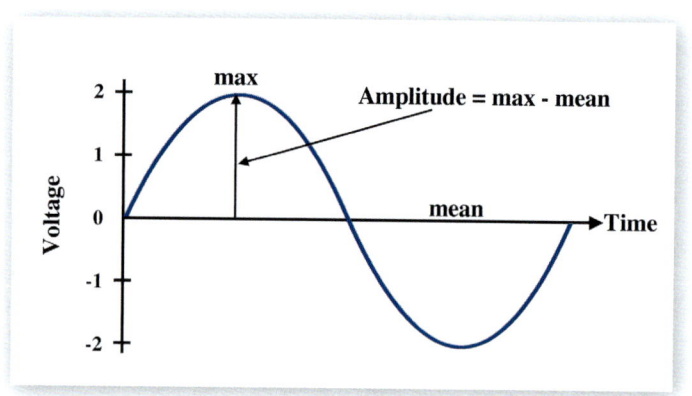

Fig. 24 **Defining the amplitude equation**

Now you should notice that the wave depicted is symmetric about the baseline, therefore, the distance from the top of the wave (the maximum) to the middle point of the wave (the mean) is the same as the distance from the bottom point of the wave to the mean. Therefore the amplitude can be defined as the distance from the mean to the maximum, or the distance from the minimum to the mean. This fact is illustrated in *Figure 25*.

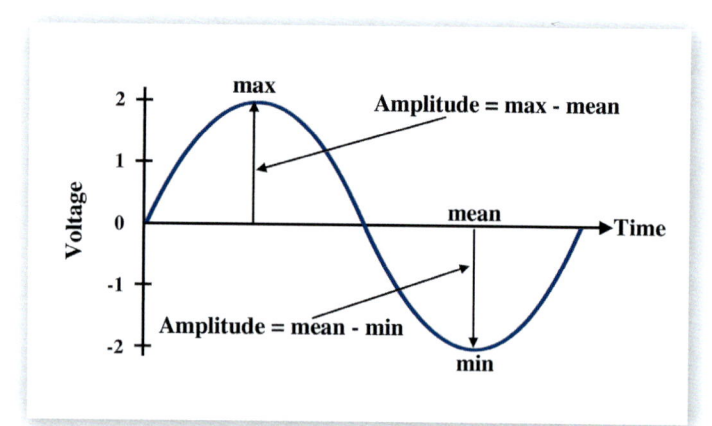

Fig. 25 **Defining the amplitude equation**

You should also notice that there is yet one more method of calculating the amplitude from the following graph. Again, since the wave is symmetric about the mean, the amplitude can also be derived by taking half of the total distance from the maximum to the minimum, as illustrated in *Figure 26*.

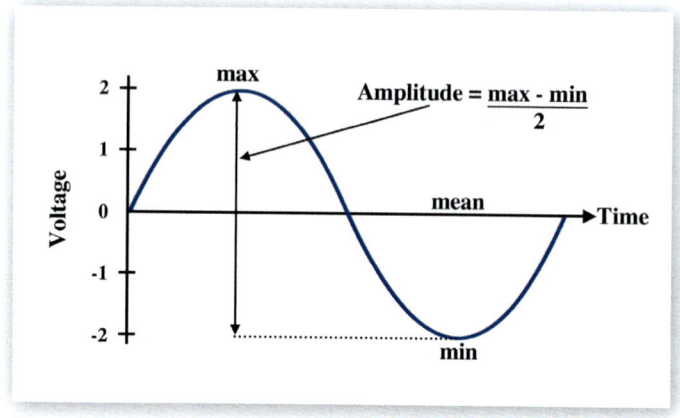

Fig. 26 **Defining the amplitude equation**

Therefore, there are "three" methods of calculating the amplitude which we will combine together into this one form:

$$Amplitude = (max - mean) = (mean - min) = \frac{(max - min)}{2}.$$

We will use some examples to further illustrate how to calculate the amplitude.

◊ *Example:*

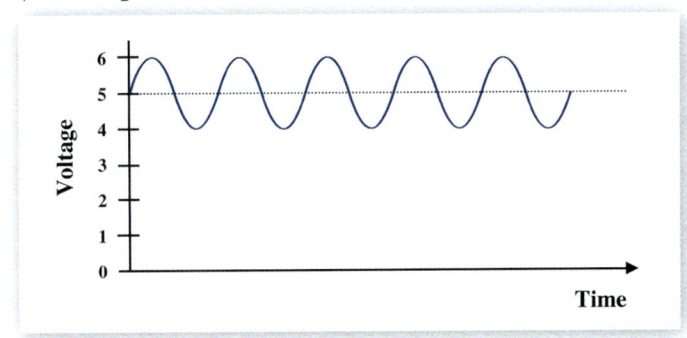

Amp = mean - min = 5 - 4 = 1 Volt
or
Amp = max - mean = 6 - 5 = 1 Volt
or
Amp = (max − min)/2 = (6 − 4)/2 = 1 Volt

◊ *Example:*

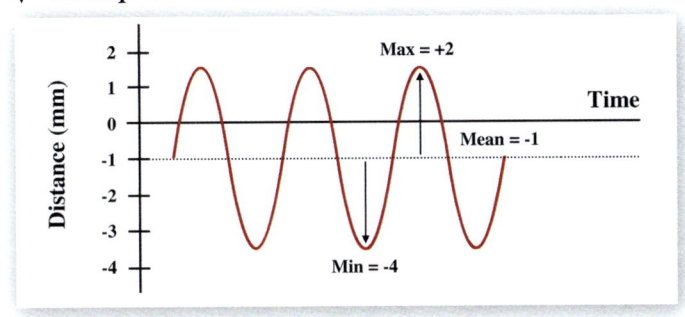

Amp = mean - min = -1 - (- 4) = 3 mm
or
Amp = max - mean = 2 - (-1) = 3 mm
or
Amp = (max − min)/2 = (2 - (-4))/2 = 3 mm

KEY CONCEPT

The amplitude is a measure of the strength or size of a physical quantity. Voltage is a measure of electrical amplitude.

9. Addition of Waves

The final topic in this section relates to wave addition. As with most of the topics discussed within this chapter, the full import of what is being taught will only be realized with progression through the book. With respect to ultrasound, understanding wave addition is fundamental to understanding the operation of phased array transducers. Wave addition is needed to grasp the concept of how ultrasound beams are steered and focused electronically. You might at this point think that this information is not that critical since you most likely don't have plans to design an ultrasound system or an ultrasound transducer anytime soon. However, understanding wave addition is critical for a very different reason than you would most likely guess.

The ability to determine flow direction in spectral and color Doppler is contingent upon understanding how different image formats are produced by different transducer types. If you do not understand how an image is produced, you will never truly be able to determine the direction of blood flow. In addition, there are some artifacts associated with the inability to make waves add up "perfectly" to create an ideal beam. You will learn that this limitation results in a very real artifact called grating lobes. Again, the ability to understand this artifact is directly related to understanding how multiple waves add together from phased array transducers. These concepts will also be employed in advanced processing and imaging techniques such as pulse inversion harmonics, compound imaging, retrospective dynamic transmit focusing, and color persistence.

9.1 Constructive Interference (In Phase Waves)

For now, we will content ourselves with just learning the basic principles of wave addition. Let us assume you directed two waves in the exact same direction, with exactly the same frequency and the same amplitude. You would naturally expect the resulting wave to be twice as big.

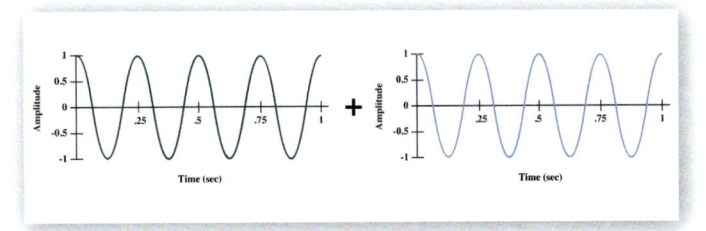

Fig. 27 **Two waves identical in amplitude, frequency, and phase**

Note that these two signals are called "in phase" because both waves reach peaks and cross the zero line at the exact same time. In other words, if the peaks and zero-crossing always align, there is no phase difference between the waves, and the waves are called "in phase."

Adding two signals which are in phase results in "constructive interference." As the name suggests, constructive interference occurs when two waves interact so as to produce one larger wave. In this example, *Figure 27*, the two waves used are identical in frequency, amplitude, and phase. Since each wave has the same amplitude, the resulting wave has twice the amplitude of either wave individually. This effect of pure constructive interference is demonstrated in the following figure, *Figure 28*.

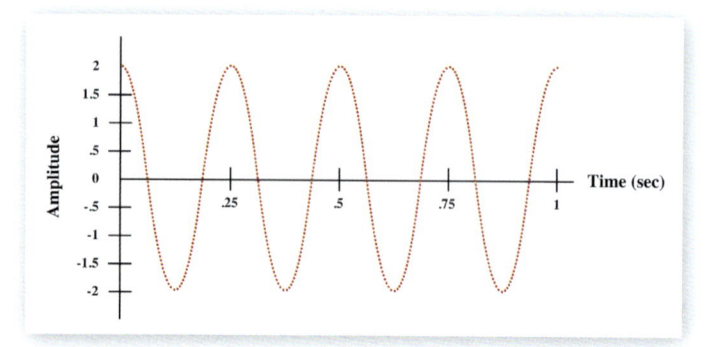

Fig. 28 **Constructive interference from two in phase waves**

9.2 Destructive Interference (Out of Phase Waves)
Now compare what would happen if you took the exact same two waves except shifted one of the waves in time so that the positive peaks of one wave aligned with the negative peaks of the other wave, as depicted in *Figure 29*.

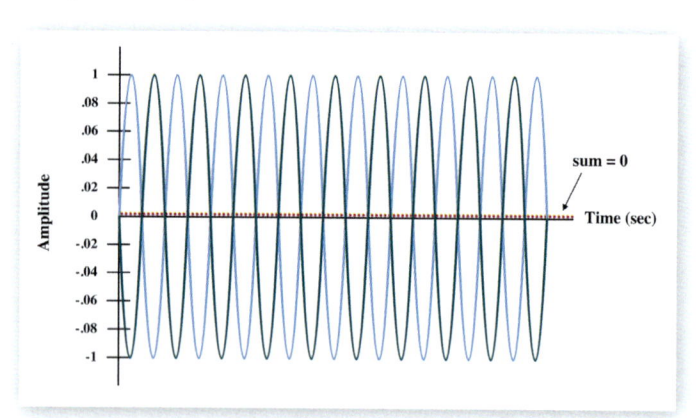

Fig. 29 **Destructive interference**

When two waves are aligned such that the peak of one wave aligns with the minimum of the other wave, the waves have a phase difference of 180° and are said to be completely "out of phase."

Notice that the two completely out of phase waves interact and cancel each other out. When two waves are purely out of phase, the result is not surprisingly termed destructive interference. In this case, since the amplitudes were identical, the net result is a complete cancellation.

9.3 Partial Constructive (or Partially Destructive) Interference
We have just demonstrated the case in which two waves are perfectly aligned in time (perfectly in phase) and when two waves are perfectly out of phase. In the first case, pure constructive interference occurred whereas in the second case, pure destructive interference occurred. Consider the much more commonly occurring case where the waves are out of phase with respect to each other, but not perfectly out of phase (less than 180 degrees). Common sense tells you that we should expect an effect somewhere between constructive and destructive interference. The next example demonstrates what happens if you take the exact same two waves as in the previous examples, except shift one wave in time so that the positive peaks are neither completely aligned nor anti-aligned to the positive peaks of the second wave.

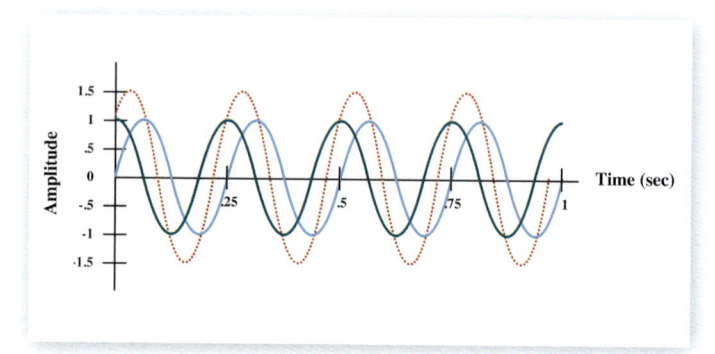

Fig. 30 **Partially constructive interference**

In this case, the two waves add only partially constructively, such that the new wave is not as "big" as when the two waves were in phase, and not as small as when the two waves were completely out of phase. This type of interference can also be called "partial destructive interference." Which term is used is inconsequential, but may reflect whether you are a pessimist or an optimist.

In this example, the two waves were created to be out of phase by 90 degrees (in fact they should look familiar to you as the sine and the cosine). Of course it is possible for the two waves to be out of phase by a phase shift such as 37 degrees or 98 degrees etc. As the phase shift gets smaller, approaching 0 degrees (or in phase), the interference becomes more and more constructive. Similarly, as the phase shift gets larger and larger (approaching 180 degrees) the interference becomes more and more destructive.

The examples given here demonstrate the concept of partially constructing interference using two waves. Of course this concept can be extrapolated to include many waves simultaneously. Pure constructive interference would occur when all of the waves were perfectly in phase. Pure destructive interference would occur when all of the waves were completely out of phase. In the ultrasound world, the much more likely scenario is not pure constructive or pure destructive interference, but rather a whole range of varying phase delays between the many waves resulting in partial constructive interference.

View ONLINE Clarifying Clip

> **KEY CONCEPT**
>
> The concept of constructive and destructive signal interference is foundational to ultrasound and many medical techniques. This concept will help explain such concepts as how transducers produce images, how certain artifacts in imaging occur, and how many more advanced imaging techniques such as color persistence, frame averaging, compound imaging, and retrospective dynamic transmit focusing work.

10. Exercises and Conceptual Questions

View ONLINE Exercises & Conceptual Questions

LEVEL 2: Board Level

11. Relating Wave Characteristics to Application and Relevance in Diagnostic Ultrasound

In Level 1, we developed the rudimentary understanding of waves as a general phenomenon. Although all of the material covered in Level 1 is applicable, there was no effort made to relate these concepts and parameters with actual scanning. This approach is intentional since a foundation must be built before we can hope for an understanding of greater complexity.

The task is now to relate those general parameters of Level 1 with the relevance to diagnostic ultrasound and ultimately the importance of how well you can control system parameters to perform a good clinical study. The wave parameters discussed and the concepts taught in this chapter are the foundation to all later chapters. Therefore, we will need to make a great effort to ensure that a thorough understanding is developed. To facilitate this understanding, this section will include many numerical examples. Additionally, you should make certain to complete all of the conceptual questions and exercises as a means of testing your readiness to progress on to Level 2 of later chapters.

12. Wave Characteristics and Parameters

12.1 Frequency and Period
Perhaps the wave parameter first thought of when scanning a patient is the operating, or transmit frequency. Specifically, the operating frequency refers to the frequency at which the transducer crystal vibrates. This vibrational energy is then coupled into the body as a sound wave, compressing and decompressing the tissue.

◊ *Example:*
> If a 2 MHz transducer is used, the sound wave compresses and decompresses the tissue 2 million times per second. Since the period is the reciprocal of the frequency, a 2 MHz wave has a period of
>
> $$Period = \frac{1}{f} = \frac{1}{2\ MHz} = 0.5\ \mu sec.$$

12.2 The General Term Frequency
In reality, the term "frequency" is a general term which can refer to any periodic event. There are many different frequencies such as the operating or transmit frequency (as we just described), the pulse repetition frequency, the frame frequency (usually called the frame rate), the Doppler shifted frequency, etc. If the term frequency is used in ultrasound without any qualifying words like "pulse repetition", "frame", or "Doppler", then it is generally presumed that the frequency being referenced is the operating frequency.

Classifications of Sound

What Sound is Not
Although many people would define "sound" as something that can be heard, this definition is unequivocally ambiguous. Even from person to person there is variation as to what frequencies can be heard. Also, with age, hearing decreases, especially at the higher frequency ranges. What is heard by one person may not be heard by another. Therefore, without any significant discussion of physics, this definition is already flawed.

Sound is a longitudinal mechanical wave of any frequency. It is useful to further define sound into various classifications.

The Human Audible Range
The human audible range is usually defined as any sound wave with a frequency between 20 Hz to 20 kHz. In reality, very few adults can hear frequencies anywhere close to 20 kHz. In general, the highest frequencies heard by most adults is below 17 kHz and quite frequently well below 15 kHz. Not surprisingly, humans classify sound ranges according to the human audible range. By adding a prefix to the word sound, we can then specify a specific range of frequencies. For example, the prefix "infra" means "below" so infrasound is sound below human hearing, or below 20 Hz. The prefix "ultra" means "above" so ultrasound is any sound above human hearing, or above 20 kHz.

At this point you must make a distinction between ultrasound and diagnostic ultrasound. Diagnostic ultrasound is a subset of ultrasound. Specifically, diagnostic ultrasound refers to the range of frequencies useful for medical evaluation.

The Diagnostic Range (Non-invasive)

The diagnostic range is usually specified as the range of frequencies from 2 MHz to about 18 or 20 MHz. Clearly from these numbers, interpreting the terminology "diagnostic range" requires certain assumptions. When the term "diagnostic frequencies" or "diagnostic range" is used there is generally a tacit assumption that only non-invasive, transcutaneous ultrasound is being referenced. There are certainly applications of diagnostic ultrasound that utilize frequencies higher than 20 MHz. It is important to realize that the range of frequencies considered useful for diagnostic ultrasound changes with advancements in technology. Not many years ago, the diagnostic range was considered about 2-12 MHz. It is fully anticipated that with time, this range will again increase. We will further discuss these points later in this section.

Classifications of Sound

Putting the information of the last few paragraphs together in one table yields:

Infrasound	0 Hz - 20 Hz (below human audible)
Audible	20 Hz - 20 kHz (human audible)
Ultrasound	>20 kHz (above human audible)
Diagnostic	2 MHz - 20 MHz (approximate conventional diagnostic range)

Table 2 **Defining sound ranges**

Figure 31 presents this data graphically.

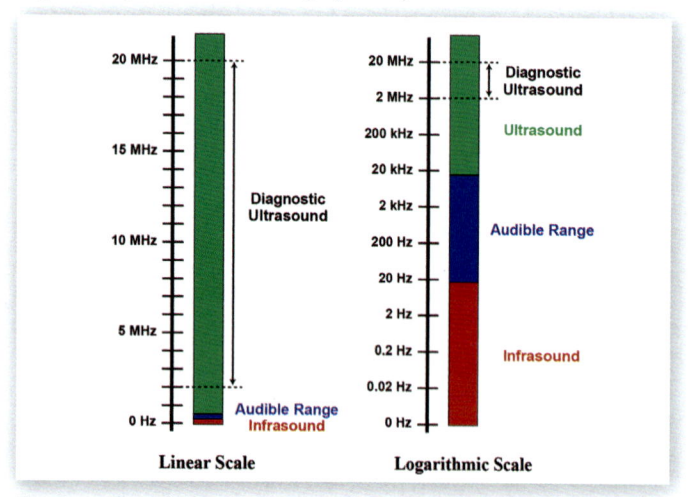

Fig. 31a **Classification of sound (linear and logarithmic graphs)**

Note: The two scales in Figure 31a give the exact same information. Recall that logarithmic graphs are good for dealing with a large dynamic range. Because of the large dynamic range of this data, notice how the logarithmic scale presentation is much easier to decipher than the linear scale presentation.

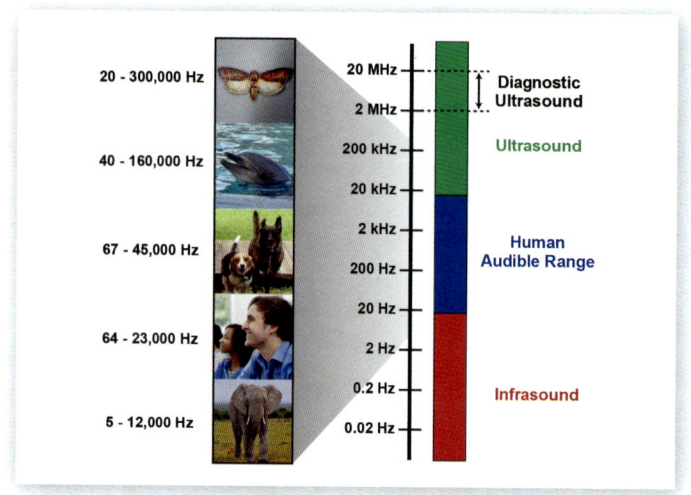

Fig. 31b **Classification of sound (audible ranges)**

KEY CONCEPT

The "sound ranges" are referenced to the human audible range.

CHECKPOINT: Exam Tip

Conventional diagnostic ultrasound commonly uses frequencies between 2 MHz and 20 MHz although lower frequencies are sometimes used (in some Doppler applications and with harmonic imaging) and some higher frequencies are used (such as for imaging small parts, intravascular ultrasound, and dermatology).

Why 2 MHz to 20 MHz?

In general, conventional diagnostic ultrasound does not commonly use frequencies much below 2 MHz because of poor detail resolution. From the wavelength equation, we know that a lower frequency results in a longer wavelength. We will learn in later chapters that longer wavelengths result in a diminishing ability to resolve structures close together and to discern fine detail. At some point, the resolution is considered so poor that there is little reason to acquire data. The frequency of 2 MHz, is generally the limit of acceptable resolution. However, there are exceptions. Some newer harmonic techniques will transmit at frequencies lower than 2 MHz and receive at frequencies near or above 2 MHz. Also, there are some applications of Doppler which do not require high resolution, but do require extraordinary sensitivity, and therefore utilize frequencies below 2 MHz (generally around 1.6 or 1.8 MHz).

The upper limit of 20 MHz is dictated by the inability of higher frequency sound to penetrate deep into the patient. In Chapter 3, the concept of attenuation will be fully discussed. For now, you should realize that the diagnostic frequency range really demonstrates one of the classic trade-offs on diagnostic ultrasound: resolution versus penetration.

Just as there are exceptions to using frequencies below 2 MHz, there are obvious exceptions to using frequencies above 20 MHz. For small parts imaging, if the imaging is very superficial, it is now common to exceed the 20 MHz range.

Intravascular Ultrasound (Frequencies Above the Typical Diagnostic Range)

Another example of when higher frequencies are used for diagnostic ultrasound is intravascular ultrasound. Intravascular ultrasound (IVUS) began in the late 1980s and, depending on the application, uses frequencies generally ranging from 20 to 40 MHz. The primary goal of intravascular ultrasound is to assess vessel walls and help characterize plaque morphology. The transducer is either a single rotated element or a very small phased array. The transducer, contained within a sheath, is attached to the end of a catheter usually less than 1 mm in diameter. The high frequencies are desirable for maximal resolution. Since the imaging depths are so shallow, and since there is no air interface, these high frequencies are tenable.

Uses of IVUS include:

- assessment of lesion calcium
- vessel and lesion dimensions
- confirmation of atherosclerotic plaque
- plaque morphology and plaque assessment for vulnerability
- adequacy of stent deployment

The following image of *Figure 32*, demonstrates an IVUS image from a coronary artery.

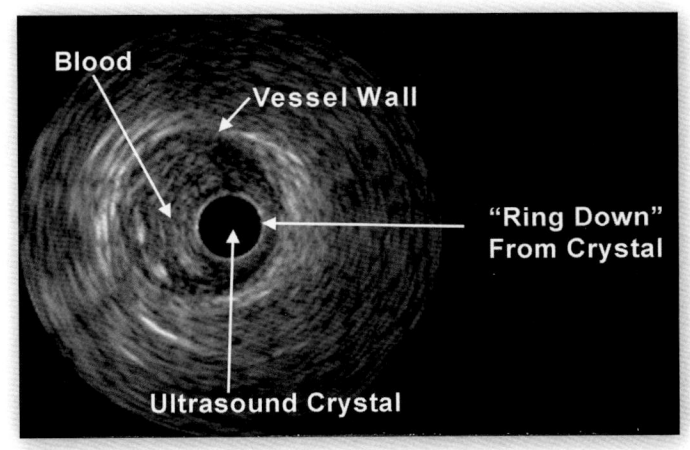

Fig. 32 **Intravascular Ultrasound (IVUS) image of a coronary artery**

Therapeutic Ultrasound (Physiotherapy and Focused Ultrasound)

Therapeutic ultrasound (physiotherapy) has been in use for many years, and has been increasing in efficacy. Therapeutic ultrasound is used to increase blood flow and manage several soft tissue conditions such as muscle spasm, tendonitis, and bursitis. Additionally, therapeutic ultrasound is used to reduce joint contractures, scar tissue, and pain as well as to promote wound healing. The typical frequency range for therapeutic ultrasound is between 0.5 MHz and 3.0 MHz, and most commonly, a frequency close to 1 MHz is used. Beam intensities range from about 0.25 W/cm^2 to as high as 2.5 W/cm^2 resulting in tissue temperature rises as high as 4 degrees Celsius up to depths of about 5 cm.

In recent years, the term therapeutic ultrasound has also started to include some very exciting acoustic surgical techniques based on using high intensity ultrasound. High-intensity focused ultrasound (HIFU) or now more commonly referred to as simply focused ultrasound, has shown promise for selective destruction of tissue volumes such as cancerous lesions in the liver, kidney, breast, and prostate. By using extremely high intensity beams, large temperature increases are possible. By focusing the beam, the energy can be concentrated on the diseased tissue while sparing the healthy surrounding tissue. The frequencies commonly used for HIFU are from 0.5 MHz to about 10 MHz with transmit intensities as high as 1,500 W/cm^2. These high intensities can raise the local temperature above 56 degrees Celsius, and are allowed to exist for a few seconds. Focused ultrasound is discussed in detail in a later chapter.

Relation to Future Topics

As mentioned at the beginning of this chapter, one of the goals is to help the student learn the material in the context of why each piece matters and of how the pieces interrelate. The following list indicates the various topics which will build from the concepts and discussion contained in this section on frequency:

1) penetration
2) types of reflection
3) resolution
4) harmonics
5) appropriate transducer selection for imaging and for Doppler
6) frequency fusion (compounding)

12.3 Propagation Velocity

General

In Level 1, we discussed the meaning of the propagation velocity, and that it is primarily determined by the properties of the medium through which the wave is propagating. Perhaps one of the most maligned topics in ultrasound physics has been the discussion of exactly what properties of the medium affect the propagation velocity and how. In an effort to streamline the topic, it is frequently oversimplified such that what the student memorizes no longer agrees with what is observed when scanning a patient. For anyone who then tries to apply what they are learning with what they are clinically seeing there is a very disturbing disconnect. In the upcoming sections, we will discuss both the reality and overly simplified approach.

Terminology: Elasticity, Compressibility, Stiffness, and Bulk Modulus

There are many terms that are commonly used when referring to the properties of the medium that determine the propagation velocity. Many of the terms are related and, although each has a specific, differentiating physics meaning, for the purposes of diagnostic ultrasound, some of these differences can be ignored. Note that these concepts will be discussed in greater detail in Chapter 15 because of the relevance to newer ultrasound approaches which utilize shear and strain waves. For now, we will focus on the basic terminology as relates to longitudinal waves and more conventional ultrasound.

Elasticity

The term elasticity refers to the ability of a solid object to return to its original shape after distortion by a force. For example, if a mechanical vibration distorts a crystal's dimensions, the elasticity is a measure of that crystal material's ability to return to its original "un-deformed" shape.

Compressibility

The compressibility of a material is a measure of how much the volume of the material changes for a given distorting force (pressure). A high compressibility implies that the material can be compressed to a much smaller volume than a low compressibility material, for the same given force (pressure). For the purposes of ultrasound, it is generally presumed that a compressible material is elastic and vice versa.

Stiffness (Inelasticity)

In ultrasound, the term "stiffness" is commonly used to imply the inverse of elasticity or compressibility. Therefore, a stiff material is a material which cannot be compressed much. Since the prefix "in" means not, an inelastic material is a material which is "not" elastic and hence, stiff.

Bulk Modulus

The bulk modulus is formally defined as the decrease in the ratio of the stress to the strain, where the stress is defined as the change in the pressure applied, and the strain is defined as the percent change in volume which occurs as a result of the stress (as pictured in *Figure 33*). Looking at the equation, it should be easy to imagine that stiff materials would require a lot of pressure to achieve a small percent change in volume. Therefore, when a material is stiff, the bulk modulus becomes large, when a material is more elastic, the bulk modulus is a smaller value. In essence, for simplicity, we will simply relate the bulk modulus with the material "stiffness," or the inverse of compressibility. Therefore, a low compressibility material would have a high bulk modulus.

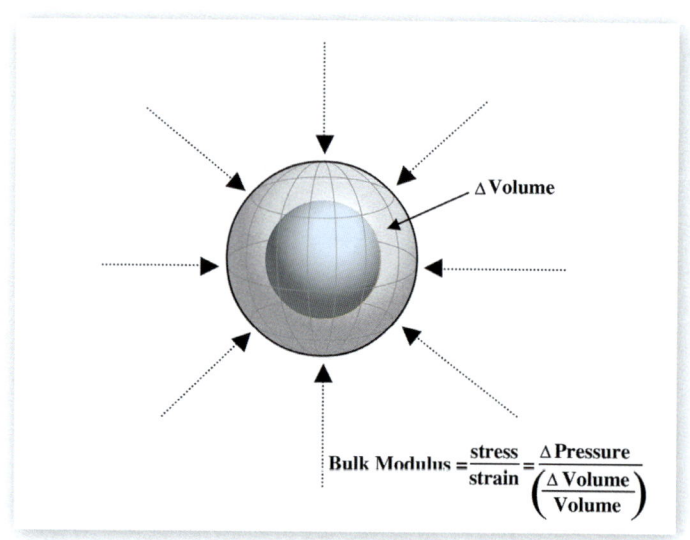

Fig. 33 **Changing volume with pressure**

$$\text{Bulk Modulus} = \frac{\text{stress}}{\text{strain}} = \frac{\Delta \text{Pressure}}{\left(\frac{\Delta \text{Volume}}{\text{Volume}}\right)}$$

Table Relating Terminology

The following table should help put all of these terms into perspective.

High Bulk Modulus	incompressible	inelastic	stiff
Low Bulk Modulus	compressible	elastic	not stiff

Table 3 **Bulk modulus and related terms**

Note: Although technically these terms are not completely equivalent, for the purposes of ultrasound, the lack of rigor is acceptable.

The Propagation Velocity Analogy

It has already been stated that the propagation velocity is determined by properties of the medium, and not by the frequency of the wave. We will use a classic physics analogy to determine what parameters of the medium will affect the propagation velocity.

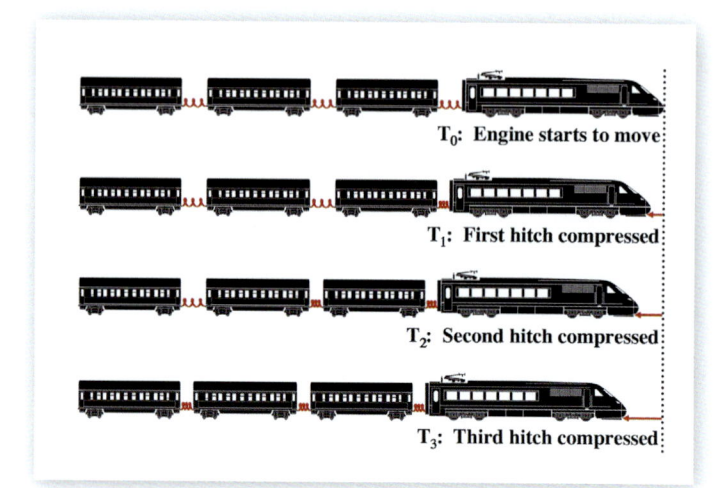

T_0: Engine starts to move
T_1: First hitch compressed
T_2: Second hitch compressed
T_3: Third hitch compressed

Fig. 34 **Train in reverse and compression**

Consider a situation in which a long train is sitting in a station and needs to go in reverse. From time zero of *Figure 34* (T$_o$) you will notice that the hitch between each pair of cars is drawn as an uncompressed spring. As depicted in the diagram, at time T$_o$, the train starts to back up. Because there is slack in the hitch between the engine and the first car there is a time delay from when the engine first starts to move and when the first car starts to move (time T$_1$). Once the first car starts to move, there is another time delay until the slack between the first and second car is removed. Once the slack is compressed out (time T$_2$), the second car starts to move. In this manner, the longitudinal compression wave travels from the engine until it reaches the last car of the train, resulting in movement of the last car. Before the train started to move, you could consider the train as compressible because of the slack between each car. Once the train starts moving, you would hear a series of "clangs" that represents the time when the slack between each hitch has been compressed out and the train becomes a rigid object.

The speed with which the wave propagates from one car to the next is clearly dependent on the amount of slack between each car. If there is a lot of slack, then the speed will be slow, as more time is required for the previous car to move a greater distance to compress out the slack. This concept is depicted in *Figure 35*.

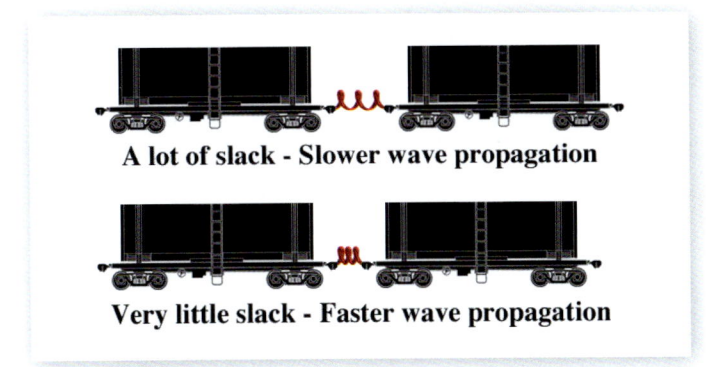

Fig. 35 **Compressibility and propagation velocity**

You can also imagine that the time required to compress out the slack between the hitches will depend on the mass of each car. If the train is unloaded, each car will be easier to accelerate, and the car will begin to move more quickly. Instead, if the train is heavily loaded, more time will be required to accelerate each car and the wave velocity through the train will be slower.

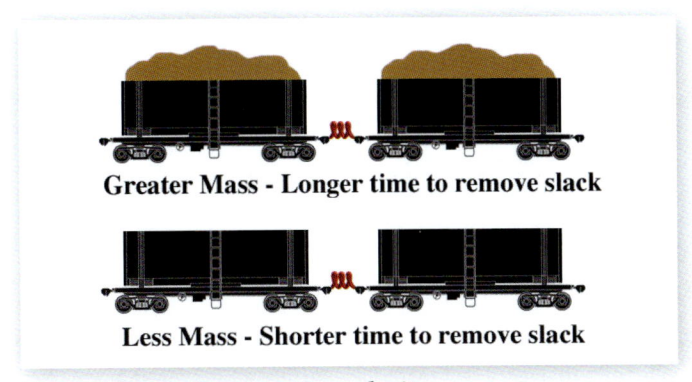

Fig. 36 **Mass and propagation velocity**

Interestingly, if you carefully analyze this analogy, it will become clear that the velocity of the train engine is actually slower than the wave propagation velocity. Referring to *Figure 37*, notice that in the time it took the engine to move the short distance of 3 meters, the wave has propagated from the engine of the train to the end of the fourth car or 30 meters. Let's imagine that this propagation occurred over a 1 second time period. The velocity of the train is therefore 3 meters/second whereas the wave propagation velocity is 30 meters/second. For this example, the wave propagation velocity is actually 10 times greater than the velocity of the train.

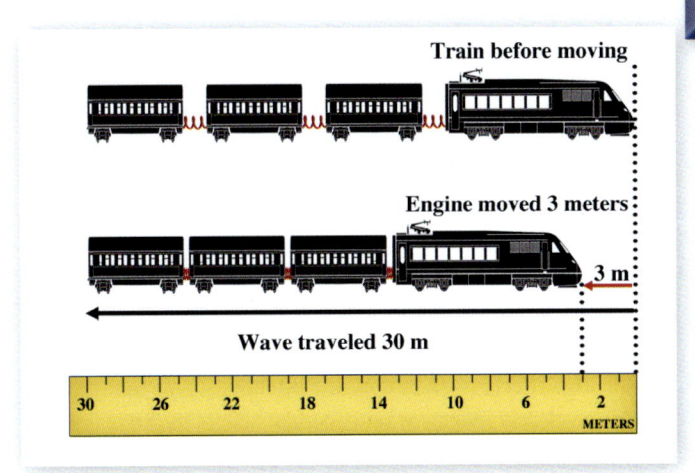

Fig. 37 **Wave velocity versus train velocity**

Relating the Analogy to the Speed of Sound

In our train analogy, the train cars represent the molecules of a medium, and the compressible hitches between the cars represent the molecular bonds. From our analogy, the "slack" in the hitches is analogous to the compressibility of the medium, and the mass of the train cars is analogous to the density of the medium.

From our analogy, we know that an increase in density results in a decrease in propagation velocity, presuming that the slack in the hitches was not changed. We would therefore expect to see an inverse relationship between the propagation velocity and the density of the material.

$$propagation\ velocity\ (c) \propto \frac{1}{density\ (\rho)}.$$

However, this is not the entire story. As we will see, unlike the train analogy described, a change in density in a material usually results in a change in the compressibility of the material as well.

From our analogy, we also know that if the slack between the train cars (the compressibility) is increased, the propagation velocity will decrease, presuming that there is no change in the density (train load). We would therefore expect an inverse relationship between the propagation velocity and the compressibility of a material. Again, this is not the whole story.

$$\text{propagation velocity } (c) \propto \frac{1}{\text{compressibility}}.$$

In both cases of our analogy, a presumption was made that a change in one parameter did not affect the other parameter. Specifically, it was presumed that changing the density did not affect the compressibility, and that a change in compressibility did not affect the density. This is where the analogy breaks down. Let's modify our analogy slightly so that it better reflects reality. Let's imagine that if a train is designed to be very heavily loaded, it is likely that the hitches will be designed with less compressibility (similar to how heavy duty vehicles have stiffer shock absorbers). Now, when a train has a heavier load, it also is less compressible and we must consider that the two effects work in opposite directions. This modification now more closely reflects what generally occurs in the real world. For the materials commonly found in the body, a change in density is accompanied by a much greater change in the compressibility.

View ONLINE Clarifying Clip

View ONLINE Animation and Image Library

Putting the Pieces Together to Create the Equation
We have determined that the speed of sound is determined principally by two parameters, the density of the material, and what we have referred to as the compressibility of the material (also related to the stiffness of the material or the bulk modulus). In physics, the most precise way of defining the relationship is to use the bulk modulus (related to the inverse of the compressibility). So we know:

$$\text{propagation velocity } (c) \propto \frac{1}{\text{density } (\rho)}$$

and

$$\text{propagation velocity } (c) \propto \frac{1}{\text{compressibility}} \Rightarrow (c) \propto \beta_{modulus}.$$

Without proof, we will just state that the relationship between the propagation velocity and both the density and the bulk modulus is a square root. Therefore we have:

$$c = \sqrt{\frac{\beta_{modulus}}{\rho}}.$$

In other words, as the bulk modulus of a material increases (assuming no change in density) the propagation velocity increases. As the density increases (assuming no change in stiffness), the propagation velocity decreases.

Propagation Velocities for Various Materials
The following table lists the approximate propagation velocities for a range of materials from gases to solids.

Medium	Propagation Velocity
Gases	
Air (0 degrees C)	331 m/sec
Air (25 degrees C)	347 m/sec
Helium (0 degrees C)	972 m/sec
Hydrogen (0 degrees C)	1286 m/sec
Liquids	
Methyl alcohol (0 degrees C)	1130 m/sec
Methyl alcohol (25 degrees C)	1145 m/sec
Water (0 degrees C)	1405 m/sec
Mercury (25 degrees C)	1450 m/sec
Water (25 degrees C)	1495 m/sec
Ocean water (25 degrees C)	1530 m/sec
Solids	
Lead	1322 m/sec
Rubber	1600 m/sec
Gold	3240 m/sec
Copper	3560 m/sec
Brass	4700 m/sec
Aluminum	5100 m/sec
Stainless steel	5790 m/sec
Diamond	12000 m/sec

Table 4 **Propagation Velocities**

Discussion of Values in the Materials Table
As you can see from the above table, the propagation velocity for gases tends to be the lowest of the three states. In general, the propagation velocity for most gases is below 1,000 m/sec. From the table, it is clear that the propagation velocity in a gas changes with temperature. As the temperature increases, the propagation velocity increases. The propagation velocity for fluids is generally higher than for gases, and usually above 1,000 m/sec, but lower than 2,000 m/sec. The propagation velocity for fluids also shows temperature dependence.

For solids, there is a very large range of propagation velocities. More compressible materials like rubber have much lower propagation velocities than very stiff materials like diamonds. You should notice that the propagation velocity in most metals tends to be above 3000 m/sec. This fact should not be too surprising given the high stiffness of metals. The one clear exception given in the table is the material of lead. Although lead is relatively dense, it has a low bulk modulus, resulting in a relatively low propagation velocity (in comparison with other metals). This low bulk modulus is not too surprising when you consider how lead can be easily molded (deformed) and shaped.

Because metal objects are sometimes introduced into the body (needles for biopsy, prosthetic valves, stents), it is recommended that you remember that the velocity in metals tends to be relatively high.

What Affects Velocity Most in the Body

From the equation of Section 12.3.5, and from *Table 4*, it is easy to be misled with respect to expectations for propagation velocities in the body. From the equation, since the propagation velocity is dependent on the square root of both the bulk modulus and density, you might presume that both parameters have equal effects. Similarly, since most people think of the body as comprised of solids, you might infer that propagation velocities through the body would be more consistent with the upper end of the propagation velocity table. This thought process is where the biggest mistakes are made. Because of high fluid content, most tissues in the body (excluding lung and bone) tend to behave more like fluids than solids. In reality, for most materials found in the body, those that are slightly denser have a significantly higher bulk modulus (much less compressible, or much stiffer). Therefore, materials that are denser generally have much higher propagation velocities than materials that are less dense. This seems to contradict the relationship in the equation that the propagation velocity is inversely related to the density. However, just as we had to adjust our train analogy, we need to adjust our thinking. If it were possible to increase the density without increasing the stiffness of a tissue, then the relationship would hold as anticipated. Since for tissues in the body, increased density always implies an increase in bulk modulus, more dense tissues have higher (not lower) propagation velocities.

> **KEY CONCEPT**
>
> An increase in density usually results in an increase in stiffness (bulk modulus) thereby resulting in a higher propagation velocity.

Propagation Velocities in the Body

The following table lists the approximate propagation velocity for sound through many different biological materials. Note that these values can only be approximate since tissue composition varies from patient to patient, and in some cases, even by direction of sound propagation relative to the orientation of the tissues (for example: along the axis of the bone vs. across the bone or oriented with the muscle fibers vs. across the muscle fibers). If you look in the published literature regarding sound velocities through various tissues, you will see that a range of velocities are given for each tissue type.

Medium	Propagation Velocity
Air (25 degrees C)	347 m/sec
*Lung (inflated)	950 m/sec
Fat	1440 m/sec
Water (25 degrees C)	1495 m/sec
Brain	1510 m/sec
"Soft Tissue"	average 1540 m/sec
Liver	1560 m/sec
Kidney	1560 m/sec
Blood	1578 m/sec
*Diaphragm	1588 m/sec
Muscle	1588 m/sec
*Nerve	1630 m/sec
Skin	1700 m/sec
*Bone (cortical)	3515 m/sec
*Bone (max)	4080 m/sec

* values from https://itis.swiss/virtual-population/tissue-properties/database/acoustic-properties/speed-of-sound/

Table 5 **Propagation Velocities in the Body**

The following table (*Table 6*), demonstrates the relationship that generally exists for tissue in the body.

↑ ρ ⇒ Bulk modulus increases (incompressible, inelastic, stiff) ⇒ increases c
↓ ρ ⇒ Bulk modulus decreases (compressible, elastic, not stiff) ⇒ decreases c

Table 6 **Relating Density (ρ), Bulk Modulus and Propagation Velocity (c) in the Body**

> **KEY CONCEPT**
>
> Notice that higher density mediums have higher propagation velocities.

Discussion of Values in the Biological Table

As you can see from *Table 5*, the propagation velocities of the "biomaterials" (excluding bone and lung) are generally close to the propagation velocity of sound in water. Lung, when inflated, is comprised primarily of low density air, is very compressible and hence has a lower propagation velocity than other biological materials. Similarly, higher density bone is very incompressible. As a result of the high bulk modulus, the propagation velocity in bone is very high in comparison to other biological materials such as liver, kidney, or brain. The propagation velocity in water (at 25 degrees C) is close to 1500 m/sec. You will notice that many tissues have propagation velocities which, as a percentage, vary only slightly from this value. The propagation velocity for "soft tissue" is actually an approximate average velocity in the body presuming that the sound does not propagate through an air-filled cavity, a fluid-filled cavity, or bone. In reality, there is no specific tissue that comprises "soft tissue".

In the materials table (*Table 4* of section 12.3.7) we saw that the propagation velocity for gases and fluids varies with temperature. Although the propagation velocity in tissue varies with temperature, the normal range of variance is very small. We can therefore ignore temperature variation on propagation velocity in the body with very little introduction of error.

> **Author's Note:**
> **Density and Propagation Velocity**
>
> One of the greatest sources of confusion in ultrasound relates to how density affects propagation velocity. This concept has been taught incorrectly in multiple books for many years. As mentioned throughout the text, these authors, and hence the exam, ask the effect of a change in density on the propagation velocity. The reality is that more dense mediums almost always have higher propagation velocities, the opposite of what is taught in most physics books. This is because these authors have assumed that the density can be changed without changing the stiffness (bulk modulus) of the medium, a situation that does not generally match reality.
>
> *Table 7* shows what would happen in the real world for each situation (some not realistic but matching what other authors have written and some realistic). The realistic situations are highlighted in blue and the non-realistic (theoretical) situations are not highlighted.

Density	Stiffness/Bulk Modulus			Propagation Velocity
↑	+	NO CHANGE	⇨	↓
↓	+	NO CHANGE	⇨	↑
↑	+	↑	⇨	↑
↑	+	↓	⇨	↓
↓	+	↑	⇨	↑
↓	+	↓	⇨	↓

Table 7 Realistic (blue shaded) vs. Theoretical: the impact of density on propagation velocity

The Propagation Velocity Assumed by the Ultrasound System

Ultrasound systems assume a propagation velocity of 1540 m/sec to determine depth of structures. By measuring the time between the transmit event and the returning echoes, depth can be calculated using the distance equation. Given that the propagation velocity is assumed (1540 m/sec), and the time of travel (time of flight) is measured, the distance can be calculated. Since ultrasound is based on reflection, the distance traveled is actually twice the depth of the structure causing the reflection (sound travels to the structure and reflects back to the transducer, commonly referred to as the "roundtrip effect"). Therefore, by solving the distance equation and accounting for the roundtrip effect, the depth of structures in the body can be depicted in an ultrasound image.

Of course, the accuracy of the depth depiction is predicated on the assumed velocity of 1540 m/sec. When the velocity is other than 1540 m/sec, the depth prediction is not accurate (referred to as speed error artifact). Fortunately, the variance in propagation velocities, as a percentage, for most tissues varies relatively little and the associated errors are not too significant. However, whenever the propagation velocity varies more significantly, as occurs when scanning air filled regions, large fluid-filled cavities, bone, and virtually any man-made object in the body, the errors can become quite significant.

Relation to Future Topics

Knowledge of the propagation velocity through various materials in ultrasound is important for many reasons. Principally, the propagation velocity affects:

1) the depth prediction accuracy (speed error artifact)
2) the wavelength (and hence any parameter affected by the wavelength)
3) axial resolution
4) refraction and refraction related artifact
5) beam aberration

> **CHECKPOINT: Exam Tip**
>
> For general ultrasound imaging the system assumes a propagation velocity of 1540 m/sec.

12.4 Wavelength

The Equation and its Importance

In Section 1 we learned that the wavelength is determined principally by two parameters, the frequency of the wave, and the propagation velocity through the medium. With respect to ultrasound, the wave frequency is the transducer frequency, often referred to as the operating frequency.

The wavelength equation is one of two fundamental equations which dictate diagnostic ultrasound behavior. As we will learn in Chapter 3, the wavelength, in part, determines the type of reflection that occurs. Also, as we will learn in Chapter 4, the wavelength affects the resolution of the image in the axial direction (along the axis of the beam). Since both of these aspects of ultrasound are so critical, it is expected that you will be very familiar with the equation, what affects the wavelength, and how to calculate the wavelength.

Control of the Wavelength
Since the wavelength affects two critical parameters for ultrasound (reflection and resolution), it should make sense that we will want to analyze how the wavelength can be controlled.

When we analyze the equation, we consider how changes in frequency and propagation velocity affect the wavelength. Increasing the propagation velocity causes the wave to be "stretched out", increasing the wavelength (proportionality). Increasing the frequency dictates that there are more cycles for the same time period, or a shortening of the wavelength (inverse proportionality).

Recall that the propagation velocity is determined strictly by the properties of the medium. The operating frequency is determined strictly by the source. Therefore, one of the two parameters which determines the wavelength, the propagation velocity, is completely out of the control of the sonographer when imaging. Ironically, although the frequency is "chosen" by the user, the real world issue of penetration tends to restrict how much freedom the sonographer gets to exercise. As a result, with conventional ultrasound modalities, the sonographer has only a little control over the very important parameter of the wavelength.

Calculating the Wavelength
Calculating the wavelength from the wavelength equation is facilitated greatly by a thorough understanding of the metric table. The reduction in calculation complexity is illustrated by the following examples.

◊ *Example 1:* Calculate the wavelength for a 10 MHz operating frequency presuming a medium of "soft tissue".

$$f = 10\ MHz$$
$$c = 1540\ m/\sec$$
$$\lambda = ?$$

Using the equation: $\lambda = \dfrac{c}{f} = \dfrac{1540\ m}{10\ MHz * \sec} = \dfrac{154\ m}{1 M \dfrac{1}{\sec} * \sec} = 154\ \mu m$

(Recall that the metric table is based on reciprocals. A mega (M) in the denominator is equivalent to a micro (μ) in the numerator.)

◊ *Example 2:* Calculate the wavelength for a 2 MHz operating frequency presuming a medium of bone.

$$f = 2\ MHz$$
$$c = 4080\ m/\sec$$
$$\lambda = ?$$

Using the equation: $\lambda = \dfrac{c}{f} = \dfrac{4080\ m}{2\ MHz * \sec} = \dfrac{2040\ m}{1 M \dfrac{1}{\sec} * \sec} = 2040\ \mu m$

◊ *Example 3:* Calculate the wavelength (λ) in soft tissue using a 5 MHz transducer.

$$f = 5\ MHz$$
$$c = 1540\ m/\sec$$
$$\lambda = ?$$

Using the equation: $\lambda = \dfrac{c}{f} = \dfrac{1540\ m}{5\ MHz * \sec} = \dfrac{1540\ m}{5 M \dfrac{1}{\sec} * \sec} = 308\ \mu m$

Relation to Future Topics
As already mentioned, the wavelength is a critical parameter and will be discussed throughout the book in relation to many other topics. Specifically, the wavelength will be important for the following topics:

1. Types of reflection and signal strength
2. Types of reflection and artifacts
3. Resolution
4. Harmonics

KEY CONCEPT

The wavelength equation is important because:

- the wavelength affects the resolution
- the wavelength affects the reflection that occurs

12.5 Amplitude
In addition to the formal definition of the maximum variation from its mean, we learned in Level 1 that amplitude is a measure of size or loudness. The term "amplitude" is general, and can be used in reference to measuring changes in the four acoustic variables or for measuring changes in the electrical variable of electromotive force (voltage). Although the term amplitude can be used to assess the degree of change in any of the four acoustic variables, since these changes are relatively small, this application of amplitude is rarely

made. Usually, when referring to amplitude in ultrasound, the term is being used in reference to the transmit voltage which drives the transducer crystal elements.

Control of Electrical Amplitude and Transmit Gain

The control of the transmitted signal amplitude is achieved through the "transmit power" setting control on the ultrasound system. As discussed in the upcoming sections, although amplitude and power are different, there is a relationship between these two parameters. As a result, the control of the transmitted signal amplitude generally has many names depending on the equipment manufacturer. Some examples are acoustic power, output power, transmit, transmit gain, power gain, transmit voltage, acoustic amplitude, output intensity, acoustic intensity, and the acoustic output.

Although these many different names can be confusing, the confusion can be minimized by realizing that all of these terms (in one form or another) express the concept of how big the output signal is in terms of an amplitude or a power-related term. When the "transmit power" setting is increased, the amplitude of the transmit voltage which drives the transducer is increased.

Effect on Acoustic Pressure Field

As will be discussed in Chapter 5, a higher amplitude drive signal (voltage) to the transducer results in a greater mechanical distortion of the transducer crystal. This increase in distortion implies a stronger acoustic wave in the body. For a longitudinal wave such as sound, a higher amplitude wave implies a greater degree of compression and a greater degree of rarefaction. For our transverse depiction of a sound wave, this increase in amplitude is displayed as a taller wave, where the taller peak represents a higher compression, and the lower peak represents a greater rarefaction.

Relationship to Acoustic Power

The electrical voltage signal is a relatively easy parameter to physically measure. In comparison, measuring the acoustic amplitude of the pressure field is considerably more challenging. In the chapter on quality assurance (Chapter 11) the techniques for measuring acoustic pressure fields will be discussed. For now, it will suffice to know that the process is complex, difficult, and time consuming. Ultimately, it is desirable to have some method by which to relate a change in the transmit voltage (amplitude) to the possible benefit or risk to the patient.

For electrical signals, the power is proportional to the voltage of the signal (amplitude) squared. Power is defined as a measure of the rate at which energy is transferred or the rate at which work is performed and has units of Watts. If a transducer is run at a higher power, it should not be too surprising that the acoustic energy produced (the wave) will also have a higher power. This fact is important for at least two major reasons:

1. A higher power is related to a stronger ultrasound signal (improved signal-to-noise ratio resulting in a better image)

2. A higher power is also related to an increased risk of bioeffects (tissue damage) to the patient

In other words, driving the transducer with a higher transmit voltage will result in higher power waves which potentially produce better images because of increased penetration, but with a potential increase in the risk of bioeffects.

Since both of these parameters are of great interest to us, we would like to have an easy method of assessing relative improvement in the signal and relative increased risk from bioeffects. Recalling that it is very challenging to measure the acoustic pressure field, we will instead look for a relationship between the acoustic power and the transmit voltage. Since a higher voltage implies a higher electrical power, and a higher electrical power implies a higher acoustic power, we will relate the acoustic power to the electrical voltage as:

$$Power \propto (Voltage)^2$$
or, in general,
$$Power \propto (Amplitude)^2$$

This non-linear relationship is important since it expresses the fact that a small increase in transmit voltage produces much faster changes in the delivery rate of acoustic energy into the patient. In terms of increased sensitivity, when stronger signals are desirable, this relationship is obviously good news. In terms of increased risk of bioeffects, this relationship is clearly not so great. (You will learn in Chapter 9 that the risk of bioeffects, although possible, have never been confirmed with appropriate use of ultrasound).

The following example will help demonstrate the relationship between amplitude measurements and power measurements.

◊ **Example 1:** If the amplitude is increased by a factor of 5, what happens to the power?

$$Power \propto (Amplitude)^2$$
$$Original\ Power \propto (Original\ Amplitude)^2$$
$$New\ Power \propto (5 \times Original\ Amplitude)^2$$

So the new power is 5^2, or 25 times the original power.

◊ **Example 2:** If the transmit voltage is increased by a factor of 6, what happens to the power?

$$Power \propto (Amplitude)^2$$
$$Original\ Power \propto (Original\ Amplitude)^2$$
$$New\ Power \propto (6 \times Original\ Amplitude)^2$$

So the new power is 6^2, or 36 times the original power.

Note that voltage is a measure of amplitude.

◊ **Example 3:** If the amplitude is decreased by a factor of 3, what happens to the power?

$$Power \propto (Amplitude)^2$$
$$Original\ Power \propto (Original\ Amplitude)^2$$
$$New\ Power \propto (\frac{1}{3} \times Original\ Amplitude)^2$$

So the new power is $\left(\frac{1}{3}\right)^2$, or $\frac{1}{9}$ times the original power.

Note: Stating that the new power is 1/9 the original power is mathematically the same as stating that the power has decreased by a factor of 9.

> **KEY CONCEPT**
>
> Turning the transmit power knob increases or decreases the transmit voltage used to drive the transducer to create the sound waves which penetrate the body.

Relationship to Acoustic Intensity

Although assessing relative changes in acoustic power based on changes in the electrical amplitude is easier than directly measuring the acoustic power, it is not the best indicator of sensitivity or of the risk of bioeffects. Power is a general statement about the rate at which work is performed (energy transferred). However, for ultrasound it is possible to spread this energy transfer over a large region or a small region of the body. Clearly, if the same amount of energy is spread over a large region, neither the sensitivity nor the risk of bioeffects will be as high as when the energy is distributed over a smaller region. This fact leads to the definition of another related parameter referred to as the intensity.

> **KEY CONCEPT**
>
> Acoustic intensity describes how the sound wave power is distributed over the beam area.

The intensity is a measure of the concentration of force (power) per area. To determine the equation we will develop the mathematical relationship through a few scenarios.

Scenario 1:
Assume there are two flashlights with identical beams, but flashlight A has a much brighter bulb (higher power) than flashlight B. Which flashlight beam has a higher intensity?

Clearly the higher power results in a more intense beam, given that both flashlights have the same beam shape. Therefore, the relationship between the intensity and the power is proportional or:

$$Intensity \propto Power$$

Scenario 2:
Assume there are two flashlights with identical bulbs (same power), but flashlight A spreads the light over a broader beam (larger beam area) than flashlight B. Which flashlight beam has a higher intensity?

Since the power for flashlight A is spread over a larger area, the beam is more diffused, and hence, has a lower intensity. As the beam area increases maintaining the same power, the intensity decreases, which is an inverse proportionality, or:

$$Intensity \propto \frac{1}{Beam\ Area}$$

By combining the two relationships into one equation, we have:

$$Intensity = \frac{Power}{Beam\ Area}$$

Since the unit for power is Watts, and the units for area in the metric system is based on meters squared, the unit for intensity is $\frac{Watts}{m^2}$.

However, since square meters is relatively enormous in comparison with normal beam areas for ultrasound, the units are usually expressed using the prefix of centimeters, or $\frac{Watts}{cm^2}$.

The following examples are provided to further illustrate the relationships between amplitude, power, and intensity.

◊ **Example 1:** If the power is increased by a factor of 5, what happens to the beam intensity?

$$Intensity \propto Power$$
$$Original\ Intensity \propto Original\ Power$$
$$New\ Intensity \propto 5 \times Original\ Power$$

So the new intensity is 5 times the original intensity

Note: As with all relative math questions, an assumption is made that no other variable is changed. In this case, the presumption is that the beam area is not changed as the power is changed.

◊ *Example 2:* If the transmit voltage is increased by a factor of 6, what happens to the beam intensity?

$$Intensity \propto Power \propto (Amplitude)^2$$
$$Original\ Intensity \propto (Original\ Amplitude)^2$$
$$New\ Intensity \propto (6 \times Original\ Amplitude)^2$$

So the new intensity is 6^2, or 36 times the original intensity.

Note: That the power is proportional to the amplitude squared. Since the intensity equals the power divided by the area, the intensity is also proportional to the amplitude squared.

Mathematically, we can write:

$$Intensity = \frac{Power}{Beam\ Area} \propto \frac{(Amplitude)^2}{Beam\ Area}.$$

◊ *Example 3:* If the beam area is doubled, what happens to the intensity?

$$Intensity \propto \frac{1}{Beam\ Area}$$
$$Original\ Intensity \propto \frac{1}{Original\ Beam\ Area}$$
$$New\ Intensity \propto \frac{1}{2 \times Beam\ Area}$$

So the new intensity is $\frac{1}{2}$ original intensity.

Note: Stating the intensity is half of the original intensity is the same as stating that the intensity has been decreased by a factor of 2.

KEY CONCEPT

High intensities generally result in better sensitivity but also result in an increased risk of generating bioeffects.

Relation to Future Topics

The concepts related to amplitude, power, and intensity are pervasive in ultrasound. The following is a partial list of the topics which are related:

1) common intensity measurements and risk of bioeffects
2) mechanical index and cavitation
3) receiver gain and compensation (TGCs)
4) attenuation
5) sensitivity
6) signal-to-noise ratio
7) non-linear effects and harmonics

13. Decibels (dB)

13.1 The Need for Decibels

We have just learned that acoustic intensity is proportional to the power, and that power is proportional to the square of the amplitude. In Chapter 3 we will learn that the rate at which the signal intensity decreases while traveling through the body (attenuation) is very non-linear. Non-linear attenuation almost guarantees that the range of signal intensities will be very large since the wave at shallow depths will have a much higher intensity than at deeper depths. As a result of the very non-linear attenuation, we will have a need for a non-linear means by which to assess the changes in signal intensity or power.

13.2 The Definition of Decibels

In Chapter 1: Mathematics, we learned a powerful non-linear mathematical tool which is very useful for compressing large ranges of data. That tool is the logarithm. The term we use to refer to relative changes in signal power (or intensity) is decibels. A decibel is defined as a logarithmic power ratio. Since you have already learned how to calculate a logarithm, converting from a ratio to decibels is relatively straightforward.

Notice that in the definition we used the term "power ratio". A ratio implies division of two numbers. Specifically, the power ratio entails taking the ratio of an initial and a final power. In ultrasound, this power is produced by driving a transducer with an excitation voltage. The acoustic power into the patient can be changed by changing the transmit voltage through the power output control. Within the patient, the power changes as the sound travels and interacts with the tissue. Therefore, we can see that there are two distinct mechanisms by which the power is changed.

13.3 The Equation for Decibels

In terms of the power ratio used to calculate decibels, the initial power is the acoustic power before whichever change occurs (changing the power control or attenuation in the body). Obviously, the final power is the resulting acoustic power after the change has occurred (after changing the power control knob or the attenuation from traveling in the body). Putting the definition of decibels into equation form we have:

<u>Power form</u>
$$dB \triangleq 10 * log\left(\frac{P_f}{P_i}\right)$$

Where:

P_f = Power Final
P_i = Power Initial

The power ratio is also often referred to as the power factor or the power gain factor. This terminology should be intuitive since the ratio of the final power to the initial power is the gain. The following equation manipulation demonstrates this fact.

Note: The symbol ≜ stands for the words "is defined as."

$$P_f = Gain * P_i$$

dividing both sides by the initial power yields:

$$\frac{P_f}{P_i} = Gain$$

13.4 Applying the Equation for Decibels
The following examples illustrate how the equation is applied.

◊ **Example:** If the power is increased by a factor of 2, what is the increase in power in dB?

We are given that $\frac{P_f}{P_i} = 2$, since the problem states the power was increased by a factor of 2. Plugging this information into the power form of the equation yields:

$$10 * log\left(\frac{P_f}{P_i}\right) = 10 * log(2) = 10 * 0.3 = 3 \; dB.$$

◊ **Example:** If P_f = 10 Watts, and P_i = 1 Watt, what is the increase in power in dB?

We are given that $P_f = 10 \; W$ and $P_i = 1 \; W$

Therefore $\frac{P_f}{P_i} = \frac{10 \; W}{1 \; W} = 10$

Plugging this information into the power form of the equation yields:

$$10 * log\left(\frac{P_f}{P_i}\right) = 10 * log(10) = 10 * 1 = 10 \; dB.$$

◊ **Example:** If the power is decreased by a factor of 100, what is the decrease in power in dB?

We are given that $\frac{P_f}{P_i} = \frac{1}{100}$, since the problem states the power was decreased by a factor of 100. Plugging this information into the power form of the equation yields:

$$10 * log\left(\frac{P_f}{P_i}\right) = 10 * log\left(\frac{1}{100}\right) = 10 * -2 = -20 \; dB.$$

So the power was decreased by 20 dB.

It is critical that you notice that the answer format is a decrease of 20 dB and not a decrease of -20 dB. Since the question asks "for the decrease", the answer must be in the format of "the decrease is ..." Since the word decrease already implies a minus sign, you cannot include the minus sign, or you will have created a double negative. If the question had asked for the change, the answer would be -20 dB, since the word change does not imply negative or positive.

13.5 The Amplitude Form of the Decibel Equation
As mentioned earlier, measuring acoustic power is very difficult, whereas knowing the actual transmit voltage is relatively straight forward. As a result, we would like to have a way of relating the amplitude to decibels. It is important to note that decibels is always a logarithmic power ratio. To develop the "amplitude form" we will apply the relationship between power and amplitude that we have already learned earlier in this chapter, as well as a fact about logarithms discussed in the previous chapter. Specifically:

1) Power is proportional to the amplitude squared.
2) Taking the logarithm of a product (two or more factors in a multiplication problem) is equivalent to the sum (addition) of the logarithms of each factor individually.

We will start with our equation definition of logarithms and make substitution based on the two facts above.

$$dB \triangleq 10 * \left(log_{10} \frac{P_f}{P_i}\right)$$

but $\frac{P_f}{P_i} = \left(\frac{A_f}{A_i}\right)^2$

substituting yields:

$$dB = 10 * \left(log_{10}\left(\frac{A_f}{A_i}\right)^2\right) = 10 * \left(log_{10}\left(\frac{A_f}{A_i} * \frac{A_f}{A_i}\right)\right)$$

$$dB = 10 * \left(log_{10}\left(\frac{A_f}{A_i}\right) + log_{10}\left(\frac{A_f}{A_i}\right)\right) = 10 * \left(2 * log_{10}\left(\frac{A_f}{A_i}\right)\right)$$

$$dB = 20 * \left(log_{10}\left(\frac{A_f}{A_i}\right)\right)$$

This derivation leads us to what is commonly referred to as the "amplitude form" of the decibel equation.

Amplitude form

$$dB \triangleq 20 * log\left(\frac{A_f}{A_i}\right)$$

Where:
A_f = amplitude final
A_i = amplitude initial

Similar to the power form, the ratio of the initial and final amplitude is referred to as the amplitude ratio, amplitude factor, or gain factor.

13.6 Why Two Forms and When to Use Which Form

First, we must state unequivocally that both of these forms of the decibel equation are equivalent. Twenty times the log of the amplitude ratio is equivalent to ten times the log of the power ratio. The reason why it is useful to know both forms is that we sometimes know information about power or intensity (such as Watts or Watts/cm^2), whereas other times we know information about the amplitude (such as Volts or any unit which is a measure of the four acoustic variables). If you are given information about a change in amplitude, you can use the amplitude form, or you can compute $[A_f/A_i]^2$ and then use the power form. Because the likelihood of making a simple math error increases with the requirement to square a ratio, most people choose to use the amplitude form which already compensates for converting amplitude into power.

The following examples illustrate how the amplitude form of the equation is applied.

◊ **Example:** If the initial transmit amplitude is 0.1 Volts and the transmit amplitude is increased by a factor of 100, what is the final amplitude, and what is the change in dB?

We are given that $A_i = 0.1\ V$ and that the amplitude is increased by a factor of 100. From this gain factor we can determine that
$$A_f = 0.1\ V * 100 = 10\ V$$
In reality we don't need this information since the problem already gives us the amplitude factor:
$$\frac{A_f}{A_i} = 100$$

Plugging this into the amplitude form of the equation yields:
$$20 * log\left(\frac{A_f}{A_i}\right) = 20 * log(100) = 20 * 2 = 40\ dB.$$

Note: That we could also have solved this problem by converting the amplitude factor into a power factor by squaring and then using the power form of the equation instead, as follows:

$$\text{Since } Power \propto (Amplitude)^2$$
$$\frac{P_f}{P_i} \propto \left(\frac{A_f}{A_i}\right)^2$$

So an amplitude of 100 is the same as a power factor of
$$100^2 = 10,000$$
$$\text{or } \left(\frac{A_f}{A_i}\right) = 100 \Rightarrow \frac{P_f}{P_i} = 10,000$$

Plugging this information into the power form equation yields:
$$10 * log\left(\frac{P_f}{P_i}\right) = 10 * log(10,000) = 10 * 4 = 40\ dB$$

and we get the same answer as when we used the amplitude form.

◊ **Example:** If the acoustic pressure field is decreased by a factor of 10, in decibels, what is the change in power?

Since pressure is a measure of amplitude, we will use the amplitude form. The problem tells us that the amplitude has decreased by a factor of 10, or:
$$\frac{A_f}{A_i} = \frac{1}{10}$$

Plugging this information into the amplitude form of the equation yields:
$$20 * log\left(\frac{A_f}{A_i}\right) = 20 * log\left(\frac{1}{10}\right) = 20 * -1 = -20\ dB.$$

Since the question asks for the change, the answer is -20 dB.

KEY CONCEPT

Decibels express a ratio of power through logarithmic compression. Any parameter in ultrasound which results in a change in power is measured in decibels including transmit power, attenuation, receiver gain, and compression.

View ONLINE Clarifying Clip

13.7 Exercises and Conceptual Questions

View ONLINE Exercises & Conceptual Questions

14. Comparing Frequency with Amplitude

14.1 Frequency and Amplitude are Disjoint

In the mathematical sense, the term "disjoint" means having no elements in common. In other words, if two topics are disjoint, the two topics are completely separate or unrelated. It is imperative for you to keep the concepts of frequency and amplitude separate in your mind. This distinction will become critical when reviewing Doppler. The propensity to intermix the concepts of frequency and amplitude leads to much confusion when performing, interpreting, or optimizing Doppler.

With respect to sound, the frequency corresponds to the pitch. In comparison, the amplitude refers to the volume, or the loudness of the sound.

> Frequency ⇒ Pitch
> Amplitude ⇒ Volume

14.2 Graphical Representation

The following two graphs demonstrate how frequency can be changed independently of amplitude and amplitude can be changed independently of frequency.

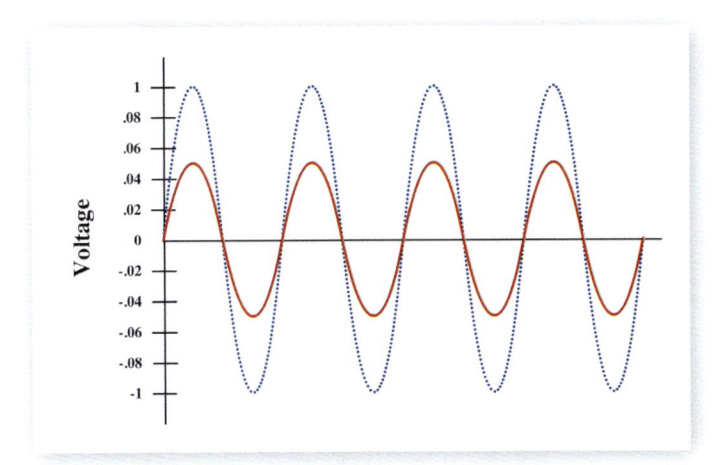

Fig. 38 **Same frequency but different amplitudes**

The graph of *Figure 38* depicts two waves that have the same frequency, but different amplitudes. For these two waves, the sound would have the same pitch, but the solid line would be softer and the dotted line would be louder.

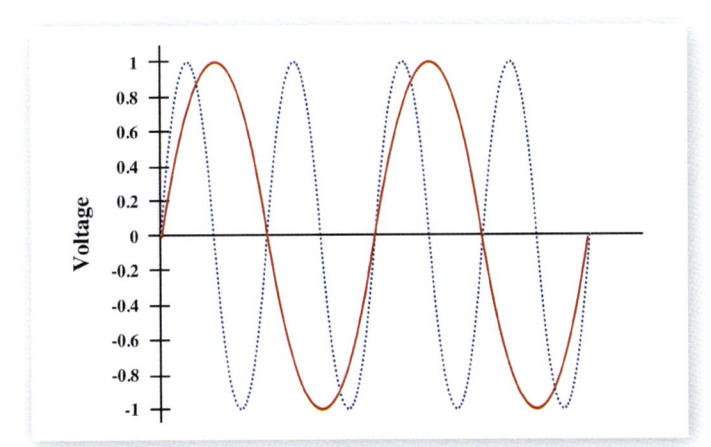

Fig. 39 **Same amplitude but different frequencies**

In comparison with the previous graph, the graph in *Figure 39* depicts two waves that have the same amplitude, but different frequencies. For these two waves, the sound would be of different pitches. The dotted line represents a sound that would have a higher pitch, and the solid line represents a sound that would have a lower pitch. The loudness of the two waves would be approximately the same, presuming that the person listening has the same sensitivity to both frequency ranges.

14.3 Exercises and Conceptual Questions

View ONLINE Exercises & Conceptual Questions

COMMON MISCONCEPTION: Waves

MISCONCEPTION: *If the density increases the propagation velocity decreases.*

Explanation:
From the equation for the propagation velocity, it would appear that a higher density would result in a lower propagation velocity (an inverse relationship). The reality is that higher density mediums almost always have higher (not lower) propagation velocities (as seen in the propagation tables on pages 58-59). This confusion comes from the fact that variables within an equation are usually independent of each other (a change in one variable does not result in a change of the other variable). The variables in the propagation velocity equation are dependent, which means that for most mediums, a higher density implies a much higher bulk modulus, and hence, a higher, not lower propagation velocity.

CHAPTER SUMMARY: Waves

- Waves transfer energy from one location to another location.
- Waves are generally broken into one of two classifications: mechanical waves which need a medium to propagate, and electromagnetic waves which can propagate through a medium but do not necessarily need a medium to exist.
- Sound is a mechanical wave.
- The fact that sound is a mechanical wave indicates the physical interaction which occurs between the medium and the wave.
- Mechanical waves can propagate either in transverse or longitudinal mode.
- A transverse wave results in the particles moving perpendicular to the wave direction.
- A longitudinal wave propagates by a series of compressions and rarefactions back and forth in the same direction as the wave propagation direction. Sound is a longitudinal wave.
- As the wave propagates, interactions with the medium cause changes measurable in four quantities called the acoustic variables.
    - Pressure
    - Density
    - Temperature
    - Particle motion (distance)
- Understanding the parameters which characterize a wave is important to understand ultrasound system controls, how to improve image quality, and how to reduce risks of bioeffects.
- The frequency of the wave represents the number of compressions (or rarefactions) which occur per second (unit is Hz = 1/sec).
- The period is the reciprocal of the frequency (units in sec).

$$P = \frac{1}{f}$$

- The frequency (and hence the period) are determined strictly by the wave source.
- The propagation velocity of a wave (c) is determined by the properties of the medium, independent of the frequency used.
- The propagation velocity is determined by the square root of the bulk modulus divided by the density.
- An ultrasound system presumes the propagation velocity to be 1540 m/sec (an approximate average propagation velocity, excluding bone and lung, commonly referred to as "soft tissue").
- For biological materials, a higher density usually translates into a significantly higher bulk modulus, increasing the propagation velocity.
- There are many terms which are used in place of the bulk modulus. The stiffness is proportional to the bulk modulus which is inversely related to the compressibility. Therefore, as the stiffness increases, the compressibility decreases and the propagation velocity increases. The inverse also holds true. As the stiffness decreases, the compressibility increases and the propagation velocity decreases.
- The wavelength is a critical parameter which is determined both by the frequency (determined by the source) and the propagation velocity (determined by the medium).
- You must know the wavelength equation

$$\lambda = \frac{c}{f}$$

- On some credentialing exams you may be asked to solve the wavelength equation in terms of given numbers.
- On a drawing, the period and the wavelength appear to be the same parameter. Be careful to pay attention to whether the horizontal axis represents time or distance.
- The amplitude of a wave is defined as the maximum variation of a variable from its mean

$$Amplitude = max - mean = mean - min = \frac{max - min}{2}$$

- The units for the four acoustic variables and voltage are all measures of amplitude.
- Power is proportional to the amplitude squared. This non-linear relationship expresses the fact that small increases in amplitude result in significant increases in power (if the amplitude is tripled, the power increases by a factor of 9)

$$Power \propto (Amplitude)^2$$

- Intensity is defined as the power divided by the area

$$Intensity = \frac{Power}{Area}$$

- Since intensity is proportional to the power, and the power is proportional to the amplitude squared, increasing the amplitude (voltage) by a factor of 3 increases the intensity by a factor of 9.

- The intensity is an important parameter since it gives a better indication of the signal strength (and the risk of bioeffects) than just the power or the amplitude.

- Amplitude and frequency are measures of independent parameters (amplitude and frequency are disjoint). In terms of sound, amplitude is a measure of loudness whereas frequency is a measure of pitch.

- Sound is subdivided into classifications based on the human hearing range (audible range).

- Sound below 20 Hz is referred to as infrasound.

- Sound above 20 kHz is referred to as ultrasound.

- Diagnostic ultrasound is a further subdivision of ultrasound which specifies the approximate useful range for conventional, non-invasive ultrasound (typically stated as 2-20 MHz although frequencies higher and lower are sometimes used.)

- The top of the diagnostic frequency range is restricted by penetration.

- The lower range of the diagnostic frequency range is restricted by resolution.

- Since the dynamic range of signals returning from the body is extraordinarily large, non-linear data compression in the form of logarithms is used.

- Decibels is a definition based on logarithms and are defined as a logarithmic power ratio:

$$dB \triangleq 10 * log\left(\frac{P_f}{P_i}\right)$$

- The amplitude form of decibels is applied when the changing parameters are given as measures of amplitude instead of power (voltage or any of the units for the acoustic variables). The amplitude form is:

$$dB \triangleq 20 * log\left(\frac{A_f}{A_i}\right)$$

- You should know that a factor of 2 change in power is equivalent to 3 dB: since $10 * log(2) = 10 * 0.3 = 3$ dB.

- You should know that a factor of 2 change in amplitude is the same as a factor of 4 change in power (since power is proportional to amplitude squared) which is equivalent to 6 dB since $20 * log(2) = 20 * 0.3 = 6$ dB.

ONLINE EXTRAS

For additional support material and to view your completion progress, visit:
www.pegasuslectures.com/6thEdExtras

Extras by Chapter include:
- Animations
- Videos
- Additional Images
- Clarifying Clips
- Supplemental Exercises
- Conceptual Questions

See page x of Preface for access instructions

Attenuation

Chapter 3

WHY DO WE STUDY THIS?

▶ The mechanisms of attenuation are what make ultrasound "work or not work".

▶ Identifying the mechanisms of attenuation is essential in understanding how and why system controls are used, the source of artifacts, and how advanced topics such as harmonic and contrast imaging are used.

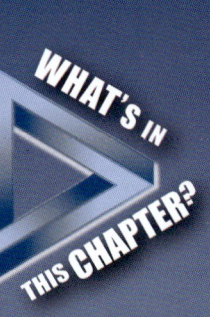

WHAT'S IN THIS CHAPTER?

LEVEL 1 — BASIC ULTRASOUND PHYSICS
Concepts of absorption, reflection, and refraction, their relationship to the angle of incidence, angle of reflection, and angle of transmission and the impact on the ultrasound image are introduced.

LEVEL 2 — BOARD LEVEL
Level 1 concepts are expanded with a focus on the clinical impact and the resulting diagnostic ultrasound image.

LEVEL 3 — ADVANCED TOPICS
A deeper understanding of Level 2 concepts is developed including how to determine the maximum imaging depth for a specific frequency transducer.

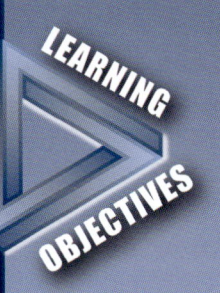

LEARNING OBJECTIVES

▶ Describe how absorption, reflection, and refraction impact the level of attenuation in tissue, the inferior structures, and the resulting image

▶ Define Snell's law and the clinical importance of understanding when refraction occurs

▶ Apply ultrasound terminology to describe plaque echogenicity and surface characteristics

▶ Identify the importance of the critical angle

▶ Understand that absorption not only decreases signal strength, but also serves as the foundation for understanding thermal bioeffects

Chapter 3
Attenuation

1. Attenuation

Attenuation can be defined as a decrease in wave amplitude (or intensity) due to the mechanical wave interaction with the medium. The word attenuation implies a decrease, so when referring to attenuation, a negative sign is not used. Stating that a signal has been attenuated by 10 dB is the same as saying the signal has been reduced or decreased by 10 dB, or changed by -10 dB. It is incorrect to state that the signal was attenuated by -10 dB, since this sentence now has a double negative.

A comprehensive understanding of the mechanisms for attenuation is crucial for understanding diagnostic ultrasound. They are precisely what makes ultrasound work and not work. Without understanding attenuation effects, it is impossible to understand how and why the controls of an ultrasound system work (Chapter 6), the sources of artifacts (Chapter 8), the advanced topics of harmonic imaging, contrast imaging (Chapter 10), and future ultrasound developments.

We will divide the topic of attenuation into three subtopics, each subtopic corresponding to a physical or mechanical interaction with the medium. Specifically, we will subdivide attenuation into the categories of:

- Absorption
- Reflection
- Refraction

2. Absorption

Absorption is a conversion of energy from the sound wave into heat within the medium. The fact that energy is lost to heat within the tissue should be intuitive from our description in Chapter 2 of how a mechanical wave propagates. As the wave encounters the molecules (particles) of the medium, some of the energy is transferred. This transfer of energy is responsible for the particle displacement which results in compression and rarefaction. As with moving any physical entity, energy is required. How much of the wave energy is lost to heat through this interaction is dependent on the molecular interactions within the medium and the frequency of moving (compressing) the medium.

2.1 Absorption and Viscosity

The molecular interaction is sometimes referred to as the viscosity of the medium. A high viscosity medium implies that the molecular attraction within the medium is high, requiring greater energy to move the molecules within the medium. (Viscosity is formally discussed in Chapters 12 and 13.) Therefore, higher viscosity mediums result in greater energy losses to heat through absorption than lower viscosity mediums.

2.2 Absorption and Frequency Dependence

If the frequency of the wave is increased, the amount of energy lost to heat increases. This fact should be intuitive since an increased frequency implies that the molecules are being "moved" more times per second. A simple demonstration of this mechanical interaction is rubbing your hands together. If you rub your hands together a few times per second, not much heat is generated. If instead you rub your hands together many times per second (higher frequency) significantly more heat will be produced. Therefore, higher frequency waves lose energy faster to heat through absorption than lower frequency waves.

> **KEY CONCEPT**
>
> Absorption is the conversion of energy from the wave into heat within the body. Higher viscosity mediums and higher transmit frequencies result in increased absorption rates.

3. Reflection

Reflection is formally defined as the phenomenon of causing a propagating wave to change direction such that some of the wave energy does not continue to propagate forward. More simply stated, reflection implies a change in energy propagation direction such that some of the energy returns in the general direction of the source.

Reflection is the foundation for diagnostic ultrasound. Unlike x-ray, which is based on transmitted energy, diagnostic ultrasound is based on receiving and processing the reflected energy. There are different types of reflection. Understanding the various types of reflection forms the foundation for understanding how to best utilize the imaging capabilities of ultrasound while simultaneously minimizing the number of mistakes leading to possible misdiagnoses.

The concept of reflection is certainly not new to any of us. Every one of us sees examples of reflection every day. Some examples include the reflection from looking in a mirror, seeing the reflection of car headlights off street signs, seeing the sunlight shimmering off a river or pond, and even hearing echoes from buildings or mountains. In fact, nearly everything we see is based on reflection of some sort. The easiest way to understand the aspect of reflection which is important to diagnostic ultrasound is to relate the concepts to everyday occurrences with which we are already familiar. We will begin by considering how the different types of reflection occur based on the geometry of the interaction.

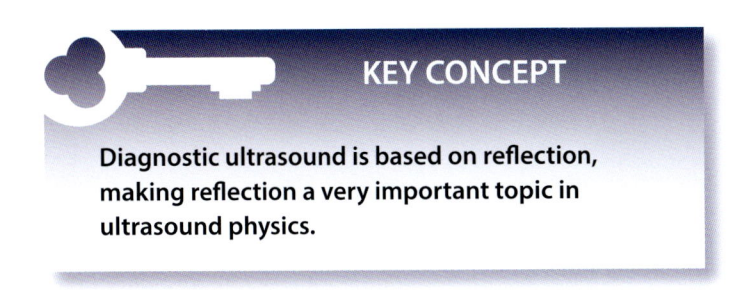

KEY CONCEPT

Diagnostic ultrasound is based on reflection, making reflection a very important topic in ultrasound physics.

3.1 Geometric Aspects of Reflection

Defining Terms

The Angle of Incidence

Before discussing the types of reflection, we must define a system which standardizes an understanding of the wave direction relative to the reflecting structure. With respect to reflection, the angle formed between the wavefront and the interface of the reflecting structure is called the incident angle (angle of incidence).

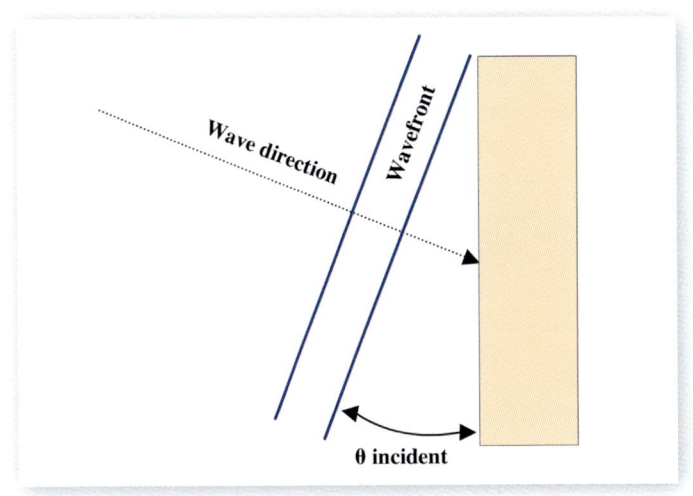

Fig. 1 **Measuring the incident angle**

Note: As defined, the incident angle is not the same as the angle formed between the wave propagation direction and the interface of the reflecting structure. In fact, these two angles are complements (add together to equal 90 degrees.) To make this point clear, we will need to discuss the difference between the wavefront and the wave direction.

Wavefront Versus Wave Direction

As the name suggests, the wavefront is the front surface of a wave. In contrast, in an undisturbed region of the wave, the wave direction is always perpendicular to the wavefront. The fact that the wave propagation direction is perpendicular to the wavefront is pretty intuitive if you consider your experience at the beach. If you are standing on shore, the wave direction is coming into shore, but the wavefront is perpendicular to the wave direction, and parallel to the shoreline.

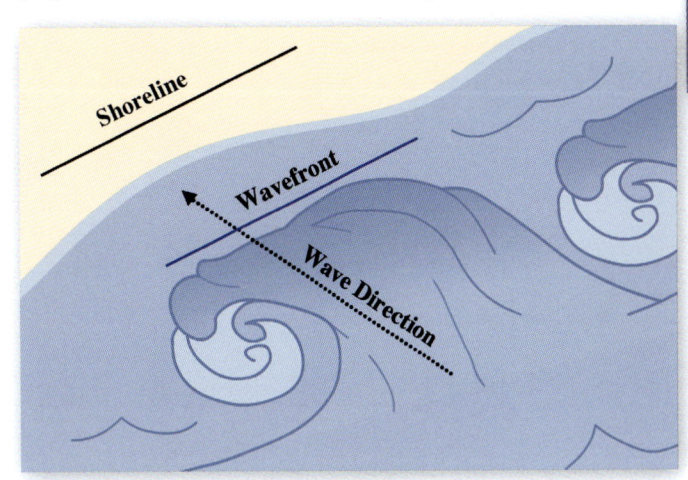

Fig. 2 **Wave direction and wavefront**

How to Define The Incident Angle Referenced to the Wave Direction

Since the wavefront and the wave direction are perpendicular (90° apart), the incident angle can also be measured as the angle formed between the line perpendicular to the reflecting structure (called the normal line) and the wave direction. *Figure 3* demonstrates why both approaches to measuring the incident angle are equivalent. (If you recall similar triangles from geometry, the following figure demonstrates why these two approaches are equivalent.)

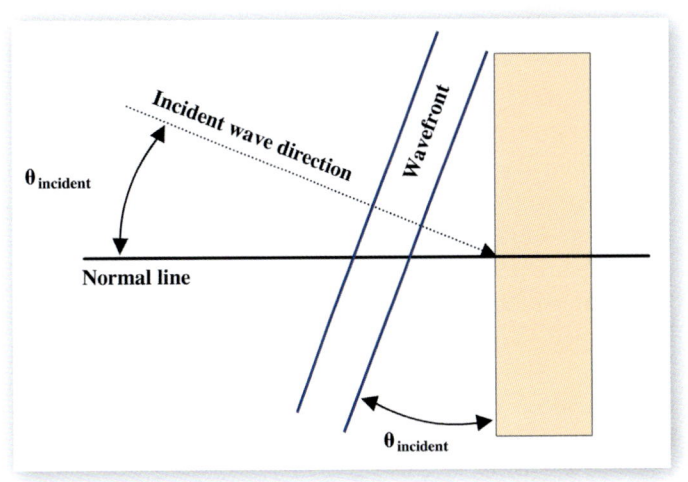

Fig. 3 **The incident angle**

Normal Incidence

The term "normal incidence" implies that the wavefront is parallel to the reflecting structure, or that the wave direction is parallel to the normal line. In other words, with normal incidence, the angle formed between the wave direction and the normal line is zero degrees. Normal incidence is illustrated in *Figure 4*. Note that this concept is often confused by students. A zero degree incidence is equivalent to saying that the wave direction (beam) is perpendicular (90°) to the interface.

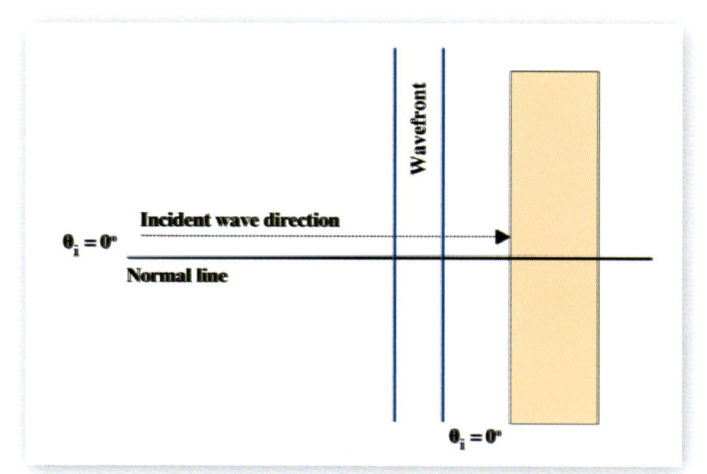

Fig. 4 **Normal incidence**

Figure 5 is intended to clarify how the incident angle is specified when using a transducer.

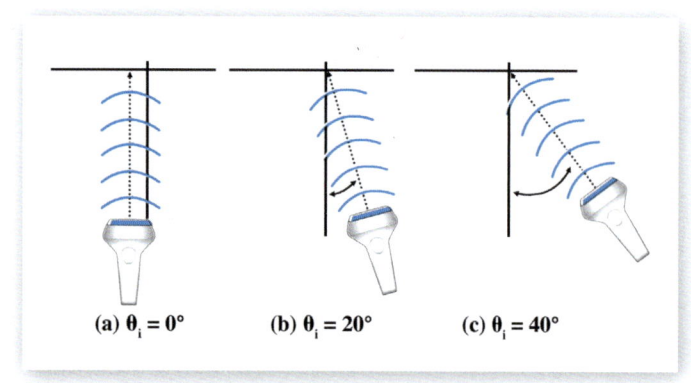

Fig. 5 **Various incident angles**

KEY CONCEPT

The incident angle is the angle formed between the wavefront and the reflecting surface. Since picturing the wavefronts is more challenging than picturing the wave direction when producing an ultrasound image, the incident angle is usually specified relative to the wave direction instead of the wavefront. Therefore, the incident angle is the angle formed between the beam direction and the line normal (perpendicular) to the reflecting surface.

View ONLINE Animation and Image Library

The Angle of Reflection

The angle of reflection is measured using the same method as the angle of incidence, except using the reflected wavefront instead of the incident wavefront. Just as there are two equivalent ways of specifying the incident angle, there are two equivalent ways of specifying the reflected angle. For specular reflection, the angle of incidence is always equal to the angle of reflection. This fact is well known by anyone who has ever played billiards (pool) or racquetball. Of course in both of these examples, the presumption is made that the reflecting surface is smooth and that there is no spin involved, imparting angular momentum which would affect direction.

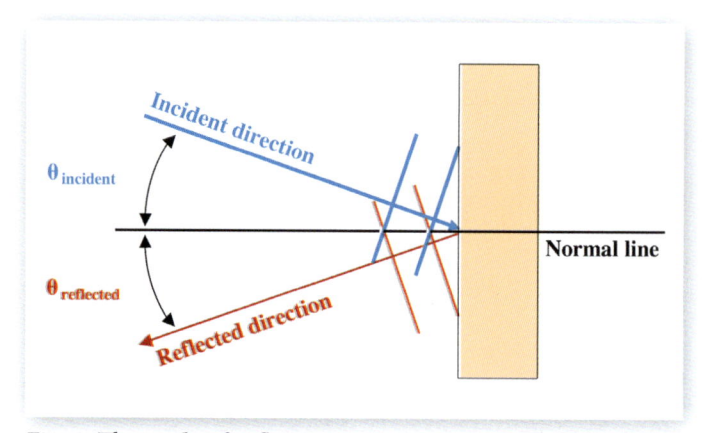

Fig. 6 **The angle of reflection**

The Angle of Transmission

As we will learn, at an interface or boundary between two different mediums, it is common to have a percentage of the wave energy reflect and a percentage of the wave energy that continues propagating through the second medium, referred to as the transmission percentage. Like the incident angle and the reflected angle, the transmission angle is also measured with respect to the angle formed by the wavefront and the reflecting surface. Of course, for the transmission angle, the angle is measured between the wavefront of the transmission wave and the reflecting surface. As with the incident angle and the reflected angle, this approach is equivalent to making the angular measurement between the transmitted wave direction and the line normal to the structure. *Figure 7* depicts all three angles in one diagram.

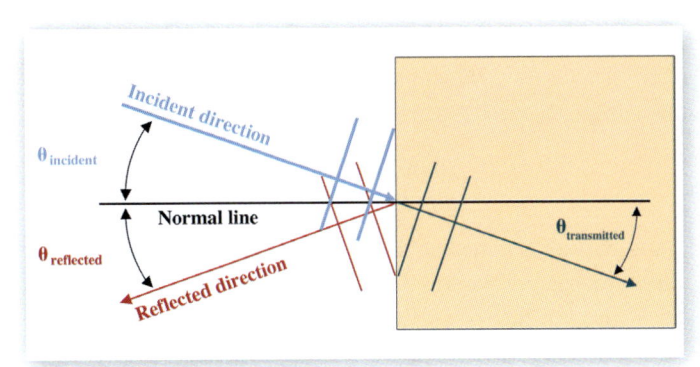

Fig. 7 **Angle of transmission**

Specular Reflection

The word specular refers to a "mirror-like" reflection. Specular reflection occurs from a surface which is large and smooth relative to the wavelength of the wave. Some common examples are light from a mirror, reflections on the calm, smooth surface of a pond, and reflections from polished metal surfaces. For specular reflection, the angle of incidence always equals the angle of reflection. Therefore, the incident angle can dramatically affect where the reflection will appear. This angle dependence is one of the most critical parameters to understand regarding specular reflection.

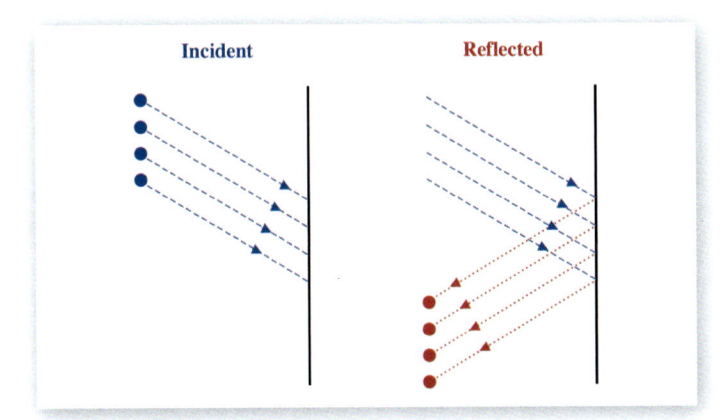

Fig. 8 **Specular reflection**

KEY CONCEPT

Specular reflection is highly angle dependent. Whenever specular reflectors exist, you should immediately assess the angle of incidence to the specular reflector. The incident angle will help you determine the path the reflection will take (the angle of incidence equals the angle of reflection).

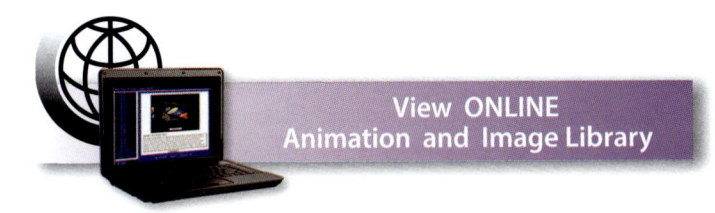

View ONLINE Animation and Image Library

(Back) Scattering

In contrast with specular reflection, scattering occurs when the reflecting surface is rough with respect to the wavelength. The resulting reflection is redirected in many different directions, hence the name "scattering". An example of scattering is the reflection of light from a shower glass door or the diffuse light that reflects back from a textured metal surface. Unlike specular reflection, scattering has little angular dependence.

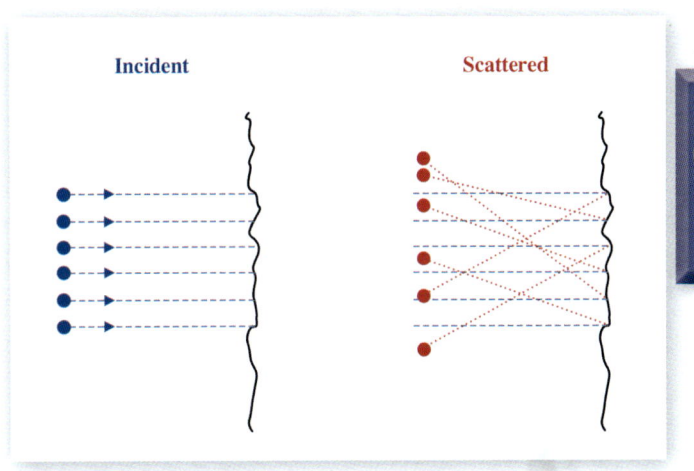

Fig. 9 **Back scattering**

View ONLINE Animation and Image Library

Rayleigh Scattering

Rayleigh scattering occurs when reflecting structures are very small with respect to the wavelength. Since the wavelength depends on the frequency, Rayleigh scattering is also frequency dependent. As the frequency of the wave increases, the wavelength decreases, making the structure look effectively larger. As a result, Rayleigh scattering increases with increasing frequency. Some common examples of Rayleigh scattering are light off the air molecules in the atmosphere and sound reflecting from red blood cells (RBCs).

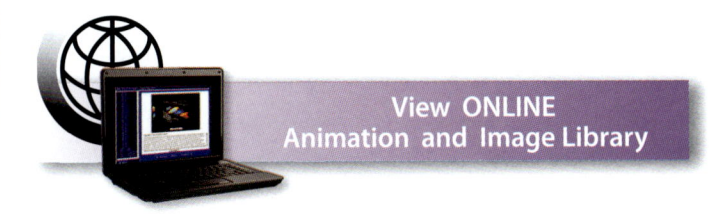

View ONLINE Animation and Image Library

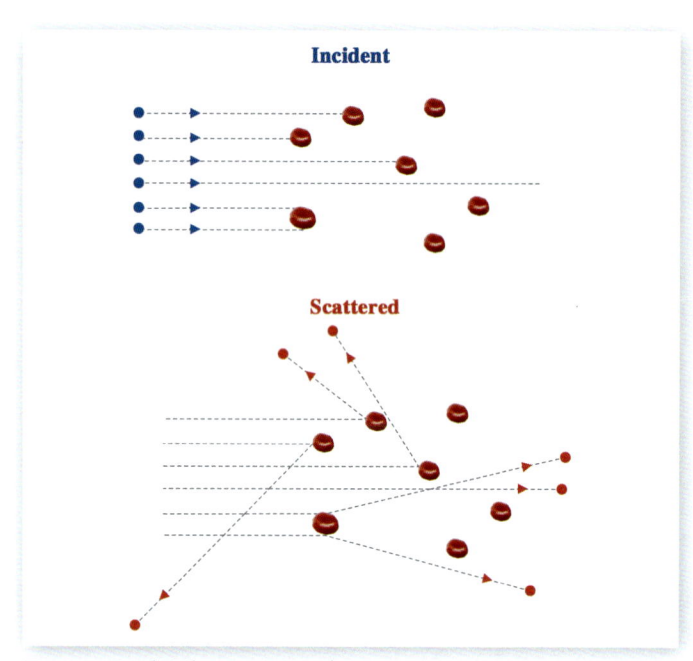

Fig. 10 **Rayleigh scattering**

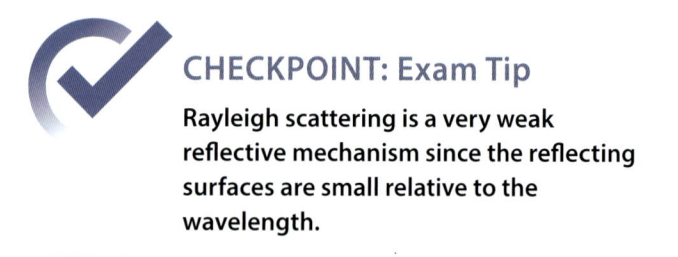

> **CHECKPOINT: Exam Tip**
>
> Rayleigh scattering is a very weak reflective mechanism since the reflecting surfaces are small relative to the wavelength.

3.2 Acoustic Aspects of Reflection

If we return to our definition of a sound wave as a transfer of energy through mechanical interaction, we will discover the foundation for understanding reflection, based on the acoustic parameters of the mediums. Recall that energy transfers as molecules are imparted with energy, causing compression. In this description, no mention is made of varying particle sizes or varying density in the undisturbed medium. Therefore, there is a tacit assumption that all of the particles are similar in size and the density uniform. The question is, what would happen if that assumption were not true?

Momentum Analogy

Imagine that you are playing marbles. Consider the difference when you roll a small marble at a very large marble (an aggie), versus rolling a small marble at another small marble. We will assume that you are a very good shot and can hit the target marble head on.

When the two marbles are of similar size, there is a significant transfer of energy from the rolled marble into the stationary marble. The result is that most of the momentum will be transferred to the small stationary marble and it will begin to roll. In comparison, when the small marble collides with the much larger marble, the large marble barely moves, but the small marble strongly reflects.

Defining the Acoustic Impedance

In physics, the momentum is determined by multiplying the mass of an object by its velocity, or:

$$momentum = m \times v$$

For molecules of a medium being mechanically displaced through wave propagation, we will replace the velocity of the marble with the velocity of the wave, c. Instead of referring to the mass of the marble, we will refer to the density of the molecules, ρ. Now the "momentum" transfer for a sound wave propagating through a medium will be related to the density times the propagation velocity. This term is given the name "acoustic impedance" denoted by the letter Z. Therefore, the acoustic impedance of a material is defined as:

$$Z = \rho \times c$$

The units for the acoustic impedance can be simply determined by multiplying the units for density (mass per volume) with the units for the propagation velocity (distance per time).

$$\text{units for } Z = \frac{kg}{m^3} * \frac{m}{sec} = \frac{kg}{m^2 sec}$$

This unit has been given the name of Rayls, or

$$1 \frac{kg}{m^2 sec} = 1\ Rayl.$$

In the upcoming sections, we will see how the change in acoustic impedance from medium to medium or within a medium will affect the amount of reflection that occurs.

Impedance Mismatch Analogy

Now let's change our analogy so that we are rolling 100 marbles towards a paper wall. When the marbles are rolling through the air, there is no reflection. Since the air is relatively homogeneous (constant throughout), there is no change in impedance and hence, no reflection. However, when the marbles encounter the paper wall, a transfer of momentum can occur. Imagine that the marbles are rolled hard enough such that only 27 of the 100 reflect back from the paper wall. If 27 are reflected back, 73 rolled right through the paper. In other words, there is a conservation of energy. All of the marbles either reflect back or transmit through. The reason for the reflection is clear, the paper wall represents a difference (mismatch) in impedance relative to the air.

Now repeat the process rolling 100 marbles but replace the paper wall with a cardboard wall. When the marbles encounter the cardboard wall, more will reflect back and fewer will transmit through. Since the cardboard represents a greater impedance mismatch, there will be more reflection and less transmission (similar to our momentum analogy). If the cardboard wall is replaced by a concrete wall, you can safely imagine that all of the marbles will reflect and none will transmit through the wall. In other words, as the impedance mismatch increases, the amount of reflection increases.

Conservation of Energy

From the impedance mismatch analogy, we saw that the reflected number of marbles plus the transmitted number of marbles equals the incident number of marbles. At an interface between two different mediums, the momentum was conserved and all of the energy was either reflected or transmitted. This analogy is actually a bit simplified because it ignores any energy lost to heat during the collision. In other words, if we assume that there is no energy lost to absorption, at an infinitesimal boundary between two mediums, the reflected energy plus the transmitted energy will equal the energy that arrived at that boundary. Written mathematically:

$$\text{Reflection \%} + \text{Transmission \%} = 100\%.$$

Therefore, making the presumption that there is no energy conversion to heat, calculating the reflection percentage also yields the transmission percentage simply by subtracting from 100% of the energy at that interface.

> **KEY CONCEPT**
>
> The acoustic impedance (Z) is a measure of amplitude and has units of Rayls. At a boundary, when there is a large difference in impedances (a large acoustic impedance mismatch) a large reflection occurs.

Reflection Equation

From our analogy, we can start to build an equation which will determine the percentage of reflection that will occur at an interface between two different mediums. First, we know that the amount of reflection increases with an increase in acoustic impedance mismatch. In other words, if the acoustic impedance of medium 1 is significantly different than the acoustic impedance of medium 2, there will be a large reflection.

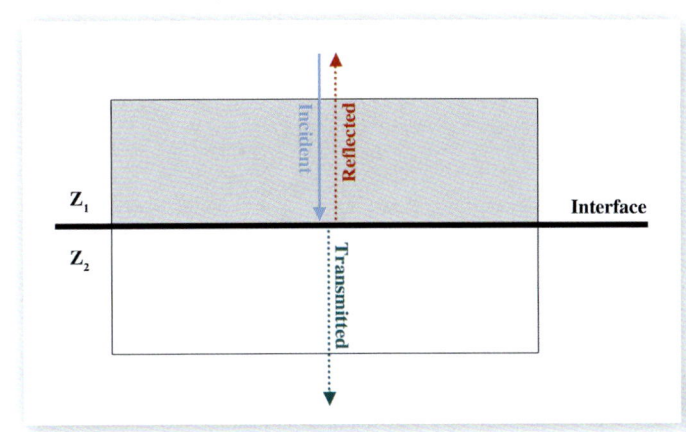

Fig. 11 **Reflection and transmission**

Mathematically, a difference is represented by the operation of subtraction. Therefore, the reflection will depend on the difference in impedances or:

$$\text{Reflected} \propto (Z_2 - Z_1).$$

We would like to have a reference for our calculation of the reflected energy. The most common approach to giving a mathematical reference is to divide by a total to convert into a percentage. Therefore, by dividing by the total impedance, we will now have a percentage of reflection, or:

$$\% \text{ Reflected} \propto \frac{(Z_2 - Z_1)}{(Z_2 + Z_1)}.$$

The last step is to determine the percentage of power and energy that is reflected. Since the acoustic impedance is a measure of amplitude, to convert an amplitude to power, the amplitude expression must be squared. Squaring the amplitude expression now yields the expression for percentage reflected energy, or:

$$\% \text{ Reflected} = \frac{I_{reflected}}{I_{total}} = \left[\frac{Z_2 - Z_1}{Z_2 + Z_1}\right]^2.$$

As with our analogy, this equation presumes that the angle between the wavefront and the interface is 0 degrees (incident angle of 0 degrees which is the same as saying that the wave direction is perpendicular to the interface). There is a more complex form of the equation which accounts for oblique incidence discussed in Level 3. For now, this simplified form will be sufficient and useful in helping you intuitively realize how reflection and transmission occur.

Transmission Equation

We have already stated that presuming no absorption, the reflected energy plus the transmitted energy equals all of the energy at an interface. The simplest way to calculate the transmission percentage is to calculate the reflection percentage and subtract from 100% (or in decimal form to subtract from 1).

$$\% \, Transmitted = \frac{I_{transmitted}}{I_{total}} = 1 - \left[\frac{Z_2 - Z_1}{Z_2 + Z_1}\right]^2$$

Applying the Concept of Acoustic Impedance Mismatch
The equations just derived show how the acoustic impedance mismatch is used to determine what percentage of the incident wave will be transmitted and what percentage will be reflected at an acoustic interface. When there is a large difference between the acoustic impedances of the two interfacing materials, there will be a large reflection and, correspondingly, a small transmission. When there is no acoustic impedance mismatch at a boundary, there will be no reflection and 100% transmission at that boundary. These two situations are illustrated in the following examples.

◊ *Example:*

What happens if $Z_2 = Z_1$ (no impedance mismatch)?

$$Z_2 = Z_1 \Rightarrow \left[\frac{Z_2 - Z_1}{Z_2 + Z_1}\right]^2 = \left[\frac{0}{2Z}\right]^2 = 0 \Rightarrow \{No \, Reflection\}$$

In other words, if there is no acoustic impedance mismatch there will be no reflection, or, equivalently, 100% transmission.

◊ *Example:*

What happens if Z_2 is much greater than Z_1, $(Z_2 >> Z_1)$?

$$(Z_2 >> Z_1) \Rightarrow \left[\frac{Z_2 - Z_1}{Z_2 + Z_1}\right]^2 \approx \left[\frac{Z_2}{Z_2}\right]^2 = 1 \Rightarrow \{100\% \, Reflection\}$$

If Z_2 is significantly greater than Z_1, $Z_2 - Z_1$ is effectively equal to Z_2. For example 1000 – 1 is almost equal to 1000. Similarly, $Z_2 + Z_1$ is also almost equal to Z_2.

KEY CONCEPT

The percentage reflection calculation based on acoustic impedance mismatch is the second fundamental equation that governs diagnostic ultrasound (which means that we know with great certainty that you will be tested on the concept underlying the equation).

4. Refraction

4.1 Refraction Defined
Up to this point, we have concentrated on the reflected energy. Presumably, any transmitted wave at an interface between two media would continue traveling in the same direction as before traversing the interface. This presumption is incorrect. Refraction is effectively the bending of the wave at an interface of two media. Refraction occurs due to a change in propagation velocity when the wave is incident at an angle other than normal (0 degrees). The phenomenon of refraction is most commonly visualized by placing a spoon or pencil into a glass of water in bright sunlight. Since light travels at different velocities in the water, glass, and air, there is a bending of the light rays, making the spoon appear bent in the water.

4.2 Visualizing Refraction
As depicted in *Figure 12*, assume that the propagation speed in medium 2 is higher than in medium 1. The resulting transmitted beam will bend to the right. The reason for this bending is shown by following the wavefront over time. While the entire wavefront is within medium 1 (from time t_1 through t_4), the propagation direction remains unaffected. Between times t_4 and t_5, the left edge of the wavefront travels through the interface and begins traveling at the faster velocity of medium 2. Note that during this time period, the right portion of the wavefront is still in medium 1, and is still traveling at the slower velocity, hence traveling a shorter distance. The difference in distances traveled during this time period is indicated by the varying length arrows.

By connecting the tips of these arrows, the new wavefront at time t_5 is visualized. You should note that this wavefront is now bent. Between times t_5 and t_6, the right edge of the waveform also transitions from the slower speed to the higher speed, but still travels a shorter distance than the left, which has spent the entire time period at the higher propagation velocity of medium 2. Between times t_6 and t_7, the entire wavefront is in the faster medium 2, and hence, the entire wavefront travels a uniform distance. Recall from earlier in this chapter (Section 3.1) that the wave direction is always perpendicular to the wavefront. By drawing the line perpendicular to the new wavefront at any time after time t_5, the new wave direction is depicted and refraction is apparent. In essence, the refraction is a distortion of the wavefront caused by one side of a wavefront traveling at a faster rate than the other side of the wavefront.

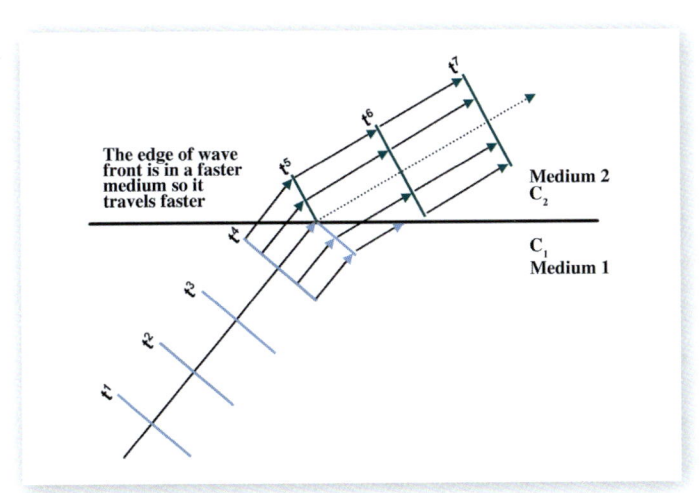

Chapter 3: Attenuation

Fig. 12 **Refraction**

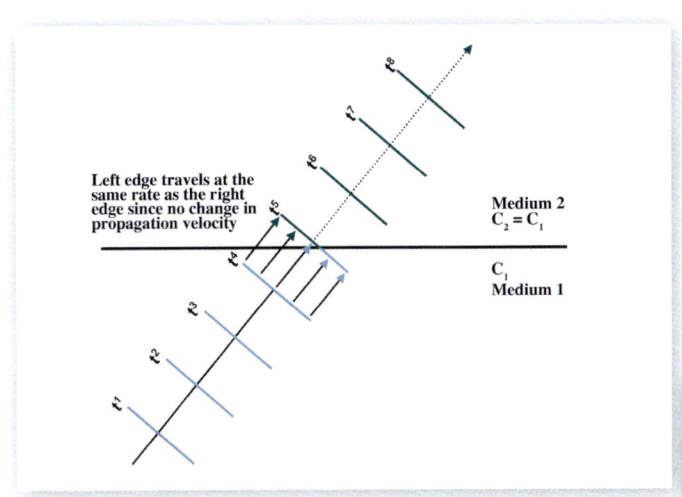

Fig. 13 **No refraction if no change in propagation velocity**

View ONLINE Animation and Image Library

In this example, notice that the incident angle was oblique (other than 0 degrees) and that there was a change in propagation velocities between the two interfacing mediums. We will now consider what happens when either one of these two conditions does not hold.

CHECKPOINT: Exam Tip

Refraction is a bending of the beam as the beam crosses an interface, with a change in propagation velocity when the incident angle is non-zero.

4.3 Oblique Incidence but No Change in Propagation Velocities

Imagine in the last example if the propagation speeds were equal in both mediums, or $c_1 = c_2$. As depicted in *Figure 13*, even though the left edge of the wavefront arrived at the interface between the two mediums earlier than the right edge, since there was no change in propagation velocity, the left edge would continue to travel at the same rate as the right edge of the wavefront. Since the entire wavefront is traveling at the same velocity, there is no disparity in distance traveled which would distort the wavefront. As a result, there is no refraction. Therefore, for refraction to exist, there must be a change in propagation velocities between the two interfacing mediums. Clearly, the greater the difference in propagation velocities, the greater the degree of refraction that can occur.

4.4 Normal Incidence (Incident angle = 0°)

Imagine now if a wave has normal incidence to an interface between two mediums, and that the propagation velocities are significantly different. Will there be any refraction?

Before we illustrate this example, we will again review what it means to have a normal beam. Since there are so many different ways of expressing this concept, this is usually a point of confusion for many students.

As expressed earlier in this chapter, the angle of incidence, the angle of reflection, and the angle of transmission can be measured two different ways. In general, since the wave direction is easily depicted as a ray (an arrow tipped line), the preferred method for measuring the angle is between the wave direction relative to the line normal (the line which is perpendicular to the interface). In other words, when a sound beam direction of travel is perpendicular to an interface, (90°), the incident angle is 0°. If the direction of travel is 30° to the interface, then the angle of incidence is 90° - 30° = 60°. These two examples are depicted in *Figure 14* and *Figure 15*.

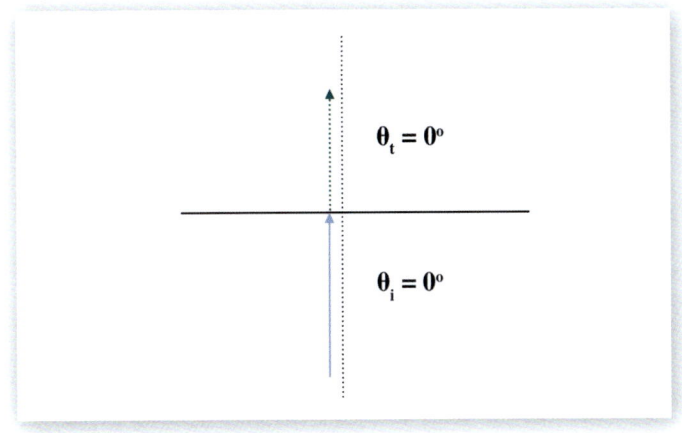

Fig. 14 **Normal incidence**

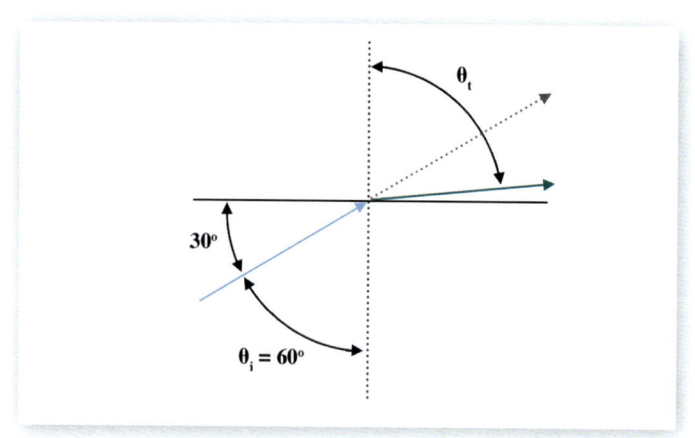

Fig. 15 60° incidence

The key is to pay particular attention to the wording. All of the following statements are equivalent

- Normal incidence
- Beam perpendicular to the interface
- Beam orthogonal to the interface
- Beam at 90 degrees to the interface
- 0 degree incident angle
- Wavefront parallel to the interface

We are now ready to determine the outcome of a beam at normal incidence with an interface with varying propagation velocities.

For this example, from *Figure 16*, it is clear that the propagation velocity in medium 2 is higher than the propagation velocity in medium 1. This fact is demonstrated by the wavefronts being drawn farther apart in time in medium 2 than in medium 1.

Note: As the wavefront approaches the interface, since the wavefront is parallel to the interface, the entire wavefront reaches the interface at the same time. The result is that the entire wavefront accelerates at the same time. As a result, there is no distortion of the wavefront, and because the wave is allowed to travel faster, there has been no redirection of the wave. In other words, when there is normal incidence, there is no refraction.

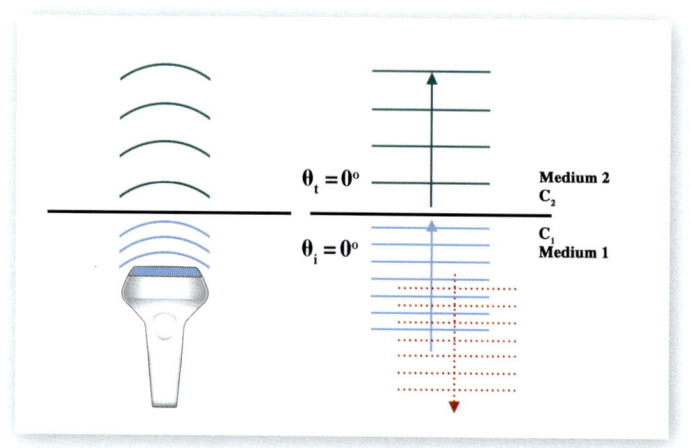

Fig. 16 **No refraction with normal incidence**

4.5 Snell's Law

The Equation

Not surprisingly, there is a mathematical expression which predicts when refraction will occur, and to what degree. The rule which predicts the amount of refraction is called Snell's law. From our discussions above, it should be evident that Snell's law will involve the propagation velocity in the incident medium and the propagation velocity in the transmitted medium (the medium into which the wave propagates as it crosses the interface). Also, it should not be surprising that Snell's law will also involve the incident angle. Snell's law relates the ratio of the propagation velocities with the ratio of the sines of the incident and transmitted angles, or:

$$\text{Snell's law:} \quad \frac{c_i}{c_t} = \frac{\sin(\theta_i)}{\sin(\theta_t)}.$$

Snell's law can be written in many different forms by simple mathematical manipulation as discussed in Chapter 1: Mathematics. For example, all of the following forms express Snell's law:

$$c_i \bullet \sin(\theta_t) = c_t \bullet \sin(\theta_i)$$

$$c_i = c_t \bullet \frac{\sin(\theta_i)}{\sin(\theta_t)}$$

$$\frac{c_i}{\sin(\theta_i)} = \frac{c_t}{\sin(\theta_t)}$$

Figure 17 puts all of the pieces discussed to this point together, illustrating the terms referenced in Snell's law.

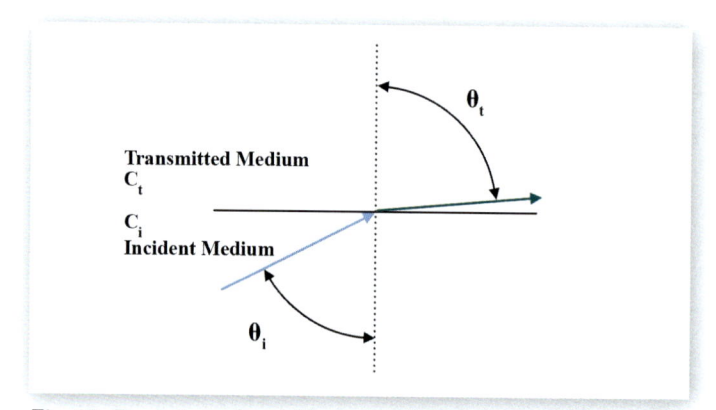

Fig. 17 **Depiction of variables in Snell's law**

Note: Snell's law determines the presence and amount of refraction; it does not tell what percentage of the incident beam energy is transmitted and what percentage of the beam energy is reflected. The amount of reflection and transmission is determined by the acoustic impedance mismatch.

Determining Degrees of Refraction from the Transmission Angle

Another common point of confusion is determining when there is refraction from the application of Snell's law. Quite simply, refraction exists when the transmitted angle does not equal the incident angle, or $\theta_i \neq \theta_t$. (The greater the difference between the incident and transmitted angles, the greater the amount of refraction.) Consider the following two diagrams.

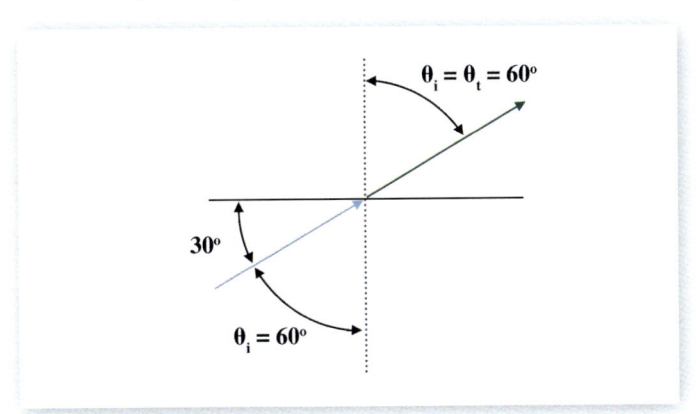

Fig. 18 **No refraction**

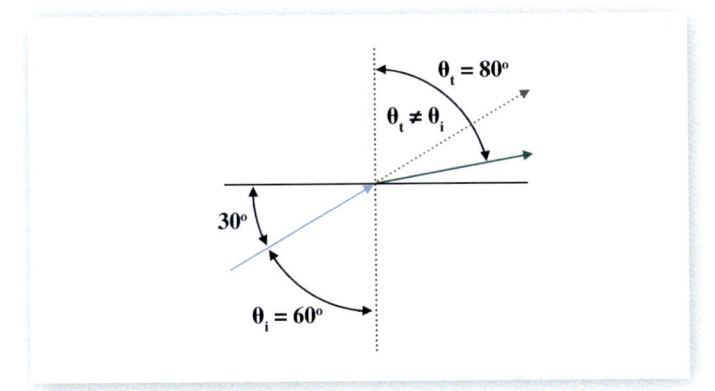

Fig. 19 **20° of refraction**

In the first example, *Figure 18*, the transmitted angle is equal to the incident angle. For these two angles to be equal, the wave direction cannot have changed as the wave crossed the interface, and hence, there is no refraction. In the second example, *Figure 19*, the transmitted angle is larger than the incident angle by 20 degrees. In other words, the wave direction has been changed by 20 degrees. Clearly, the greater the difference between the incident angle and the transmitted angle, the greater the amount of refraction.

It is unfortunate that sometimes the transmitted angle is also referred to as the refraction angle. This nomenclature is poor since a transmitted angle may exist when there is no refraction. As illustrated, in *Figure 18*, the transmitted angle is 60 degrees. Referring to this angle as the refraction angle is very confusing since, in this case, there is no refraction. Within this text, we will always refer to the angle on the transmitted side as the "transmitted angle" and avoid the confusion associated with naming that angle the "refraction angle".

> **KEY CONCEPT**
>
> Snell's law allows for the calculation of refraction. Since refraction depends on a difference in propagation velocities and a non-zero degree incident angle, the equation involves the propagation velocity in the incident and transmitted mediums, and involves the angles (sine of the angle discussed in Chapter 1: Mathematics) in the incident and transmitted mediums.

4.6 The Critical Angle

We have already seen that there can be no refraction if the incident angle is 0 degrees, or if there is no change in propagation velocity across an interface. Clearly, as the change in propagation velocity increases, or as the beam gets farther away from normal incidence, the amount of refraction will increase. It is possible to get so much refraction that none of the incident beam will transmit across the interface, causing total internal reflection. The incident angle at which total internal reflection occurs is called the critical angle.

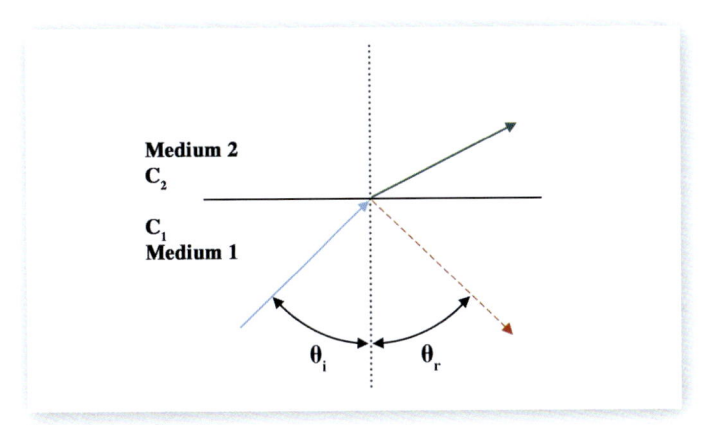

Fig. 20a **Refraction**

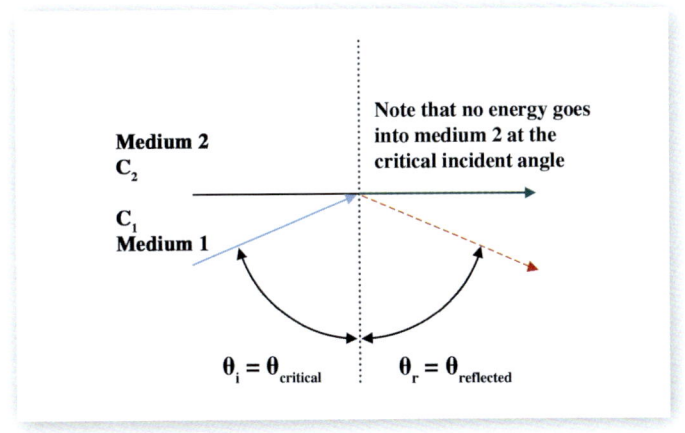

Fig. 20b **Critical angle**

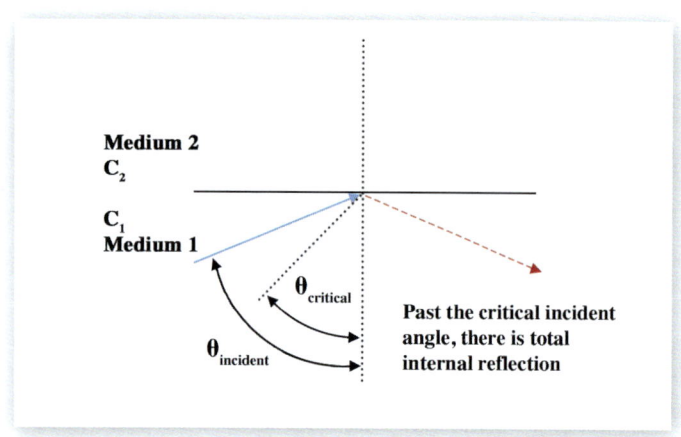

Fig. 20c Total internal reflection

Notice that in *Figure 20a*, the incident angle is smaller than the critical angle, so there is still some transmission, albeit refracted. In *Figure 20b*, the incident angle exactly equals the critical angle, resulting in the refracted beam traveling along the interface between the two media. In *Figure 20c*, the incident angle is larger than the critical angle resulting in total internal reflection.

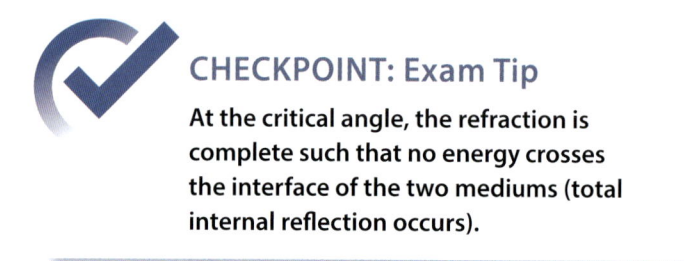

CHECKPOINT: Exam Tip

At the critical angle, the refraction is complete such that no energy crosses the interface of the two mediums (total internal reflection occurs).

View ONLINE Clarifying Clip

5. Conceptual Questions

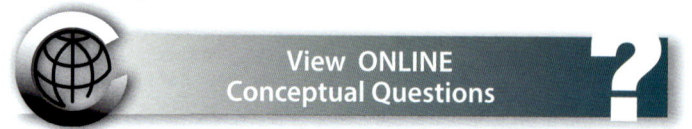

View ONLINE Conceptual Questions

LEVEL 2: Board Level

6. Ultrasound Terminology

6.1 Echogenicity

Echogenicity refers to the strength and/or type of the signal reflection. There are at least five terms which are used to refer to the strength of the echo.

Anechoic:
No echogenicity
(no reflected signal)

Example: fluids, blood, bile, and serous fluids

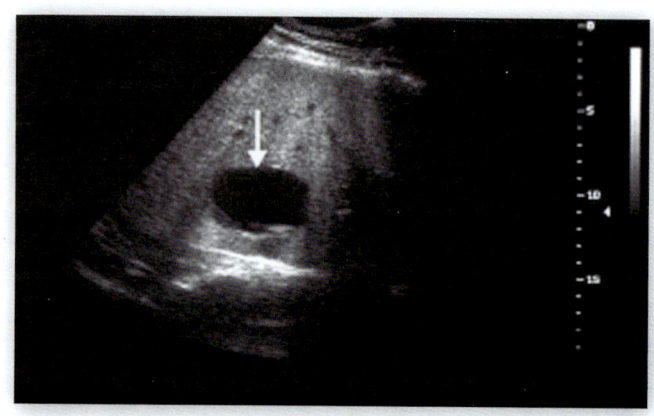

Fig. 21a Anechoic mass (cyst) in the liver

Hypoechoic:
Low echogenicity
(low level reflected signals)

Example: fatty plaque, some masses

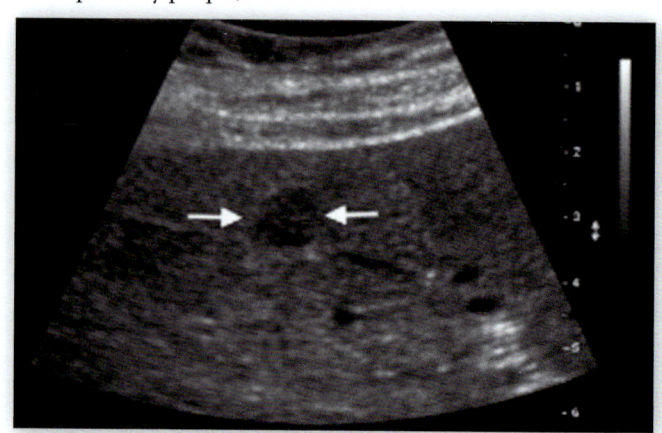

Fig. 21b A small (5-6 mm) hypoechoic mass in the liver compatible with metastatic disease

Hyperechoic:
High echogenicity
(moderate to high reflected signals)

Example: fibrous plaque, any specular reflectors

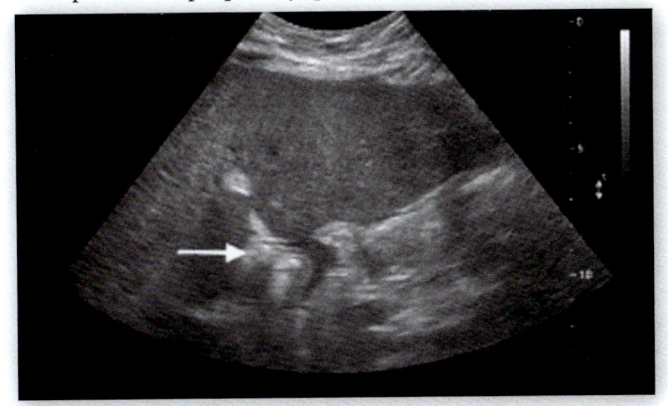

Fig. 21c **Transverse view through a normal liver with a hyperechoic or echogenic area in the liver which is from the ligamentum teres**

Calcified:
Strongly echogenic usually with acoustic shadowing

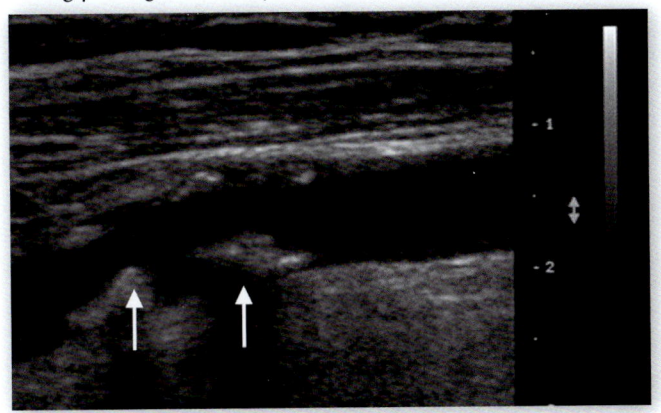

Fig. 21d **Calcified plaque with acoustic shadowing at the origin of the internal carotid artery**

Complex:
Mixed echogenicity with or without acoustic shadowing

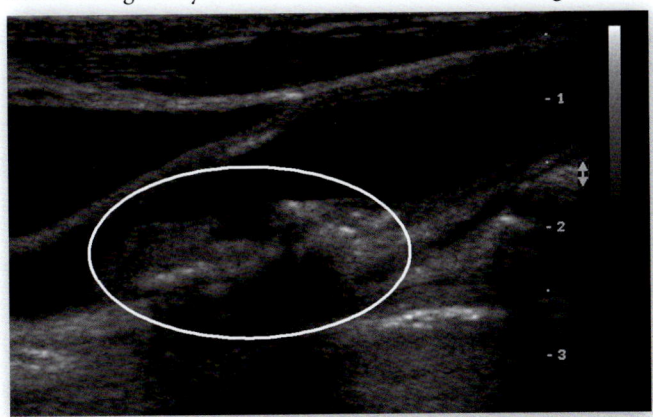

Fig. 21e **Complicated plaque with multiple levels of echoes at the origin of the internal carotid artery**

6.2 Uniformity

There are two terms which are used to refer to how uniform the signal appears. Homogeneous, or homogeneity, implies that the signal is relatively uniform. Heterogeneous, or heterogeneity, implies that there is variation within the signal. These terms can be applied to any aspect of the image including the characteristic appearance of tissue, thrombus, plaque, etc. They become very important when referring to plaques since heterogeneous plaques tend to be less stable and have a greater risk of hemorrhage and creating embolic events.

It is also important to realize that the terms for "uniformity" refer to the appearance of the image and not the actual characteristic of the tissue itself. If a tissue were truly homogeneous, it would appear black since there would be no reflection based on the absence of an acoustic impedance mismatch (as occurs with fluids). When a structure appears homogeneous in an image, it really implies that the variation within the medium is uniform, not that the medium itself is purely uniform.

View ONLINE Animation and Image Library

6.3 Plaque Surface Characteristics

a) **Smooth:** Continuous intimal surface, tends to be less symptomatic and more stable

b) **Irregular:** Discontinuous intimal surface, tends to be more symptomatic and less stable (more likely to embolize)

7. Attenuation Rates

7.1 Table of Attenuation Rates

As a result of scattering, refraction, and absorption, the intensity of the ultrasound beam decreases as it travels through the medium. Since scattering and absorption increase with frequency, the amount of attenuation is frequency dependent as well as depth and medium dependent.

Soft tissue attenuation rate:	0.5 dB/(cm-MHz)
Muscle attenuation rate:	1.0 dB/(cm-MHz)
Blood attenuation rate:	0.125 dB/(cm-MHz)

Table 1 **Attenuation Rates**

Notice how the values in the table are exact multiples of each other.

They have been simplified so as to be easier to remember and apply. A more complete and precise table exists in Level 3.

Note: The denominator is comprised of two different units, cm and MHz. Be sure not to confuse the dash in the denominator with subtraction. Look carefully at the examples below to make sure that you understand this notation.

7.2 Calculating Approximate Attenuation
Perhaps the biggest cause of error in calculating the attenuation is not paying close enough attention to whether the problem is asking for a roundtrip attenuation, or a one-way attenuation. The following examples will illustrate how the difference in wording indicates one-way versus roundtrip measurement.

◊ **Example:** In soft tissue, what is the attenuation of a 5 MHz ultrasound beam at a depth of 10 cm?

$$\left(\frac{0.5 \text{ dB}}{cm\text{-}MHz}\right) \times (10 \text{ cm}) \times (5 \text{ MHz}) = 25 \text{ dB attenuation}.$$

Note: The wording expresses "at a depth of 10 cm" and does not imply roundtrip. As a result, the total distance traveled is 10 cm, not 20 cm.

◊ **Example:** In soft tissue, what is the attenuation of a 5 MHz ultrasound beam imaging to a depth of 10cm?

$$\left(\frac{0.5 \text{ dB}}{cm\text{-}MHz}\right) \times (20 \text{ cm}) \times (5 \text{ MHz}) = 50 \text{ dB attenuation}.$$

Note: In contrast with the first example, the second example implies a round-trip calculation. To image a structure at a depth of 10 cm implies that the beam must travel 10 cm to the structure and reflect back another 10 cm. The total distance traveled is 20 cm.

7.3 Interpreting Calculated Attenuation
In the last example, we calculated an attenuation of 50 dB. Recall that decibels are a logarithmic power ratio. As a review of logarithms, we will translate the answer of 50 dB back into an intensity (which is directly related to power) ratio.

$$-50 \text{ dB} = 10 \log\left(\frac{I_f}{I_i}\right)$$

$$-\frac{50}{10} = \log\left(\frac{I_f}{I_i}\right)$$

$$10^{(-5)} = \frac{I_f}{I_i}$$

$$\frac{1}{100,000} = \frac{I_f}{I_i}$$

In other words, the beam intensity for imaging a 10 cm depth is 1/100,000 the original beam intensity. Recall that in this problem we assumed "soft tissue" only and no muscle, a relatively unlikely scenario. The attenuation rate in muscle is greater than the attenuation rate in soft tissue. Since it is likely that there would be some muscle when imaging through a depth to 10 cm, the calculated attenuation of 50 dB is likely lower than the attenuation in reality.

Given the result of this calculation, it should be evident why you are not likely to use a 5 MHz transducer imaging at a 10 cm depth. Since attenuation is frequency dependent, using a higher frequency would result in even more attenuation. This example illustrates the first half of the classic trade-off in ultrasound between attenuation and resolution.

Note: The word attenuation means a decrease and implies a negative sign.

> **KEY CONCEPT**
>
> Since attenuation is nonlinear, attenuation rates are measured in decibels (see logarithms in the Chapter 1: Mathematics and decibels in Chapter 2. Since attenuation is dependent on depth and frequency, attenuation rates are measured in decibels (dB) per cm (depth) and MHz (Frequency).

8. Absorption in the Body

In Level 1 we discussed how absorption is the conversion of wave energy into heat. There are two critical points to be made about absorption which will be discussed in 8.1 and 8.2.

8.1 In Soft Tissue, Absorption is the Dominant Factor Creating Attenuation
Rephrased, this statement means that within "soft tissue", more of the energy is lost to heating the tissue than is redirected through reflection or refraction. This fact is important for two reasons. First, absorption reduces the amount of the energy there is to reflect, reducing penetration and signal strength. Second, since the energy being absorbed causes tissue heating, there is a potential risk of thermal tissue damage, or thermal bioeffects.

8.2 Absorption Increases Exponentially with Increasing Frequency
This point is critical since it tells you something about the rate at which energy is absorbed. Recall from the math section that an exponential relationship means that small changes in one variable cause much larger changes in the related variable. In this case, a

slight increase in the transmit frequency, or operating frequency, will cause significantly more absorption. This fact should be well known to you, since there is always significantly less penetration using a higher frequency transducer than a lower frequency transducer while imaging (assuming conventional imaging techniques). Also, the fact that the rate of attenuation is exponential with increasing frequency will help determine the processing steps and control adjustments necessary on the imaging system. Therefore, this concept will be important for understanding system operations discussed in Chapter 6.

8.3 Fluids and Absorption

Fluids tend to absorb less sound energy than soft tissue. Recall from Level 1 that the energy loss to heat is related to the density and viscosity of the medium. In general, fluids have lower densities and lower viscosities than tissues. Water has a very low absorption rate.

This fact is important since:

1. Fetal imaging involves scanning through amniotic fluid which is primarily water.
2. Pelvic scanning usually involves scanning through a full bladder.
3. Scanning through a fluid-filled cystic structure changes the attenuation rate relative to nearby tissue (producing what is generally referred to as enhancement artifact).
4. Sound attenuation in a fluid is lower than in tissue, so when scanning through a fluid-filled region, the thermal index models may underestimate the maximum temperature rise (discussed in Bioeffects).
5. Imaging of fluid-filled phantoms for Doppler do not necessarily accurately mimic the behavior of true in vivo scanning (discussed in Quality Assurance).
6. Whales can communicate very long distances in water, as much as 600 to 1,000 miles. (Maybe this will not be on any exam, but it is still neat to know.)

KEY CONCEPT

There are two critical points you should know about absorption:

1) absorption is the dominant form of attenuation in soft tissue

2) absorption increases exponentially with increasing frequency and increasing depth (which explains why attenuation rates are measured in dB/(cm – MHz))

You should also know that fluids tend to absorb very little, and that higher absorption rates lead to a greater risk of producing a bioeffect related to temperature increase (thermal).

9. Reflection in the Body Based on Geometric Conditions

9.1 Specular Reflection

In Level 1 we discussed three distinct types of reflection which can occur at an interface, or boundary. Specular reflection is the strongest reflective mode, but is highly angle dependent. Therefore, a distinction must be made between the strength of the reflection and the strength of the reflection received back to the transducer. For specular reflection, if the reflected angle returns the signal back in the receiving path of the ultrasound transducer, then specular reflection will yield the strongest signals. In contrast, for a pure specular reflector, if the reflection angle directs the reflected signal away from the receive path of the transducer, then no signal will be registered.

Notice that we referred to a "pure" specular reflector. A pure specular reflector results in only specular reflection and virtually no scattering at all. In practical terms, most structures in the body are not pure specular reflectors, generating some scattering as well. In essence, you can think of reflection as a spectrum of effects.

Examples of Specular Reflectors

Some examples of relatively strong specular reflectors are:

- The diaphragm
- Boundaries between organs
- Vessel walls
- Heart walls
- Valve leaflets
- Calcifications
- Fascial sheathing
- The surface of bones and tendons
- The surface of a fluid-filled or air-filled cavity
- Prosthetic valves
- Biopsy needles and catheters
- Pacemakers and pacemaker wires
- Some prosthetic implants

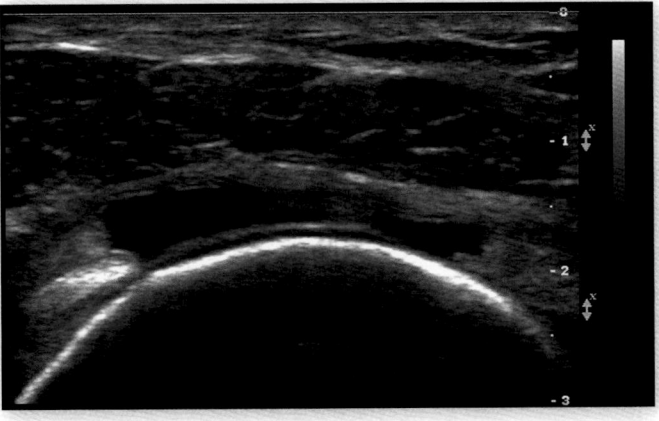

Fig. 22a **Specular reflection from the humeral head in the shoulder**

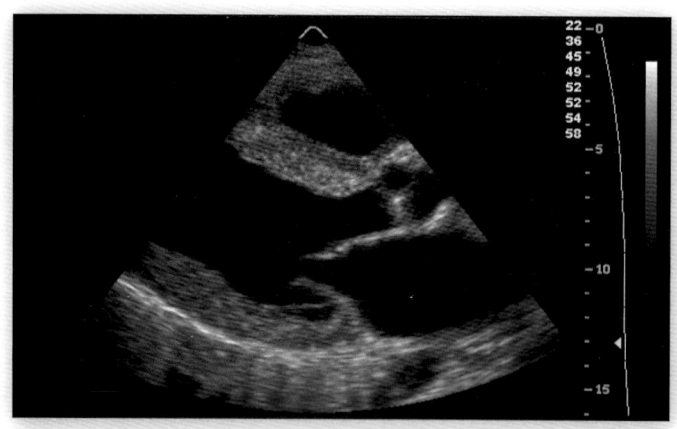

Fig. 22b **Specular reflection from the anterior leaflet of the mitral valve and aortic valve cusp**

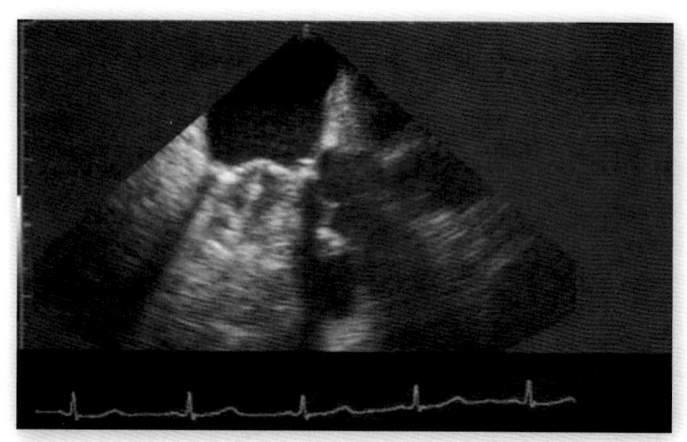

Fig. 22c **Specular reflection from a prosthetic mitral valve**

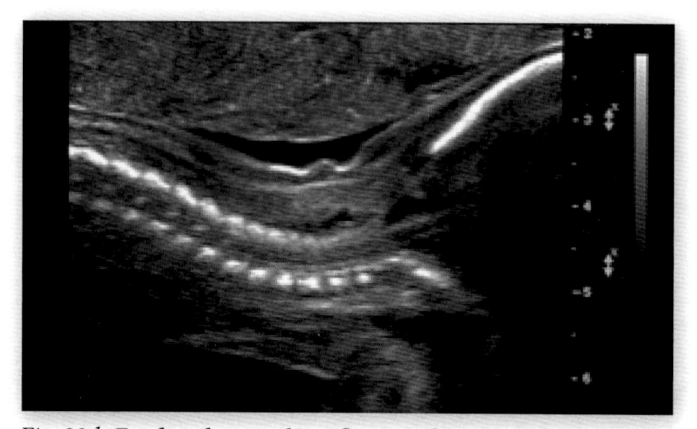

Fig. 22d **Fetal neck: specular reflections from spiny processes and the cranial bone**

Specular Reflection: A Principal Source of Imaging Artifacts

Although the formal discussion of artifacts is in Chapter 8, for now, it is valuable to develop the relationship between the mechanism of specular reflection and the concept of artifactual data. As you will learn, artifacts will sometimes lead to a conclusion that disease is present when it is not, or that disease is absent when it really is present. Either way, a wrong conclusion is reached which certainly does not help the patient. From understanding the physics of the mechanisms which cause the artifacts, these mistakes can often be avoided.

The primary mechanism for generating imaging artifacts is specular reflection. Note that this statement is not the same as stating that specular reflection is the only source for imaging artifacts. There most certainly are other mechanisms besides specular reflection as the source of imaging artifacts. It cannot be overstated that the direction of specular reflection depends heavily on the angle of incidence. Therefore, the first and most important point for understanding imaging artifacts is assessing the incident angle with respect to specular reflecting structures.

Identifying Specular Reflection Based Artifacts (Step-by-Step)

Step 1:
When imaging, or viewing an ultrasound image, the first step should always be to identify the structures which potentially could generate specular reflections, principally in the relative near field. In general, the relative near field refers to structures that are 5 cm deep or shallower. Although specular reflectors deeper than 5 cm can cause artifacts, because of the increased path length to deeper structures, attenuation and timing will tend to reduce the severity of these effects. Whenever specular reflectors are present in the relative near field, you can be pretty certain that some imaging artifacts will be present.

Step 2:
Once specular reflectors have been identified, the second step is to determine the angle of incidence formed between the wave direction (ultrasound beam) and the surface of the specular reflectors. This step requires that you understand how ultrasound images are created using different transducer types and imaging formats. Viewing the exact same structures, the image appearance and even presence of specular reflection-based artifacts will vary significantly depending on the imaging format being used (unsteered linear, steered linear, curved linear, or sector – discussed in Chapter 5).

Step 3:
The third step is then to assess where the specular reflection will travel and the propensity for this energy to produce an artifact. To successfully complete this step, you must become familiar with the primary mechanisms which can cause specular related artifactual images and structures. Fortunately, based on the physics, there are really only two mechanisms, specifically a redirection of the beam from the presumed straight path, and reverberation. Both of these mechanisms are formally discussed in Chapter 8. As a note, although there are only a few mechanisms, unfortunately, the names for these artifacts has generally developed from their appearance in the image, and not based on the mechanism of creation. As a result, there are many names for artifacts based on how they appear, all which have the same mechanism of creation. As if recognizing and minimizing artifacts is not challenging enough, the problem is compounded by

a myriad of names such as ring down artifact, comet tail artifact, mirroring artifact, multi-path artifact, etc. (discussed in Chapter 8).

Step 4:
Given that there is a likely source and mechanism of artifact in an image, the next step should be to vary the incident angle. In general, structures that are real should maintain the same relative location within the image no matter the angle. When artifacts based on specular reflection exist, a change in angle usually causes a change in either appearance or relative location of structures. It is important to realize that changing the angle may introduce new artifacts. Therefore, repeating the steps listed above is necessary each time the angle is changed. This change in angle can be achieved by changing the steering (for transducers with steering capability – see Chapter 5), rocking the transducer (both heel-to-toe and elevationally), and using a different imaging window.

This methodical process should become routine for every imaging or interpretation session. Without a methodical, physics based approach as just introduced, artifacts are often unrecognized. The result can be inaccurate or even completely incorrect diagnoses. The goal is to reduce these errors by reducing the very complex situation of imaging to manageable, somewhat controllable, understood steps.

Note: It is strongly suggested that you reread this step-by-step process as you begin studying Chapter 8 on artifacts.

> **KEY CONCEPT**
>
> **Most (but not all) imaging artifacts are caused by specular reflection. Since specular reflections are highly angle dependent, one of the best techniques for determining if there are imaging artifacts is to change the incident angle.**

9.2 Scattering in the Body

Speckle and "Tissue Texture"
In part, the appearance of tissue texture in an ultrasound image is created by scattering. As discussed in Level 1, scattering occurs when the surface characteristics of the tissue are "rough" with respect to the wavelength. In other words, when the variation in the tissue texture is larger than the wavelength, the wave energy is scattered. In essence, each region of tissue acts as its own transmitter, scattering signals in many different directions. Since the distance from each point in the tissue to different locations on the transducer face is different, there are small time delays between the receiving of these reflections. When these signals are added together, there is some partial constructive and destructive interference, resulting in larger and smaller signals. The result is the appearance of a "speckle" pattern, giving the impression of tissue texture.

With increasing frequency, the wavelength decreases. As the wavelength decreases, the different distances from each point in the tissue to the transducer face becomes a larger percentage of the shorter wavelength. As a result, the waves go from constructive interference to destructive interference over a smaller region. The result is a finer speckle pattern, as is generally perceived when using higher frequency transducers. *Figures 23a* and *23b* demonstrate the difference in speckle pattern when imaging thyroid tissue. Note that speckle and speckle reduction techniques are discussed in Chapter 8.

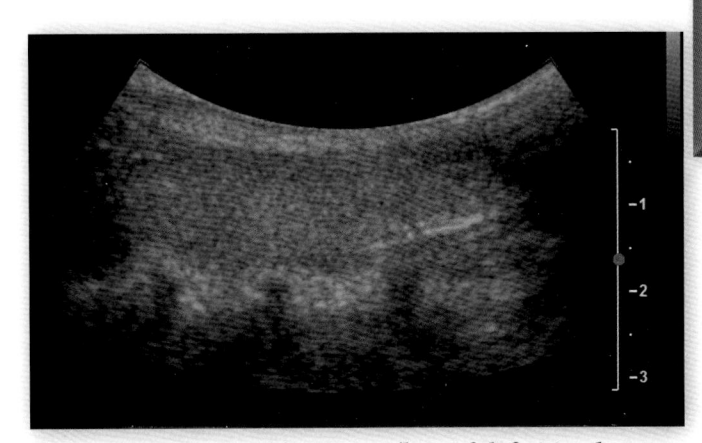

Fig. 23a **Coarse speckle pattern (loss of definition between muscle and gland)**

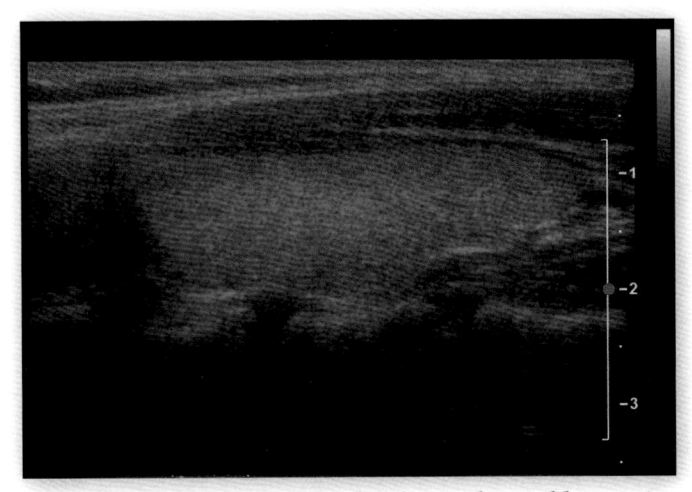

Fig. 23b **Fine speckle pattern (neck muscles visible anterior to thyroid)**

> **KEY CONCEPT**
>
> **Apparent tissue texture is really an artifact based on constructive and destructive interference (see Chapter 2: Waves) which produces speckle patterns. Many new technologies reduce speckle in the image often improving visualization of low level structures.**

Examples of Scattering in the Body
Whereas the interface between organs tend to produce primarily specular reflection, the tissues themselves generally produce scattering. Heart muscle, skeletal muscle, liver parenchyma, and kidney, are all good examples of tissues that primarily cause scattering.

9.3 Rayleigh Scattering

Wavelength Relative to Red Blood Cells (RBCs)
The diameter of a red blood cell is typically 6 to 8 µm. From Chapter 2, we learned that the wavelength for diagnostic ultrasound at 5 MHz is about 308 µm. At 10 MHz, the wavelength decreases to 154 µm. Even at this very high imaging frequency, the wavelength is still much, much larger than the size of a red blood cell. Since Rayleigh scattering occurs when the reflectors are very small with respect to the wavelength, reflection from blood is predominantly Rayleigh.

Some Consequences of Rayleigh Scattering
Excluding pure specular reflection at an angle which results in no energy reflected back to the transducer, Rayleigh scattering is clearly the weakest reflective mechanism for imaging. As we will learn in the upcoming sections, the acoustic impedance of the RBCs is relatively close to the acoustic impedance of plasma, further exacerbating this weak reflection. For conventional imaging frequencies, the reflection from blood is a much weaker signal than the reflection from tissue. The result is that blood pools generally appear dark in an ultrasound image. Although there are conditions where blood visualization occurs (see spontaneous contrast in Chapter 7), it is not the norm.

Since Rayleigh scattering is a weak reflective mode, for Doppler based techniques, it is absolutely critical that all precautions be taken to maximize signal strength. In essence, this requires that lower frequencies be used for almost all Doppler imaging. The only exceptions to this rule are when the imaging is relatively superficial. As discussed previously, as the frequency increases, the wavelength decreases, making the red blood cells "appear" larger, thereby increasing the amount of scattering. In fact, Rayleigh scattering predicts that the amount of scattering increases as the fourth power of the frequency. For superficial imaging, this relationship between frequency and increased scattering implies that using a higher frequency will produce a stronger Doppler signal. However, penetrating through more tissue for deeper imaging, the increased attenuation more than dominates the increased scattering, resulting in weaker signals. As a result, for deeper Doppler imaging, if the frequency used is too high, there may be inadequate signal strength to accurately detect blood flow.

> **KEY CONCEPT**
>
> Rayleigh scattering is a weak reflective mechanism. Since Doppler relies primarily on Rayleigh scattering from red blood cells, every effort should be made to optimize sensitivity when performing Doppler imaging.

9.4 Reflection in the Body Based on Acoustic Aspects

9.4.1 The Acoustic Impedance Mismatch
In Level 1 we determined that the percentage of reflection (for normal incidence) is governed by the equation:

$$\% \; Reflected = \frac{I_{reflected}}{I_{total}} = \left[\frac{Z_2 - Z_1}{Z_2 + Z_1} \right]^2.$$

Of course the reality is that the beam is not always normally incident to all structures. In Level 3, the equation which predicts percentage reflection for non-normal incidence is given. For intuitive understanding (and for board level questions), knowing the equation only for normal incidence is acceptable. At varying angles, the percentage reflection decreases. Therefore the equation for normal incidence gives an upper bound on the percentage of reflection.

The Acoustic Impedance
Before we begin applying the reflected energy equation, we should review what determines the acoustic impedance of a material. The acoustic impedance is calculated as $Z = \rho \times c$. Recalling that more dense materials generally have a higher bulk modulus (lower compressibility), we would expect dense materials to also have a higher propagation velocity. As a result, more dense materials generally have much higher acoustic impedances because both the density and the propagation velocity are increased.

Consider the difference in acoustic impedance between a ceramic material and tissue. The density and propagation velocity of a stiff crystal will be significantly higher than that of tissue. Therefore, the acoustic impedance of the crystal will be much greater than the acoustic impedance of the tissue.

In Level 3, a table of acoustic impedances is listed for general knowledge and for further developing intuitive reasoning.

Examples

◊ **Example 1:** Given that the acoustic impedance of a PZT crystal is 38 MRayls, and the acoustic impedance of tissue is approximately 2 MRayls, how much reflection will occur at the interface of a crystal put directly on this tissue?

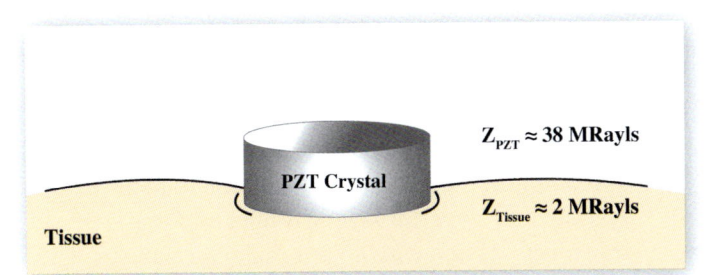

Fig. 24 **Acoustic impedance mismatch between PZT and tissue**

The reflection at the interface between the crystal and the tissue is calculated by plugging the impedance values into the reflection percentage equation developed in Section 3.2.5. Ideally, there would be 100% transmission into the patient and no reflection at the surface.

$$\% \text{ Reflected} = \left[\frac{38 \text{ MRayls} - 2 \text{ MRayls}}{38 \text{ MRayls} + 2 \text{ MRayls}}\right]^2 = \left[\frac{36}{40}\right]^2 = \left[\frac{4 \times 9}{4 \times 10}\right]^2 = \left[\frac{9}{10}\right]^2 = 0.81$$

Note: Since the expression is squared, it does not matter which is considered to be medium 1 and which is considered to be medium 2.

So at the surface, 81% of the energy is reflected right back into the transducer. This is the same as stating that only 19% of the energy is transmitted into the patient, a far cry from the desired 100%. If this seems bad, the situation is actually worse than it already appears. As the sound propagates into the body, most of the sound will be absorbed, and only small fractions of the non-absorbed remaining percentage (from the 19%) will reflect back. On return, that small fraction then encounters the same acoustic impedance mismatch, this time going from the low impedance of the tissue to the higher impedance of the crystal. The result is 81% of that very small percentage will be reflected right back into the body and only 19% will be received by the crystal.

$$\text{Roundtrip} = 0.19 \times 0.19 = 0.036 \text{ or } 3.6\%$$

Effectively only 3.6% of the signal that is not absorbed and which reflects back from the very small mismatches within the tissues is received, which is essentially 0. This fact serves as the motivation for designing transducers with a material that is affixed to the front of the crystal called a matching layer.

◊ **Example 2:** As just demonstrated, since the acoustic impedance mismatch between a crystal material and tissue is so great, there is very poor transmission into and out of the patient. By adding an intermediate material called a matching layer, the effective mismatch can be reduced to improve efficiency in both directions. Imagine that a matching layer with an acoustic impedance of 10 MRayls is placed between the crystal and the patient. What is the net effect?

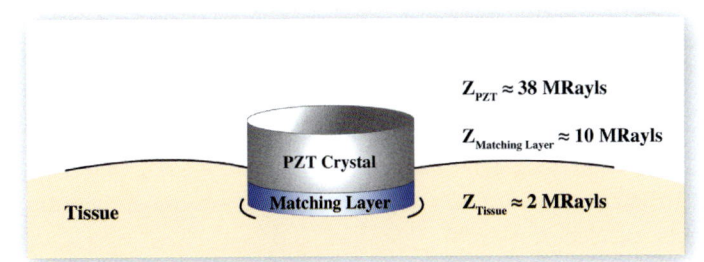

Fig. 25 **Impedance matching**

To solve this problem we will have to perform two calculations. The first calculation will determine the percentage of energy which is transmitted into the matching layer. The second calculation will determine the percentage transferred from the matching layer to the patient.

$$\% \text{ Reflected} = \left[\frac{38 \text{ MRayls} - 10 \text{ MRayls}}{38 \text{ MRayls} + 10 \text{ MRayls}}\right]^2 = \left[\frac{28}{48}\right]^2 = \left[\frac{4 \times 7}{4 \times 12}\right]^2 = \left[\frac{7}{12}\right]^2 = 0.34$$

So 100% - 34% = 66% of the energy transfers into the matching layer. We now need to calculate the transmission efficiency into the patient.

$$\% \text{ Reflected} = \left[\frac{10 \text{ MRayls} - 2 \text{ MRayls}}{10 \text{ MRayls} + 2 \text{ MRayls}}\right]^2 = \left[\frac{8}{12}\right]^2 = \left[\frac{4 \times 2}{4 \times 3}\right]^2 = \left[\frac{2}{3}\right]^2 = 0.44$$

So 56% of the energy that penetrates into the matching layer is transmitted into the patient. Since only 66% of the total transmitted energy made it into the matching layer, we must multiply the two percentages to get the overall efficiency of transfer.

$$\text{Overall one way percentage} = 0.66 \times 0.56 = 0.37 \text{ or } 37\%$$

Again, since on return, the signal encounters the same mismatch, we must square this percentage or:

$$\text{roundtrip percentage} = 0.37 \times 0.37 = 0.14 \text{ or } 14\%$$

Although 14% is not wonderful, it is almost 4 times greater than the overall transmission efficiency without a matching layer (3.6% as calculated in the previous example).

◊ **Example 3:** In the last two examples there is an implicit assumption that is not true. Although there is no mention made, the assumption must be that there is no air trapped between the surface of the transducer and the surface of the skin. For this example, given that air has an acoustic impedance of approximately 0.0004 MRayls, let's remove the artificial assumption and see what happens.

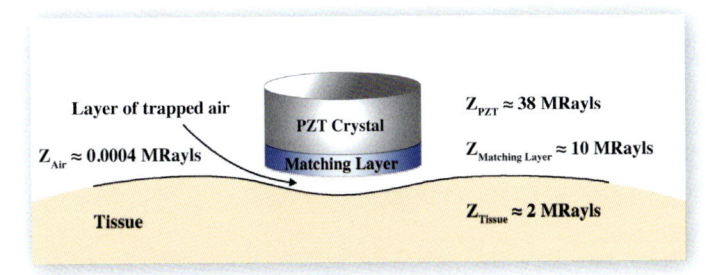

Fig. 26 **High impedance mismatch with air**

To fully solve the problem, we would need to perform the calculation three times, one for each interface. However, since the mismatch between the matching layer and the air is so enormous, we can pretty quickly answer this question practically by stating that there will be virtually 100% reflection at the air to matching layer interface, resulting in no transmission. For completeness sake, we will perform the calculation anyway.

Note that the first calculation was already performed in Example 2. So we already know that 66% of the transmitted energy is transferred to the matching layer. Now let's calculate the percentage transferred from the matching layer into the air boundary.

$$\% \ Reflected = \left[\frac{10 \ MRayls - 0.0004 \ MRayls}{10 \ MRayls + 0.0004 \ MRayls}\right]^2 = \left[\frac{9.9996}{10.0004}\right]^2 = 0.9998 \ or \ 99.98\%$$

100% - 99.98% = 0.02% of the energy is transferred from the matching layer to the air. We now need to calculate the transmission efficiency into the patient from the air.

$$\% \ Reflected = \left[\frac{2 \ MRayls - 0.0004 \ MRayls}{2 \ MRayls + 0.0004 \ MRayls}\right]^2 = \left[\frac{1.9996}{2.0004}\right]^2 = 0.9992 \ or \ 99.92\%$$

So 0.08% of the energy that penetrates into the air is transmitted into the patient. Since only 66% of the total transmitted energy made it into the matching layer, and only 0.02% made it from the matching layer into the air, and then only 0.08% of that made it into the patient, we must multiply the three percentages to get the overall efficiency of transfer.

$$Overall \ one \ way \ percentage = 0.66 \times 0.0002 \times 0.0008 = 0.0000001$$
$$or \ 0.00001\%$$

Again, since on return, the signal encounters the same mismatch, we must square this percentage or:

Roundtrip percentage = $0.0000001 \times 0.0000001$ = Essentially 0%.

This example clearly demonstrates the need for using gel when imaging. The role of gel is to eliminate any air that can be trapped at the interface, causing an enormous acoustic impedance mismatch that is virtually insurmountable for imaging.

Note: The low acoustic impedance of air could be easily anticipated by considering the equation which predicts acoustic impedance. The density of air is extremely low. The propagation velocity in air, relative to stiffer materials like tissue or the matching layer, is also extremely low. The result is that the acoustic impedance of air is extremely low.

KEY CONCEPT

The acoustic impedance of a transducer crystal is much higher than the acoustic impedance of tissue, which would result in very little transmission of sound into the patient from the transducer and out from the patient back into the transducer. A "matching layer" (or layers) is built into the transducer design with an intermediate acoustic impedance to improve efficiency of sound transmission both into and out of the patient.

◊ *Example 4:* Imagine that there is a large mass in a kidney with an acoustic impedance of 1.64 MRayls. Presuming that the acoustic impedance of the surrounding kidney tissue is 1.62 MRayls, calculate the percentage reflection from normal incidence to the mass.

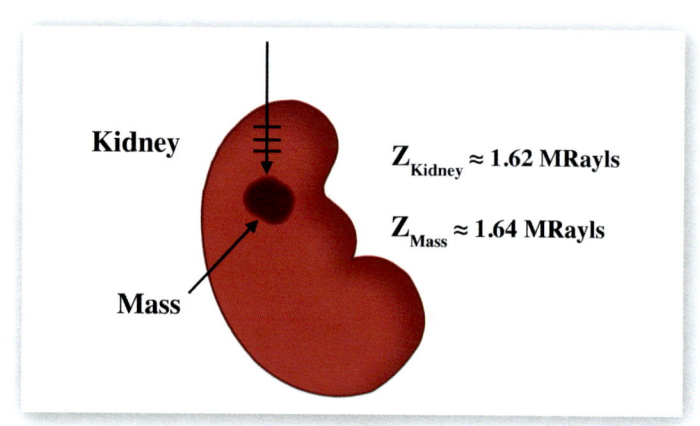

Fig. 27 Small impedance mismatch

This time we want to know the reflected percentage at the interface between the kidney and the mass. Plugging in the values for the mass and the kidney yields:

$$\% \ Reflected = \left[\frac{1.64 \ MRayls - 1.62 \ MRayls}{1.64 \ MRayls + 1.62 \ MRayls}\right]^2 = \left[\frac{0.02}{3.26}\right]^2 = 0.0038 \ or \ 0.38\%$$

Since this is a very small percentage reflection, there is a chance that this mass will not be visualized, regardless of the size of the mass. This exercise demonstrates a very important lesson about ultrasound in specific and testing in general, "just because you do not visualize something, doesn't mean that there isn't anything there."

◊ *Example 5:* For the following image of a vertebral artery, what percent of the beam that reaches the vertebral spinous process bone is transmitted deeper, given that the acoustic impedance of the bone is approximately 6.7 MRayls, and the surrounding tissue has an acoustic impedance of approximately 1.7 MRayls (assuming no absorption within the bone)?

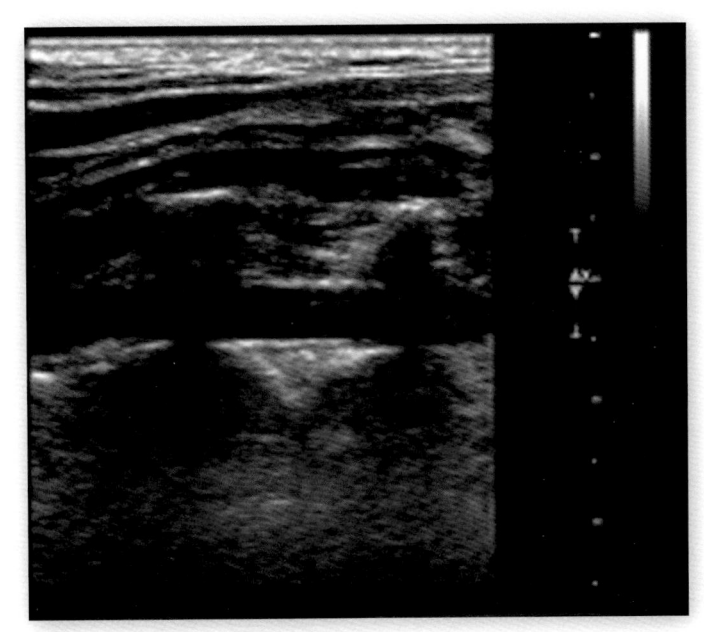

Fig. 28 **Shadowing from bone**

This time we want to know the transmission percentage after two interfaces, the anterior and posterior aspect of the bone to tissue interfaces. Since the mismatch is the same on either side, we will solve the equation once and then apply the results a second time. Plugging in the values for the bone and the tissue yields:

$$\% \text{ Reflected} = \left[\frac{6.7 \text{ MRayls} - 1.7 \text{ MRayls}}{6.7 \text{ MRayls} + 1.7 \text{ MRayls}}\right]^2 = \left[\frac{5}{8.4}\right]^2 = 0.35 \text{ or } 35\%$$

So the transmission past the anterior aspect of the bone is approximately 65%. After the posterior aspect, 35% of the remaining energy will again reflect back leaving:

$$\text{Transmission percentage deeper than bone} = 0.65 \times 0.65 = 0.42 \text{ or } 42\%.$$

Excluding the absorption within the bone, a total of 58% of the energy that reached the anterior aspect of the vertebral artery has reflected back from either the anterior or posterior interface with the tissue. If you then consider the fact that absorption in bone is approximately five to fifteen times greater than the attenuation in tissue, you should now have a good appreciation why a shadow is created below most bony structures.

> **KEY CONCEPT**
>
> The mere fact that a mass is large does not guarantee that it can be well visualized in ultrasound. When the acoustic impedance of the mass is close to the acoustic impedance of the surrounding tissue, there may not be enough contrast to visualize the mass.

Considering Tissue as an Infinite Series of Small Mismatches

We can consider the body as being comprised of an infinite number of reflecting boundary surfaces, or small acoustic impedance mismatches. The most obvious boundaries are the transitions from one organ to another, such as blood vessel wall to lumen, or heart wall to chamber, kidney to liver, etc. However, we can also consider every organ as being comprised of infinitesimally thin layers or boundaries, each of which will have various types of reflection. The type of reflection which occurs at each of these boundaries will clearly impact the amount of energy reflected back to the transducer. Additionally, the small acoustic impedance mismatches at each of these boundaries will determine what percentage of the incident energy will be reflected.

The strength of the signal clearly depends on how much of the wave energy is reflected back to and received by the transducer: the stronger the backscatter, the stronger the signal. However, there is a limited amount of energy within the wave. If there is too much reflection at any one boundary, or at multiple boundaries collectively, then there will not be enough energy to visualize any of the deeper boundaries. In reality, we are therefore relying on there being enough of an acoustic impedance mismatch to produce a strong reflection so as to be visualized, but not so much reflection such that deeper tissue is in the "shadow" of the stronger reflecting tissue. As we will learn in later sections, when there is an excessive amount of attenuation from a more superficial structure, the artifact called shadowing is visualized (an artifact in which structures below the strongly attenuated structured are either poorly visualized, or not visualized at all).

Standoffs and Water-Path Scanners

For "water path scanners" an acoustic standoff or water standoff is used between the transducer crystal(s) and the patient. The acoustic standoff pad is often made of a gel that may or may not be reusable. This approach is generally used when it is desirable to image broad areas, especially with superficial structures. Standoffs are also advantageous for allowing better angles to superficial specular structures, since very little energy is lost within the standoff. The one disadvantage is the acoustic impedance mismatch at the surface of the pad which produces a ring down effect.

Important Points About Scattering, Specular Reflections, and Rayleigh Scattering

1. A truly homogeneous medium would produce no echoes (anechoic) since there would be no acoustic impedance mismatch. Fluids tend to be relatively homogeneous and hence, anechoic (no echoes).

2. Tissues are never "truly homogeneous" and, hence, produce varying degrees of echogenicity. Since the interface between various organs tends to be "specular" in nature, in general,

the best B-mode (2D) images are produced when the angle of incidence is normal to the surface of the organs (vessels) being imaged.

3. Most tissue in the body is "rough" with respect to the wavelength of diagnostic ultrasound, producing scattering. It is the scattering which gives the apparent tissue texture to ultrasound.

4. Specular reflectors are most often the cause of imaging artifacts. Some examples of very strong specular reflectors are bones, the diaphragm, and gas bubbles.

5. Specular reflections from large, smooth surfaces are very angle dependent and may not be received back to the transducer if the angle of incidence is not normal (beam direction perpendicular to the structure's smooth surface). As a result, small variations in the incident angle can cause significant changes in both the display intensity, and any associated artifacts. Knowledge of this fact is critical for minimizing the presence of specular reflection based image artifacts.

6. A good example of a Rayleigh scatterer is blood. The red blood cells (RBCs) are very small relative to the wavelength used in diagnostic ultrasound.

7. Rayleigh scattering is a very weak reflection mechanism. Additionally, the acoustic impedance of the RBCs is relatively close to the acoustic impedance of the plasma. As a result, the echoes from the blood pool are very weak. This fact creates some extra difficulty when performing spectral and color Doppler.

8. Fresh thrombus is not always identifiable using ultrasound. The reflected signal energy from a fresh thrombus is usually very low since a fresh thrombus is comprised of aggregated red blood cells. Recall that Rayleigh scattering occurs from structures which are small relative to the wavelength.

9. As frequency increases, the wavelength decreases, making the surfaces within the body appear rougher; as a result, the amount of scattering increases with increasing frequency. In addition, absorption increases with increasing frequency. As a result, since more ultrasound energy is scattered and absorbed at high frequency, penetration decreases (less energy is transmitted).

10. The range of reflected signal amplitudes (signal dynamic range) can vary widely from specular reflectors to Rayleigh scatterers. As a result, compression is necessary to accommodate the much smaller dynamic range of the human eye. This compression has the potential to "hide" small variations in signal which may be critical. Extreme care must be taken to guarantee that no signals have been "compressed out". This will become a motivating factor for understanding compression and system controls.

> **CHECKPOINT: Exam Tip**
>
> Refraction artifact results in a lateral displacement of structures within an image such that either two structures are displayed side-by-side where only one truly exists, or a structure appears in the wrong location, laterally shifted from the actual location.

10. Refraction in the Body

10.1 Effects of Refraction

As expressed in Level 1, refraction is a change in beam direction caused by a distortion of the wavefront. This distortion occurs when a wave traverses an interface between mediums of varying propagation speeds at an angle such that the wavefront is not parallel to the interface (normal incidence). The effects of refraction in imaging are numerous. The principal effects are:

- Edge shadowing
- Displacement of a structure in the image laterally
- Artifactual second image (actual structure exists in correct position and artifactual replica exists laterally displaced from actual structure)
- Loss of signal intensity from dispersion of beam
- Degradation in lateral resolution

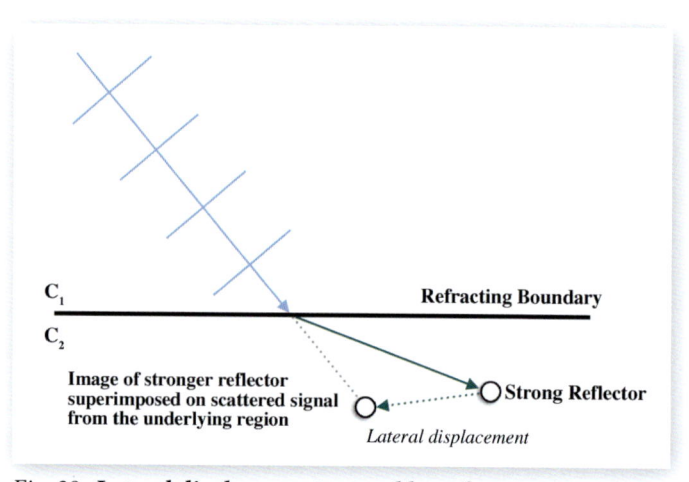

Fig. 29 **Lateral displacement caused by refraction**

Ultrasound always presumes that the reflections returning to the transducer came from the steered direction. If a transmitted beam is pointing straight ahead, then the reflections are presumed to come from structures straight ahead. If the beam is angled at thirty degrees, then the reflections are presumed to come from structures along the path of 30 degrees. In *Figure 29*, notice that since the beam direction was refracted, the echoes that return are not from the presumed direction, but from an angularly displaced path. When the reflected signal encounters the interface, the beam is again refracted and returned to the transducer. Since the transducer presumes that the data emanated from the original transmitted direction, the reflection is drawn laterally displaced from its true source.

You should also note that in this case, the propagation velocity in medium 2 is faster than in medium 1. This fact can be determined by analyzing the direction in which the beam was bent. *Figure 30* illustrates this point.

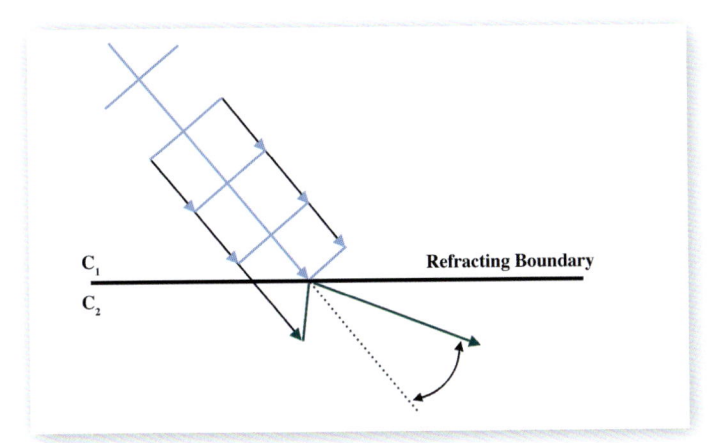

Fig. 30 **Determining refraction direction**

Notice that the "page left" edge of the wavefront encounters the interface before the "page right" edge of the wavefront. If the propagation velocity in medium 2 is higher than in medium 1, the left edge travels farther than the right. When the resulting points of the wavefront are connected, the new wave direction is as shown. Therefore, the propagation velocity in medium 2, for this case, is higher than the propagation velocity for medium 1.

This change in velocity is important to recognize since the depth a structure is displayed depends on the flight time of the ultrasound. Recall that ultrasound always presumes a propagation velocity of 1540 m/sec. Therefore, if a higher velocity medium is encountered, the flight time is decreased. Interestingly, in this case, since the beam was bent, the flight path is longer but the propagation velocity is faster. The longer flight path would increase the time, but the higher velocity works to decrease the time. Since these two errors work in opposite directions, the resulting structure is displaced almost purely laterally. If the beam was bent, but the propagation velocity was not increased, the increased path length would result in the artifact being drawn deeper as well as being laterally displaced. This fact is demonstrated in *Figure 31* and *Figure 32*.

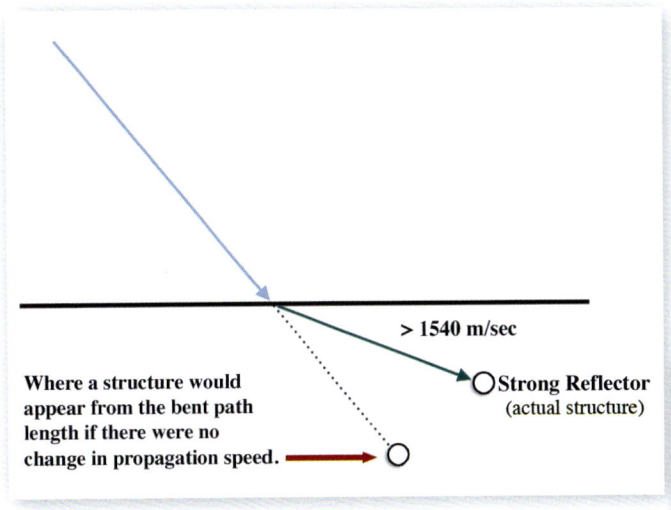

Fig. 31 **Lateral and depth displacement**

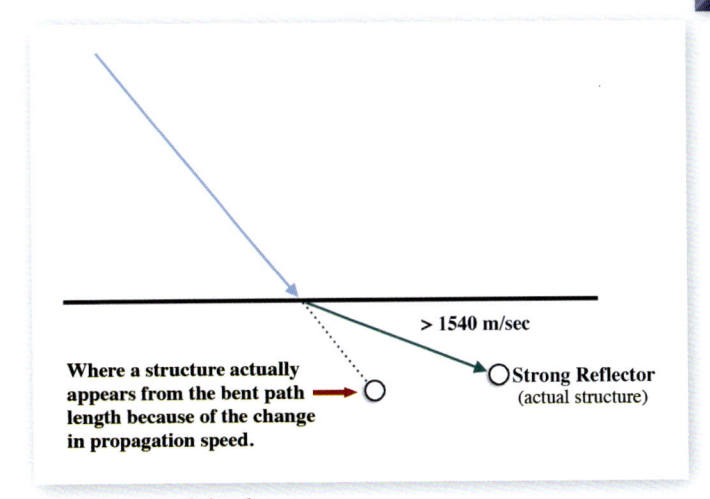

Fig. 32 **Lateral displacement**

Notice that in the hypothetical situation of *Figure 31*, since the flight path from the bent beam is longer than if the structure were on the presumed axis of the beam, and since the propagation velocity remained the same, the overall time for the echo to return is increased. A longer flight time implies a deeper structure. Therefore, the drawn structure is displayed too deep because of the increased time, and laterally displaced because of the bent beam. In *Figure 32*, although the flight path is longer, the velocity increased. The increased time of the flight path offsets the decreased time of the increased velocity. Therefore, the structure is drawn at the same depth, but laterally displaced because of the bent beam.

10.2 The Critical Angle and Refractive Shadowing

With refraction artifact, there is a lateral displacement as a result of the beam refraction. Another artifact associated with refraction is acoustic shadowing (sometimes referred to as edge shadowing or refractive edge shadowing). As the name suggests, a "shadow" is a dark region in the ultrasound image. We have already discussed the fact that greater than normal reflection can result in shadowing, since there is less energy to insonify inferior structures. We can now consider what refraction situations would result in shadowing.

Consider *Figure 33* in which a beam is incident at an angle far from 0 degrees (non-normal incidence). Because there is a change in propagation velocity at the interface, the beam will be refracted as shown. In many cases, the critical angle is achieved, at which all of the energy of the wave is internally reflected, and none transmitted into the interfacing medium. Since most or all of the energy is directed away from the original axis of the beam, there is very little, if any, energy to insonify the deeper region along the original beam axis. The result is either weak reflection or no reflection from this region. When there is a very weak signal or no signal present, the image appears close to black or black. Hence, regions of shadowing occur in the image.

Refractive shadowing is very common whenever viewing vessels, cystic structures, gas bubbles, prosthetic devices, and bones.

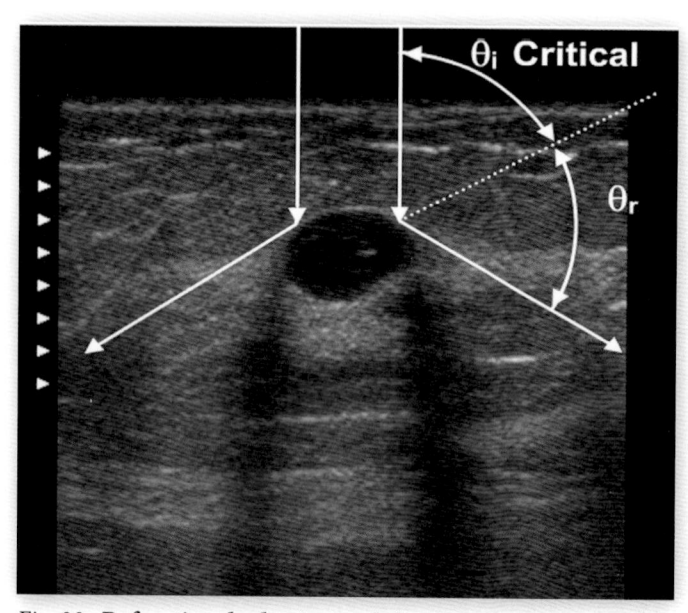

Fig. 33 **Refractive shadowing and the critical angle**

10.3 Applying Snell's Law

In Level 1 we learned that Snell's law predicts the presence of refraction and the degree of refraction. From the equation, we know that a greater disparity in propagation velocities will increase the degree of refraction. From the equation, we also know that a larger incident angle will also increase the degree of refraction that occurs. The following examples of the application of Snell's law should further demonstrate the concepts which have been discussed to this point.

◊ *Example 1:*

Applying Snell's Law with Normal Incidence

The fact that no refraction occurs with normal incidence can easily be shown by applying Snell's law as in the following example.

How much refraction occurs for normal incidence ($\theta_i = 0°$)?

$$\text{Snell's law:} \quad \frac{c_i}{c_t} = \frac{sin(\theta_i)}{sin(\theta_t)}$$

Rewrite the equation in terms of the known variable.

Multiply both sides by $sin(\theta_t)$: $\frac{c_i}{c_t} \times sin(\theta_t) = sin(\theta_i)$.

Since the $sin(\theta_i) = sin(0°) = 0$,

$$\frac{c_i}{c_t} \times sin(\theta_t) = 0.$$

And since it is not physically possible for the propagation velocity to equal 0,

$$sin(\theta_t) = 0$$
$$\text{and } (\theta_t) = 0°.$$

Since the transmit angle, θ_t, equals the incident angle, θ_i, the beam has not changed direction, and hence, there is no refraction.

◊ *Example 2:*

Applying Snell's Law with Equal Propagation Velocities

The fact that no refraction can occur if the propagation velocities are equal at an interface (regardless of the incident angle) can also easily be demonstrated using Snell's law.

$$\text{Snell's law:} \quad \frac{c_i}{c_t} = \frac{sin(\theta_i)}{sin(\theta_t)}$$

If $c_i = c_t$, then $\frac{c_i}{c_t} = 1$

Therefore: $\frac{sin(\theta_i)}{sin(\theta_t)} = 1.$

Multiplying both sides by the $sin(\theta_t)$ yields:

$$sin(\theta_i) = sin(\theta_t),$$
$$\text{therefore, } \theta_i = \theta_t.$$

As already discussed, if the incident angle equals the transmitted angle, there has been no bending of the beam, and hence, no refraction.

◊ *Example 3:*

Applying Snell's Law and the Critical Angle

At the critical angle, all of the beam travels along the surface of the interface, implying a transmitted angle of 90 degrees. Therefore, if Snell's law predicts a transmitted angle of 90 degrees, the critical angle has been reached. For this example we will calculate the critical angle between a tissue to bone interface. We will assume that the propagation velocity in tissue is the soft tissue value of 1540 m/sec. For bone we will presume the approximate average of 4080 m/sec.

The last step of this problem requires finding the inverse sine of an angle. From the unit circle you learned in Chapter 1: Mathematics, you may not get the exact angle, but you can get close enough.

$$\text{Snell's law: } \frac{c_i}{c_t} = \frac{sin(\theta_i)}{sin(\theta_t)}$$

We would like the incident angle by itself, so we will multiply both sides by the $sin(\theta_t)$,

$$\frac{c_i}{c_t} \times sin(\theta_t) = sin(\theta_i)$$

Plugging in the values yields:

$$\frac{1540 \frac{m}{sec}}{4080 \frac{m}{sec}} \times sin(90°) = sin(\theta_i)$$

$$\frac{154}{408} \times 1 = sin(\theta_i)$$

$$0.37 = sin(\theta_i) \Rightarrow \theta_i = 22°$$

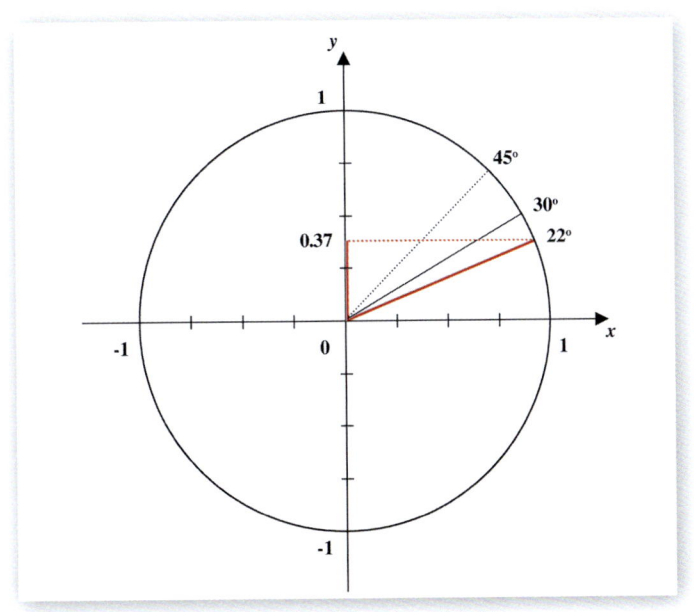

Fig. 34 **Estimating the angle with a sine of 0.37**

Imagine how disconcerting total internal reflection can be. If the angle between the ultrasound beam direction and a structure in the body is far enough away from perpendicular, no ultrasound energy or little ultrasound energy travels distal to that interface. The result, as already explained, is that structures can be drawn at incorrect locations or appear as acoustic shadowing in the ultrasound image. This is one of the principal reasons that 2D, or B-mode imaging, is best performed with the incident beam perpendicular to the structure. This same artifact can also cause spectral and color Doppler signals to drop out. As always, you must assess the angle between specular reflectors and the incident beam to determine the likelihood and type of artifact which can exist.

Note: The critical angle has been reached when the calculated transmitted angle is 90°.

10.4 Important Points about Refraction

1. The incident angle is measured relative to the (normal) line perpendicular to the interface.

2. There is no refraction if the ultrasound beam has normal incidence (the beam direction is perpendicular, orthogonal, or 90° degrees) to the interface between two media.

3. A perpendicular beam implies that the incident angle is 0°.

4. There is no refraction if there is no change in propagation velocity across the interface of two media.

5. As the difference in propagation speeds increases, and as the angle gets further away from normal incidence, the amount of refraction increases.

6. There is an angle of incidence at which there is no transmission and 100% internal reflection occurs. This angle is called the critical angle.

7. At the critical angle, the transmission angle is 90°.

8. Refraction is considered an artifact which can cause objects to be drawn at the wrong location (primarily laterally displaced) or not even drawn at all.

9. Refraction can cause loss of signal strength, and cause acoustic shadows in a 2D image.

10. Refraction can also cause a loss of Doppler signal strength, and at the critical angle, can even make the Doppler spectrum or color Doppler disappear.

11. Exercises and Conceptual Questions

View ONLINE Exercises & Conceptual Questions

12. Review of Attenuation

1. Attenuation is dependent on both the characteristics of the wave and characteristics of the medium.

2. Attenuation represents a transfer of energy (a change in any of the acoustic variables) through absorption (conversion of sound to heat) and scattering represented by reflection and refraction.

3. Absorption is the conversion of wave energy into heat and is the dominant form of attenuation in soft tissue.

4. Attenuation through absorption increases exponentially with higher operating frequencies. Attenuation in soft tissue is approximately 0.5 dB/(cm-MHz) and in muscle is approximately 1 dB/(cm-MHz).

5. The amount of energy reflected is determined by the acoustic impedance mismatch, the incident angle, and the type of reflection.

6. Ignoring absorption, the sum of transmitted energy and reflected energy equals the incident energy (energy is conserved).

7. We consider three categorizations of reflection: specular, scattering, and Rayleigh scattering.

8. Specular reflection is dependent on "smoothness" and size of the reflector relative to the wavelength. Specular reflection is highly angle dependent.

9. Scattering occurs from surfaces which are "rough" relative to the wavelength.

10. Rayleigh scattering occurs when the reflectors are small relative to the wavelength. Rayleigh scattering is a very weak reflective mechanism.

11. The acoustic impedance (with units of Rayls) equals the density times the velocity.

12. The percentage of reflection and transmission at a normal interface can be determined by the equations:

$$Z = \rho \times c.$$

$$\text{reflection \%} = \left[\frac{Z_2 - Z_1}{Z_2 + Z_1} \right]^2 \cdot 100\%$$

$$\text{transmission \%} = \left[1 - \left[\frac{Z_2 - Z_1}{Z_2 + Z_1} \right]^2 \right] \cdot 100\%$$

13. There is a very undesirable trade-off between improving resolution and decreasing penetration due to increased attenuation at higher frequency imaging. Harmonic imaging (discussed in Chapter 10) is an attempt to minimize this trade-off.

14. Refraction is determined by Snell's law:
$c_t (\sin \theta_i) = c_i (\sin \theta_t)$.

LEVEL 3: Advanced Topics

13. Table of Acoustic Values

The following table lists the density, propagation velocity, acoustic impedance, and absorption rates for various materials. You should note that the attenuation rate is specified at a frequency of 1 MHz. For the simplified material of Level 2, the attenuation rates were rounded off, and specified as being a simple linear relationship between increase in frequency and increase in logarithmic attenuation. In reality, the frequency relationship is considerably more complex and is highly dependent on properties of the material. Some materials demonstrate relationships as low as the square root of the frequency, whereas others demonstrate relationships proportional to the square of the frequency. The treatment of these frequency dependencies is not included here.

Material	Density (ρ) $\frac{kg}{m^3}$	Velocity (c) $\frac{m}{sec}$	Impedance (z) $MRayls = \frac{1 \times 10^6 \, kg}{m^2 \times sec}$	Absorption (a) $\frac{dB}{cm}$ (@1 MHz)
Air	1.2	330	0.0004	12
Castor oil	950	1500	1.4	0.95
Water	1,000	1484	1.52	0.0022
Fat	920	1450 - 1480	1.35	[0.63]
Brain	1030	1510 - 1560	1.55 - 1.66	[0.75]
Kidney	1040	1560	1.62	-
Lung	400	500 - 650	0.26	[40]
Liver	1060	1570	1.64 - 1.68	[1.2]
Spleen	1060	1570	1.65 - 1.67	-
Muscle	1070	1560 - 1580	1.65 - 1.74	[0.96 - 1.4]
Blood	1060	1560 - 1580	1.62	[0.15]
Bone	1380-1810	4080	3.75 - 7.38	[14.2 - 25.2]
Aluminum	2700	6400	17	0.18
Brass	8500	4490	38	0.020
Mercury	13,600	1450	20	0.00048
Stainless Steel	7840	5790 m/sec	45	0.4

Table 2 **Acoustic parameters** (Principal source: <u>Medical Imaging Signal and Systems</u> by Prince and Links, Prentice Hall 2006)

Note: The gray area of the table represents the values used in determining the approximate average of "soft tissue."

14. Reflection and Transmission Percentage for Non-normal Incidence

The equation developed for determining the percentage reflection was based on the assumption that the incident angle was 0 degrees. The general equation is given by:

$$\% \text{ Reflected} = \frac{I_{reflected}}{I_{incident}} = \left[\frac{Z_2 \cos(\theta_1) - Z_1 \cos(\theta_2)}{Z_2 \cos(\theta_1) + Z_1 \cos(\theta_2)}\right]^2$$

The transmitted percentage can then be generated by subtracting the fractional reflection from 1, or:

$$\% \text{ Transmitted} = 1 - \left[\frac{Z_2 \cos(\theta_1) - Z_1 \cos(\theta_2)}{Z_2 \cos(\theta_1) + Z_1 \cos(\theta_2)}\right]^2$$

$$\% \text{ Transmitted} = \frac{(Z_2 \cos(\theta_1) + Z_1 \cos(\theta_2))^2}{(Z_2 \cos(\theta_1) + Z_1 \cos(\theta_2))^2} - \frac{(Z_2 \cos(\theta_1) - Z_1 \cos(\theta_2))^2}{(Z_2 \cos(\theta_1) + Z_1 \cos(\theta_2))^2}$$

By expanding both expressions and subtracting the expression simplifies to:

$$\% \text{ Transmitted} = \frac{4 Z_1 Z_2 (\cos(\theta_1))(\cos(\theta_2))}{(Z_2 \cos(\theta_1) + Z_1 \cos(\theta_2))^2}.$$

Note: The process of mathematically simplifying is made easier if you remember the rule about differences of squares from algebra.

From these general equations, the specific equations for normal incidence are easily generated by plugging in a value of 0 degrees for the incident and transmitted angles. Recall that the cosine of 0 degrees is 1.

$$\% \text{ Reflected} = \left[\frac{Z_2 \cos(0°) - Z_1 \cos(0°)}{Z_2 \cos(0°) + Z_1 \cos(0°)}\right]^2 = \left[\frac{Z_2 \times 1 - Z_1 \times 1}{Z_2 \times 1 + Z_1 \times 1}\right]^2 = \left[\frac{Z_2 - Z_1}{Z_2 + Z_1}\right]^2$$

To calculate the transmission percentage, instead of introducing another equation, we used the conservation theorem to subtract the reflection percentage from 100%. This approach works fine, but for the purists who enjoy equations, the general form of the transmission equation above can also be simplified by plugging in for the cosine of 0 degrees yielding:

$$\% \text{ Transmitted} = \frac{4 Z_1 Z_2}{(Z_2 + Z_1)^2}.$$

15. Matching Layer

Let us return to our matching layer example of Level 2. What is the ideal acoustic impedance for the matching layer given the impedance of the crystal at 38 MRayls, and the acoustic impedance of the tissue at 2 MRayls?

The following table shows the effective percent transmission for matching layers of acoustic impedances ranging from 37 MRayls to 3 MRayls, assuming a crystal impedance of 38 MRayls and a tissue impedance of 2 MRayls.

Matching Layer Impedance (Z) (MRayls)	Transmission % One way	Transmission % Round trip
37	19.46%	3.79%
36	19.93%	3.97%
35	20.42%	4.17%
34	20.92%	4.38%
33	21.44%	4.60%
32	21.98%	4.83%
31	22.54%	5.08%
30	23.11%	5.34%
29	23.71%	5.62%
28	24.32%	5.91%
27	24.95%	6.22%
26	25.60%	6.55%
25	26.27%	6.90%
24	26.95%	7.27%
23	27.66%	7.65%
22	28.38%	8.06%
21	29.12%	8.48%
20	29.87%	8.92%
19	30.64%	9.39%
18	31.41%	9.86%
17	32.18%	10.36%
16	32.95%	10.86%
15	33.70%	11.36%
14	34.43%	11.85%
13	35.12%	12.33%
12	35.74%	12.77%
11	36.26%	13.15%
10	36.65%	13.43%
9	**36.85%**	**13.58%**
8	36.78%	13.53%
7	36.33%	13.20%
6	35.33%	12.48%
5	33.55%	11.26%
4	30.64%	9.39%
3	26.04%	6.78%

Table 3 **Matching layer example: assuming match for 38 MRayls to 2 MRayls**

From *Table 3*, we see that the highest efficiency is achieved when the matching layer has an impedance greater than 8 and a little less than 9 MRayls. This solution can be calculated by taking the geometric mean of the impedances to be matched. In this example:

$$\text{Best Matching Impedence} = \sqrt{Z_{crystal} * Z_{tissue}}$$
$$= \sqrt{76 \text{ MRayls}^2}$$
$$= 8.7 \text{ MRayls}$$

16. Two Matching Layers

The optimal impedance for dual matching layer design can be calculated by solving this set of simultaneous equations as follows:

$$Z_{ML1} = \sqrt{Z_{crystal} * Z_{ML2}}$$
$$Z_{ML2} = \sqrt{Z_{tissue} * Z_{ML1}}$$

Starting with the ideal impedance for matching layer 1, square both sides to get:

$$(Z_{ML1})^2 = Z_{crystal} * Z_{ML2}$$
$$Z_{ML2} = \frac{(Z_{ML1})^2}{Z_{crystal}}$$

By substitution:

$$\frac{(Z_{ML1})^2}{Z_{crystal}} = \sqrt{Z_{tissue} * Z_{ML1}}$$

Square both sides to get:

$$\frac{(Z_{ML1})^4}{(Z_{crystal})^2} = Z_{tissue} * Z_{ML1}$$

Simplifying yields:

$$(Z_{ML1})^3 = Z_{tissue} * (Z_{crystal})^2$$

$$Z_{ML1} = (Z_{tissue})^{\frac{1}{3}} \cdot (Z_{crystal})^{\frac{2}{3}}$$

To solve for the ideal impedance of the second matching layer we begin with substitution:

$$Z_{ML1} = \sqrt{Z_{crystal} \cdot Z_{ML2}} = (Z_{tissue})^{\frac{1}{3}} \cdot (Z_{crystal})^{\frac{2}{3}}$$

Square both sides to yield:

$$Z_{crystal} \cdot Z_{ML2} = (Z_{tissue})^{\frac{2}{3}} \cdot (Z_{crystal})^{\frac{4}{3}}$$

$$Z_{ML2} = \frac{(Z_{tissue})^{\frac{2}{3}} \cdot (Z_{crystal})^{\frac{4}{3}}}{Z_{crystal}}$$

$$Z_{ML2} = (Z_{tissue})^{\frac{2}{3}} \cdot (Z_{crystal})^{\frac{1}{3}}$$

For the example given:

$$Z_{ML1} = (Z_{tissue})^{\frac{1}{3}} \cdot (Z_{crystal})^{\frac{2}{3}} = (2 \text{ MRayls})^{\frac{1}{3}} \cdot (38 \text{ MRayls})^{\frac{2}{3}}$$
$$= 14.24 \text{ MRayls}$$

$$Z_{ML2} = (Z_{tissue})^{\frac{2}{3}} \cdot (Z_{crystal})^{\frac{1}{3}} = (2 \text{ MRayls})^{\frac{2}{3}} \cdot (38 \text{ MRayls})^{\frac{1}{3}}$$
$$= 5.34 \text{ MRayls}$$

Let's now calculate the efficiency using two "ideal" matching layers and compare with the efficiency of using one "ideal" matching layer.

$$\text{Reflection}_{ML1} \% = \left[\frac{Z_2 - Z_1}{Z_2 + Z_1}\right]^2 = \left[\frac{38 - 14.24}{38 + 14.24}\right]^2 = 0.21$$

So the transmission percentage is 79%

$$\text{Reflection}_{ML2} \% = \left[\frac{Z_2 - Z_1}{Z_2 + Z_1}\right]^2 = \left[\frac{14.24 - 5.34}{14.24 + 5.34}\right]^2 = 0.21$$

So the transmission percentage is 79%

$$\text{Reflection}_{tissue} \% = \left[\frac{Z_2 - Z_1}{Z_2 + Z_1}\right]^2 = \left[\frac{5.34 - 2}{5.34 + 2}\right]^2 = 0.21$$

One way, the overall transmission percentage is:

$$0.79 \times 0.79 \times 0.79 = 0.49$$

So the roundtrip efficiency is given by $(0.49)^2 = 0.24$, or 24%

Compared with the highest efficiency achievable with a one matching layer design, the overall efficiency (roundtrip) almost doubles.

17. Determining the Maximum Imaging Depth from the Dynamic Range

In general, the maximum imaging depth for an ultrasound system is determined by the overall sensitivity of the system. When the reflected signal is commensurate with the level of thermal noise of the system, there is very little that can be done to adequately detect the signal. There are some adaptive techniques which rely on the coherence of the signal and the random nature of noise to adaptively improve signal detection. For these techniques, the goal is to identify noise from signal and then remove the noise through statistical or masking techniques.

These techniques aside, a general rule of thumb is that the maximum attenuation still allows adequate signal detection between 65 and 80 dB. Whereas there might be situations where more dynamic range can be supported (depending on the imaging situation, the efficiency of the transducer, noise floor of the system, and intensity limiting models to restrict the likelihood of bioeffects), 80 dB of attenuation is usually significant enough to warrant changing the imaging approach.

The calculation can be easily made to determine the maximum imaging depth for a specific transducer frequency, if we presume 80 dB maximum input dynamic range and an attenuation rate of approximately $\frac{1 \text{ dB}}{\text{cm} \times \text{MHz}}$, one way. (Of course, the result will vary from reality if our assumptions about attenuation or system dynamic range are incorrect.) For a 5 MHz transducer, the calculation is:

$$80 \text{ dB} = \frac{1 \text{ dB}}{\text{cm} \times \text{MHz}} \times (2 \times \text{Maximum Imaging depth (cm)}) \times 5 \text{ MHz}$$

$$\frac{80 \text{ dB}}{10 \text{ dB}} = 8 \text{ (cm)} = \text{Maximum Imaging depth (cm)}.$$

Not surprisingly, since we are starting with the assumption that the attenuation in decibels is linear with increasing frequency, we would get a maximum imaging depth of 4 cm at 10 MHz. Note that stating that the rate of attenuation with increasing frequency changing linearly with decibels is not the same as stating that attenuation varies linearly with frequency. This point should be obvious if you consider the fact that decibels is already a non-linear measurement.

COMMON MISCONCEPTION: Attenuation

MISCONCEPTION: *Attenuation is bad.*

Explanation:
Recall that reflection is a form of attenuation. Without reflection, diagnostic ultrasound would not function. Whereas excessive attenuation can cause imaging problems, some attenuation is necessary to create an ultrasound image. Additionally, many newer techniques use differences in attenuation as a means of identifying tissue characteristics.

COMMON MISCONCEPTION: Attenuation

MISCONCEPTION: *40 dB is twice as much power as 20 dB.*

Explanation:
Decibels are logarithmic, and hence very non-linear. 40 dB represents a power factor of 10,000 whereas 20 dB represents a power factor of 100. Therefore, 40 dB represents 100 times more power than 20 dB. Similarly, 20 dB (a power factor of 100) represents 10 times more power than 10 dB (a power factor of 10).

CHAPTER SUMMARY: Attenuation

- Attenuation implies a decrease in signal strength and occurs through absorption, reflection, and refraction.
- Absorption is the conversion of energy into heat within the medium.
- Absorption is the dominant form of attenuation in "soft tissue."
- Absorption increases exponentially with increasing frequency.
- Fluids tend to absorb energy much less than tissue.
- Bones absorb at a significantly higher rate than "soft tissues."
- The type of reflection that occurs at an interface depends on the wavelength relative to the surface geometry.
- If the surface is large, smooth, and flat with respect to the wavelength, specular reflection occurs (mirror-like reflection).
- If the surface is rough with respect to the wavelength, scattering occurs.
- If the reflecting structures are small relative to the wavelength (such as occurs with red blood cells) Rayleigh scattering occurs.
- Specular reflection is highly angle dependent and also the primary cause of most imaging artifacts.
- Rayleigh scattering is a very weak reflection mechanism.
- The amount of scattering increases with increasing frequency. Since the wavelength decreases as the frequency increases, the surface appears "rougher", increasing scattering.
- Although scattering intensifies with increasing frequency, absorption increases even faster with higher frequency. This is the reason you should use lower frequencies for Doppler unless imaging very superficial blood flow.
- The amount of reflection that occurs at an interface is determined by the acoustic impedance mismatch across the interface.
- The acoustic impedance of a material is given by the density times the propagation velocity:

$$Z = \rho \times c$$

- Higher acoustic impedance mismatches produce greater reflection.

- You should know the equation for percentage energy reflection based on acoustic impedance mismatch:

$$\text{Reflection \%} = \left[\frac{Z_2 - Z_1}{Z_2 + Z_1}\right]^2.$$

- The amount of transmission is simply calculated as 100% minus the reflected percentage.

$$\text{Transmission \%} = 100\% - \text{Reflection \%}$$

- Because of the large acoustic impedance mismatch between the relatively low impedance of tissue and the relatively high impedance of a crystal, a matching layer is used to improve efficiency.
- The matching layer (or layers) has an intermediate impedance between the impedance of the tissue and the crystal.
- Refraction refers to the bending of a beam that occurs at an interface when there is a change in propagation velocity between two interfacing media where the beam is incident at an angle other than normal.
- Snell's law predicts the amount of refraction that will occur:

$$\frac{c_i}{c_t} = \frac{\sin(\theta_i)}{\sin(\theta_t)}$$

- As the propagation velocities differ by increasing amounts, and as the incident angle is further from normal, the refraction increases, ultimately achieving a critical angle at which total internal reflection occurs.
- Attenuation rates give an approximation for the decreasing signal power as depth and frequency of operation change.
- The attenuation rate for soft tissue (one-way) is approximated to be 0.5 dB per cm and per MHz of the transmit frequency.

$$\text{Soft tissue attenuation} \approx \frac{0.5 \text{ dB}}{\text{cm} * \text{MHz}}$$

- The attenuation rate for muscle (one-way) is approximated to be 1 dB per cm and per MHz of the transmit frequency.

$$\text{Muscle attenuation} \approx \frac{1 \text{ dB}}{\text{cm} * \text{MHz}}$$

Note: Notationally, there are many ways of expressing the depth and frequency dependence of the attenuation rate. You should have noticed that many different formats have been used throughout the book to make you familiar with the various notations.

$$\left(\frac{dB}{cm \cdot MHz} = \frac{dB}{cm * MHz} = \frac{dB}{cm \times MHz} = \frac{dB}{cm - MHz} \right)$$

ONLINE EXTRAS

For additional support material and to view your completion progress, visit:
www.pegasuslectures.com/6thEdExtras

Extras by Chapter include:
- Animations
- Videos
- Additional Images
- Clarifying Clips
- Supplemental Exercises
- Conceptual Questions

See page x of Preface for access instructions

Pulsed Wave Operation

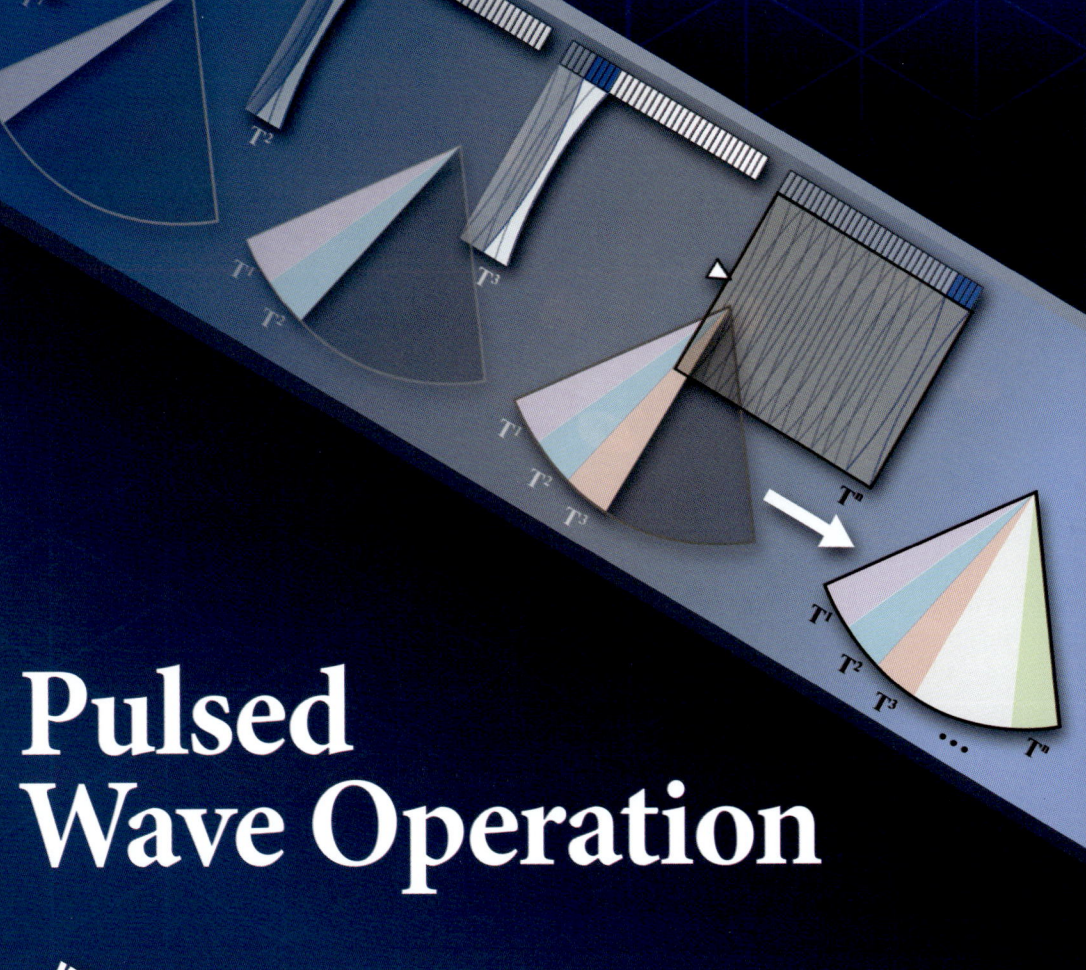

Chapter 4

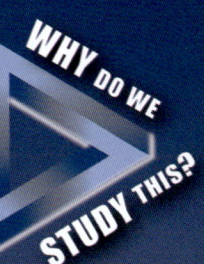

WHY DO WE STUDY THIS?

▸ Pulsed wave sets the foundation for the timing of all ultrasound modalities except CW Doppler and determines the axial resolution.

▸ The timing directly affects temporal resolution, image generation techniques, the risk of thermal bioeffects, the maximum allowed transmit voltage, and the maximum detectable Doppler velocities.

WHAT'S IN THIS CHAPTER?

LEVEL 1 — BASIC ULTRASOUND PHYSICS
The various pulsed wave definitions and the relationships between these parameters are introduced.

LEVEL 2 — BOARD LEVEL
The PW parameters are associated to the practical application in ultrasound, building the foundation for understanding the trade-offs that exist in how images are produced.

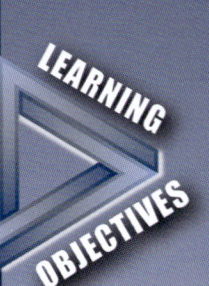

LEARNING OBJECTIVES

▸ Describe the advantages and disadvantages of pulsed and continuous wave operations

▸ List the various pulsed wave parameters

▸ Define the PW parameters that impact axial resolution

▸ Explain the relationship between imaging depth, pulse repetition period, and pulse repetition frequency

▸ Learn how to determine frame times and frame rates and understand the relation to temporal resolution

Chapter 4
Pulsed Wave Operation

1. Motivation for Using Pulsed Wave (PW)

In continuous wave operation, both the transmit and the receive are simultaneous and continuous. To simultaneously transmit and receive, there must be two transducers, one to transmit and one to receive. To avoid having to hold two separate transducers, a single transducer is "divided" into two halves; one half to continuously transmit and the other half to continuously receive. As a result of the continuous receive, echoes are received from all depths simultaneously, rendering it impossible to tell from where the echoes originated. This lack of range specificity, referred to as range ambiguity, is the greatest limitation of continuous wave operation.

1.1 Range Ambiguity and Continuous Wave (CW)

To demonstrate the problem of range ambiguity, consider *Figure 1*. In this example a continuous sound source transmits a signal toward some mountains in the distance. In time, the sound waves reach the first mountain and start to produce echoes. Meanwhile, since the sound source continues to produce wavefronts, new wavefronts continue to arrive producing more echoes. In time, the second mountain is also reached. The reflections from mountain 2 are also continuous. As time passes, the continuous stream of echoes from mountain 2 intermixes with the continuous stream of echoes from mountain 1. This process continues such that the reflection from mountain 3 also intermixes with the echoes from mountain 1 and mountain 2. As a result, there is a reflection, but there is no way of distinguishing the origin of the intermixed reflections. In other words, there is no range specificity.

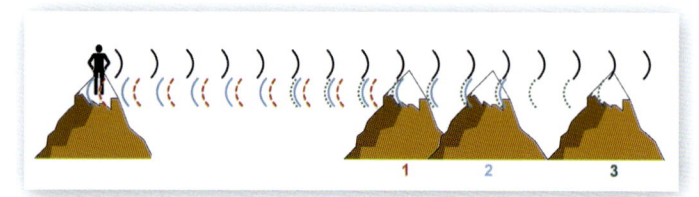

Fig. 1 **Echoes return from all mountains intermixed using a continuous wave (CW)**

View ONLINE Animation and Image Library

1.2 Range Specificity and Very Short Pulse

Imagine if instead of continuously transmitting and receiving, the transmitter were repeatedly pulsed on and then off as in *Figure 2*.

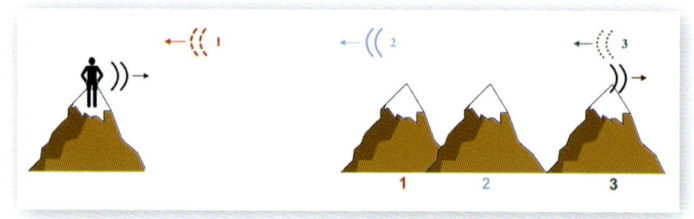

Fig. 2 **Echoes are separated in time using a pulsed wave (PW)**

Notice now that the echoes from each of the three mountains are separated in time. Obviously, the first returning echo comes from mountain number 1. The second echo returns from mountain number 2, and the third derives from mountain 3. Because each of these echoes are separated in time, it is now possible to distinguish, or "resolve" each of the mountains. Additionally, by knowing the propagation speed of sound, the distance can also be calculated by measuring the time between transmitting and the echoes returning. Of course, since the time of travel (flight) is a based on a roundtrip, a factor of 2 must be built into the calculation of the distance from the observer to the mountains.

View ONLINE Animation and Image Library

KEY CONCEPT

CW inherently has no ability to resolve the location of reflectors in depth (no range resolution). For this reason almost all ultrasound is performed using pulsed waves instead of continuous waves.

1.3 Range Specificity and Longer Pulse Pulsed Wave (PW)

In the first example, using continuous wave there was no range resolution. In the short pulsed mode of the second example there was very good resolution. What would happen if in pulse mode the pulses lasted for a longer period of time, as demonstrated in *Figure 3*? Would the resolution be as good?

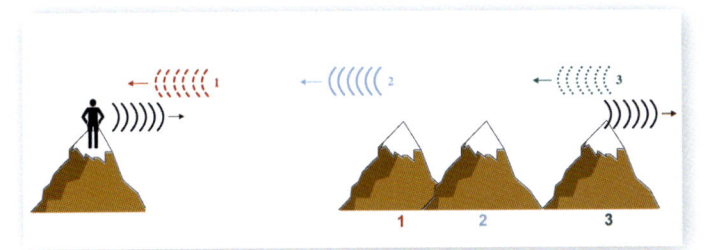

Fig. 3 **Longer pulse but still three distinct echoes**

Notice that because the pulse is now longer, the echoes from each of the mountains are also longer. As a result, the echoes from each of the three mountains are less distinct. In essence, there is less separation in time between each of the returning echoes from each of the mountains.

However, in *Figure 3*, there are clearly three distinct echoes, and hence, all three mountain peaks have been resolved. So in this case, the resolution was still adequate to determine the number of mountains and location of each. What would happen if the pulse became just a little bit longer in time?

1.4 Range Ambiguity and a Longer Pulse

In *Figure 4*, the transmitted pulse has become even longer. As a result, the echoes from each mountain have also become longer.

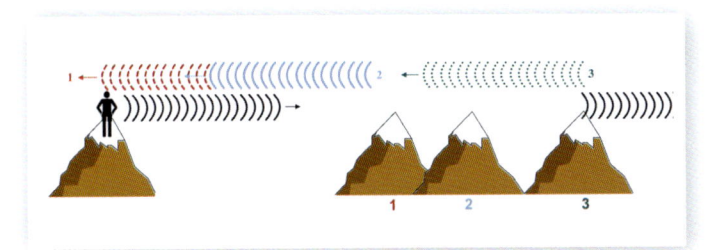

Fig. 4 **Loss of range resolution for mountains 1 and 2**

Notice how there is no longer a separation in time between the echoes from the first and second mountain. Since the echoes are no longer distinct, the two mountains will be detected as only one big mountain. There is no longer adequate range resolution to resolve these two structures. You should also notice that although the echoes from mountain 2 and mountain 3 are very close together, they are still distinct. As a result, the third mountain is resolved relative to the first two mountains. The question should now be, "why could mountain 3 be distinguished from mountain 2 but not mountain 1 from mountain 2?" The answer is quite simple, it is easier to resolve (distinguish between) structures that are farther apart than structures that are closer together. Since the distance separating mountain 2 from mountain 3 is greater than the distance separating mountain 1 from mountain 2, it is easier to resolve the third mountain from the second mountain than it is to resolve the second mountain from the first.

View ONLINE Animation and Image Library

KEY CONCEPT

The ability to resolve structures in depth gets better as the pulse becomes physically shorter.

2. Pulsed Wave Definitions

We have just seen that range resolution is the motivation for creating a pulsed wave modality (PW). With the exception of continuous wave Doppler, diagnostic ultrasound is performed in the pulsed mode. Given that the wave will now be turned on and off, there are additional time-related parameters needed to specify the pulse timing. Additionally, since the pulsed wave will occupy physical space in the medium, there will be some new distance-related parameters needed to specify the physical length of the pulse. Therefore, the next few sections are devoted to defining these time and length-based parameters for pulsed wave operation.

2.1 Time-Related Pulsed Wave Definitions

Pulse Duration (PD)

As the name suggests, the Pulse Duration is the amount of time for which a transmit pulse lasts. Note that the use of the word duration is very helpful since it indicates time. *Figure 5* depicts the parameter referred to as the pulse duration.

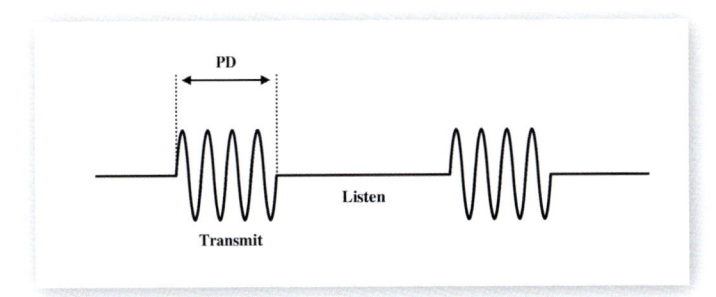

Fig. 5 **Pulse duration**

Pulse Repetition Period (PRP)

Again, if you pay attention to the naming convention, it will be significantly easier not to confuse this term with other similar sounding terms. As suggested by the name, the pulse repetition period (PRP) refers to the time until a transmit pulse is repeated. *Figure 6* depicts the parameter referred to as the pulse repetition period.

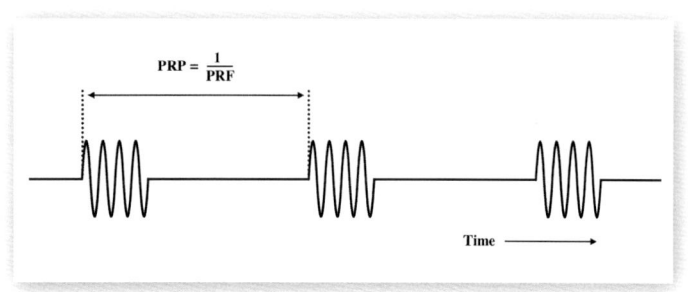

Fig. 6 **Pulse repetition period**

In Chapter 1: Mathematics and Chapter 2, we learned the fundamental reciprocal relationship between time and frequency. Therefore, the reciprocal of the pulse repetition period is called the pulse repetition frequency (PRF), as depicted in *Figure 6*. These relationships are expressed below.

Pulse Repetition Period: time from the start of one pulse to the start of the next pulse.

$$PRP = \frac{1}{PRF}$$

Pulse Repetition Frequency: number of pulses that occur per time.

$$PRF = \frac{1}{PRP}$$

CHECKPOINT: Exam Tip

The pulse repetition period (PRP) is the time between each transmitted pulse. Since time is reciprocal to frequency, the pulse repetition frequency (PRF) is the reciprocal of the PRP.

Duty Factor (Duty Cycle)

Referring to *Figures 5* and *6*, it should be clear that the pulse refers to the transmission of energy as a wave. Therefore, the pulse duration indicates the time that work is being performed by the source. As you will see in later sections, it will be beneficial to develop an expression for the percentage of time that work is actually being performed. To make this point clear, we will use an analogy.

Let's say that you work 2 days of the week. Your pulse duration (the time you work) is 2 days. The pulse repetition period (the time until you repeat the work process), is 7 days, or 1 week.

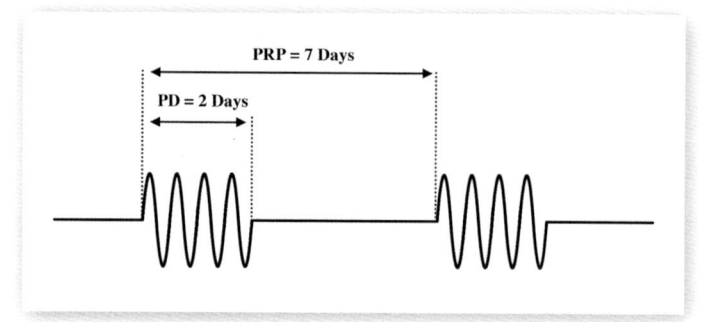

Fig. 7 **Work week duty factor example**

Therefore, to calculate your duty factor (the percentage of time you work), you would simply divide the 2 days by the 7 days, or:

$$Duty\ Cycle = \frac{2\ Days}{7\ Days} = 0.29\ or\ 29\%.$$

From this analogy, it should be relatively clear that for PW operation, the duty cycle equals the time the source is transmitting energy divided by the time until the process is repeated or:

$$Duty\ Factor = \frac{PD}{PRP}$$

Clearly, the largest duty factor is 1 (or 100%). When the duty factor is 1, it implies that the source is always transmitting, which is the definition of continuous wave. Therefore, for a pulsed wave, the duty factor must always be less than 1.

Since the duty factor is proportional to the pulse duration, anything which increases the pulse duration also increases the duty factor (presuming no change to the pulse repetition period). In *Figure 8*, notice that the second transmitting scheme has a longer pulse duration than the first transmitting scheme related to the increased number of cycles in the pulse. The result is a higher duty factor.

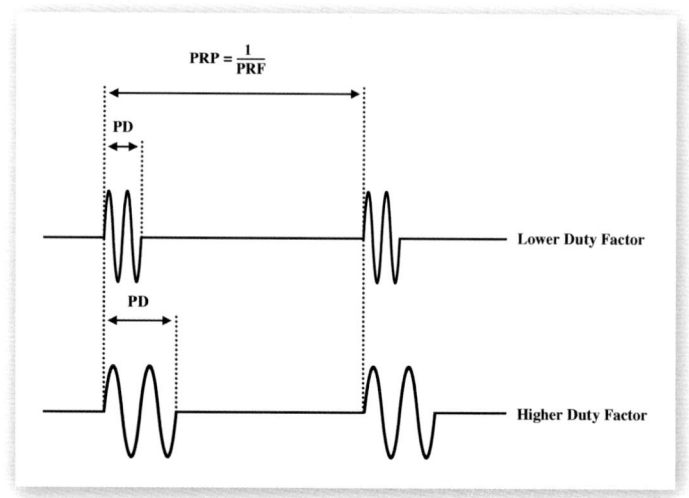

Fig. 8 **Longer pulse duration increases the duty factor**

The duty factor is also inversely related to the pulse repetition period (PRP). Therefore, by increasing the PRP, the duty factor decreases (presuming a constant pulse duration). Notice in *Figure 9* that both transmitting schemes have the same pulse duration, but that the second scheme has a shorter PRP. A shorter PRP, for a fixed PD results in an increase in the duty factor.

KEY CONCEPT

The duty factor represents the percentage of time the system is actively transmitting energy into the patient. Higher duty factors relate to a greater buildup of heat, and hence, a greater risk of thermal bioeffects.

2.2 Distance-Related Pulsed Wave Definitions

Spatial Pulse Length (SPL)

From our analogies, we have already referred to what is known as the "pulse length." *Figure 11* displays the pulse length in a more conventional drawing method without mountains and reflections present. Unfortunately, the word "length" is sometimes used in reference to time (duration is a more accurate word for time). Therefore, to make certain that there is no ambiguity in the terminology, the word "spatial" is often added as a modifier for the term pulse length. Since "spatial" indicates physical dimension, the term "spatial pulse length" leaves no possible confusion with a temporal measurement.

This naming convention is especially important since, pictorially, the spatial pulse length appears to be the same as the pulse duration. As warned in Chapter 2, you must pay careful attention to the parameter being measured. Although on a still image the two parameters look identical, the pulse duration (PD) is a measure of time and the spatial pulse length (SPL) is a measure of distance.

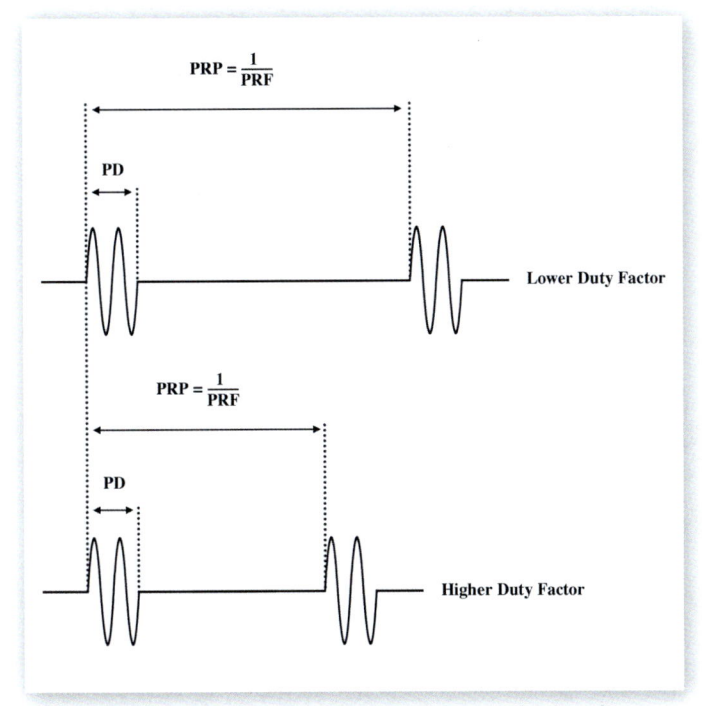

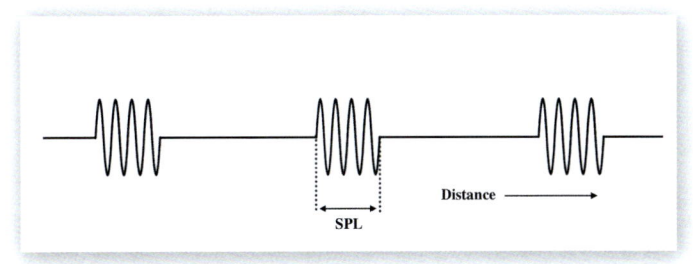

Fig. 9 **Shorter pulse repetition period increases the duty factor**

The following is a numerical example to illustrate how the duty factor is calculated:

◊ ***Example:***
Calculate the duty factor if the pulse duration is 2 msec and the pulse repetition period is 10 msec.

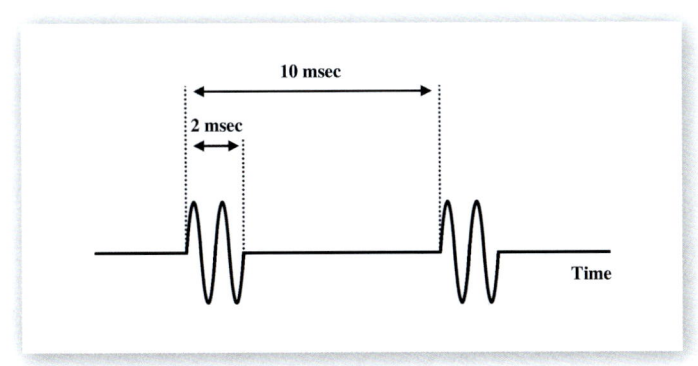

Fig. 10 **Duty factor: numeric example**

$$\textit{Pulse Duration } (PD) = 2 \text{ msec}$$
$$\textit{Pulse Repetition Period } (PRP) = 10 \text{ msec}$$
$$\textit{Duty Factor} = \frac{PD}{PRP} = \frac{2 \text{ msec}}{10 \text{ msec}} \bullet 100\% = 20\%$$

Fig. 11 **The spatial pulse length**

The Spatial Pulse Length and Range Resolution

From the previous range specificity examples in Section 1.2-1.4, it is clear that as the spatial pulse length increases, the range resolution degrades. In the limit, as the pulse length becomes infinite as in continuous wave (CW), there is no range resolution. By further analyzing the situations described above we can determine the equation which specifies the ability to resolve two structures separated in depth (range resolution).

In the pulsed range specificity examples you should have noticed that the separation between the echoes was always twice the distance between the two mountains. To make certain that you understand why the factor of two exists, we will use *Figure 12*. At time 1, the transmit pulse has reached mountain number 1, and an echo is produced. During the time required for the transmit pulse to travel to the second mountain, time 2, the echo from the first mountain has been traveling in the opposite direction. Since the speed of sound is the same in both directions, the reflected pulse from the first mountain has traveled the same distance back to the source (a distance of x) as the transmitted sound has traveled away from the source (a distance of x). Therefore, the separation between the first echo and the second echo is x + x, or 2x.

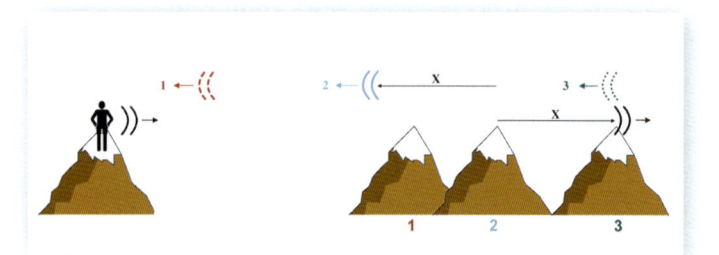

Fig. 12 **Range resolution and the spatial pulse length**

The factor of 2 increase in separation distance is often referred to as the roundtrip effect, since sound has to travel to a structure and then back in a reflective mode. In terms of resolution, if there is no separation between the echoes from two distinct objects, then only one object is detected. Since the separation between echoes is twice the distance between the structures, the resolution equals half of the pulse length. If the pulse length is greater than twice the separation distance between two structures, the echo from the first and second structures will connect into one long echo. Therefore, the equation which specifies the range resolution is:

$$\text{Range resolution} = \frac{\text{spatial pulse length}}{2}$$

View ONLINE Animation and Image Library

Other Names for Range Resolution
There are three other names commonly used to refer to range resolution:

- Depth resolution
- Axial resolution
- Longitudinal resolution

In this textbook we will interchange between the names so as to build familiarity and comfort with the various nomenclatures.

> **CHECKPOINT: Exam Tip**
> The axial resolution (also called range, depth, or longitudinal resolution) is limited by the spatial pulse length divided by two (because of the roundtrip effect).

3. Relating Wave Parameters and Pulsed Wave (PW) Parameters

3.1 The Difference Between a Wave Parameter and a PW Parameter

A principal source of confusion in ultrasound is the distinction between wave parameters and pulsed wave parameters. As just described, the pulse wave parameters are associated with the fact that the wave is pulsed on and off. In contrast, the wave parameters (as defined in Chapter 2) are specific characteristics of the wave itself. When using waves in a pulsed wave mode, both sets of parameters are applied. Within the pulse, the wave parameters such as operating frequency, period, wavelength, propagation velocity, and amplitude apply. The pulsed wave parameters define the duration of the pulse, how often the pulse is repeated, and the spatial length the pulse occupies in the medium. Sections 3.2 and 3.3 will help you to make these distinctions as well as develop the mathematical relationships which link these parameters.

3.2 Time-Related Wave Parameters and PW Parameters

Pulse Duration (PD) and Period (P)
The frequency of a wave (often referred to as the operating frequency) expresses how many compressions and rarefactions occur per time. The reciprocal of the frequency, the period, is the time between one compression and the next compression (or between successive rarefactions). The frequency (and period) is therefore determined by the vibrational rate of the crystal. In contrast, the pulse duration is the entire time the crystal is vibrating, creating the wave. *Figure 13* shows the relationship between the period and the pulse duration.

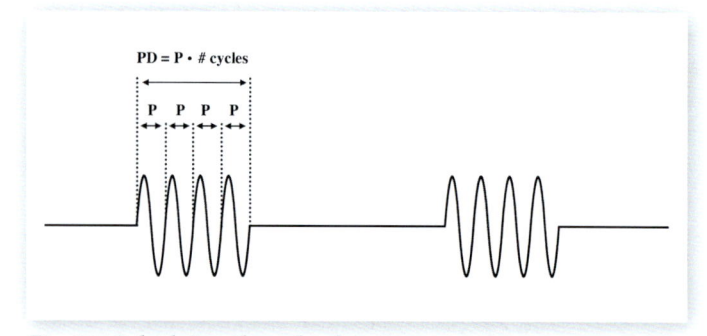

Fig. 13 **Calculating the pulse duration**

From *Figure 13*, it is clear that the pulse duration is related to the period of the wave and the number of cycles in a pulse. In *Figure 14*, there are four cycles in the pulse. As a result, the pulse duration equals the time for one cycle (the period) multiplied by the number of cycles in the pulse (in this case four). In general form, the PD can be determined by:

$$Pulse\ Duration = Period \times \#cycles$$

◊ *Example:*

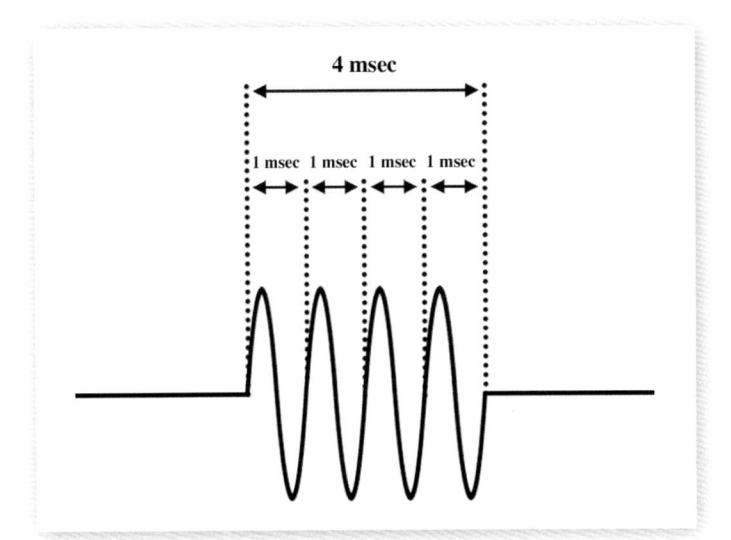

Fig. 14 Pulse duration: numerical example

In *Figure 14*, there are 4 cycles per pulse and the period is 1 msec, so the pulse duration is:

$$PD = 4 \times 1\ msec = 4\ msec.$$

PRP (and PRF) and Propagation Velocity and Imaging Depth

As specified, the pulse repetition period is the time between transmitting pulses. In practical terms, the determinant for how often a transmit will be repeated is the time it will take for the sound wave to travel the required roundtrip distance. This travel time is, as expressed by the distance equation learned in Chapter 1: Mathematics, affected by the imaging depth and the propagation velocity. In general situations, the PRP is therefore a function of the propagation velocity and the imaging depth. However, in ultrasound we presume a fixed propagation velocity, which effectively leaves the imaging depth as the only parameter that affects the PRP, and hence, the PRF.

Duty Factor and Wave Parameters

From a first glance, it would be easy to assume that since the duty factor is the ratio of the transmit time (PD) to the pulse repetition time (PRP), that the duty factor is purely determined by the pulsed wave parameters, and is not impacted by the wave parameters. This assumption is incorrect since it neglects the fact that the pulse duration is related to the period and the period is a wave parameter.

Consider *Figure 15*:

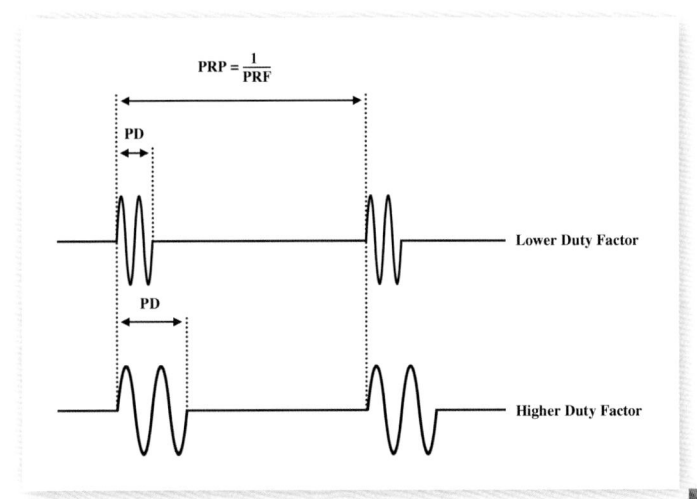

Fig. 15 Effect of period on duty factor

Notice that both of these transmitting schemes have two cycles per pulse and the same PRP; however, since the period is longer in the second scheme, the pulse duration is longer. Since the duty factor is proportional to the pulse duration, a longer pulse duration results in a higher duty factor.

3.3 Distance-Related Pulsed Wave Definitions

Spatial Pulse Length and Wavelength

Both wavelength and spatial pulse length are measures of distance. Just as there is a relationship between the period and the pulse duration, there is an analogous relationship between the wavelength and the spatial pulse length. The wavelength is a wave parameter and the spatial pulse length is a pulse wave parameter. The wavelength is the physical distance between compressions within a medium. In contrast, the spatial pulse length is the entire physical distance the pulse occupies in the medium at a given instant. *Figure 16* depicts this relationship.

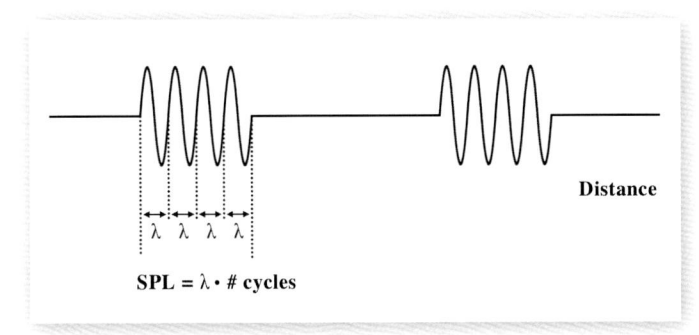

Fig. 16 Determining the SPL

From *Figure 16* it is clear that the equation relating the wavelength and the spatial pulse length is:

$$Spatial\ pulse\ length = \lambda \times \#cycles$$

Note that the spatial pulse length depends on the wavelength, and the wavelength depends on the propagation velocity and the operating frequency, as expressed by the wavelength equation. Therefore, changes in either the propagation velocity or the operating frequency will result in a change in spatial pulse length, presuming no changes to the number of cycles in the pulse.

$$\text{Recall}: \lambda = \frac{c}{f}$$
$$\text{Since } SPL \propto \lambda$$
$$SPL \propto c \text{ and } SPL \propto \frac{1}{f}$$

Axial Resolution

The axial resolution was shown to equal the spatial pulse length divided by 2. Since the spatial pulse length depends on the wavelength, which in turn depends on the propagation velocity and the frequency of operation, the axial resolution must also depend on the propagation velocity and the frequency of operation. As the frequency increases, the wavelength decreases, reducing the spatial pulse length, yielding better resolution. Similarly, if the propagation velocity decreases, the wavelength is shortened, reducing the spatial pulse length, thereby improving the axial resolution. Remember, with respect to resolution, smaller numbers are always better.

> **KEY CONCEPT**
>
> The spatial pulse length is determined by the wavelength and the number of cycles in the pulse. Fewer cycles and shorter wavelengths result in shorter spatial pulse lengths, improving axial resolution.

4. The Foundational Drawing for Pulsed Wave

The saying is that a picture is worth a thousand words. In the case of keeping straight and understanding pulsed wave operation, this adage is an understatement. *Figure 17* combines the parameters we have just learned into one figure. You will also note that for convenience sake, all parameters related to time will be drawn above the baseline and all parameters related to distance will be drawn below the baseline.

In Level 2, there will be additions to this figure with specific explanations of how each of these parameters affects diagnostic ultrasound. For now, it is suggested that you make certain you can draw this figure with the book closed (an especially helpful skill when taking a credentialing exam).

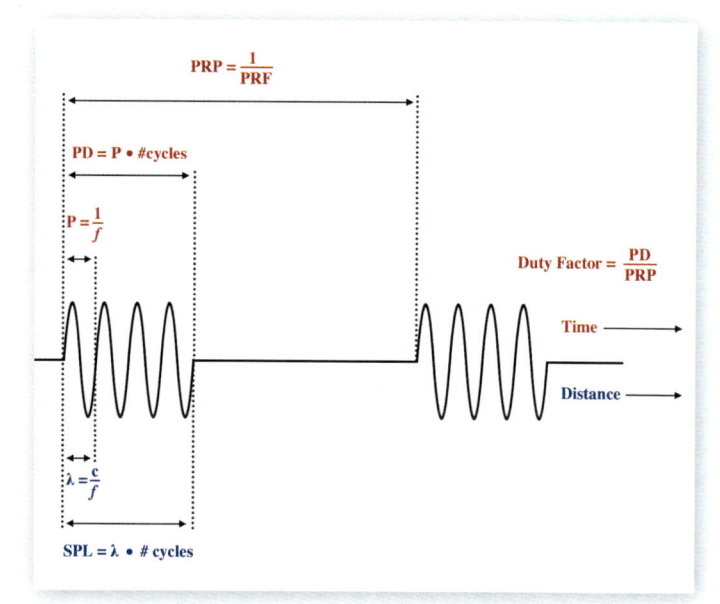

Fig. 17 **Foundational drawing for PW operation**

5. Pulsed Wave and the Need to Understand Timing

Whenever you think about pulsed wave operation, you should be thinking about timing. Pulsed operation is defined by parameters that specify the timing of when to turn on and off the transmitted wave. The timing aspects are very important for two major reasons:

1. Effect on ability to detect changes in time referred to as temporal resolution (including aliasing)
2. Effect on risk of causing damage to tissues referred to as bioeffects.

Recall that the motivation for creating a pulsed wave modality was to overcome the fundamental limitation of no range specificity as results from continuous wave operation. Of course, with the benefits there must come some trade-offs. The fundamental trade-off is a potential degradation in temporal resolution. Temporal resolution is the ability to detect (resolve) changes in time. In other words, by pulsing the wave on and off, the timing has been affected, potentially restricting the ability to detect quickly changing events.

Another related outcome of changing the timing is a variance in energy distribution into the patient. By turning the transmit signal on and off, very different heating situations are created than when the transmit is left on continuously. As a result, the amplitude of the signal will need to be varied depending on the pulsing situation. In general, short pulses will be allowed higher amplitudes whereas long pulses will be forced to use smaller amplitudes. The high amplitude short pulses will have a different risk of bioeffects than the lower amplitude long pulses. Therefore, from the standpoint of analyzing bioeffects, the timing parameters of pulsed wave will become very important.

LEVEL 2: Board Level

6. Definitions for Pulse Wave Related Imaging Parameters

As with any discipline, half of the battle is developing fluency in the language and terminology. Since there are so many terms that can potentially be used to refer to similar concepts, we will define the terms necessary for understanding the application of pulsed wave techniques.

1. **Pulsed wave**
   Any modality which turns the transmitter on and off periodically so as to reduce range ambiguity. Note that pulsed wave refers not only to PW Doppler, but also color Doppler, 2D imaging, 3D imaging, and M-mode.

2. **Acoustic beam**
   A single transmit event in a specific direction and the associated echoes. Although the term "acoustic line" is sometimes used, a more appropriate description is a beam since the word "line" implies one dimension, whereas a sound beam clearly has three dimensions. This distinction is now even more important since plane wave imaging is becoming more common (see Chapter 6, Part II).

3. **Receive beam**
   The returning echoes registered over time by the system from a single transmit event before the next transmit event occurs as dictated by the imaging depth.

4. **Display line**
   A display line (or image line) is the data displayed on the screen that corresponds to a single direction within the patient. For "simple" ultrasound imaging applications, there is a one-to-one correspondence between transmitting and receiving a single beam and the displayed data in the image. For more complex modes, there may be multiple acoustic beams to form one display line (as in color Doppler), or multiple display lines from one acoustic beam (as in parallel processing and plane wave imaging).

5. **An image**
   The received data for a specific time period formatted as a picture, covering the area of interest in the patient. Other terms often used are a frame, a scan, or a scan region.

6. **Frame time**
   The time required to transmit and receive the required number of beams until the desired region of the patient is scanned (also referred to as the scan time, acoustic scan time, or acoustic frame time).

7. **Frame rate**
   The reciprocal of the frame time, equivalent to the number of "images" generated per second. A better name for this parameter is the frame frequency, since this name indicates the reciprocal nature with respect to the frame time.

8. **Sampling rate**
   The frequency at which signals are detected or "assessed". The sampling rate determines the maximum frequency detectable without aliasing as governed by the Nyquist criterion (discussed in detail in Chapter 6, Part I). As with the frame rate, a more intuitive name is the sampling frequency.

7. PW and Image Generation

Most ultrasound is performed using pulsed, not continuous wave. There are a tremendous number of applications each of which has specific requirements. As a result, there are many different ways of using PW transmit and receive events to generate ultrasound data.

As already mentioned, when you think about pulsed wave operation, you should be thinking about timing. How PW is used to generate ultrasound data affects the timing, which in turn affects the ability to accurately detect and depict motion, referred to as temporal resolution. The timing also has an impact on the distribution of heat over time generated by absorption of the sound energy by tissue (discussed in detail in Chapter 9: Bioeffects). For these two reasons, we must review in more detail the timing considerations of applied PW.

7.1 Non-Scanned Modalities

As suggested by the name, non-scanned modalities transmit in the same direction repeatedly over time. The earliest medical applications of ultrasound were non-scanned modalities. Since with non-scanned modalities the energy is being transmitted in the same direction repeatedly, the transmit power in these modes tend to be limited by the risk of thermal bioeffects (tissue damage caused by excessive heat). The most commonly used ultrasound modalities which are non-scanned are CW Doppler, PW Doppler, M-mode, and the almost extinct early mode of ultrasound called A-mode.

In just the last few years, (discussed in additional detail in Chapter 5, Part I), a new, non-scanned approach for generating 2D and 3D images using plane waves or diverging waves has been created resulting in further complexity in what constitutes a non-scanned modality. So, whereas determining whether a certain ultrasound modality was scanned or non-scanned used to be as simple as answering if there was an image or not, that characteristic is no longer a valid differentiator. Simply put, a non-scanned modality is when each successive transmit is in the same direction as the previous transmit.

Figure 18a demonstrates the non-scanned modality of PW Doppler. A Doppler line is transmitted at time 1, time 2, time 3, and repeatedly in the same direction until the PW is turned off.

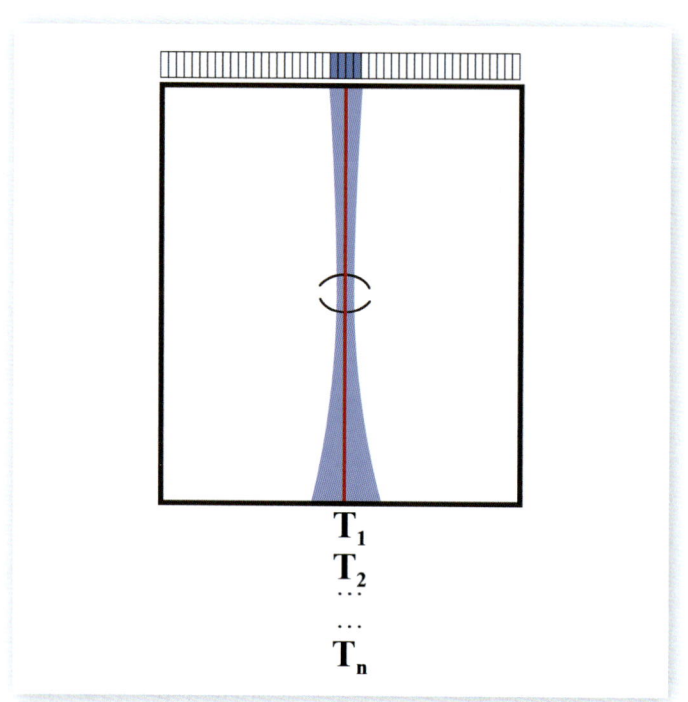

Fig. 18a **Non-scanned modalities (PW Doppler) transmits repeatedly in same direction over time**

Figure 18b demonstrates how an entire 2D image can be generated from a single transmit event, with each successive frame generated by transmitting in the same direction as the previous transmit.

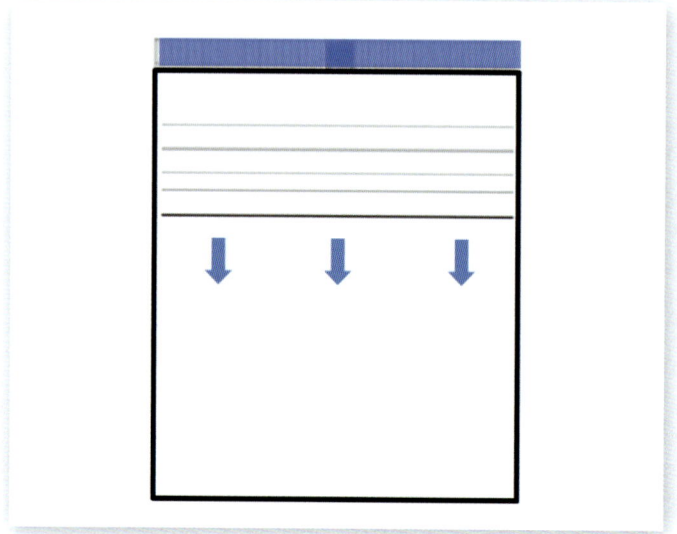

Fig. 18b **Non-scanned 2D image created by plane wave imaging (in this simple case, the entire image is generated from a single transmit)**

7.2 Scanned Modalities

A scanned modality implies that over time, sound energy is transmitted in a controlled pattern in different directions, insonifying a two or three-dimensional region. Note that the primary distinction is that unlike for non-scanned modalities, successive transmits for scanned modalities are transmitted in a different direction to acquire data corresponding to a different physical region of the image plane.

The three common ultrasound modalities that represent a scanned modality are:
1. Sequentially generated 2D imaging (B-mode)
2. Sequentially generated color flow imaging
3. 3D imaging

Until just the last few years, ultrasound images were always generated sequentially as scanned modalities. Again, it is important to stress that an image is a scanned modality when the image is built up sequentially over time using multiple transmitted beams, not when plane waves are used with ultrafast imaging (see Chapter 5, Part II).

Figure 19a demonstrates how an unsteered linear image is sequentially generated by transmitting multiple beams distributed over both time and space. At time 1 (T_1), the first beam is transmitted, generating the left-most region of the image. At time 2 (T_2), the second beam is moved over just slightly, creating the next region in the image. Over time, the entire region of interest is scanned, generating a two-dimensional image. When the end of the frame area is reached (T_n), the process is repeated starting with line 1 again.

View ONLINE Animation and Image Library

In the early 1990s, a variation on the above sequential image generation was created. The variation is called parallel processing and worked in a similar fashion, but instead of having a one-to-one correspondence between transmitted beams and received beams, a wider transmit beam was created and more than one receive beam was generated.

Parallel processing is really a scanned modality that results in fewer transmit beams to reduce the time needed to generate an image. As shown in *Figure 19b*, a wide beam is transmitted at time T_1. From this wide transmit beam, more than one receive beam is generated. Once the echoes are received, another wide beam is transmitted at time T_2, and the process repeated until time T_n, when the desired region has been scanned. The wider the transmit beam, the fewer beams that need to be transmitted to insonify the region of interest in the patient. The wider beams are sometime referred to as a "zone." Parallel processing will be discussed in further detail in Chapter 6.

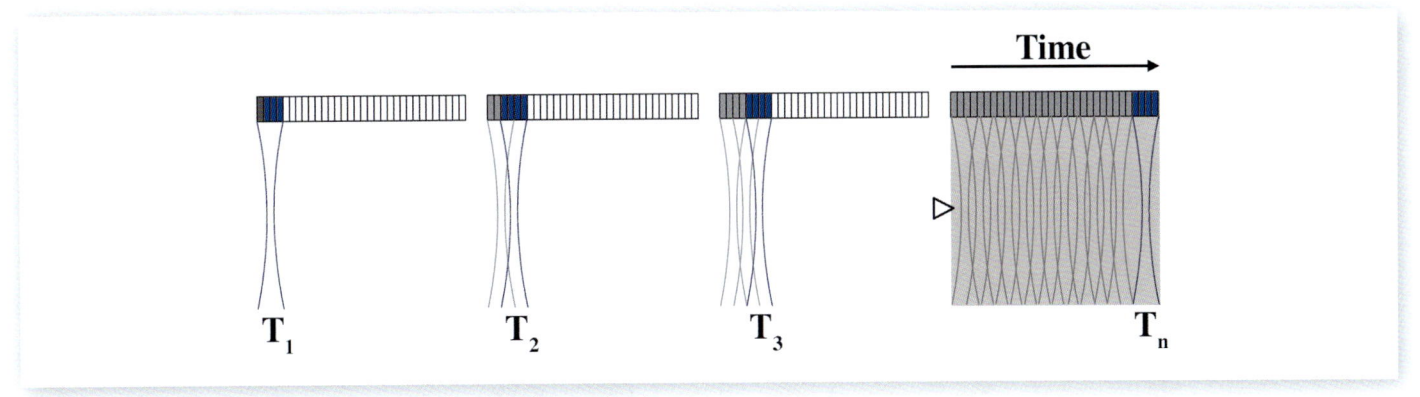

Fig. 19a Scanned modalities (images are "built up" over time)

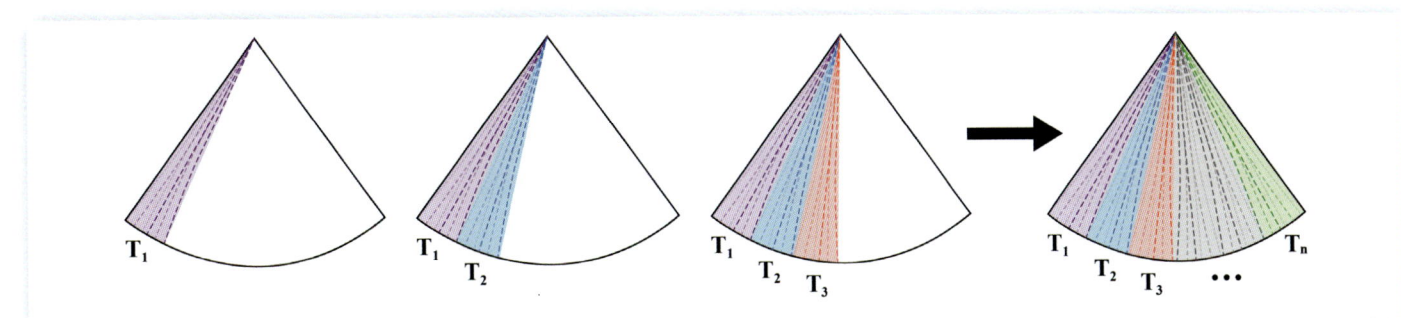

Fig. 19b Parallel processing, a scanned modality which reduces the time needed to generate a frame (by sequentially transmitting fewer, wider beams than conventional sequential imaging); note in this figure the "n" colorized zones represent the wide transmit beams comprised of multiple receive beams (represented by the dotted lines)

8. Relating PW Parameters to Ultrasound

We have thus far defined the PW parameters in the general sense, without giving many specific references to application in ultrasound. To fully appreciate the significance of these parameters, we must make the association between the practical application in ultrasound and the theoretical descriptions.

8.1 The Pulse Duration

Not all pulses are the same. For diagnostic ultrasound, the pulse duration varies significantly with the imaging modality being employed. To achieve the specific requirements for each application, the transmit pulses must vary. As a result, a pulse in 2D will look very different than a pulse for color Doppler, which will vary with respect to a pulse in PW Doppler.

We have already learned that the pulse duration is the product of the period and the number of cycles in the pulse. The period (reciprocal of the operating frequency) is determined by the user relative to the imaging situation. When scanning to a shallow depth on an easy to image patient, a higher frequency can be chosen. When scanning to deeper depths, or when scanning a difficult to image patient, a lower frequency must be chosen. But the pulse duration is also determined by the number of cycles in the pulse. You will notice that there is no control on the ultrasound system called "number of cycles in the pulse." So how is the number of cycles controlled?

To some extent, the number of cycles in a pulse is a function of the modality you choose. For reasons that will be discussed throughout the upcoming sections, in 2D imaging, a very short pulse duration is generally desired. As a result, when 2D imaging is activated, the system attempts to produce pulses with as few cycles as possible. In comparison, pulsed Doppler generally requires a longer pulse. Therefore, when PW Doppler is activated, the system naturally produces pulses with more cycles. This fact is illustrated in *Figure 20*.

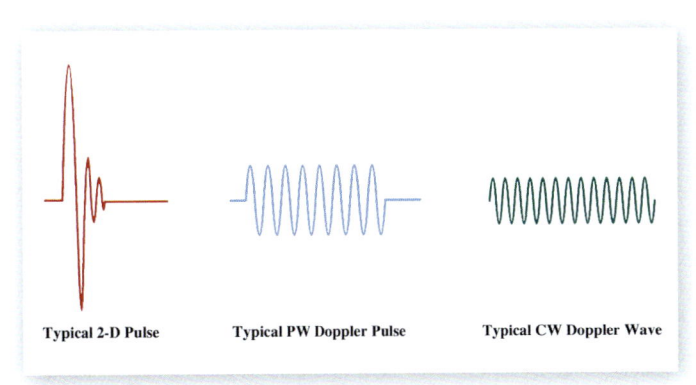

Typical 2-D Pulse   Typical PW Doppler Pulse   Typical CW Doppler Wave

Fig. 20 Pulse characteristics for various modes

Notice how the 2D pulse only has a few cycles but a very large amplitude, the pulsed wave Doppler pulse has many cycles and a much smaller amplitude, and CW Doppler is continuous with an even lower amplitude. As you will learn in the Doppler chapter, in PW there is a control, the sample volume (gate) size, which allows the user to determine the number of cycles desired in the pulse. As the sample volume size is increased, the number of cycles in the transmit pulse is increased, and PW begins to approximate CW for which the transmit is continuous (virtually infinite pulse duration).

> **KEY CONCEPT**
>
> Pulses for 2D imaging tend to have very few cycles. Pulses for color and pulsed wave Doppler tend to have more cycles. Continuous wave Doppler obviously has continuous cycles for as long as the CW is activated.

8.2 The Pulse Repetition Period and the PRF

Dependence on the Imaging Depth

In Sections 3 and 4, we learned that the PRP is related to both the propagation velocity and the distance of travel. Since for ultrasound machines a propagation velocity of 1540 m/sec is assumed, the maximum achievable PRP is therefore dependent only on the imaging depth. If the imaging depth is increased, then the time to and from the target is increased, which lengthens the PRP. Because of the reciprocal relationship between time and frequency, the PRF is simply the reciprocal of the PRP. Therefore, the principal determinant of the maximum achievable PRF is the imaging depth.

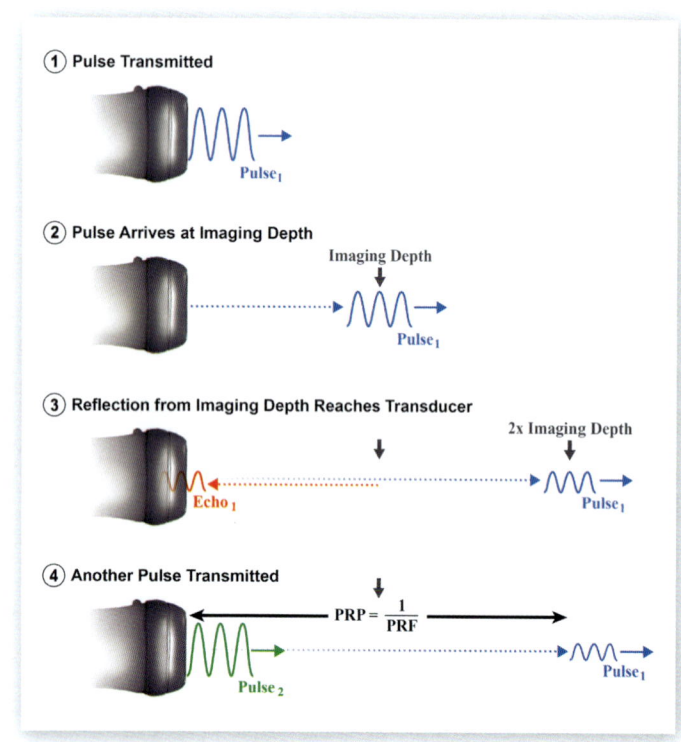

Fig. 21 Imaging depth and PRP

In practical terms for ultrasound, the PRP is really the same as the time required to transmit a single "beam" of data and receive the associated echoes. The sequence of events is as follows:

Time 1: a pulse is transmitted
Time 2: transmit pulse arrives at desired imaging depth
Time 3: echo from desired imaging depth is received back at the transducer
Time 4: another pulse is transmitted, repeating the process, creating another beam of data

View ONLINE Animation and Image Library

Given that the PRP and PRF are determined by the imaging depth, we can now calculate actual PRP and PRF values. In Chapter 1, we learned that imaging 1 cm required 13 μsec presuming a propagation velocity of 1540 m/sec. (Recall that imaging 1 cm requires a travel of 2 cm which by the distance equation takes 13 μsec.) Therefore, to calculate the line time (the PRP), we must multiply the imaging depth by 13 μsec, or:

$$acoustic\ line\ time\ (PRP) = \frac{13\ \mu sec}{cm} \times imaging\ depth\ (cm)$$

Sample Calculations

With this general equation, we are now ready to calculate some real world values.

◇ **Example 1:**
What is the minimum PRP if the imaging depth is 8 cm?

$$acoustic\ line\ time\ (PRP) = \frac{13\ \mu sec}{cm} \times 8\ (cm) = 104\ \mu sec \approx 0.1\ msec.$$

◇ **Example 2:**
What is the maximum PRF if the imaging depth is 8 cm?

$$acoustic\ line\ time\ (PRP) = \frac{13\ \mu sec}{cm} \times 8\ (cm) = 104\ \mu sec \approx 0.1\ msec.$$

$$PRF = \frac{1}{PRP} = \frac{1}{0.1\ msec} = 10\ kHz$$

◇ **Example 3:**
What is the maximum PRF if you need to image to a depth of 10 cm?

Our approach to calculating a PRF is, of course, to first calculate the PRP. Once we know the PRP, the PRF will be obtained by simply taking the reciprocal of the PRP.

Let's imagine for a moment that to solve this problem, you have forgotten that every 1 cm of imaging depth requires 13 μsec. We will therefore need to use the distance equation to determine the line imaging time (PRP). First, because of the roundtrip effect, imaging to a depth of 10 cm is the same as the sound traveling a distance of 20 cm. Second, we know the speed of sound in soft tissue is 1540 m/sec. By the distance equation we can determine the time necessary for an ultrasound pulse to travel 20 cm roundtrip.

$$\text{distance} = \text{rate} \times \text{time}$$

rewriting for time by dividing both sides by the rate yields:

$$\text{time} = \frac{\text{distance}}{\text{rate}}$$

plugging in the values for distance and rate yields:

$$\text{time} = \frac{20\ cm}{1540\ \frac{m}{sec}} = \frac{0.2\ m}{1540\ \frac{m}{sec}} = \frac{0.2\ sec}{1540} \approx 130\ \mu sec = 0.13\ msec.$$

So the minimum amount of time between firing a pulse and firing the next pulse, for an imaging depth of 10 cm is 130 μsec, or 0.13 msec.

Note: Either form of the answer is acceptable. Recall from Chapter 1: Mathematics that there are an infinite numbers of ways of writing each number.

To determine the PRF, we take the reciprocal of the PRP, or:

$$PRP = 0.13\ msec$$
$$PRF = \frac{1}{(PRP)} = \frac{1}{(0.13\ msec)} = 7.69\ kHz.$$

KEY CONCEPT

The PRF (the reciprocal of the PRP) is determined by the propagation velocity and imaging depth. Deeper imaging depths result in lower PRFs.

The Use of the Words Maximum and Minimum

In the problems just solved, you will notice that the pulse repetition periods calculated were referred to as the minimum PRP, and the pulse repetition frequencies calculated were referred to as the maximum PRF. "Minimum" was used with respect to the PRP since we calculated the absolute minimum time that could be used between transmitting pulses for the desired imaging depth without creating ambiguity. In other words, for an 8 cm imaging depth, there is no choice but to wait at least 104 μsec until the next transmit occurs, but there is no reason that we cannot simply wait longer and just not use the data from later in time (from deeper depths). As you will learn in later chapters, there are times where the minimum PRP (maximum PRF) is not used for a given depth. The two common situations where the minimum PRP is not used are in pulsed wave Doppler so as to achieve lower Doppler scales, and with superficial imaging to reduce the amount of artifact caused by range ambiguity. Both of these topics will be discussed in detail in their respective chapters.

Not surprisingly, the reciprocal of a minimum time is a maximum frequency. Hence, the reciprocal of the minimum PRP yields the maximum PRF.

8.3 The Spatial Pulse Length

Frequency and Pulse Length

For 2D imaging, one of the most important indications of image quality is the detail resolution. From the thought experiments with a sound source on a mountain, we ascertained that the longitudinal resolution (axial, range, or depth) is equal to the spatial pulse length divided by 2, or:

$$\text{Axial resolution} = \frac{\text{spatial pulse length}}{2} = \frac{\lambda \bullet \#cycles}{2}.$$

and

$$\lambda = \frac{c}{f}.$$

From the equation, it is clear that better resolution (a smaller number) can be achieved by either a shorter wavelength and/or fewer cycles in the pulse. Since we have no control over the propagation velocity, the one way to achieve a shorter wavelength is to increase the transmit frequency. Of course, you can only adjust the frequency in as much that there is still adequate penetration.

Since increasing the frequency to achieve a shorter wavelength is not always an option, we need to assess the other option: reducing the number of cycles in the pulse.

Cycles and Pulse Length

For 2D and 3D imaging, the reality is that you do not have any control over the number of cycles in the pulse. Since the system is designed to optimize resolution in modalities where resolution matters most, activating 2D or 3D automatically results in the fewest possible cycles for a given transducer and system. In other words, by design, the system will automatically give you the best axial resolution possible for the transducer and imaging system chosen.

Backing (Damping) Material

Since resolution is so important in 2D and 3D imaging, the transducer is driven with a very short pulse. However, as anyone who has ever rung a bell or listened to a tuning fork knows, a single impulse can produce a very long ring time (many cycles). Therefore, since a single electrical impulse stimulating a transducer to ring naturally produces many cycles in the generated acoustic pulse, the axial resolution will naturally be poor.

To overcome this problem, transducers are designed with a special block of material called either a backing or damping material. The purpose of the damping material is to decrease the natural resonance of the crystal so that fewer cycles are produced. By decreasing the number of cycles in the pulse, both the pulse duration and the spatial pulse length are decreased. *Figure 22* demonstrates the difference between an undamped and damped crystal when driven with a single impulse.

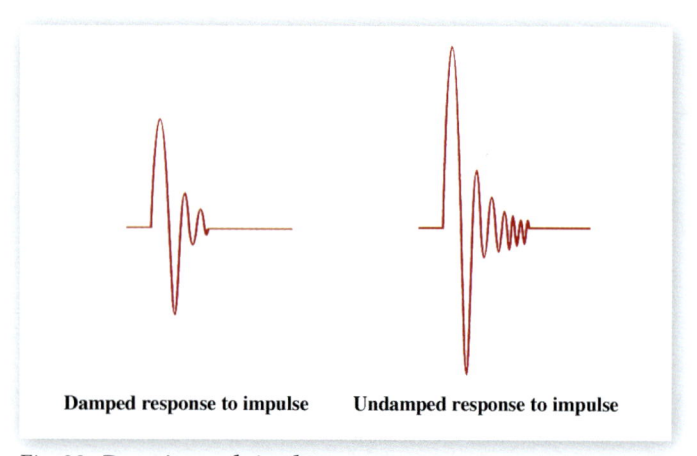

Fig. 22 **Damping and ringdown**

KEY CONCEPT

Damping (backing) materials are used in transducer design to reduce the number of cycles which would result from the natural resonance of the transducer crystal.

8.4 Using the PRP (Line Time) to Calculate the Frame Time (and Frame Rate)

Temporal Resolution and Non-Scanned Modalities
For non-scanned modalities, the ability to accurately detect changes with time is simply related to the PRF. After every transmit period there is a listening period. Therefore, the frequency of the transmitting pulses (PRF) is the same as the frequency of listening (or sampling). Since the PRF indicates how frequently you are receiving data, the PRF dictates the fastest changing signal detectable. So, for all pulsed non-scanned modalities the time resolution is strictly related to the PRF, and hence the PRP.

Consider the situation which an M-mode line is set with a maximum depth of 8 cm. From our earlier example in section 8.2 (example 2), we calculated the PRP to be 104 μsec for an imaging depth of 8 cm (8 x 13 μsec/cm). This means that the time between repeating each sample M-mode line 104 μsec.

Now consider a situation in which an image is generated all at once from a single transmit event as shown in *Figure 23*, with an imaging depth of 8 cm.

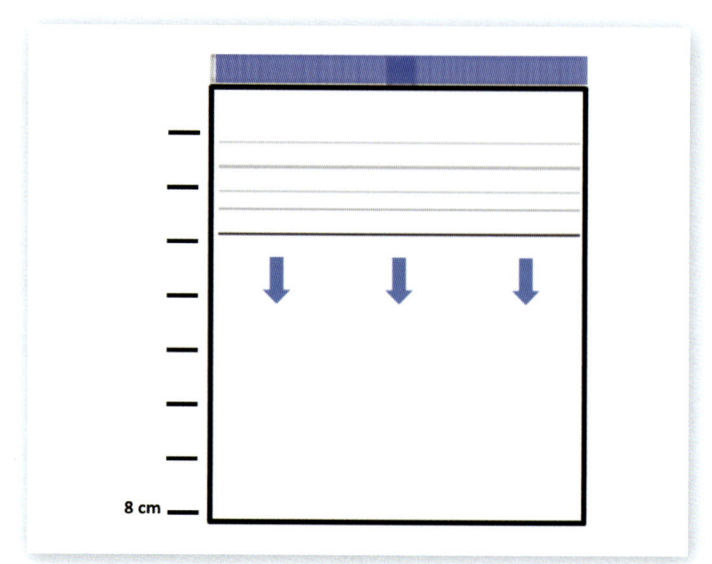

Fig. 23 **Calculating the frame time for a plane wave (non-scanned 2D image)**

Again, the time required for the sound to propagate to a depth of 8 cm and reflect back is 104 μsec. Since the entire frame is created during that single transmit event, the frame time is simply 104 μsec.

Temporal Resolution and Scanned Modalities
For scanned modalities, there is another timing restriction besides the line time (PRP). In comparison with non-scanned modalities which re-transmit an acoustic line in the same location, a scanned modality "spends" time looking over a scan region before returning back to the same location. Therefore, the time between successively looking in the same location is not determined just by the line time, but is also determined by the number of lines transmitted in the entire frame.

Consider *Figure 24*, an example of a sequentially generated 2D image. Let's assume that the imaging depth is set to 8 cm, and let's further presume that there are 200 lines in a single frame. How much time elapses between successive transmits in the same location of the frame? In other words, what is the time to produce a frame such that an individual line is repeated?

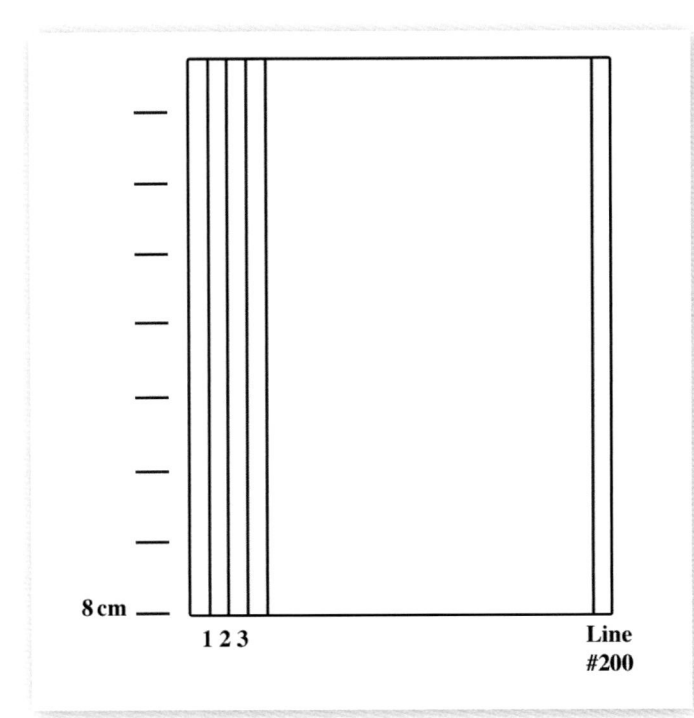

Fig. 24 **Calculating the frame time for a sequentially generated (scanned) 2D image**

From our earlier example in section 8.2 (example 2), we calculated the PRP to be 104 µsec for an imaging depth of 8 cm. All 200 lines of the frame must be transmitted until the initial line in the same location will be repeated. Therefore, the total time is (for ease of calculation, 104 µsec is rounded to 100 µsec):

$$\text{time to complete all lines} = \frac{104 \; \mu sec}{1 \; line} \cdot \frac{200 \; lines}{frame} \approx \frac{20{,}000 \; \mu sec}{frame} = \frac{20 \; msec}{frame}.$$

Frame Time and Frame Rate

In the above example, the time to produce a frame (the frame time) is 20 msec. Using the reciprocal relationship between time and frequency, the frame frequency is calculated from the frame time. The term "frame rate" is an alternative way of saying the "frame frequency". This nomenclature is often confusing because the word "rate" is also often used to refer to the speed with which something travels as well as a frequency. Unfortunately, the term frame rate seems to have become ubiquitous, even though the term frame frequency is more illustrative and accurate. Whenever you see the term frame rate, replace the word "rate" in your mind with the word "frequency." Regardless of the terminology, the frame rate is simply the reciprocal of the frame time, or:

$$\text{Frame rate (frequency)} = \frac{1}{\text{Frame time}}$$

For the previous example, the frame rate is:

$$\text{Frame rate (frequency)} = \frac{1}{\text{frame time}} = \frac{1}{20 \; msec} = 0.05 \; kHz = 50 \; Hz$$

Frame Time (Frame Rate) Equation

So from this example, we see that calculating a frame time is mathematically quite simple:

$$\text{Frame time} = \frac{Time}{Line} * \frac{\#Lines}{Frame}$$

This equation is just a mathematical way of stating common sense. Imagine if you have to perform a repetitious job of mowing your square lawn. If it takes 3 minutes to make one pass with the lawn mower and it takes 30 passes to cover the entire lawn, then it will take 30 * 3 minutes or 90 minutes to mow your whole lawn. In other words, the total time equals the time to perform a part of the job (time/line) multiplied by the total number of times that part of the job has to be performed (lines/frame).

Recalling that the line time (PRP) is calculated as:

$$\frac{Time}{Line} = \frac{13 \; \mu sec}{cm} * \text{Imaging depth} \; (cm)$$

This equation can be written in another form which builds in the calculation of the line time as:

$$\text{Frame time} = \frac{13 \; \mu sec}{cm} * \frac{\text{Imaging depth} \; (cm)}{Line} * \frac{\#Lines}{Frame}$$

Frame Rate Examples

◊ **Example 1:**
The depth is set to 10 cm and there are 128 lines per frame. What is the maximum frame rate?

$$\text{Frame time} = \frac{13 \; \mu sec}{cm} * \frac{10 \; cm}{Line} * \frac{128 \; Lines}{Frame} = 16.64 \; msec$$

$$\text{Frame rate} = \frac{1}{\text{Frame time}} = \frac{1}{16.64 \; msec} = 60.1 \; Hz$$

◊ **Example 2:**
The depth is set to 8 cm and there are 100 lines per frame. What is the maximum frame rate?

$$\text{Frame time} = \frac{13 \; \mu sec}{cm} * \frac{8 \; cm}{line} * \frac{100 \; Lines}{frame} = 10{,}400 \; \mu sec = 10.4 \; msec$$

$$\text{Frame rate} = \frac{1}{\text{Frame time}} = \frac{1}{10.4 \; msec} \approx 0.1 \; kHz = 100 \; Hz$$

◊ **Example 3:**
What would happen to the frame time and the frame rate if you doubled the number of image lines in the previous example?

Doubling the number of image lines doubles the frame time since the frame time is proportional to the number of lines.

Doubling the number of image lines halves the frame rate since the frame rate is inversely proportional to the frame time. So, the frame rate will drop to 50 Hz.

◊ *Example 4:*
The depth is set to 8 cm and there is a single transmit (line) per frame (plane wave image). What is the maximum fame rate?

$$Frame\ time = \frac{13\ \mu sec}{cm} \cdot \frac{8\ cm}{Line} \cdot \frac{1\ Line}{Frame} = 104\ \mu sec$$

$$Frame\ rate = \frac{1}{Frame\ time} = \frac{1}{104\ \mu sec} \approx \frac{1}{0.1\ msec} = 10\ kHz$$

◊ *Example 5:*
The depth is set to 8 cm and parallel processing is employed such that there are 15 zones (wide beams) transmitted to create the image. What is the maximum fame rate?

$$Frame\ time = \frac{13\ \mu sec}{cm} \cdot \frac{8\ cm}{Line} \cdot \frac{15\ Lines}{Frame} = 1,560\ \mu sec$$

$$1,560\ \mu sec = 1.56\ msec$$

$$Frame\ rate = \frac{1}{Frame\ time} = \frac{1}{1.56\ msec} = 0.64\ kHz = 640\ Hz$$

KEY CONCEPT

The frame time is determined by the imaging depth and the number of transmitted lines used to produce the image. As the depth increases the frame time increases. As the number of lines increases, the frame time increases. As the frame time increases, the frame rate (frequency) decreases, implying fewer frames are produced per second.

View ONLINE Clarifying Clip

8.5 Comparing Temporal Resolution for Scanned and Non-Scanned Modalities

From our examples in Section 8.4 (examples 1-5), it should be obvious that the frame rate is always much slower than the PRF for scanned modalities. For the third example, the PRF is 10 kHz and the frame rate is 50 Hz. This fact is common sense since the PRF is related to the time to transmit a single line whereas the frame rate is related to the time to transmit an entire scan (or frame) of lines. As a result, non-scanned modalities whose temporal resolution is governed by the PRF have far better temporal resolution than scanned modalities whose temporal resolution is governed by the frame rate.

This fact is clearly exhibited by comparing the results of example 2 with example 4. Both have a depth of 8 cm, but the non-scanned case (plane wave imaging) has a significantly higher frame rate than the scanned case (100 sequential lines to comprise an image). Also note how parallel processing improves the frame rate by reducing the frame time, as shown in example 5.

9. Color Doppler, Frame Rate, and Temporal Resolution

9.1 General
Color Doppler as a scanned modality is perhaps the most challenging of the pulsed wave modalities to fathom. This is because color Doppler has some of the characteristics of spectral Doppler, some of the characteristics of 2D imaging, and some characteristics unique to color Doppler. As a result, both 2D and Doppler techniques must be understood to fully understand color Doppler.

To understand color theory, the starting point is the Doppler equation. Therefore color theory will be developed in Chapter 7 after the development of the Doppler equation. For understanding the temporal aspects of color Doppler, the starting point is the basic premise that color Doppler gives an estimate of the mean velocity

9.2 Creating a Color Scan
Sequentially generated 2D transmits an acoustic line in a given direction and then moves over and transmits acoustic lines until a scan is created. Spectral Doppler transmits acoustic lines repeatedly in the same direction to produce a spectrum. Color Doppler is a hybrid of these two techniques. In order to register a mean Doppler shift, color must transmit multiple acoustic lines in the same direction. These multiple acoustic lines are generally referred to as a "color packet" or "color ensemble". The packet size can vary (generally between 4 and 12 inclusively).

From this ensemble of lines, a mean velocity can be estimated for each depth along the line. Once an estimate has been produced to create a single display line, the packet is then reproduced in a neighboring region, producing a mean estimate at that location. This process is repeated until the desired region is scanned. Once the desired region is scanned, the process is repeated, producing a second frame of color, etc.

Figure 25 demonstrates the generation of one color display line from a packet of transmitted acoustic lines. At time 1 (T_1), the first acoustic line is transmitted and then received. At time 2 (T_2), another pulse is transmitted in the same direction as the previous acoustic line of T_1. This process is repeated until the entire packet is complete.

As drawn in *Figure 25*, the packet size (ensemble length) is 5. From these 5 acoustic lines, the mean velocity is estimated at each depth location along the line, and one display line is generated

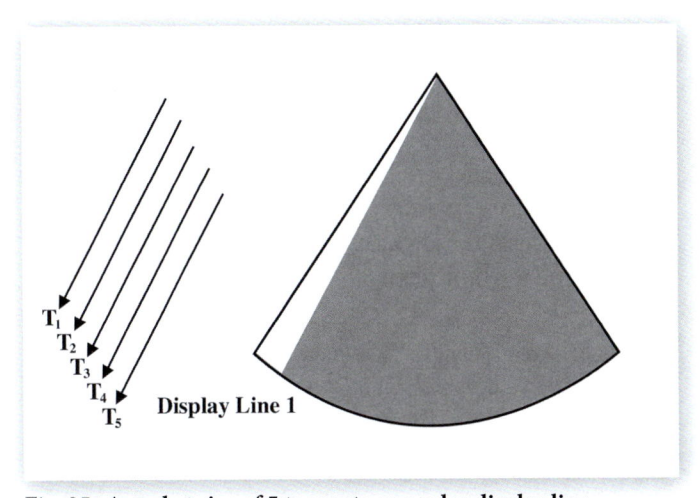

Fig. 25 **A packet size of 5 to create one color display line**

9.3 Calculating the Color and Overall Frame Rate

In essence, within a packet, color Doppler is a non-scanned modality. To produce the color image, a collection of color packets are scanned across the patient. In other words, the acoustic lines which constitute a packet are non-scanned, but then to produce a frame, the packets are scanned. Consider how much more time is required to produce a color scan than to produce a standard 2D image. Every display line of a color image requires an entire packet of color lines. Therefore, to calculate the frame time, you must multiply the number of display lines by the packet size, or:

$$\text{color frame time} = \frac{\text{time}}{\text{packet line}} * \frac{\text{packet lines}}{\text{display line}} * \frac{\text{display lines}}{\text{frame}}$$

Logistically, color Doppler images are never displayed without a 2D reference image. Therefore, the overall frame time is the sum of the 2D frame time and the color frame time.

The following example illustrates these concepts:

◊ **Example :**

Presume an imaging depth of 8 cm. Using a color packet size of 9, if there are 100 display lines in an image, what is the frame rate?

We will first calculate the 2D frame time:

$$\text{2-D frame time} = \frac{13\ \mu sec}{cm} * \frac{8\ cm}{line} * \frac{100\ lines}{frame} = \frac{10.4\ msec}{frame}$$

Note: This is the same problem as Example 2 in Section 8.4.

Now we will calculate the color frame time:

$$\text{color frame time} = \frac{104\ \mu sec}{\text{packet line}} \cdot \frac{9\ \text{packet lines}}{\text{display line}} * \frac{100\ \text{display lines}}{\text{frame}}$$

$$\approx \frac{90{,}000\ \mu sec}{frame} = \frac{90\ msec}{frame}.$$

Note: We could have also arrived at this result by just multiplying the 2D frame time by 9. This should make sense since there are 900 acoustic lines in the color frame and only 100 acoustic lines in the 2D frame.

The overall frame time is the sum of the color and 2D frame times, or:

$$\text{color frame time} = \frac{90\ msec}{frame} + \frac{10\ msec}{frame} = \frac{100\ msec}{frame},$$

and the overall frame rate is:

$$\text{overall frame rate} = \frac{1}{\text{frame time}} = \frac{1}{100\ msec} = 0.01\ kHz = 10\ Hz.$$

9.4 Color and Poor Temporal Resolution

From this example, we see that the frame rate dropped from 100 Hz when performing only 2D imaging to 10 Hz with color imaging. This result should make sense since every color display line represents a packet of acoustic lines, each of which requires time to travel. As a result, sequentially generated color Doppler is considered to have the worst temporal resolution of the ultrasound modes. As we will learn in later chapters, this problem of poor temporal resolution has been partially addressed by techniques such as parallel processing and ultimately ultrafast imaging (plane wave and related techniques).

9.5 Choosing a Packet Size, the Trade-Off

In the early days of color Doppler imaging, most systems presented the user with a relatively accessible control which allowed for direct adjustment of the color packet size. With time, the advent of soft keys, better preset designs, and significantly more imaging functions (with the need for even more controls), the control for the packet size became buried in a sub-menu, and sometimes even bundled in with other color settings. As a result, it has become significantly more challenging, on most systems, to identify the color packet control. To find this, the user now has three options: consult the user manual, ask the clinical specialist from the manufacturer of the equipment, or "dig around" in the software menus.

Even before making the decision to change the color packet size, the question must be asked if the trade-off is desirable. Choosing a larger packet size produces smoother color, with less color noise, and improved sensitivity to weak signals, but obviously sacrifices temporal resolution. Conversely, decreasing the color packet size increases the frame rate, but potentially decreases color smoothness and color sensitivity.

> **KEY CONCEPT**
>
> A single color Doppler display line requires transmitting multiple acoustic lines (a packet). As a result, producing color images requires much more time than creating a 2D image of the same physical size. A larger color packet size produces better color sensitivity but at the expense of temporal resolution. In general, color Doppler has the worst temporal resolution of the ultrasound modalities.

10. Optimizing Frame Rate and Temporal Resolution

When good temporal resolution is critical, there are a series of steps which can be taken to increase the frame rate. As we have already seen many times, improving one aspect of an ultrasound image almost always involves a trade-off. For temporal resolution, improvement comes at the expense of detail resolution, a much smaller scan region, or both. Of course not all types of imaging require high frame rates, and therefore do not warrant any degradation in detail resolution. Quite simply the criterion for deciding is: the faster the changes that need to be detected, the more frame rate matters. Therefore, imaging a liver or pancreas requires little temporal resolution, whereas imaging a shunted flow or a pediatric heart generally requires optimal temporal resolution.

The following list outlines the steps which can be taken to increase frame rate, thereby potentially improving the temporal resolution:

1. Narrow color box size (color sector)
2. Decrease color box depth
3. Activate parallel processing (likely defaulted to on)
4. Decrease color packet size
5. Decrease color line density
6. Narrow 2D image size (2D sector)
7. Decrease 2D depth

11. Typical Values and Ranges for Wave and PW Parameters

The following table illustrates the typical values and ranges for conventional ultrasound imaging. For most credentialing boards, you are expected to recognize typical values.

	Parameter	Determined by:	Value (range)	Specific Mode
Wave	Operating frequency (f)	source	2 MHz – 20 MHz	All
	Period (P)	source	0.5 µsec – 0.05 µsec	All
	Wavelength (λ)	$\lambda = \dfrac{c}{f}$	77 µm – 770 µm	2D
			154 µm – 770 µm	PW Doppler
	Propagation velocity (c)	medium	337 m/sec – 4080 m/sec	All
Pulse Wave	Pulse Duration (PD)	$PD = P \times (\#\,cycles)$	0.1 µsec – 1.0 µsec	2D
			0.4 µsec – 16 µsec	PW Doppler
	Pulse Repetition Period (PRP)	$13\,\mu sec \times$ depth	13 µsec – 260 µsec	All
	Pulse Repetition Frequency (PRF)	$\dfrac{1}{PRP}$	77 kHz – 3.85 kHz	All
	Duty Factor	$\dfrac{PD}{PRP}$	< 1%	2D
			1% - 10% (varies significantly)	PW Doppler
			100%	CW
	SPL	$SPL = \lambda \times (\#\,cycles)$	154 µm – 1540 µm	2D
			0.6 cm – 2.5 cm	PW Doppler
Frames (Sequential)	Frame Time	$= \dfrac{time}{line} \cdot \dfrac{\#\,lines}{frame}$	5 msec – 100 msec	2D
		$= \dfrac{time}{line} \cdot \dfrac{total\,\#\,lines}{frame}$	10 msec – 600 msec	Color
	Frame Rate	$\dfrac{1}{frame\,time}$	200 Hz – 10 Hz	2D
			100 Hz – 8 Hz	Color
Frames (Plane Wave)	Frame Time	$= \dfrac{time}{line}$	32 µsec – 320 µsec	2D
		$= \dfrac{time}{line} \cdot \dfrac{total\,\#\,lines}{averaged}$	5 msec – 12.5 msec	Color
	Frame Rate	$\dfrac{1}{frame\,time}$	30,000 Hz – 3,000 Hz	2D
			200 Hz – 80 Hz	Color

Table 1 **Ultrasound related parameter table: typical values and ranges**

12. The Foundational Drawing for Pulse Wave Revisited

We are now ready to update the pulsed wave diagram we began in Level 1. The ability to draw *Figure 26* from memory is critical to demonstrate knowledge of pulsed wave operation. Furthermore, the ability to draw *Figure 26* for any of the credentialing exams is invaluable.

> **KEY CONCEPT**
>
> The PW diagram is very helpful in answering many questions related to waves, pulsed waves, axial resolution, PRFs and temporal resolution, and duty factor.

$$PRP(msec) = \frac{1}{PRF(kHz)} = 13\left(\frac{\mu sec}{cm}\right) \cdot I.D. \left(\frac{cm}{line}\right)$$

$$PD = P \cdot \#cycles$$

$$P(\mu sec) = \frac{1}{f(MHz)}$$

$$Duty\ Factor = \frac{PD}{PRP}$$

$$\lambda = \frac{c}{f}$$

$$SPL = \lambda \cdot \#\ cycles$$

$$Axial\ Resolution = \frac{SPL}{2}$$

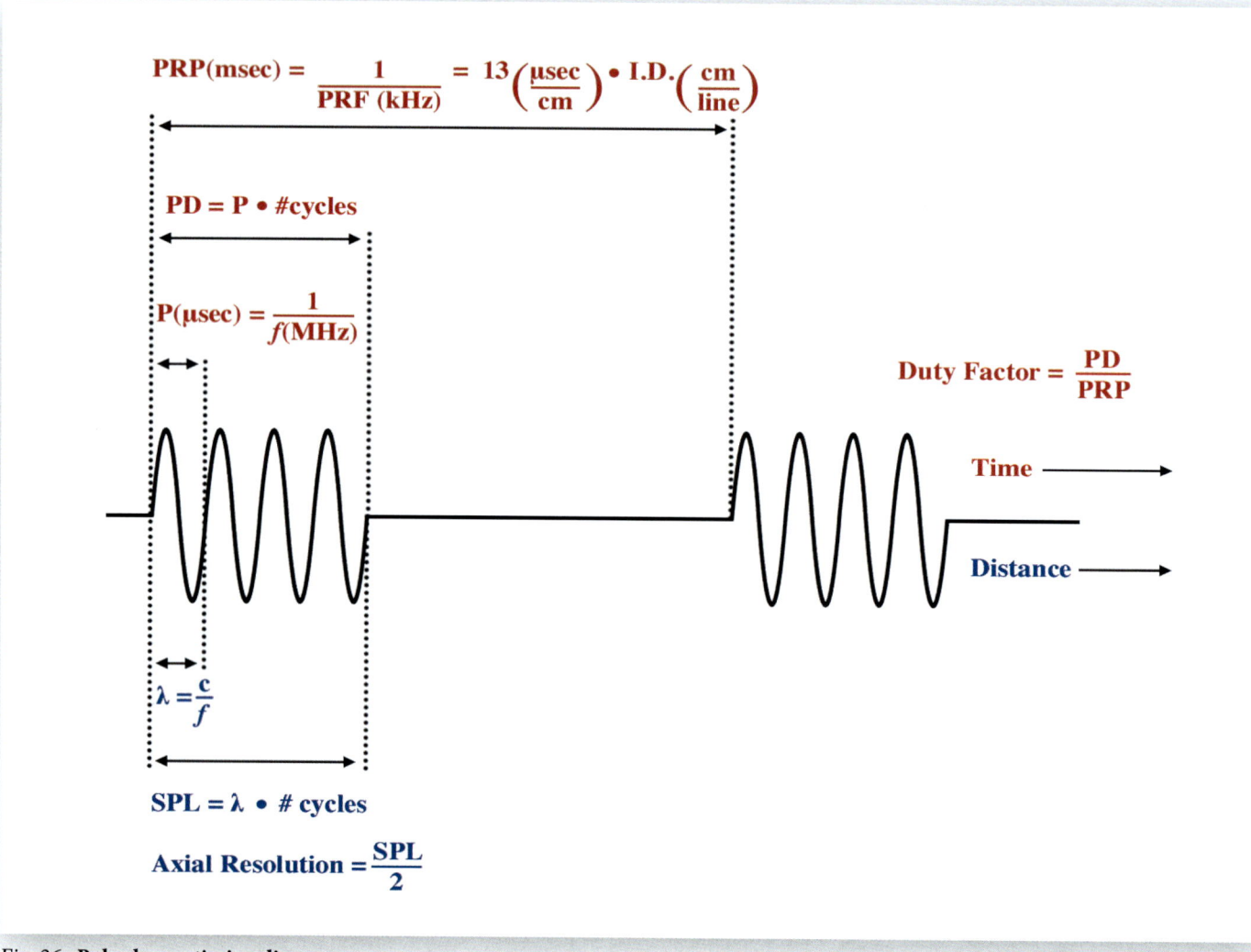

Fig. 26 **Pulsed wave timing diagram**

Figure 26 will be addressed again when discussing bioeffects. Clearly, the timing issues and duty factor will have direct consequence on the likelihood of bioeffects. Therefore, there will be future additions to this already information laden diagram.

13. Bandwidth

13.1 Bandwidth Defined

In recent years, there has been considerable talk about bandwidth in just about every arena of life. We hear about cell phone bandwidth, cable television bandwidth, digital satellite bandwidth, internet bandwidth, etc. There is also considerable talk about bandwidth in ultrasound.

Specifically, bandwidth is defined as the useful range of frequencies over which anything can operate. There are many different types of bandwidth. There is transducer bandwidth, transmit bandwidth, receive bandwidth, system receiver bandwidth, display bandwidth, etc. In general, you must specify the bandwidth to which you are referring.

13.2 Pictorial Representation of Bandwidth

Figure 27 represents a graph of a transducer bandwidth. Notice that the horizontal axis represents increasing frequency and the vertical axis represents the response sensitivity or signal amplitude. For this graph, the sensitivity is specified in decibels.

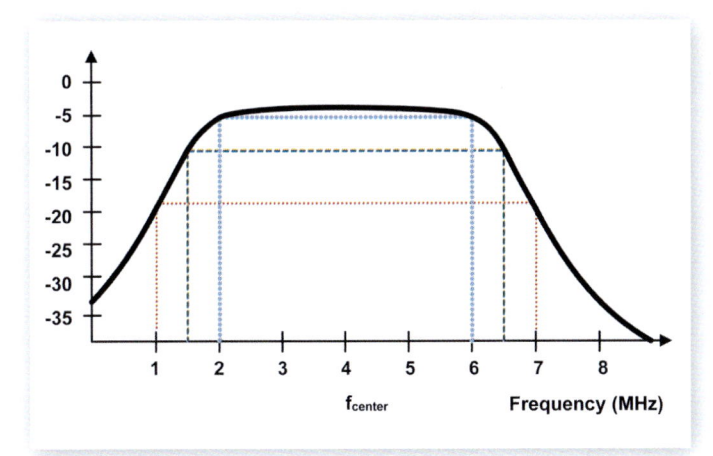

Fig. 27 **Bandwidth**

From this graph, we see that at frequencies below 2 MHz there is relatively little sensitivity. Similarly, at frequencies above 6 MHz there is little sensitivity. But how sensitive is sensitive enough? To discuss bandwidth accurately, the attenuation points must be specified as demonstrated below.

The 6 dB bandwidth point is the range of frequencies that exist between the two corner frequencies at which the signal sensitivity is decreased by 6 dB. For the above example, the signal has decreased by 6 dB at 6 MHz and at 2 MHz. The 6 dB corner frequencies are 6 MHz and 2 MHz. Since there is a range of 4 MHz between these two corner frequencies, we would say that the 6 dB bandwidth is 4 MHz, or:

-6 dB bandwidth = (6 – 2) MHz = 4 MHz.

Similarly, the 10 dB bandwidth point is the range of frequencies that exists between the two corner frequencies at which the signal sensitivity is decreased by 10 dB. For the above example, the signal has decreased by 10 dB at 6.4 MHz and at 1.6 MHz. The 10 dB corner frequencies are 6.4 MHz and 1.6 MHz. Since there is a range of 4.8 MHz between these two corner frequencies, we would say that the 10 dB bandwidth is 4.8 MHz, or:

-10 dB bandwidth = (6.4 - 1.6) MHz = 4.8 MHz.

For engineering purposes, we will generally specify at least two or three different bandwidth points, so as to more accurately characterize the response of the system we are measuring. For completeness, see if you can derive the 20 dB bandwidth and corner frequencies from the graph in *Figure 27*.

-20 dB bandwidth = (7 – 1) MHz = 6 MHz

13.3 Bandwidth Calculation

From the above example, we see that the bandwidth is defined as the maximum corner frequency minus the minimum corner frequency for a specified attenuation rate, or:

bandwidth (BW) = maximum frequency - minimum frequency.

13.4 Fractional Bandwidth

For transducers, a much more commonly used metric is the fractional bandwidth. As the name suggests, the fractional bandwidth is determined by dividing the bandwidth by the operating frequency.

$$\text{fractional bandwidth (FBW)} = \frac{\text{bandwidth}}{\text{operating frequency}}$$

Consider *Figure 27* assuming that the operating frequency is the same as the center frequency (f_c). The 6 dB fractional bandwidth would be (4 MHz / 4 MHz) or 100%. Note that the 4 MHz in the numerator represents a range of frequencies, while the 4 MHz in the denominator represents a single frequency in the center of the band. Transducers are considered to be broadband when they have more than approximately an 80% fractional bandwidth. The bandwidth in the figure would represent a broadband design.

13.5 Quality Factor

The quality factor gives the exact same information as the fractional bandwidth and is the reciprocal of the fractional bandwidth:

$$\text{quality factor (QF)} = \frac{1}{\text{fractional bandwidth}} = \frac{\text{operating frequency}}{\text{bandwidth}}.$$

There has been an implicit assumption that broader bandwidth is better. Although, in general, wider bandwidth is better, there are cases when more bandwidth has no real advantage. Let us consider when wide (or broad) bandwidth and high fractional bandwidth are useful.

13.6 The Value of Greater Bandwidth

Flexibility
A wide bandwidth transducer offers flexibility, since it can be operated at different frequencies. The user is allowed to choose an operating frequency within the band that is best suited for the modality and the specific patient. This ability to run at different frequencies is often called "frequency agility" or "multi-Hertz." Additionally, this flexibility allows for the B-mode image to be created at a higher frequency while simultaneously performing color and spectral Doppler at lower frequencies.

The ability to operate at lower frequencies for Doppler-based modalities is critical since the reflection from the blood can be very weak due to Rayleigh scattering (discussed in Chapter 3). Increased attenuation at higher frequencies further weakens these signals, making them potentially non-diagnostic. The following diagram represents a broadband transducer which can be used as a multi-Hertz transducer. For less required penetration but better resolution, the higher frequency band is used. For greater penetration, the user switches to a lower operating frequency, utilizing the lower range of the overall bandwidth. Of course there is a corresponding degradation in resolution.

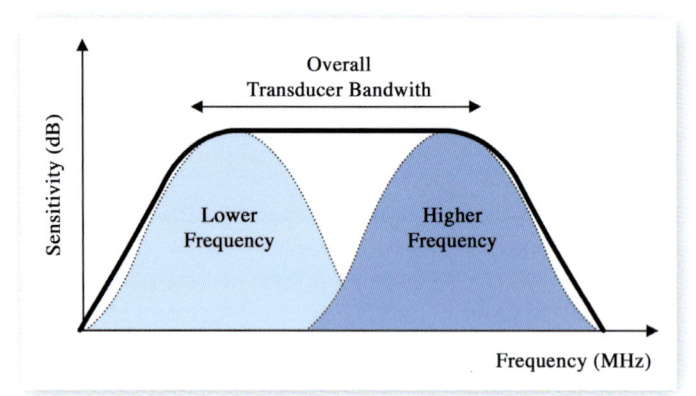

Fig. 28 **Multi-Hertz operation**

Note that using the entire bandwidth at the same time, without any advanced techniques, is not desirable. For easy to image patients, the poorer resolution data from the low frequency data will arrive simultaneously with the better resolution higher frequency data, degrading the best possible image quality. By using just the higher frequency bandwidth, the longer wavelength reflections will be absent and hence, there will be better resolution. For difficult to image patients, where penetration is critical, using the full bandwidth is again not ideal.

In order to minimize the risks of bioeffects, we are only allowed to transmit so much energy into the patient. Any energy that is being transmitted at the higher frequency reduces the amount of energy that can be transmitted at the lower frequency range. As a result, if we transmit over the entire bandwidth, we are not allowed to transmit with as much power at the lower frequency, which yields the most penetration. Therefore, for penetration, it is better to transmit using the lower frequency range and not be restricted by the transmitting of energy in a range that will not penetrate well.

KEY CONCEPT

The bandwidth refers to the range of frequencies over which a device can function. Wide bandwidth transducers can operate over a wide range of frequencies.

Dynamic Frequency Tuning (Sliding Receive Filters)

Broad bandwidth is useful for a technique called "dynamic frequency tuning" or "sliding receive filters." If a high frequency is used, a high resolution image is achieved in the near field. If a low frequency is used the resolution is worse, but there may be significantly more penetration. Dynamic frequency tuning attempts to optimize both resolution and penetration. The concept behind "dynamic frequency tuning" is to transmit over the whole bandwidth and then change, or "slide" the receive frequency from higher to lower with increasing depth. In this way, the echoes from the near field are very high resolution while there is still some lower frequency energy from the deeper regions. The greater the bandwidth, the greater the range over which the filters can slide, or be "dynamically tuned."

The diagram in *Figure 29* represents the use of dynamic frequency tuning. The echoes that return from the shallowest depths still have a fair amount of high frequency energy. So as to preserve high frequency resolution, only the high frequency band is received, ignoring the echoes from lower frequencies. In the figure, the high frequency band is designated as BW_1.

As the signals return from deeper depths, later in time, the high frequency attenuates faster than the lower frequency energy. Therefore, there would be inadequate penetration at the higher frequency band. Instead, filters in the receivers shift to receive a lower frequency band, designated as BW_2. The same process is repeated for signals arriving later and later. The net result is good resolution in the near field and relatively good penetration in the far field. In this diagram, the image was broken into four bands. In reality, the system slides the receive filters continuously, not in four discrete steps, so there are no major discontinuities as in the figure drawn.

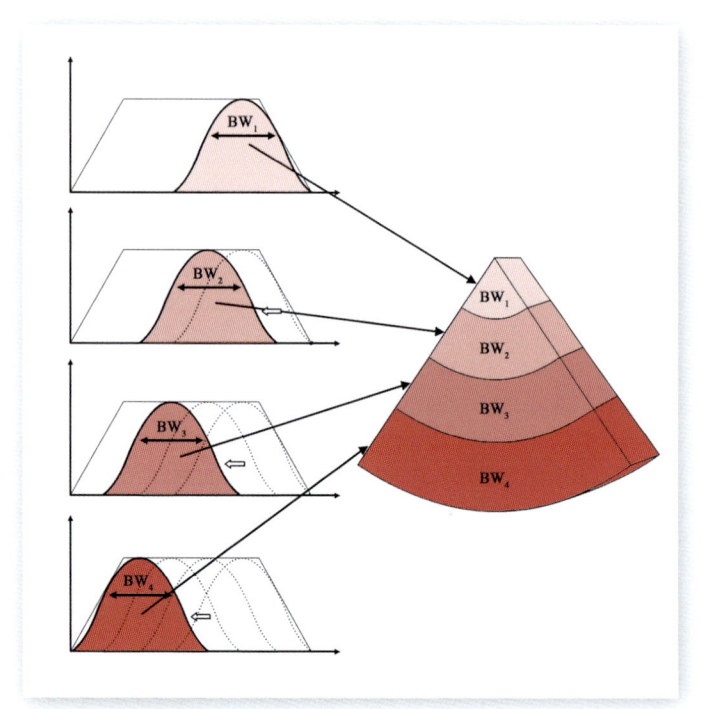

Fig. 29 **Dynamic frequency tuning**

> **KEY CONCEPT**
>
> Dynamic frequency tuning uses wide bandwidth in transmit and then by sliding the receive filters, allows higher frequency echoes to produce the image in the near field and lower frequency echoes to produce the image in the far field.

Harmonic Imaging
Third, broad bandwidth is useful for harmonic imaging. As will be discussed in Chapter 10, in second harmonic imaging, the transmit is performed at the fundamental frequency and the receive is performed at twice the fundamental frequency. This can obviously only be achieved if the transducer has enough bandwidth to operate proficiently at both of those frequencies.

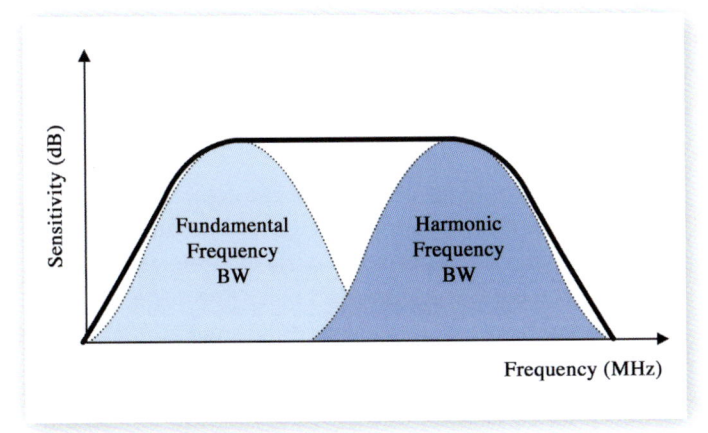

Fig. 30 **Use of bandwidth for harmonic imaging**

Frequency Fusion (Frequency Compounding)
Fourth, broad bandwidth is useful to allow for many different types of parallel processing techniques. These techniques typically involve transmitting over a broad range of frequencies and then receiving and processing the beam at two or more different narrower frequency bands. The different frequency bands are each processed to produce images which are then fused together. This technique can therefore result in better overall image quality.

CW Doppler and Bandwidth
Is there ever a time when more bandwidth is not helpful? The answer is yes. CW Doppler requires very little bandwidth. Therefore, if given a choice (as in *Figure 31*) between a narrower bandwidth and more sensitivity (A), or a broader bandwidth and less sensitivity (B), the more sensitive transducer A would be much better for CW Doppler. Also, which of the two transducer designs would you believe to be better when penetration is needed? Although transducer A has less bandwidth, at low frequencies there is significantly better penetration. Since high frequency energy does not help with penetration, transducer A is clearly better in this case as well.

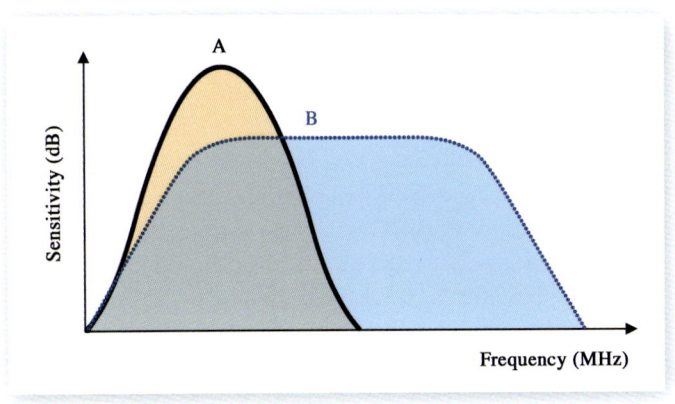

Fig. 31 **More bandwidth is not always better**

14. Pulse Duration (Width) vs. Bandwidth

14.1 The Reciprocal Relationship
We have already learned that time and frequency have a reciprocal relationship. A long time corresponds to a low frequency and a short time corresponds to a high frequency.

If the impulse response of a transducer is short (short pulse duration), the transducer will have a wide bandwidth:

$$\left(\frac{1}{small\ number} = big\ number \right)$$

If the impulse response of the transducer is long, the transducer will have a narrow bandwidth:

$$\left(\frac{1}{big\ number} = small\ number \right)$$

The following figure demonstrates the reciprocal relationship between the pulse duration and the bandwidth of a transducer.

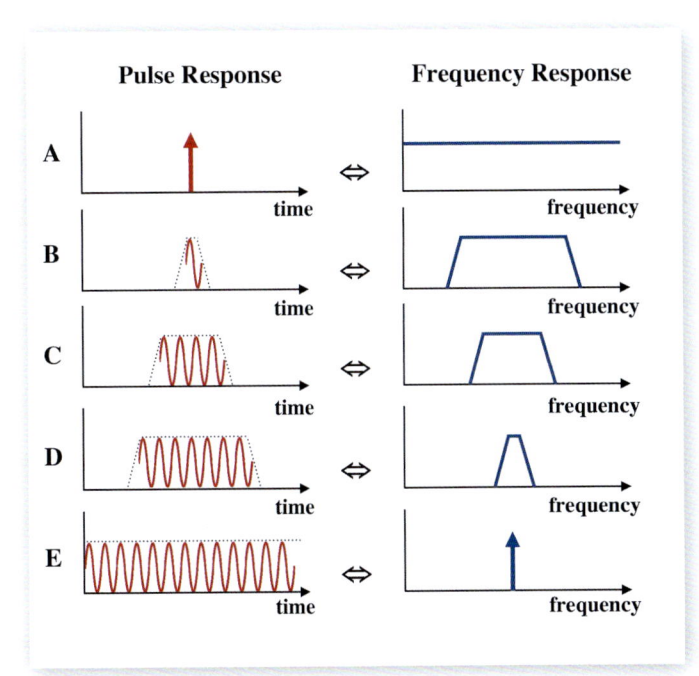

Fig. 32 **The relationship between pulse duration and bandwidth**

Referring to the various scenarios depicted, you should see demonstrated the inverse relationship between the time and frequency domain. In case A, the time response is infinitesimally short, creating an infinitely wide bandwidth. Although an infinitesimally short ring time is not possible, it is very instructive to show the inverse relationship with bandwidth. Earlier in this chapter (Section 8.3.3) we discussed the use of a backing material to decrease the number of cycles in a pulse so as to reduce the spatial pulse length, improving axial resolution. We now see that there is another advantage of the use of a backing material. By decreasing the number of cycles in the pulse, the pulse duration is also shortened, increasing the bandwidth.

The term "pulse width" is sometimes used in place of the term "pulse duration." This naming choice is less desirable since the meaning is less discernible. In this sense, the word "width" is referring to how wide a pulse looks when pictured as a drawing over time. This definition is slightly more intuitive for engineers and physicists who are used to measuring time parameters on an oscilloscope, but much less for sonographers. My suggestion is to use the term pulse duration, but be familiar with the term pulse width in case you are asked by someone a little less sensitive to inconsistencies in terminology.

> **KEY CONCEPT**
>
> A shorter pulse duration results in a broader bandwidth. Using a backing material reduces the number of cycles in the pulse, decreasing the pulse duration, increasing the bandwidth.

14.2 The Meaning of the Operating Frequency and Bandwidth Relationship

Notice in Case B of *Figure 32*, that if the transducer is only allowed to ring for a single full cycle there is extremely broad bandwidth. This demonstrates another very important point: a transducer is always operating at a range of frequencies centered around the operating, or "center" frequency, and never just at one frequency. In other words, when we say that we are using an operating frequency of 4 MHz, we are really saying that the center of the bandwidth is 4 MHz, and that we are using a range of frequencies centered around 4 MHz. If resolution is critical, as it is in B-mode imaging, then the bandwidth is generally quite wide. If resolution isn't as critical, as in CW Doppler, then the bandwidth can be quite narrow.

14.3 Bandwidth Required for Doppler

Notice in Case D of *Figure 32* that if the transducer rings for a long time, as it does with a large sample volume in PW Doppler and in continuous wave, then there is very little bandwidth. In essence, the widest bandwidth is necessary for B-mode imaging, followed by color Doppler, spectral PW Doppler, and then CW spectral Doppler.

15. Exercises and Conceptual Questions

View ONLINE Exercises & Conceptual Questions

> **COMMON MISCONCEPTION: Pulsed Wave Operation**
>
> **MISCONCEPTION:** *PW has no range ambiguity.*
>
> *Explanation:*
> Pulsed wave operation does not have perfect range specificity (some range ambiguity always exists). Range ambiguity exists in all pulsed modalities including radar for speed detection, radar for airplanes, PW Doppler, Color Doppler, 2D imaging, etc.
>
> This ambiguity occurs because the echo from the previous transmitted pulse (from deeper in the medium) returns simultaneously with the echo from the current transmitted pulse (from shallower in the medium). In fact, this range ambiguity is actually exploited to create the Doppler modality referred to as High PRF (HPRF) Doppler.

> **COMMON MISCONCEPTION: Pulsed Wave Operation**
>
> **MISCONCEPTION:** *Changing the transmit frequency changes the PRF.*
>
> *Explanation:*
> The pulse repetition frequency (PRF) is the reciprocal of the pulse repetition period (PRP). The PRP is determined by the time it takes for sound to travel to the specified imaging depth and back to the transducer (13 microseconds multiplied by the imaging depth in cm). Since the speed of sound is independent of the transmit frequency, changing the transmit frequency has no effect on the PRP, and hence, no effect on the PRF.

COMMON MISCONCEPTION: Pulsed Wave Operation

MISCONCEPTION: *More (broader) bandwidth is always better.*

Explanation:
Broad bandwidth is very useful for many advanced applications. However, for deep imaging (improved penetration) a high sensitivity at a low operating frequency is more important than increased bandwidth. (This fact is depicted in *Figure 31*)

CHAPTER SUMMARY: Pulsed Wave Operation

- Continuous waves have no ability to resolve structures separated in depth.
- Pulsing is a technique which yields the ability to resolve structures separated in depth.
- For resolution, smaller values are better.
- The shorter the pulse, the better the depth resolution. Depth resolution is also referred to as longitudinal, axial, radial, or range resolution.
- The longitudinal resolution equals the spatial pulse length divided by 2.

$$\text{Axial Resolution} = \frac{SPL}{2}$$

- The factor of 2 derives from the fact that the roundtrip effect is helping to separate the echoes from objects at varying depths.
- Because of the desire to use pulsed wave to achieve some axial resolution, many parameters which describe the pulse must be defined.
  - The time the pulse lasts is called the pulse duration (PD)
  - The pulse duration is determined by the period multiplied by the number of cycles in the pulse:

  $$PD = P \bullet \#cycles$$

  - The time between transmit events (from the start of one pulse until the pulse is repeated) is called the pulse repetition period (PRP)
  - The PRP is determined primarily by the imaging depth and is equal to the imaging depth (in centimeters) multiplied by 13 μsec per cm:

  $$PRP = ID(cm) \times \frac{13\ \mu sec}{cm}$$

  - The pulse repetition frequency is simply the reciprocal of the PRP:

  $$PRF = \frac{1}{PRP}$$

  - Typically PRF values are in the kHz range
- The ratio of the PD to the PRP is referred to as the duty factor. The highest value the duty factor can reach is 1 or 100% which indicates CW.

$$DF = \frac{PD}{PRP}$$

- The duty factor is an indicator for the risk of thermal bioeffects.
- The physical length the pulse occupies in the medium is called the spatial pulse length (SPL).
- The SPL is equal to the wavelength multiplied by the number of cycles in the pulse.

$$SPL = \lambda \bullet \#\ cycles$$

- A backing or damping material is used to shorten the number of cycles in a pulse from a transducer.
- By reducing the number of cycles in the pulse, the pulse duration is decreased which results in an increase in the bandwidth.

- By reducing the number of cycles in the pulse, the spatial pulse length is decreased which results in improved axial resolution.
- A scanned modality implies that over time the acoustic beams are transmitted in different directions.
- A non-scanned modality implies that over time the acoustic beam is repeatedly transmitted in the same direction.
- Non-scanned modalities present greater thermal risks than scanned modalities.
- The frame time is the product of the time to produce an individual acoustic line and the number of lines in the frame.

$$\text{Frame time} = \text{PRP} \times \frac{\text{\# lines}}{\text{frame}}$$

- The frame rate (better termed the frame frequency) is simply the reciprocal of the frame time.

$$\text{Frame rate} = \frac{1}{\text{Frame time}}$$

- Higher frame rates result in better temporal resolution.
- Color Doppler generally has the worst temporal resolution since each display line of color is comprised of an entire "packet" or "ensemble" of acoustic lines.
- The bandwidth is defined as the range of frequencies over which a device can operate.
- The fractional bandwidth is defined as the bandwidth divided by the center frequency or the operating frequency.

$$FBW = \frac{BW}{f_c}$$

- The quality factor is the reciprocal of the fractional bandwidth.

$$QF = \frac{1}{FBW}$$

- Broadband transducers can be used for many techniques such as harmonic imaging, dynamic frequency tuning, and frequency fusion (compounding).
- A short impulse response (pulse duration) implies a broad bandwidth. A long pulse duration implies a narrow bandwidth.
- CW Doppler requires very little bandwidth, whereas 2D imaging requires significant bandwidth.

ONLINE EXTRAS

For additional support material and to view your completion progress, visit:
www.pegasuslectures.com/6thEdExtras

Extras by Chapter include:
- Animations
- Videos
- Additional Images
- Clarifying Clips
- Supplemental Exercises
- Conceptual Questions

See page x of Preface for access instructions

Transducers
(Piezoelectric)

Chapter 5 — Part I

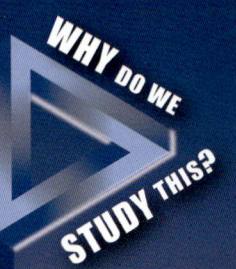

WHY DO WE STUDY THIS?

▷ To create ultrasound images, sound waves must be both transmitted and received.

▷ A variety of transducers have been designed to meet the specific requirements of each type of imaging. Until recently, all ultrasound transducers were based on the piezoelectric effect.

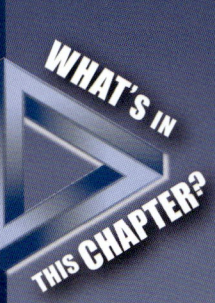

WHAT'S IN THIS CHAPTER?

LEVEL 1 — BASIC ULTRASOUND PHYSICS
The basics of transducers, the piezoelectric effect, and beam characteristics are discussed.

LEVEL 2 — BOARD LEVEL
Details the evolution of ultrasound transducers from single crystals and mechanical steering through complex 1-D and 2D phased arrays with electronic focusing and steering to wireless transducers.

LEVEL 3 — ADVANCED TOPICS
Develops in greater detail the concept of the piezoelectric effect and compares the crystal structure of standard PZT ceramics with PMN-PT (single) crystals.

LEARNING OBJECTIVES

▷ List the beam parameters and how each affects ultrasound images
▷ Explain the piezoelectric effect
▷ Describe the evolution of transducers, being able to explain why each advancement was made
▷ Identify the underlying principle of phasing used with phased array transducers
▷ Define the process by which sequential images are generated
▷ Draw and explain the basic block diagram of a transducer

Chapter 5 – Part I
Transducers (Piezoelectric)

Introduction

Ultrasound is changing at a rapid pace. Whereas new technologies are revolutionizing certain aspects of ultrasound, many existing technologies have advantages for certain applications. This means that for at least the foreseeable future, both older and newer technologies will coexist. If history is any teacher, older technologies will persist to a great enough extent that ultrasound practitioners will need to be familiar with both the older and new technologies for at least the next eight to ten years. This of course makes learning more complicated. To deal with both older and newer technologies, Chapter 5 is now divided into effectively two chapters. Part I discusses basic transducer theory, piezoelectric transducers, sequential imaging, and the evolution of piezoelectric transducers. Part II deals with CMUT technology, a transducer technology that represents much of the future.

In Chapter 2 we discussed waves and the parameters that define a sound wave useful for diagnostic testing. In Chapter 3, we discussed the interaction that occurs between the mechanical wave of sound and the medium, responsible for ultimately returning the signal back for interpretation. In Chapter 4, we discussed various timing schemes so as to achieve the desired axial resolution as well as the basics of image formation. You will note that there was no discussion specific to the device responsible for producing these waves which interact with the patient to produce time variant signals for processing and interpretation. The approach not to discuss this topic is very deliberate. It is very difficult to discuss the specifics of a complex device before you understand the requirements for the device. Since we now know some of the parameters that are desirable for a wave, we are now ready to discuss these devices called transducers and how transducers are used to produce basic images.

The subject of "transducers" is very broad. Since there are many different types of transducers and many different applications for transducers, we will start by discussing in Level 1 the basic principles of piezoelectric transducers and general theory. Level 1 is designed to teach the rudimentary principles without encumbering the reader with specifics about transducer application in clinical ultrasound. Once the general aspects are understood, Level 2 will discuss specific piezoelectric transducer designs, advantages and disadvantages of various technologies, and applications, and different approaches to generating basic, sequentially-generated ultrasound images. Level 2 will be structured in a unique manner, following the technology development path from the early days through the current designs. By splitting the material into two distinct sections (the theory in Level 1, and the application in Level 2), we will hopefully reduce the amount of confusion which arises from the many permutations and interactions between the types of transducers, the application of various transducer types, the benefits and limitations to each design, and the desired features and technology that drove future designs. As already mentioned, the most recent designs based on CMUT technology will be discussed in Chapter 5, Part II.

The importance of learning about transducers must be stressed. Aspects of the transmitted wave directly affect the quality of the scan, what modalities can be performed, and the risk of bioeffects. Since the transducer and transducer design directly affect the beam, it is logical that understanding transducer theory and function will be critical to performing a good clinical diagnostic ultrasound test on a patient.

1. Transducer Basics

1.1 Transducers Defined
A transducer is any device which converts energy from one form to another. Using the meaning of the prefix in the definition, a transducer is a device which converts energy across the device from one form to another form. There are many forms of transducers in the world. Do not make the mistake of defining the word too narrowly to only mean "ultrasound" transducers.

1.2 Examples of Transducers

◊ ***Examples:***
- microphones
- stereo speakers
- temperature sensors (thermocouples, thermistors)
- light bulbs
- lasers
- eyes
- ears
- nerves

1.3 Ultrasound Transducers and Bi-directionality

To be specific, an ultrasound transducer converts electropotential energy (voltage) into mechanical vibration (sound or pressure) as well as converts mechanical vibrations back into electrical energy. This fact implies that the same transducer can potentially be used to both send out a signal into the patient (transmit) and receive a signal from the patient (receive), in juxtaposition to a system where a separate device is required for each. You will note that not all of the examples of transducers given above can operate bi-directionally. Light bulbs don't convert photons back into electrical energy and ears certainly do not convert electrical impulses from the brain back to sound waves that emanate from the ear. The fact that an ultrasound transducer can work bi-directionally (exhibits reciprocity) is a fortuitous benefit.

> **KEY CONCEPT**
>
> A transducer is any device which converts one form of energy to another form of energy. Ultrasound transducers convert electrical energy into mechanical energy (sound) and the returning mechanical energy back into electrical energy.

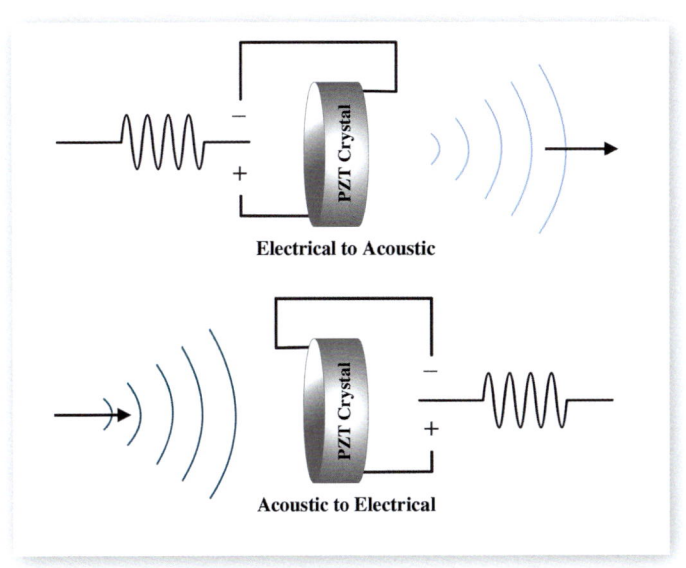

Fig. 1 **The piezoelectric effect**

2. Ultrasound Transducers Mechanisms of Operation

Until very recently, ultrasound transducers were all based on the piezoelectric effect. The piezoelectric effect was discovered by the Curie brothers in the early 1880s. Since the earliest days of ultrasound, piezoelectric materials were chosen to serve as the source of the sound waves.

2.1 The Piezoelectric Effect

The piezoelectric effect is a phenomenon by which an electric field (voltage) results when certain crystal materials are mechanically deformed. By reverse piezoelectric effect (reciprocity), a varying electric field also produces mechanical deformation of the crystal.

Simply put, when you drive a crystal with a voltage, it resonates mechanically at some characteristic frequency. When you vibrate the crystal mechanically at some characteristic frequency, a voltage is produced. *Figure 1* depicts the basic conversion back and forth (bi-directionally) between electrical energy and acoustic energy.

2.2 The Piezoelectric Mechanism

A simplified description is provided here in Level 1, but in Level 3 of this chapter, there is a formal discussion of the piezoelectric effect. (Hopefully, you will be intrigued enough by the interesting aspects of piezoelectricity to venture into Level 3 for the more complete description.)

All atoms and molecules of a material are bound together with electrical binding forces. This fact is well known since it is the foundation of nuclear energy. For crystals which exhibit the piezoelectric effect, the molecules are dipolar. As the name suggests, molecules that are dipolar have two poles, one pole which is positive and the other which is negative.

If electrodes (electrical contacts) are placed across the crystal with a voltage potential applied, the poles of the molecules will shift to align with the polarity of the electrodes. Remembering that "opposites attract" (like magnetic poles) the negative poles rotate toward the positive electrodes and the positive poles align with the negative electrodes.

For *Figure 2a*, since the negative electrode is placed on the left side, the positive poles rotate to the left. When this rotation occurs, the molecules are now slightly farther apart, causing an expansion of the crystal. If instead, as demonstrated by *Figure 2b*, the polarity of the voltage is reversed, the molecules will rotate to the right, resulting in a closer spacing of the molecules, causing the crystal to contract. If the voltage potential is then eliminated, the molecules will then shift back to their normal alignment and spacing, "shrinking" back to the original dimension *Figure 2c*. Therefore, by varying the electrical field, a mechanical "distortion" of the crystal occurs.

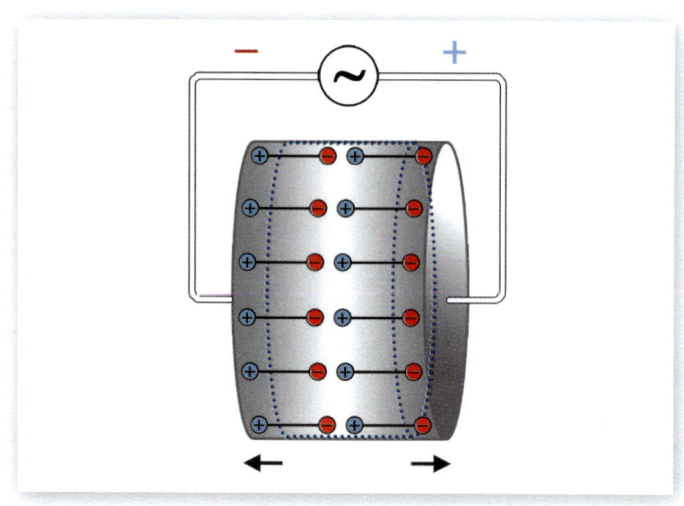

Fig. 2a **Expansion**

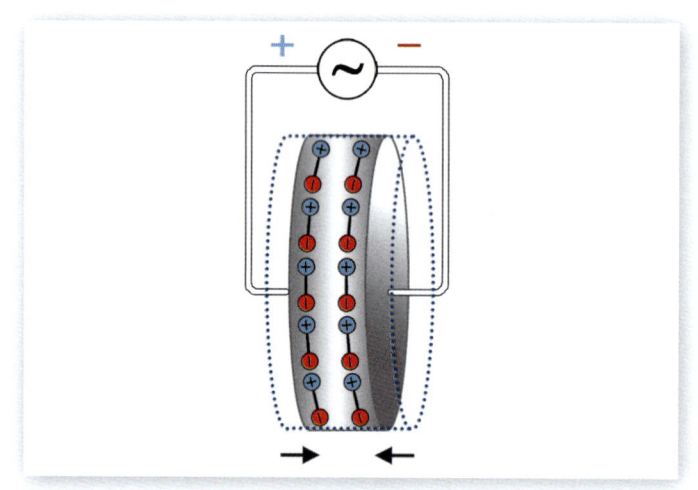

Fig. 2b **Contraction**

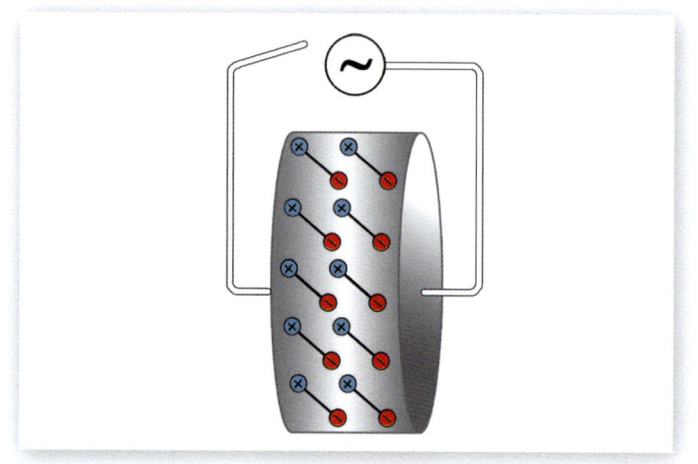

Fig. 2c **At rest**

The result is that a varying electrical field produces a physical change in the dimension of the crystal. If the crystal is then placed against a medium, the physical vibration can be coupled into that neighboring medium. As discussed earlier, how much of that vibration is transferred depends on the acoustic impedance mismatch between the crystal and the medium.

An analogy for this phenomenon is applying a force to two blocks connected by a spring. If a force is applied on the two blocks in opposite directions, the spring will be stretched and the blocks will be farther apart than the resting condition. By releasing the force on the objects, the two objects will recoil towards each other, but because of momentum, the objects will actually get closer together than the original separation distance. As a result, the two blocks will start traveling away from each other, oscillating until finally coming to rest at the same separation distance as the resting condition.

How far these objects are separated, and how long the oscillation occurs depends on the force applied, the mass of the blocks, and the properties of the interconnecting spring. Just as the mechanical resonance is related to the parameters of the spring, the resonance of the crystal is related to the parameters of the crystal. Clearly, a single impulse will cause the crystal to ring at a resonant frequency producing multiple cycles.

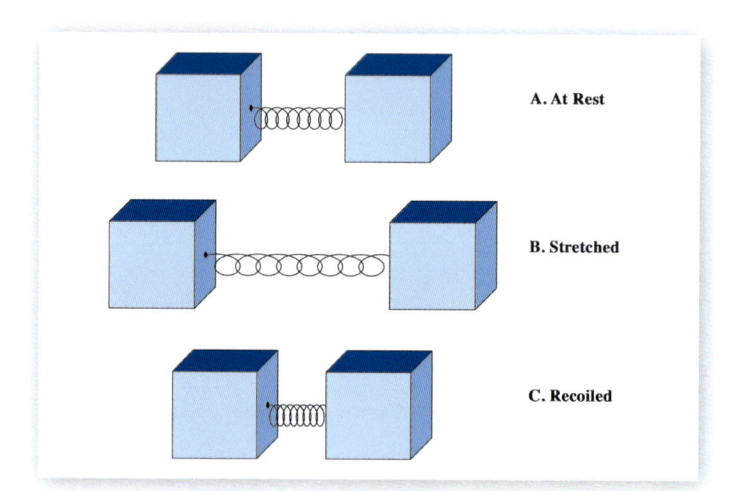

Fig. 3a **Block analogy of crystal oscillation**

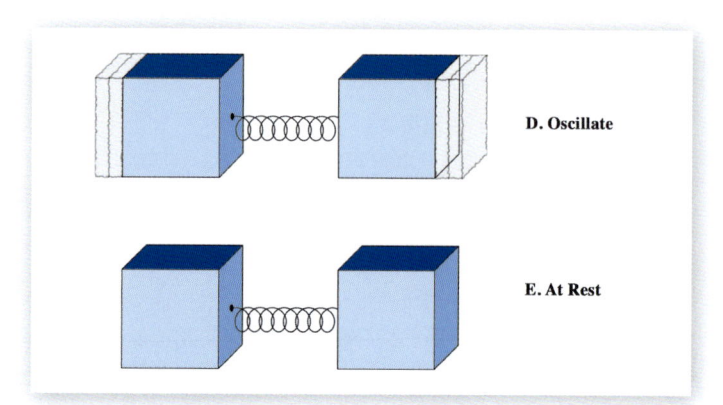

Fig. 3b **Block analogy of crystal oscillation**

From both our analogy and our description of the piezoelectric effect, we can imagine that applying a stronger electrical field will produce a greater mechanical distortion. In essence, the amplitude of the acoustic energy is related to the amplitude of the electrical signal driving the crystal. To produce a higher amplitude acoustic signal (pressure field), a higher voltage is applied to the crystal.

2.3 Natural Piezoelectric Materials

The most notable naturally occurring piezoelectric material is quartz (SiO_2). The original work done with piezoelectric properties by Pierre and Jacque Curie in the latter 1880s was using quartz. Quartz is commonly used today in many electrical devices for its piezoelectric properties. Confirmation of this fact is as simple as looking at the advertising for most battery operated watches. The battery is the source of the electrical energy, and the quartz acts as a very well calibrated vibrational source for measuring time. Quartz is also commonly used as a clock system for many electronic circuits. Part of the reason quartz is used so frequently in electronic circuits is because of its very reliable and controllable behavior. Quartz is regularly controlled to be consistent to better than 1 part in 10^8. Also, quartz as a natural piezoelectric material has a relatively high efficiency of conversion referred to as the coupling coefficient (in thickness or piston mode). The coupling coefficient is a measure of efficiency of conversion between electrical and mechanical signals. There are other naturally occurring materials such tourmaline, topaz, sugar cane, Rochelle salts (sodium potassium tartrate tetrahydrate), and even bone, but when is the last time you heard someone marketing their watch as Rochelle salt or bone activated?

2.4 Manufactured Piezoelectric Materials

There are many materials which can be manufactured that can exhibit the piezoelectric effect. Some examples are barium titanate, lead zirconate titanate, barium lead zirconate, lead metaniobate, and polyvinylidene fluoride (PVDF). Now that you have seen a partial laundry list of would be contenders, the material most commonly chosen for ultrasound transducers has been lead zirconate titanate (PZT). PZT became the material of choice for medical applications because of:

- High coupling coefficient (efficiency)
- High frequency of natural resonance
- Very good repeatable characteristics for stable designs

One issue with the use of PZT as the crystal material in medical applications is its relatively high impedance. Generally, the impedance of PZT ranges from around 30 to 40 MRayls, depending on the type of PZT used. Since the impedance of tissue is so much lower, this high impedance results in a significant acoustic impedance mismatch with the patient. As we learned in Chapter 3, a large acoustic impedance mismatch results in poor transmission. This large mismatch becomes the motivation for the use of a matching layer. Although other materials such as PVDF have much lower impedances, around 4 MRayls for PVDF, the coupling coefficient is much lower, resulting in inadequate sensitivity. You will note that although quartz has a relatively high coupling coefficient as a naturally piezoelectric material, its coupling coefficient is about one tenth that of PZT. As a result, quartz is never used as the piezoelectric material for ultrasound transducers which need extraordinary sensitivity. Newer transducers are now making use of a combination of materials called composites to address some of these issues. Composite materials are discussed in Level 2 of this chapter.

2.5 Poling

In our example in Section 2.2, we started with the assumption that all of the poles of the molecules were nicely aligned, with the positive poles pointing in one direction and the negative poles pointing in the other. The efficiency of piezoelectric materials can be improved through a process called "poling." The process of poling involves placing the crystal material into a specialized oven at extremely high temperatures. The increased temperature, allows the molecules to "slide" more freely, such that the molecules can move and realign. A large electrical field is introduced so that the molecules adopt a well behaved pattern where the positive poles align in one direction and the negative poles align in the other direction. In other words, each molecular dipole is now aligned in a specific orientation which enhances the physical distortion that occurs with an applied varying electric field. The temperature is reduced with the strong electrical field still applied. When the material is removed from the large electrical field at lower temperatures, the molecules remain in the new orientation.

2.6 Curie Point

As mentioned, Pierre and Jacque Curie worked with quartz in the latter part of the 1800s. As a result, the temperature at which a material will lose its poling and hence, efficiency as a piezoelectric material, is called the Curie temperature. The Curie temperature for PZT is approximately 300° Celsius. The probability of mistakenly heating a material close to or beyond its Curie point is extremely low (300° Celsius is 572° Fahrenheit). However, as you will learn later throughout this chapter, the process of transducer construction utilizes materials such as epoxies, which will break down well before the Curie point, causing delamination and overall destruction to your transducer. For this reason, you should make certain not to autoclave any transducer, unless you desire a very expensive paperweight.

KEY CONCEPT

Some materials such as quartz naturally exhibit the piezoelectric effect. Other materials are manufactured to exhibit the piezoelectric effect such as PVDF and PZT. The manufactured materials are generally put through a process called poling which makes use of heating the material beyond its Curie temperature and then applying a strong magnetic field so as to improve the piezoelectric efficiency of the material. PZT has long been a material of choice because of its repeatable characteristics and high efficiency.

3. Frequency of Operation and Crystal Dimension

3.1 Pulse Wave
As stated in the introduction to this chapter, one of the reasons for waiting to cover the topic of transducers until this point was so that the most important parameters for ultrasound application would be recognizable. One of the fundamental wave parameters discussed was the operating frequency. In Chapter 2, we stated that the operating frequency is determined by the source. It is now time to discuss that source. For pulse wave operation, the frequency of operation depends primarily on the thickness of the piezoelectric material and the propagation velocity within the piezoelectric material. The following illustration demonstrates how a pulsed electrical signal is converted into a pulsed acoustic signal. In case A, the crystal is thicker, resulting in a longer time for the crystal to fully expand and contract. In the expansion state, the transducer compresses the neighboring medium. Therefore, a slow compression rate implies a longer period and hence, a lower frequency. In case B, the crystal is half as thick as in case A. As a result, the crystal can expand and contract twice as fast.

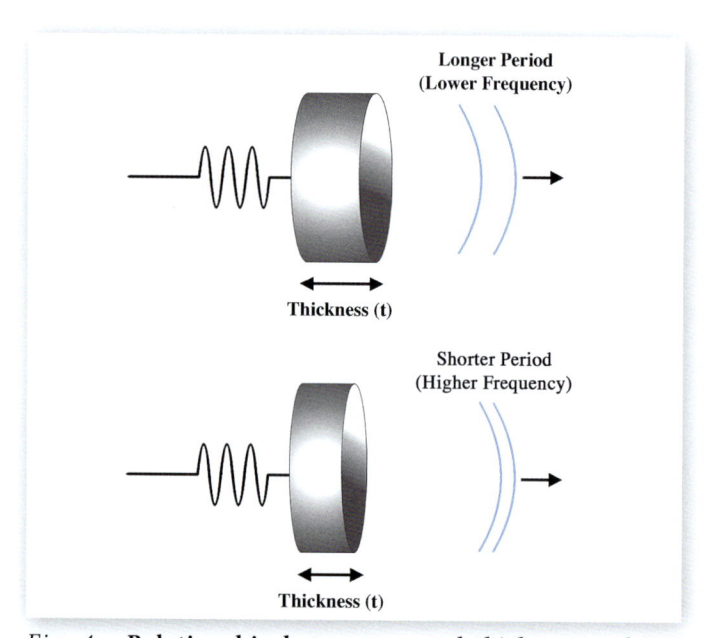

Fig. 4 **Relationship between crystal thickness and PW operating frequency**

So for pulsed operation:

$$f_0 \propto \frac{1}{thickness}$$

Now imagine that there are two crystals identical in thickness but one crystal has a higher propagation velocity than the other crystal. The higher propagation velocity implies that the material can expand and contract faster, reducing the time between compressions (the period). Since the frequency is the reciprocal of the period, a shorter period implies a higher operating frequency. Therefore, the operating frequency is proportional to the propagation velocity, or:

$$f_0\,(MHz) \propto Propagation\ Speed\ in\ Crystal\,(C_{crystal})$$

So the equation for the operating frequency in PW must express a proportional relationship with the propagation velocity in the crystal, and an inverse relationship with the thickness of the crystal. Before we write the equation, we must consider one more aspect of the physical situation. When the crystal expands, it expands in two different directions. Only half of the motion is in the direction of the coupled medium. Therefore, there is a constant factor of 2 in the denominator to account for this expansion. The equation is therefore:

$$f_0\,(MHz) = \frac{Propagation\ Speed\,(mm/\mu sec)}{2 \cdot (thickness)\,(mm)}.$$

You will notice that the units for each of the variables have been fixed to a specific format. By forcing the units to be in millimeters per microsecond and millimeters, the frequency will have the units of MHz. Although you do not have to force the units as suggested here, it does make calculations a little bit easier and more readily solved in your head.

3.2 Continuous Wave
In contrast with pulse wave operation, in continuous mode the ultrasound frequency is determined by the frequency of the transmit signal or, equivalently, the drive voltage frequency of the pulser. For continuous wave, although the crystal has a natural resonant frequency, the constant driving of the crystal by the drive voltage overrides the natural response. The result is that the frequency of the transducer will match the frequency of the transmit voltage.

So for continuous operation:

$$f_0 = Transducer\ Frequency = Drive\ Voltage\ Frequency.$$

Note that although the frequency of operation is determined by the frequency of the drive voltage, for sensitivity reasons, we would never choose to run a transducer outside its natural bandwidth. If a transducer naturally resonates with a 4 MHz bandwidth centered around 6 MHz, we would run it in CW as high as 8 MHz and as low as 4 MHz, but not usually above or below that range since the transducer would be very inefficient.

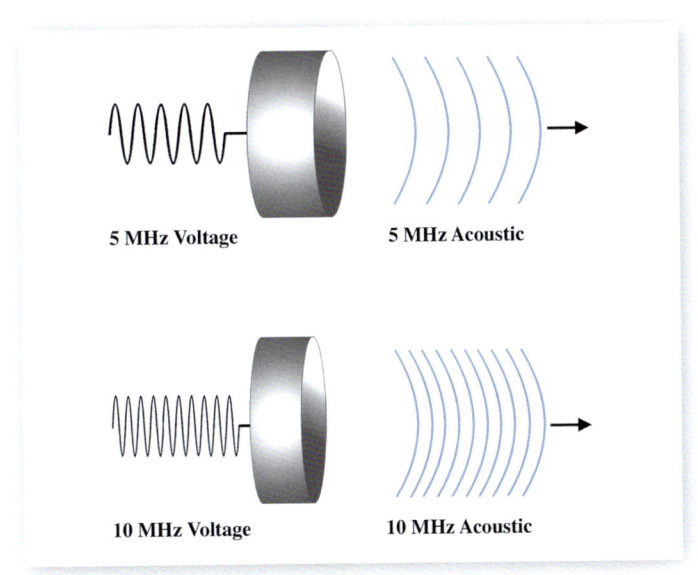

Fig. 5 CW operating frequency

KEY CONCEPT

For piezoelectric transducers, the operating frequency of a crystal is determined differently when transmitting continuously than when operating in a pulsed modality. For continuous wave, the frequency of operation is determined by the frequency of the electrical signal driving the crystal. For pulsed wave, the frequency is determined by the propagation speed of sound in the crystal (proportionally) and by the crystal thickness (inversely).

4. Impulse Response of a Transducer

In Chapter 4, when discussing bandwidth, we learned that, like a bell, when a transducer is driven with a single impulse, a resonance occurs, and more than a single cycle of mechanical vibration is produced. The response of a transducer to a single, short duration pulse is called the transducer's impulse response. When the transducer has a long impulse response, there are many cycles in the pulse which leads to a long spatial pulse length and degraded axial resolution. With a short impulse response, there are fewer cycles in the pulse and improved axial resolution. Ideally, we would have perfect control of the pulse parameters to make it as short as desired when resolution is critical.

Figure 6 demonstrates some actual pulse responses for two different transducer designs.

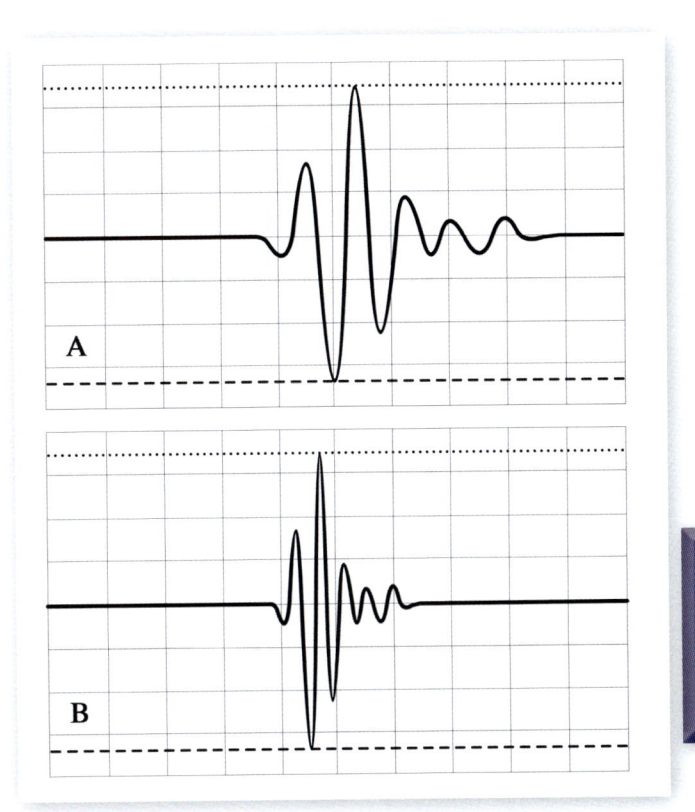

Fig. 6 Pulse response for a 2 MHz (A) and a 4 MHz (B) transducer

You will notice that both of these transducers produce more than one cycle when driven with a single transmit pulse (impulse). You will also notice that the pulse actually grows in amplitude and then decays over time. In the first case (A), the period is 0.5 μsec, so the operating frequency is close to 2 MHz. In the second case (B) the period is approximately 0.25 μsec, so the operating frequency is close to 4 MHz.

KEY CONCEPT

How a crystal responds to a single, short electrical impulse is referred to as the crystal's impulse response. Since there is a natural resonance, the impulse response generally has more than one cycle, increasing the spatial pulse length which results in degraded axial resolution.

5. Beam Characteristics with a Simple, Single Disc Transducer

5.1 Simple, Single, Disc Transducers

Now that we understand the basic principles, theory, and components of a transducer, we can assess the "beam characteristics" produced by a simple transducer. The simple single disc shaped transducer was the first transducer produced and used in ultrasound. Transducers with this simple design are still in use today. Whereas many transducer designs are now much more complex – with multiple elements, all of the concepts discussed for the simpler design are instructive in developing the foundation for understanding the more complex designs.

Physical Dimensions of the Transducer

First, we must identify the physical dimensions of the transducer. For the simple, round transducer there are clearly two important geometric parameters, the diameter (D), and the thickness (t).

- The diameter plays a major role in determining the beamwidth.
- The thickness plays a role in determining the transducer operating frequency for piezoelectric transducers.

You must make certain to not confuse these two parameters as each affects very different aspects of the sound beam.

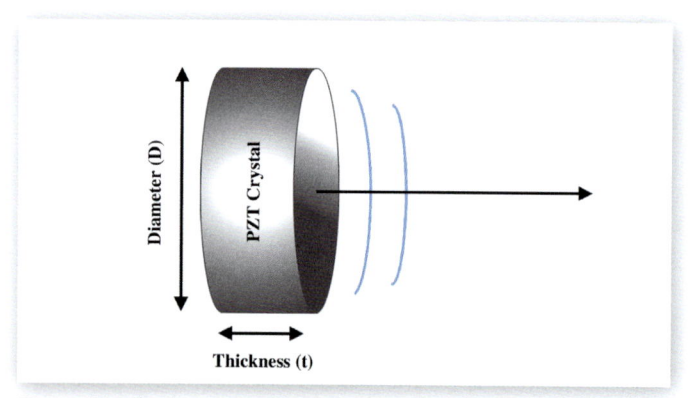

Fig. 7 **Single disc crystal dimensions**

The Beam Shape

The dimensions of the beam, or beam shape, is basically the region in the patient through which the sound wave propagates. As a result, you will notice that quite frequently, with respect to ultrasound waves traveling, you will see the word "beam" used interchangeably with the idea of a traveling wave over time. For example:

"As the wave travels through the body, there is more attenuation at deeper depths."

or

"As the beam travels through the body, there is greater attenuation at deeper depths."

Both of these sentences express the same idea, using different terminology. To be precise, the beam is the path the wave travels, whereas the wave is the energy which is traveling.

CW and Beam Shape

With continuous wave, the beam is continuous and the beam shape can be visualized all at one time like a beam of light from a flashlight (see *Figure 8*). The "beam" begins as the width of the transducer converges to a narrower region and then diverges. As long as the flashlight is left on, the beam retains this consistent shape.

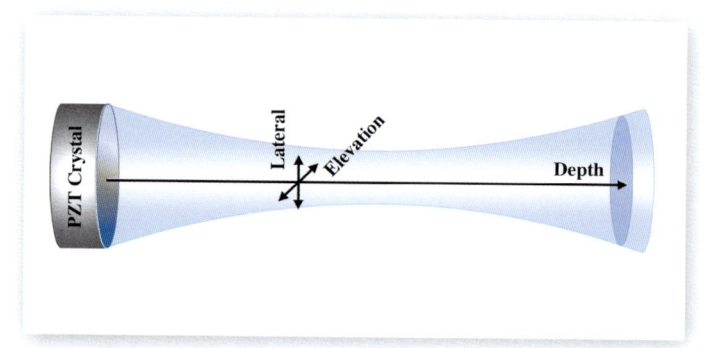

Fig. 8 **Beam shape**

PW and Beam Shape

It is generally easier to understand the dimensions of a continuous wave beam than dimensions of a pulsed wave beam. Unlike CW, the beam shape is not "present" all the time in pulsed wave. For pulsed wave, the beam shape represents the general shape that is created as the pulse travels over time. The "beam" emanates from the transducer face as the width of the transducer (T_1 in *Figure 9*). If you were to take a "snapshot" a short period of time later (T_2), the wave pulse will obviously have traveled to a deeper depth, and the beam will physically cover a slightly narrower area (converging). A little later in time (T_3), the wave would again have traveled deeper, and the beam would continue to converge until it reaches the minimum width. Later still in time (T_4), the beam will start to diverge, and continue to diverge over time (T_N).

represents the direction in which the compression and rarefaction propagate. For pulsed wave, the depth represents the direction in which the pulse length is measured.

Beamwidth: Lateral (azimuthal, side-by-side, transverse, angular)

For a round crystal, the beamwidth is symmetric in both planes (lateral and elevation). As we will see for non-symmetric crystals, the beamwidth will be different in the lateral and elevation planes. For now, since both dimensions are equal with a round crystal, we will just refer to the lateral dimension. Unfortunately, just as there are many different terms referring to the depth of the beam, there are many terms which refer to the lateral dimension of the beam, such as: azimuthal, side-by-side, transverse, and angular. Fortunately, the term most commonly used is "lateral".

5.3 The Natural Focus

As we have seen from the beamwidth pictures, *Figures 8* and *9*, the beam converges at a specific depth and then diverges from this specific depth. The depth at which the beam reaches its narrowest beamwidth is called the "natural focus." The region shallower than the natural focus is referred to as the near field, near zone, or the Fresnel zone. The region deeper than the natural focus is referred to as the far field, the far zone, or the Fraunhofer zone.

These simple disc transducers are often referred to as "unfocused," since nothing has been added to affect the "natural focus" of the transducer. Be careful not to confuse the concept of an "unfocused transducer" with the absence of a natural focus. Even the beam pattern for an "unfocused" transducer naturally converges and then diverges from the point referred to here as the natural focus. A focused transducer is a transducer in which a technique has been employed to either move or allow the focus to be moved to a depth other than the natural focus.

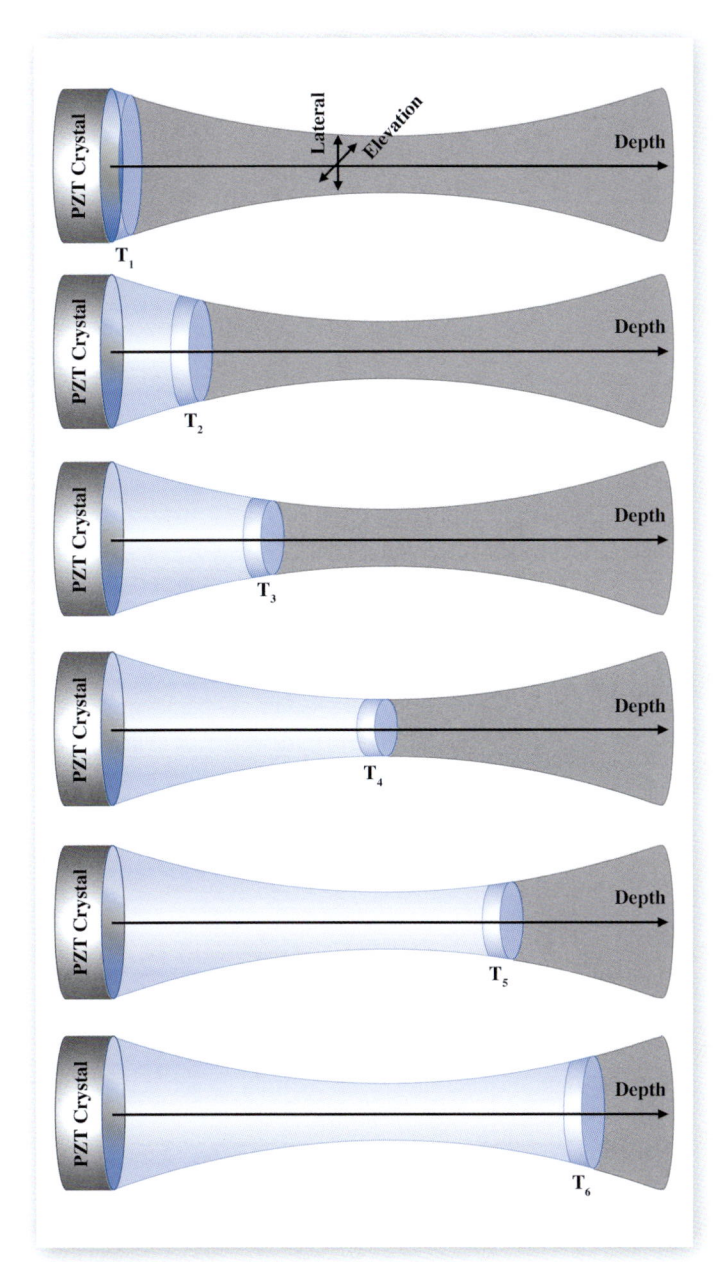

Fig. 9 **Beam shape swept over time in PW**

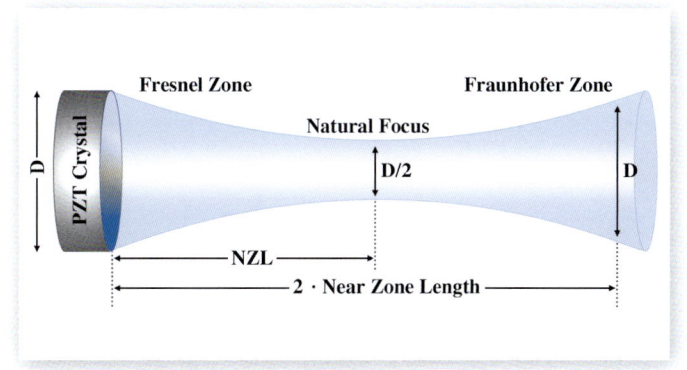

Fig. 10 **Basic beam characteristics**

5.2 The Beam Parameters

Depth (axial, longitudinal, radial, range)

The direction of a beam away from the transducer is referred to as the axis of the beam, the depth direction, the longitudinal direction, or the radial direction. Regardless of the terminology used, this dimension is the direction in which the wave is propagating (continuous wave or pulsed wave). As a longitudinal wave, the depth

For the unfocused transducer, notice that the beamwidth is approximately ½ the crystal diameter at the focus. Also notice the symmetry of the beam. At twice the focal depth, the beam returns to approximately the same diameter as the crystal diameter. As the depth increases the beam continues to diverge.

$$\text{Beamwidth} = D/2 \text{ at the focus}$$

$$\text{Beamwidth} = D \text{ at } 2 * \text{focal length}$$

Note: The beam profiles drawn are extremely simplified from reality. In reality, the beams are not neatly defined by distinct boundaries within which wave energy exists, and outside of which no energy exists. Furthermore, the near field of the beam is extremely complex, with rapidly varying pressures. Therefore, these simplified drawings are to serve as a tool to help explain general principles, and not as absolute truths. In Level 2, a more realistic beam profile is given.

5.4 Varying the depth of the Natural Focus

There are two parameters which principally affect the depth of the natural focus, the operating frequency and the diameter of the crystal. Somewhat counter-intuitively, a higher frequency produces a deeper focus for a fixed crystal diameter. A larger diameter crystal, for a fixed operating frequency also increases the depth of the natural focus. The following diagram depicts how a larger crystal produces a deeper focus (for the same operating frequency).

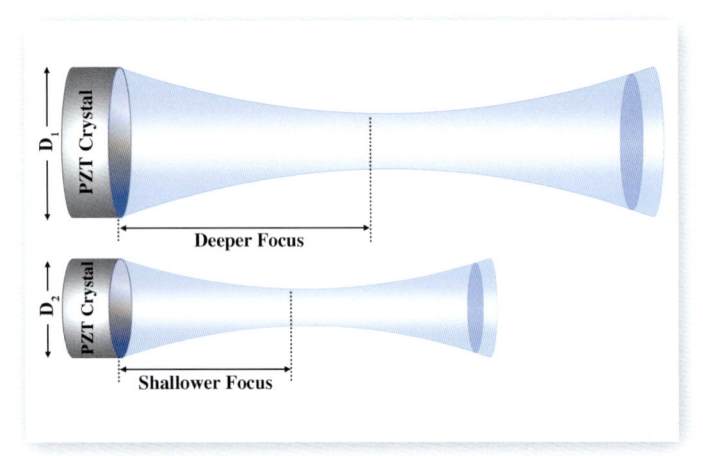

Fig. 11 A larger diameter results in a deeper focus (for the same operating frequency)

5.5 Depth of Focus (Focal Depth) and Equation

As we have just learned, the distance from the surface of the transducer to the natural focus is called the "focal depth" or the "Near Zone Length" (NZL).

The Near Zone Length is given by the equation:

$$NZL = \frac{D^2}{4\lambda}$$

In general, students learn the above equation in a slightly modified form. The reason for modifying this equation is that through a substitution and an assumption about the medium, the equation can be rewritten in a form that can be calculated in your head. We will transform this equation as follows:

Recall:

$$f * \lambda = c \Rightarrow \lambda = \frac{c}{f}$$

Substituting yields:

$$NZL = \frac{D^2}{4\left(\frac{c}{f}\right)} = \frac{D^2 f}{4c}$$

If we assume $c = 1540$ m/sec then:

$$NZL = \frac{D^2 f}{4c} = \frac{D^2 f}{4 \times 1540 \frac{m}{sec}} = \frac{D^2 f}{6160 \frac{m}{sec}} \approx \frac{D^2 f}{6000 \frac{m}{sec}}$$

Now if we force the units for the frequency to be in MHz and the units for the crystal diameter to be in mm, we will be able to ignore the units in the numerator since a milli squared is the reciprocal of a mega, or: $(10^{-3})^2 \times 10^6 = 1$.

This allows us to rewrite the equation as

$$NZL \approx \frac{D^2 \,(mm) \bullet f_0 \,(MHz)}{6000 \, m}.$$

Now if we multiply both sides by 10^{-3}, or milli we get:

$$NZL \,(mm) \approx \frac{D^2 \,(mm) \bullet f_0 \,(MHz)}{6}.$$

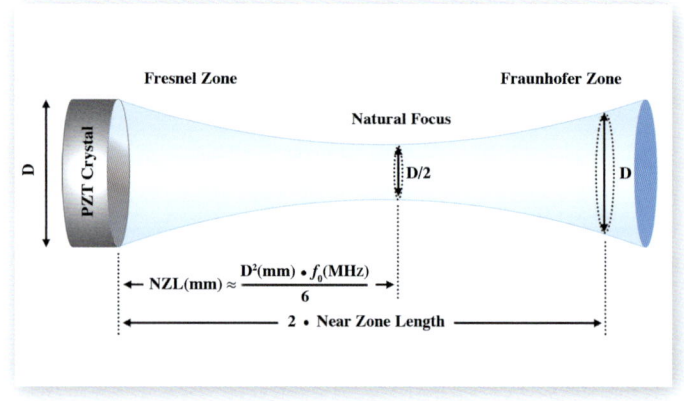

Fig. 12 Near Zone Length approximation

Using the Modified Equation

Perhaps the best way to illustrate how to apply the modified equation is through example.

◊ *Example:*
At what depth would the natural focus be for a 3 MHz transducer with a diameter of 1 cm?

The first step is to convert the diameter from cm to mm, since the modified form requires the diameter to be written as mm. In Chapter 1, we learned how to convert between units. Since mm is a smaller unit than cm, the number in front of mm must be larger than 1. Between mm and cm there is one decimal shift. Therefore, we must move the decimal point 1 place to make the number larger or, 1 cm = 10 mm.

Since the operating frequency is already in MHz, no conversion is necessary.

Plugging these numbers into the equation yields:

$$NZL\ (mm) \approx \frac{D^2 f}{6} = \frac{10^2 \times 3}{6} = 50\ mm = 5.0\ cm.$$

Notice that once the diameter and frequency are converted to the appropriate form, the units can be ignored. You should also note that this problem could be solved by using the unmodified equation as follows:

$$NZL = \frac{D^2}{4\lambda} = \frac{D^2}{\left(4\frac{c}{f}\right)} = \frac{D^2 f}{4 \times 1540 \frac{m}{sec}}$$

$$= \frac{(1\ cm)^2 \times 3\ MHz}{6160 \frac{m}{sec}} = \frac{0.0001\ m^2 \times 3\ MHz}{6160 \frac{m}{sec}}$$

$$= 0.0487\ m = 48.7\ mm = 4.87\ cm.$$

This example demonstrates how the modified form of the equation simplifies the calculation. Because this modified form assumed a propagation velocity of 1540 m/sec, it can only be appropriately applied in soft tissue.

Effect of Aperture on NZL

From the equation $NZL\ (mm) \approx \frac{D^2\ (mm) \cdot f_0\ (MHz)}{6}$ we know that the NZL is proportional to the square of the diameter, or $NZL \propto D^2$.

As demonstrated in the example below, if the diameter of one crystal is twice the diameter of the second crystal, the corresponding near zone length will be four times greater. In other words, by increasing the diameter by a factor of 2, the depth of the natural focus increases by a factor of 4.

When you compare the two different beams from the two different crystals from *Figure 13*, you should notice that the smaller crystal achieves a much narrower beam at shallower depths. You should also notice that the larger crystal achieves not only a significantly deeper focus, but also a narrower beam at relatively deeper depths. As we will learn in the upcoming sections, small diameter crystals are good for superficial imaging, and large diameter crystals are better for deeper imaging.

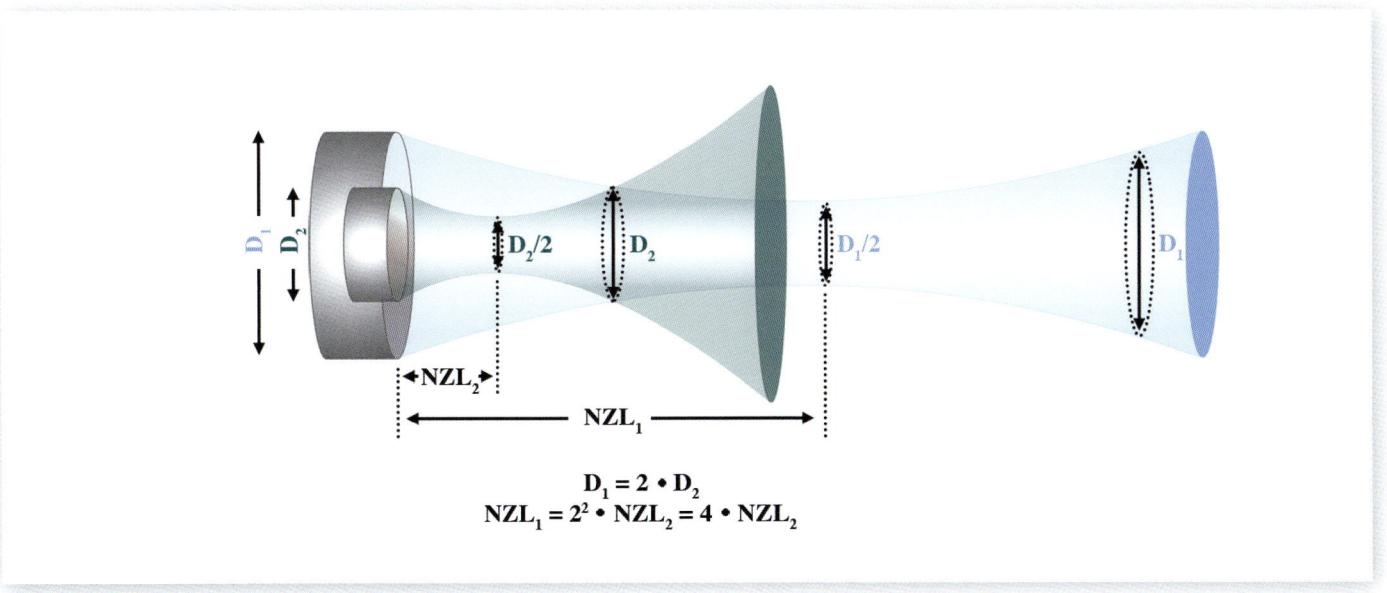

$$D_1 = 2 \cdot D_2$$
$$NZL_1 = 2^2 \cdot NZL_2 = 4 \cdot NZL_2$$

Fig. 13 **Effect of diameter on focal depth**

Effect of Frequency on NZL

From the equation:

$$NZL(mm) \bullet \frac{D^2(mm) \bullet f_0(MHz)}{6}$$

we know that the NZL is proportional to the operating frequency, or $NZL \propto f_0$. If the operating frequency of the second crystal is twice the operating frequency of the first crystal, the corresponding near zone length will be two times greater. In other words, by increasing the operating frequency by a factor of 2, the depth of the natural focus increases by a factor of 2, as shown in *Figure 14*.

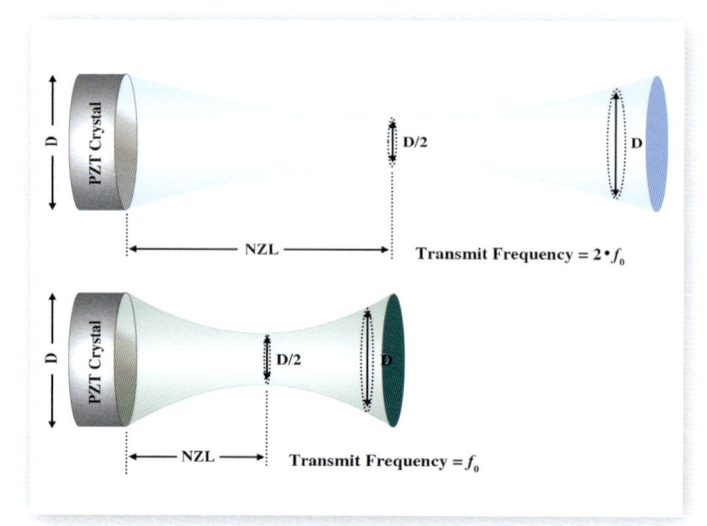

Fig. 14 **Effect of frequency on focal depth**

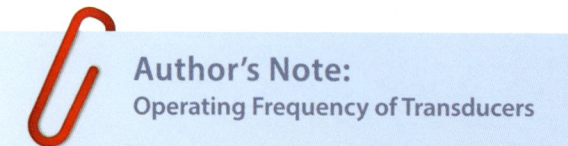

> **Author's Note:**
> **Operating Frequency of Transducers**
>
> Although a deeper focal depth results from using a higher operating frequency, the use of higher frequency also results in increased attenuation. To improve penetration, attenuation through absorption must be minimized. Therefore, because of the increased attenuation, transducers are generally designed with lower operating frequencies, and larger diameters instead.

5.6 Depth of Field (Focal Region)

The depth of field, also referred to as the focal region, refers to the general region above and below the focus where the beam is approximately the same width. For beams that converge and diverge quickly, there is a very short (or shallow) depth of field. For beams that converge and diverge slowly, there is a very broad (or deep) depth of field. *Figure 15* demonstrates the difference between a shallow and broad depth of field.

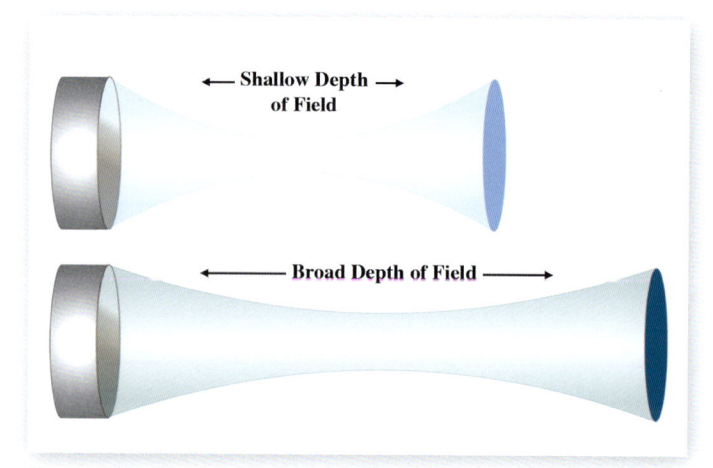

Fig. 15 **Shallow and broad depth of field**

Just as shorter pulse lengths produce better axial resolution, narrower beams produce better lateral resolution. When the depth of field is shallow, there is a very small range over which the intensity and lateral resolution remain relatively constant. When the depth of field is broad, there is a much longer region over which the lateral resolution and the intensity (ignoring attenuation affects) remain relatively constant.

The concept of depth of field is often compared with taking pictures with a camera. If a close-up picture is taken, the camera aperture will be set very small, yielding a very shallow focus with a very short depth of field. The result is a very "narrow beam" which produces extremely high resolution for objects at, or very near to the focal depth. However, since the beam converges and diverges very quickly, any objects that are shallower or deeper than the focus tend to be blurred. Think about a picture you have seen such as a bee in a field of flowers, or a close-up of an individual in a crowd of people in which the close object shows incredible detail, whereas everything in the background is blurry. In comparison, if the focus is set much deeper, the detail resolution is certainly lost, but objects at many different depths are now in focus.

This same concept applies in ultrasound. If there is a very shallow depth of field, only a very short depth range will have very good lateral resolution.

5.7 True Beam Shapes

More than once, we have made reference to the fact that the beam profiles are highly simplified. The following beam profile (*Figure 16*) is illustrative of the complexity of a true beam.

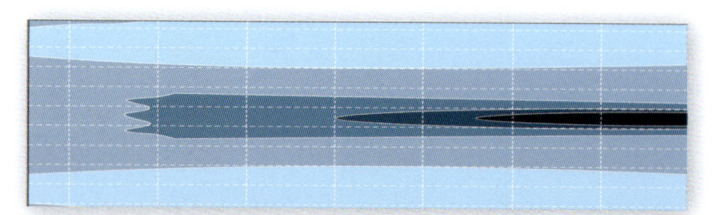

Fig. 16 **Actual beamplot: lighter shades equal higher intensities**

5.8 Changing Intensity from Beam Convergence and Divergence

Recall in Chapter 2 that the beam intensity was defined as the power divided by the beam area. In the most simplistic world, from this definition, the highest intensity of the beam would always exist at the focus. This should make sense since the focus is the region of the beam where the area is the narrowest. Since the intensity is inversely related to the beam area, a smaller area results in a higher intensity.

In reality, this analysis is overly simple and most frequently incorrect. There are two reasons why this analysis is not correct:

- This analysis incorrectly presumes that there is no change in power with depth (ignores attenuation effects).
- This analysis relies on the overly simple beam models that we have drawn in order to make discussion of beams easier and the topic less threatening.

A better analysis would take both of these facts into account leading to the conclusion that the highest intensity must be either at the focus or shallower than the focus, and usually shallower than the focus. We know that realistically there will always be attenuation when the beam is propagating through the body. Therefore, the power is not constant at each depth, but rather decreasing with depth. Therefore, the two parameters that determine the intensity are working in opposite directions in the near field. From an area standpoint, the intensity is increasing as the beam is converging. From a power standpoint, the intensity is decreasing as the depth is increasing. Which of these two parameters dominates depends on the rate of convergence in comparison with the rate of attenuation.

Also, we cannot ignore the fact that the beam is not such a simple, symmetric, well-defined shape with constant behavior everywhere within, especially in the near field. In the near field, there are all sorts of beam intensity variations as constructive and destructive interferences occur.

KEY CONCEPT

The simplest beam shapes result from symmetric, round crystals. Although many transducer elements are now rectangular or part of an array, discussing the beam characteristics of the simple round disc helps develop an understanding for the more complex cases. For an "unfocused" crystal, the beam naturally starts out the dimension of a simple crystal and then narrows in the near field (also called the Fresnel zone) to a point called the natural focus. Past the natural focus the beam diverges creating what is called the far field or Fraunhofer zone. A deeper natural focus occurs when the operating frequency is increased and/or when the crystal diameter is increased.

Why This Point Matters:

If you are asked where the highest intensity occurs on a board exam, you must assume the oversimplified approach and answer "at the focus". However, clinically, you should realize that this is incorrect. The reason why this fact matters is twofold:

1. *Frequently sonographers make the mistake of not moving the transmit focus deeper for difficult-to-image patients, leading to poor signal-to-noise and decreased clinical value.*

    Unlike the near field, in the far field, both the beam dimension and the power are working to change the intensity in the same direction. In the far field, the beam is continuously diverging, decreasing the beam intensity. Also, as the depth increases, there is more attenuation, again making the beam less intense. The result is clear, in the far field, the beam intensity drops precipitously. Therefore, when the focus is left too shallow, significant signal is lost. This fact is often overlooked by many sonographers.

2. *There are times when putting the transmit focus a little deeper than the actual region of interest will improve signal strength in the region of interest.*

    There are two reasons why this approach might slightly improve sensitivity. First, the highest intensity is almost always a little shallower than the focus. Second, when you place the focus deeper, the system is usually allowed to increase the maximum transmit power. This increase is allowed since the beam is presumed to be not as focused at the shallower depths, which is most likely where the power restriction occurs. This technique still may not result in beautiful images for the more "difficult-to-image" patients but might make the difference between a diagnostic and non-diagnostic scan.

Note that some systems do not have a transmit focus. The reason for this will be discussed later in this chapter.

> **KEY CONCEPT**
>
> Although exam questions often state that the highest intensity is at the focus, the reality is that the highest intensity of a beam is generally shallower than the focus. In the near field, there are two parameters working against each other. As the beam narrows, the power is distributed over a smaller area, serving to increase the intensity. However, attenuation decreases the power with depth, serving to decrease the intensity. Therefore, the highest intensity is generally somewhere between the skin where the power is the highest, and the focus, where the area is the smallest. Practically speaking, when penetration is critical, it is best to place the focus slightly lower than the region of interest to achieve optimal sensitivity.

6. Limitations of the Simple Crystal

Let's consider what some of the problems and limitations would be if we tried to use the simple crystal just described as a transducer on a patient.

First, if this transducer were to be used directly on a patient with no other modifications, it would not function at all. The acoustic impedance of a crystal such as PZT is extremely high relative to tissue. Recall from Chapter 3, a large acoustic impedance mismatch results in a large reflection and very little transmission. When the large reflection occurs at the transducer/patient interface, there is little energy coupled into and out of the patient. The result would be virtually no penetration. Clearly, the transducer design must be modified to ameliorate this situation.

Second, as demonstrated in Section 4, the impulse response of a simple crystal may have many cycles, leading to a long spatial pulse length and poor axial resolution. Without some modification, the simple crystal we have discussed will clearly have suboptimal axial resolution.

Third, we have just learned that the focus of the simple transducer is determined by the operating frequency and by the crystal diameter. What if the natural focus is not at the desired depth? With the current specified design there is no way to affect the focus. There are at least two major reasons why having a "fixed" focus can be detrimental. As we will learn later in this chapter, the lateral and elevation resolution are determined by the beamwidth; the wider the beamwidth, the worse the resolution. Since the beam reaches a minimum width at the focus, the best lateral resolution occurs at the lateral focus. Similarly, the best elevation resolution occurs at the elevation focus.

The second reason is related to the beam intensity. As we learned in Chapter 3, the beam intensity is inversely proportional to the beamwidth. As the beamwidth increases, the intensity decreases. If the beam intensity decreases, there is less reflected signal power. Eventually the signals will be too weak to be detected. As a result, a deeper focus allows for better penetration. Clearly, the ability to control focus is desirable for improved imaging.

Fourth, the simple transducer described is only capable of imaging straight ahead. In essence, there is no way of visualizing anything which is not directly under the transducer face. With this design, the only way a region of the body can be scanned is to physically move the transducer over the region of interest. This limitation makes it very difficult to interpret complex geometries and disease states. Clearly, it is highly desirable to have a mechanism which allows our beam to be "steered" in different directions so that a scan can be created.

The next three sections discuss methodologies to address the issues of impedance mismatch, poor impulse response, and a simple method to set a fixed focus at a depth shallower than the natural focus. As will be discovered in Level 2, the desire to have a variable focus and the ability to steer to create an image will together drive the evolution of transducer technology.

> **KEY CONCEPT**
>
> A simple crystal has many limitations including a very high acoustic impedance (resulting in poor signal coupling into and out of the patient), a fixed focal depth, potentially a long spatial pulse length (many cycles in the impulse response), and no ability to steer other than straight ahead. These limitations lead to more complex transducer designs as described in the upcoming sections.

7. Minimizing the Acoustic Impedance Mismatch

7.1 High Impedance Piezoceramics

Recall that the acoustic impedance of a material is given by the equation $Z = \rho * c$. For any piezoceramic crystal both the density and the propagation velocity will be very high, hence, the acoustic impedance will be extremely high. In comparison, tissue has a much lower density and a significantly lower propagation velocity. As a result, the impedance of tissue is significantly lower. For example, the acoustic impedance of most forms of PZT is greater than 35 MRayls, while the acoustic impedance of tissue is typically less than 2 MRayls. Since the amount of reflection is proportional to this mismatch, we clearly need to find another manner in which to couple the energy from the crystal into the patient.

7.2 Matching Layer

A matching layer is used to minimize the acoustic impedance mismatch between the high impedance of the transducer crystal and the low impedance of the tissue. In essence, the matching layer is a thin layer of material attached to the front crystal of the transducer. The material is chosen such that it has an acoustic impedance lower than that of the crystal, and higher than that of the tissue. As the sound propagates from the crystal to the matching layer, there is more transmission (i.e., less reflection) than if the interface had been directly to tissue. Then, as the sound propagates from the matching layer to the tissue, there is still more transmission because of the closer impedance match. (See Chapter 3: Section 9.4 for matching layer calculations.) Note that this technique also helps minimize the reflection back into the body of the returning echoes.

Many transducer designs now use multiple matching layers. Obviously each successive matching layer (in the direction from the crystal towards the patient) has a lower impedance so as to better match the crystal impedance to the tissue impedance.

7.3 Quarter Wavelength Thickness

Since both interfaces of the matching layer represent relatively large acoustic impedance mismatches, a significant percentage of reflection can occur. Additionally, a fair amount of this energy will ping back and forth between the surfaces creating multiple echoes (reverberation artifact) of the matching layer itself. If these reverberations are not somehow canceled, the image will be full of bright white reverberation echoes. Therefore, unless a method to overcome this problem is employed, by decreasing the inefficient coupling, we have introduced a new problem, perhaps just as insidious.

By controlling the thickness of the matching layer, this reverberation problem can be significantly reduced. The ideal thickness for a conventional matching layer scheme is quarter wavelength. In other words, the matching layer should have the thickness of a quarter of the wavelength of the operating frequency. The reason for this thickness is based on the idea of constructive and destructive interference.

Since a full wavelength is 360 degrees, a quarter wavelength represents 90 degrees. If the thickness of the matching layer is quarter wavelength, the wave at the far surface of the matching layer (the patient side) will be 90 degrees out of phase with the wave at the first surface (interface between the crystal and matching layer). On its return path back from the far interface, the wave is delayed another 90 degrees. Therefore, when the matching layer thickness is quarter wavelength, the reflection which occurs from the patient side of the matching layer is out of phase by half a wavelength with the reflection which occurs at the interface between the crystal and the matching layer. As we learned in Chapter 2: Waves, waves which are out of phase by half a wavelength (180°) add destructively and cancel. This is the ideal situation since we clearly want any reflection from the surfaces of the matching layer to cancel out. This destructive interference is illustrated in *Figure 17*.

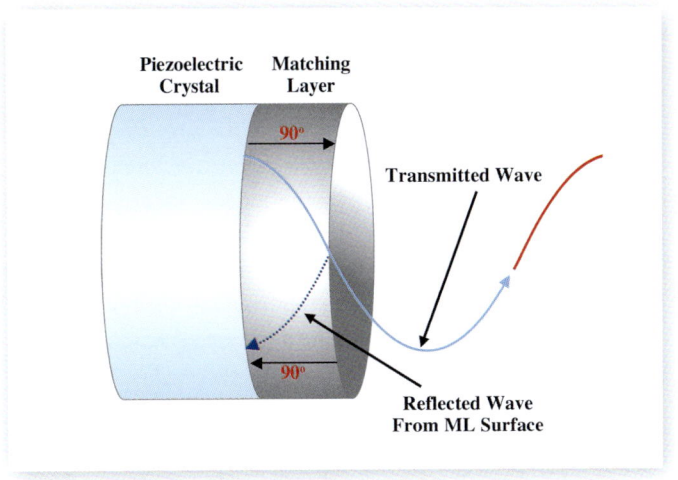

Fig. 17 Cancellation of wave reflection for $\frac{\lambda}{4}$ matching layer

7.4 Composites with Lower Acoustic Impedances

Many of the composite materials are now designed to have much lower acoustic impedances than PZT, improving the acoustic coupling factor. As discussed earlier, other piezoelectric materials that had lower impedances than PZT and hence, better matched to tissue, also had much lower efficiency. As a result, even though these materials had less of an acoustic impedance mismatch with tissue, they were just not sensitive enough to be used. The use of polymers with much lower impedances in composite designs reduces the severity of the mismatch between the crystal and the patient. This does not mean that matching layers are still not needed; it means that since smaller steps exist, better matching can be produced.

CHECKPOINT: Exam Tip

A matching layer is a thin layer (ideally a quarter wavelength thick) with an impedance lower than that of the piezoelectric crystal but higher than that of the tissue. In essence, a matching layer behaves like stairs between two floors of a building. Without stairs, it is difficult to safely pass through the large height differential between the upper and a lower floors. Similarly, a matching layer "reduces" the acoustic impedance mismatch between the high impedance crystal and the low impedance tissue, improving the transmission efficiency into and out of the patient. Newer composite materials tend to have better transmission efficiency (coupling factor) than PZT, as PZT intrinsically has a very high acoustic impedance.

8. 2D Image Planes

Even though we refer to an image as two-dimensional, there are really three dimensions (planes) in the scan. The three corresponding imaging planes are axial, lateral, and elevation as pictured below. The elevation plane has been, in general, the "forgotten plane" since, until 3D imaging, there has been no direct visualization of the elevation plane. With greater adoption of 3D imaging, the elevation plane is beginning to receive more consideration. Many imaging mistakes are made because people neglect the elevation plane.

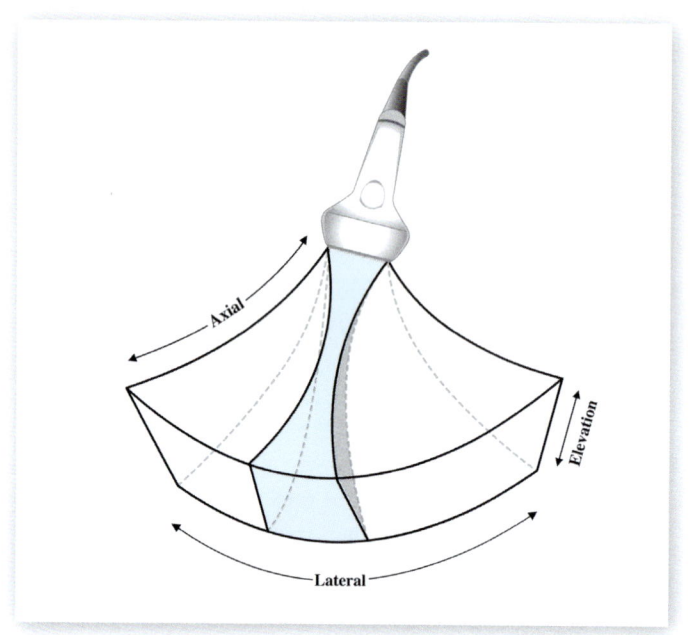

Fig. 18 **Scan dimensions**

There are multiple names used to refer to these imaging planes, especially the axial and lateral planes.

Lateral:
- azimuthal
- side-by-side
- transverse
- angular

Axial:
- radial
- depth
- longitudinal
- range

Elevation:
- slice thickness

9. Detail Resolution

9.1 General

Detail resolution refers to the ability to resolve physical tissue characteristics in each of the three physical dimensions (lateral, axial, and elevation). With respect to detail resolution, there are really two different considerations. The first consideration is whether or not two neighboring structures can be differentiated. For example, imagine imaging two side-by-side structures separated by a small distance. Inadequate lateral resolution would result in the presentation of one large structure instead of two side-by-side smaller structures. This concern regarding resolution is the more obvious consideration.

When discussing resolution, most people think only of cases this extreme, not realizing the second important consideration. It is important to realize that ultrasound generally has much higher requirements than just merely identifying structures as distinct from one another. Frequently, as occurs when measuring valve leaflets, nuchal fold thickness, intima media thickness (IMT), etc., the accuracy of the measurement also matters. When the accuracy of a detail measurement is limited by the beam characteristic(s), resolution is considered suboptimal. In our discussions of the three different resolutions which collectively comprise the broader category of "detail" resolution you should consider not only the extreme limit (as specified by the equations) but also the practical consideration of associated measurement errors.

9.2 Axial Resolution

Definition
Axial resolution is defined as the ability to distinguish between two structures in the axial (longitudinal, radial, depth, or range) dimension. The axial resolution specifies the smallest physical measurement possible along the axis of the beam. When the axial resolution is inadequate, measurements made along the beam axis appear larger than reality.

Determining the Axial Resolution Limit
Recall that Chapter 4 began with a discussion on "range" resolution. In fact, the reason for creating a pulsed wave modality was to overcome the inability to resolve structures in depth in the continuous mode. If you recall, we demonstrated that a shorter spatial pulse length resulted in better resolution. We will now review those results with the intention of relating the pulse requirement with transducer design and construction.

Consider what happens when a transmit pulse encounters two objects separated in depth by a distance of "x". To distinguish the two separate objects, the reflected echoes from the first and second objects must be distinct in time and must not connect. For the echoes to connect, the echo from the second object would have to return while the pulse train was still insonifying the first object. This can only happen if the pulse train length (SPL) is twice as long as the separation between the two objects. In other words, the roundtrip effect helps to separate the echoes between objects, hence, the axial resolution is half the spatial pulse length. (Remember that a smaller number is always better for resolution since a smaller number implies the ability to resolve structures which are closer together.)

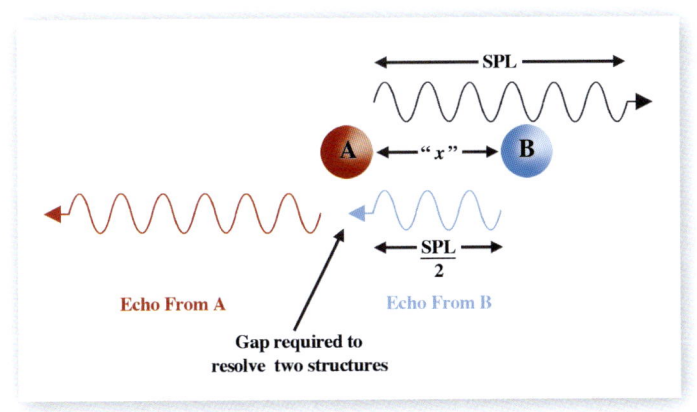

Fig. 19 **Axial resolution**

The axial resolution is determined by the spatial pulse length:

$$\text{Axial Resolution} = \frac{\text{Spatial Pulse Length}}{2}.$$

Backing Material

In Chapter 4 we learned that the spatial pulse length is determined by both the number of cycles within the pulse and the wavelength. We know that the wavelength is inversely proportional to the operating frequency. As a result, using a higher operating frequency results in better axial resolution. However, increasing the frequency to achieve better axial resolution is often not an option because of the required imaging depth (the size of the patient).

The other method of shortening the spatial pulse length (so as to improve the axial resolution) is to decrease the number of cycles within the pulse. A backing material is used to shorten the ring time of a transducer, thereby decreasing the number of cycles within the pulse. Fewer cycles within the pulse decreases the spatial pulse length. Also, as an aside, recall that fewer cycles within a pulse decreases the pulse duration and thereby increases the bandwidth.

The backing material shortens the ring time by absorbing some of the ring energy. For piezoelectric transducers, the backing material generally is made from a powdered tungsten mixed into an epoxy resin. By changing the composition and thickness of the backing material, various degrees of damping can be achieved. A higher damping leads to a shorter pulse, improving the axial resolution. However, since some of the energy is absorbed into the backing material, the efficiency of the transducer decreases. As a result, the quality factor of the transducer is said to decrease. Recall that the quality factor is the reciprocal of the fractional bandwidth as defined in Chapter 4.

> **CHECKPOINT: Exam Tip**
>
> The axial resolution limit is approximately equal to half of the spatial pulse length (SPL). Shorter SPL's result in better axial resolution. A shorter SPL results from a shorter wavelength (high operating frequency) and fewer cycles in the pulse. To reduce the number of cycles in the pulse a backing (damping) material is used. The backing material absorbs some of the energy decreasing the ring time, but also decreasing the amplitude thereby decreasing the transducer quality factor.

9.3 Lateral Resolution

Definition

Lateral resolution is defined as the ability to resolve two structures in the lateral dimension (side by side, angular, transverse, or azimuthal). For a specific depth, the lateral resolution specifies the smallest physical measurement possible in the lateral, or side-by-side, aspect of the image. Since the beamwidth varies with depth, the lateral resolution also varies with depth.

Determining the Lateral Resolution Limit

Consider what happens if a beam is wide enough so that two side-by-side structures are insonified simultaneously. The echoes from both objects add together and there is no way of distinguishing between the two objects, as shown in the figure below. In contrast, if the beam is narrower than the separation between the two objects, there is no way both objects could ever reflect from the same beam, and therefore no way that the two objects could ever mistakenly appear as one structure.

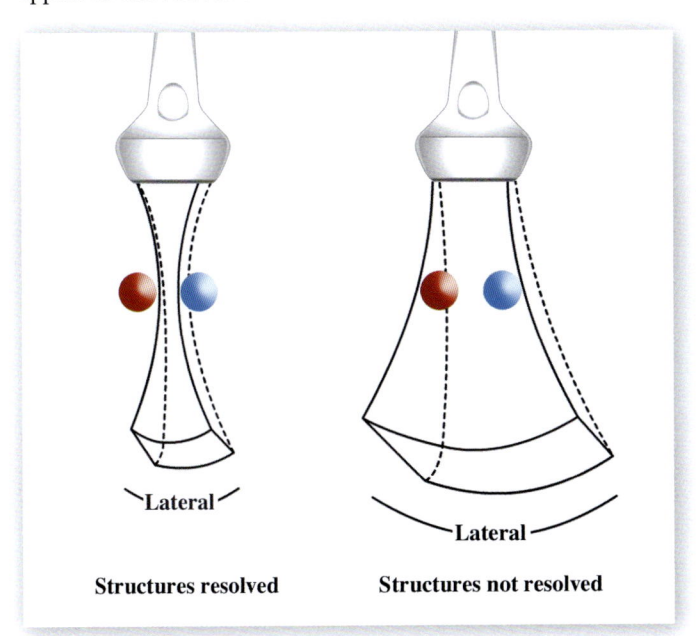

Fig. 20 **Lateral resolution and lateral beamwidth**

From these observations, it is evident that the best lateral resolution occurs with narrower beams and that the lateral resolution is defined by the beamwidth.

Lateral resolution = Lateral beamwidth

Changing the Focus

For many applications the natural focus of a transducer is inadequate or suboptimal. Besides changing the physical size of a crystal to affect the beam diameter, five different focusing schemes have been developed and utilized, such as:

1) mirrors
2) lenses
3) curved elements
4) electronic focusing
5) retrospective gating

Of these five techniques, only four are actually frequently employed. The use of an acoustic mirror, although possible, has not been a popular technique employed in ultrasound, therefore, we will constrain ourselves to discussing the four remaining techniques. Of these four techniques, electronic focusing and retrospective gating can only be achieved when there are multiple transducer elements, referred to as an array. Therefore, electronic focusing will be discussed when we cover the topic of array transducers in Level 2 of this chapter. Retrospective gating requires the use of multiple beams and, therefore, will be discussed in Chapter 6, Part I. This leaves two techniques to consider for a simple transducer, a lens and curving the surface of the crystal itself. In reality, both of these techniques function in the same manner, with the only difference being that the lenses' approach requires the addition of another material while the curved elements' approach is created from the crystal material itself.

Lenses

The idea of an acoustic lens is quite simple. Just as occurs with optics and light waves, the sound waves can be caused to converge more quickly than would occur naturally, producing a shallower focus. Of course, if the beam focuses at a shallower depth, the beam also begins to diverge at a shallower depth. Lenses have been used extensively for ultrasound transducers for many years, and are still frequently used. However, newer crystal materials, and newer styles of transducers are reducing the need for lenses. The ability to eliminate lenses is desirable since lenses result in another acoustic impedance mismatch between the matching layer and the patient and are generally very absorptive. The result is a decrease in efficiency and potential surface heating of the transducer.

Fig. 21 **Use of lenses for focusing**

Curved Surface

Piezoelectric material generally tends to be very brittle. As such, generating a curved surface to behave like a lens is extremely challenging, and up until recently, was less commonly employed than attaching an acoustic lens. More recently, with the advent of more flexible composite materials, the curved surface approach is becoming more widely utilized. Using a curved crystal surface to act as the lens eliminates the additional acoustic impedance mismatch and the extra source of absorption that the lens introduces.

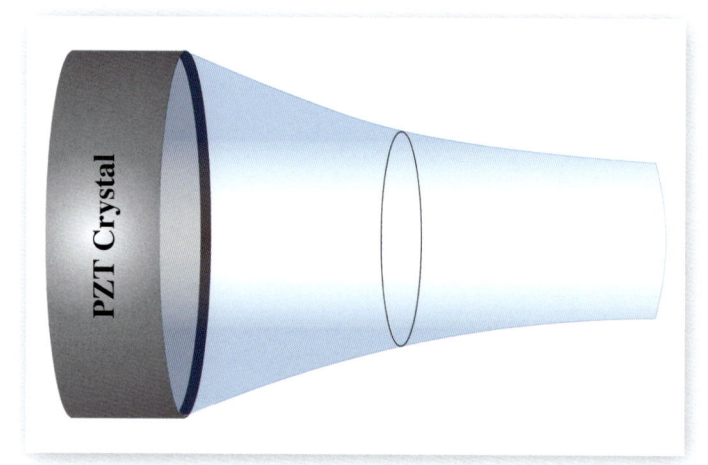

Fig. 22 **Use of curved surface for focusing**

Diffraction Limiting

Another important point is that all of the focusing techniques can only affect the transmit beamwidth in the near field relative to the natural focus. Beyond the near field, the beam is diffraction limited, and there is no way in which to get the waves to constructively and destructively interfere so as to create a narrower beam. If a deeper focus is required, the only practical solution is to use a larger transducer diameter.

> **CHECKPOINT: Exam Tip**
>
> The lateral resolution is limited by the beamwidth. Narrower beams produce better lateral resolution. For a specific beam, the best lateral resolution occurs at the lateral focus (and the best elevation resolution occurs at the elevation focus). Since the natural focus may be deeper than optimal for certain imaging scenarios, focusing techniques have been created to vary the focus in the near field (the focus cannot be varied in the far field because the beam is already diverging, or diffraction limited). Of the five techniques discussed in this chapter, the most powerful are the variable focusing techniques (electronic focusing and retrospective gating) as the other techniques are fixed focusing techniques (not under user control).

9.4 Elevation Resolution

Definition

The elevation resolution is determined by the beamwidth in the elevation plane. Just as the lateral resolution is limited by the lateral beamwidth, the elevation resolution is limited by the beamwidth in the elevation dimension. For a specific 2D imaging depth, the elevation resolution specifies the smallest physical region which will impact the image in the slice thickness (elevation) aspect of the image. Since the elevation beamwidth varies with depth, the elevation resolution also varies with depth. The elevation resolution is best where the beam is narrowest in the elevation dimension, referred to as the elevation focus.

Determining the Elevation Resolution Limit

With respect to the limit to elevation resolution, the discussion is analogous to the discussion for the lateral resolution, of course related to the beam dimensions in the elevation plane instead of the lateral plane.

Elevation Resolution = Elevation Beamwidth

Changing the Focus

The same techniques for changing the focus in Section 9.3 apply to changing the focus in the elevation direction. Practically speaking, many transducers are designed using a different technique to focus the beam laterally than to focus the beam elevationally. The specifics will become clear in the upcoming sections which detail the different design techniques for each type of transducer.

9.5 Detail Resolution Summary

Detail resolution is the collective name for the axial resolution, lateral resolution and the elevation resolution. Although the individual components have already been discussed, each is included again here so as to be put into context of a 2D scan. The following figures will serve as a review and means by which to see all three components of detail resolution simultaneously.

Lateral Resolution

Lateral resolution is defined as the ability to resolve two structures as well as the limit to measurement accuracy in the lateral dimension of an image or volume (side-by-side, angular, transverse, or azimuthal).

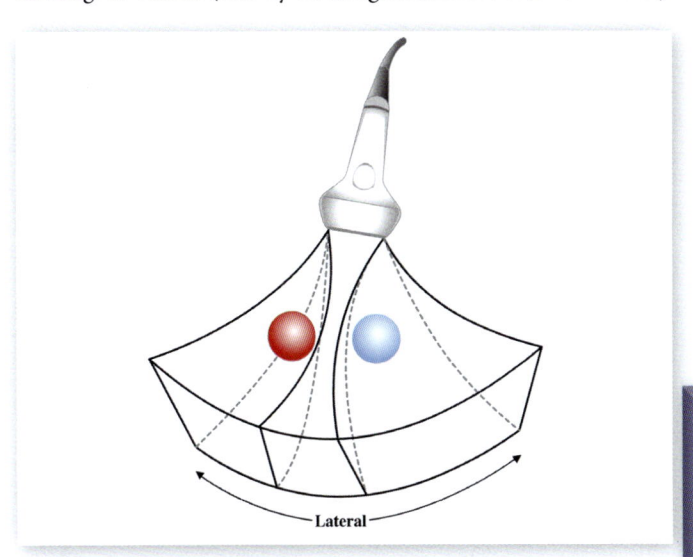

Fig. 23 **Lateral resolution**

Lateral Resolution = Lateral Beamwidth

Elevation Resolution

Elevation resolution is defined as the ability to resolve two structures as well as the limit to measurement accuracy in the elevation dimension in a 3D image. In a 2D image, the elevation resolution determines the image "slice thickness" which can result in visualizing within the image structures in front of or behind the desired imaging plane.

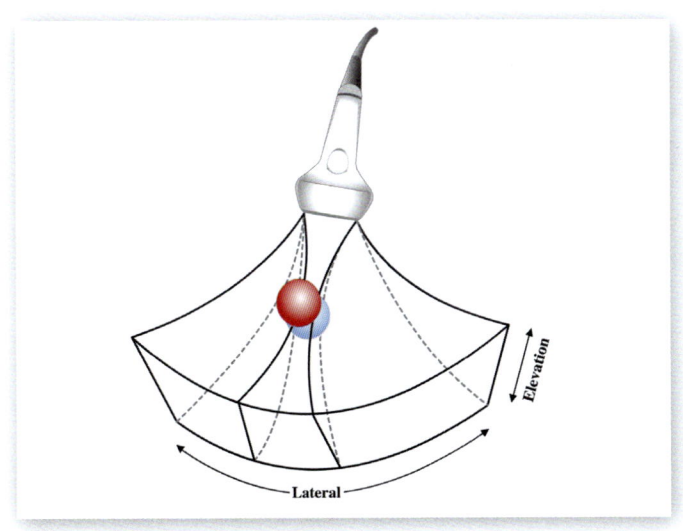

Fig. 24 **Elevation resolution**

$$\text{Elevation Resolution} = \text{Elevation Beamwidth}$$

Axial Resolution

Axial resolution is defined as the ability to resolve two structures as well as the limit to measurement accuracy in the axial dimension of an image or volume (depth, longitudinal, or range). The axial resolution is determined by the spatial pulse length. Because of the roundtrip effect, the axial resolution is a factor of 2 better than the spatial pulse length.

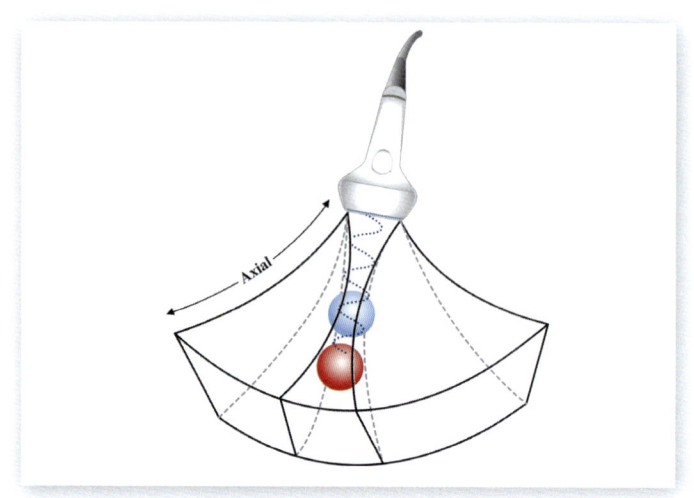

Fig. 25 **Axial resolution**

$$\text{Axial Resolution} = \frac{SPL}{2}$$

10. Transducer Block Diagrams

In the preceding sections, we have learned many requirements for a piezoelectric transducer. The following block diagram model is a valuable didactic tool. You should be able to explain the functionality of each of the components with this model.

Piezoelectric Transducer Model

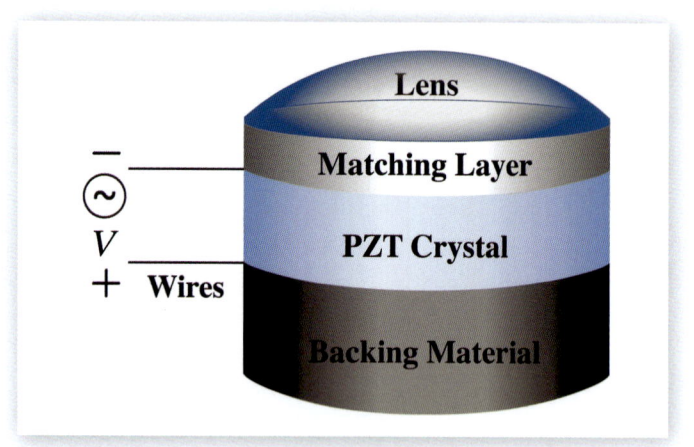

Fig. 26 **Simple transducer block diagram**

Piezoelectric crystals: Convert electropotential (voltage) into acoustic waves and acoustic waves back into voltage

Backing material: Shortens spatial pulse length improving longitudinal resolution

Matching layer: Minimizes the acoustic impedance mismatch from crystal to tissue and tissue back to crystal

Transmit/receive signal: Varying voltage which creates the transmit and is processed to create an image in receive mode

Wires: Transmit - delivers voltage to crystal Receive - delivers echo voltage to system receivers

Lens: Helps to focus beam (for 2D arrays in the elevation plane)

11. Exercises

View ONLINE Conceptual Questions

KEY CONCEPT

A deeper natural focus occurs when the operating frequency is increased (linearly proportional) and when the crystal diameter is increased (proportional to the square of the diameter). Unlike the simple single disc-shaped crystals, for multi-element transducers (arrays), the user can essentially change the "diameter" by turning on or turning off elements. This technique allows for variable focusing. Although changing the frequency can also affect the focus, this approach is less beneficial as using a higher frequency results in more attenuation which reduces sensitivity at deeper depths.

LEVEL 2: Board Level

12. Transducer Evolution Overview

In the early days of ultrasound, a single disc-shaped crystal transducer was used. These simple transducers could essentially be used in one of two ways, either to register Doppler shifts and produce corresponding audio, or to record changes in reflectivity and present a modality called A-mode. These simple transducers could only look straight ahead, and could only view a different region of the body by being manually angled. In essence, this was a one-dimensional scanning technique. Over time came the desire to have the ability to look at more than one region "simultaneously", or at two-dimensional data. The first step in the process was to create a modality called static B-scan. Although not exactly a "real-time" process, the static B-scan allowed for the building up of an image over time by manually "sliding" the transducer across the patient. The depth aspect was produced with the one-dimensional technique, and the lateral dimension of the imaging was created through the manual motion of the transducer across the patient. Relative to modern imaging, this process was extremely crude, but relative to blind imaging, this was the beginning of a revolution in medicine.

From the limits of static B-scans, came the motivation to create an "automated" system that could generate images without the sonographer physically dragging the transducer to create the second dimension of data. Mechanical transducers were produced, in which the simple crystal was now attached to the head of a motor. By wobbling the motor at various angles, an angular region of the body could now be swept over time.

As with all mechanical systems, there were many issues and limitations. Because of the many limitations, there was a desire to create a system which would not require moving parts to create a two-dimensional scan. This desire led to the creation of array transducers using a technique called phasing. An entire family of phased array transducers has been created so as to meet the specific requirements of different types of scanning. Because these arrays have multiple elements in one dimension, these transducers are referred to as 1-D arrays. For all of the unbelievable flexibility and power of 1-D arrays, there are still a few fundamental drawbacks. Specifically, 1-D arrays cannot change the focus in the elevation direction (the direction orthogonal to the lateral direction), and 1-D arrays cannot automatically acquire data in the third dimension to create three-dimensional scans.

Around the early to middle part of the nineties, the first 1.5 D array was created. This transducer had three elements in the elevation direction. In comparison with the lateral dimension which generally has 64 or more elements, three elements will certainly not give the same degree of flexibility. Therefore, even though there was more than one element in the elevation direction, it was termed a 1.5-D array. The multiple elements in the elevation direction could be turned on all together, making an effectively larger "diameter" transducer in elevation, or only the center element turned on, creating a smaller "diameter" transducer. Recalling from the equation learned earlier in this chapter, the focal depth is proportional to the square of the diameter. Therefore, this new style transducer allowed for two different focal depths in elevation.

Of course the story does not end with 1.5-D arrays. The desire to have a completely variable focus in elevation is certainly compelling, but by itself did not motivate the giant leap from 1.5-D technology to 2D array technology. Instead, the desire to have a non-manual, non-mechanical approach to creating three-dimensional imaging drove the technology. A 2D array has multiple elements in both the lateral and elevation direction, allowing for both steering and focusing virtually anywhere in a three-dimensional volume below the transducer.

Currently, most of the transducers used in ultrasound are 1-D and 2D arrays. Today, although the majority of transducers currently are based on piezoelectric crystal designs, more CMUT-based designs exist. So, while the basic transducer format is not likely to change significantly, transducer evolution will certainly continue as this technology is advanced and benefits are realized.

We will now use this technological evolutionary path as the outline for discussing the operation, utility, strengths, and weaknesses of the various transducers from each generation. As we arrive at the limits of a technology, we will use those limits to contextualize the desire for a new technology that can overcome those constraints. Therefore, as with the advancement of technology, the limitations at each stage will become the driving factor for discussing and understanding each successive generation.

13. The Pedof (Blind, Doppler Only Transducer)

These simple round transducers are still in use, most often referred to as a pedof, a pencil probe, or a blind Doppler probe.

Single Element, Blind, Pedof, Pencil, or (Doppler Only Transducer)

Fig. 27 **Pencil probe beam**

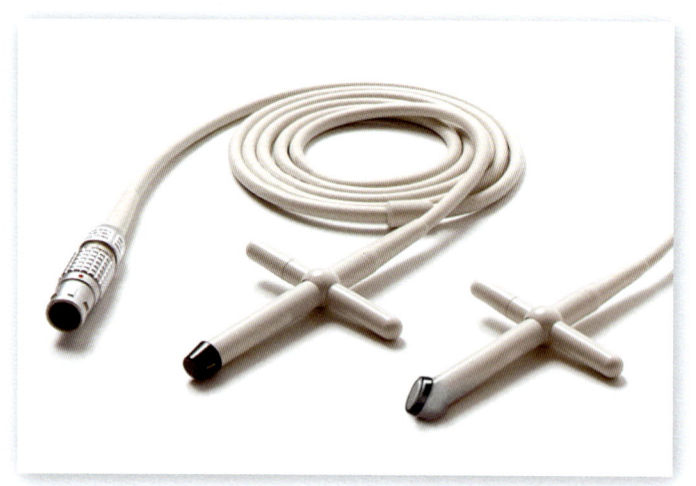

Fig. 28 **Pedof transducers**

Advantages:
- Usually extremely sensitive in Doppler since designed specifically for Doppler
- Relatively inexpensive to make
- Relatively inexpensive electronics necessary (single channel system)
- Small footprint allowing for insonation in smaller areas such as between ribs and suprasternal notch

Discussion
In the past few years, one of the biggest benefits most often overlooked was the superior sensitivity of these transducers for performing Doppler. Since the bandwidth requirements for Doppler are very low in comparison to the requirements for 2D imaging, these transducers can generally be peaked for sensitivity in a very small frequency range (a high Quality Factor.) The result has been superior sensitivity in the narrow band of operation. Unfortunately, fewer and fewer people routinely use the Pedof probes since there is no associated image, requiring more expertise. Whether or not these transducer designs persist as more sensitive depends on whether or not ultrasound manufacturers roll the new generation of more sensitive piezocomposite materials, new matching layer technologies, and new production processes into these transducers. If so, then these transducers will probably continue to be the most sensitive probes for Doppler. If not, then the newer technology used for imaging transducers will eventually surpass the performance of the existing pencil probes.

Major Limitation Leading to a New Technology
If ever there was an obvious issue to tackle, this one is it. Since these transducers cannot produce an image, there was a desire to find a means by which to scan two-dimensional space.

> **CHECKPOINT: Exam Tip**
> Pencil probes have the advantage of being relatively inexpensive and having very good sensitivity for Doppler. The disadvantages are no ability to produce an image and a fixed focus.

14. Creating a 2-Dimensional Scan Sequentially

The obvious question is, how do you take a single, narrow beam and create a 2-dimensional image? The first solution was to build up the image sequentially (piece-by-piece) over time. It is important to note that there are many different methods of sequential image generation, each of which will be discussed throughout this section on transducer evolution. For now, we will focus on the basic underlying principles.

Fortuitously, the speed of sound in tissue is high enough that many beams can be transmitted and received fast enough so that it appears to the human eye as if a complete image is generated in real time. For sequential image generation, a narrow beam is transmitted and received from a specific direction. This first sound beam creates the first line in the displayed image. Then, the next transmitted beam is pointed toward a neighboring location. Again, the echoes are received to form the second line of the image. There are many different techniques for how the successive beams can be "pointed" in different directions. The process is repeated continuously until the desired region of the patient is scanned, creating a single image, or frame, as depicted in *Figure 29*. Once the frame is completed, the process can be started over to create more frames over time.

In *Figure 29*, the image is built up sequentially. Time (T_1) represents the first transmitted beam which results in line 1 (L_1) of the image. The transducer is moved or "pointed" in a different direction and the acoustic line at T_2 is transmitted and received resulting in image line L_2. This process is repeated "N" times until the entire desired scan region is covered, generating a single image or frame.

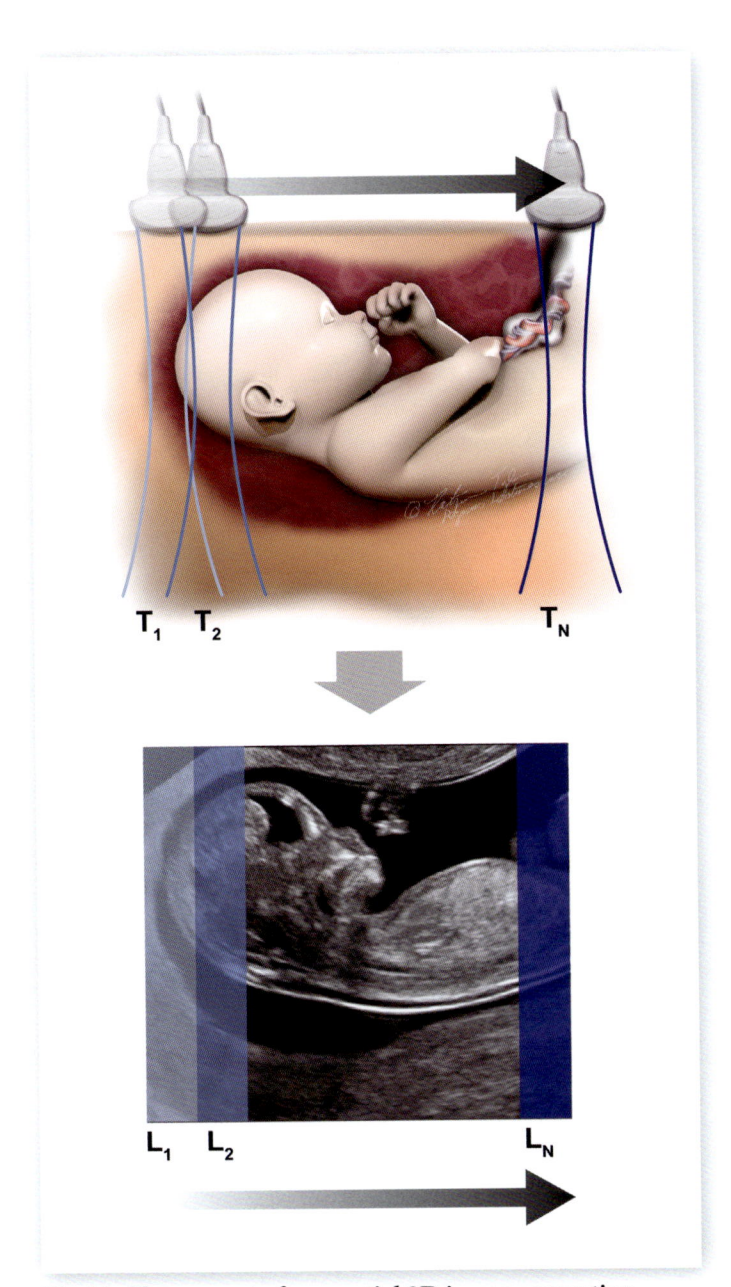

Chapter 5 | Part I: Transducers (Piezoelectric) 153

Fig. 29 **The concept of sequential 2D image generation**

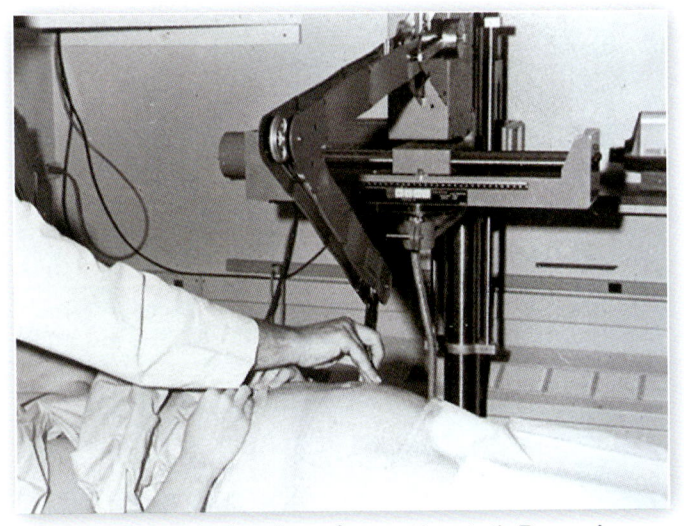

Fig. 30 **Picker articulated arm for creating static B-scan images**

For cardiac imaging, a static B-scan is not very practical because of the presence of ribs which make transducer movement challenging and cause acoustic shadows. This obscures cardiac structures. Although more practical for vascular and abdominal scanning, the quality of a B-scan was very limited. Additionally, a static sweep generated a single image which is clearly not ideal for assessing the movement of structures. These limitations led to the desire to have an automated, non-manual approach to creating a scan. At this point, the path diverges for cardiac imaging relative to vascular and abdominal imaging.

16. Mechanical Steering

Another approach to sequential 2D image generation is based on mechanical movement of the transducer. For the cardiac branch of imaging, there were two specific requirements: the ability to create a scan in an automated fashion, and a method to create useful images in the presence of ribs. The first approach which met both of these requirements was a mechanical sector transducer.

When a transducer is referred to as "mechanical" the term applies to how the beam is steered to create the image. As depicted in *Figure 31*, a mechanical image is produced by actuating the motor to point the transducer crystal in different directions over time.

At Time 1, the crystal is pointed to the farthest left of the image. Once the appropriate acoustic line time has expired (based on the imaging depth), the crystal is pointed in another direction and a second transmit pulse is produced (Time 2). When the signal has been received from the imaging depth, the process is repeated until the entire scan region, as specified by the user, is scanned. When the entire frame is produced (Time N), the motor returns the crystal to pointing in the first direction and the entire process is repeated.

View ONLINE Animation and Image Library

15. Static B-Scan

One of the earliest approaches to generating sequential 2D images was to manually drag the transducer in the lateral dimension, creating what was called a static B-scan. To create the image in a controlled fashion, the transducer was attached to an articulated arm which both controlled movement and tracked transducer location.

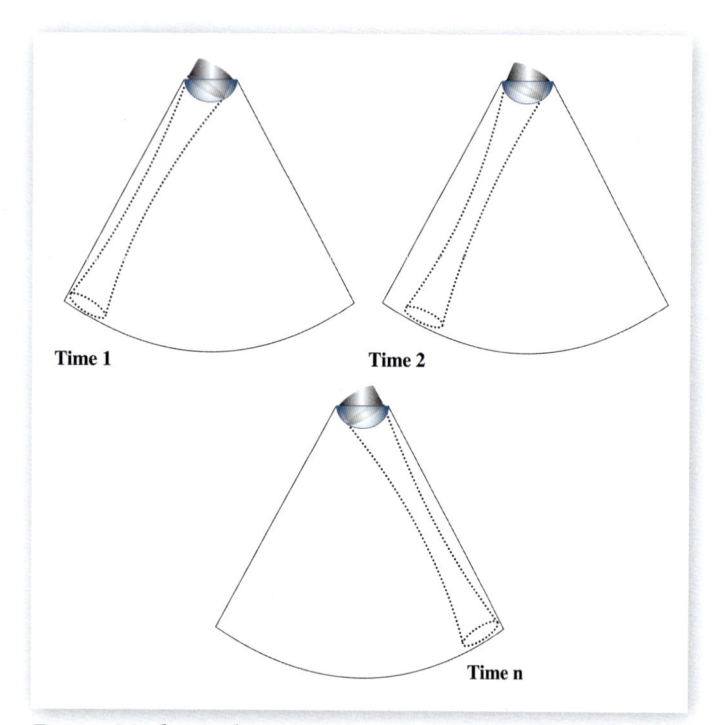

Fig. 31 **Mechanical steering**

Obviously, air is a poor choice because of its extremely low acoustic impedance which would cause a catastrophic impedance mismatch. Usually, these transducers were filled with a very viscous grease, or more commonly, a viscous oil. Of course, if any air got into these transducers, the large impedance mismatch resulted in acoustic shadowing in the region below the air bubble. Extracting the air bubbles with a syringe refill kit was challenging and time consuming, and usually was left to the person in the lab who became sufficiently frustrated with the shadow in the image. To avoid refilling the transducer, people would generally try to angle the transducer so that the air bubble rose to the upper corner, causing the shadow only along the edge of the image instead of in the middle of the image.

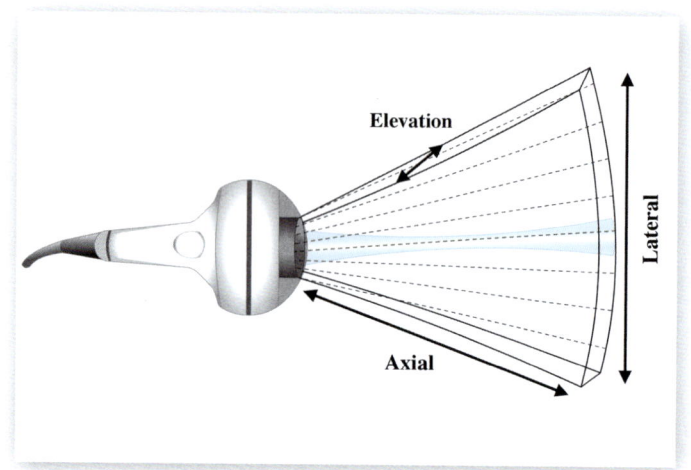

Fig. 32 **Mechanical sector scan**

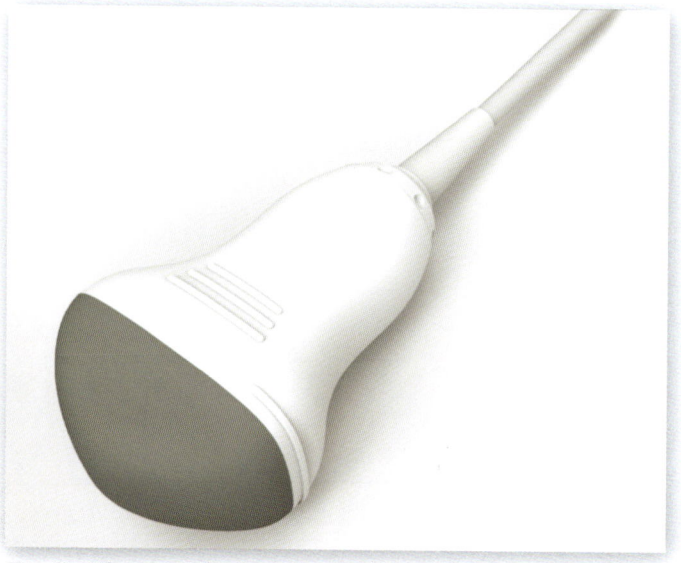

The sector name is given because of the image shape produced. A sector is a wedge of a circle. The sector shape was produced specifically to deal with the issues of limited access because of the presence of ribs. Since bone represents an extremely large acoustic impedance mismatch, a source of specular reflection, significant absorption, attempting to view the heart through ribs results in large acoustic shadows. To overcome this issue, a small transducer footprint is used and the beams are allowed to fan out with depth. This approach results in a narrow near field and a much broader far field, or a sector shape.

Conventional mechanical transducers had a dome over the top of the crystal. The image produced was similar to a sector image but with a rounded top where the dome exists. The reason for this dome was very practical and was based on the need to maintain patient contact. Since a motor wobbles a crystal back and forth, it is very difficult to maintain skin contact. By putting the crystal behind the dome, the dome stayed in constant contact and the crystal can wobble within the dome. Of course, the presence of the dome resulted in the issue of what material could exist around the crystal that would allow sound to propagate and also allow the crystal to be mechanically steered.

Fig. 33 **Photograph of mechanical curved array transducer**

Description:
- Used for 2D imaging, M-mode, Doppler, and color Doppler
- Creates a sector image with a "curved top"
- Single crystal (sometimes split into two halves for CW Doppler or a second small crystal off to the side dedicated for Doppler).

- Transducer steered by wobbling motor, rotating crystal, or mirrors
- Beam is symmetric in elevation and lateral planes
- Usually designed to have a broad depth of field
- Usually designed to have a very deep focus

Disadvantages:
- Fixed focus for transmit
- Fixed focus for receive
- Parts wear out (mechanical wear)
- Parts break (somewhat fragile)
- Motion artifacts
- Limited temporal resolution
- Very little imaging flexibility
- Air pockets in gel causing acoustic shadowing

Advantages: (relative to phased arrays)
- Relatively inexpensive to make
- Relatively inexpensive electronics necessary (single channel system)

Discussion
The majority of mechanical transducers are now either relegated to a shelf or a museum for those who want to trace the history of ultrasound. In the latter years of their existence, mechanical transducers were usually designed for lower cost systems, or limited applications.

Major Limitation Leading to a New Technology
For mechanical transducers, the limitation of a fixed focus led to a technology to provide variable focus. This technology spawned the mechanically steered annular array.

> **KEY CONCEPT**
>
> The term mechanical refers to a transducer that is motorized to steer to produce an image. Mechanical transducers are rarely used today, but are still valuable to study so as to understand the motivation and importance of later technological advancements.

17. Mechanical Annular Array

For an annular array, the single round crystal was diced into a series of concentric rings, but the image was still produced by mechanically steering the crystal. The concept of an annular array is quite simple: if varying the diameter of the crystal varies the focus, then build a transducer with a variable diameter. The diameter is varied simply by turning on and off rings. If only the center disc is turned on, then the focus is very shallow. If the next outer ring is activated, then the diameter is larger and the focus is deeper. If the fourth ring is activated, then the focus will be considerably deeper, as indicated in *Figure 34*.

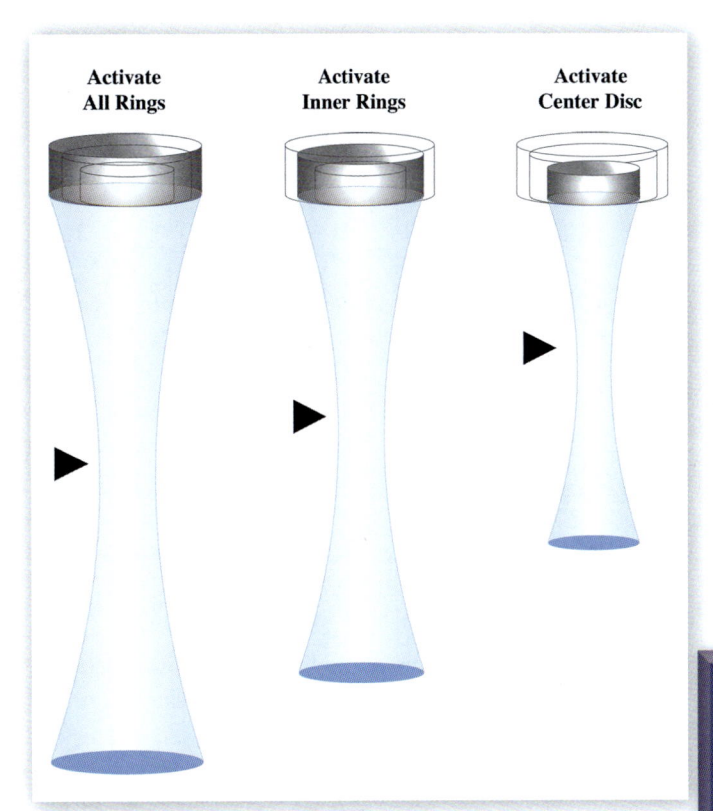

Fig. 34 **Mechanical annular array (varying focus)**

View ONLINE Animation and Image Library

Recall that the focus is proportional to the square of the diameter. Therefore, by having many concentric rings, the focus can be varied from very shallow to very deep.

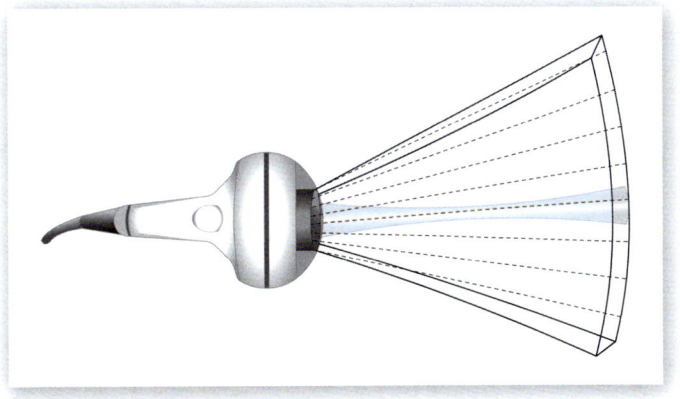

Fig. 35 **Mechanical annular array scan**

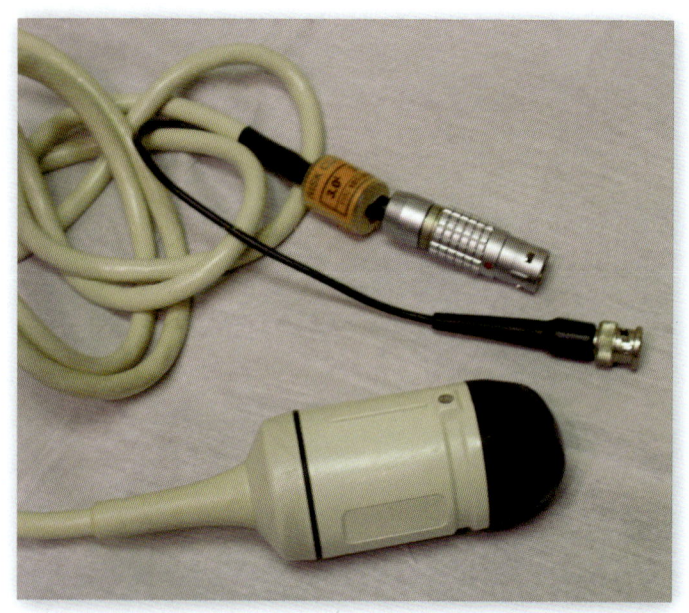

Fig. 36 **Photograph of a mechanical annular array transducer**

Description:
- Used for 2D imaging, M-mode, Doppler, and color Doppler
- Creates a sector image with a "curved top" (same shape as simple mechanical sector)
- Multiple concentric "ring" elements
- Transducer steered by wobbling motor, rotating crystal or mirrors
- Beam is symmetric in elevation and lateral

Disadvantages:
- Parts wear out (mechanical wear)
- Parts break (somewhat fragile)
- Motion artifacts
- Limited temporal resolution
- Excessive grating lobe artifacts common (grating lobes discussed in Chapter 8: Artifacts)
- More expensive to make than single element mechanical transducers
- More expensive electronics necessary (one channel for each ring element)

Advantages: (relative to single element mechanicals)
- Variable focus in the lateral direction
- Variable focus in the elevation direction
- Variable depth of field

Discussion
In principle, annular arrays represented a large advance in technology, providing a variable focus both laterally and elevationally. In practice, these transducers did not find great favor since they were generally prone to bad grating lobe artifacts. As will be formalized in Chapter 8: Artifacts, grating lobes refer to the fact that wave energy does not really form one narrow beam as indicated by our over simplified beam drawings. Instead wave energy radiates in many directions producing weaker "beams" in varying directions.

Because of constructive and destructive interference, the beam goes through higher and lower intensities with varying angles. All transducers have some degree of grating lobe artifact. To reduce the prevalence of grating lobe artifacts, transducers are designed with tight spacing between elements (the element spacing is referred to as the "pitch"). From a production standpoint, it is very difficult to cut small concentric rings into a disc of material. In order to accommodate the manufacturing process, the ring spacing for annular arrays was generally larger than ideal, exacerbating the grating lobes.

Grating lobes results in a lateral displacement or a lateral overlaying of data. As an example, many times people imaging with an annular array would visualize an artifactual kidney overlapped with the actual kidney. As a result of this issue, annular arrays never became as "big" as expected.

One very unique feature of annular arrays is the fact that when a ring is turned on and off, both the lateral and elevation directions are affected. Until the advent of 2D arrays, an annular array was the only transducer capable of controlling the elevation focus. (1.5-D-arrays offered a choice in the elevation dimension, but certainly not to the same degree as multi-ring annular arrays.)

Major Limitation Leading to a New Technology
In addition to the bad grating lobes specific to annular arrays, mechanical transducers in general have many undesirable features. From the movement of the crystal, there tends to be a lateral smearing effect which degrades the lateral resolution. Additionally, in color Doppler, the motion artifact results in bright flashes of color. For the simple mechanical transducer, there is also a fixed focus. All of this is compounded by the fact that the mechanical parts tend to wear out and break, and often the dome oil would leak out and be replaced by air. The desire to create a scan with no moving parts, and the desire to have a variable focus led to the concept of phasing and phased array transducers.

Therefore, both the linear switched array path for vascular and the mechanical approach for cardiac led to the same requirement of the ability to steer without moving parts and the ability to change the focus. Before we discuss the family of phased array transducers, we will first need to consider the technique of phasing and how it can be used to both steer and to focus.

The first incarnation of this new approach resulted in a technology called a linear switched array. In order to understand a linear switched array, we will need to first discuss the idea of linear sequencing as a scanning technique.

18. Sequencing

The narrow apex of a sector image is less than ideal for vascular and abdominal imaging. The desire to have a broad near field as well as no moving parts led to another approach to sequential 2D image generation referred to as sequencing. Sequencing was (and still is) commonly used with large linear and curved linear arrays. Sequencing refers to exciting groups of elements in a specific pattern to scan a region. Since the geometry of these transducers is large (in the lateral direction), the lateral dimension of the scan can be accomplished without transducer movement.

Referring to the images of *Figure 37*, notice how the first beam is created by exciting the first group of elements at time T_1. Once the echo has returned from the depth of interest (determined by the depth knob setting), a second beam is transmitted, at time T_2, by exciting a second grouping of elements, creating a laterally displaced beam. Continuing in this manner, groups of elements are fired in a linear sequence creating a scan region. The width of this scan region is determined by the user by setting the scan or "image" size on the screen. Once the end of the scan or frame is reached T_N, the first group of elements is again excited and the process repeated.

> **KEY CONCEPT**
>
> When large arrays are used, only a sub group of the elements (referred to as the aperture) are activated so that the lateral beamwidth does not become too large resulting in poor lateral resolution. Each beam is narrow such that building up an image requires transmitting and receiving a sequence of beams over time.

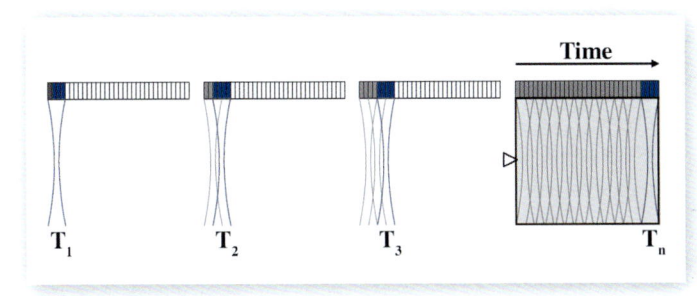

Fig. 37 **Sequencing**

View ONLINE Animation and Image Library

19. Linear Switched Array

One of the first transducers to employ the sequencing approach for image generation was called a linear switched array. As the name suggests, a linear switched array consisted of a group of elements which could be turned either on or off through electronic switches. These transducers were physically large and consisted of many elements (generally 200 elements or more). These transducers did not have any steering capability; therefore, the image shape was always rectangular. The large lateral dimension of the transducer was to provide a large field of view. These switched linear array transducers are no longer used, but the principle of sequencing is still used commonly in newer phased array linear and curved linear transducers.

Description:
- Used for vascular 2D imaging, Doppler, and color Doppler (Linear Switched Array obsolete now)
- Creates a rectangular image
- Multiple rectangular crystals arranged linearly
- Elements fired in a specific sequence to create image
- Beam is not necessarily symmetric in elevation and lateral planes

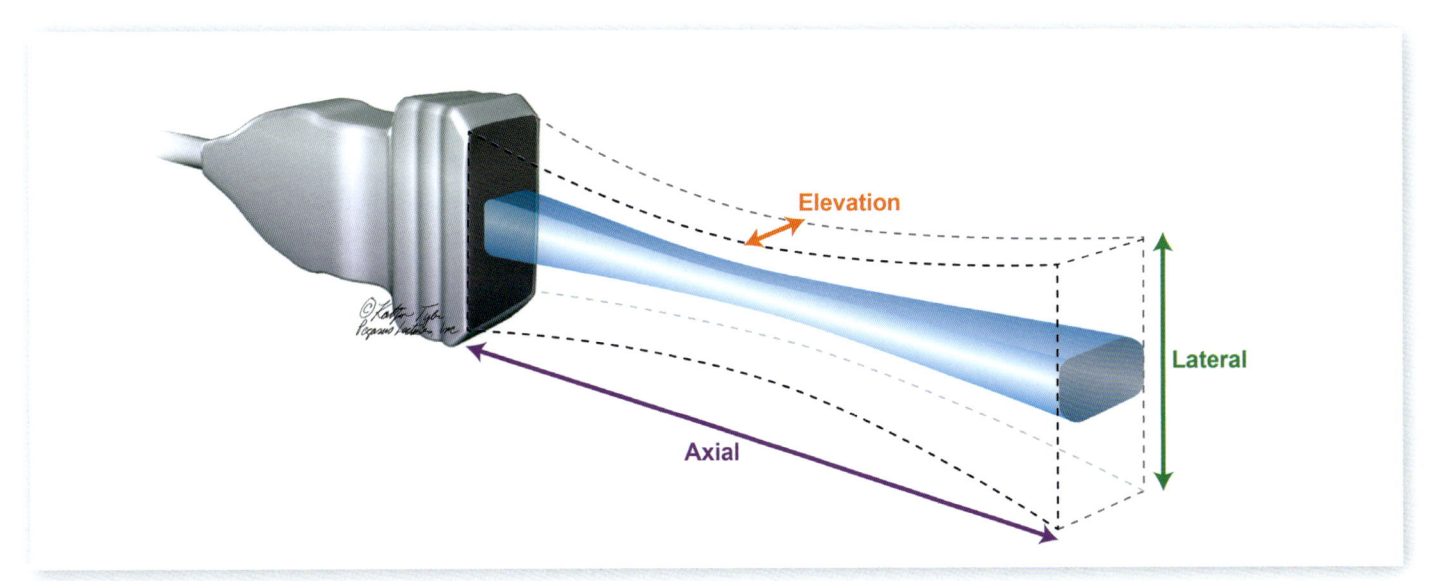

Fig. 38 **Linear switched array**

Disadvantages:
- Fixed transmit focus
- Fixed receive focus
- No image steering capabilities (must look straight ahead)
- More expensive to make than single element mechanical transducers
- More expensive electronics necessary (potentially one channel for each element)

Advantages: (relative to single element mechanicals)
- Allows for creation of a wide linear image in near field (good for vascular)

Discussion

Linear transducers produced now are phased linear and not switched linear arrays. Even the smallest, least expensive systems nowadays have circuitry to perform phasing and electronic focusing. Therefore, there is no motivation or cost benefit to producing transducers that can only be sequenced. Even if the steering through phasing is never used for conventional 2D imaging, as with modern curved linear transducers, the phasing can be used to steer the Doppler appropriately. However, since the sequencing mechanism discussed is routinely used for curved linear and phased linear arrays, it is useful to have reviewed this transducer type.

Major Limitation Leading to a New Technology

Switched linear transducers had no steering capability. As a result, when viewing a diving vessel, other than manually rocking the transducer, there was no ability to change the angle to better capture the specular component of the reflection. The lack of steering was also problematic since most imaging artifacts are based on specular reflections which are very angle dependent. Furthermore, the ability to achieve good color filling and accurate Doppler measurements requires control over Doppler angles. For these reasons, there was a motivation to create a new technology with the ability to steer the ultrasound beam in directions other than straight ahead. This led to the phased array concept and a whole family of transducers within this family.

> **KEY CONCEPT**
>
> Early vascular imaging was produced by linear switched arrays. These transducers produced wide rectangular images but could only be steered manually (by angling the probe).

20. Electronic Steering

20.1 Creating an Array

The ability to steer electronically requires an array. An array is a transducer comprised of multiple "elements" which can operate together or be controlled separately to transmit and receive signals. Imagine starting with a rectangular block of piezoelectric crystal, but cutting that block into a series of smaller "elements" as shown in *Figure 39*. The process of cutting is referred to as "dicing" and the gap that is generated by the dicing is referred to as the "kerf." Each element can now serve as a transmitter and as a receiver.

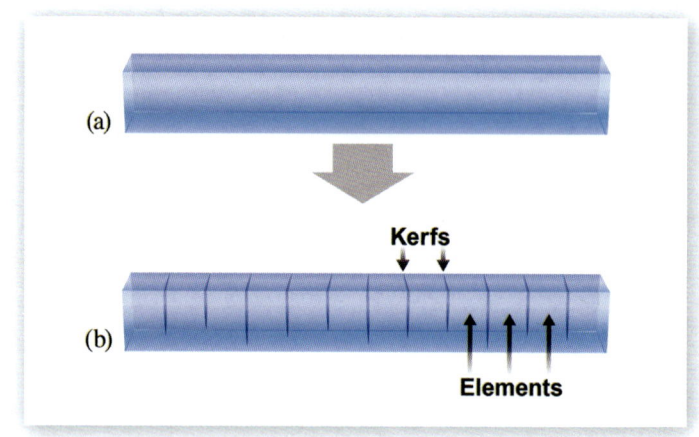

Fig. 39 **Creating a multi-element transducer through dicing**

In *Figure 39*, (a) shows a rectangular single crystal block; (b) depicts the same block after dicing to create a "kerf" to form multiple elements which together constitute an array. Notice that the kerfs are cut to different depths to reduce the amount of "crosstalk," or communication, between the elements.

20.2 Understanding the Term Phase

The term "phase" is used to determine a time reference.

◊ *Example:* "We are in phase 3 of a 10 phase building proposal."

◊ *Example:* "Your hair is too long. You listen to noise and call it music. Your friends are rude, and you think you know everything." (Parent's perception of teenage phase)

For waves, a phase difference is the amount of time shift necessary to make two waves align. Recall that, in Chapter 2, we discussed phase differences between waves and how the phase affected wave addition. When two waves are in phase, the resulting wave has a significantly higher amplitude resulting from constructive interference. When two waves are completely out of phase (180°), there is cancellation or destructive interference. As is more often the case, when two waves are partially out of phase, the resultant wave has an amplitude somewhere between the sum of the two individual waves.

To create constructive and destructive interference, multiple waves are necessary. A transducer array is simply a collection of smaller transducers that can be used together collectively to form a dynamic, variable transducer. We can therefore think of each transducer element as a mini transducer. Each element acts as an individual wave source. A collection of "elements" can be driven in concert to create many waves simultaneously.

Electronic steering is achieved by using small time or phase delays between the excitation pulses to each of the transducer elements within the array.

Electronic steering eliminates all of the disadvantages of mechanical steering. The fact that electronic steering requires an array leads to some further advantages such as the ability to vary the focus through changing the aperture as well as by phasing (the aperture is the active area of transducer being used), the ability to perform parallel processing, and many other advanced processing techniques. The major disadvantage of a phased array is cost. Creating a phased array transducer is considerably more complex and costly than the more simple mechanical transducers.

20.3 Electronic Steering for Transmit

To steer a beam electronically, tiny time shifted excitation pulses are applied to each element of the aperture. (The aperture is the portion or "window" of the transducer elements which is being utilized.)

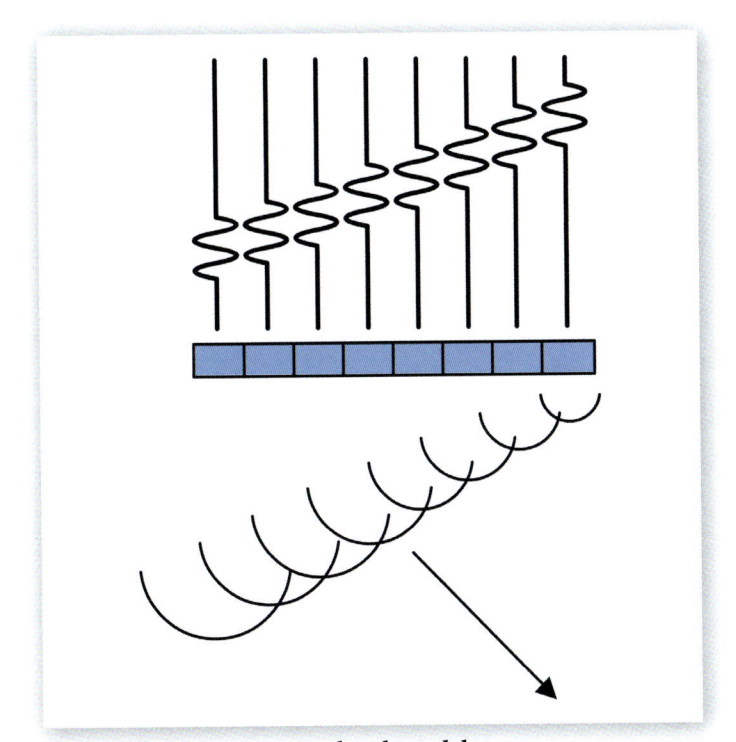

Fig. 40 **Electronic steering by phase delays**

Figure 40 demonstrates the concept of applying a phased delay voltage profile to a group of elements within a transducer. The zigzagged line represents the voltage pulse for an individual transducer element. The difficulty of presenting time in a static picture again presents itself. In this case, time is represented by the "distance" between the transducer element and the voltage pulse. The farther away the zigzagged line, the later in time the pulse will arrive at the element. Therefore, since the pulses are not all at the same "distance" from the elements, the picture represents time differences, or "delays" between the voltages driving each of the elements.

By using Huygens' principle we can predict how each of the individual wavefronts will add to construct a beam and in what direction that beam will travel. Huygens' principle states that all points on a wavefront can be treated as point sources producing spherical secondary wavelets, whose tangential surface predicts the new position of the wavefront over time. (Note that from this principle, the laws of reflection and refraction can also be determined.) In essence, each transducer element acts as an individual transducer producing a spherical wave. Because of the time delays, each individual wave is at a different distance from the transducer face at a given moment in time. The wavefronts of each of these spherical waves begin to overlap producing more constructive interference. Eventually, with depth, the spherical waves start growing to the point where the overlap decreases more and more, resulting in less and less constructive interference. At any time, the spherical wavefronts can be connected to demonstrate the wave direction and behavior.

In this example, notice that the new beam direction is no longer perpendicular to the transducer face. The phase delays between the excitation pulses to each of the elements result in delayed waves. The delayed wavefronts add such that the "main beam" is at an angle to the transducer face that matches the transmit phase delay profile. In essence, time delays are being used to make the transducer "appear" as if it were facing a different direction.

20.4 Electronic Steering for Receive

Just as we would like the ability to transmit a beam in a specific direction, we also would like to receive a beam from that same specific direction. In other words, if we would like the transmit signal to go in a specific direction, we would like to listen from that same direction, and not just from echoes returning from straight ahead.

The same delay principles that apply to transmitting apply to receive and receiving. Notice in *Figure 41* that the path length from point "x" to element #1 is different than the path length to element #8. Therefore, if we want the signals that arrive from point "x" to all 8 elements to add up correctly as one signal, we will have to use a delay profile on the received signals from each element. In this case, since the path length is longer to element #1 than to element #8, we must delay element #8 more than element #6, which requires a greater delay than element #5, etc. Again, time is indicated as distance away from the transducer element. Since the transmit pulse for element #8 is farther away than the pulse for element #6, there is a greater delay for element #8.

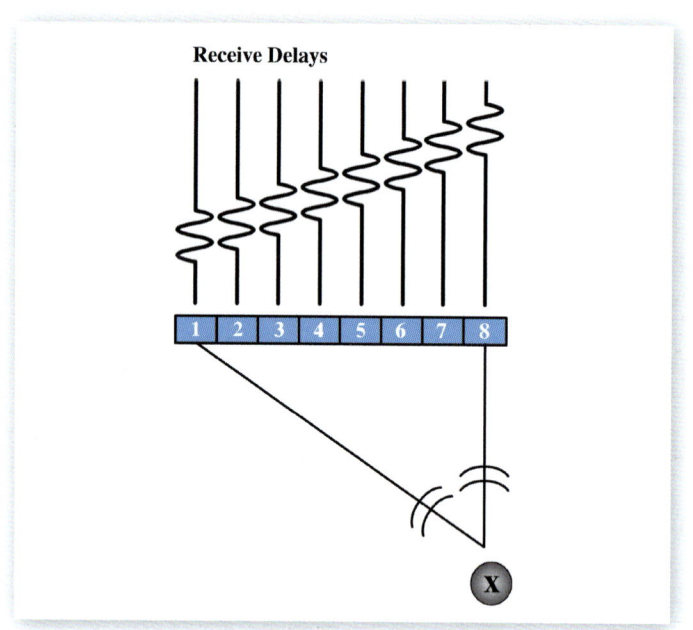

Fig. 41 **Receive delay profile**

> **KEY CONCEPT**
>
> Electronic steering is achieved by using small phase delays between the excitation pulses that drive the elements of a phased array transducer. Electronic receiving is also achieved by applying phase delays to signals received by each of the active elements of the phased array transducer. The advent of electronic steering revolutionized ultrasound and is still the basis of many imaging techniques today. Electronic steering allows for varying incident angles resulting in improved image acquisition and control of imaging artifacts. Additionally, electronic steering allows for significantly improved Doppler and color Doppler performance when flow is parallel to the skin surface.

20.5 Electronic Focusing for Transmit

Phase delays are also used to focus transmit and receive beams. We will start with the simple case of focusing an "unsteered" beam.

This first transmit profile is flat implying that there is no delay to the transmit pulse driving any of the elements. As a result, this "delay" profile would transmit straight ahead. Notice that the resulting transmitted wave takes on a planar profile and is referred to as a "plane wave." This delay profile and plane wave may not seem that important, but in recent years this has become the foundation for ultrafast imaging and shear wave elastography (SWE) imaging.

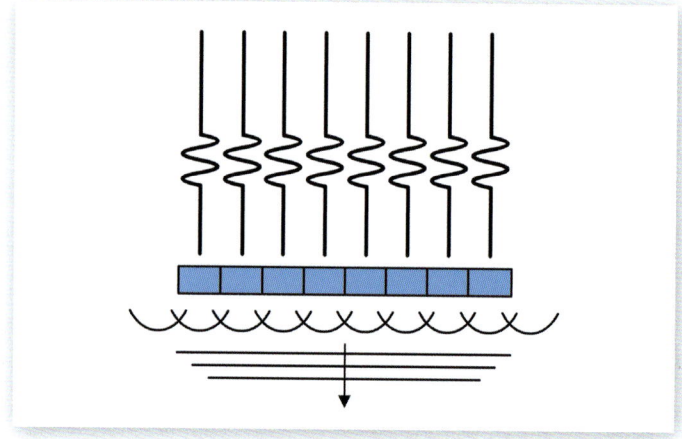

Fig. 42 **Unsteered and unfocused beam**

Now consider if we change the above profile to a profile that is parabolic as shown in *Figure 43*. The end elements are driven earliest in time, so the spherical wavefronts from these two elements travel the farthest for a given period of time. The next two inner elements were driven a short time later, so the associated spherical wavefronts will be a little shallower. The element in the center of the transducer was transmitted last, and hence, the associated spherical wave has traveled the shortest distance. We can again use Huygens' principle to demonstrate the wave direction and behavior over time.

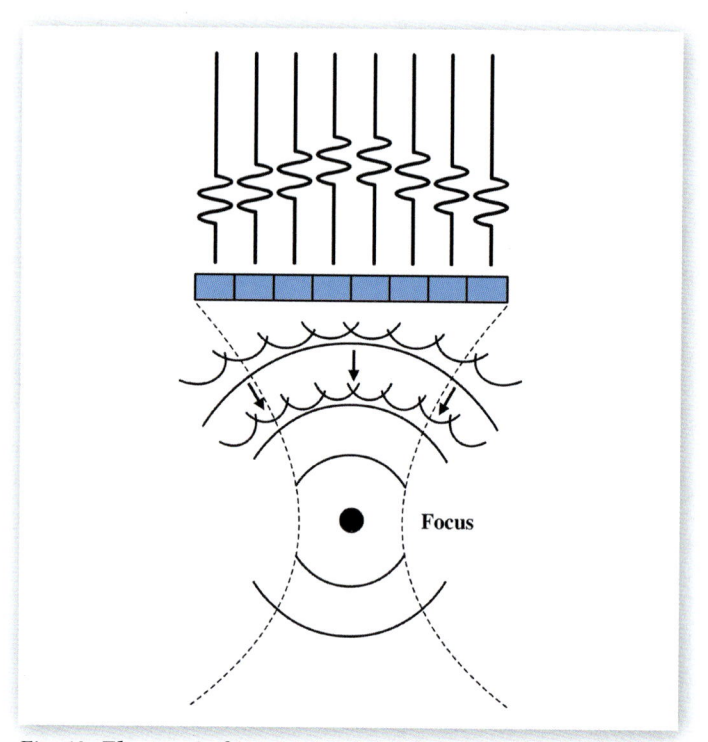

Fig. 43 **Electronic focusing**

When the tangent to each spherical wave is connected, the beam is clearly converging to a point. If you imagine these wavefronts later in time and draw the tangent to the spherical wavefronts, as indicated by the two curved lines at the bottom of the image, it is clear that the beam is now diverging. In other words, by using small time delays (phase delays), the beam is now focusing.

To decrease the focal depth, a more "severe" phase profile can be used. For a deeper focal depth, a less severe profile can be used. If no profile is used, the result is the natural focus of the transducer and transducer lens. Recall that it is not possible to improve focusing beyond the natural transducer focus for a given transducer aperture and operating frequency. Past the focus the beam is "diffraction limited," which basically says that the beam is bending away or diverging from the center line of the beam.

View ONLINE Animation and Image Library

20.6 Electronic Focusing for Receive
Just as the same delay profile was applied on receive steering as for transmit steering, the same delay profile can be applied to focus a receive beam as for transmitting a focused beam.

20.7 Focusing and Steering Together
Not surprisingly, there will be times when we will want to both steer and focus. To both steer and focus, all that is needed is to add the delay profile from the steer to the delay profile that achieves the focus. The following figure demonstrates how a steering and a focusing profile can be added to achieve a steered and focus beam.

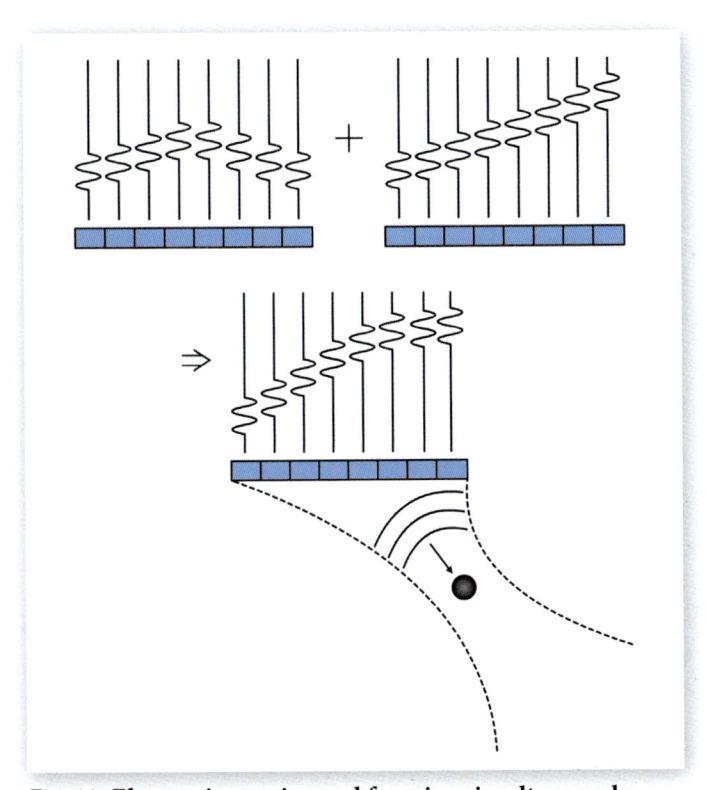

Fig. 44 **Electronic steering and focusing simultaneously**

Again by using Huygens' principle, we can see that the beam is now directed at an angle from the transducer face, and the beam is converging to, and diverging from a point. As we will see with phased array transducers, steering and phasing simultaneously is very common.

View ONLINE Animation and Image Library

KEY CONCEPT
The same technique of varying time delays for electronic steering is also employed for electronic focusing. With phased array transducers, the system varies the transmit focus to the desired depth indicated by the user primarily by changing the applied delay profile. The focus can also be changed by changing the number of active elements (the transmit aperture).

21. 1-D Phased Array Sector

The phased array sector transducer, like the mechanical sector, was designed for rib access. These transducers typically have between 64 and 128 elements, although transducers with fewer or more elements certainly exist. The frequency range for these transducers depends on the intended application. For adult cardiac imaging, these transducers generally run as low as 2 MHz and as high as 4 MHz in conventional imaging mode. Quite frequently, the Doppler frequency will be set at or below the lowest imaging frequency, generally not going lower than about 1.8 MHz. For small adults and children, the Doppler frequency range is generally from 3.5 MHz to 5 MHz, and for pediatric imaging, the Doppler frequency range is typically from 5 MHz to about 8 MHz. Note these frequency ranges are approximate and vary from ultrasound company to ultrasound company.

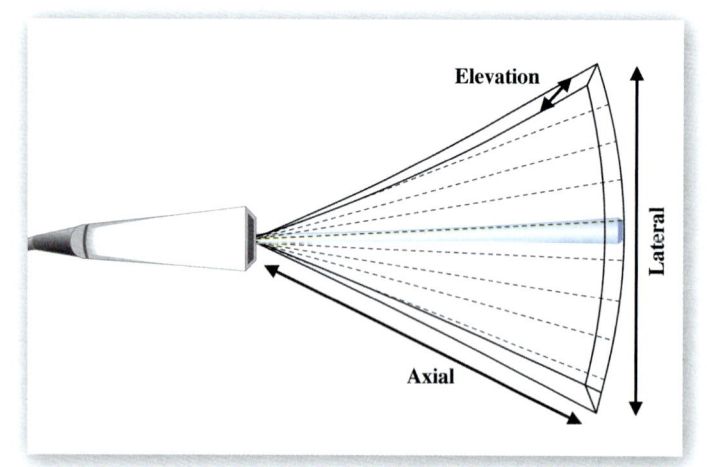

Fig. 45 **Sector scan**

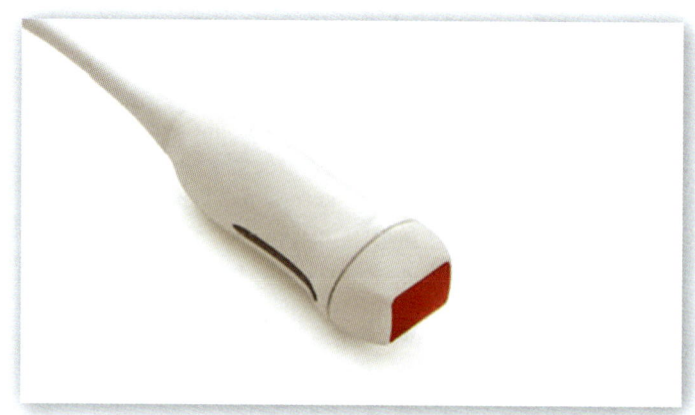

Fig. 47 **Sector transducer**

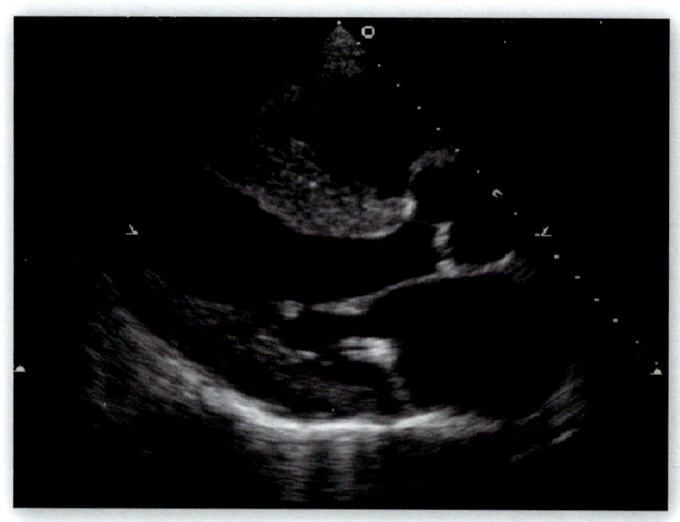

Fig. 46 **Sector image**

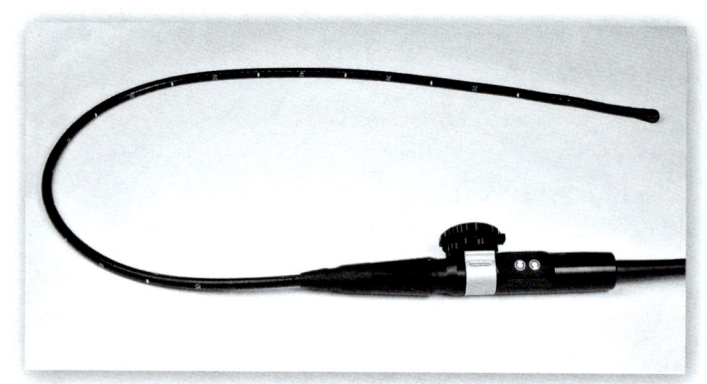

Fig. 48 **TEE (sector format)**

Description:
- Used for 2D imaging, M-mode, Doppler, and color Doppler
- Creates sector image with small footprint for rib access
- Multiple square or rectangular elements in a row (64 to 128 elements common)
- Transducer is steered electronically by phasing in lateral dimension
- Variable transmit focus by electronic phasing in lateral dimension
- Continuous variable receive focus by electronic phasing in lateral dimension
- Lens used to create the appropriate fixed elevation focus for intended use
- Beam usually not symmetric in elevation and lateral dimensions

Disadvantages: (relative to mechanical)
- More expensive to make than single element mechanical transducers
- More expensive electronics necessary (potentially one channel for each element)

Disadvantages: (relative to 2D arrays)
- Fixed elevation focus
- No steering in elevation dimension (to perform 3D, must manually or mechanically steer in elevation)

Advantages: (relative to single element mechanicals)
- Variable focus in the lateral dimension
- Motion artifacts and problems related to mechanical parts are eliminated
- Flexibility to perform parallel processing and other advanced processing techniques

Discussion
The sector image for this type of transducer is produced purely by phase delays. It is very important that you understand how the image is actually formatted so that you will understand the angle formed between the steered beam and the structures at each location in the image. This knowledge is critical to truly understanding, predicting, and controlling artifacts. Furthermore, the only way to ever truly understand direction of flow is to first understand how the image is created. This fact will become evident in Chapter 7: Doppler when flow direction is discussed. For now, we will learn how an image is created in a sector format.

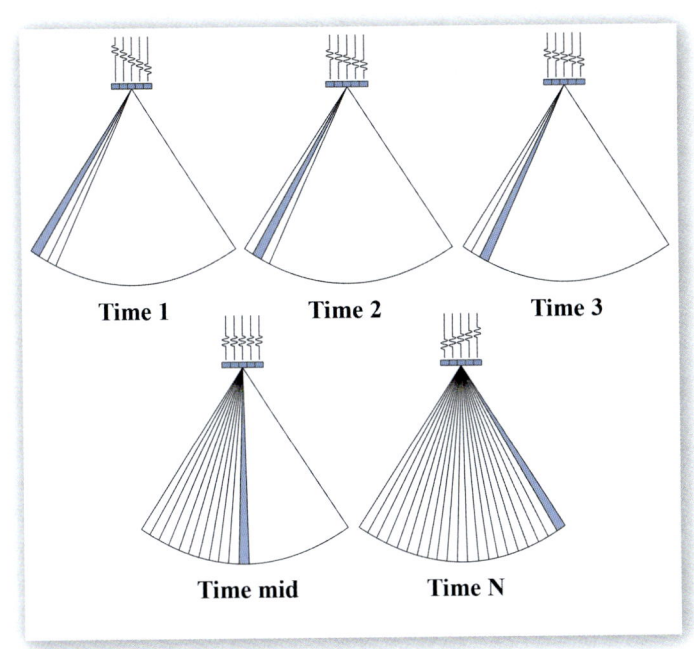

Fig. 49 **Creating a sector scan**

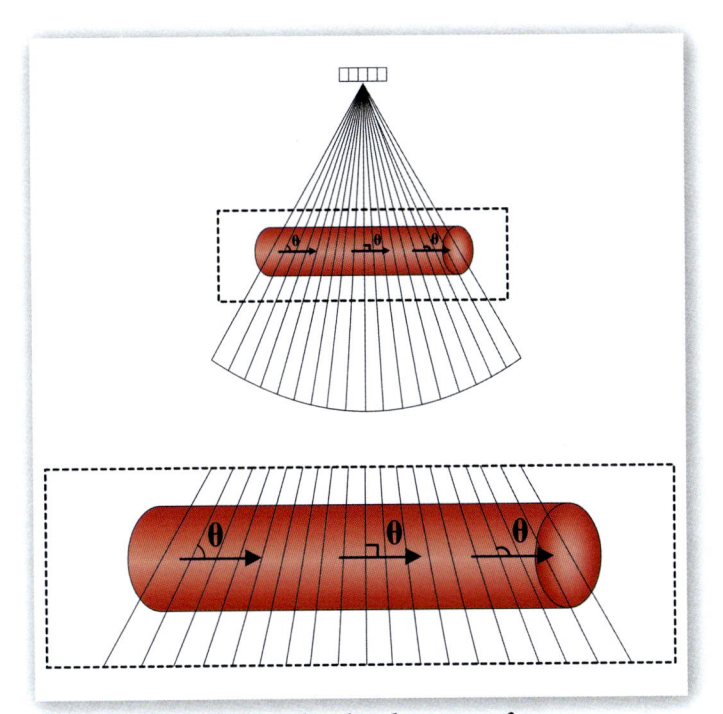

Fig. 50 **Varying flow angle related to sector format**

Notice in *Figure 50* that although the structure drawn is straight, with no bends, kinks, or twists, the angle formed between the beam and the structure varies across the entire length of the structure. For the given figure, the only place where the beam is normal to the structure is at the very center line of the image. Of course, if the angle of the structure were diving, normal incidence would no longer occur along the midline.

Notice that each beam is created by firing a group of elements. The waves from each of the elements propagate into the body and constructively interfere to produce a beam pattern. As we learned earlier in the chapter, by using time delays, the beams can be forced to add constructively in a direction other than straight ahead from the transducer. Referring to *Figure 49*, notice that at Time 1, a delay profile is used to steer the beam toward the left (page left) side of the image. Since it takes time for sound to propagate into and out of the body, the system must wait 13 μsec per imaging cm until transmitting the next neighboring beam. As the echoes return in time, the receiver continuously changes the time delays so as to focus at each location along the receive line.

Once the required line time has transpired, the second beam is created using a slightly more gradual delay profile. Again, the receive delay profile is continuously varied to maximize sensitivity to each specific depth and improve lateral resolution as much as possible. This process is repeated until eventually the beam required is straight ahead of the transducer. (Labeled 'Time mid' in *Figure 49*.) You should notice that since this beam does not need to be steered, the phase delay profile is flat. Past this midpoint (to the right of the midline), the phase delay profile is reversed so as to create steering in the opposite direction as the beams on the left side of the image. When the right edge of the sector is reached and the echoes received, the process repeats with the retransmission of line 1.

Major Limitation Leading to a New Technology

1-D phased array transducers have been the workhorse for ultrasound for many years. Because of the many elements and the ability to customize a design to meet the needs of a specific application such as vascular, OB, etc., there were not that many limitations that forced a new paradigm in transducer design for many decades. Instead, iterative improvements were made to increase sensitivity, increase bandwidth, and to allow for many new imaging and processing techniques. However, there is one major limitation to all 1-D phased array transducers, the inability to control the elevation direction by focusing or steering. The desire to control elevation so as to produce 3D images with no moving parts becomes the motivation for 2D arrays. Additionally, phased arrays using piezoelectric crystals are extremely complex to construct and hence expensive to manufacture.

22. 1-D Linear Phased Array

Whereas sectors were designed with rib access in mind, linear transducers were produced for vascular applications where contact must be maintained with a relatively flat surface such as the neck and legs. The linear phased array is the technology that replaced the linear switched array. These transducers are physically large and usually consist of 200 to 300 elements or more. In reality, with linear phased array, the switching and sequencing aspects of a linear switched array still are utilized. The difference is that a phase array linear can also be phased to create steering and focusing when desired. As a result, we will need to consider this transducer when both steered and unsteered to fully appreciate the functionality.

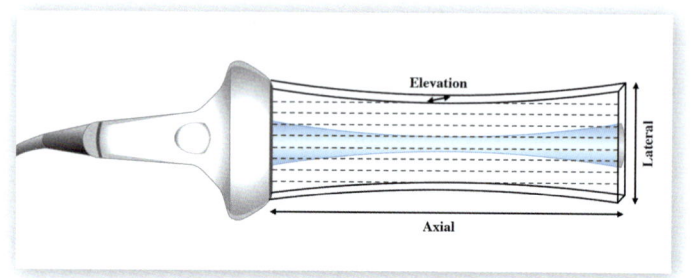

Fig. 51 **Linear scan**

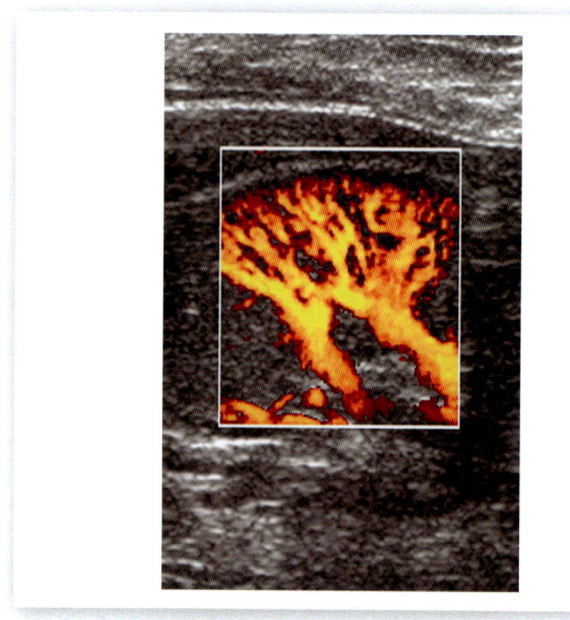

Fig. 52 **Linear image**

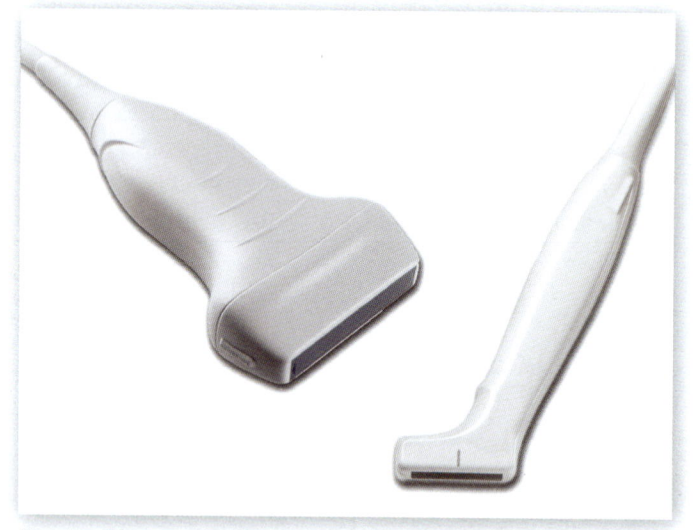

Fig. 53 **Linear transducers**

Description:
- Used for 2D imaging, Doppler, and color Doppler
- Rectangular image created by sequencing
- Parallelogram image created by phasing each group of sequenced elements
- Multiple rectangular elements in a linear array (200 to 300 elements common)
- Transducer steered electronically by phasing in the lateral dimension
- Variable receive focus by electronic phasing in the lateral dimension
- Dynamic receive focus in the lateral direction
- Lens used to create the appropriate fixed elevation focus for intended use
- Beam usually not symmetric in elevation and lateral dimensions

Disadvantages: (relative to mechanical)
- More expensive to make than single element mechanical transducers
- More expensive electronics necessary (potentially one channel for each element)

Disadvantages: (relative to 2D arrays)
- Fixed elevation focus
- No steering in elevation direction (to perform 3D must manually or mechanically steer in elevation)

Advantages: (relative to single element mechanicals)
- Variable focus in the lateral direction
- Allows for creation of a wide linear image in the near field
- Flexibility to perform parallel processing and other advance processing techniques

Discussion
In terms of image generation, there are three different ways in which linear transducers are used. When unsteered, the image is created through sequencing, just as the switched linear array operated. When the image is steered, then a combination of phasing and sequencing is used. A third mode, called trapezoidal scanning, creates wings to the image by phasing, and produces the center part of the image through sequencing. We will start with the simplest of these three modes which is unsteered imaging.

Unsteered Imaging
Although the mechanism for an unsteered linear transducer is the same as for a switched linear transducer, we will repeat the discussion, but with more detail to serve as the foundation for discussing steered linear images.

Referring to *Figure 54*, notice how the first beam is created by exciting the first group of elements at time T_1. Notice that all of the elements in the group are excited at the same time, with no phase delay between the pulses for each element. The flat delay profile results in a beam which propagates straight ahead. Once the echo has returned from the depth of interest (determined by the depth knob setting), a second beam is transmitted, at time T_2, by exciting a second grouping of elements, creating a beam laterally displaced. Again note that all of the elements within the second group are excited at the same time, with no phase delays. Therefore, the beam is transmitted straight ahead and parallel to the first beam. Continuing in this manner, groups of elements are fired in a linear sequence creating a scan region of parallel beams. The width of this scan region is determined by the user by setting the scan or "image" size on the screen. Once the end of the scan or frame is reached (T_N), the first group of elements is again excited and the process repeated.

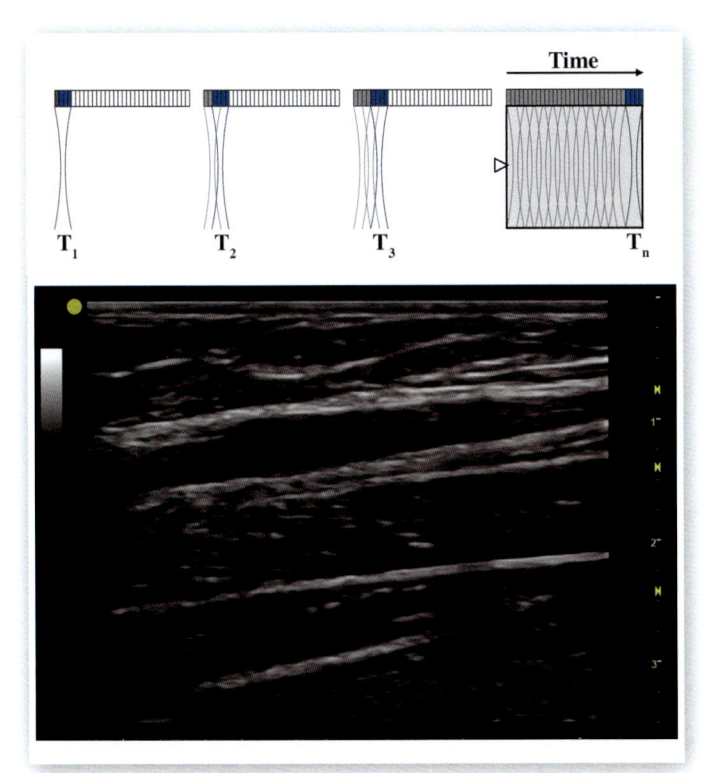

Fig. 54 **Unsteered image of a normal basilic vein produced by sequencing**

View ONLINE Animation and Image Library

Steered Image

A steered linear image is also produced by sequencing. However, to achieve the desired steering angle, phasing is used. Referring to *Figure 55*, notice that when the first group of elements is activated, not all of the elements are pulsed at the same time. Instead, a phase delay results in some elements being pulsed earlier than others. As we have learned in the earlier section on phasing, this phase delay results in a constructive interference such that the main beam now travels at an angle relative to the transducer face. Once the echo has been received from the imaging depth, the next group of elements in the "sequence" is activated. Of course, it is desired that the beam created by the second group of elements be parallel to the first beam. Therefore, the same phase delay profile is applied to the second group of elements as was applied to the first. This process repeats across the entire array until the entire frame is complete, and the process repeats to produce another frame. Therefore, a steered linear image requires both sequencing and phasing to create the desired image.

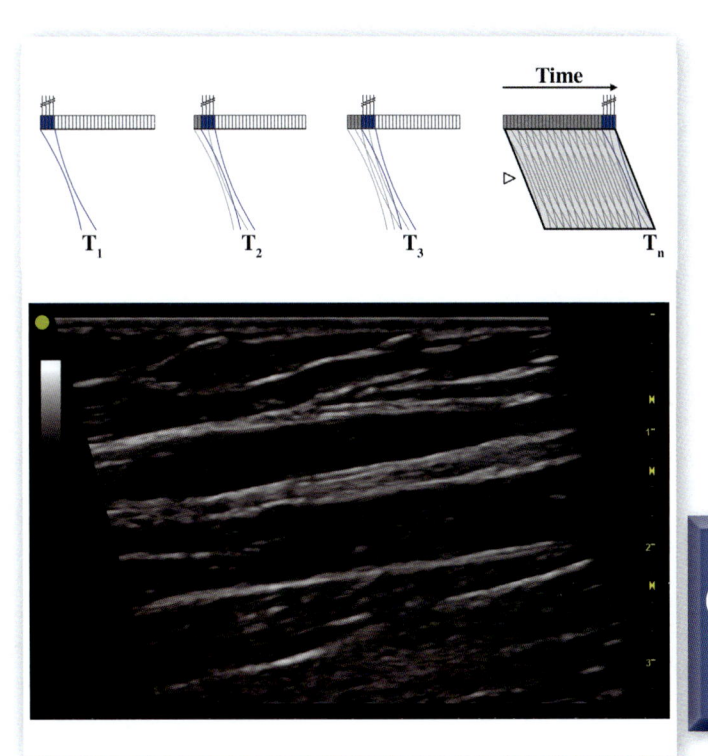

Fig. 55 **Steered linear image of a normal basilic vein produced by phasing and sequencing together**

View ONLINE Animation and Image Library

Note that not all ultrasound systems allow the user to steer the 2D image, as shown in *Figure 55*. Also note that the mechanism for steering a color Doppler image with a linear phased array follows the same approach as for creating a 2D image. Notice in *Figure 55* that the 2D image is steered to the right while the color Doppler image in *Figure 56* is steered to the left. In general, the optimal steering direction for the color Doppler is in the opposite direction as optimal direction for the 2D image. The reason is based on the fact that the beam direction is generally best when perpendicular to the vessel walls (called normal incidence) to capture the specular component of the reflection for 2D imaging, whereas, as you will learn in Chapter 7: Doppler, the worst possible Doppler results when the beam direction is perpendicular to the flow direction.

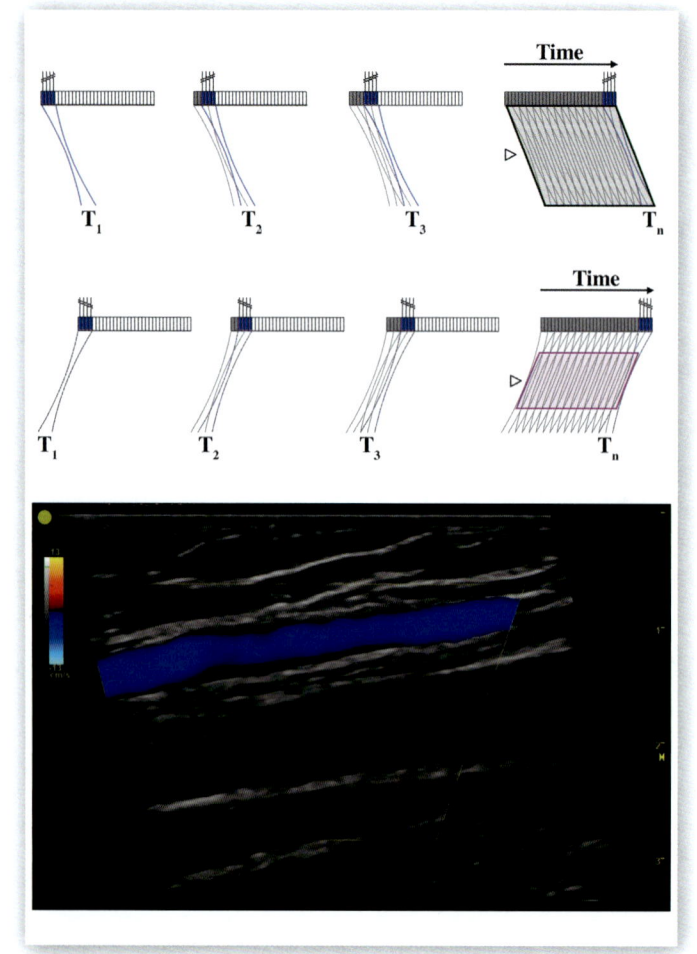

Fig. 56 Steered 2D and color Doppler image of a normal basilic vein

Trapezoidal Scanning

Trapezoidal scanning results in an extended field of view by creating an image that is trapezoidal in shape. (There is nothing like stating the obvious.) However, what is probably not so obvious is that trapezoidal scanning is produced by treating the linear array as if it were two different transducers. To produce the left and right "wings" of the image, a portion of the array is treated as a sector transducer. To produce the center portion of the image, the array is treated as an unsteered linear. *Figure 57* demonstrates how trapezoidal scanning is achieved. Notice that the image demonstrates both a trapezoidal format (2D image) and a steered image (color Doppler).

Author's Note:
Linear Arrays and Phasing

Even when a linear phased array is not using phasing for steering, phasing is still used for focusing on transmit and dynamic (continuous) focusing on receive. Also note that no matter what the format, a linear image always has a region of the image on top and bottom that are flat and parallel.

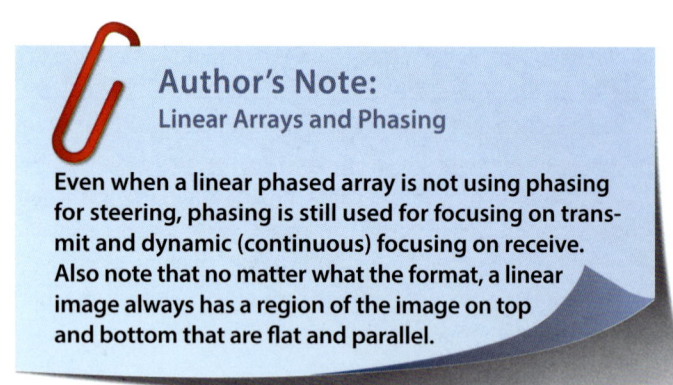

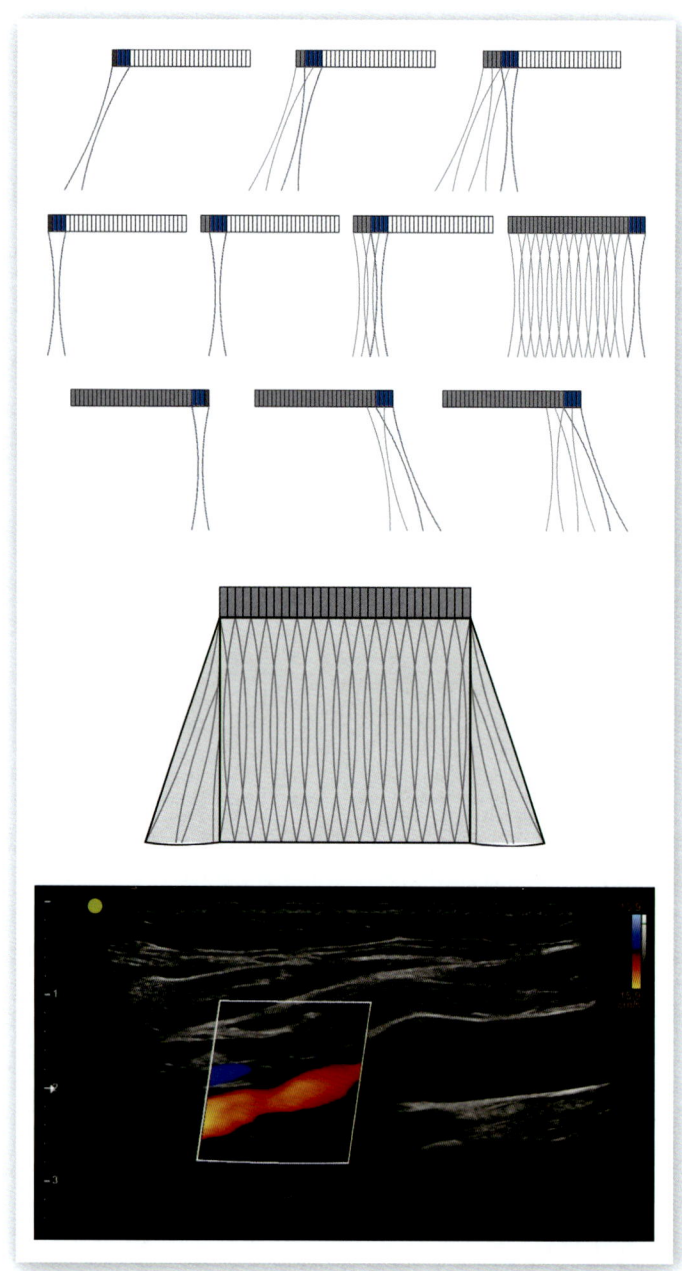

Fig. 57 Trapezoidal 2D image (with steered color box) of a normal carotid artery

View ONLINE Animation and Image Library

Major Limitation Leading to a New Technology

Like the 1-D array sector, the main limitation is the inability to control the elevation plane for focus and 3D imaging.

23. 1-D Curved Linear Phased Array

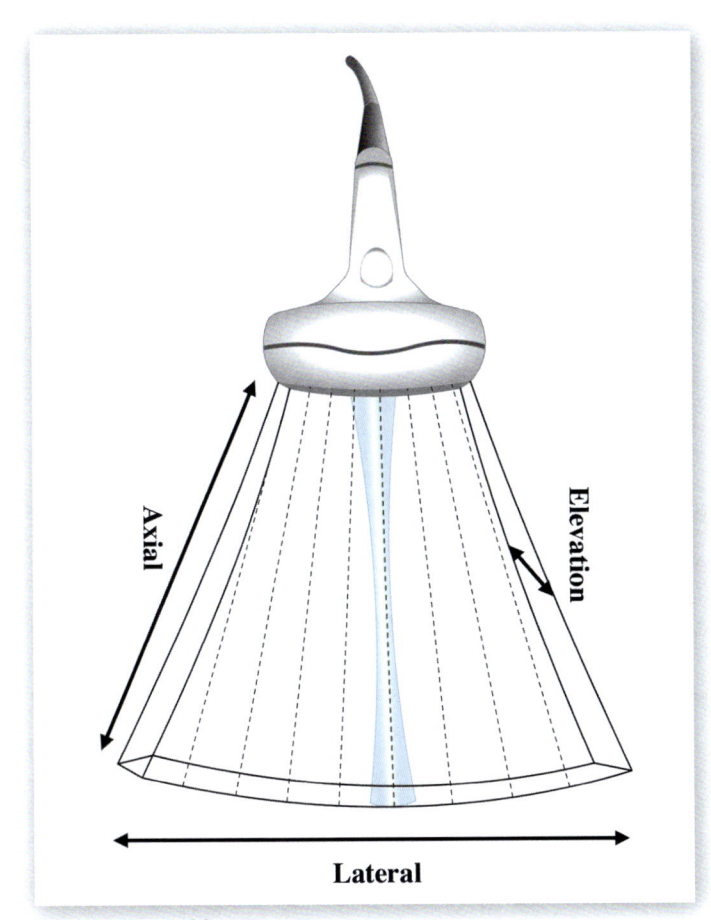

Fig. 58 **Curved linear scan**

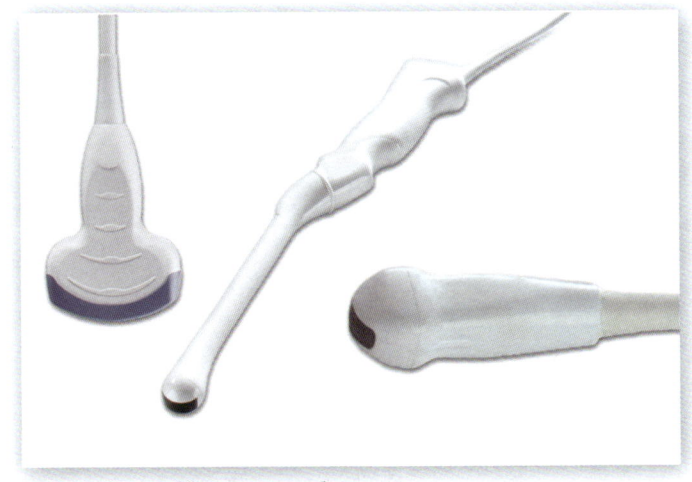

Fig. 59 **Curved linear transducers**

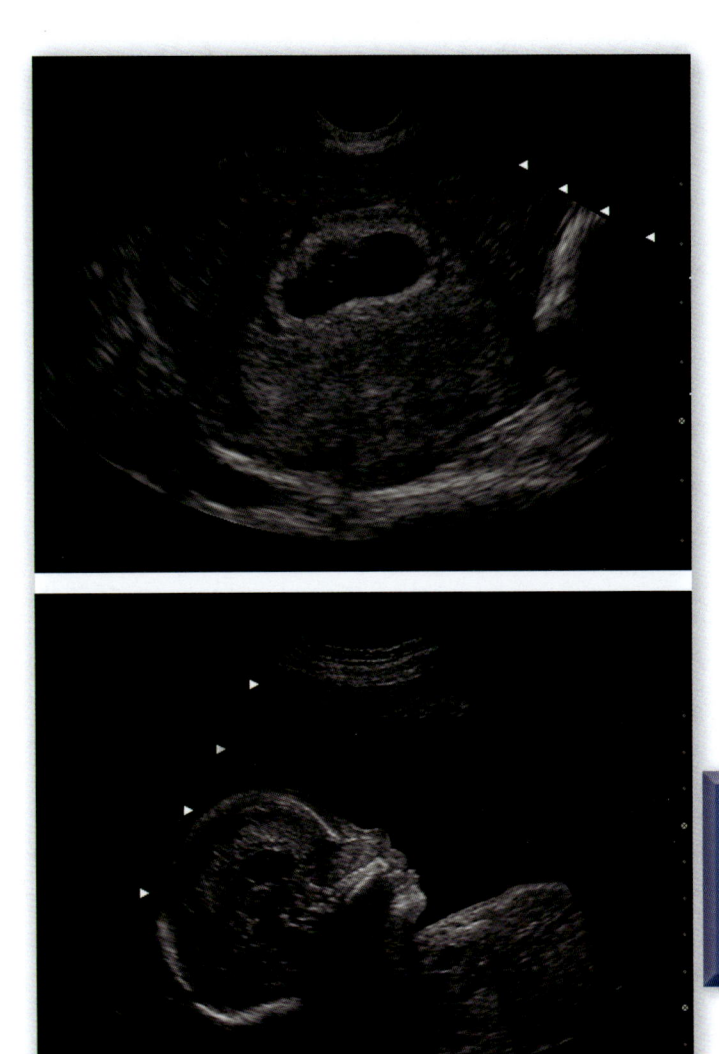

Fig. 60 **Curved linear images**

Curved Linear Array

Description:
- Used for 2D imaging, Doppler, and color Doppler
- Curved image created by sequencing
- Multiple rectangular elements in a curved linear array
- No steering necessary – geometry creates desired scan shape
- Variable receive focus by electronic phasing in lateral dimension
- Dynamic receive focus in lateral dimension
- Beam usually not symmetric in elevation and lateral dimensions

Disadvantages: (relative to mechanical)
- More expensive to make than single element mechanical transducers
- More expensive electronics necessary (potentially one channel for each element)

Disadvantages: (relative to 2D arrays)
- Fixed elevation focus
- No steering in elevation dimension (to perform 3D must manually or mechanically steer in elevation)

Advantages: (relative to single element mechanicals)
- Variable focus in the lateral dimension
- Allows for creation of an extremely wide linear image in near field
- Flexibility to perform parallel processing and other advanced processing techniques

Discussion
For conventional 2D imaging a curved linear image is produced by sequencing only. We will not review sequencing since it was already discussed in detail in Section 22. The image shape is produced by the curvature of the front of the transducer. Larger arrays produce larger images, with the curvature of the image matching the transducer curvature.

Since the image shape is produced by sequencing only, students often ask, "Then why do we call this a phased array transducer?" The answer is primarily that phase delays are used to control the transmit focus and dynamic receive focus. Also, the phasing is used to achieve appropriate angles to perform Doppler. Additionally, as we will learn in Chapter 6: System Operation, techniques such as compound imaging will use steering to create curved linear images. Therefore, even though a conventional image is not produced using phasing, phasing is still used.

Major limitation leading to a new technology
Like the 1-D array sector, the main limitation is the inability to control the elevation plane for focus and 3D imaging.

24. Plano Concave (Hanafy Lens)

24.1 1-D Arrays and Sub-optimal Elevation Control
A common limitation to each of the 1-D phased array transducers has been the inability to control the beamwidth in the elevation dimension (fixed elevation focus). Recall that the beam starts wider, converges to its narrowest point at the focus, and then diverges past the focus. Also recall that for 2D images, there is no direct visualization of the elevation data. In the ideal case, the elevation beam would be very narrow and uniform over depth. But as just mentioned the beam naturally converges and then diverges resulting in: degraded elevation resolution, lower intensity (as the beam diverges), and increased slice thickness artifact (representation of tissues either in front of or behind the desired imaging plane). For 1-D arrays, electronic control is only possible in the lateral direction. Therefore, most 1-D arrays are designed with a lens to focus the beam elevationally. The depth of the focus is generally determined by the application of the specific transducer design. For example, if a transducer will generally be used for depths ranging from the surface to 3 cm, the elevation focus would likely be set at about 2 cm, giving good overall resolution and sensitivity over the range of interest. Of course, as the depth range over which a transducer functions increases, the "optimal" depth for the elevation focus becomes less obvious and more consequential.

24.2 Hanafy Lens
In section 9, we discussed the concept of curving the surface of a transducer to affect focus. The discussion dealt mainly with the geometric aspects of how the focus would converge at a depth shallower than the natural focus, as determined by the degree of curvature employed. However, if the transducer is constructed such that the center of the element is thinner than the edges of the elements, another effect occurs. Recall that the resonance of a crystal is inversely related to the crystal thickness (as thickness increases, operating frequency decreases). With a Hanafy lens (named after its inventor Amin Hanafy), the crystal is thicker along the crystal edges (in the elevation dimension) and thinner in the middle (as seen in *Figure 61*). The consequence of this varying thickness is that there are different resonances across the crystal surface, with higher frequencies generated in the middle section and lower frequencies generated by the thicker outer aspects of the crystal. In other words, the Hanafy lens construction results in a single element producing a wider bandwidth of transmit frequencies from a single transmit pulse. The net result is a beam that has a much broader field of view in the elevation plane. In essence, the lower frequency from the outer aspects of the crystal help maintain the beam from diverging as much in the far field as would occur from a using a smaller diameter with higher frequency. Conversely, the higher frequency from the center helps promote a narrower high frequency beam in the near field. Through signal processing techniques, the system optimizes the received data essentially creating a narrower and more uniform elevation beam. Siemens is the primary company that utilizes Hanafy lenses in some of their transducer designs.

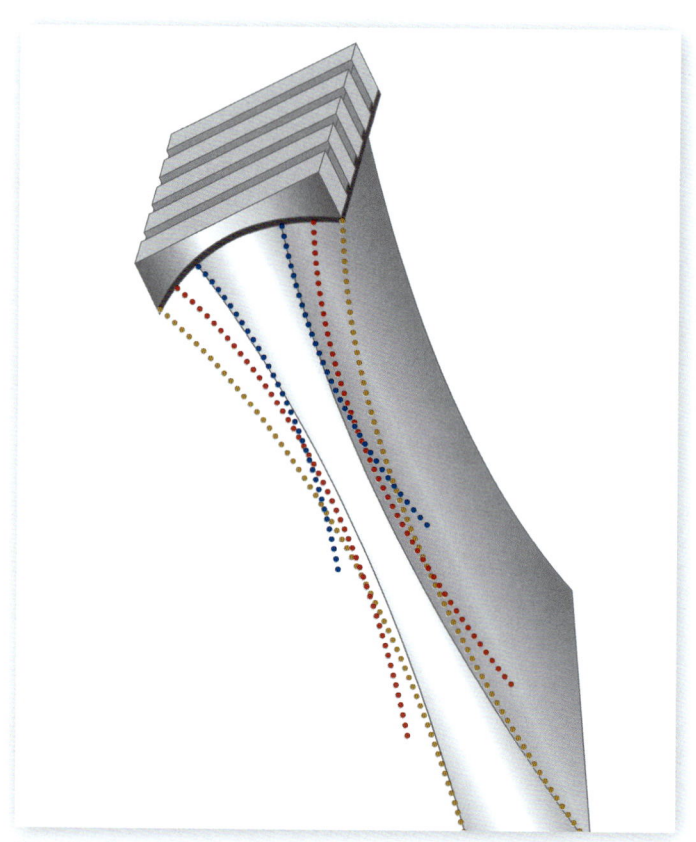

Fig. 61 **Hanafy lens technology**

25. Multi-dimensional Arrays

25.1 1.5-D Arrays

As we have already seen, a 1-D array has multiple elements arranged in a line to create 2D images. One of the greatest limitations of a 1-D array is a fixed elevation focus. The Hanafy lens attempts to address this limitation through varying element thickness, resulting in a wideband transmit. Another approach to overcoming the limitation of a fixed elevation focus is the use of a 1.5-D array. A 1.5-D array has more than one element in the elevation direction, which results in some, albeit limited, flexibility for elevation control. The following figure demonstrates the design of a 1.5-D array.

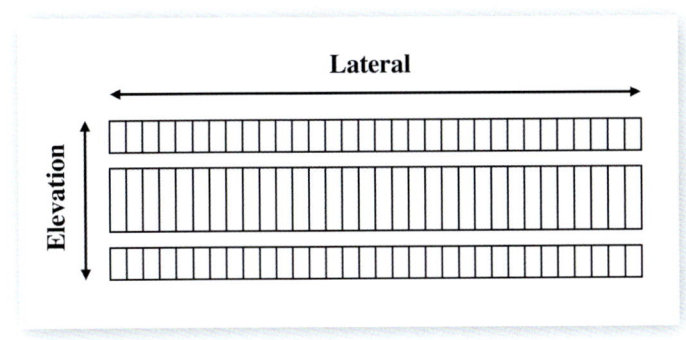

Fig. 62 **1.5-D array**

Discussion

A 1.5-D array allows for either the center row of elements to be used alone, or for the outer two groups of elements to be linked and turned on as well. If just the center aperture is used, the elevation focus is relatively shallow. If the outer group is activated as well, then the elevation focus becomes deeper.

Since any transducer format can be made as a 1.5-D array, we will not reiterate the purpose and function of sectors, linears, and curved linears.

Major Limitation Leading to a New Technology

With the advent of 1.5-D arrays there is some control in the elevation direction, but that control is limited. Additionally, the inability to create an automated 3D image still remains. Therefore, there is a desire for another generation with these capabilities, or 2D arrays.

25.2 2D Arrays

Recall that phased array transducers were developed in response to the limitations of mechanical transducers. The resulting transducers were called 1-D arrays, since their design was an array of elements along a line, or in one dimension. As listed in the disadvantages of phased array transducers, 1-D transducers have a fixed elevation focus and no elevational steering capability. 2D arrays overcome these limitations, affording elevation focus and steering as well as lateral control.

As with most new technologies, limitations existed when the first 2D array matrix transducers were created. In early iterations, only some of the 2D array elements could be used at one time, referred to as a "sparse matrix design." Using only a small fraction of their elements, these sparse matrix 2D arrays generated considerable grating lobe artifact as well as low acoustic output power. Around 2002, Philips released a fully populated 2D array with 2800 elements. As part of the design, micro-beamforming was created by adding special electronics, (multiple specialized chips called ASICs), into the handle to allow for the active use of all transducer elements. The micro-beamformer contained circuitry to control the signals applied to groups of elements ("patches") for the array transducer, and to process echo signals received by the elements of each group. Micro-beamforming in the probe advantageously reduces the number of conductors in the cable between the probe and the ultrasound system mainframe. There are now multiple manufacturers producing 2D arrays that generally contain between 2,000 and 9,000 elements. The technology of 2D arrays can be applied to all imaging formats including sector, linear, and curved-linear transducers.

The obvious advantages for 2D arrays are an ability to reduce slice thickness related artifacts, and electronically produce 3D and 4D images. Since with 2D arrays there are multiple transducer elements in the elevation plane, the elevation focus can be varied to reduce artifacts associated with elevation beamwidth. Additionally, with multiple elements in the elevation and lateral dimensions, electronic phasing can be used to steer both elevationally and laterally so that entire volumes can now be interrogated without moving the transducer. By micro-beamforming, the newer 2D arrays allow for higher power output and reduced grating lobe artifacts relative to sparse 2D arrays.

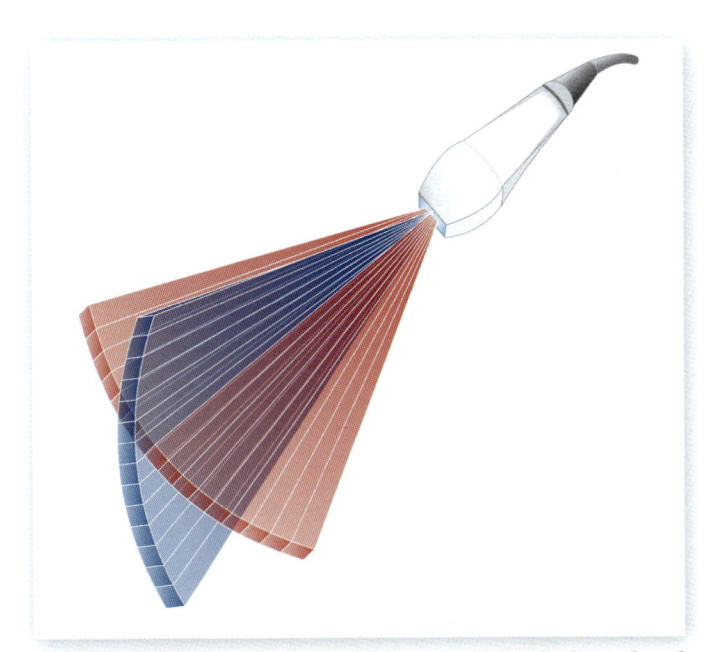

Fig. 63a **2D arrays can steer and focus in both the lateral and elevation planes**

Fig. 63b **2D arrays are capable of scanning 3D volumes**

Of course, there is always a trade-off to each benefit. A significant issue with creating 3D images from 2D arrays is the relatively long time required to sequentially create a 3D image. The low frame rate is especially problematic in dynamic imaging situations such as cardiac imaging. This limit in temporal resolution with sequential image generation will lead to a new image generation technique (discussed in Part II of Chapter 5). With respect to 2D arrays, the increased complexity leads to increased cost. Not only is the transducer acoustic stack more complex and difficult to manufacture, but the cable, electronics built into the transducer, and the processing power are more complex and costly as well. However, following Moore's law (which predicted exponential improvement in electronic-related capabilities with time), the increased computing power required becomes relatively less and less expensive, reducing the impact of this disadvantage.

Fig. 64 **This figure demonstrates a 2D array (matrix); the arrows indicate a human hair** *(Courtesy of Philips Medical Systems)*

26. Piezocomposite Materials

In the early days of ultrasound, PZT was used almost exclusively for transducer design. With the ever present desire to create transducers with greater bandwidth and improved sensitivity, more exotic approaches are now used to engineer the crystal material. A composite is generally a mixture of a polymer and piezoceramic material. One approach to create a composite material crystal is to take a block of piezoelectric material and dice it into a series of "posts". Usually the dicing cuts through about 80% of the thickness of the block. The posts are then embedded in a polymer matrix like an epoxy. Depending on the materials used, the manufacturing process, and the desired characteristics of the crystal, different ratios of polymer and piezoceramic materials will be used. To give an idea on the element spacing, for a 5 MHz transducer, the "pitch" (separation between elements) is typically about 0.1 mm. This small pitch is important to try to minimize excitation modes in directions other than the desired "piston" mode which is towards the face of the transducer, and to reduce the amount of energy that exists in the grating lobes of the beam. Once the epoxy has cured, the uncut side of the block is ground off. Electrodes are then added and the material is polarized through poling.

The result of these new composite materials has been the birth of ultra-wide bandwidth transducers. These newer transducers make performing harmonic imaging (discussed in Chapter 10: Contrast and Harmonics) feasible. In addition to wider bandwidth, the lower impedance of the polymer provides a better match to tissue. In comparison to the impedance of PZT (35-40 MRayls), the impedance of many polymers is around 8-12 MRayls. This lower impedance implies that the addition of a matching layer (or layers) provides significantly better "matching" than with PZT crystals.

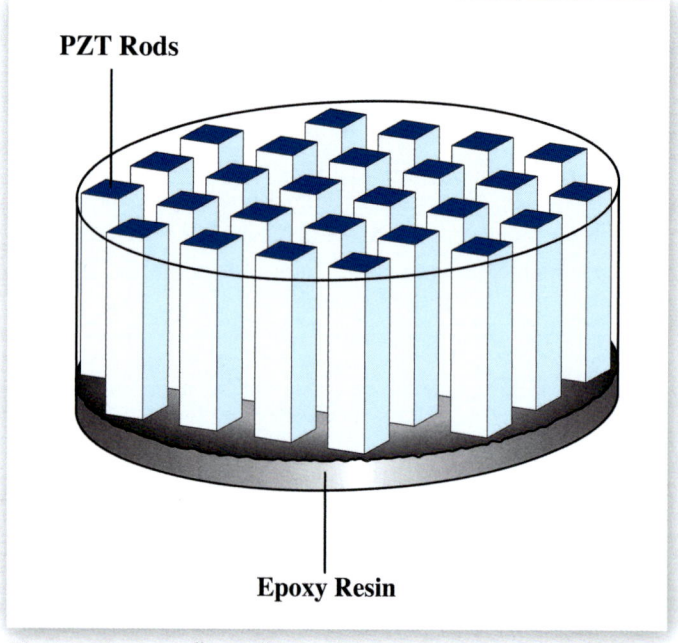

Fig. 65 **2D array "posts"**

27. PMN-PT (Single) Crystals

In the early 1970s some Russian and Japanese scientists discovered that lead magnesium niobate-lead titanate could be used to create a new piezocrystal with extremely uniform crystal structure (see Level 3 for more detail). These uniform crystals could achieve significantly better polarization than PZT crystals. However, there was considerable difficulty in growing crystals larger than a few millimeters, limiting application in the ultrasound field. In the 1990s research work led to a new technology to grow larger crystals exhibiting this improved electro-mechanical efficiency. The result was a significantly more efficient piezoelectric crystal that significantly impacted ultrasound imaging. Clinical trials comparing these new PMN-PT crystals against the older generation resulted in better image quality with significantly better penetration in obese and difficult to image patients. This new technology received different names from different companies. Philips refers to this technology as Purewave, and GE refers to their version as XDClear. Mindray, Siemens, and Canon all refer to this technology as single crystal.

Regardless of the multiple, confusing names, the benefits of using PMN-PT are many. Since the conversion efficiency is so much higher, lower voltages are required to obtain the same intensity transmit signals. The result is that less surface heat is generated, allowing for higher transmit powers in certain modes in which the transducer temperature becomes a limiting factor. The improved conversion efficiency also means that smaller signals become detectable (improved signal-to-noise ratio resulting in better sensitivity). Additionally, these transducers have broader bandwidths, allowing for greater penetration for deep imaging while still allowing for better resolution for more superficial imaging. In essence, these transducers significantly outperform most earlier piezoelectric designs.

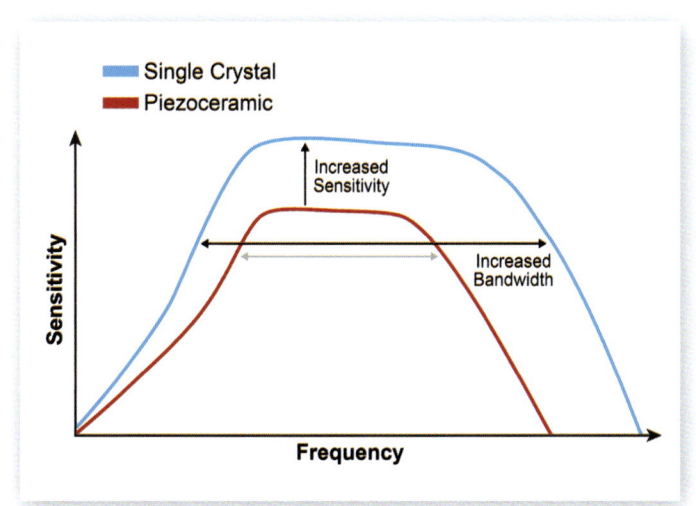

Fig. 66 **PMN-PT (single) crystals exhibit broader bandwidth and increased sensitivity relative to piezoceramic materials**

28. Wireless Transducers

Most transducers have attached cables that induce stress on the hand, wrist, arm, and shoulder of the person scanning. People have asked why a wireless transducer could not be produced. The answer for many years was that technology could not support the bandwidth necessary to transmit so much data. Additionally, since the ultrasound signals returning back from the patient are so small, the signals themselves would be corrupted by noise in the transmission. In recent years, with advances in circuitry, manufactures have been able to include amplifiers and micro-beamformers into the transducer itself. The result is a much more stable signal and a lower bandwidth demand. Additionally, with improvements in Bluetooth technology, wireless transducers now exist.

The transducer shown in *Figure 67* has both a 7.5-10 MHz linear array (right side) and a 3.5-5 MHz curved linear (convex) phased array (left side). The transducer connects wirelessly to either an iPhone or iPad for image display as shown in *Figure 68*. Notice how all of the controls are controlled through the iPad screen.

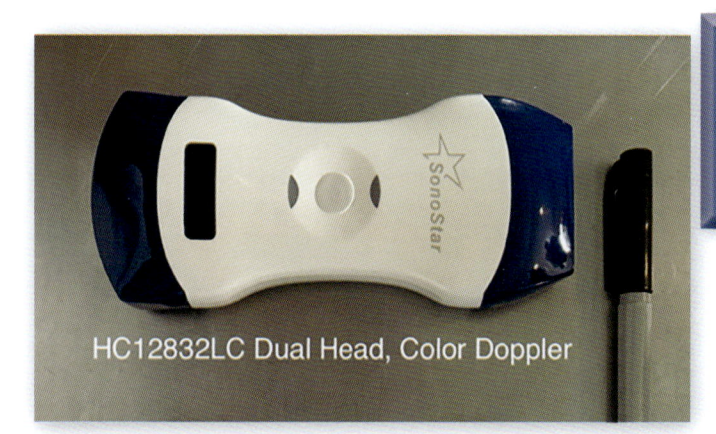

Fig. 67 **Sonoque (Sonostar) dual head wireless transducer**

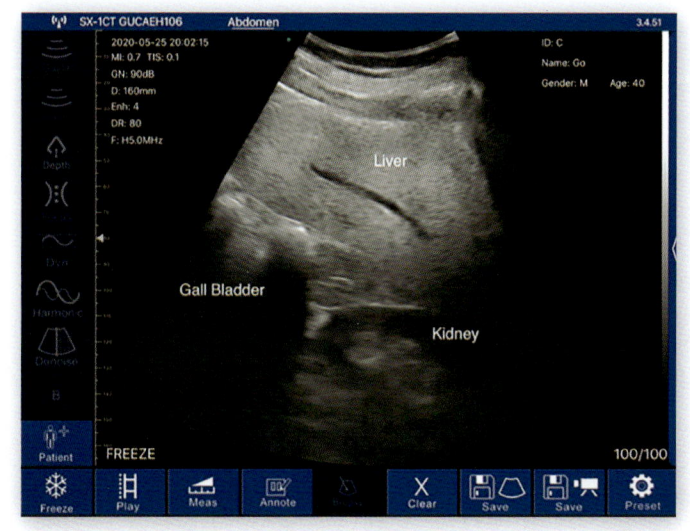

Fig. 68 **Curved linear image created by a Sonostar transducer**

Fig. 69 **Acuson Freestyle L13-5 (5-13 MHz) linear phased array transducer (and rechargeable battery)**

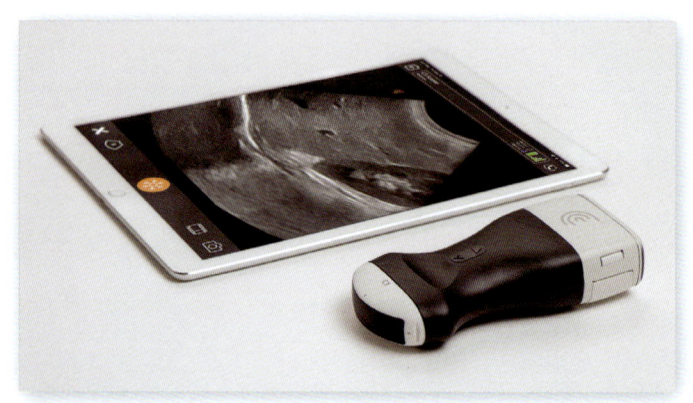

Fig. 70 **Clarius C3 HD Multipurpose (2-6 MHz) wireless transducer**

The transducer shown in *Figure 69* is used for abdominal, musculoskeletal, OB/GYN, small parts, and vascular imaging. Note the controls on the transducer which allow some system adjustments directly from the transducer. The transducer shown in *Figure 70* is used for abdominal, lung, and OB/GYN imaging.

29. Important Concepts for Transducers

Near field (Fresnel): The area between the face of the transducer and the beam focus.

Far field (Fraunhofer): The region past the focus.

Focus: Where the beam reaches its minimum diameter.

Focal region (Depth of field): Region over which the beam is most tightly focused.

Detail Resolution: Ability to distinguish between two objects in any of the three dimensions: axial, lateral, or elevation.

Operating frequency (f_o): The center frequency of the transmit bandwidth.

f_o (pulsed mode): Determined by crystal thickness and speed of sound in crystal material:
$$f_0 = \frac{c}{2 \cdot (thickness)}.$$

f_o (continuous mode): Determined by the frequency of the drive (transmit) voltage.

For many applications the natural focus of a transducer is inadequate or suboptimal. As a result many different focusing schemes have been developed to make the focus shallower such as:

1) Lenses
2) Curved elements
3) Electronic focusing
4) Mirrors

Most 1-D array transducers actually use a combination of these techniques so that a transducer design is optimized for a specific application.

◊ *Examples:*

- Curved linear arrays (CLA's) use a lens, curved elements, and electronic focusing.
- Phased arrays use a lens and electronic focusing.
- Mechanical transducers generally use a lens and possibly a mirror or mirrors.

As we already have discussed, there are a few very compelling reasons to desire a variable focus. Of the four techniques listed above, only electronic focusing allows for variable focusing. The other three techniques all result in a fixed focus. In essence, you can change the focus from the natural focus of a transducer by adding a lens to the design; however, since there is no easy way to change the lens on the transducer, the focus is now fixed by the lens.

30. Exercises and Conceptual Questions

View ONLINE Exercises & Conceptual Questions

LEVEL 3: Advanced Topics

31. The Piezoelectric Effect

31.1 Use of Piezoelectric Materials
The piezoelectric effect found its first application in the early 1900s with sonar for submarines. Since then there have been myriad applications including piezoelectric buzzers, phonograph cartridges (the stylus for records), piezoelectric igniters for gas grills and small engines, clocks for electronic circuits, reflectometers to sense defects and flaws in metal structures such as airplane wings, sensing devices to warn vehicles of objects when backing up, and of course, ultrasound.

31.2 Crystal Structures
Virtually all metals, most ceramics, and some polymers crystallize when transitioning from liquid to solid form. When people think about crystals, the common perception is that crystals are precious minerals with numerous, somewhat translucent, relatively clear facets. For material scientists, the term crystal implies that the atomic or molecular arrangement is regular and repeated so that no matter in what direction within the material you travel, the same arrangement (pattern) exists. This repeated pattern in all three dimensions is generally referred to as three-dimensional periodicity. The smallest repeatable pattern of molecules is called a cell. There are many different geometric organizations (cells) possible for molecules to interlink such as cubic cells, tetragonal cells, orthorhombic cells, and hexagonal cells. How the molecules "pack" to form these various cell geometries depends on the type of bonds that occur between the molecules of the particular material and the number of molecules interconnecting. The term lattice is used to refer to space arrangement of the periodicity of a crystal. Therefore, the lattice constant is the edge dimension of the cell.

31.3 Intermolecular Bonds
As mentioned, the cells are comprised of various arrangements of bound molecules. Unlike the bonds within the molecules, the bonds between molecules are much weaker. Specifically, intramolecular bonds which hold a molecule together are much higher energy bonds than the intermolecular bonds that hold multiple molecules together. The relatively weak intermolecular bonds allow for the molecules to have some degree of movement when acted upon by some stress.

31.4 Polarization
There are some molecules which exist in a permanent state of polarization. For these molecules, the "center of mass" for the positive and negative charges of the molecule are not coincident, thereby creating a negative pole and a positive pole. In essence, one side of the molecule possesses a greater positive charge distribution and the other side has a greater negative charge distribution, creating what is called a dipole. Unless something breaks down the bond which holds the molecule intact, the dipole is permanent.

When a group of molecules are interconnected in a cell, the cell itself can have a polarization. Similar to how a dipole exists in an individual molecule, when the center of the collection of molecular dipoles is not in the center of the cell, a cell dipole exists. Now recalling that the intermolecular bonds are relatively weak, when the temperature rises above a certain point for a given molecular material, the molecules will arrange more uniformly into more symmetric cells, reducing the polarization of the cell. Below that temperature, called the Curie point, the molecules shift slightly within the cells, increasing the distance between the positive and negative poles, referred to as the dipole distance "d". The change in the dipole distance is very small, on the order of thousandths of a nanometer. The fact that the molecular cell structure changes with temperature is the foundation for the procedure of "poling" which was briefly described in Level 1 of this chapter, and further described a little later in this section.

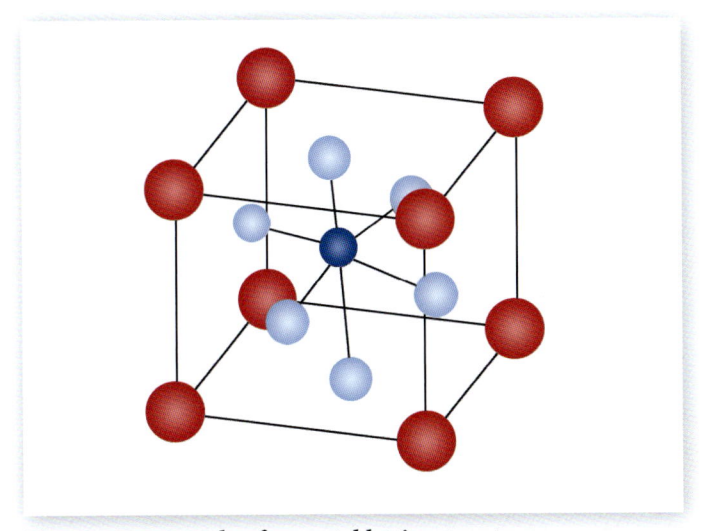

Fig. 71 **An example of a crystal lattice structure**

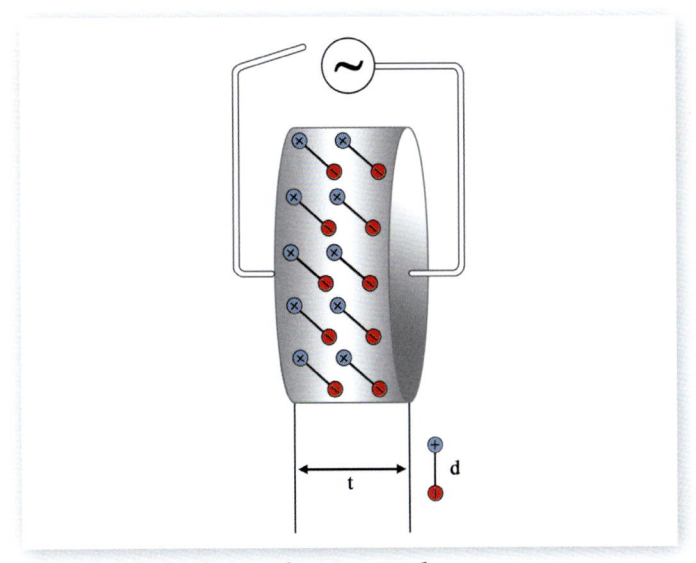

Fig. 72 **Polarized piezoelectric crystal**

Figure 72 depicts a crystal structure with polarized cells. Let's presume that the dipole distance in the "unperturbed state" has a length of "d". If you apply a voltage across the electrodes of the crystal, then the dipole length increases, as the positive and negative poles move towards the charged electrodes. Notice in the figure below, *Figure 73*, the negative distribution moves towards the positive electrode and the positive distribution moves toward the negative electrode. Since the dipole distance has increased, there is an expansion in the physical dimension of the crystal.

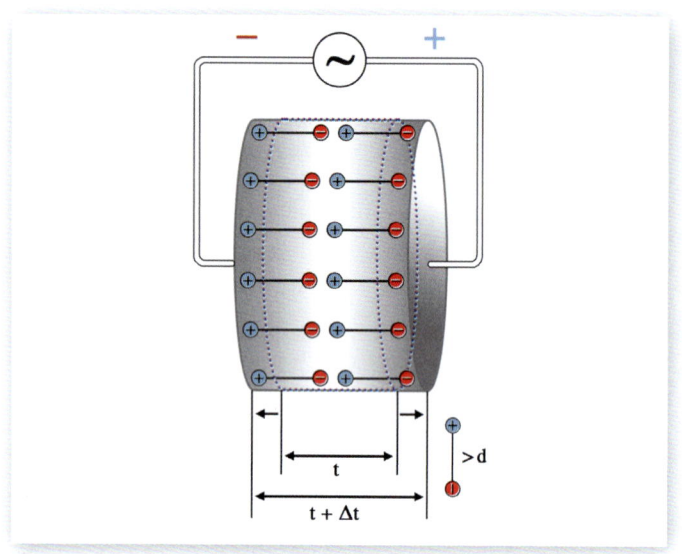

Fig. 73 **Crystal expansion**

If you reverse the polarity of the voltage applied across the electrodes, then the poles of the molecular cells are repelled, decreasing the dipole length. This causes a contraction of the material, as indicated in *Figure 74*.

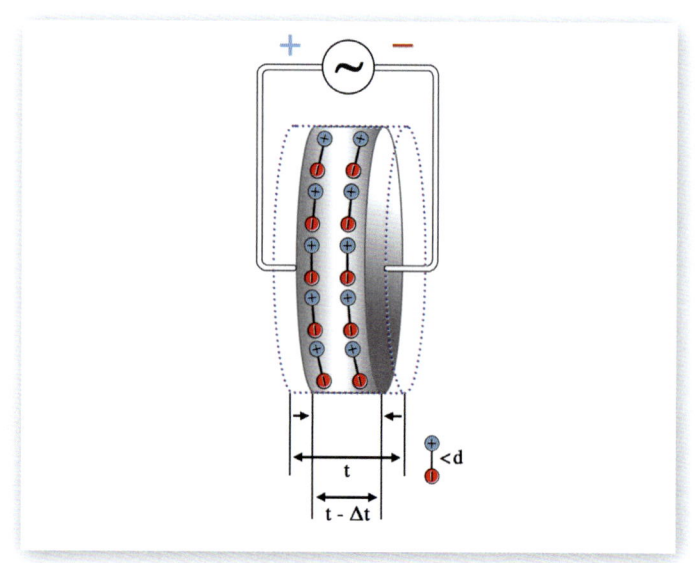

Fig. 74 **Crystal contraction**

In the process so far described, we have seen how an applied voltage can cause a physical deformation of the crystal dimension. In a reverse manner, if you mechanically compress the material, a voltage is produced. When a stress is induced to mechanically compress the material, the dipole length is shortened. Since the positive and negative charge distributions are forced closer together, there is an increase in the repulsive forces, creating an excess of charge. By measuring the excess charge from the attached electrodes, there is now a voltage change associated with the mechanical compression. A greater applied stress results in a greater strain and a larger excess of charge, or a larger measured voltage.

In our discussion in Level 1, we described poling as a process which made materials more efficient as a piezoelectric material. In reality, many materials that are ferroelectric are made piezoelectric through poling. Ferroelectric materials shrink when a voltage is applied, no matter what the polarity of the applied voltage. In contrast, a piezoelectric material can be made to both expand and contract.

Through the process of poling, the molecules reposition slightly to form a more uniform polarization. When the molecules shift, the dipole distance is shortened, decreasing the crystal size. Once removed from the electric field and high temperature, the molecules remain in their new locations, in essence, leaving the crystal in a "shrunken" form. Now when a voltage is applied, it is possible to make the crystal expand from the "shrunken" state or, depending on the polarity of the voltage applied, to further shrink. In other words, by poling the material, the material has been converted from a ferroelectric material to a piezoelectric material.

32. Newer Technologies

32.1 New Crystal Growth Technology

Even in our more in-depth treatment of poling, we have ignored some fundamental issues. From our treatment of poling, the presumption might be that all molecules align within the piezoceramic material during the process of poling, resulting in a relatively homogeneous transducer element. In reality, when crystals grow, there are discontinuities which develop at the molecular level referred to as grain boundaries. These grain boundaries act as imperfections such that perfect pole alignment is not achievable. At best, approximately 70% of the dipoles align, reducing the mechanical coupling coefficient (conversion coefficient from mechanical to electrical and electrical to mechanical energy). Over the last 40 years, the significant improvement in transducer performance has stemmed primarily from researching and designing new materials in conjunction with advances in matching layer technology. Very little success had been achieved relative to making more uniform crystals that would achieve higher polarization percentages.

As mentioned in Level 2, in the early 1970s some Russian and Japanese scientists discovered a new piezocrystal with extremely uniform crystal structure, PMN-PT crystals. These uniform crystals could achieve significantly better polarization resulting in much higher electro mechanical efficiency than with standard PZT ceramics. The following figure illustrates how grain boundaries of conventional crystals lead to less efficient poling than ideal.

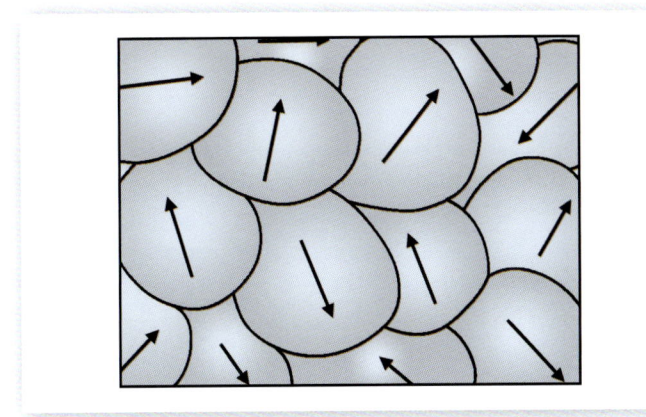

Fig. 75a **Crystal grain boundaries (notice imperfect alignment)**

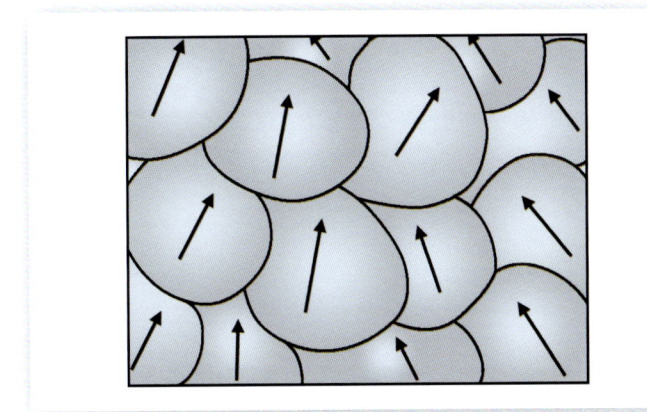

Fig. 75b **Crystal after poling (notice better but still imperfect polarization)**

The following figures illustrate actual crystal images under magnification. You will notice that the "conventional" PZT ceramic (*Figure 76*) exhibits many grain boundaries whereas the new technology (*Figure 77*) is completely uniform.

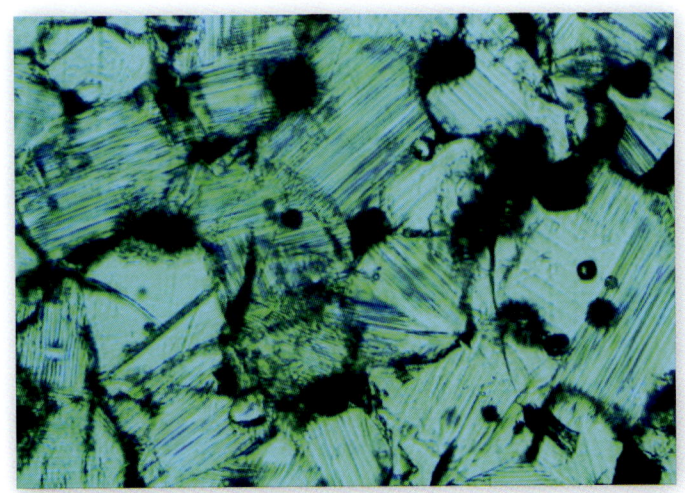

Fig. 76 **PZT ceramic (grain boundaries and imperfections evident)**

Fig. 77 **New technology (Completely uniform crystal structure)**

View ONLINE Animation and Image Library

*Crystal Growth Comparison

"To prepare conventional PZT ceramics, fine powders of the component metal oxides are mixed and then heated to form a uniform powder. The powder is mixed with an organic binder and baked into a dense polycrystalline structure. To produce Pure-Wave crystals, the fine ceramic powder is formed using a process similar to PZT powders; however the rest of the process is unique. The powder is then melted into liquid in a platinum crucible at 1400° C using a specially designed high temperature furnace with a precisely controlled temperature profile. To nucleate the crystal from the melt at the desired orientation, a seed crystal is pulled (or drawn) away from the melting zone slowly (less than 1 mm/hour) and the crystal is grown layer by layer atomically to form a homogeneous crystal "boule" or cylinder. Boules are orientated along the desired crystallographic orientation(s) to maximize the crystal properties and then sliced into multiple wafers."

Fig. 78 **Wafer and a crystal boule**

The result of this new uniform crystal structure is reported to be an increase in coupling efficiency by as much as 68% to 85%.

Furthermore, because of the uniform crystals structure, very wide bandwidths are achieved.

(*Excerpt and images reprinted with permission by Philips Medical Systems.)

> **✗ COMMON MISCONCEPTION: Transducers**
>
> **MISCONCEPTION:** *The highest beam intensity occurs at the focus.*
>
> **Explanation:**
> An overly simplistic analysis of the intensity equation leads to the conclusion that the highest intensity occurs at the beam focus. This would be true only if there were not attenuation such that the power remained constant with depth. Since the signal attenuates with depth but the power concentration increases towards the focus, the highest intensity is generally above the focus. For this reason, with respect to improving penetration, it is often better to set the focus for slightly deeper than the region of interest.

> **✗ COMMON MISCONCEPTION: Transducers**
>
> **MISCONCEPTION:** *2 MHz is 2 MHz.*
>
> **Explanation:**
> Just because two transducers both operate at 2 MHz, does not mean that both function the same at 2 MHz. In transducer design, there is often a trade-off between broader bandwidth and increased sensitivity. This trade-off is, to a degree, specified by the quality factor. Imagine a scenario in which one transducer has a very high Q factor at 2 MHz (very sensitive in the frequency ranges surrounding 2 MHz) and a second transducer has very broad bandwidth but with much lower sensitivity at 2 MHz. For imaging deep in a patient, and for non-superficial Doppler, the high Q factor transducer would, in this case, significantly outperform the broad bandwidth transducer.

CHAPTER SUMMARY: Transducers (Piezoelectric)

- A transducer is anything which converts one form of energy to another form of energy.
- An ultrasound transducer converts electropotential energy to mechanical, and mechanical energy to electropotential energy via the piezoelectric effect.
- The process of poling is used to enhance the piezoelectricity of a crystal.
- If a crystal is heated beyond the Curie temperature (300 degrees Celsius for PZT), the crystal can lose its piezoelectric properties.
- Lead zirconate titanate (PZT) historically has been the crystal material of choice for ultrasound transducers.
- Composite materials achieve greater conversion efficiency with less of an acoustic impedance mismatch than standard PZT crystals.
- Transducers may be single or multi-element, fixed focused or phased, mechanically or electronically steered.
- The field of view of a transducer is broken into two ranges: the near field (Fresnel) and the far field (Fraunhofer).
- The transition between the near and far field occurs at the focal depth. The focus is where the beam width is narrowest (best resolution and presumed highest beam intensity).
- Transducers can be run in continuous or pulsed mode. In continuous mode, the transmit frequency is determined by the frequency of drive voltage. In pulsed mode, the operating frequency is determined by both the propagation speed and the thickness of the element.

$$f_0 \, (MHz) = \frac{\text{Propagation Speed} \, (mm / \mu sec)}{2 \bullet (thickness) \, (mm)}$$

- The Near zone length (NZL = distance to focus) is proportional to the diameter of the transducer squared and also proportional to the frequency of the transducer.

$$NZL \, (mm) \approx \frac{D^2 \, (mm) \bullet f \, (MHz)}{6}$$

- The actual beam pattern in the Fresnel zone is extremely complex. For an unfocused transducer, a simple ap-

- proximation assumes that the beam tapers from the diameter of the transducer at skin level to 1/2 the diameter at the focal distance or NZL.
- The beam diverges in the Fraunhofer zone. The beamwidth increases from approximately 1/2 the diameter of the transducer at a distance of one NZL to the diameter of the transducer at a distance twice the NZL.
- A wider transducer aperture (opening or active region) creates a narrower beamwidth in the far field. Also, the higher the frequency, the narrower the beam in the far field.
- Focusing by use of lenses, mirrors, curved elements, and electronic phasing can decrease the beamwidth, but only in the near field (Fresnel Zone). In the far field, relative to the natural focus, the beam is diffraction limited.
- Generally, a longer near zone length (deeper focus) leads to greater depth of field. Larger apertures give a broader depth of field.
- The longitudinal resolution is determined by the spatial pulse length:

$$\text{Longitudinal Resolution} = \frac{\text{Spatial Pulse Length}}{2}$$

- The lateral resolution is determined by the lateral beamwidth:

$$\text{Lateral Resolution} = \text{Beamwidth}$$

As previously discussed, the beamwidth varies with depth, implying that the lateral resolution varies with depth for a given transducer.

- The elevation resolution is determined by the elevation beamwidth:

$$\text{Elevation Resolution} = \text{Elevation Beamwidth}$$

- A transducer consists of:
  - an element or multiple elements across which a voltage is applied
  - a backing material used to decrease the spatial pulse length
  - a matching layer or multiple matching layers to reduce the amount of reflection which results from a large acoustic impedance mismatch
  - an acoustic lens (or other focusing techniques) which reshapes the beam so as to provide a more optimum beam width per specific application
  - a pair of wires for each element to conduct the driving voltage and the return echo voltage from and to the system
- A 1-D phased array has multiple elements in the lateral direction which can be turned on or off and/or phased to steer and focus laterally.
- 1-D arrays produce two-dimensional images.
- A sector phased array produces a scan in a sector format purely by phasing the elements to steer at various angles.
- The sector format was produced specifically for rib access.
- A linear phased array can be operated in a few different ways to produce a scan.
- For non-steered 2D imaging or color imaging, sequencing is used.
- For steered 2D imaging (some systems can steer 2D images) and steered color images, a combination of sequencing and phasing is used.
- Curved linear phased array transducers produce images purely by sequencing.
- A 2D array has multiple elements in both the lateral and elevation direction which can be turned on or off and/or phased to steer and focus both laterally and elevationally. 2D arrays can produce two-dimensional or three-dimensional images.

ONLINE EXTRAS

For additional support material and to view your completion progress, visit:
www.pegasuslectures.com/6thEdExtras

Extras by Chapter include:
- Animations
- Videos
- Additional Images
- Clarifying Clips
- Supplemental Exercises
- Conceptual Questions

See page x of Preface for access instructions

References

Woo, J. (1998). *Obstetric Ultrasound History Web*. Ob-Ultrasound.net. http://www.ob-ultrasound.net/articulated-arm.html. (Figure 30)

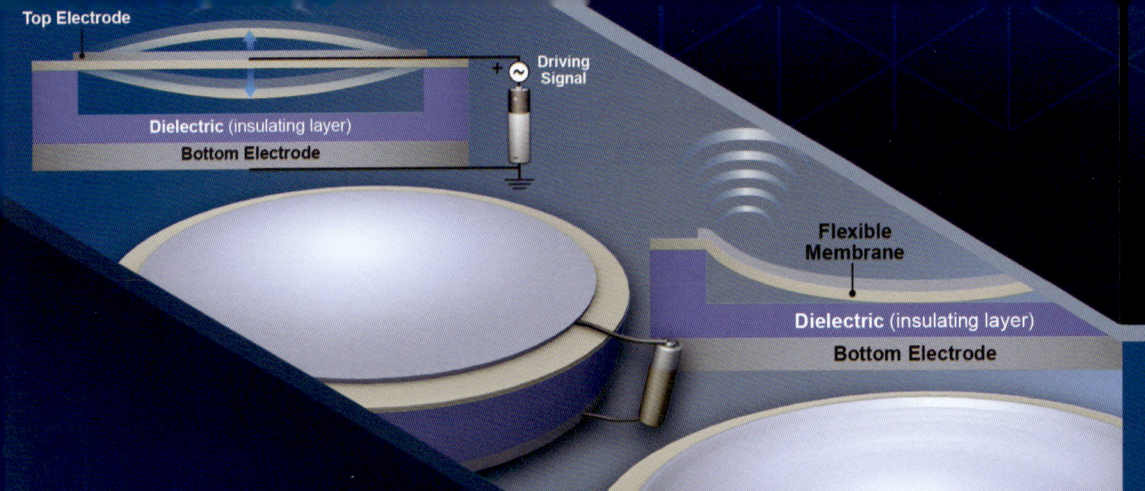

Transducers
(CMUT)

Chapter 5 Part II

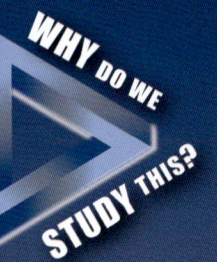

WHY DO WE STUDY THIS?

▸ Capacitive Micromachined Ultrasonic Transducer (CMUT) technology is in the process of revolutionizing ultrasound.

▸ CMUT is reducing cost, increasing operating frequency ranges, and creating new paradigms for ultrasound transducers and clinical applications.

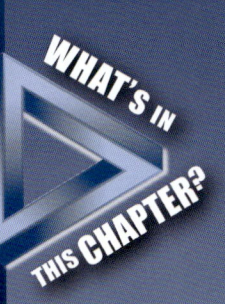

WHAT'S IN THIS CHAPTER?

LEVEL 1 — BASIC ULTRASOUND PHYSICS
The basics of CMUT theory are developed, starting with the underlying principle of capacitance, progressing through how a single capacitive cell produces sound, and concluding with a basic block model of a CMUT cell.

LEVEL 2 — BOARD LEVEL
Continues the transducer evolution of the previous section, showing how CMUT can be used as the foundation not only for 1-D and 2D arrays, but also for miniaturized array transducers that scan virtually the entire body.

LEARNING OBJECTIVES

▸ Explain the concept of capacitance and how it is calculated

▸ Describe how varying the changing electric field of a capacitor can be used to create sound

▸ List the main components of a capacitive cell

▸ Explain how multiple cells can act as an "element," and how a group of these elements can constitute a transducer array

▸ List the advantages of CMUT relative to piezoelectric transducers

Chapter 5 – Part II
Transducers (CMUT)

Introduction

This chapter continues the topic of transducers discussing a technological change that is once again revolutionizing ultrasound: CMUT technology. As mentioned in Part I of Chapter 5, up to the present day, ultrasound transducers have functioned on the piezoelectric principle discovered by the Curie brothers in the 1880s. Theses transducers improved in bandwidth and sensitivity over the last five decades, but always brought with them tremendous cost, manufacturing complexity, and restricted design formats. However, a new technology, called CMUT, which has been showing promise since the early 1990s is finally ready to truly impact ultrasound. In Level 1 of this chapter, the basics of CMUT theory are developed. In Level 2, we will continue the transducer evolution of the previous chapter, showing how CMUT can now be used as the foundation not only for 1-D and 2D arrays, but also for miniaturized arrays, transducers that scan virtually the entire body, and even potentially wearable devices.

1. Capacitive Micromachined Ultrasonic Transducer (CMUT)

The concept of sound resulting from vibration of a material is the same regardless of the mechanism that creates the vibration. CMUT technology was first invented in the 1990s with significant research performed at Stanford University. The new technology excited everyone in the field, holding promise of incredible design flexibility, significant decreases in manufacturing complexity and related cost, and improved performance. Significant fabrication and integration challenges limited the use of this technology for nearly three decades.

In recent years, CMUT technology has become a viable alternative to using piezoelectric materials for ultrasound transducers. Like piezoelectric materials, mechanical vibrations are produced by varying the applied electrical field. Also, like piezoelectric materials, when CMUT transducers are mechanically vibrated, they produce a varying electrical field. Unlike piezoelectric materials, the varying electric signal does not result from variations in the crystal structure of the material, but rather from a change in the capacitance of the device. For this reason, a basic understanding of capacitance is necessary to develop an understanding of CMUT transducer functionality.

1.1 Capacitance and Capacitors

Electrical capacitance is defined as the stored electrical charge when a potential difference (voltage) is applied between electrical conductors.

$$C = \frac{q}{V}$$

In circuit design, the devices used to store this charge are called capacitors. In a sense, capacitors act like "small" batteries to apply electrical current (flowing charge). Capacitors (*Figure 1*) can be used for many applications such as stabilizing and filtering noise from power supplies, creating filters to pass or reject certain signals, or supply extra current when a sudden, short duration increase is needed such as in a defibrillator or camera flash.

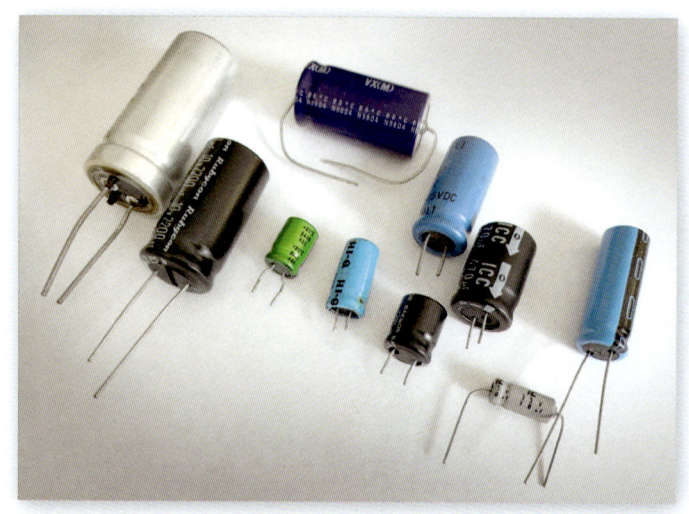

Fig. 1 **Various types and sizes of capacitors used in circuit design**

> **KEY CONCEPT**
>
> **CMUT technology is based on the concept of creating and detecting sound through a variable capacitor.**

1.2 Fundamentals of Capacitance

Figure 2 shows the basic schematic of a capacitor. A capacitor, in its most basic form, consists of two electrical conductors separated by a gap. In this example, the conductors are two parallel plates. By applying a voltage across the two plates, an electrical charge is built up over the area of the conductors producing an electric field (as expressed in the equation: C = q/V). In between the two conducting plates any poor conductor of electricity (insulating) material) can exist. In the simplest design, the plates are separated by a layer of air.

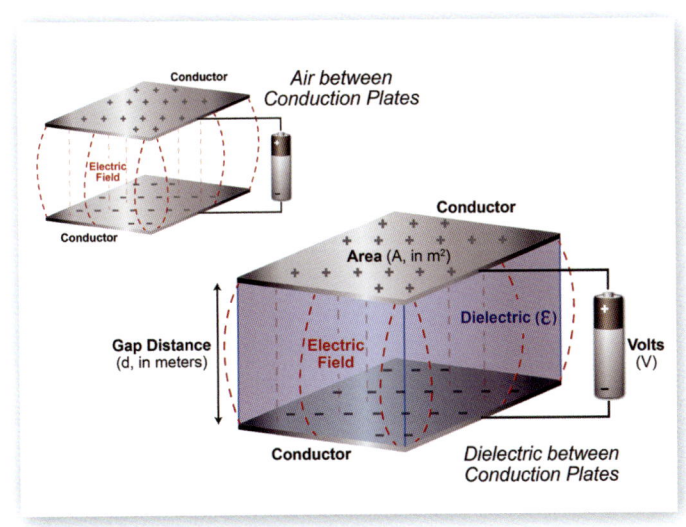

Fig. 2 **Basic parallel plate capacitor**

Using the basic parallel plate capacitor design with air between the conducting plates, the capacitance equation can be written in terms of the properties of the materials as follows:

$$C = \frac{\varepsilon_o A}{d}$$

Where: C = capacitance in Farads
ε_o = permittivity of free space
A = plate area (m²)
d = plate separation distance (m)

As seen from the equation, the capacitance is proportional to a property of free space (vacuum) called the permittivity. The permittivity is a measure of the resistance to an electric field. Frequently, an insulating material called the dielectric layer is put in place of the vacuum between the two plates. The simplest dielectric material is air. Air has a relative permittivity only slightly higher than that of a vacuum. By replacing the air with a dielectric material of a higher relative permittivity, the capacitance can be made greater for the same size plates and area. These dielectric materials are usually solids. For example, using waxed paper allows for a capacitance approximately 2.5 times greater than using air for the same size capacitor. When using a dielectric layer, the equation must take into account the relative permittivity of the material relative to free space so that the equation becomes:

$$C = \frac{\kappa \varepsilon_o A}{d}$$

Where: κ = relative permittivity of the dielectric

Note: By measuring the permittivity relative to free space, the equation for a capacitor with a dielectric material is virtually the same as one with a vacuum, with the simple addition of the κ factor.

So you should be asking yourself, "why should I care about how a capacitor works?" The simple answer is that the concept of capacitance and varying electric fields is the foundational principle behind the new CMUT technology which is revolutionizing the field of ultrasound.

1.3 Basic CMUT Theory (Non-Collapse Mode)

CMUT technology is based on the concept of creating a series or network of variable capacitors (cells) which operate together to function as a transducer. We will begin by considering a single cell of the network. As specified in Section 1.2, a simple capacitor consists of two plate conductors separated by a distance, "d", with a vacuum and/or dielectric material between, and an applied voltage. *Figure 3* is a schematic drawing of a single capacitive cell. Note the similarity between this drawing and the basic capacitor depiction of *Figure 2*.

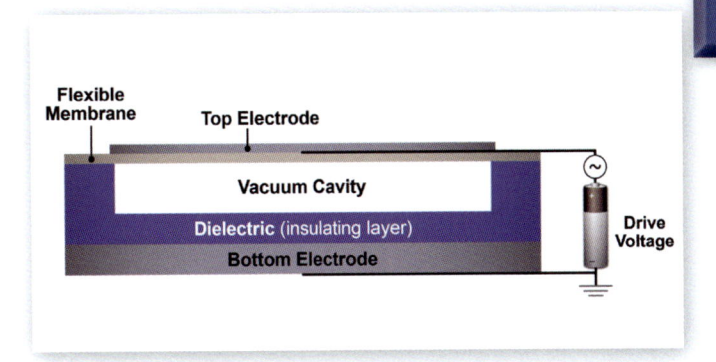

Fig. 3a **CMUT single cell cross-section (2-dimensional slice depiction)**

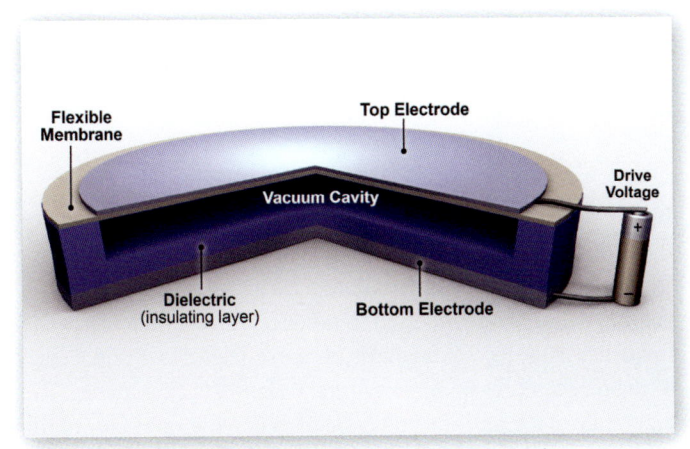

Fig. 3b **CMUT single cell (3-dimensional depiction)**

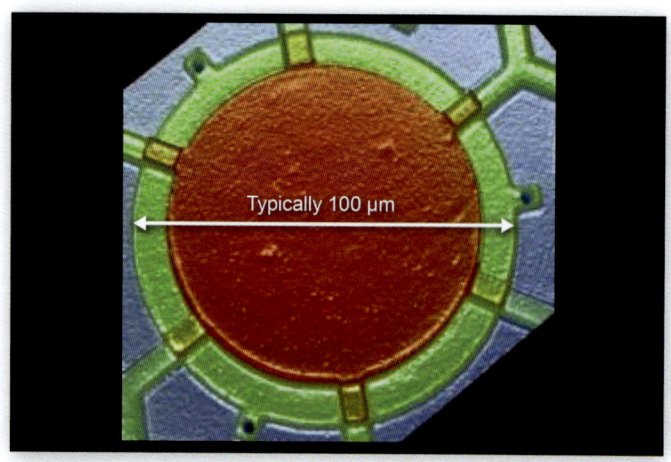

Fig. 3c **Actual photograph of a CMUT cell** *(Courtesy of R. van Schaijk, Phillips Innovation Services)*

Notice that the top electrode of the capacitor is on a flexible membrane and that the bottom electrode is fixed. By carrying the drive voltage, the top electrode can be displaced towards or away from the bottom electrode, in essence, varying the capacitance. By causing the flexible membrane on top to move back and forth, a vibration is created that serves as a transmit signal. In other words, the varying electric signal is converted to a mechanical vibration by allowing the top electrode of the capacitor to be displaced from its at-rest position (*Figure 4a*). The frequency of the generated wave is determined by the frequency of the drive voltage.

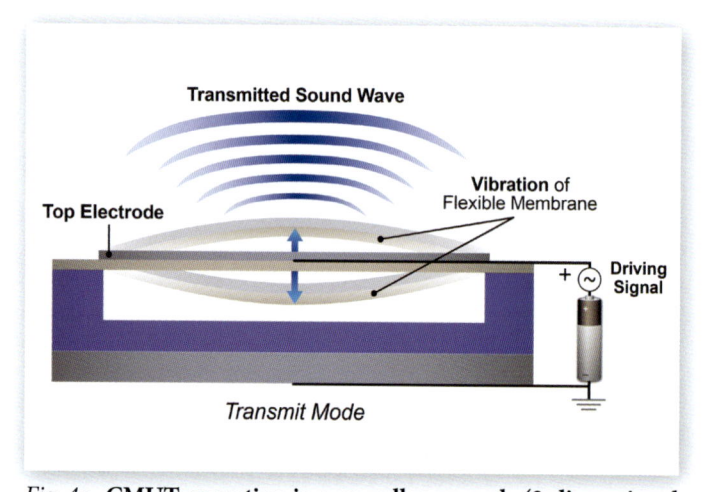

Fig. 4a **CMUT operation in non-collapse mode (2-dimensional slice depiction)**

In reverse, when a sound wave vibrates the flexible membrane of the CMUT cell, the capacitance fluctuates, creating a varying electric field (*Figure 4b*). The variation in electric field is detected as a varying voltage and processed to produce ultrasound images. The frequency of the received signal is, of course, related to the frequency of the mechanical signal causing the variation in capacitance. The amplitude of the received voltage is related to the amplitude of the reflected sound waves interacting with the flexible membrane.

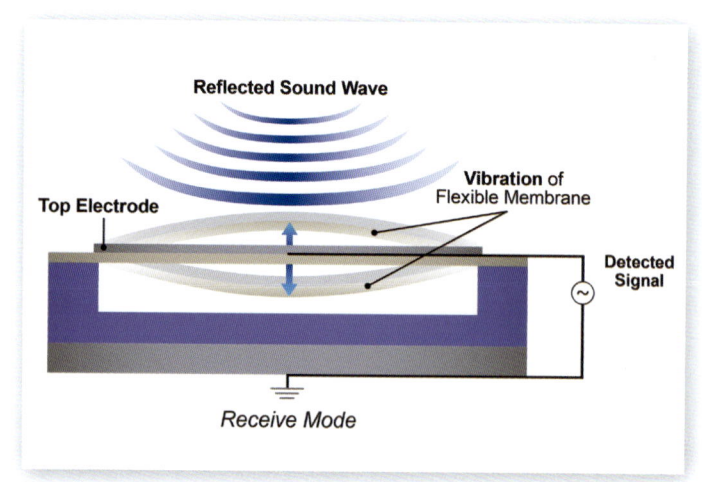

Fig. 4b **CMUT in receive mode (2-dimensional slice depiction)**

View ONLINE Animation and Image Library

KEY CONCEPT

In receive mode, when the flexible membrane of a CMUT cell vibrates, the distance between the electrodes changes, producing a varying electrical signal. The larger the displacement, the stronger the signal. For transmit mode, applying a varying signal results in vibrations of the flexible membrane.

1.4 Collapse Mode

Although many of the technological advancements in terms of fabrication techniques, materials used, and tuning of electrical properties are well beyond the scope of this book, one advancement, referred to as collapse mode, is so important that it warrants mention. As depicted in previous figures, the highest amplitude signal was generated from the center of the flexible membrane, the region with the greatest displacement. In collapse mode, a bias (DC) voltage is applied so that the center of the flexible plate is attracted to the bottom electrode and comes in actual contact with the top of the insulating material (*Figure 5a*).

As seen in *Figure 5b*, this mode of operation leaves only the outer ring free to vibrate with varying drive voltages (in transmit mode) and with varying mechanical vibrations (in receive mode). Because the effective distance between the top plate and the bottom plate is smaller, the resulting electric field is higher. The result is that the CMUT cell is more efficient both in transmit and receive mode, making the transducer significantly more sensitive. Operation in collapse mode also has the effect of shifting the operating frequency up from non-collapse mode. Therefore, by varying the bias voltage, the frequency of operation is tunable, with a higher bias voltage resulting in a higher operating frequency (*Figure 6*). Collapse mode has made CMUT technology not only valuable for ultrasound imaging, but also makes high intensity focused ultrasound (HIFU) techniques (see Chapter 18: Focused Ultrasound) viable with the same transducer.

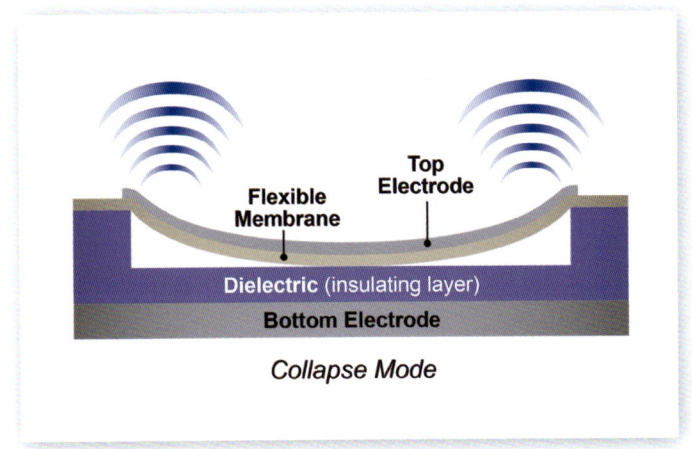

Fig. 5a **CMUT operating in collapse mode (2-dimensional slice depiction)**

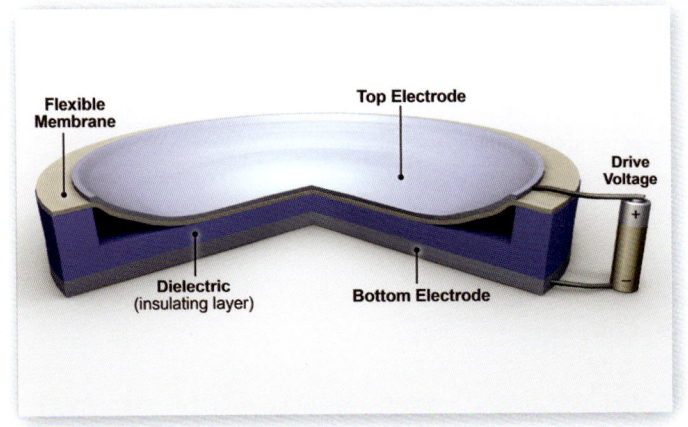

Fig. 5b **CMUT operating in collapse mode (3-dimensional depiction)**

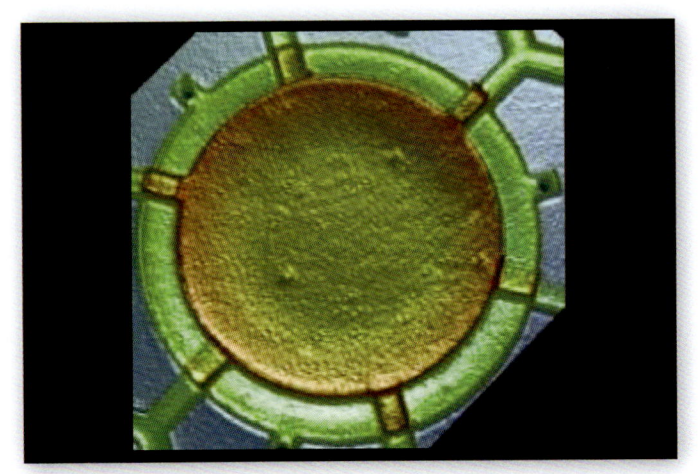

Fig. 5c **Actual photograph of a CMUT cell in collapse mode**
(*Courtesy of R. van Schaijk, Phillips Innovation Services*)

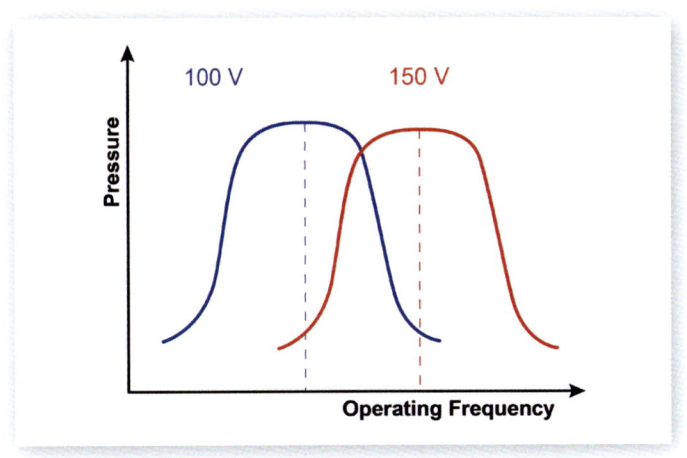

Fig. 6 **CMUT bias voltage effect on operating frequency**

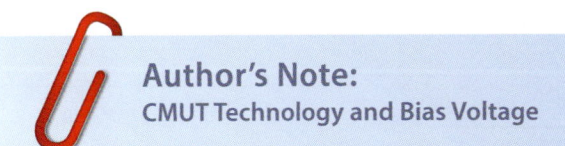

Author's Note:
CMUT Technology and Bias Voltage

CMUT technology allows for frequency tuning by controlling the bias voltage. A higher bias voltage results in a greater region of collapse and a higher operating frequency.

KEY CONCEPT

Collapse mode improves the efficiency of a CMUT in both transmit and receive mode. Collapse mode also increases the frequency of operation and makes the operating frequency "tunable." A higher bias voltage results in a higher operating frequency.

View ONLINE Clarifying Clip

2. CMUT Acoustic Impedance Matching

For piezoelectric transducers we discussed the poor coupling efficiency of sound into and out of the patient because of the large acoustic impedance mismatch between the high impedance of the crystal material and the low impedance of the tissue. This mismatch results in the use of a matching layer or layers of intermediate impedance(s) so as to improve coupling efficiency. CMUT transducers have an inherent advantage over piezoelectric materials in that the acoustic impedance of the flexible membrane tends to be very close to that of tissue. As a result, the impedance mismatch between the front surface of a CMUT and the patient is small and there is generally no need for the use of a matching layer (or layers).

3. Acoustic Window and Bandwidth

Although a matching layer is not needed for CMUT, a material must be put over the cells to act as a barrier between the patient and the CMUT cells. This material is referred to as an acoustic window. Ideally, the acoustic impedance of the acoustic window will be close to that of the membrane and tissue, and have a low absorption rate.

Two materials that are currently used are polydimethylsiloxane (PDMS) and polybutadiene rubber (PBR). PDMS is a material commonly used for underwater acoustic applications because it has an acoustic impedance (approximately 1.5 MRayls) and a propagation velocity (approximately 1500 m/sec) very close to that of water. Recall from Chapter 3 that most tissues have an acoustic impedance of approximately 1.6 MRayls, making PDMS a very good impedance match for transducers in the lower frequency range. PBR has many different formulations but also has advantageous acoustic properties including low acoustic absorption rates up to over 25 MHz, thereby making it a good candidate for an acoustic window material.

Figure 7 shows the bandwidth comparison of a commercial PZT-based probe with a CMUT-based probe using PBR for the acoustic window. Notice the significant difference in fractional bandwidth: 80% for a commercial PZT-based probe versus 107% for a CMUT-based probe using PB for the acoustic window.

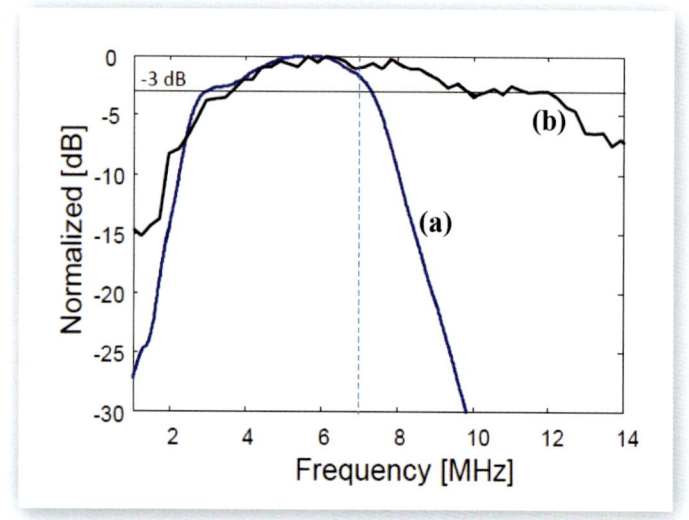

Fig. 7 **Bandwidth comparison of (a) commercial PZT-based probe with (b) CMUT-based probe** *(Adapted from MEMS and Micro Devices, R. van Schaijk, Phillips Innovation Services)*

4. Backing Material

For piezoelectric transducers, we learned the importance of using a backing material. The new CMUT technology also requires the use of a backing material. As you will learn in greater detail in Chapter 8: Artifacts, ultrasound is predicated on the assumption that sound travels to a target and back to the transducer only once. If the sound reverberates between structures, including part of the transducer itself, structures will appear multiple times in the image, creating an artifact referred to as reverberation. Reverberation artifact is a significant reason why backing material is critical for CMUT technology. Since the impedance mismatch between air and the silicon substrate at the back of the CMUT cell is so high, significant reflections from the back surface of the CMUT cell toward the front surface occur, resulting in reverberation artifacts within the ultrasound image. The backing material is critical for absorbing, or redirecting, this energy.

Since this technology is relatively young, there is significant research into optimizing the backing material design, with associated patents being filed. Some approaches entail creating a "refractive" path that redirects the energy from returning back toward the front surface and patient. Other approaches are very similar to the concept discussed in terms of matching layers for piezoelectric transducers. In essence, the problem is the same whether occurring at the front surface or back of the transducer: large impedance mismatches result in large reflections and poor transmission. By creating backing materials that better match to the silicon substrate, more energy can be coupled into the backing material, reducing the energy reflected back toward the front surface, thereby reducing reverberation artifacts.

5. Focusing

In Part I of Chapter 5, we discussed four different techniques for focusing. The same focusing techniques can be used for CMUT technology as discussed for piezoelectric crystals. Note that one of the great advantages of CMUT technology is design flexibility. Collections of CMUT cells can be networked on a flexible, curved surface that can effectively act as a lens. This approach will be further discussed in Level 2 of this chapter.

6. CMUT Transducer Model

Recall from Chapter 5, Part I the importance of the block diagram models as a didactic tool. You should be able to explain the functionality of each of the components for the CMUT model. You should also make note of the similarities and differences between the piezoelectric and CMUT models.

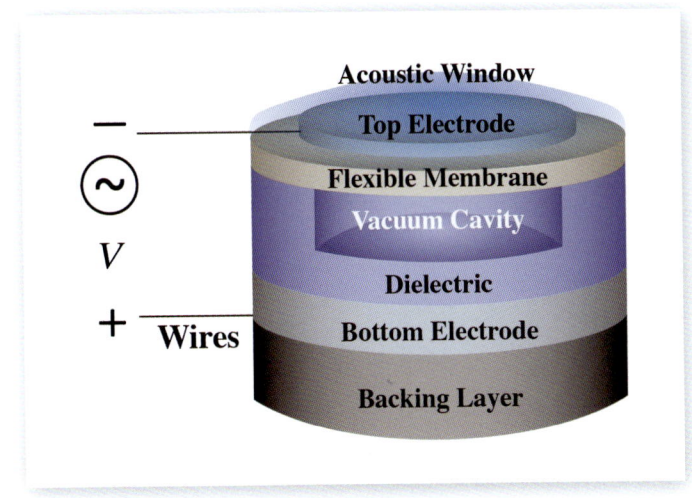

Fig. 8 **CMUT transducer block diagram**

Acoustic Window:	Interface layer between patient and CMUT surface. Ideally matched in impedance to patient, with low absorption rate
Electrodes:	Basic components of the capacitor which hold electrical charge to create an electric field
Dielectric Layer:	Used to increase capacitance and keep electrodes from shorting in collapse mode
Wires:	Transmit – delivers voltage to capacitive cell Receive – delivers echo related voltage to system receivers
Transmit/receive signal:	Consists of a DC bias voltage "V" (tunes transmit frequency in collapse mode) and a varying signal which creates the transmit signal and is processed to create an image in receive mode
Backing material:	Shortens spatial pulse length, improving longitudinal resolution and absorbs reflections, reducing reverberations

KEY CONCEPT

Because of the low acoustic impedance of the flexible membrane on the surface of a CMUT cell, no matching layer is needed.

LEVEL 2: Board Level

7. CMUT Transducers

As mentioned throughout the last sections, the manufacturing process for piezoelectric transducers is very complex, requiring many delicate and time consuming steps, many of which must be performed by hand. In addition to the labor intensive process, the materials are very expensive, especially for the newer "single crystal" materials, and the process is prone to wide variations in performance, resulting in transducers that do not always fall within specifications, and therefore result in a percentage of waste and even more cost. As mentioned in Level 1, research into capacitive micromachined ultrasound transducers began in the early 1990s as a promising technique to reduce the labor intensive, expensive, complex production of ultrasound transducers.

In Level 1, we learned about how an individual capacitive cell could both produce and detect sound waves. Although the theory was proven very early on, creating reliable fabrication methods to produce ultrasound array transducers took many years. The first generation CMUT was developed in 1994. The first commercially available ultrasound CMUT transducers were produced by Hitachi in 2009 with applications for breast imaging. The second commercial release came eight years later in 2017 by Butterfly Network Inc. and by Kolo Medical, a spinoff company from the Stanford researchers. With mass production of CMUT, we are now poised for yet another revolution in ultrasound.

7.1 CMUT Arrays (1-D)

For piezoelectric crystals, the smallest part of a transducer capable of producing or receiving sound is called an "element." For CMUT technology, the smallest part of the transducer is an individual cell. In Section 1.3 we saw that an individual capacitive cell is typically about 100 μm and almost always less than 500 μm, clearly too small to operate as an ultrasound transducer on its own. In fact, recall that we learned that the near zone length is related to the diameter squared. So for a 100 μm (0.1 mm) diameter cell, with an operating frequency of 6 MHz, the natural focal depth would be at approximately 0.01 mm (0.001 cm), clearly too shallow to be functional for diagnostic ultrasound. Additionally, the area of the transducer face is so small that there would be low intensity transmit and receive signals. To be useful, a collection of cells operate together to perform a function similar to an element of a piezoelectric crystal. Therefore, an entire array of elements (each a collection of cells) are needed to comprise a transducer with a reasonable focal depth and sensitivity.

One of the many great advantages of CMUT technology is the flexibility allowed in creating different format transducers. *Figure 9b* shows a "simple" 64 element 1-D array using CMUT technology. Note the similarity between this design and the standard piezoelectric array shown in *Figure 9a*. Of course the major difference is that instead of each element existing as a single block of piezoelectric crystal, each "element" consists of an entire array of capacitive cells.

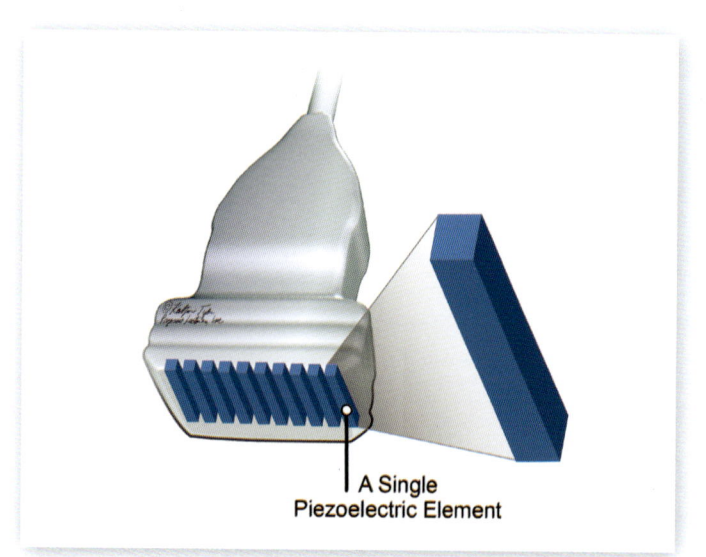

Fig. 9a **Schematic drawing showing a PZT-based 1-D array**

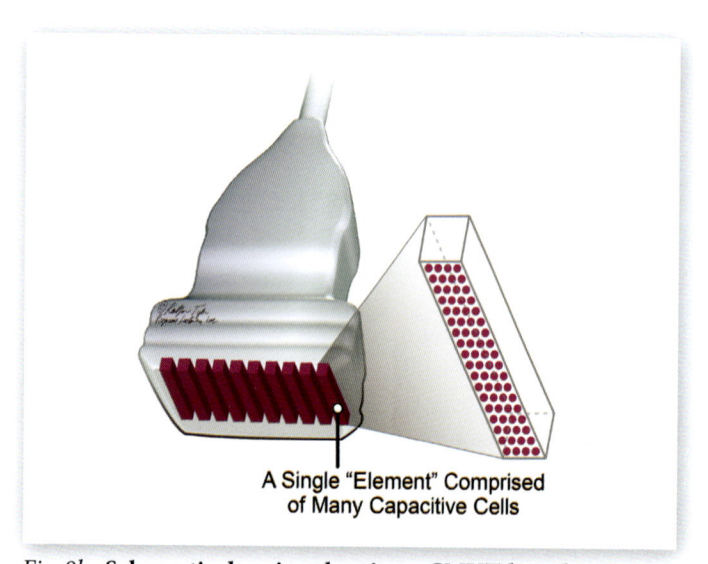

Fig. 9b **Schematic drawing showing a CMUT-based 1-D array**

Figure 10 shows an actual 1-D CMUT transducer that operates at a center frequency of 8.5 MHz with a fractional bandwidth of 80% (4.8 MHz to 11.2 MHz). This particular transducer has a collapse voltage of 50 V DC and has a maximum pressure output of 3.5 MPa. (Specifications courtesy of Philips Innovation Services).

Fig. 10 **8.5 MHz (center frequency), 96 element 1-D CMUT imaging transducer** *(Courtesy of Philips Innovation Services)*

In *Figure 11* below, (a) shows the surface of an actual 64 element CMUT array; (b) shows an expanded view of the CMUT array that shows a portion of six of the elements of the array; and (c) shows a further expanded view that depicts the individual cells that function collectively to comprise an element of the array.

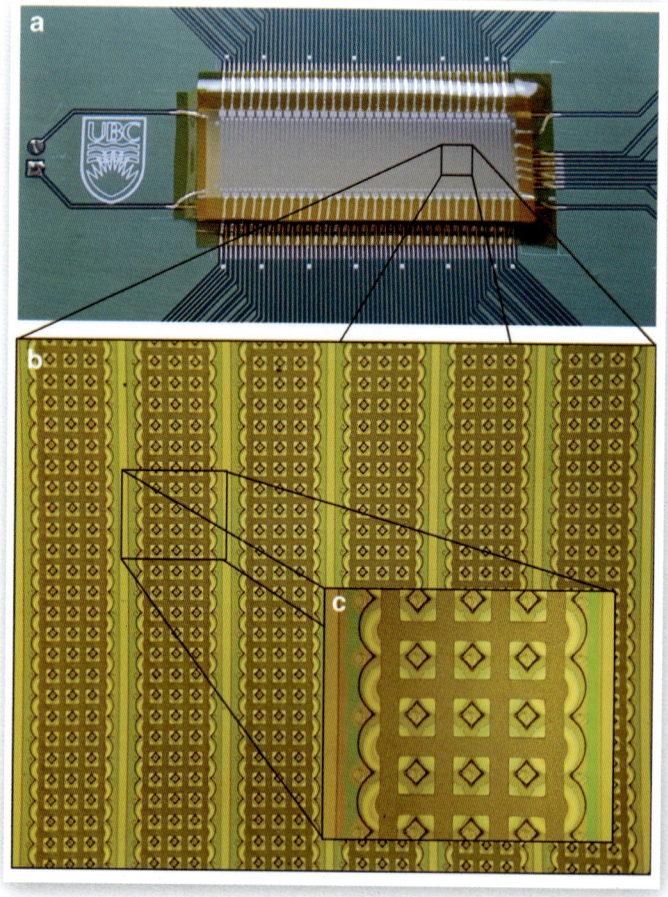

Fig. 11 **64 element CMUT 1-D array** *(Courtesy of C.D. Gerardo, E. Cretu, and R. Rohling)*

7.2 CMUT Matrix Arrays (2D)

Analogous to how 2D (matrix) arrays are constructed using piezoelectric crystals, CMUT technology can be employed. *Figure 12* shows a conceptual schematic of a CMUT matrix transducer. Notice that there are multiple elements in both the lateral and elevation direction. Like the piezoelectric array, this pattern allows for tremendous imaging freedom including the ability to focus and steer both laterally and elevationally as well as to produce real-time 3D images.

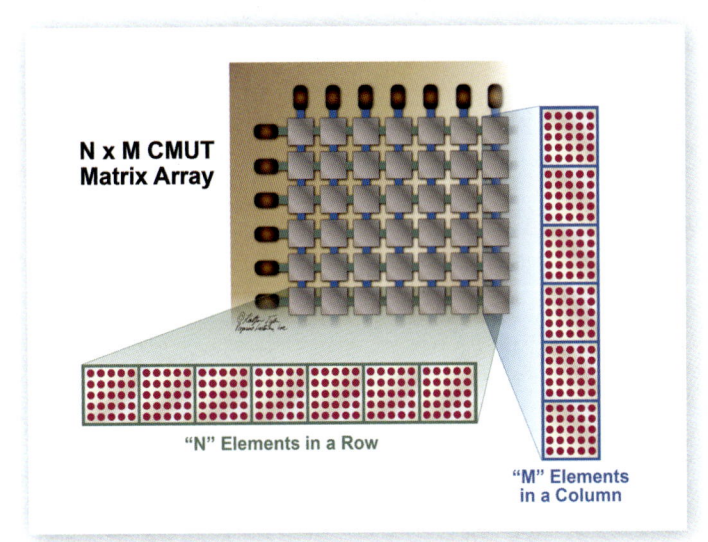

Fig. 12 **Graphical representation of an N x M CMUT (2D) Array**

Figure 13 shows an 18 x 18 CMUT 2D array. Notice that an individual cell is connected both to a "line" in the lateral dimension and to a "line" in the elevation dimension.

Fig. 13 **An 18 x 18 CMUT 2D Array** (*Courtesy of Philips Innovation Services*)

7.3 CMUT Advantages

There are many advantages that CMUT technology offers relative to piezoelectric crystals. CMUT technology is built onto silicon wafers or into application-specific integrated circuits (ASICS). Although the tooling necessary to create these manufacturing processes is extremely expensive, once completed, transducers can be rapidly mass produced at relatively low cost without the fastidious hand work required for crystal technology. A large advantage of being built into an ASIC is that many different form factors can be created, including different shapes to meet specific needs and miniaturization. Capacitive cells in the same array can be designed for different frequency operation as well as the fact that frequency tunability allows for the same cells to be run at different frequencies. For example, for greater penetration while still producing very high resolution near field imaging, the elements of the outer edge can be run at a lower frequency while the elements in the middle are run at a higher frequency (*Figure 14*) giving CMUT arrays a natural, programmable way to create the same effect as the Hanafy lens discussed earlier.

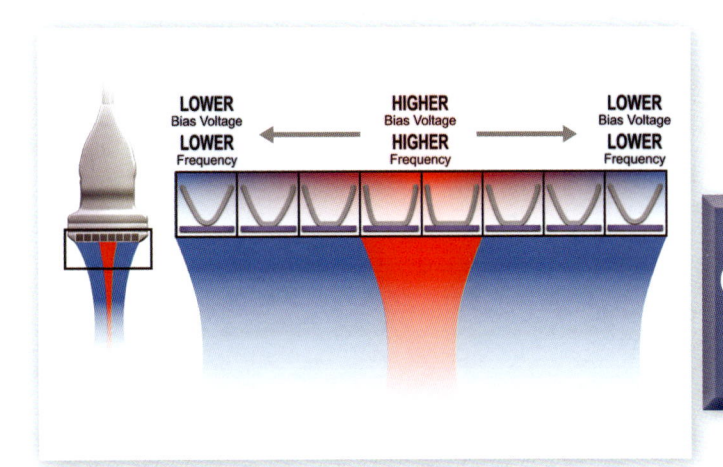

Fig. 14 **Dynamic frequency control using CMUT**

CMUT allows for dynamic control over frequency of operation, even for the potential to have some elements transmit at different frequencies at the same time.

Benefits of CMUT:
- Faster and less expensive to manufacture
- Higher percentage yield (less variability from transducer to transducer)
- Higher frequency applications
- Extremely flexible – can be used in any form factor or shape including micro-miniature device (like catheters) and has the potential to be used in flexible sheets (potential wearable devices)
- Efficiency close to PZT ceramics (but currently much less than single crystal)
- Lower acoustic impedance – better matching to patient without the need for match layer(s)
- Extremely wide bandwidth – can use same transducer at very wide range of frequencies (tunable by controlling bias voltage in collapse mode); note that, in collapse mode, the DC bias voltage plus the AC (transmit) voltage is limited by the dielectric breakdown voltage; this limit reduces the maximum transmit signal,

potentially limiting performance at the higher frequencies of the bandwidth
- Ability to include cells that are optimized for different frequencies in the same array
- Tremendous operational flexibility such as ability to simultaneously transmit with different frequencies on different parts of the array
- Lead-free so RoHS compliant (Restriction of the Use of certain Hazardous Substances in Electrical and Electronic Equipment)
- Less heat production than piezoelectric crystals allowing for higher transmit powers in higher duty factor modes (like CW, PW, and color Doppler) which are often restricted because of transducer surface heating; also an advantage for invasive ultrasound such as ultrasound catheters and endoscopic imaging arrays
- Same transducer can potentially be used for both diagnostic ultrasound and therapeutic ultrasound (See Chapter 18: Focused Ultrasound)

CMUT allows for complex, miniaturized form factors. *Figure 15* shows an actual CMUT catheter. Notice the size relative to the head of a match shown in the inlay of the photograph.

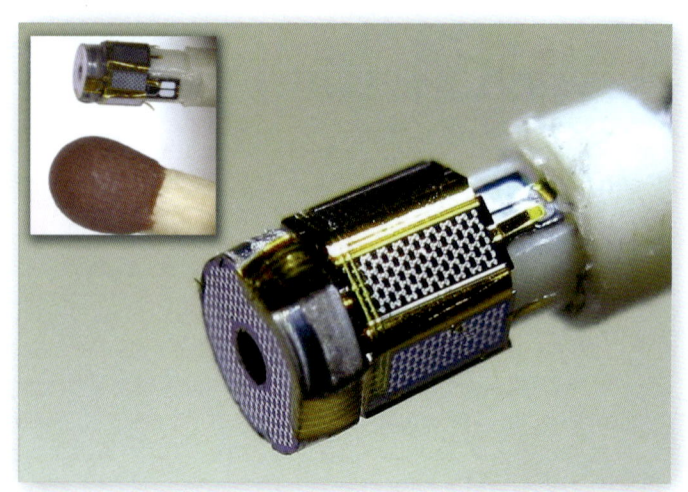

Fig. 15 **A miniature CMUT catheter** *(Courtesy of Philips Innovation Services, MEMS and Micro Devices: Rob van Schaijk)*

One of the advantages mentioned above is the tremendous flexibility in transducer form factor. Because the CMUT cells can be constructed into virtually any shape and onto flexible layers, the possibility of creating large, wearable transducers or transducers that potentially wrap over the top of the abdomen can now be imagined. Unlike rigid PZT-based designs, CMUT designs will likely be possible to solve virtually any geometry.

In the future, it might be possible to create "wearable" imaging devices. *Figure 16* shows a proof of concept in which four CMUT sector arrays were built into a single flexible strip connector. The strip of transducers was laid over a CIRS imaging phantom producing the ultra-wide image as displayed.

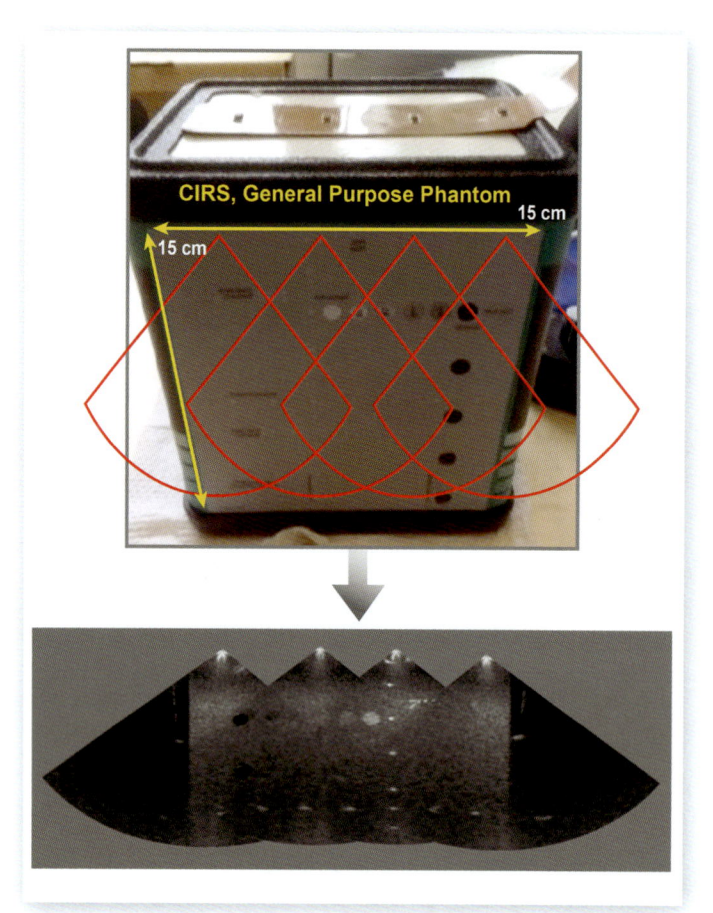

Fig. 16 **Concept showing 4 CMUT sector arrays built into a single flexible strip connector** *(Courtesy of Philips Innovation Services, MEMS and Micro Devices: Rob van Schaijk)*

7.4 Application of Increased Bandwidth

It is instructive to consider how the specifications of CMUT transducers is changing the field of ultrasound. From the list of benefits, we have seen that one of the greatest advantages is the extraordinary wide bandwidth. Many of the advantages of increased bandwidth will become apparent in later chapters as we discuss applications.

One of the greatest benefits of increased bandwidth is the ability to use the same transducer for both easy and difficult to image patients. With the extremely wide bandwidth offered by CMUT, some companies are suggesting that a single transducer can be used for "whole body imaging." Butterfly, Inc. now offers a single probe solution for scanning adult and pediatric patients including but not limited to cardiac, abdomen, small parts, vascular, and lungs. The transducer is rechargeable and connects to a tablet or phone. *Figure 17* shows the Butterfly transducer (a) and a cutaway image showing the CMUT stack that comprises the 2D array and the associated surface mount electronics inside the handle (b).

Chapter 5 | Part II: Transducers (CMUT)   189

frequency of 30 MHz. The bandwidth used by this transducer ranges from 22 to 38 MHz.

The result of being able to image at frequencies above 20 MHz is that there are now many new superficial imaging applications, including dermatology. The images in *Figures 18b*, *18c*, and *18d* (more available online) were created by the KOLO L38-22 transducer.

Fig. 17a **Photograph of a Butterfly transducer with tablet**

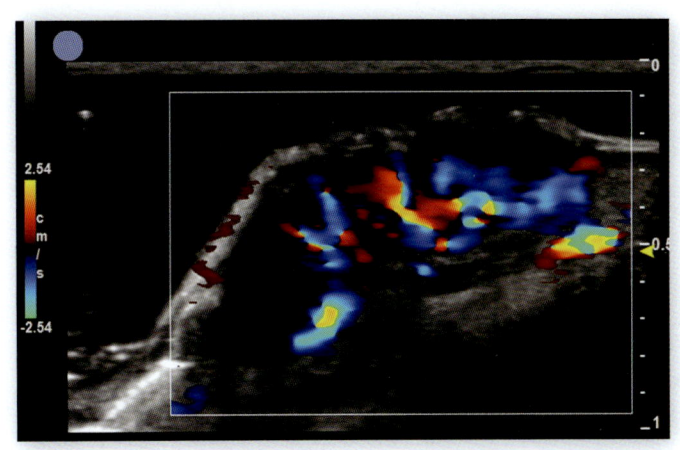

Fig. 18b **Color Doppler image of a squamous cell carcinoma** *(Courtesy of Kolo Medical, Inc.)*

Fig. 17b **Cutaway of a Butterfly transducer showing CMUT "stack" and associated electronics**

Another significant advantage is the ability to perform extremely high frequency imaging. Recall that higher frequency results in less penetration but improved resolution. *Figure 18a* shows a KOLO L38-22 transducer and corresponding bandwidth graph with a center

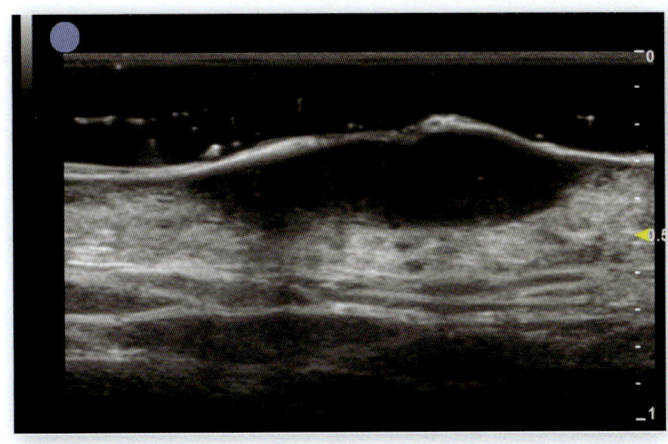

Fig. 18c **2D image of a basal cell carcinoma** *(Courtesy of Kolo Medical, Inc.)*

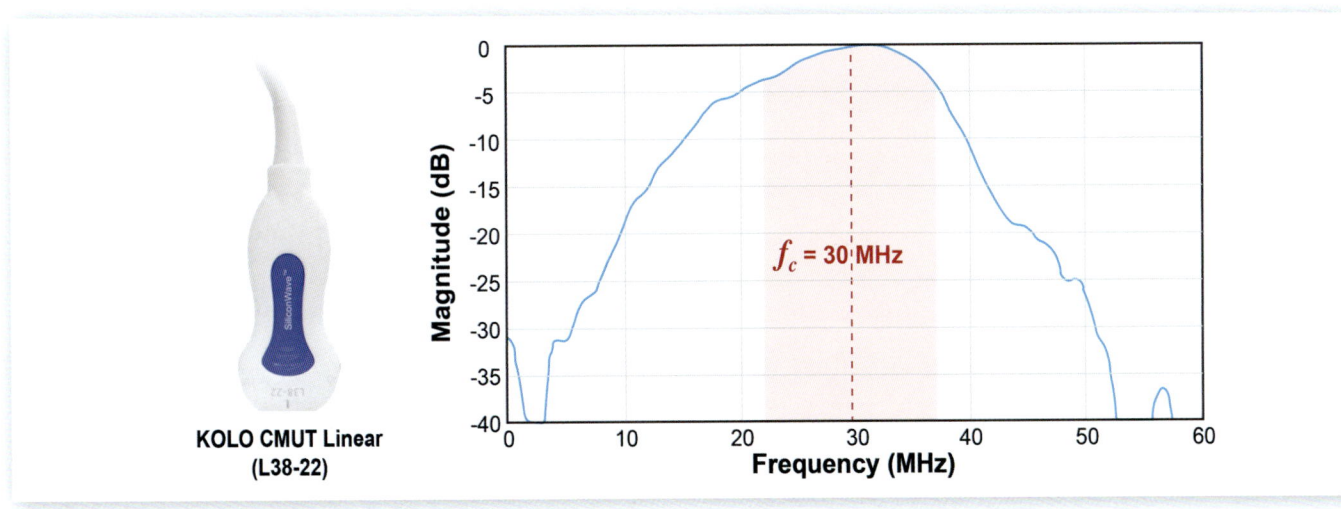

Fig. 18a **A KOLO CMUT linear (L38-22) transducer and associated bandwidth plot showing the center frequency of 30 MHz and the usable bandwidth (from 22 to 38 MHz)**

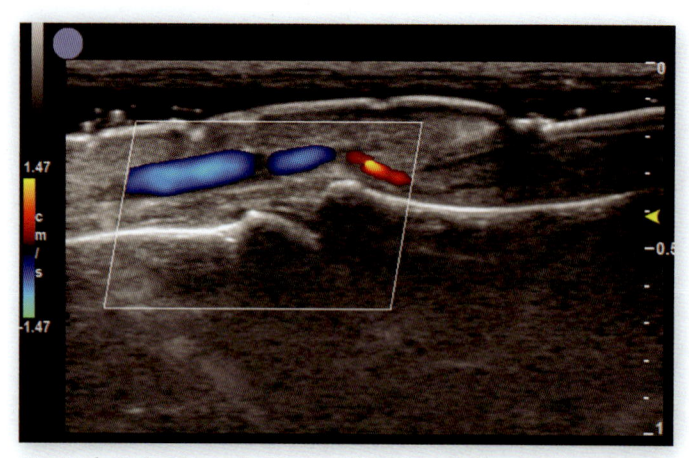

Fig. 18d **Color Doppler image of a normal fingernail structure**
(Courtesy of Kolo Medical, Inc.)

View ONLINE Animation and Image Library

8. Conceptual Questions

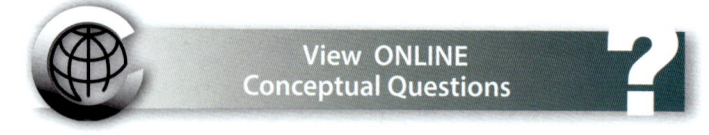

View ONLINE Conceptual Questions

ONLINE EXTRAS

For additional support material and to view your completion progress, visit:

www.pegasuslectures.com/6thEdExtras

Extras by Chapter include:
- Animations
- Videos
- Additional Images
- Clarifying Clips
- Supplemental Exercises
- Conceptual Questions

See page x of Preface for access instructions

CHAPTER SUMMARY: Transducers (CMUT)

- CMUT represents an alternative to piezoelectric materials for producing and receiving sound waves.
- CMUT technology is based on the concept of creating a series or network of variable capacitors (cells) which operate together to function as a transducer.
- A capacitor is basically a means of storing charge (energy).
- In its basic form, a capacitor consists of two electrical conductors separated by a gap.
- The capacitance is proportional to the plate area and inversely related to the plate separation distance.
- The capacitance can be increased by replacing the air gap with a dielectric material.
- The bottom electrode is fixed and a flexible membrane is attached to the top electrode.
- With a varying electric field, the top electrode attached to the flexible membrane vibrates, producing sound (transmit mode).
- When the flexible membrane and top electrode vibrate from sound, a varying electric field is produced (receive mode).
- A single capacitive cell is the smallest component of a CMUT capable of producing and receiving sound.
- Like piezoelectric materials, CMUT cells can be operated in CW or PW mode.
- By applying a DC bias voltage, the center of the flexible membrane and top electrode is deflected toward the bottom electrode, coming in contact with the insulating material creating "collapse mode."
- By using collapse mode, CMUT transducers become more efficient than normal mode both for transmission and receiving.
- By varying the bias voltage the operating frequency becomes tunable.
- Because of the low impedance of the flexible membrane, there is a good impedance match to tissue, and matching layers generally are not needed with CMUTs.
- Although a matching material is not needed, an acoustic window material is needed to act as a barrier between the CMUT cell and the patient.
- To reduce reverberation artifact between air and the silicon substrate, a backing material is important in CMUT design.
- In addition to the same techniques used for piezoelectric transducers, CMUT cells can be networked on a flexible, curved surface for focusing.
- A collection of capacitive cells can be grouped to perform a similar function as a piezoelectric element (the smallest component of a piezoelectric transducer capable of producing and receiving sound).
- Because of the controlled manufacturing process, CMUTs tend to result in less variation from transducer to transducer than piezoelectric transducers.
- CMUT technology results in tremendous design flexibility and significant reductions in manufacturing cost.
- CMUT designs allow for reliable high frequency designs, resulting in new fields for ultrasound such as dermatology.
- CMUT potentially allows for the same transducer to be used for diagnostic and therapeutic applications.
- Because of the extraordinary bandwidth, companies such as Butterfly now propose that a single transducer can be used to images the entire body.
- CMUT opens up the possibility for large-scale production, for large transducers, and for wearable ultrasound devices in the future.

References

Gerardo, C. D., Cretu, E., & Rohling, R. (2018). Fabrication and testing of polymer-based capacitive micromachined ultrasound transducers for medical imaging. *Microsystems & nanoengineering, 4*(1), 1-12.

van Schaijk, R. Phillips Innovative Services (2020). Photographs used with written permission. *(Figures 3c and 5c)*

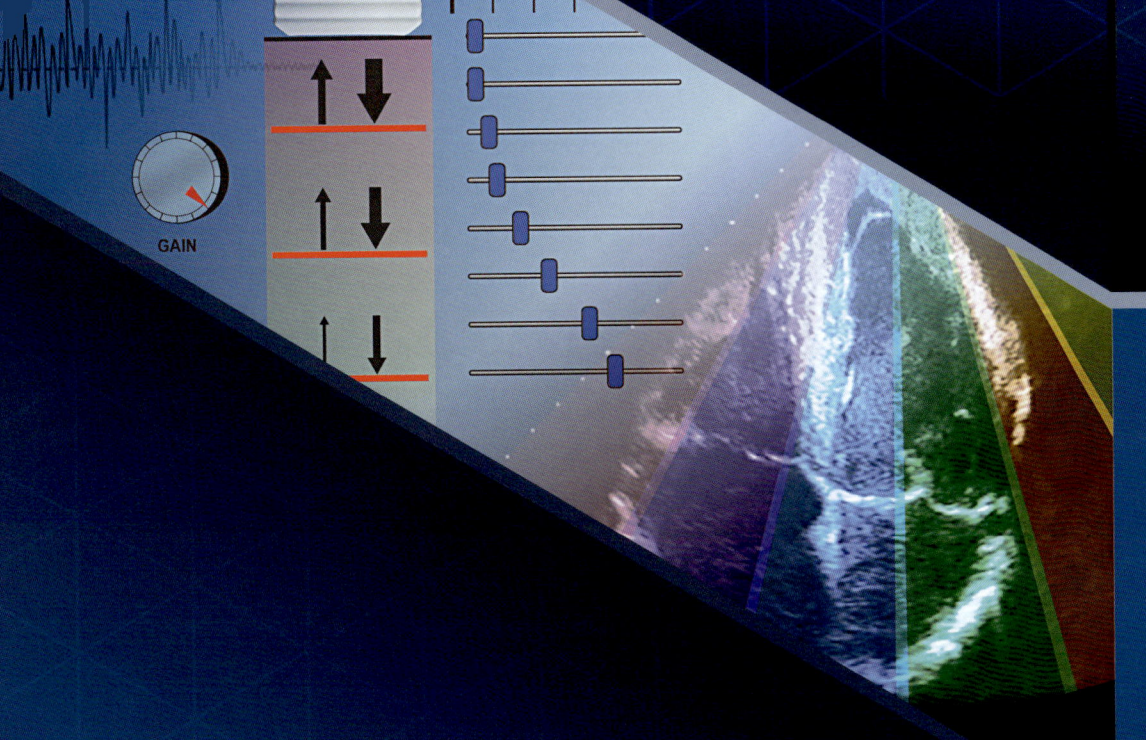

Chapter 6
Part I

System Operation
(Fundamentals)

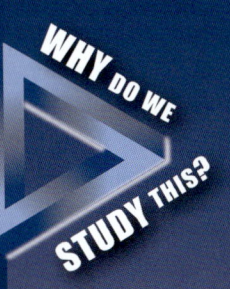

WHY DO WE STUDY THIS?
- System operation connects the concepts learned to this point to explain the basics of how a system transmits sound waves, captures reflections, and generates an image.
- By understanding the basic principles of image generation, it is much easier to understand the fundamental imaging controls of an ultrasound system.

WHAT'S IN THIS CHAPTER?

LEVEL 1 — BASIC ULTRASOUND PHYSICS
The basic functions of an ultrasound system are introduced, leading to an explanation of how received signals are processed to generate images.

LEVEL 2 — BOARD LEVEL
Basic system controls and their effects on images are detailed in relation to how images are created, optimized, stored, and displayed.

Level 3 — ADVANCED TOPICS
The concepts of video formats, compression algorithms (codecs), and concepts related to human perception are discussed.

LEARNING OBJECTIVES
- List the core processing functions required to create an ultrasound image
- Explain the difference between true and apparent signal-to-noise
- Describe how beam former evolvement has advanced ultrasound
- Describe how signals are displayed and stored, including the basics of monitors
- Identify the limitations of human perception

Chapter 6 – Part I
System Operation (Fundamentals)

Introduction

There are three great challenges with writing a chapter on system operation. The first challenge is that ultrasound is now at a crossroad with technology changing rapidly so that image generation is fundamentally very different for newer systems than many existing systems in the field. Over some period of time, the existing older systems will be replaced with systems using the newer technology, but in the interim, ultrasound practitioners will need to understand both the old and new paradigms.

The second difficulty is that advanced features are being released at a very rapid rate. Teaching advanced features to students before they have learned basic functions will be frustrating for the student and likely not very successful. To address these two issues, Chapter 6, like Chapter 5, is now divided into Parts I and II. Part I will deal with basic system features whereas Part II will deal with more advanced system features.

The third challenge is related to the lack of consistent terminology from one ultrasound provider to the next. The same basic function on System A will most likely have a very different name than the exact same technology on System B. This discrepancy in naming presents a problem since not everyone uses the same system. As much as possible, I have attempted to use generic, yet descriptive names for the system functions, only using a specific manufacturer's name when there is no other competing technology, when the name used by a specific company leads to a more "intuitive" understanding of the technique, or because the name itself has become a standard (like the use of the word Kleenex in reference to a disposable facial tissue).

Even with dividing system functions into two chapters, in many ways this chapter is really still two chapters joined by a common purpose. Level 1 focuses on the basic functions of an ultrasound machine while simultaneously integrating all of the material in the earlier chapters into one cohesive topic. Level 2 deals with system operation from the standpoint of user interaction to make the system function. Level 1 is designed to teach the basic physics of what an ultrasound system must do to process acoustic data to create an image. Level 2 is designed to teach the basics of what the sonographer needs to do with the system and the choices faced to make an image.

1. The Basic Processes of Real-Time Imaging

There are six core functions that an ultrasound system must perform:

1. Transmit beams
2. Receive beams
3. Process the returned data
4. Perform measurements on the processed data
5. Display the processed data
6. Store the processed data

Of course each of these core functions can be further dissected into processes, and those processes again subdivided, but that level of discussion is beyond the scope of this book for ultrasound practitioners.

In the following sections, we will discuss each of these functions as an integral part of creating an image. The process of discussing the core functions will force us to integrate the material from the previous five chapters. To assist us with this task, we will start by learning related terminology and definitions, followed by a functional block diagram, relaying the links of each chapter to the current topic.

2. Important System Definitions

Many engineering terms are used to describe system performance and specifications. Many of these terms are often misused, leading to confusion and often misleading people in the ultrasound field, especially when in the market to purchase new equipment. Understanding these terms should help clarify some of the incredible functionality provided by current ultrasound systems. For continuity, many of the terms defined below will be redefined in the following sections so as to allow integration with related concepts. At the conclusion of the section you should be able to define the following terms:

- Transmit power
- Dynamic range
- Signal
- Noise and noise floor

- Signal-to-noise ratio (SNR)
- Compression
- Pre-processing
- Post-processing

> **Author's Note:**
> **Definitions of New Material**
>
> The astute reader will note that a few of the definitions discussed below include references to Level 2 material. These references would, in an ideal world, not take place until the topic was discussed. Alas, we have found ourselves with a chicken and an egg dilemma. We cannot discuss new topics without defining the terminology, and we cannot define the terminology without discussing the technologies these terms describe.

2.1 Transmit Power

There are many different names used to refer to the transmit power. Some of the names frequently used are acoustic power, output power, transmit gain, power gain, acoustic gain, output intensity, transmit voltage, and output voltage.

The transmit power knob controls the amplitude of the excitation voltage which drives the transducer. A higher voltage corresponds to a higher amplitude mechanical oscillation of the crystal or electrode (for CMUT). The result is a higher amplitude sound wave. Since the power is proportional to the amplitude squared, a higher amplitude wave corresponds to a significantly higher power wave. Also, since the beam intensity is related to the power, higher power results in a more intense beam. Using a more intense beam results in stronger returning echoes. Clearly, if not enough transmit power is used, the returning echoes can be too weak and the signal inadequate.

Using a higher intensity has another potential consequence. If the intensity were to get too high, tissue damage (bioeffects) could result. Clearly, it is desirable to use the minimum amount of transmit power necessary to get good clinical results.

> **KEY CONCEPT**
>
> Ultrasound manufacturers generally create different names for the same functionality. Consequently, the underlying system functions are often confused. As much as possible, generic terminology (related to the underlying engineering terms are used) but with some of the company specific names listed for cross reference.

2.2 Dynamic Range

Dynamic range is the ratio of the maximum to the minimum amplitude of any quantity, or more simply, the ratio of the biggest signal to the smallest signal.

The term dynamic range can be applied to many different areas. To be clear, the dynamic range to which you are referring should be specified. For example:

Input dynamic range: Ratio of the maximum input signal to the minimum possible input signal

Output dynamic range: Ratio of the maximum to the minimum output signal

Display dynamic range: Ratio of the maximum to the minimum display signal

Gain dynamic range: Ratio of the maximum to the minimum applicable gain

In general, when speaking about ultrasound, if there is no specific qualifier to the term "dynamic range" the default interpretation is the input dynamic range. A formal definition for the input dynamic range of an ultrasound system is: "the range of signal amplitudes a system can receive and process accurately."

> **CHECKPOINT: Exam Tip**
>
> Receiver gain and transmit power are completely different mechanisms. The transmit power affects the amplitude of the signal going into the patient. The receiver gain only affects the signal after it has returned from the patient. As a result, increasing the transmit power increases the risk of bioeffects, whereas increasing the receiver gain incurs no risk to the patient.

2.3 Signals, Noise, and Signal-to-Noise Ratio (SNR) Definitions

Signal: Any phenomenon desired to be measured

Noise: Any unwanted signal(s)

Noise floor: The amplitude level below which no signals are visible because of the presence of noise

Signal-to-noise Ratio: The amplitude of the signal divided by the amplitude of the noise

What is Signal, What is Noise, and What Determines a Good SNR

For ultrasound imaging, the "signals" are the reflections from the tissues that are converted into images. For spectral Doppler, the signals are the Doppler shifts that are processed into the Doppler spectrum displaying the range of velocities over time. In both of these cases, noise presents as random white speckle in either the image or the Doppler spectrum. The noise is primarily generated within the electronics and for the most part is completely independent of the signals being generated.

The signal-to-noise ratio is what specifies the signal quality, and hence, how much faith should be put in the data. A higher signal-to-noise ratio implies a better imaging situation and, excluding artifacts, more trustworthy data. A useful analogy to explain the concept of signal, noise, and SNR comes from considering what happens when listening to an FM radio station while driving your car. When you are close to the radio station antenna, the music (the signal) is clear and can be heard well even with low volume settings (amplification). As you drive farther away from the antenna, the signal gets weaker and you have to turn the volume up. Eventually, you get to a point where you start to hear random popping and cracking (noise). Turning up the volume makes not only the bits of music breaking through louder, but it also makes the noise louder. When you were close to the antenna, the SNR was very good. As you drive farther away, the SNR degrades until eventually, the SNR becomes poor as the signal (music) is dominated by the noise (popping and cracking).

Note that a high amplitude signal by itself does not necessarily guarantee a good signal-to-noise ratio (SNR). For example, a relatively strong signal could be masked by inordinately strong noise. Therefore, even though the signal is strong, in the presence of significant noise, the ratio is still not very good. Conversely, a low amplitude signal does not necessarily imply poor signal-to-noise (although much more likely). If the signal is relatively weak but the noise floor is very low, then the ratio may still be relatively good. Overall, the desired situation is to have much greater signal strength than noise strength. Compare the three situations as depicted in *Figure 1*. The first example, (A), demonstrates a very high amplitude signal and a low noise floor, or good signal-to-noise. Example (B) has the same high amplitude signal but very high noise therefore presenting poor signal-to-noise. Example (B) can result from very high amplitude noise in the presence of a high amplitude signal, or more commonly from high amplification of a weak signal. Example (C) demonstrates a low noise floor but a very weak signal, thereby again producing a poor signal-to-noise ratio.

(A) Good SNR: High amplitude signal and low amplitude noise

(B) Poor SNR: High amplitude signal and high amplitude noise

(C) Poor SNR: Low amplitude signal and low amplitude noise

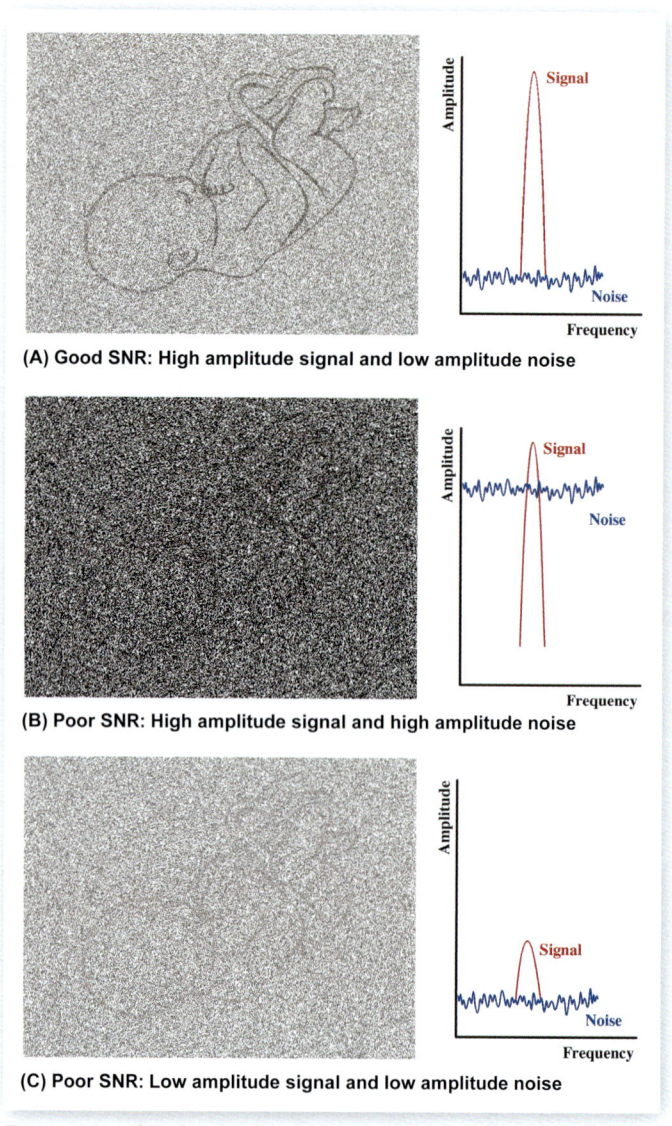

Fig. 1 Graphical representation of signal-to-noise ratio

Apparent SNR, Gain, and True SNR

It is important to note that increasing the receiver gain does not improve the signal-to-noise ratio. Unless an electronic circuit is saturated (overgained such that some component of the signal is at the maximum circuit voltage), increasing amplification increases both the signal and the noise by the same amount so that the ratio stays the same. Although the true "SNR" may not change with gain, the apparent SNR might. This concept is perhaps one of the most often misunderstood concepts related to signal optimization. The confusion is derived from the fact that a certain amount of gain is necessary to make the signal bright enough so that it can be well visualized on the display within the dynamic range of both the display and the human eye. If the gain does not map the signal into this signal range, the signal will appear weak. However, this appearance is not because the signal is inadequate relative to the noise, but rather that the monitor and observer do not have the sensitivity to adequately detect the signal. By increasing the gain, both the signal and the noise are amplified the same amount, leaving the SNR unchanged. However, the signal now appears stronger giving the user the appearance of improved SNR, hence the term "apparent SNR". In other words, if the gain is too low the signal might appear weak, even if there is good signal-to-noise. From our earlier radio analogy this is like having a good radio signal but the volume set too low so that the music is not that audible. By turning up the volume, the signal sounds stronger, even though it is still the same signal.

Referring to *Figure 2*, note that there is a horizontal line just below 2 labeled "Weakest Visible Signal (Dark Black)." In this model any signal with an amplitude below this level would appear too dark and would not be visualized to the human eye. Notice also the line at 4 labeled 'Brightest Detectable Signal (Bright White)." Any signal with an amplitude higher than this would appear so bright that it could not be differentiated from other bright signals. Now notice that both examples have identical signal-to-noise ratios. However, in case A, since the signal amplitude is close to the visibility threshold of the human eye, the signal is barely perceptible. In comparison, by amplifying the signal, as shown in case B, the peak signal is now close to the upper limit of the visibility range and appears bright white.

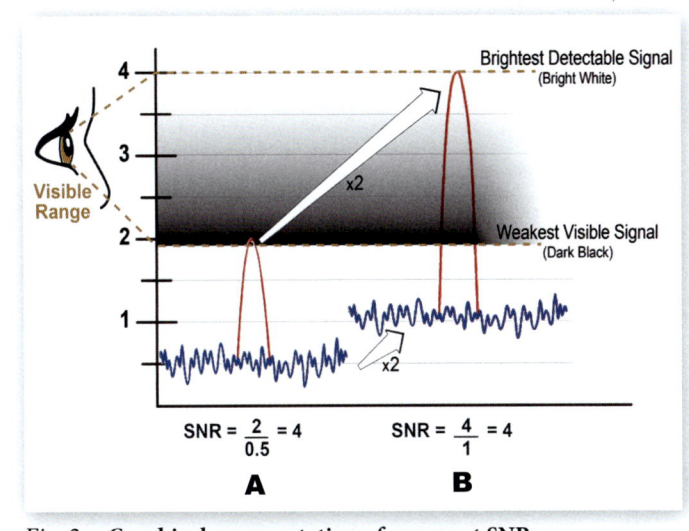

Fig. 2 Graphical representation of apparent SNR

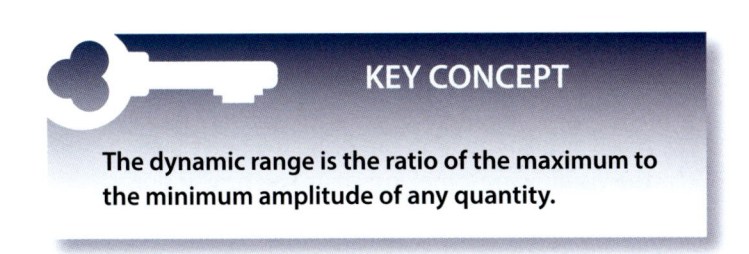

View ONLINE Clarifying Clip

KEY CONCEPT

The dynamic range is the ratio of the maximum to the minimum amplitude of any quantity.

Relating SNR, Noise Floor, and Apparent SNR
Ultrasound Images

The images in *Figure 3* through *Figure 5* are of a transverse carotid artery with various signal-to-noise ratios and varying apparent signal-to-noise ratios. Comparisons between images are very important to grasping the concept of signal-to-noise and how to recognize adequate signal.

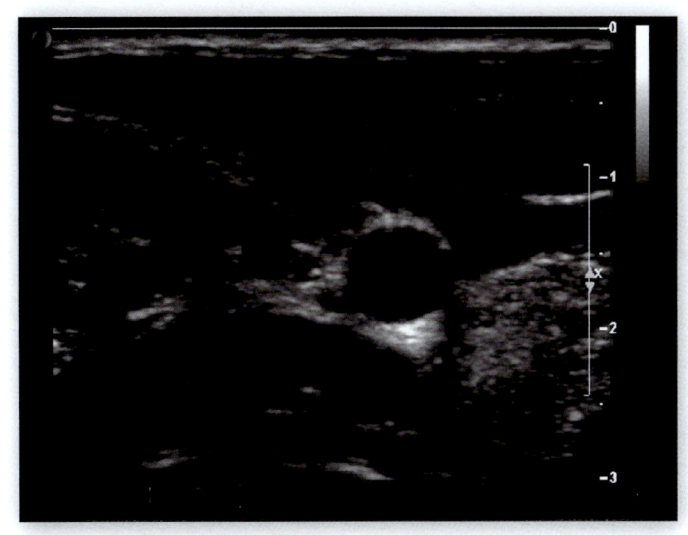

Fig. 3a **Signal appears weak**

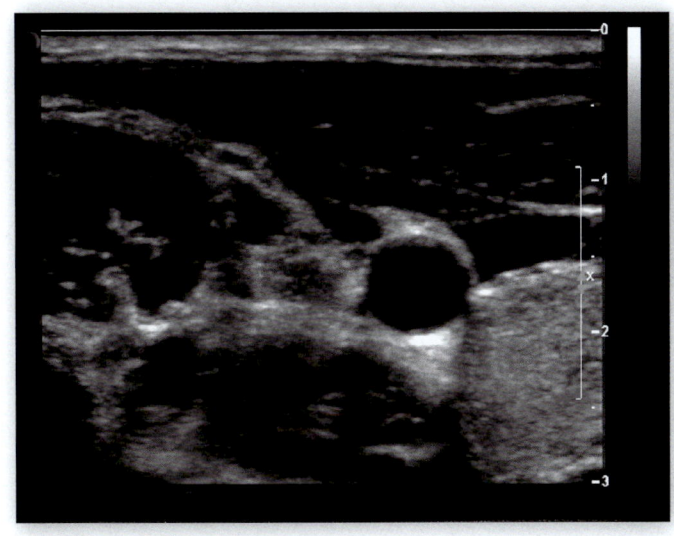

Fig. 3b **Signal appears strong**

Figure 3a was created using the same transmit power as *Figure 3b* but with a lower receive gain. Therefore, *Figures 3a* and *3b* have the same signal-to-noise ratio (SNR). However, the image of *Figure 3a* has a much lower apparent SNR than *Figure 3b*. Since *Figure 3a* has a lower overall receiver gain, many of the signal intensities are mapped to values below the visual threshold. The image in *Figure 3b* is analogous to the graphical representation of case A in *Figure 2*. In comparison, *Figure 3b* has a high enough gain so that most signals fall within the visual dynamic range. In other words, the same information is actually contained in both images, but that information is only apparent in *Figure 3b* and not *Figure 3a*. *Figure 3b* is analogous to the graphical representation of case B in *Figure 2*.

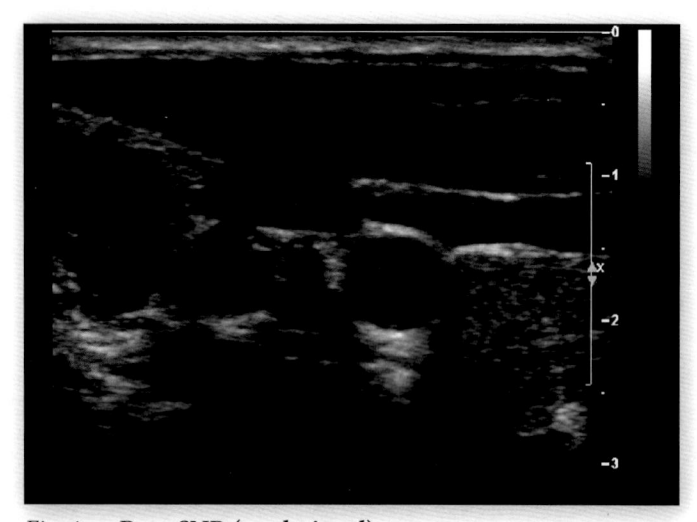

Fig. 4a **Poor SNR (weak signal)**

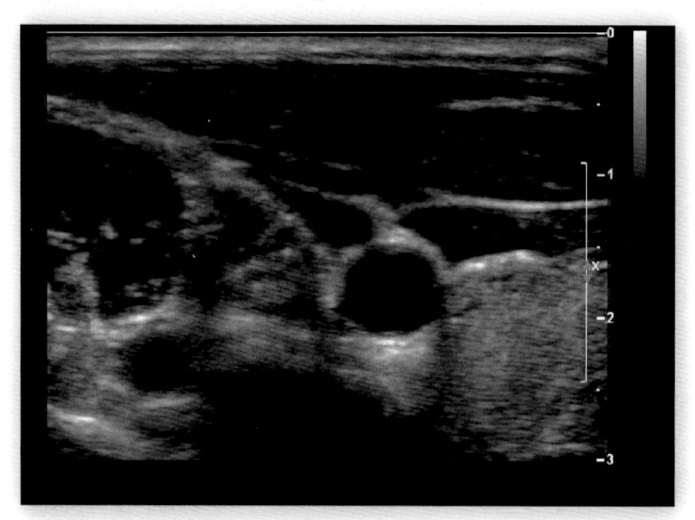

Fig. 4b **Good SNR**

In contrast to *Figures 3a* and *3b*, *Figure 4a* was created using a much lower transmit than *Figure 4b*. As a result, only the strongest signal components of *Figure 4a* are visible in the image. Since the image was created with relatively low receiver gain, the noise floor is below the visual range so no noise is apparent in the image. Yet, the signal-to-noise ratio is clearly poor.

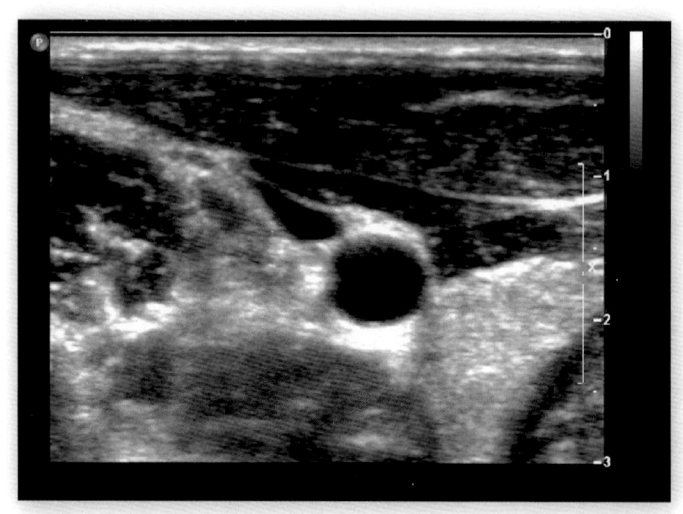

Fig. 5a **Transmit too high but good SNR**

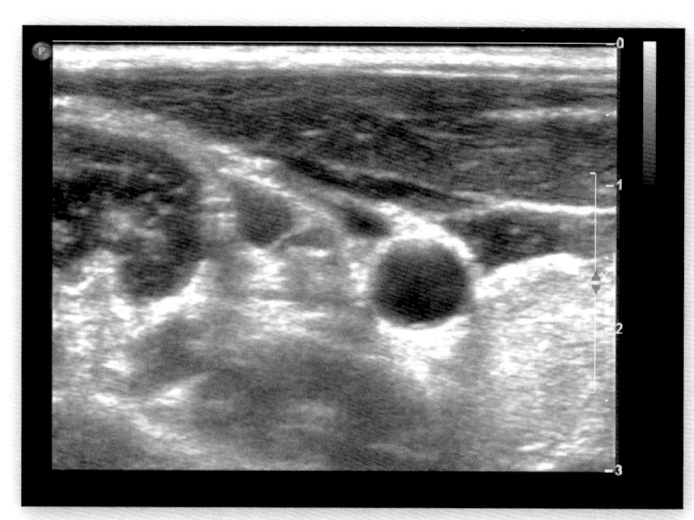

Fig. 5b **Receive gain too high, SNR good but apparent SNR worse**

Figure 5a has a much higher transmit power and a much lower receive gain than *Figure 5b*. As a result, *Figure 5a* has a better SNR than *Figure 5b*. Notice how the lumen of the carotid is somewhat ill-defined in *Figure 5b*, whereas the lumen is virtually noise free in *Figure 5a*. Throughout the entire image of *Figure 5b*, the high amplitude receive gain has mapped the noise floor into the visual range so that some of the noise obscures some signal components. In marked contrast, the lower gain of *Figure 5a* has resulted in the noise floor remaining below the visual threshold such that no noise is apparent in the image. For *Figure 5b*, since the SNR is good, reducing the receiver gain would improve the apparent SNR by forcing some of the noise below the visual threshold. Because the SNR is good, not much gain is necessary to drive the signal into the visual range. However, as the signal becomes weaker and weaker as occurs with deeper imaging, more receiver gain is necessary to drive the signal into the visual range. As depicted in example (B) of *Figure 1*, weaker signals with more receive gain results in the noise becoming apparent within the image.

KEY CONCEPT

A good image requires a good signal-to-noise ratio (signal amplitude much larger than noise amplitude). By changing system settings it is possible to make a good signal-to-noise image look bad, leading to the concept of apparent signal-to-noise ratio. Because of the limited dynamic range of the human eye and of monitors, decreasing or increasing the receiver gain may make the signal appear very weak or very noisy. When the gain is set too low, the image will appear dark, giving the impression of a weak signal. Increasing the receiver gain too high can bring the noise into the visible range, making an image appear noisy. Apparent SNR is also affected by the compression setting chosen.

Sources of Noise

As already stated, noise is any undesired signal. There are many sources of noise. Let us consider a few:

Electronic noise: Nothing in this world comes for free. The electronics used to amplify the tiny returning echoes add random signals (or thermal electronic noise). This added energy is created by random excitations of electrons within the electronics. The amplitude of these signals is very small; however, when you use a high receiver gain you will see this noise as random white speckle on the image or in your Doppler spectrum. In color Doppler, electronic noise shows up as random color pixels.

Clutter: Large returning echoes from structures that obliterate weaker signals. Examples include large specular reflections in imaging, valve clicks in spectral Doppler, etc.

Haze: There are many types of haze. Sometimes haze is created by returning echoes from sidelobes (discussed in Chapter 8). Haze may be created by poor transducer to skin contact or by beam aberration (distortion) from tissue characteristics. All cardiovascular sonographers have seen the haze associated with imaging through the lung.

Electrical interference: It is possible for transducers or ultrasound machines to receive energy emanating from other electrical devices or electromagnetic waves such as radio transmissions. The energy may be carried through the air or potentially down the power line to the system. This energy often shows up as a bright "flashlight" down the middle of an image, a "barber pole-like" flashing, or as bright white horizontal or zigzagging lines in spectral Doppler referred to as "Doppler tones".

Clutter One Moment May Be Signal the Next

Although clutter signals are often classified as noise, these signals are characteristically different than electronic noise, haze, and electrical interference. The fundamental difference is that "clutter" signals are related to anatomical structures and true reflections whereas the other forms are produced by sources outside the body or as an artifact. Therefore noise to one person may be signal to someone else. For example, the blood echoes during spectral Doppler are often obscured by the "clutter" signals which result from the surrounding tissue and wall motion. However, when performing tissue Doppler, the very clutter signals that were filtered out as noise are now the desired signal. This is somewhat reminiscent of the age old battle between parents and their children relative to their taste in music. Noise to one is pure harmony to the other.

2.4 Pre-processing and Post-processing

Conventional Definitions

The term processing refers to any conditioning of a signal in an attempt to interpret or improve the display of that signal. The terms pre-processing and post-processing are specifically defined below.

Pre-processing: Signal conditioning that occurs in real time and cannot be removed from an image once acquired (i.e. cannot be changed once the image is frozen.)

Post-processing: Any processing which can be changed after the data is acquired such as data compression, colorization, and reject. Post-processing can be performed on frozen data as well as live imaging.

Changes in the Pre-processing and Post-processing Paradigm

Ultrasound systems keep advancing, moving the point at which post-processing takes place earlier and earlier in the chain. The consequence is that many of the functions that could not be performed on frozen data only a few years ago can now be adjusted post acquisition. The determination of what functions fall before or after this point is generally determined by how early in the processing path the data is stored. The earlier the data is stored, the more of the functions that become post-processing.

3. Analog to Digital (A/D) Conversion

Most physical signals and movements in the world are analog. Analog signals are continuous in time and can exist in an infinite number of states. All biological signals are analog. If you monitor blood flow, EKGs, pressure waveforms, and back scattered energy in ultrasound, all of these signals will be analog. *Figures 6* and *7* illustrate two different analog signals. The first graph represents a low frequency content signal, since it varies slowly with time. The second graph represents higher frequency signal content since the signal changes relatively quickly with respect to time.

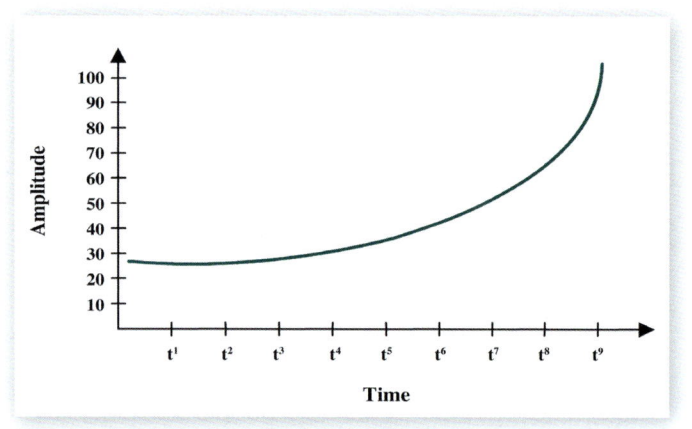

Fig. 6   **Slowly varying analog signal**

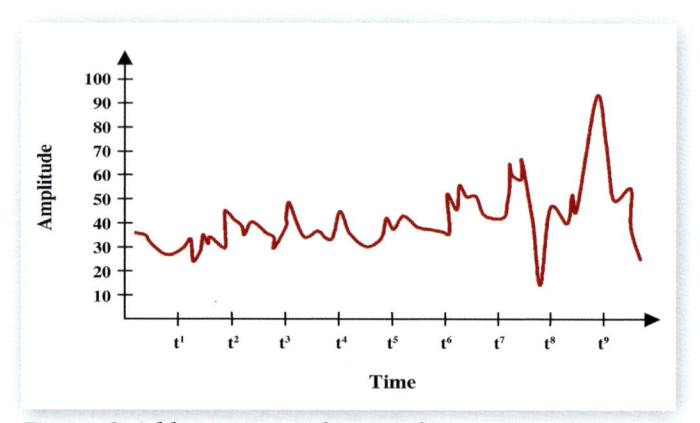

Fig. 7   **Quickly varying analog signal**

For many reasons, continuous (analog) signals are difficult to process and store. Most biological signals and communication signals require significant processing, usually involving many steps. A special circuit must be designed to perform each of these processing steps when the signal is processed in the analog domain. If instead, these signals are converted into discrete values represented as a time series of numbers (digital signals), then a single math processing circuit can be used to perform most of the processing steps. Thus there is a motivation to creating a specialized electronic circuit whose job it is to convert signals from continuous to discrete time values.

In order to convert the signals, an electronic circuit called an analog to digital converter (A/D) is used. In essence, an A/D converter takes periodic samples of the continuous analog signal and outputs numbers that are proportional to the signal at the moment of "sampling." The A/D converter uses a clock signal to tell it when to sample the signal. Every time the clock "ticks", the analog signal is sampled, and the digital number is stored as a binary number (This is illustrated in *Figures 8-10*).

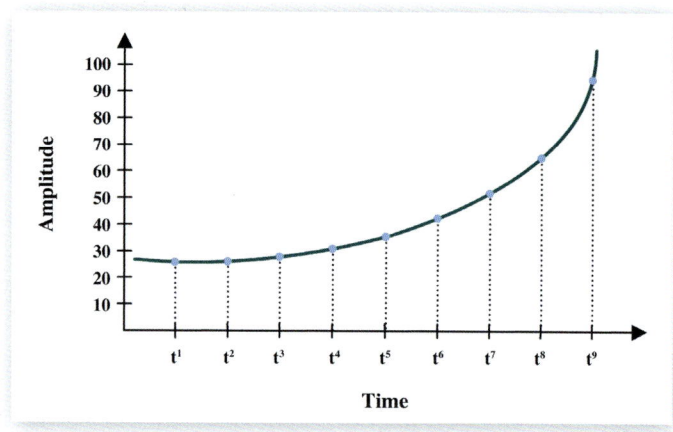

Fig. 8   **Graphical representation of sampling**

Fig. 9   **The sampling clock**

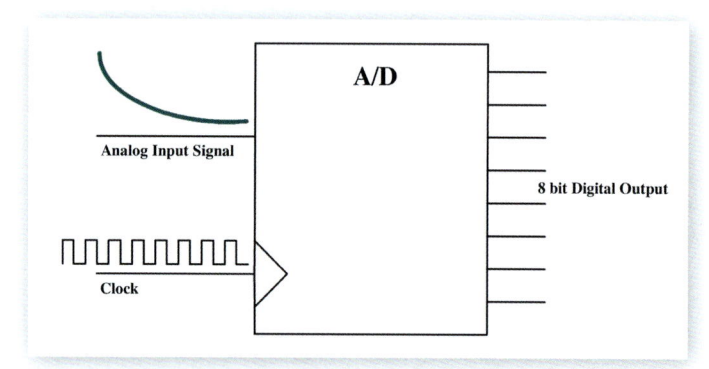

Fig. 10   **8-bit A/D converter**

The digital signal is therefore just a list of binary numbers at discrete time intervals.

Note: Comparing Figures 11 and 12, the reconstructed signal looks relatively similar to the original analog signal. This faithful representation of the signal after conversion does not always hold. We will now consider a case in which the reconstructed signal will not faithfully represent the original analog signal.

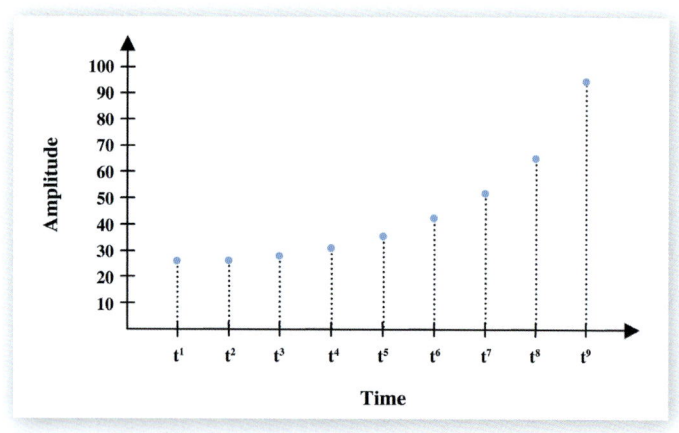

Fig. 11   **Graphical representation of a digital signal**

Ultimately, once the signal has been detected, converted, and processed, it will need to be displayed. Even if the data sent to the display is in the digital format, a reconversion from digital to analog takes place such that the data displayed is analog. If all goes well, the "reconstructed signal" has retained the important information of the original analog signal.

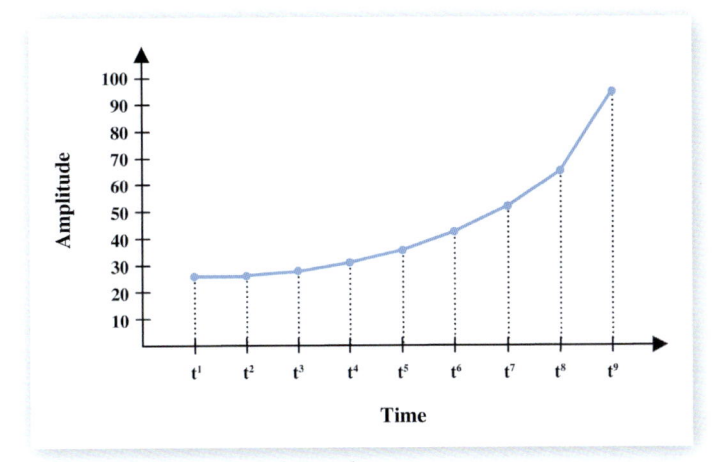

Fig. 12   **Reconstructed signal**

Now let's repeat the sampling and reconstruction process on the "quickly varying analog signal" as was just done on the "slowly varying analog signal" (See *Figures 13-16*).

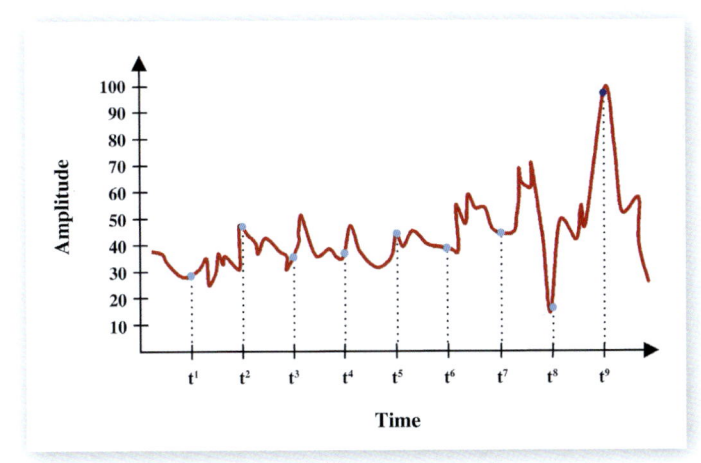

Fig. 13   **Sampling of a quickly varying analog signal**

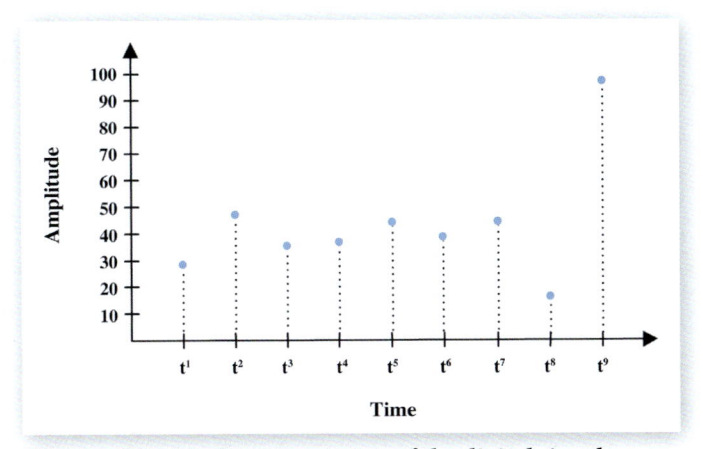

Fig. 14   **Graphical representation of the digital signal**

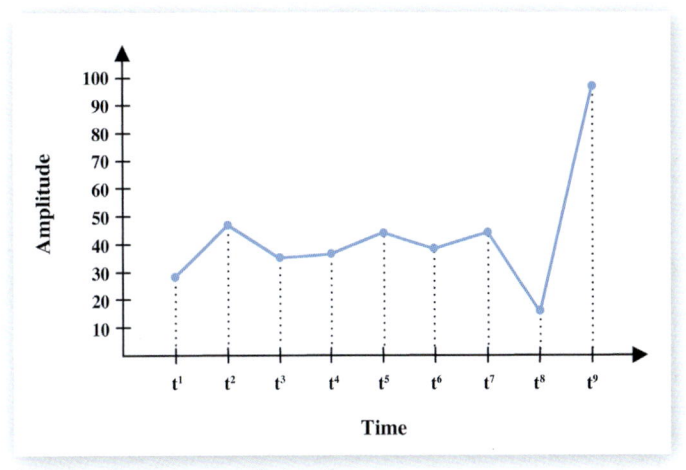

Fig. 15   **Reconstructed signal**

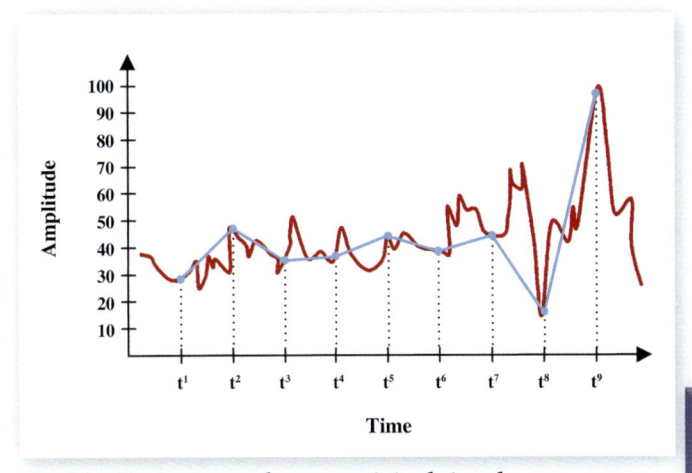

Fig. 16   **Reconstructed versus original signal**

In this case notice how poorly this "reconstructed" signal reflects the variations of the original signal. Although the general shape is correct, there certainly are many quick changes within the original signal which are missing in the reconstructed signal. Clearly, in the process of sampling and reconstructing, much information has been lost. You should now consider why sampling at the same rate worked quite well for a more slowly varying signal (a signal with lower frequency content) than for a more quickly varying signal (a signal with higher frequency content).

In order to preserve the higher frequency energy within the quickly varying signal, the sampling rate must be increased. In essence, the faster a signal varies (the higher the frequency of the signal), the faster the sampling rate must be to preserve the information within the signal. How fast the sampling must be to make an accurate reconstruction is called the Nyquist criterion (discussed in the next section).

All signals coming from the body are analog and must be received as analog signals. Therefore, the very first stage of all ultrasound systems must be analog. The reason for converting analog signals into digital signals in ultrasound, and most other electronic systems, is to make it easier to process the signals for measurements and display. For ultrasound, digitizing the signals makes it easier to perform scan conversion, analysis and measurement, post-processing, and data storage.

> **KEY CONCEPT**
>
> Most biological signals are analog (continuous in time), requiring analog detection. Because mathematical processes can more easily be applied to discrete values at discrete time intervals, most circuits convert signals from analog to digital formats. High quality conversion requires that the sample rate (the rate at which the analog signal is assessed) be fast relative to how fast the signal is changing. Additionally, high quality conversion requires having enough range (dynamic range) to represent the varying analog signal amplitudes.

3.1 Nyquist Criteria

As just discussed, when a signal changes faster (contains high frequency content), the sampling per time must be faster for an accurate reconstruction of the signal. Undersampling a signal (sampling too slowly) results in a poor reconstruction which loses too much of the original information. For an accurate reconstruction, the minimum rate at which you must sample is called the Nyquist criterion. The Nyquist criterion states that the sampling frequency must be at least twice the highest frequency in the signal.

$$\text{Nyquist}: f(max) = \frac{f_{sampling}}{2}$$

One way of demonstrating the Nyquist criterion is to sample a sine wave and then to do a reconstruction. If the frequency of the reconstructed signal is not the same as the initial analog signal, Nyquist has been violated, as seen in *Figures 21* and *22*.

◊ **Example:** 2 Hz signal sampled at 25 Hz

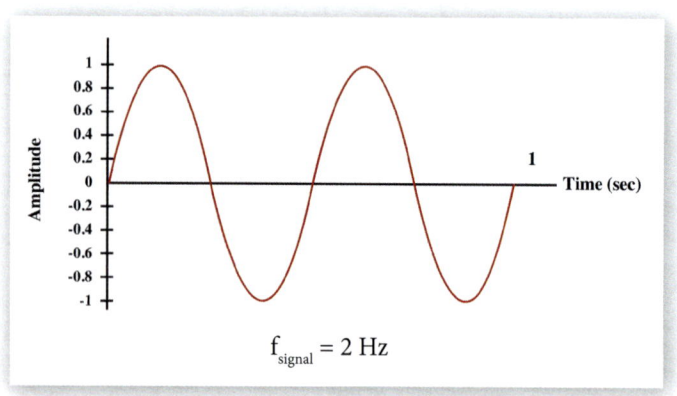

Fig. 17   **Original analog signal before sampling**

$f_{sampling}$ = 25 Hz (25 samples/sec)

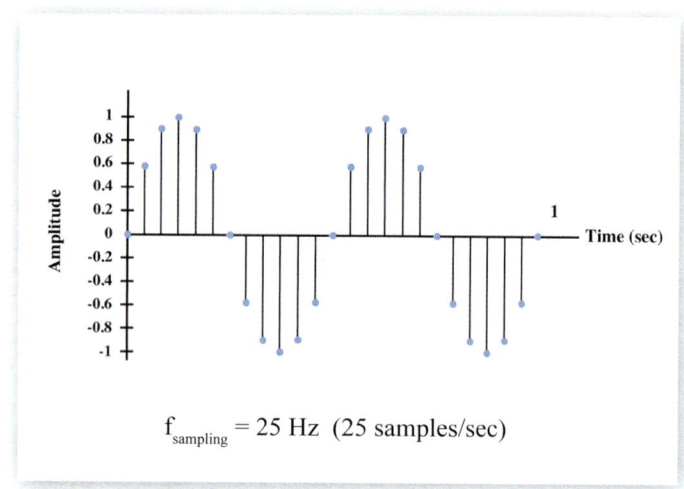

Fig. 18   **Sampled signal**

$f_{reconstructed}$ = 2 Hz

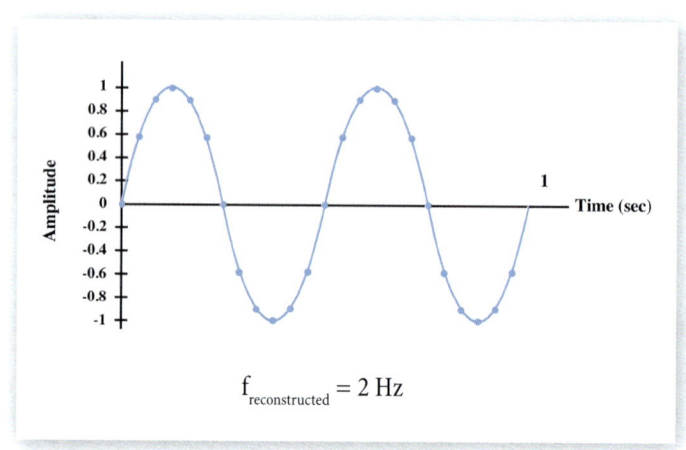

Fig. 19   **Reconstructed signal**

In *Figures 17-19*, however, the sampling rate satisfies the Nyquist criterion, since the sample rate of 25 Hz is faster than twice the signal frequency (2 x 2 Hz = 4 Hz). As a result, the reconstructed signal has the correct (same) frequency as the original signal.

◊ **Example:** 2 Hz signal sampled at 2 Hz

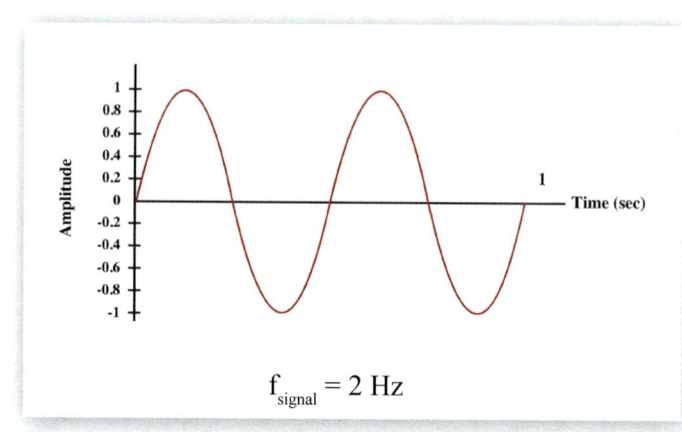

f_{signal} = 2 Hz

Fig. 20   **Original analog signal before sampling**

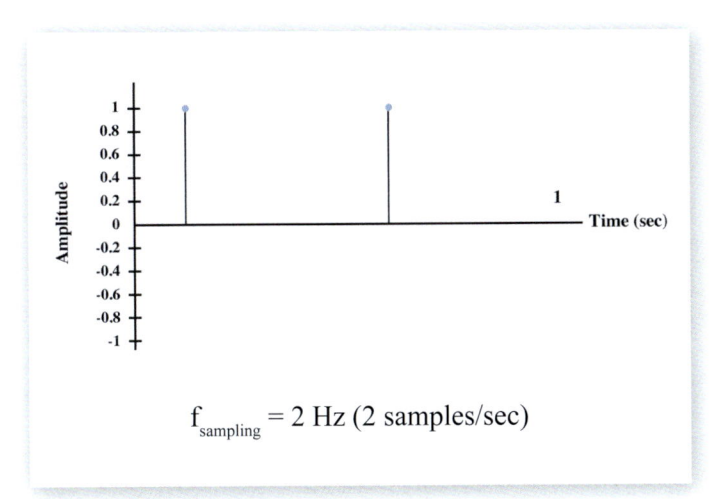

Fig. 21 **Sampled signal** — $f_{sampling} = 2$ Hz (2 samples/sec)

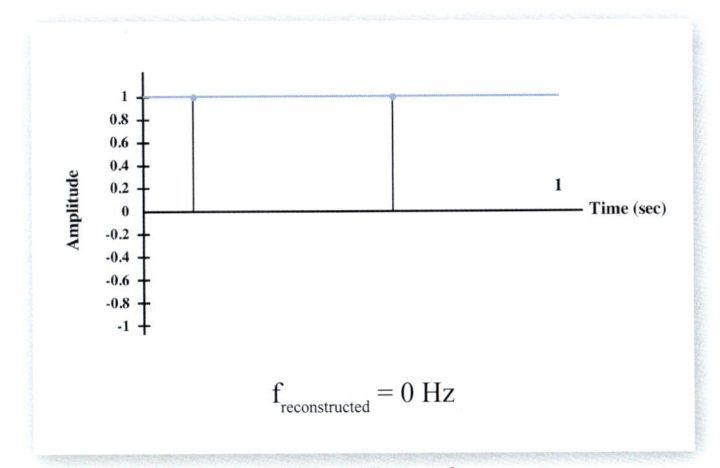

Fig. 22 **Reconstructed (aliased) signal** — $f_{reconstructed} = 0$ Hz

Clearly, the reconstructed signal in *Figure 22* misrepresents the original signal depicted in *Figure 20*. This demonstrates a violation of the Nyquist criterion, because the sampling rate of 2 Hz is not at least twice 2 Hz, or equivalently 4 Hz.

◊ **Example:** 2 Hz signal sampled at 4 Hz

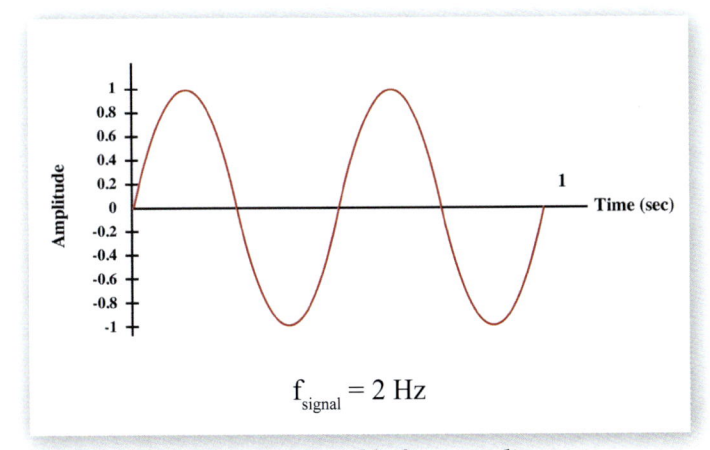

Fig. 23 **Original analog signal before sampling** — $f_{signal} = 2$ Hz

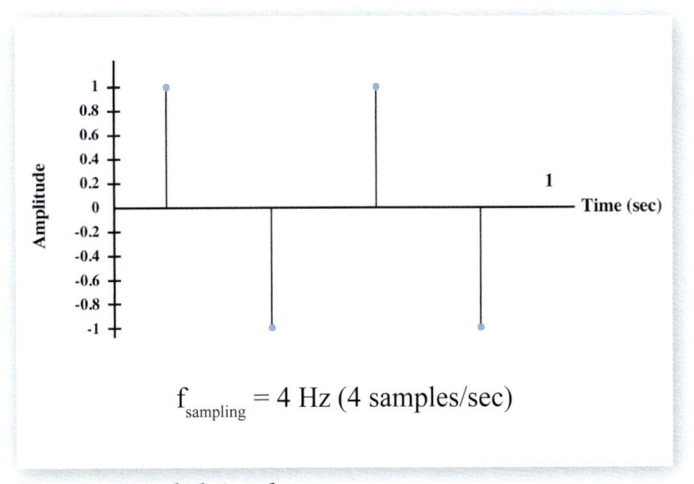

Fig. 24 **Sampled signal** — $f_{sampling} = 4$ Hz (4 samples/sec)

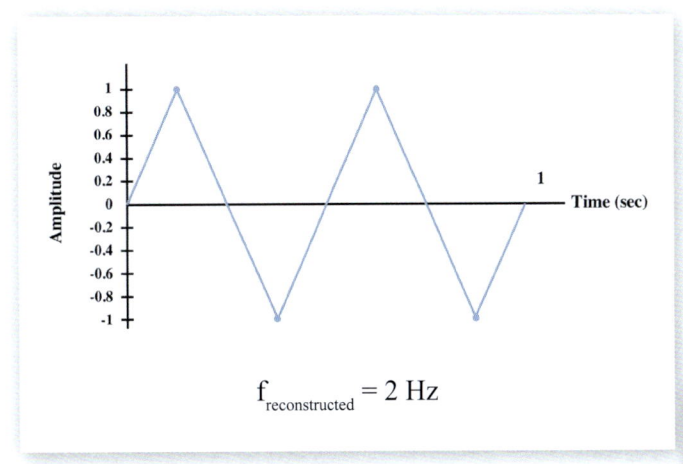

Fig. 25 **Reconstructed signal** — $f_{reconstructed} = 2$ Hz

In *Figures 23-25*, the Nyquist criterion was satisfied. Notice how the frequency of the reconstructed signal is the same as that of the original analog signal (2 Hz) as shown in *Figure 23*.

View ONLINE Clarifying Clip

View ONLINE Animation and Image Library

◊ Example:

Watch what happens if you sample at the wrong frequency:

$$f_{signal} = 9 \text{ Hz}$$
$$f_{sampling} = 8 \text{ Hz}$$
$$f_{reconstructed} = 1 \text{ Hz}$$

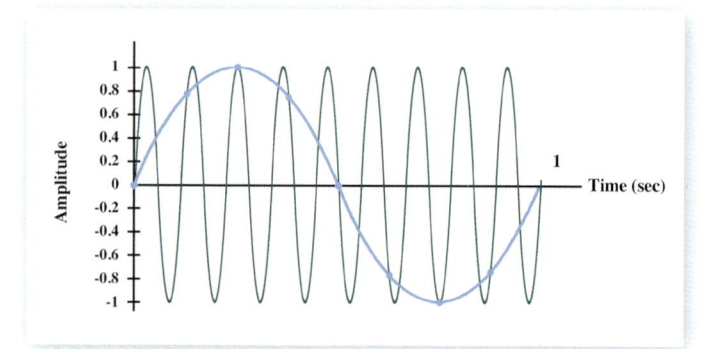

Fig. 26 **Aliasing**

Not only do you inaccurately recreate the original signal, but you create a signal at the wrong frequency. When the Nyquist criterion is violated, an artifact called aliasing occurs. You have most likely seen many examples of aliasing in life including old western movies in which the wagon wheels appear to spin in the wrong direction. In these films, the sample rate is related to the frame rate of the film. So when the frame rate of the film is not twice as fast as the frequency of the wheel, aliasing occurs, giving the appearance of the wheels varying speeds and even reversing.

For ultrasound, the concept of aliasing is important in order to understand temporal artifacts (ability to correctly distinguish changes in time) in imaging and in order to understand limits in velocity detection in spectral and color Doppler. Temporal artifacts in imaging occur when the frame rate is not high enough with respect to changes that are occurring within the body. Doppler artifacts occur when the Doppler sampling rate is not fast enough with respect to the frequency shift which results from moving structures such as red blood cells. A further discussion of Nyquist as it relates to Doppler modalities and artifacts is in Chapter 7.

If there is one thing that aliasing should teach us it is that you can't necessarily trust everything you perceive with your senses. This fact is very important because quite frequently, the limiting factor in ultrasound is not the ultrasound equipment or the physics of sound interacting with the body, but rather the limitations of the human senses to perceive reality.

View ONLINE Animation and Image Library

> **CHECKPOINT: Exam Tip**
>
> The Nyquist Criterion specifies that to accurately determine the frequency of a signal, the signal must be sampled at least twice as fast as the signal is changing. In essence, to detect a single cycle, at least two samples are required so that both the maxima (largest point) and the minima (minimum point) are captured.

4. Basic Functions of a System (Simplified)

4.1 Putting the Pieces Together

An ultrasound system begins by creating a transmit waveform. The waveform characteristics are determined by the system control settings, transducer selection, and presets that you, the user, select. The pulser then interprets all of the settings to determine the initial amplitude, frequency, and mode (2D, CW Doppler, PW Doppler, etc.) of the excitation voltage. For phased array systems, the pulser must determine the type of image generation (sequential, planar, multiple beam, etc.) and also produce the time or phase delays necessary to create the image as specified. The different ways in which images can be generated will be discussed in greater detail in Part II of Chapter 6.

As discussed in Chapter 5, when the transducer is driven with an electropotential waveform (voltage), the energy is converted into an acoustic wave. This acoustic wave is coupled into the body and is reflected, refracted, and absorbed as it travels through the body. Some of the acoustic energy is reflected back to and received by the transducer. The transducer converts this energy into an electropotential signal (voltage) which is then sent to the system receiver.

The system receiver processes the small electrical signals, detecting changes that result from interactions within the patient and conditioning the signals for conversion, measurement, and display. The conditioned and detected signals are then passed to a processing engine (usually referred to as a scan converter). The job of the scan converter is to take the streaming data and convert it into a format that can be measured, stored, and displayed. Besides the basic function of scan conversion, at this stage, there are usually many user controllable options, allowing the user to dictate how the conversion and formatting are to take place.

Once the data has been converted into a scan, the user is allowed to measure the data in various ways such as distance measurements, area measurements, volume measurements, rise times, etc. Although the user is viewing the image on the display at the time of making the measurement, the measurement is actually occurring on the data stored within the scan converter. (This is why the "measurement" function box is pictured before the "display" function in the

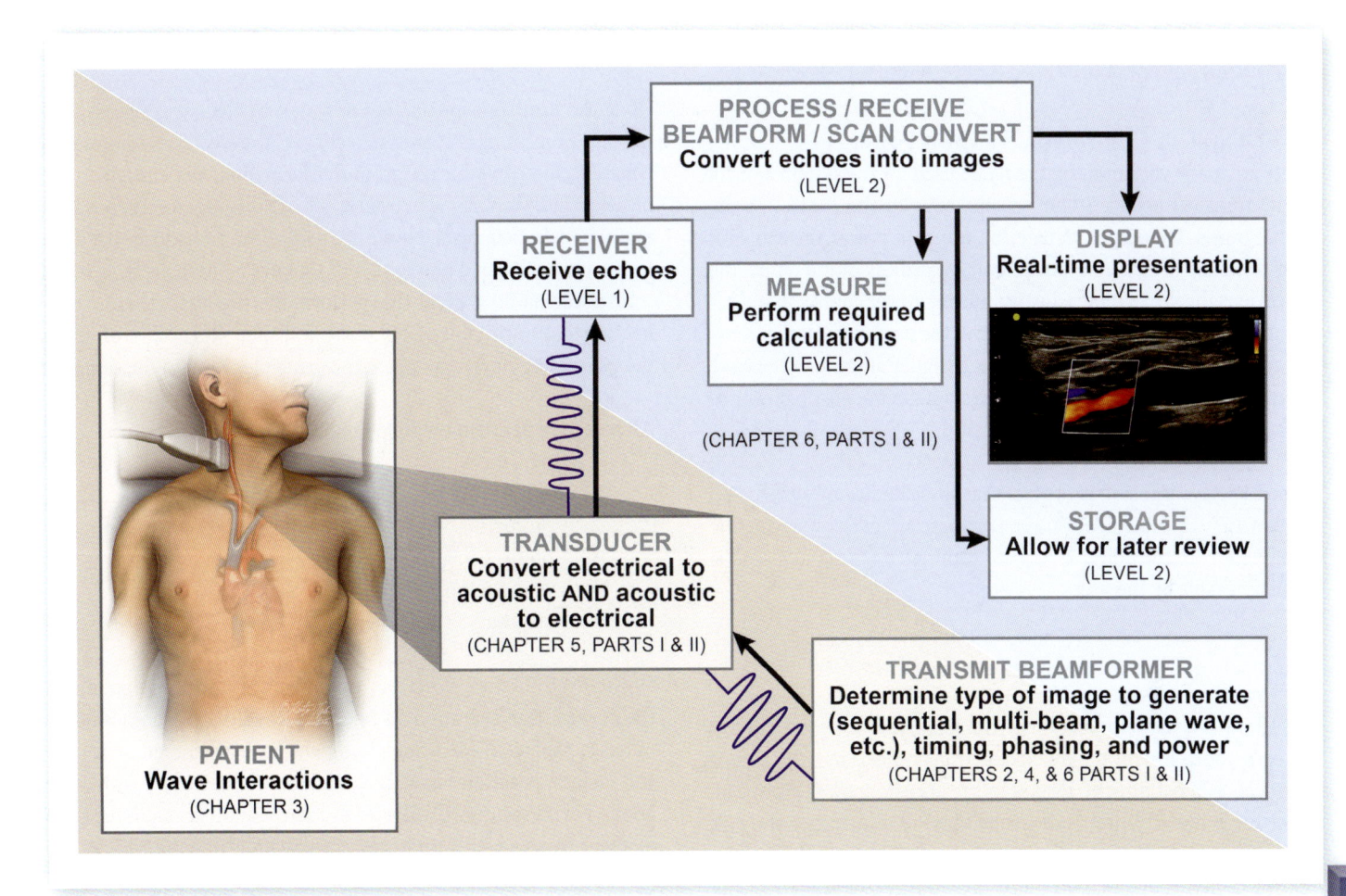

Fig. 27 **Basic functional block diagram**

diagram of *Figure 27*.) Both the image and the measurements are then displayed for real-time viewing, while simultaneously being sent for storage if desired.

We will now cover the functional blocks of the transmit beamformer and the receiver in more depth. Since the processing functions are more specifically related to clinical applications, the functional blocks, starting with processing, will be covered in Level 2. In Level 2, we will also further develop some specific receiver functions in terms of clinical applications.

> **KEY CONCEPT**
>
> The distinction between pre-processing and post-processing is that pre-processing cannot be changed once an image or video loop is acquired; whereas post-processing can be changed on already acquired data. The distinction between which processes are considered pre and post are blurring as technology is allowing for data storage earlier in the processing path, converting some processing techniques from pre-processing to post-processing.

5. Transmit Beamformer

5.1 Function

The role of the transmit beamformer is to create transmit pulses of the appropriate amplitude and with the appropriate phasing and timing to drive the transducer so as to meet the clinical objective of the person performing the ultrasound scan. The transmitter is capable of producing a virtually infinite number of electrical waveforms to drive the various transducers used in ultrasound. Clearly, the transmitter must be able to produce continuous voltage electrical signals as well as pulsed signals. When the signals are pulsed, the transmitter must be capable of producing different operating frequencies (f_o), shorter and longer pulses (PD), and more frequent and less frequent pulses (PRF). In addition, the transmitter must be able to change the amplitude of the voltage, resulting in a change in acoustic power into the patient. When driving a phased array, the transmitter must create many excitation pulses simultaneously. In order to focus or steer, the transmitter must produce these simultaneous excitation pulses with small time delays between each pulse (phase delays are discussed in Chapter 5, Part I, Level 2). As we have already learned in the pulsed wave chapter, the timing for the transmitter is determined primarily by the imaging depth control. The phasing is determined by the desired focus and by the type of scan required. The amplitude of the transmitted signal is controlled directly by the user through the transmit power knob.

5.2 The System Control for Transmit Power

There are many variations on the name used for the system control of the transmit power. Some systems refer to the control as the output power, the output voltage, the transmit power, the transmit voltage, or the acoustic output power. Regardless of the name, the function is the same. Increasing the output power control increases the amplitude of the voltage which drives the transducer. If the transducer is driven with a higher voltage, a higher amplitude pressure is produced. A higher pressure implies a higher acoustic power in the patient and hence, a higher intensity.

To add to the confusion is the fact that some dedicated systems do not have a user control for power. For these systems, by setting the imaging preset, the power level is determined by the system and is not changeable by the user.

5.3 Practical Concerns

There are at least two very important reasons why you should concern yourself with the role of the transmitter. First, the risk of bioeffects is most directly related to the acoustic power produced. Since the acoustic power is controlled by the transmitter, the risk of bioeffects is linked to the transmit power control. The second reason is that the signal strength is also directly related to the acoustic power. A higher acoustic output results in a stronger signal. Therefore, when imaging to greater imaging depths, turning up the acoustic power usually results in greater penetration.

> **KEY CONCEPT**
>
> With increasing system functionality, many system controls have been added. As a result, some controls have become less obvious than with earlier ultrasound systems. The transmit power control is sometimes its own control, sometimes tied in with another function such as receiver gain, and on other systems controlled through a soft key or from within a software menu. For each system you will need to do some investigation to determine where and how you control the transmit power. Additionally, the transmit power is often tied into presets, such that changing a preset may result in a change in output power, depending on how the preset has been configured.

6. Receiver

Once the acoustic signals are converted to electrical signals, significant processing is required to convert the electrical signals into coherent, interpretable ultrasound information. Depending on the ultrasound system, some or even much of the initial receive processing may now take place physically within the transducer itself. As we saw in both Part I and Part II of Chapter 5, there are now many transducer-based systems that perform this processing before connecting to generic tablets of phones for display. Regardless of where the processing now takes place, the principles remain the same.

All receivers perform the following five operations:

1. Amplification
2. Compensation
3. Compression
4. Demodulation
5. Rejection

Of the five functions described, really only four are designed into the system. The "operation" of rejection is really a misnomer for an undesirable fact of electronics with which we are forced to live. We will include rejection as a fifth operation for consistency with other books. Furthermore, we will need to address another major function of all receivers which is often neglected in most other textbooks, the process of analog to digital conversion.

> **KEY CONCEPT**
>
> The receiver is responsible for "receiving" the signals from the transducer and applying the processing necessary before converting the signals into an image. The receiver is actually only part of the ultrasound system front end, which, in addition to the five receiver functions listed, also performs analog to digital (A/D) conversion and beamforming.

6.1 Amplification (Receiver Gain)

Need for Amplification

Amplification means to make bigger or to multiply. Amplification is necessary because the returning signals from the body are too small to be adequately processed within the electronics or visualized on a monitor. Amplification is partly under user control and partly under system control. Because the signals are so small, an enormous amount of amplification is necessary. Since a certain amount of gain is always necessary no matter what the imaging situation, there is always some amount of gain which is automatically applied by the system. Since there is no way of knowing a priori how large the signal returning from the patient will be, the user is allowed to add further amplification by changing the receiver gain knob.

Amplification of the RF Signal

The following diagrams demonstrate the application of gain (amplification). The first diagram *(Figure 28)* shows a low-level radio frequency (RF) signal of a blood vessel. (The signal is called an RF signal since the operating frequency is in MHz, which is in the range of frequencies used for radios.) The low-level signal represents the vessel lumen (blood pool).

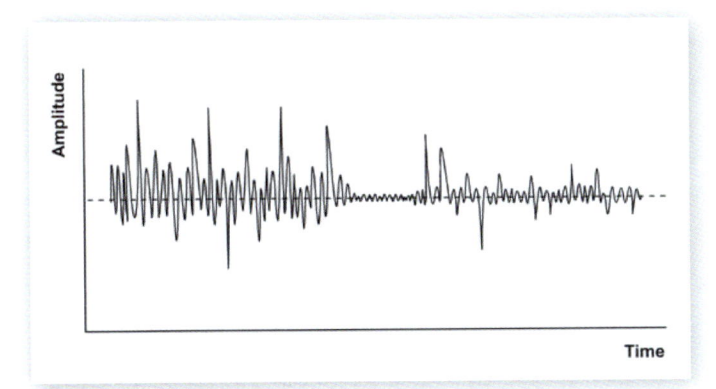

Fig. 28 **Raw RF signal**

Figure 29 shows the same RF signal after amplification (shown in red as an overlay). Notice how all of the characteristics of the amplified signal are the same as the un-amplified signal except for the amplitude. Amplification should preserve all other characteristics of a signal. If a signal is overamplified, distortion will occur. In terms of an ultrasound image, distortion appears as signal where no signal should be present. This distortion is usually relatively evident since overgained signals look excessively bright.

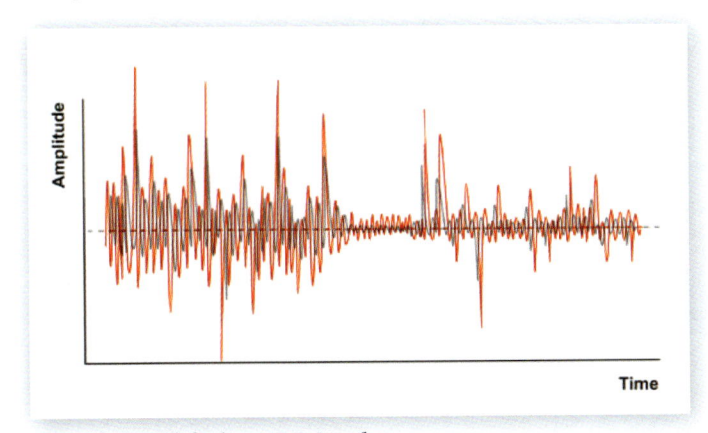

Fig. 29 **Amplified raw RF signal**

The System Control

Unlike the transmit control, there are fewer naming variants for the receiver gain. The common names are gain, receiver gain, and amplification. Increasing the receiver gain increases the amount of amplification of the received signal and does not affect the acoustic intensity in the patient. Returning to our radio analogy, the transmit is analogous to the radio station using a larger and more powerful broadcast antenna whereas the receiver gain is like the volume knob on the radio. Imagine if the radio station increased the transmitted radio signal in the middle of a song. The larger transmitted signal would mean a larger received signal. A larger signal implies that the volume would get louder, even without you increasing the radio volume. In fact, if the transmitted signal increases too much, you may find yourself having to decrease the volume (as commonly occurs when watching TV and a commercial is aired). In contrast, turning up the receiver gain is like increasing the volume on the radio. The transmit signal is unaffected, just the amplitude of the already received signal is increased.

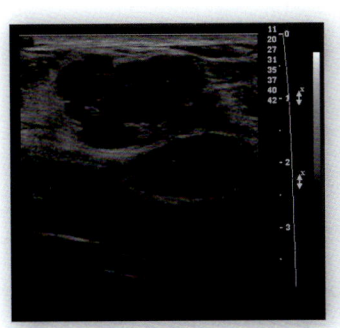

Fig. 30a **Severely undergained**   *Fig. 30b* **Badly undergained**

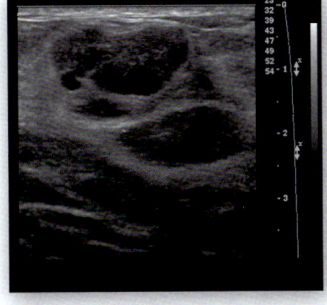

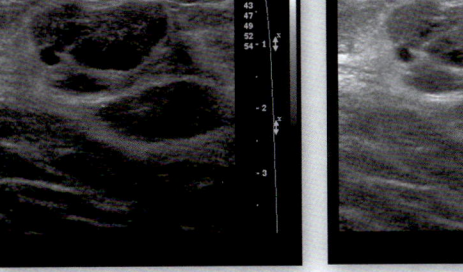

Fig. 30c **Undergained**   *Fig. 30d* **Appropriately gained**

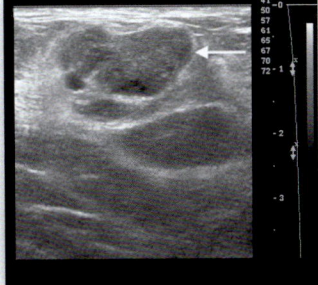

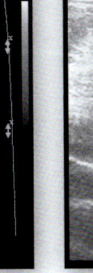

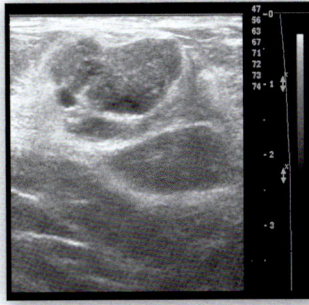

Fig. 30e **Optimally gained**   *Fig. 30f* **Slightly overgained**

View ONLINE Animation and Image Library

The images of *Figure 30* are of a fibroadenoma of a breast (indicated by the arrow in *Figure 30e*). Each frame represents an increase in amplitude by a factor of 2 (+6 dB) from the previous frame such that the amplitude *Figure 30f* is 32 times greater (+30 dB) than the image of *Figure 30a*. Notice that in the earlier frames, the signal amplitude is so low that only the very near field and strongest specular reflectors are visualized. As the amplitude is increased, more of the stronger breast tissue echoes are visualized. In *Figure 30d*, the receiver gain is now high enough so that the weaker signals from the mass are becoming visible. The gain of *Figure 30e* is now appropriate so that the signals from the breast tissue and the mass are visible simultaneously. The image of *Figure 30f* is overgained as evidenced by the extremely bright near field resulting in a loss of ability to distinguish the boundaries of the mass from the superficial breast tissue.

> **KEY CONCEPT**
>
> The receiver gain, or amplification, is really another term for multiplication. Increasing signal amplification implies that all signal and noise amplitudes are multiplied. Since the normal convention for grayscale images is that higher amplitude values are displayed as brighter grayscale shades, amplification essentially makes the entire image appear brighter.

6.2 Compensation (Time Gain Compensation)

The Role of TGC

The term compensation is very descriptive. Compensation refers to the application of increased amplification (gain) to compensate for attenuation with depth. Since attenuation increases with depth, compensation increases the gain with increasing depth to normalize the amplitude of the returning echoes.

On most ultrasound systems, the controls which compensate for increasing attenuation with depth are called the TGC (time gain compensation). In past days there were systems which referred to these controls as DGC (depth gain compensation) or SGC (swept gain compensation). The term TGC has become the default name.

Figure 31 shows conceptually how TGC controls function. Part (a) represents a transducer on a "patient". This patient is very particular in that there are four identical structures (red lines) at uniform depth increments. The down arrows represent the transmit signal at each of the four depths. Notice how the transmit signal attenuates with depth. The up arrows represent the reflected signals. Notice that the reflected signal is always lower in amplitude than the transmit signal at each of the four structures. Part (b) graphically represents the amplitude of the echoes for the reflectors at each of the four depths. Since all four reflecting structures are identical, in the ideal world, the echoes of all four structures would have the same amplitude. Because of increasing attenuation with distance traveled in the

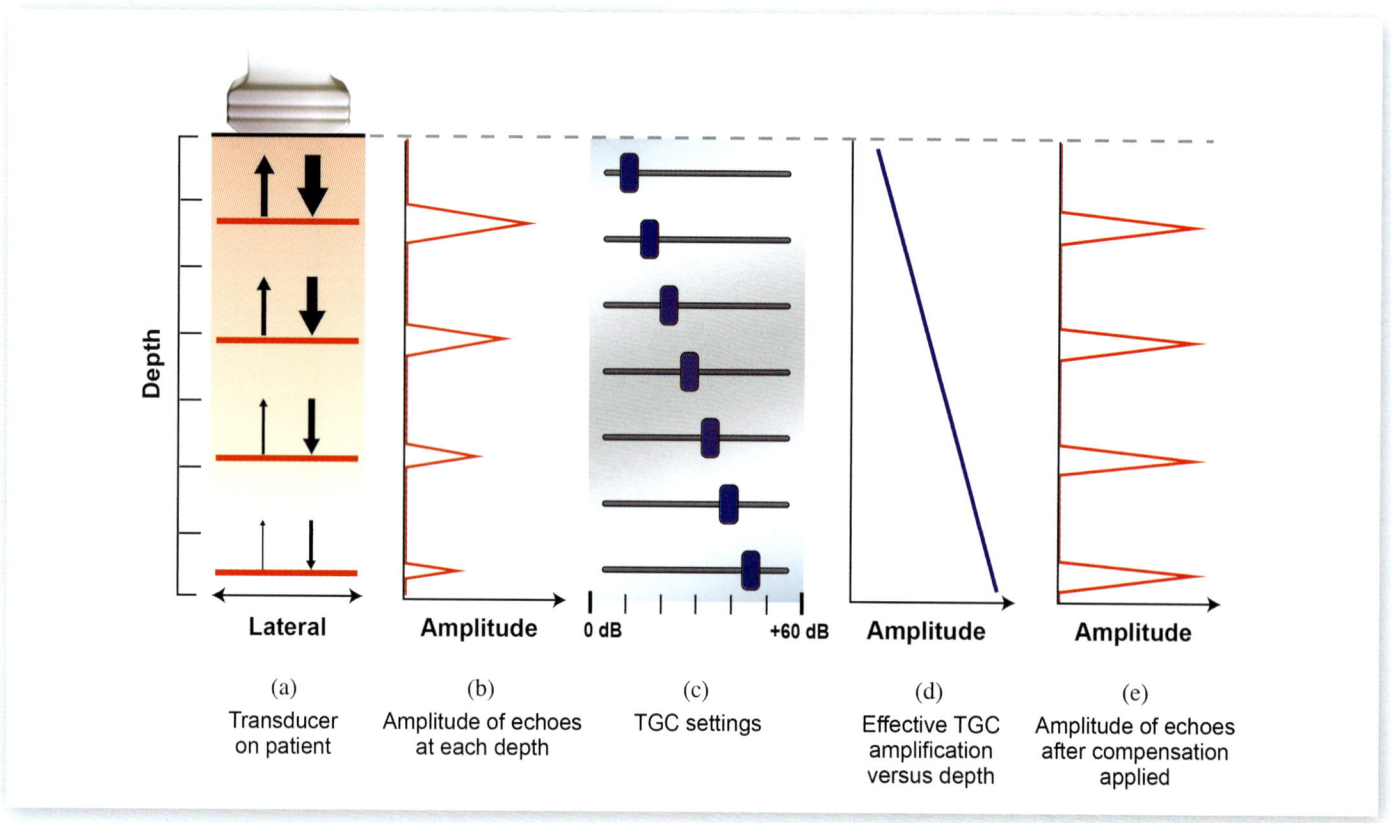

(a)	(b)	(c)	(d)	(e)
Transducer on patient	Amplitude of echoes at each depth	TGC settings	Effective TGC amplification versus depth	Amplitude of echoes after compensation applied

Fig. 31 Conceptual functional diagram of TGCs

patient for both the transmit signal and for the return signal, each successive echo is lower in amplitude. *Figure 31* part (c) represents the TGC setting that would be used to compensate for the increasing attenuation with depth. The slider at the top affects the echoes that arrive earliest in time, or equivalently from the shallowest depths. Each successive slider affects a deeper region. So the bottom slider represents significantly more gain (compensation) than the shallowest slider. Part (d) graphically represents the gain profile relative to depth, showing the least compensation for shallowest echoes, and the most compensation for the deepest echoes. Note how the shape of the effective amplification matches the TGC profile. Part (e) represents the signals of (b) after the gain of (d) has been applied. In essence the echoes from (b) are multiplied by the amplification graph of (d) to produce (e). Notice that now the amplitudes of all four structures are the same (compensated).

Compensation of the RF Signal

Whereas *Figure 31* shows the conceptual application of TGC controls, *Figure 32* demonstrates the application of TGC controls to an actual RF ultrasound signal. The signal shown in black represents the uncompensated RF signal (as also shown in *Figure 29*). The red colored signal (overlaid) represents the compensated signal. Notice that the signals from later in time (right side of the graph) were amplified more than the signals from earlier in time (shallower depth). The result is that for the compensated signal for the tissue below the blood vessel (low-level echoes at about the middle) are now similar in amplitude to the tissue above the blood vessel.

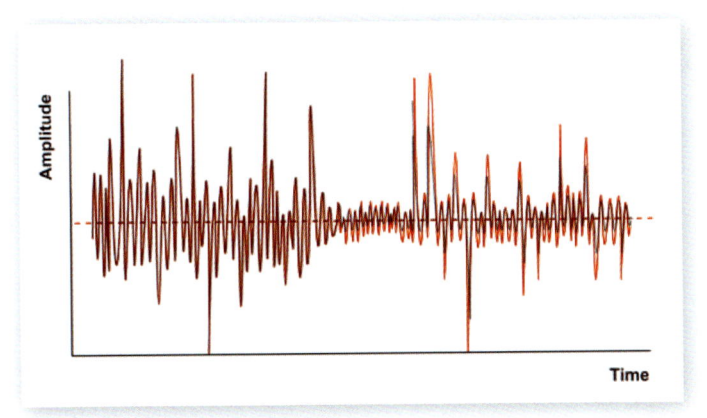

Fig. 32 **Compensated RF signal**

The Relationship Between TGCs and Receiver Gain

Note that compensation is really the same as amplification, except TGC gain is broken into individual bands or zones over depth. Turning up the receiver gain is equivalent to sliding all of the TGC sliders (also referred to as "pots", (short for potentiometers)) up at the same time. The following *Figures 33* and *34* illustrate this concept.

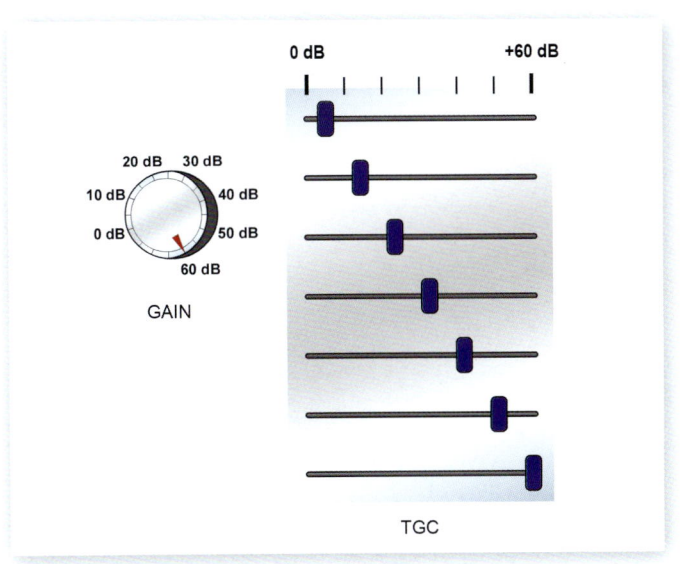

Fig. 33 **Maximum total gain = 120 dB**

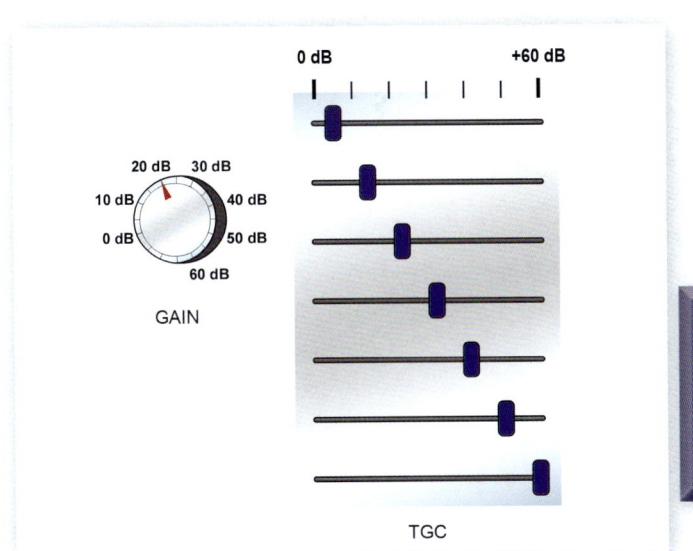

Fig. 34 **Maximum total gain = 80 dB**

In *Figure 33*, the total gain for the top of the image is 60 dB from the overall gain plus 5 dB from the top TGC slider. For the bottom of the image the total gain is 60 dB from the overall gain plus 60 dB from the bottom TGC slider. For each of the depths represented by the sliders between the top and bottom, the overall gain is between the 65 dB of the top and the 120 dB of the bottom. In comparison, for *Figure 34*, the TGC profile is the same, but the overall gain is set to 20 dB. Therefore the top of the image has an overall gain of 25 dB and the bottom of the image has an overall gain of 20 dB plus 60 dB, or 80 dB.

Depth and TGC Zones

Most systems have 8 to 10 TGC slider controls. The imaging depth is subdivided into uniform depth zones, such that each slider represents a specific zone. For example, if the depth is set to 8 cm and there are 8 sliders, then each TGC represents 1 cm of depth on the image.

Similarly, if the depth is set to 6 cm, then each slider represents

$$\frac{6 \text{ cm}}{8 \text{ sliders}} = \frac{3}{4} \text{ cm} = 0.75 \text{ cm}.$$

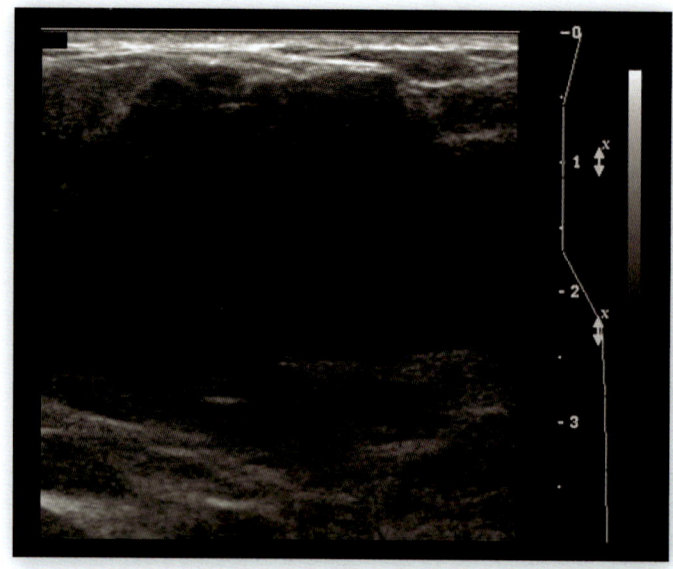

Fig. 35a **Mid-range TGCs too low**

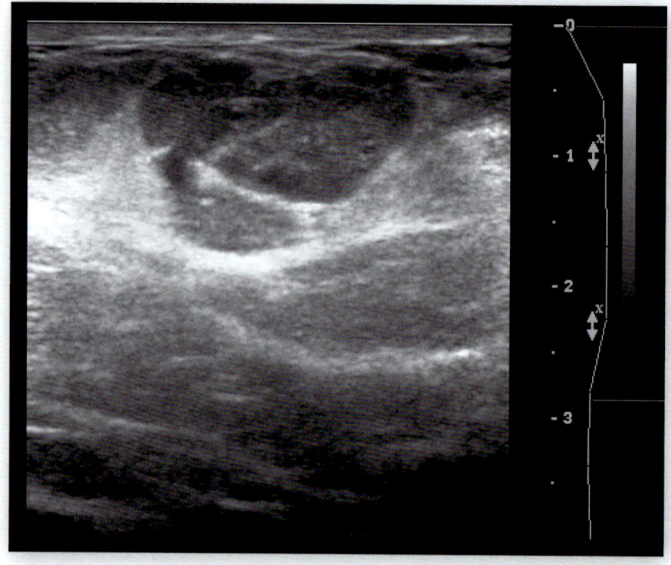

Fig. 35b **Mid-range TGCs too high**

These two images of *Figure 35a and 35b* of the same fibroadenoma as displayed in *Figure 30a* through *Figure 30f* demonstrate the effect of inappropriate TGC positioning. In *Figure 35a* the center TGC sliders are set too low resulting in under gaining in the depth range from slightly shallower than 1 cm to about 2.5 cm. In contrast, *Figure 35b* demonstrates the effects of over gaining the mid-region. In Level 2, we will relate TGC profiles to clinical situations.

> **CHECKPOINT: Exam Tip**
>
> Compensation is depth-dependent gain, to "compensate" for the fact that signals from deeper in the body experience greater attenuation than signals returning from shallower depths.

6.3 Compression

Dynamic Range

To understand the concept of compression, we must first discuss the concept of dynamic range. Dynamic range refers to the ratio of the maximum to the minimum amplitude of any quantity. Dynamic range can be used to specify the ratio of the largest to the smallest echoes from a patient, the largest to smallest signal an A/D converter can process, the largest to smallest brightness levels of a monitor, the largest to smallest signal the human eye can detect, the largest to smallest signal the human ear can hear, or even the ratio of the maximum to minimum amount in your bank account. Since dynamic range represents a ratio of two numbers, a large signal does not necessarily represent a very large dynamic range. For example, if the maximum signal is 10 Volts and the minimum signal is 2 Volts, the dynamic range is only 5 to 1. In comparison, if the maximum signal is only 1 Volt, but the minimum signal is 1 mV, then the dynamic range is 1,000 to 1.

Every one of our senses has a maximum dynamic range. For example, at the lower end of the spectrum, you may have the tactile ability to feel the weight of a grain of sand but not an individual molecule. On the upper end, it is unlikely that you are able to distinguish the difference between piles of sand dumped on you weighing 10,000 pounds versus 20,000 pounds.

The signal dynamic range (ratio of maximum to minimum echo amplitudes returning from the patient) is generally much larger than the display dynamic range (the range of signals a monitor can display). In fact, the display dynamic range generally well exceeds the visual dynamic range (the range of signals visible to the human eye at one instant in time). Therefore, although there is a big problem with the signal occupying a much larger range than what can be displayed on the monitor, there is an even bigger problem in that the monitor can display a larger dynamic range than what the eye can see.

Compression and Dynamic Range

Compression is the general term for any technique which maps a larger dynamic range into a smaller dynamic range. Because of the great disparity between the dynamic range of the eye and the reflected signals, compression must be performed to map the enormous signal dynamic range into the significantly smaller dynamic range of the human eye.

Figure 36 demonstrates a simple compression scheme where a range of 10:1 is mapped to a smaller range of 2:1.

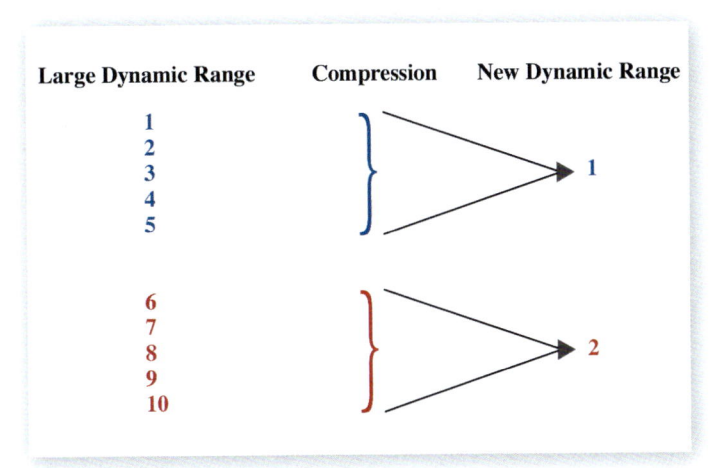

Fig. 36 Simple compression map

Effects of Compression and Information Loss

Notice that the process of compression depicted in *Figure 36* distorts the data such that some information is lost. In the uncompressed range, there is an obvious difference between the number 6 and the number 10. However, after applying the above compression scheme, both values would be mapped to the same value of 2. Of course there are an infinite number of compression schemes and techniques possible. Different compression schemes will have different levels of loss. The term compression is also used to refer to digital data storage such as in a picture archiving and communication system (PACS). You will sometimes hear of lossless compression schemes for data storage. Whereas it may be possible to create lossless compression schemes for data storage, in general it is not possible to create a lossless compression scheme for compressing signal levels into brightness levels visible by the human eye. With that said, it is possible that the signal loss is inconsequential relative to the interpretation at times.

For brightness mapping, the only time a lossless scheme would be possible is in the rare case when a signal has so few levels so as to require less dynamic range than the capability of the human eye. Therefore, compression is effectively always needed, and is an integral part of making ultrasound images that are interpretable by humans. The fact that information can be "compressed" is very important because it warns us that there is a limitation with ultrasound (and most imaging techniques). It is certainly possible that an important signal could be "compressed" out of visibility relative to the surrounding tissue or medium.

In Level 2, we will demonstrate some specific approaches to compression and further discuss the ramifications on clinical practice and practical application.

Compression of the RF Signal

To comprehend the effect of compression, the diagram of *Figure 37* compares the uncompressed data of *Figure 29* (shown in black) to the log compressed signal (overlaid in red). Notice that for *Figure 37* the lowest amplitude signals (in the middle of the graph) were little changed but that amplitude of the larger signals were reduced. As a result, the ratio of the biggest signal to the smallest signal has been reduced. For this example the compression ratio is only about a factor of two. You should also notice that another approach to compression would be to amplify the smaller signals more and the larger signals less, since this would also reduce the ratio of the largest to the smallest signal.

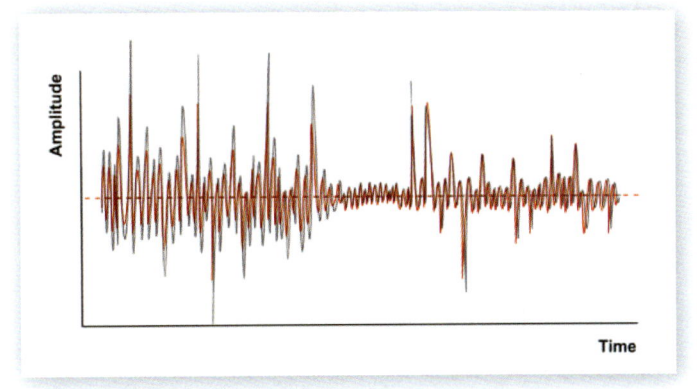

Fig. 37 Log compressed RF signal

Compression is a critical function for diagnostic ultrasound. It is important to understand that there are many different functional areas of the system which perform a degree of "compression." The receiver function of compression is not under the control of the user but is specified by the system design team. This pre-processing function should not be confused with the compression function which occurs later in the signal processing path and is controllable by the user. This later compression could be called "video compression," since it compresses the appearance of the displayed grayscale. In Level 2 of this chapter, we will further discuss the role of compression and the possible implications for diagnostic accuracy.

> **KEY CONCEPT**
>
> Compression is a very complex and extremely critical topic. Compression is necessary to reduce the signal dynamic range. In an ultrasound system compression is actually performed at different stages in the processing. Some compression is done in the receiver (not under user control) and then some compression (video compression) is controlled by the user as a post-processing technique. A consequence of reducing the dynamic range through compression is that some signal information may be lost.

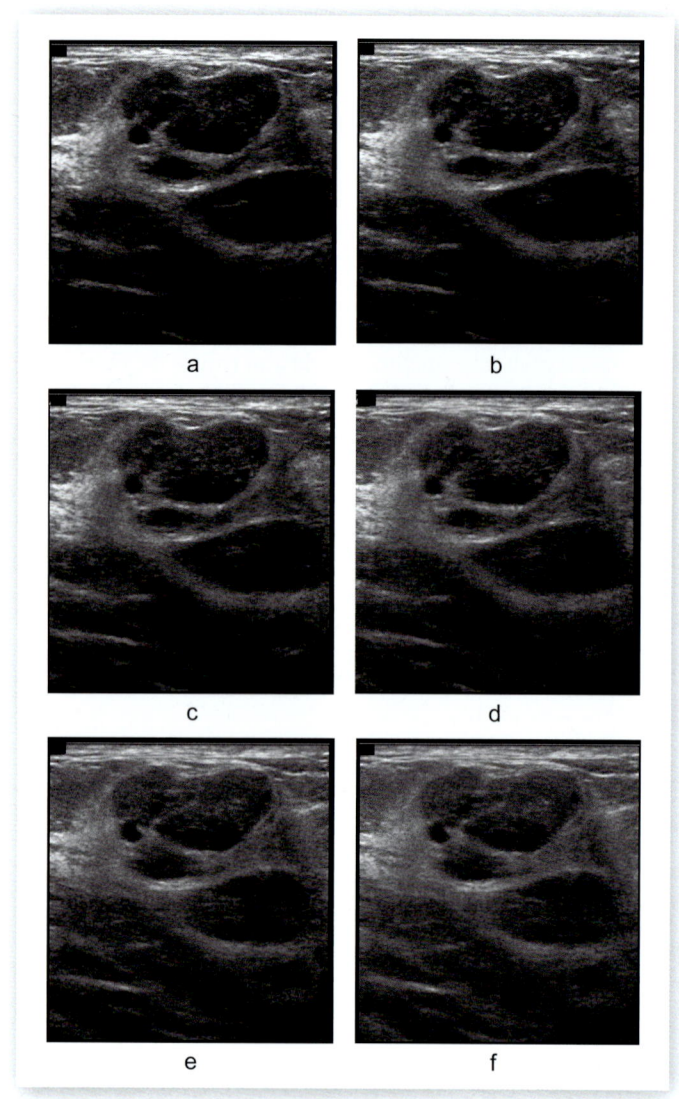

Fig. 38 **Various compression maps**

The vignette of *Figure 38* displays the same fibroadenoma with six different compression settings. Notice that the compression in *Figure 38a* shows the most contrast, mapping the lower level signals to darker shades of gray and black. Each successive map displays less contrast by mapping the lower level signals to lighter shades of gray. In *Figure 38f*, notice that the image is considerably "softer" than *Figure 38a*, displaying the low level echoes within the mass as well as the bright white echoes from the breast ligaments and subcutaneous skin.

View ONLINE Animation and Image Library

6.4 Demodulation

Modulation and Demodulation

The word "modulate" means to change or modify. Recall that sound is a mechanical wave, implying a physical interaction with the medium. As the wave propagates through the medium, the interaction causes changes (modulations) in the wave. Therefore, demodulation is the process by which the modulations of the wave are removed or detected. Hence, demodulation is often called "signal detection." For ultrasound signals, demodulation consists of two stages: rectification and "smoothing" or envelope detection. As a result, the process of demodulation is also commonly referred to as envelope detection. Rectification and smoothing effectively remove the transmit (RF) signal from the return echo, leaving just the modulation caused by the interaction with the tissue as shown in *Figure 40*.

Rectification

Rectification converts the negative components of a signal into positive components (changes a signal from being bipolar to unipolar). As shown in *Figure 39*, the original signal before rectification is in black; the rectified signal is in red. Notice how the black signal below the baseline is now flipped to be above the baseline in the rectified (red) signal.

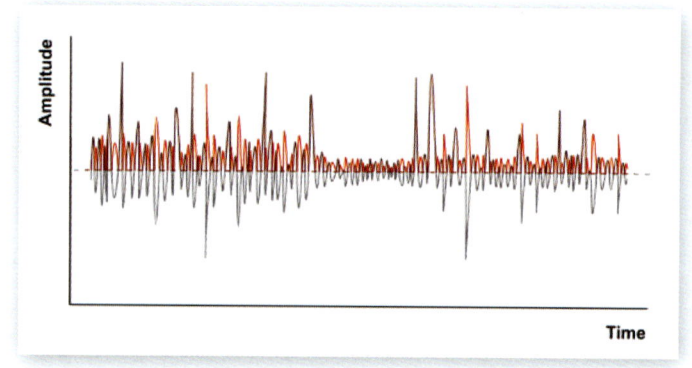

Fig. 39 **Rectification of RF signal**

Envelope Detection (Smoothing)

Once rectification has occurred, the process of envelope detection basically traces the signal peaks and valleys while simultaneously applying some averaging or smoothing. The following figure illustrates the process of envelope detection.

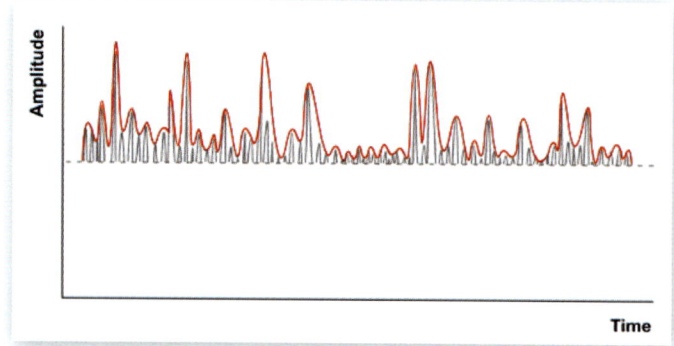

Fig. 40 **Envelope detection of RF signal**

The Detected Signal and A-mode

Figure 41 demonstrates the resultant "detected" or "demodulated" signal. The demodulated signal is the same as the early modality of A-mode. In *Figure 41*, the area of low amplitude represents low reflectivity. As was learned in Chapter 3, low reflectivity results from a low acoustic impedance mismatch, or equivalently, a relatively "homogeneous" medium. The most likely medium which would produce such a low signal return is a fluid. As mentioned earlier, in the figure below, this region pertains to a vessel lumen (region of blood within a vessel).

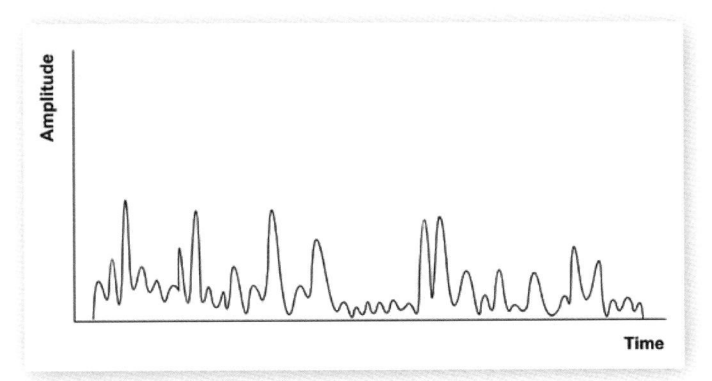

Fig. 41 **Demodulated signal (A-mode)**

6.5 Reject

Nothing in life is perfect. Unwanted noise can be added to the signal through the body, transducer, cable, and system electronics. Generally these noise signals are smaller than the desired signals and can be suppressed. Rejection effectively sets a threshold below which signals will not be visible on display.

Figure 42 demonstrates how a reject function would work, if one actually existed in the receiver.

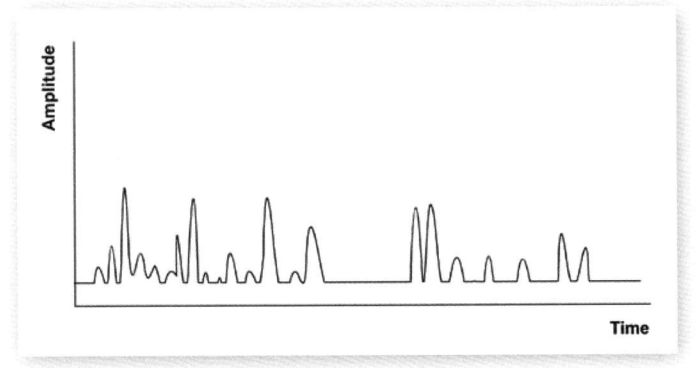

Fig. 42 **Demodulated signal after rejection**

In reality, this reject threshold is not actually actively set in the receiver but rather is just the limit of the sensitivity of the system. Engineers who design receivers do not actively set a reject level to limit low-level signals. Instead, a level is reached below which the signals are not detected. This level is referred to by design engineers as the noise floor. Designers go through extraordinary efforts to push the noise floor of the electronics as low as possible while still preserving the required signal input dynamic range and amplification. The reason it is desirable to have the noise floor as low as possible is greater system sensitivity. The lower the noise floor, the smaller the signals that can be detected.

> **KEY CONCEPT**
>
> As the mechanical sound wave propagates through the body, the body changes, or modulates, the sound wave. Demodulation is the process of detecting these changes by removing the original transmitted signal from the returned signal. This process is generally performed in two stages: rectification and smoothing (or envelope detection).

7. A-mode (Amplitude mode)

7.1 A-mode Display

In the early days of ultrasound, signal detection was essentially where the processing stopped. The demodulated signal was presented on a screen as a waveform with amplitude on the vertical axis and time (or depth as related through the distance equation) on the horizontal axis. This modality was called amplitude mode (A-mode), for the obvious reason that signal amplitude was displayed. In terms of the signal in A-mode, when there is a large acoustic impedance mismatch, there is a large reflection, and hence, there is a high amplitude signal. When there is a small mismatch, the reflected signal is smaller, and a lower amplitude signal is detected. Therefore, the vertical axis of the data can be referred to using many related terms such as the acoustic impedance mismatch, the signal reflectivity, the amplitude, or the signal strength.

7.2 Interpreting an A-mode

The following figure demonstrates a real A-mode taken from a radial artery for a research project.

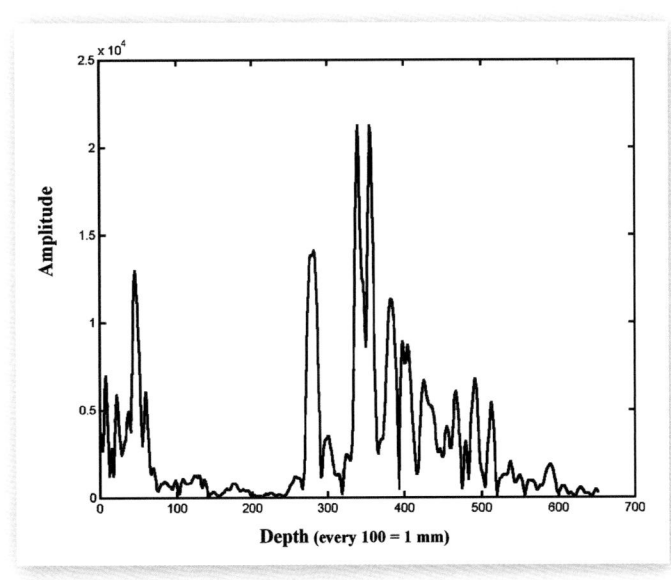

Fig. 43 **A-mode of a radial artery**

In the A-mode example of *Figure 43*, note the lower amplitude reflections in the range from about 80 to about 275. This lower amplitude reflection corresponds to a relatively "homogeneous" medium, in this case the blood pool within the artery. Notice the exceptionally high amplitude signals just before and after this region. These high amplitude signals represent the large acoustic impedance mismatches associated with the anterior and posterior artery walls. The large echo at about 350 corresponds to the specular reflections from tendon and fascial sheathing. Many students when first viewing this A-mode mistakenly identify this strong reflection as the reflection from bone. If this reflection were from bone, we would anticipate "shadowing" resulting in virtually no signal from deeper depths. Since this shadow is not present, we can be relatively certain that the reflector is not bone. You should also notice the increasing attenuation with increasing depth (from 400 to 650). Here we can clearly see the need for compensation.

7.3 The Use of A-mode

A-mode is rarely used as a modality with the exception of a few ophthalmic applications (*Figure 44*) which have been replaced in most offices with B-mode (2D) and even 3D imaging. Although rarely used, there is a benefit to understanding A-mode. As we will learn in Level 2, modern ultrasound images are really the compilation of many A-modes presented in grayscale. Therefore, the principles which govern A-mode govern B-mode (brightness mode also referred to as 2D imaging).

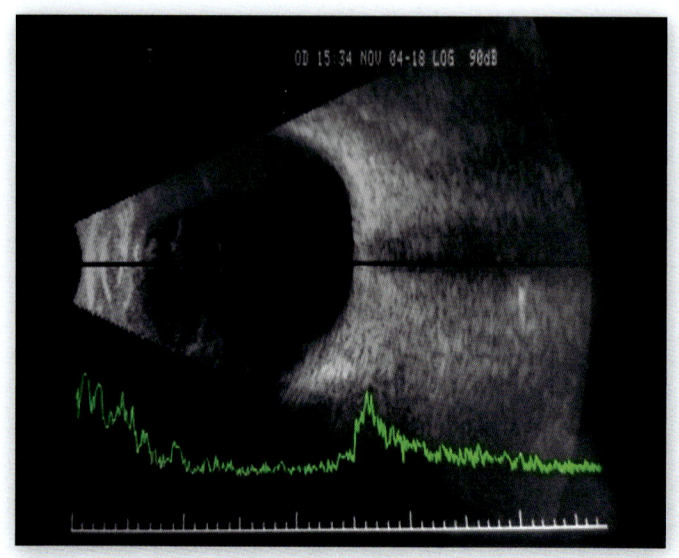

Fig. 44 **A-mode of the human eye (green tracing) with corresponding B-mode image for correlation** *(Image used with permission from Ophthalmology Rounds)*

> **KEY CONCEPT**
>
> Although data is rarely presented in an A-mode format, the concepts of A-mode still serve as the underlying principles of B-mode: stronger reflectors result in higher amplitude signals, and weaker reflectors result in lower amplitude signals.

8. Exercises

View ONLINE Exercises

LEVEL 2: Board Level

9. System Block Diagram

In years past, ultrasound systems were more standard in their design such that the block diagram was a fairly good representation of the major functions and the partitioning of these functions. With the greater adoption of application-specific integrated circuits (ASICS) along with more portable ultrasound systems, the partitioning is no longer as standardized. For example, many of the functions found in the box labeled "Receiver" may now be found within the transducer itself instead of a system box. Whereas the functions still exist in all ultrasound systems, the partitioning now varies significantly. So your focus should be more what each subsystem does and why it is needed rather than where the subsystem exists.

The system block diagram in *Figure 45* displays most of the major functions performed by an ultrasound system, with a notable exception that there is no explicit depiction of a phase engine when phasing is needed. For the simplified block diagram, the "phase engine" responsible for creating the phase delay profiles operates in both the pulser and the receiver. Clearly, no attempt was made to include all of the system features and all of the less fundamental processing techniques. Inclusion of every feature would render the block diagram complex beyond measure and virtually useless as a didactic tool. Instead, we will discuss the basic processing techniques one by one throughout Part I of this chapter and we will cover the advanced features in Part II.

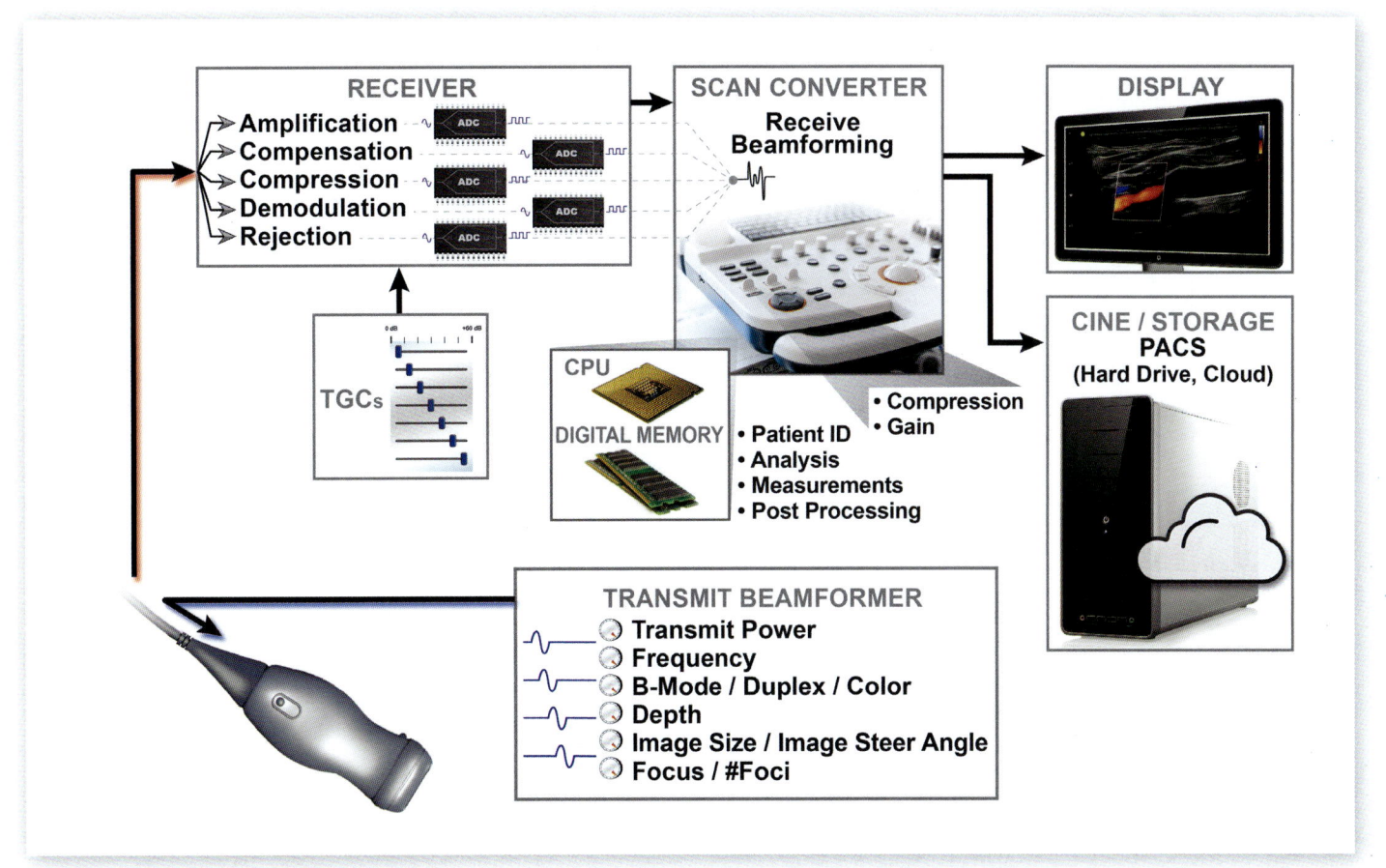

Fig. 45 **System functional block diagram**

10. Transmit Beamformer

10.1 Transmit Beamformer Function
The role of a transmit beamformer is to determine all of the characteristics of the transmit signals that drive the transducer elements. From the setting of many controls (discussed throughout Section 11), the beamformer calculates the transmit amplitude, the number of cycles in the transmit pulse (unless continuous wave), the timing between pulses, the number of elements and which elements to make up the transmit aperture, and the phasing for each element. The phasing can be used to create narrow beams for sequential imaging, wide beams for multi-beam acquisition (MLA) also known as parallel processing, defocused beams, multiple simultaneous beams for multi-line transmit (MLT), and plane waves. The phasing also can be used to create steering, focusing, and any combination thereof. You will learn more about how the beamformer functions in Section 15, when we discuss the receive beamformer.

Figure 46 provides an example of the multiple beams used to create a cardiac image. Note that the beamwidths are highly exaggerated by the six color overlays (a typical full-sized sequential image would have more than 200 transmitted lines).

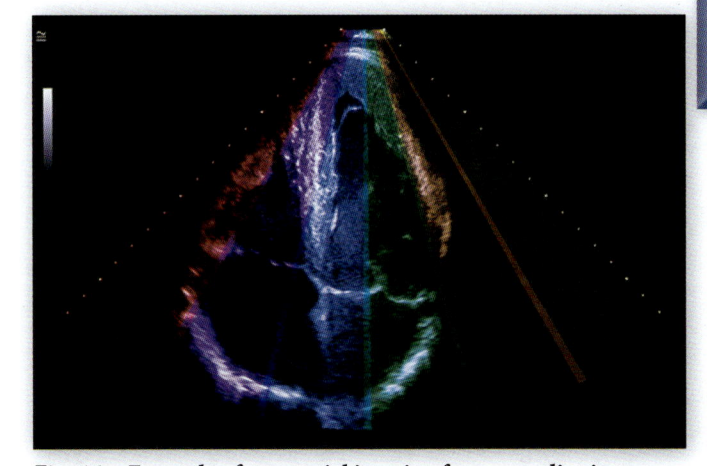

Fig. 46 **Example of sequential imaging from a cardiac image**

10.2 Transmit Aperture and Apodization
Typically, not all elements of a transducer are used at the same time. The group of active elements being used at any moment are referred to as the aperture (similar to the opening of the camera when taking a picture). In order to improve the beam shape by reducing the grating lobes, a technique called apodization is often used. This technique involves varying the voltage from element to element of the aperture. Typically, the voltage is highest for the elements in the center of the aperture, and lower for the elements at the edges of the aperture.

Figure 47 provides an example of a focused beam with an apodization profile. As shown in Chapter 5, the focusing is the result of the delay profile. Notice that the amplitude of the excitation pulses (voltages) is highest at the center element and lowest near the edge elements of the transmit aperture.

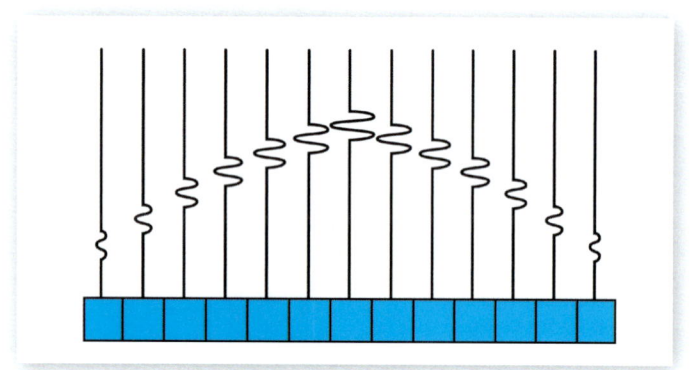

Fig. 47 **Apodization waveform profile**

> **KEY CONCEPT**
>
> The signal created to drive the transducer is determined by a myriad of system settings including the transducer type, the transmit frequency, the transmit power, the method for generating the image (sequential, multi-line acquisition (MLA), multi-line transmit (MLT), ultrafast (plane or defocused wave)), focus (if applicable), and which imaging modalities are desired.

11. Controls that Affect Transmit and Power Distribution

11.1 Transducer Frequency and Transmit Power

Within the block labeled "Beamformer" there is displayed a series of system controls. Each of these controls affects the transmitted pulse and hence the power distribution in the patient, either over time, or over space. The effects of changing the transmit power are the most evident. A higher transmit power implies the generation of a higher acoustic power and hence, a higher intensity sound beam. The effects of choosing a different frequency of operation may not be quite as evident. Recall that higher frequency waves are absorbed at much greater rates than lower frequency waves. Therefore, at the very least, we would anticipate that higher frequency transducers will potentially have restrictions regarding power so as to limit thermal issues within the tissue, most specifically on the near field (shallower imaging depths).

11.2 Imaging Modalities, Image Generation, Image Size, and Transmit Power

The decision to perform a 3D scan versus a 2D scan, versus duplex (color and 2D) versus Doppler, or M-mode etc. also affects power. The reason the modality affects power is related to two different aspects of the image creation: the duty factor and whether or not the modality is scanned or non-scanned. If longer pulses are desired (such as occur in color Doppler, PW Doppler, and of course, CW Doppler), the duty factor increases and the transmit power must be accordingly decreased. Since non-scanned modalities concentrate the energy in the same location from acoustic beam to acoustic beam, there is again a greater risk of thermal issues. As a result, the maximum allowed transmit power must again be decreased by the system to assure safety.

The interaction between imaging mode and power has become even more complex with the addition of non-sequential image generation modes such as ultrafast plane wave and defocused transmit. Transmitting narrow beams for sequential imaging clearly results in different power distribution than transmitting broader beams for multi-beam imaging or unfocused beams which insonify the entire imaging regions at once. Similarly, changing the image size also changes the scan region, potentially affecting the power. For sequential imaging, a smaller image size implies a more rapid scanning of the region (higher frame rate) and hence, a greater risk of thermal bioeffects. Therefore, as the scan size is decreased, the maximum transmit power may decrease. In reality, unless the image size is drastically reduced, this parameter rarely has a significant impact on the transmit power. The reason is that for a scanned modality, mechanical bioeffects are still much more likely. As you will learn in Chapter 9, the risk of mechanical bioeffects is related to the peak rarefactional pressure and not the time distribution of the signal. The bottom line is that many imaging controls affect the allowed maximum transmit power and there is an inverse relationship between the maximum transmit voltage and the frequency at which the transmit events occur.

> **KEY CONCEPT**
>
> There is an inverse relationship between the maximum transmit voltage and the frequency at which the transmit events occur.

11.3 Imaging Depth and Transmit Power

Changing the imaging depth changes the duty factor and hence, affects the maximum transmit power allowed. A shallower imaging depth implies a higher duty factor (a shorter line can be repeated more frequently than a longer line). A higher duty factor implies that a lower maximum transmit power is allowed.

11.4 Focus and Transmit Power

For systems that have transmit focus controls, changing the transmit focus can directly affect the acoustic power. By changing the depth of focus, the beamwidth and beam pattern can be altered significantly. Setting a shallower focus usually results in a decrease in the maximum allowed transmit power. This decrease is the consequence of having the beam come to a narrow focus at shallow depths at which not much attenuation has yet occurred. In contrast, with a deep focus, the beam converges in the far field where the signal has already been significantly attenuated. Therefore, a deeper focus generally allows the system to increase the maximum transmit voltage without increasing risk to the patient. This fact was also discussed in Chapter 5 when reviewing the concept of focusing.

Some systems do not have a transmit focus control, while other systems have the control only in certain image generation modes. When an image is being created sequentially, with focused transmitted beams, the system will present a focus control. The focus control usually appears as a sideways 'caret,' or what looks like a greater than ">" or less than "<" sign from mathematics (see *Figures 48-50*). Whenever a system creates images non-sequentially, either through a group of broad unfocused beams or defocused beams, the transmit focus control will not exist.

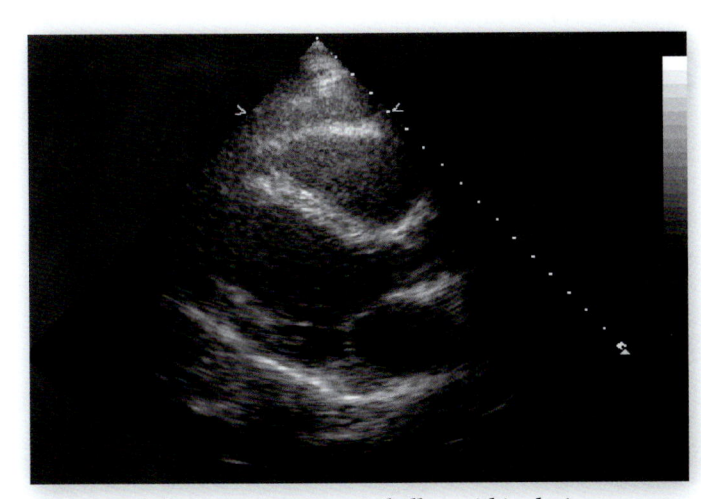

Fig. 48 **Focal zone positioning too shallow within the image sector**

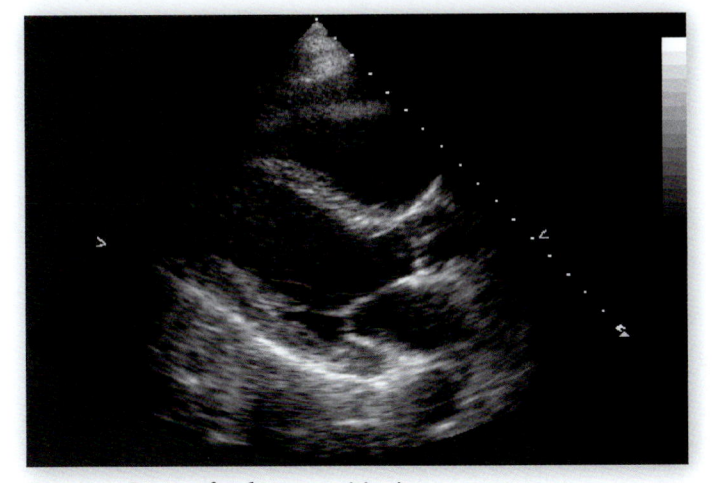

Fig. 49 **Correct focal zone positioning**

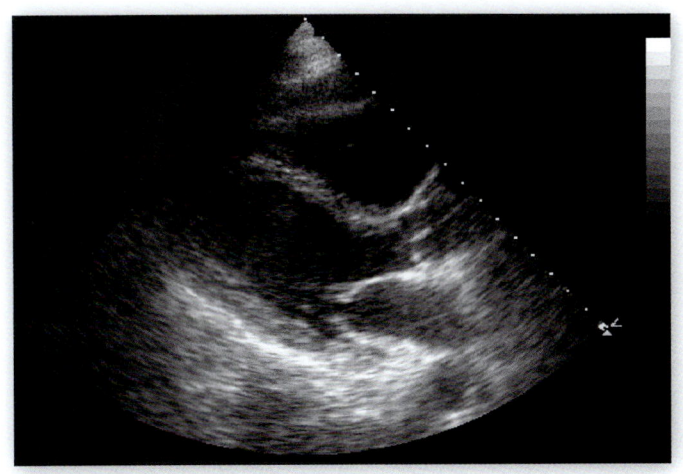

Fig. 50 **Focal zone positioning too deep within the image sector**

View ONLINE Animation and Image Library

12. TGC and Gain Revisited

12.1 Internal TGC Profiles

In Level 1, we discussed the role of amplification and the role of compensation through TGCs. Although not explicitly stated, in Level 1, the reader most likely assumed that the TGC controls are completely under the control of the sonographer. Furthermore, from the examples given, we would presume that the dynamic range of the TGC is generally 60 dB. This is not completely true. Because of the enormous dynamic range of signals returning from deeper depths relative to shallower depths, the amount of compensation required is generally more than 60 dB. As a result, when designing the ultrasound machine, the user is generally given 60 dB of TGC range and then more compensation is applied which is not under the control of the user. The amount of this internal TGC depends on the application, transducer being used, frequency, etc. It is certainly not uncommon to apply 30 dB or more of compensation before the user ever touches a TGC slider. The reason this internal TGC is applied is basically to make the TGC sliders more responsive and not overly sensitive. Imagine if a TGC slider represented 100 dB of gain instead of 60 dB as demonstrated in *Figure 51*. Even the slightest movement of the slider could result in significant changes in the brightness associated with that TGC. For the example given, in *Figure 51*, the same movement of the second slider results in 10 dB change in comparison to 17 dB change in *Figure 52*. By performing some of the required TGC before allowing user control, the user is allowed a control with less range per travel and a more easily managed control.

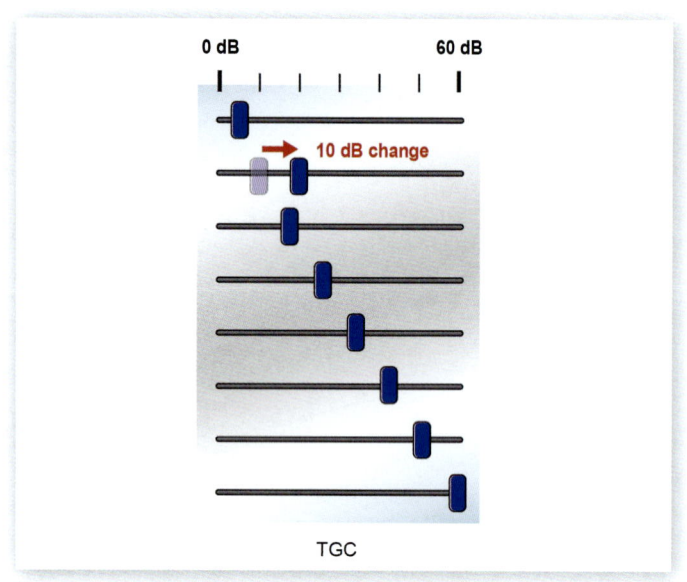

Fig. 51 TGC profile with 60 dB dynamic range

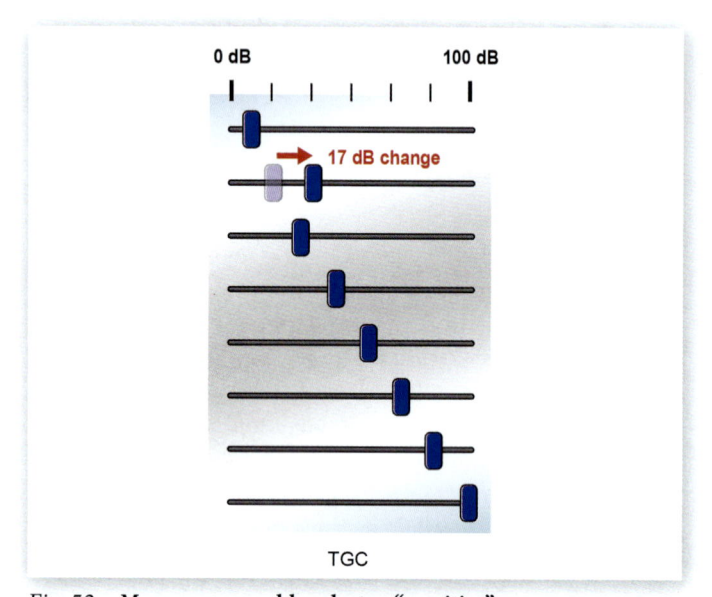

Fig. 52 More range would make too "sensitive"

In general, this "behind the scene" compensation does not present any significant issues since there is so much range on the TGC controls for the user to dictate. However, this fact does not always hold true for color imaging.

12.2 Internal Color TGC Profiles

In color imaging, the TGC control is entirely internal. Excluding adaptive processing which is now utilized more commonly, the TGC profile for color is based on assumed attenuation. The assumed attenuation is based on the imaging depth, frequency of the transducer, and the preset which tells the system information about the region of the body being scanned. For example, the internal TGC profile for a pediatric 5 MHz cardiac transducer will most certainly be different than the internal TGC profile for a 5 MHz linear transducer being used for vascular studies. With that said, there is absolutely no guarantee that the color TGC profile internally set is correctly for all patients all of the time. Unlike 2D, the user does not have any control which can correct for an "inappropriate" internal TGC profile. Since color data does not indicate signal strength (unlike 2D which displays signal strength as "brightness"), when the internal TGC is incorrect for a specific patient, the problem can be masked by decreasing or increasing the overall color gain. However, there are times when the presence of color noise speckle will be apparent in only one depth region of the image while the rest of the color image is correctly gained. Conversely, one region of color may drop out when the rest of the color image appears to be correctly gained. The source of both of these problems is the internal TGC profiles. The problem is rare, but existent. Systems that are now setting the color TGC adaptively avoid this problem, as long as their algorithms are using the correct parameters for the existing imaging situation.

12.3 "Pre-compensated" TGC Profiles

There is also a TGC feature on most ultrasound systems that is user selectable. This control is referred to as pre-compensated TGC control (not to be confused with an adaptive or autocorrect TGC control). The concept behind a pre-compensated TGC profile is that an algorithm was used to determine the best guess for the appropriate TGC profile, and the entire TGC profile is applied internally. As a result, if the TGC profile assumed is perfectly correct for the patient being imaged, the TGC profile of the sliders on the system will need to be perfectly flat and in the middle. If the "guessed at" profile over-compensated or under-compensated at any particular depth, then the TGC slider for that zone will be increased or decreased to "compensate" for the incorrect internal compensation. *Figure 53* demonstrates a compensated TGC profile with a patient for whom the internal profile was ideal. In comparison, *Figure 54* demonstrates a compensated TGC profile with a patient for whom the profile was a little off in zones 3, 4, 7, and 8.

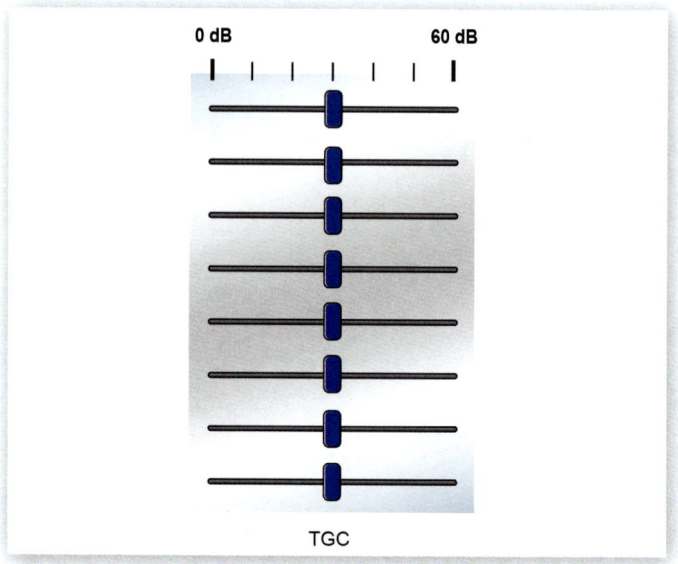

Fig. 53 **Starting point using "pre-compensated" TGCs**

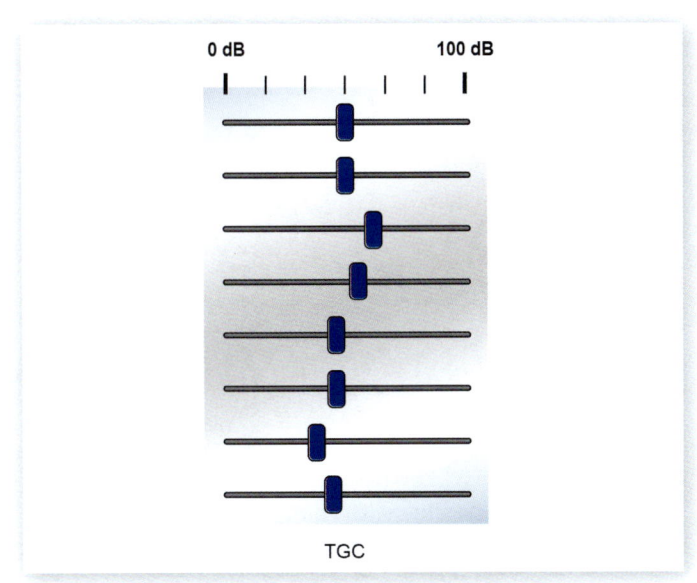

Fig. 54 **Adjusting "pre-compensated" TGC controls**

Note that unlike "uncompensated" TGC profiles, compensated TGC profiles tend to be relatively centered and may jog back and forth with depth.

12.4 TGC Controls and Imaging Scenarios

For completeness, we will now review the TGC controls for various imaging situations. For these examples we will presume conventional TGC function and not "pre-compensated" TGCs. These examples are very important for two reasons: first you should understand the operation of TGCs for proper imaging, and second because you may still be expected to know this information when taking credentialing exams.

◊ **Example 1:** The following TGC profile resulted from the user setting another system control incorrectly. What control was set incorrectly, how was it set, and what would the corresponding ultrasound image look like in the near field?

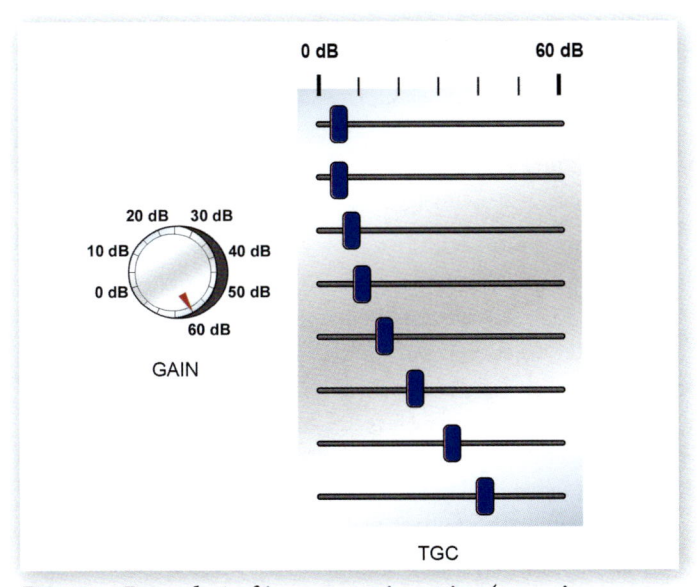

Fig. 55 **Example 1 of incorrect gain setting (assuming uncompensated TGC)**

Answer: (please see online Clarifying Clip)

View ONLINE Clarifying Clip

View ONLINE Animation and Image Library

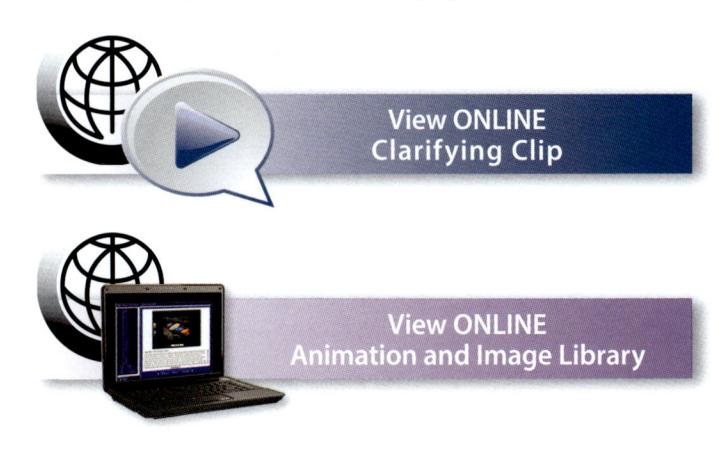

◊ **Example 2:** The following TGC profile resulted from the user setting another system control incorrectly. What control was set incorrectly, how was it set, and what would the corresponding ultrasound image look like in the near field?

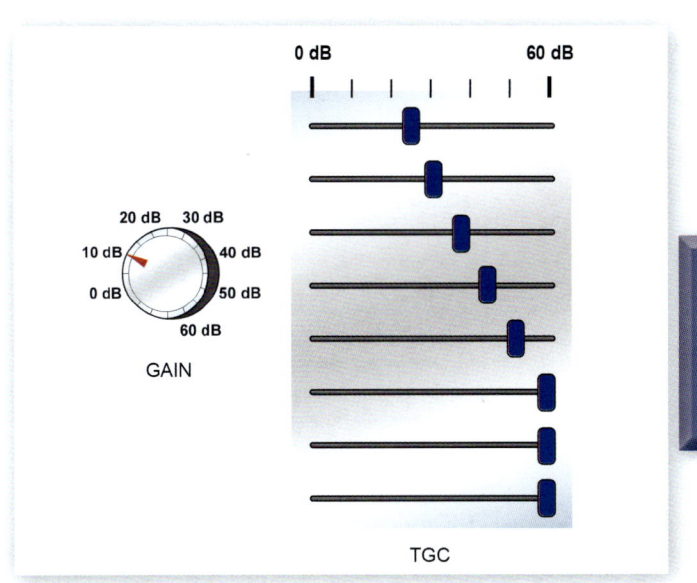

Fig. 56 **Example 2 of incorrect gain setting (assuming uncompensated TGC)**

Answer: (please see online Clarifying Clip)

View ONLINE Clarifying Clip

View ONLINE Animation and Image Library

12.5 Appropriate Use of Receiver Gain with TGCs

You should think of the overall gain control as the course adjustment and the TGC sliders as the fine adjustment for compensation. By starting with the TGC profile in an increasing arc from top to bottom, you can then position the overall gain so that the overall image appears close to the right amplification. Then you should go back and "tweak" the TGC sliders so as to optimize the gain for each depth. When the overall gain is set correctly, you should have adequate range at both the top and the bottom of the TGC sliders so that neither one is "pegged". As long as neither extreme of the TGC slider zones is pegged, using a little more receiver gain and backing down all of the TGC sliders a little, or vice versa, really has no effect on the image.

◊ *Example:* Which of the following two TGC profiles (*Figure 57* or *Figure 58*) would represent the appropriate profile for a higher frequency transducer? (Assume you are imaging the same patient.)

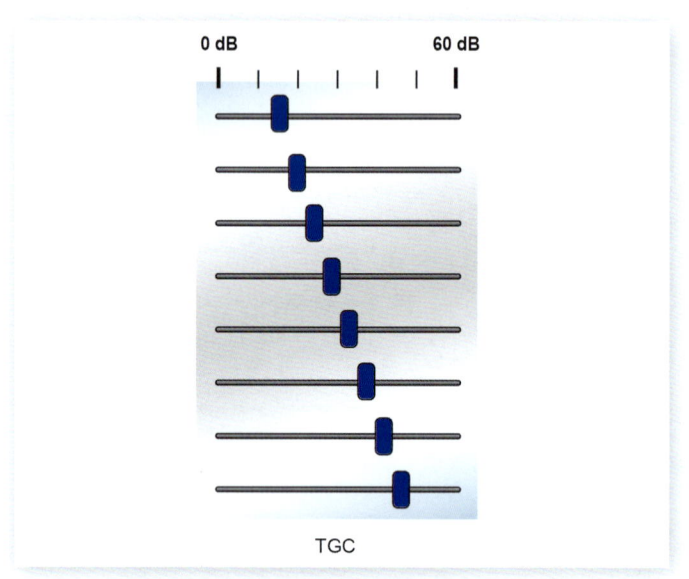

Fig. 57 **Sample TGC profile for transducer**

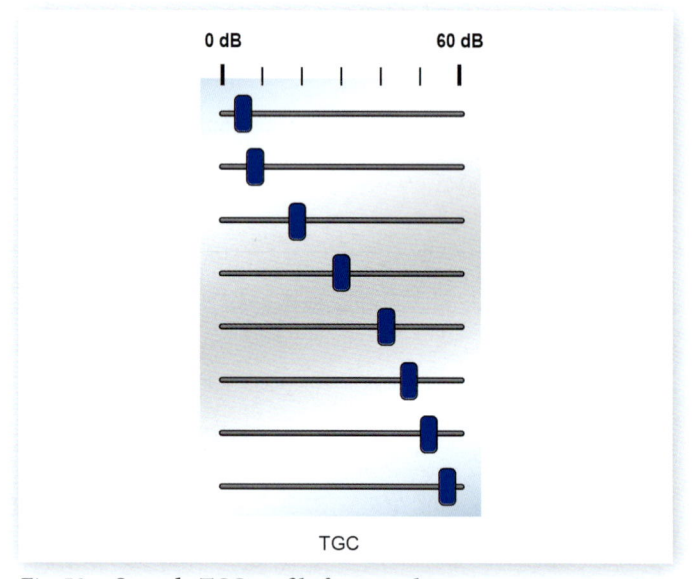

Fig. 58 **Sample TGC profile for transducer**

Answer: (please see online Clarifying Clip)

View ONLINE Clarifying Clip

KEY CONCEPT

Time gain compensation (TGC) is depth dependent gain to compensate for depth dependent attenuation. TGC can be completely system controlled, as occurs with color Doppler or when using adaptive processes, or partially controlled by the system through the use of internal TGC profiles and pre-compensated TGC profiles. With internal TGC profiles and pre-compensated profiles, the user is allowed to change the TGC profile by sliding knobs that subdivide the image into depth dependent zones.

13. Analog to Digital Conversion

13.1 Analog Received Signal and Digital Conversion

The signals transmitted into the body and the returning echoes from the body are analog signals. Since the echoes are analog, all ultrasound signals must be received as analog signals. In all ultrasound systems designed in the last 30 years or more, these received analog signals are converted into digital signals. The process by which a signal is converted from analog to digital is not surprisingly referred to as A/D conversion (read A-to-D conversion), and was discussed previously.

Since all ultrasound systems convert from analog to digital format, the data output to the beamformer from the front end of every system is in a digital format. Therefore, the beamforming and scan conversion processing that takes place in the ultrasound system is generally performed on digital data.

13.2 The Motivation for Converting from Analog to Digital

The motivation for converting the signals from analog to digital is that digital formats make the functions of beamforming, grayscaling, memory storage, and post-processing significantly easier and cheaper. Once a signal is converted into digital format, the signal exists in a numeric representation instead of continuous voltage levels. As an analog voltage, every processing step requires a dedicated circuit. In contrast, since digital signals are numeric, the same math engine can be used to perform multiple calculations. For ultrasound some of the desired calculations are related to grayscale mapping and compression, tissue colorization, automatic boundary detection, elastography and strain measurements, and spatial and time-based measurements.

Because math processing functions can be used on signals no matter what the source of the signal, the same electronic math engine can be used in an ultrasound machine as in a computer, a navigation system, or a gaming system. For many people, the term math engine is pretty foreign, but terms like CPU (Central Processing Unit), GPU (graphics processing unit), and the company specific names of an Intel, AMD, and Nvidia are instantly recognizable. Of course, there are some math engines that are more powerful than others, offering greater processing potential, faster processing, parallel processing of data, and a greater feature set (more mathematical functions). In the world of electronics there are as many choices for processors and dedicated math processors as there are types of vehicles. As designers, the engine we choose is based on the complexity of the system, the desired functionality, the power consumption of the processor, and the cost allocated for more computational horsepower.

14. Scan Conversion

Scan conversion is a very complex process that involves multiple functions. Before discussing the actual process and the myriad variants, we must first develop a conceptual understanding of how we can transition from amplitude mode to something that looks like a 2D representation of the tissue being imaged.

14.1 Paradigm Shift: From A-Mode to B-Mode

At the conclusion of Level 1, we discussed A-mode presentation. Relative to today's standards, A-mode seems like a primitive and crude diagnostic tool. However, this comparison isn't completely fair. The more appropriate comparison is A-mode relative to the non-invasive alternatives of the time of which there really were none other than extrasensory perception or guessing, neither of which are very reliable. Therefore, even as a one-dimensional technique, A-mode represented a giant step forward in medicine. However, it obviously did not take long for the medical field to want a two-dimensional technique. Creating a two-dimensional image presented many new challenges. In the transducer section we already discussed how 2D scans could be created manually first, then mechanically, and finally electronically. However, even after making the changes required to the transmit signals, the transducers, and the receiving electronics, there was still a major impediment; how to display two-dimensional data.

Until recent years, 2D images were always generated sequentially: line by line. For each acoustic line transmitted into the patient, the output from the system front end is a digital representation of an A-mode line. In scanned modalities, each successive acoustic line results in another A-mode line from a different region of the body. Consider if a scan consisted of 250 lines. Can you imagine if you had to review 250 A-mode lines of data virtually simultaneously, especially when all 250 A-modes would be changing in time (from frame to frame)? Clearly what was needed was a paradigm shift. A new method of displaying data was required so that the spatial content of the data could be interpreted as well as the amplitude content of the data. This paradigm shift was the inception of B-mode (brightness mode often referred to as 2D imaging).

14.2 Creating a Sequential B-mode From Multiple A-modes

The conversion of A-mode to B-mode required an entirely new approach. In A-mode, the amplitude was presented simply as the height of the waveform on a graph. In brightness mode, each amplitude is mapped to a grayscale level or brightness. For conventional imaging maps, a high amplitude signal is mapped to a bright white level. Weaker signals are mapped to a gray, very weak signals are mapped to dark gray, and the absence of signal is mapped to complete black. (Inverted grayscale maps exist but are rarely used in ultrasound and almost never used with 2D images.)

In *Figure 59a,* a single A-mode line is converted into a brightness mapped individual line. Notice that the horizontal axis represents depth and the vertical axis represents signal amplitude. The depth is divided into small depth increments and the amplitude assessed. Since the very shallowest signal is low amplitude, the very first pixel of the brightness mode line is dark gray. The second depth division is only a slightly higher amplitude, so the second pixel is only slightly brighter. Notice that the pixel which represents the very high amplitude signal is presented as bright white. In this manner, the entire A-mode line is converted until all of the B-mode pixels are colorized.

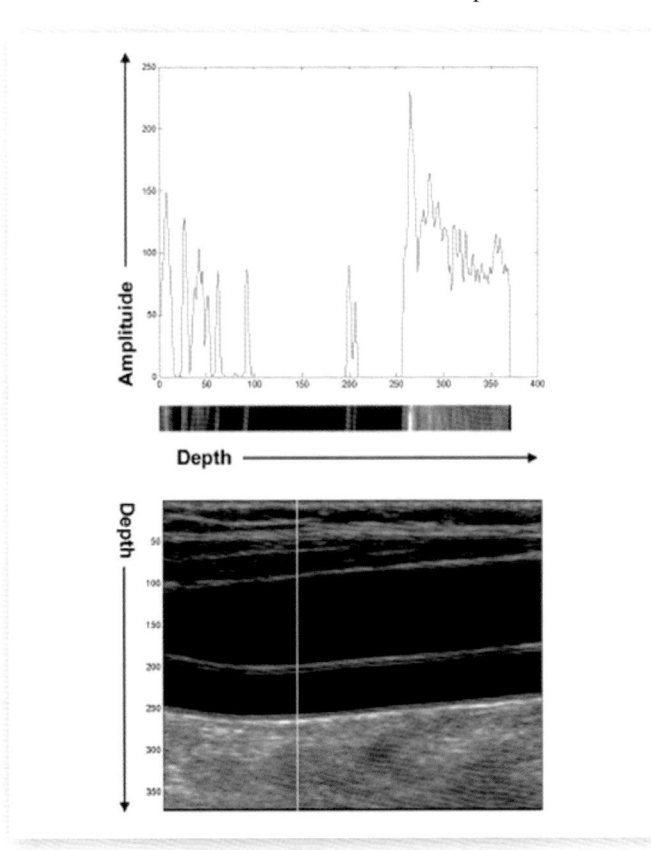

Fig. 59a **Creating B-mode from A-mode**

Figure 59a demonstrates how the vessel walls of the jugular vein and carotid artery are clearly delineated from the respective lumens in the A-mode image.

Figure 59b demonstrates how the reverberations within the jugular vein appear in the A-mode image (the large reflections and spikes in the region of approximately 130 to 220 on the horizontal axis of the A-mode). For comparison, notice how the A-mode is relatively free of echoes in the same region in *Figure 59c*.

We just showed the process for converting an individual A-mode line of data into grayscale values. Based on this concept, you can now understand how a B-mode image is created. By sequentially transmitting a series of adjacent A-mode lines, converting each to brightness mode, and then placing the collection of grayscale lines next to each other, a B-mode (2D) image is generated.

14.3 The Role of the Scan Converter

There are three core functions of the scan converter: beamforming the data received from each of the elements to form received beams, converting these A-mode lines into B-mode lines, and then organizing the successive lines of data into a formatted image. The role of conversion from A-mode to B-mode has just been described. The roles of beamforming and of formatting the data are very complex. Because of the complexity of modern beamformers, and because it is helpful to think about image formats when discussing beamforming, we will first discuss image formatting.

In order to format an image correctly, the scan converter must keep track of which lines of data should be presented at what location on the screen. Once a frame is complete, the scan converter is sent an end of frame "flag" which warns the scan converter that the next line received is the first line of the next frame. In the simplest case, a scan converter can simply break the A-mode lines into discrete depth increments, create a pixel and display that pixel. However, there are many more complex situations which require significantly more processing. For example, consider the case of a sector scan in comparison to a linear scan.

14.4 Polar Scan Conversion and Lateral Distortion

For a linear scan, each depth increment of each A-mode line represents the same physical size in the image. In essence, the linear image is simply a uniform grid. In contrast, for a sector or curved-linear image, the near field is narrower than the far field. Since, for conventional imaging, there are the same number of acoustic lines which constitute the data in the near field and in the far field, the "grid" size is not uniform from the top of the image to the bottom of the image. These comparisons are illustrated in *Figure 60*.

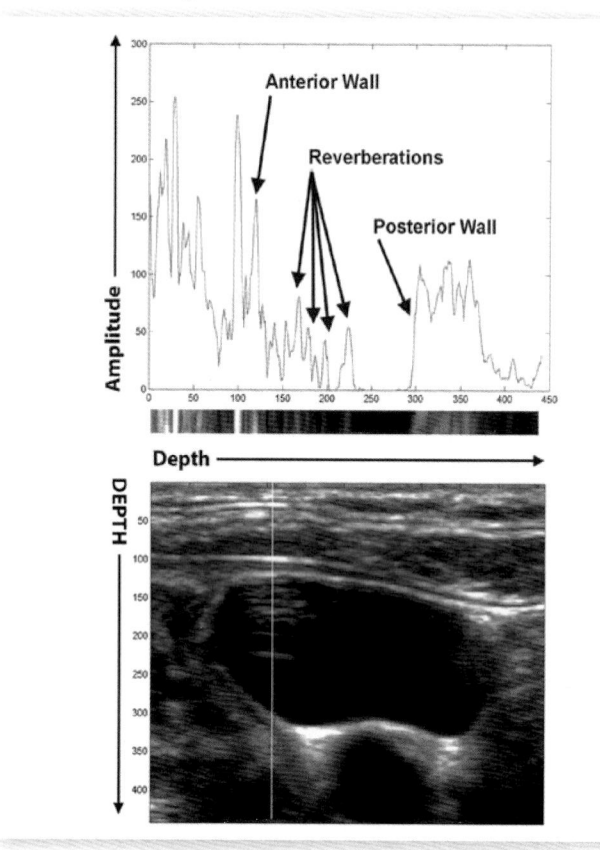

Fig. 59b   **Creating B-mode from A-mode**

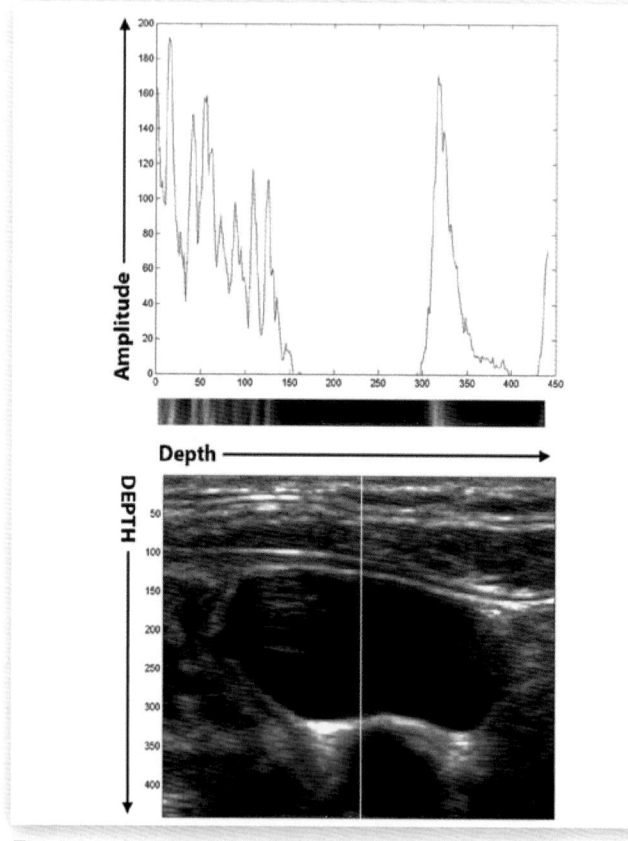

Fig. 59c   **Creating B-mode from A-mode**

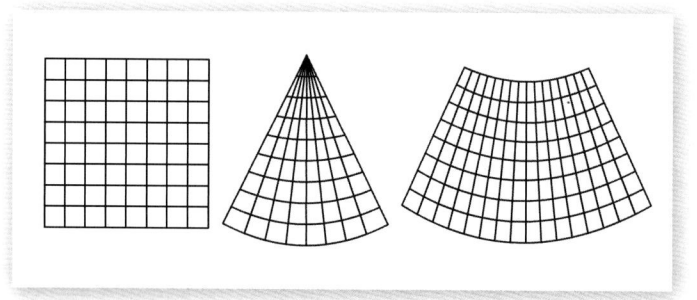

Fig. 60   **Grid sizes for different imaging formats**

For a sector, in the near field, there are many lines which essentially cover the same region of the patient. In the far field, as the beams "fan out" an individual line must cover a much wider area. Therefore, the width of the image created by the first line from shallow depths certainly cannot be the same width as the converted data from the deeper depths. As a result, the data must go through a conversion from a linear coordinate system to a polar coordinate system. In essence, a polar coordinate system makes it easy to map points onto rings of a circle. Since a sector image is really a portion of a circle, a polar coordinate system is better suited than a linear system to plot data. As a result of the complex format, there is not a simple method of converting signals into uniform sized grid boxes as for a linear image. Extremely complex algorithms are required to transform the collection of lines into this format while best preserving lateral resolution and keeping the image looking uniform. Depending on the line spacing (also referred to as the line density), this polar coordinate conversion often results in a lateral distortion (banana shaped pixel effect) of the data. In the earlier days of ultrasound this scan conversion distortion was much more pronounced, especially in color Doppler imaging. Now with narrower beams, higher line densities, and improved processing this distortion has been decreased, but not completely eliminated.

> **KEY CONCEPT**
>
> Scan conversion is the process of converting lines of data into an image format. This process requires a grayscale mapping from an amplitude (A-mode) to a brightness level (B-mode). Additionally, the scan converter must assign the grayscale values to pixel locations on the screen, resulting in an image.

15. The History of Beamformers

The beamformer is really a powerful math engine that performs calculations which control how transmits are performed and how received data is phase delayed and summed in order to create coherent lines of ultrasound data. The beamformer is basically the heart and soul of modern ultrasound systems. In the early days of ultrasound, with single crystal elements used to create scans, there was no need for a beamformer. The data for each display line of data came from a single element (a single channel). With the advent of phased arrays, in the mid 1970s, each transducer element was connected to a system channel (a processing chain capable of processing acoustic data received from a single transducer element). With multiple elements being used for transmitting and receiving, multiple channels were now required. Having multiple channels resulted in the need for electronics to delay the signals appropriately channel by channel and then sum the collection of signals from each channel into one line of data. This process of delaying and summing is often abbreviated as "DAS."

In the early days of phased arrays, the delays and summation were performed using analog circuits. The signal from each channel was delayed using an analog circuit and then summed into a single analog line of data. After the delaying and summing, the analog line was converted to digital. Since all of the signals were already summed into an individual line, only one A/D converter was necessary (*Figure 61*). Although this method worked very well, there was very little flexibility, and adding more channels (to connect and control more transducer elements) was very expensive. Initial systems had only 32 channels. By the early 1980s systems were starting to increase the channel count to allow for running larger transducers with more closely spaced elements (smaller pitch). Having more elements allowed for greater steering and focusing and improved sensitivity. Have a closer pitch allowed for a better beam with fewer grating lobes (see Chapter 8: Artifacts). By the mid 1980s most systems had 128 or 256 channels. Of course, in time, higher end systems incorporated 512 channels.

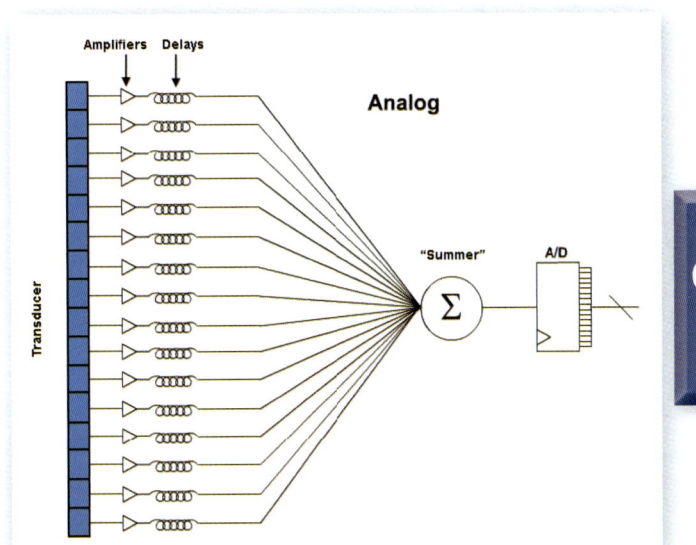

Fig. 61 **Depiction of 16-channel analog receiver**

Notice in *Figure 61* that the delays and summing is performed by an analog to digital conversion and that this design requires only a single A/D converter.

The next step in the evolution was a digital beamformer. A digital beamformer implies that both the delays and summing are performed using math engines on digital data instead of using analog circuits on the analog signal. The idea is that by beamforming digitally, there can be significantly more flexibility in terms of how time delays and summing takes place. Initially, digital beamformers resulted in a large increase in cost, power consumption, and heat generation, making small scanning rooms quite warm. For the delays on each channel to be performed digitally, every channel had to be converted from analog to digital (*Figure 62*). In other words, 256 A/D converters were required to have 256 channels. Whereas using digital beamformers before the 1990s was possible, the high cost made digital beamformers impractical. Around this time, the quality of A/D converters improved while the cost decreased, making digital beamformers practical. Like the introduction of phased arrays, digital beamforming resulted in a revolution in ultrasound that paved the way for 1.5 and 2D arrays, compound and harmonic imaging, and many other ultrasound enhancements.

Notice in *Figure 62* that each channel has its own A/D converter, converting the analog signal to digital before the delays and summing are applied.

Digital beamformers continued to advance as a result of improvements in electronics including faster and multi-core processors and application specific integrated circuits (ASICs) as well as new techniques based on the expanding capabilities of the digital beamformer. In the early part of the 2000s, Zonare released a system that utilized a software-based beamformer to perform what they called "zone imaging." This pushed the concept of parallel processing to a new level, resulting in significantly higher frame rates. In 2010, a company called SuperSonic Imagine released an ultrasound system that utilized graphics processing units (GPUs) as a means of dramatically increasing the beamformer capability, making ultrafast imaging and shear wave imaging possible. GPUs are used extensively in the gaming world, and the increase in performance in tandem with the decrease in cost has resulted in a tremendous increase in the ability to perform parallel processes as is needed in math intensive beamforming.

The timeline of *Figure 63* displays the history of the beamformer relative to other significant changes that periodically revolutionized ultrasound. You will notice that many of the major changes in ultrasound were enabled by technology advancements in processing capabilities.

Specific image generation and comparisons will be discussed in Part II of Chapter 6, since many of the newer techniques rely on other advanced imaging techniques beyond the scope of Part I.

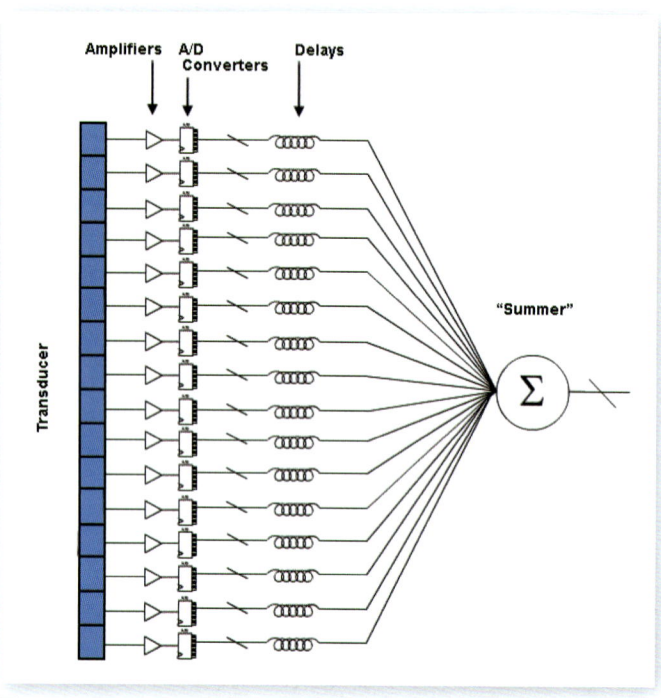

Fig. 62 **Depiction of 16-channel digital beamformer**

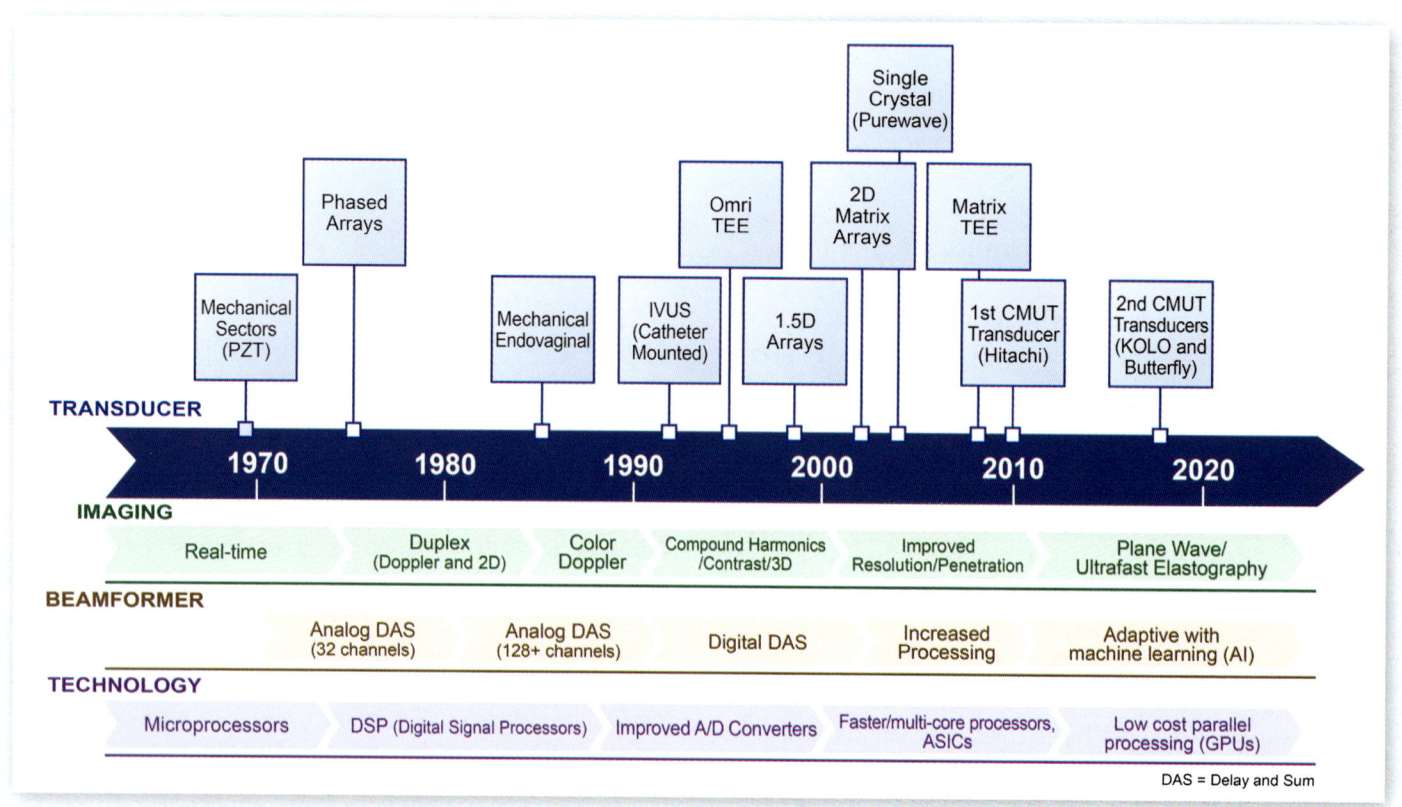

Fig. 63 **Timeline of transducer technology**

16. Pre-processing and Post-processing Revisited

In Level 1 we defined pre-processing and post-processing before discussing the role of the scan converter. With an understanding of scan conversion, it is now easier to make a clear distinction in these two terms. Any process which occurs before the scan conversion and data storage is considered a pre-processing technique. Therefore, any process that can be performed on the stored data after conversion is referred to as a post-processing technique. This is precisely why post-processing techniques can be performed after freezing the data whereas pre-processing techniques cannot be changed. Once the signals are converted into an image, there is generally not a way to reverse and redo the non-linear processes that were performed before the image conversion occurred. What processes occur before scan conversion depends on the system design. Many systems are storing the data earlier in the processing path, allowing for more of the processes that once were considered pre-processing to now become post-processing techniques. In time, as memory becomes less expensive and as storage capacity per physical size continues to increase, it is likely that systems will eventually store raw (RF) data (amplified unprocessed received echoes), making this distinction of pre-processing and post-processing disappear. Virtually all of the processing techniques and tools discussed in the upcoming section are currently post-processing on most ultrasound systems.

Since what is considered pre and post-processing varies from system to system, it is important to acquaint yourself with your specific system. The easiest way to determine pre vs. post-processing is to simply freeze and image and then attempt to change controls. Any control that can be changed on a frozen image is a post-processing technique.

- A control which fundamentally determines how the image is formed (such as transmit frequency, transmit power, compound imaging (discussed in Part II of Chapter 6), transmit focus, plane wave vs. sequential image, harmonic image, etc.) is a pre-processing technique.
- Controls such as TGC, speckle reduction, and edge enhancement are pre-processing on some systems and post-processing on other systems.
- Controls such as compression (grayscale), basic image display controls (such as flip, invert, size on screen, single to dual display, etc.), and colorization (chroma maps) are post-processing on all, or nearly all systems.

17. Compression

17.1 Compression: A Multi-Stage Process
In Level 1 we learned about the "receiver" function of compression. The compression which occurs in the system front end is not under user control. However, not all of the compression applied to the ultrasound signals occurs in the system front end. Because of the extraordinary dynamic range of the signals, and because of the relatively small dynamic range of the human eye, extraordinary compression is required. Understanding the reasons that the compression is distributed throughout the system can lead to some very important clinical results. Before we can discuss the clinical ramifications, we must first develop a better understanding of the dynamic range constraints that the compression must address.

17.2 Dynamic Range of 2D Echoes
The dynamic range of the reflected signals from a patient is very large. For 2D imaging, the signal range is typically 80 dB or more. For Doppler, the dynamic range is significantly greater. Remember that decibels are logarithmic, so 80 dB represents an extraordinary range. For review:

$$20 \times \log\left(\frac{A_{biggest}}{A_{smallest}}\right) = 80 \text{ dB}.$$

Dividing both sides by 20 yields:

$$\log\left(\frac{A_{biggest}}{A_{smallest}}\right) = 4.$$

(The base is 10 - recall if not expressly written, we assume a base of 10.)

$$\log_{10}\left(\frac{A_{biggest}}{A_{smallest}}\right) = 4.$$

Solving the logarithm yields:

$$\left(\frac{A_{biggest}}{A_{smallest}}\right) = \frac{10^4}{1} = 10,000:1.$$

Therefore 80 dB implies that the largest signal is 10,000 times larger than the smallest signal. If you recall the concepts of Chapter 3, you should have a good foundation for understanding why this enormous range exists. Recall that the strength of a reflection is based on the acoustic impedance mismatch. Further, you should realize that specular reflection for normal incidence produces strong reflections back to the transducer. Additionally, the echoes from shallower depths will have experienced much less attenuation than echoes from deeper depths. The combination of these effects results in some echoes being much stronger than other echoes. As just seen, it is not uncommon for some received signals to be 10,000 times larger than other signals.

17.3 Dynamic Range of the Human Eye
The dynamic range of the human eye is a fascinating subject. The human eye has extraordinary dynamic range, capable of seeing very bright objects such as the sun, and very faint objects such as the distant stars hundreds of thousands of light years away. To see such an enormous dynamic range, the eye adaptively controls the pupil in order to visualize a wide range of brightness levels. However, even with this tremendous adaptive control, the human eye can see fewer than 64 shades of gray, or 64 to 1 brightness levels at one instant. In other words, although the eye can see an enormous range

of brightness levels, it can only distinguish between fewer than 64 shades at a specific instance.

Let's convert 64 shades into decibels so that we have a comparison with the dynamic range of the signal.

$$20 \times \log\left(\frac{64}{1}\right) = ?\ dB$$

Since 64 is a power of 2, and we have memorized the log of 2, we can solve for the log of 64 by using our rule that logarithms convert multiplications into additions of logs or:

$$20 \times \log\left(\frac{64}{1}\right) = 20 \times \left[\log(2 \times 2 \times 2 \times 2 \times 2 \times 2)\right]$$
$$= 20 \times \left[\log(2) + \log(2) + \log(2) + \log(2) + \log(2) + \log(2)\right]$$
$$= 20 \times \left[0.3 + 0.3 + 0.3 + 0.3 + 0.3 + 0.3\right] = 20 \times 1.8 = 36\ dB$$

Therefore, the "instantaneous" dynamic range of the eye is less than 36 dB, but the signal range is generally greater than 80 dB. In the linear world, the human eye can see fewer than 64 shades of gray simultaneously whereas the signal occupies more than 10,000 levels. This enormous difference in dynamic range is precisely the reason why logarithmic compression is needed.

To demonstrate the limits of the human eye, look at the three "color bars" presented in *Figure 64*. In the bottom bar, it is relatively easy to distinguish all the rectangles of various brightness levels. In the middle bar, discerning each rectangle is slightly more challenging. In the last example, it is improbable that you can distinguish all 64 shaded rectangles. If you change the room lighting, you may find different results.

Fig. 64 **Grayscale and visual dynamic range**

17.4 Why the System Allows for Compression in the Back End of the System

Some amount of compression is always performed in the back end of the system under the control of the user. To distinguish between the compression in the front end of the system and the compression of the back end of the system under user control, we will adopt the term "video compression." The reason some compression is under user control is related to the fundamental limitation associated with compression. When data is compressed, there is generally a loss of information. It is conceivable that the very signal that needs to be detected for an accurate clinical diagnosis could be compressed out, and hence, not recognized. The following example will illustrate this point. This same question was asked in Chapter 3 when dealing with contrast resolution as it relates to acoustic impedance mismatch.

Imagine that a large mass exists. If the system controls are set correctly, will it always be visualized?

The answer to this question is still "No". This answer does not simply imply that a user can incorrectly set system controls resulting in an inability to detect a mass or a thrombus. Instead, this is a statement that ultrasound has limitations based on real physics. Consider *Figure 65*. On the left side of the diagram, there is a large range of amplitudes which represents the signal dynamic range. On the other side of the diagram, there is a much smaller range representative of the instantaneous dynamic range of the human eye. Within the signal range, there are marks indicating the reflection amplitude from the mass and the reflection level from the tissue surrounding the mass. Notice that there is a distinction between these two signal amplitudes. In order to visualize the reflected signals in real time (as opposed to developing films at different grayscale levels and reviewing the information as a collection of different "exposures"), the large dynamic range must be mapped into the smaller dynamic range of the eyes. In the process of compressing the two signals, the difference between the reflection from the mass and the reflection from the surrounding tissue is reduced, potentially to the point where the distinction either no longer exists, or is no longer perceptible to the human eye. Therefore, it is quite possible that the mass will not be visualized because of the compression scheme chosen.

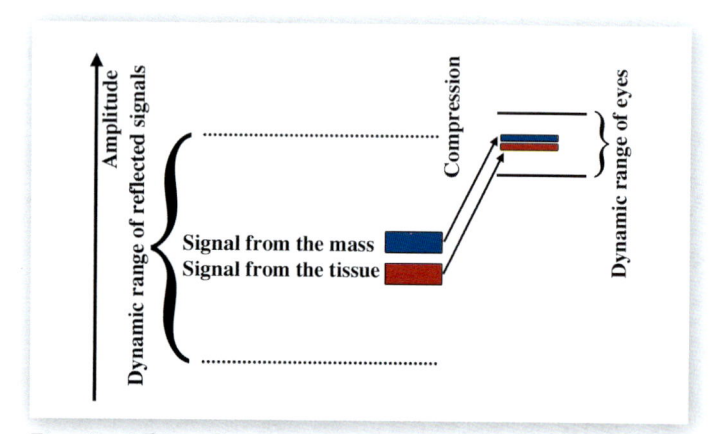

Fig. 65 **Effects of compression**

17.5 Compression Controls on the System

Since there is no way of knowing a priori when the compression will potentially expunge the very data needed, a dilemma exists. For physics-based practical reasons we have no choice but to compress the data; however, this leads to the possible situation of not presenting adequate contrast resolution such that important characteristics in an image may be missed. As a result, the system is designed to give the user many different compression mapping schemes from which to choose. Each compression map still compresses the data, but does so using a different mathematical mapping. In essence, some maps may be more aggressive in compressing higher level signals leaving more dynamic range for the mid-level and low-level signals. Some maps may have much more contrast, attempting to preserve a greater distinction between strong and weak signals. Recall that the function of compression must be logarithmic since the dynamic range is so large.

The following figures (*Map 1* through *Map 6*) show the results of various compression maps on a cardiac image and a vascular image. The image on the left is an apical 4-chamber cardiac image of a normal heart. The image on the right is a popliteal vein with a thrombus. The graph between the images represents the compression mapping used to produce the associated image. Note that the horizontal axis is the signal strength and the vertical axis is the output display intensity, ranging from 0 to 255. A value of 0 is pure black and a value of 255 is pure white.

View ONLINE Clarifying Clip

KEY CONCEPT

As noted previously, compression is necessary to reduce large signal dynamic range (typically greater than 80 dB) closer to the dynamic range of the human eye (less than 36 dB or fewer than 64 shades of gray simultaneously). Not changing the compression maps (referred to by different manufacturers as compression, post-processing, grayscale, and dynamic range) can result in loss of data. In cases where there is little contrast between structure and surrounding tissue (such as fresh thrombus and masses), the non-linear mapping of different compression maps can make structures virtually appear or disappear.

Apical 4-Chamber   **Compression Maps**   **Popliteal Vein Thrombus**

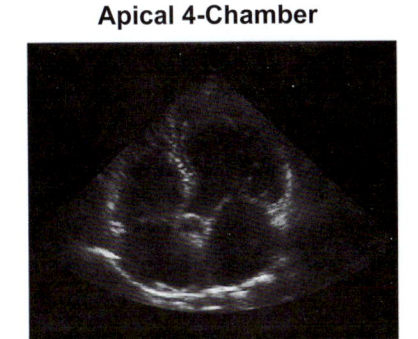

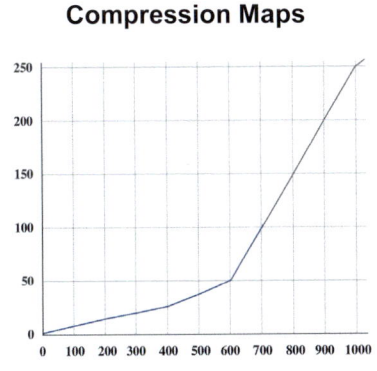

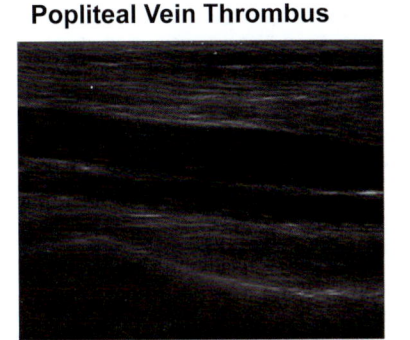

Map 1: Most dynamic range dedicated for higher-level signals. Weak signals and noise mapped out.

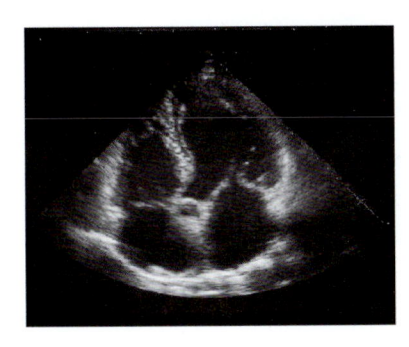

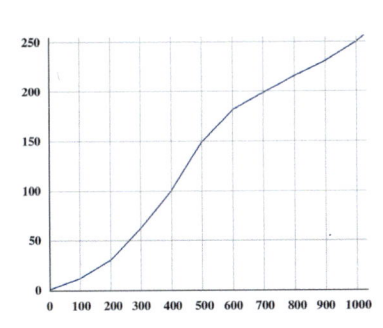

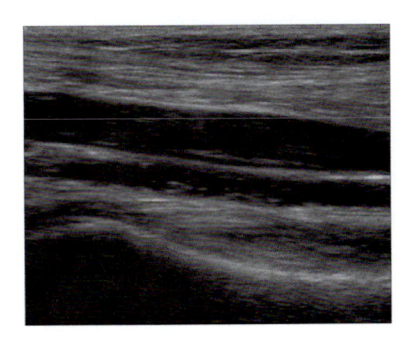

Map 2: Most dynamic range in mid-level signals. Low-level signals not very apparent.

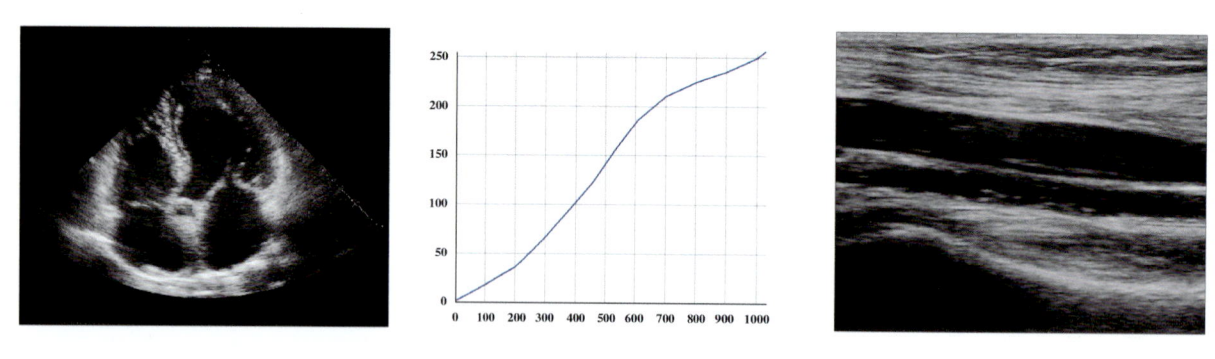

Map 3: Transition begins earlier so that weaker signals become more apparent.

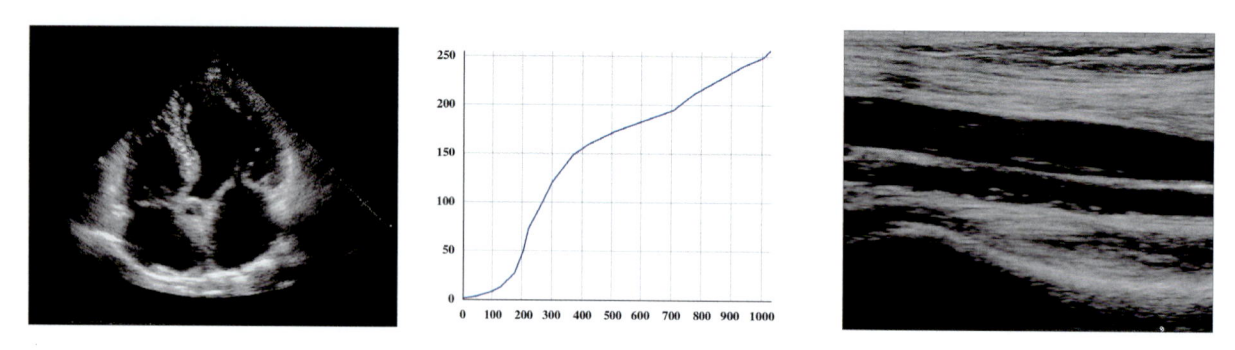

Map 4: Low-levels mapped out, rapid transition for mid-level signals.

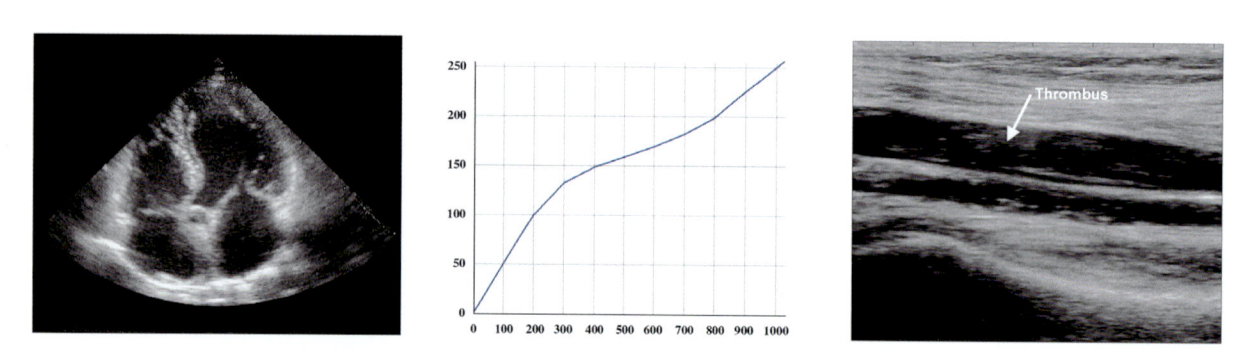

Map 5: Rapid transition to display weak level signals. Less dynamic range in mid-range.

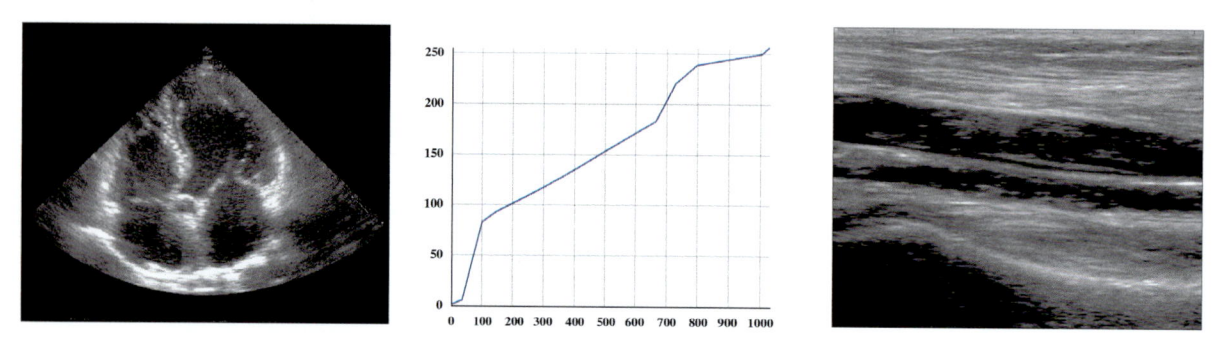

Map 6: Extremely rapid transition to display weak level signals. Very little dynamic range in mid-range.

Notice how *Map 5* and *Map 6* demonstrate the thrombus in the popliteal vein whereas the thrombus is not visualized using *Maps 1* through *4*. However, for the cardiac image, *Maps 5* and *6* somewhat obscure the valves and myocardial borders. The point is that there is clearly no perfect map for all patients and all applications.

The entire compression and grayscale mapping process is very complex since the very process of assigning grayscale levels is a non-linear compression scheme. As we will learn, a monitor is capable of producing more grayscale level signals than the eye can detect simultaneously. Also, the display brightness of the monitor is non-linear, further compounded by the fact that the eye's sensitivity to brightness is non-linear and variable with ambient light. If you are starting to get the impression that there are many variables which affect your ability to detect signals "accurately", you are catching on.

Because of the critical importance to these maps, there is usually more than one set of controls which affect the compression mapping. For example, a system may have a knob control called compression and then a family of post-processing curves. Of course, every ultrasound company has their own name for these functions further exacerbating the confusion. The following list represents some of the most common names used by systems to refer to this compression mapping:

- Compression
- Dynamic range
- Grayscale
- Post-processing (curves or maps)
- (Display) contrast

17.6 Using Compression Controls Correctly

The effects of compression can be very dramatic on the display and potentially can lead to misdiagnosis. Most people choose a processing setting they find visually appealing and then tend not to change the compression settings very often. This approach can lead to many mistakes. Proper use of compression is to periodically vary the compression settings, especially when there is a greater likelihood of low reflective echoes such as the presence of a fresh thrombus. This changing of the controls will only add a few seconds to the scan time, but can make a significant difference to the few patients on which a mass or thrombus would have otherwise been missed.

The different compression mappings shown in *Figure 66* and *67* make the difference between missing or detecting the thrombus in each vessel. The appropriate compression maps enhance the low-level echoes so that the thrombus is visualized. Notice the value of color Doppler in *Figure 67* to confirm the existence of a thrombus.

Color Doppler images are included in the Online Animation and Image Library, demonstrating how the thrombus is affecting flow through the popliteal vein.

View ONLINE Animation and Image Library

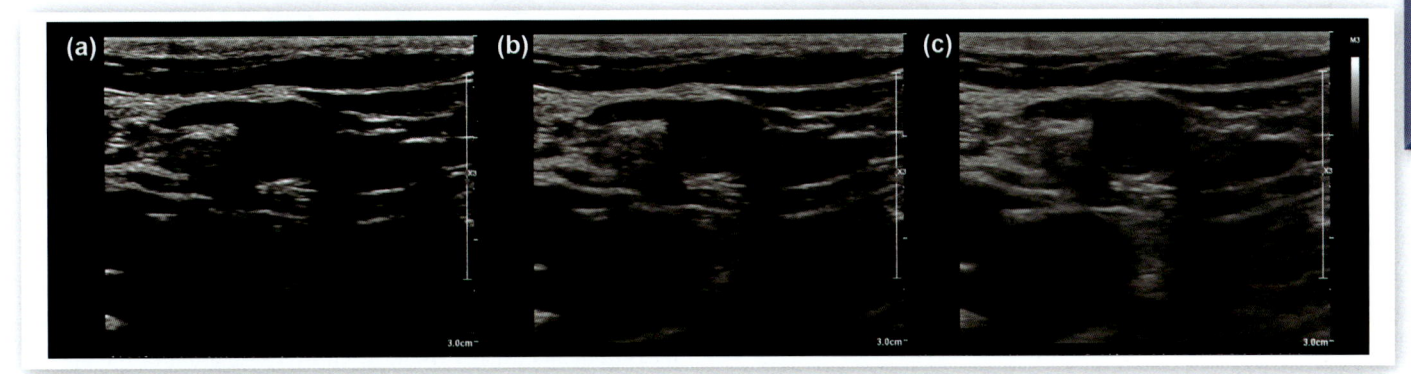

Fig. 66 Greater saphenous vein in the same patient at different compression settings; note how the compression setting affects visualization of the thrombus with (a) dynamic range: 45, (b) dynamic range: 58, and (c) dynamic range: 70

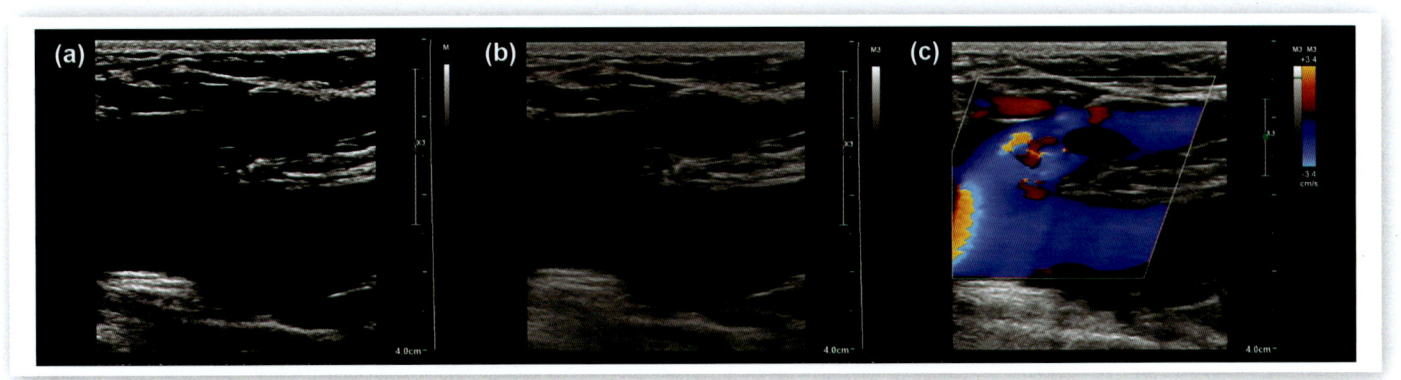

Fig. 67 Saphenofemoral junction in the same patient at different compression settings; note how the compression setting affects visualization of the thrombus with (a) dynamic range: 40, (b) dynamic range: 68, and (c) color Doppler confirming presence of thrombus

18. Tissue Colorization

We will soon learn that the dynamic range of the eye is much less than the dynamic range of the video monitor, which in turn, is significantly less than the signal dynamic range, making the human eye usually the limiting factor in dynamic range visualization. However, our treatment of the dynamic range of the eye thus far has been restricted to the ability to distinguish between grayscale levels. By including color hues, the dynamic range of the eye is extended. The use of colorization maps is intended to improve visualization when significant dynamic range must be preserved. Most systems offer an assortment of maps ranging from "wheat" colors through blues, pinks, and greens. How much these maps help depends on the specific imaging situation, the compression maps chosen, and the color mapping scheme itself. For the existing mapping schemes there often does not appear too dramatic a change, although there are times when color maps makes it easier to distinguish low-level signals.

View ONLINE Animation and Image Library

19. Measurements

The measurements and analysis packages reside in the back-end software. Since the data is stored in a digital format in the memory of the back end, it is possible to freeze the data, scroll back in imaging time, and place calipers. What you see on the screen is just the calipers, but the process is actually a reverse mapping technique. You can think of the image as a grid as was illustrated in Section 14.4. With the placement of the calipers, the system now has a pair of coordinates (x and y, or r and θ for polar coordinate systems), as well as a time coordinate. These coordinates are then referenced against the scan converted data coordinates. In this way, the specific value for the signal at that location can be identified if desired. More often, the cursor is placed in two or more locations and a geometric measurement is made. Since the system knows the physical dimensions of the image, these measurements can be converted in actual distance, area, or volume measurements.

19.1 Area Measurements

There are two different approaches to area measurements with conventional 2D imaging. One approach is to trace the desired region and the system performs an integration to determine the area. The other approach is to indicate a radius of a presumed round structure by setting the calipers and performing an area calculation based on the area equation. Caution must be taken with both of these approaches to minimize the amount of error in the assessed area term.

Tracing an Area

Besides poor tracing skills, the greatest source of error in an area tracing is incorrect angle in the 2D image. *Figure 68a* demonstrates graphically how angle can affect area measurements.

Scenario 1:

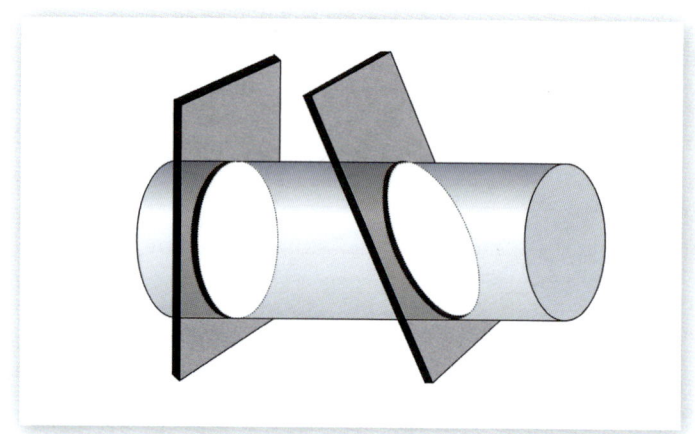

Fig. 68a **Area overestimation**

Scenario 2:

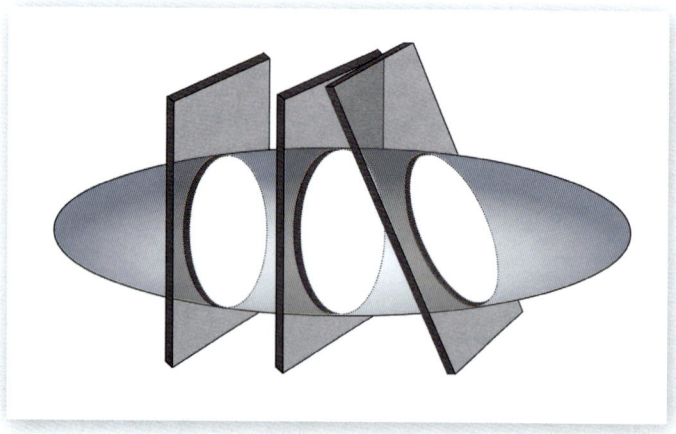

Fig. 68b **Area over and underestimation**

For the uniform cylindrical shape such as a blood vessel, off-axis measurements usually result in an overestimation of the area as indicated by *Figure 68a*. As long as the beam intersects both the anterior and posterior wall of the vessel, underestimation from angle is not possible.

In comparison, for area measurement tracings of objects that are not uniform in cross-section such as heart chambers and diseased vessels, there are two different sources of error: location and angle. Clearly, even if the image plane is perpendicular to the structure, the cross-sectional area measured is dependent on location. For this example, there is a larger cross-sectional area in the middle of the object than at either end. The other error source is related to angle. As in the previous example, off-axis beams tend to increase the cross-sectional area.

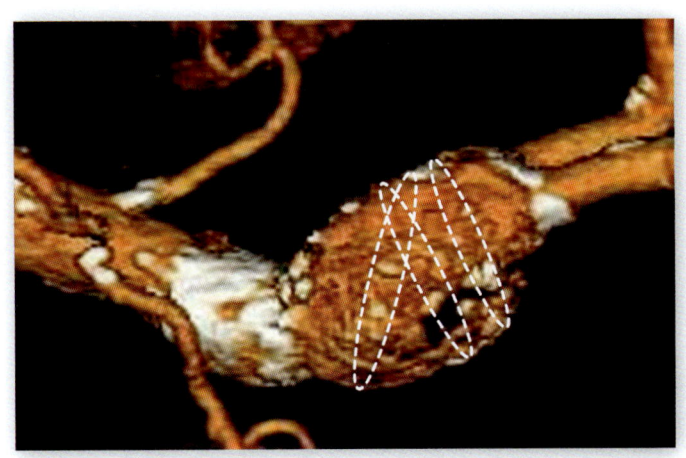

Fig. 69 3D spiral CT of an abdominal aortic aneurysm (possible measurement errors)

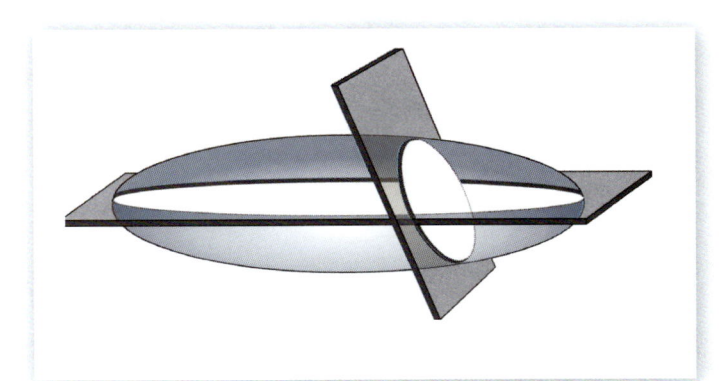

Fig. 70 Longitudinal plane and area underestimation

Along the longitudinal axis of the nonuniform cross-sectional object, there are again two distinct sources of error: location and angle. If the imaging plane does not intersect this object in the center, then the area measurement will naturally be smaller. In this case, if the angle is incorrect, the area measurement will be smaller than reality. In the cardiac world, when this occurs when viewing a chamber, the image is said to be "foreshortened."

Calculated From the Radius

Just as with tracing, angle effects can be a significant source of error in area measurements calculated from a radius. Recall that area is a two-dimensional measurement whereas the radius is only a one-dimensional parameter. As discussed in Chapter 1: Mathematics, the area is proportional to the radius squared, or: $Area \propto r^2$. Therefore, any error in the radius measurement is squared to produce the area calculation. This source of error is depicted in *Figure 71*.

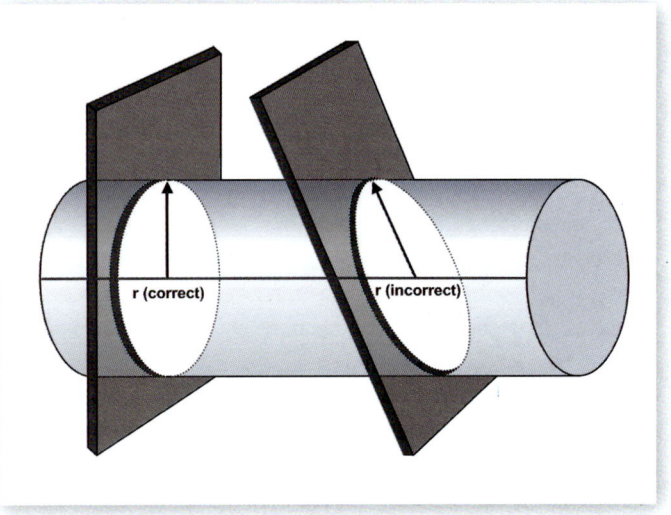

Fig. 71 **Errors in radius measurement are squared for area**

KEY CONCEPT

Careful thought should always be given to error sources when making measurements. Inappropriate visualization based on contrast, sensitivity, or angle can result in incorrect measurements. Furthermore, calculations based on measurements will often represent even greater error sources, when the calculated parameter is non-linearly related to the measured parameter. For example, a 10% underestimation error in a radius represents a 19% underestimation error in calculated area.

20. Video Display and Monitors

Almost all ultrasound systems are now using Liquid Crystal Display (LCD) monitors (including LED – see below). Before the proliferation of LCD technology, most monitors were driven by cathode ray tube (CRT) technology.

20.1 Cathode Ray Tube (The Olden Days)

As already mentioned, the older technology utilized for ultrasound monitors was the cathode ray tube (CRT). A CRT emits electrons which are scanned across a coated screen. The screen is coated with a phosphorescent layer which "glows" when excited by electrons. By changing the electron density, regions on the screen can be made to glow more or less brightly. A short time after excitation, the phosphorescent glow begins to decay, requiring another excitation to refresh the image. For color monitors, there are actually three cathode ray tubes, one for red, one for green, and one for blue (RGB). All three beams converge on the inside of the screen to form a color image. In general, CRTs are bulky and heavy, consuming more energy than many newer technologies and thereby producing more heat.

20.2 Liquid Crystal Displays (LCD)

The detailed principles behind how an LCD (and LED) monitor functions are beyond the scope of this book and likely beyond the interest of most readers. As such, the discussion of LCD monitors will be limited to a very rudimentary overview, the specifications, features, and limitations as related to ultrasound interpretation. Note that understanding the basic overview is helpful in understanding the advantages and disadvantages of LCD monitors.

Understanding the basics of how an LCD (which includes LED) monitor works requires that we consider one of the limitations of a CRT. With a CRT, the fields of lines were drawn and then refreshed, such that between refreshes, the image decays out. This means that if you were able to slow down the display refresh, you would see part of an image just updated, one line actively being drawn, and some of the image dark, waiting to be refreshed. The result is that CRT monitors often flicker. In contrast, an LCD display does not "draw" lines of a field, implying a very different image paradigm, and very different issues relating to ultrasound interpretation.

Understanding a conventional LCD display conceptually is relatively simple. There is a light that always stays on, and a grid of controlled "doors" in front of the light that either open to let the light show, or close, to keep the region dark. In front of the light source, a thin plastic layer is placed to diffuse the light so that it becomes uniform (so that no part of the screen is brighter or darker than any other part). Clearly, the description of a grid of "doors" was overly simplified. Additionally, there is more than one technology for creating the "light gate keeping doors." The grid of doors really consists of a series of layers with a grid of clear electrodes sandwiched between them (as shown in *Figure 72*). The layers consist of a light polarizing sheet, a layer of liquid crystals sandwiched between electrodes, and an oppositely polarized sheet in front. The liquid crystals have a very cool property by which the crystal molecule will twist or untwist when an electric field is applied. When the crystal molecule twists, it acts to change the polarization of the light so that it aligns with the front polarizing layer, allowing the light to show. When the electric field is not applied, the light is incorrectly polarized to traverse the front polarizing plate, and the region stays dark. Since the light is always on, it is possible that some light can escape reducing the monitor contrast ratio (the ratio of the brightest white to the darkest black that can be displayed). Producing color adds a little more complexity to be discussed below.

A picture element, or "pixel," represents the smallest region of the display. As with CRTs, the pixel size can potentially limit detail resolution. Clearly, as the pixel size increases, the resolution potentially degrades. To some degree, the pixel size is determined by the number of lines per area. Although a beam is not being swept across the screen in lines like a CRT, the grid of electrodes does determine the number of horizontal lines that comprise an image. Higher definition is clearly achieved when there are more lines per area.

For LCD displays, each pixel is divided into three sub pixels by color filters, resulting in a red, green, and blue sub pixel. By controlling the amount of light that goes through each sub pixel, full color images can be generated. If each subpixel can be represented by 256 different intensities, there are 256 x 256 x 256, or 16,777,216 different colors

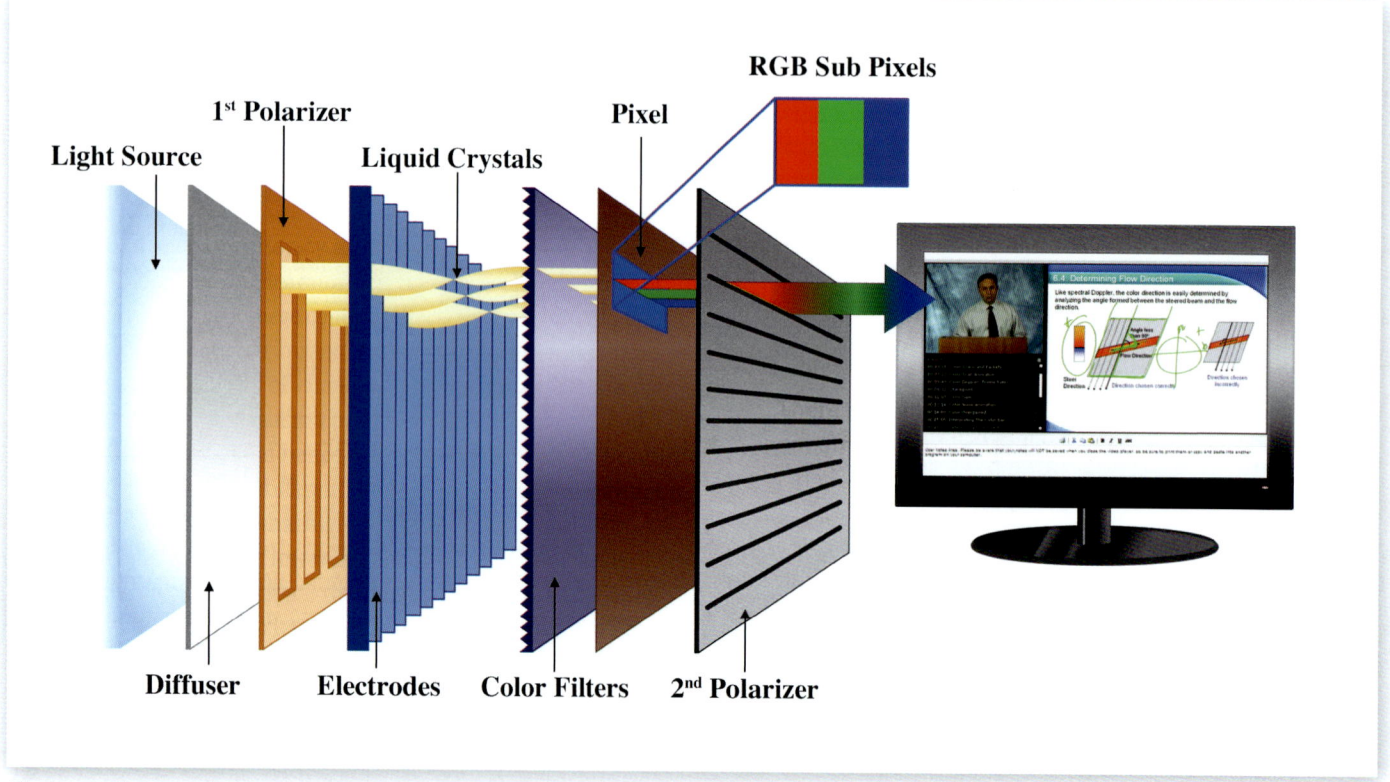

Fig. 72 Diagram showing how an LCD display works

possible. Again since the light source is always on, there is no refresh needed (as needed for CRT monitors) which means that flicker is less of an issue. For CRT monitors, low monitor frame rates implied a potential limitation to temporal resolution. Although LCD pixels do not need to be "refreshed" there are still two factors that contribute to limiting the temporal resolution of an image on an LCD display. First, it takes a finite amount of time to force a liquid crystal to change its shape to go from blocking light to passing light, or passing light to allowing light. This time is referred to as the response time. When the response time gets slow enough a phenomenon called ghosting can occur. When the response time becomes slower than about 16 msecs (60 Hz), the human eye will detect some of the previous image still on the screen while the new image is updating. The second restriction is related to the electronics that drive the electrodes. Most electronics are now designed to operate at 60 Hz or faster, so that the electronics do not become the limiting factor.

20.3 Monitor Frame Rates and Why They Matter

Most LCD/LED monitors currently operate at 60 Hz (higher frame rate monitors discussed in Level 3). In Chapter 4 we learned how to calculate the acoustic frame rate. Since temporal resolution is directly impacted by frame rate, there was considerable discussion as to how to best optimize the acoustic frame rate. Notice that we are now making a distinction between the frame rate for the monitor and the frame rate at which we gather images (the acoustic frame rate). In some of the examples we calculated, for 2D imaging we were able to realize frame rates of about 100 Hz, and with some newer technologies, frame rates in the kHz. However, there is now an obvious issue. Even if we are able to generate 100 frames per second, most monitors can only display 60 frames per second. Additionally, even if the monitor could display faster than 60 Hz, the "human eye" is limited to about 60 Hz detection (see more in Level 3).

The following figures demonstrate the importance of display frame rate. As shown in *Figure 73a*, the acoustic frame rate (30 frames per second) is less than the monitor display rate (60 Hz) which results in middle frames being "interpolated" to create 60 display frames per second. In *Figure 73b*, the acoustic frame rate matches the monitor display rate, so there is a one-to-one correspondence between acoustic frames and displayed frames. *Figure 73c* shows an acoustic frame rate higher than the monitor display rate such that two of every three acoustic frames must be dropped in the display.

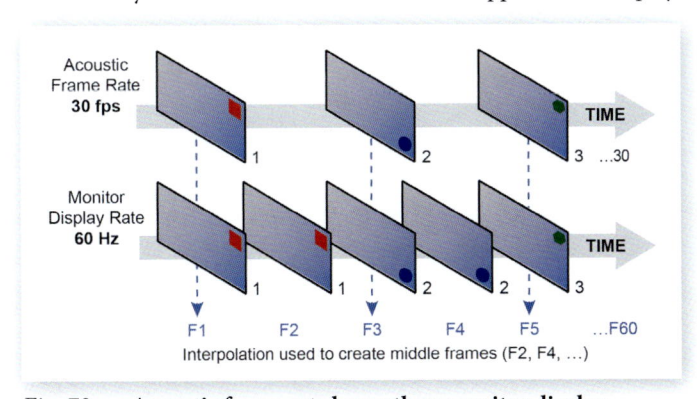

Fig. 73a **Acoustic frame rate lower than monitor display**

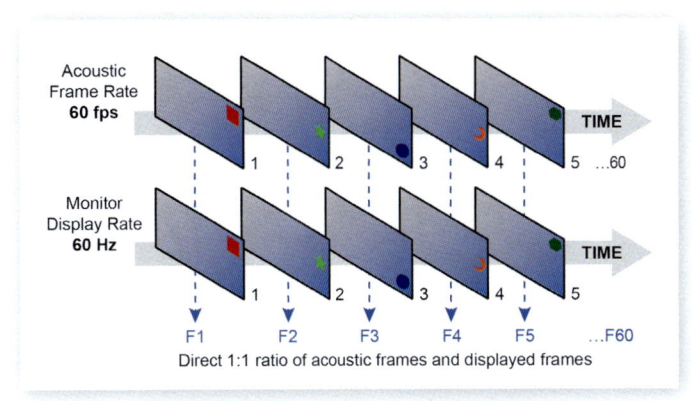

Fig. 73b **Acoustic frame rate matches monitor display**

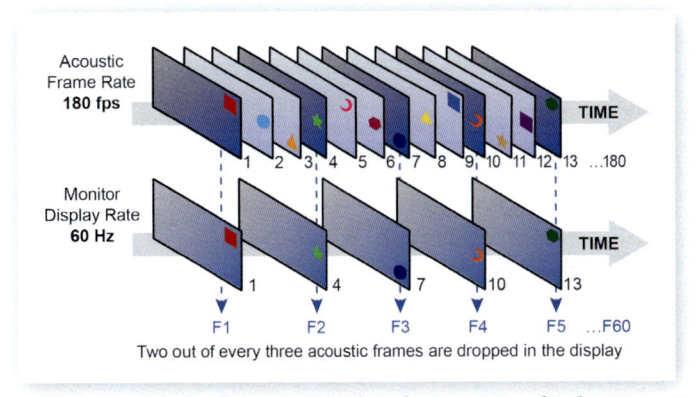

Fig. 73c **Acoustic frame rate higher than monitor display**

Consider the following situation. What happens if the acoustic frame rate is 180 Hz and the monitor display rate is 60 Hz (as shown in *Figure 73c*)? The answer is only every third frame is displayed on the monitor and two of every three frames are never displayed. You can imagine situations in which a short duration event takes place and is captured in only one of the 180 frames. Given that not all frames are displayed on the screen, this event may never be displayed. In other words, the limiting factor to the temporal resolution might be the monitor itself, and not the acoustic scan time. This situation brings up the question of why we would ever want acoustic frame rates above 60 Hz if the monitor is usually limited to 60 Hz, and furthermore, if we as humans cannot detect faster changes than that anyway. The answer is in cine loop review (discussed in Section 22) and non real-time analysis of the data.

20.4 LED and LCD

In reality, both LED and LCD monitors use liquid crystal displays. This means that all LED monitors are LCD monitors, but not all LCD monitors are LED monitors. The naming system is very unfortunate and confusing. As described above, all LCD monitors make use of some fascinating properties of liquid crystals which exhibit some behaviors of solids and some behaviors of liquids. The difference between an LED LCD monitor (called simply LED) and a non-LED LCD monitor (called an LCD monitor) is the source of the backlight. LCD monitors use a fluorescent backlighting source. LED monitors use light emitting diodes as the backlighting source.

20.5 LCD Advantages and Disadvantages

The following table displays the relative advantages of LED versus LCD monitors. Note that LCD monitors overall have some limitations such as limited contrast ratio (greatest difference between brightest white and blackest black), limited viewing angle (side to side), limited viewing angle (from above and below), limited color range, and ghosting. Finally, since the properties of liquid crystals vary with temperature, LCD monitors tend to vary with cold and heat. Medical monitors, which are more expensive than consumer versions, have a closed feedback system to monitor and compensate for the display luminosity based on temperature over time so as to be compliant with DICOM standards (see Level 3 for further discussion).

LCD	LED
Shorter lifespan (30,000 hours)	Longer lifespan (50,000 hours)
Less expensive	More expensive (price difference decreasing over time)
Burn-in is not an issue	Burn-in can occur
Slightly thicker and heavier	Slightly thinner and lighter
Resolution not as high	Supports 4K resolution
Includes mercury (disposal is an environmental issue)	Does not contain mercury
Consumes more power; Generates more heat	More economical to run; Less heat generated
Lower contrast resolution	Better contrast and color quality

Table 1 **Comparison of conventional LCD and LED monitors**

20.6 Subdividing Horizontal Lines into Pixels

The smallest division of a horizontal display line is called a pixel. Since an image already consists of horizontal lines, the pixels subdivide the screen into a grid. A high pixel density (number of pixels per inch) potentially will yield better detail resolution than a low pixel density.

Fig. 74a **Larger pixels (worse resolution)**

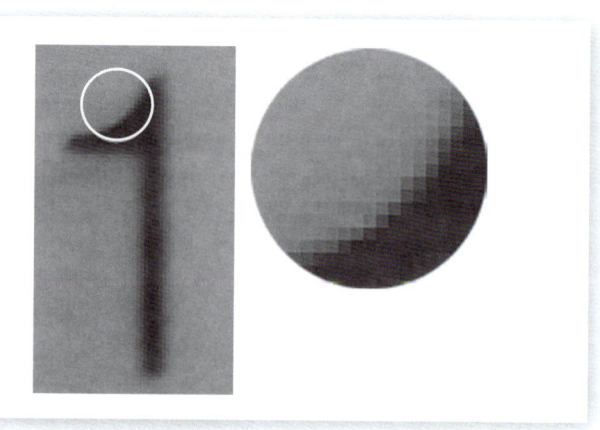

Fig. 74b **Smaller pixels (better resolution)**

Notice that the pixel size is smaller in *Figure 74b* than in *Figure 74a* resulting in better resolution.

CHECKPOINT: Exam Tip

For the credentialing exams it is important to note that the smallest physical division of a monitor's display is called a pixel. Do not confuse this with the smallest division of a binary number, or the smallest division of an A/D converter's output which is referred to as a bit.

Pixels and Brightness Levels

As mentioned in Section 20.2, for LCD displays, the monitor contrast is determined by the light brightness as well as the ability to block that light from reaching the front of the display. In the simplest terms, the monitor contrast ratio is simply the ratio of the brightest white possible relative to the darkest black possible. The luminance (light intensity) of the monitor or other device is commonly measured in candelas per square meter (yes, related to the light from a candle), with the unit of a "nit" defined as one candela per square meter, or:

$$1\frac{cd}{m^2} = 1\ nit$$

So imagine a system that is at full brightness is measured at 1,000 nits, and at full darkness is measured at 1 nit. This system would claim a contrast ratio of 1,000:1.

We often use the concept of layers to express the contrast ratio of a monitor. Imagine that each pixel can be represented by multiple "layers" which can either be illuminated or left dark. Since there are two choices for each layer (light or dark), each layer is often likened to the binary counting system and the concept of a bit. You can imagine if there are eight layers and all eight layers are lit up, that pixel will appear very bright. In comparison, if the top three layers are lit up, but the bottom five are dark, that pixel will appear as a gray hue. Note that the brightness would be different if the bottom three layers are lit up as opposed to the top three layers. If the bottom three layers are lit, then the pixel will be a much darker shade of gray. If all eight layers are dark, then the pixel will be pure black. *Figure 75* demonstrates this concept.

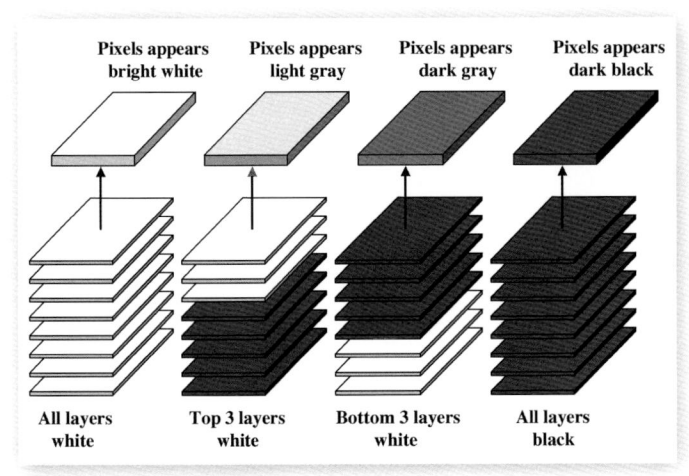

Fig. 75 **Pixel brightness**

20.7 Relating Brightness Levels to Binary

If we rename each layer with the name "bit", we can see how the binary number system now describes the total number of grayscale levels possible. Let's assume there is only one layer, or a 1 bit display. There are two choices, either light up the bit (1) or leave it dark (0). Since there are only two color levels, this type of display is called a bistable display. In the very early days of ultrasound, bistable displays were used. Although still periodically referred to on credentialing exams, bistable displays were also the tools of Moses, and no system today would dream of using a bistable monitor.

Imagine that a pixel were represented by two bits (two layers). The choices are shown in *Figure 76*.

Fig. 76 **4 gray levels with 2-bits**

Therefore a 2-bit display can present four varying brightness levels, or four "shades of gray". If a three-bit display existed, the number of possible gray levels would be represented by the following combinations:

000	Dark black
001	Very dark gray
010	Dark gray
011	Gray
100	Lighter gray
101	Very light gray
110	Almost white
111	Bright white

By now the pattern should be clear. The number of gray levels possible is just the number 2 raised to the power equal to the number of bits.

$$\text{gray levels} = 2^{\text{bits}}$$

$$1 \text{ bit} \Rightarrow 2^1 = 2 \text{ shades (bi-stable)}$$
$$2 \text{ bits} \Rightarrow 2^2 = 4 \text{ shades}$$
$$3 \text{ bits} \Rightarrow 2^3 = 8 \text{ shades}$$
$$4 \text{ bits} \Rightarrow 2^4 = 16 \text{ shades}$$
$$8 \text{ bits} \Rightarrow 2^8 = 256 \text{ shades}$$

Earlier in this chapter we discussed the fact that the human eye is capable of seeing fewer than 64 shades of gray. Therefore, the absolute minimum number of gray levels desired in a monitor must be at least 64, which requires 6 bits, or a contrast ratio of 64:1. Even though the human eye can only see 64 shades of gray simultaneously, all medical grade monitors have a contrast ratio of 750:1 (more than 9 bits) and commonly 1,000:1, or 10 bits. The question is "why?"

20.8 Brightness Levels and Ambient Light

The term ambient light refers to the background light which surrounds us. When in a sunshine filled room, the ambient light is very high. When in a room with no windows and no lights on, there is low ambient lighting. Every time a reference to the dynamic range of the eye was made, you will notice that the word "instantaneous" was used as a modifier. As mentioned earlier, the eye adjusts adaptively to the ambient lighting. In the presence of high ambient lighting, the pupil constricts, allowing the eye to discriminate between brighter shades of gray. When the ambient lighting is low, the pupil dilates, allowing the eye to detect and discriminate between low-level signals. Since there is no way of guaranteeing that the ambient light will always stay constant, the monitor must be able to produce brighter levels when the system is used in high ambient light and lower level signals when the system is used in lower ambient light.

The fact that the eye behaves differently with differing ambient light is important for two reasons:
1. If the monitor is not adjusted correctly for the ambient light, weak signals can be missed.

2. Data stored to external devices may not be calibrated to what is appearing on the screen in high ambient light, leading to either very bright or very dark stored studies, inconsistent with what was visualized while scanning.

View ONLINE Animation and Image Library

The first of these two points, is precisely why monitors are supposed to be calibrated for the ambient lighting condition. Many systems now have self-calibrating monitors which use sensors to determine ambient light and calibrate luminosity. For systems that do not have self-calibrating monitors, the calibration procedure should be learned. Calibration procedures are specific to each manufacturer but usually are very similar and entail adjusting the monitor contrast and brightness until the bottom of a calibrated color bar just fades into the background screen. This calibration should occur every time there is a change in ambient light, as well as at least every 6 months since the luminosity of a monitor tends to change over time.

21. Data Storage

21.1 Data Storage Devices
Data storage can be internal or external. Internal storage is to a system hard drive, similar to any computer or laptop. External storage can be accomplished through data ports such as USB ports. As with a computer device, the data can be stored to an external memory device such as an external hard drive or a USB flash drive. The other option for external data is through the internet to a PACS and/or cloud storage. PACS stands for picture archiving and communication system and is now the standard in most practices. The PACS system includes a secure network for transmission of patient information, a workstation for interpreting and reviewing images, and an archive for storage and retrieval of both the clinical study and the report. The storage can be on a dedicated hospital server, a dedicated remote (at another location) server, or in the Cloud. The standard format for data stored to a PACS is DICOM. A PACS offers many advantages including:

- A controlled method for both archiving and retrieving patient data (interpreting physician can quickly access past studies)
- Electronic image integration (interpreting physician can access other types of studies)
- Remote access for telemedicine or for data sharing (which reduces the number of studies needed on patients)
- Standardization of reports
- Workflow management

21.2 DICOM
Digital Imaging and Communication in Medicine (DICOM) is an agreed upon file standard used in medical imaging. DICOM is used to manage, send, store, and print information. Modern medical imaging devices including ultrasound, X-ray, CT, and MRI all use DICOM as the standardized file output. A DICOM file consists of a header file and the stored images. The header file includes a series of standardized tags that include patient information, imaging procedure, and the parameters that describe the image itself. The file is stored using a lossless compression scheme such as JPEG2000, although other compression techniques that offer a higher compression ratio are constantly being researched.

The purest data is what is seen on the ultrasound system. The only method which currently exists for storing this data in an uncompressed and unadulterated format is through the use of DICOM. DICOM is a standard format agreed upon by ultrasound manufacturers to allow ultrasound images from any system to be viewed on any ultrasound or DICOM reading station. There are three possible methods for storing these DICOM images:
- Store to the ultrasound system's hard drive
- Store to a magneto optical disk
- Store to a external hard drive or computer memory via an Ethernet port

There are two potential disadvantages to DICOM. First, to preserve lossless compression, the compression ratio is not very high, so DICOM data still requires large amounts of memory. As memory is becoming less expensive, this issue is diminishing. Second, DICOM images are only viewable by DICOM readers and not by standard viewing software on laptops or PCs. For viewing on standard laptops and computers without DICOM software, DICOM images are translated into another digital format such as JPEG or TIFF. Once the images are converted from DICOM to any compressed format, there is the potential for some loss of data.

22. Data Storage (Internal)

22.1 Cine (Cine Loop) Review
When the scan converter is processing each line and formatting for display, the processed, formatted data is temporarily stored in a large bank of digital memory. This data is stored until the block of memory is full. When full, the oldest data in the memory is written over first so that the most recent data is always resident. This memory, in conjunction with the ability to review the data in this memory, are referred to as cine loop review. When reviewing cine loop, once all of the stored data is displayed, the video loops back to the beginning, starting over with the oldest data, hence the name cine loop review.

22.2 Purposes for Cine Review
There are many purposes for cine review:
1. It allows the user to review complicated images in slow time.

2. It allows the user to compare frames and changes with time.
3. It allows the user to go back and find the best image for measurement purposes.
4. It provides a non-real-time approach to overcoming the limited frame rate of the monitor and the limit to human perception.

As mentioned, a typical monitor frame rate is 60 Hz for LCD monitors. The ability to accurately detect changes temporally is restricted by the pixel response time. In situations where the acoustic frame rate is higher than the monitor frame rate, some frames cannot be displayed. The cine loop generally stores all frames such that in review, frames that were not viewed in real time can be viewed in "slow time." In other words, cine loop review provides a non real-time solution to a temporal resolution limit imposed by the monitor. Of course, if the acoustic frame rate is lower than the monitor, then there are no "unviewed" frames stored in the cine loop memory. In this case, the video driver of the system interpolates the data so that the monitor always has data to display.

22.3 The Recording Length of a Cine Memory

How much imaging time can a cine loop hold? This question is always challenging to answer. The memory size is determined by the hardware design. However, the number of seconds or minutes of video that can be stored is determined by both the memory size and the data rate. The data rate is dependent on the acoustic frame rate. For a slow frame rate, the memory can hold a longer time record. For a faster frame rate, the memory can store a shorter time record. Hypothetically, let's say that a system can hold 1,000 frames of data. If the frame rate is 10 Hz, then the memory can hold 100 seconds worth of data. If on the other hand the frame rate is 1,000 Hz, then the memory can only store 1 second worth of data. Many systems now allow you to set the maximum amount of time to store data in the cine loop memory (of course not to exceed the maximum memory size).

23. Zoom (Res Mode, Magnification)

23.1 Acoustic Versus Non-acoustic

The function of zooming data, sometimes referred to as res mode (for resolution) or magnification can be performed by two fundamentally different techniques. One approach is a non-acoustic approach. The non-acoustic zoom allows the user to place a "zoom" box over the area of interest to be displayed larger on the screen and then essentially stretches the data to the new display size. The term non-acoustic is used since no new sound beams are used to generate the larger displayed image. The other approach is an acoustic approach. With an acoustic zoom, the user again is allowed to place a zoom box over the region of interest, but instead of just stretching the data, the system changes the transmit beam profile so as to potentially improve the resolution of the image. The term acoustic therefore refers to the fact that new acoustic beams were transmitted to achieve the larger display. We will discuss both of these approaches in more depth.

23.2 Non-acoustic Zoom (Read Zoom)

A non-acoustic zoom can be applied either for frozen data or in real time, hence, a non-acoustic zoom is a post-processing technique. Many texts have referred to this type of zoom as a "read zoom," implying that the data is "read" from the memory after scan conversion. Fundamentally, the resolution of a non-acoustically zoomed image does not change. Whatever resolution exists in the image before zooming is the same resolution that exists after zooming. Despite this fact, there are still benefits to a non-acoustic zoom. When there are small structures which need to be measured or visualized, by zooming the structure and surrounding region, it becomes easier to place calipers and make potentially more accurate measurements. If the resolution is poor, then the zoomed image will appear very fuzzy and no advantage will be perceived. On the other hand, if the image has good resolution, by displaying larger, more detail may be perceived and appreciated. It is precisely for this reason that the term "perceived resolution" is frequently used. Perceived resolution implies that the true resolution really hasn't changed, but our perception of the resolution has changed. *Figures 77b* and *78b* depict non-acoustic zooms.

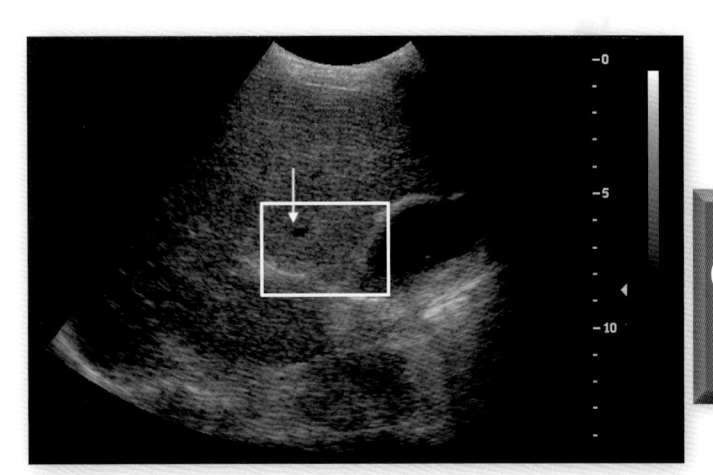

Fig. 77a   **A small liver lesion of 1 mm**

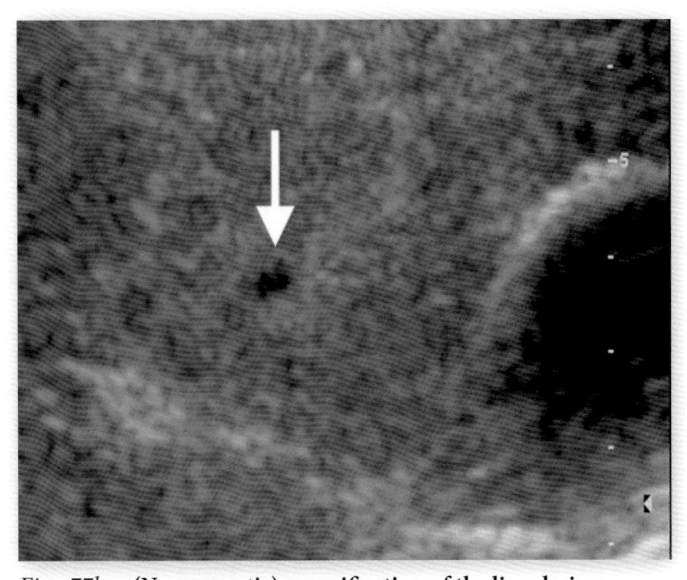

Fig. 77b   **(Non-acoustic) magnification of the liver lesion**

23.3 Acoustic Zoom (Write Zoom)

An acoustic zoom cannot be applied to frozen data. Once the image is generated, it is not possible to change the transmitted or receive beam profiles so as to change the resolution of the image. Acoustic zooming is commonly referred to by most texts as a "write zoom" or "write magnification", implying that new data is written to the memory post scan conversion. When an acoustic zoom is employed, the system decides how best to transmit and receive the beams in the region of interest so as to provide optimal resolution. The following diagram illustrates how an acoustic zoom works.

Figure 79 demonstrates how a conventional linear image is created. The dotted lines represent individual beams which comprise the frame. When the user places a zoom box within the reference image, the system recalculates how best to transmit and receive the beams so as to provide optimal detail resolution. As shown in *Figure 79*, only the lines within the desired zoom region need to be transmitted. Also, since the maximum depth of interest within the zoom region is 6 cm, the line time is shortened from 130 µsec to 78 µsec. To achieve better lateral resolution, the line density is increased, with narrower transmitted beams. An increase in line density increases the frame time. In this case, the decrease in frame time associated with the smaller scan region and decreased depth will more than compensate for the increase in frame time associated with the higher line density. As a result, the frame rate (the reciprocal of the frame time) will increase. *Figure 80b* demonstrates how the new smaller scan region outlined in *Figure 80a* is displayed in a larger format.

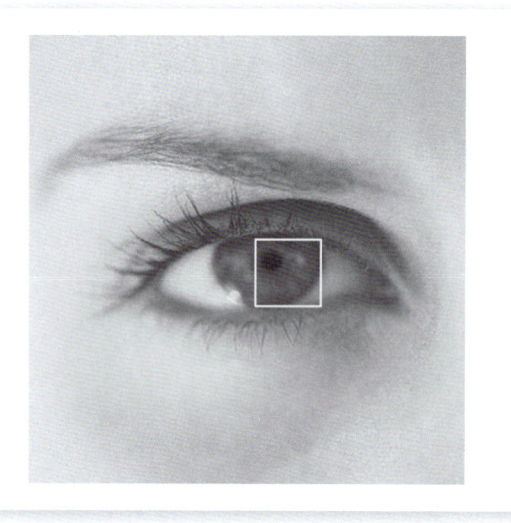

Fig. 78a **An eye**

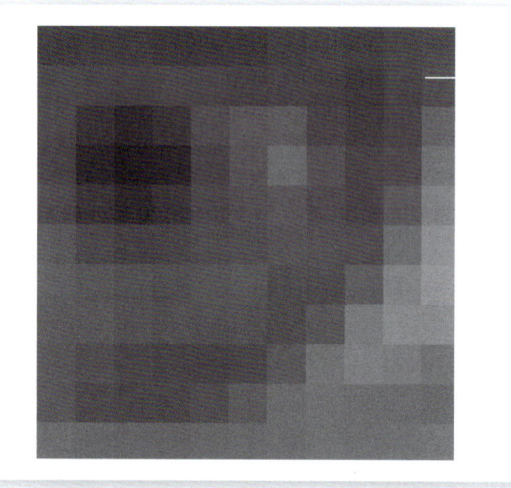

Fig. 78b **(Non-acoustic) magnified zoom region**

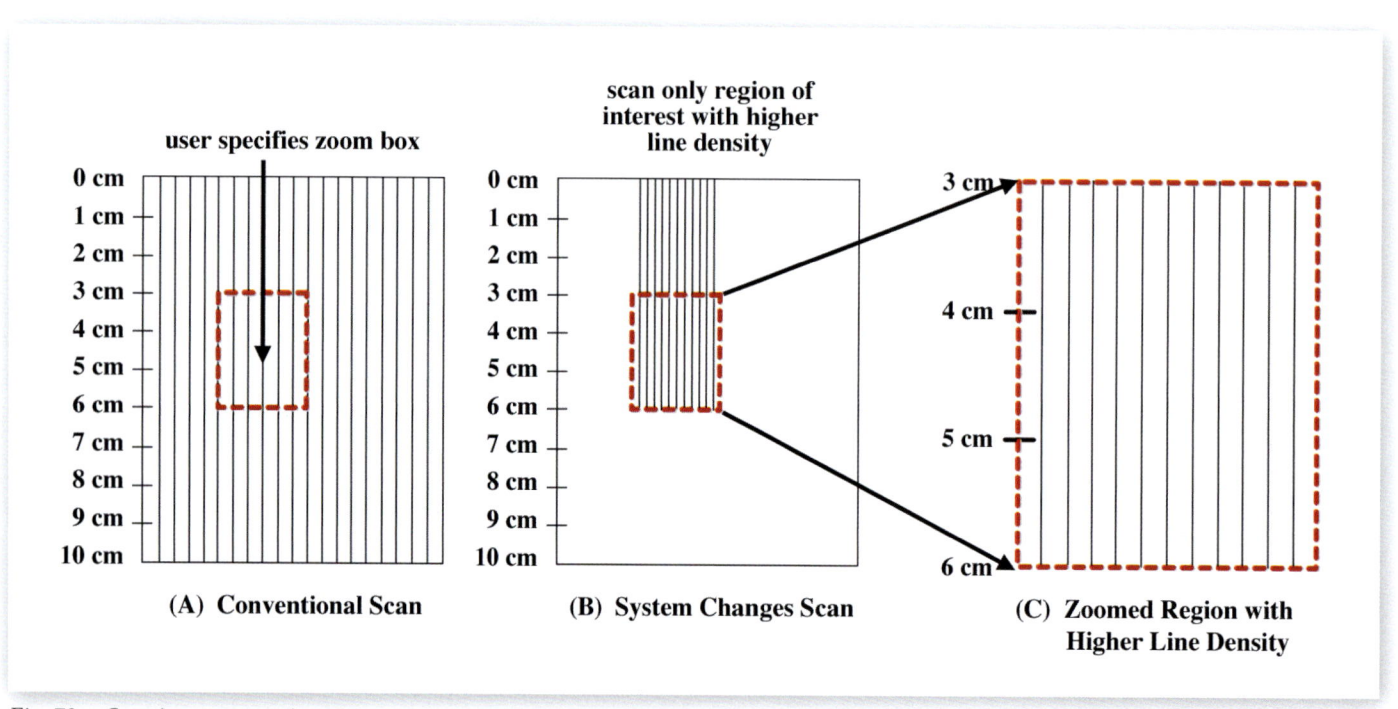

Fig. 79 **Creating an acoustic zoom**

(A) Conventional Scan

(B) System Changes Scan

(C) Zoomed Region with Higher Line Density

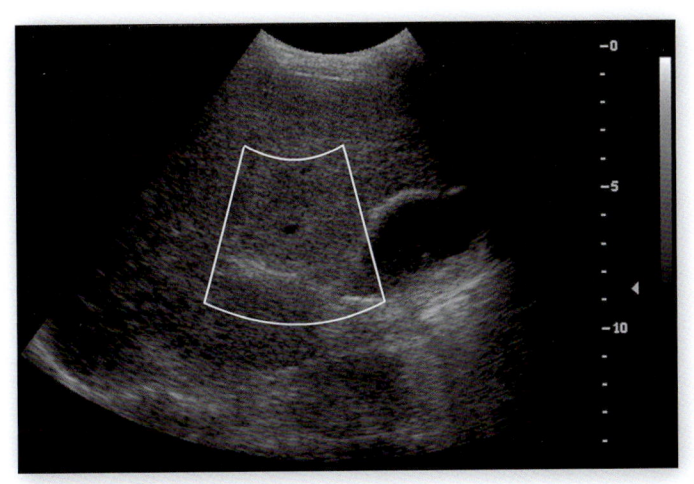

Fig. 80a **A small liver lesion of 1 mm**

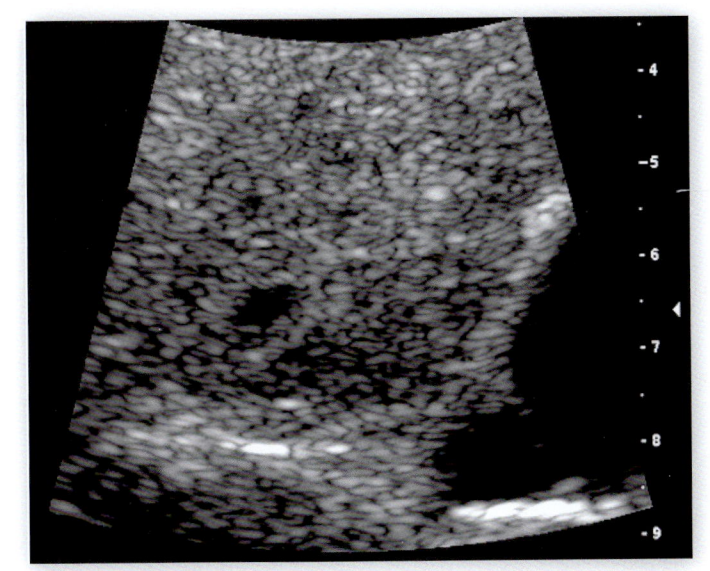

Fig. 80b **Acoustic (write) zoom**

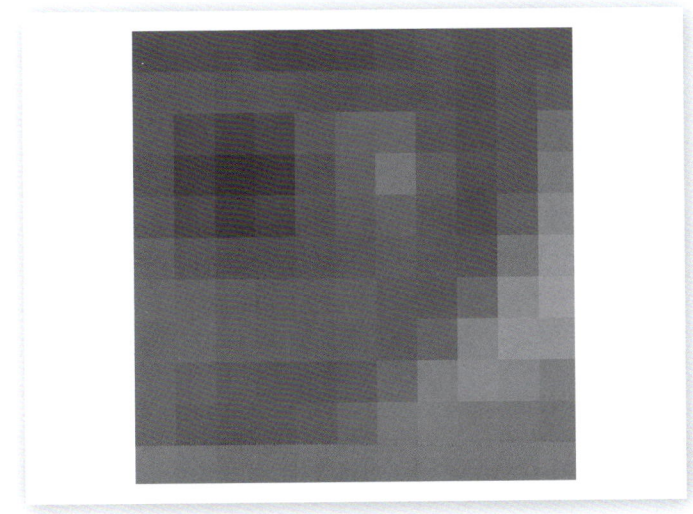

Fig. 81 **Non-acoustic (read) zoom**

Fig. 82 **Acoustic (write) zoom**

Notice the difference in resolution between the non-acoustic images of *Figures 77a* and *80a* and the acoustic images of *Figures 77b* and *80b*. In the past years, greater differences existed between acoustic and non-acoustic zooms for ultrasound images. With technology advances, the quality of the non-acoustic zoom is now only slightly inferior, generally, to the quality of an acoustic zoom.

CHECKPOINT: Exam Tip

A read zoom is a post-processing technique (can be done on a frozen image) which does not affect the true image resolution. A write zoom is a pre-processing technique (cannot be performed once the data is frozen) and potentially can improve image resolution.

24. Ultrasound Modes

The following is a summary of ultrasound modes and their abbreviations.

A-mode	Amplitude mode
B-mode	Brightness mode
C-mode	Constant depth mode
M-mode	Motion mode

A-mode has already been discussed in Level 1. B-mode has been discussed throughout all of Level 2 (and will be further discussed in Part II of Chapter 6, including 3D and 4D). That leaves C-mode and M-mode for discussion.

24.1 C-mode (Constant Depth Mode)

For constant depth mode, the ultrasound system electronics employ the distance equation to turn the receiver electronics on and off (gating) so as to listen to echoes returning only from a specific depth. This technique can be used to acquire an image slice at a particular depth by moving the transducer back and forth over the patient and developing the image over time (this technique is rarely, if ever, used). The most obvious application of a C-mode is PW Doppler. In PW Doppler, the user places the Doppler gate at the specific depth of interest. The system electronics gate out all echoes except those returning from the desired depth. The topic of PW Doppler will be covered extensively in Chapter 7: Doppler.

24.2 M–Mode (Motion Mode)

Motion mode (used commonly for cardiac imaging and for determining fetal heart rate) is a special case of B-mode. In M-mode, a single acoustic line is repeatedly transmitted in the same direction (non-scanned modality). As in B-mode, the returning echo amplitudes are converted to brightness along the line depth. As time passes, these repeated lines are displayed side-by-side, displaying the motion changes over time. Therefore the horizontal axis displays time while the vertical axis displays depth. The motion is determined by your eyes correlating the continuity of certain echoes from one line to the next, as demonstrated in the M-mode of a mitral valve of *Figure 83*.

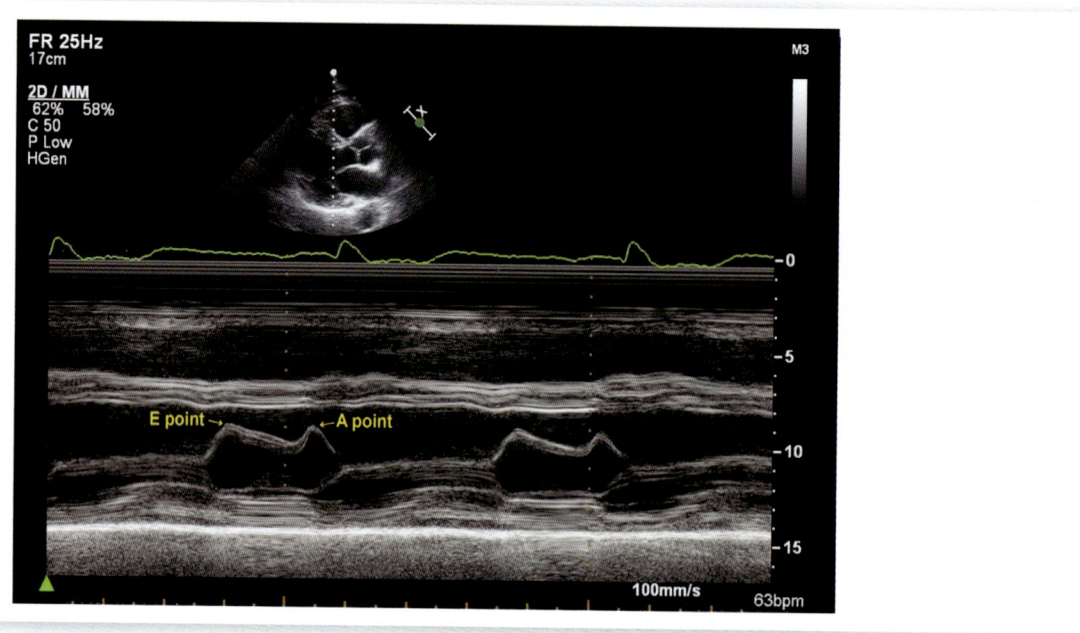

Fig. 83 **M-mode in the parasternal long-axis view; the E point and A point represent mitral valve (MV) anterior leaflet motion during diastole**

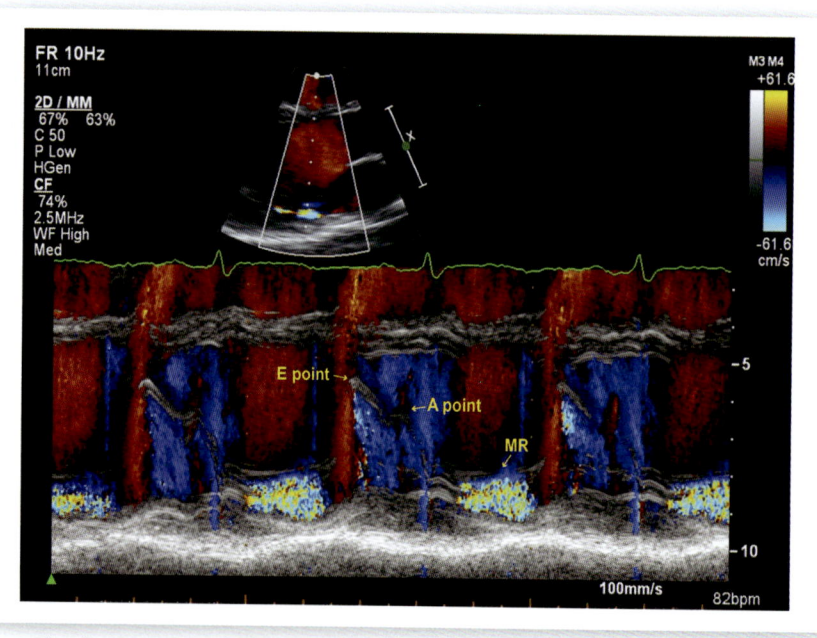

Fig. 84 **Combined M-mode and color Doppler overlay in the parasternal long axis view; mitral regurgitation (MR) is displayed during systole when the MV is closed**

Color M-mode also exists in which flow is presented simultaneously with the motion image. Color M-mode uses color maps in the same manner as color Doppler such that flow directionality can be determined.

24.3 Real-Time Imaging
Real-time imaging implies that all the ultrasound lines are being transmitted, recorded, processed and displayed so as to appear instant and continuous in time. Even though there is a finite amount of time required to build up an entire image, the process happens so fast that "persistence of vision" makes the image appear continuous. In other words, your eyes do not have the temporal resolution to see the change of one frame to another. The advantage of a real-time scan mode is the ability to appreciate motion such as the movement of heart valves and wall motion.

25. Exercises and Conceptual Questions

View ONLINE Exercises & Conceptual Questions

LEVEL 3: Advanced Topics

26. Digital Formats and Compression

26.1 Data Compression and Decompression (CODEC)
The term codec comes from combining the end of the word "encode" with the beginning of the word "decode." A codec is used to encode a media file into a compressed format and/or to decode the compressed format so that the media can be played. A codec is valuable to reduce the size of the file so that less memory is required and so that the file can be transferred more quickly. There are two types of codecs, lossless and lossy. A lossless codec implies that when the file is decompressed, the file is identical to the original file. In contrast, lossy codecs result in decompressed files that approximate the original file, but are not exact.

Ideally, there would be no loss in data quality with compression/decompression. The reality is that there is a significant trade-off: higher compression ratios generally lead to smaller files but more distortion and loss of data fidelity. There are virtually hundreds of codecs used today to compress digital data. Each codec takes different approaches in an attempt to maximize compression while minimizing loss (a decrease in video quality). Regardless of the approach taken, virtually all video compression schemes result in some video quality degradation. If the loss is not readily apparent during real-time playback, then the degradation is generally considered acceptable. However, with medical applications where the playback may be halted and measurements made from a single frame, the video loss that was not apparent in real-time may now become a significant problem, altering or even rendering the diagnosis incorrect. As a result, the compression used must be very carefully chosen to guarantee that the clinical characteristics necessary for the diagnosis have not been improperly altered.

26.2 Video Formats Versus Codec
There is so much confusion between what constitutes a video format, also referred to as a "wrapper" or "container," and what constitutes a video codec that it is instructive to briefly discuss the differences.

A video format is actually a standard which includes the audio and video codecs and the metadata such as subtitles, closed captioning, and preview images. Multiple codecs can belong to an individual format. AVI, .mp4, .mov, and .wmv are actually formats and not specific compression schemes. Within the same video format, it is possible to have videos that were created using different codecs. As a result, two AVI's of the same video, but using a different codec, will not necessarily be the same.

The following table was originally derived in the previous edition from a table included in a website article entitled: *Digital Video, MPEG and Associated Artifacts*, by Shanawaz A. Basith and Stephen R. Done, at the Departments of Computing & Electrical Engineering, Imperial College, London. *Table 2* presents some of the video formats that exist as well as their respective benefits and drawbacks. For this edition, older formats have been deleted and newer formats have been added.

26.3 Comparison of Video Formats

FORMAT	CHARACTERISTICS
Audio Video Interleave AVI	• Developed by Microsoft and IBM • Uncompressed files yield a high quality video but results in large file sizes (requiring a lot of storage space) • Plays on almost all systems because of Microsoft's omnipresence; can be viewed with standard Windows Players such as Windows Media Player • From the Internet, the entire file must be downloaded before it can be viewed • Does not contain pixel aspect ratio such that videos sometime appear spatially distorted (stretched or squeezed) • Menus/chapters not supported • Usage and support are diminishing
Advanced Systems Format ASF Windows Media Video WMV	• WMV is a compressed video file format that uses many different proprietary codecs from Microsoft, often wrapped in the Advanced Systems Format (ASF) • Produces extremely small file sizes but usually at the significant expense of video quality • ASF provides digital rights management • WMV files can also be placed inside AVI or Matroska containers • WMV files require Windows Media Player to be installed on viewing system • Can be streamed over internet, allowing viewing before entire file is downloaded when using Windows Media Server • Provides high compression with good video quality • Usage and support are diminishing
Apple QuickTime MOV	• With lower compression settings, purported to have best video quality, however resulting files sizes are large • Requires Apple QuickTime player – there is a version for MAC and Windows • MPEG-4 files will run in QuickTime Player since it uses the same standard as MOV format • Can be streamed over internet, allowing viewing before entire file is downloaded when using QuickTime Streaming Server • Standard for professional video editing
Motion Pictures Experts Group MPEG-2	• A descendent of MPEG-1 with more efficient audio compression • Used for content distribution on DVDs • Used commonly for digital television broadcast • Can decode and play MPEG-1 video streams • From the Internet, the entire file must be downloaded before it can be viewed, since the files are so large • Uses H.262 codec
Motion Pictures Experts Group MPEG-4	• Patented collection of methods specifying compression of video and audio • Encompasses many of the features of MPEG-2 • Supports digital rights management • Files most commonly encoded with H.264 or H.265 • Currently a popular standard for internet streaming
Matraska MKV	• Developed by CoreCodec, Inc. and named after Russian nesting dolls • Very flexible with the ability to contain almost any video or audio format • Can hold a large number of video, still pictures, and audio tracks • Metadata cam be edited without rewriting entire files • High compression and good video quality • Playback limitations on some devices
WebM	• Optimized for web operation with secured storage of structured data • Uses Google codecs VP8 and VP9 • WebM can be used under HTML5 without the need for additional plugins • Very good compression and video quality • Allows for interactive and responsive design

Table 2 **Comparisons of video formats**

26.4 A Partial List of Codecs

The list of video codecs could by itself fill a book. We will include the names of a few that may be most recognizable for edification. Some of the most popular codecs include H.264/AVC, H.265/HEVC, H.266/VVC, AV1, and VP9.

Viewing this list leads to the natural question: "why are there so many codecs?" The answer is twofold: ever evolving approaches to increase compression while maintaining or increasing quality and market factors. Each codec has a special ability to handle certain types of graphics, but at a different cost. The bottom line is, each of these codecs represent a different trade-off in quality for varying amounts of compression. In other words, a codec that is virtually perfect for compression of slow action movies may be terrible for ultrasound data. The marketing reason is a little more straightforward. Some of these codecs require the payment of royalties, such as H.264. Some codecs, like AV1, were created as open-source alternatives.

To better understand the trade-offs, it is valuable to review some of the basic theory supporting various compression algorithms.

27. Compression Algorithms and Techniques

To fully appreciate the video degradation that can result from compression algorithms, it is imperative to first develop a rudimentary understanding of the basic theory behind some of the compression approaches. The following is a list of many (but not all) of the theories on which compression algorithms are based.

- Truncation
- Run Length Encoding (RLE)
- Indexing or Lookup Table
- Spatial Interpolation
- Temporal Interpolation
- Mathematical Transforms
- Statistical Approaches
- Motion Detection

It is instructive to consider the theory of each approach, but please realize this is only a top-level description.

27.1 Truncation

Perhaps one of the simplest approaches is based on truncation. Quite simply truncation involves throwing away some data to reduce the data size. Truncation attempts to compress the data by preserving the most significant data and eliminating only the least significant data. However, there is certainly no way for the algorithm to know which information is critical and which is not. The advantage of a truncation scheme is simplicity to develop and implement.

27.2 Run Length Encoding (RLE)

As the name suggests, run length encoding involves looking for repetition of data (runs), measuring the length of the runs, and encoding the length. Perhaps this approach is most easily understood with a simple example. The following data:

| 2 | 2 | 2 | A | B | B | B | B | B | 1 | 1 | 1 | 1 | 1 | 1 | 1 | C | C | C | C |

would be encoded as:

| 2 | 3 | A | 1 | B | 5 | 1 | 7 | C | 4 |

which is only 10 digits in the compressed form as opposed to the 20 digits in the uncompressed form, or a compression ratio of 2:1.

Note that the run length encoded data really presents the data as paired information in which the first value represents the actual data, and the second value represents the number of pixels (length of the run) that have that same value in a row. So,

| 2 | 3 |

indicates that the value of 2 was repeated 3 times. Then,

| A | 1 | B | 5 |

indicates that the value of A existed only once before the value of B was repeated 5 times.

From this demonstration, it is clear that RLE can reduce the size for the data needed to represent a frame. The process is then repeated frame by frame so that there is significantly more reduction over the entire video. RLE can also be extended to work in two dimensions (over an array), further improving compression ratios.

However, run length encoding is only truly beneficial when there is significant repetition of values within a data set. When the data varies significantly within a frame, there is very little, if any data reduction. In fact, if the data varies enough, the data size could conceivably become larger (as demonstrated below).

| 2 | 1 | 3 | A | B | B | 2 | B | D |

would be encoded to:

| 2 | 1 | 1 | 1 | 3 | 1 | A | 1 | B | 2 | 2 | 1 | B | 1 | D | 1 |

In this case the compressed data is represented by 16 digits whereas the original data is represented in only 9 digits.

The benefit of RLE is that it is a *lossless* compression scheme, preserving the original video quality. The reality is that RLE by itself rarely results in enough file size reduction to be used in diagnostic ultrasound, since there is significant variance in standard ultrasound signals.

27.3 Indexing (Lookup Table)

The concept behind indexing is that even if data spans a large range of values, not necessarily every value will exist within the data. As a result, the data at each pixel could then be encoded into a smaller value requiring less memory. However, to decipher the code, a table or "index" would be necessary, translating the encoded sequences back to their original values for accurate display. This process is much less than trivial and again has the limitation that if there are many distinct values within the data set, then the compression savings may be minimal or even non-existent.

27.4 Spatial Interpolation

The concept behind spatial interpolation is that each frame can be reduced in size by looking at neighborhoods within the frame. The presumption is that there is some correlation between pixels within a neighborhood, and therefore some of the pixels can be eliminated, reducing the data size. When decompressing the data, the algorithm then makes mathematical attempts to reconstruct the values of the pixels that were decimated to reproduce the entire image. Perhaps an example would best demonstrate this technique:

Original Data

| 2 | 3 | 2 | 2 | 1 | 9 | 9 | 5 | 5 | 4 | 1 | 1 | 6 | 6 | 2 | 1 | 0 | 8 | 9 |

Compressed Data

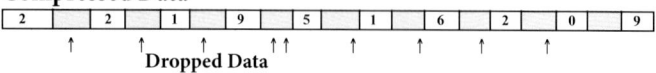

| 2 | 2 | 1 | 9 | 5 | 1 | 6 | 2 | 0 | 9 |

↑ ↑ ↑ ↑↑ ↑ ↑ ↑ ↑
Dropped Data

Since the light gray squares are skipped, there is half as much data to transmit, in this example, representing a compression ratio of 2:1. For playback, the system then takes the compressed data and attempts to interpolate the missing values as follows:

Interpolated Data

| 2 | 2 | 2 | 1.5 | 1 | 5 | 9 | 7 | 5 | 3 | 1 | 3.5 | 6 | 4 | 2 | 1 | 0 | 4.5 | 9 |

Note that this interpolation scheme is not very complex and as a result generates some significant errors (differences between the interpolated values and the original data). More complex non-linear interpolation schemes can be used, but the bottom line is that there will be some amount of error no matter what decompression interpolating algorithm is used. For this simple demonstration case, the error is represented by the difference between the original data and the interpolated data as given in the following array:

Error Data

| 1 | 0.5 | 4 | 2 | 1 | 2.5 | 2 | 0 | 3.5 |

27.5 Temporal Interpolation

The concept behind temporal interpolation is very similar to spatial interpolation except that the data is interpolated over time instead of over physical space. Simplistically viewed, every other frame could potentially be dropped during compression. During decompression, the decompression algorithm would interpolate a frame by looking at the previous and next frame. The interpolated frame would hopefully be close to the original frame that was dropped. Of course, non-linear behavior in the data can represent significant problems for this technique. Techniques to overcome the interpolation errors include sending information that tells the decompression algorithm how to reduce the interpolation error in each frame. Of course, the more accurate this correction, the more data is sent, and the smaller the effective compression rate.

27.6 Mathematical Transforms

Another approach is to mathematically transform the data into a complementary data space. On playback, the inverse transform is applied to try to restore the data. Depending on the data and the transform, this approach can yield large compression ratios. However, there is no single transform that will work well for all different types of video. The computational power and speed necessary to perform the transformations can become a constraint, although this is less and less of an issue as computing power continues to increase at decreased costs. Additionally, there is no guarantee that approximations needed to make the transform solvable do not add significant error into the video. One example of a mathematical transform that can be used is a Discrete Fourier Transform (DFT).

27.7 Statistical Approaches

The use of statistics to characterize data for compressional savings has become a greater reality with faster and more powerful processors. The basic concept is that since some values will occur more frequently in the data than other values, a code can be used to represent the more commonly occurring values. Since the code for the values requires less memory than the actual value, there is a space savings. However, since the codes must be deciphered by the decompression algorithm, the code must also be transferred, somewhat diminishing the space savings.

27.8 Motion Detection

Perhaps one of the most powerful techniques is based on the ability to sense motion and compress accordingly. The basic concept is that from frame to frame, many pixels will have remained static and only objects or structures that are moving need to be encoded. As an example, imagine if there was a video of the trajectory of a ball against a black background. In each of the frames, the black background remains the same and only the position of the ball changes. A motion-based algorithm would look ahead in the frames to see what regions of each frame have changed and encode the data for just those regions. In this example, the only part of the frame that would change is the new location of the ball and the old location of the ball. The data can then be sent as key frames which identify the overall image and motion frames with motion vectors that identify the parts of the image that are moving and how much from frame to frame. This technique is extremely powerful and is able to achieve significant compression ratios. As a result, this technique is commonly used (in conjunction with other techniques) by most compression algorithms. However, there are certainly a few issues, which become more significant with more complex time variation in the video signal. For example, to detect motion, the algorithm must grid the video into a series of blocks. The algorithm then analyzes each block for changes from frame to frame. If the block is considered "unchanged" then the same block is repeated. When change is identified, the new block is displayed in the new frame. The problem with this technique is two-fold: first, how much of a change constitutes motion, and second, how big or small is the block. When very small changes are recognized within a block, the compression algorithm might decide the changes are not substantial enough to label as motion. This introduces errors into the compressed video. Furthermore, the block size introduces even further quantization errors. As a result, for very well-behaved video, this technique achieves impressive compression ratios with no significant video degradation. Conversely, when there is great variation within a frame and from frame to frame, as occurs with ultrasound data, this algorithm can introduce significant errors.

27.9 Combining Algorithms

Most codecs use a combination of techniques, with various weightings on each. For example, a codec designed for simple time transitions with little variation from pixel to pixel within the image can allow the user to very heavily weight spatial, temporal, and motion techniques. If data has significant variance from pixel to pixel but not from frame to frame, then a codec which does more temporal encoding will have greater benefits than spatial approaches. Again, the bottom line is that no codec is perfect, and all that have significant compression ratios will have losses.

28. Digital to Digital Format Conversion

Multiple (Iterative) Compressions

Since virtually all digital formats involve compression, converting from one digital format to another digital format implies that the data goes through at least two compressions. Performing multiple (iterative) compressions on the same data (iterative compressions) is a recipe for significant video loss. People who are trained to process video for a living know that it is critical to preserve the video in its purest form and then experiment with which compression algorithm will yield the best compression ratio while preserving the critical characteristics and quality of the video being processed.

The reason that iterative processing is potentially so catastrophic to video quality is that compression effects are very non-linear. The relatively non-linear errors generated from one compression scheme can grow exponentially when the second compression scheme assumes those errors as actual data. The following images demonstrate how much distortion can occur from applying multiple digital compression schemes.

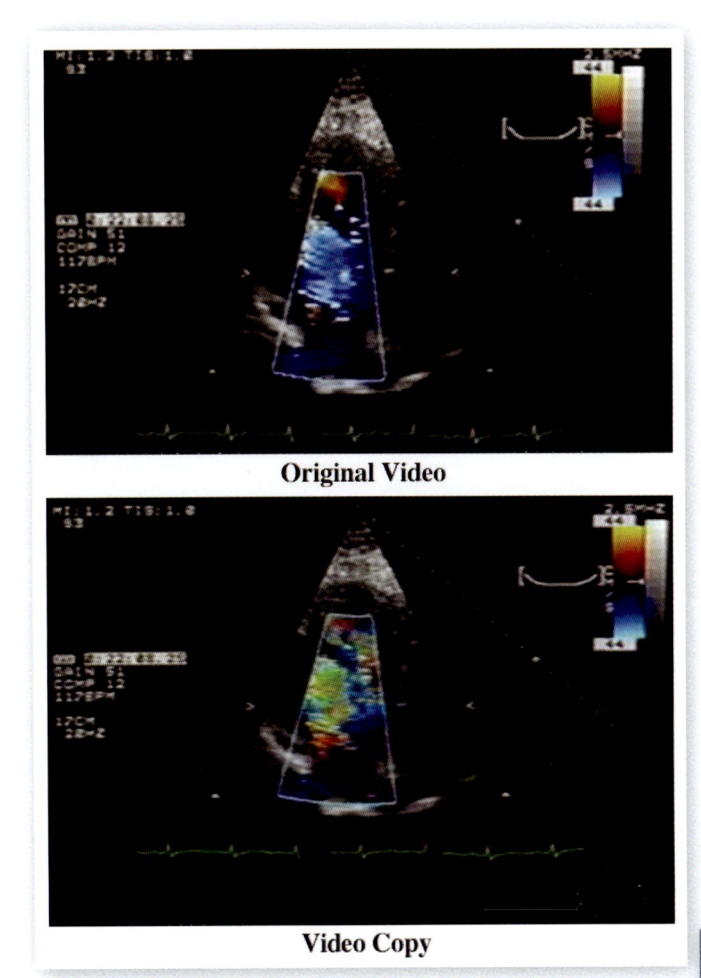

Fig. 85 **Distortion from iterative digital conversions**

Note that although these two frames represent the same frame of data, there has been some temporal distortion through the compression scheme such that the flow is no longer representative of the flow actually visualized. It is highly recommended that for clinical review, data never be utilized that has gone through multiple compressions. The rule of thumb should always be to use data that is as close to the source data as possible.

29. More About Monitors

29.1 OLED and QLED Monitors

In our discussion of LED monitors we talked about two different methods of creating backlighting, fluorescent for LCD monitors and LEDs for LED monitors. Televisions and cell phones are now using two new technologies which have begun to filter down to monitors: OLED and QLED. OLED stands for "organic light emitting diode" and QLED stands for "quantum light emitting diode." Currently monitors which use these technologies are pricey, but with time, the price will come down leading to more adoption.

QLED monitors use nanoparticles referred to as quantum dots to act as color and light filters. These monitors offer brilliant color saturation even in very bright ambient light. Currently, this type of display suffers from two problems that, unless rectified, make QLED monitors unlikely in the field of ultrasound. Specifically this technology has limited viewing angles and limits on its ability to produce a dark black hue. For dark colors, QLED screens have to dim the backlighting, making it difficult to create a pure black color.

OLED displays use carbon-based organic materials that emit light when electricity is applied. OLED monitors hold a lot of promise for ultrasound. Unlike other LCD monitors, OLEDs do not use back lighting. Every pixel is supported by a miniature LED light. When activated, the LED pixel lights up, and when not activated, it remains dark. This fact means that there is not the level of light leakage that occurs with backlit systems, resulting in dramatic contrast ability. Furthermore, OLEDs have very rapid response times, ideal for ultrasound, and of course gaming. Besides better refresh rates and higher contrast than LCD monitors, OLED monitors offer better viewing angles, are thinner and lighter, and consume less power. OLEDs have another advantage in that they can be made flexible, and even potentially transparent. The biggest problem with an OLED display is "burn-in" or image retention. Another potential drawback is that individual pixels that are activated more frequently will dim faster than pixels that are activated less frequently.

29.2 Frame Rates and Human Perception
In Level 2 we briefly discussed the fact that the "human eye" generally cannot perceive above 60 Hz, implying that there is not really a need for monitors with higher refresh rates than 60 Hz. Yet, there are monitors with higher rates including 120 Hz, 144 Hz, 165 Hz, 180 Hz, 200 Hz, and even 240 Hz. So the questions are "why?" and "is there ever a reason to invest more money to purchase a monitor with rates higher than 60 Hz?". The answers are complicated – but the bottom line is, probably not unless you are a world class gamer or if the screen is being used for virtual reality.

29.3 Flicker Fusion and Perception
The way we perceive the world is limited. Some fluorescent lights flicker at a rate of 120 times per second, but this flickering is not perceptible to most of us. The rate at which flicker becomes imperceptible and the source seen as continuous is referred to as flicker fusion. The original work on this phenomenon was published by Selig Hecht and Emil Smith from Columbia University back in 1935. The most germane part of their research to concerns about flicker in the ultrasound image are the results displayed in the graph of *Figure 86*.

This graph has brightness on the x-axis and the critical frequency on the y-axis (the frequency at which the flicker was perceived as continuous). The different color line plots correspond to different diameter light sources measured in degrees. At 2 and smaller, the light size is small enough to encompass a portion of the retina that is rod-free. For the larger diameters both the cones and rods are activated, partially explaining why the plots are diameter dependent. From this graph we can see that at 19 degrees (which is consistent with viewing a monitor) there is a plateau of the flicker fusion rate just below 60 Hz. Notice that at lower levels of illuminance, the rate drops to frequencies well below 60 Hz.

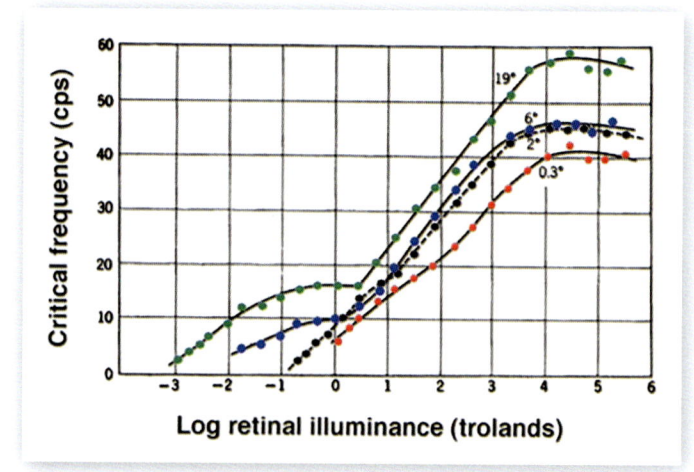

Fig. 86 **Critical flicker frequency as a function of retinal illuminance and stimulus size (0.3°, 2°, 6°, and 19°)**

As a result of this data, we generally state that humans cannot actively perceive flicker past 60 Hz. The exact rate varies by person (each data point on the graph represents an average of three complete runs with at least two measurements per intensity).

29.4 Flicker Fusion as an Advantage
The fact that we are limited as to perceiving less than 60 Hz makes media such as movies, television, and video games possible. Many movies are produced at 24 frames per second, yet to us, the movie looks smooth and continuous. Yet, as mentioned above, some monitors (for a high enough price) can be purchased that far exceed 60 Hz refresh rates. For video that contains rapid changes, it is possible that artifacts will be apparent at frame rates of 30 Hz. For most people, at 60 Hz, artifacts associated with motion are not noticeable.

29.5 Unconscious and Conscious Sensing of Flicker
It turns out that although we cannot consciously detect flicker at 60 Hz, at least some portion of the brain is capable of detecting the flicker. Studies have been done that show that flicker rates can cause fatigue and even headaches, even when the flicker is not perceived. One study, performed in 1995, showed that students performed worse with flicker rates of 120 Hz than the higher rates achievable with electronically ballasted fluorescent lights (most compact fluorescent lights refresh at between 10,000 and 40,000 cycles per second). I recall reading a book about perception and autism written by Temple Grandin in which she explained that she, and many others on the spectrum are able to perceive the refresh rates of older fluorescent bulbs, and how debilitating this lighting can be.

29.6 When 60 Hz is Not Enough
In the last few years, virtual reality (VR) has become more prevalent. For years, VR was limited by processing power and technology.

Researchers have found that frame rate is very important for VR. Using VR at frame rates of 60 Hz, many people experience motion sickness as there is a discrepancy between the visual and vestibular cues in the brain. In essence, motion results in a greater sensitivity to frame rate. Scenes that would not be problematic when stationary become problematic with head and/or body movement. When neurons from the medial superior temporal area of the visual cortex sense a mismatch, the result is disorienting. Michael Abrash, the chief scientist for Oculus VR had originally found that a frame rate of 90 Hz or greater was needed to eliminate the sensitivity to motion. Since then, by controlling the visual cues that elicit motion, some VR systems, including Oculus Quest have refresh rates of only 72 Hz. The bottom line is that there is no hard and fast rule that applies to all situations. The refresh rate that is needed depends on the application, the visual media, and how the user is interacting with that media.

> **COMMON MISCONCEPTION: System Operation**
>
> **MISCONCEPTION:** *The ideal compression is set once to achieve a specific grayscale appearance.*
>
> You will find that many labs rarely, if ever change the compression (dynamic range, grayscale, post-processing curves) once a preferred image appearance has been determined. As was explained earlier in this chapter, this can lead to missing masses and thrombus. The compression should be adjusted up and down to determine if anything appears or disappears in the image. If a change is appreciated, then further testing needs to be performed to verify whether the structure in question is real or artifactual.

> **COMMON MISCONCEPTION: System Operation**
>
> **MISCONCEPTION:** *Increasing receiver gain improves sensitivity.*
>
> A distinction must be made between the true signal-to-noise ratio and the apparent signal-to-noise ratio. Since for 2D images, signal strength is represented by display brightness, any control which affects the displayed brightness (such as receiver gain) appears to affect sensitivity. However, unlike increasing transmit power, using a higher receiver gain (amplification) does not increase the signal-to-noise ratio. Amplification results in an increase in the amplitude of both the signal and noise components, preserving the signal-to-noise ratio. In other words, if you increase the receiver gain, not only does the signal appear "stronger" but so too does the noise. This fact does not imply that receiver gain is not a useful function. Without receiver gain, even very strong signals would be well below the visual threshold of the human eye, and hence, undetectable. Note that if a signal is very weak, turning up the receiver gain will just produce a brighter, but still noisy image.

> **COMMON MISCONCEPTION: System Operation**
>
> **MISCONCEPTION:** *Using more receiver gain and lower TGCs is better than using lower receiver gain and higher TGCs.*
>
> The receiver gain and TGC controls are both methods of amplification. The only difference is that TGC amplification is subdivided into depth zones. Therefore, increasing the receiver gain by 10 dB is identical to increasing all of the TGC sliders by 10 dB. The only problem with setting the gain too high or too low occurs when there is inadequate TGC to adequately compensate the image. If you set the gain too high, you will run out of TGC range in the near field, resulting in the near field image being too bright. Conversely, if you set the receiver gain too low, the deeper TGC zone will be pegged and the far field will not be gained enough, making the image appear too dark.

> **COMMON MISCONCEPTION: System Operation**
>
> **MISCONCEPTION:** *Monitors do not need more than 36 dB (fewer than 64 shades) because of the human eye limit.*
>
> Although it is true that the human eye can see less than 36 dB (64 shades of gray) simultaneously, the human eye has an incredible adaptive range, being able to see brighter values in brighter ambient light, and lower intensity signals in lower ambient light. The monitor must be able to display the brighter whites and the darker grays to accommodate for variations in room lighting

CHAPTER SUMMARY: System Operation (Fundamentals)

- It is important to understand terms such as signal, noise, signal-to-noise ratio, and dynamic range.
- Clinically, it is critical that you understand what parameters can be changed to improve signal-to-noise and how to identify good SNR.
- For most exams, the system is divided into two main subsystems: the receiver (better named the front end) and the scan converter (better named the back end).
- The receiver consists of five basic functions:
  - Amplification
  - Compensation
  - Compression
  - Demodulation
  - Rejection
- The purpose of amplification is to map the very small signals which return from the patient into a higher voltage range which can be visualized on a monitor.
- Compensation (time gain compensation (TGC)) is amplification divided into depth regions so that greater amplification can be applied to signals from deeper depths which have experienced greater attenuation than signals from shallower depths.
- The dynamic range of signals returning from the patient span an enormous dynamic range (DNR). To reduce the DNR, a compression scheme is used.
- The Nyquist criterion dictates that the sample rate must be at least twice as fast as a frequency to be detected. Sampling slower than the Nyquist criteria results in aliasing.

$$Nyquist : f(max) = \frac{f_{sampling}}{2}$$

- Since sound is a mechanical wave, as the radio frequency (RF) signal propagates through the body, the interaction with the body changes or modulates the RF signal.
- Demodulation is the process of removing the transmitted radio frequency signal (RF) from the modulated returned echoes.
- The output of demodulation is the early ultrasound mode of amplitude mode (A-mode).
- Rejection is a process by which all levels below a threshold are eliminated.
- The back end of the ultrasound system includes the function of the scan converter which converts the scan of A-mode lines into an interpretable image called brightness mode (B-mode).
- The scan converter aligns the A-mode lines of data into the appropriate image format as well as converting amplitudes into grayscale levels (brightness).
- The principles which are used to interpret an A-mode are the same principles which are used to interpret a B-mode image. Higher amplitude result in brighter pixels, lower amplitudes correspond to darker pixels.
- Transmit power changes SNR and also the potential risk of bioeffects.
- The focus affects power distribution. Adequate SNR may not be achieved if the focus is incorrectly set.
- If appropriate gain settings are not used, resulting in apparent poor SNR, higher transmit power than necessary may be used.
- As well as scan conversion, the back end of the system is responsible for data storage.
- The memory in which the image data is stored internally in the system is usually referred to as the cine loop memory.
- Cine loop allows for both real-time and non-real-time playback of data.
- Data storage can be internal or external to the ultrasound system. Internal storage is to the system hard drive. External storage can be through the internet to a PACS or server through a data port to an external hard drive or other memory device.
- Digital storage quality does not degrade when copied as long as the digital format is not changed. Extreme caution must be exercised to not apply additional compression schemes to already compressed data.
- DICOM is a "lossless" standard digital format agreed upon by the medical device manufacturers.
- The human eye does not have adequate dynamic range to visualize (all at one time) the dynamic range that exists in ultrasound signals returning from the body.
- Additional compression is performed under control of the user in the back end of the system to further compress the dynamic range into the visible range (DNR of the human eye).
- Since all non-lossless compression schemes have the potential for loss of information, care must be taken to verify that disease processes are not missed or misinterpreted.

- Error in two-dimensional measurements can be the result of poor tracing, incorrect angles, or image artifact.
- If the area measurement is generated from a one dimensional radius measurement, care must be taken since any error in the radius is squared in the calculation of the area.
- The same problems exist in three-dimensional measurements as exist in two-dimensional measurements.
- The monitor itself can be the limiting factor in terms of detail resolution, contrast resolution, and temporal resolution, although this is now rare with high quality LCD monitors.
- You should understand the basic principles of monitors.
- You should know the correct calibration procedure to adjust the brightness and contrast (Gamma curves) of the monitor relative to the ambient light.

ONLINE EXTRAS

For additional support material and to view your completion progress, visit:

www.pegasuslectures.com/6thEdExtras

Extras by Chapter include:
- Animations
- Videos
- Additional Images
- Clarifying Clips
- Supplemental Exercises
- Conceptual Questions

See page x of Preface for access instructions

References

Abrash, M. (2014). *What VR Could, Should, and Almost Certainly Will Be Within Two Years*. Steam Dev Days. http://media.steampowered.com/apps/abrashblog/Abrash%20Dev%20Days%202014.pdf.

Hecht, S. and Smith, E.L. (2008). *Critical flicker frequency as a function of retinal illuminance and stimulus size*. Columbia University. http://www.scholarpedia.org/article/File:Flicker_fusion_fig3.jpg. (*Figure 85*)

Hecht, S., & Smith, E. L. (1936). Intermittent stimulation by light: VI. Area and the relation between critical frequency and intensity. *The Journal of general physiology, 19*(6), 979-989.

Ilg, U. J. (2008). The role of areas MT and MST in coding of visual motion underlying the execution of smooth pursuit. *Vision research, 48*(20), 2062-2069.

Izhikevich, E. M. (2013, April 2). *Flicker Fusion*. Scholarpedia. http://www.scholarpedia.org/article/User:Eugene_M._Izhikevich/Proposed/Flicker_fusion.

Mineault, P. (2020, March). *What's the maximal frame rate humans can perceive?* xcorr:comp neuro. https://xcorr.net/2011/11/20/whats-the-maximal-frame-rate-humans-can-perceive/.

Pavlin, CJ. (2004). *Ultrasound Biomicroscopy*. Ophthalmology Rounds. https://www.intechopen.com/books/novel-diagnostic-methods-in-ophthalmology/a-brief-overview-of-ophthalmic-ultrasound-imaging. Photograph used with permission. (*Figure 44*)

Veitch, J. A., & McColl, S. L. (1995). Modulation of fluorescent light: Flicker rate and light source effects on visual performance and visual comfort. *International Journal of Lighting Research and Technology, 27*(4), 243-256.

Wikipedia. (2020, May 5). *Nyquist-Shannon Sampling Theorem*. Wikipedia. https://en.wikipedia.org/wiki/Nyquist%E2%80%93Shannon_sampling_theorem.

Chapter 6
Part II

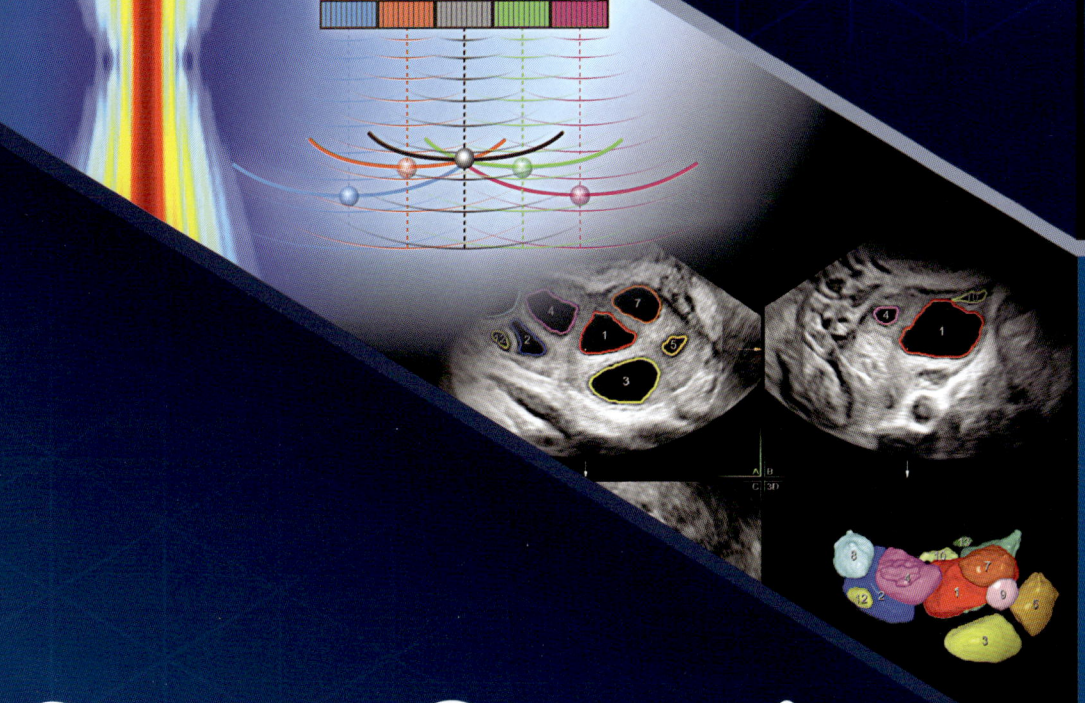

System Operation
(Advanced)

WHY DO WE STUDY THIS?

- Sequentially generated imaging is inherently temporally limited, but increased processing power and speed allows for new image generation techniques.
- New techniques allow for increased frame rates, averaging, improved resolution, better signal-to-noise, and reduction of artifacts.
- Studying advanced system operation reveals the trade-offs between advanced system controls and optimal image quality.

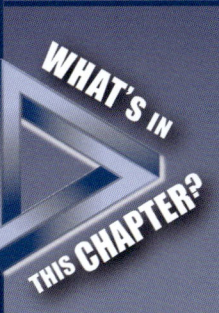

WHAT'S IN THIS CHAPTER?

LEVEL 2 — BOARD LEVEL

Limitations of conventional sequential image generation are considered along with signal-to-noise and contrast. A discussion of the theory of averaging follows including benefits and trade-offs. Temporal resolution is used to segue into the benefits of various image generation techniques. Consideration of signal processing follows, including improving image quality with speed of sound correction and adaptive processing, and a discussion of advancements in 3D imaging, extended field of view, and CT/MR/PET fusion imaging. The chapter concludes with a discussion regarding artificial intelligence and its application in ultrasound.

LEARNING OBJECTIVES

- Explain the concept and benefits of averaging in imaging
- List and describe the many new image generation techniques
- Identify the trade-offs associated with various image generation techniques
- Describe the benefits of image processing techniques
- Define some of the benefits of 3D imaging
- Describe the application of fusion imaging
- Define the basic principles of AI and describe the use of AI in ultrasound

Chapter 6 – Part II
System Operation (Advanced)

Introduction

As technology advances, the world of ultrasound is becoming paradoxically both simpler and more complex. The simplicity comes from advancements which use processing power to automatically improve image quality, make measurements, and in some cases, even tell the user which way to move the transducer and when a quality image has been achieved (artificial intelligence, or AI). The increasing complexity comes from the increasing number of methods to generate images so as to overcome specific limitations and the expanding number of applications for which ultrasound is now being used. In the earliest days, images were generated by manually moving a transducer. With the advent of phased array transducers, sequential, single focus transmit image generation became the foundation of imaging for nearly fifty years. The desire to create better real-time 3D imaging, to perform elastography, and for improved temporal information regarding motion and flow has resulted in myriad different approaches to image generation, increasing the complexity of learning ultrasound and how to optimally obtain images.

Throughout many of the chapters we have discussed the various types of resolution and the associated parameters and trade-offs. Usually, to improve one imaging characteristic, another characteristic must be sacrificed. For this reason, ultrasound practitioners need to understand all of the parameters of ultrasound, the associated physics, and the consequences as well as the advantages of changing system parameters.

With advancing technologies, ideas that have existed for years have become feasible, producing new imaging advantages, and almost certainly, new trade-offs. Understanding the physics of the various types of resolution and the associated trade-offs becomes even more critical as we discuss more advanced system functions since most, if not all of the advanced imaging tools were designed to overcome specific limitations. Unfortunately, just about every change made to optimize one parameter results in a potentially negative change in a different parameter. For example, using a larger transmit aperture (more elements for transmit) results in greater penetration and an effectively narrower beam at deeper depths, but a broader beam in the near field with a corresponding decreased lateral resolution. It can honestly be said that ultrasound is all about trade-offs – and the trade-offs are based on ultrasound physics.

1. Resolution and Trade-Offs

We have already learned that temporal resolution is related to the time required to generate an image, referred to as the frame time, and is inversely related to the frame rate. We know that detail resolution is comprised of three different components: lateral, axial, and elevation. Both the lateral and elevation resolution are limited by the width of the beam in the corresponding dimension whereas the axial resolution is related to one half of the spatial pulse length. We have learned that the signal-to-noise ratio is determined by many different parameters and is a major determinant of sensitivity and penetration. We have also learned that contrast resolution determines whether or not there is enough of a difference in the grayscale between adjacent tissues so that the tissues can be differentiated. In addition to these forms of resolution, there are many different artifacts which can obscure an image or lead to incorrect conclusions, discussed extensively in Chapter 8. We will consider some of the fundamental trade-offs between attempts to reduce resolution limitations and the consequential changes to other parameters. This general information is summarized in *Table 1*. These concepts will be used throughout the next sections in the discussion of technology advancements and advanced system functions.

1.1 FOV, Line Density, and Temporal Resolution

Since for sequentially generated images, the time to create a frame is linearly related to the number of transmit lines, the only way to increase the frame rate is to decrease the number of transmitted lines. For conventional sequential image generation, fewer lines can be achieved two ways: a smaller field of view (FOV) or a lower transmit line density. By keeping the same line density while setting the image size smaller, the number of required lines is reduced, thereby reducing the corresponding frame time. Reducing the image size by a factor of two, reduces the number of transmitted lines by a factor of two, thereby decreasing the frame time by a factor of two, and increasing the frame rate by a factor of two. The trade-off is clearly FOV vs. temporal resolution. The other approach is to leave the FOV fixed but decrease the line density. Decreasing the line density can be achieved by transmitting slightly wider beams so that fewer beams are required to cover the same FOV. Of course, transmitting fewer beams requires less time and hence improves temporal resolution. Wider beams result in a degradation in lateral resolution; so the

Change	POSITIVE Effect	NEGATIVE Effect
Increase the Number of Image Lines (keeping line density constant)	Expanded field of view to appreciate larger regions of interest within the patient	Increased frame time, decreasing temporal resolution
Narrower Beams (keeping FOV same size)	Using narrower beams potentially improves the lateral resolution	To keep the FOV the same size, a higher line density is required, increasing frame time, decreasing temporal resolution
Larger Transmit Aperture	Increases focal depth, increasing penetration depth (improved SNR at depth). Because the beam focus is deeper, the beam is narrower in the immediate far field than when using a smaller aperture. This narrower beam further improves penetration and improves lateral resolution at these deeper depths.	The larger aperture results in a wider beam width in the near field, resulting in decreased lateral resolution (in the near field). Additionally, transmitting over a larger aperture can potentially increase the risk of bioeffects by increasing the acoustic pressure field.
Line/Frame Averaging	Line/frame averaging improves the signal-to-noise ratio, improving sensitivity. For frame averaging, if the samples are decorrelated (transmitted from different angles), speckle is reduced, improving contrast resolution.	When more lines are transmitted to increase the number of samples in the average, the frame time increases, decreasing temporal resolution

Table 1 Trade-offs associated with various changes to increase resolution

trade-off with changing line density is between lateral and temporal resolution. In other words, there is an inherent trade-off that exists between temporal resolution and lateral resolution and temporal resolution and field of view (FOV).

(FOV) giving a smaller region of clinical information. The other approach is to decrease the line density by increasing the beam width, thereby compromising lateral resolution.

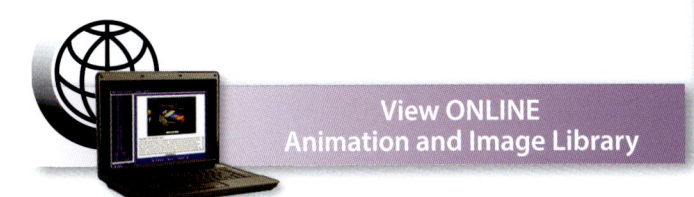

Fig. 1 FOV and line density trade-offs to increase frame rate (temporal resolution) with sequential image generation

As shown in *Figure 1*, by reducing the number of transmitted lines, the frame rate increases. One approach is to decrease the field of view

KEY CONCEPT

System optimization and varying imaging generation techniques are really about trade-offs. Virtually every technique is an approach to reduce the effects of a limit in resolution or reduce the presence of an artifact. Since improving one parameter generally results in a change in a different parameter, optimization requires a thorough understanding of the underlying physics principles.

1.2 Transmit Focal Depth, Transmit Aperture, Sensitivity, and Lateral Resolution

As we learned in Chapter 5, the transmit focus is the region of the narrowest beam and best lateral resolution and is a function of both the aperture of the transducer and the phased delay profile. Additionally, the highest sensitivity is generally at or just shallower than the transmit focal depth, with the beam intensity decreasing rapidly with increasing depth beyond the focal depth as the beam diverges. Using a smaller aperture results in a shorter focal depth, and hence, improved lateral resolution in the near field. This improvement in the near field comes at the cost of a weaker overall signal deeper than the focus because of the fewer elements in the aperture and the more rapidly diverging beam. This fact implies that there is both a decrease in sensitivity (deeper than the focus) and a degradation in lateral resolution.

1.3 SNR and Contrast Resolution vs. Temporal Resolution

Almost always of concern when imaging is whether there is adequate signal strength and adequate contrast resolution for visualization and differentiation of tissues and structures. One way to improve poor signal-to-noise and to improve the contrast ratio is to use averaging. There are many different ways to average (as you will learn in the next section) but, as always, there are associated trade-offs which usually impact some desired parameter, and quite often, temporal resolution. Many averaging techniques require transmitting additional acoustic lines, increasing the frame time, and hence decreasing temporal resolution.

2. Averaging Techniques

2.1 Theory of Averaging

In a perfect world, there would be no noise present in any image, and averaging techniques would have no benefits and no purpose. However, since noise is an omnipresent reality, averaging concepts are applied in many different medical imaging techniques including ultrasound.

Speckle Reduction

One advantage of averaging techniques is the reduction in speckle within an image. Speckle is extensively discussed in Chapter 8 as it relates to artifacts, but is briefly included here for context and completeness. As considered in Chapter 8, speckle results from coherent wave interference resulting in a grainy (speckle pattern) appearance in the image. The result of the speckle pattern is a reduction in both contrast and detail resolution potentially obscuring anatomical structures, including abnormal masses. The reduction of speckle can therefore significantly impact image quality. The image of *Figure 2* shows how the reduction in speckle improves visualization of structures within a sagittal image of a uterus.

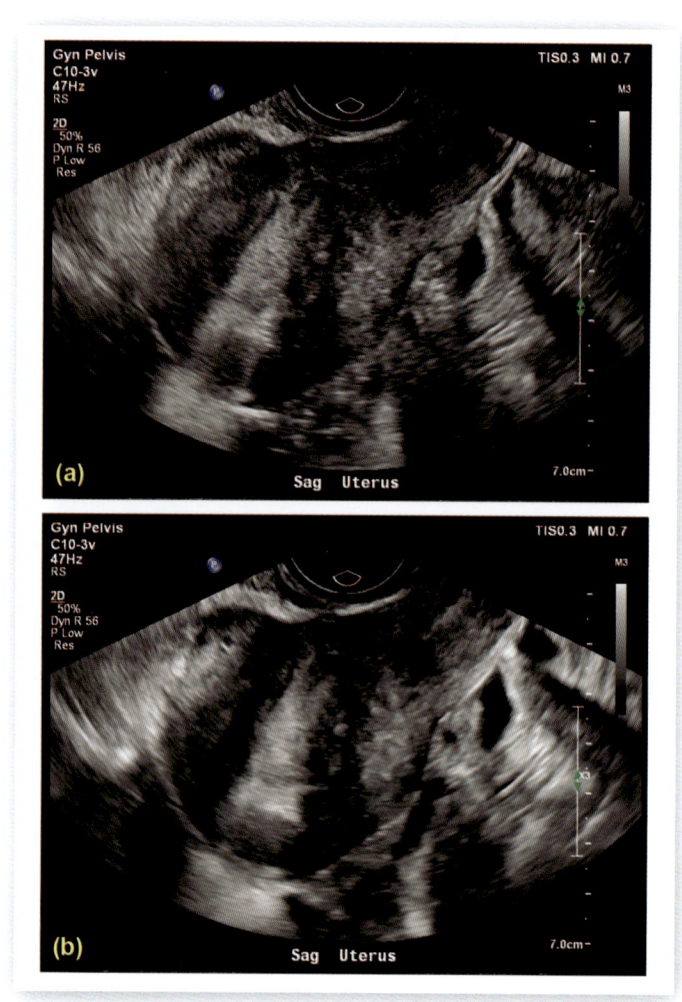

Fig. 2 **Sagittal image of uterus exhibiting speckle reduction from averaging techniques off (a) and on (b)**

Improvement in SNR

Signal averaging is based on the idea that the signal-to-noise ratio can be improved by adding noisy signals together when the signals are correlated (in phase) and the noise is random. This concept should sound familiar since it is the same concept you learned in Chapter 2 regarding constructive and destructive interference. The following diagram of *Figure 3* demonstrates a weak signal in the presence of noise. Note that thermal noise as exists in electronics is completely random. In other words, there is no way of predicting exactly what the noise will be like from one instant to another.

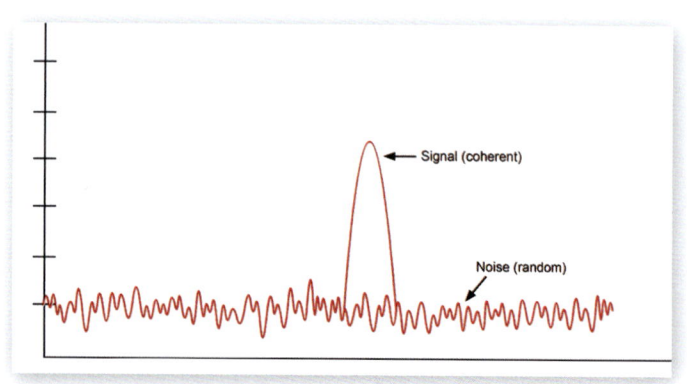

Fig. 3 **Graphical representation of SNR**

Now imagine that, in addition to the signal of the previous figure, another sample is taken at a slightly different moment in time. Because the sample was taken so close in time, the signal will still be in phase (coherent) but the noise characteristics will have changed, since noise is completely random. If the two images are then added together, the signal from the first image and the signal from the second image will add constructively, producing a resultant signal with an amplitude twice the amplitude of each individual signal. The random noise will add only partially constructively. At some points the two noise samples will be in phase, at other points the noise samples will be out of phase, and most of the time, any two samples will be somewhere in between. The result is that the noise amplitude will also grow, but not as fast as the rate at which the signal grows, improving the signal-to-noise ratio. The situation (before addition) is depicted in *Figure 4* while the result (after addition) is depicted in *Figure 5*.

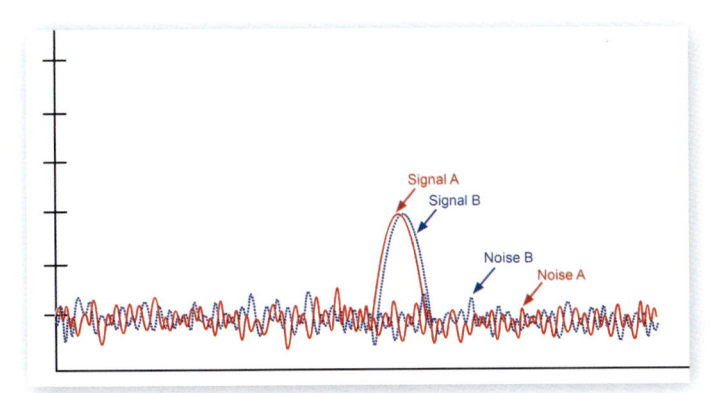

Fig. 4 **Two signals before addition**

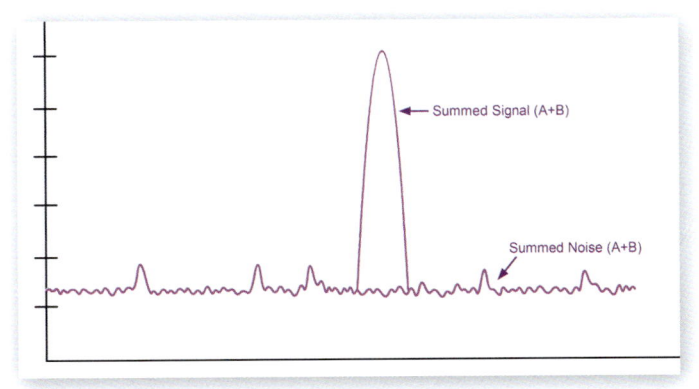

Fig. 5 **Resulting signal after addition with improved SNR from signal coherence**

Calculating the Improvement in SNR

Figure 5 demonstrates the advantage of adding the two signals together. Each successive addition adds the signal constructively and the noise only partially constructively, resulting in increasing improvement in the signal-to-noise ratio. Therefore, if *n* images are added together, the new signal will be *n* times larger than the original signal because of the pure constructive interference (signal coherence). However, when the same *n* images are added together, the noise adds up partially constructively and partially destructively, or at a rate of $\sqrt{n}$. Therefore, the SNR increases by:

$$\text{Improvement in SNR} = \frac{n}{\sqrt{n}} = \sqrt{n}.$$

Applying the above rule, if two images are added together, the SNR improves by a factor of 1.4 (the square root of 2). If nine images are averaged together, the SNR improves by a factor of 3.

The following vignette of images demonstrates the improvement achieved in signal-to-noise through averaging. *Figure 6a* is virtually free of all noise. *Figure 6b* has considerable noise. *Figures 6c, 6d,* and *6e* are the resulting images from averaging 2 frames, 9 frames, and 16 frames, respectively. Notice how the noise speckle pattern becomes finer and the signal strength increases relative to the noise strength. In this example, the signal intensity is kept at about the same brightness so that the improvement would be apparent in the decrease in noise amplitude.

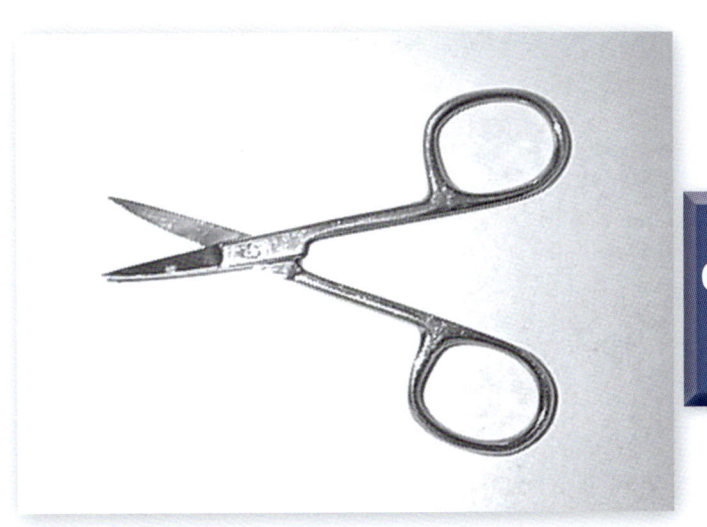

Fig. 6a **Image of scissors with no noise**

Fig. 6b **Image of scissors with significant noise**

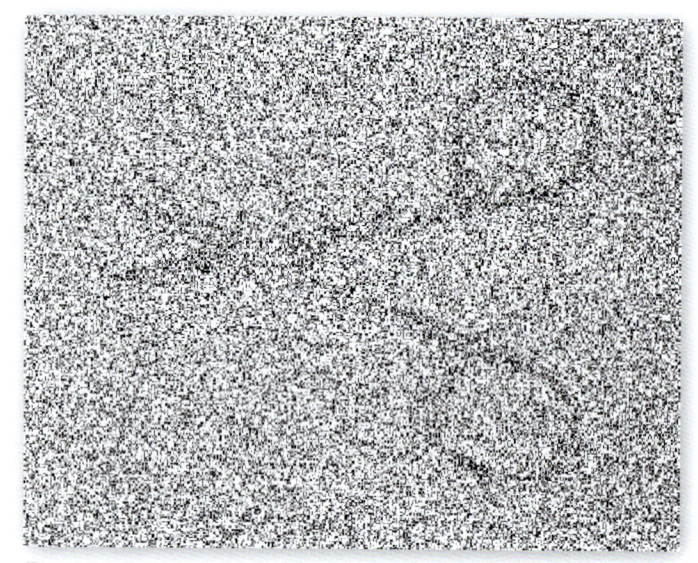

Fig. 6c **2 images averaged (SNR improved by a factor of 1.4)**

Fig. 6d **9 images averaged (SNR improved by a factor of 3)**

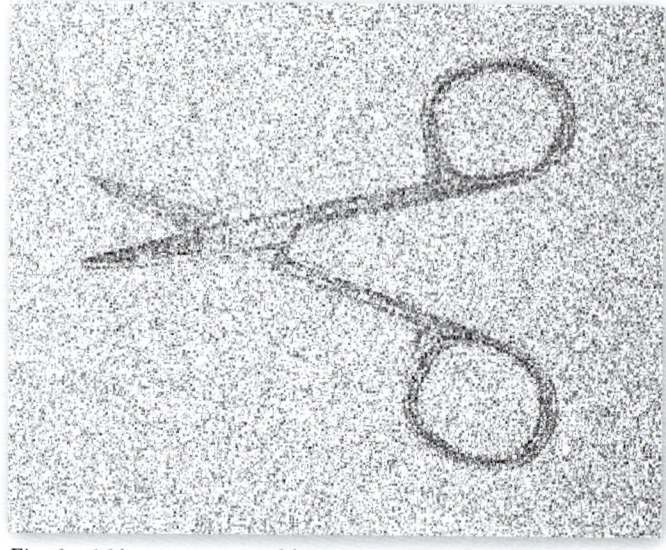

Fig. 6e **16 images averaged (SNR improved by a factor of 4)**

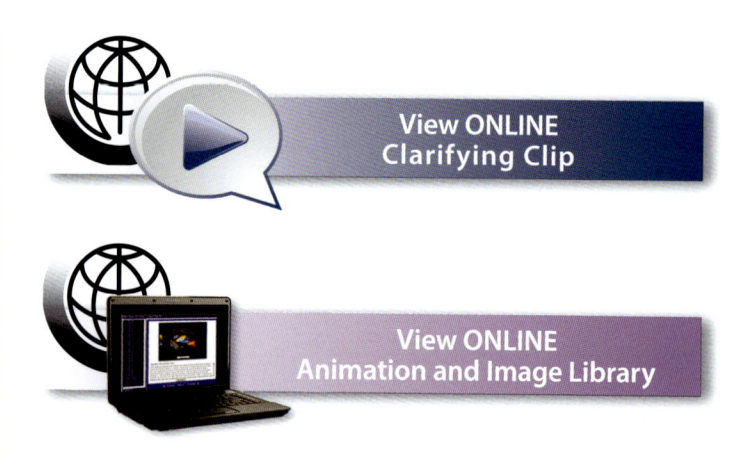

2.2 Line Averaging

Some ultrasound modes are based on line averaging. Color Doppler is an example of when line averaging is utilized. As you will learn in Chapter 7, the number of acoustic lines used in the average to produce a single color line is referred to as the "packet size" or "ensemble length." From what we have just learned about signal-to-noise improvement from averaging, you should now recognize the trade-off with packet size. A larger packet size improves the color sensitivity (larger SNR) but at the expense of temporal resolution. In addition to color Doppler, the SNR of non-steered modalities like spectral Doppler and M-mode benefit from line averaging. Additionally, as you will learn in the Chapter 10, pulse inversion harmonics uses two acoustic lines to generate each display line, improving the SNR by a factor of approximately 1.4.

2.3 Frame Averaging

Frame averaging is also extensively used in ultrasound. Unlike line averaging in which a frame is produced after the averaging, frame averaging is performed by adding together already complete images. Because of the time required to generate full frames sequentially, frame averaging works best when imaging relatively static structures. This method of course can be problematic when the time to generate a frame is long enough to allow for significant motion to occur. In these cases, the signal will no longer be in phase from frame to frame, which means the signal gain is not achieved. Furthermore, the technique will lead to temporal distortion in these cases. For these reasons, frame averaging has historically been used much more extensively for vascular, abdominal, and small-part imaging, and very little for cardiac imaging. For frame averaging to work well for cardiac imaging, the frame times must be reduced from the relatively long durations which result from sequential imaging.

KEY CONCEPT

There are many ultrasound techniques based on averaging. As long as the sample rate is fast enough relative to changes in the signal, each signal sample will add in phase, leading to pure constructive interference. The image noise should be completely random such that when averaged together it adds neither purely in phase nor purely out of phase, or partially constructive interference. The result is that when adding together multiple frames (of relatively slow moving structures) the signal increases at a faster rate than the noise, improving the signal-to-noise ratio (by the square root of the number of frames averaged).

2.4 Spatial Compound Imaging

Spatial compound imaging, or simply "compound imaging," is a frame averaging technique. Multiple images are created over time and then averaged to create one image. These multiple images are formed at varying angles, as depicted in *Figure 7*. The first release of this technology by ATL was referred to as Sono CT™. Since ATL is now part of Philips, this technique is still referred to as Sono CT™ on Philips ultrasound systems. GE refers to this technique as CrossXBeam™, while Canon refers to their version as ApliPure™ and Mindray refers to their version as iBeam™. Siemens uses the term compound imaging, which has now become the generic term for this technique. As usual, every company has a different name for essentially the same technology.

Benefits to Compound Imaging

There are three primary benefits to compound imaging. The first advantage is an improvement in SNR from adding multiple image frames together (as discussed in the previous section). The second is speckle reduction (also discussed above). The third advantage is related to the reduction of specular reflection related artifacts (see more detailed explanation in Chapter 8).

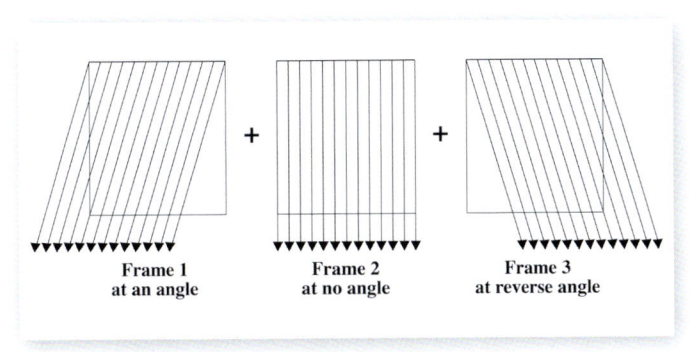

Fig. 7 **Compound imaging with three frames**

By creating image frames at multiple angles, the specular compo-nents which cause artifacts, such as reverberation and shadowing, are present in only some of the image frames. When these image frames are added together, the specular reflection related artifacts are decreased, potentially disappearing. Compound imaging tends to reduce the amount of reverberation and shadowing present in an image. *Figure 7* demonstrates how three images might be created at varying angles for a compound image.

To understand how artifacts can be diminished, imagine a structure perpendicular to the beams of frame two, as shown in *Figure 8*. Because of the 0° incident angle, this structure would then be a likely source of reverberation artifact. However, in frame 1 and frame 3, since the incident angle to the structure is no longer 0° (the beam direction is not perpendicular), the specular component is not reverberated between the structure and the transducer, and the artifact is either lessened or weakened. As a result, the artifact will not be as visible in the compounded image as it would in the non-compounded image.

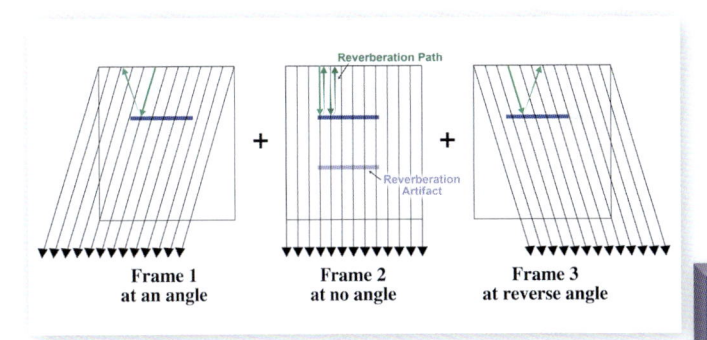

Fig. 8 **Frame angulation of compound imaging reduces reverberation artifact**

Consider another situation in which there is a highly attenuative structure in the middle of the field of interest. Because of the high attenuation rate, we would expect acoustic shadowing below the structure. Notice in *Figure 9* that the location of the shadow varies for each of the frames created because of the varying transmitted angle. When averaged together, the shadowing becomes weaker and potentially disappears. In some cases, the shadowing may be weaker than what would be visualized with compound imaging off, but may be spread over a wider region. The reason is best visualized by looking at the images in *Figures 10* and *11*.

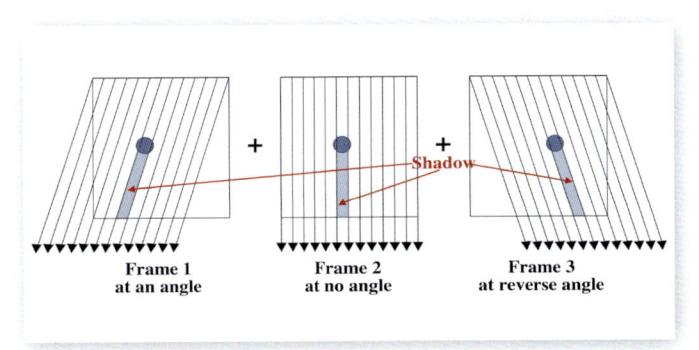

Fig. 9 **Frame angulation reduces acoustic shadowing artifact**

The images in *Figure 10* demonstrate the beam transmission pattern with a shallow focus for a single beam (conventional imaging), three beams, five beams, and nine beams. From the images, the varying incident angles between the beams are evident. The images in *Figure 11* show the same number of transmitted beams but now with a deeper focus. The complex patterns generated explain how and why artifacts can vary and often disappear when using compound imaging relative to conventional imaging.

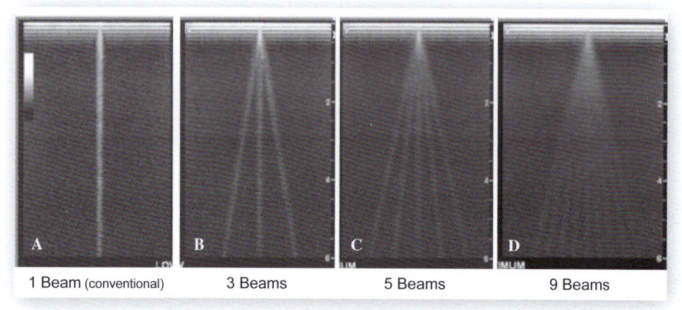

Fig. 10 **Varying beams with shallow focus**

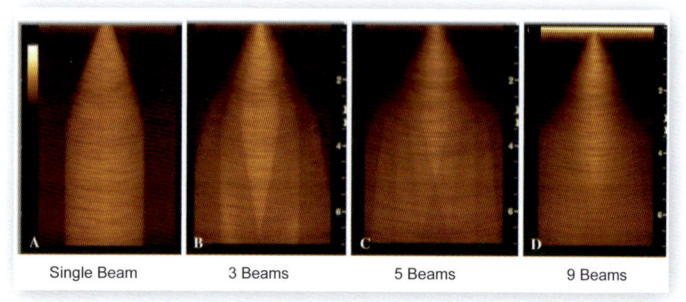

Fig. 11 **Varying beams with deep focus**

The images in *Figure 12* show the difference in refractive edge shadowing in conventional and compounding imaging. Note that we can tell the compound image is comprised of three averaged frames. Also note how the compound shadows are faint relative to the shadow of the conventional image.

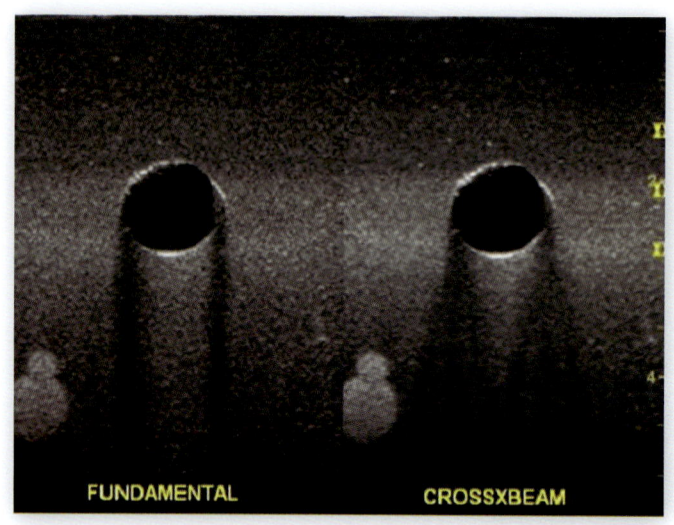

Fig. 12 **Breast phantom images showing differences in refractive edge shadowing resulting from conventional ("fundamental") and compounding ("crossxbeam") imaging**

Frame Rate and Temporal Resolution Degradation

As illustrated above, compound imaging is usually performed using between three and nine images. So that the frame rate does not degrade, a buffering technique is used in which the oldest frame of data is replaced with the newest frame of data, maintaining the same frame rate as conventional imaging. This type of data buffering is referred to as "first-in, first-out," or FIFO.

For example, imagine that compound imaging with six frames is activated, such that the last six frames are used in each new frame displayed (see *Figure 13*). As each new frame is produced, it replaces the oldest frame (taken at the same incident angle) in the buffer. Therefore, as each new frame is produced, a new average is calculated and a new compounded frame displayed. As a result, there is no change in frame rate. However, this is not to say that there is no degradation in temporal resolution. Any time an averaging technique is used, short duration events have the potential to be "averaged out" and hence, not displayed.

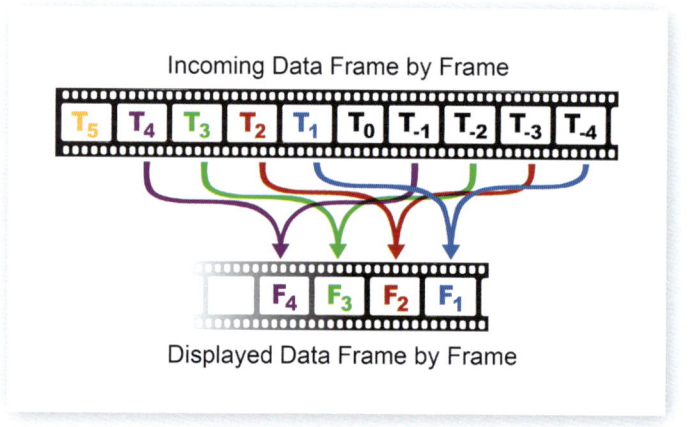

Fig. 13 **Concept of FIFO buffering used to preserve frame rate in frame compound imaging**

In the example shown in *Figure 13*, six frames are averaged per display frame. Notice that the display frame (F_2) is generated by including the frame of T_2 and removing the oldest frame that was used to generate frame 1 (T_{-4}). Similarly, for the third display frame (F_3), the newest frame in time is added and the oldest frame in time is deleted. In this manner, as each new frame is captured, a new averaged frame is displayed, thereby preserving the frame rate.

Imagine that nine frames are averaged together. Now imagine if a short duration event occurred and was captured in one of the nine frames. In our model above, improvement in SNR came from having the same signal in all frames resulting in a constructive interference (also referred to as signal coherence). In this case, if the signal is only present in one frame, when added with the other eight cases, there will be a destructive interference with the short duration signal, which will diminish the amplitude of the signal. Unless the signal has a very high amplitude, the short duration signal will not be visualized.

KEY CONCEPT

Compound imaging is an averaging technique. Multiple frames are transmitted at varying angles and then averaged together. The result is a decrease in many specular reflection-based artifacts and an improvement in the signal-to-noise ratio. This technique cannot be employed when sequentially imaging highly dynamic structures.

Imaging Examples

The following series of images demonstrate some of the advantages of spatial compound imaging. In many cases, the reduction in artifacts along with the increase in contrast and signal-to-noise ratio result in better visualization of structures or pathology that otherwise might be missed, underappreciated, or challenging to confirm. There are times when a thrombus which is not visible with standard imaging becomes visible with compound imaging and other times when artifacts which appear like a thrombus are eliminated by compound imaging.

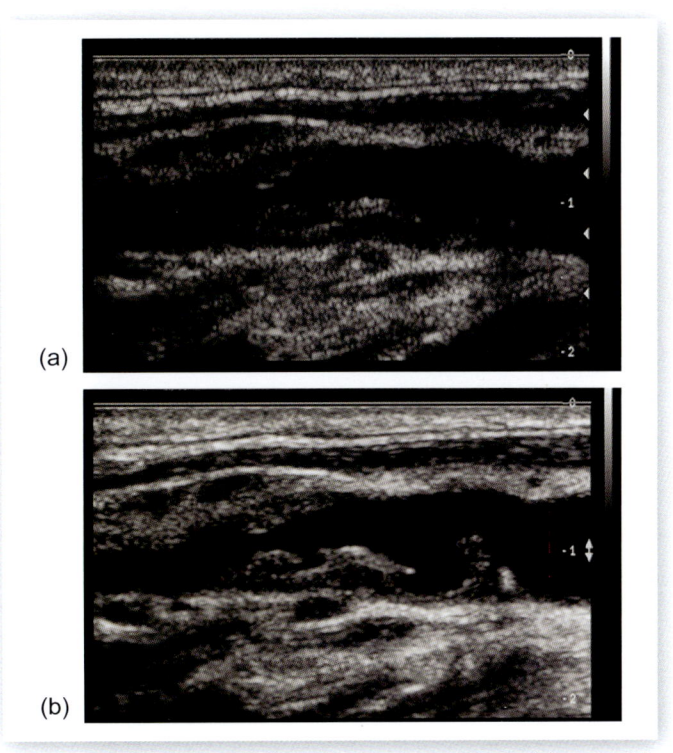

Fig. 15 **Image of a carotid artery stenosis without (a) and with (b) spatial compound imaging; note the improved border definition of the irregular plaque surface**

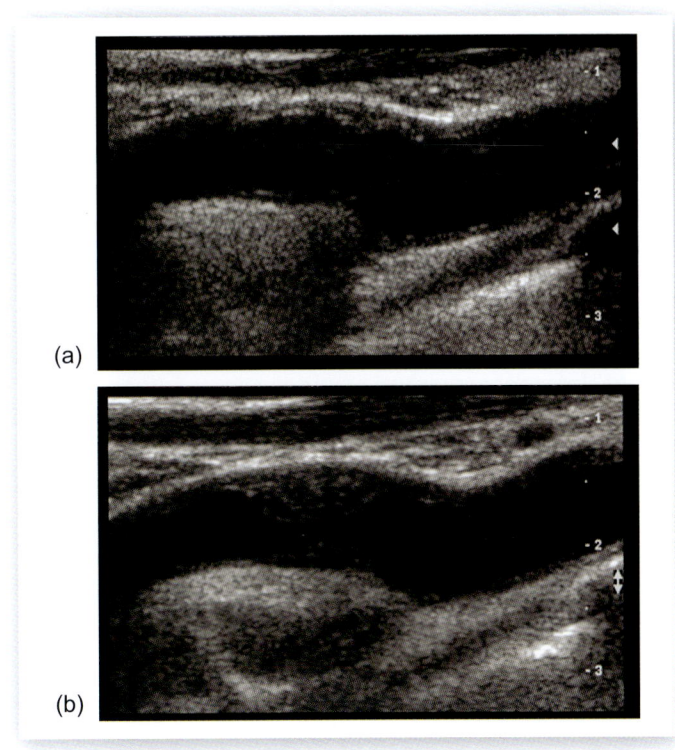

Fig. 14 **Image of a carotid artery with a plaque without (a) and with (b) spatial compound imaging; note the significantly improved plaque visualization with spatial compound imaging**

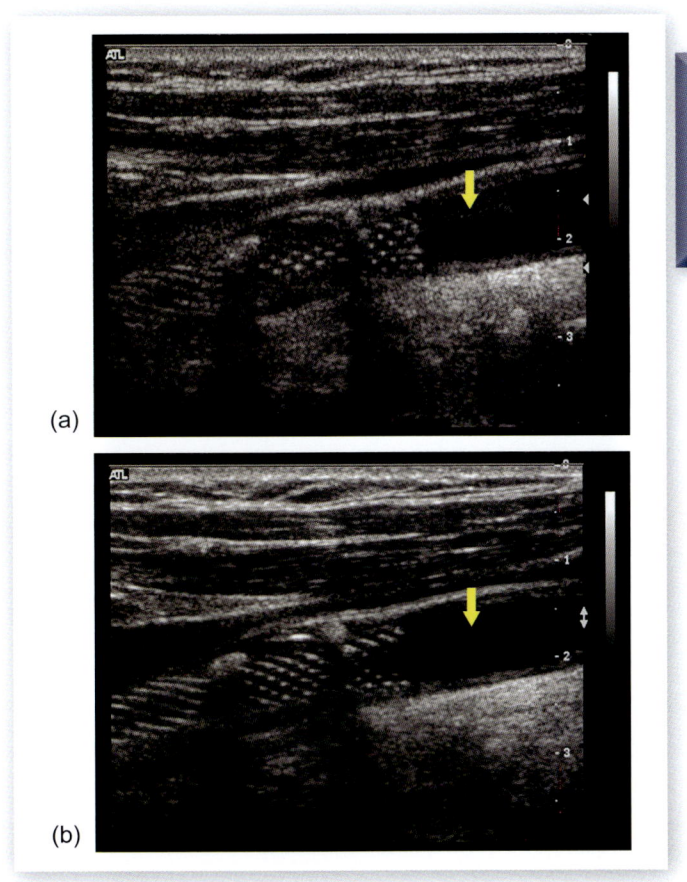

Fig. 16 **Image of a carotid artery stent without (a) and with (b) spatial compound imaging; note the improved visualization of the stent and reduction of grating lobe artifact (arrow) with compound imaging**

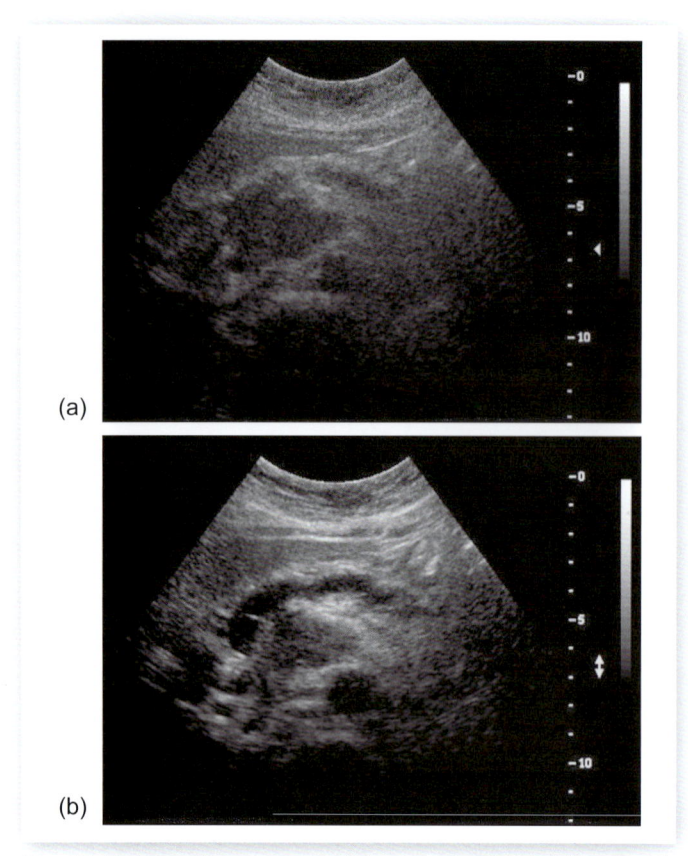

Fig. 17 **Image of a pancreas with cancer without (a) and with (b) spatial compound imaging; note the improved visualization of the mass in pancreas head**

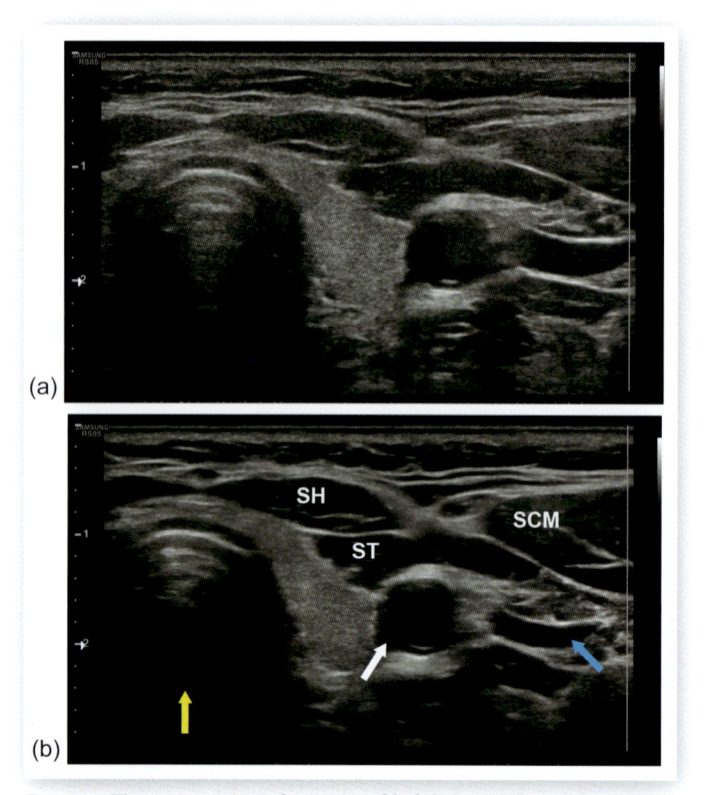

Fig. 18 **Transverse/axial image of left lobe of thyroid without (a) and with (b) spatial compound imaging; note the reduction of reverberation (yellow arrow) and improved definition of the walls of the carotid artery (white arrow) and jugular vein (blue arrow)**

In addition to the reduced reverberation in the trachea and reduced noise and improved border definition of the carotid artery and partially compressed jugular vein seen in *Figure 18* (b), the structures surrounding the thyroid are easier to visualize. Structures visualized include the sternohyoid (SH), sternothyroid (ST), and the sternocleidomastoid (SCM) muscles.

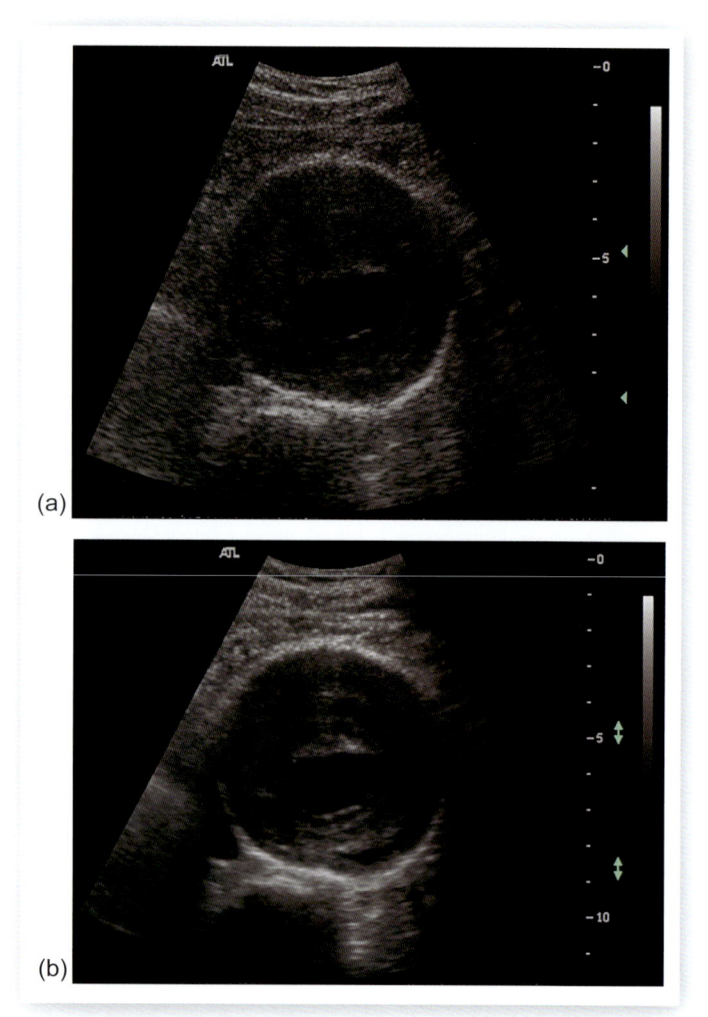

Fig. 19 **Image of abdominal aortic aneurysm without (a) and with (b) spatial compound imaging; note the improved visualization of the lateral walls of the aorta with the use of spatial compound imaging**

View ONLINE Animation and Image Library

2.5 Frequency Compounding (Fusion)

In Chapter 4 we briefly mentioned frequency fusion (compounding) as one of the benefits afforded by broadband transducers. The technique entails transmitting with a broadband signal and then simultaneously parallel processing more than one image, each at a different receive frequency, and then combining the images to create one resultant image. A very detailed discussion also exists in Chapter 8 as relates to the reduction of speckle within an ultrasound image. For completeness of system processing functionality, frequency fusion will also be included here.

Be careful not confuse spatial compound imaging with frequency compound imaging. As discussed earlier, compound imaging is based on averaging frames of data taken over time at varying angles. Conversely, frequency compounding (fusion imaging) implies that multiple images created using different frequencies are combined, or fused, to produce a single image.

Unlike compound imaging, the fused frames are captured and processed simultaneously (in parallel), not sequentially in time. As a result, frequency fusion does not have any degradation in temporal resolution, even when used with sequential image generation techniques, and can be used while imaging dynamic systems. In order to generate multiple images in different frequency bands, the broadband signal received is parallel processed as two or more simultaneous narrower bandwidth images. Therefore, two or more images are produced of the same structures, at the exact same moment in time, but at different frequencies. As we have learned, lower frequency imaging generally supplies greater penetration whereas higher frequency imaging generally results in finer resolution. The fusing of the images allows for improved texture within the composite image while providing superior penetration in comparison to conventional imaging.

From the processing perspective, the technique of frequency compounding can become very complicated when you consider the possibility of fusing fundamental images, harmonic images at different frequencies, harmonic and non-harmonic images, etc. Ultrasound manufacturers can provide many different frequency fusion maps, each created for different imaging situations and applications. Of course, each company calls their process by a different name.

The following pair of images demonstrates the advantages of frequency fusion imaging.

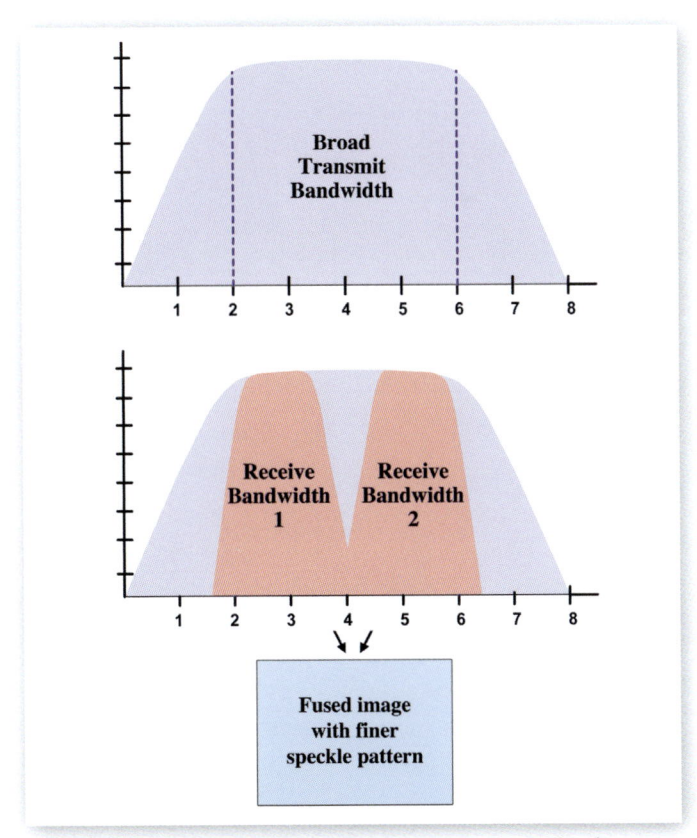

Fig. 20 **Frequency fusion; the fused image is a weighted average of two or more images generated at different frequencies**

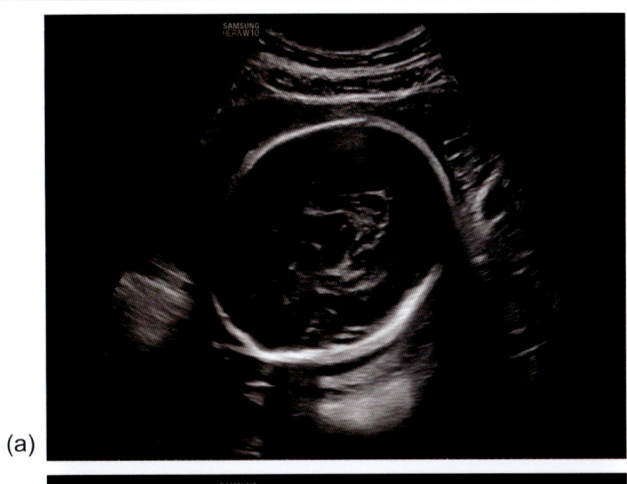

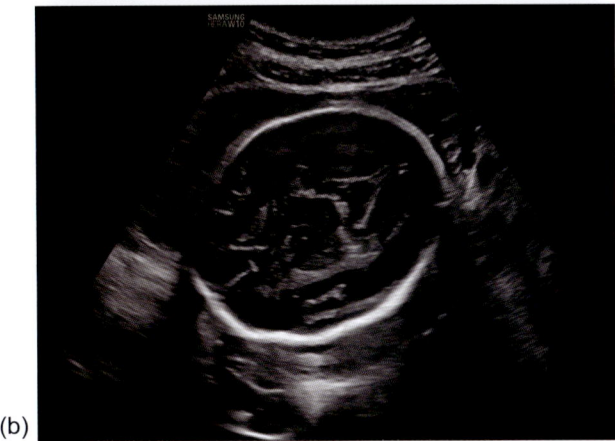

Fig. 21 **Fetal skull image comparing (a) conventional imaging with (b) frequency fusion imaging** *(Courtesy of Samsung: HERA W10 with ShadowHDR™)*

KEY CONCEPT

Frequency fusion entails averaging two or more images created at different frequencies. The benefits are based on the concept that the lower frequency image(s) can provide better penetration whereas the higher frequency image(s) can provide better resolution. By fusing the images together, better texture results than would be produced using only a lower frequency, and better penetration is achieved that would result from using only a higher frequency.

2.6 Image Persistence

Persistence also refers to an "averaging" technique. Like compound imaging, the goal of persistence is to reduce noise thereby giving the appearance of improved SNR. There are two fundamental differences between a persistence technique and a spatial compounding technique:

- The angle is not changed between frames.
- A weighted average is applied to each frame so that newer frames "count" for more than older frames.

The word persistence implies a continued presence. The algorithms for persistence can vary significantly from vendor to vendor. There are two main parameters that are varied:

1. How many frames are averaged together
2. The weighting function applied to each frame

To make this clear, we will consider an example.

High persistence = $0.1 * f_{n-3} + 0.2 * f_{n-2} + 0.3 * f_{n-1} + 0.4 * f_n$

Low persistence = $0.4 * f_{n-1} + 0.6 * f_n$

To understand this example, we will need to define a few terms. Each "f" term represents a frame at a given time. The term (f_n) represents the current frame. Therefore, the term (f_{n-1}), represents the frame just previous to the current frame. The multipliers in front express what percentage of the frame to add to the composite frame. In the "high persistence" example, the current frame is being affected by the previous three frames. The displayed frame will be 10% of the frame which existed three frames previously, plus 20% of the frame which existed two frames previously, plus 30% of the frame just previous, plus 40% of the current frame. In comparison, the low persistence example adds 40% of the previous frame to 60% of the current frame.

As mentioned earlier, there are many different algorithms that can be used to create the effect of persistence. It is not likely that any two companies chose to implement persistence in the same manner. Persistence will become a more important topic when color flow is discussed (see Chapter 7) since persistence is quite commonly employed with color Doppler imaging.

2.7 Spatial Averaging

Spatial averaging is another technique which attempts to reduce random noise through averaging. In contrast to the previous techniques which average data from different frames, spatial averaging looks at small local regions within the same frame. *Figure 22* illustrates this concept.

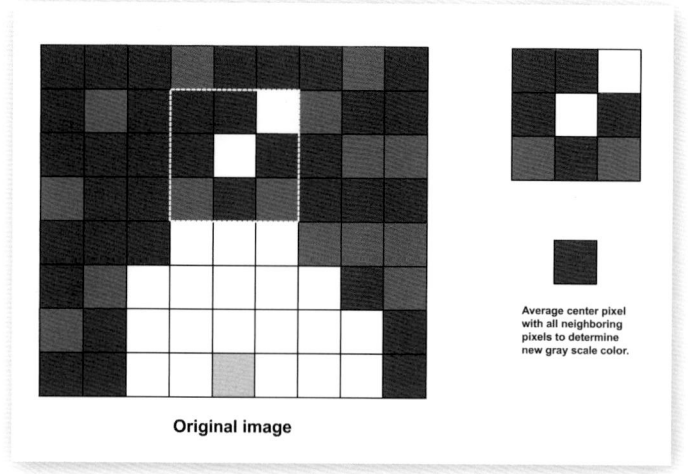

Fig. 22 **"Pre-smoothed" original image**

In *Figure 22*, the "smoothing" algorithm is demonstrated for the pixel in the center of the region enclosed within the dotted white box. The center pixel is averaged with all of the surrounding pixels and re-colorized. Since most of the neighboring pixels are dark, the center pixel is changed from white to a dark gray. This same process is performed pixel-by-pixel across the image, smoothing the image. *Figure 23* represents the smoothed image after averaging is applied to all pixels.

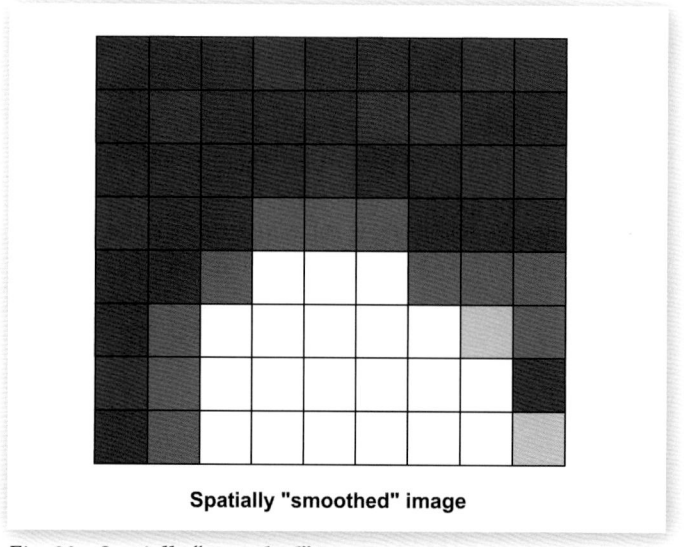

Fig. 23 **Spatially "smoothed" image**

The image appears "less noisy" from the fact that averaging tends to reduce noise. In this case, by adding multiple pixels together, the incoherence of the noise tends to add destructively. In comparison, wherever there is signal, the neighboring pixels are also most likely signal, which add constructively. On many systems, this technique is called spatial smoothing, spatial filtering, or spatial averaging. These spatial averaging techniques have been used in ultrasound for many years, although with improved computing power, much more complex algorithms are now employed.

> **KEY CONCEPT**
>
> Spatial averaging is a method to reduce noise in the image by "smoothing" the data based on neighboring pixels. By averaging a region of pixels together, areas of signal dropout or noise can potentially be reduced or even eliminated.

3. Receive Focusing Techniques

3.1 Continuous Dynamic Receive Focusing

Although conventional imaging can only create a single transmit focus per acoustic line, an infinite number of receive foci are possible. To understand this fact, you must consider the fundamental difference between transmitting a line and receiving a line for 2D imaging. Transmitting is an active, momentary function, whereas receiving is a passive, more continuous, function.

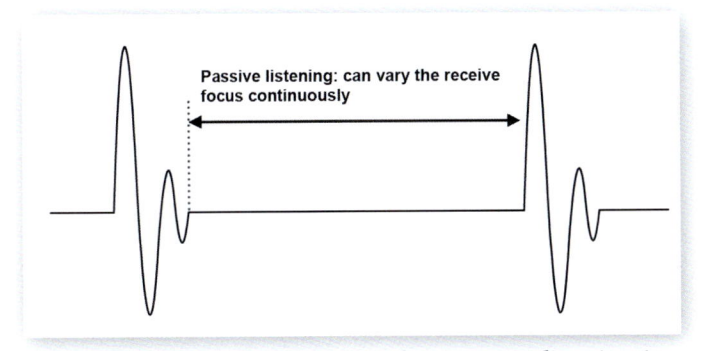

Fig. 24 Continuous focusing occurs during passive listening time

During the pulse duration (transmit period), the system actively dictates the parameters of the wave which propagate into the patient, including the focal depth. For conventional imaging, calculations are performed to vary the timing of the transmit pulse for each element so that a single focus at the depth specified by the user is achieved. Once the waves from each element start traveling within the medium, the system no longer has any control of the wave characteristics. In essence, a process is started in motion, and whatever happens, happens. In comparison, the receiver is turned on as soon as the transmitting ends, and generally remains on until the next transmit event occurs. During the receive time, the system is free to change any receive parameters desired. As a result, it is possible for a system to dynamically change the receive focus based on the depth of the signal returning. For the earliest arriving signals (signals from the shallowest depths), a very shallow receive focus is set. As the signals arrive later in time, the delay profile is changed so that the focus is at the depth of the signal. In this way, the receive beam is as "narrow" as possible, improving the lateral resolution.

Figure 25 demonstrates how dynamic receive focusing is performed. Notice that there are two mechanisms which can be used in conjunction to affect the receive focus: changing the active window of the transducer, and changing the delay profile. At time 1, notice that the effective aperture is very small and the delay profile is very steep. Recall that a small aperture produces a very shallow focus. Also recall that a steep delay profile also results in a shallow focus. At time 2, the aperture is larger and the delay profile is less severe. At time 3, the aperture is even larger and the delay profile is very shallow. Finally, at time 4, the full aperture of the transducer is being used for receive and the delay profile is essentially flat, hence focusing at the natural focus of the transducer.

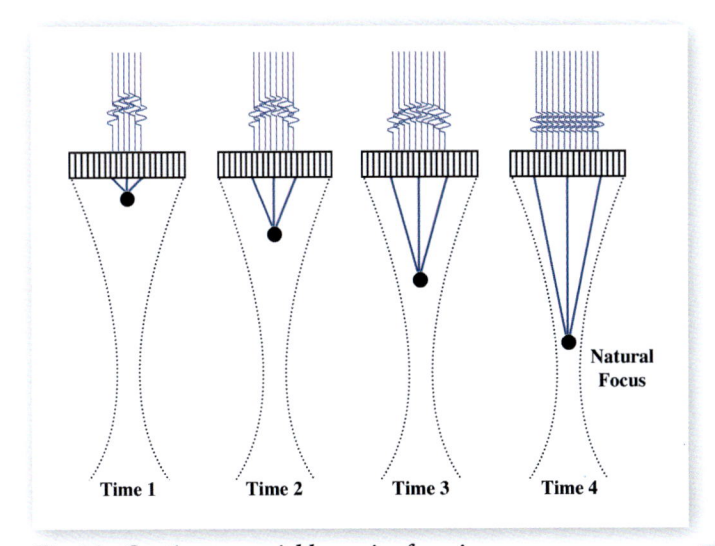

Fig. 25 **Continuous variable receive focusing**

In our demonstration of dynamic receive focus in *Figure 25*, there are four discrete receive foci displayed. In reality, the system can continuously vary the aperture and delays so as to achieve a nearly continuous receive focus. The only trade-off to running continuous receive focusing is that more computing power and processing speed is required. In the earlier years of ultrasound, with analog beamformers, the cost to perform continuous dynamic receive focus was too high. In later years, digital beamformers and improvements in technology have made this increase in "horsepower" inconsequential such that dynamic receive focusing is performed on all systems, all of the time.

4. Effective (Composite) Beam

When we first discussed beam shapes in Chapter 5, we discussed only the transmit beam shape associated with a single focus. That beam had the characteristic "hourglass" shape converging toward and then diverging from the focus. As just discussed, with the advent of digital beamformers with greater processing power, it became possible to create a variable focus receive beam referred to as dynamic receive focusing. Unlike the transmit beam, the receive beam could therefore be in focus at all depths. With a fixed focus transmit, the lateral resolution is detrimentally affected by the transmit beams at

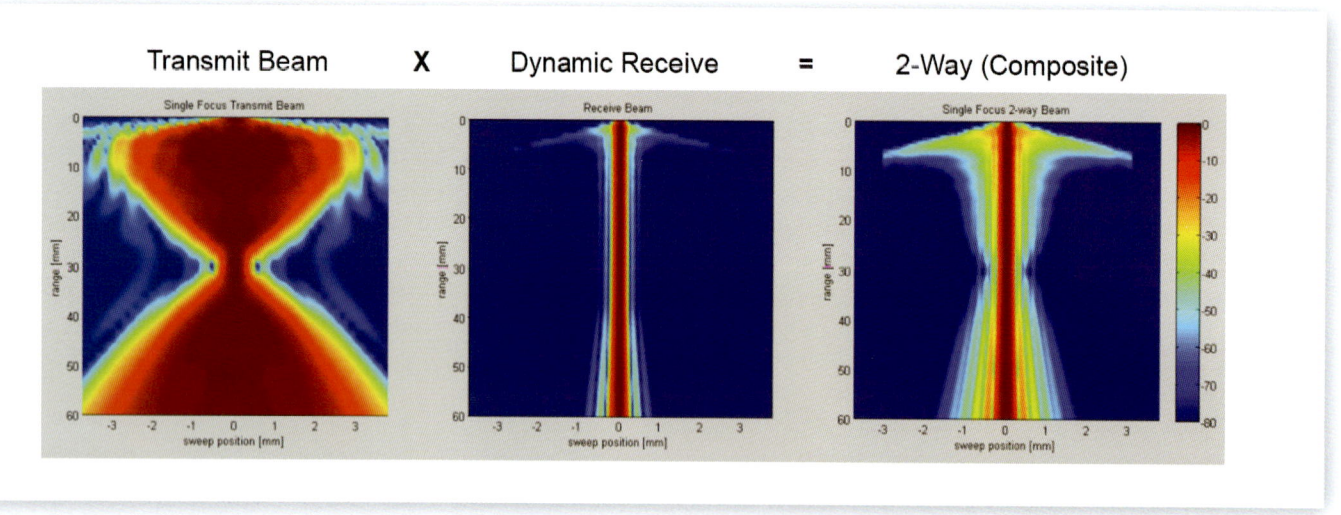

Fig. 26 **Composite (2-way beam) for single focus transmit resulting from the hourglass-shaped single focus transmit beam focused at 3 cm (30 mm) depth combined with the continuous dynamic focus receive beam; note the composite beam is narrowest at the depth of the transmit focus and overall wider than the receive beam, resulting in a degradation in lateral resolution** *(Courtesy of Mindray)*

depths not at or near the focal depth, but improved at all depths by the dynamically received focused beam. Considering the effect of both the transmit and the receive beams simultaneously leads to the concept of the effective, or composite, beam. The effective beam is essentially the mathematical "product" of both the transmit and the receive beams. Therefore, when the transmit and receive beams are both very narrow, the effective beam is very narrow, yielding excellent lateral resolution. When one or both beams become wider, the composite beam becomes wider, resulting in a decrease in lateral resolution. This concept is depicted in *Figure 26*.

The images of *Figure 26* are simulated beam plots which indicate beam intensity. As dictated by the color bar to the right side of the figure, there is an 80 decibel difference between the highest plotted intensities of dark red (labeled 0 dB) and the lowest intensity signal of dark blue (labeled – 80 dB). As we can see from this figure, being able to create a narrower transmit beam would result in a narrower composite beam, improving lateral resolution. The upcoming section will discuss approaches for achieving improved transmit focus.

5. Transmit Focusing Techniques

5.1 Active Single Focus

In Chapter 5, we developed the concept of the classic, hourglass shaped transmit beam. Active single focus is the transmit technique used to create sequential images. For many years, this single focused, relatively narrow beam has been the foundation of diagnostic ultrasound. As shown from the composite beamplot of *Figure 27*, the lateral resolution is best at the transmit focus and degraded at all other depths.

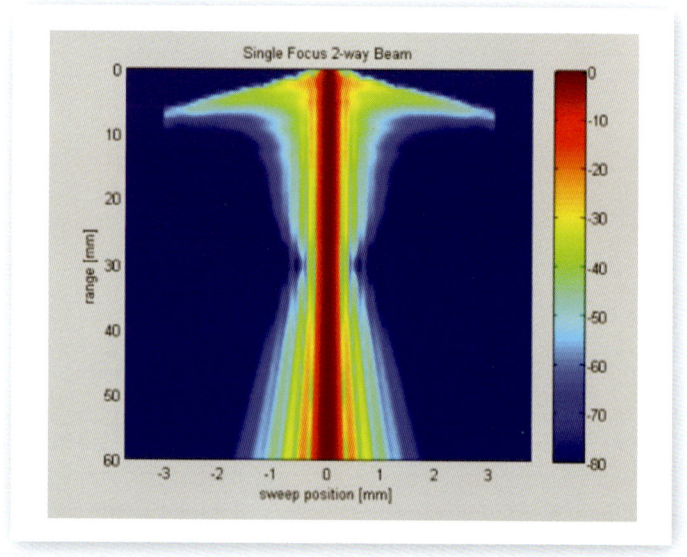

Fig. 27 **Composite (2-way beam) for single focus transmit** *(Courtesy of Mindray)*

Better lateral resolution at a specific depth can be achieved by moving the focal depth up or down in the image. Of course, the consequence of the moving the single focus up or down in the image is that the lateral resolution improves at the depth of the new focal depth and degrades at the depth of the previous focal depth. The biggest drawback to this approach of single active focus is, of course, the fact that only one depth is optimally focused and that there is limited temporal resolution related to the sequential nature of building up images line by line.

5.2 Multiple Transmit Foci

Better lateral resolution than what can be achieved with conventional (single focus) imaging is often required. Multiple transmit foci is an approach to improve lateral resolution by transmitting multiple beams in the same direction with varying focal depths, and then splicing the zone of best resolution from each of the beams together to form one single, effectively, narrower beam.

For phased array transducers, we learned that focusing can be achieved electronically by varying the phase delay to each of the elements of the transmit aperture. For conventional, single pulse transmission, it is only possible to have one focus per acoustic line (transmit). In other words, once the beam starts to diverge within the patient past the focus, there is no way to make the beam physically start to converge again. It is, however, possible to build a display line as the composite of multiple transmits at different times, each with a different focus, as indicated in *Figure 28*.

Referring to *Figure 28*, imagine if the system transmitted and received Transmit 1 with a very shallow focus, but then did not display the received data as the display line. Instead, the system now transmits and receives a second line, Transmit 2, with a deeper focus but in the same direction as Transmit 1. Again, the received data is not displayed. The system then transmits and receives a third line, Transmit 3, with an even deeper focus. The system now has three received lines of data, one short line with a shallow focus, one intermediate line with an intermediate focus, and one deep line with a deep focus. The narrowest portions of each of these three receive beams are then spliced together to form one effectively "narrow" display line. The display line therefore becomes the composite of multiple acoustic lines. In essence, we can think of the transmit line which creates the image as a composite of the multiple foci used to generate the image (in this case three foci). The result is superior lateral resolution as demonstrated by the resulting "Effective Transmit" beam in *Figure 28*.

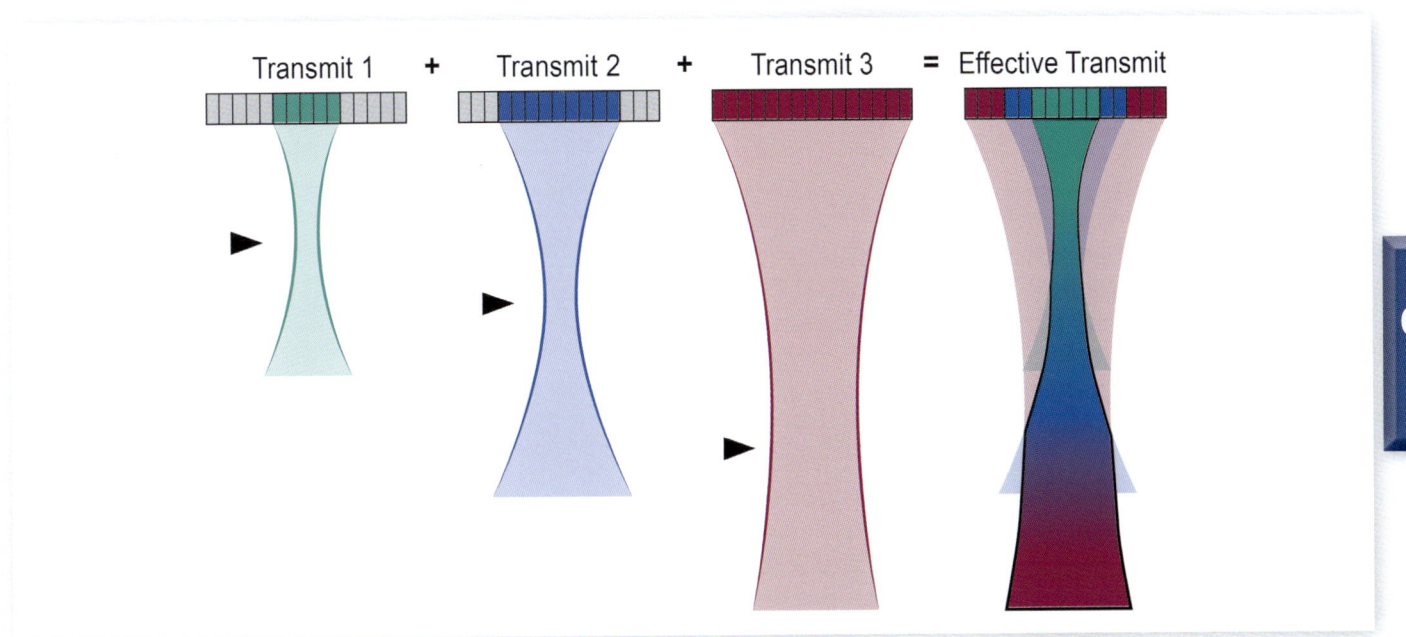

Fig. 28 **Multiple transmit foci**

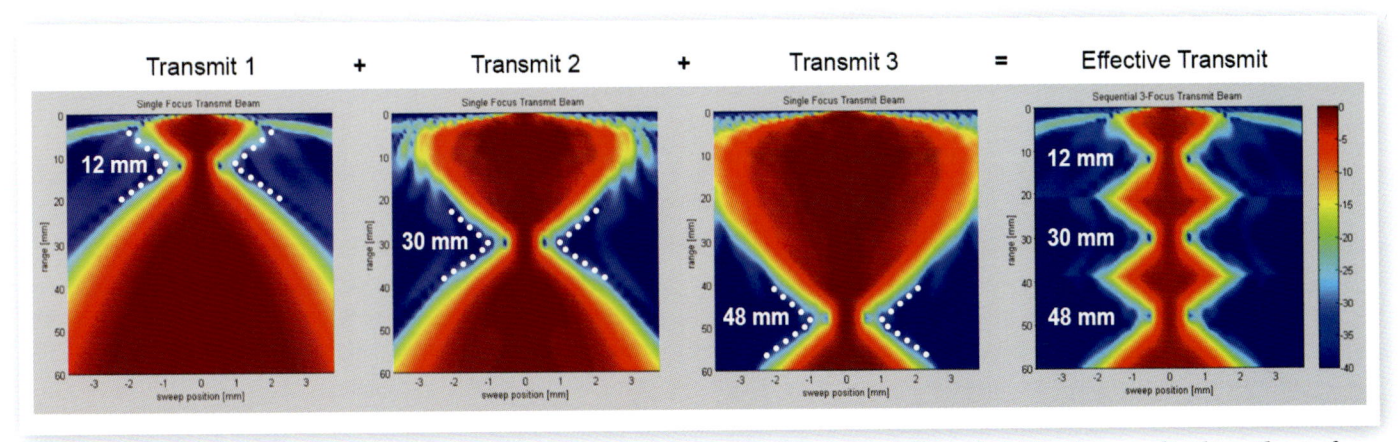

Fig. 29a **Multiple (three) foci composite beam; three separately transmitted beams at different focal depths are spliced together to form the "Effective Transmit" beam** (*Modified from images courtesy of Mindray*)

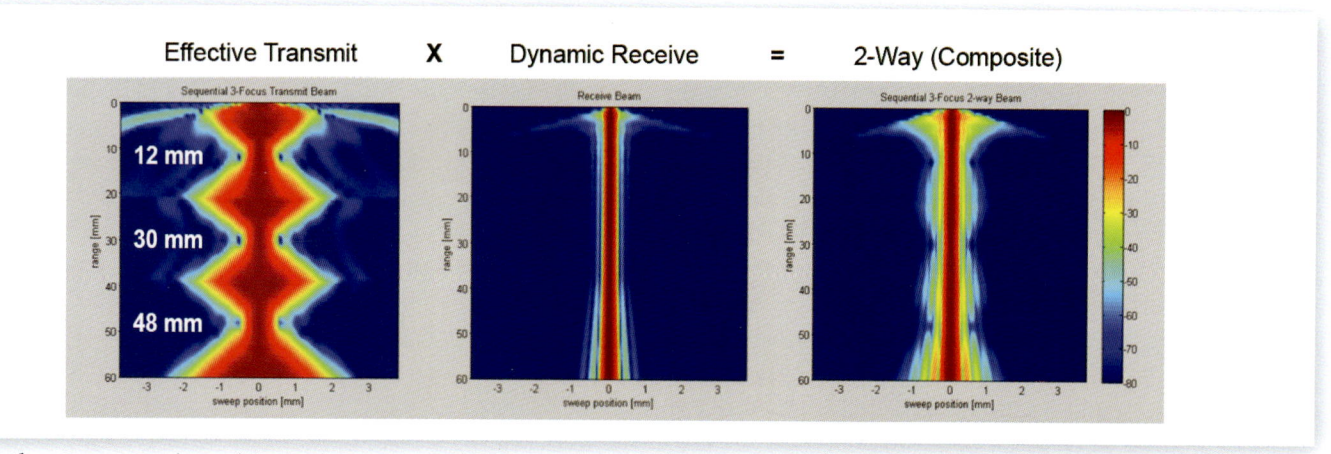

Fig. 29b **Composite (2-way) beam that results from the multi-foci transmit beam and a continuous dynamic focused receive beam** *(Modified from images courtesy of Mindray)*

Figure 29a demonstrates the simulated beam plots of a multi-focal transmit. As shown in *Figure 29b*, we can now create the two-way composite beam and compare the effective overall beam width using the multi-focal approach with the single focus approach. Notice that the two-way composite beam is narrower for the multi-focal beam than for the single focus beam, resulting in the desired improvement in lateral resolution.

Degraded Temporal Resolution

Keeping with the theme that virtually all benefits come at the expense of trade-offs, we can now consider the impact of transmitting multiple beams to generate a single display line of the image. The improved lateral resolution that results from transmitting multiple transmit foci is achieved at the expense of a longer time to create an individual display line, and hence, a longer time to produce an acoustic frame. Since the frame time is the reciprocal of the frame rate (frequency), a longer frame time implies a lower frame rate and a degradation in temporal resolution. Increasing the number of foci, further improves lateral resolution, but at the expense of temporal resolution. Therefore, the use of multiple foci is generally restricted to applications in which temporal resolution is not as critical as improved lateral resolution. For example, breast and liver imaging commonly use as many as eight foci, whereas adult echo generally restricts the maximum foci to two, and pediatric echo rarely, if ever, uses more than one focus.

Clearly, the more transmit foci used, the longer the time to produce a line, and the greater the effect on the temporal resolution. Additionally, deeper multiple foci impact the temporal resolution more than shallower multiple foci. Although the display line time is affected by the number of foci, you cannot simply multiply the standard line time by the number of foci to determine the multiple foci line time; this approach will overestimate the line time, and hence, will overestimate the frame time. The reason for this overestimation is illustrated in *Figure 30*.

With an imaging depth set at 10 cm, with three transmit foci as displayed in *Figure 28*, the time to produce the composite line is clearly not the same as transmitting three 10 cm lines. Since only the very shallowest portion of the first line is being used, there is no sense in receiving signals from the full imaging depth. In this case, the line time is based on receiving signals from the maximum depth of 4 cm. For the second transmit, only the mid-range data is to be used. Again there is no sense in receiving signals from depths that will not be used. In this case, signals are received to the maximum depth of 7 cm before the third line is transmitted. Since the deepest portion of line three is used in the composite line, the entire line time is used.

For completeness, we will perform the calculation to show the difference in line times.

$$\text{Composite time} = \underbrace{\frac{13\,\mu sec}{cm} \times 4\,cm}_{\text{1st Line}} + \underbrace{\frac{13\,\mu sec}{cm} \times 7\,cm}_{\text{2nd Line}} + \underbrace{\frac{13\,\mu sec}{cm} \times 10\,cm}_{\text{3rd Line}}$$

The single line time for a 10 cm line is 130 μsec. In comparison, this composite from three foci requires 273 μsec, significantly more time than a single line, but not nearly three times as much. As more foci are added, more lines are required, and the composite line time increases. Also, as each of the foci are placed lower in the image, the associated transmit line becomes longer, increasing the composite time.

Figure 31 is a multi-focal image of a cyst phantom with tissue mimicking material. Notice that there are nine transmit foci used, producing very good lateral resolution in the midfield. Also note that the resolution in the near field is good, but is not as good as the resolution in the focal region. The improved lateral resolution in the midfield is evident by comparing the "cystic" structures in this region with those of the near field. You should also notice that the resolution degrades past the focus until the cysts are barely identifi-

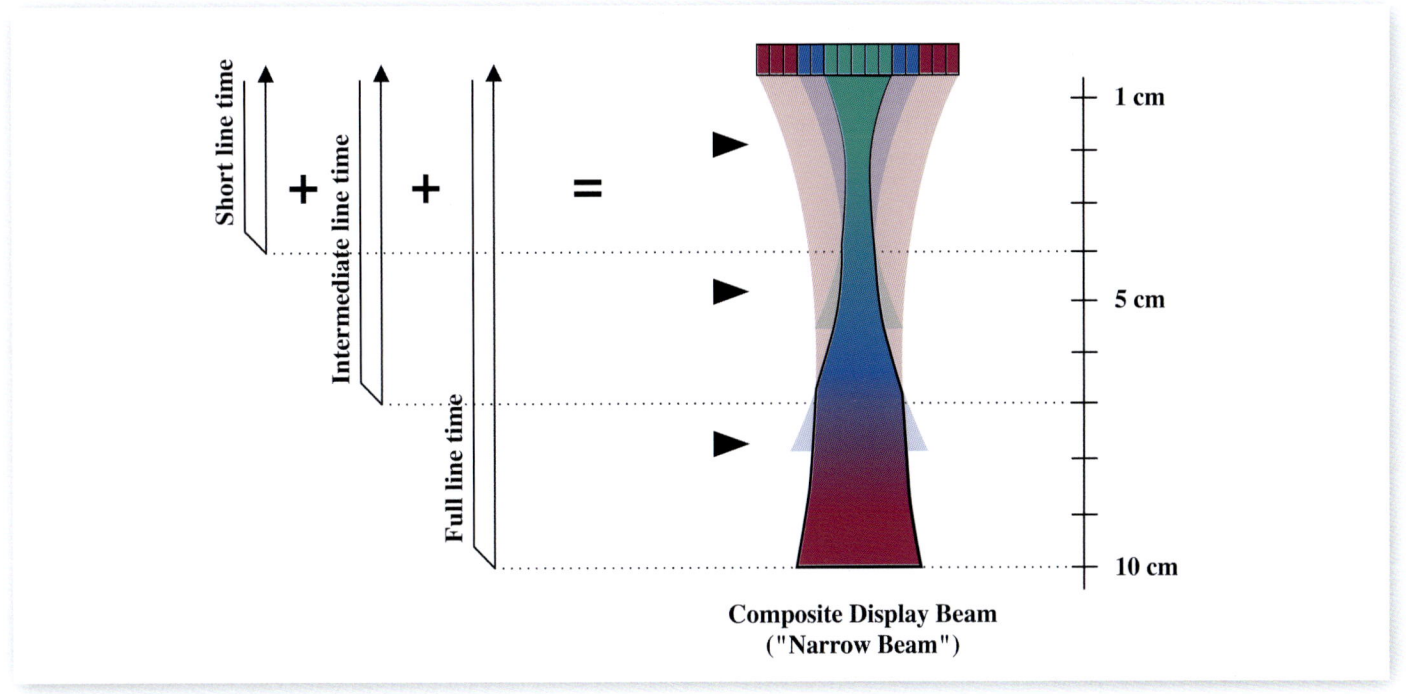

Fig. 30 **Temporal resolution and multiple foci**

able. This degradation at depth is a function of not simply the lack of lateral resolution but also of decreased sensitivity resulting from both attenuation and beam divergence in the far field.

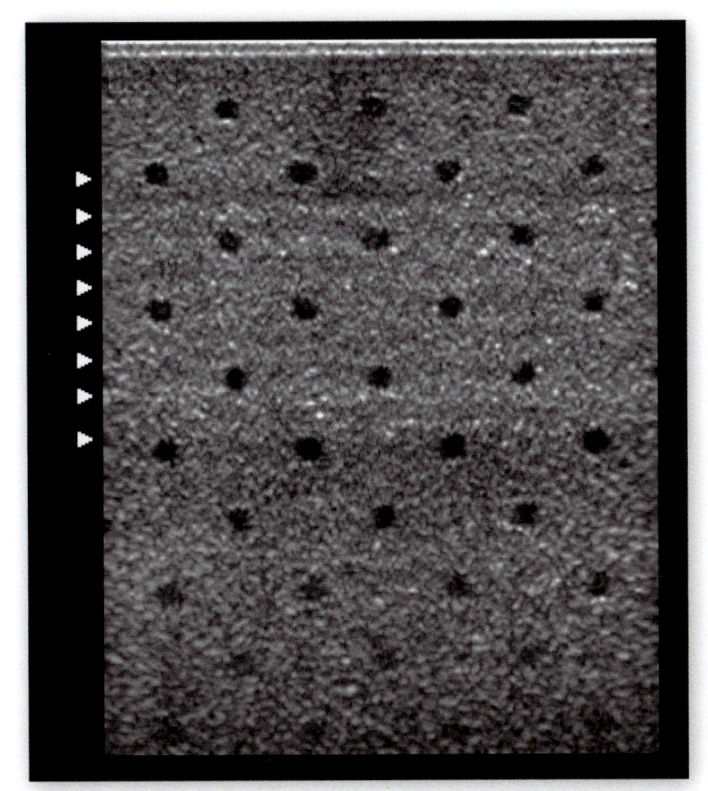

Fig. 31 **Multiple foci image of a phantom displaying "banding" noise**

Banding Noise

Referring to the same cyst phantom image, notice that within the focal region there is some banding which is caused by imperfect fusing of the multiple transmitted lines (brighter echoes stretched laterally across the image). This problem is common with multiple foci. The source of this artifact is related to the change in system parameters that occurs when changing focus. Specifically, setting a deeper focus may increase the number of elements used in the aperture to increase the focal depth and may change the maximum transmit power allowed based on the beam intensity. Changes in either of these parameters will affect the uniformity of the returning echo. Whenever there is a discontinuity in the received echo, there will be a discontinuity in the displayed image.

5.3 Dynamic Transmit Focusing, Retrospective Gating, and Synthetic Aperture

One of the greatest enabling advancements in beamforming has been the ability to perform retrospective dynamic transmit focusing. Dynamic transmit focusing allows for improved lateral resolution as well as allowing for significant improvements in temporal resolution, contrast resolution, and signal-to-noise ratio (increasing penetration). The concept of "retrospectively transmit focusing" is somewhat confusing since the effect is achieved by applying time delays and apodization (amplitude weighting) to received data (not the transmit signal), leading to the question, how is this actually a transmit focusing technique?

The answer to the question relies on a principle taught in Chapter 2: Waves, on which we have relied many times, the concept of linear superposition achieved through constructive and destructive interference. The idea of linear superposition is that you can create a synthetic transmit aperture retrospectively by appropriately adding together signals received at differing times from two or more individual elements (discussed in more detail below).

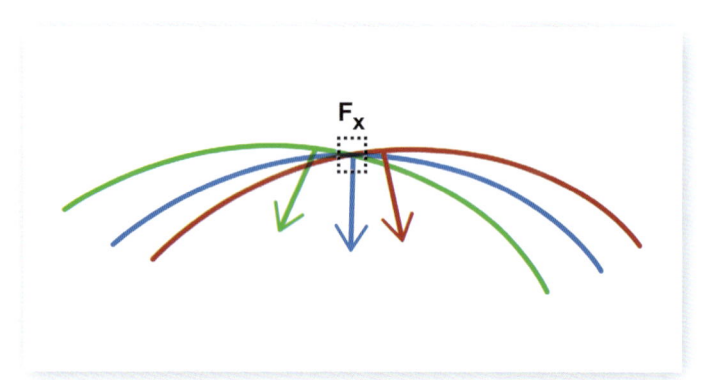

Fig. 32 **Superposition of three wavefronts generated from different apertures at different times; added together, a focused pixel at F_X is generated; note there is no other location at which the wavefronts are coincident (focused) at the same moment in time**

Although there are many different approaches to retrospective transmit focusing, all are based on the idea of storing massive amounts of data received element by element over time, and then, based on a geometric model, retrospectively, adding the signals by basically reversing time. *Figure 33* shows how three wavefronts at different times can be superimposed to focus at two different locations. From this diagram, you can imagine how each focused point in the image would require the superposition of the wavefronts at different times.

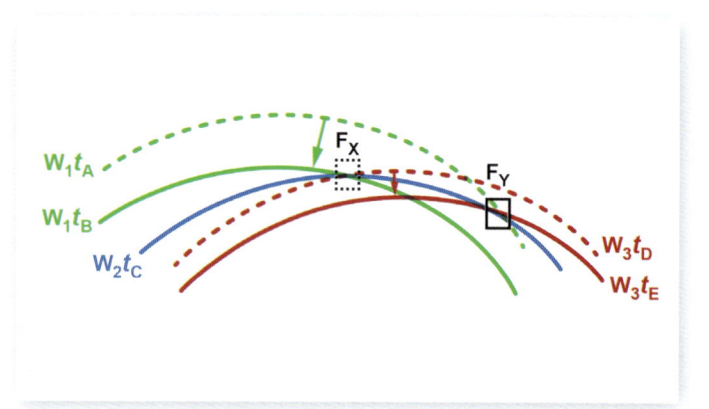

Fig. 33 **Retrospective focusing; focused point F_X results from the superposition of wavefronts $W_1 t_B$, $W_2 t_C$, and $W_3 t_D$; also note at point F_Y these three wavefronts are not coincident, and hence not focused; to achieve focus at F_Y wavefront 1 must be captured earlier in time ($W_1 t_A$), wavefront 2 captured at the same time ($W_2 t_C$), and wavefront 3 captured later in time ($W_3 t_E$)**

By adding together the dynamic transmit focusing technique with the dynamic receive focusing techniques, improved lateral resolution results. Compare the composite beam of *Figure 34* with that of *Figure 29b* for multi-focal transmit, and *Figure 26* for single transmit focus. Notice that the composite beam is narrower, implying improved lateral resolution.

The result of dynamic transmit and dynamic receive focus together can result in significantly better lateral resolution as seen in *Figure 35* which compares phantom images using conventional single line focus with dynamic receive focus (a) and both dynamic transmit and receive focus (b).

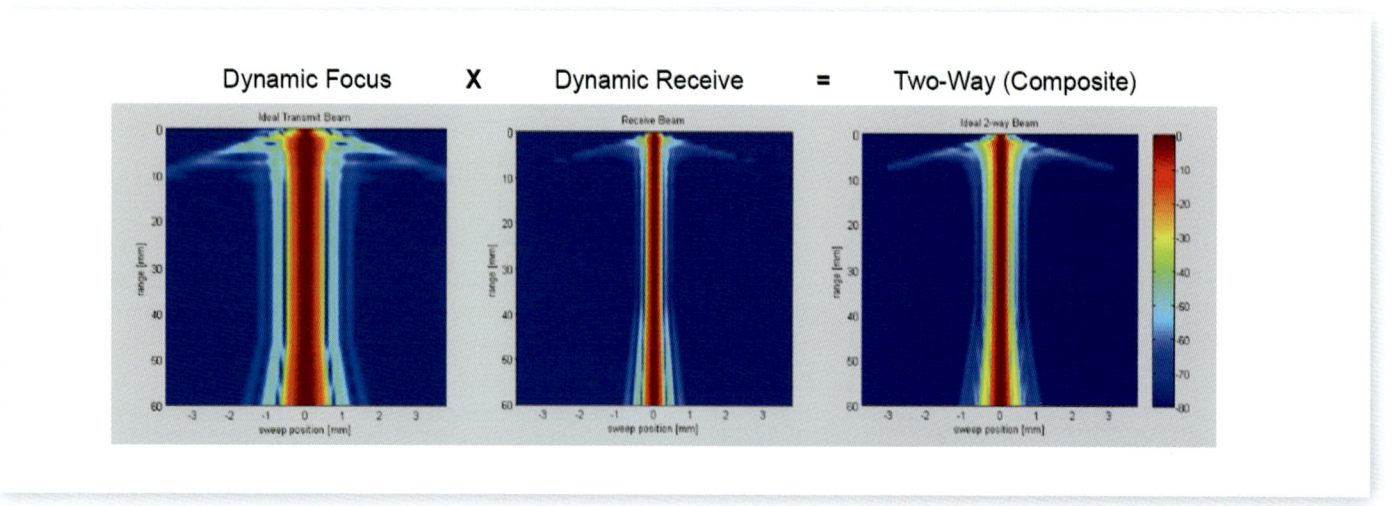

Fig. 34 **Ideal beamplot showing effect of dynamic transmit and dynamic receive focus resulting in a narrower composite beam with improved lateral resolution** *(Modified from images courtesy of Mindray)*

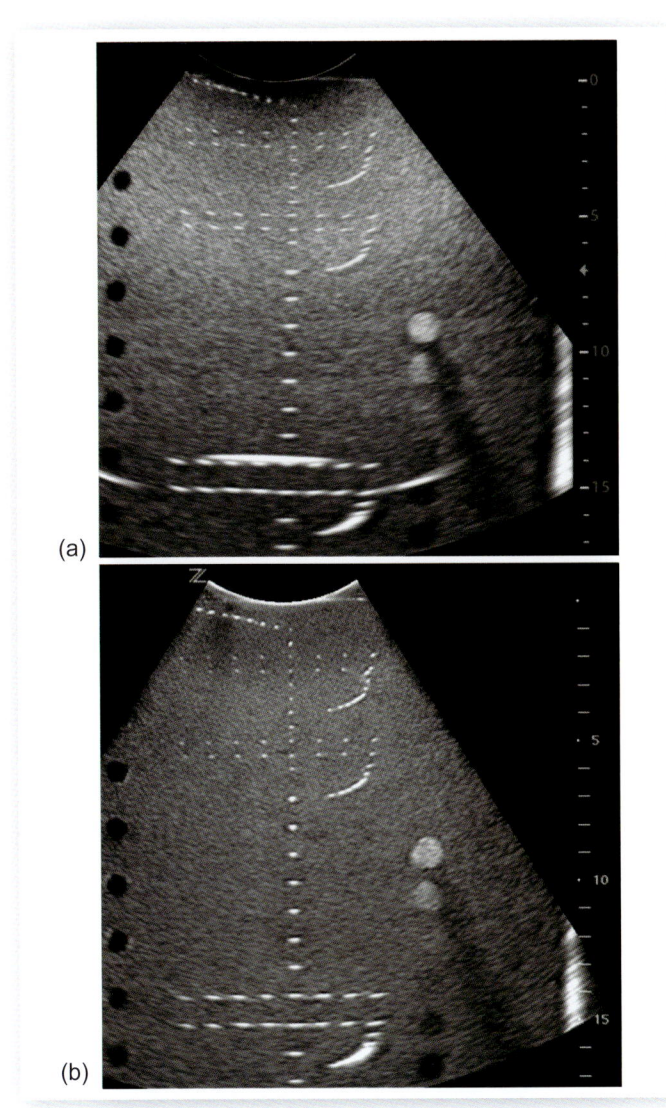

Fig. 35 **Single versus dynamic transmit focus; image (a) uses conventional imaging with a single transmit focus per line and dynamic focusing on receive; image (b) uses dynamic transmit and receive focusing, resulting in superior lateral resolution** *(Courtesy of Mindray)*

Synthetic Aperture and How it Works

The term "synthetic aperture" refers to the "effective" aperture created by adding signals from individual elements. The synthetic aperture is the equivalent aperture that results from including each of the summed individual elements. We learned in Chapter 4 about Huygens' principle and the idea of how spherical waves from different elements can add to create a stronger beam. The idea behind synthetic aperture is that instead of transmitting each of the individual wavelets at the same time and allowing them to physically interact in the body, the same effect can be generated by adding each of the individual wavelets that were transmitted separately. In this way, the aperture that would generate the super-positioned signal is synthetically created by adding the individual components together. In essence, by adding the appropriately time delayed and amplitude weighted signals from each of the individual elements activated at different times, each pixel of the image can be "focused" as if the transmit had originally been focused at that specific location.

Different Synthetic Aperture Approaches

The original theory of synthetic aperture is that a single element would be used for transmit and then all of the elements of the array used for receive. This approach would result in an image of the entire scan region, but with poor SNR since the transmit power would necessarily be so much less than the transmit power that results from using a large aperture. However, each of the other elements could then be used sequentially and each of the resulting full images averaged together to produce an image with very good SNR. Although this approach works, there is the obvious drawback of limited temporal resolution. This fact then led to the idea of using a virtual source with more than one element in the subaperture comprising the synthetic aperture. For this approach, a point is chosen as the effective point source relative to the transmitting array. There are three basic approaches when used:

- Focused waves (virtual source in front of the array)
- Plane waves (virtual source at infinity)
- Diverging waves (virtual source behind the array)

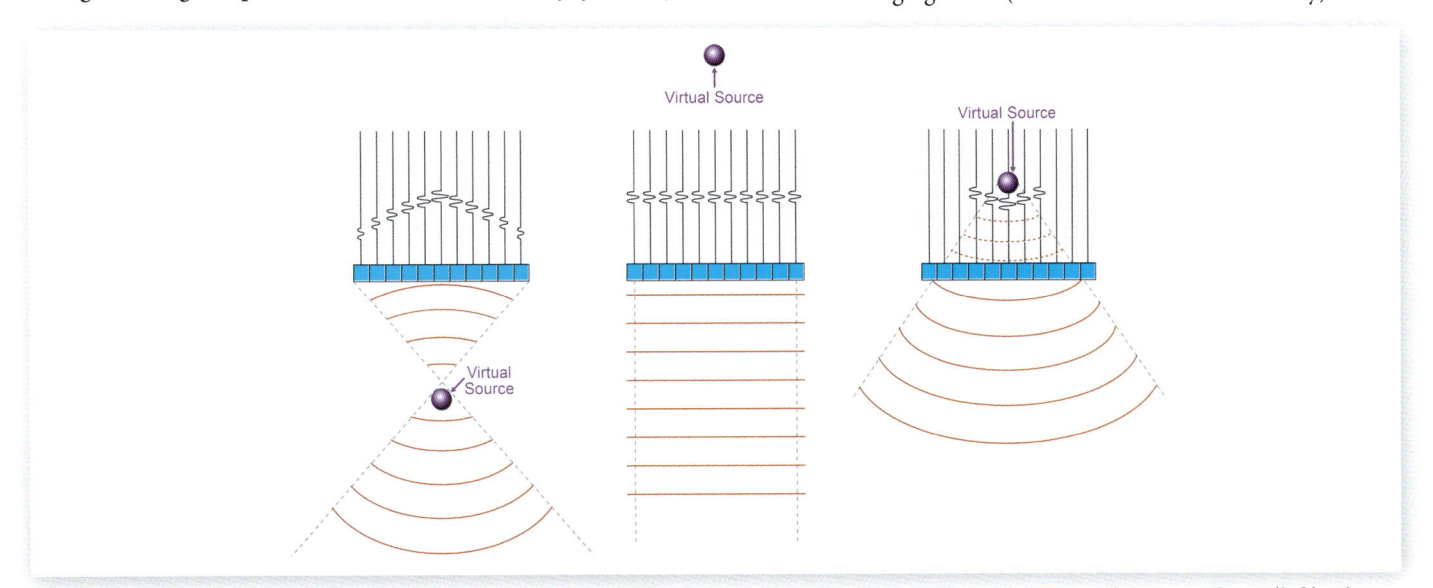

Fig. 36 **Three geometric approaches to retrospective focusing; focused waves with virtual source in front of the transducer (left), plane wave imaging with virtual source at infinity (middle), and diverging waves for which the virtual source is behind the phased array (right)**

Note that time delays are calculated relative to path length differences to the focal point when the virtual source is in front of the transducer.

To achieve the transmit focus, the beamformer then must apply varying delays to effectively remove the path length differences from each element to the specific virtual source point. By also applying the time delays for the dynamic receive focusing, the image is now focused both on transmit and receive.

The following figure illustrates how multiple elements can be used to create synthetic apertures with diverging waves (virtual focus behind the array). Each dot represents the focused received data for each of the synthetic apertures used. We can see that there is an overlap between the corresponding wavefronts of the five apertures used along the center line. By using a weighted summation of the data from each of the 5 points shown, the data at the black point is retrospectively transmit focused.

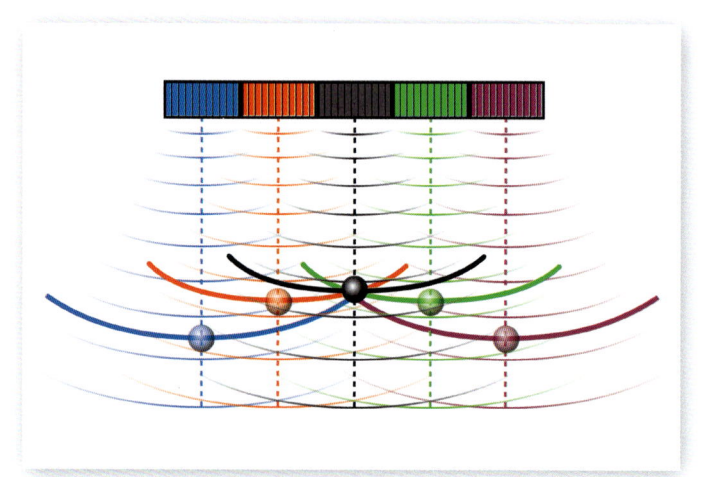

Fig. 37 **Synthetic aperture imaging with virtual focus behind the array to create diverging waves**

Notice, in *Figure 37*, the overlap between the five bold wavefronts coincident at the center of the image (black dot). By storing the signal over time from every location for each aperture, a summing can take place, resulting in a retrospective transmit focusing.

KEY CONCEPT

For conventional transmitting pulses, only one focus can be achieved per transmit. Multiple transmit foci are created by sequentially transmitting beams with different focal depths in the same direction and then splicing the best resolution data from each beam to form one effectively narrower beam. The result is improved lateral resolution at the expense of frame time, hence degrading temporal resolution. Multiple transmit foci should not be used in very dynamic imaging situations such as when viewing a pediatric heart.

6. Image Generation Techniques and Trade-Offs

6.1 Sequential (Single Line Transmit and Single Line Receive)

Although we have already discussed the technique of generating images sequentially using a single transmit focus per line, we will again review the methodology for a few reasons. First, we will look at the approach with respect to the limitations instead of just what it provides. Second, recapitulating the technique here gives context to how each of the other image generation approaches differ, both in terms of the specific image generation methodology and in terms of the limitations and trade-offs.

In Chapter 5, Part I, we learned about sequential image generation, a technique that has dominated clinical ultrasound for the last four to five decades. A single focused beam is transmitted, and a single line is received. The beam is then pointed in a new direction (either by sequencing, phasing, or both) and another line is produced. This sequential process is repeated until the entire field of view (specified by the scan region set by the user) is insonified, creating a single frame. The process is then repeated to produce each successive frame. This sequential approach to image generation requires very complex phase delay control to steer and focus beams both on transmit and on receive. The benefit of this tried and true imaging approach is relatively good spatial and contrast detail.

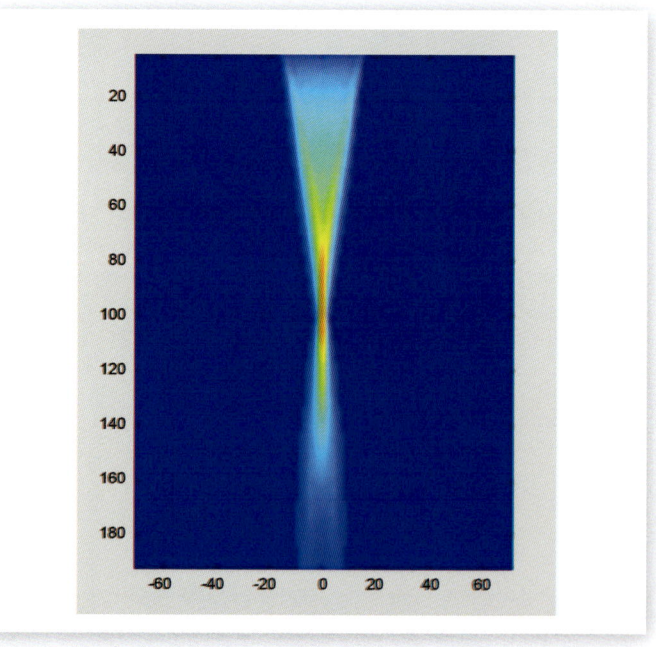

Fig. 38 **Single focus beam used for conventional sequential image generation; note the high intensity and narrower beam width at and near the focus, with lower intensities and wider beam width in the near and far field** *(Courtesy of Verasonics)*

View ONLINE Animation and Image Library

For many years, sequential image generation was generally considered adequate for ultrasound imaging. Because of the relatively high speed of sound in tissue (1540 m/sec on average), a collection of acoustic lines could be transmitted and received over the region of interest quickly enough so as to appear real time. As discussed in Chapters 4, 5, and 6: Part 1, temporal resolution is a measure of the ability to accurately detect changes that occur over time. For ultrasound, the temporal resolution is primarily determined by the rate at which images can be generated (assuming the display monitor can keep up with the acoustic frame rate).

The first ultrasound modality that routinely was limited by inadequate temporal resolution was color Doppler. As you will learn in more detail in Chapter 7, color Doppler requires transmitting multiple acoustic lines to create a single color display line. As a result, the time to create a color frame is significantly higher than the time to generate a basic 2D image of the same size. As we learned earlier, time and frequency are reciprocals, implying that a higher frame time, implies a lower frame rate. Since color Doppler often suffers from poor temporal resolution, the user has always been obligated with knowing the parameters that most significantly impact the frame time so that the frame rate could be optimized.

Other imaging modalities besides color Doppler, that similarly rely on creating a single image from more than a single transmit event, also suffer temporal resolution issues. These modalities, such as multiple transmit foci, compound imaging, and strain imaging, also require specific optimization skills from the sonographer generating the image and specific understanding by those interpreting the images. But even standard 2D imaging can be impacted by limited temporal resolution as discussed in the next section.

As shown in previous chapters, optimizing ultrasound is about trade-offs. Usually, to improve one imaging characteristic, another characteristic must be sacrificed. For this reason, ultrasound practitioners need to understand all of the parameters of ultrasound, the associated physics, and the consequences as well as the advantages of changing system parameters. One of the classic trade-offs is between field of view (image size), spatial resolution, and temporal resolution.

As discussed in Section 1.1, since for sequentially generated images, the time to create a frame is linearly related to the number of transmit lines, the only way to increase frame rate with sequential image generation is to decrease the number of transmitted lines. To increase the frame rate for sequential imaging, either the field of view can be decreased or the line density can be decreased. The decreased FOV has the obvious disadvantage of appreciating a smaller region of the anatomy. Decreasing the line density requires transmitting and receiving wider beams. Wider beams result in a degradation in lateral resolution; so the trade-off with line density is between lateral and temporal resolution.

Given the temporal resolution limitation and the associated trade-offs to improve temporal resolution with conventional sequential imaging, other approaches need to be considered.

We have briefly made mention of other techniques in which there is not a one-to-one correlation between the acoustic lines transmitted and the lines displayed, the most obvious of which is color Doppler, discussed thoroughly in Chapter 7. With respect to 2D imaging, there are now many different image generation techniques that do not follow the simple rule of one display line per one transmit event. With technological advancements, ideas to overcome the associated limitations that have existed for many years have now become feasible. These new techniques result in many new advantages, and almost certainly, new trade-offs. The upcoming sections discuss the many different ways of producing an image, revealing both the associated advantages and disadvantages. As you study about each approach, think about the trade-offs involved and the desired benefit serving as the underlying motivation. A table is included at the end of the section to summarize this very complex topic.

6.2 Ultrafast Imaging: General
Ultrafast imaging refers to any image generation methodology which results in significantly faster frame rates than conventional, sequential image generation. Whereas sequentially generated 2D frame rates are generally below 100 Hz (frames per second), ultrafast image techniques result in frame rates frequently in the kHz range (as much as 100 times faster). The path to achieving higher frame rates is complex and involves many image generation techniques, combining many of the concepts we have learned throughout this chapter.

6.3 Multi-Line Acquisition (MLA)
6.3.1 General
Multi-line acquisition (MLA) refers to any imaging technique for which more than one receive line is generated simultaneously. MLA techniques have been in existence for many years but in recent years have significantly benefited from technology advancements such as increased processing speed and dynamic focusing techniques.

6.3.2 Parallel Processing
In an effort to increase frame rate and improve temporal resolution, the concept of parallel processing was created. The concept is relatively simple. Instead of transmitting very narrow beams from which a single receive beam is generated, a wider transmit is generating and more than one receive beam is created. By receiving more than one beam simultaneously, fewer transmits are required to scan the same field of view, reducing the frame time and improving temporal resolution. The first parallel processing system was released between 1990 and 1991. As a designer of the hardware for the parallel receive channels, I have intimate knowledge of the difficulties that had to

be overcome. This early system allowed for two receive beams from one transmit beam.

As illustrated in *Figure 39*, the transmit beam is produced slightly wider than normal. When receiving the data, the transducer is electronically divided into two parallel groups of receiver channels and associated elements. One group of channels is dedicated to receiving, processing and beamforming one beam, while the other group simultaneously processes and forms the second beam. These two simultaneous receive beams must then be sent to the back end for scan conversion and display. A second transmit is then steered in the next required direction of the scan and the process repeated. As a result of this parallel processing, twice as many receive beams are generated in the time required to transmit the same number of acoustic beams, thereby doubling the imaging frame rate.

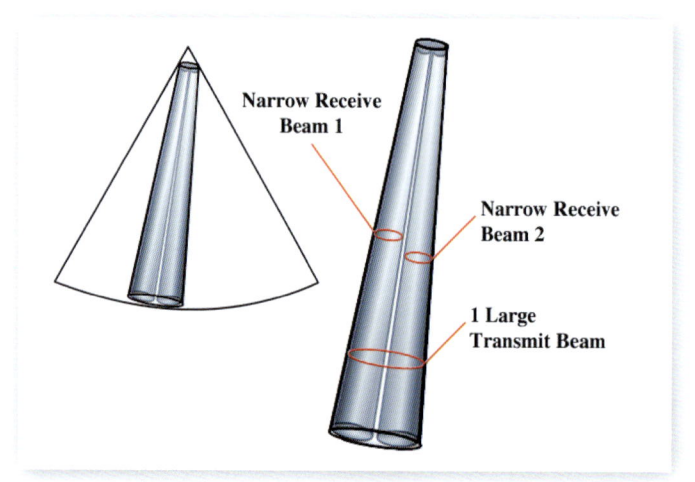

Fig. 39 **Multiple (two in this case) receive beams per transmitted beam (parallel processing)**

The early system was designed to work only for color Doppler, since color Doppler generally has the worst temporal resolution of the sequentially generated modalities. One of the difficulties was making sure that the two receive channels were perfectly balanced so that the color Doppler image was uniform and did not look striped (referred to as a grouping or "corduroy" artifact).

The concept of parallel processing was extended beyond the initial approach. Whereas initial parallel processing involved creating two received beams from one wider transmitted beam, more advanced parallel processing progressed to four or more received beams per transmit. This increase in the simultaneous number of received beams (increasing frame rate) of course came at the expense of losing the benefits that result from transmitting with a narrower beam, namely, some lateral resolution. The decreased lateral resolution is the consequence of the wider transmit beam which results in a wider effective (2-way composite) beam, as shown in *Figure 40*. In these initial systems, the ability to parallel process required duplicated hardware channels to form the parallel receive beams. This increase in hardware channels resulted in increased complexity and cost. With the introduction of digital beamformers with greater processing power, the processing could be performed without replicating entire portions of the system.

The other issue related to MLA image generation is the existence of grouping artifacts. As shown in *Figure 41*, the beams generated from the lateral aspects of the wider transmit beam have an overall lower intensity than the beams generated from the more central portion of the beam. The result is lower sensitivity that appears in bands in the image, separated by the width of the parallel processing groupings.

Notice, in *Figure 41*, the intensity of the beams generated by the lateral aspect of the unfocused beam (R_1 and R_8) is significantly lower than the intensity of the beams generated by the more central portion of the beam. The result will be the appearance of non-uniform brightness in the image associated with each group of receive beams.

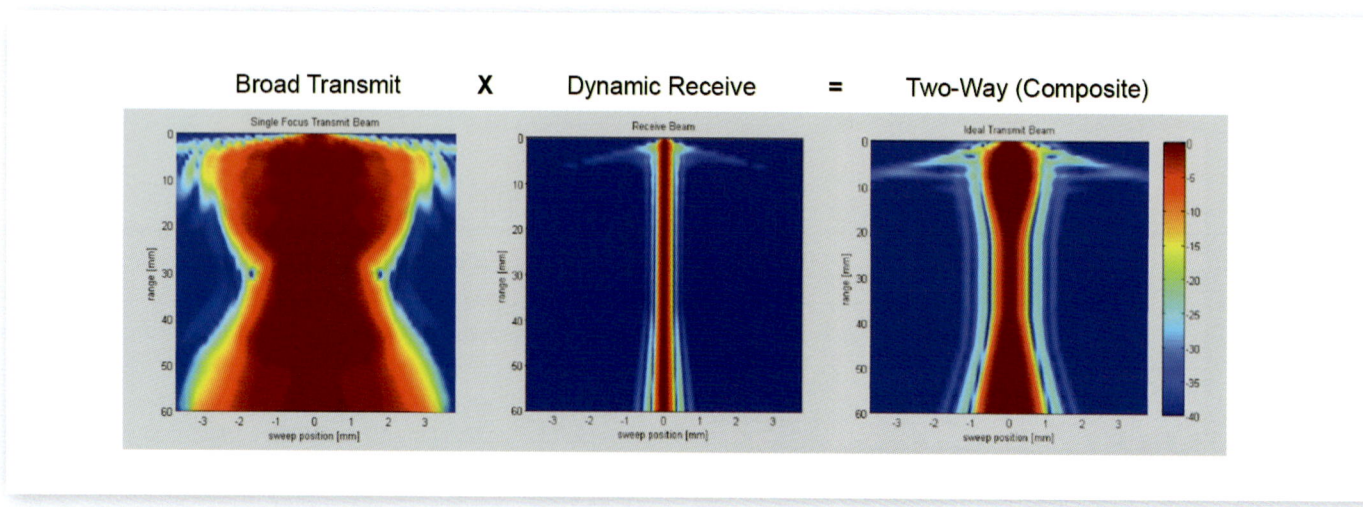

Fig. 40 **Effect of a non-focused wide transmit beam on the composite beam and lateral resolution; note the dynamic receive focus improves lateral resolution, but the effective beam is still relatively wide** *(Modified from images courtesy of Mindray)*

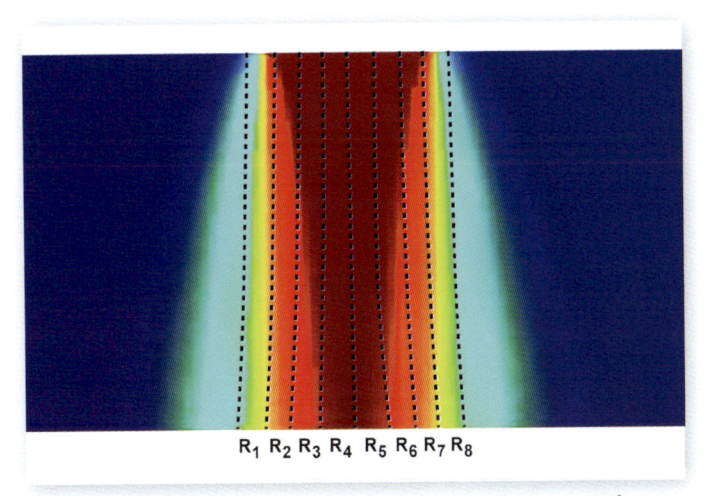

Fig. 41 Unfocused transmit and the creation of group artifact

> **KEY CONCEPT**
>
> The technique of parallel processing is based on transmitting a "fatter" than normal beam and then receiving and processing the data simultaneously over the wider zone as multiple beams. Since more than one beam is received and processed at the same time, scanning a region can be completed more quickly, increasing the frame rate.

6.3.3 Zone Imaging

With the increase in processing speed came the ability to perform even higher order parallel processing. The concept was to convert the signal earlier in the path so that the beamforming could be achieved completely on digital data. Digital beamforming with fast enough processors meant that complex, multiple hardware channels were no longer needed to create parallel receive beams. Ultimately, this approach led to transmitting very wide beams, referred to as zones, and receiving many more beams simultaneously. Not surprisingly, this approach was referred to as "zone" imaging and was first released by Zonare, now part of Mindray. With zone imaging there is no longer a transmit focus. With zone imaging, frame rates increased significantly, often as much as fifteen fold. Today, there are multiple systems that now use the concept of "zone" imaging. For these systems, you will not see a transmit focus on the image, and generally recognize higher imaging frame rates (than what is achieved by systems that are still using focal techniques on transmitted beams). As mentioned, the downside to using wider transmit beams is a loss in lateral resolution which results from the wider transmitted beam.

Many systems now perform dynamic, retrospective transmit focusing (as discussed in Section 5.3) to overcome the lateral resolution limitation which otherwise would result from creating a very wide (zone) transmit beam. In conjunction with dynamic receive focusing, the two-way beam is very narrow and approaches an ideal beamwidth.

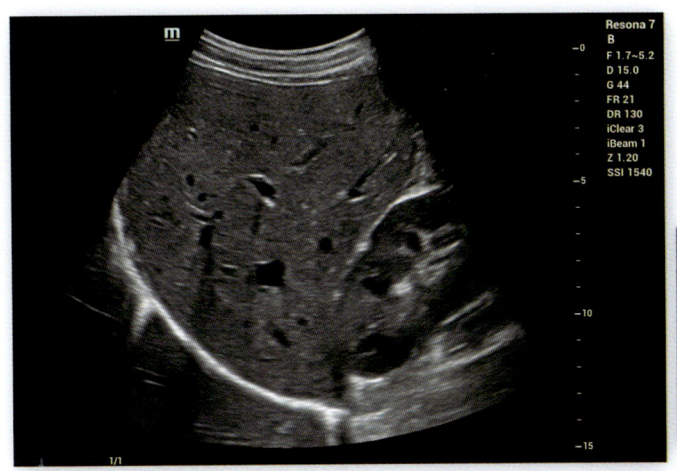

Fig. 43 **Zone image of the right lobe of a normal liver and right kidney using dynamic retrospective transmit focusing resulting in good detail of structures both in the near and far field; note there is no focal zone indicated** *(Courtesy of Mindray)*

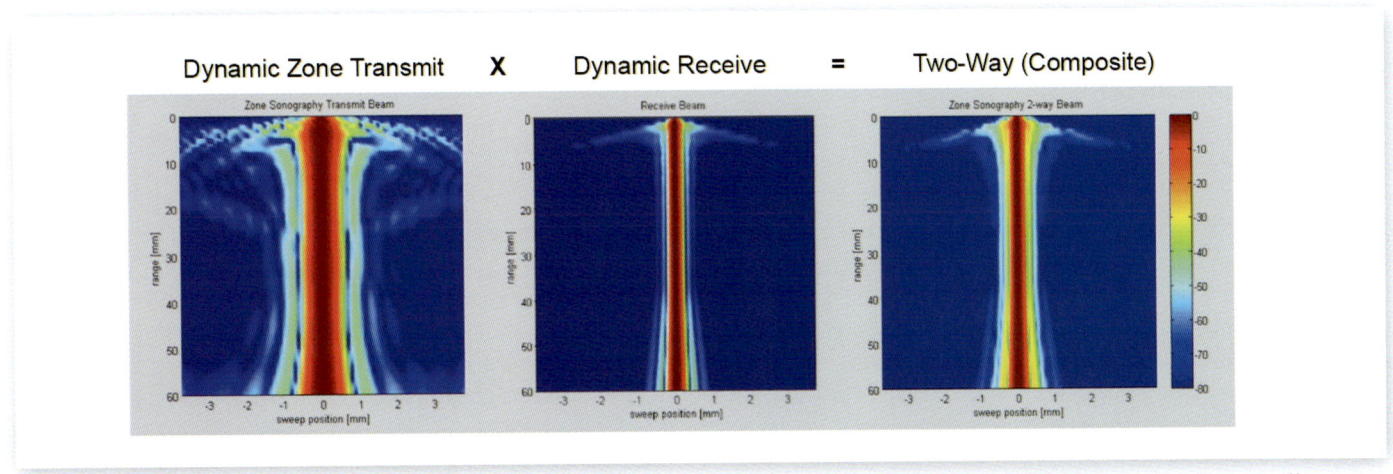

Fig. 42 **Composite beam which results from a dynamic retrospective focusing of a broad beam transmit (zone) and a dynamically receive focused beam** *(Courtesy of Mindray)*

6.4 Multi-Line Transmit (MLT)

Whereas MLA refers to multiple simultaneous receive lines (acquisition), multi-line transmit (MLT) refers to multiple simultaneously transmitted lines. The concept of MLT is that the temporal resolution can be improved by transmitting multiple lines in different locations at the same time. After receiving the echoes from the multiple transmitted lines, the next group of lines is transmitted and received (as shown in *Figure 44*). The sequence is repeated until the entire image is scanned and the process is started over.

Figure 44 shows an example in which four beams are transmitted simultaneously resulting in four zones in the image. The result is that the frame time is decreased by a factor of four, increasing the frame rate by a factor of four.

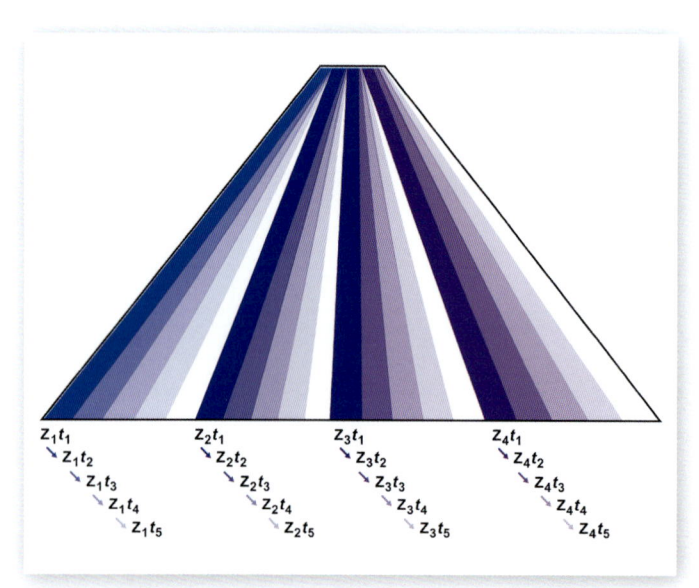

Fig. 44 **Multi-line transmit with four lines transmitted simultaneously; note that in this example each zone is comprised of five transmit events (t_1 through t_5)**

One of the greatest challenges with MLT image generation is the suppression of crosstalk between the simultaneous beams. Applying apodization on the dynamic transmit and receive focusing helps reduce some of the crosstalk and grating lobes but negatively impacts lateral resolution. There are digital beamforming approaches used to reduce the issue of crosstalk and grating lobes, but these approaches are beyond the scope of this book.

Of course, all MLT approaches require that there be multiple lines acquired simultaneously. It is also possible to simultaneously transmit multiple broader beams, receive more than one beam per transmit (MLA of each MLT beam) and employ dynamic retrospective focusing so as to further increase the frame rate.

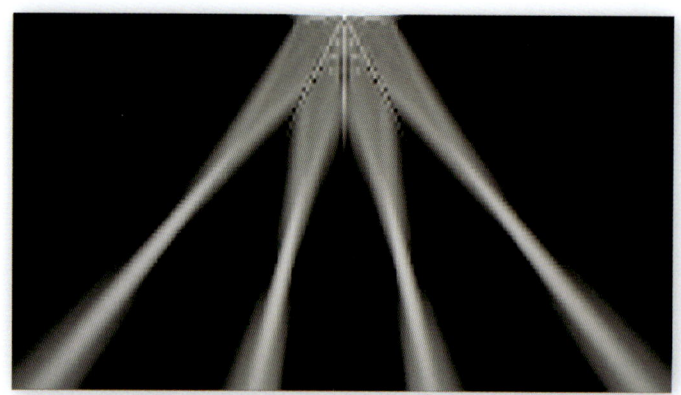

Fig. 45 **MLT beamplot with four simultaneously transmitted beams** *(Courtesy of MDPI Journal of Applied Sciences)*

6.5 Plane Wave and Diverging Wave

The idea of creating images from transmitted plane waves is certainly not new, but really only became feasible with dramatic increases in processing speeds and data storage. The idea is straightforward: send out a single plane wave to insonify the entire region of interest and then receive in parallel as many beams as desired to constitute an image. This approach became practical with the development of powerful general processing units (GPU's) commonly used in the gaming industry. The concept of creating an entire image from a single transmitted plane wave is illustrated in *Figure 46* and better appreciated by watching the corresponding animation.

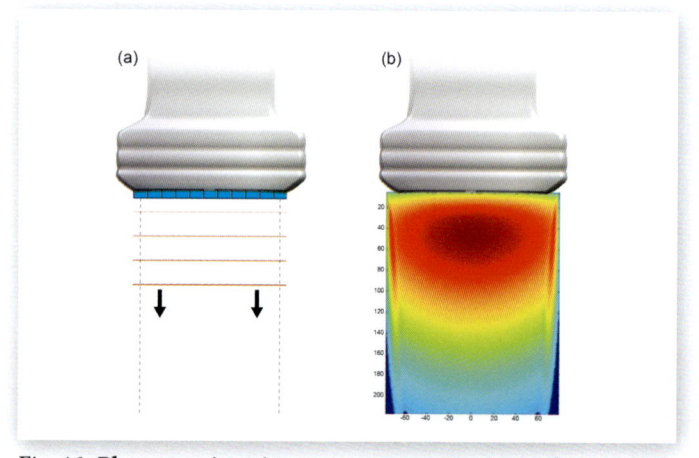

Fig. 46 **Plane wave imaging generates an entire image from a single transmit event, resulting in extremely high frame rates (ultrafast imaging); schematic drawing (a) and simulated beamplot showing acoustic pressure field of a plane wave (b)**

Using a transmitted plane or diverging wave, an entire image can be generated in the time it takes to create a single line of conventional, sequential ultrasound with a single transmit focus. Employing plane/diverging waves with ultrafast processing results in extraordinarily high frame rates relative to what has been standard in ultrasound. For example, at an imaging depth of 8 cm, an entire image can be generated in 104 microseconds, resulting in a frame rate of almost 10 kHz (as shown in the calculation below):

$$Planar_{FT} = 13\,\frac{\mu sec}{cm} \times 8\,\frac{cm}{frame} = 104\,\frac{\mu sec}{frame}$$

$$\Rightarrow Frame\ Rate = \frac{1}{104}\,\frac{frames}{\mu sec} \approx 0.096\ MHz = 9.6\ kHz$$

For comparison with conventional ultrasound built up line by line, we will do the calculation assuming the same imaging depth of 8 cm and making the very reasonable assumption of an image width that requires 300 transmitted beams to constitute a single frame.

$$Conventional_{FT} = 13\,\frac{\mu sec}{cm} \times 8\,\frac{cm}{line} \times 300\,\frac{lines}{frame} = 31{,}200\,\frac{\mu sec}{frame} = 31.2\,\frac{m\,sec}{frame}$$

$$\Rightarrow Frame\ Rate = \frac{1}{31.2}\,\frac{frames}{m\,sec} \approx 0.032\ kHz = 32\ Hz$$

Not surprisingly, if a single plane/diverging wave is used to create an entire image, the frame rate would be 300 times faster than an image created using 300 consecutive transmits.

The problem with using a single plane/diverging wave to create an image is that there is a loss in detail and contrast resolution. This loss results from not having a focused transmit beam. The comparison images of *Figure 47* demonstrate the degradation that results from a single plane wave in contrast with a conventionally generated image. As you can see, the extremely high frame rate comes at the expense of desired image quality.

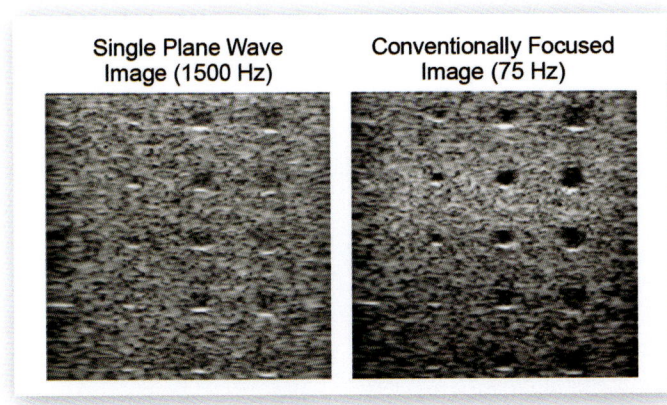

Fig. 47 **Comparison of 4 cm deep plane wave image of an imaging phantom with conventionally focused sequential image; the frame rate of the plane wave image is 1500 Hz versus 75 Hz; note the increased frame rate is a trade-off in contrast and sensitivity** *(Courtesy of Intechopen.com)*

The solution to this degradation issue is signal averaging. As discussed in Section 2.1, the averaging of multiple decorrelated and in phase images results in an improvement in the signal-to-noise ratio by the square root of the number of images being averaged. Therefore, instead of presenting an image from a single planar transmit wave, multiple images are averaged together. The idea is virtually identical to the concept behind spatial compound imaging discussed in Section 2.4. A series of plane waves at varying angles are transmitted and the resulting images from each transmitted plane wave are averaged to present a single display image.

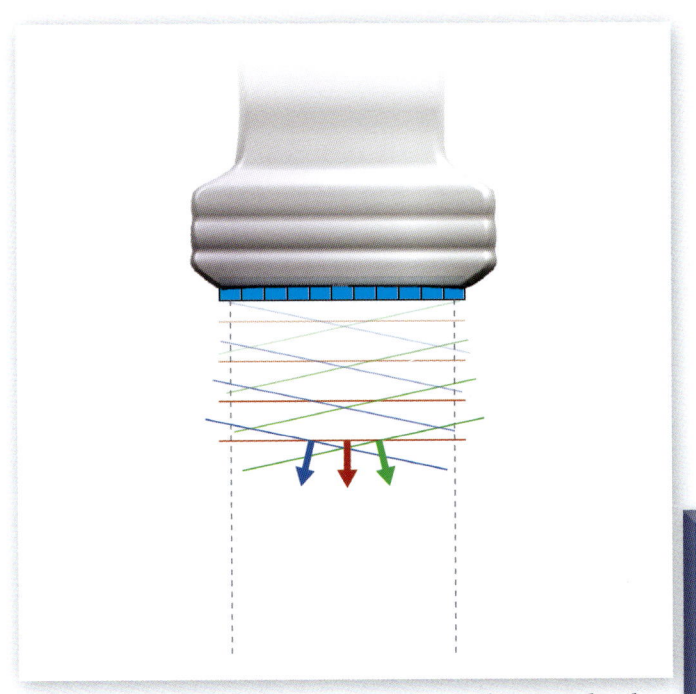

Fig. 48 **Compounded plane wave imaging; in this example, plane waves at three different angles are transmitted and averaged together resulted in improved contrast**

As the number of images used in the average increases, the signal improves while the effective frame rate decreases. This means that for planar wave imaging there is a trade-off between the signal-to-noise ratio and the contrast resolution versus the frame rate. However, since frame rates for a single image are so high, very high signal-to-noise ratios can be achieved while still resulting in significantly higher frame rates than achievable with conventional ultrasound imaging.

Figure 49 compares varying number of compounded planar waves. Notice that as the number of angles increases, the frame rate decreases but the contrast and the signal-to-noise ratio improves.

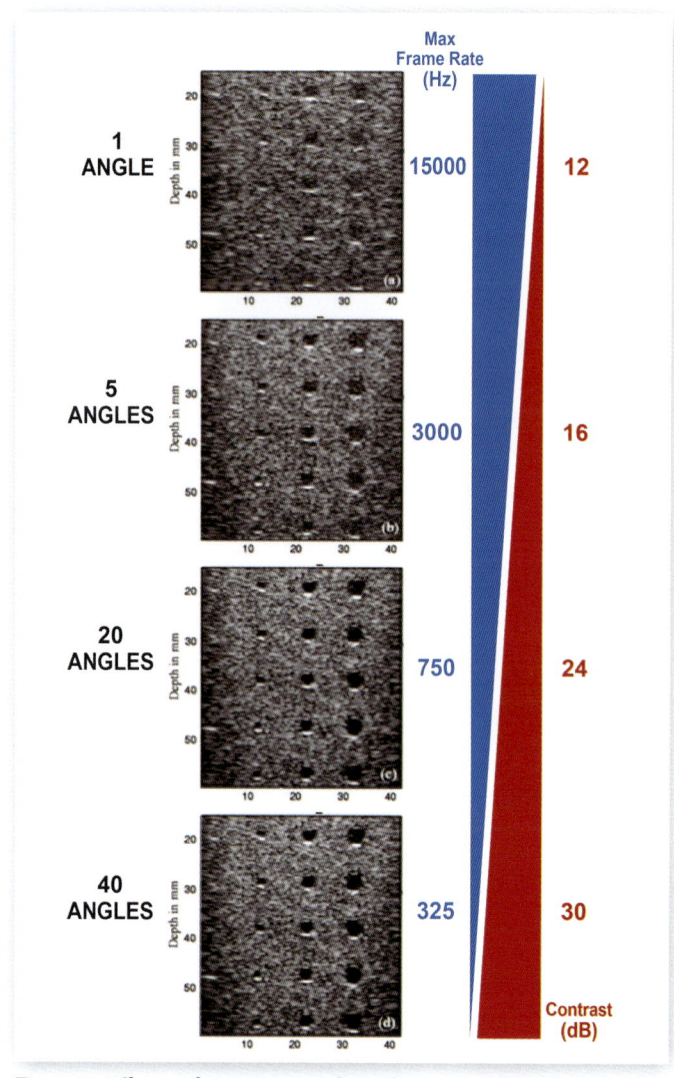

Fig. 49 **Effects of varying number of compounded planar waves** *(Courtesy of Intechopen.com)*

It is useful to compare the difference between compound plane wave imaging and single focus imaging. The following series of images shows the relative poor signal of a single plane, but with extraordinary frame rate (12.5 kHz), the improvement with seven and then forty-one tilted planes with corresponding decreased frame rates, and the conventional approach of 128 sequential beams each with a single transmit focus. Notice that not only is the resolution of the conventional approach poor in comparison to the multi-planar approach, but also the frame rate is the lowest.

In *Figure 50*, image A is generated by a single plane wave with relatively poor resolution and contrast but an extraordinarily high frame rate of 12.5 kHz. Image B shows a composite image generated from compounding 7 tilted plane wave images. Notice the improved contrast and resolution with a corresponding decrease in frame rate to 1.8 kHz. In C, the composite image has been generated from compounding 41 tilted plane wave images. In this case there is not an appreciable difference in resolution or contrast because of the relatively low attenuation in the imaging phantom, but notice that the frame rate has decreased to 300 Hz. Finally, D shows a conventional 128 line sequentially generated image with a single transmit focus per each line. Notice the relatively poor resolution and the frame rate of only 100 Hz.

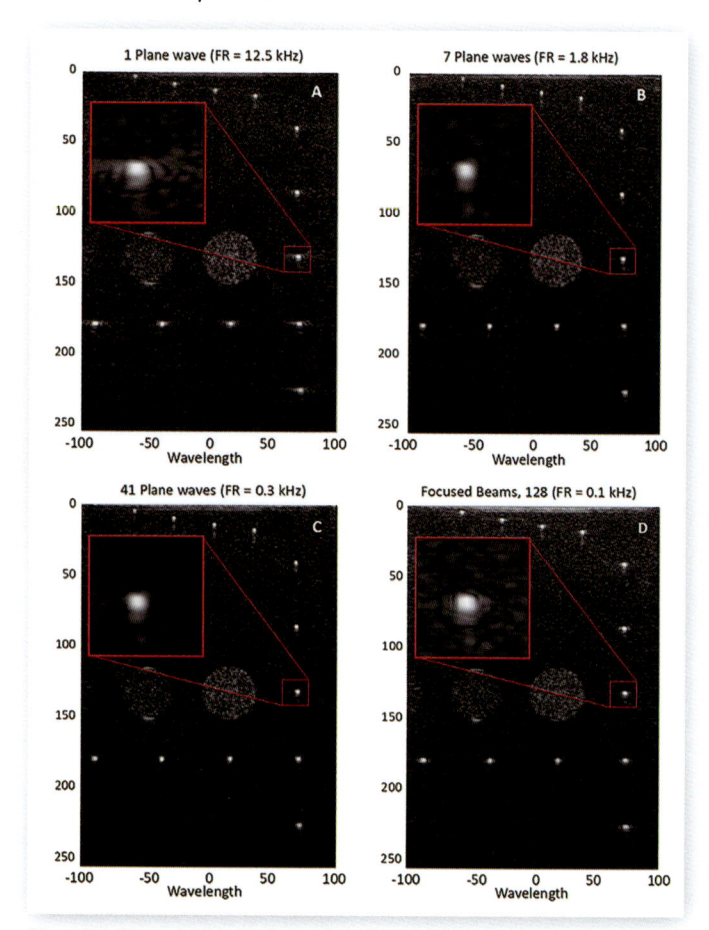

Fig. 50 **Comparison of single plane wave imaging with single focused conventional sequential imaging** *(Courtesy of Verasonics)*

It is also useful to compare the benefits of compounded planar wave images with multi-focal transmit techniques. Using the dynamic retrospective transmit focusing and even 40 angles, the frame rate can still be about 10 times greater than with the multi-focal zone approach. Notice that the lateral resolution, contrast resolution and sensitivity are similar or better with the compounded multi-planar approach.

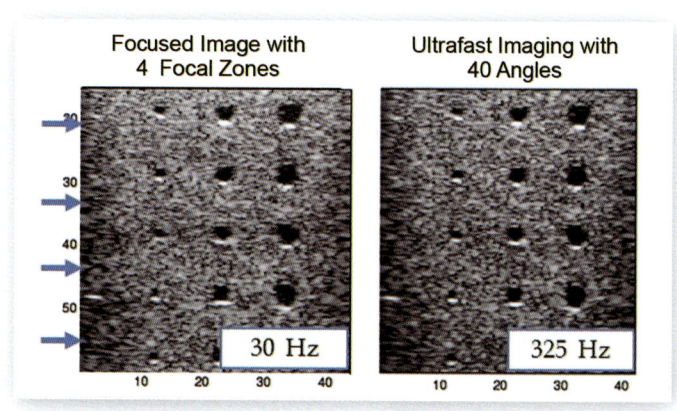

Fig. 51 **Comparison of multi-focal transmit with multi-planar compound imaging** *(Courtesy of Intechopen.com)*

It is valuable to note that, as of now, sector transducers cannot do plane waves well. Similarly, divergent wave imaging is limited because of restrictions on the mechanical index (MI) due to transducer surface temperature limits. Harmonic imaging is also more challenging with divergent and retrospective transmit than with fundamental imaging. The lower MI non-linearly reduces the harmonic signal (discussed in Chapter 10) and makes it challenging to create a broad beam. As a result, the faster frame rate choices in cardiac are not as advantageous as the focused choices, but research is still under way.

Benefits of Ultrafast Imaging

Besides the obvious increase in 2D imaging frame rates, there are many other realizable benefits of ultrafast imaging:
- By trading off some of the extremely high frame rates, improvement in contrast resolution can be achieved
- Color Doppler frame rates can be significantly increased
- Sensitivity and color smoothness can also be improved by trading off some of the higher frame rate
- Multiple spectral Doppler sample volumes can be processed simultaneously
- Shear wave imaging (see Chapters 15 and 16) can be achieved
- These modes are the basis for 3D frame rate and IQ improvements

6.6 Comparison of Image Generation Approaches

The ability to rapidly process large amounts of data has facilitated improved beamforming techniques which make new image generation approaches feasible. To make comparison of the various approaches easier, *Figure 52* compares the transmit beams used for each technique.

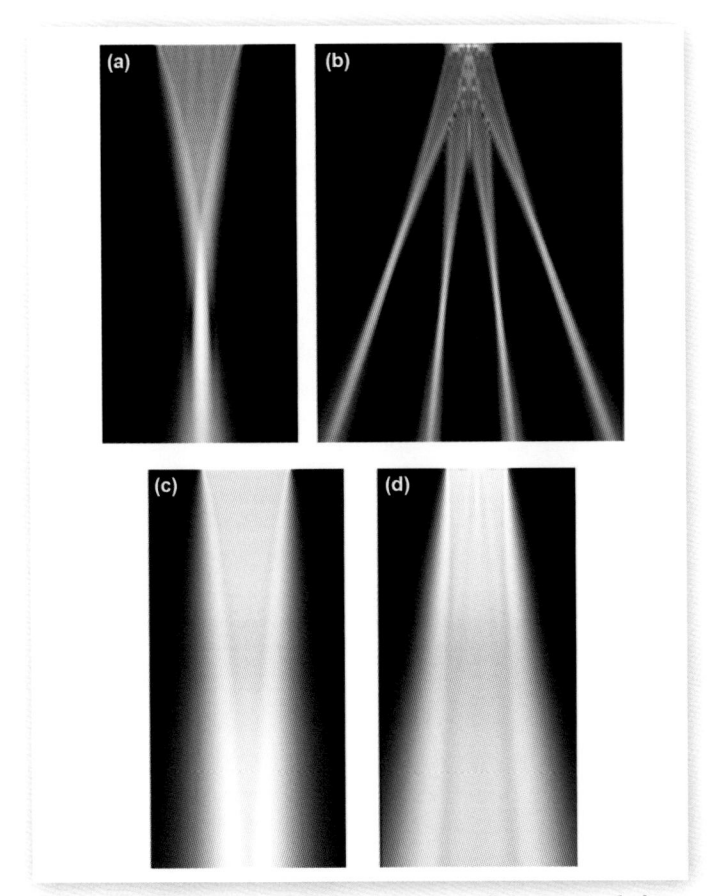

Fig. 52 **Beamplot comparisons of transmit techniques; single focus (a), multi-line transmit (b), plane wave transmit (c), and diverging beam transmit (d)** *(Adapted from multiple sources[1])*

Technique	Advantages	Disadvantages
Dynamic receive focus	Improved lateral resolution	Increased processing power required
Single focal sequential	Good detail resolution	Limited temporal resolution
Multi-focal sequential	Improved lateral resolution	Degraded temporal resolution
Multi-line acquisition (MLA)	Increased temporal resolution	• Decreased lateral resolution unless retrospective focusing also employed • Grouping artifact
Multi-line transmit (MLT)	Increased frame rate	Grating lobes and crosstalk between simultaneously transmitted beams
Synthetic aperture (single element)	Ability to create high resolution focus both for transmit (retrospectively) and receive	• Image from a single element has poor SNR • Creating image from multiple single aperture firings to improve SNR has temporal resolution similar to single transmit focus
Synthetic aperture (multiple elements)	• Ability to create high resolution focus both for transmit (retrospectively) and receive • Better SNR than single element synthetic aperture	Requires massive amounts of processing power
Retrospective transmit focus	Improved lateral resolution (good lateral resolution not just at single or multi-focal depths)	Processing power requirements
Compounded plane / diverging wave (with retrospective transmit focus)	• Improved temporal resolution • Potential for increased contrast resolution	Grating lobe artifacts and associated image degradation

Table 2 **Comparison of image generation techniques**

7. Extended Field of View/Panoramic Imaging

In Chapter 5, we learned about various image formats which are dictated by the physical footprint of the transducer. Large linear and curved linear arrays are able to produce much larger fields of view than smaller sector transducers. The motivation behind the trapezoidal format was to further extend the field of view beyond the conventional linear image. The idea of panoramic imaging is essentially to dramatically extend the field of view by physically moving the transducer across the patient to build up a 2-dimensional image over time.

The basic concept of acquiring an image by physically moving a transducer across a region of the patient should sound familiar as the technique called B-scan used to create 2D images in the very early days of ultrasound. However, unlike B-scans, panoramic imaging uses very complex processing to correlate returning data with data already received to draw an accurate representation of the imaged anatomy. By looking at 2D correlations, repeated lines can be dropped and actual successive lines can be displayed in the correct orientation. With B-scans, the quality of the data was extremely dependent on the rate of sweeping as well as the uniformity of the sweep speed.

Panoramic imaging is somewhat immune to variations in sweep speed since repeated data is detected and not displayed. However, a sweep speed that is too fast will still present a problem as missed or motion blurred data which cannot be fixed through processing. The result is an extended field of view that can potentially display a whole organ, or the whole organ in relation to neighboring structures (see *Figure 53*). As with most ultrasound technologies, each company has their own name for the feature. Philips refers to this technique as panoramic imaging, the name that has become the default. Canon refers to this technology as Panoramic View. Siemens refers to their version as SieScape. GE refers to their version as LOGICView, and Mindray refers to their version as iScape.

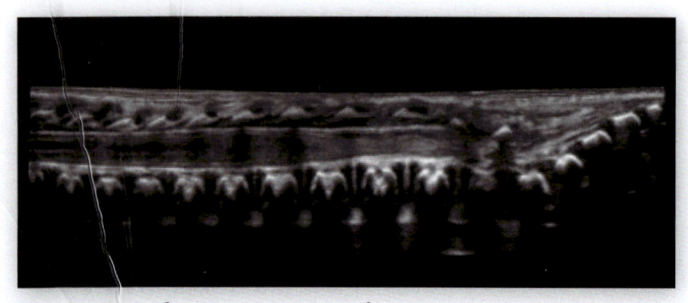

Fig. 53 11 inch panoramic view of spine

The benefits of panoramic imaging are mostly related to the ability to see large or long anatomical structures, as well as to see structures in the context of neighboring structures. The applications are primarily in vascular, abdominal, OB/GYN, small parts, and musculoskeletal imaging. Most systems allow for both linear and angular translation so that imaging around curved anatomy is possible.

The following series of images further illustrate the advantages of panoramic imaging. In *Figure 54*, the extended field of view helps to show the location of the fracture in the foot relative to the entire bone.

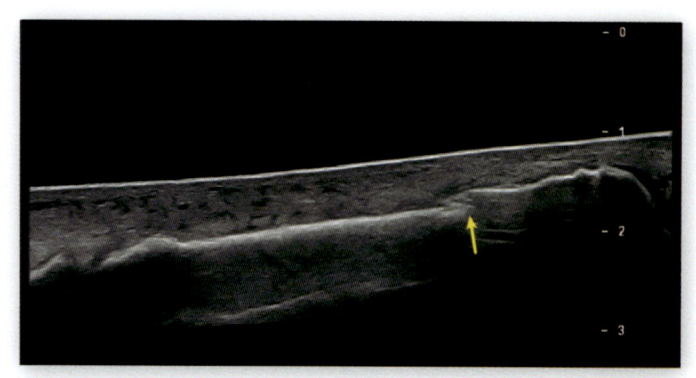

Fig. 54 **Entire length of dorsal aspect of 5th metatarsal using panoramic imaging; there is a fracture present (arrow)**

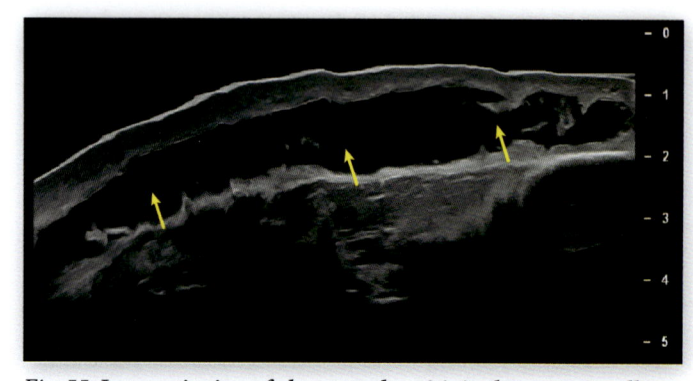

Fig. 55 **Long-axis view of olecranon bursitis in the posterior elbow; the panoramic view helps capture the location and entire size of the fluid collection (arrows)**

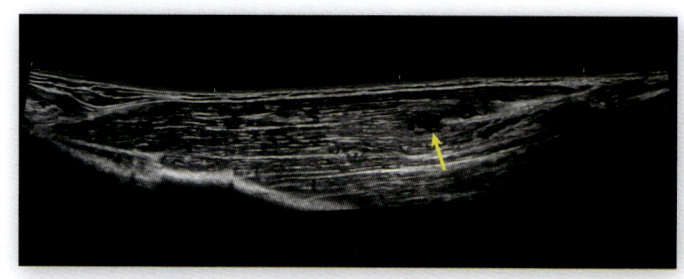

Fig. 56 **Long-axis view of biceps muscle in the anterior upper arm; panoramic view demonstrates the entire length of the muscle and shows precisely where the tear is located (arrow) at the myotendinous junction**

View ONLINE Animation and Image Library

8. Adaptive Processing / Auto-Optimize

As this chapter has clearly illustrated, there are a plethora of system parameters under the control of the user. To produce an optimized image, changing any one system parameter often results in a need to change another system parameter because of the complex interaction between the controls. For example, increasing the receiver gain may result in the need to adjust the video compression (dynamic range) to get optimal grayscale (contrast) visualization. Adaptive processes attempt to reduce the amount of user interaction necessary to achieve optimum images. Note there is also an extensive discussion of adaptive processes in Chapter 8 as it relates to decreasing the artifact of beam aberration.

As the name suggests, adaptive processes "adapt" the system settings automatically based on the characteristics of the received signals. At the core of all adaptive processes is an analysis algorithm which mathematically determines the detected signal characteristics. By measuring many signal characteristics and by performing statistical analyses, the algorithm can use the results to change system parameters "intelligently" to improve the image presentation. This second part of the algorithm is referred to as the enhancement phase.

Different companies use different proprietary algorithms and most companies now offer an adaptive optimization for B-mode imaging, color Doppler, and spectral Doppler. Of course, each ultrasound company has a different name for their technique. Mindray refers to their technology as iTouch, Philips calls their version intelligent scan (iSCAN) and XRES, Siemens calls their technique native tissue equalization (NTEQ), Canon refers to this technology as Quick Scan, and GE refers to their approach as automatic optimization (AO) or automatic tissue optimization (ATO).

Most adaptive (one-touch techniques) adjust receiver gain, time gain compensation, and the video compression or dynamic range of the image. The makers of ultrasound generally claim that this technique allows for less user to user variability as well as greater consistency in repeat scans, in addition to fewer system interactions, thereby reducing imaging time. There are certainly times when using an adaptive processing technique can result in improved images with more consistent results. However, as with virtually all technologies, these techniques cannot be perfect, and hence should be turned off and turned back on to make sure that an improvement in the image has resulted.

Figure 57 shows both an un-optimized image and the resulting image from application of an auto optimization technique. *Figure 58* shows the image of a cirrhotic liver optimized manually (a) and by an adaptive process (b). Notice that in (b) the reverberation artifact is reduced and the liver architecture is better appreciated and more uniform, especially in the far field. Also notice that there is less artifact in all the regions of fluid.

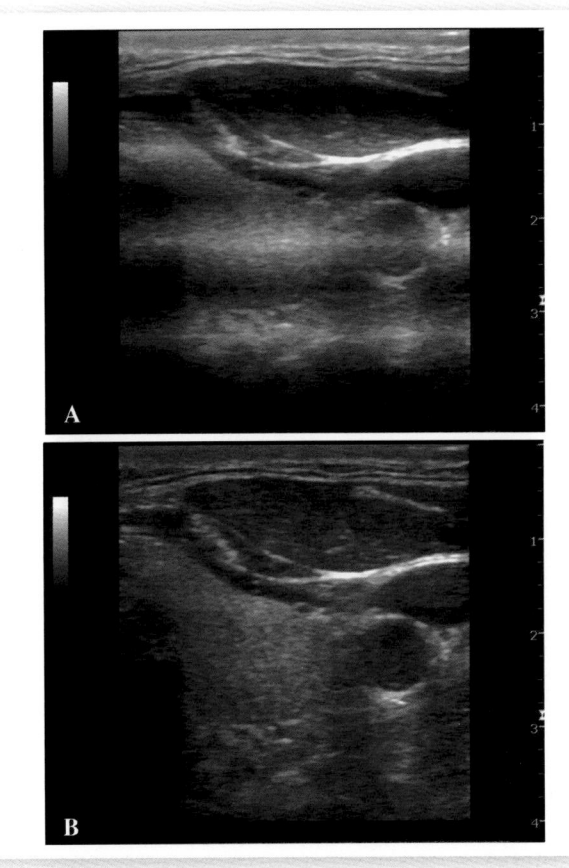

Fig. 57 **Images of a normal thyroid comparing an unadjusted image with many system parameters set incorrectly (a) with the auto corrected image (b)**

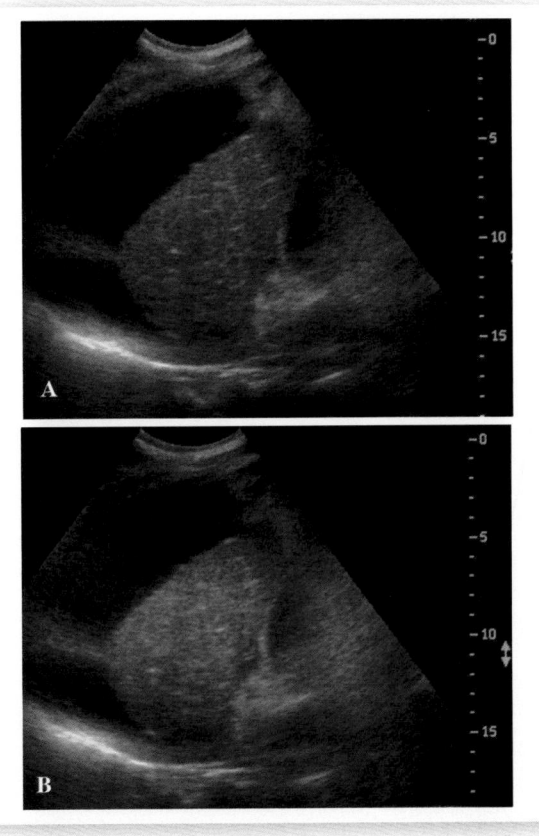

Fig. 58 **Images of a cirrhotic liver with ascites comparing an image optimized manually (a) with an adaptive auto corrected image (b)**

Many systems now combine several functions to provide optimization for specific imaging situations. For example, one system allows the user to set a region of interest box. The system adaptively changes many system parameters to optimize the image within the ROI. Since the ROI does not include the entire image, the transmit power can be increased within the smaller region and then decreased outside the region to still comply with power restrictions. The increase in transmit improves the signal-to-noise ratio within the ROI. To improve the lateral resolution, the line density can also be increased similar to the manner in which the line density is often increased when performing an acoustic (write) zoom. In addition to the changes to the transmit power, adaptive processing is applied within the ROI to enhance the contrast to improve visual differentiation of structures.

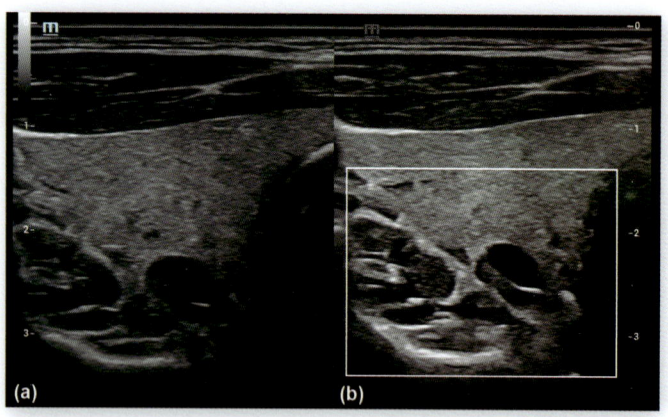

Fig. 59 **Image of a thyroid mass without (a) and with (b) selective adaptive processing** *(Courtesy of Mindray)*

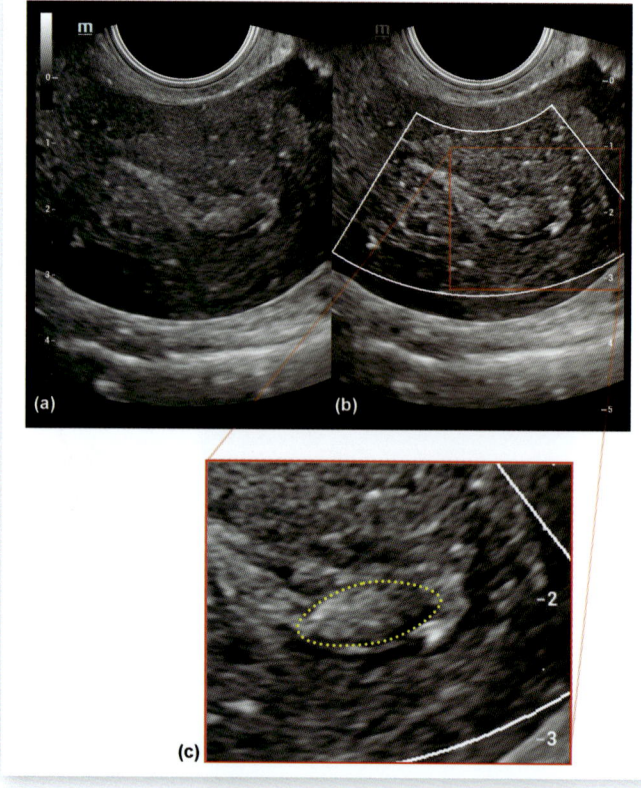

Fig. 60 **Endovaginal image of a retroverted uterus without (a) and with (b) selective adaptive processing; the additional detail allowed visualization of the endometrial polyp (c)** *(Courtesy of Mindray)*

In *Figure 59*, image (b) more clearly documents the septation in the thyroid mass. Additionally, the more echogenic, solid components within the nodule are noticeable with the adaptive processing. Similarly, *Figure 60* image (b) displays the echogenic endometrium with more detail, thereby allowing better visualization of the endometrial polyp (outlined in yellow) in the close up of (c). The polyp was initially missed when imaging on a system not utilizing the adaptive processing. Both *Figures 59* and *60* used HD Scope imaging.

Other systems have combined adaptive real-time image enhancement to reduce speckle, haze, and clutter artifacts with algorithms to enhance border detections between structures. The processing is fast enough to be applied in real-time imaging. The following image captures illustrate the results of this adaptive process (which can be better visualized by watching the online content).

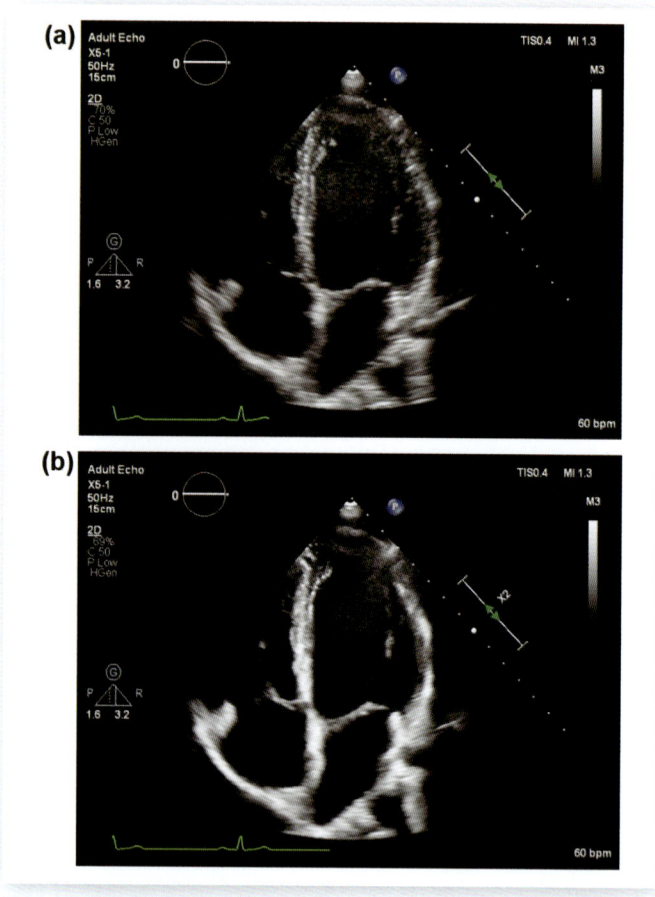

Fig. 61 **Apical 4-chamber cardiac view without (a) and with (b) adaptive XRES technology applied**

View ONLINE Animation and Image Library

9. Sound Speed Compensation

As with the discussion above regarding adaptive processing, speed of sound correction is also treated more extensively in Chapter 8 (Section 6) in terms of reducing artifacts related to beam aberration.

As we learned very early in Chapter 2, ultrasound assumes a speed of sound of 1540 m/sec. However, this "soft tissue" velocity is simply an average and varies with tissue types, and from patient to patient even for the same tissue type. Since the wavelength calculations are affected by the propagation velocity (recall the all-important wavelength equation),

$$\lambda = \frac{c}{f}$$

correct phase delays for appropriate focusing and steering is impacted by the propagation velocity. In other words, as sound propagates through tissues with differing propagation speeds, that path time varies from the assumed travel time. This difference in time results in a blurring of the echoes and a loss in resolution. To accommodate for the differing travel times, different time delays are required to get signals traveling from the same structure in the body along different paths to different transducer elements to add in phase.

Sound speed compensation is any approach which attempts to correct for differences in propagation speed from the assumed 1540 m/sec in order to improve signal coherence. There are some non-adaptive approaches, but with ever increasing processing power, retrospective adaptive processes are becoming more common. The result of sound speed compensation is increased signal correlation which results in improved penetration, improved contrast resolution, and improved detail resolution. Notice the significant improvement in image with sound speed compensation as shown in the following phantom images.

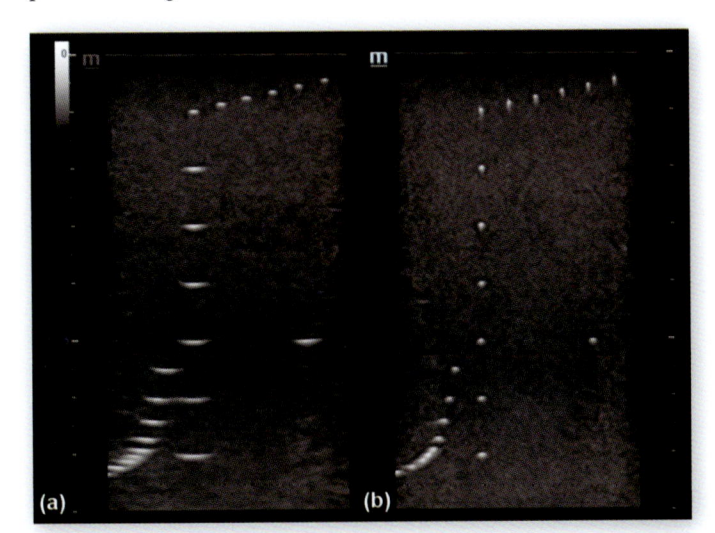

Fig. 62 **Phantom pin image without (a) and with (b) speed sound compensation** *(Courtesy of Mindray)*

In *Figure 62*, image (a) used a propagation velocity of 1580 m/sec whereas image (b) adaptively adjusted the speed of sound used in the wavelength and delay calculations to 1449 m/sec. Notice the significantly improved lateral resolution and image uniformity.

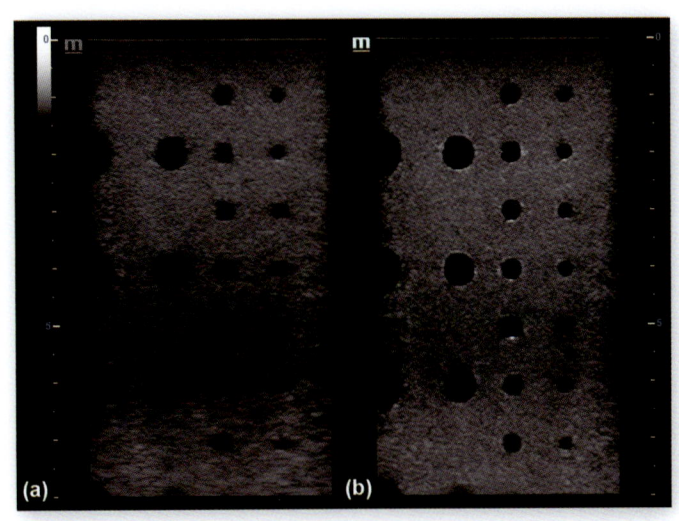

Fig. 63 **Cyst phantom image without (a) and with (b) speed sound compensation; note the significantly improved contrast resolution and ability to detect structures at depth** *(Courtesy of Mindray)*

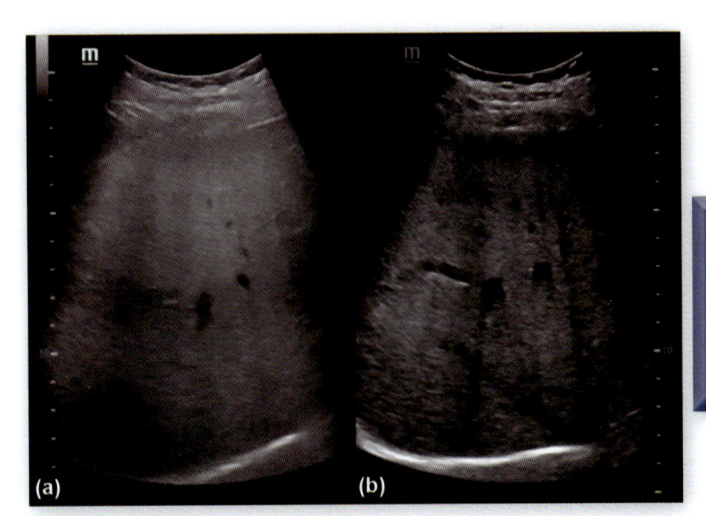

Fig. 64 **Image of fatty liver without (a) and with (b) sound speed correction** *(Courtesy of Mindray)*

View ONLINE Animation and Image Library

10. 3D Imaging

As suggested by the name, 3D imaging provides information not just in the lateral and depth direction, but also in the elevation direction. For the most part, all of the concepts that relate to 2D imaging relate to 3D imaging, with the addition of elevational control which causes further issues regarding temporal resolution. In the early days of

3D imaging, a volume was generated by building up an image over time as a 1-D transducer was scanned across the patient. Today, 2D imaging is performed almost exclusively with two-dimensional transducers, with multiple elements both in the lateral and elevation directions. Control over elements in two dimensions of course increases complexity of transmit and receive beamformers as well the processing needed to generate volume images.

To obtain complete structural information, all three dimensions of that structure must be imaged and viewed. One image which could simultaneously display all three dimensions would be ideal. Great strides have been made recently in acquiring and displaying three-dimensional images. Some companies refer to 4D imaging as the presentation of 3D imaging over time. Since most companies now offer real-time 3D, we will just refer to real-time 3D imaging as 3D.

Acquiring three-dimensional information is difficult because of the increased time requirements to gather acoustic data in the third (elevation) dimension. Displaying this information is also challenging because our normal display modes really only have two physical dimensions: depth and width, and a third perceived dimension of brightness. For 2D images, all three of these display dimensions are already used. Depth and width of the image correspond to depth and width in the patient. The third dimension of brightness (hence the name brightness mode) is utilized to demonstrate changes in tissue reflectivity.

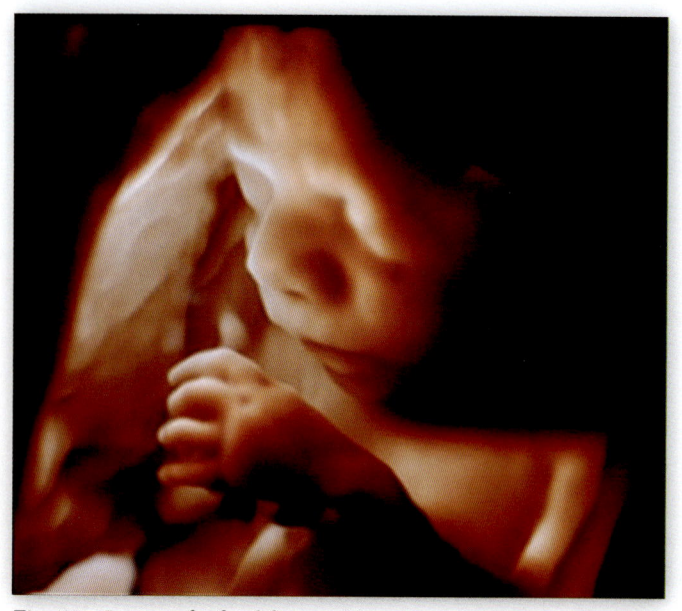

Fig. 65 **Image of a fetal face and hand using 3D/4D surface rendering technology; this technology demonstrates the "flashlight" appearance to brighten the left side allowing for more realistic facial features** *(Courtesy of Philips)*

Using A-mode to display a two-dimensional image has the same difficulty as using a B-mode to display a three-dimensional image: there are not enough display dimensions. The most common current approach to displaying three physical dimensions is to develop a light-shaded perspective with slight rotation of the image. Other approaches include a "wire mesh" presentation, or user determinable orthogonal (perpendicular) 2D slices. There are now companies who are experimenting with virtual reality headsets to view and interact with 3D images. In the future, three-dimensional holograms will probably become the display of choice, but this technology may be long coming.

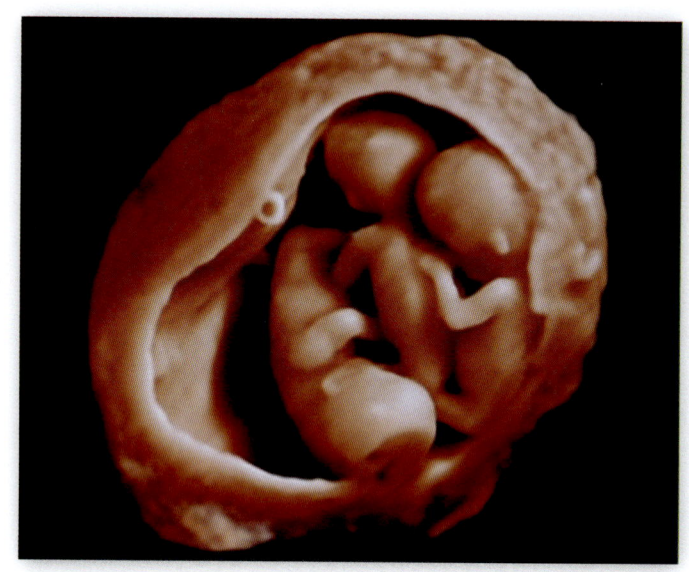

Fig. 66 **Image of 1st trimester triplets using 3D/4D surface rendering technology** *(Courtesy of Philips)*

From the image in *Figure 66*, all three fetuses appear to be in one sac. Two fetal heads are seen towards the top of the image and one fetus has its head toward the bottom of the image.

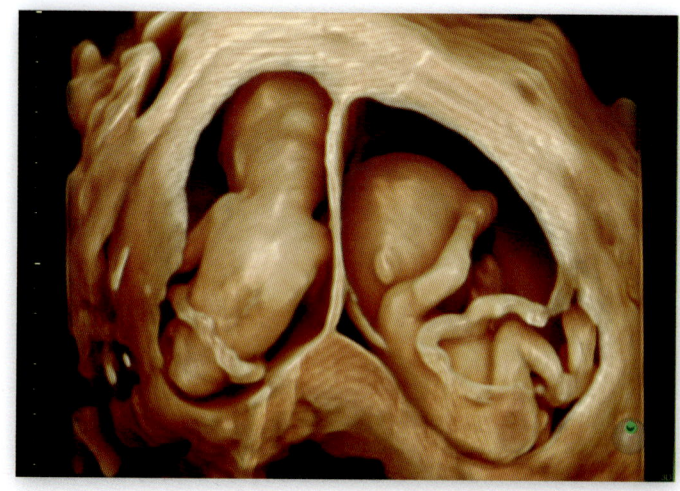

Fig. 67 **Image of 1st trimester twins using 3D surface rendering technology** *(Courtesy of GE)*

In *Figure 67*, one twin's back can be seen with its umbilical cord on the left side. The other twin is displayed from a side view demonstrating its ear, arm, umbilical cord, and leg. The rendering technology enables clear visualization of the twins being in two separate gestational sacs.

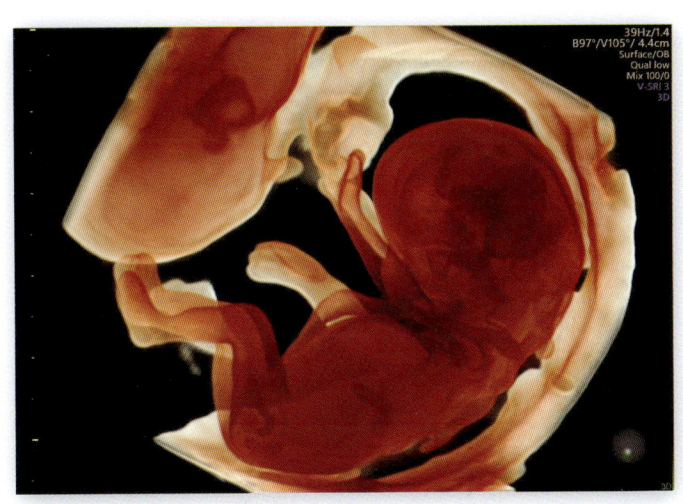

Chapter 6 | Part II: System Operation (Advanced) 283

Fig. 68 **Image of 1st trimester fetus using 3D transparent rendering technology which allows for visualization of the external and internal structures** *(Courtesy of GE)*

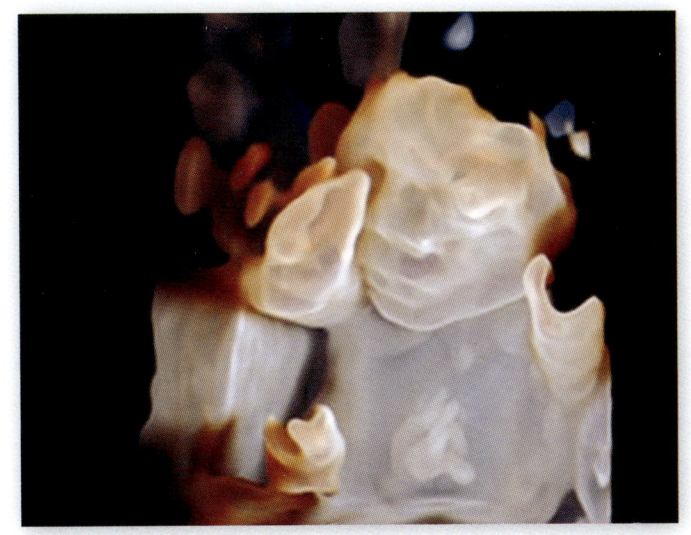

Fig. 69 **Image of a fetus using 3D/4D transparent rendering technology; the fetal face is displayed at the top of the image, with the fetal heart visualized below in the thorax** *(Courtesy of Philips)*

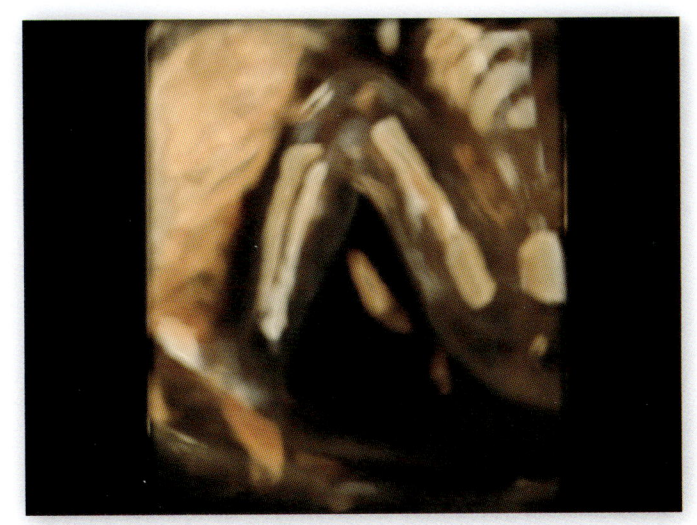

Fig. 70 **Image of a fetal thigh and lower leg using 3D/4D transparent rendering technology which allows bony structures to be accented while muting the surface of other tissues** *(Courtesy of GE)*

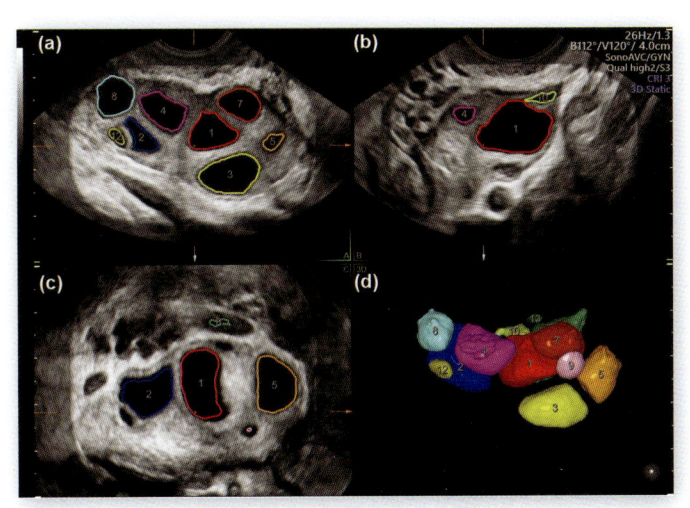

View ONLINE Animation and Image Library

Fig. 71 **Images of an ovary using 3D technology in which the follicular volumes have been calculated** *(Courtesy of GE)*

In *Figure 71* above, the system has automatically color-coded, numbered, measured, and calculated the follicular volumes from the 3D volume dataset. Image (a) is the ovary's longest axis; (b) is a transverse axis (90° clockwise rotation); (c) is a 90° forward rotation from the longest axis, and (d) demonstrates the color-coded, numbered follicles with the ovarian tissue subtracted for improved visualization. This technology is used in fertility clinics to assess follicular growth for reproductive planning purposes.

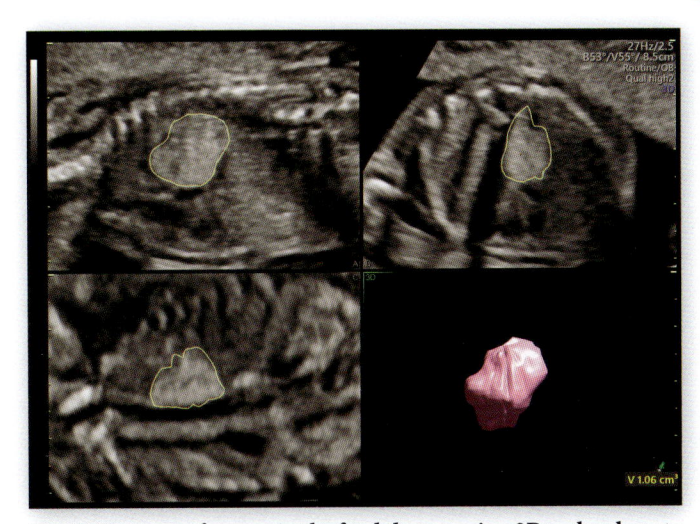

Fig. 72 **Images of a mass in the fetal thorax using 3D technology to calculate the volume of this irregularly shaped structure** *(Courtesy of GE)*

Two-dimensional calculations of irregularly shaped structures using length • height • width measurements are not as accurate as those available using 3D technologies. In order to calculate the volume of the mass in *Figure 72*, the user traces the structure in variable increments of rotations to create the 3D tracing and allow for more accurate volume measurement. In this case, the top left image displays the sagittal fetal thorax with fetal head to the left side of the display. The top right image displays the transverse fetal thorax (90° clockwise rotation). The bottom left image displays the coronal fetal thorax (90° forward rotation from the sagittal plane). The bottom right image demonstrates a clay rendering of the thoracic mass with the volume calculation of 1.06 cm³ displayed.

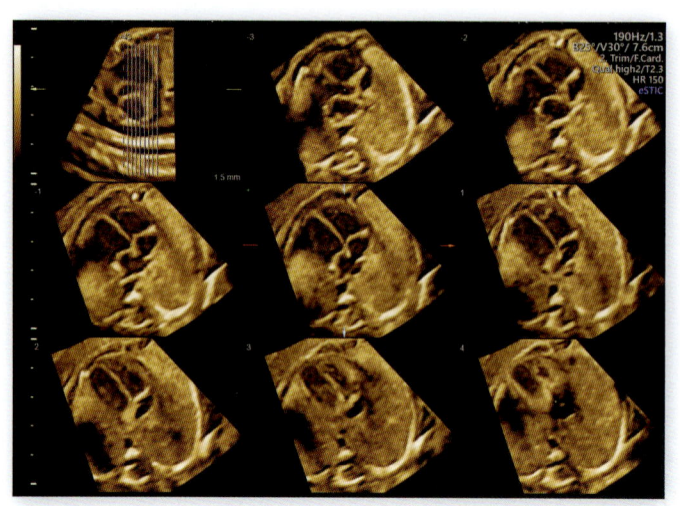

are also valuable such as being able to control the location of the lighting source, making assessment of closures and other repairs easier to make.

The limitations of 3D imaging are still predominantly related to frame rate, but with increasing computing power and new image generation techniques, the temporal resolution issues have been decreasing significantly. As the issues related to generating and displaying 3D images are resolved, 3D will become a much more extensively used tool in ultrasound.

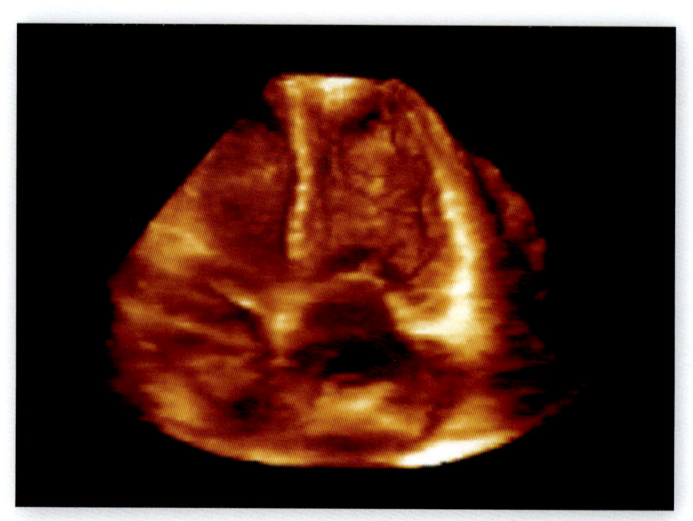

Fig. 73 **Images of a 2nd trimester fetal heart using a multi-slice 3D/4D technology** *(Courtesy of GE)*

Fig. 74 **3D apical 4-chamber image**

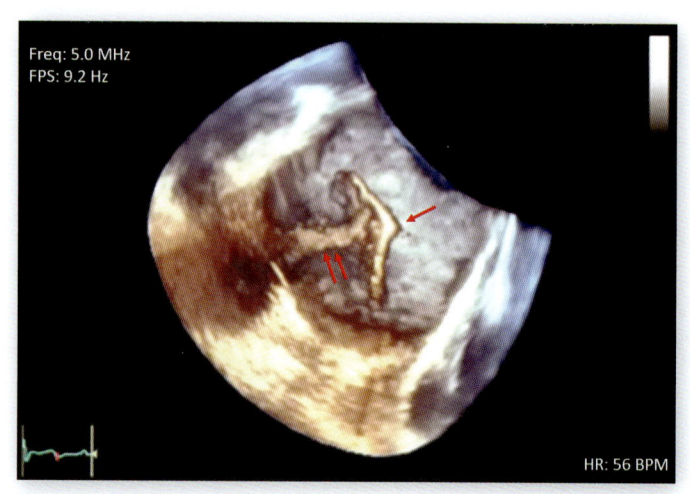

In *Figure 73*, with the exception of the reference image in the top left corner, all of the remaining displayed images are in the same plane (90° clockwise rotation from the reference image). The reference image displays the fetal heart with the fetal head to the left of the image and the fetal spine on the bottom of the image. The lines through the reference image correlate to the numbers on the other images. Each slice is separated at a distance of 1.5 mm. Slice numbered "-3" is toward the fetal head, whereas slice numbered "4" is towards the fetal abdomen. This multi-slice technology allows the full depth of the anatomy to be displayed as one image. To appreciate the cardiac motion, view the full video online.

**View ONLINE
Animation and Image Library**

Fig. 75 **3D image of the deployment of an Amplatzer septal occluder device; note the open device (single arrow) in the left atrium and the catheter (double arrows) extending through the opening of the interatrial septum**

In cardiac applications, 3D imaging has become extremely valuable for assessing structural interventions. First, the 3D imaging techniques provide structural views that allow surgeons to plan interventions and the ability to better determine whether devices will fix a given problem and what size device is needed. 3D imaging has also helped advance many transcatheter repair techniques. Many of the new visualization techniques for displaying 3D data

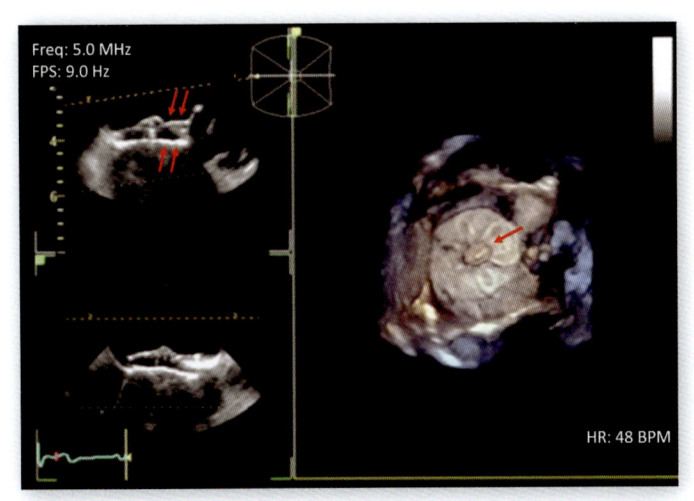

Fig. 76 **3D image (en face) of a deployed Amplatzer septal occluder device (arrow); note the 2D images to the left showing the cross-sectional views of the device displaying the two discs (double arrows) indicating appropriate seating**

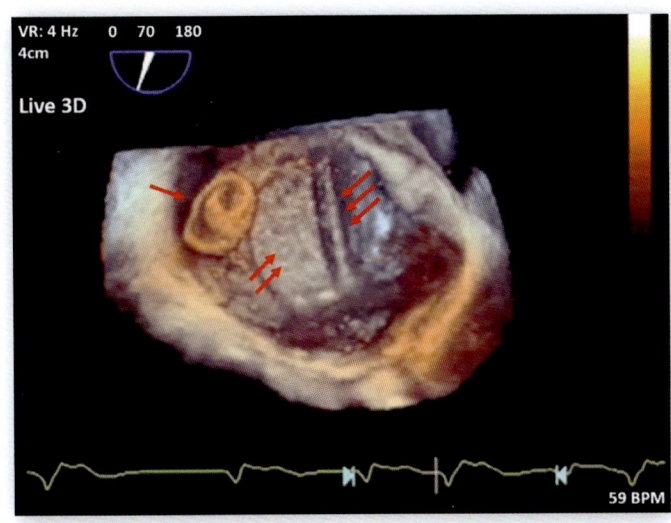

Fig. 77 **3D image an Amplatzer septal occluder device (single arrow) encroaching upon a mechanical bileaflet prosthetic mitral valve, restricting movement; note one disc (double arrows) in the closed position with the other disc (triple arrows) open**

The valve in *Figure 77* can be better appreciated in the corresponding online video.

View ONLINE Animation and Image Library

11. Fusion (Modalities)

Fusion is a technology by which two imaging modalities can be linked together (co-registered) for simultaneous comparison. Ultrasound images or contrast enhanced ultrasound images (CEUS) are generally fused with images from computed tomography (CT), magnetic resonance (MR), and positron emission tomography (PET). Many systems allow for fusion with both 2D and 3D ultrasound imaging.

Fundamentally, the concept is to take the results of two different imaging technologies and mathematically link the images together so that structures visualized in one image correspond to the structures displayed in the fused image. For ultrasound fusion, this approach is generally done by uploading the comparison volumetric image (CT/MR/PET) to the system and then performing a registration and calibration procedure with either stored or live ultrasound imaging.

There are many different approaches to correlating the images. Some techniques are manual with an increasing number of manufacturers offering automatic approaches but with a user ability to manually correct or optimize the co-registration. One of the co-registration approaches is to identify a specific structure in the reference image and then find the corresponding structure in the ultrasound image. Once confirming that the imaging planes of the two comparison modalities are matched, another point is then usually identified somewhere else in both images. This allows the system to calibrate the two images in three-dimensional space, including determining the scaling so that movement within the ultrasound image can be linked to the corresponding image from the reference (CT/MR/PET) 3D volume. Once the images are fused, the reference image display changes synchronously with the changing ultrasound image with transducer movement.

Many systems offer an electromagnetic method for registration thereby allowing for monitoring the transducer position and movements. This process entails a device to produce a magnetic field (magnetic field generator), a magnetic sensor which connects to the transducer, and potentially a fiducial marker which is placed on the patient. The magnetic field generator is placed near the patient so that a magnetic field exists around the region being scanned. As the magnetic sensor (attached to the transducer) is moved within the magnetic field, the change in electric field is sensed by the ultrasound system. In this manner, movement relative to the known location (referenced to the location of the fiducial marker) can be determined. By tracking the direction and distance of movement of the transducer, the corresponding reference (CT/MR/PET) fused image is changed to match the image of the ultrasound system either in the side-by-side image, the overlaid (fused) image, or both.

Fusion technology is currently being used for many different regions of the body including the brain, breast, liver, prostrate, kidney, musculoskeletal, and vascular imaging. Another application for fusion imaging is electromagnetic needle tracking for imaging guided biopsies. In this application, a magnetic sensor is embedded within the needle for more accurate needle placement.

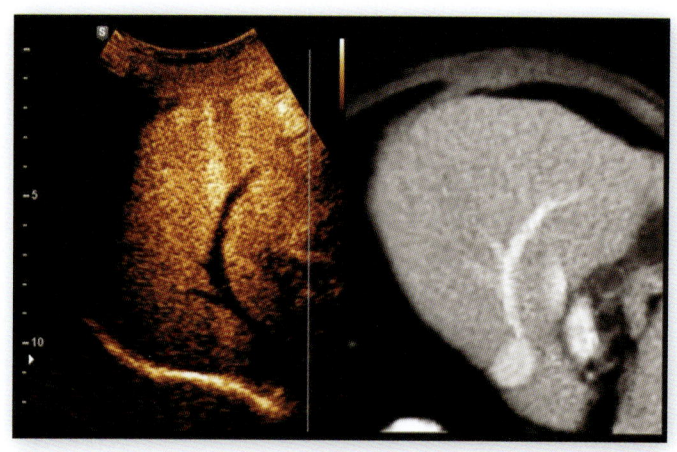

Fig. 78 Dual display fusion imaging of a liver with ultrasound (with sepia tint) on the left and CT on the right; these images are synced so when the sonographer scans throughout the liver (left), the CT anatomy displayed is correlated in real time

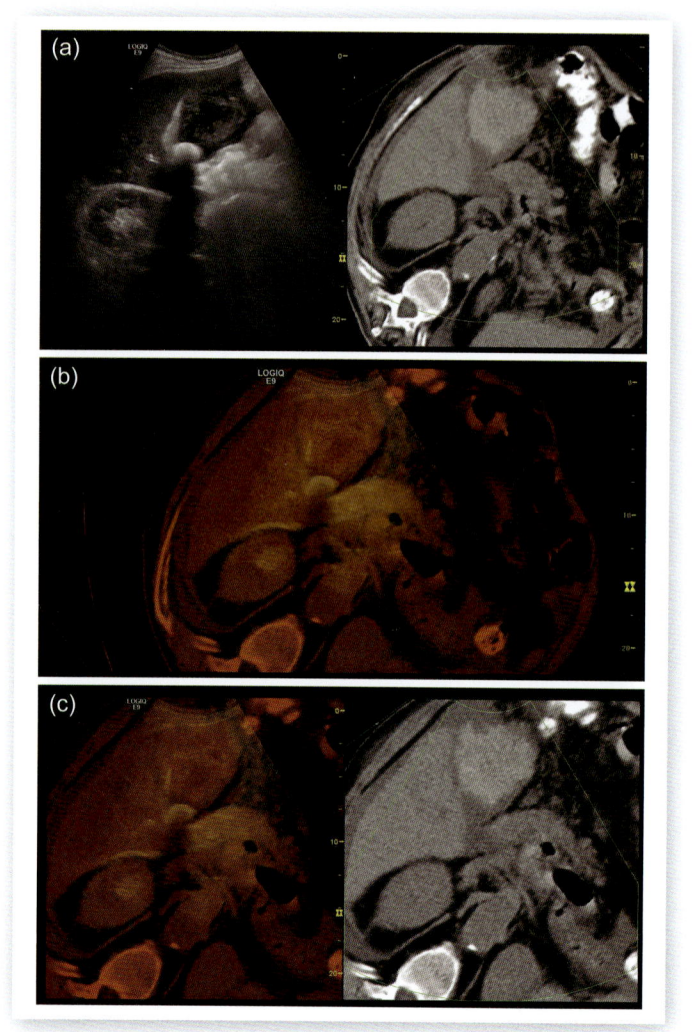

Fig. 79 Fusion image of an ultrasound and CT image of a liver and kidney; dual display (a), overlaid format (b), and dual display with CT overlay on left (c)

In the fusion images of *Figure 79*, the CT image is synced with the ultrasound such that changes in the ultrasound image results in a corresponding change in the displayed anatomy of the CT image.

Image (a) shows the dual display. Notice the green box on the CT image (left) corresponding to the field of view of the ultrasound image. Image (b) shows the overlaid format with CT image (with sepia tint) displayed in the background. Finally, (c) shows dual display with CT image on the right and overlaid image on the left.

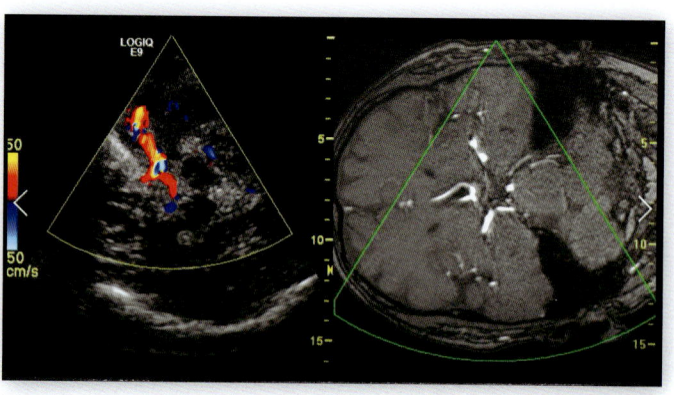

View ONLINE Animation and Image Library

Fig. 80 Dual display fusion image of the Circle of Willis in an adult brain with MRI image displayed on the right and color Doppler ultrasound on the left; the white areas in the MRI indicate the blood vessels of the Circle of Willis

Blood flow for *Figure 80* can be better appreciated in the corresponding online video.

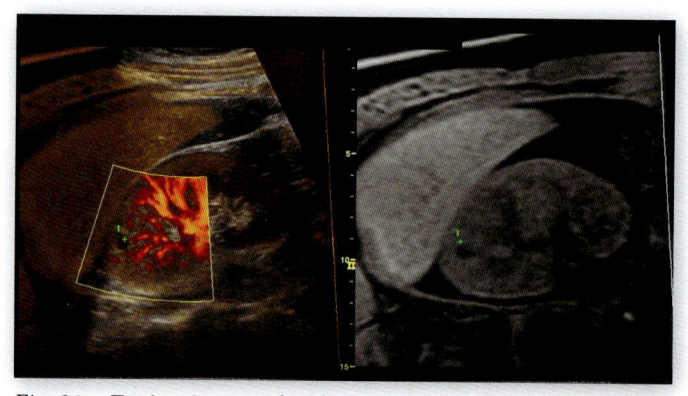

View ONLINE Animation and Image Library

Fig. 81 Fusion image of right kidney with MRI displayed on the right and MRI (with sepia tint) overlaid with color Doppler ultrasound on left; a mass is seen at the crosshairs (tagged "1")

The mass in the right kidney of *Figure 81* is observed in real time in both images using a fusion tracking feature which allows the sonographer to ensure they are scanning the same mass/lesion as indicated in the MRI even if there is shadowing in the ultrasound image. The ability to observe color flow in real time is unique to ultrasound and not possible with MRI nor CT.

View ONLINE Animation and Image Library

Company	Name for Fusion Technology
Canon	Smart Fusion
Esaote	Virtual Navigator and Fusion Imaging
GE	GPS/Fusion
Mindray	iFusion
Philips	PercuNav
Samsung	S-Fusion
Siemens	eSie Fusion

Table 3 **Fusion technology naming conventions by company**

Benefits of Fusion Imaging
The benefits of using fusion imaging include:
- Enhanced visualization of lesions and structures that are difficult to appreciate in one of the two modalities
- Corroboration of image findings (reduction in false positives)
- Real-time image guidance for interventional procedures
- Lack of radiation for both patient and staff with repeated imaging
- Improved needle placement accuracy for procedures and biopsies

Most of the limitations with fusion imaging are related to ease of use and accuracy of registration. As the process for co-registration of the images becomes more automated with improved algorithms and increased processing power, the ease of use problem is becoming less of an issue.

One of the more significant issues with accuracy of registration is the fact that ultrasound is a live imaging modality which visualizes patient changes with respiration whereas CT, MR, and PET all capture an image during a breath hold. With respiration, organs potentially change orientation and size. Many systems now try to compensate algorithmically for the organ deformation so as to better link the live ultrasound data to the static comparison volume image. Additionally, since the comparison image may have been captured using a different imaging plane and with the patient in a different orientation when being scanned, some systems will resample the reference volume set and interpolate the values (sometimes referred to as "reslicing") to better improve the registration match.

As with other technologies, every company has their own specific branding of this technology. *Table 3* offers a partial list of fusion technology names. Some companies have more than one name for the technology, depending on the platform.

> **CHECKPOINT: Exam Tip**
>
> Be careful to avoid confusing frequency fusion with fusion imaging. Frequency fusion is a weighted frame averaging technique of two or more ultrasound images generated at different frequencies. Fusion imaging refers to simultaneous displays of ultrasound images with another reference modality.

12. Resolution Summary

With the advancements of new image generation techniques, fully understanding resolution has become more complex. The chart of *Figure 82* on the following page is intended to encapsulate the complexities associated with resolution.

13. Artificial Intelligence (AI)

13.1 What is AI?
Artificial intelligence (AI) is the name for a broad category of approaches that allow computer systems to make decisions about input data that generally would require human intelligence and decision making. In essence, AI is the ability of a system, based on a hardware and software combination, to produce results that emulate what a well-informed human would decide given the same input of information.

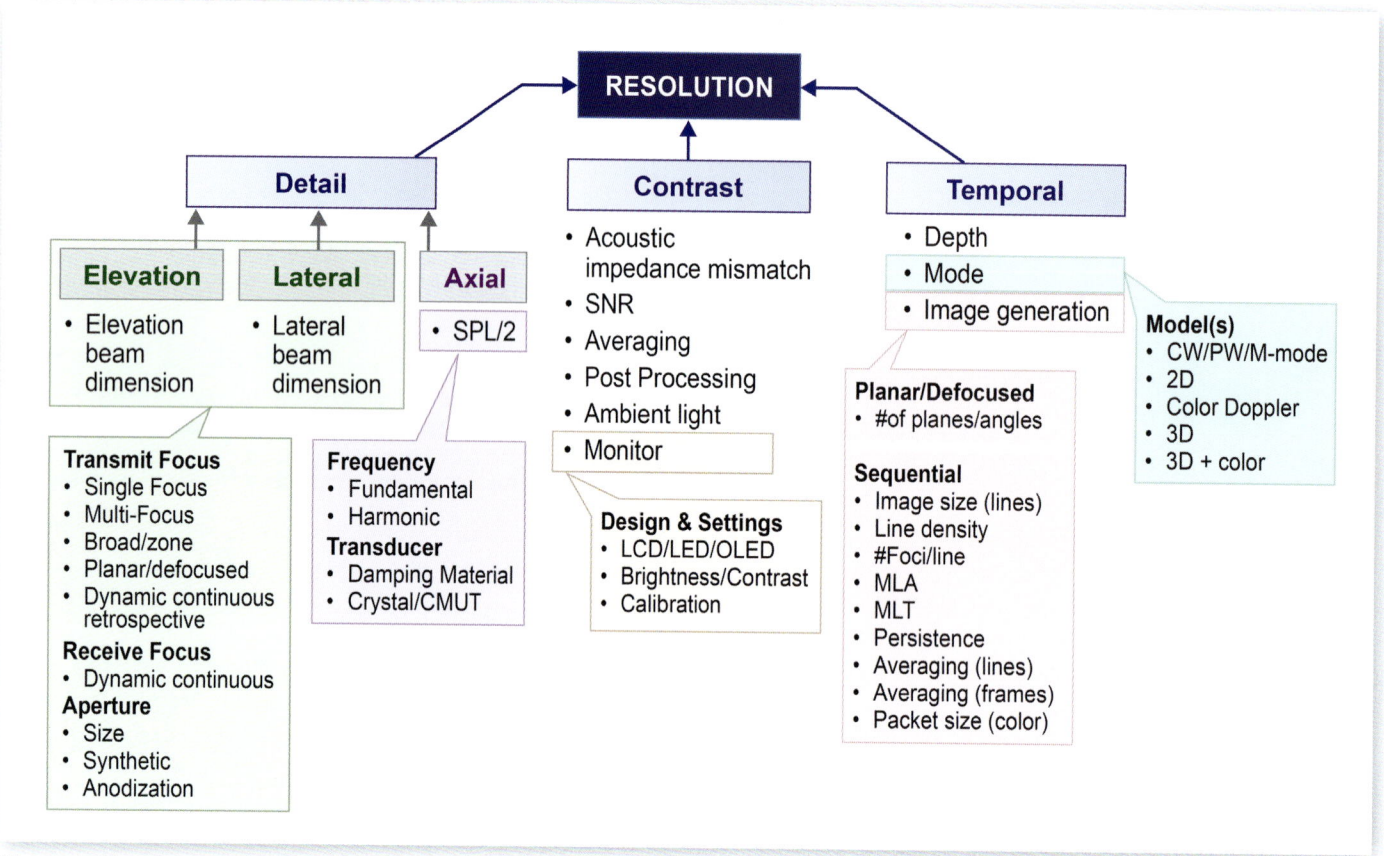

Fig. 82 **Compilation of resolution factors**

13.2 A Brief History of Artificial Intelligence and Its Rapid Growth

Although some people will argue that the concept of artificial intelligence stretches back to early philosophers, scientists, and mathematicians who imagined that at some point machines would be capable of performing calculations, most people tend to believe that the first major step for AI came when in 1950, Allen Turing, famous for breaking the German Enigma code during World War II, published "Computing Machinery and Intelligence," which asked the foundational question if machines can think. In 1952, a computer scientist named Arthur Samuel created a program which learned how to play the game of checkers. A few years later in 1956, John McCarthy held a summer conference at Dartmouth College which revealed a problem-solving program by the Research and Development (RAND) Corporation considered by many to be the first artificial intelligence program created. At this conference, the term artificial intelligence (AI) was coined and adopted. From this point forward, AI has had a "checkered" history in the sense that expectations kept exceeding capabilities as a result of limited data storage and computing power. In essence, advancements would be made that would then stall out as technology limits were reached. One of the interim high points is well known, when IBM's "Big Blue" was able to defeat the world-renowned chess champion, Gary Kasparov, in 1997.

Each start and stop brought AI to a much higher level, but the technology limits kept the AI from going mainstream until the development of highly powerful graphics processing units (GPUs) – the development of which is driven by the gaming industry and its need for highly sophisticated graphics drawn-redrawn at high speed for action games and the same technology responsible for the extreme advances that have recently taken place with beamforming and image processing. With this new technology, clusters of GPUs and dedicated chipsets could be created to perform parallel processing of enormous amounts of data quickly. This capability was the critical step needed for AI to become a widespread technology. These days, virtually everyone is exposed to AI every day. This exposure comes from phone answering services, Google searches, the use of technology assistants such as Alexa and Siri, and vehicle driving assist functions (lane departure, blind spot detection, automatic breaking, etc.) Self-driving vehicles have been in test for years now, and are believed to be just around the corner. AI is also now used to mine "Big Data" with dramatic impact on marketing and entertainment. Just do a few Google searches and watch how the algorithms start customizing the ads which appear based on what AI thinks is of interest to you.

13.3 Categorizations of AI
To fully detail the current state of AI is beyond the scope of this textbook, but the core concepts are discussed.

There are multiple ways of breaking down artificial intelligence. One approach leads to two simple categories: "Narrow" or "Weak" AI and "Artificial General Intelligence" (AGI) or "Strong" AI. This categorization is based on the constraints of the AI approach. For example, weak AI is generally focused on accomplishing a specific task, and is constrained by specific rules. In comparison, strong AI is the ability of AI to solve virtually any type of problem, with very few constraints. Strong AI implies a form of intelligence that is essentially indistinguishable from the intelligence of humans. Currently, the artificial intelligence programs which exist are all considered weak AI – with AGI, as of now, an aspirational goal that some argue may never be realizable.

Another categorization system divides AI into four categories:
1. **Reactive machines**: systems that can react to a current situation, but have no ability to utilize past experiences to influence present or future responses. IBM's Big Blue of 1997 is an example of a reactive system.
2. **Limited memory**: systems based on machine learning models which can use stored information or events to affect current and future responses. Autonomous vehicles which utilize both pre-programmed information and data regarding the environment input from sensors to output responses exemplify a limited memory AI system.
3. **Theory of mind**: systems that have decision making capability indistinguishable from that of a human, capable of adapting responses based on the emotional state of the person with whom there is interaction. Although there has been some progress toward this type of AI in which robots can sense and respond with a semblance of emotion, true theory of mind AI is not yet in existence.
4. **Self-awareness**: system that not only can adapt to emotional and situational changes, but is also capable to think for itself, with self-created desires, thoughts, and emotions. This is the type of AI that appears in many movies in which humans are at risk of extermination by machine dominance (Matrix anyone?).

13.4 Methods Utilized in Artificial Intelligence
Whereas the field of artificial intelligence is still advancing rapidly, a few basic approaches are commonly used. Techniques within AI are commonly associated with machine learning, deep learning, and neural networks.

13.4.1 Machine Learning
Most AI programs today are based on machine learning. The basic concept of machine learning is that the system is fed a large amount of input data of which it uses statistical techniques to analyze and learn from the data, without having a specific program dictating what the software needs to do. In other words, machine learning represents the ability of a system to learn how to perform a task rather than being programmed specifically to perform the task. For example, an image recognition program can learn to recognize the difference between male and female faces by analyzing a large number of images of males or females. Once the system is trained, the systems can look at any new image and output whether it believes the person in the image is male or female. Many voice recognition systems are based on machine learning.

Machine learning is generally classified into "supervised" and "unsupervised" learning. For supervised learning, the input datasets on which the system trains are labeled, indicating the relevant features. Once the system is trained, the system can then apply these labels to characteristics identified within new input data. In contrast, unsupervised learning implies that the system is trained on unlabeled data, and instead given algorithms on which to base recognition of specific characteristics within the data.

13.4.2 Deep Learning
Deep learning is a subset of machine learning. Deep learning is a more complex machine learning in which the system can process unstructured data from more than one source, analyze that data, and use the results to solve new problems. Currently, deep learning always involves the use of artificial neural networks (described in next section). Deep learning systems are capable of performing more than just a specific task. This capability comes from the use of algorithms that allow the system to apply learning across more than just one application. Examples of deep learning machines are self-driving vehicles, personal assistants, and facial recognition programs (like the ability to sort pictures in a system based on the picture's subject, location where taken, person/people in the photo).

13.4.3 Artificial Neural Networks (ANN)
As just mentioned, all deep learning systems currently utilize artificial neural networks. These networks are designed to loosely imitate the human brain structure. The network consists of a neural net with algorithms that link the layers of the net together. At its most basic level, the neural net consists of three layers of data:
- Input layer
- Hidden layer
- Output layer

The input layer is the data being analyzed. The hidden layer, (or layers) conceptually represents a characteristic associated with the data. The output layer represents the results or conclusion of the system. A weighting function maps the data from the input layer to the hidden layer, and another weighting function maps the hidden layer to the output. The hidden layer can consist of more than one layer with corresponding weighting functions that map between each layer. When the system is trained, a large number of datasets with known outcomes are input into the system. The weighting functions between each of the layers are iteratively changed to minimize the error of the system. At the end of the training, the weighting functions now allow the system to map input data to the correct output a percentage of the times. If the training is highly successful, then the percentage of times correct is very high. The quality of the mapping depends on the type of network used, the complexity of the mapping, and the number and quality of the datasets used to train the system.

13.5 AI in Ultrasound

Although there are already many AI applications within ultrasound, it is still early in the AI adoption curve for medicine and ultrasound. It is anticipated that within a few years, many more applications of AI systems applications will be readily available in the market. The discussion of AI in ultrasound will be broken down into three different categories:

- AI for improvement in work efficiency
- AI used in the acquisition of ultrasound images
- AI in the interpretation of ultrasound images

13.5.1 AI and Work Efficiency in Ultrasound

A great advantage of AI is its ability to perform efficient scheduling and assess large amounts of data to determine which studies should be performed based on patient history, symptoms, and prior studies. Additionally, AI can be used to automate the process of taking a progression of images needed to document whether or not a patient has a specific illness. With the ability to autodetect structures within an image, both labeling and measurements can be performed automatically, reducing study times. Also, with AI, the system can automatically perform image storage and develop thorough patient reports for analysis.

The following list summarizes current work enhancement features of AI:

1. Facilitates patient scheduling
2. Automates the process of taking progression of images
3. Autodetects structures in the image
4. Auto image storage for reports and analysis

Following are two examples illustrating auto-labeling and auto-measurements based on AI. *Figure 83* is an image of a fetal head generated by a GE Voluson system using a technology referred to as SonoCNS. This AI-based application automatically identifies the appropriate planes of the fetal head volume acquired by the sonographer, and then automatically performs the measurements. The result is a reduction in keystrokes and scan time as well as less variation in measurements between users than when performed manually.

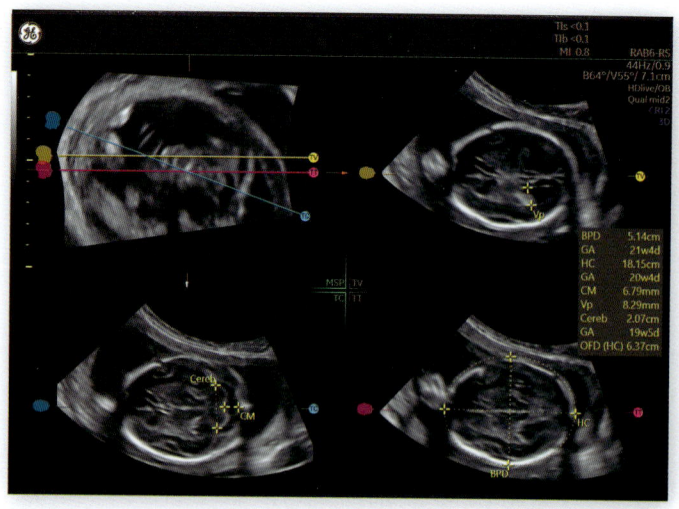

Fig. 83 **AI-assisted measurements of a fetal head using the SonoCNS application** *(Courtesy of GE Healthcare; Voluson™ is a trademark of GE Healthcare)*

Figure 84 is an example of the mitral valve Navigator A.I. (MVNA.I.) used on the Philips EPIQ system. The system assesses a live 3D volume of the mitral valve, and through a series of steps generates a list of mitral valve measurements and calculations. Again, this AI process reduces the time to acquire intensive measurements previously performed by hand, as well as standardizing results.

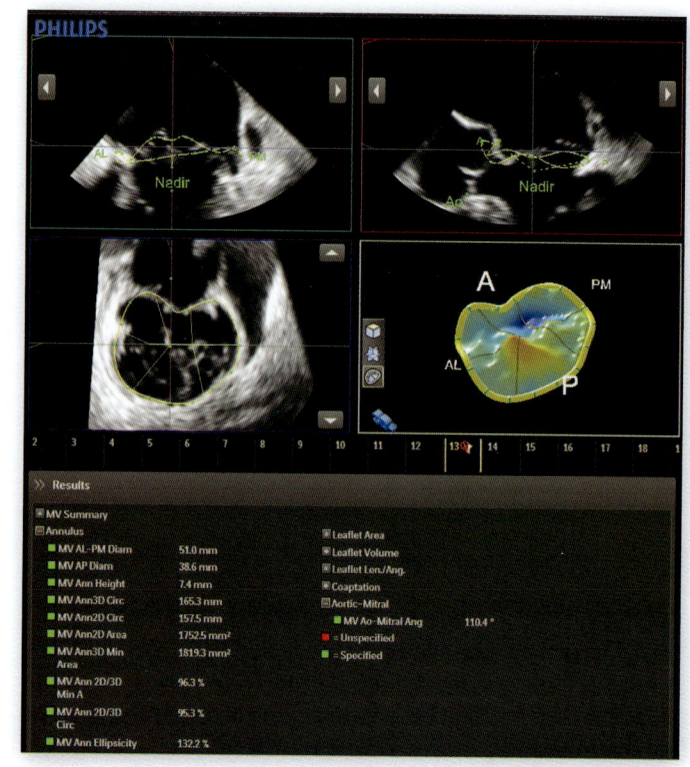

Fig. 84 **AI-assisted measurements of a mitral valve using Philips' MVNA.I. application** *(Courtesy of Koninklijke Philips N.V.)*

13.5.2 AI and Image Acquisition

There are many ways in which AI can be used to assist in image acquisition. As seen in *Figures 85* and *86*, one method is automatic selection of 2D images from 3D volume sets. This function can significantly decrease study time, since conceivably, a 3D volume of a region can be acquired and then the appropriate 2D slices automatically selected for measurements. Another potential AI feature is the ability to assist a sonographer in image optimization. A trained system can generate and display a quality index which tells the user when the image quality is poor or high enough quality as well as imaging suggestions to improve clinical assessment.

AI is also now providing the ability for "untrained" or lightly trained people to perform ultrasound and generate clinical images. This guidance capability extends the utility of ultrasound into emergency rooms, medical transport, field hospitals, etc. where personnel with ultrasound expertise may not exist. An example of this type of system is produced by Caption Health.

As shown in *Figure 85*, a portion of the screen indicates the location of where to place the ultrasound transducer as well as transducer orientation. When the transducer is placed near the correct area from which to acquire a high quality image, directions on how to acquire the scan are given. In the upper left corner is a quality meter which indicates when the image is of high quality. Once the correct image is obtained, automatic storage occurs and certain calculations are automatically generated. Whereas this system was the first to receive FDA clearance for ultrasound guidance in some limited applications, it assuredly will not be the last, and the number of approved applications will certainly grow rapidly.

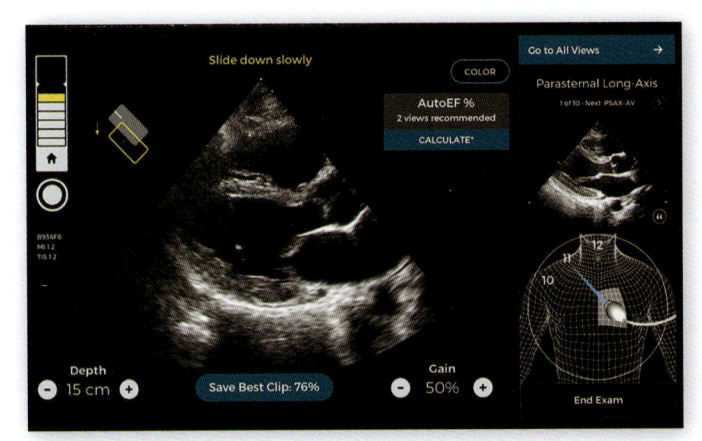

Fig. 85   **AI-assisted placement of transducer for scanning a PLAX view of the heart** *(Courtesy of Caption Health)*

13.5.3 AI-Assisted Image Interpretation

As discussed previously, one of the strengths of AI is its ability to be trained for assessment of image characteristics. Through deep learning, systems can be trained to differentiate normal from abnormal tissue and assist in identifying masses and lesions. These systems can be employed both on ultrasound systems or in reading stations when images are reviewed. Many research papers have been published which show varying degrees of success in automatic detection of abnormalities as well as classification such as breast cancer. Clearly, as these systems advance, they will provide greater consistency in study interpretation, decreased wait time for exam results, with the expectation that fewer false positives and false negatives will occur. At the very least, these systems serve as an aid for interpreting physicians with less experience, and can act like a "second opinion."

As shown in *Figure 86*, AI systems can detect possible lesions for assessment. For this particular system, the user is presented with multiple possible tracings of the auto-detected lesion. Once the user selects the desired tracing, the system automatically generates a classification (in this case the Thyroid Image Reporting and Data System, TI-RADS) and the probable diagnosis.

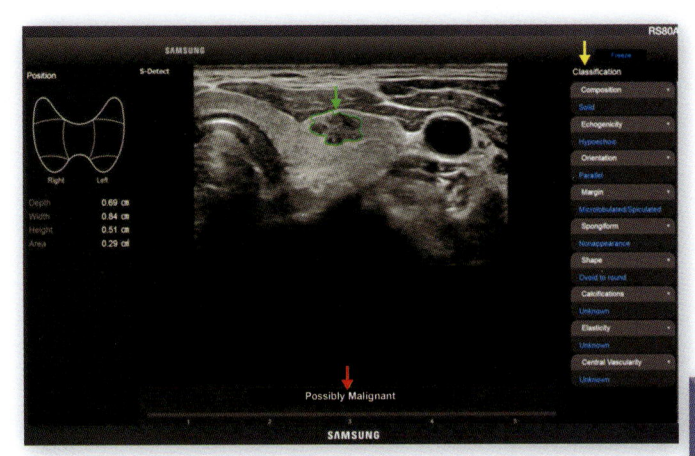

Fig. 86   **AI assessment (red arrow) of a possibly malignant thyroid lesion (green arrow/outline) showing TI-RADS classification (yellow arrow)** *(Courtesy of Samsung RS80A with S-Detect™)*

In the previous example, classification of characteristics of the lesion were used to assist in the diagnosis. In other cases, the diagnosis assistance is based on calculations, as shown in *Figure 87*.

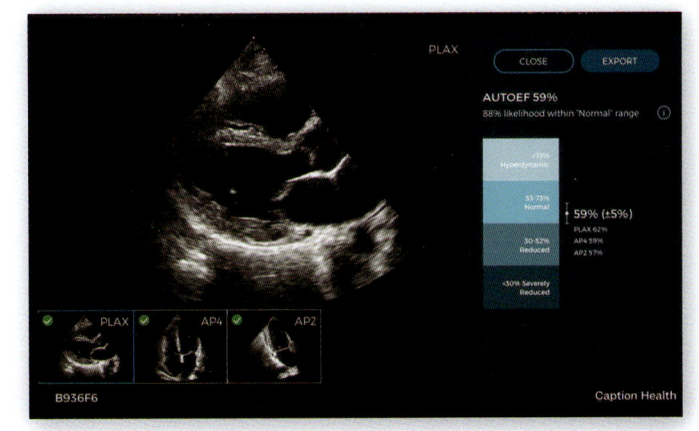

Fig. 87   **Auto-calculation and interpretation of the cardiac ejection fraction; note that, for this system from Caption Health, there is an indication of the sensitivity of the test (88% likelihood within 'Normal' range)** *(Courtesy of Caption Health)*

View ONLINE Animation and Image Library

13.6 The Future of AI

One can imagine a day when there is a global healthcare system that looks at all medical tests performed (including ultrasound), results of these tests, patient symptoms, family history, genetic risk factors, etc. and then outputs recommended testing and/or a more comprehensive diagnosis. The system could then look for drug interactions, optimization of individualized drug specific regimens, early detection of disease for earlier intervention, etc. Testing will be much more specific and capable of more quickly converging on diagnosis. Treatment will also become much more specific, taking into account the unique characteristics of the individual. Monitoring of treatment efficacy will likely become routine, resulting in diagnosis and treatment modifications, improved outcomes, and improved treatment models (more deep learning). There will also be an impact on ultrasound practitioners and the role of physicians, but exactly what those changes will be are unclear and the topic of much debate.

14. Conceptual Questions

View ONLINE Conceptual Questions

COMMON MISCONCEPTION: System Operation

MISCONCEPTION: *Math is not important to pass the exam.*

The mathematical concept of constructive and destructive signal interference is foundational to ultrasound and many medical techniques. This concept helps to explain such concepts as how transducers produce images, how certain artifacts in imaging occur, and how many more advanced imaging techniques work such as color persistence, frame averaging, and compound imaging.

COMMON MISCONCEPTION: System Operation

MISCONCEPTION: *Compound imaging results in a lower frame rate.*

Paradoxically, the frame rate for compound imaging is usually the same as the frame rate for conventional imaging, but compound imaging still suffers degradation in temporal resolution. The frame rate for compound imaging generally remains high since the average is updated by replacing the oldest frame of data with the newest frame of data. Therefore, a new "average" is displayed for each new frame of data that is acquired. So why is there a potential degradation in temporal resolution? Since a compound image is produced by averaging together multiple frames of data, events which occur in only one or two frames can essentially be "averaged out." Therefore, the degradation in temporal resolution with compound imaging is not the result of a lower frame rate, but rather the direct result of the averaging effect.

> **COMMON MISCONCEPTION: System Operation**
>
> **MISCONCEPTION:** *Compound imaging is the same as frequency compounding.*
>
> Although both frequency compounding and (spatial) compound imaging are techniques which reduce speckle artifact and improve signal-to-noise ratio, these two techniques achieve these results through different mechanisms. Compound imaging reduces speckle by averaging multiple images acquired over time. Since the images are acquired over time, this approach is not well suited for dynamic imaging situations such as adult or pediatric echo. However, since many images can be used in the average, the reduction in speckle and improvement in SNR is often significant. In contrast, frequency compound generates multiple images by parallel processing different bandwidths from a wide bandwidth received signal. Since the frames are acquired simultaneously, there is no degradation in temporal resolution. However, the improvement in speckle reduction and SNR is generally less impressive with frequency compounding than with compound imaging since fewer frames are generally used in the average.

> **COMMON MISCONCEPTION: System Operation**
>
> **MISCONCEPTION:** *Frequency fusion is the same as fusion imaging.*
>
> Frequency fusion (compounding) is an averaging technique by which frames produced using different transmit frequencies are combined together to improve speckle characteristics. Fusion imaging is a technique by which an ultrasound image is synced to a reference image (usually CT, MR, or PET) and then displayed simultaneously, such that changes in the ultrasound image by moving the transducer result in a corresponding change in the reference image plane.

> **COMMON MISCONCEPTION: System Operation**
>
> **MISCONCEPTION:** *Spatial averaging is the same as spatial compounding (spatial compound averaging).*
>
> Spatial averaging is a technique which smooths data pixel by pixel by considering the value of neighboring pixels. Spatial compound averaging (spatial compounding) is a frame averaging technique which is based on the concept of constructive and destructive interference and reduces speckle, increases signal-to-noise ratio, and reduces many artifacts based on specular reflection.

CHAPTER SUMMARY: System Operation (Advanced)

- Ultrasound optimization ultimately requires trade-offs. Successful optimization requires understanding how changing system parameters affects all aspects of the image.
- Detail resolution is the collective name for axial resolution, lateral resolution, and elevation resolution.
- Temporal resolution is limited by whichever process of image generation, display, or interpretation is the slowest. This can be the acoustic time to scan a frame (acoustic frame time), the time to display the frame (monitor frame rate), or the highest detection rate of the human eye (less than 60 frames per second).
- Contrast resolution is the ability to distinguish varying tissues based on brightness.
- For sequentially generated images, temporal resolution improvements come at the expense of the field of view or the lateral resolution.
- The advent of digital systems with increased processing power has made many new processing techniques economically and technologically feasible. Some of the many techniques facilitated by digital architectures include:
  - Parallel processing (MLA)
  - Multi-line transmit (MLT)
  - Frequency (fusion) compounding
  - Dynamic receive focusing
  - Retrospective transmit focusing
  - Plane/diverging wave imaging
  - Synthetic aperture
  - Fusion imaging
- Averaging is an important technique for improving the signal-to-noise ratio (SNR) and decreasing the speckle within an image.
- The gain in SNR from averaging is related to the concept of constructive and destructive interference.

- Constructive interference occurs when two or more waves are in phase (0° phase shift) such that the maxima and minima of all waves align and add to create one larger wave.
- Destructive interference occurs when two waves are purely out of phase (180° phase shift) such that the maxima of one wave aligns with the minima of the other wave, causing a complete cancellation of the wave amplitude.
- Partial constructive interference (for optimists) or partial destructive interference (for pessimists) results when two or more waves are not completely in or out of phase. The resultant wave has an amplitude smaller than the sum of the individual amplitudes.
- Spatial compound imaging (compound imaging) is a frame averaging technique which reduces noise and artifacts generally produced by angle dependent reflection (specular reflection).
- To maintain the frame rate when performing spatial compounding, a "FIFO" approach is taken in which the oldest frame is removed as each new frame is produced and added to the average.
- Spatial compound imaging can often reduce artifacts and improve the contrast resolution so that structures that otherwise would be missed (masses, thrombus, etc.) are visualized.
- Frequency compounding (fusion) is a technique by which two or more frames created at different transmit frequencies are combined (fused) so as to produce an image with improved speckle characteristics relative to the lower frequency image and improved penetration relative to the higher frequency image.
- Image persistence is a weighted averaging technique usually used in color Doppler.
- Spatial averaging is a noise reduction technique which adjusts each pixel's value by considering the neighboring pixel values.
- There are effectively two beams, a transmit beam and a receive beam whose product forms the composite (2-way) beam. Ultimately, the lateral resolution depends on the composite beam's width.
- For decades ultrasound has been based on using a single active transmit focus per line and sequential image generation.
- The single transmit focused beam has an hourglass shape which has degraded lateral resolution at depths farther from the focal depth.
- Multiple transmit foci results in an effectively narrower composite beam, improving lateral resolution at the expense of temporal resolution.
- Synthetic aperture uses the principle of superposition to add signals from varying elements at different times to effectively create a larger aperture.
- Dynamic retrospective transmit focusing essentially reverses time to add together the signals from the same location in the body to different elements as if the transmit had been originally focused at that location.
- Ultrafast imaging is any technique which results in significantly faster frame rates than the conventional sequential image generation approach.
- Parallel processing is a multi-line acquisition (MLA) technique to help improve temporal resolution by increasing the acoustic frame rate.
- Creating a wider transmit beam to allow for MLA would result in an improved temporal resolution at the expense of a wider two-way (composite) beam, deleteriously impacting the lateral resolution.
- Using dynamic retrospective focusing with MLA (parallel processing) does not result in a loss in lateral resolution.
- Another image generation approach to improve temporal resolution is to transmit more than one line at different locations simultaneously (MLT).
- The biggest drawback to MLT imaging is crosstalk between the transducer elements and grating lobes which degrade the image quality.
- Plane and diverging wave image can result in an entire image from a single transmit event – the time it takes to produce a single line of a sequential image.
- The SNR and contrast of a single plane wave image is not very good, but the frame rate is extraordinary.
- Multi-planar imaging uses the concept of spatial compounding planes at different angles to improve the SNR and contrast of single plane imaging.
- Multi-planar imaging, with dynamic receive and dynamic retrospective focusing can produce images with increased sensitivity and contrast while still preserving significantly higher frame rates than conventional sequential imaging.
- The increased temporal resolution affords the ability for improved 3D image acquisition as well as shear wave imaging.
- Panoramic imaging is a signal processing technique that allows for dramatic increases in the normal field of view (FOV) by correlating images from a translated transducer to scan out a large region of the patient.

- Adaptive processing is a two stage process by which a signal is mathematically analyzed and then displayed through an algorithm intended to intelligently enhance the display.
- Sound speed compensation is an adaptive process to adjust for actual varying speed of sound through different tissues so as to reduce beam aberration and improve focusing.
- 3D imaging extends a 2D image in the elevation plane so that an entire volume can be represented.
- Fusion imaging allows for a comparison of live ultrasound imaging (including contrast enhanced ultrasound (CEUS)) simultaneously with an uploaded reference image from another imaging modality such as CT, MR, or PET scanning.
- Artificial intelligence is advancing rapidly as a result of increased memory and processing speed
- Using machine learning, deep learning, and various forms of neural networks and algorithms, AI is capable of performing many tasks previously only possible by humans.
- Although still in the early stages, AI is already impacting ultrasound in terms of increased work efficiency, improved image acquisition, and image interpretation.

ONLINE EXTRAS

For additional support material and to view your completion progress, visit:
www.pegasuslectures.com/6thEdExtras

Extras by Chapter include:
- Animations
- Videos
- Additional Images
- Clarifying Clips
- Supplemental Exercises
- Conceptual Questions

See page x of Preface for access instructions

References

[1] Images modified and compiled from multiple sources including Verasonics and open source articles courtesy of MDPI Journals

Anyoha, Rockwell. (2017, August 28). *The History of Artificial Intelligence: Can Machines Think?*. Harvard. https://sitn.hms.harvard.edu/flash/2017/history-artificial-intelligence/.

Bae, S., & Song, T. K. (2018). Methods for grating lobe suppression in ultrasound plane wave imaging. *Applied Sciences, 8*(10), 1881.

Bercoff, J. (2011). Ultrafast ultrasound imaging. *Ultrasound imaging-Medical applications*, 3-24.

Bottenus, N. (2018). Comparison of virtual source synthetic aperture beamforming with an element-based model. *The Journal of the Acoustical Society of America, 143*(5), 2801-2812.

Bradley, C. (2008). Retrospective transmit beam formation. ACUSON SC2000 volume imaging ultrasound system. *Mountain View, California, https://www.siemens.com.tr/i/Assets/saglik/Whitepaper_Bradley.pdf*.

Built In. (2021). *Artificial Intelligence*. https://builtin.com/artificial-intelligence.

Cikes, M., Tong, L., Sutherland, G. R., & D'hooge, J. (2014). Ultrafast cardiac ultrasound imaging: technical principles, applications, and clinical benefits. *JACC: Cardiovascular Imaging, 7*(8), 812-823.

Demi, L. (2018). Practical guide to ultrasound beam forming: Beam pattern and image reconstruction analysis. *Applied Sciences, 8*(9), 1544.

Heath, Nick. (2020, December 11). *What is AI? Everything you need to know about Artificial Intelligence.* ZDNet. https://www.zdnet.com/article/what-is-ai-everything-you-need-to-know-about-artificial-intelligence/.

Jedrzejewicz, T., Napolitano, D., DeBusschere, D., Chou, C. H., & McLaughlin, G. Two-Way Continuous Transmit and Receive Focusing in Ultrasound Imaging.

Lee, M. W. (2014). Fusion imaging of real-time ultrasonography with CT or MRI for hepatic intervention. *Ultrasonography, 33*(4), 227.

Matrone, G., & Ramalli, A. (2018). Spatial coherence of backscattered signals in multi-line transmit ultrasound imaging and its effect on short-lag filtered-delay multiply and sum beamforming. *Applied Sciences, 8*(4), 486.

Nikolov, S. I., Kortbek, J., & Jensen, J. A. (2010, October). Practical applications of synthetic aperture imaging. In *2010 IEEE International Ultrasonics Symposium* (pp. 350-358). IEEE.

Philips. *Obstetrics and gynecology ultrasound.* https://www.philips.iq/en/healthcare/solutions/ultrasound/obstetrics-and-gynecology-ultrasound.

Polichetti, M., Varray, F., Béra, J. C., Cachard, C., & Nicolas, B. (2018). A nonlinear beamformer based on p-th root compression—application to plane wave ultrasound imaging. *Applied Sciences,* 8(4), 599.

Reynoso, Rebecca. (2019, March 27). *4 Main Types of Artificial Intelligence.* G2. https://learn.g2.com/types-of-artificial-intelligence.

Tanter, M., & Fink, M. (2014). Ultrafast imaging in biomedical ultrasound. *IEEE transactions on ultrasonics, ferroelectrics, and frequency control, 61*(1), 102-119.

Tong, L., He, Q., Ortega, A., Ramalli, A., Tortoli, P., Luo, J., & D'hooge, J. (2019). Coded excitation for crosstalk suppression in multi-line transmit beamforming: Simulation study and experimental validation. *Applied Sciences, 9*(3), 486.

Wu, G. G., Zhou, L. Q., Xu, J. W., Wang, J. Y., Wei, Q., Deng, Y. B., ... & Dietrich, C. F. (2019). Artificial intelligence in breast ultrasound. *World journal of radiology, 11*(2), 19.

Doppler

Chapter 7

WHY DO WE STUDY THIS?

▶ Spectral Doppler provides a means of quantitatively measuring velocity with respect to time.

▶ Blood flow can be assessed from Doppler spectral waveform characteristics, parameters calculated from the velocity measurements, and from color flow visualization.

▶ Collectively, Doppler provides information necessary to assess systemic hemodynamics and perfusion of organs.

WHAT'S IN THIS CHAPTER?

LEVEL 1 — BASIC ULTRASOUND PHYSICS
General Doppler theory and fundamental principles are discussed.

LEVEL 2 — BOARD LEVEL
We examine how Doppler systems function, including the difference between sequentially generated color and ultrafast Doppler. We also discuss Doppler waveforms, spectral Doppler, and color Doppler.

LEVEL 3 — ADVANCED TOPICS
Detailed information is provided on angular errors, wall filtering, and associated effects on flow appreciation, including vector flow (V Flow) imaging as a tool for assessing wall shear stress (WSS).

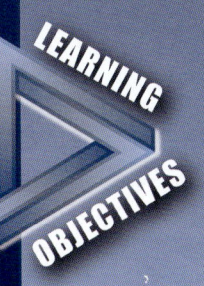

LEARNING OBJECTIVES

▶ Define the Doppler effect and Doppler equation

▶ Describe the parameters which affect the Doppler shift

▶ Identify processing steps in generating spectral and color Doppler

▶ Explain the system controls impacting Doppler signals

▶ Describe the difference between sequentially generated and ultrafast color Doppler

Chapter 7
Doppler

Introduction

One of the principal requirements of diagnostic ultrasound is to determine the characteristics and velocity of blood flow. The analysis is performed by multiple Doppler modalities that include spectral Doppler, waveform Doppler, audio Doppler, and color flow Doppler imaging. It is essential to understand that everything you have learned about sound waves, transducers, etc., holds true for Doppler, with the addition of a new effect – a frequency shift called the Doppler effect. The Doppler effect has been used for many years as the mechanism by which blood flow is detected, measured, and monitored noninvasively within the body.

Doppler is one of the most powerful techniques used in ultrasound, but also the tool most underutilized and misinterpreted. A Doppler spectrum contains a wealth of information for the person who has learned the theory of Doppler, the practical application, and the relationship to the hemodynamic situations being assessed. This chapter focuses on the fundamentals of Doppler. By itself, the fundamentals of Doppler are less than half of the whole story. To fully appreciate the significance of Doppler and Doppler measurements, you must review the principles of fluid dynamics and hemodynamics. In essence, you should consider this chapter as part of a trilogy which includes Chapters 12 and 13.

Most students have an inherent understanding of why we want the ability to generate ultrasound images of structures in the body. Nearly everyone has seen an image of a fetus, and as well, can naturally intuit the value in being able to see if there are abnormalities to kidneys, the liver, or heart tissue. The value of "seeing" blood flow is likely more esoteric. As such, before we begin discussing Doppler theory, it is helpful to develop an appreciation for why assessing parameters associated with blood flow can be clinically helpful.

The health of tissue is dependent on an adequate blood supply. When tissue is not adequately perfused (supplied blood), it becomes ischemic (lacking in oxygen needed to meet metabolic demand), and if left long enough in this state, can lead to tissue death (necrosis). Assuring adequate tissue perfusion is therefore requisite to assuring healthy organs, and ultimately, the well-being of the entire individual. As discussed in Chapters 12 and 13, blood flow represents the volume of blood that passes a particular point for a given time period. For example, if five liters are propelled out of the heart through the aorta in one minute, we would say that the cardiac output flow is 5 liters/min. Doppler does not give a direct measurement of volumetric flow. Color Doppler allows for visual perception of where blood is flowing, the mean velocity of that flow, and a qualitative assessment of whether the flow is normal or abnormal based on knowledge of normative flow for each specific organ. Spectral Doppler gives a direct measurement of blood velocity relative to time, not a direct measurement of volumetric flow.

Although Doppler does not give direct volumetric flow measurements, based on the appearance of the color Doppler and based on calculations derived from the spectral waveforms and comparisons with expected velocities, informed decisions can be made about the volumetric flow. In fact, there are many Doppler velocity related parameters and calculations that are used to assess volumetric flow such as the peak velocity, acceleration, deceleration, Doppler indices (ratios), velocity time integral (VTI), and time-averaged mean velocities (TAMV). In essence, we can use Doppler to determine if there are increases or decreases in blood flow associated with vessel narrowing (stenosis), blockage (occlusion), increased (compensatory) flow, shunting, aneurysmal changes, rupture, or any other change in vascularization. So, as you can see, there are many reasons why understanding Doppler is essential. *Figures 1* and *2* give a hint of what is to come.

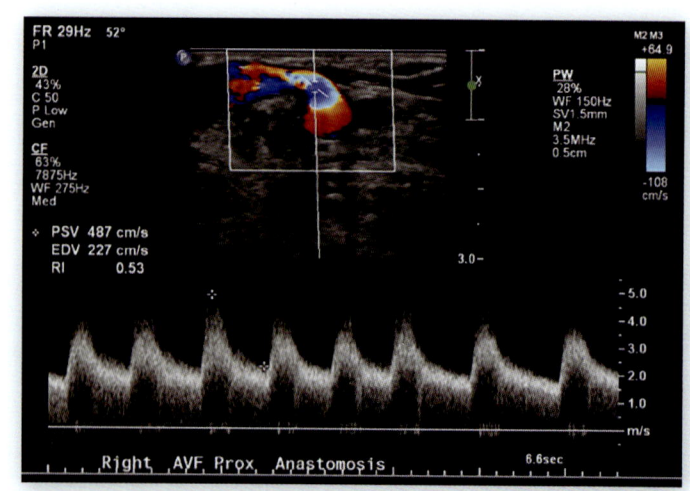

Fig. 1 **Color and spectral Doppler of an arteriovenous fistula at the site of the connection demonstrating very high velocity flow**

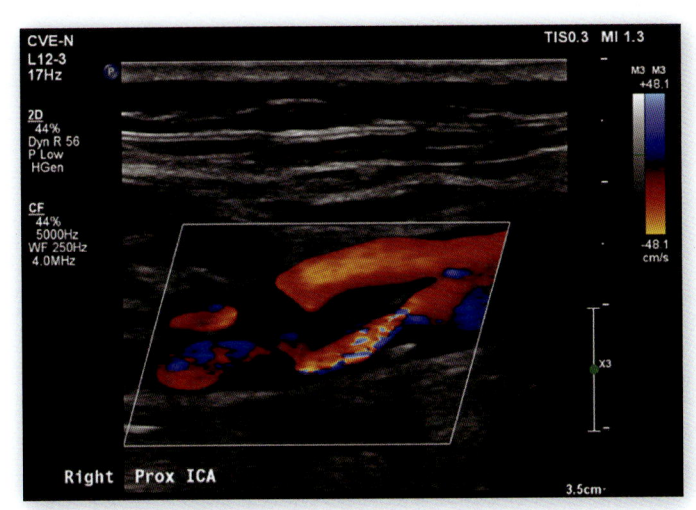

Fig. 2 Color Doppler of the carotid bifurcation leading to the external and internal carotid arteries demonstrating stenotic flow at the origin of the ICA

So how do you learn to create and understand color Doppler images and Doppler spectra? The starting point is learning the Doppler effect.

1. The Doppler Effect

1.1 Change in Frequency

The Doppler effect is an apparent shift in frequency of an interrogating wave caused by relative motion between an observer and an object. This noticeable frequency shift is actually the result of changes that occur to the wavelength because of the relative movement. In other words, if a wave (with a given wavelength) reflects from an object which is moving, the wavelength of the reflected wave will be different than the original wavelength. Specifically, if the object moves toward the observer (wave source) then the wavelength will be shorter than the original wavelength; whereas, if the object moves away from the observer, then the reflected wave will have a longer wavelength. Since a shorter wavelength represents a higher frequency, motion toward the observer produces a higher frequency than the original wave. Conversely, movement away from the observer produces a lower frequency than the frequency of the transmitted wave.

1.2 The Doppler Thought Experiment

To understand the Doppler effect we will use the classic example of a moving train blowing its whistle and two observers.

Scenario 1: Stationary Train

Let's begin by considering a stationary train blowing its whistle. There are two observers, observer A and observer B, on either side of the train equal distance away. As the whistle blows, it produces a series of compressions and rarefactions at uniform time increments. As we learned in Chapter 2, the time increment between each compression (the period) is determined by the frequency of the whistle. Over time, the waves propagate radially away from the stationary train. For the figure below, the rings surrounding the train represent the propagating mechanical sound waves over time. The solid circles represent the peak wave compressions, and the white regions in between represent rarefactions. Also recall that the distance between these compressions is called the wavelength.

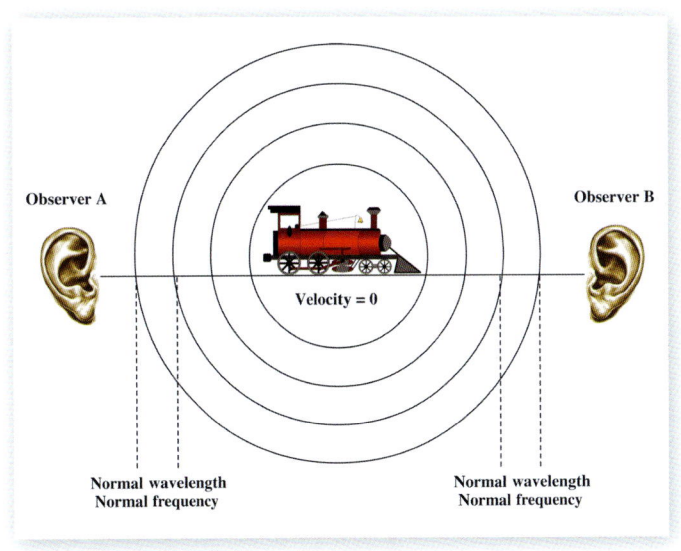

Fig. 3 No Doppler shift: stationary train

Eventually, the radiating wave reaches both observers. Since the wavelengths of the wave that reaches each observer is identical, both observers will hear the same pitch (frequency) whistle.

Scenario 2: Moving Train

Now let's modify the situation. The train is currently traveling at a velocity (v) directly toward observer B, and directly away from observer A. Again, we must imagine time and motion from our still drawing. When the train reaches the same location as in the scenario with the stationary train, it blows the same whistle. Again the whistle produces a series of compressions and rarefactions separated uniformly in time. However, between the time of emitting the first compression and the second compression, the train has moved some distance toward observer B. This movement results in the wavefronts in front of the train being closer than if the train had been stationary. Similarly, the wavefronts will be separated by a greater distance behind the train than if the train had been stationary.

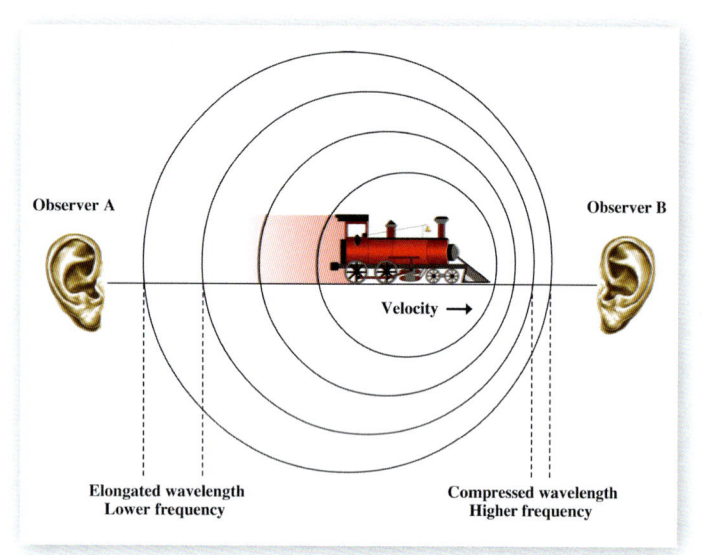

Fig. 4 Doppler shift: train moving with velocity "v" toward observer B

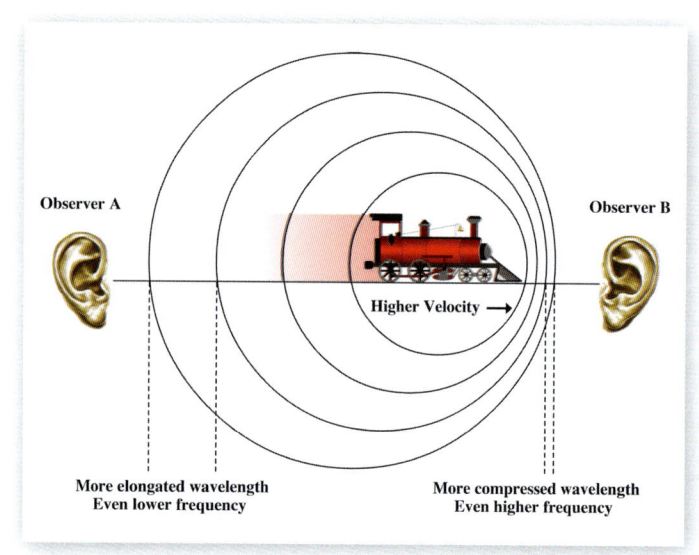

Fig. 5 Greater Doppler shift: as velocity increases, Doppler shift increases

Effectively, the wavelength was compressed toward observer B, and decompressed (elongated) relative to observer A. Since a shorter wavelength represents a higher frequency, observer B hears a higher pitch whistle than when the train was stationary. Conversely, since a longer wavelength implies a lower frequency, observer A hears a lower pitch whistle than when the train was stationary. This change in frequency for both observers is the Doppler effect.

Observer B hears an even higher pitched whistle, and observer A hears an even lower pitch whistle than in *Scenario 2*.

View ONLINE Animation and Image Library

View ONLINE Animation and Image Library

KEY CONCEPT

The Doppler effect is an apparent change in frequency which results from a change in wavelength because of motion between a source and an observer. The Doppler effect is exemplified by the change in pitch that occurs as a high speed train or car at a racetrack approaches and then speeds past.

Scenario 3: **Faster Train**
Now let's modify the situation by increasing the train's velocity. As in *Scenario 2*, when the train reaches the same location midway between the two observers, the train blows its whistle. In the time between the sound wave compressions, the train is moving. Since the velocity of the train is higher than in *Scenario 2*, the distance traveled during the period will increase. The compression of the wavefront toward observer B will be greater than in *Scenario 2*. Similarly, the elongation (decompression) of the wavefront toward observer A will also be greater than in *Scenario 2*.

1.3 The Relationship Between Velocity (v) and the Doppler Shift

In essence, the train's motion as a percentage of the wavelength is greater when the train moves with a higher velocity than when it moves with a slower velocity. The result is a greater compression of the wavelength toward the observer and a greater decompression of the wavelength away from the observer. The greater the compression, the greater the apparent change in frequency, or equivalently, the greater the Doppler shift. Mathematically, we can write the relationship between the train's velocity (v) and the Doppler frequency shift f_{Dop} as:

$$f_{Dop} \propto v$$

> **KEY CONCEPT**
>
> The Doppler shift is proportional to the relative velocity. The Doppler shift increases as the velocity increases.

1.4 Wavelength (λ) and the Doppler Effect
In our description of the Doppler effect, you should have noticed that the change in frequency resulted from a change in the wavelength caused by relative motion. Therefore, it should not be surprising that the parameters which affect the wavelength also affect the Doppler shift. In Chapter 3, we derived the wavelength equation which dictates that the frequency and the propagation velocity determine the wavelength, and hence, affect the Doppler shift. If you don't recall this equation, this might be a good time to review Chapter 3.

1.5 Relative Motion
In Chapter 1: Mathematics, a considerable effort is made to highlight the distinction between absolute and relative. In our definition of the Doppler effect, the fact that the motion is described as "relative" is no accident. One of Einstein's famous theorems was about the inability to determine absolute motion. Without a reference frame, it is not possible to determine whether the observer is moving or the train is moving.

Imagine if we changed our *Scenario 2* such that the train was stationary and the observers were moving instead. Observer B moves toward the train with velocity v and observer A moves away from the train with the same velocity v. For observer B, the distance between wavefronts will be compressed because of the decreasing distance between the train and the observer. Conversely, the wavefronts will be elongated for observer A because of the increasing distance between the train and the observer. Therefore, the exact same effect occurs as when the train was moving instead of the observers.

When the distance between the source and the observer is increasing, the relative motion is "away" and a decompression occurs. When the distance between the source and the observer is decreasing, the relative motion is "towards" and a compression occurs. Compression leads to a higher frequency, and hence, a positive frequency shift whereas decompression leads to a lower frequency and a negative frequency shift.

1.6 The Relative Shift
If there is one area that catches people, it is making the distinction between the word shift and the word frequency. The problem yet again comes down to paying attention to the difference between a relative term versus an absolute term. The term "shift" implies a relative relationship. A shift can be positive or negative. Like the word "change," a greater shift does not tell direction, only amount. A faster velocity will result in a greater frequency shift. Note that there is no way of knowing whether the shift was positive or negative unless we know about the relative motion. If the relative motion is towards, then a greater shift implies an increasingly higher frequency. If the relative motion is away, then a greater shift implies an increasingly lower frequency.

1.7 Determining the Relative Doppler Shift Numerically
The Doppler shift is the relative difference between the detected frequency and the transmitted frequency. Mathematically, this is expressed as:

$$f_{Dop} = f_{detected} - f_{transmitted} = \Delta f.$$

From this equation notice that when the detected frequency is higher than the transmitted frequency, the Doppler shift is positive. Let's add some numbers to our previous train example to illustrate the relative nature of the Doppler effect. Imagine that the train's whistle was transmitted with a frequency of 2 MHz. Our observers will now have to be ultrasound listening devices since 2 MHz is well above human hearing.

In *Scenario 1*, the absolute frequency detected by both ultrasound observers is 2 MHz. The shift is the difference between the transmitted and received detected frequencies. In this case, the Doppler shift for both observer A and observer B is zero and there is no Doppler effect.

$$f_{Dop} = f_{detected} - f_{transmitted} = 2 \text{ MHz} - 2 \text{ MHz} = 0.$$

In *Scenario 2*, suppose ultrasound observer A detected an absolute frequency of 1.98 MHz while observer B detected an absolute frequency of 2.02 MHz.

The Doppler shift for observer A is:

$$f_{Dop} = f_{detected} - f_{transmitted} = 1.98 \text{ MHz} - 2 \text{ MHz} =$$
$$-0.02 \text{ MHz} = -20 \text{ kHz}.$$

The Doppler shift for observer B is:

$$f_{Dop} = f_{detected} - f_{transmitted} = 2.02 \text{ MHz} - 2 \text{ MHz} =$$
$$+0.02 \text{ MHz} = +20 \text{ kHz}.$$

Note that both observer A and observer B detected a frequency shift of 20 kHz. The difference is that observer A detected a negative frequency shift whereas observer B detected a positive frequency shift.

1.8 Exercises
So far we have learned that the Doppler shift is proportional to the relative velocity. Let us now consider a few scenarios to test our understanding.

2. Relationships in the Doppler Equation

2.1 Velocity (v) and Wavelength (λ)
From the experiments we have conducted, we have learned that the Doppler effect is principally caused by a change in wavelength caused by motion relative to an observer. As the relative motion increases, the Doppler effect also increases. This proportional relationship makes sense since a higher velocity implies a greater distance traveled during the period. Since the effect is caused by the relative distance change as a percentage of the wavelength, anything which results in a greater relative distance will result in a greater percentage change.

To illustrate this point, imagine that the wavelength is 10 meters. Now consider what happens if a train moves two meters instead of one meter during the period. One meter is 10% of the wavelength whereas two meters is 20% of the wavelength. Clearly, the greater distance results in a greater change. Since the distance traveled is related to the velocity, we again arrive at the relationship discovered earlier that the Doppler shift is proportional to the velocity, or $f_{Dop} \propto v$.

2.2 Wavelength (λ) and the Transmit Frequency (Operating Frequency f_0)
The wavelength equation dictates that there is an inverse relationship between the wavelength and the operating frequency:

$$\lambda = \frac{c}{f}.$$

Since the Doppler effect is determined by the wavelength, and since the wavelength is affected by the operating frequency, we know (by the transitive property) that the Doppler effect must be affected by the operating frequency. Now all we need to do is to determine the mathematical relationship between the Doppler shift and the operating frequency.

Consider what happens to the wavelength if the operating frequency increases. Since there is an inverse relationship, as the operating frequency increases, the wavelength decreases. Now recall that the Doppler effect is caused by the percent relative change in the wavelength caused by the train's motion. Therefore, as the wavelength decreases, the Doppler effect increases. As we did in Section 2.1, we will use a numerical example to make this point clear (See *Figure 6*).

For a given operating frequency, imagine that the wavelength is 10 meters. Now further imagine that the train moves one meter during a period of time (the distance between the red and the blue wavefront), equivalent to 10% of the wavelength. Now presume that the operating frequency is doubled. Since there is an inverse proportionality between the operating frequency and the wavelength, if the operating frequency doubles, the wavelength is reduced by a factor of 2.

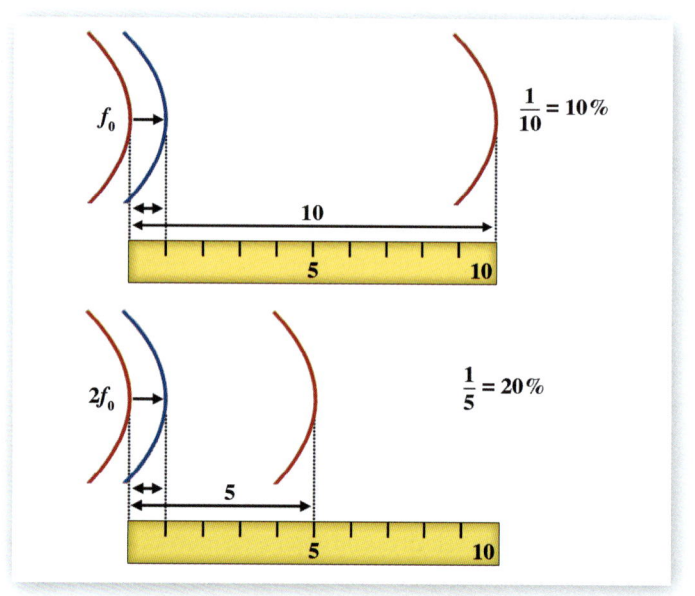

Fig. 6 Effect of frequency on the Doppler effect

Therefore, at the higher operating frequency the wavelength is reduced from 10 meters to 5 meters. The train's velocity is independent of the frequency of its whistle, therefore the train still moves 1 meter during the same period of time. One meter relative to a 5 meters wavelength now represents 20%, or a doubling in the Doppler effect relative to the lower operating frequency. Therefore, as the operating frequency increases, the Doppler shift increases. Mathematically, this is written as:

$$f_{Dop} \propto f_0.$$

2.3 Wavelength (λ) and the Propagation Velocity (c)

The wavelength equation also dictates that there is a direct relationship between the wavelength and the propagation velocity:

$$\lambda = \frac{c}{f}.$$

Again, since the Doppler effect is determined by the wavelength, and since the wavelength is affected by the propagation velocity, we know (by the transitive property) that the Doppler effect must be affected by the propagation velocity. Now we need to determine the mathematical relationship between the Doppler shift and the propagation velocity.

Consider what happens to the wavelength if the propagation velocity increases. Since there is a direct relationship, as the propagation velocity increases, the wavelength increases. Again recall that the Doppler effect is caused by the percent relative change in the wavelength caused by the train's motion. Therefore, as the wavelength increases, the Doppler effect decreases. As we just did with illustrating the effect of the operating frequency, we will use a numerical example to make this point clear.

For a given propagation velocity, imagine that the wavelength is 5 meters. Now further imagine that the train moves 1 meter during a period of time, equivalent to 20% of the wavelength. Now presume that the propagation velocity is doubled. Since there is a direct proportionality between the propagation velocity and the wavelength, if the propagation velocity doubles, the wavelength is doubled.

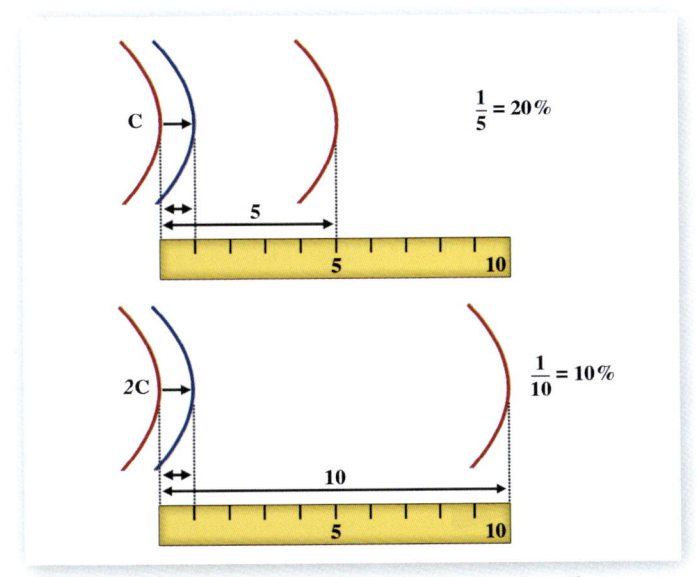

Fig. 7 **Effect of propagation velocity on the Doppler effect**

Therefore, at the higher propagation velocity, the wavelength is increased from 5 meters to 10 meters. The train's velocity is independent of the propagation velocity of the whistle, therefore the train still moves 1 meter during the same period of time. One meter relative to a 10 meters wavelength now represents only 10%, or half of the Doppler effect that occurred with a lower propagation velocity.

Therefore, as the propagation velocity increases, the Doppler shift decreases. Mathematically, this is written as:

$$f_{Dop} \propto \frac{1}{c}.$$

2.4 Roundtrip Effect

In each of our thought experiments so far, the Doppler effect was measured by the observer. However, in ultrasound, the measurement is not made by the observer but rather by measuring the reflected frequency back to the transducer. In other words, there is a roundtrip effect that must be considered. In essence, as the wave travels to the moving structure, there is an associated shift. The structure then acts as the source of the reflected wave. Recall that movement by the source or by the observer both cause a frequency shift. Therefore, since the structure is moving as it reflects the wave back to the transducer, there is a doubling effect. As a result, we should expect to see a factor of two in the mathematical expression which determines the Doppler shift (the Doppler equation).

> **KEY CONCEPT**
>
> Since the Doppler effect is related to a change in wavelength, the parameters which determine the wavelength must be variables in the Doppler equation. Therefore, from the wavelength equation we know that changes to the operating frequency, f, and changes to the propagation velocity, c, affect the Doppler shift.

3. A Simplified Doppler Equation

3.1 Equation with No Angle Effects

As we saw in the various scenarios, the Doppler shift can be positive or negative depending on the direction of motion relative to the observer. In the examples we have analyzed, the relative motion was either directly toward or directly away from an observer. For now, we will deal only with this simplified case. In Level 2 we will add the next level of complexity which expresses mathematically what happens when the motion is neither directly towards nor directly away from the source (in ultrasound, the source is the transducer).

Cognizant of this simplification, if we combine all of the relations we have just discussed into one equation, we arrive at a simplified form of the Doppler equation:

$$f_{Dop} = \frac{2 f_0 v}{c}$$

where:

f_{Dop} = Doppler shifted frequency
f_0 = transmit frequency
v = velocity of target through medium
c = speed of interrogating beam through medium
(c = 1540 m/sec for sound in tissue)

Notice that the absolute equation expresses all of the following relationships.

$$f_{Dop} \propto v.$$

$$f_{Dop} \propto f_0.$$

$$f_{Dop} \propto \frac{1}{c}.$$

Notice that the factor of 2 which accounts for the roundtrip effect is not demonstrated in the relationships. Recall from Chapter 1: Mathematics that relationships exist between variables. The number 2 is a constant, and hence, cannot change in response to changes with other variables.

3.2 Simplified Numeric Form

In many textbooks you may see a further simplified form in which an assumption is made for the propagation velocity, and the assumed value plugged into the equation. Assuming a propagation velocity of 1540 m/sec, the equation can be rewritten as:

$$f_{Dop} = \frac{2 f_0 v}{c} = \frac{2 f_0 v}{1540 \frac{m}{sec}} = \frac{f_0 v}{770 \frac{m}{sec}}.$$

Author's Note:
The Doppler Equation

I am not a big proponent of learning the Doppler equation in this simplified numeric form, since it usually leads to pure memorization instead of intuitive understanding of the equation and its application. I believe that seeing the variable for propagation velocity in the equation is a reminder that the Doppler effect is wavelength-related and that the wavelength is determined by both the operating frequency and the propagation velocity. This simplified, numeric form is included here so that no confusion develops should you see the equation written in this form in any other literature. You should realize that this equation still presumes that the direction of motion is either directly toward or directly away relative to the observer, and therefore does not take into account angle effects.

3.3 Examples of Doppler Relations Applied

◊ **Example 1:**
For a given interrogating frequency, if the velocity triples, what happens to the Doppler shift frequency?

Answer:
Since the Doppler shift is proportional to the velocity ($f_{Dop} \propto v$) a tripling of the velocity implies a tripling of the Doppler shift.

◊ **Example 2:**
For a specific target velocity, if the transmit frequency is decreased by a factor of 1.63, what happens to the Doppler shift frequency?

Answer:
Since the Doppler shift is proportional to the operating (transmit) frequency ($f_{Dop} \propto f_0$) a decrease in the operating frequency by a factor of 1.63 implies a decrease in the Doppler shift by a factor of 1.63.

◊ **Example 3:**
Assuming no other changes, if the propagation velocity increases by a factor of 1.1, what happens to the Doppler shift frequency?

Answer:
Since the Doppler shift is inversely proportional to the propagation velocity ($f_{Dop} \propto \frac{1}{c}$), an increase in the propagation velocity by a factor of 1.1 implies a decrease in the Doppler shift by a factor of 1.1.

◊ **Example 4:**
If the transmit frequency is changed from 2 MHz to 10 MHz, what happens to the Doppler shift frequency?

Answer:
Since the Doppler shift is proportional to the operating (transmit) frequency ($f_{Dop} \propto f_0$) an increase in the operating frequency by a factor of 5 implies an increase in the Doppler shift by a factor of 5.

◊ **Example 5:**
Using 2 MHz, the measured Doppler shift was -3 kHz. If the transmit frequency is changed from 2 MHz to 4 MHz, what will the Doppler shift frequency be?

Answer:
Since the Doppler shift is proportional to the operating (transmit) frequency ($f_{Dop} \propto f_0$), an increase in the operating frequency by a factor of 2 implies an increase in the Doppler shift by a factor of 2. Since the original

Doppler shift frequency was -3 kHz, the new Doppler shift frequency is -6 kHz.

In the case of diagnostic ultrasound, the target is usually red blood cells and the observer is the transducer. However, any motion which occurs, such as wall motion, respiration, transducer movement, etc., will cause a frequency shift.

4. Solving the Doppler Equation for Velocity

The simplified Doppler equation is expressed in terms of the Doppler shift frequency. Since, in general, the Doppler shift is the measured parameter, what we would like to calculate is the velocity. To express the equation in terms of velocity, all that is needed is to manipulate the equation. As discussed in Chapter 1: Mathematics, the rules for equation manipulation are simple: whatever you do to one side of the equation you must also do to the other side of the equation. So by using the property of reciprocals we can manipulate the equation as follows:

$$f_{Dop} = \frac{2 f_0 v}{c}$$

$$f_{Dop} \times \frac{c}{2 f_0} = \frac{2 f_0 v}{c} \times \frac{c}{2 f_0}$$

$$v = \frac{c \times f_{Dop}}{2 f_0}.$$

Remember, this equation is simplified and does not contain angle correction.

KEY CONCEPT

Since the Doppler effect is perceived as a change in frequency, the equation is generally written with respect to the Doppler frequency shift. However, the parameter of interest is really the blood velocity. Therefore, using basic rules of algebra, we manipulate the Doppler equation to a form that relates the parameters relative to the velocity.

5. Conceptual Questions

View ONLINE Conceptual Questions

LEVEL 2: Board Level

6. Completing the Doppler Equation

6.1 Removing the "Directly Toward or Directly Away" Assumption

When we derived the Doppler equation, we took note that the Doppler shift would change depending on where the observer was located relative to the moving train. We then made the assumption that the motion was always either directly toward or directly away, so as to simplify the Doppler equation. Real world conditions pretty much guarantee that the flow direction we measure in the body is frequently not directly towards or directly away from the transducer. The probability of flow directly toward or away is more probable in cardiac imaging and much less probable in vascular studies. Even in the cardiac imaging, there is a plethora of times where the "direct" assumption will not hold. Therefore, we will now remove this assumption and develop the mathematical correction for angle in Doppler.

6.2 Relative Motion and Angle

Recall that in our first thought experiments, observer A and observer B saw inverse frequency shifts. Observer A experienced a negative shift and observer B experienced a positive shift. In the figure below, we will use a -1 to represent a negative shift and a +1 to represent a positive shift.

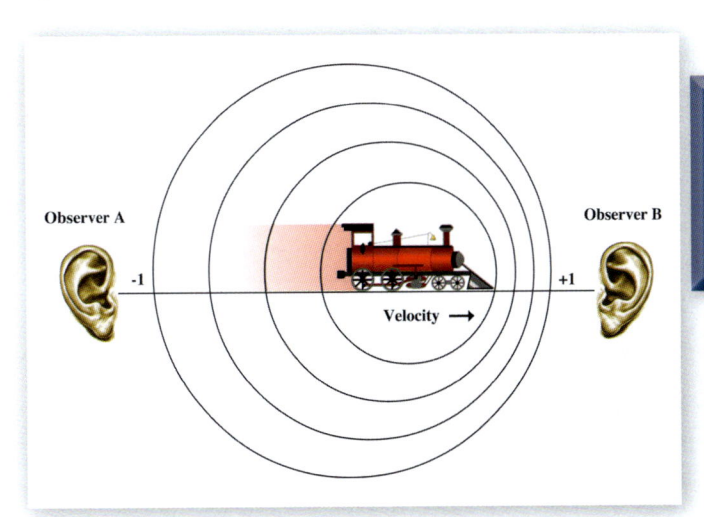

Fig. 8 **Positive and negative frequency shifts**

Because the train is coming directly toward observer B, we will call the angle between the motion of the train and the observer B 0 degrees. In contrast, the train is moving directly away from observer A. We will therefore call the angle between the train's direction of motion and observer A 180 degrees. Imagine now if we were to add a third observer, C, as indicated in *Figure 9*. Observer C is located at 90 degrees relative to the train's direction of motion. At the very instant when the train first starts blowing the whistle, the train is neither going toward (decreasing the distance to) observer C nor going away from (increasing the distance to) observer C. Since there is no motion toward or away relative to observer C, they experience no change in the frequency.

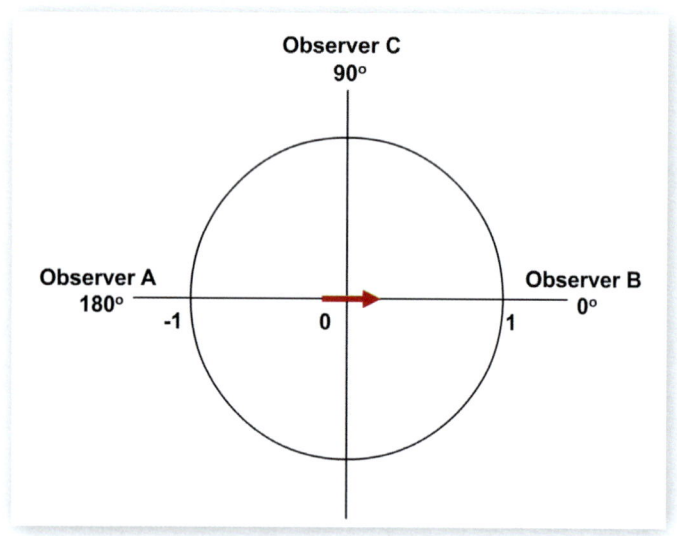

Fig. 9 **Doppler angle dependence**

You should already be familiar with a mathematical function which expresses this very relationship between angle and perceived effect. This mathematical function is called the cosine of the angle. Not surprisingly, since the Doppler effect is a based on motion relative to an observer, the angle between the observer and the motion affects the Doppler effect. In Level 1, we started with the assumption that the motion was either directly towards or directly away. We can now add the cosine term to the Doppler equation yielding:

$$f_{Dop} = \frac{2 f_0 v}{c} \cos(\theta).$$

where:

f_{Dop} = Doppler shifted frequency
f_0 = transmit frequency
v = velocity of target through medium
c = speed of interrogating beam through medium (c = 1540 m/sec for sound in tissue)
$\cos(\theta)$ = mathematical correction for angle effect
θ = insonification angle (or angle to flow)

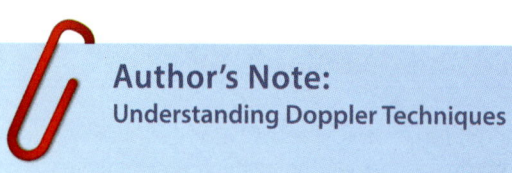

Author's Note:
Understanding Doppler Techniques

Understanding this equation is the foundation for understanding all Doppler techniques. There is a wealth of information within the mathematical relationships expressed within this equation.

CHECKPOINT: Exam Tip

The Doppler effect is based on relative motion. When the motion between the source and the observer is such that the distance becomes smaller, a positive shift occurs. Conversely, when the motion results in an increasing distance, a negative shift occurs. When the motion is not directly towards, 0° (maximal positive shift), or directly away, 180° (maximal negative shift), the Doppler shift decreases as predicted by the cosine of the angle.

7. Doppler Shifts from Red Blood Cells

7.1 The Rayleigh Scattering/Frequency Paradox

In Chapter 3 we discussed types of reflection, referring to specular, scattering, and Rayleigh scattering. The criterion for when Rayleigh scattering occurs is when the diameter of the reflector is small relative to the wavelength of the interrogating wave. For red blood cells (RBCs), the typical diameter is approximately 7 µm, and the thickness about 2 µm, whereas the typical wavelength for diagnostic ultrasound ranges from 154 µm (at 10 MHz) to 770 µm (at 2 MHz). With respect to these numbers, we can be quite certain that red blood cells meet the requirement for Rayleigh scattering. Since Rayleigh scattering is such a weak reflective mode, extra caution must be taken in choosing the appropriate operating frequency for performing Doppler studies.

In Chapter 3 we also introduced a paradox. Since the amount of scattering increases with increasing frequency (as the frequency increases, the wavelength decreases making the structures appear larger relatively), it would be presumed that a higher frequency would produce stronger Doppler signals. In fact, Rayleigh scattering is related very non-linearly to the frequency. The amount of scattering is related to the frequency to the fourth power. This relationship implies that changing from a 3 MHz to a 6 MHz operating frequency should increase the amplitude of the Doppler signal by a factor of 16 (the factor of 2 increase in frequency raised to the fourth power). However, the reality is that higher frequencies for most imaging situations produce weaker Doppler signals. Therein lies the paradox.

The problem is that increasing the frequency increases reflectivity, but also results in significantly increased attenuation. Therefore, these two effects work inversely, and the increased attenuation with higher frequency very quickly dominates the increase in reflectivity.

7.2 The Optimal Frequency for Doppler

The following graph demonstrates the "optimal" Doppler frequency versus Doppler depth in cm. Since very few systems allow for Doppler below a frequency of 1.8 MHz, you will notice that past the depth of 5 cm, the optimal frequency is artificially fixed at 1.8 MHz.

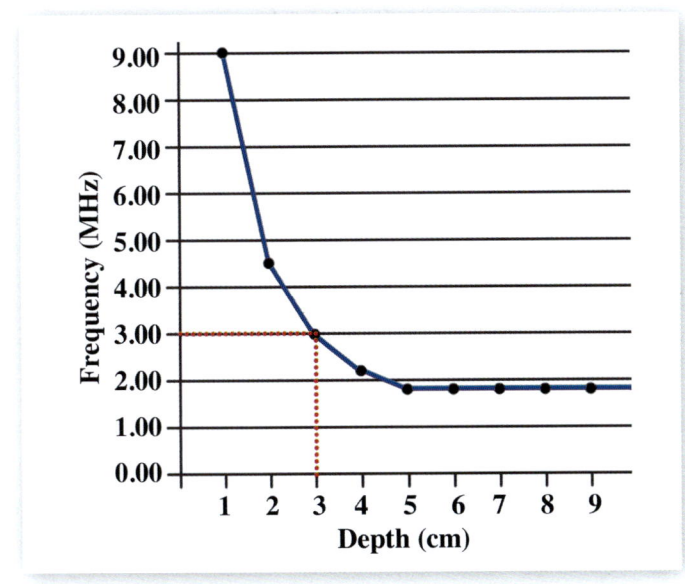

Fig. 10 **Optimal Doppler frequency versus depth of Doppler**

Shallower than 1 cm, the optimal Doppler frequency is 9 MHz; from 1 cm to 2 cm, the optimal Doppler frequency drops below 5 MHz. By 5 cm, the optimal frequency is actually at the limit of how low most ultrasound systems produce transducers for Doppler. Therefore, excluding very superficial imaging, the lowest Doppler frequency possible should be used to optimize sensitivity.

> **Author's Note:**
> **Assumptions on Doppler Frequency**
>
> To create the graph of *Figure 10*, certain assumptions about attenuation and blood reflectivity had to be made. Although there are no assumptions that will be absolutely true for all patients and situations, absolute predictive value is not the purpose or requirement of this graph. Instead, this graph is intended to serve only as a guideline for appropriate frequency selection and a warning that errors can occur when the frequency used for Doppler is even slightly higher than optimal.

7.3 Red Blood Cell Aggregation and Reflectivity

Most theoretical work analyzing the reflective behavior of ultrasound from blood concludes that in reality it is not the individual RBC that acts as the source of the reflection but rather the interference that results from the point source scattering from the inhomogeneities in the RBC concentration. The reflected spherical waves from an individual RBC are small enough so as to be undetectable by ultrasound; however, the constructive interference of spherical waves from multiple blood cells increases the signal strength. Also, changes in blood cell concentration give rise to larger reflections than could be attributed to a collection of individual RBCs. The responses are presumed to be the reason for the increase in amplitude in the presence of turbulence relative to laminar flow of blood with the same hematocrit. In general, there is a weak correlation between the number of red blood cell scatterers and the reflected energy. With aggregation, as occurs in low flow states, the reflectivity increases. This fact is also in support of the theory that changes in cell concentration are responsible for the reflectivity of blood.

7.4 Rouleaux and Spontaneous Contrast

In low shear flow states, red blood cells tend to aggregate, creating what is referred to as rouleaux flow. A rouleaux refers to a small row or coil of coins, or anything which forms a similar coiled shape. With respect to blood, the erythrocytes (red blood cells) actually change their shape and form an adhesion to other erythrocytes. The chain of connected red blood cells resembles a coil and hence the name rouleaux. Since a rouleaux becomes larger with respect to the wavelength, the reflectivity tends to increase. In some imaging situations, rouleaux formation can lead to the visualization of blood within a 2D image. This appearance is often described as "smoke" or "spontaneous contrast". The conditions under which spontaneous contrast becomes more likely are related to low-volumetric flow, high hematocrit, low shear, and the interrogating frequency (high frequency). The presence of "spontaneous contrast" can therefore be indicative of a greater likelihood of a hemodynamic problem such as increased risk for embolism or thrombus, or can be perfectly normal. With the increased use of higher frequency imaging through harmonics (discussed in Chapter 10), "spontaneous contrast" has become much more commonplace. Still, it is useful to recognize that there are times when the presence of "smoke" is a warning that increased risk exists.

The following image of *Figure 11* demonstrates rouleaux formation in venous flow in a varicosed great saphenous vein. Harmonic imaging was used, increasing the visibility of the blood pool in this image.

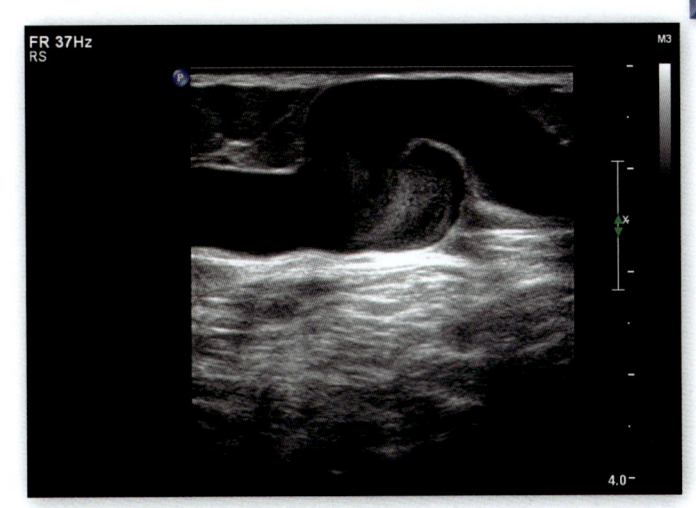

Fig. 11 **Rouleaux resulting in spontaneous contrast (visualization of blood) in a varicosed great saphenous vein (GSV)**

Figure 12 shows a dramatic case of rouleaux formation which results from low shear in the left atrium of a patient after a mitral valve repair using an Alfieri stitch. The Alfieri stitch, intended to reduce significant mitral regurgitation, inadvertently and effectively sutured the mitral valve closed.

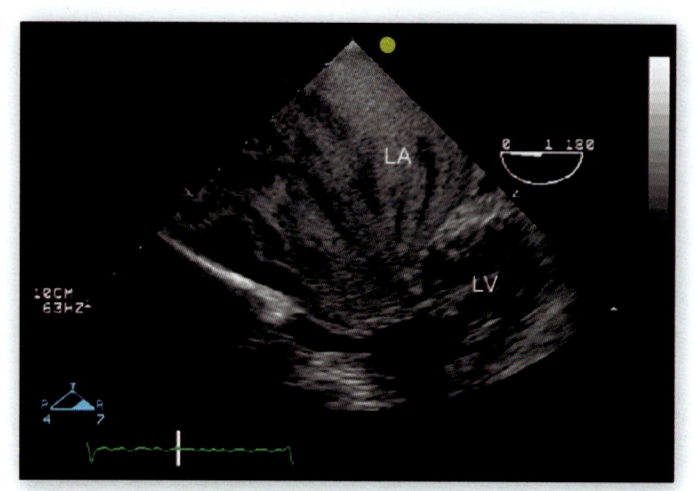

Fig. 12 Transesophageal (TEE) image of left atrium with flow incapable of passing through a mitral valve repair (Alfieri stitch) which resulted in the valve effectively being sutured shut; the low flow state created rouleaux formation

View ONLINE Animation and Image Library

KEY CONCEPT

For Doppler from red blood cells deeper than 3 cm, the optimal transmit frequency is below 3 MHz. At shallower depths, higher frequencies produce stronger Doppler signals because of increased reflectivity. At deeper depths, lower frequencies produce stronger Doppler signals because of the increased absorption that occurs with higher transmit frequencies.

8. Identifying the Doppler Angle (Insonification or Insonation Angle)

8.1 Standardized Angle Determination

The Doppler angle is defined as the angle that is formed between the observer's line of sight and the direction of the target object. In terms of ultrasound, this angle is often referred to as the insonification angle or the angle of insonation, measured between the beam steering direction and the direction of the flow. The ability to correctly identify the insonification angle (Doppler angle) is critical for many reasons including:

1. The ability to determine flow direction.
2. The ability to assess Doppler measurement accuracy.
3. The ability to minimize Doppler error sources.
4. The ability to assess likelihood of artifact-related issues such as spectral broadening.

8.2 Examples of Insonification Angles

The following series of diagrams indicate how the Doppler angle is determined.

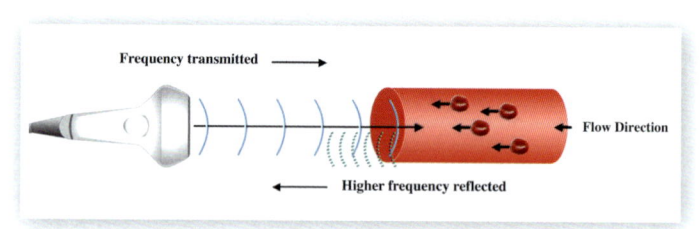

Fig. 13 Doppler insonification angle = 0^0

Figure 13 illustrates measuring the angle between the beam direction and the flow direction. Since there is no angular displacement between the two directions, the angle is specified as 0°, or directly towards the transducer.

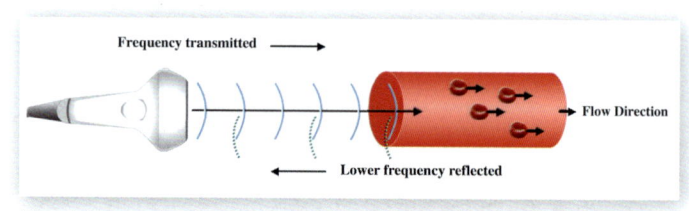

Fig. 14 Doppler insonification angle = 180^0

Figure 14 represents the exact opposite of *Figure 13*, since the blood flow is directly away from the transducer beam, or 180°.

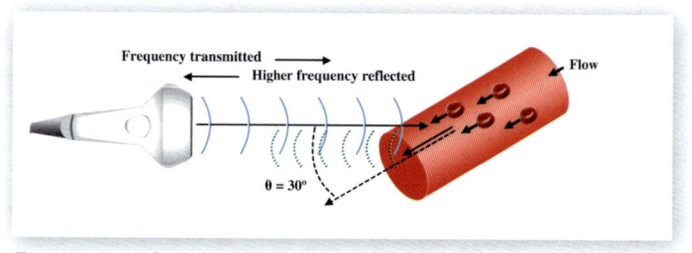

Fig. 15 Doppler insonification angle = 30^0

In *Figure 15* the angle is measured between the flow direction (where the flow is going to - indicated by the arrowhead) and the beam direction. Since the angle is less than 90 degrees, and since the cosine of an angle less than 90 degrees is positive, this represents a positive frequency shift. However, you will note that the flow is not directly toward the transducer, hence, the shift detected will be less than 100%. Recalling that the cosine of 30° is 0.86, we know that only 86% of the true shift is detected.

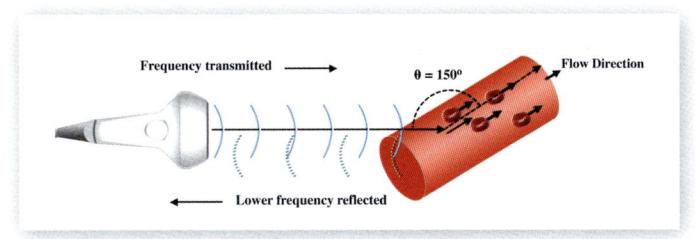

Fig. 16 **Doppler insonification angle = 150⁰**

As shown in *Figure 16* the angle is measured between the flow direction (where the flow is going to, indicated by the arrowhead) and the beam direction. You need to pay particular attention to the difference between this case and the previous case represented by *Figure 15*. Although the angle formed between the vessel and the ultrasound beam is the same, the angle to flow is not the same. Since the flow is now in the opposite direction within the vessel, the angle to flow must be different. By drawing the angle between the head of the flow (the flow arrowhead) and the beam direction, it is clear that this angle is now greater than 90 degrees. Since the cosine of an angle greater than 90 degrees is negative, this represents a negative frequency shift. However, you will note that the flow is not directly away from the transducer, hence, the shift detected will be less than 100%. Recalling that the cosine of 150° is 0.86, we know that only 86% of the true shift is detected. Therefore, the same shift is detected as when the angle was 30 degrees, except now the shift is negative instead of positive.

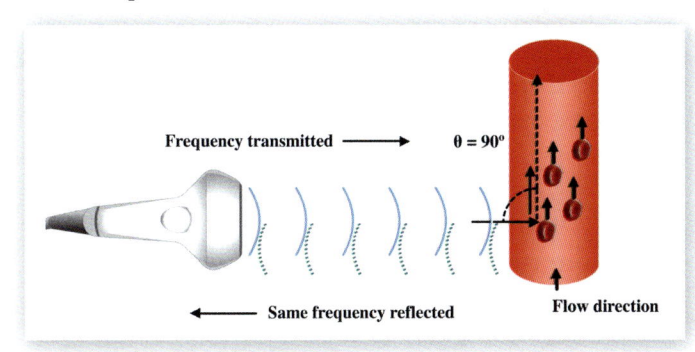

Fig. 17 **Doppler insonification Angle = 90⁰**

In *Figure 17* the angle to flow is 90 degrees. With a 90 degree insonification angle, there is no motion towards or away from the transducer and hence, no Doppler effect. The cosine of 90° is 0 and the Doppler equation predicts the absence of a shift at 90°. In other words, if the insonification angle equals 90°, or is close to 90°, then there is no Doppler shift:

$$\cos(90°) = 0 \Rightarrow f_{Dop} = \frac{2f_0 v}{c}(0) = 0.$$

(So even though the target is moving, you have not detected this movement!)

Author's Note:
Insonification Angle

The ability to determine the angle to flow is relatively straightforward given that you are taught the standardized definition of the insonification angle. The ability to determine flow direction, measurement accuracy, minimize error sources, and assess artifact related issues is also relatively straightforward given that you have reviewed basic trigonometry. In lieu of this understanding, you will be relegated to "techniques" which only give the right answer some of the time in very specific cases.

Reviewing the Cosine
Because of the cosine dependence of the Doppler effect, it is important that you review the behavior of the cosine. Specifically, you should make certain that you can calculate the cosine of the basic angles (0°, 30°, 45°, 60°, 90°) and their equivalent angles in quadrant II (120°, 135°, 150°, 180°). Additionally, you should know for what range of angles the cosine is positive and for what range of angles the cosine is negative. Later in this chapter, we will analyze the slope of the cosine function as a means of assessing error and measurement accuracy. If you are not comfortable with determining the cosine of various angles, it is highly recommended that you review Chapter 1: Mathematics. (Isn't it great how your earlier work is now paying dividends?)

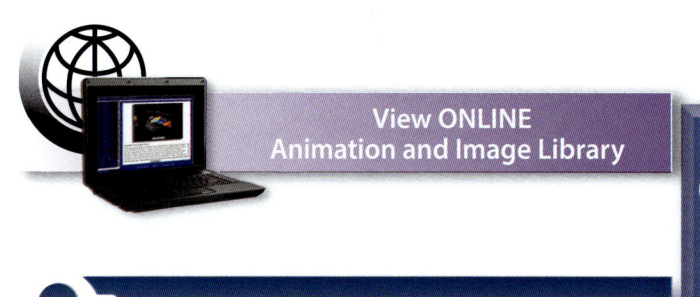

View ONLINE Animation and Image Library

KEY CONCEPT

The Doppler insonification angle (or simply Doppler angle) is measured between the flow direction and the beam direction. The ability to identify the Doppler angle is the only method of always correctly determining flow direction with spectral and color Doppler.

8.3 The Effects of Angles Greater and Less Than 90°
One of the principal reasons you must be able to identify the Doppler angle is to determine blood flow direction in the body. When the Doppler angle is less than 90°, a positive shift occurs and the spectrum is displayed as positive velocities. When the Doppler angle

is greater than 90°, a negative shift occurs and spectrum is displayed as negative velocities, implying that the flow is in the opposite direction. Although the standard display is to present positive velocities above the Doppler baseline (reference line that represents a velocity of 0 m/sec), you must be careful as there are many times in which the spectrum is inverted such that positive velocities (flow at angles less than 90°) are displayed below the baseline.

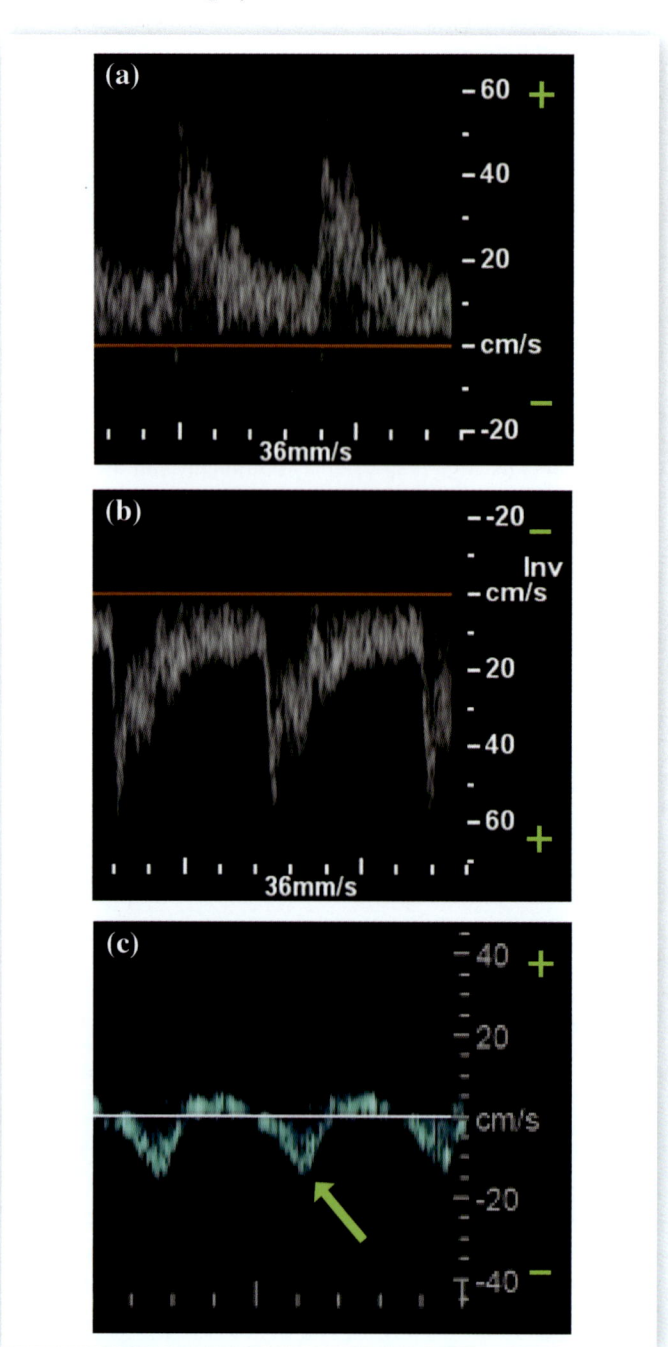

Fig. 18 **Positive velocities (angles < 90°) shown above the baseline (a) and below the baseline because of spectral invert (b); Negative velocities (angles > 90°) indicated by green arrow (c)**

Look carefully at the spectrums in *Figure 18*. As seen in *(a)*, positive velocities (angles less than 90°) are presented above the baseline. In *(b)*, positive velocities are displayed below the baseline because spectral inversion has been activated (noted by "Inv"). In *(c)*, the green arrow indicates that the flow has a negative velocity (angle greater than 90°).

9. Exercises

View ONLINE Exercises

10. Spectral Doppler System Operation

10.1 The Value of a Block Diagram

Just as we reviewed a high-level system block diagram as the foundation for discussing system operation for 2D imaging, we will use a high-level block diagram of how Doppler functions. At the highest level, the block diagram for a pedof (pencil, blind, Doppler-only transducer) is very similar to the block diagram for performing Doppler with a phased array transducer. (With the exception of the beamforming functions for phased arrays, the core functions are the same.) Therefore, instead of going through the process twice, we will use the same diagram for both Doppler systems.

The value of the block diagram will not derive from your ability or inability to design a Doppler circuit, or even memorize the diagram and draw it yourself. Rather, the value derives from the block diagram serving as means of integrating all of the various aspects and controls related to spectral Doppler. As you review each Doppler function and process, you should relate the function to its location in the block diagram, and then ultimately to the controls that exist on your ultrasound system.

10.2 Why You Need to Also Know About Analog Waveform and Unidirectional Doppler

The block diagram described here is for a high-end, bidirectional, spectral Doppler. There are lower complexity approaches which provide waveforms and use less precise techniques such as zero-crossing detector schemes. These simpler devices are now becoming less common, and are now frequently only found as dedicated, stand-alone Doppler devices. As a result, we will concentrate much more heavily on what you will use most of the time in the clinical world. However, for two reasons we will point out how a simpler device operates:

1. If you perform vascular studies, there is a chance you might use an analog waveform Doppler and you should be aware of the definition and limitations of an analog waveform Doppler.
2. You may be still expected to know about unidirectional Doppler and analog waveform Doppler techniques on credentialing exams.

10.3 The Doppler Block Diagram

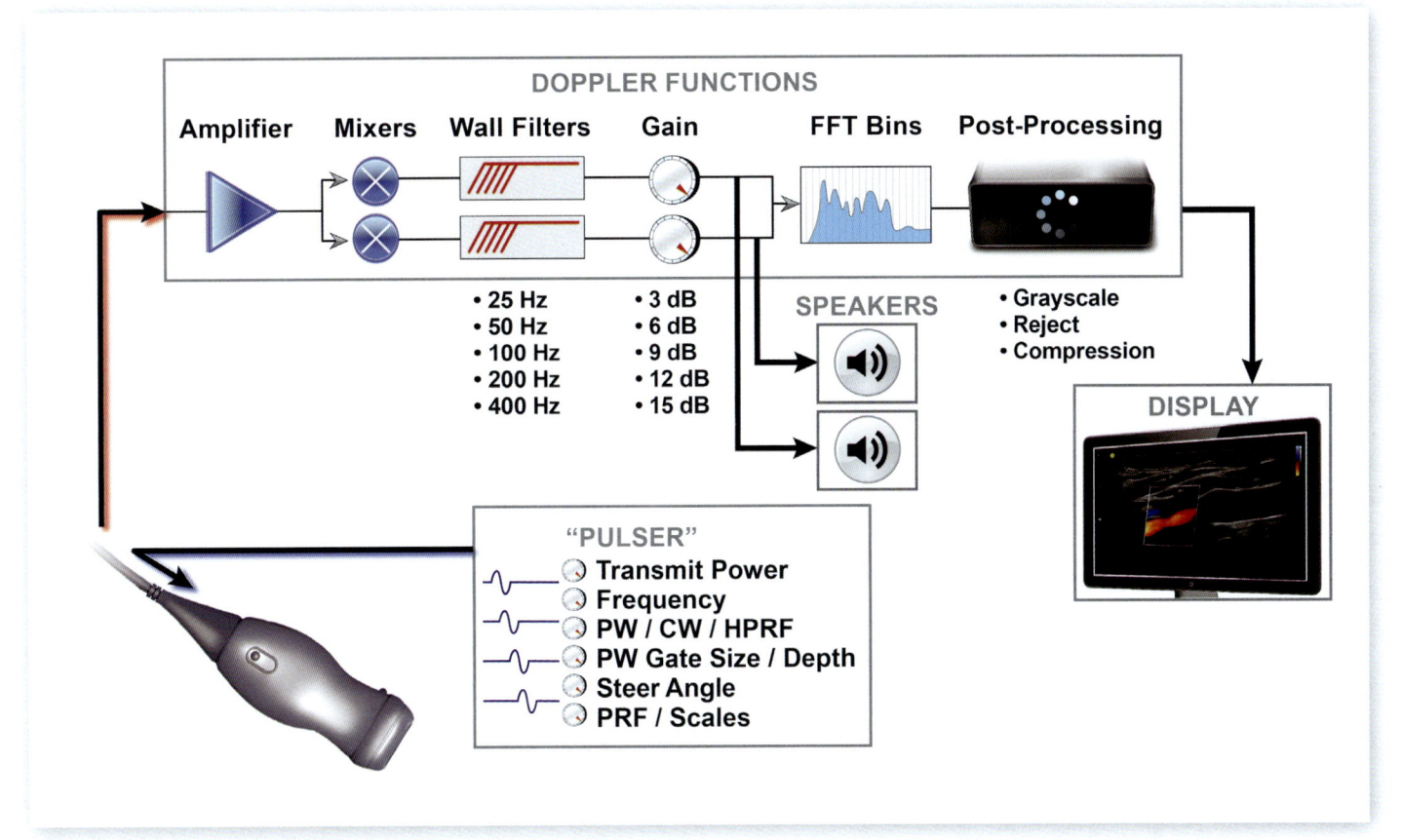

Fig. 19 The Doppler block diagram

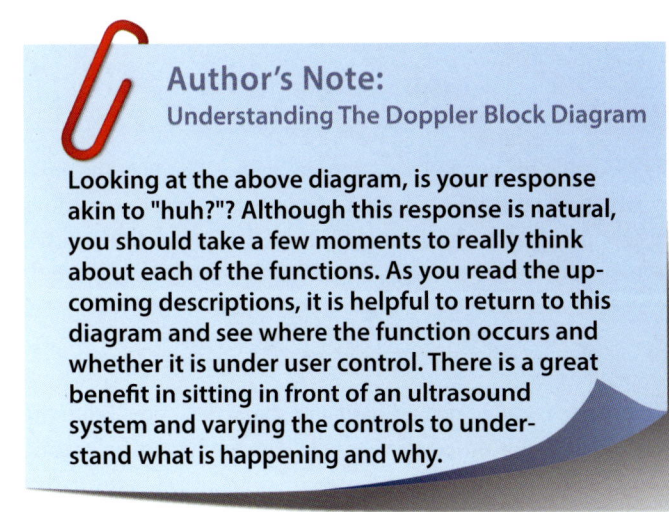

Author's Note:
Understanding The Doppler Block Diagram

Looking at the above diagram, is your response akin to "huh?"? Although this response is natural, you should take a few moments to really think about each of the functions. As you read the upcoming descriptions, it is helpful to return to this diagram and see where the function occurs and whether it is under user control. There is a great benefit in sitting in front of an ultrasound system and varying the controls to understand what is happening and why.

As indicated on the block diagram, the user chooses the operating frequency by selecting a transducer (and sometimes a button push as well). The user then selects whether they want to perform PW, CW, or high PRF (HPRF). By changing the power control, the user determines what percentage of the maximum allowed transmit power will be transmitted. If PW is chosen, the user determines the PW gate depth and gate size. By changing the scales, the user determines if a PRF lower than the maximum PRF is desired. (This concept will be discussed in Section 13.) If the transducer is a phased array, the user is also able to steer the Doppler beam in the desired direction (for both CW and PW). From all of these settings, the system then decides the parameters in the transmit sequence. The following diagram illustrates how the parameters might vary depending on the user's selections.

11. The Processes Involved in Spectral Doppler

Note: The term after each title in this section refers to the function name on the block diagram.

CHECKPOINT: Exam Tip

The timing between the transmit pulse and the Doppler gate (listening time) is referred to as the pulse repetition period, the reciprocal of the pulse repetition frequency (PRF).

11.1 Transmit Ultrasound Into the Body: (Pulser)

The transmit characteristics are determined by many parameters.

Case 1:
Reference pulse wave

Case 2:
Increase the transmit power and leave all the other parameters

Case 3:
Decrease the Doppler scales (PRF)

Case 4:
Increase the transmit frequency

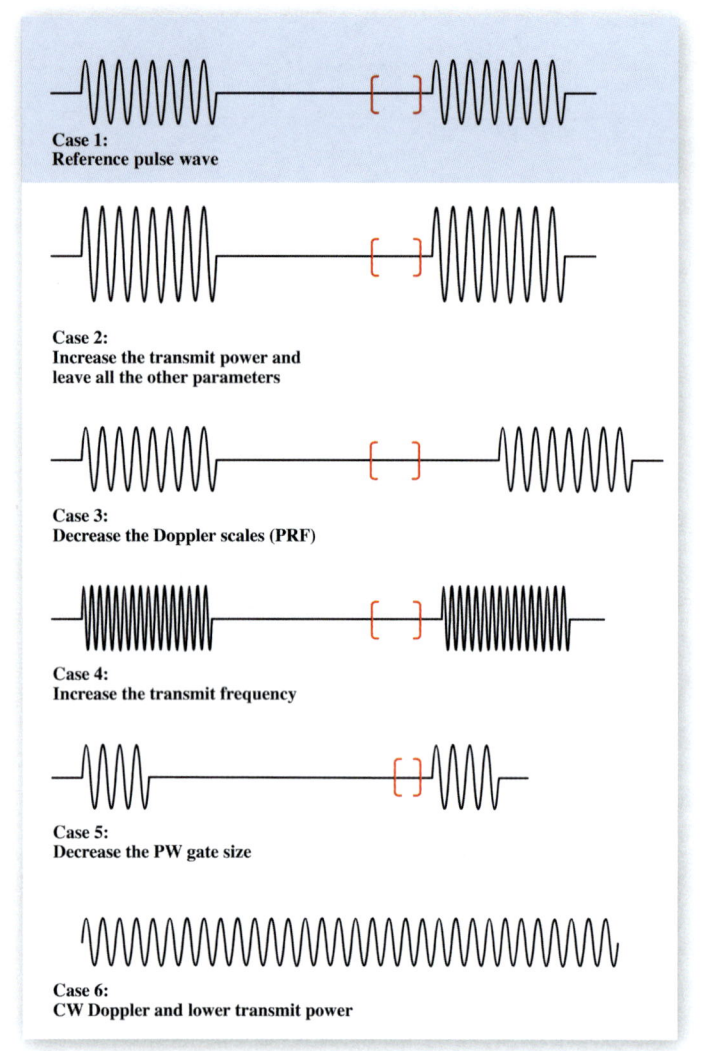

Case 5:
Decrease the PW gate size

Case 6:
CW Doppler and lower transmit power

Fig. 20 Variations in transmit sequence (compare each case with Case 1 to visualize which system change was made)

11.2 Frequency Shift from Moving Blood

As we have already discussed, through the Doppler effect, a frequency shift occurs proportional to the velocity when the ultrasound wave insonifies any moving structures such as valves, vessel walls, cardiac walls, blood cells, etc. The ultrasound frequency shifts by an amount dictated by the Doppler equation:

$$f_{Dop} = \frac{2 f_0 v}{c} \cos(\theta).$$

Unlike our train example, there is not one source of Doppler shifts, but many sources. In addition, unlike the single train, there are many moving red blood cells. The red blood cells are not necessarily all traveling at the same speed, and the angle to flow is not necessarily constant throughout the Doppler sample volume. As a result, there is not one Doppler shift but an entire range of frequency shifts, also referred to as a spectrum. Notationally, we will represent the sum of all of the frequency shifts using the mathematical symbol for summation, or:

$$\pm \sum f_{Dop}.$$

where the plus and minus in front of the symbol indicates that the shifts can be both positive (towards) and negative (away). Typically, these Doppler shifts are on the order of -10 kHz to +10 kHz. However the shifts can be much higher, as indicated by the Doppler equation. In pediatric settings, in which higher frequency transducers are used and higher velocity flows are sometimes detected, the Doppler shifts can reach as high as ± 50 kHz.

11.3 Amplification: (Amplifier)

When the reflected echoes are received, the amplitude of all of the echoes is very low, therefore amplification is necessary. The amplification in the receiver is not under user control (user-controlled amplification takes place later in the processing chain). Typically 40 dB to 60 dB of gain is applied before any other processing occurs. For phased systems, the beamformer has the extra task of steering and focusing the returning echoes by applying the appropriate phase delays to the signals from each transducer element and then summing the channels together.

11.4 Doppler Shift Detection: (Mixers)

The returning signal is a combination of back-scattered data from tissue and frequency-shifted data from the moving targets. The signals reflected from stationary structures are still at the same frequency as the transmit frequency. Therefore, the combination of signals returning can be notationally written as:

$$\underbrace{f_0 \text{ (MHz)}}_{\text{Stationary Structures}} \pm \underbrace{\sum f_{Dop} \text{(kHz)}}_{\text{Moving Structures}}.$$

Since Doppler is interested in determining the velocity of the moving structures, the reflected signals from the stationary structures are subtracted from the combined signal, leaving just the shifted frequencies from the moving structures:

$$\underbrace{\pm \sum f_{Dop} \text{(kHz)}}_{\text{Moving Structures}}.$$

This process is called demodulation or signal detection. From the old radio days, this process is also called "heterodyning" or "mixing to baseband."

The mixing to baseband is performed using two channels in what is called quadrature detection. A quadrant of a circle is 90°. Quadrature detection signifies that the information is detected at two different phases, 90° apart. This separation is created by multiplying the received Doppler signal by the sine and cosine. (As we learned in Chapter 1: Mathematics, the sine and the cosine have a phase separation of 90°.) Later in the Doppler processing, the channels are rotated another 90° resulting in a phase separation of 180°. Since 180° represents exact opposite directions, forward flow is now distinguished from reverse flow. Therefore, the reason for quadrature detection is to separate the signal into its forward and reverse components so that flow directionality is known.

Early Doppler systems did not perform the quadrature detection and as a result yielded unidirectional Doppler. In these systems, both flow towards and away from the transducer would be represented above the baseline, as demonstrated in *Figure 21*. Fortunately, the days of non-directional (unidirectional) Doppler have been extinct for many years. *Figure 22* demonstrates a bidirectional Doppler waveform of a femoral artery. This waveform was generated by a zero-crossing detection Doppler circuit. For a pure frequency, the frequency can be detected by counting the number of times the signal crosses through the baseline (zero). With many simultaneous frequencies (as commonly occurs when measuring blood flow), a zero-crossing yields a value loosely related to a mean velocity (root mean squared velocity). For comparison, *Figure 23* demonstrates a typical spectral Doppler waveform for a femoral artery.

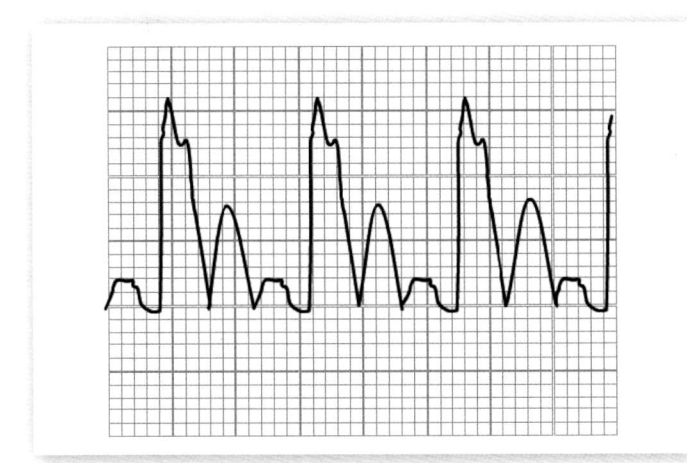

Fig. 21 **Unidirectional Doppler waveform**

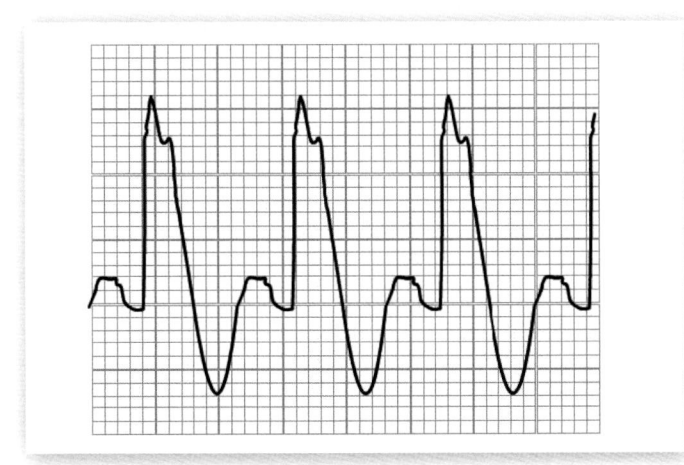

Fig. 22 **Bidirectional Doppler waveform**

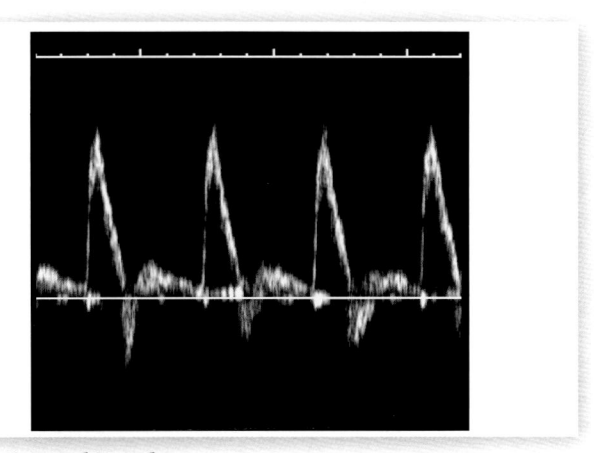

Fig. 23 **Spectral Doppler**

11.5 Wall Filtering

Dynamic Range of Doppler

In Chapter 6, we discussed how the large dynamic range of the returning signals presented such an enormous problem. In that section, we learned that the dynamic range of the signal typically spanned more than 80 dB. In comparison, the situation is much worse for Doppler. Depending on the imaging situation, the dynamic range may be as great as 140 dB in PW Doppler and 160 dB in CW Doppler. As way of review, we will convert 160 dB into the equivalent signal ratio.

$$20 \times \log\left(\frac{A_{biggest}}{A_{smallest}}\right) = 160 \text{ dB}$$

Dividing both sides by 20 yields:

$$\log\left(\frac{A_{biggest}}{A_{smallest}}\right) = 8$$

(The base is 10 - recall if not expressly written, we assume a base of 10)

$$\log_{10}\left(\frac{A_{biggest}}{A_{smallest}}\right) = 8$$

Solving the logarithm yields:

$$\left(\frac{A_{biggest}}{A_{smallest}}\right) = \frac{10^8}{1} = 100,000,000 : 1$$

This calculation shows that the largest signals returning in CW Doppler can be one hundred million times larger than the smallest signals. This is problematic for two reasons. First, recall that human visible dynamic range is less than 36 dB (fewer than 64 shades of gray simultaneously), so there is an enormous dynamic range issue. Second, the signals from blood that we care about are unfortunately the signals most likely at the very bottom of the dynamic range (weakest). If we do not eliminate the enormous signals from stronger reflectors (referred to as clutter), there will be no way of detecting the tiny signals associated with the Rayleigh scattering of the blood. Before we discuss a solution, we need to first understand the source of the problem.

Clutter Signals

Recall that any relative movement between target and transducer will create a Doppler shift. In addition to blood flow - wall motion, valve motion, respiration induced movement, transducer movement, etc., will create Doppler shifts. These Doppler shifts are usually much bigger in amplitude than the amplitude of the associated blood signals because of the specular nature of these reflectors. These high amplitude signals from relatively stationary, strongly reflecting structures are generally referred to as "clutter" signals.

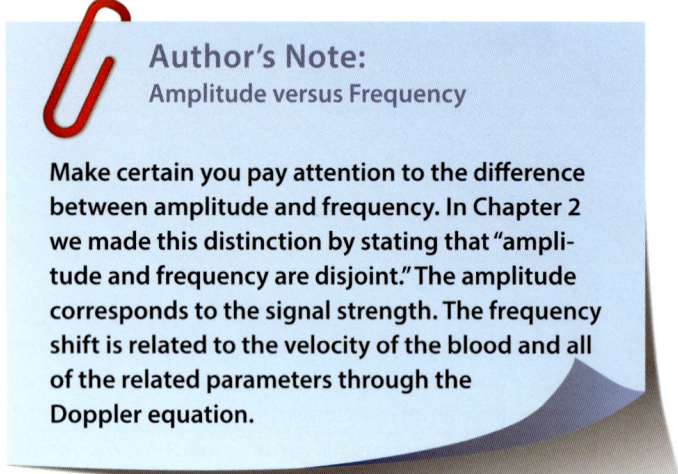

> **Author's Note:**
> **Amplitude versus Frequency**
>
> Make certain you pay attention to the difference between amplitude and frequency. In Chapter 2 we made this distinction by stating that "amplitude and frequency are disjoint." The amplitude corresponds to the signal strength. The frequency shift is related to the velocity of the blood and all of the related parameters through the Doppler equation.

Graphic Depiction of Dynamic Range Issues

Figure 24 illustrates the dynamic range issues associated with processing Doppler data.

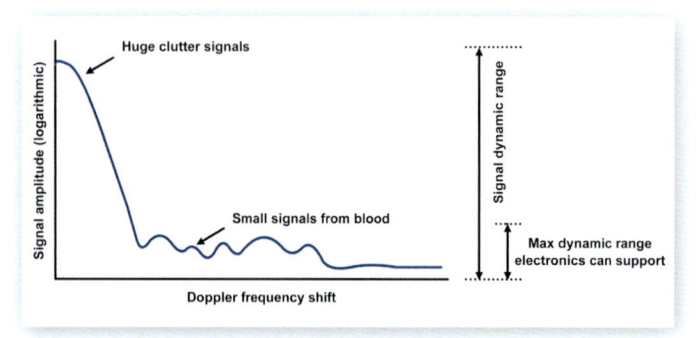

Fig. 24 **Doppler dynamic range and clutter**

Notice how the (clutter) signals at the lower Doppler frequency shifts are extremely high amplitude, and much larger in amplitude than the signals from the blood flow. Also note that the overall signal dynamic range (the ratio of the biggest signal to the smallest signal) is much larger than the dynamic range of the electronics. If we were to consider the dynamic range of the human eye, that range would be even smaller than the supportable dynamic range of the electronics. Since the dynamic range of the Doppler signal is much larger than the dynamic range supported by the electronics and much larger than the dynamic range visible to the human eye, something must be done with the large clutter signals.

Wall Filter Theory

Luckily, the reflectors that cause these enormous clutter signals usually move slowly relative to most blood flow. From the Doppler equation, we know that low velocities result in low frequency shifts. Therefore, if we discriminate signals based on their frequency shifts, we have the potential to filter out the clutter signals. The technique for filtering out these clutter signals is called wall filtering. Wall filters allow the user to attenuate the lower frequency shift (velocity) signals which are usually the highest amplitude signals. By reducing or eliminating the high amplitude signals, the signal dynamic range is reduced.

Graphic Depiction of Wall Filters

Wall filters are high pass filters. As the name suggests, high pass filters allow the high frequency signals to pass through while rejecting the lower frequency signals. A high pass filter is designed to have a specific cutoff frequency. The cutoff frequency is the breakpoint frequency above which the signal frequencies are passed, and below which the signal frequencies are attenuated.

Figure 25 depicts the relation of the wall filter to the signal data.

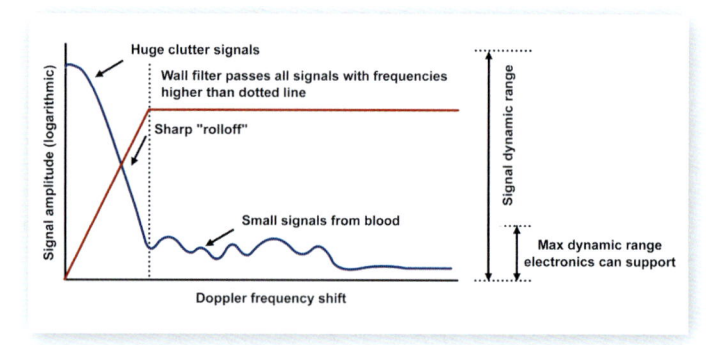

Fig. 25 **Applying a wall filter**

Notice that the red line represents the function of the wall filter. The dotted line indicates the frequency below which signals are attenuated and above which signals are passed. The frequency at which the attenuation begins is commonly referred to as the "corner" frequency or "cutoff" frequency of the wall filter. Signals with frequency shifts above this corner are multiplied by 1, or passed through unchanged (hence the name "high pass" filter). Frequencies below the corner frequency are multiplied by a number less than 1. As displayed graphically, the lower the frequency below the corner frequency, the lower the multiplier applied. Note that the filter drawn in this diagram has a very sharp "roll-off," implying that frequencies just below the corner are attenuated a fair amount. If the roll-off were more gradual (slower slope), then more of the signals with frequencies below the corner would still pass through the filter, albeit with a lower amplitude (weaker signal displayed).

View ONLINE Animation and Image Library

CHECKPOINT: Exam Tip

Wall filtering is a technique to reduce dynamic range by decreasing signals (multiplying by a number less than one) with frequency shifts below the wall filter setting. In spectral Doppler, wall filters are "high pass" filters since signals with frequency shifts higher than the wall filter setting are "passed" through.

Effects of Wall Filters

Once the wall filter has been applied, if the wall filter corner frequency is set appropriately, then the signal dynamic range should be significantly reduced. The following diagram depicts the reduced signal dynamic range after the wall filters are employed.

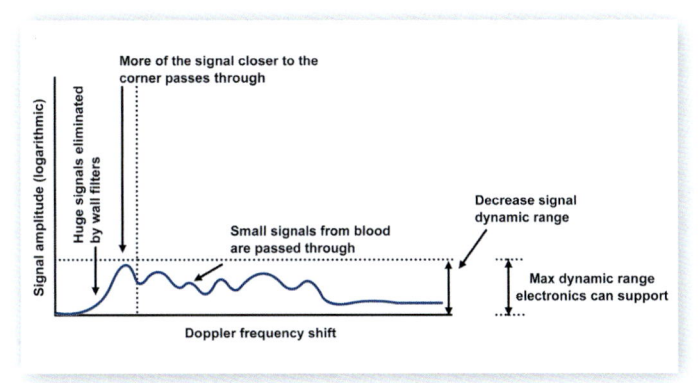

Fig. 26 Reduced dynamic range after wall filters

Author's Note:
Dynamic Range and Wall Filters

The dynamic range is greatly reduced by attenuating the large clutter signals at the lower frequency shifts. Also note that the wall filter is not a pure reject filter, and therefore still allows larger signals closer to the corner frequency to pass through, although with a much lower amplitude. The result is a much smaller dynamic range which now can be more easily processed by the system and visualized by the human eye.

Wall Filter Appearance on Doppler Spectrum

In spectral Doppler, the effect of the wall filters is visualized as black bands around the baseline of the spectrum. This black band represents the low frequency signals that were attenuated and mapped to very low amplitudes.

Figure 27 demonstrates the effects of changing the wall filter. As the corner frequency of the wall filters is increased, this black band becomes broader. The wall filters also affect the Doppler audio signal. As the wall filters are increased, less of the base frequencies are audible, allowing only the higher frequency signals to be heard.

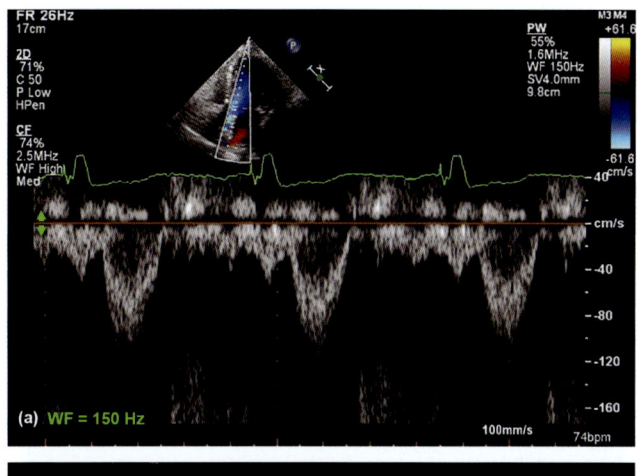

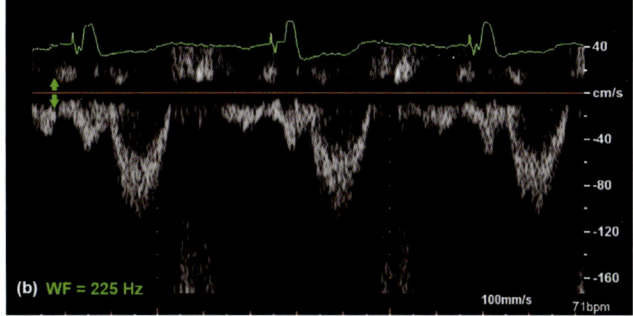

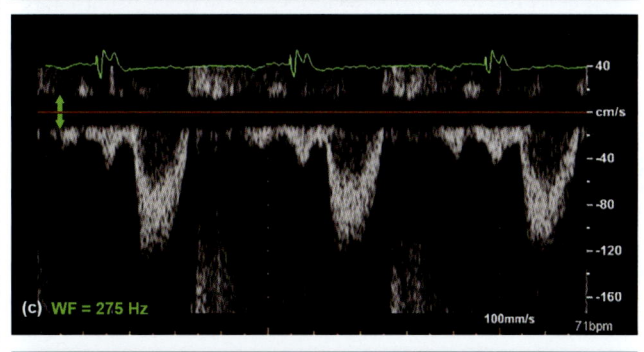

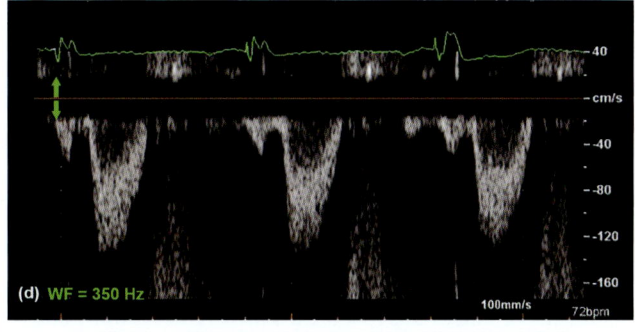

Fig. 27 **Spectral appearance of changing the wall filter (WF)**

When comparing the spectrums of *Figure 27*, notice how more of the signal is progressively removed from around the baseline as the wall filters are increased (double green arrow). The wall filters also affect the audio, such that more of the bass frequency components are removed, allowing only the higher frequency audio signals to pass through.

Appropriate Wall Filter Settings for Various Clinical Applications

Different applications require different wall filter settings. For example, venous Doppler detection generally requires the ability to detect lower frequency shifts than arterial Doppler studies. As a result, the wall filters must be set to a lower cutoff frequency for venous Doppler studies, or the desired venous signals may actually be eliminated by the wall filter.

Typical ranges for wall filters are from about 10 Hz to as high as 1600 Hz. Venous Doppler is usually performed with wall filters of 50 Hz or less. Arterial studies are usually performed at 50 Hz to 100 Hz (unless a low flow state exists). Adult echo typically uses a range of 200 Hz to 600 Hz, while pediatric echo typically uses a range of 600 Hz to 800 Hz.

Effect of Operating Frequency on Wall Filter Settings

An important point is that the operating frequency affects what wall filter settings should be used. From the Doppler equation, we know that the Doppler shift is proportional to the operating frequency. For the same velocity, using a higher operating frequency results in a higher frequency shift. Assume a reflector is moving at a velocity such that it produces a Doppler shift of 40 Hz when using a 2 MHz transducer. Also assume that the wall filters are set at 50 Hz, so that these "clutter" signals are eliminated. Now imagine that the transducer frequency is changed to 4 MHz. The exact same reflector velocity will now create a Doppler shift at 80 Hz and the 50 Hz wall filter will pass the clutter through. This fact is the principal reason why pediatric Doppler generally uses higher cutoff wall filters than adult Doppler.

Saturation of Wall Filters

Note that if the wall filters are set too low, saturation of the electronics will occur. When the electronics saturate, there is a very distinct bright band symmetric about the baseline, usually from top to bottom of the spectrum (see *Figure 28*). Additionally, the audio will have a characteristic loud thump or banging sound. Saturation occurs when the signals are amplified to the level of the voltage rails of the electronics. In essence, the electronics can only handle a certain voltage dynamic range. If the signals become larger than the maximum of this range, then the circuit saturates and the electronics ring. During this ringing phase, the Doppler circuit is not really working. The result is that the desired Doppler spectrum is obscured by the "clutter" signal.

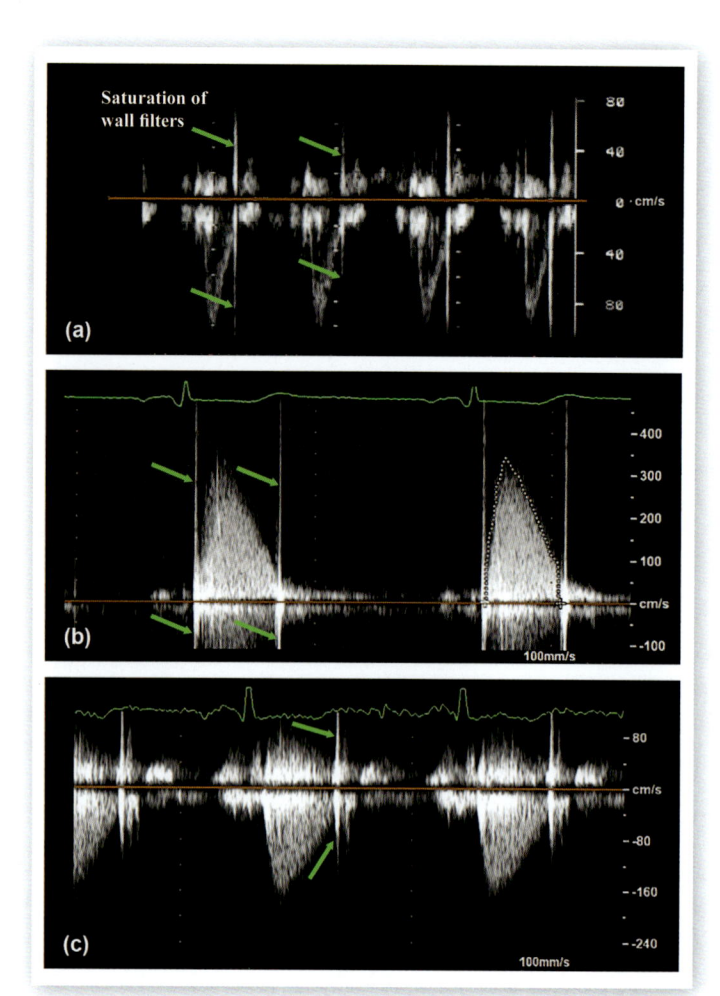

Fig. 28 **Wall filter saturation (arrows)**

> **KEY CONCEPT**
>
> If wall filters are set too low, the Doppler circuit saturates producing loud audio thumps and bright white spikes symmetric about the Doppler baseline. If the wall filters are set too high, the desired Doppler signal may be eliminated, giving the appearance of no flow.

11.6 Variable Gain: (Gain)

Recall that some amplification is applied in the receiver. However, since the wall filters are applied after the receiver functions, the amplification must be limited so that the large clutter signals do not saturate the circuit. Once the large clutter signals have been removed by the wall filters, more amplification can be applied. Since the echoes from the blood are so small, the signal must be significantly amplified to be in an appropriate range for viewing. For conventional Doppler processing techniques, this amplification is referred to as the "Doppler gain" and is controlled by the user.

As with all "gain" related controls on the system, the Doppler gain is logarithmic. By this point, you have hopefully become accustomed to the idea that since the attenuation is non-linear, the amplification controls are most usable if designed to perform non-linearly as well.

Figure 29 demonstrates the need for amplification of the Doppler signal after wall filtering.

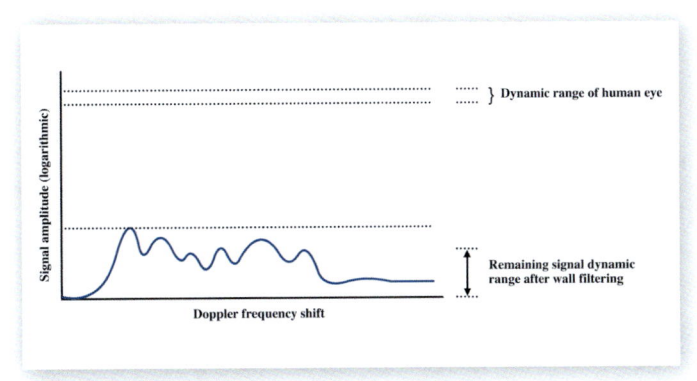

Fig. 29 **Reduced dynamic range after wall filters**

As seen in *Figure 29*, note that there are really two existing issues that must be overcome. First, even the highest amplitude signal is less than the visual threshold as indicated by the dynamic range of the human eye. This fact is precisely why user-controlled amplification is applied at this point in the processing chain. Second, even though we have reduced the dynamic range by wall filtering, the dynamic range of the signal is still significantly greater than the dynamic range of the eye. Not unlike 2D, this dynamic range issue will force the need for compression.

> **Author's Note:**
> **Interpreting Doppler Audio**
>
> Learning to interpret Doppler audio is very valuable. There is a wealth of information in the audio signal. In general, I recommend that anyone teaching Doppler should first focus only on Doppler audio without a spectral display. Begin with normal studies until the student can identify the characteristics of the normal blood flow for each study type. Next, progress to audio only from abnormal studies. Once students have mastered the audio, then allow them to correlate what they see spectrally with what they hear audibly. The next step is to allow the students to see the 2D or B-mode image in addition to the spectrum and the audio. The last step is to allow the students to see color Doppler in conjunction with the image and the spectrum.

11.7 Audio: (Speakers)

The signals are "cleaned up" to drive the speakers. Since the frequency shifts of diagnostic ultrasound are generally within the audio range (± 10 kHz), you can "detect" the different blood velocities as different frequencies with your ears. If the detection is performed in quadrature, as discussed earlier) forward flow is presented in one speaker channel and reverse flow is presented in the other channel. As a result, stereo separation is useful to help distinguish signal phasicity.

11.8 Analog to Digital Conversion (A/D)

In addition to hearing, there is a definite desire to see and quantify the Doppler spectrum. The human ear is capable of hearing multiple frequencies simultaneously, and detecting the presence of various frequency ranges. If this were not the case, it is not likely that many of us would ever listen to music. Recall that the output of the mixing process was an entire spectrum of frequency shifts associated with the flow situation. In order to display all the different velocities (the spectrum) so that the signal characteristics can be interpreted visually, more work must be done to the signal for spectral Doppler than for audio Doppler.

In order to perform an FFT (Section 11.9), post-processing (Section 11.10), and store the spectrum into digital memory for analysis and measurement, the analog Doppler signal must be sampled and converted from an analog signal to a digital signal. We have discussed the process of A/D conversion multiple times so that there is no need to repeat the discussion here. Just as with 2D imaging, one of the principal differences between a digital and analog Doppler system is when the analog to digital conversion occurs. Analog Doppler systems perform the conversion right after the wall filtering and amplification, whereas digital systems can convert just before or just after the mixing process.

11.9 Fast Fourier Transform (FFT)

The Fast Fourier Transform is a mathematical technique for separating a spectrum into its individual frequency components. The following figure illustrates graphically the role of FFT processing.

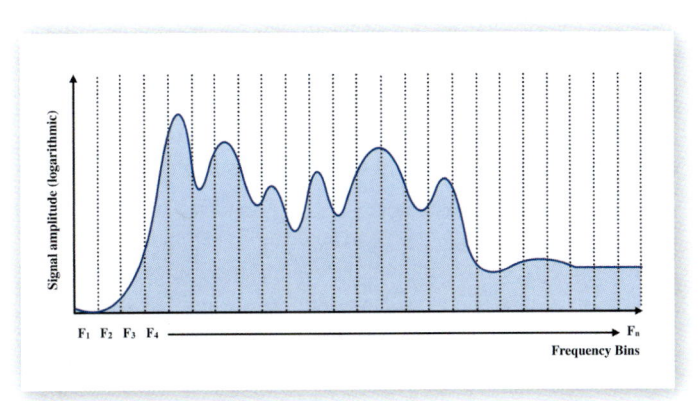

Fig. 30 **FFT processing**

Notice that the full range of frequency shifts is divided into individual frequency bins. Each bin corresponds to a narrow range of frequency shifts, which by the Doppler equation, can be converted into a calculated velocity. Clearly the lowest frequency bin corresponds to virtually zero velocity. The last bin, F_n, corresponds to the Nyquist limited maximum detectable Doppler frequency (discussed in Section 13.6). In addition to dividing the summation of frequencies into individual frequency bins, the FFT also determines how much energy, if any, is in each frequency bin. The energy in the bin is weakly related to the number of red blood cells traveling at that particular velocity. If a bin has no signal, then no blood cells were detected with that particular frequency shift. If a bin has a large signal, then it is presumed that there were many blood cells which caused the associated frequency shift.

Notice in the graphical representation of the FFT process in *Figure 30* that the first two bins (F_1 and F_2) have no signal. This absence of signal is the result of the applied wall filtering. If the wall filter were increased, more of the lowest bins would have no signal, or virtually no signal.

Author's Note:
Wall Filters and Reflections

Any structure which moves creates a Doppler shift. This is why wall filters are needed – to remove the large reflections (clutter) which come from moving reflectors which have much higher amplitudes than the signals returning from moving blood cells.

11.10 Post-processing (Compression and Reject or Grayscale)

As was demonstrated in *Figure 29*, (Section 11.6), the Doppler signals still span a greater dynamic range than the visible dynamic range, even after wall filtering. Just as was needed for 2D images, compression is employed to further reduce the dynamic range. The compression maps for Doppler are non-linear. Care must be taken to make certain that weak signals are not compressed out just as can occur with 2D images. Since the compression maps occur after the Doppler data has been stored, compression is a post-processing technique. In other words, the compression of the Doppler spectral data can be changed on frozen data as well as in real time.

Names for spectral Doppler compression are very similar to the names used for compression mapping for B-mode, including compression, grayscale, dynamic range, video compression, and post-processing curves. Some systems also have a function called reject which sets the threshold, below which signals are mapped to black. For systems with both controls, compression and reject together determine the mapping of signal amplitudes to brightness on the screen.

11.11 Display

The Doppler display actually demonstrates three quantities on a two-dimensional display. Frequency shift (or equivalent velocity through the Doppler equation) is displayed on the vertical axis. Across the horizontal axis, time is swept. Most systems allow the user to change the time base of the sweep, also referred to as the sweep speed. Higher sweep speeds result in less time displayed on the horizontal axis such that only two cardiac cycles might appear whereas in a lower sweep speed four or five cardiac cycles might be visualized. The third axis is "imaginary" and represents the amplitude. Amplitude display is achieved by the variations in brightness levels.

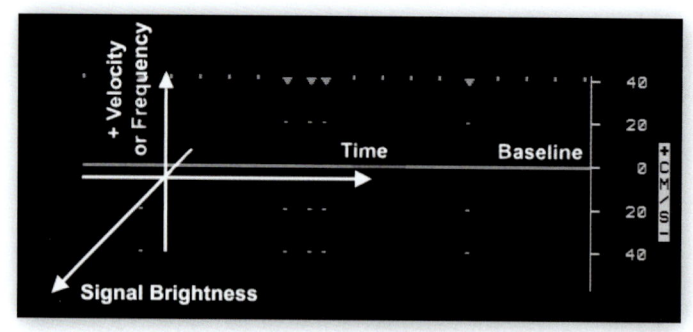

Fig. 31 The display axes of spectral Doppler

KEY CONCEPT

The Doppler spectrum displays time on the horizontal axis and velocity (or frequency shifts) on the vertical axis. The brightness of the spectrum is somewhat indicative of signal strength which is related to the number of blood cell scatterers.

12. Frequency vs. Amplitude

Earlier in this chapter we reiterated the fact that amplitude and frequency are disjoint (or independent). In other words, knowing the frequency tells you nothing about the amplitude and vice versa. This concept is very important for Doppler. The frequency shift in Doppler is dictated by all the terms in the Doppler equation [f_o, v, c, $\cos(\theta)$]. The amplitude of the signal is determined by the scattering properties of the blood. In other words, the wavelength relative to the size of the RBCs, the number of RBCs, discontinuities in concentration of the blood cells, as well as the attenuation properties of the tissue through which the ultrasound beam travels all contribute to the strength of the signal. The velocity of the blood determines the frequency shift, NOT the amplitude or strength of the signal. The following four Doppler spectra demonstrate the disjoint nature of frequency and amplitude.

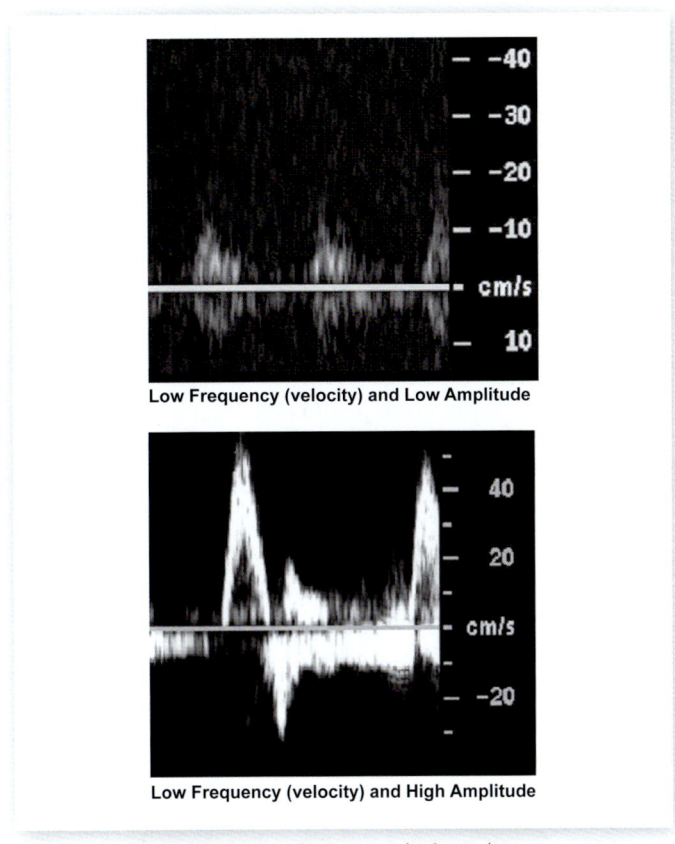

Fig. 32a **Amplitude versus frequency (velocity) in a spectrum**

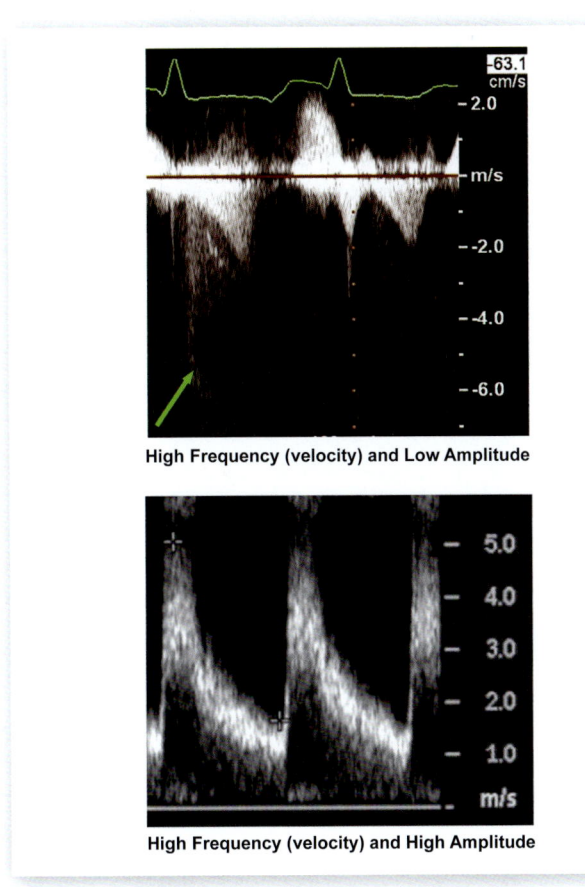

Fig. 32b **Amplitude versus frequency (velocity) in a spectrum**

13. PW vs. CW Comparison

13.1 Trade-Offs
Ultrasound, like life, is all about trade-offs. The winner is the person who trades off what they don't need for what they do need. The loser is someone who doesn't understand that there is a trade-off, or worse yet, gives up something needed for something not needed. PW and CW Doppler both exist as ultrasound modalities since each has a primary benefit and a primary drawback.

13.2 Timing and Basics of CW Doppler
Continuous wave Doppler is performed by one crystal or group of elements continuously transmitting while a second crystal or group of elements continuously receives the echoes. Since the transmit is continuous, there are echoes being generated from all depths simultaneously. Hence the receiver continuously receives echoes from all locations at once.

Although CW receives from all depths simultaneously, there is a region of maximal sensitivity related to where the transmit and receive beam best overlap (see *Figure 33*). Note that when performing CW Doppler, most systems represent this region of overlap with a diamond placed on the Doppler steering line. When you move the diamond up or down, the system changes the focusing such that the best overlap occurs at the depth of the diamond.

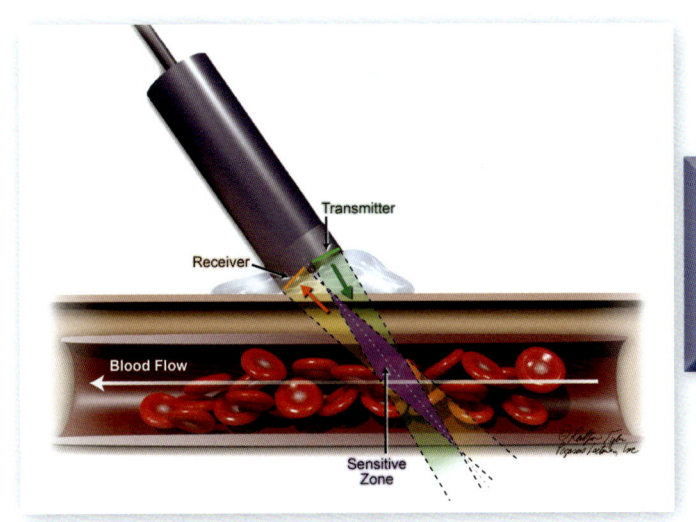

Fig. 33 **Transmit angle for CW Doppler**

13.3 Timing and Basics of PW Doppler
In contrast to CW Doppler, PW Doppler is performed by transmitting a pulse on either a single crystal or a group of crystals followed by a "dead time" or "dead period." During this dead period, the system is neither transmitting nor receiving. The dead period is really the roundtrip propagation time required for the pulse to arrive at and reflect back from the depth of interest as specified by the Doppler gate location placed by the user.

Recall that 1 cm imaging depth requires 13 μsec travel time, so the dead time until listening can begin is simply the gate depth in centimeters multiplied by 13 μsec. When the "dead time" has transpired, the crystal or group of elements are allowed to receive the echoes. The transition from using a crystal or an element as a transmitter to receiver is achieved through the use of a T/R switch. (You can probably guess what T and R stand for.) The switch changes the connection of the element from the transmit circuit to the receive circuit. During the "dead time" the T/R switch is open and the echoes are not registered. Therefore, echoes from depths shallower than the gate are not received.

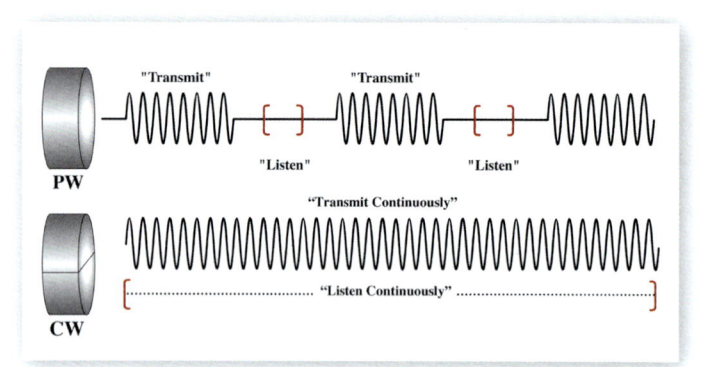

Fig. 34 **Comparison of PW and CW transmit and listen**

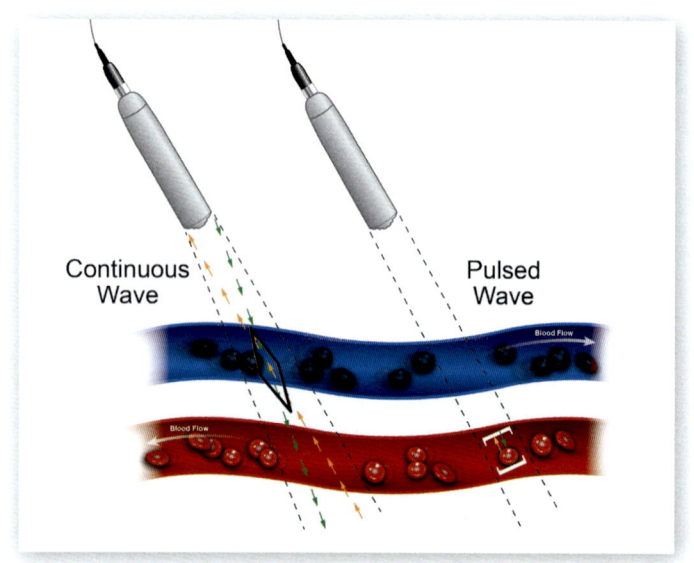

Fig. 35 **PW and CW Doppler comparison**

13.4 Range Specificity: Advantage PW
The fundamental advantage of PW over CW is good range specificity. In fact, the motivation for creating the more complex approach of PW was the inability of CW to offer any range resolution.

There are two fundamental misconceptions that we must address concerning CW versus PW and range specificity.

1. ***Misconception: When using CW Doppler, there is no means by which to create range specificity.*** Other modalities can be used in conjunction with CW to effectively create range specificity. Although there is no range specificity in CW as a modality by itself, the use of other modalities in conjunction with CW effectively yields range specificity. For example, if you are "Dopplering" flow through a stenotic valve or stenosed vessel, and the image and/or color Doppler shows that there is only one narrowed region in the area of the CW Doppler beam, then the peak velocity obtained can pretty safely be attributed to that specific region in the image.

2. ***Misconception: PW Doppler does not suffer any range ambiguity.*** PW offers good range specificity, not perfect range specificity. If you notice, the fundamental advantage of PW relative to CW was written as "good" range specificity, not perfect range specificity. Contrary to popular misconception in the field, PW Doppler always suffers from some range ambiguity. In fact, every Doppler modality based on pulsed wave operation suffers from range ambiguity including 2D imaging, color Doppler, M-mode, and PW spectral Doppler. This range ambiguity is responsible for artifacts which are rarely identified. The range ambiguity is so predictable that the Doppler modality called HPRF Doppler was created specifically by exploiting the range ambiguity artifact. Range ambiguity and HPRF Doppler will be discussed thoroughly in Section 18.

13.5 Aliasing: Advantage CW
The fundamental advantage of CW relative to PW is no aliasing. In Chapter 6, Part I, we discussed the Nyquist criterion as the phenomenon that occurs when a signal is sampled below the Nyquist limit. For CW, since the receiver is always "listening" the sampling rate is essentially infinite. For PW Doppler, "listening" occurs intermittently, when the receivers are turned on. We have already learned in Chapter 4 that the time between repetitions of the transmit pulse is called the pulse repetition period (PRP). In the figure below, we see that the time between "listens" is the same as the time between "transmits." Therefore, the time between "listens" is also referred to as the PRP. Expressed as a frequency, the reciprocal of the time between "listens" is referred to as the pulse repetition frequency.

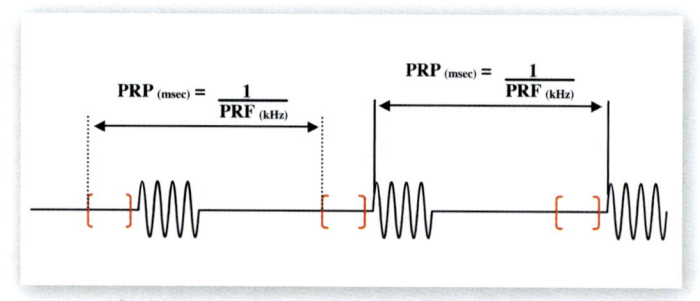

Fig. 36 **The listening rate in PW is the PRF**

CHECKPOINT: Exam Tip

PW has the advantage of good range specificity (signals are received primarily from the Doppler gate location) whereas CW has virtually no range specificity. Conversely, CW can detect virtually unlimited velocities whereas PW suffers from aliasing.

13.6 The Maximum Detectable Frequency Shift in PW

For consistency with the language used to describe the Nyquist criterion, we will refer to the time of "listening" as "sampling." Therefore, the frequency at which sampling occurs in PW Doppler is the PRF. We know that by the Nyquist criterion, the maximum detectable frequency is half of the sample rate.

Therefore, for PW Doppler, the Nyquist limit is the PRF divided by 2. Since the frequencies we are sampling are the Doppler shift frequencies, we can write the relationship between the maximum detectable frequency shift and the occurrence of aliasing simply as:

$$f_{Dop}(\text{maximum}) = \frac{PRF}{2}.$$

From this equation it is evident that higher frequency shifts are more likely to cause aliasing. Fortunately, we have already learned the Doppler equation which dictates what causes higher Doppler frequency shifts. According to the Doppler equation, higher velocity flow, higher operating frequencies, lower propagation velocities, and insonification angles closer to 0 degrees or 180 degrees all result in higher Doppler frequency shifts. From this equation, it is also evident that lower PRFs are more likely to cause aliasing. We learned in Chapter 4 that the PRP, and hence the PRF, are determined by the depth. (The propagation speed theoretically also affects the PRF, but from a practical standpoint, since the system always assumes 1540 m/sec, the propagation velocity is no longer treated as a variable but instead as a constant.) A deeper imaging depth requires a longer line time, resulting in a longer PRP and a lower PRF. As a result, we can now compile a table which expresses when aliasing is most likely to occur.

CHECKPOINT: Exam Tip

According to the Nyquist Theorem (discussed in Chapter 6, Part I) the maximum detectable frequency is half of the sampling rate. For PW Doppler, the sampling rate is the PRF. Therefore, Nyquist dictates that the maximum detectable Doppler shift is equal to half of the PRF.

13.7 Parameters Affecting Aliasing in PW Doppler

Related Parameter	Parameter Affecting Aliasing
Doppler Shift	Higher velocity of blood
	Insonification angle closer to 0° or 180°
	Higher transmit frequency
PRF	Deeper gate depth

Table 1 Increased likelihood of aliasing for PW Doppler

Note: Although this table was included for completeness, it is hoped that you will analyze the Doppler equation and the physical situations which control the PRF to arrive at the same conclusions on your own.

13.8 Appearance of Aliasing in a Doppler Spectrum

The following Doppler spectrum of *Figure 37* demonstrates aliasing. When true aliasing occurs, it is not possible to increase the Doppler scales any more so as to unwrap the true peak velocity. Aliasing appears in the spectrum as a "wrapping" of the signal from either the top of the spectrum to the bottom of the spectrum or vice versa. Flow toward the transducer (presuming spectral invert is not on) will extend to the top of the spectrum and then continue at the bottom of the spectrum.

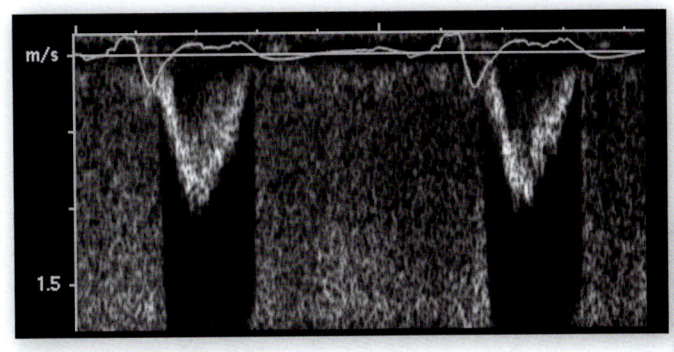

Fig. 37 **Doppler aliasing**

The following Doppler spectrum in *Figure 38* is often referred to as aliasing, but is really just a "display alias." A display alias implies that the signal is wrapped in the spectrum but can actually be "unwrapped" by increasing the scales or shifting the Doppler baseline. For the specific spectrum of *Figure 38*, the display alias can be unwrapped simply by shifting the baseline all the way down to the bottom of the scales.

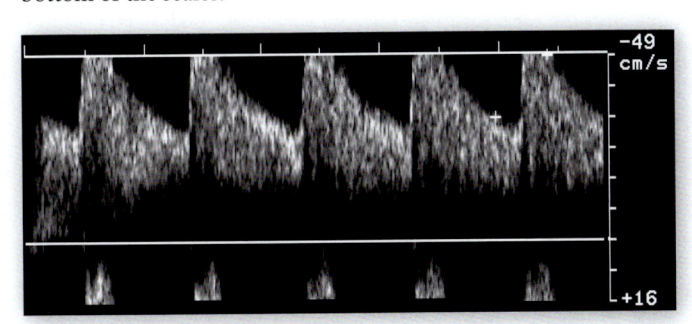

Fig. 38 **Doppler "display" alias**

The concept of display aliasing is further illustrated by Figure 39. Note that in (a), the aliased component on the top of the spectrum has a velocity slightly greater than 10 cm/sec. In (b), a depiction of what the spectrum would look like if it were possible to add 10 cm/sec to the bottom scale setting is shown. Even without shifting the baseline, it is possible to determine the peak velocity accurately by simply adding the velocity of the aliasing component to the velocity of the cutoff portion as depicted in (b). We can now see that the true peak velocity is slightly greater than 30 cm/sec.

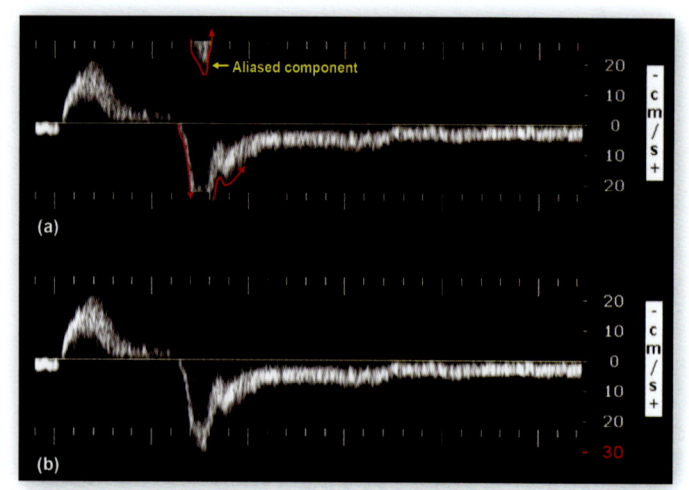

Fig. 39 Doppler display alias (a) with modified scale to visualize true peak velocity (b)

13.9 Practical Limit in CW Doppler and Aliasing

In reality, there is a practical limit imposed on the sampling rate of CW Doppler, but by design, this limit is so high that it rarely becomes a limiting factor clinically. Since the listen is continuous in CW Doppler, the receiving of the CW signal does not limit the ability to detect Doppler shift frequencies as with PW Doppler. Recall that in the processing of Doppler, the signal is converted from analog format to digital format. The A/D converter samples the analog signal at the frequency determined by the sampling clock. If the sample rate of the A/D converter is 50 kHz, then the analog signal conversion would be half of that or 25 kHz. Since it is possible in some extreme cases to achieve Doppler shifts as high as 50 kHz, the 50 kHz converter would cause aliasing in CW. In order to avoid aliasing for a 50 kHz Doppler shift, the converter would have to convert at a rate of at least 100 kHz. In earlier days, there were very few technologies capable of producing higher conversion rate A/D converters. As a result, the cost of the high speed converters was prohibitive. However, following Moore's law of technology advancement, converters with conversion rates much higher than 100 kHz now cost essentially pennies. Therefore, the A/D converter rate is pushed up high enough so as to never be a practical concern in CW Doppler anymore.

13.10 Changing the Scale in PW Doppler

As a review of the concept of reciprocals, the reciprocal of a maximum is a minimum. The maximum PRF is the reciprocal of the minimum PRP. The minimum PRP is determined by the gate depth.

In other words, since we can't make sound travel any faster into the body than 1540 m/sec, the time we must wait for the reflection to return to the transducer is purely a function of the depth. If the gate is set deep, then the time for the echo to return will be longer than when the gate is set at a shallow depth. Unfortunately, as a sonographer, you do not have the power to make all blood flow occur at shallow depths. As a result, long PRPs are possible and probable, implying low PRFs. The low PRFs lead to greater likelihood of aliasing in PW Doppler. Specifically if the PRF is not at least twice the Doppler frequency shift, aliasing occurs.

Let us consider the converse case. What if the maximum PRF is much higher than twice the Doppler frequency shift detected? The following spectrum of *Figure 40* demonstrates this situation.

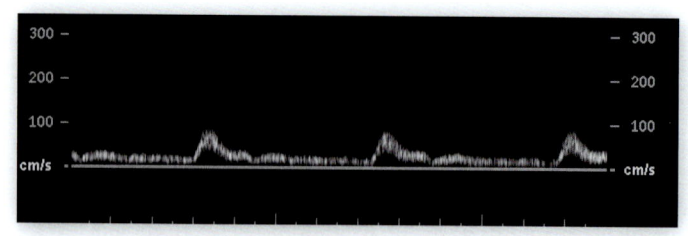

Fig. 40 Doppler scales too high

The ability to accurately measure the velocity of this spectrum is clearly compromised by the scale being too high. With the high scale setting, even a slight difference in cursor placement means a significant difference in the measured velocity. If the Doppler scale (PRF) is lowered, the spectrum will appear as a greater percentage, and hence more appropriately scaled. *Figure 41* demonstrates the same signal with the Doppler scale lowered.

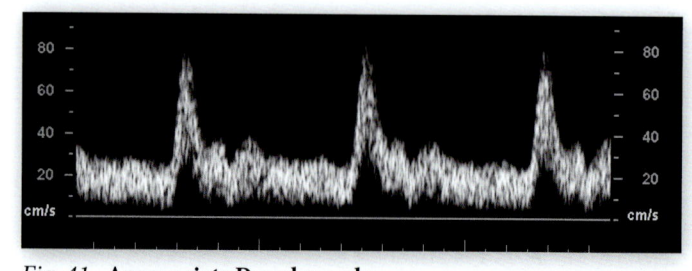

Fig. 41 Appropriate Doppler scale

View ONLINE Animation and Image Library

To demonstrate what physically happens when the scales are changed, we will return to our pulse wave picture. Let's imagine that the depth is set so that the maximum PRF is 8 kHz as shown below.

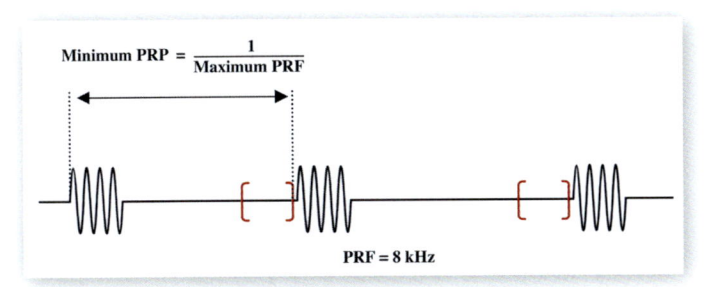

Fig. 42 Minimum PRP (no dead time)

Now imagine that the user wants to decrease the Doppler scale so as to make the spectrum a more appropriate percentage of the scale as just shown with the two spectrums of *Figures 40* and *41*. A lower PRF is achieved by increasing the gate depth. However, the gate depth, although under user control, must be placed wherever the flow to be measured exists. Therefore, we need a way to increase the PRP without changing the gate location. The following figure, *Figure 43*, demonstrates how this can be achieved.

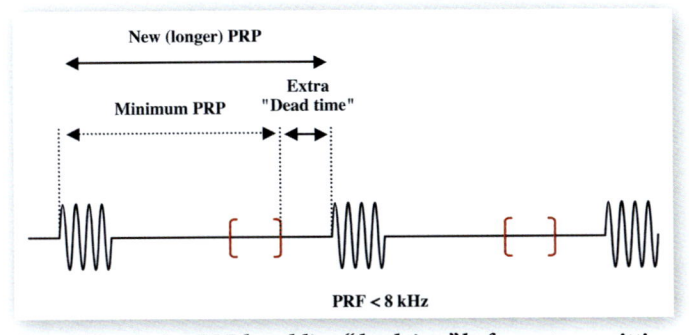

Fig. 43 Increasing PRP by adding "dead time" before retransmitting

Notice that additional "dead time" has been added after the Doppler gate, but that the time between the transmit and the Doppler gate remains unchanged. This means that the Doppler gate is still listening to signals from the same depth as in the previous example. However, since the time between transmits has now increased (similarly the time between listens has increased), the PRF is now lower. If the PRF is lower, the maximum detectable frequency shift is now lower which means that the Doppler signal now occupies a larger percentage of the displayed spectral frequency range. If the Doppler scales are lowered again, more dead time is added repeatedly until the desired PRF is reached.

When the Doppler scales are increased, the exact opposite process occurs. Each time the scale is increased, some of the extra dead time between the Doppler gate and the next transmit pulse is removed. Eventually, all of the dead time is removed and the maximum scale (for that particular depth) is reached. If aliasing is still occurring, there are only a few choices:

1. Use a lower frequency transducer.
2. Find a view that results in a shallower gate depth to interrogate the same flow.
3. Use CW Doppler.
4. Use HPRF Doppler (described later in this chapter).

14. The Maximum Detectable Velocity

In Section 13.6 we developed the equation which specifies the maximum detectable frequency shift as dictated by the Nyquist criterion. Although Doppler displays can present either the Doppler frequency shift or the velocity on the vertical axis (and some systems allow for both simultaneously), velocity has pretty much become the norm. We would therefore like to be able to convert the maximum detectable frequency shift into an expression for the maximum detectable velocity.

We will start with the Doppler equation. We will presume that no variables are changing so that we can write that the maximum Doppler shift detectable is directly related to the maximum velocity detectable, or:

$$f_{Dop}(\text{maximum}) = \frac{2f_0 v(\text{maximum})}{c} \cos(\theta)$$

Solving for v (maximum detectable) by manipulation yields:

$$\frac{c \times f_{Dop}(\text{maximum})}{2f_0 \cos(\theta)} = v(\text{maximum})$$

Since we have another expression for the maximum detectable Doppler shift frequency according to Nyquist,

$$\left(f_{Dop}(\text{maximum}) = \frac{PRF}{2} \right),$$ we can substitute as follows:

$$\frac{c \times PRF}{4 \times f_0 \cos(\theta)} = v(\text{maximum})$$

We now have an expression which relates the maximum detectable velocity to the system parameters that are known when scanning. Specifically, we know the relationship between the maximum detectable velocity and the transmit frequency and the PRF. Not surprisingly, this equation shows that as the PRF increases, the maximum detectable velocity increases. Also evident is the fact that as the operating frequency increases the maximum detectable velocity decreases. This inability to detect higher velocities with higher frequency transducers is yet another reason why Doppler should be performed with lower transmit frequencies.

The following table demonstrates the maximum detectable velocities for imaging depths from 10 cm to 20 cm, using varying transmit frequencies. Shading has been used to break the velocity ranges into bands of 10 cm/sec.

Depth (cm)	PRP (msec)	PRF/2 (kHz)	f_0 = 2.0 MHz	f_0 = 2.5 MHz	f_0 = 3.0 MHz	f_0 = 3.5 MHz	f_0 = 4.0 MHz	f_0 = 5.0 MHz
10	154.87	3.2	124.3	99.4	82.9	71.0	62.1	49.7
11	167.86	3.0	114.7	91.7	76.5	65.5	57.3	45.9
12	180.84	2.8	106.4	85.2	71.0	60.8	53.2	42.6
13	193.83	2.6	99.3	79.5	66.2	56.8	49.7	39.7
14	206.82	2.4	93.1	74.5	62.1	53.2	46.5	37.2
15	219.81	2.3	87.6	70.1	58.4	50.0	43.8	35.0
16	232.79	2.1	82.7	66.2	55.1	47.3	41.3	33.1
17	245.78	2.0	78.3	62.7	52.2	44.8	39.2	31.3
18	258.77	1.9	74.4	59.5	49.6	42.5	37.2	29.8
19	271.75	1.8	70.8	56.7	47.2	40.5	35.4	28.3
20	284.74	1.8	67.6	54.1	45.1	38.6	33.8	27.0

Table 2 Max detectable velocity (± cm/s) for given transmit frequencies (f_0)

Author's Note:
Inclusion of Overhead Time

The observant reader will have noticed that the PRP listed is greater than the imaging depth multiplied by 13 μsec per cm.

A certain amount of overhead is necessary for setting up each transmitted line. This "overhead" time has been included so as to yield more accurate line time estimates.

KEY CONCEPT

Since the Doppler shift is proportional to the operating frequency, a lower operating frequency results in a lower Doppler shift, decreasing the likelihood of aliasing.

15. Spectral Windows and Modal Flow

15.1 The Presence of a Spectral Window

Notice in the PW spectrum of *Figure 44a* that there is a spectral window (the open area between the spectrum and the baseline). The sample volume is 0.05 cm. In this case, the sample volume is small relative to the diameter of the vessel and is placed in the center of the vessel. Since most of the blood traveling through the sample volume is traveling at the same velocity, there is relatively little spread around the mean velocity. The presence of a spectral window indicates the presence of laminar flow. However, the absence of a spectral window may or may not indicate turbulence (see *Figure 44c* and Chapter 13: Hemodynamics). Caution must be taken not to over interpret this criterion in the absence of a spectral window.

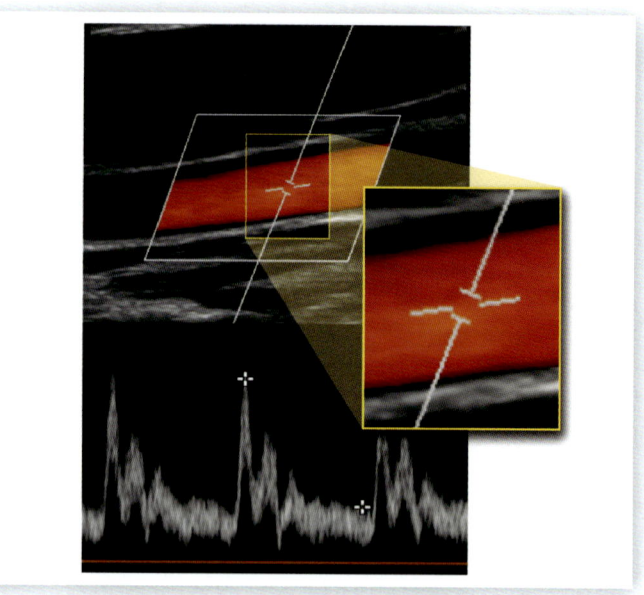

Fig. 44a A small PW Doppler sample volume in the centerstream of laminar flow demonstrating a spectral window

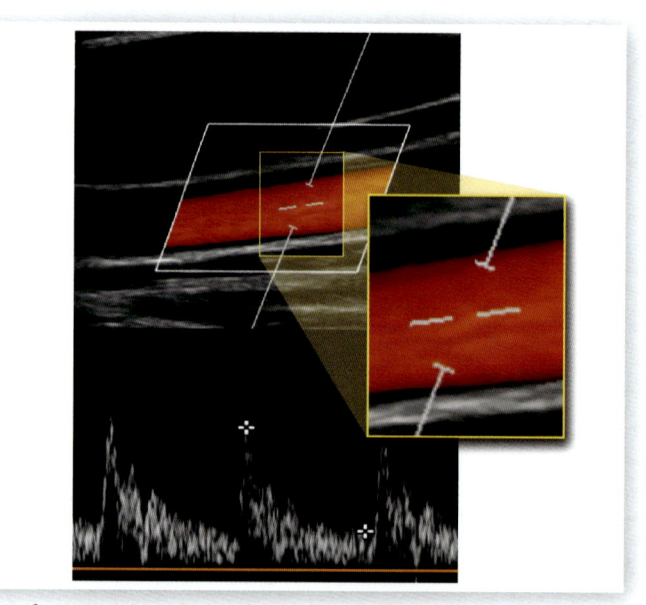

Fig. 44b A PW Doppler with a larger sample volume demonstrating the spectral window diminished with the detection of lower velocities close to the vessel wall

For example, the spectrum in *Figure 44b* is taken from the exact same vessel but using a larger sample volume. In this case, the sample volume incorporates the lower velocity flow that exists close to the vessel wall as well as the higher velocity of the centerstream. Note how the spectrum is filled in at lower velocities (closer to the baseline) from the slower blood velocities registered along the vessel walls. It is important to realize that moving a small sample volume close to the wall will also fill in the spectral window. A spectrum with little or no spectral window similar to this spectrum would be created using CW Doppler, which is effectively an infinitely large PW sample volume.

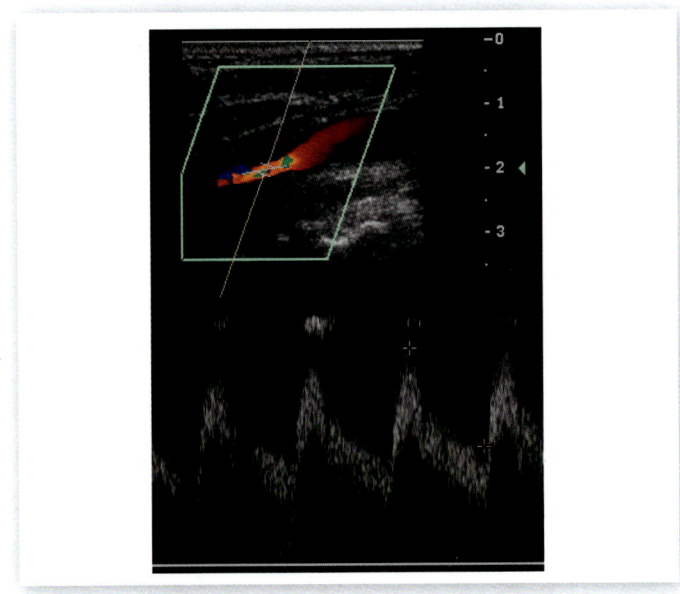

Fig. 44c **Diminished spectral window as the result of post-stenotic turbulence**

15.2 Spectral Doppler Modal Flow

In mathematics, the mode refers to one of the three different types of averages (mean, median, and mode). People tend to be more familiar with the mean and median, and less so with the mode. The mode is simply the most often occurring value in a data set. For spectral Doppler, the modal flow usually refers to a visual spectral envelope that appears brighter than the rest of the spectrum. This brighter portion of the spectrum corresponds to the range of velocities at which a majority of the blood is traveling.

The ability to visually appreciate the modal flow is dependent on not over or under gaining the Doppler signal and using the appropriate grayscale (compression/dynamic range setting). Modal envelopes are more common in CW than in PW because of the fact that multiple flow patterns along the entire CW Doppler line are often detected. However, there are hemodynamic situations that result in a modal flow from a single flow location. In these cases, the flow is usually being constrained by frictional and viscous forces so that more of the flow is traveling at a lower velocity, and a smaller portion of the blood is traveling at a higher velocity, as can happen with stenoses.

Figure 45 shows three separate CW Doppler tracings of right ventricular infundibular obstruction and pulmonary valve regurgitation. In (a), the modal envelope is dagger-shaped due to dynamic obstruction, and the lighter envelope is the result of regurgitation. For (b), lower gain and lower dynamic range result in the dagger shape envelope's enhancement and loss of the regurgitation envelope. In (c), higher gain and dynamic range result in the loss of the modal envelope and the blending of both envelopes into one signal.

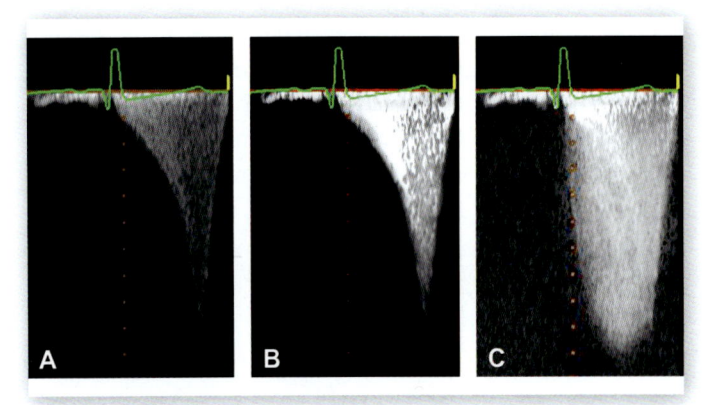

Fig. 45 **Three separate CW Doppler tracings of right ventricular infundibular obstruction and pulmonary valve regurgitation viewed differently based on changes to gain and dynamic range**

In *Figure 46*, the CW Doppler of an aortic valve shows modal flow both before (a) and after angulation (b). After angulation, the distinction between the two flow envelopes is minimized.

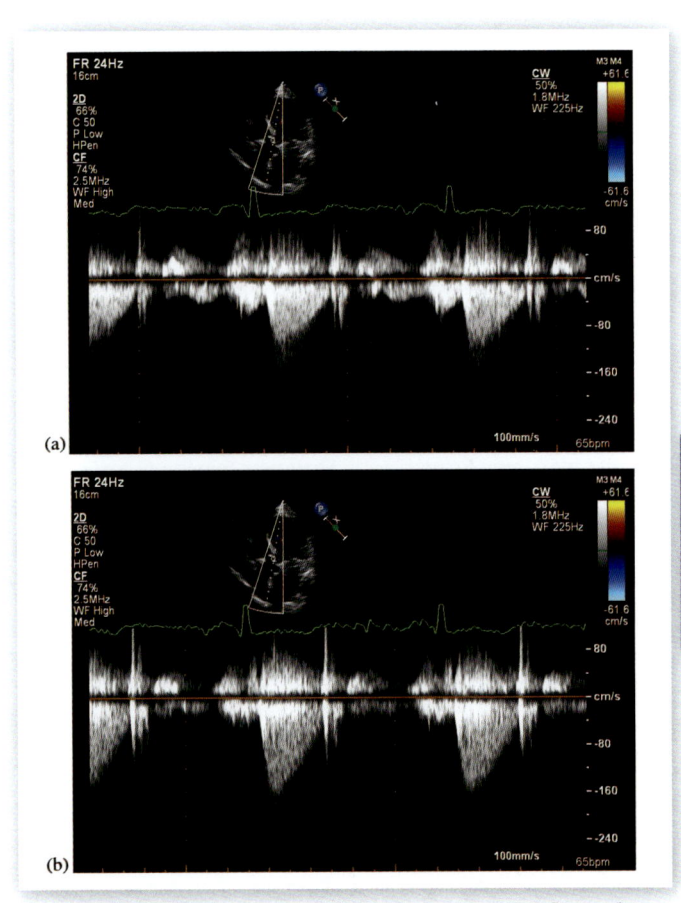

Fig. 46 **CW Doppler of aortic valve showing modal flow velocity before (a) and after angulation (b)**

Figure 47 shows three CW Doppler tracings through the aortic valve and LVOT. In (a), appropriate gain and compression are set to appreciate modal flow representing elevated LVOT velocity and elevated aortic velocity (lighter envelope and higher velocity). For (b), an inappropriate gain is set so that the modal envelope is lost. In (c), inappropriate gain and compression settings show that only the LVOT envelope is appreciated. Note that this would likely lead to a misinterpretation of this spectral envelope representing the aortic peak velocity and a misreading of the peak by nearly a factor of 2.

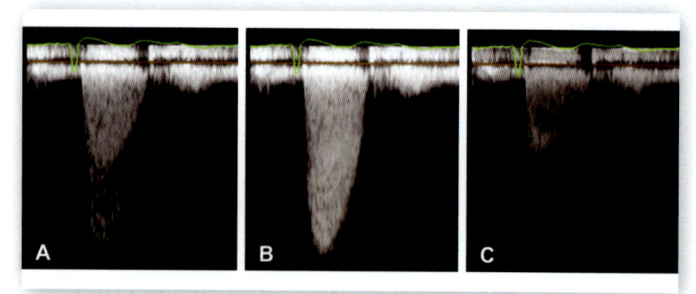

Fig. 47 **CW Doppler through aortic valve and LVOT with appropriate (a) versus inappropriate gain and compression settings (b), (c)**

For more on spectral interpretation, please see Chapter 13: Hemodynamics.

16. PW Versus CW Comparison

PW	CW
Good range resolution Not perfect: see range ambiguity	**No range specificity** Unless derived from other modalities
Aliasing: limited maximum detectable velocity Nyquist limited	**Virtually unlimited maximum detectable velocity** (High A/D converter rate is limit)
Deeper maximum focus Can use full-aperture since transmit and receive are separated in time	**Shallower maximum focus** Can only use half aperture since transmit and receive are concurrent
Possible to visualize spectral window for laminar flow For small sample volumes in the center of large healthy vessels, with appropriate gain and insonification angle, spectral window exists	**Rarely visualize spectral window** Low and high velocities are received simultaneously so filling to baseline is normal
Greater potential sensitivity Can use full aperture for transmit and receive; also, not as restricted by thermal issues	**Potentially less sensitive** Usually less sensitive than PW, but depends on gate size, alignment to flow, thermal limits, depth of focus, etc.
Less restricted by thermal bioeffect risks Lower I_{SPTA}	**More restricted by thermal bioeffect risks** Higher I_{SPTA} implies potentially lower sensitivity

Table 3 **PW versus CW comparison**

17. PW Range Ambiguity

17.1 Dispelling the Myth
PW Doppler is often assumed to have perfect range resolution. This statement implies that the Doppler signal from a PW Doppler can only emanate from the desired Doppler gate depth. This statement is not true. In reality, standard PW Doppler always receives signals from depths which correspond to multiples of the pulse repetition period (PRP). This artifact has been well understood in radar for many years and is called range ambiguity.

17.2 The Mechanism that Causes Range Ambiguity
We will use *Figure 48* to illustrate the cause of this artifact. Assume that the first transmit pulse occurs at time T_0. From time T_0 to time T_1, the sound has traveled from the transducer to the desired gate depth. From time T_1 to time T_2, the transmit pulse continues to travel within the medium to the 1st ambiguous gate depth. Simultaneously the echo from the desired gate depth returns to the transducer. At time T_2, since the echo from the first transmit is received, a second transmit pulse is fired. From time T_2 to time T_3, the pulse from the second transmit pulse has reached the desired gate depth. Simultaneously, the echo of the first transmit pulse has traveled from the 1st ambiguous gate location and arrived at the Doppler gate location. The 1st ambiguous gate echo from the first transmit is added to the echo from the desired Doppler gate of the second transmit. From time T_3 to time T_4, this combined echo returns to the transducer. At time T_4, the echo is received and the third transmit occurs. The process continues such that every subsequent echo is really a sum of echoes from multiples of the roundtrip distance that the sound travels in the time between transmits, or the pulse repetition period, (PRP). Hence PW Doppler is actually always receiving echoes from multiple gates at the same time. (Watching the range ambiguity animation in 6e Online Extras should make this concept easier to grasp.)

View ONLINE Animation and Image Library

17.3 Range Ambiguity and Mitigating Factors
Given that this artifact always exists in PW Doppler, there are two very important questions to answer: "How often does this artifact occur and go unrecognized?" and "How can you tell when this artifact is affecting the Doppler spectrum?"

This artifact affects the Doppler spectrum frequently and is almost always unrecognized. There are, however, mitigating factors which reduce the occurrence or severity of the range ambiguity artifact in

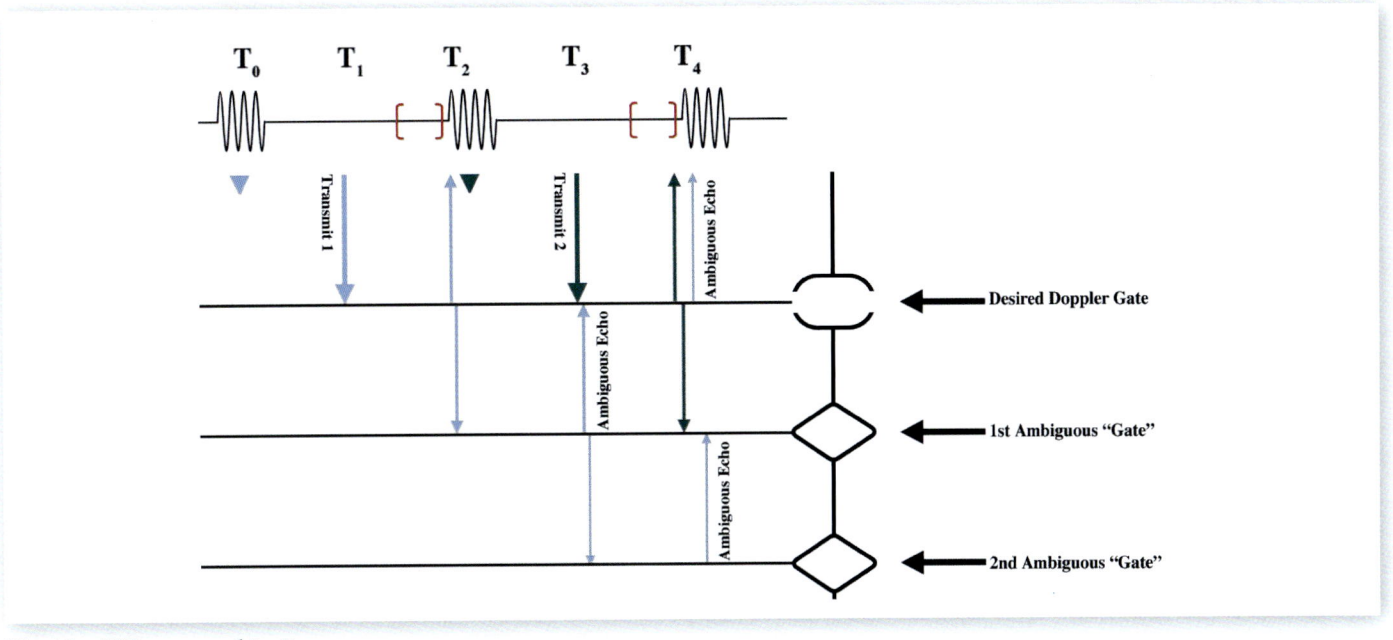

Fig. 48 **PW range ambiguity**

PW Doppler, such as:

1. There may be no blood flow at the ambiguous gate locations.
2. The signals from the ambiguous gates are generally weaker than from the desired Doppler gate.
3. There is more attenuation from deeper depths.
4. Electronic (phased) transducers focus the beam at the Doppler gate, making the beam more diffuse (less intense) at the ambiguous gate locations. (This is not true for fixed focus transducers which generally experience range ambiguity worse than phased array transducers.)

17.4 Risk Factors

The greatest risk of range ambiguity occurs when the Doppler gate is shallow. When the Doppler gate is shallow, the ambiguous gate locations are still relatively shallow. The resulting echoes from these ambiguous locations may be strong enough to affect the Doppler spectrum. This problem is exacerbated when mechanical transducers are used. Since mechanical transducers have a fixed focus, usually as deep as possible, the beam cannot intentionally be made more diffuse at the ambiguous gate location. As a result, attenuation due to beam divergence cannot be utilized to help discriminate signals from the desired gate location and the ambiguous gate location. With the passage of time, mechanical transducers are becoming less and less common such that this risk factor is decreasing over time.

17.5 Determining if Range Ambiguity is Present

The easiest way to ascertain whether or not range ambiguity is present is to change the PRF (Doppler scales). Changing the Doppler scales should only scale the Doppler spectrum (stretching or shrinking) but not change the basic characteristic of the spectrum.

Changing the PRF changes the PRP and hence, the location of the ambiguous gate. If changing the scale results in a change in the characteristic shape of the spectrum, range ambiguity is present.

> **KEY CONCEPT**
>
> Although PW has good range specificity, it is not perfect. All pulsed modalities have some range ambiguity which results from receiving signals from an earlier transmit with signals from the current transmit.

18. HPRF Doppler

18.1 Using the Trade-Offs

As we have just learned, PW generally has good range resolution but is prone to aliasing. CW has virtually no range resolution but virtually unlimited maximum detectable velocities. High pulse repetition frequency Doppler (HPRF) is a compromise of these two modes. HPRF Doppler intentionally utilizes the artifact of range ambiguity to increase the maximum detectable velocity without aliasing, at the expense of some range resolution.

18.2 Using Range Ambiguity to Create HPRF Doppler

In PW, the minimum PRP (maximum PRF), is determined by the Doppler gate depth. A deeper gate results in a longer travel time and hence, a lower maximum PRF. The first schema depicted in *Figure*

49 shows standard PW Doppler with a relatively deep Doppler gate depth such that the PRF is relatively low. Note that the beam is focused at the Doppler gate depth. The second schema depicts standard PW Doppler with a shallower gate depth. Note that the ambiguous gate happens to align with the desired gate depth of the first schema. Since the gate depth is shallower, the PRF is higher than the first schema. Note that the beam focus is again set at the Doppler gate depth. The third schema demonstrates how high pulse repetition frequency (HPRF) Doppler functions. HPRF uses the timing of the shallower gate depth with the focusing of the deeper depth to achieve higher PRF with improved sensitivity at the desired depth.

> **KEY CONCEPT**
>
> HPRF Doppler takes advantage of the ever present range ambiguity which exists in PW Doppler to allow for higher detectable velocities than are achievable with standard PW Doppler.

19. Doppler Insonification Angle and Error Sources

19.1 Cardiac and Alignment with Flow

Since the Doppler effect is angle dependent, modern systems allow for angle correction of Doppler measurements. In cardiac, the insonification angle is presumed to be 0 degrees or 180 degrees such that 100% of the Doppler shift is detected, and no correction is needed. For vascular Doppler, the angle can vary considerably, and angle correction is commonly employed.

In cardiac imaging, because of the number of different imaging windows (apical, parasternal, sub-costal, and the suprasternal notch) as well as the ability to move to different intercostal spaces, the ability to achieve insonification angles close to either 0 degrees or 180 degrees generally holds true. When the angle deviates from these ideal angles, the angular error is small enough relative to other error sources in ultrasound so as to be ignored. However, there are times when the angle to flow deviates more than normal where the velocities recorded will have enough error so as to be significant. To fully understand the relationship between the angle and the velocity measurement accuracy, we will need to review the cosine function.

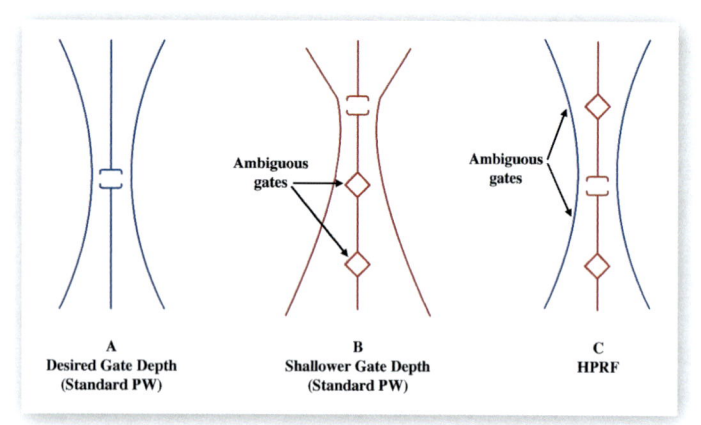

Fig. 49 **Range ambiguity exploited to create HPRF Doppler**

Note that the diamonds on the HPRF Doppler steer line demonstrate the locations of the ambiguous gates.

The value of HPRF Doppler is the ability to achieve higher PRFs at deeper gate depths. The trade-off is that HPRF allows for some range ambiguity shallower than the Doppler gate to achieve the higher PRF. Therefore, HPRF Doppler has range ambiguity both above and below the desired gate location. Standard PW also has range ambiguity, but the ambiguous gates are only at locations deeper than the desired gate depth. In HPRF, the "ambiguous" gate locations are usually indicated by diamonds on the steer line. If the diamonds do not overlay any regions of flow, then no extraneous flow is being registered and there is no source for problems or confusion. If these diamonds overlay a region of low-velocity flow, then there is also not likely a significant issue since there must be high velocity in the actual Doppler gate or HPRF would not be activated in the first place. The only real issue occurs when the diamond overlays a region where there are also very high velocities. By changing the scales, the location of the ambiguous gates (represented by the diamonds) can be moved in the hopes of registering only the high velocity flow from the desired gate location. On most systems, the activation of HPRF is automatic when the user increases the Doppler scales past the depth-restricted limit. When HPRF is activated, all systems notify the user with the display of the diamonds and many systems usually add the title HPRF above the spectrum.

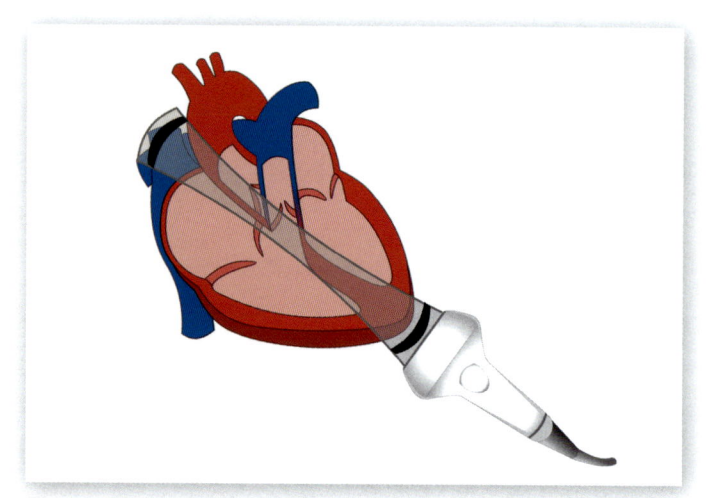

Fig. 50 **CW Doppler beam alignment with ascending aorta (180°)**

19.2 Vascular Doppler and the Need to Angle Correct

Before reviewing the cosine, we should also discuss the prevalence of angle errors in vascular Doppler. Unlike cardiac, vascular Doppler applications frequently are restricted to views where the vessel is parallel to the skin surface. The result is a less than optimum angle formed between the beam and the flow. In fact, quite frequently, without steering or transducer angulation, the insonification angle is the worst possible, 90 degrees. Through steering and angulation, angles of 60 degrees or less are generally achievable. Since the cosine of 60 degrees is only 0.5, clearly, angle correction is going to be a critical component of an accurate assessment.

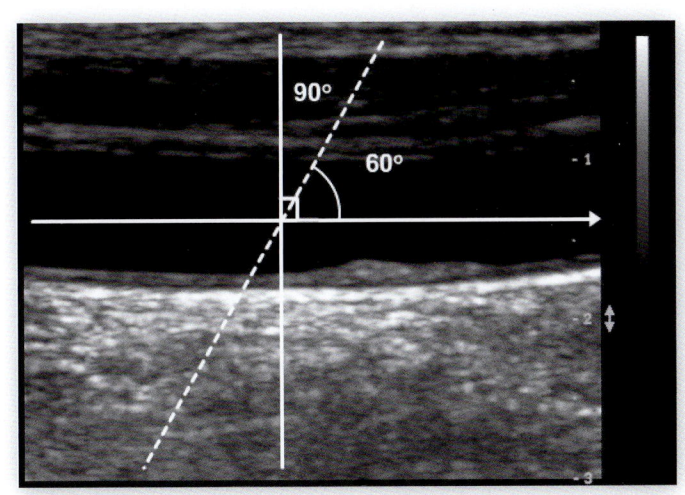

Fig. 51 **With no steering, Doppler angle to flow is commonly close to 90°**

19.3 Angle Correction and the Doppler Angle

Angle correction is performed by the ultrasound system based on information from the sonographer. For angle correction, the sonographer aligns a flow indicator with the presumed direction of blood flow through the Doppler sample volume as seen in *Figure 52a* The ultrasound system can then determine the angle that is formed between the blood flow direction and the Doppler steering angle (*Figure 52b*), and then use the cosine of that angle in the Doppler equation to correct the calculated blood flow velocity.

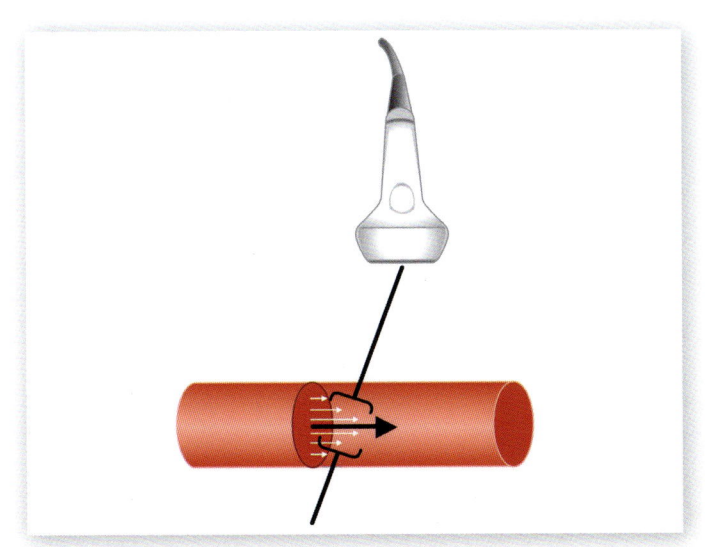

Fig. 52a **User aligns flow indicator with presumed blood flow direction**

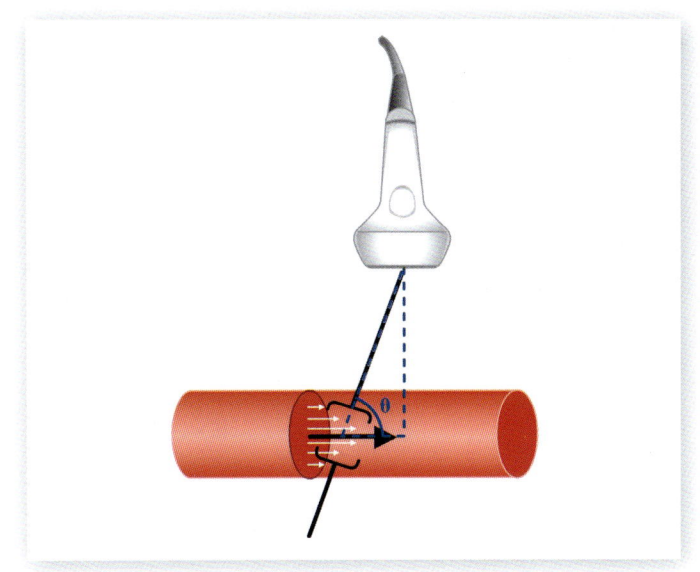

Fig. 52b **System determines Doppler angle from basic geometry**

If the Doppler indicator is not correctly aligned with the blood flow direction (*Figures 52c* and *53a*), the system is in essence told the wrong angle to calculate the correction. In these cases, the Doppler shift is determined by the actual angle to flow but the correction is by a different angle, and hence incorrect. Because the cosine function is non-linear with angle, a 5 degree error in setting the flow indicator from flow truly at 60 degrees creates a larger percentage error than the a 5 degree error relative to a an actual angle of 50 degrees. These errors will be further explained in the following sections.

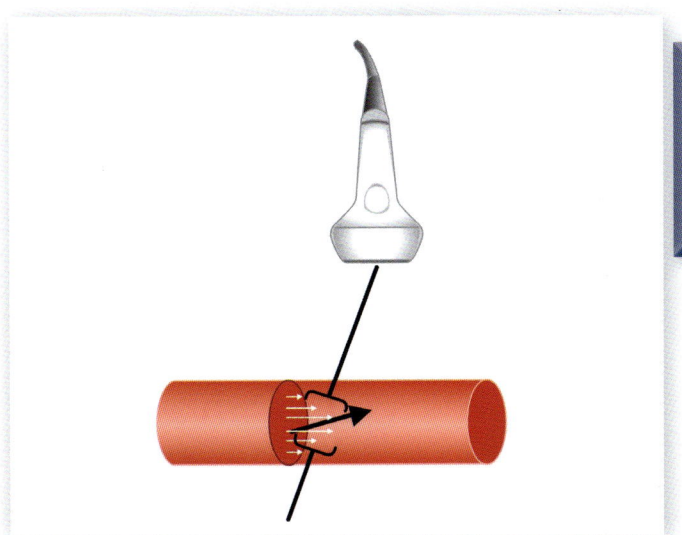

Fig. 52c **Angle correction introduces error when the flow indicator is not aligned correctly with the true flow direction**

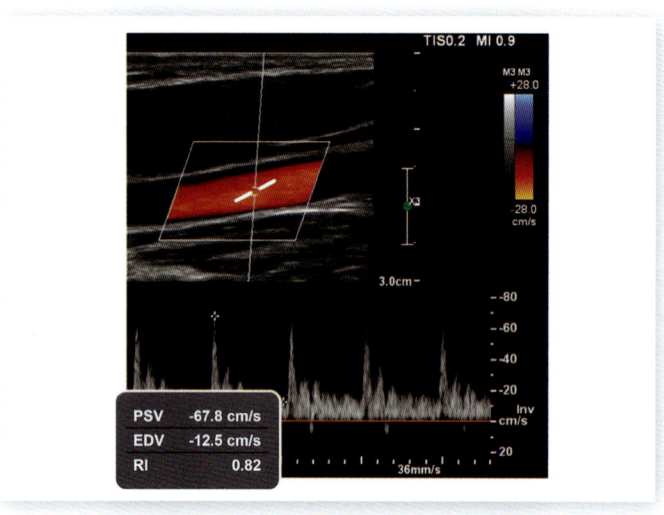

Fig. 53a   Flow indicator not correctly aligned to flow

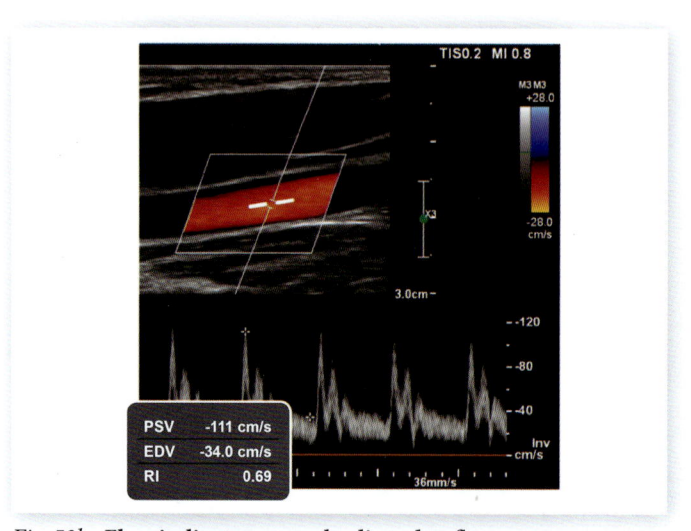

Fig. 53b   Flow indicator properly aligned to flow

When comparing *Figures 53a* and *53b*, note that the peak systolic velocity error is nearly 40%.

Review of the Cosine
In Chapter 1: Mathematics we discussed the details of the cosine for various angles. The following is a plot of the cosine of the angle (y-axis) versus varying angles (x-axis).

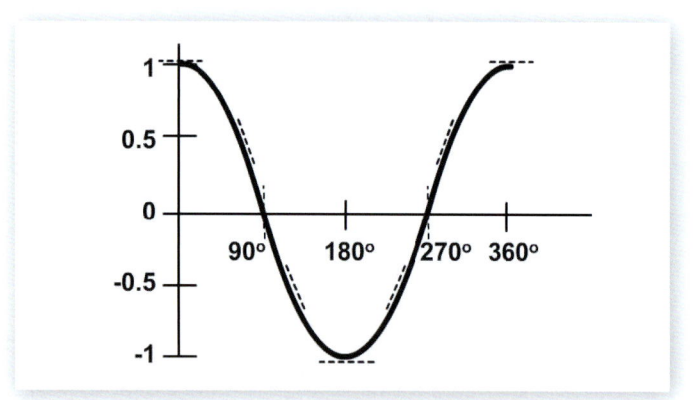

Fig. 54   The slope of the cosine function and error

From the shape of the cosine curve, the non-linear aspect of the cosine is evident. Notice that the rate of change of the cosine is very slow at angles close to zero degrees. The rate of change is determined by the slope and is indicated by the dotted tangential lines on the graph. In other words, for small deviations in angles around zero degrees, the associated measurement error is relatively small. Notice that as the angle becomes larger, the rate of change increases (slope steepens). The rate of change reaches a maximum at 90 degrees, where the cosine itself reaches zero. The registered Doppler shift will be zero at an angle of 90 degrees or will be close to zero when the angle is close to 90 degrees because of the rejection caused by the wall filters. Therefore, regardless of the true velocity, the system will yield a velocity of zero, implying infinite error. As the angle progresses from 90 degrees towards 180 degrees, the rate of change decreases. At 180 degrees, the slope flattens out, and the error associated with angular error is as small as it was at 0 degrees.

19.4 Peak Velocity and Pressure Gradient
The peak velocity measurement is usually made so that a pressure gradient can be calculated (discussed in Chapters 12 and 13). The pressure gradient is calculated from the modified Bernoulli's equation, by squaring the peak velocity. Any error in the peak velocity thereby is squared, making the error in the pressure gradient increase even more rapidly with increasing velocity error. Since the angular error associated with the cosine is non-linear, and the pressure gradient relationship is non-linear, it is imperative that you understand how significant "small angular errors" can become.

19.5 Angle Correction Error (5 Degree Table)
Table 4 demonstrates the velocity error and the pressure error associated with only a 5 degree error in angle correction, relative to various insonification angles from 0 degrees to 80 degrees. The first column (white) represents the assumed insonification angle. The second column (yellow) represents the cosine if the actual Doppler angle to flow is 5 degrees smaller than the presumed angle represented in Column 1. Similarly, the third column (green) represents the cosine if the actual Doppler angle to flow is 5 degrees greater than the presumed angle of Column 1. Column 4 (light red) represents the associated percentage overestimation in velocity. Column 5 (gray) represents the associated percentage underestimation in velocity. Column 6 (orange) represents the associated percentage overestimation error in the calculated pressure, and the last column (light purple) represents the associated percentage underestimation in the calculated pressure.

Assumed Angle	Cosine		% Velocity		% Pressure	
Degrees	Actual Angle Smaller by 5°	Actual Angle Larger by 5°	Over-estimation	Under-estimation	Over-estimation	Under-estimation
0	0.99619	0.99619	-0.38%	-0.38%	-0.76%	-0.76%
10	0.99619	0.96593	1.16%	-1.92%	2.32%	-3.80%
20	0.96593	0.90631	2.79%	-3.55%	5.66%	-6.98%
30	0.90631	0.81915	4.65%	-5.41%	9.52%	-10.53%
40	0.81915	0.70711	6.93%	-7.69%	14.35%	-14.79%
50	0.70711	0.57358	10.01%	-10.77%	21.01%	-20.37%
60	0.57358	0.42262	14.72%	-15.48%	31.60%	-28.56%
70	0.42262	0.25882	23.57%	-24.33%	52.69%	-42.73%
80	0.25882	0.08716	49.05%	-49.81%	122.15%	-74.81%

Table 4 **Angle correction error (5 degree error)**

This table represents the errors that result from an angular error of only 5 degrees. You should note that even if you were always capable of specifying the insonification angle within 5 degrees in the lateral plane, (which is not probable), you still have not accounted for the angular error in the elevation plane. As you can see from the table, as the insonification angle gets larger, the error grows extremely rapidly. In fact, at larger angles, there are other error sources which have not been accounted for such as spectral broadening (discussed in Chapter 8: Artifacts). The take home lesson is that extreme care must be made when assessing Doppler angles. Effort should be made to completely interrogate the vessel to make certain of the appropriate alignment in the elevation direction. Additionally, it should be clear how even well-performed studies can have significant error sources which must be accounted for when interpreting.

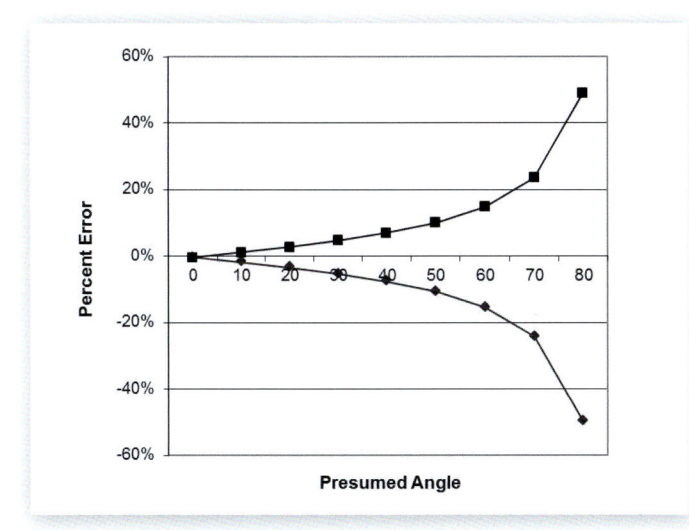

Fig. 55a **Velocity over and underestimation**

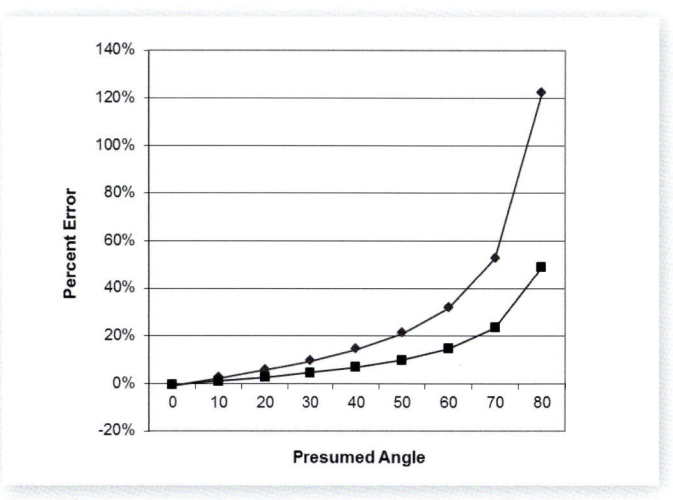

Fig. 55b **Pressure and velocity overestimation with a 5 degree error relative to presumed angle**

In Level 3, another table is included which demonstrates the effects of a 10 degree error in angle.

History of 60 Degrees

Angle correction is a very misunderstood topic. For vascular studies, a Doppler angle of 60 degrees has become the default setting. The history of how and why 60 degrees was first chosen is not well known with newer generations of ultrasound professionals. This history is included in an online component for those who are interested.

View ONLINE Animation and Image Library

KEY CONCEPT

Since the Doppler shift is angle dependent, when the Doppler angle is other than 0° or 180°, the calculated velocity would be less than the actual velocity. By the user indicating the Doppler angle, the system can calculate the cosine of the angle and correct the calculated velocity.

19.6 Exercises

View ONLINE Conceptual Questions

20. Color Flow

20.1 The Blessing and the Curse

The addition of color imaging to ultrasound has been both a blessing and a curse. On the one hand, color is an invaluable tool that generally makes detecting disease simpler and faster. Unlike spectral Doppler (a non-scanned modality), color offers a wonderful survey tool to quickly assess a large region of the patient. These are the blessings, now for the curse. Color does not give full spectral information. Color Doppler yields only an estimate of the mean velocity. There are many hemodynamic situations where the mean will appear normal whereas the spectral Doppler will indicate the presence of disease. The temptation to over-interpret color information is great. Color is certainly a powerful, useful, and even indispensable tool, but rarely should color Doppler be used as the sole means of assessing severity of disease, if ever. As long as this fact is always part of the equation, the curse goes away and color becomes what it should be, a powerful tool that corroborates the findings of all other modalities being utilized.

Studying color Doppler, like studying much of ultrasound, is becoming more complicated as new technologies are emerging. Similar to what we learned in Chapter 6, Part II, there are now two fundamentally very different paradigms for generating color Doppler ultrasound images. The first paradigm is sequential generation, the technique that has been around since the inception of color Doppler. Because this technique builds up an image line by line, this approach has severely limited temporal resolution. The second approach is based on using diverging or plane waves to create ultrafast images. With the passing of time, the expectation is that much (but not all) of color Doppler will be done using the ultrafast approach, although currently, sequential color Doppler is more common. Because the trade-offs between the approaches are so different, to make the correct trade-offs, you must know which paradigm is implemented whenever you are scanning.

Some concepts are common to both paradigms, whereas some concepts are specific to only one approach. For clarity, a reference to sequential or ultrafast imaging is made only in those sections where a concept is specific to one approach and not the other. When not specified, the concept is common to both approaches.

> **CHECKPOINT: Exam Tip**
> Color Doppler yields mean velocity information over the color box region.

21. Color Doppler Versus Spectral Doppler

21.1 Differences in Gating Techniques for Doppler Modalities

Color Doppler uses the Doppler effect and then correlates the frequency shifts recorded to estimate the mean flow velocity and variance. In juxtaposition to spectral Doppler, color Doppler has a distinct advantage of providing flow information over a large spatial area, whereas spectral Doppler provides information along a specific line or within a specified gate range. Color is able to provide this spatial information because of two distinct differences with respect to how spectral Doppler is performed. First, color Doppler is a scanned modality, whereas spectral Doppler is a non-scanned modality. The scanning in color Doppler produces the lateral dimension not present in spectral Doppler. Second, after producing the transmit pulse, color Doppler listens with a series of "range gates" which span the entire time until the next transmit pulse is produced. In this way, color receives pixel-by-pixel information to determine the spatial data for the depth direction. *Figure 56* demonstrates the difference between pulsed wave Doppler, CW Doppler, HPRF Doppler, and color Doppler.

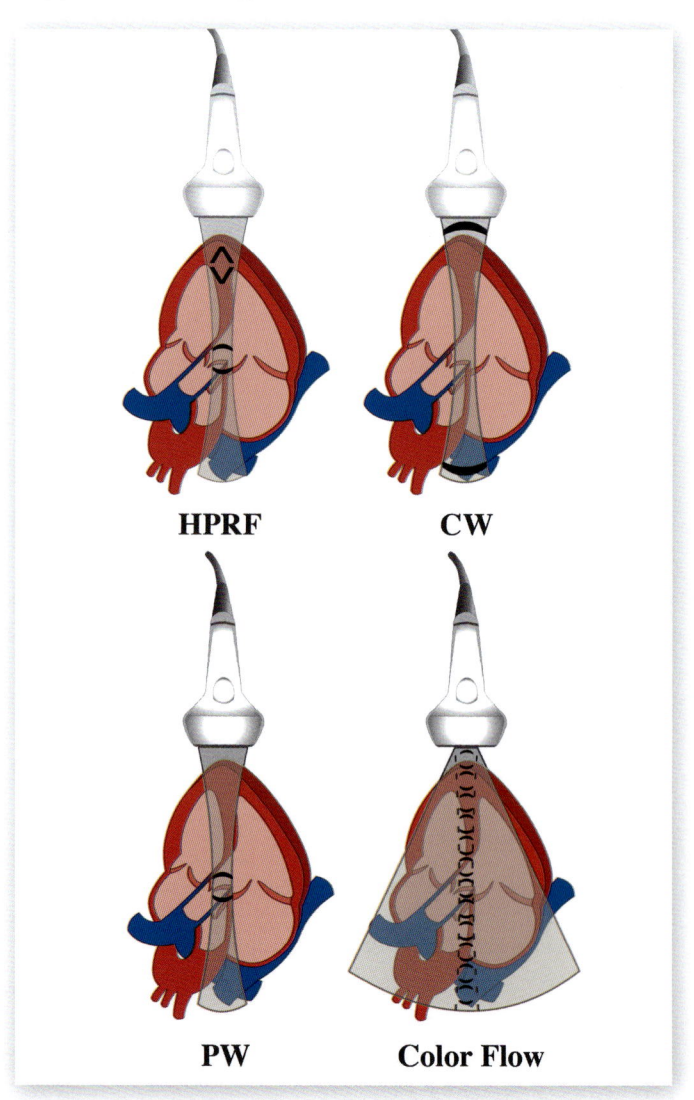

Fig. 56 Comparison of "receive gates" for HPRF, CW, PW, and color flow Doppler

Although color provides information over spatial dimensions, color does not provide peak velocities, velocity gradients, or spectral broadening characteristics. Note that no FFT is performed on color Doppler. In spectral Doppler, an FFT is performed so that spectral analysis and quantification can be performed. In color Doppler, no FFT is performed since there are not enough data samples per individual location (color is a scanned modality) and furthermore there would be no way of displaying the results. In spectral Doppler, the physical display axes are frequency and time. For color Doppler, the two physical display axes are the spatial coordinates of depth and width. For spectral Doppler, the imaginary third axis is amplitude; for color it is a mean velocity estimate.

22. Overview of How Sequential Color Doppler is Performed

22.1 Multiple Approaches

Until recently, color Doppler images were always generated sequentially. Just as there are now multiple non-sequential methods of generating 2D images as a means to increase frame rate (see Chapter 6, Part II), there are now non-sequential methods of generating color Doppler images. As such, we will need to discuss multiple approaches to color image generation. This of course makes learning color Doppler more complex than in the past. The good news is that regardless of how the beams are transmitted to create the color data, the color processing steps, for the most part, remain the same. How the beams are transmitted to generate the color Doppler data will have a direct impact on the color frame time and rate, and hence the temporal resolution. It will therefore be important to know how the color Doppler image is being generated to know how to optimize the image and to understand the trade-offs. As of the publication date, most color is still generated sequentially, as it has been for many years. However, with time, it is expected that non-sequential (higher frame rate) Doppler will become much more common.

22.2 Similarities of Color to Spectral Doppler and 2D Imaging

In terms of ultrasound processing, color Doppler is perhaps the least understood. This lack of understanding likely stems from the fact that color Doppler behaves in some aspects like spectral Doppler, in some aspects like 2D, and in other aspects like neither. Like 2D, color Doppler creates an image by repeatedly generating lines of data from the same direction to create what is called a color packet (or color ensemble). For sequential color Doppler, the packets are then scanned across the body to produce a frame. For plane wave generated color Doppler (ultrafast), the packet does not need to be scanned since the entire color region is scanned at one time. (This will be explained in more detail in Section 23.) So in some sense, color data is produced like spectral Doppler data in that a single line is transmitted repeatedly in the same direction (non-scanned). In another sense, color data is produced like a 2D image since packets of acoustic lines are either scanned across the body or generated in large sections at a time. Furthermore, color Doppler relies on Doppler frequency shifts like spectral Doppler but also relies on spatial information to produce an image, like 2D. Unlike spectral Doppler, color Doppler produces an estimate of the mean velocity, not a full distribution of signals. Unlike 2D imaging, the signal intensity is not interpretable from the brightness of a pixel on the color image.

22.3 Color Overview

Figure 57a shows a duplex image (color and 2D) and how within the color box region, a pixel can be represented by color or by a grayscale value, but not by both simultaneously. In the regions of the image encoded as blue (and red), the color signal was stronger than the 2D grayscale threshold so that color is presented. In regions inside the color box but outside the vessel lumen, the grayscale value is stronger than the threshold such that grayscale is presented. The green arrow indicates the general direction of flow within the vessel.

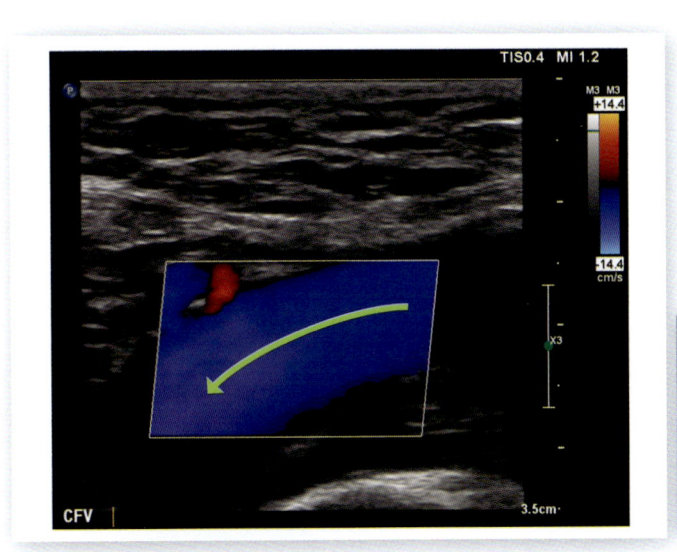

Fig. 57a **A duplex image (color Doppler and 2D) with flow (green arrow) away from the transducer (right to left on screen)**

Figure 57b demonstrates the concept of how color Doppler is generated within the color box region. Acoustic lines are transmitted at an angle to match the steering of the color box. Each line is subdivided into smaller regions and Doppler shifts assessed within each color "pixel." In this case the flow is "away" from the transducer as indicated by the white overlaid arrow.

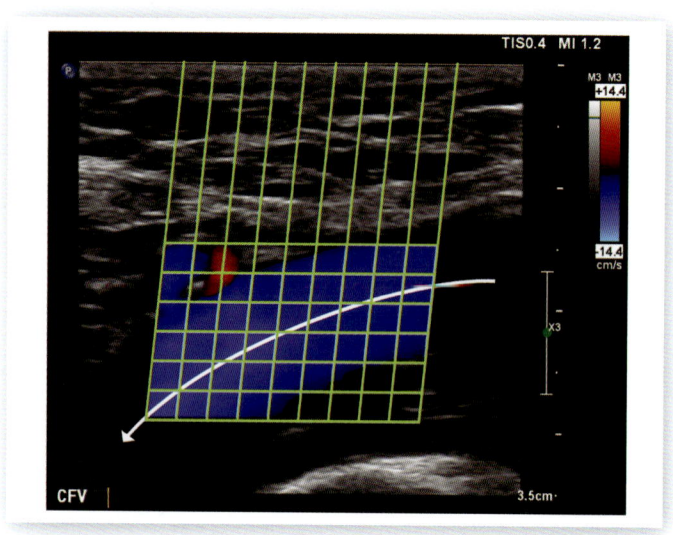

Fig. 57b Lines added to color box image to demonstrate the concept of how color Doppler images are generated

22.4 Creating a Sequential Color Scan

In sequential color Doppler, the color image is produced by transmitting a single line in a specific direction and then repeating that single line a number of times (usually between 4 and 12) creating what is called a packet. The Doppler information is obtained by a series of range gates within each acoustic line of the packet. A correlation is then performed using each of the lines within the packet to yield an estimated mean velocity at each range gate along the line (where each successive range gate in time corresponds to deeper depths). The direction of the line is then changed and a new packet is then transmitted in the new direction. The same correlation process is repeated, and a new transmit direction chosen until eventually information is acquired from the scan region in the area of interest.

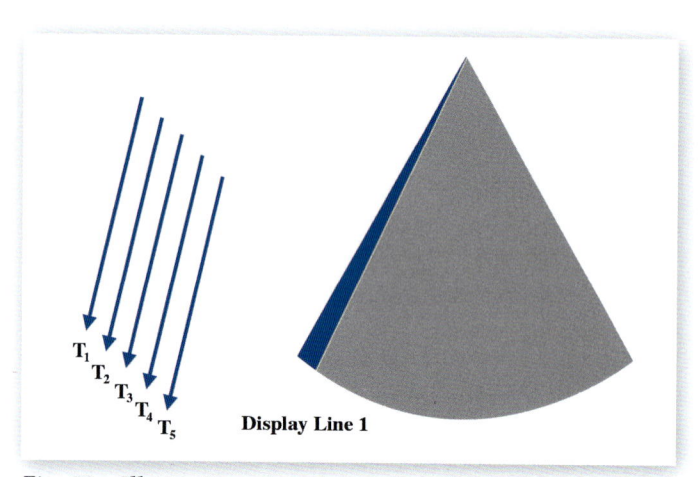

Fig. 58 Illustration of a color packet of five acoustic lines to produce one color display line

View ONLINE Animation and Image Library

22.5 Temporal Resolution and Sequential Color

In Chapter 4, we learned how to calculate the acoustic frame rate. At that time, we made reference to the fact that sequential color Doppler has the worst temporal resolution of all the ultrasound modalities. From the description of how a scan is created, the reason should now be clear. Since every color line displayed on the screen represents an entire packet of acoustic lines, creating an entire color scan requires many more acoustic lines than creating an entire conventional 2D scan. As a result, a higher frame time results in a lower frame rate (frequency). A lower frame rate implies a greater likelihood of not capturing a short duration event. For this reason, color Doppler is generally not well suited for determining timing parameters or timing accuracy.

22.6 Color Display and Velocity Interpretation

The processing of color data is really a series of steps. Once a packet has been transmitted and a correlation performed, the data is filtered and colors assigned on a pixel-by-pixel basis based on a color scale or color bar. The color bar is really a "key" which relates detected mean frequency shifts with a color. When a certain color is displayed on the screen, the user can then look at the color scale to determine approximately what mean frequency shift corresponds with that color. As we have already shown through the Doppler equation, the frequency shift can be translated into a velocity measurement. However, interpreting velocity from color Doppler can be somewhat misleading since the frequency shift detected is greatly affected by the angle formed between the ultrasound beam and the flow direction (the insonification angle). As a result, if the angle is close to 0 degrees or 180 degrees, the velocity displayed can be relatively close to the true mean velocity. However, as the angle varies and becomes closer to 90 degrees or 270 degrees, the velocity displayed can be only weakly related to the true mean velocity.

Toward and Away

Since it is desirable to know direction as well as velocity, the color bar has a plus and minus direction. The plus direction implies that the flow is toward the transducer, or equivalently that the insonification angle is less than 90 degrees. The negative direction implies that there is a negative frequency shift and that the insonification angle is greater than 90 degrees. If no plus and minus are indicated on the scale, and there is no text such as "color invert" then the plus is assumed to be on top and the minus assumed to be on the bottom. In the center of the color bar is a black band which represents the baseline and the color wall filters. If no frequency shift is detected or a low frequency is detected but filtered out, there is an absence of color in the image.

How the System Applies a Color Map

The way in which the color map is applied by the system is to look pixel-by-pixel across the scanned color region. Each pixel is assessed for whether or not there is a signal above a color noise threshold, and if so, what is the associated frequency shift. If the signal is too weak (below the color noise threshold) no color will be assigned to that pixel. In other words, even if there is motion, if the signal is too weak, then the pixel will present as black, which may then be misinterpreted as the absence of flow. If the signal is stronger than the threshold, the frequency shift and direction is compared against the maximum frequency shift of the color scale (the Nyquist limit) and a color assigned. In essence, the display of color images goes through a digital "go, no go" process. Once a signal is determined to be above the threshold, increasing the signal amplitude by increasing the gain causes no change in how that particular pixel is displayed.

Since color is performed over a region, the spatial distribution of the signal is often interpreted to give an estimate of many flow parameters. Color flow is widely valued because it is relatively quick and simple to appreciate global hemodynamic conditions.

> **CHECKPOINT: Exam Tip**
>
> The mean velocity in color is calculated by using correlation techniques with multiple lines. Therefore, in order to create a single line of color, multiple lines are transmitted (a color packet). Larger packet sizes improve color sensitivity but require more time, reducing the frame rate. For this reason, color Doppler generally has relatively poor temporal resolution.

23. Time-Correlated Color

23.1 Overview
Besides the Doppler-based approach to color just described, there is another approach called "time-correlated" color. Time-correlated color effectively uses the distance equation and correlates the most commonly occurring time shifts to determine blood velocity. This technique provides a modal velocity (the most commonly occurring velocity) and like color Doppler, cannot supply peak velocity quantification, flow gradients, or spectral broadening characteristics.

Mean velocities (from color Doppler) and modal velocities (from time-correlated color) generally cannot be compared with peak velocities. Both the mean and modal velocities can change with the presence of turbulence or even as the result of using different range gate sizes. In addition, using different receive gain, wall filtering, and post-processing (grayscale mapping) settings can significantly alter these measurements.

23.2 Ultrafast Doppler
Until recently, Doppler techniques have been sharply categorized as either yielding highly specific information at a localized region (spectral Doppler along a single line (CW) and at a single gate location along a single line (PW)) or very general information over a wide region (color Doppler). As a result, spectral Doppler has very good temporal resolution but only at a specific location (or along a single line). Conversely, sequentially generated color Doppler has very poor temporal resolution but provides information over a wide area. Because of the poor temporal resolution, sonographers are taught techniques to optimize temporal resolution by increasing frame rate (decreasing frame time). The optimization generally results in constraining the color box size to the narrowest width and shallowest depth necessary for flow assessment in the region of interest.

Another way of looking at the difference between spectral and color Doppler is as a trade-off between accurate velocity information (both temporally and in terms of velocity) but limited spatial information versus color which trades off velocity and temporal accuracy for spatial information. Ultrafast Doppler completely changes this paradigm. As discussed in Chapter 6, ultrafast imaging was generated as a means of overcoming temporal resolution limitations resulting from generating images sequentially, line by line. Just as 2D images can be generated using plane waves, so too can color Doppler images and spectral Doppler. We will begin by considering the generation of ultrafast color Doppler.

23.3 Ultrafast Color Doppler Compound Imaging
Like sequential color Doppler, ultrafast color Doppler generates an estimate of the mean flow velocity for display. The difference between conventional (sequential) color Doppler and ultrafast color Doppler is the frame rate. By transmitting plane waves or diverging waves, the entire scan region is insonified in the same amount of time that was required to transmit and receive a single narrow focused color line. Just like sequential Doppler, multiple samples are required at each location to generate a mean estimate for color encoding. As discussed in Chapter 6 regarding compound imaging, each of the plane waves are transmitted at a different angle in order to decorrelate the speckle so that there is improved signal-to-noise ratio when summing the different angle frames. So, just as an entire color Doppler plane wave frame angle can be generated in the time it takes to produce a single color Doppler display line for conventional color Doppler, a packet of angles requires the same time as a packet of individual focused beams. In other words, the number of angles used to generate a single color frame is analogous to the color packet size in conventional, sequential color Doppler. The easiest way to understand the differences and similarities of ultrafast compound image and sequential color image generation is to compare the figures below and the corresponding calculations.

For the simplest case, the frame rates of ultrafast color Doppler have the potential to be hundreds of times faster than conventional ultrasound as shown by the following calculations.

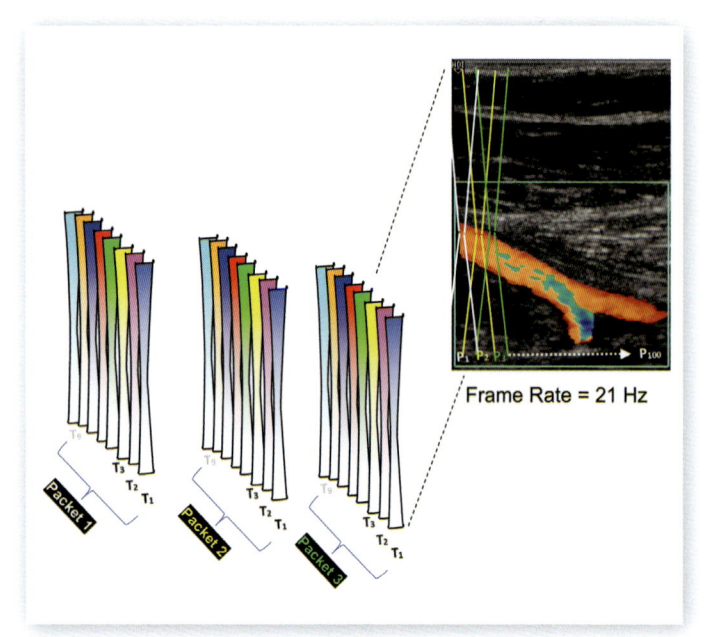

Fig. 59a **Sequential color Doppler image generation; in this case the packet size is 8 (8 transmitted lines per packet)**

Serial Color Doppler:
   Depth = 4 cm
   Image width = 100 color (packet) lines
   Packet size = 9 lines

$$Frame\ time = \frac{13\ \mu sec}{cm} \cdot \frac{4\ cm}{Line} \cdot \frac{9\ Lines}{Packet} \cdot \frac{100\ Packets}{Frame} = 46,800\ \mu sec$$

$$46,800\ \mu sec = 46.80\ msec$$

$$Frame\ rate = \frac{1}{Frame\ time} = \frac{1}{46.80\ msec} = 0.0214\ kHz = 21.4\ Hz$$

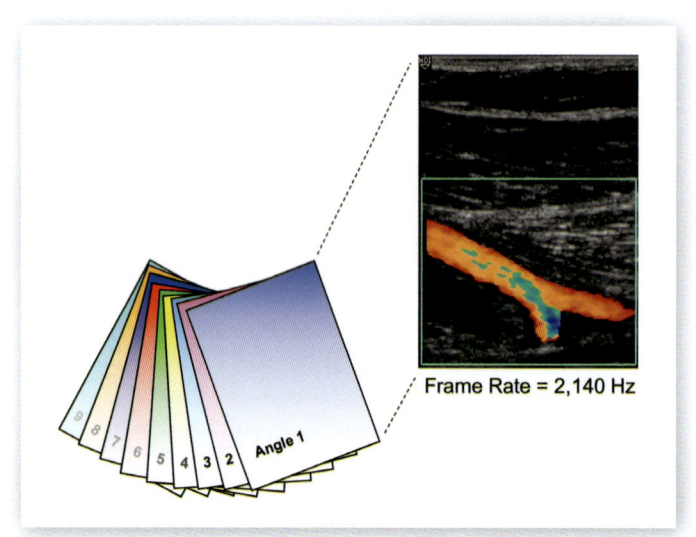

Fig. 59b **Ultrafast color Doppler image generation; in this example, 9 angled planes are used (correlating with a packet size of 9)**

Ultrafast Doppler:
   Depth = 4 cm
   Packet size = 9 "angles"
   (Note that image width does not matter.)

$$Frame\ time = \frac{13\ \mu sec}{cm} \cdot \frac{8\ cm}{Angle} \cdot \frac{9\ Angles}{Frame} = 468\ \mu sec$$

$$468\ \mu sec = 0.468\ msec$$

$$Frame\ rate = \frac{1}{Frame\ time} = \frac{1}{0.468\ msec} = 2.14\ kHz = 2,140\ Hz$$

23.4 Beamforming and Processing Requirements of Ultrafast Doppler

As previously mentioned, sequentially generated color Doppler produces one single display line at a time. As a result, the processing and data transfer rate requirements are relatively low. In comparison, ultrafast requires the ability to receive, process, and transfer entire frames of data at one time. For this reason, ultrafast imaging requires the ability to parallel process all of the lines of an image at one time as well as having fast data transfer rates to handle entire frames instead of lines.

As we discussed in Chapter 6, generating images from planar or diverging waves requires a very complex beamformer capable of performing retrospective transmit and receive focusing on data received from every element. After retrospective focusing is applied to every line in parallel, the system can generate a single beamformed image. The next step is to coherently add successive beamformed images to create a composite (compound) beamformed image. The rate at which these compound beamformed images are presented is the data frame rate. Note that when the frame rate is faster than what a monitor can present (or what the human eye can detect), cine loop review becomes useful to visualize small temporal changes in non-real-time viewing.

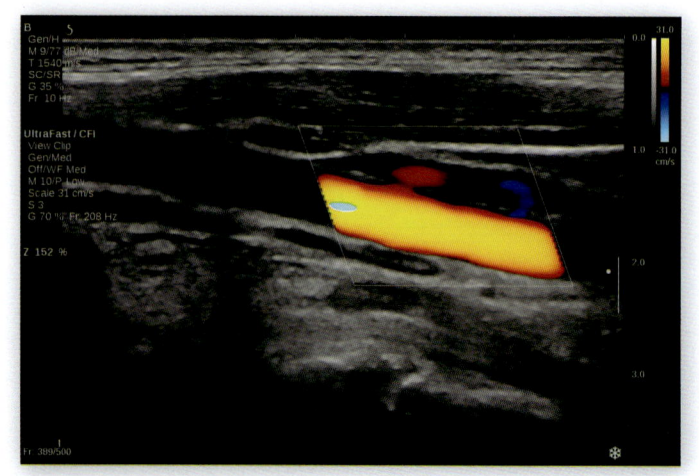

Fig. 60 **Ultrafast color Doppler image of a carotid artery** *(Image compliments of Hologic)*

Note that in *Figure 60*, which shows an ultrafast Doppler of a carotid artery, the frame rate is 208 Hz. This particular image is number 389 of 500 captured frames in the clip which must be displayed in "slow time" using cine loop since the frame rate is significantly higher than both what the monitor can display and what the human eye/brain can perceive.

23.5 Optimizing Ultrafast Color Doppler Compound Imaging

When we discussed compound imaging, we learned that the signal-to-noise ratio improves with the number of samples being averaged. In essence, a greater number of samples in the average results in a better signal-to-noise ratio. The same concept holds true for ultrafast color compound imaging. By increasing the number of angles used to generate each color frame, the sensitivity of the color can be improved. Of course, increasing the number of angles requires more time, reducing the color frame rate. But, recall from the calculation just performed that extremely high frame rates can be achieved relative to sequentially generated color Doppler. Therefore, increasing the number of angles used to generate a color frame to improve sensitivity is a good trade-off unless extremely high temporal resolution is required. In cases of very small or deep vessels, increasing the sensitivity at the expense of temporal resolution is assuredly a good trade-off.

Figure 61 offers a comparison of conventional and ultrafast color Doppler. Notice the improved sensitivity and considerably higher frame rate with ultrafast in images (b) and (d). Also notice, in (d), the ability to visualize the transient reversal of flow in the center stream while forward flow still exists near the vessel walls.

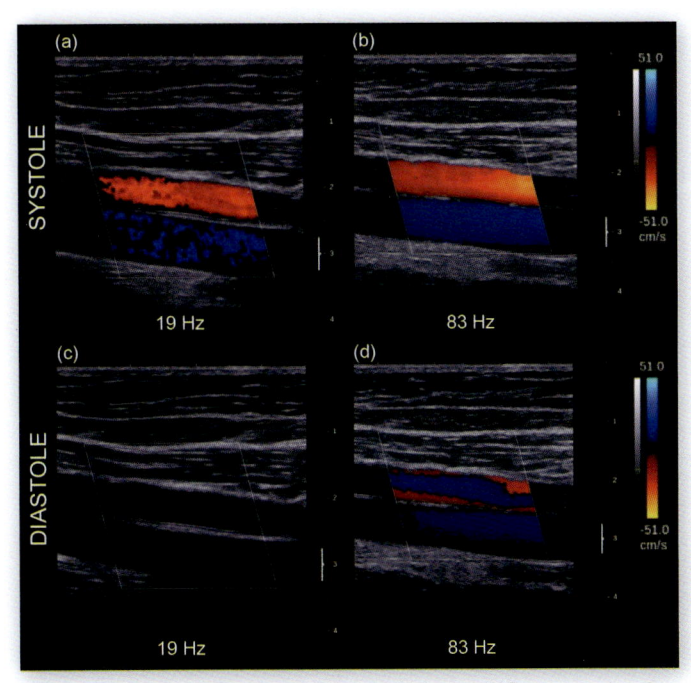

Fig. 61 **Comparison of conventional [(a) and (c)] versus ultrafast [(b) and (d)] color Doppler** *(Images compliments of Hologic)*

23.6 Ultrafast PW Doppler

One of the great advantages of ultrafast Doppler is the ability to perform retrospective PW Doppler at any location within the color image. Recall that in order to generate specific velocity information, spectral Doppler requires significantly more acoustic samples than color Doppler requires to generate mean velocity information. By increasing the angles used to constitute each frame with ultrafast imaging, there is adequate information to generate a Doppler spectrum everywhere within the image region. Again, since the data is acquired everywhere within the image, spectral Doppler can also be displayed from anywhere within the image. In fact, the French company that produced the first ultrafast imaging system, Supersonic Imagine, allows for as many as three different Doppler sample volumes simultaneously. The use model is as follows:

- Use conventional live color Doppler imaging until satisfied with imaging location
- Capture an ultrafast "clip" or data set which is generally from 2 to 4 seconds
- Review the color in "slow time" using a cine review mode
- Place a Doppler sample volume (or volumes) at desired location(s) to generate instantaneous spectrum from stored clip
- Customize Doppler:
  - Change gate location
  - Change gate size
  - Change Doppler gain
  - Change Doppler compression (grayscale setting)
  - Change angle correction

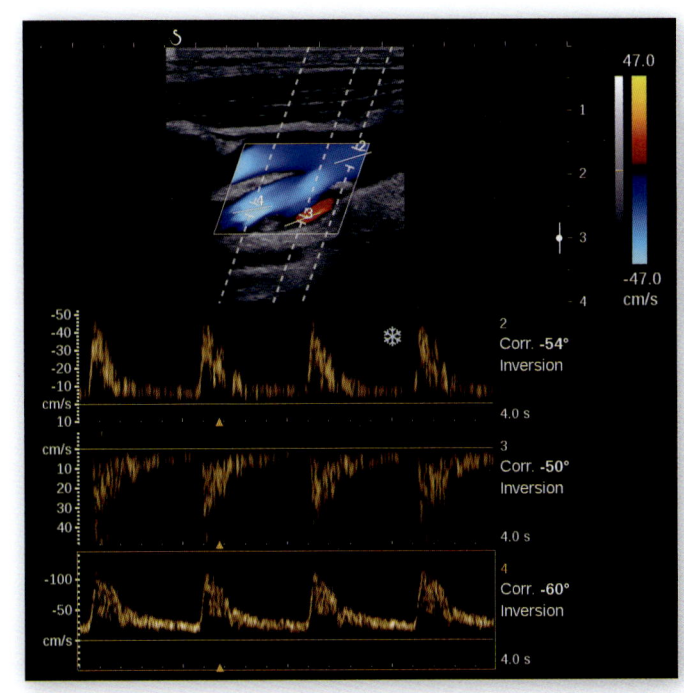

Fig. 62 **Ultrafast color Doppler of the distal carotid artery**

Figure 62 shows an ultrafast color Doppler image of the distal carotid artery. The frame rate is 89 Hz. Notice that three simultaneous spectral Doppler measurements are displayed:

(1) the top measurement (labeled 2) from the common carotid artery (CCA) just before the bulb
(2) the middle measurement (labeled 3) from the bulb
(3) the bottom measurement (labeled 4) from the internal carotid artery (ICA)

Also note that it is possible to angle correct each spectrum individually as shown to the right of each spectrum.

View ONLINE Animation and Image Library

Advantages of Ultrafast Doppler:

- Significantly higher frame rates for color are possible
- Better temporal resolution allows for appreciation of changes in flow not perceived with standard, sequentially generated color Doppler
- Improved sensitivity (by using large number of angles per frame) for low-velocity flow
- Can acquire as many measurements as desired on stored ultrafast clip by simply moving the Doppler sample volume to a new location
- Can acquire multiple simultaneous Doppler measurements (only limited by ultrasound system design – i.e. how many Doppler gates a system allows at once by design)
- The color Doppler is synchronous with the spectral Doppler (this is not true with sequentially generated color Doppler, especially as the frame time increases over large color boxes making the left and right side of the same color box potentially at different phases of the cardiac cycle)
- Allows for Doppler measurements at a later time (if the system can store the full data set)

24. Color Gain

Like the receiver gain for 2D imaging, the color gain amplifies the signal after it has been received back from the patient. Also like 2D, increasing the color gain can affect the "apparent signal-to-noise" but not the true signal-to-noise ratio since both the signal and the noise are amplified together.

Color Doppler gain behaves differently than 2D imaging and spectral Doppler gain. With 2D imaging and with spectral Doppler, increasing or decreasing the gain increases or decreases the display intensity of the signal on the screen. For color Doppler, increasing the color gain may have no visible effect on the signal over a certain range of the gain knob for certain signals. On the other hand, increasing the gain may have a profound effect on the amount of color displayed.

This behavior is very different than 2D or spectral Doppler for which an increase in gain results in an increase in display intensity no matter what the imaging situation. For color Doppler, a pixel is either colorized or not based on whether the color signal exceeds an amplitude threshold. Thus, at a certain location in the image, if the color signal amplitude is higher than the color threshold, the pixel is colorized. If the signal amplitude is lower than that same color threshold, the pixel is not colorized. The implications of this approach are very important to recognize. Since different color shades are used to represent mean velocity and not signal amplitude, with color Doppler there is no direct display parameter that indicates signal strength (unlike spectral and 2D imaging for which brightness indicates signal strength). As a result, if there is very poor signal-to-noise when producing a color image (weak color signals), there may be no apparent effect on the color image over a wide range of gain increase. Similarly, very strong color signals may show no change in appearance over a wide gain range. Therefore, setting the color gain appropriately requires some skill and technique as will be discussed in the upcoming section.

24.1 Setting the Appropriate Color Gain

As alluded to in the previous section, appropriate setting of color gain is dependent on the imaging situation. In essence, the approach to setting the color gain differs when dealing with very strong color signals than when dealing with weak signals because of sensitivity issues. When the color signal is weak and sensitivity is a potential issue, the correct way to set the color gain is to increase the color gain until noise speckle just becomes apparent within the image, and then to decrease the color gain until the color speckle just disappears. At this point, the color gain is set for optimal sensitivity. When increasing the color gain, the color noise will appear as random speckles of both colors of the color bar distributed randomly throughout the color box, especially in regions where no flow exists (i.e. over tissue). This technique maps the weak color signals just above the color noise floor to amplitudes just above the color threshold, while still suppressing the color noise floor itself. Therefore, weak signals are presented as flow, but color noise is still below the threshold, and hence, not displayed. In these cases, if the color gain is set too low, color dropout can occur, giving the artifactual appearance of no or limited flow.

When the color signals are high amplitude (such as when imaging superficial blood flow) the above technique will result in overgaining at gain levels well before visualizing color speckle. When the color signals are strong, the receiver gain should be reduced so that the color flow signals do not overlap the non-flow regions (an artifact referred to as color blossoming or color bleeding). To understand how this artifact occurs, you must recall that transmit pulses generally have a "tail". The effect of this tail is that the spatial pulse length is longer than ideal, resulting in reduced axial resolution. With color, this color tail results in color signals extending beyond the posterior aspect of the actual flow region. Since the amplitude of the tail is weaker than the main cycles within the pulse, the signal amplitude is weaker than the true flow signals acquired from within the actual flow region. If the receiver gain is turned up too high, these weaker signals from the pulse tails are mapped above the color threshold and presented as flow bleeding over the actual tissue. Therefore, when overgaining occurs for stronger color signals, the color signals tend to bleed into neighboring regions, making the color region appear larger than reality. The solution is to reduce the color receiver gain until the amplitude of these artifactual signals drops below the color threshold but keep the gain high enough so as to preserve the amplitude of the true color signals above the color threshold. Of course, if the color gain is set too low, color dropout will occur, giving the artificial appearance of limited or no flow.

The following panel of images (*Figure 63a*) demonstrates the presence of moderate noise speckle, excessive noise speckle, and then appropriate color gain so that noise speckle is absent. The panels of *Figure 63b* show the effects of low, high, and appropriate gain in the presence of strong color signal.

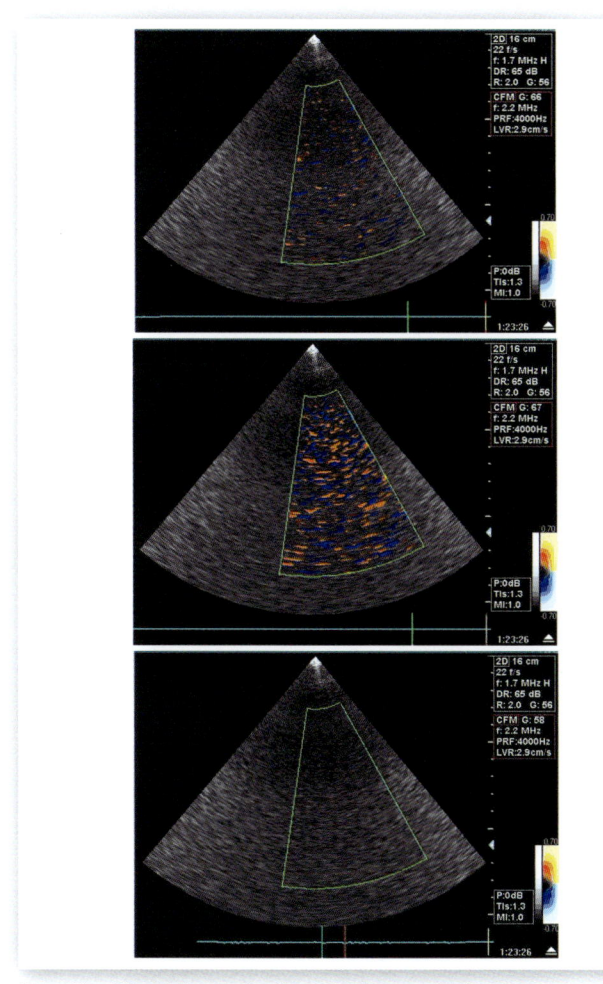

Fig. 63a The color noise floor (color speckle)

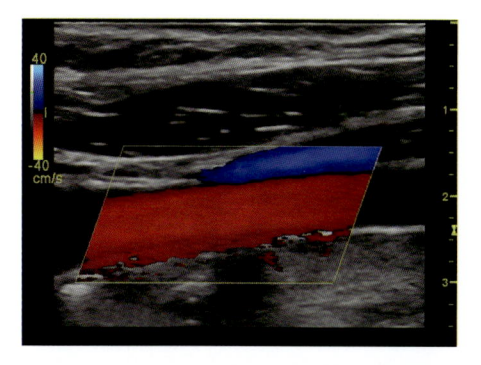

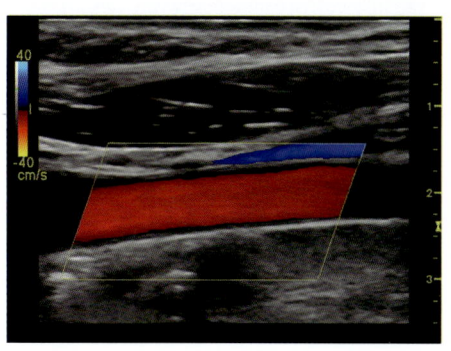

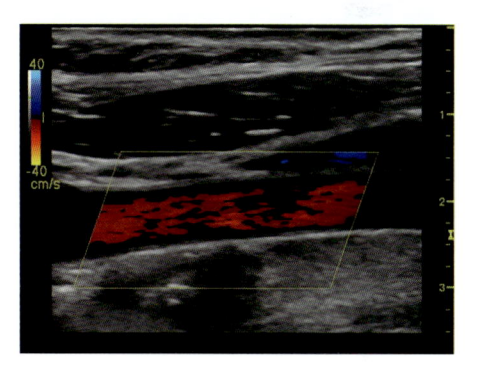

Fig. 63b Overgain, appropriate gain, and undergain

KEY CONCEPT

Unlike 2D and spectral Doppler which display signal strength through grayscale (brightness), color Doppler does not directly display signal strength. Color Doppler is a threshold-based technique. When the amplitude of the color signal exceeds a specified threshold, the pixel is displayed as color. When the amplitude of the color signal is below the threshold, no color is displayed and the grayscale value from the 2D image is presented.

25. Interpreting the Color Bar Relative to Spectral Doppler

Recall that directionality is known from the Doppler equation by determining if the Doppler shift is positive or negative relative to the operating frequency. Flow towards the transducer creates a positive frequency shift, while flow away from the transducer creates a negative frequency shift. In spectral Doppler, the direction is indicated by whether the flow is presented above or below the baseline, unless spectral invert is activated, which results in flow towards the transducer displayed below the baseline and flow away from the transducer displayed above the baseline. For color Doppler, directionality is indicated by the colors on the color bar. Using the figure below, you should note the similarities between the color bar and the display parameters of the Doppler spectrum.

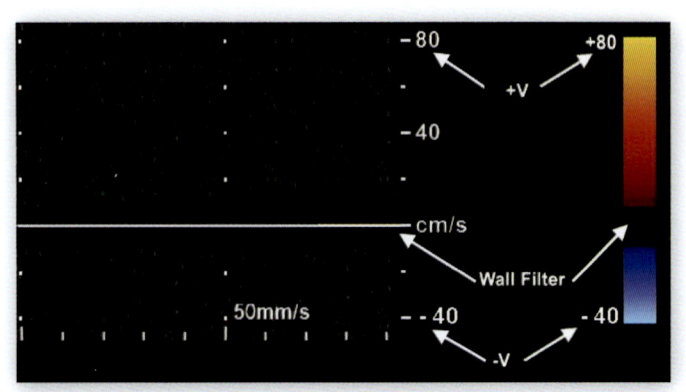

Fig. 64 **Color bar relation to spectral display**

26. Color Invert and Aliasing

Just as with invert on spectral Doppler, attention must be paid to whether or not the color invert is on, so as to appropriately determine flow direction. For the color bar in *Figure 64*, since color invert is not on, flow towards the transducer is represented by the color above the baseline (red in this case). In spectral Doppler, higher velocity flows are represented higher above the baseline. Similarly, as the velocity increases, the color transitions up the color bar (from shades of red to shades of yellow for this color bar). If the velocity, or, equivalently, frequency shift, goes beyond the maximum detectable velocity or frequency shift, aliasing occurs. With spectral Doppler, when aliasing occurs, the spectrum wraps over the top and returns from the bottom. Similarly, with color Doppler, the color representation wraps from the color at the top of the color bar to the color which appears at the bottom of the color bar (yellow to light blue). Obviously, the reverse occurs if the flow aliasing occurs in the opposite direction.

27. Color Wall Filters

27.1 Wall Filter and Color Scale Integration

In spectral Doppler, separate controls are given for both the wall filters and the PRF (Doppler scales). The user is therefore allowed to change either of these parameters independently from the other. In sequential color Doppler, all systems build the function of wall filtering into the PRF knob. In other words, by changing the color PRF (Nyquist limit), the wall filter is also (usually unwittingly) changed. As a result, increasing the color scale increases the corner frequency of the color wall filter. Similarly, decreasing the Nyquist limit on the color bar (PRF) decreases the corner frequency of the color wall filter. Whereas changing the PRF affects the wall filters in sequentially generated color, as you will soon learn, this relationship does not have to hold for ultrafast Doppler. For ultrafast Doppler, it is possible to completely separate the wall filters from the color PRF, just as is done with spectral Doppler.

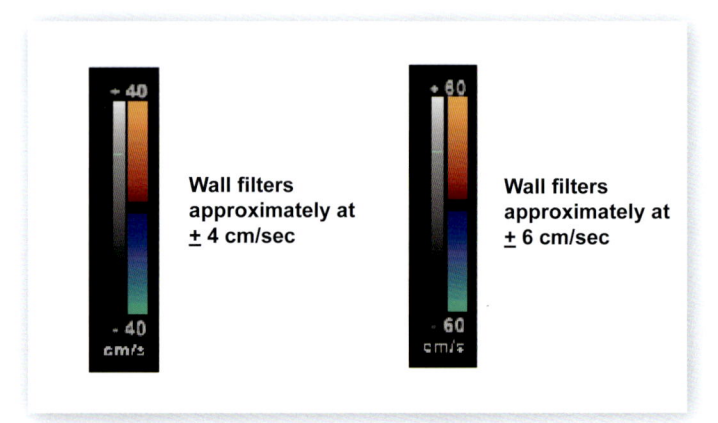

Fig. 65 **Wall filters as a percentage of color scales**

> ✓ **CHECKPOINT: Exam Tip**
>
> When trying to detect low-velocity flows with color, you must make certain to lower the color scale. If you do not lower the color scales, the integrated wall filters will be too high, and will eliminate the very signals you are trying to detect.

27.2 The Absence of Color

As already mentioned, for color Doppler, the wall filters are represented as the black band in the center (around the baseline) of the color bar. This black band represents that either the flow was not detected (velocity or frequency shift of 0), or that the detected velocity signal (or frequency shift) was low enough such that they were eliminated by the wall filters. Therefore, a black area on a color image could be the result of no flow, an angle at or close to 90°, or low frequency shifts rejected by the wall filters. Additionally, a black region could represent an area where the signal was too weak to be detected by the color Doppler circuitry or too weak to overcome the noise threshold (poor signal-to-noise). It is critical to understand that a black region within a region where there is blood does not necessarily represent blood that is static. *Figure 66* demonstrates how changing the scales (which affect the wall filters) can dramatically affect visualization of flow. In *Figure 66*, the flow is in the portal vein.

the center is approximately 10% of the Nyquist limit.

This value represents that the highest mean velocity detectable is 61.6 cm/sec toward the transducer. Flow directly toward the transducer with a mean velocity of 61.6 cm/sec would be displayed as yellow according to this color scale.

The black band vaguely expresses the fact that signals with detected velocities in this range are not likely to be visualized (colorized as black). However, weak signals at higher velocities also may not be visualized because the color wall filters do not have a sharp corner frequency like spectral wall filters (as discussed in the upcoming paragraphs and graphs.)

This value represents that the highest mean velocity detectable is 61.6 cm/sec away from the transducer. Flow directly away with a mean velocity of 61.6 cm/sec would be displayed as aqua, according to this color scale.

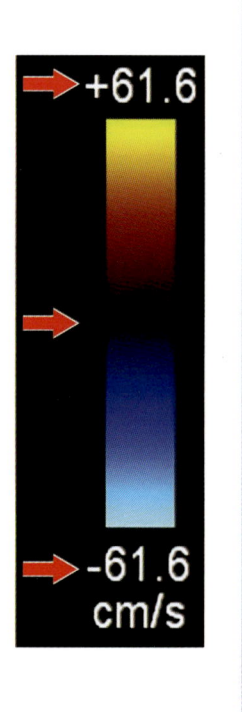

Fig. 67 **Interpreting the color bar (sequential color Doppler)**

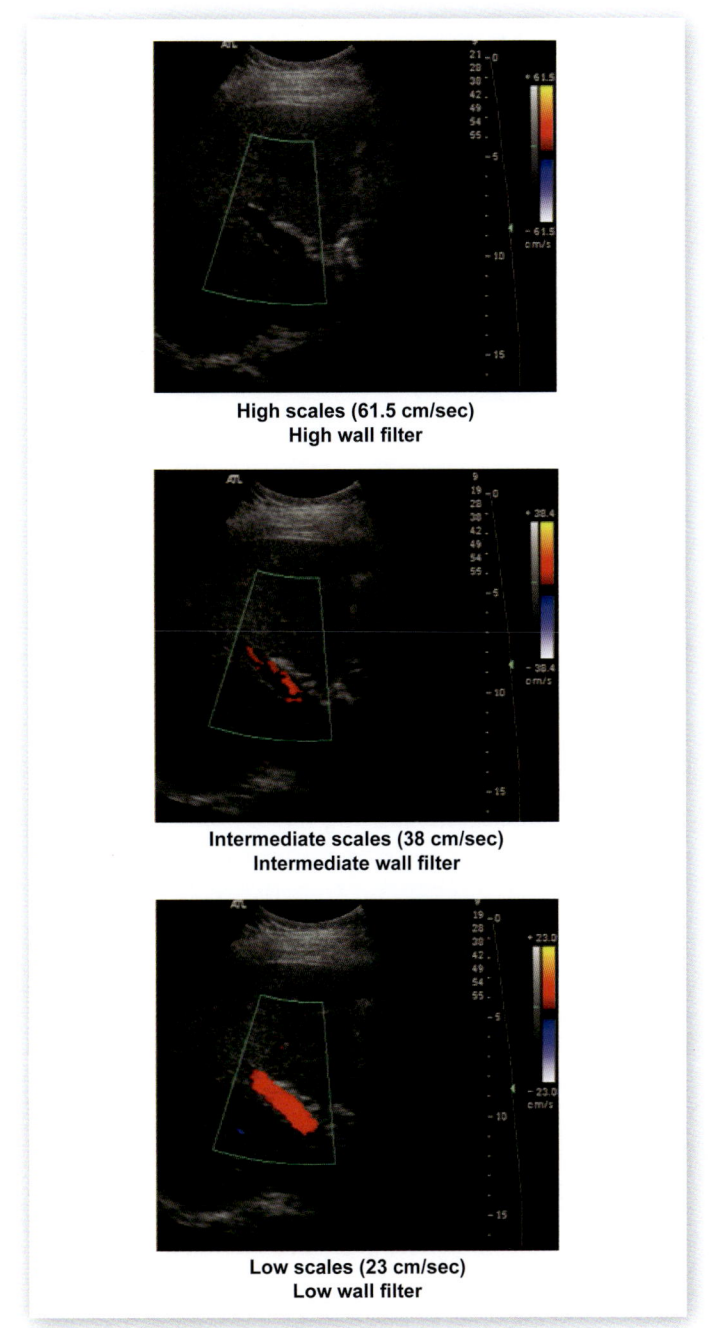

Fig. 66 **Color wall filter effects**

Some systems allow the user to adjust the wall filter percentage. In other words, the user can determine at what percentage of the PRF the wall filter corner frequency is set. For example, imagine that filter setting 1 represents 10% and filter setting 2 represents 20%. If the PRF is set to ± 100 cm/sec, the first wall filter setting would put the wall filter corner at ± 10 cm/sec, whereas the second wall filter setting would set the wall filter at ± 20 cm/sec. If the PRF were changed to 150 cm/sec, the filter 1 setting would set the wall filters at ± 15 cm/sec, and the filter 2 setting would result in the wall filters being set at ± 30 cm/sec.

27.3 Interpreting the Color Bar Relative to Nyquist and the Wall Filters

The following color bar illustrates how a typical color bar is interpreted relative to the Nyquist limit (PRF) and the color wall filter in sequentially generated color Doppler. Notice that the black band in

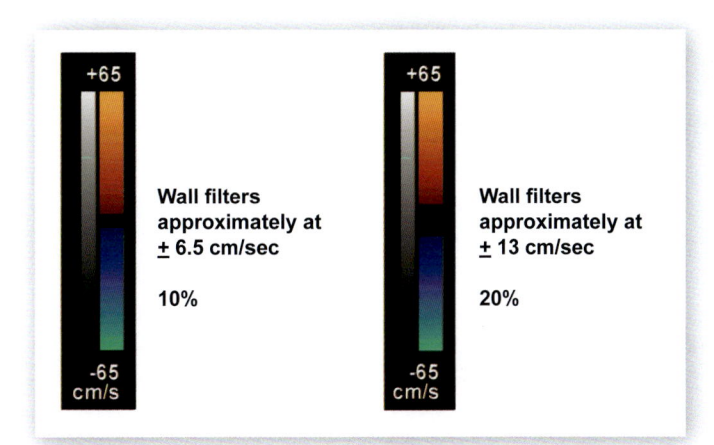

Fig. 68 **Variable percentage of Nyquist wall filter control**

View ONLINE Animation and Image Library

KEY CONCEPT

Like spectral Doppler, color Doppler uses high pass wall filters to reduce dynamic range by eliminating signals at lower frequency shifts. Unlike spectral Doppler, color wall filters are affected by the color scale settings (PRF). Increasing the color scales increases the wall filter setting, potentially eliminating lower mean velocity flow. Some systems have a secondary control which allows the user to determine how aggressively the wall filters attenuate.

28. Determining Flow Direction in Color Doppler

28.1 Why Colors Change Even When Velocity Doesn't

Figure 69 demonstrates how flow in a straight vessel, with no flow disturbance can be displayed with colors at either end of the color bar just by variations in the angle between the observer line and the flow direction (the insonification angle). Because a sector transducer steers the beam at different angles to create an image, the steering direction is different across the entire image. As a result, the angle to flow changes across a straight vessel.

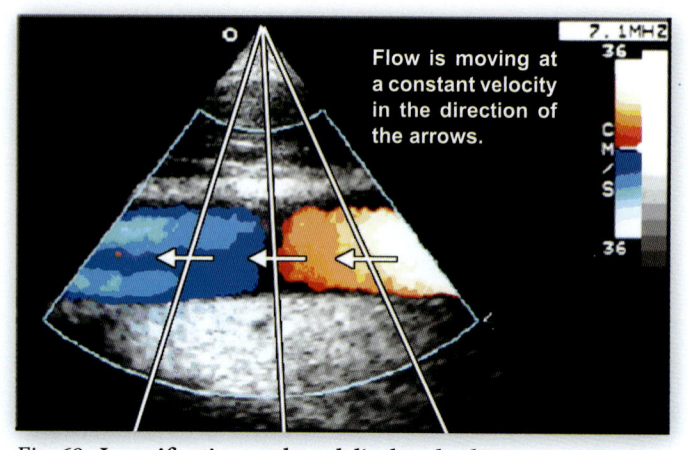

Fig. 69 Insonification angle and displayed color

Notice how in the center of the vessel, there is a black band, or color dropout. This color dropout exists not because there is an absence of flow, but because the insonification angle is close to 90 degrees and because the wall filters are eliminating low frequency shifts at that particular location in the image. On the far extreme right of the vessel notice that the velocity displayed looks higher (lighter hues) than the velocity closer to the center (darker red). Similarly, notice how the flow just to the left of the center line of the image looks as if it is traveling more slowly (darker blue hues) than the flow farther to the left side of the image (lighter blue hues). This perception of changes in velocity is purely the result of the angular effects, and not because there is an actual change in velocity within the vessel.

View ONLINE Animation and Image Library

CHECKPOINT: Exam Tip

Color Doppler images are frequently included on credentialing exams. Besides asking about the color dropout related to insonification angle, the direction of flow is commonly asked. In the upcoming sections, we will learn how to correctly interpret flow direction, regardless of image shape, steering versus non-steering, aliasing, and even tortuosity.

28.2 Defining the Doppler Insonification Angle

In Section 8.2, we specified that the Doppler insonification angle is always measured between the head of the flow (where the flow is going to) and the steered beam direction. Since color is a Doppler technique dependent on the same equation as spectral Doppler, the angle to flow in color is measured the same way as in spectral Doppler. Any approach to determine color Doppler direction which does not start out with recognizing the true insonification angle is a "trick" which will lead to mistakes, not just on exams but also in the clinical world. The insonification angle must be properly identified since the angle is precisely what determines how color is presented on the system. Unlike "trick" techniques sometimes used (which only work for non-aliased flow in a non-tortuous vessel using a sector transducer), this technique will work for non-steered linear images, steered linear images, curved-linear images, sectors, and even in the presence of tortuosity.

28.3 Cosine Revisited

Once the angle is correctly identified, determining the directionality is a relatively straightforward task. When the angle to flow is less than 90 degrees, the flow direction is considered toward the transducer. Since the cosine of an angle less than 90 degrees is positive, the flow will be presented in whatever color is associated with the plus sign on the color bar. (If no plus sign exists, the color on top is assumed to be positive.) When the insonification angle is greater than 90 degrees, the cosine is negative and hence the color of the flow will match the colors associated with the negative sign on the color bar.

Figure 70 demonstrates the use of color invert, imaging the same flow during the same phase of the cardiac cycle.

> **Author's Note:**
> Do Not Presume BART
>
> Be careful not to presume that red always means towards the transducer and that blue always indicates away from the transducer (often referred to as "BART" for blue away, red toward). There are an infinite number of color maps possible, and the mere application of color invert can reverse what you have come to expect.

28.4 Determining Flow direction: Step-by-Step Approach

Step 1. Determine the Steering Direction Throughout the Image

The first step to determining flow direction is identifying the steer directions throughout the image. Changing the steer direction alters the insonification angle and hence, can easily result in flow perceived as "towards" becoming flow perceived as "away." This need to be able to determine steer direction in an image was one of the motivating factors for learning how different transducers function. From an image, the color steer angle can be determined by looking at the direction of the color box or color sector. The steer angle can also often be determined by looking for color dropout where the insonification angle equals 90°.

The following images demonstrate how the steering direction is indicated for various image formats. Note that in each image, three or four locations were arbitrarily chosen to assess the steering directions. Notice how the color steering direction is dictated by the color box in each example.

(See *Figure 71, Determining the steering direction*)

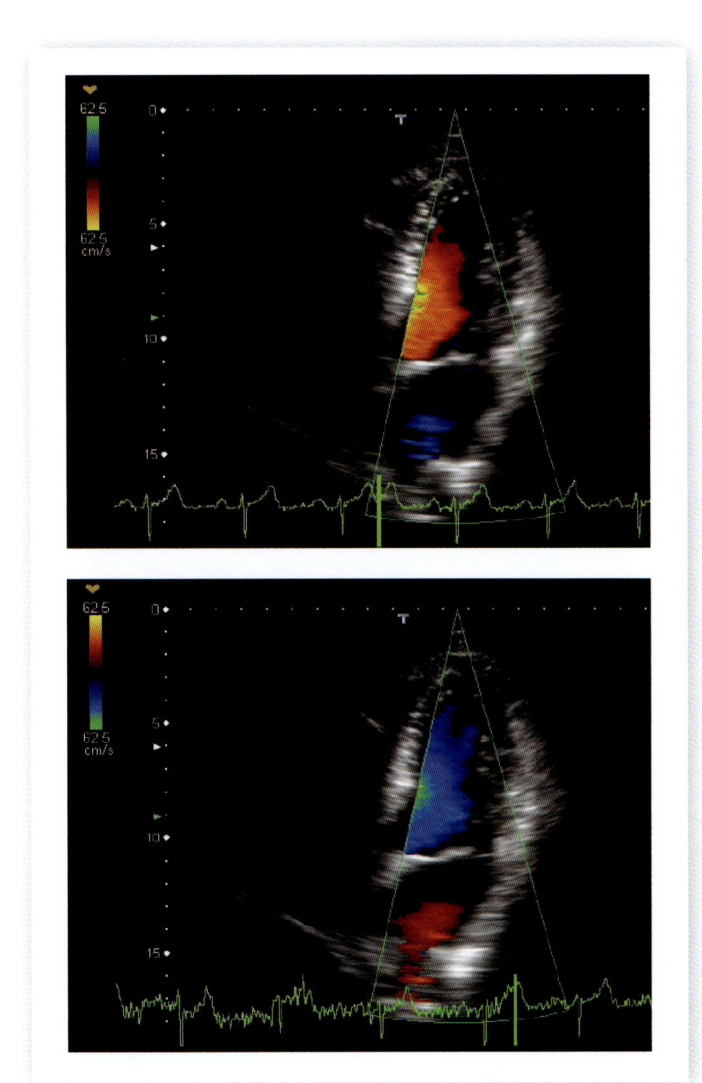

Fig. 70 **Color invert**

View ONLINE Animation and Image Library

TEE Transducer (Sector Image)

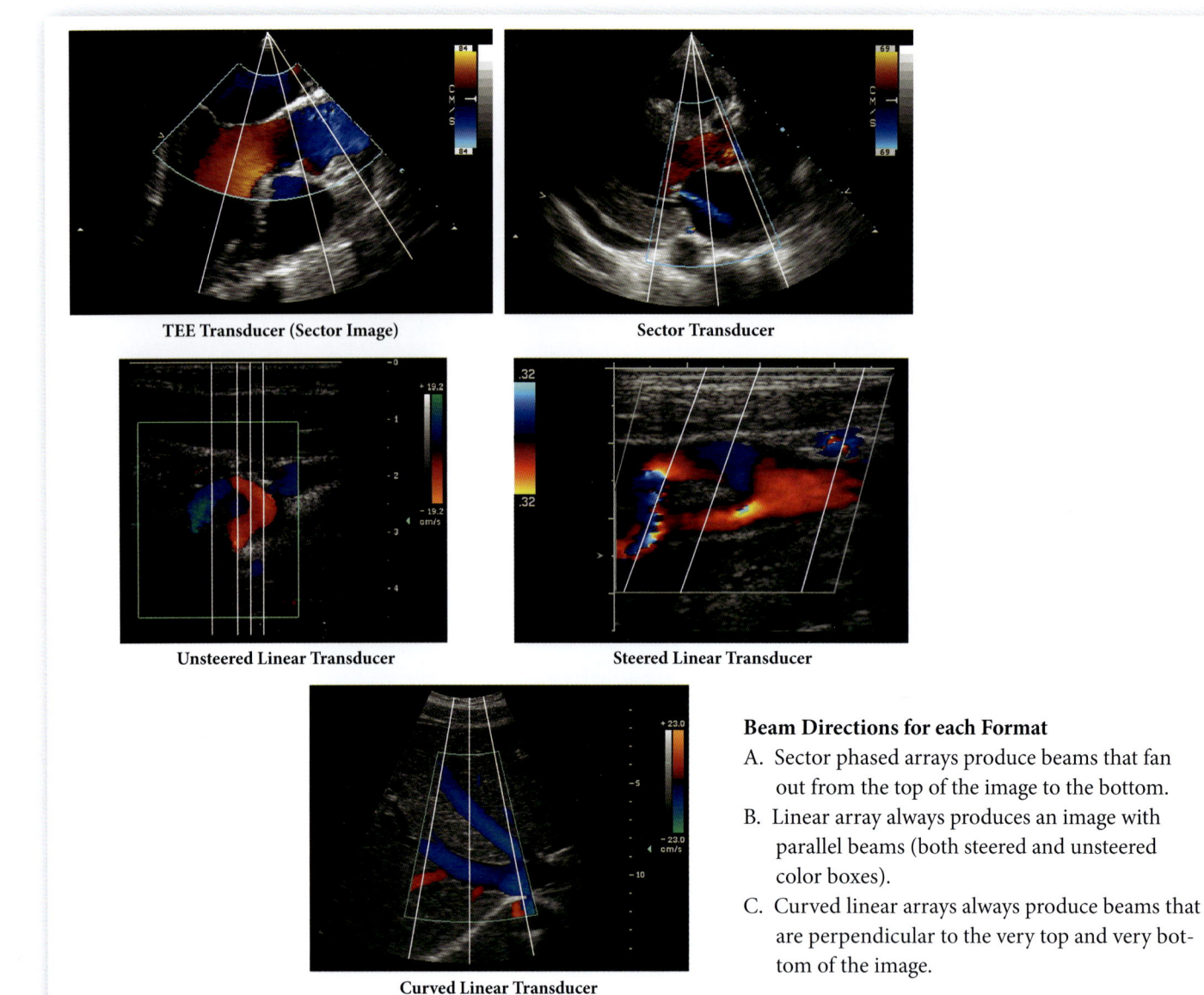

Sector Transducer

Unsteered Linear Transducer

Steered Linear Transducer

Curved Linear Transducer

Beam Directions for each Format
A. Sector phased arrays produce beams that fan out from the top of the image to the bottom.
B. Linear array always produces an image with parallel beams (both steered and unsteered color boxes).
C. Curved linear arrays always produce beams that are perpendicular to the very top and very bottom of the image.

Fig. 71 **Determining the steering direction**

Step 2. Draw Directionless Flow Indicator Lines
In Step 1 we specified the steering direction. Since the angle to flow is formed between the steering direction and the flow direction, we now need to indicate the direction of flow. We will perform this step in two stages by first drawing in directionless flow lines and then assessing actual flow direction.

(See *Figure 72, Directionless flow lines*)

Step 3. Read the Color Bar
The color bar is the "legend" or "key" which dictates the presentation color for positive and negative shifts. First check to make sure that color invert is not activated. If color invert is activated, then you must find the color which is associated with the positive sign. If color invert is not on, then the color on the top of the bar represents flow "toward" the transducer, or an angle that is less than 90 degrees. You must also now assess the "negative" direction color from the color bar.

Chapter 7: Doppler **347**

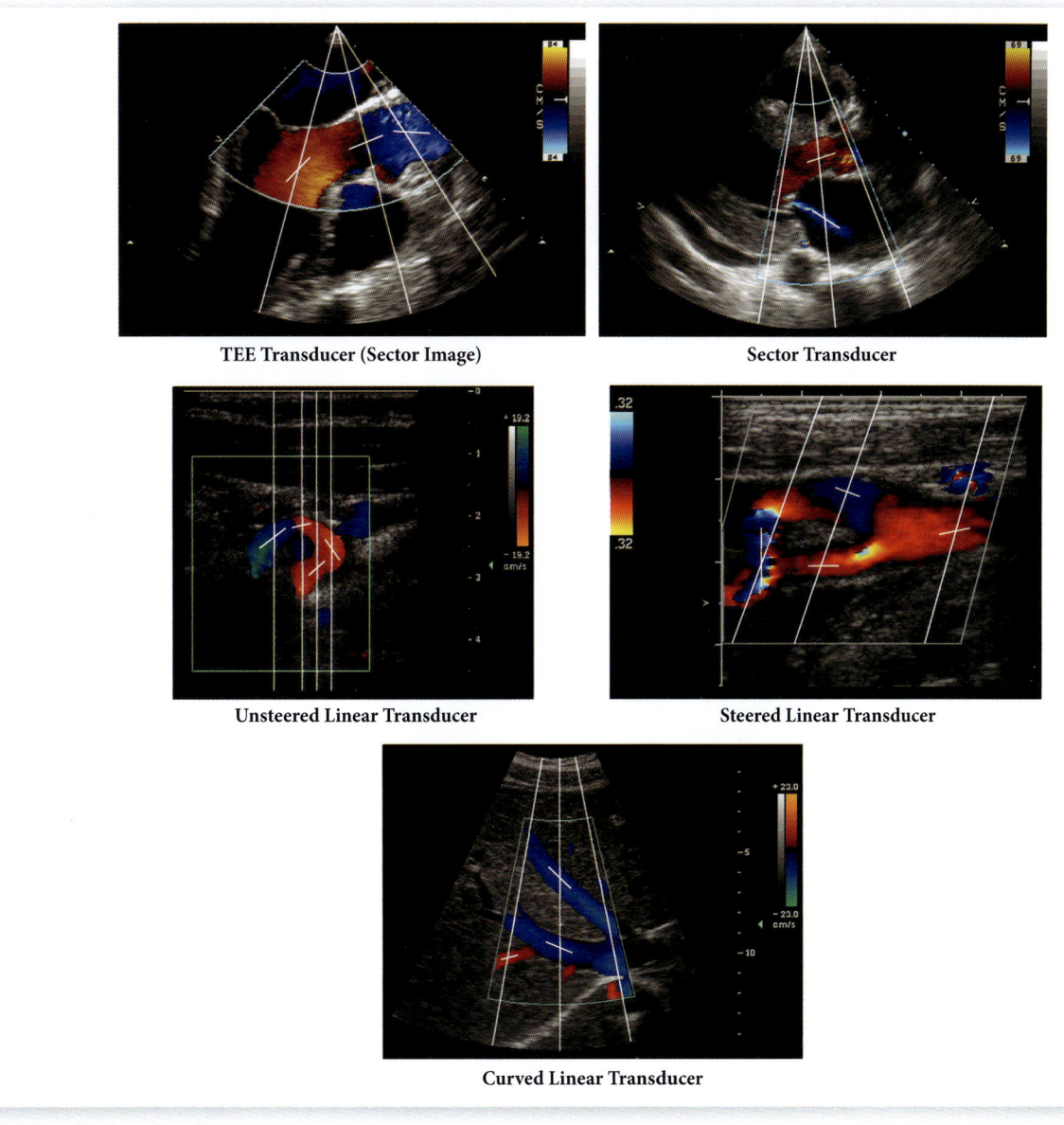

TEE Transducer (Sector Image) Sector Transducer

Unsteered Linear Transducer Steered Linear Transducer

Curved Linear Transducer

Fig. 72 **Directionless flow lines**

Step 4. Assign Directions (Arrowheads)

Within the image, find the regions that are presented in the "positive" colors. Excluding aliasing (discussed in a moment), the angle that is formed between the steer line and the flow indicator must be less than 90 degrees. Therefore, you can now add the arrowhead on the side of the flow indicator that results in an angle less than 90 degrees. Similarly, find the negative colors in the image. Again excluding aliasing, you should now be able to add a directional arrow to the flow indicator, since these angles should be greater than 90 degrees.

Remember – the insonification angle at a point in an image is always measured between the arrow head back toward the line of sight (steering line) from the transducer.

(See *Figure 73, Assign flow directions*)

348 LEVEL 2 Board Level

TEE Transducer (Sector Image)

Sector Transducer

Unsteered Linear Transducer

Steered Linear Transducer

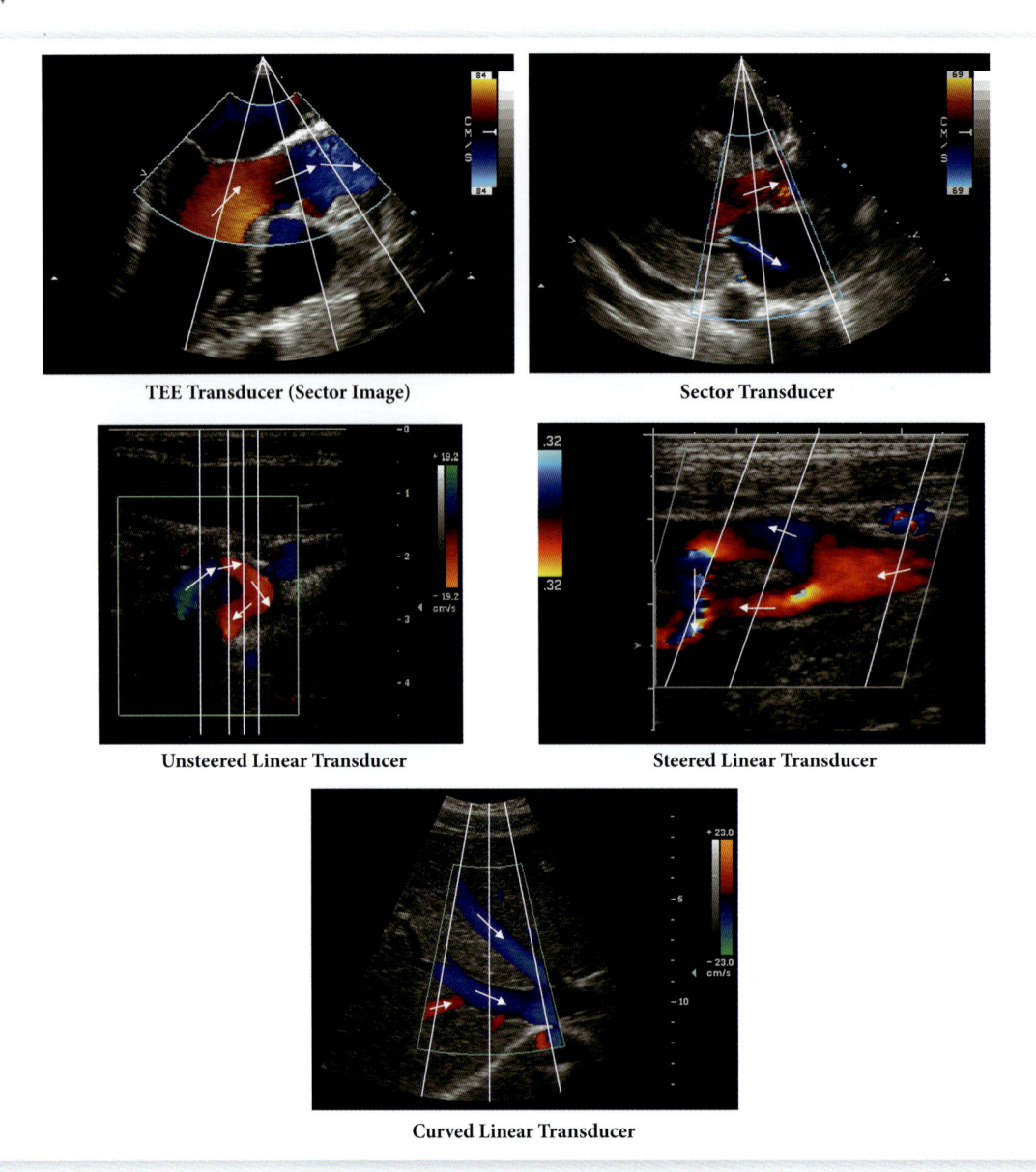

Curved Linear Transducer

Fig. 73 Assign flow directions

View ONLINE Animation and Image Library

KEY CONCEPT

Recall that the Doppler insonification angle (or simply Doppler angle) is measured between the flow direction and the beam direction. When the angle is less than 90° the flow is depicted by the color of the color bar indicated as positive flow (often referred to as flow "towards"). When the angle is greater than 90° but less than 180°, the flow is depicted by the color of the color bar indicated as negative flow (or flow "away").

Step 5. Recognizing Aliasing and Applying Common Sense

Within the steered linear image of *Figure 73*, you will notice that the flow indicator farthest to the left is actually an angle much greater than 90 degrees. From the color scale, this region of flow should be presented as red. However, the flow is blue and the flow direction indicated is correct. The reason is simple; there is aliasing occurring. The reason for this aliasing is twofold: first, the flow has gone around a corner which requires acceleration, and second, the angle to flow has become almost 180 degrees. Recall that the greatest Doppler shifts are recorded at 0 degrees and 180 degrees. A higher Doppler shift implies a greater likelihood of aliasing. The other insonification angles specified are very close to 90 degrees where very little shift is recorded. Therefore, it should make sense that aliasing would occur in this one location.

You must always consider the reasons why higher Doppler shifts can be detected in assessing the likelihood of aliasing as well as the color scale setting. Low color scales are much more likely to result in aliasing than high scale settings. In addition to angular effects, geometric flow conditions such as a narrowing, a corner, and being closer to the center-stream all result in higher velocities which should result in higher frequency shifts.

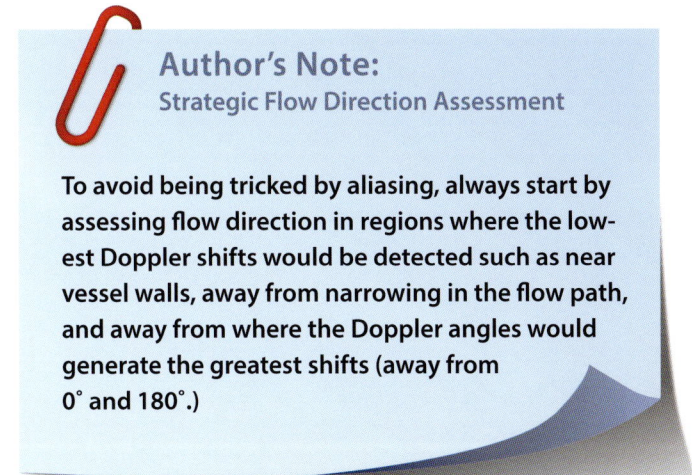

> **Author's Note:**
> **Strategic Flow Direction Assessment**
>
> To avoid being tricked by aliasing, always start by assessing flow direction in regions where the lowest Doppler shifts would be detected such as near vessel walls, away from narrowing in the flow path, and away from where the Doppler angles would generate the greatest shifts (away from 0° and 180°.)

Consider the following examples:

◊ **Example 1:** Starting with *Figure 74a*, we notice that the image was created by a linear transducer and the color box is steered. We also notice that the color scales are not that high and that the vessel is tortuous with areas of acceleration. By quick assessment we also see regions of the vessel which are encoded with colors on either side of the color bar, indicating a high likelihood of aliasing. As a result, we will want to start by assessing the flow direction in areas less likely to alias such as angles closer to 90°, longer, straight sections, and near vessel walls.

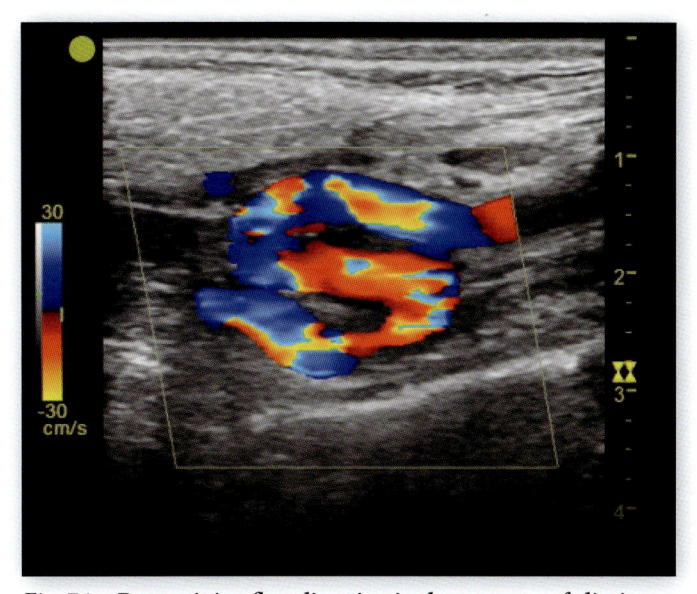

Fig. 74a **Determining flow direction in the presence of aliasing as a result of tortuosity (original image)**

Answer:
Step 1: Draw or imagine steering lines (in this case parallel to the color box) as shown in *Figure 74b*.

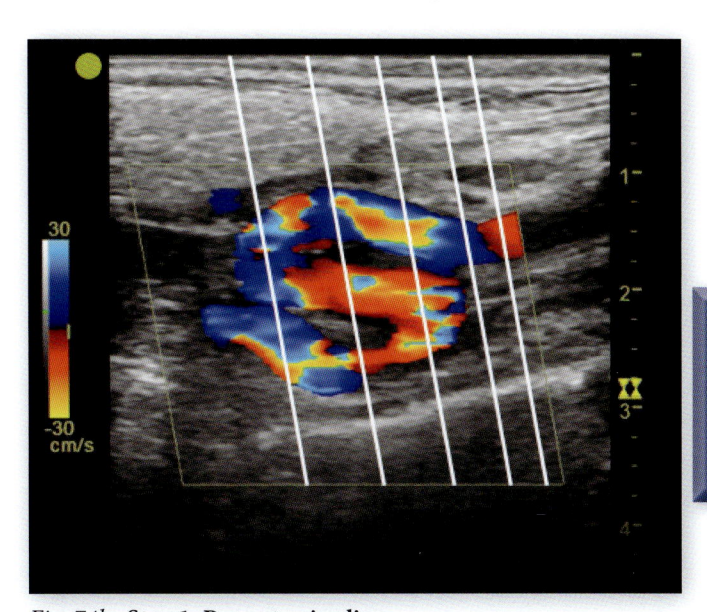

Fig. 74b **Step 1: Draw steering lines**

Step 2: Draw or imagine directionless flow line indicators as shown in *Figure 74c*.

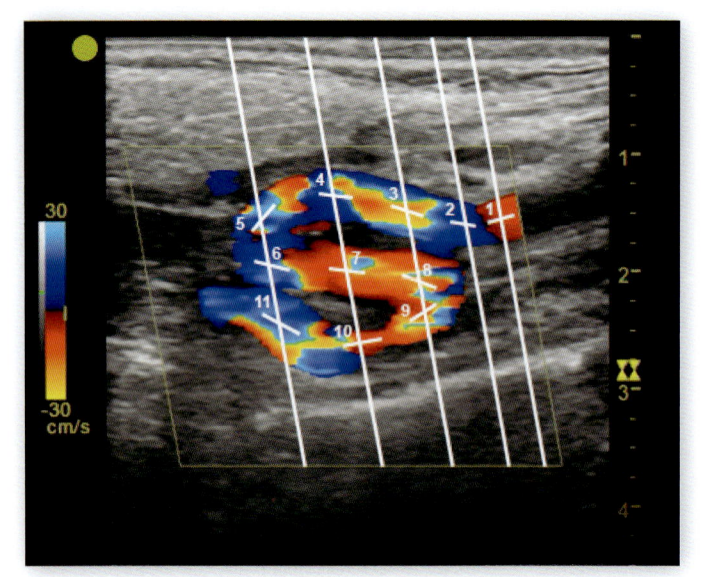

Fig. 74c **Step 2: Draw directionless flow line indicators**

Step 3: Refer to the color bar which indicates that unaliased flow at angles less than 90° will be present in hues of blue to aqua whereas unaliased flow at angles greater than 90° will present as hues of red to yellow.

Step 4: Assign direction (arrowheads). In this case, we want to start by looking at flow regions 1, 2, 4, 7, and 10, initially avoiding the remaining regions since the angles are either getting closer to 0 or 180 degrees and/or there is a bend in the vessel causing acceleration (both increasing the likelihood of aliasing).

Region 1: If we draw the arrow from screen right to screen left, the angle between the arrowhead and the line of sight from the transducer is slightly greater than 90° and should be encoded as red, as it is. Therefore, we are pretty certain that flow is moving from right to left at this point.

Transition from region 1 to region 2: Notice that there is a dark region indicating no flow detected as occurs when the angle is at or close to 90°.

Region 2: Again, if we draw the arrow from right to left, the angle (between the arrow head and line of sight from transducer) is now slightly less than 90° and should be encoded as blue. Since the color displayed matches what the color bar indicates, the flow direction was specified correctly.

Region 4: Since flow is contiguous, we would expect the flow to still be moving from right to left. Drawing in the arrowhead, the angle is slightly less than 90° indicating that the flow should be blue, matching reality. Note that the color just proximal (before) region 4 is yellow, as a result of aliasing.

Region 7: Since the vessel reverses course, for flow to be contiguous, flow should now be moving from screen left toward screen right. Drawing in the arrowhead the resulting angle is just slightly greater than 90° resulting in red encoding of the flow. Just above we again see the effects of aliasing with the small aqua region.

Region 10: The vessel has again reversed course such that contiguous flow is once again from screen right toward screen left. The resulting angle is now slightly greater than 90°, indicating flow as red.

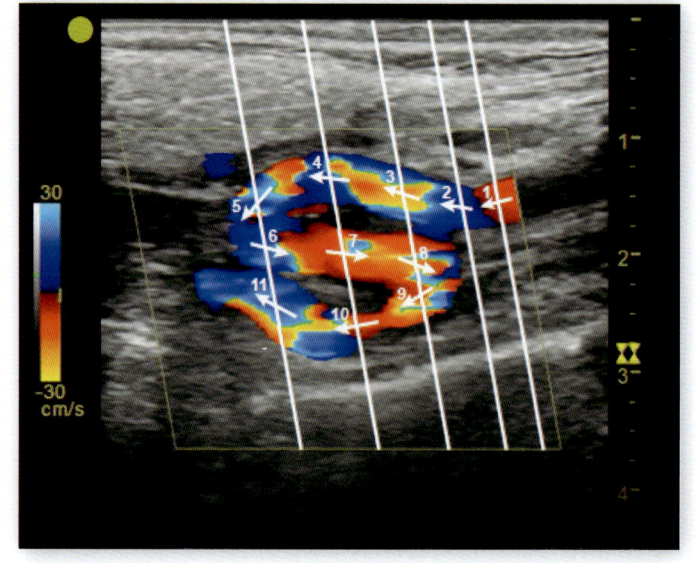

Fig. 74d **Steps 3 and 4: Assign direction (arrowheads)**

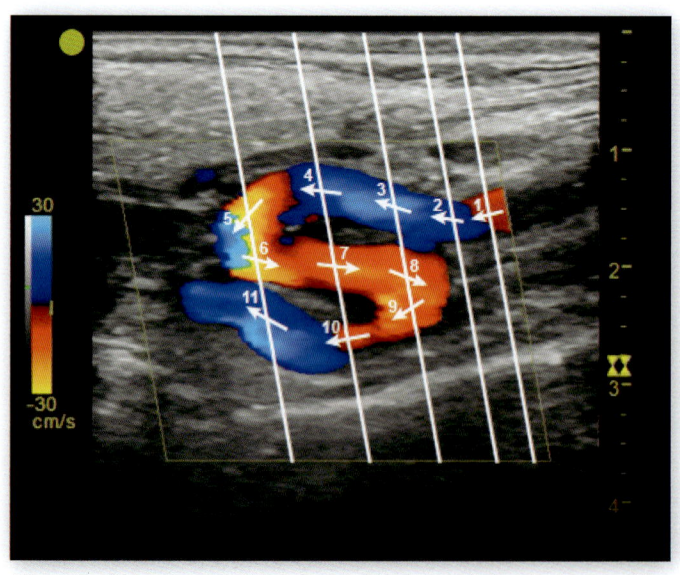

Fig. 74e **Color image of same vessel during a different phase of the cardiac cycle with arrowheads showing flow direction**

Figures 74a - 74d represent the vessel during peak systole, when the flow velocity is highest. Now let's look at *Figure 74e* which represents the same vessel but during a different phase of the cardiac cycle. Notice that as a result of the lower pressure, there are lower velocities and significantly less aliasing throughout the image. Note that at peak systole, the flow would look more like *Figure 74e* simply by increasing the color scales.

◊ **Example 2:** Starting with *Figure 75a*, we notice that, like the previous example, this image was produced by a linear transducer and that the color box is steered. We also note that the color scales are very low, increasing the likelihood of aliasing. A quick glance at the color image confirms that there is likely aliasing since we are seeing both colors of the color bar simultaneously in the same region of flow. As a result, we must again be careful to start by assessing a segment of the vessel away from where aliasing is more likely. Since the velocity is generally higher in the center of the vessel, we should assess near the vessel wall, where the flow is constrained.

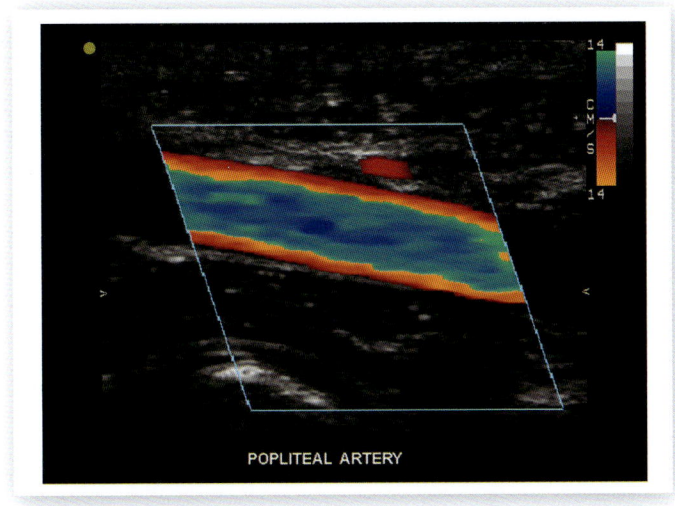

Fig. 75a **Determining flow direction with center stream aliasing (original image)**

Step 1: Draw or imagine steering lines (in this case parallel to the color box) as shown in *Figure 75b*.

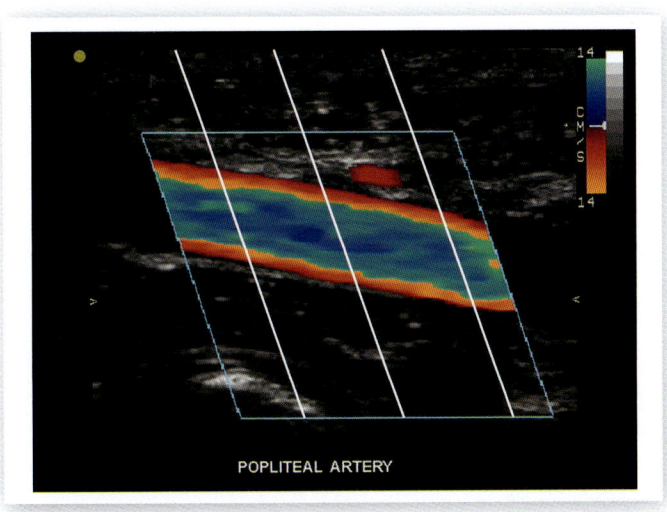

Fig. 75b **Step 1: Draw steering lines**

Step 2: Draw or imagine directionless flow line indicators as shown in *Figure 75c*. (Note we will assess near the vessel wall, not in the center of the vessel.)

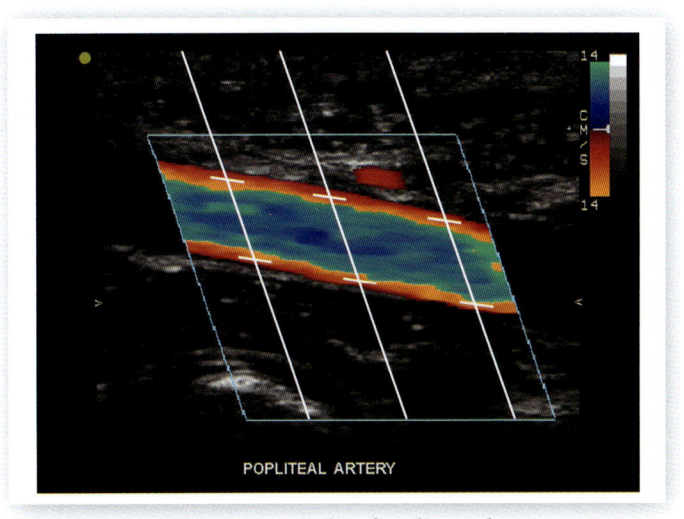

Fig. 75c **Step 2: Draw directionless flow line indicators**

Step 3: Refer to the color bar which indicates that unaliased flow at angles less than 90° will be present in hues of blue to aqua whereas unaliased flow at angles greater than 90° will present as hues of red to orange.

Step 4: Assign direction (arrowheads). If the flow is traveling from screen left toward screen right, the angle (between the arrowhead and the line of sight from the transducer) is greater than 90°, implying that the flow should be encoded as red, matching reality. Therefore, the flow is moving from screen left toward screen right.

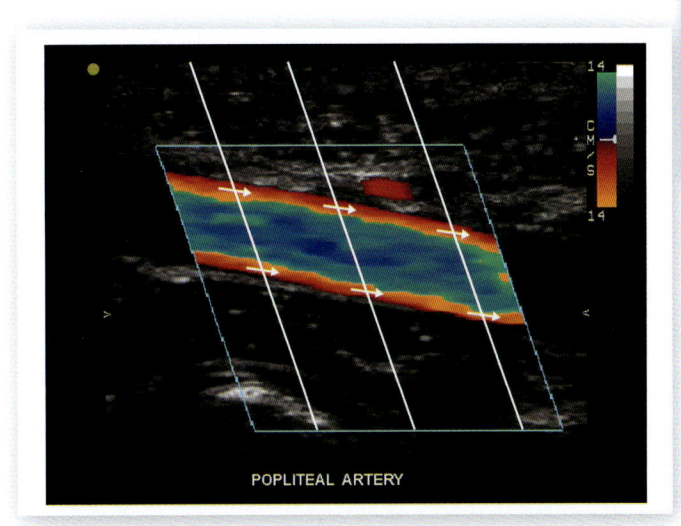

Fig. 75d **Steps 3 and 4: Assign direction (arrowheads)**

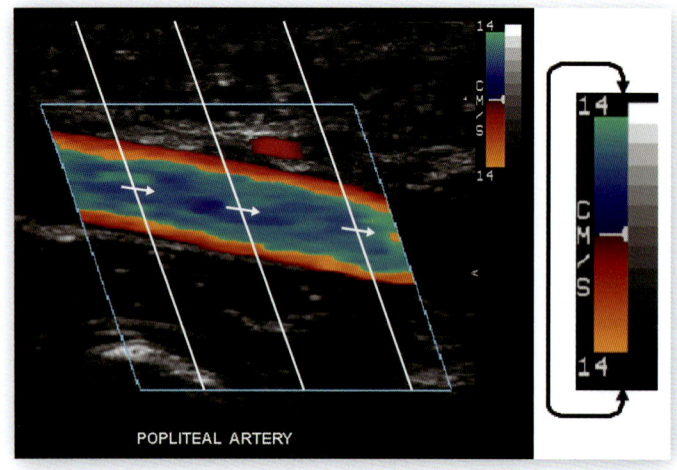

Fig. 75e **Notice that, although the Doppler angle is greater than 90°, the color in the centerstream does not match the color indicated by the color bar because of aliasing (aliasing indicated by the arrows wrapped around color bar)**

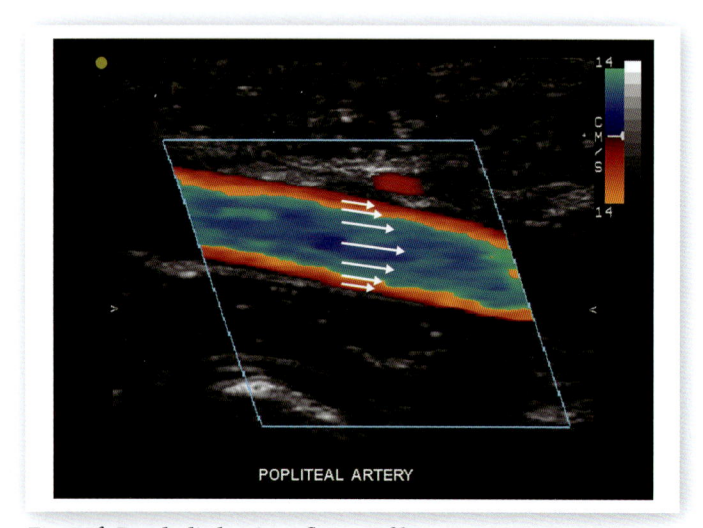

Fig. 75f **Parabolic laminar flow profile**

Note that without paying attention to aliasing, the flow direction in this image would be misinterpreted. Notice in *Figure 75e* that in the center of the vessel the flow is depicted as aqua and dark blue even though the angle formed between the steering direction and the flow is greater than 90°, which according to the scale should be red. Clearly, if you do not pay attention to the warning signs, you would incorrectly assess that flow is moving from screen right to screen left.

Figure 75f illustrates how the color encoding is indicating a parabolic laminar flow profile. With increasing distance from the vessel wall, notice that the color hue lightens, representing higher velocities as indicated by the color scale, and is still consistent with the flow direction indicated. Only in the more central regions of the vessel where the higher velocity flow occurs does the color seem "inconsistent" with the drawn color direction. In fact, at the very center of the vessel where the highest velocities occur, even darker hues of blue are reached, which is a clear indication that the color has wrapped back around the color bar, hence, aliasing.

Figure 76 shows aliasing that occurs with higher velocity flow of mitral regurgitation. Notice that the color aliasing actually helps by making the regurgitant flow stand out in the image.

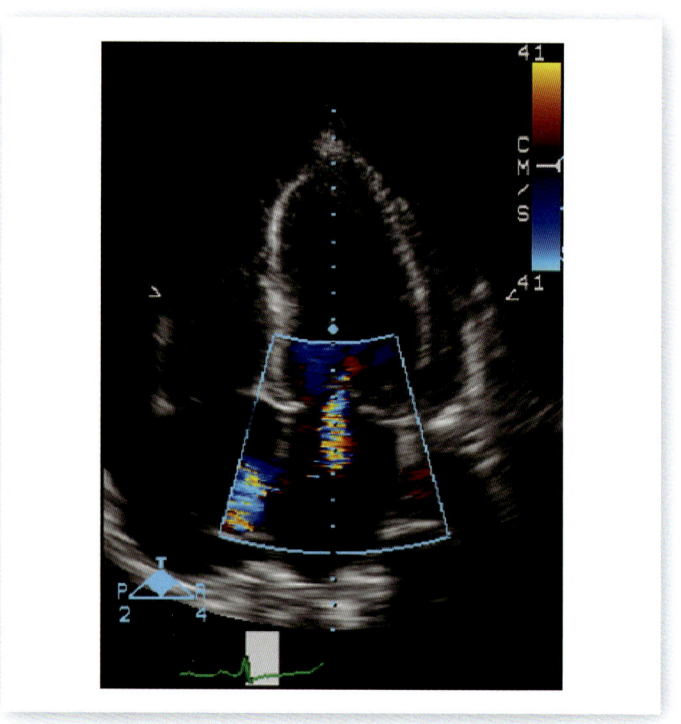

Fig. 76 **Aliased mitral regurgitation**

View ONLINE Animation and Image Library

28.5 Direction of Flow in the Body

We have just learned how to determine flow direction within a color Doppler ultrasound image. The next step is to use that information to make the determination of which way the flow is traveling within the body. The terms "antegrade" and "retrograde" are commonly used to refer to blood moving in the direction expected and in the opposite direction, respectively. For example, if assessing a carotid artery, the expected direction is flow toward the brain. Therefore, flow traveling toward the head in the carotid artery system is considered antegrade, whereas flow traveling away from the head would be considered retrograde.

Once you determine the direction of flow from an ultrasound image, determining flow direction in the body requires the use of specific paradigms or conventions. Every ultrasound transducer has a physical indicator which is used as part of the convention. This indicator if often referred to as a "notch" or "dot." The physical indicator on the transducer corresponds to a displayed indicator on the ultrasound image. The indicator on the ultrasound image is often a dot, but is commonly a company logo. Although there are plenty of exceptions, including some cardiac views (see *Table 5*), the general scanning convention is the transducer is positioned on the patient such that the physical notch is pointing toward either the patient's head or right shoulder.

You must learn the convention required for each type of imaging. If the convention is not followed and the transducer is flipped, the anatomy will be inverted in the image from what is expected (see *Figures 77a* and *77b*) and the flow may be assumed to be traveling in the opposite direction from reality. A few of the multiple cardiac views used are noted in the table below, providing an example of how important it is to know the correct position of the transducer notch.

Cardiac View	Transducer Notch Starting Position
Parasternal Long-Axis View	Notch pointing toward patient's right shoulder
Parasternal Short-Axis View	Notch pointing toward patient's left shoulder
Apical Four-Chamber View	Notch pointing toward patient's left shoulder
Apical Two-Chamber View	From Apical 4C view, rotate transducer approximately 30°
Subcostal View	Notch pointing toward patient's left shoulder
Suprasternal Notch View	Notch at 12 o'clock (toward patient's head)

Table 5 **Cardiac transducer notch positions**

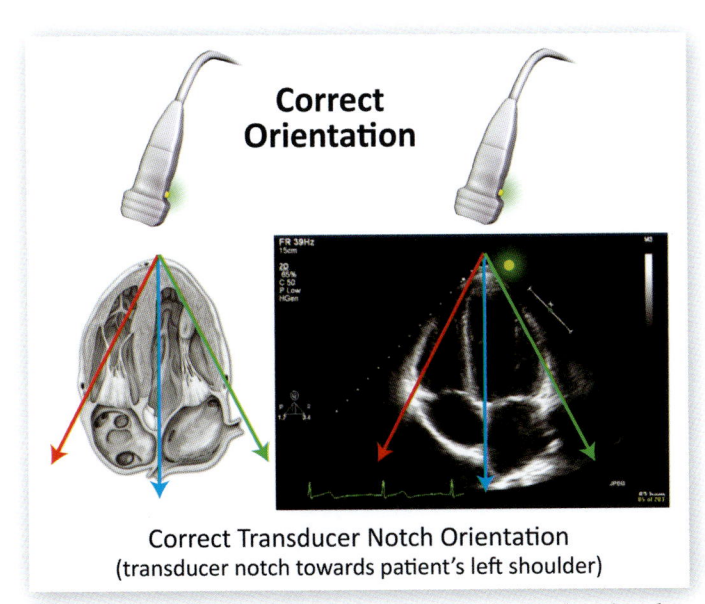

Fig. 77a **Correct transducer orientation for apical 4-chamber (A4C) view**

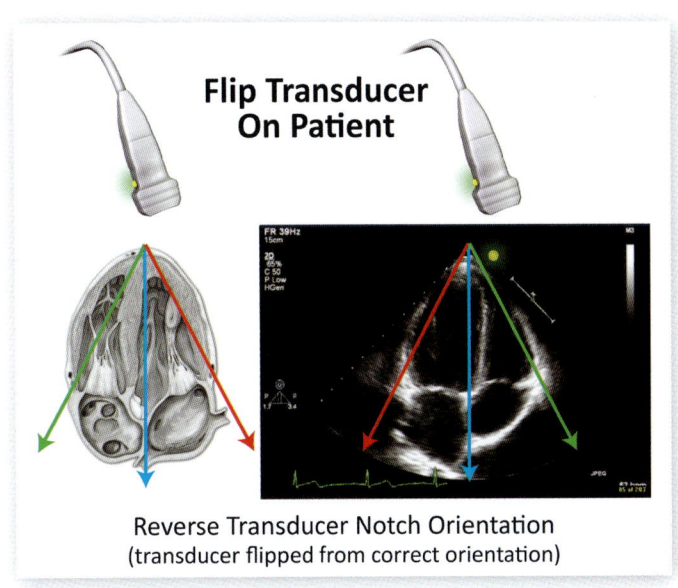

Fig. 77b **Result of flipping transducer on patient for apical 4-chamber (A4C) view**

Perhaps the best way to understand the concept of how transducer orientation can affect the view of anatomy and flow within vessels is to analyze a few examples.

◊ **Example 1:** When imaging the vertebral artery (as shown in *Figure 78*), notice that the transducer notch is pointing toward the patient's head. Since the transducer is oriented correctly, the image indicator aligns with the transducer indicator. Based on the Doppler angle, flow is from right to left (white arrow). Since the orientation notch is pointing toward the head, flow in the vertebral artery is toward the head, or antegrade.

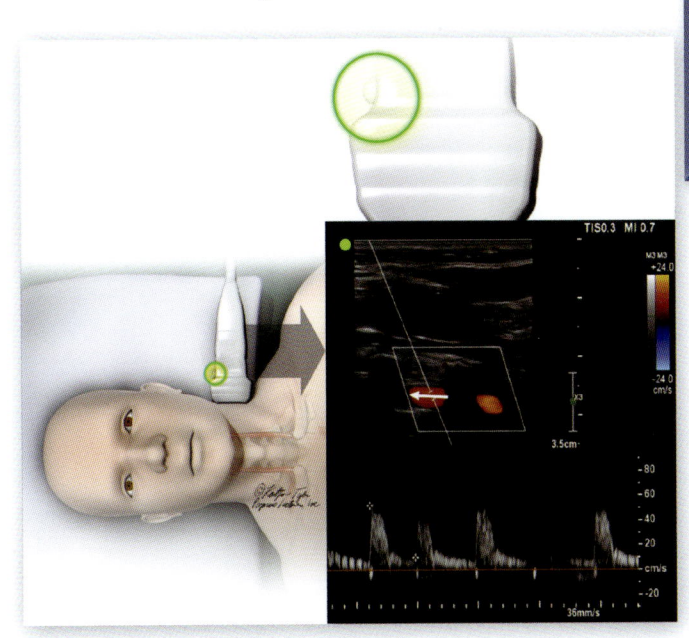

Fig. 78 **Imaging vertebral artery with notch pointed toward patient's head**

◊ **Example 2:** When examining the Doppler image of a vertebral artery in *Figure 79a*, some determinations can be made.

Question 1: Is this antegrade flow?
Question 2: Does the blue color represent antegrade or retrograde flow?
Question 3: Does the blue correspond to the spectral flow above or below the baseline?
Question 4: Why is the color only blue, but the spectrum shows flow in both directions?

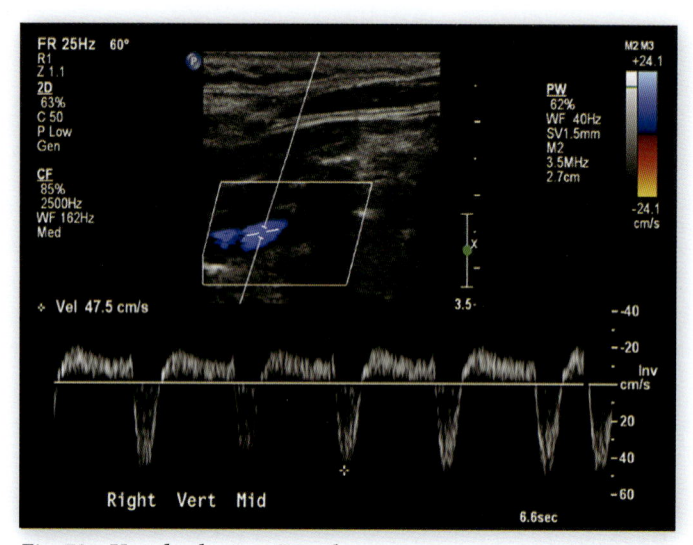

Fig. 79a **Vertebral artery Doppler**

Answer 1: As shown in the Doppler spectrum, the flow is alternating between antegrade and retrograde.
Answer 2: The blue color represents flow moving from screen right (angle less than 90°). This means that the blue flow represents flow away from the head, or retrograde, as shown in *Figure 79b*.

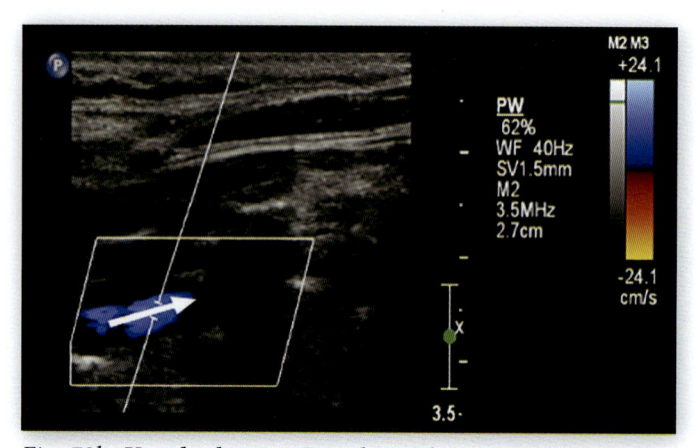

Fig. 79b **Vertebral artery Doppler with arrow indicating flow direction**

Answer 3: For this image, when the flow is moving from screen left to screen right, the Doppler angle is less than 90°. When the Doppler angle is less than 90°, the Doppler shift is positive. Positive shifts are normally shown above the baseline, but notice that spectral invert is on (as indicated by "Inv" next to the spectrum scale in *Figure 79a*). Therefore, the positive flow is shown below the baseline.

Answer 4: You must realize that the color image was captured at one instance in time, whereas for spectral Doppler, the horizontal axis is time. As explained in Answer 3, the blue color corresponds to a moment during which the spectrum was positive (displayed below the baseline because of spectral invert). If the image had been frozen when the spectrum was flowing antegrade (toward the head), the color would be encoded as red. The following figures artificially color the spectrum to match the corresponding color that would appear in the image. *Figure 80a* is the same spectral invert seen in this Doppler image, whereas *Figure 80b* shows what the spectrum would look like with inversion off.

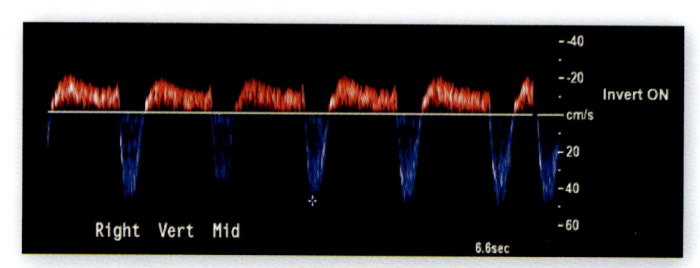

Fig. 80a **Vertebral artery spectrum with invert on**

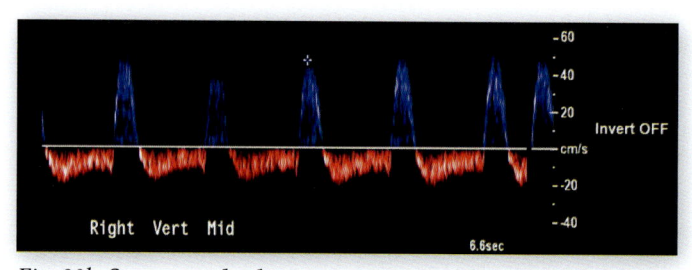

Fig. 80b **Same vertebral artery spectrum with invert off**

✓ **CHECKPOINT: Exam Tip**

In color Doppler, aliasing results in the displayed color "wrapping" around the color bar. As indicated by the Nyquist criterion, the likelihood of aliasing increases with increasing flow velocity (narrowings, increased flow, bends and kinks, etc.), decreasing PRFs (color scales), and when the angle to flow is closer to 0° or 180°.

29. Color Persistence

29.1 The Purpose and Effects of Color Persistence

In Chapter 6 we discussed "averaging techniques" with the goal of improving signal-to-noise benefits. The goal of color persistence, like the goal of 2D persistence, is to "average" frames over time so as to improve the signal-to-noise ratio. Improving the signal-to-noise ratio is especially desirable when there is poor sensitivity resulting from weak signals. Recall that in Chapter 6 we learned that persistence was usually not a pure averaging but rather followed a recipe of adding together some of the existing frame data with smaller percentages of the data from previous frames. Since the noise from frame to frame is random (incoherent), averaging (coherent) signals over time reduces the effects of the noise and increases the signal strength.

29.2 Persistence and Temporal Distortion

Of course, the trade-off with all averaging techniques is a reduction in temporal resolution. With persistence, this trade-off is often misconstrued. This confusion stems from the fact that persistence has the exact opposite effect on signals that are present in many frames than on signals that are present in only one or two frames. Signals that are present in only one or two frames generally disappear with high persistence. Conversely, signals that are present in many frames can be persisted into other frames. The reason for this difference is clear. If a signal is present in many frames and absent in only one, averaging all of the frames together will add the event into the one frame in which it was not contained. In reverse, an event which occurs in only a single frame, when averaged with the data in the other frames, makes those signals weaker or potentially disappear. As a result, by using higher persistence there is the potential to miss events which occur over a short duration, and also possibly introduce a temporal discordance, or time delay, between the actual occurrence of the event and the display of that event. For short duration events, such as non-holosystolic regurgitant jets, using too much persistence can mask the appearance of the jet, especially when the color frame rate is low. Conversely, long duration events, such as relatively continuous, uniform diastolic flow, are generally persisted into frames in which the flow doesn't actually exist. This potential for temporal distortion is another reason why timing and time duration estimates are better assessed by spectral Doppler than by color Doppler.

View ONLINE Animation and Image Library

29.3 Important Points about Persistence
- There are many different recipes which can be used for persistence. Most approaches use a time weighting function, giving more "weight" to the last frame obtained and successively less weight to each earlier frame.
- Higher color persistence is generally used when the color signal is weak and some color (speckle) noise is present.
- Higher color persistence can distort the temporal aspects of the visualized flow.
- Very short duration signals that exist for only one color frame may potentially be "persisted" out.
- Longer duration signals that persist for multiple frames may potentially be "persisted" into future frames.

> **KEY CONCEPT**
>
> Color persistence is a weighted frame averaging technique which improves sensitivity and reduces noise, but also can distort the temporal characteristics of the flow signal.

30. Color Priority

30.1 How Color Priority Works

Color priority is a threshold technique set by the user on most ultrasound systems. When an individual pixel has both a grayscale (tissue) signal and a color signal, the color priority determines if the color is displayed or the grayscale is displayed. A higher color priority setting gives preference to displaying color for a pixel that has both a color signal and a grayscale signal. Conversely, lower color priority is more likely to display a pixel in grayscale, when that pixel has both a color signal and a grayscale signal. Color priority is intended to allow the user to maximize color filling while minimizing color bleed overlaying tissue (as shown in *Figure 81*). In other words, color priority is a weighting function that votes only when a pixel has conflicting information. It is important to note that color priority does not create flow where no Doppler shift exists; it just gives more or less priority to color values in the presence of conflicting data.

30.2 Important Points about Color Priority
- Axial resolution of color is generally not as good as that of 2D so it is common for there to be a color "tail". Color priority helps reduce related tissue/color overlap.
- A higher color priority gives color higher precedence over a grayscale signal.
- Color priority will not "create" a signal where no Doppler shift was recorded; color priority just votes between competing signals at the same location.
- High 2D gain can cause color depending on the color priority setting.

- Color noise from overgaining can be minimized by color priority but this is not suggested. Color noise should be controlled by the color gain.

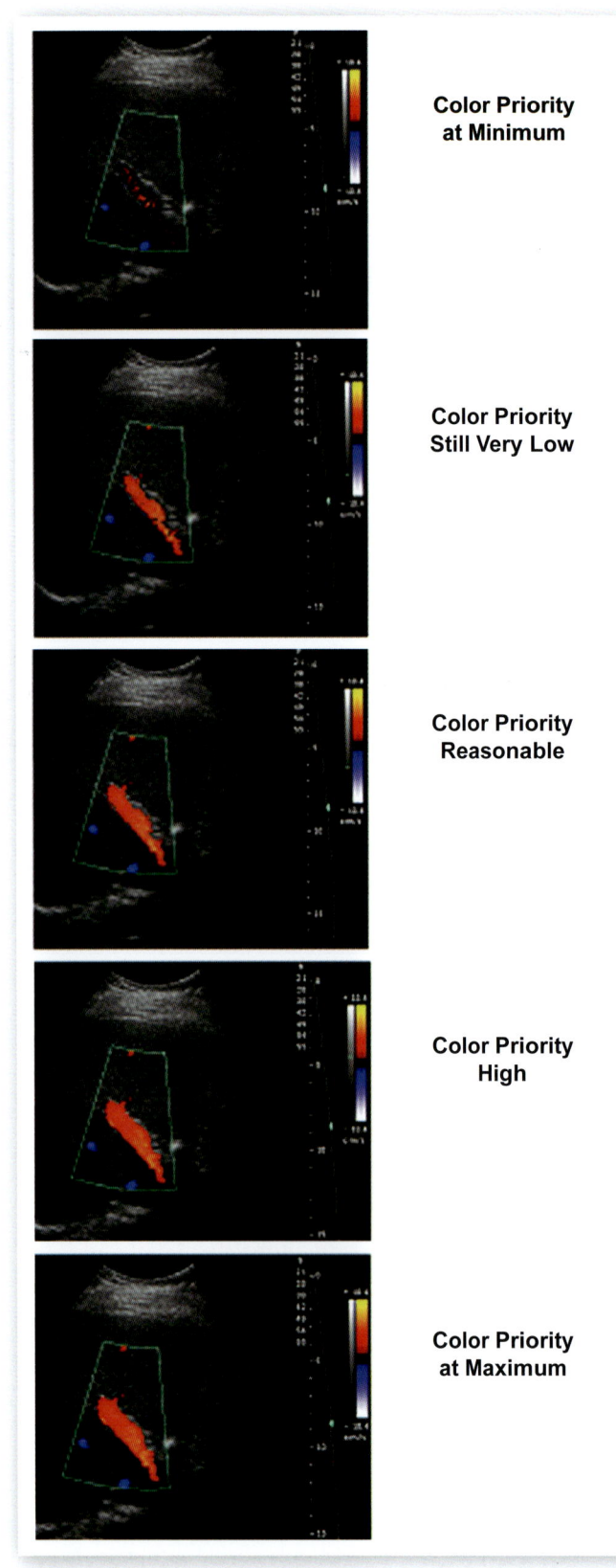

Fig. 81 **Effect of color priority**

From the images of *Figure 81*, you should notice that the high and maximum color priority only slightly "overfilled the vessel relative to the "reasonable" setting. In contrast, using too low color priority caused significant under-filling. As the signal-to-noise decreases, you should make certain to increase the color priority appropriately, or color filling will be difficult to achieve. This fact should make sense if you consider the weak reflective mechanism responsible for color Doppler signals.

> **KEY CONCEPT**
>
> Color priority allows the user to vary the threshold used to determine whether a pixel will be displayed as color or as grayscale. Increasing the color priority implies that color is given display priority unless the grayscale amplitude is higher than the threshold.

31. Color Power Doppler

31.1 Color Power Doppler Encoding

As already discussed throughout the previous sections, standard color Doppler encodes flow based on mean velocity. Direction of flow is indicated by different colors (such as red and blue) whereas velocity is indicated generally as a gradation of color (generally darker hues representing lower mean velocities and lighter hues representing higher mean velocities). Color power Doppler, also referred to as color angio, energy Doppler, amplitude Doppler, or simply power Doppler is another Doppler-based technique, but which color encodes using a different paradigm. With power Doppler, flow is encoded based on the signal amplitude, not based on the detected mean velocity. Recall that the signal amplitude (signal strength) from blood is related to the number of reflecting blood cells. Therefore, higher numbers of blood cells produce higher amplitude signals, whereas fewer blood cells produce lower amplitude signals. With color power Doppler, weaker signals are encoded with a different color hue than stronger signals, regardless of the velocity of the blood cells.

31.2 Disadvantages

When discussing a technique or technology, it is conventional to begin by discussing advantages before disadvantages. However, in this case, understanding the advantages is facilitated by first understanding the disadvantages, as the process of discussing the disadvantages further clarifies the methodology of producing color power Doppler.

Since color power Doppler encodes based on amplitude and not frequency shift information, conventional color power Doppler does not yield any velocity information, implying that neither mean velocity nor direction of flow is presented. In essence, power Doppler displays where flow exists, but does not present other important flow parameters. This lack of flow information is the primary limitation of power Doppler. There are now some ultrasound systems that display a hybrid of standard color Doppler and color power Doppler, producing directional power Doppler images.

Additionally, power Doppler is generally produced using frame averaging. Frame averaging improves the sensitivity of color power Doppler but at the expense of temporal resolution. In general, power Doppler has worse temporal resolution than standard color Doppler, which itself already suffers from poor temporal resolution. The third disadvantage to color power Doppler is related to flash artifact. Flash artifact appears as a sudden appearance of color over much or all of the color box region. The flash is the result of relative motion between the transducer and the patient (either from patient motion or movement of the transducer). Most systems attempt to reduce flash artifacts by using suppression algorithms. Although there has been significant improvement in reducing flash artifact, flash artifact is still relatively common.

31.3 Advantages

The primary advantage of color power Doppler is improved flow sensitivity, especially to low flow states. This advantage is really the result of two different processing approaches. First, color power Doppler is generally able to detect lower velocity flow since aggressive wall filtering is not required to reduce the risk of circuit saturation. Whereas color Doppler requires that low frequency shifts related to low-velocity flow must be eliminated, power Doppler can differentiate tissue signals from blood signals based on amplitude. Higher amplitude signals come from tissues, and hence can be eliminated, leaving the lower amplitude blood signals to be processed. Second, since color power Doppler does not yield any flow velocity or directional information, there is no significant need to try to improve temporal resolution. As a result, frame averaging can be employed, improving the sensitivity (signal-to-noise as discussed in Chapter 6).

The second advantage to color power Doppler is that there is much less angle sensitivity. With standard color Doppler, color dropout occurs when flow is assessed at insonification angles close to 90°. Since power Doppler encodes based on amplitude and not frequency shift, flow is usually still detected at angles close to 90°.

Figure 82 shows flow in a splenic vein when using color Doppler (A) versus color power Doppler (B). Note that in A, there is a region of dropout because of poor Doppler angle. B shows the same flow, but using color power Doppler. Note how the color power Doppler is less sensitive to angle.

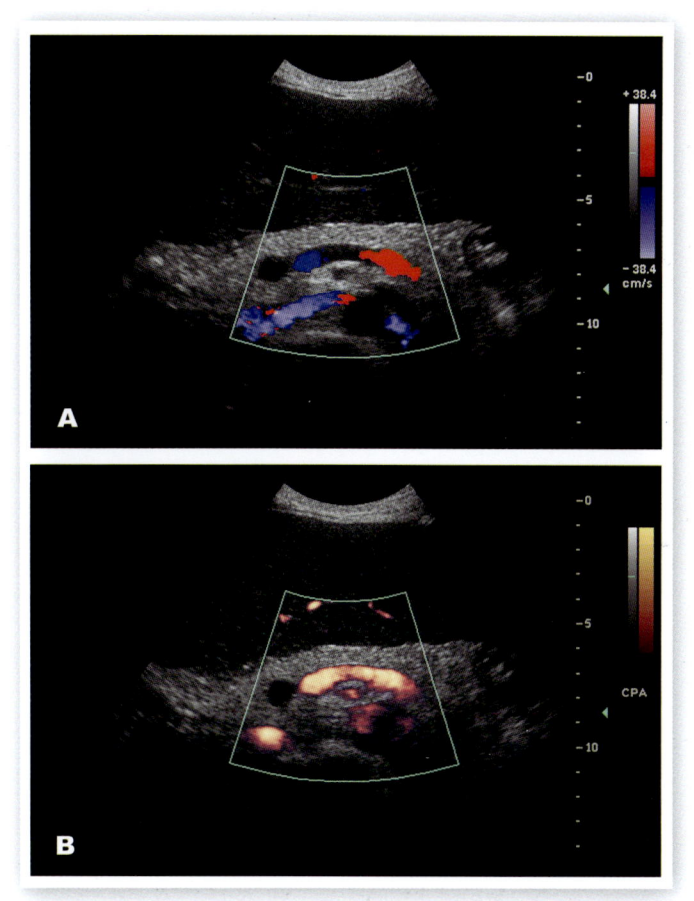

Fig. 82 **Flow in the splenic vein using color Doppler (A) compared to the same flow using color power Doppler (B)**

Because of the increased sensitivity, using power Doppler is a good choice when trying to detect low-velocity flow, or flow in very small, deeper vessels. Specifically, power Doppler is useful to confirm thrombosis or occlusion of vessels. Power Doppler is advantageous for transcranial imaging which often suffers from weak signal related to attenuation through the skull bone as well as weak signals from low flow through very small vessels. Additionally, power Doppler often improves visualization of tumors or inflammation in the prostate, testicular or ovarian torsion, and renal parenchymal flow.

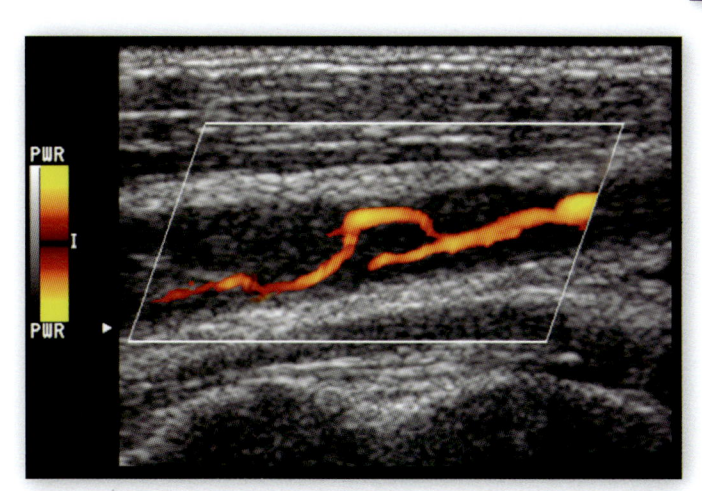

Fig. 83 **Color power Doppler showing recanalized flow in an occluded artery**

Note that power Doppler has advantages in the imaging situation presented in *Figure 83* both because of the relative angle insensitivity and the better sensitivity for detection of low-velocity flow.

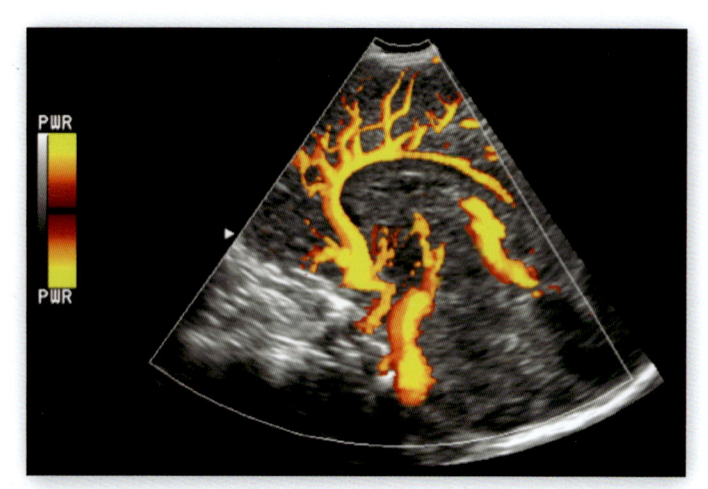

Fig. 84 **Color power Doppler image of the pericallosal artery in a neonatal head**

31.4 Directional Power Doppler

Many systems now offer a directional color power Doppler technique, overcoming one of the principal limitations of standard color power Doppler. In order to present flow direction, the system uses phase information in conjunction with the power information. *Figure 85b* illustrates directional power Doppler. Note that there are no scales presented as the phase is used only to determine direction, and not velocity. Just as with other ultrasound techniques, just about every company has a different name for their version of the technology.

- Philips: Directional Color Power Angio (Directional CPA) and Bidirectional Power Doppler
- Canon: (Directional) Color Power Doppler
- Samsung: S-Flow
- GE: Directional Power Doppler and High Definition Power Doppler (HD-Flow™)
- Mindray: Directional Power Mode (DirPower)
- Siemens-Acuson: Directional Power Doppler
- Toshiba: Directional Power Doppler Mode

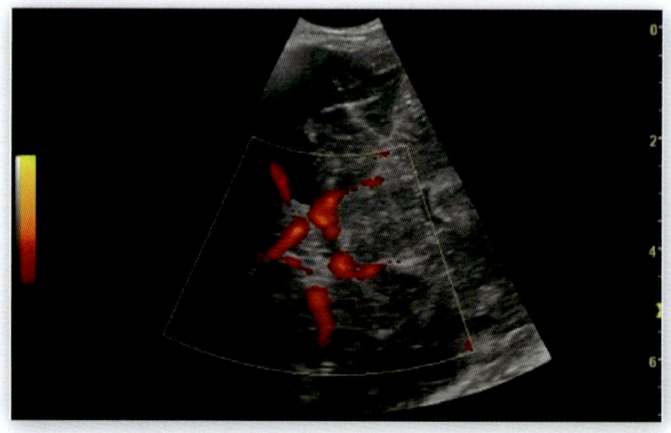

Fig. 85a **Standard color power Doppler showing the intracranial vessels of the Circle of Willis**

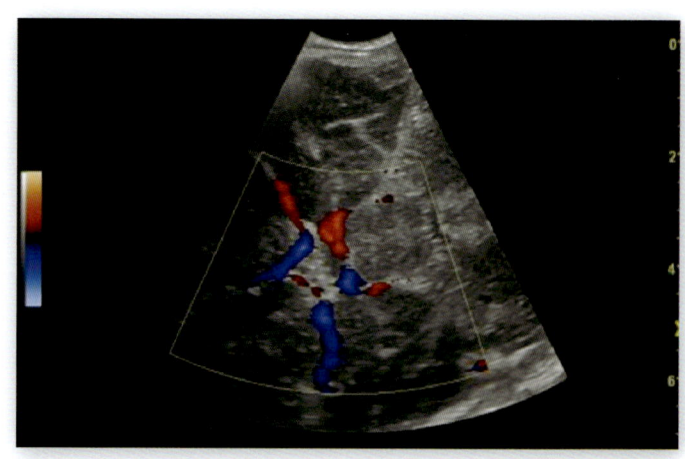

Fig. 85b **Directional color power Doppler showing the intracranial vessels of the Circle of Willis (notice there are no scale markings on the power color bar)**

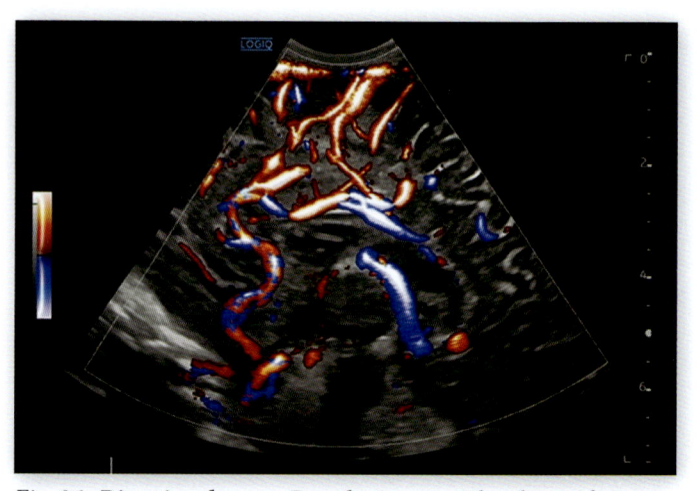

Fig. 86 **Directional power Doppler image with color surface rendering (Radiantflow™) of a neonatal brain (note there are no scale markings on the power color bar)** *(Courtesy of GE Medical)*

View ONLINE Animation and Image Library

32. Surface Rendered Color Doppler

32.1 Concept and Theory

In his PhD thesis at the University of Utah in 1975, Bui Toing Phong described a method for "illumination for computer generated pictures." The technique treats lighting sources so that images have a more realistic surface appearance. Although many other methods exist, the genius of Phong's approach is that it results in very good approximations that can be calculated very rapidly. Just as we learned that sound can reflect in different ways based on the surface charac-

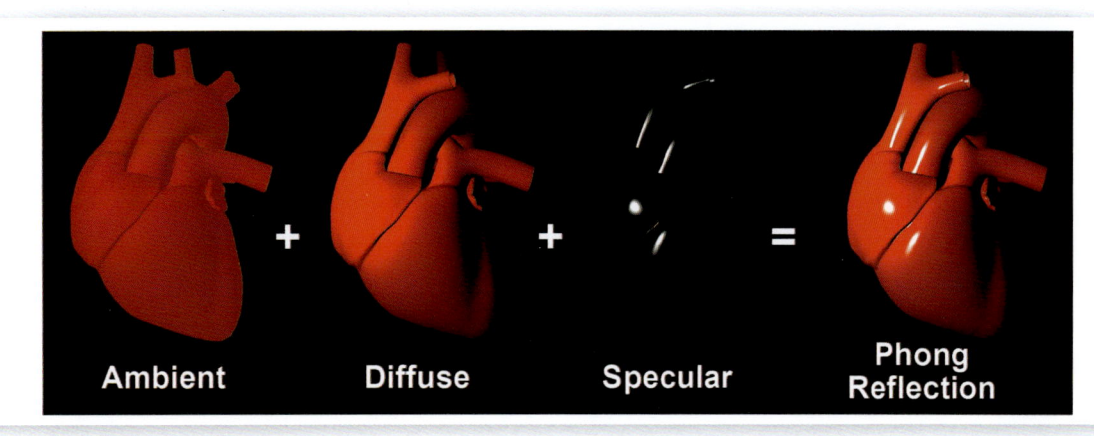

Fig. 87 **Subdivisions of Phong reflection**

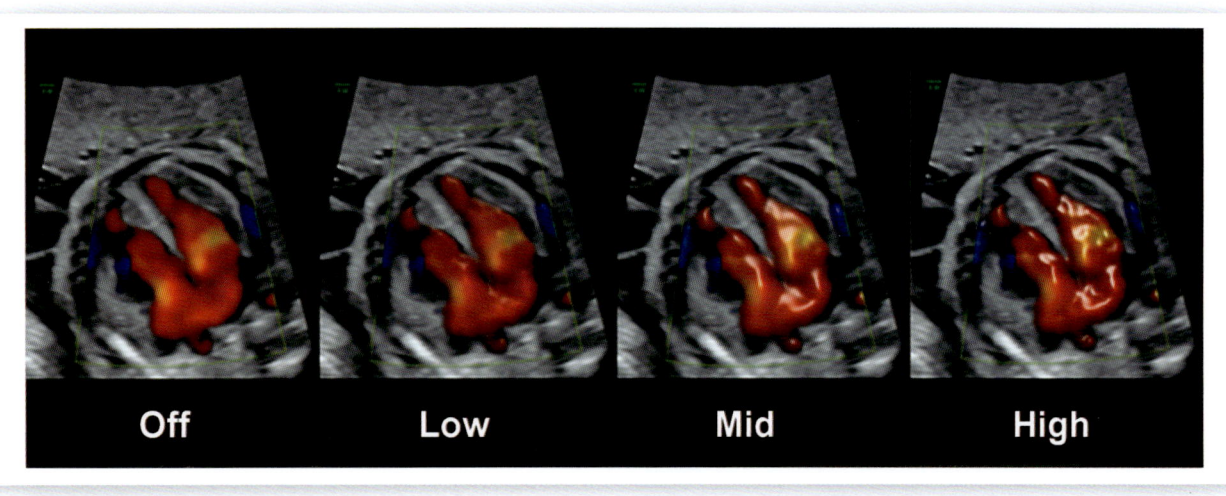

Fig. 88 **Fetal heart comparing differing degrees of surface rendering** *(Courtesy of GE using Radiantflow™)*

teristics of the reflecting surface and the wavelength(s) of the sound source, light also has different reflecting mechanisms based on the surface characteristics of the reflecting surface and the wavelengths of the light source.

Phong's approach subdivides a lighted 2D image into three sub-images, one comprised of the specular reflection, one based on the diffuse (scattering) component, and one based on the ambient lighting. When combined together, the composite image presents an image with a rendered surface that appears three-dimensional as shown in *Figure 87*.

32.2 2D Color Doppler Surface Rendering

Recently, ultrasound vendors have started using the Phong (and similar) rendering techniques to present color Doppler flow images. By applying the surface rendering technique, color images that normally appear flat and two-dimensional, now give the appearance of curvature and a simulated three-dimensionality. This 3D dimensional appearance comes from the appearance of light reflection from some surfaces, giving the perception of being raised, and the darkening hues of other surfaces, giving the appearance of being deeper set. The perception of this rendered flow sometimes facilitates appreciation of complex flow by the perceived increased dimension. Continuing the theme, each company refers to their technology with a different name such as LumiFlow™ or Radiantflow™. The images shown in *Figure 88* are examples of surface rendered flow techniques.

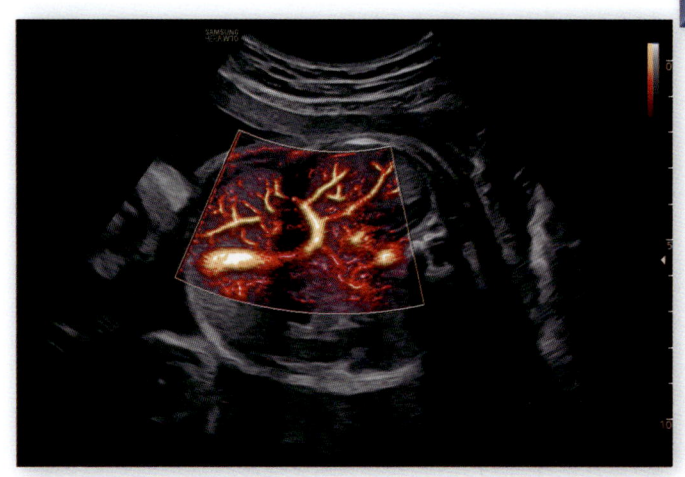

Fig. 89 **Surface rendered color of a transverse fetal abdomen demonstrating liver vasculature** *(Courtesy of Samsung: HERA W10 with MV-Flow™ and LumiFlow™)*

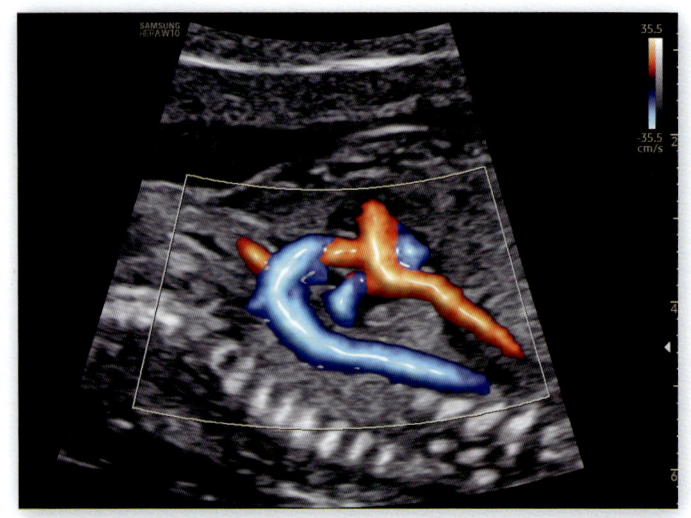

Fig. 90 **Surface rendered color Doppler image of the fetal aortic arch** *(Courtesy of Samsung: HERA W10 with LumiFlow™)*

32.3 3D Color Renderings

In addition to 2D Color Doppler surface rendering techniques, many companies are generating 3D color image renderings that make ultrasound images seem more like models than actual images. The following are a few examples of a lighting technique produced by GE called HD*live* Flow™ (not to be confused with HD-Flow™ which is the term they use for their directional power Doppler).

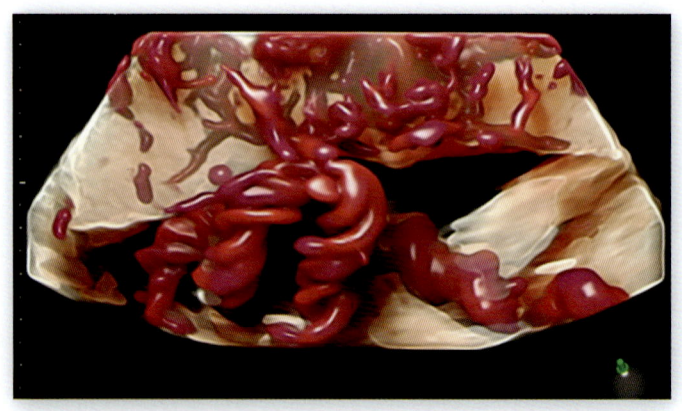

Fig. 91 **Umbilical cord placental insertion captured with HD*live* Flow™** *(Courtesy of GE)*

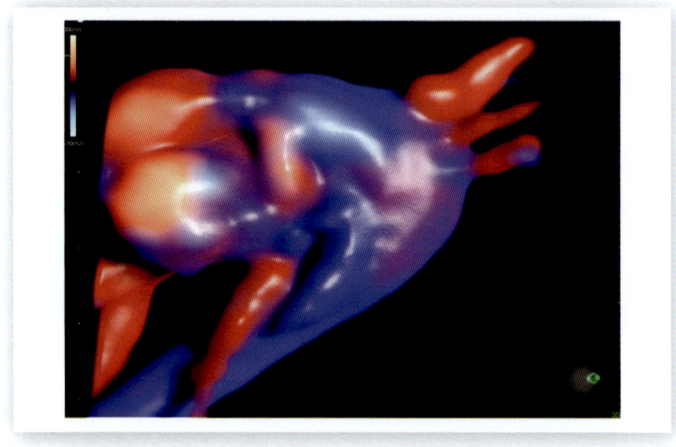

Fig. 92 **Placental fetal circulation with HD*live* Flow™** *(Courtesy of GE)*

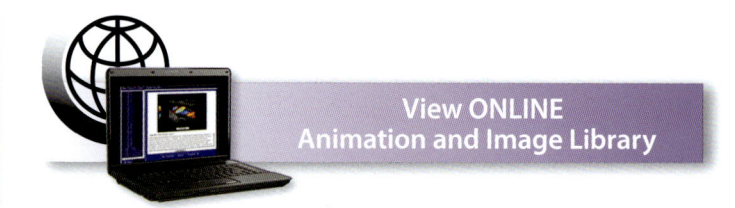

33. Slow Flow (Microvascular) Detection

33.1 Conventional Color Doppler and Wall Filters

The conventional high pass wall filters previously described discriminate solely based on frequency shift. One of the important associated lessons was that there are times when this type of wall filter can eliminate the very signal you need to detect. It is important to realize that the high pass wall filters used in both spectral and color Doppler are based on a central assumption: tissue will move more slowly than the blood and hence are separable based solely on the frequency of their Doppler shifts. In other words, to reduce the clutter from the Doppler blood signal, a high pass filter can be applied that passes (allows through) the higher frequency shifts of the blood signals and rejects the high amplitude lower frequency shifts of the tissue.

Problematically, there are times when the blood velocities are very low or when the tissue motion is excessively high, resulting in overlapping frequency shifts. This is especially true with low-flow vessels of the microvasculature. As a result, the application of the wall filters removes the low velocity signals we would like to detect or color flash artifact from the moving tissue becomes apparent. Of course, the next logical question is "why not simply reduce the wall filters so that the low frequency shift signals pass through?". The answer is quite simple: the signal from the small blood vessels is significantly lower in amplitude than the signal from the surrounding moving tissue (clutter). In fact, the blood signal is generally more than 30 dB weaker than the clutter signal, implying that the blood signal is completely undetected. The problem is very similar to trying to hear someone whisper when there is a jet engine running at full throttle. The blood signal is like the whisper, the clutter from the tissue is like the sound from the jet engine.

Figure 93 shows the effects of applying a standard wall filter. In (a), clutter (tissue) dominates and hence masks the blood signals. As seen in (b), after a standard wall filter has been applied, but the clutter and the low velocity blood signals are eliminated.

With standard color Doppler, there is another problem related to color wall filters. Specifically, we learned that to detect lower velocity flow with standard color Doppler, it is important to not only lower the color wall filters, but to also lower the color scales. The reason was explained that with conventional color Doppler, the wall filters change with the PRF (color scales). When the color scales are increased, the color wall filters also increase, resulting in an increase in the cutoff frequency of the color wall filter. The reason for this problem is very technical and has to do with how the wall filters have to be designed when there are so few samples (typically 16 or fewer, equivalent to the color packet size) per color line (see Level 3). In comparison, spectral Doppler generally has at least 64 samples per line, and correspondingly can have wall filters that operate independent of the spectral Doppler scales (PRF).

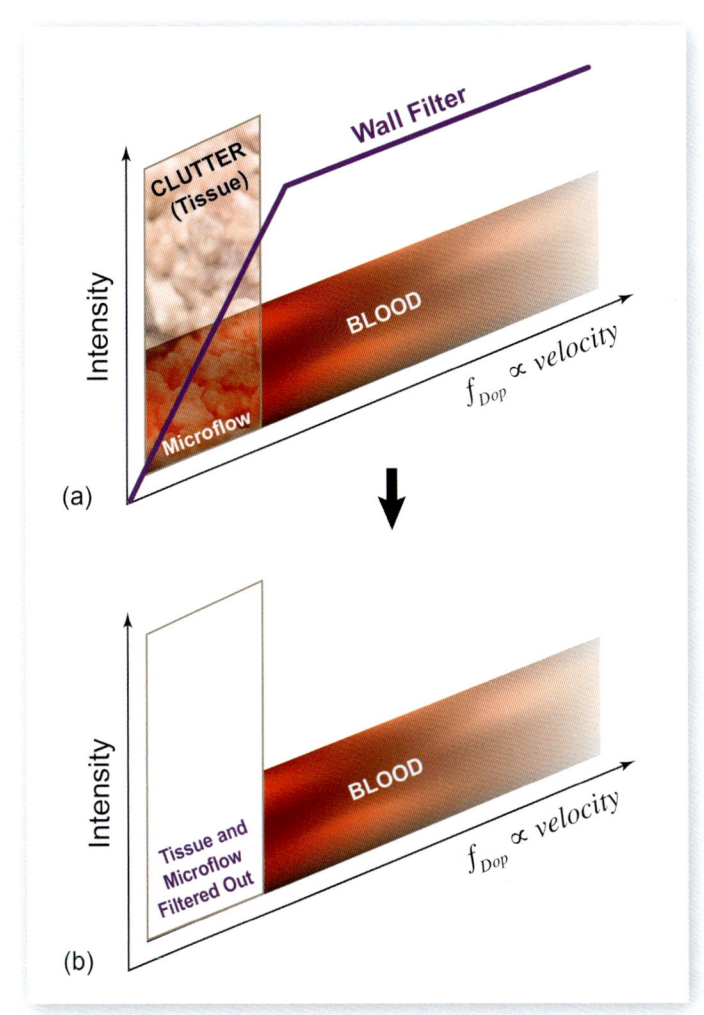

Fig. 93 **Before (a) and after (b) application of a standard wall filter which results in elimination of both clutter and low velocity blood flow signals**

Before we discuss solutions to these issues, it is valuable to discuss more in depth why detecting lower velocity flow is important. First, the ability to detect microvasculature is valuable for the detection of cancer. The term angiogenesis refers to the ability of the body to promote the growth of new blood vessels. Angiogenesis is necessary for growth and for repair such as in the healing of wounds. However, angiogenesis is also important in the growth of cancerous tumors. The ability to detect the microvasculature in tumors is very helpful in identifying cancer. Standard color Doppler, and even power Doppler, rarely have the ability to visualize the microflow associated with

angiogenesis. In many cases, contrast-enhanced ultrasound (CEUS) is needed in order to detect the vascularity of residual tumors post cancer treatment. The second reason is that ultrasound is now also being used for functional assessment, referred to as functional ultrasound, or simply fUltrasound. fUltrasound is currently being utilized in research with small animals to better understand brain function. fUltrasound is also beginning to see use intraoperatively and in neonates, in which the thick cranial bone does not present an impediment to signal strength.

33.2 Adaptive Spatiotemporal Wall Filtering

With the advent of ultrafast Doppler, an individual color line can now have the same PRF as spectral Doppler, implying that the wall filter can also be improved to match that of the spectral Doppler (the reason for which is explained in more detail in Level 3). This fact, in and of itself results in an improvement in color Doppler wall filtering performance. However, there have been even more important consequences that result from the increased frame rates. In recent years, new processing techniques have been created to increase the ability to detect low flow states, especially as exhibited in the microvasculature. To understand how these new filters function, we must refer back to foundational physics discussed in Chapter 3 and throughout the rest of the book.

Recall in Chapter 2 when we discussed the idea of phase and how in-phase signals tend to add constructively whereas partially out-of-phase signals add partially constructively. This same concept applies to the spatiotemporal coherence of signals. Spatiotemporal coherence refers to how similar the speckle pattern is from a moving reflector (or reflective region) over time. When there is a high spatiotemporal coherence, signals tend to add more constructively, whereas lower coherence results in only partial constructive interference.

Consider the difference between moving tissue and moving blood cells. Tissue movement can be the result of respiration, muscle activation, heart contraction, vessel response to pulse pressure, or even the movement of the transducer relative to the tissue. When tissue moves, it tends to return back to its prior location after a short duration of time. As tissue moves, its characteristic reflection changes very little, meaning that from frame to frame, the same (highly correlated) speckle pattern appears. This high level of coherence implies that tissue can be tracked as it moves based on statistical analysis of the speckle pattern (see speckle and speckle tracking: in Chapters 8 and Chapter 16). In comparison, as blood flows it does not return to its former position. As blood moves, the red blood cells change their arrangement over time with varying pulse pressure and vessel geometry, creating a varying aggregate, and hence a much less correlated speckle pattern. As a result, the speckle pattern of the tissue tends to be a relatively simple spatial shift over time whereas the reorganizing blood results in a varying speckle pattern. In other words, the tissue spatiotemporal pattern tends to be more coherent than the speckle pattern of the blood – and, by comparing frame to frame speckle patterns, the global motion of tissue can be distinguished from the more localized speckle patterns of flow.

Figure 94 compares spatiotemporal coherence of tissue with a blood speckle pattern. Notice that at each time interval there is very little change in the speckle pattern of the tissue in contrast with the more dramatically changing speckle pattern of the blood as a result of the changing distribution of red blood cells with time.

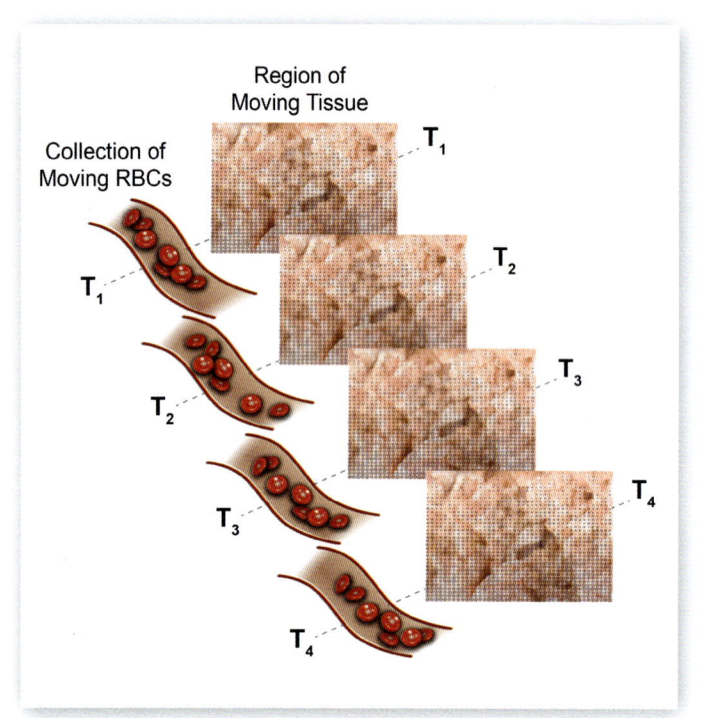

Fig. 94 **Comparison of spatiotemporal coherence of tissue vs. blood speckle pattern**

Wall filters designed to detect microflow use this difference in spatiotemporal coherence to distinguish blood signal from tissue signal so that the tissue signal can be filtered out, leaving only the low velocity blood signal. Furthermore, the tissue signals tend to be higher in amplitude and occur over larger spatial regions whereas the blood signals tend to be much lower in amplitude and much more localized, providing more distinguishing characteristics by which to separate low velocity blood signal from tissue movement. Once each part of the image is assessed for the spatiotemporal coherence, the blood signal can be mathematically "separated" from the tissue signal for filtering. Adaptive spatiotemporal wall filters can then be applied that reject signal on both spatiotemporal coherence and frequency shift. The result is a much more selective filter that allows for low velocity blood signals to be visualized, even in the presence of moving tissue.

As shown in *Figure 95*, there is a difference in the spatiotemporal coherence of the tissue and blood signals (a). By filtering along the spatiotemporal coherence axis instead of the Doppler shift axis, the tissue signals can be removed without removing the low velocity blood flow signals (b).

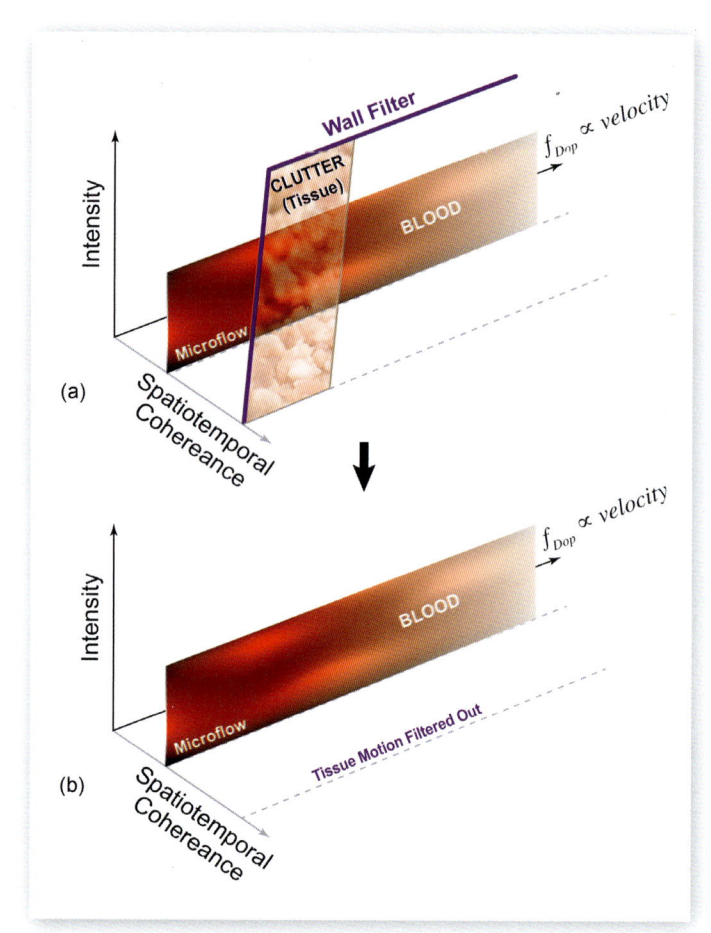

Fig. 95 **Before (a) and after (b) application of a spatiotemporal wall filter which differentiates between clutter signals and low velocity blood flow**

These adaptive spatiotemporal wall filters are usually used in conjunction with ultrafast power Doppler imaging. The ultrafast imaging provides the high number of samples necessary to create a sharper wall filter while power Doppler provides a technique which is less sensitive to angle than color Doppler. As discussed, the spatiotemporal wall filters allow for the discrimination of moving tissue, leaving the low velocity blood signal for display. Adaptive spatiotemporal filters are significantly more sensitive to detecting microflow with many studies showing a decreased need for contrast-enhanced ultrasound to detect post-treatment residual cancerous tumors. Compare the following images using color power Doppler with conventional wall filters and ultrafast power Doppler with spatiotemporal wall filtering.

The images in *Figure 96* are of an indeterminate thyroid nodule. Increased internal vascularity and ill-defined borders of a nodule may suggest an increased risk of malignancy. *Figure 96a* is a power Doppler image demonstrating a small feeder vessel entering the thyroid nodule. *Figure 96b* shows microvascular flow of the same thyroid nodule. Although power Doppler is very sensitive to detecting blood flow, notice how the adaptive spatiotemporal filtering allows for detection of even more flow within the surrounding thyroid tissue as well as enhanced vascularity within the thyroid nodule.

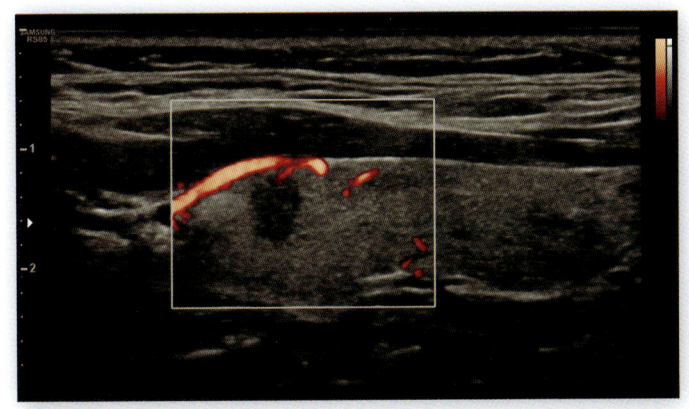

Fig. 96a **Power Doppler image of small feeder vessel entering a thyroid nodule**

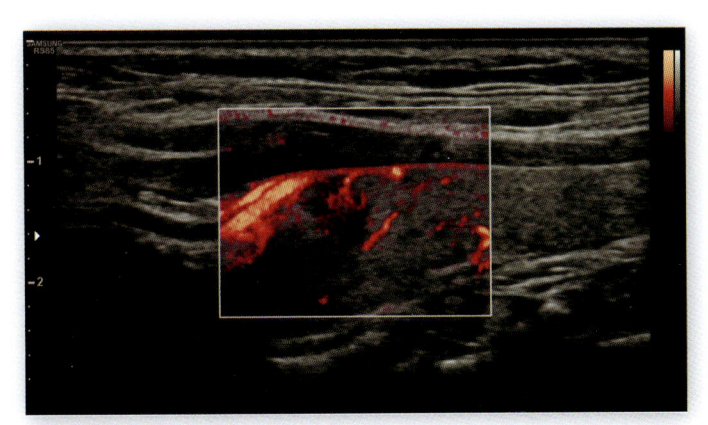

Fig. 96b **Microvascular flow of the same thyroid nodule with adaptive spatiotemporal filtering**

View ONLINE Animation and Image Library

As with most specific applications in ultrasound, each manufacturer creates their own marketing name for each function such as Supermicrovascular Imaging (SMI – Canon), MicroFlow Imaging (MFI – Philips), MV-Flow (Samsung), Superb Microvascular Imaging (SMI – Toshiba), Micro Vascular Imaging (MVI – GE), etc. The following examples show how sensitive these adaptive spatiotemporal wall filtering approaches are to detecting microvascular flow.

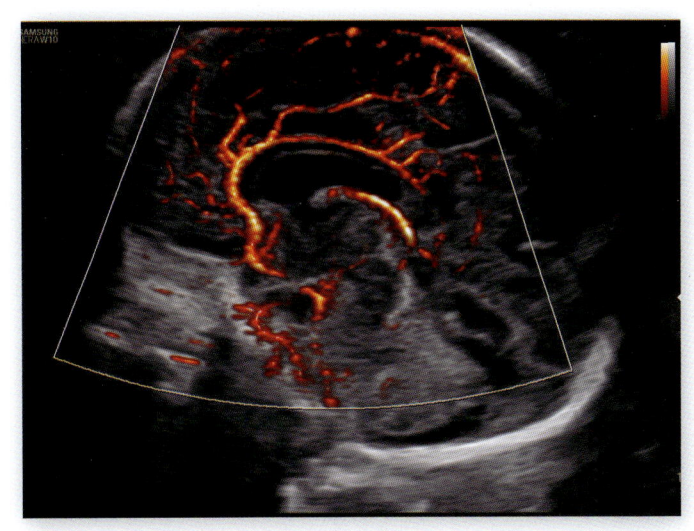

Fig. 97 **2nd trimester image of fetal brain vasculature using spatiotemporal filtering for detection of microvascular flow and color surface rendering** *(Courtesy of Samsung: Hera W10 (MV-Flow™ and LumiFlow™)*

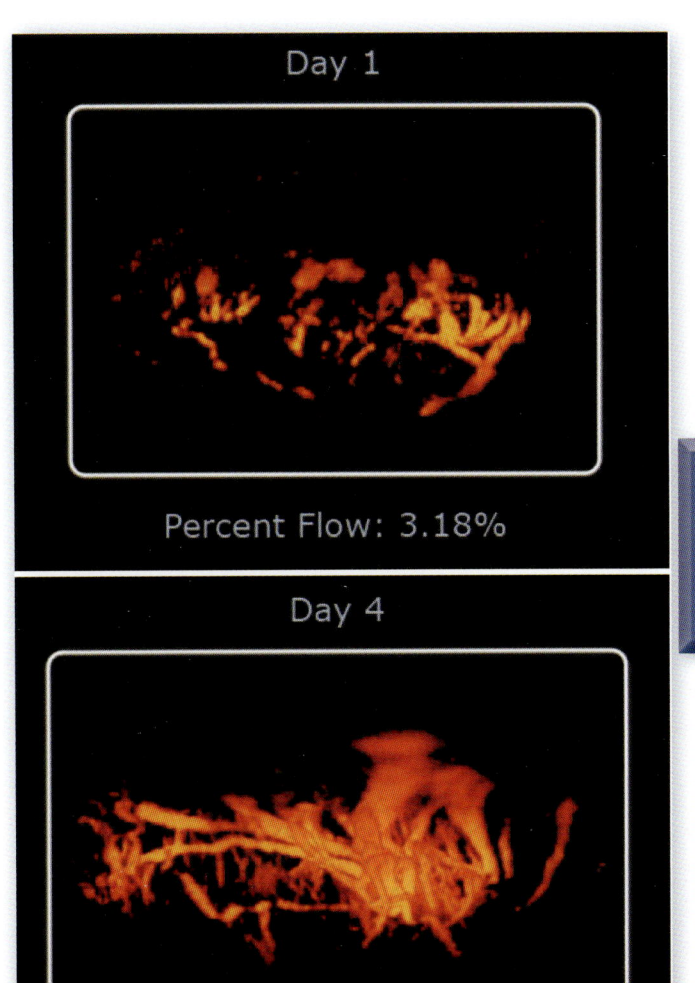

Fig. 98 **3D power Doppler image of a murine prostate tumor using spatiotemporal filtering, illustrating the rapid increase in vascularization in just three days** *(Courtesy of FUJIFILM VisualSonics, Inc.)*

LEVEL 3: Advanced Topics

34. Angle Correction Error (10 degree error)

The following table is analogous to *Table 4* in Section 19.5, except the error is now 10 degrees from the presumed angle. A 10 degree angular error is certainly possible and even quite probable given that angular alignment errors exist not only in the two viewed planes in the lateral and axial dimensions, but also in the non-visualized elevation plane.

Assumed Angle	Cosine		% Velocity		% Pressure	
Degrees	Actual Angle Smaller by 10°	Actual Angle Larger by 10°	Over-estimation	Under-estimation	Over-estimation	Under-estimation
0	0.98481	0.98481	-1.52%	-1.52%	-3.01%	-3.01%
10	1	0.93969	1.54%	-4.58%	3.11%	-8.95%
20	0.98481	0.86603	4.80%	-7.84%	9.83%	-15.06%
30	0.93969	0.76604	8.51%	-11.55%	17.74%	-21.76%
40	0.86603	0.64279	13.05%	-16.09%	27.81%	-29.59%
50	0.76604	0.5	19.17%	-22.21%	42.03%	-39.49%
60	0.64279	0.34202	28.56%	-31.60%	65.27%	-53.21%
70	0.5	0.17365	46.19%	-49.23%	113.72%	-74.22%
80	0.34202	0	96.96%	infinite	287.94%	infinite

Table 6 **Angle correction error (10 degree error)**

35. Understanding the Behavior of Color Wall Filters

35.1 Digital Filtering

Predicting the behavior of the conventional wall filters in color Doppler is much more difficult than predicting the behavior of the wall filters for spectral Doppler. Although the concept of the wall filters is the same, the electronic implementation is very different. In contrast to spectral Doppler, color Doppler wall filters are designed as pure digital filters. Usually these filters take on the form of an infinite impulse response (IIR) filter. Since the number of samples used in the filter must be small (usually around eight, corresponding to the color packet size), the filters have a very gradual roll-off. As a result, to achieve enough attenuation of the large clutter signals at the lower frequencies, the wall filters must be designed to begin attenuating at much higher frequencies than the wall filters for spectral Doppler. The significance of this fact is that the color wall filters, although designed to perform a similar function to the wall filters of spectral Doppler, behave very differently. Whereas, a spectral Doppler wall filter has a sharp corner frequency at a relatively low frequency with very steep attenuation ("roll-off"), a color wall has a much higher "corner" frequency and tends to gradually roll-off. This difference is graphically depicted in the *Figure 99*.

35.2 Comparing Spectral Doppler Wall Filters with the Color Wall Filter

The following graph depicts the differences between a bank of selectable spectral Doppler wall filters and the color Doppler wall filter which results for a specific PRF. For spectral Doppler, the wall filters can be set independent of the PRF, whereas for color Doppler, the wall filters are automatically adjusted by changing the PRF.

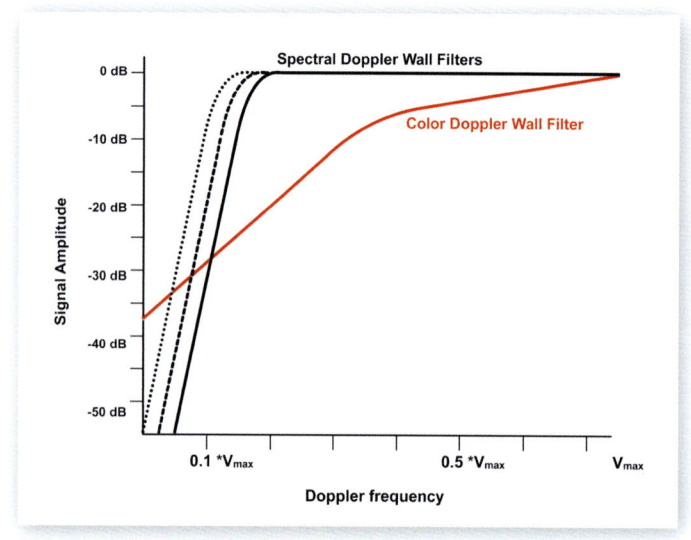

Fig. 99 **Spectral Doppler vs. Color Doppler wall filter**

The wall filters for spectral Doppler attenuate at a much faster rate ("roll-off") than the wall filters for color Doppler. The wall filter for color begins attenuating at a much higher frequency than the spectral Doppler wall filters. This higher "corner" frequency is needed for the color wall filter to compensate for the much slower roll-off. Since the attenuation rate is so much slower with the color wall filters, the corner frequency must be set higher to try to achieve adequate attenuation of the large clutter signals at the lower frequency shift ranges. As a result, color Doppler signals at lower percentages of V_{max} may or may not be displayed – depending on their signal strength. This point will be illustrated in later graphs (*Figures 102* and *103*).

35.3 Color Wall Filters and Nyquist
The following graph depicts the behavior of the color wall filters for two different Nyquist settings. The blue curve and blue labels on the x-axis represent the wall filters for a Nyquist limit half of that for the red curve and red labels on the x-axis.

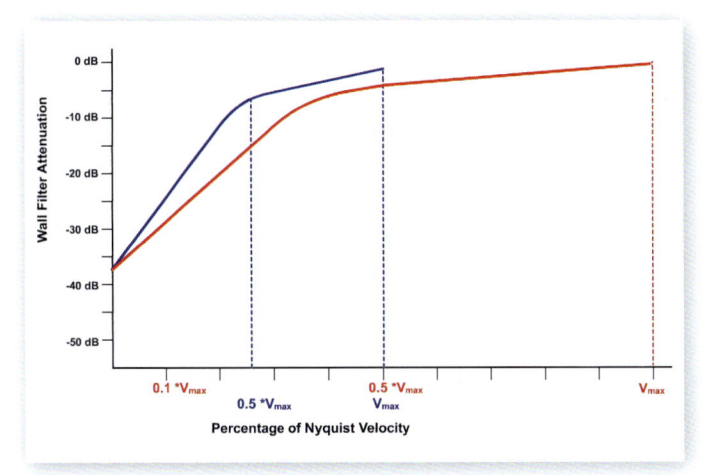

Fig. 100 **Color Doppler wall filters for two different Nyquist settings**

As the maximum detectable velocity is reduced (by reducing the PRF), the effective corner frequency of the wall filter is also reduced. A signal with a frequency shift at the second tick mark on the x-axis is attenuated very differently by the red curve (lower wall filter setting) than the blue curve (higher wall filter setting).

35.4 Effect of Signal Strength on Color Wall Filtering
It already has been shown how the wall filter affects the signal for spectral Doppler. For spectral Doppler, the wall filters are very discriminating, attenuating very rapidly below the corner frequency and passing, virtually unchanged, signals above the corner frequency. In comparison, the wall filters for color Doppler are much less discriminating. The following graph depicts the effect that the same wall filter has on two signals of different amplitudes (signal strength). Note that in both cases (the stronger signal indicated in red and the weaker signal indicated in blue), the flow conditions are identical, implying that the results ideally would be the same.

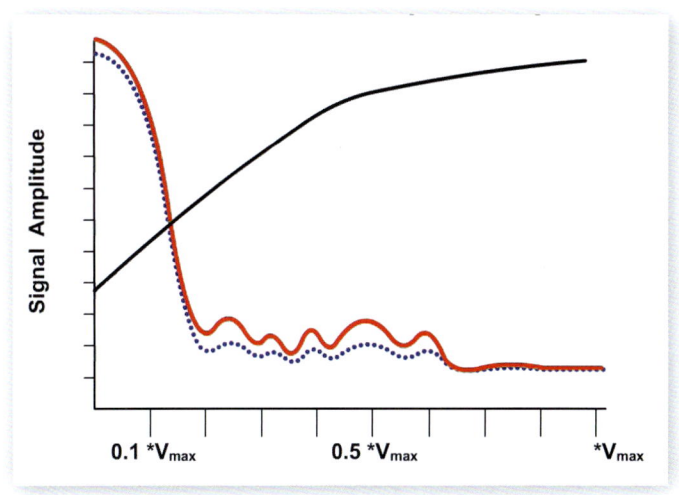

Fig. 101 **Effect of wall filters on strong and weak signals**

Again, the red solid-line signal represents a stronger signal than the blue dotted-line signal, but for the identical flow situation. A weaker signal could result from having to image deeper (larger patient), use a higher frequency transducer, use a less efficient transducer, or use of a lower transmit power.

Figure 102 depicts the same two signals after attenuation by the wall filter and some applied amplification. Using the given color bar, the resulting flows are then depicted in *Figure 103*. Since these two signals are from identical hemodynamic situations, the resulting color image, ideally, would be the same.

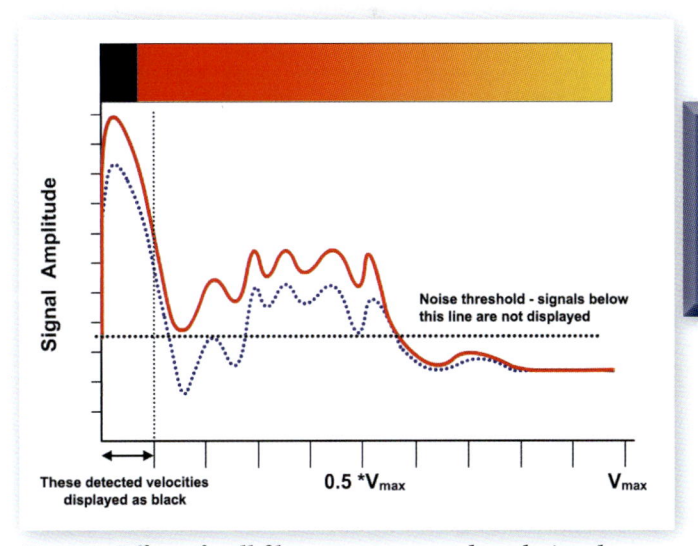

Fig. 102 **Effect of wall filters on strong and weak signals**

From this graph it is clear that the lower velocity flow of the blue dotted-line signal (just beyond the black band of the color bar) was attenuated so that the resulting signal was too weak to be displayed (below the visible threshold). In comparison, the same range of frequencies for the red solid-line signal is still above the visible threshold, and hence, is displayed.

Imagine that the signal in question represents a flow with a velocity gradient from the center of the flow to the outside edge, as commonly occurs. In this case we will depict this flow as a regurgitant jet, but any flow situation can be utilized. Since the lower velocities will be found at the outer bounds of the regurgitant jet, the result of wall filtering a weaker signal will be a smaller perceived jet area. This decrease in area is shown pictorially in the figure below:

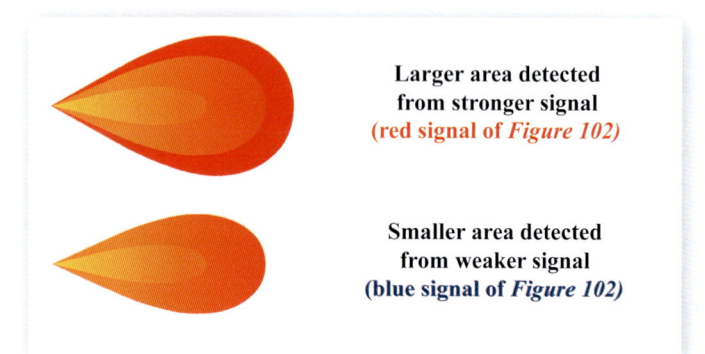

Fig. 103 **Perceived jet size and signal strength**

If we take this effect to its logical conclusion, it is clear that poor signal-to-noise can play a major role in affecting perceived color. As the signal-to-noise ratio decreases, the detected region of color decreases non-linearly. If the signal strength becomes weak enough, a color jet can be significantly underestimated or even not detected. The following figure demonstrates how signal-to-noise can affect perceived jet size.

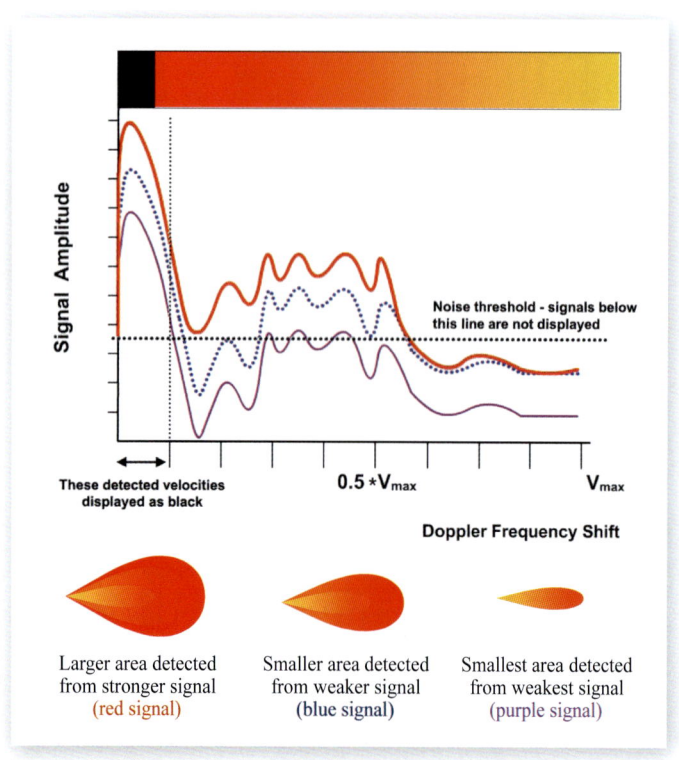

Fig. 104 **Effect of signal strength on color jet size**

As a result, we can see that there is a complex interaction between Nyquist, the color wall filter settings, the signal-to-noise and perception of color. The size of a color jet can vary considerably with any changes in an entire host of parameters. If the wall filters are set very low, then low velocity-entrained flow will inflate the perceived jet size. If the sensitivity is too low, then the perceived jet size will be smaller than "reality." The thresholding behavior of color Doppler does not serve well as a low variance, high repeatability measurement technique. Therefore, extreme caution must be taken when color measurements are made for a "numerical" assessment of severity.

CHECKPOINT: Exam Tip

Conventional color wall filters are often misunderstood. The wall filters are set as a percentage of the color scales (Nyquist setting). Increasing the color scales increases the color wall filters, therefore the color scales must be set low when trying to detect low-velocity flow in conventional color Doppler.

36. B-Flow

B-flow is a technique which directly presents the reflections from blood in real time simultaneously with echoes from tissue within a B-mode image. Generally, blood pools and vessel lumens appear dark because of the extremely low echogenicity of blood in comparison to tissue (with the exception of Rouleaux formation). As discussed in Chapter 6, with 2D images, low-level signals are mapped to black with increasing signal strength appearing as different shades of gray, and very high amplitude signals appearing bright white. In general, reflected blood signal intensities are approximately 30 dB weaker than the signal intensities from tissue (as shown in *Figure 1* of Chapter 10). In order to portray the very low-level blood reflections as visible signals, there are two major changes required relative to the conventional approaches for 2D imaging: a method for increasing blood signal strength, and a compression technique to allow for visualization of both tissue and blood amplitudes simultaneously.

36.1 Increasing Blood Signal Strength

The most obvious method to increase the blood signal strength is simply to increase the transmit power. However, increasing the transmit power is not feasible because of power limits and the risk of bioeffects (see Chapter 9). In order to increase blood signal strength, Doppler techniques increase the signal-to-noise of blood by both increasing the length of the transmit pulse and increasing signal gain through averaging by using multiple pulses within the packet size (color) or FFT (spectral Doppler). The problem with increasing the transmit pulse length is a degradation in axial resolution, and the problem with using multiple samples is decreased temporal resolution. In order to increase the blood signal-to-noise adequately, a different approach is required. B-flow uses coded excitation as a means of increasing the signal strength while simultaneously preserving good axial resolution. Coded excitation is discussed in Chapter 10, Section 15.1, in more detail, but the basic idea is that a longer coded transmit pulse is used to increase the energy in the signal, and then decoded through the use of a matched filter to produce a short effective received pulse for good axial resolution. By this approach, the blood signal can be increased adequately so as to appear above the noise floor of the electronics, and hence displayed.

36.2 B-Flow Display

The second requirement to displaying low-level blood reflections as visible signals is the ability to present both tissue and blood signal simultaneously. This display requires a special compression mapping technique which keeps the tissue signals from saturating (being displayed as too white) while simultaneously increasing the grayscale output of the blood signals. There are generally three different display formats, tissue and flow (*Figure 105*), blood flow only by tissue subtraction (*Figure 106*), and colorized flow (*Figure 107*). As discussed in Chapter 6, because of the limited instantaneous grayscale dynamic range of the human eye, color maps are a means of extending the range.

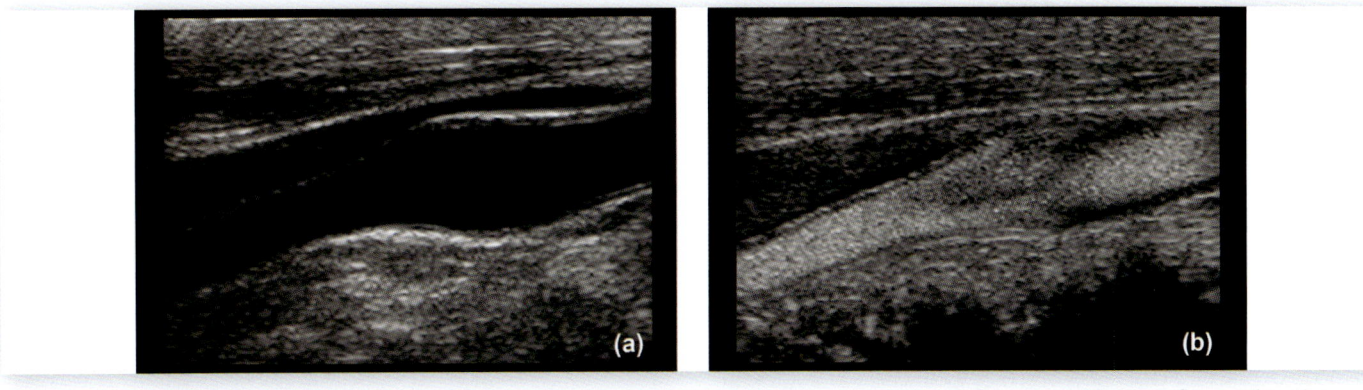

Fig. 105 **Conventional 2D image of a carotid bulb and internal carotid artery (a) compared to B-flow image showing flow within the carotid bulb and internal carotid artery (b)**

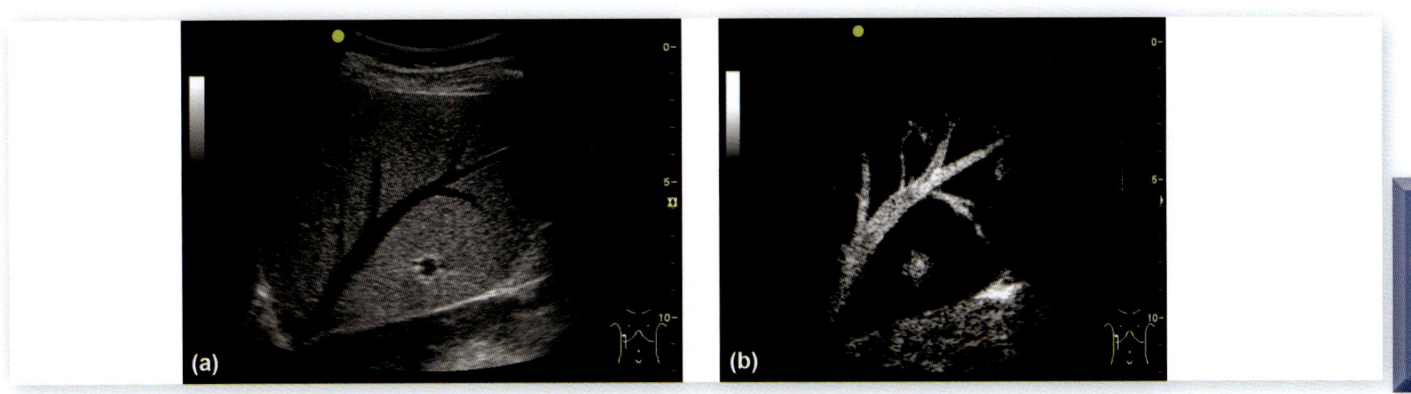

Fig. 106 **Conventional 2D image of the liver and hepatic veins (a) compared to B-flow image with tissue suppression showing flow within the hepatic veins (b); notice the resulting image looks similar to an angiogram** *(Courtesy of GE)*

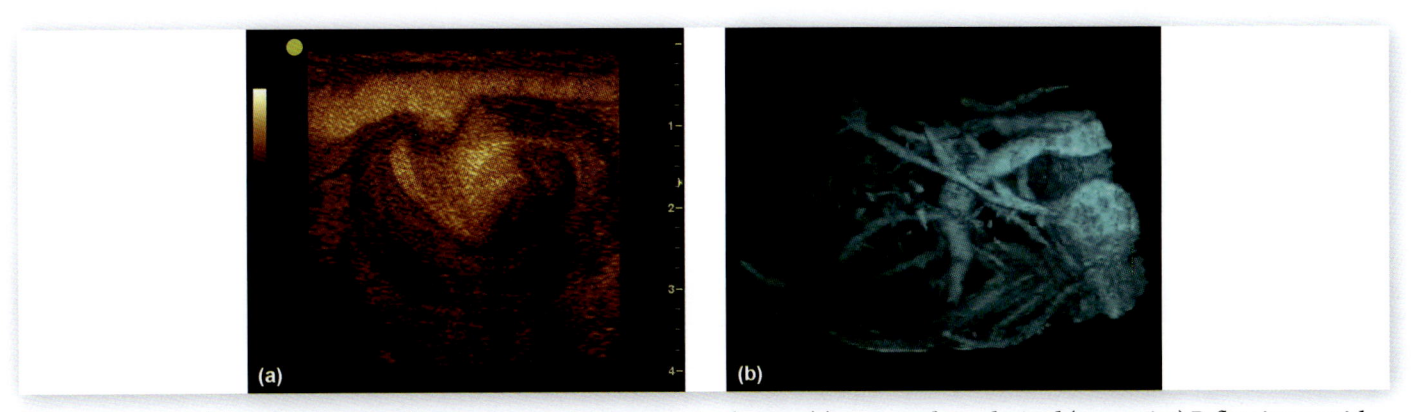

Fig. 107 **Colorized (sepia-tint) B-flow image of a pseudoaneurysm in the arm (a) compared to colorized (green-tint) B-flow image with tissue suppression illustrating liver vasculature (b)** *(Courtesy of GE)*

In addition to standard B-flow, which presents flow as grayscale, there is B-flow color mode. This mode is very similar to directional power Doppler (angio) in that flow direction is detected and the flow is presented using a directional color map. Like directional power Doppler, B-flow color does not display the flow velocity and does not suffer from aliasing.

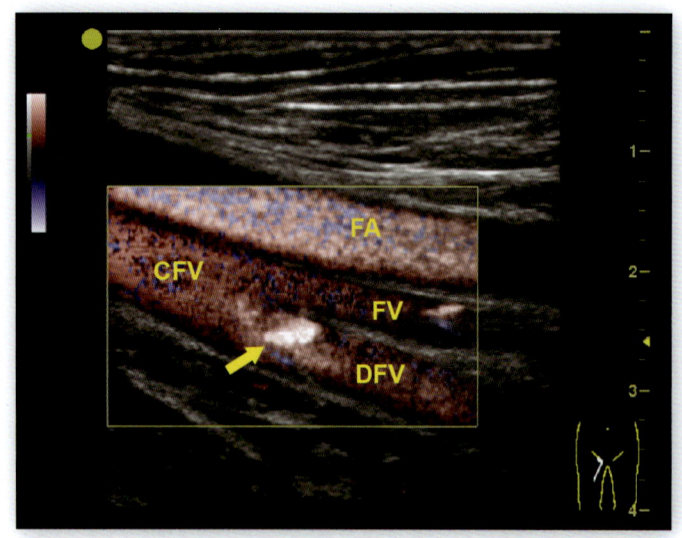

Fig. 108 B-flow color mode image of the common femoral vein (CFV) branching into the femoral vein (FV) and deep femoral vein (DFV); note the echogenic valve cusp (arrow) at the origin of the DFV (another valve cusp is present distal to the FV origin); the femoral artery (FA) is visualized anterior to the venous system

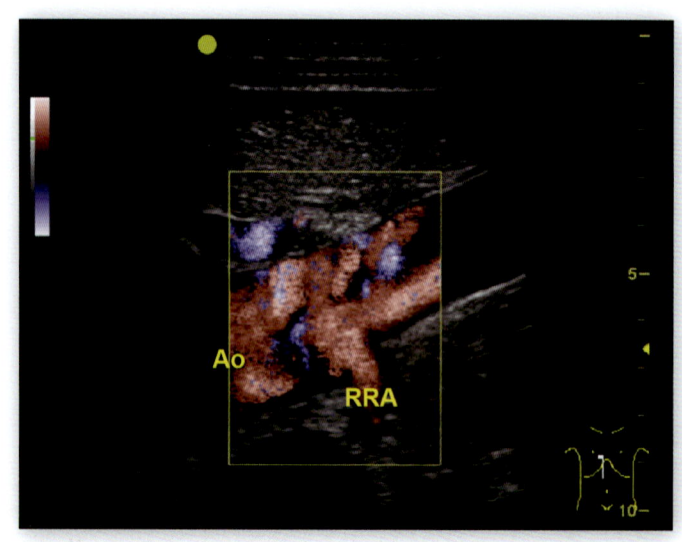

Fig. 109 B-flow color mode image of the abdominal aorta (Ao); the vessel branching off the Ao is the right renal artery (RRA)

Advantages of B-Flow

Recall that conventional color Doppler is created separately from the 2D image and then overlaid onto the 2D image. The process of overlaying images created using different techniques and with different resolutions results in many potential issues. The limitations associated with color Doppler which make B-flow advantageous at times are as follows:

- Color dropout related to Doppler angles close to 90°
- Aliasing, especially with higher velocity flow and at deeper depths
- Color blossoming artifact (color bleeds over tissue, vessel walls, soft plaque, intimal wall thickening, etc.)
- Poor temporal resolution (for sequential color Doppler)
- Inability to display very low-velocity flow (unless spatiotemporal filtering is being used)

Because B-flow is based purely on the reflected signal and is not a Doppler technique, B-flow does not suffer from color dropout associated with flow angle nor the aliasing artifact. Furthermore, since the flow is generated simultaneously with the tissue image, the overlay issues do not exist. With B-flow, the temporal resolution is the same as that of the 2D image, and the axial resolution is the same such that the flow presentation does not artifactually mask tissue signals.

37. Vector Flow (V Flow) Imaging

37.1 Representing Flow as Vectors

As we have seen, interpreting flow direction with color Doppler requires understanding of the underlying color Doppler principles. Further, the actual velocity (magnitude) of the flow is not presented, but rather, only regional mean velocities. Because of the highly limited temporal resolution, short duration changes in flow dynamics are generally not appreciated. As such, color Doppler tends to present a limited perspective on intricate, regional flow patterns.

In physics, flow is often depicted using vectors, a mathematical tool used to represent both magnitude and direction of movement. By representing flow as vectors, the limitations just discussed can be removed and complex changes in flow, both in terms of magnitude and direction can be appreciated regionally. By taking advantage of the significantly higher frame rates offered by using diverging or plane wave transmission (ultrafast imaging), intricate temporal changes can also be appreciated.

Vector flow imaging is produced by a similar process as ultrafast Doppler imaging. A series of plane waves are transmitted, each of which produces data for the entire scan region. As discussed many times previously, each of the plane waves is transmitted at a different angle and then retrospective beamforming is performed for each angled data set to focus the returning data set pixel-by-pixel. Adaptive spatiotemporal filtering is applied to distinguish regions of blood flow from regions of tissue. An autocorrelation technique is then used looking from frame to frame to determine blood direction and velocity over the entire region of blood flow (see *Figure 110*). Unlike Doppler techniques, the detection of flow is not angle dependent.

In *Figure 110*, an unspecified number of plane waves (N) are transmitted to track flow velocity in the entire flow region of a blood vessel (in this example, a carotid bifurcation). The resulting arrow lengths and color represent flow velocity, with red indicating a high velocity and green indicating a low velocity. The arrow direction represents the flow direction.

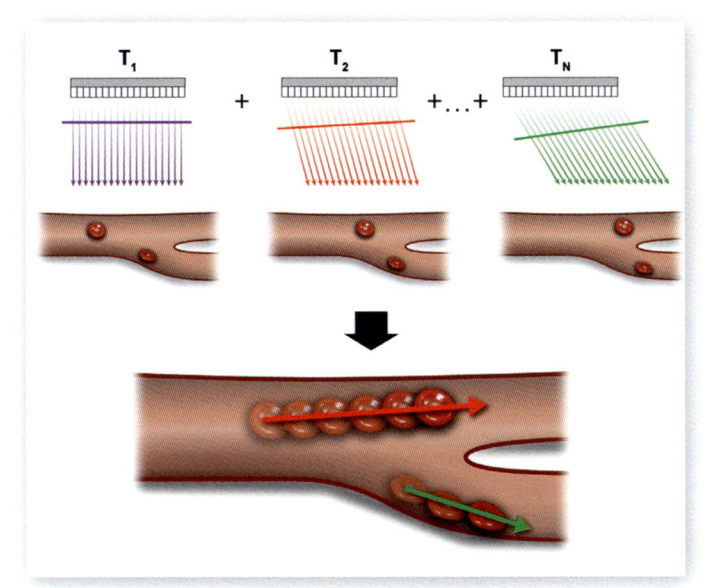

Fig. 110 **Vector flow imaging with N tilted plane waves transmitted to track flow velocity in the entire flow region and arrow lengths/color representing flow velocity and direction**

37.2 Image Interpretation

Because the frame rates are so high, typically 400 to 1200 frames per second, the use model is to acquire a cine loop of about 1.5 seconds in duration and then to review the images at a slower frame rate of about 30 frames per second (playback speed is adjustable). For the following V Flow images, the vectors are both color and length encoded. Lower velocity flow is presented as shorter arrows and dark and light blue. As the velocity increases, the arrow length increases and the color transitions to green, then yellow, then orange, with the highest velocities encoded as red.

Figure 111 offers a direct comparison of color Doppler (a) to vector flow imaging (b). This example, also of a carotid bifurcation, shows the magnitude of the velocity is encoded both by the arrow length and color.

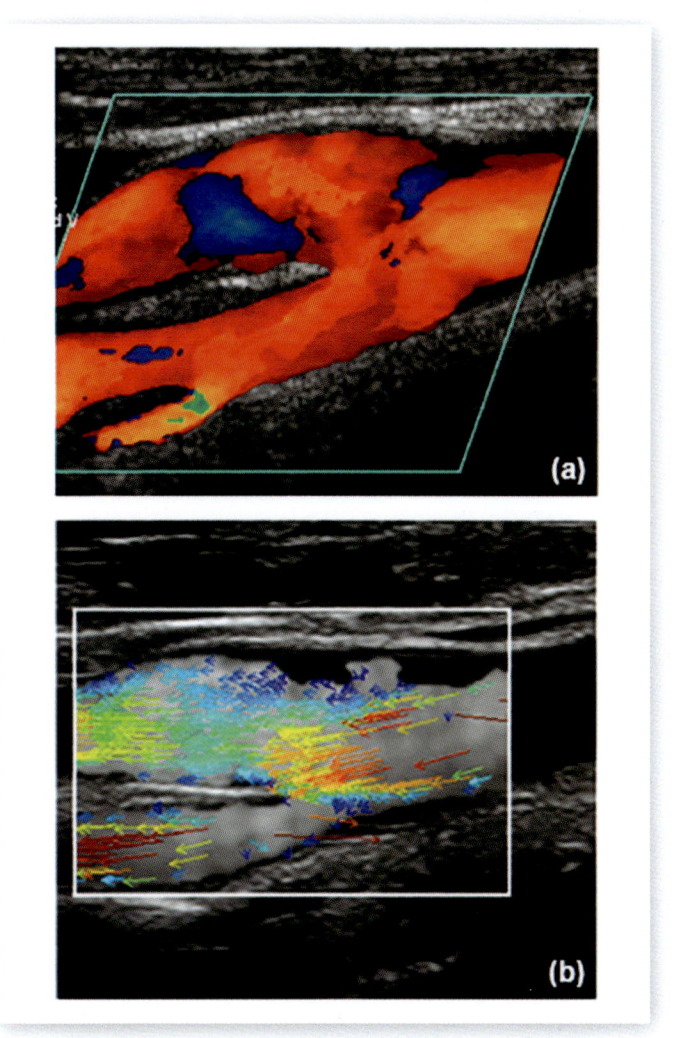

Fig. 111 **Comparison of color Doppler (a) with vector flow imaging (b) of a carotid bifurcation** *(Courtesy of Mindray)*

The following vector flow images show a common carotid artery (CCA) during different phases of the cardiac cycle (diastole and systole, respectively). Note there is a region of plaque which causes a disturbed area of flow which is more evident in systole (*Figure 112b*).

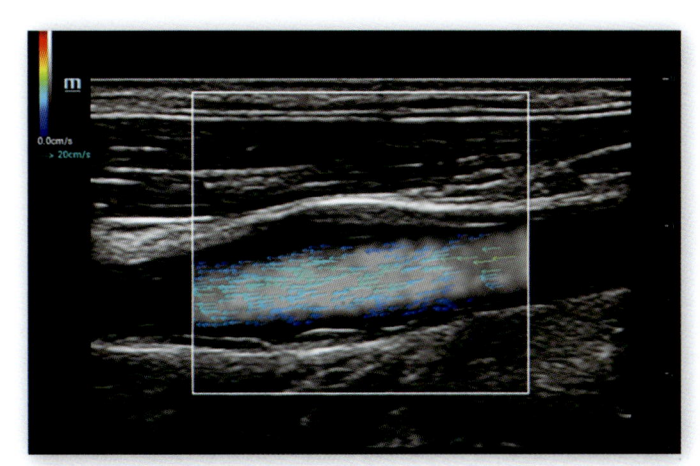

Fig. 112a **Vector flow imaging of a CCA in diastole**

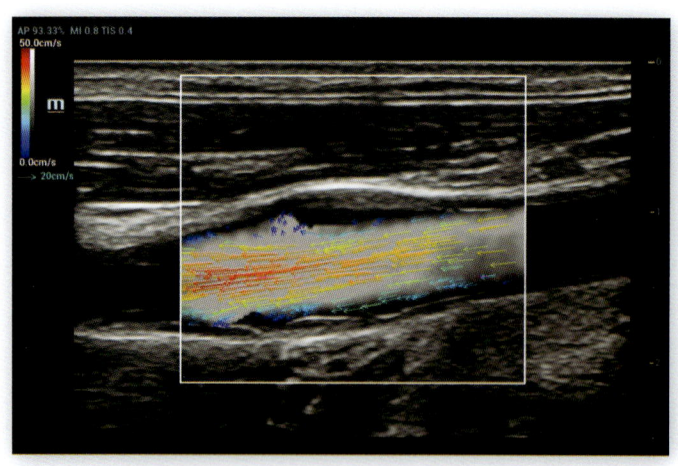

Fig. 112b Vector flow imaging of a CCA in systole; note there is a region of plaque which causes a disturbed area of flow visualized in systole (more easily visualized in the associated online video)

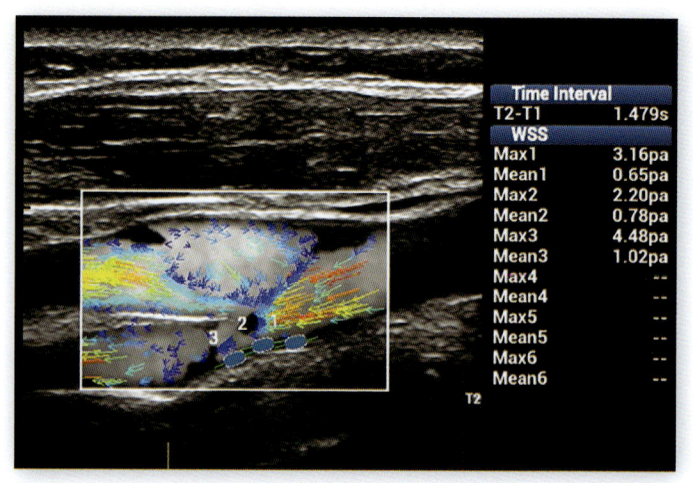

Fig. 113 Wall shear stress (WSS) measurements

View ONLINE Animation and Image Library

37.3 Calculating Wall Shear Stress (WSS)

Besides better visualization of flow dynamics, ultrasound vector flow imaging is also useful for calculating wall shear stress. Wall shear stress (WSS) is the result of the frictional force exerted parallel to the vessel wall as a result of the blood viscosity. In addition to other factors, it is currently theorized that low and oscillatory wall shear stress is one of the key factors for the development of atherosclerosis through stimulation of the inflammatory response. The wall shear stress is directly related to the blood viscosity and the change in velocity relative to the distance away from the wall surface (for a more detailed treatment of the physics of stress, see Chapter 15).

Although wall shear stress can be assessed using MRI and multi-gated PW Doppler, both techniques are limited. Not surprisingly, the PW approach is hampered by how conventional wall filters function and the resulting inability to accurately detect low-velocity flows in the vicinity of highly pulsatile vessel walls. Vector flow imaging overcomes this limitation by using adaptive spatiotemporal wall filters. Unlike multi-gated PW which assumes laminar flow profiles, vector flow imaging is able to assess shear wall stress in non-laminar conditions. Additionally, because of the ability to image an entire region at once, the wall shear stress can be calculated at a series of locations contemporaneously.

Figure 113 shows a vector flow image with wall shear stress measurements. Each numbered blue dot (1, 2, and 3 in this case) represents a region where WSS was assessed. Normal maximum values are between 1 and 7 Pascals, with values of -0.4 to 0.4 Pa indicative of a high risk of atherosclerosis.

38. Comparing Flow Detection Techniques

Table 7 (on the next page) gives a detailed comparison of various flow techniques including a summary of benefits, limitations, and what each mode displays. There is clinical value in knowing and understanding the trade-offs between these various modes as there will certainly be times when using a specific mode for assessing flow will make the difference as to whether or not clinical information is successfully acquired. Note that some applications for techniques such as V Flow are still being discovered.

39. Conceptual Questions

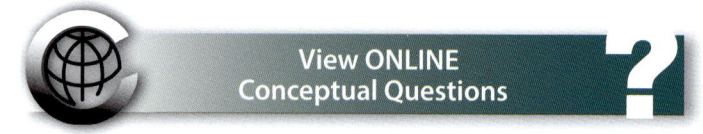

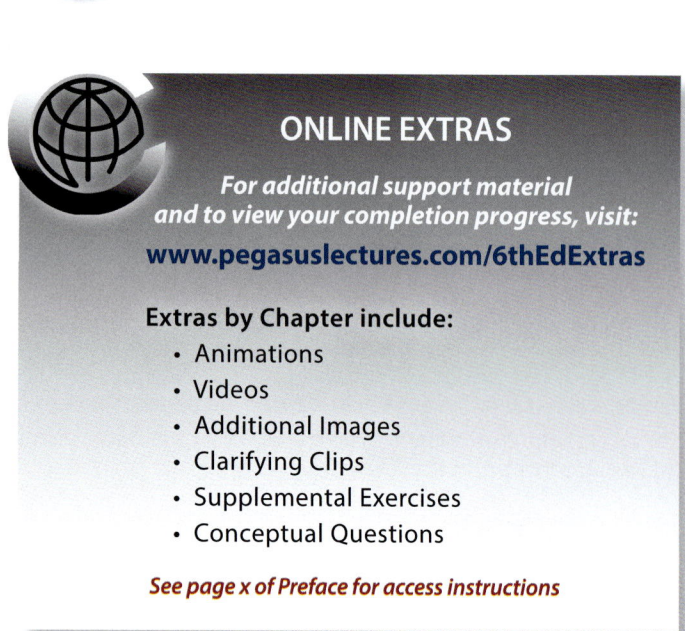

View ONLINE Conceptual Questions

ONLINE EXTRAS

For additional support material and to view your completion progress, visit:
www.pegasuslectures.com/6thEdExtras

Extras by Chapter include:
- Animations
- Videos
- Additional Images
- Clarifying Clips
- Supplemental Exercises
- Conceptual Questions

See page x of Preface for access instructions

CATEGORY	MODE	DISPLAYED	BENEFITS	LIMITATIONS
Waveform	Zero-Crossing	An analog waveform representative of the root mean squared velocity vs. time	Inexpensive	Does not yield information related to peak velocity or the range of velocities; is susceptible to noise and is angle dependent
Spectral Doppler	CW	Distribution of velocity vs. time (spectrum) captured from flow along entire Doppler line	Virtually unlimited maximum detectable velocity so no true aliasing	No inherent range specificity; is angle dependent
	PW	Distribution of velocity vs. time (spectrum) from a Doppler sample volume (and unwanted multiples of the sample volume depth)	Good range specificity (unlike CW) but range ambiguity artifact possible	Has a maximum detectable velocity related to Doppler depth and transmit frequency which when exceeded results in aliasing; has some range ambiguity artifact; is angle dependent
	HPRF	Distribution of velocity vs. time (spectrum) from a Doppler sample volume and from displayed multi-gates	Higher detectable velocities than PW (but still can have aliasing)	More frequent range ambiguity than PW, less than CW; is angle dependent
	Ultrafast PW	One or more spectrums of velocity vs. time	Can look at spectral velocity waveforms from multiple locations at the same time; can change gate location(s), size, gain, compression settings, and angle correction	Currently, ultrafast is not real time: an ultrafast clip is stored and then reviewed in "slow time"; no corresponding audio signal; is angle dependent
B-Flow	Coded Excitation 2D	Reflection from blood as well as tissue (also can display tissue suppressed B-flow to show only blood signals)	Since B-flow is not a Doppler technique it is not prone to dropout with angle, aliasing, or color blossoming; has same frame rate as 2D imaging	Qualitative method only
V Flow	Ultrafast Imaging with Autocorrelation	Blood flow velocity and direction as a vector	High frame rates allow for detection of small hemodynamic changes and the ability to calculate wall shear stress; still in research phase for applications	Still learning applications of V Flow
2D Color Doppler	Sequential Color Doppler	Color-encoded mean velocity within area of color box	Good survey tool for quick assessment of global hemodynamic conditions	Very poor temporal resolution; suffers from angle dependence, sensitivity issues (at greater depths), and blossoming artifact
	Power (Angio)	Color-encoded presence of flow based partly on signal strength (power)	More sensitive to low flow than conventional Doppler; less angle dependent than other Doppler techniques	More susceptible to motion and flash artifact than conventional color Doppler; cannot determine flow direction
	Directional Power (Angio)	Same as power (angio) but uses phase information to also encode directionality	Same benefits as power (angio) but with the ability to determine direction	Same limitations as power (angio) but with the ability to determine direction
	Ultrafast Color Doppler	Color-encoded mean velocity within area of color box	High frame rates (improved temporal resolution) and color is synchronous to spectral Doppler; can be more sensitive than sequential color Doppler by increasing angles averaged	Must review in "slow time" by scrolling through frames of stored clip; is angle dependent
	Spatiotemporal Filtered	Ultrafast color but with special wall filtering to separate slow flow signals from tissue clutter	Ability to display very low-velocity flow as occurs in microvasculature and angiogenesis	Requires high frame rates; is angle dependent

Table 7 **Comparison of various flow detection techniques**

✗ COMMON MISCONCEPTION: Doppler

MISCONCEPTION: *The specified angle must be the actual Doppler angle.*

Explanation:
For most vessels, it is anatomically impossible to obtain a 0° or 180° angle which is why angle correction is employed. When performing Doppler, the Doppler angle used for angle correction and specified on the screen is the angle formed by the Doppler steering line and the direction indicated by the flow indicator set by the user (generally used for non-cardiac applications). If the user does not correctly align the flow indicator to the flow direction, the specified Doppler angle will not be the true angle at which the Doppler shift is actually detected by the system. In cardiac applications, it is generally assumed that the user has aligned the Doppler steering with the flow so that the angle is either 0° or 180°, resulting in 100% of the Doppler shift being detected, and hence no need for angle correction. Of course, just as with angle correction in non-cardiac cases, if the Doppler line is not correctly aligned to flow, the assumed angle of 0° or 180° will not be correct, thereby introducing error.

✗ COMMON MISCONCEPTION: Doppler

MISCONCEPTION: *The Doppler angle is also called the incident angle.*

Explanation:
The angle of incidence is not measured the same way as the Doppler angle (also referred to as the Doppler insonification angle). The angle of incidence is measured between the beam direction and the line normal to an interface. When referring to images, the incident angle is referenced. The Doppler angle is measured between the flow direction and the Doppler beam direction. When referring to a Doppler based technique, it is the Doppler angle, not the incident angle which matters.

✗ COMMON MISCONCEPTION: Doppler

MISCONCEPTION: *The Doppler shift is linear with the Doppler angle.*

Explanation:
The Doppler equation expresses that the Doppler shift is linear with the cosine of the Doppler angle, not with the Doppler angle. Since the cosine, is a very non-linear function, the Doppler shift is very non-linear with the Doppler angle. For this reason, small errors in angular alignment relative to 0° result in much smaller measurement error than the same small angular error relative to 40°, which in turn is much smaller than what occurs relative to 70°, etc.

✗ COMMON MISCONCEPTION: Doppler

MISCONCEPTION: *Doppler displays flow.*

Explanation:
Flow is a volumetric term, which has units of volume per time. Doppler does not directly measure or display flow. Doppler directly displays velocity over time. From the Doppler information it is possible to calculate flow but additional information is required to perform the calculation. The calculation of flow is explained in Chapter 12: Flow Dynamics, by discussing the volumetric flow equation.

✗ COMMON MISCONCEPTION: Doppler

MISCONCEPTION: *Low color wall filter settings necessarily imply the ability to detect low-velocity flow.*

Explanation:
On all ultrasound systems, conventional color wall filters are linked to the color scales for sequentially generated color Doppler. Setting higher color scales (color PRF) automatically results in higher color wall filters. Some systems have a second control which allows the user to set wall filters more or less aggressively for a particular scale. In other words, even if the wall filters are set to "low", if the scales are high, the wall filters will still be high, and low-velocity flows might not be detected.

COMMON MISCONCEPTION: Doppler

MISCONCEPTION: *PW has no range ambiguity.*

Explanation:
Pulsed wave operation does not have perfect range specificity (some range ambiguity always exists). Range ambiguity exists in all pulsed modalities including radar for speed detection, radar for airplanes, PW Doppler, Color Doppler, 2D imaging, etc. This ambiguity occurs because the echo from the previous transmitted pulse (from deeper in the medium) returns simultaneously with the echo from the current transmitted pulse (from shallower in the medium). In fact, this range ambiguity is actually exploited to create the Doppler modality referred to as high PRF (HPRF) Doppler. Range ambiguity occurs more commonly with shallow gate depths (and with mechanical transducers). There is a simple test to determine if the detected flow is from the actual gate or from an ambiguous gate location. If the detected flow is from the specified Doppler gate depth, increasing and decreasing the Doppler scales (PRF) should result in a direct scaling (down and up) of the signal, with no changes in the waveform characteristics. If any waveform characteristic changes, range ambiguity exists.

COMMON MISCONCEPTION: Doppler

MISCONCEPTION: *Color persistence makes all events last longer.*

Explanation:
Persistence generally results in a temporal distortion. With high color persistence, events which persist for longer than the time required to acquire multiple frames will be presented for a longer duration than reality. However, for events which exist only in a frame (or possibly two), the duration is presented shorter than reality. In fact, short duration events can be "averaged" out by high persistence.

CHAPTER SUMMARY: Doppler

- The Doppler effect is caused by motion relative to an observer. Movement by either a target, the observer, or both can cause the effect.
- The Doppler effect is an apparent change in frequency caused by a change in wavelength as a result of relative motion between the target and the observer.
- The Doppler shifted frequency is the difference between the transmitted frequency and the returned frequency.
- The Doppler shift depends on the relative velocity. The faster the movement between structure and observer, the greater the shift: $(f_{Dop} \propto v)$.
- Since the Doppler effect is caused by a change in wavelength, any wave parameter which affects the wavelength also affects the Doppler shift.
- The wavelength is inversely related to transmit frequency. As the frequency increases, the wavelength decreases, making the object's distance traveled a greater percentage of the wavelength. The Doppler shift is proportional to the operating (transmit) frequency: $(f_{Dop} \propto f_o)$.
- The wavelength is proportional to the wave propagation velocity. As the propagation velocity increases, the wavelength increases, making the object's distance traveled a lesser percentage of the wavelength. So the Doppler shift is inversely proportional to the propagation velocity: $\left(f_{Dop} \propto \dfrac{1}{c}\right)$.
- Since the Doppler effect is due to motion relative to the observer, the direction relative to the observer (angle between observer and motion) affects the Doppler shift. The angle is referred to as the insonification angle. The Doppler shift is proportional to the cosine of the Doppler angle: $(f_{Dop} \propto \cos(\theta))$.

- The Doppler equation is:

$$f_{Dop} = \frac{2f_o v \cos(\theta)}{c}$$

- The Doppler angle is assumed to be 0° or 180° (parallel to flow) in cardiac scanning. The sonographer's role is to get as close to parallel to flow as possible.
- In general, Doppler modalities other than cardiac scanning should strive for a Doppler angle of 45°- 60° when possible.
- In vascular studies, the user indicates the Doppler angle by placement of the flow indicator. Proper alignment to flow is critical since error with Doppler angle is non-linear and can become very significant if not aligned correctly.
- The advantage of CW (relative to PW) is the ability to detect flow of virtually any velocity without aliasing.
- The primary advantage of PW (relative to CW) is good range specificity.
- Aliasing occurs in any pulsed mode when the Nyquist criterion is violated.
- For PW Doppler, aliasing occurs when the Doppler frequency shift is more than half of the PRF.

$$f_{Dop}(max) = \frac{PRF}{2}$$

- Although PW has good range specificity, it is not perfect. All PW modalities (including PW Doppler, color Doppler, B-mode imaging, and M-mode) suffer from range ambiguity.
- Range ambiguity results in echoes from deeper in the patient from the previous transmit line adding to the echoes from shallower depths from the current transmit line.
- Range ambiguity effects are most apparent when the imaging depth is set shallow.
- Aliasing is more likely to occur with:
  - Deep Doppler gate depths
  - Higher transmit frequencies
  - High velocity flow
  - Angles to flow closer to 0° or 180°
- Wall filters are high pass filters which reduce the signal dynamic range by eliminating low frequency signals which are generally produced by slowly moving and stationary specular reflectors ("clutter" signals).
- If the wall filter is set too low, circuit saturation occurs.
- If the wall filters are set too high when measuring low-velocity flow, the actual low-velocity flow may not be detected.
- A single color Doppler display line is produced by transmitting multiple lines (a "packet" or "ensemble") in the same direction and then correlating the data within the packet.
- To produce a sequential color scan, the process is repeated by transmitting packets at varying angles or locations across the scan region.
- Since sequential color is produced using packets of lines, the frame times are very high resulting in low frame rates.
- Low frame rates result in poor temporal resolution.
- Larger packet sizes produce smoother color with less noise, but further degrade temporal resolution.
- Color yields an estimate of the mean velocity, not the distribution of velocities as does spectral Doppler.
- Ultrafast Doppler overcomes the temporal limitations of sequentially generated Doppler by transmitting diverging or plane waves which insonify the entire region at once.
- Although planar waves sacrifice some sensitivity and lateral resolution relative to transmitting focused beams, averaging multiple angled images (compounding) compensates, resulting in potentially greater sensitivity while still producing higher frame rates.
- Determining flow direction is a process involving assessing the angle formed between the steered direction and the "head" of the flow (the direction to where the flow is going).
- If the angle is less than 90°, the flow direction is encoded with the color on the color bar that corresponds with positive frequency shifts (excluding aliasing).
- If the angle is greater than 90°, the flow direction is encoded with the color on the color bar that corresponds with negative frequency shifts (excluding aliasing).
- Aliasing must always be considered. Factors to consider are:
  - Certain hemodynamic situations which imply the likelihood of high velocities (i.e., a vessel narrowing, bending, kinking, high pressure, and small flow cross-sectional arrow areas)
  - The frequency of the transducer (higher operating frequencies alias earlier than lower operating frequencies)
  - The angle to flow (angles closer to 0° or 180° yields higher frequency shifts and therefore are more likely to alias)

- The color scale setting (aliasing is more likely to occur with lower color scales)
- Conventional color wall filters are often misunderstood. The wall filters are set as a percentage of the color scales (Nyquist setting). Increasing the color scales increases the color wall filters.
- To detect low-velocity flow in conventional color Doppler, the color scales must be set low or the wall filters will eliminate the low velocity signals.
- Unlike conventional wall filters which are frequently unable to preserve low velocity signals, spatiotemporal filters are designed specifically to detect microvasculature flow.
- Spatiotemporal filtering uses the difference in coherence between tissue and blood scatter to help differentiate between tissue signals and blood signals.
- By separating signals based on the spatiotemporal coherence first, wall filters can then be applied to remove clutter signals and preserve the much lower amplitude low frequency signals of low-velocity flow associated with microvasculature.
- Color priority is a user-controlled thresholding technique.
- Setting a higher color priority specifies that when a pixel has conflicting data (both a color signal and a 2D signal), if the 2D signal is below the threshold value, then color is displayed instead of the tissue signal. If the 2D signal is above the threshold value then the color is not displayed.
- Color persistence is a user-controlled, time-based averaging technique.
- Persistence reduces random noise through averaging.
- Persistence can potentially eliminate short duration events or possibly "persist" (extend) long duration events.
- B-flow is a technique which directly visualizes blood flow as grayscale within a 2D image.

References

Demené, C., Deffieux, T., Pernot, M., Osmanski, B. F., Biran, V., Gennisson, J. L., ... & Tanter, M. (2015). Spatiotemporal clutter filtering of ultrafast ultrasound data highly increases Doppler and fUltrasound sensitivity. *IEEE transactions on medical imaging, 34*(11), 2271-2285.

Goddi, A., Fanizza, M., Bortolotto, C., Raciti, M. V., Fiorina, I., He, X., ... & Calliada, F. (2017). Vector flow imaging techniques: An innovative ultrasonographic technique for the study of blood flow. *Journal of Clinical Ultrasound, 45*(9), 582-588.

Gijsen, F., Katagiri, Y., Barlis, P., Bourantas, C., Collet, C., Coskun, U., ... & Serruys, P. (2019). Expert recommendations on the assessment of wall shear stress in human coronary arteries: existing methodologies, technical considerations, and clinical applications. *European heart journal, 40*(41), 3421-3433.

Kang, H. J., Lee, J. M., Jeon, S. K., Ryu, H., Yoo, J., Lee, J. K., & Han, J. K. (2019). Microvascular flow imaging of residual or recurrent hepatocellular carcinoma after transarterial chemoembolization: comparison with color/power doppler imaging. *Korean journal of radiology, 20*(7), 1114.

Montaldo, G., Tanter, M., Bercoff, J., Benech, N., & Fink, M. (2009). Coherent plane-wave compounding for very high frame rate ultrasonography and transient elastography. *IEEE transactions on ultrasonics, ferroelectrics, and frequency control, 56*(3), 489-506.

Papaioannou, T. G., & Stefanadis, C. (2005). Vascular wall shear stress: basic principles and methods. *Hellenic J Cardiol, 46*(1), 9-15.

Park, A. Y., & Seo, B. K. (2018). Up-to-date Doppler techniques for breast tumor vascularity: superb microvascular imaging and contrast-enhanced ultrasound. *Ultrasonography, 37*(2), 98.

Phong, B. T. (1975). Illumination for computer generated pictures. *Communications of the ACM, 18*(6), 311-317.

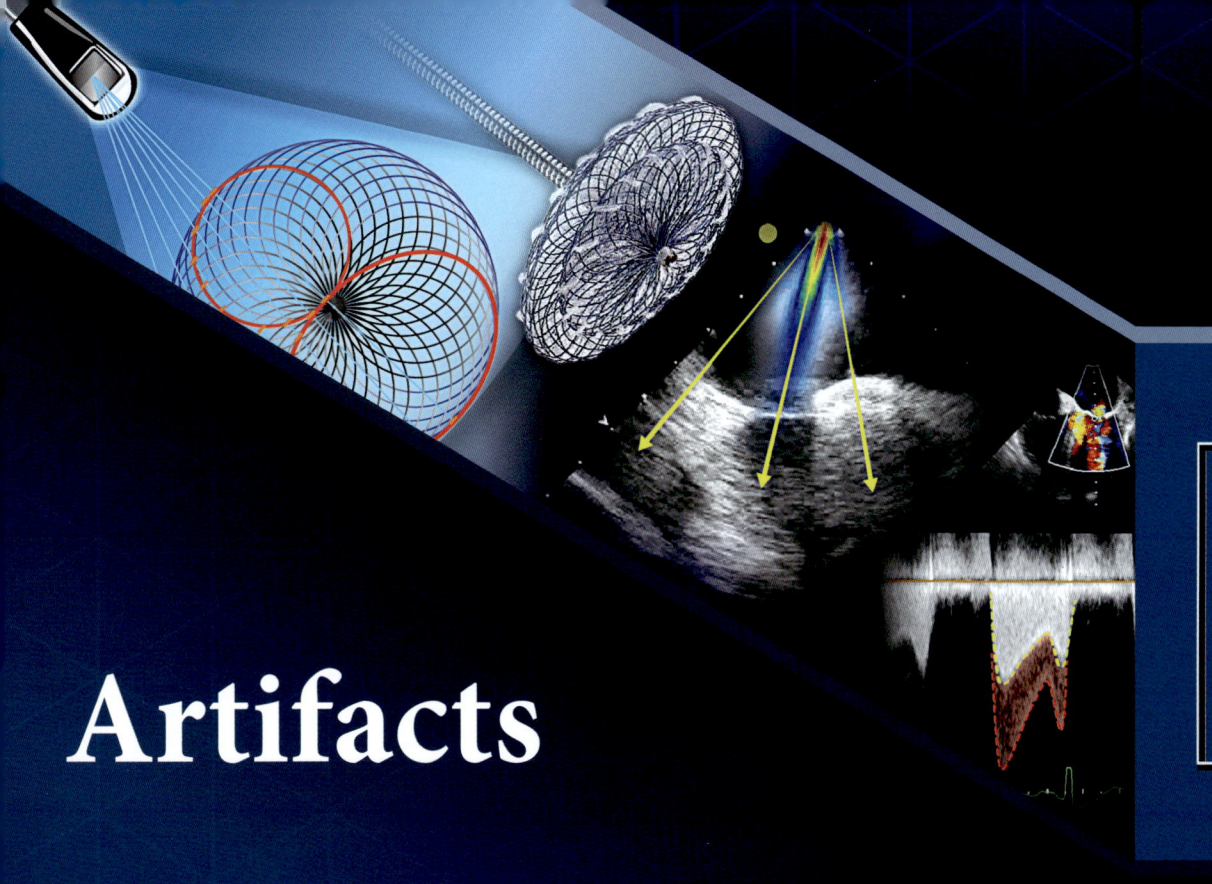

Artifacts

Chapter 8

WHY DO WE STUDY THIS?

▷ Just because you see something does not make it real - and just because you do not see something does not mean that it does not exist.

▷ Understanding and recognizing artifacts is important so as to not make clinical errors based on artifactual appearance or lack of visualization.

WHAT'S IN THIS CHAPTER?

LEVEL 2 — BOARD LEVEL
The underlying variables and assumptions of ultrasound artifacts are discussed. Techniques to recognize the source and impact of artifacts are developed.

LEARNING OBJECTIVES

▷ Identify that artifacts result from the violation of assumptions made in diagnostic ultrasound

▷ List the underlying assumptions and the associated artifacts when these assumptions are violated

▷ Recognize the primary artifacts and understand the cause of the perceived artifact

▷ Describe how artifacts can be categorized according to appearance, mechanism, and/or by modality

Chapter 8
Artifacts

Introduction

The term artifact has many different meanings even within the "narrow" field of ultrasound. The word artifact, defined as "something made through skill by man," is hardly the definition we would use in ultrasound. In its simplest form, an artifact is any representation in the image or on a spectrum which is not indicative of "truth". To quote Shakespeare and Socrates in a mixed metaphor of sorts, "therein lies the rub for what is truth but a shadow on the cave wall." In other words, "truth" and artifact are often extremely difficult to discern, and sometimes present only a shadow by which to determine "reality". In essence, determining what is "real" is often more nebulous than we would like to admit.

One thing is for sure, not all artifacts are bad. Paradoxically, some artifacts can be very useful as an indication of a very specific mechanism in the body. For example, the bright white "spike" which occurs on a cardiac Doppler spectrum, often referred to as a "valve click," is in reality an artifact caused by circuit saturation. Yet, it is a useful artifact when controlled since it helps to quickly identify timing in the cardiac cycle. Artifacts such as shadowing and enhancement can be very useful since understanding the mechanisms which cause the artifact leads to information about the associated tissues and structures. For example, shadowing may indicate the presence of a calcification and enhancement may indicate the presence of a fluid. Of course, there are other artifacts which are absolutely not useful such as susceptibility artifacts which result from receiving radio frequency signals from outside sources. These external signals from sources such as radio signals, television signals, pulse oximeters, Bovie electrosurgical units, etc., are not related to what is physically occurring in the body and therefore are not at all useful as artifacts.

Throughout the entire book we have been analyzing artifacts within the context of each chapter topic. For example, the concept of speed error was introduced when reviewing the assumed propagation velocity in Chapter 2, specular reflection as a main source of imaging artifacts and refraction-related artifacts when reviewing attenuation in Chapter 3, range ambiguity when discussing timing issues in pulsed wave operation in Chapter 4, grating lobes when discussing transducer design in Chapter 5, contrast issues and detail resolution in Chapter 6, and aliasing when discussing Doppler in Chapter 7. Great effort has been expended to make sure that the physics of the mechanisms which cause artifacts has been thoroughly taught in the previous chapters so that this chapter on artifacts can simply serve as a compilation of artifacts, rather than trying to teach all of the underlying physics in one chapter. In other words, this chapter presumes that all of the previous chapters have been read. Because understanding artifacts requires some clinical background, the entire chapter is Level 2. In an effort to make the integration of artifacts easier, we will group artifacts either by common mechanisms (source of the artifact) or by common appearance attribute (location, intensity, etc.). The result of this classification scheme is that the same artifact may be listed in more than one category. Additionally, there are many more artifact images included in the online animation and image library, intended to make identification of artifacts both more comfortable and systematic.

Before we begin categorizing artifacts, it is beneficial to consider the source of artifacts.

1. The Source of Artifacts

1.1 Assumptions for Imaging

Throughout the book you have been learning the assumptions on which ultrasound is based. Any time one of these assumptions are violated an artifact occurs. Therefore, by generating a list the various assumptions, you will have a comprehensive list of the sources of artifacts. *Table 1* applies to both imaging and color Doppler imaging except where notated in blue – these notes apply specifically to color Doppler.

As mentioned when we discussed color Doppler, color Doppler has some characteristics of imaging, some characteristics of Doppler, and some unique characteristics. *Table 2* refers to assumptions specific to color Doppler. You will note that some of these assumptions are also common to spectral Doppler, but since the artifact presentation is different in color than in spectral Doppler, these common artifacts will be listed in both *Table 2* and the spectral Doppler table (*Table 3*). Please note that specific differences are notated in blue.

UNDERLYING VARIABLE	ASSUMPTION	ARTIFACT NAME	ARTIFACT DESCRIPTION
Propagation Speed	Speed of sound is 1540 m/sec	Speed error	Structure appears deeper or more shallow than reality
		Bayonet sign	Needle appears bent when within a structure with a speed different than the assumed 1540 m/sec
Beam Path	Sound travels in a straight line	Refraction artifact	A structure appears laterally displaced, or two structures, one real and one artifactual exist side-by-side
		Refractive edge shadowing	The appearance of dark regions emanating from the edge(s) of a structure (like a vessel, cystic structure, mass, bone) that acts as a source of refraction
	Sound travels directly to and from a structure	Reverberation	Sound bouncing back and forth between two or more structures resulting in replication of the structure in depth; if movement is involved, the artifactual structures move in the same direction as the reverberating structure
		Ring Down	A special case of reverberation which occurs within an air-filled structure; image produces a bright tail inferior to structure
		Comet tail (sometimes called Twinkle artifact in color)	A special case of reverberation which occurs within a metallic or solid structure; image produces a bright tail inferior to structure
		Multi-path	Sound is redirected by a specular reflector toward another specular reflector which reflects back to the transducer; the true structure appears at the correct location and an artifactual structure appears deeper than the actual structure as a result of the longer ultrasound path
		Mirror artifact	The sound reflects from a smooth specular reflector (mirror) toward another structure and then back to the mirror before reflecting back to the transducer; the original object appears in the correct location and a second object appears symmetric about the reflecting surface (mirror); if movement is involved, mirrored objects move opposite of the direction of the actual object (just like a reflection in a mirror)
Beamwidth	The effective beam is infinitesimally thin	Lateral resolution limit	The inability to distinguish two side-by-side structures such that they appear as one wider structure
		Elevation resolution limit	The inclusion in the image of echo from tissue/structures either in front of or behind the slice being imaged
		Grating lobes	The inclusion in the image of echoes emanating from off-axis reflectors; this artifact causes a lateral translation of structures in the image such that two structures appear side-by-side when only one really exists
Pulse Length	Transmit pulse is infinitesimally short	Axial resolution limit	The inability to distinguish two structures separated in depth such that they appear as one longer structure
Attenuation	Uniform attenuation	Enhancement	Enhancement appears as a region of brighter echoes inferior to more superficial structures with less attenuation than normal; this artifact does not occur in color Doppler since color does not present amplitude information – it is either present or not (threshold-based)
		Shadowing	Shadowing is the reciprocal of enhancement and appears as a dark region inferior to a structure which attenuates more than normal; in color, shadowing is often referred to as color dropout
Contrast	Signal is large relative to noise level and different enough from surrounding signals as to be differentiated	Inadequate contrast resolution	Inadequate contrast results in structures not being visualized; when the problem is that the signal is not adequately stronger than the noise level, the structure is simply hidden by the noise; when the issue is inadequate contrast between two tissues, one of the tissues just appears as if part of the background tissue (as can happen with masses surrounded by tissue (liver, breast, kidney, etc.); this artifact does not occur in color Doppler since color does not present amplitude information – it is either present or not (threshold-based)
		Speckle	Speckle creates the apparent "tissue texture" and results from constructive and destructive interference from the reflection from tissues; lower frequency results in a more coarse pattern than higher frequency signals; this artifact does not occur in color Doppler
Time (temporal)	Signal acquisition is fast enough to detect changes in real time	Inadequate temporal resolution	Inadequate temporal resolution results in either short duration events not being visualized, or (depending on the cause of the inadequate temporal resolution) longer duration events appearing to last longer than reality; this problem is very common in color Doppler when the image is generated sequentially (line-by-line); this problem is less common in color generated using plane wave (ultrafast imaging)

Table 1 **Assumptions for Imaging (and Color Imaging) and Associated Imaging Artifacts** (*blue denotes color Doppler differences*)

UNDERLYING VARIABLE	ASSUMPTION	ARTIFACT NAME	ARTIFACT DESCRIPTION
PRF	PRF is at least twice the highest Doppler shifted frequency	Aliasing	The color bar has a black baseline which represents no detected flow, colors which represent "positive flow" (angle < 90°), and colors which represent "negative" flow (angles > 90°); similar to aliasing in spectral Doppler, when the detected mean velocity exceeds the maximum detectable mean velocity as determined by the color scales (related to the PRF) the display color will wrap around the color bar (from either the top wrapping to the bottom or the bottom to the top of the display)
	PRF not set excessively high	Color dropout	For sequentially generated color Doppler, the wall filters change with the scale (PRF) setting; by increasing the PRF, the wall filters are increased which can result in lower velocity flow being filtered out (note that this artifact exists for sequentially generated color Doppler but not for ultrafast color Doppler)
Pulse Length	Transmit pulse is infinitesimally short	Color bleed	Because the transmit pulse is not infinitesimally short, the limited axial resolution results in color "bleeding" over regions occupied by tissue; for example, color bleed in a vessel results in color being displayed over the posterior vessel wall
Receiver Gain	Color gain is not set too high	Color noise speckle	When the receiver gain is high enough that the thermal (electronic) noise is above the 2D/color threshold, the color noise becomes visible within the color image; since thermal noise is random, the color noise appears as color speckle representing both positive and negative flow directions, and usually is most evident in regions within the color box where no actual flow is present
Wall Filters	Not set too high	Color dropout	If the wall filters are set too high, lower velocity flow will be filtered out, presenting as an absence of color filling
	Not set too low	Flash artifact	If the wall filters are set too low, clutter signals (usually associated with tissue movement) will not be filtered out, resulting in large flashes of color throughout the color box region
SNR (sensitivity)	The transmit signal is strong enough and the attenuation low enough so that the signal is above the noise threshold	Inadequate sensitivity (color dropout)	When there is inadequate sensitivity, no color will be presented, even though flow exists; this dropout can exist for many reasons including transmit power set too low, inadequate penetration related to using a high frequency transmit, excessive signal absorption, reflection, or refraction

Table 2 **Assumptions Specific to Color Doppler Imaging Artifacts** *(blue denotes color Doppler differences)*

The following table (*Table 3*) represents assumptions that serve as the source of spectral Doppler artifacts.

Chapter 8: Artifacts 381

UNDERLYING VARIABLE	ASSUMPTION	ARTIFACT NAME	ARTIFACT DESCRIPTION
PRF	PRF is at least twice the highest Doppler shifted frequency	Aliasing	Aliasing occurs when the signal velocity is higher than the maximum detectable velocity of the Doppler scale (related to the PRF) such that the signal wraps around the spectral display (from either the top wrapping to the bottom or the bottom to the top of the display); a true alias implies that the true peak velocity cannot be determined
PRF	Signal is only received from the Doppler gate depth	Range ambiguity	Signal is detected from depths corresponding to multiples of the PRF and combined with the signal from the actual gate depth; there is no obvious indication in the spectrum that the signal is from an ambiguous gate location; the key to detection is to change the PRF (Doppler scales) and determine if components of the signal change (and does not simply scale up or down)
Wall Filters	The system has adequate dynamic range to process the signal dynamic range	Circuit saturation (valve clicks)	When circuit saturation occurs there is a bright white spike symmetric about the baseline that appears in the spectrum with a corresponding loud click or popping sound in the Doppler audio
Wall Filters	The wall filter is set low enough to detect the desired signals with low frequency shifts	Signal dropout	When the wall filters are set higher than the frequency shift of low-velocity flow, no signal is presented on the spectrum; for arterial blood flow, this problem more commonly occurs in diastole when lower velocities exist or during late systole/early diastole when short duration low-velocity flow reversals can occur
Doppler Angle (especially at shallow depths with larger Doppler angles)	The spectral display represents the range of existing velocities and is not artifactual spread because of geometric and transit time effects related to the Doppler angle	Spectral broadening	Artifactual spectral broadening results in a spread of the Doppler spectrum such that the peak velocity appears higher than reality and with a potential decrease in the presence of a spectral window (when a spectral window would otherwise exist)
Doppler Angle Correction	Flow indicator correctly aligned to flow	Peak velocity error	Angle correction adjusts the calculated velocity by using the cosine of the Doppler angle as indicated by the flow indictor; if the flow indicator is not truly aligned to the flow, the angle correction is incorrect, either artifactually increasing or decreasing the peak velocity measurement; since the cosine is very non-linear, the same angular error in the flow indicator setting represents significantly higher velocity measurement errors as the Doppler angle becomes larger
Signal amplitude	The signal is not overgained	Blossoming	When the Doppler signal becomes excessively high (from too high transmit or more commonly from excessive Doppler receive gain), the signal overflows the FFT bins into neighboring bins, artifactually spreading the Doppler signal and increasing the measured peak velocity
Beam path	Sound travels in a straight line	Dropout (related to refraction)	As the incident angle becomes larger (further away from 0°) and there is an increasing change in propagation velocity at a reflective interface, the amount of refraction increases until eventually the critical angle is reached at which point total internal reflection occurs; with spectral Doppler, as the amount of refraction occurs from a vessel or heart valve, the Doppler signal will decrease in strength and eventually even disappear when total internal reflection occurs
SNR (sensitivity)	The transmit signal is strong enough, and the attenuation low enough so that the signal is above the noise threshold	Inadequate sensitivity (color dropout)	When there is inadequate sensitivity, some or all of the spectrum will be absent, even though flow exists; this dropout can exist for many reasons including transmit power set too low, inadequate penetration related to using a high frequency transmit, excessive signal absorption, reflection, or refraction
Separation Between I and Q Channel	When the signal is separated into the forward and reverse channels (in phase and quadrature) none of the signal leaks from one channel to the other	Spectral mirroring	Spectral mirroring results in a replication of Doppler spectral components symmetric about the Doppler baseline; the higher the amplitude, the more likely the component will appear as a mirror (note that is it also possible to have spectral mirroring when the Doppler angle is close to 0°, as the flow may be detected as both forward and reverse flow simultaneously)

Table 3 **Assumptions Specific to Spectral Doppler Artifacts**

2. Categorizing Artifacts

2.1 Image Detail Resolution Related
We have already discussed artifacts associated with ultrasound beam characteristics generated by transducer and system designs. These artifacts are often, but not always, the limiting factor in detail resolution.

Detail resolution artifacts for 2D and color Doppler are associated mainly with:

- Limited axial resolution
- Limited lateral resolution
- Limited elevation ("slice thickness") resolution
- Beam aberration (which affects axial, lateral, and elevation resolution)

2.2 Locational Artifacts
Locational artifacts result in structures appearing either displaced in the image from the true location, or the presence of a structure or signal which does not even exist in the patient. Most of the locational artifacts can also affect detail resolution. The locational artifacts that generally affect detail resolution are indicated by an asterisk (*) in the list below.

- Refraction
- Reverberation
- Comet tail (twinkle in color)
- Ring down
- Multi-path
- Grating lobes *
- Side lobes *
- Speed error
- Range ambiguity
- Mirror images

We can further stratify the categorization by breaking down where the locational artifacts appear relative to the actual structure. The following figure illustrates the effect of each of these locational artifacts.

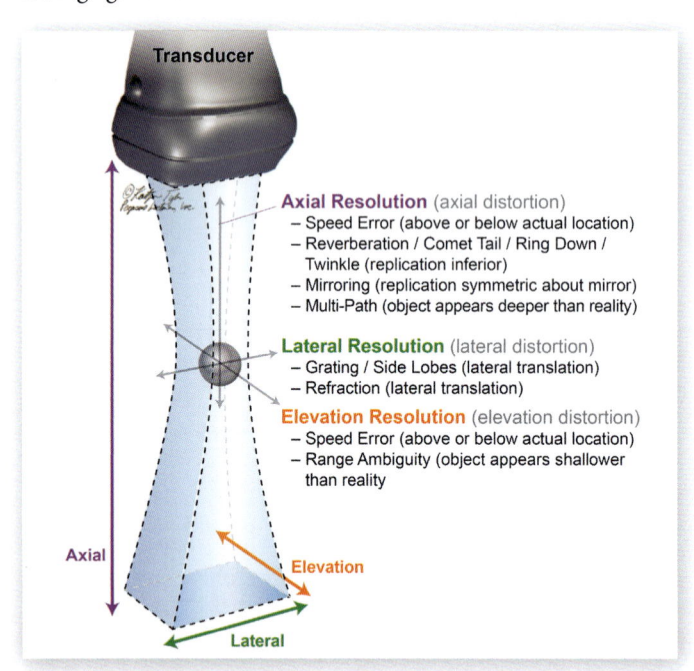

Fig. 1 Breakdown of where each type of locational artifact is presented in the image

2.3 Attenuation Artifacts
Attenuation artifacts may result in a change in intensity of the signal, and potentially the location of a signal. As a result, you will notice that some of the artifacts listed in this section are also included in the locational artifact list.

- Acoustic shadowing
- Enhancement
- Reverberation
- Comet tail
- Ring down
- Refraction
- Speckle

2.4 Phase-Related
Variations in phase can result in a defocusing effect (loss of detail resolution) as well as a pseudo tissue texture. Although these artifacts also overlap with existing categories previously listed, the mechanisms are complex enough to warrant separate treatment. In addition to considering the mechanisms, we will also consider advanced techniques developed to decrease the effects of phase-related artifacts.

- Speckle
- Beam aberration

2.5 Doppler Artifacts
Almost all spectral Doppler artifacts affect the spectrum such that error is introduced into the velocity measurement. Some artifacts tend to cause overestimation while others tend to cause an underestimation. For color Doppler, almost all artifacts result in the presence of a color signal where no signal should exist, or the absence of a color signal where color should exist.

- Aliasing (spectral and color)
- Range ambiguity (spectral and color)
- Spectral mirroring
- Spectral spread (broadening)
- Blossoming (spectral and color)
- Wall filter saturation (spectral)
- Peak velocity error (angle correction required)
- Signal dropout
- Harmonic double spectrum envelope

> **KEY CONCEPT**
>
> Artifacts can be categorized in many different ways. Perhaps the easiest way to understand artifacts is to realize that artifacts exist whenever an assumption of ultrasound is violated (such as assumed speed of sound is 1540 m/sec, if the speed of sound is not 1540, speed error artifact exists).

3. Detail Resolution

3.1 Lateral and Axial Resolution

The primary factors which limit lateral and axial resolution were discussed in detail in Chapters 4 and 5. For axial resolution, we learned that the limit is determined by half the spatial pulse length (SPL), which is determined by the wavelength and number of cycles in the pulse.

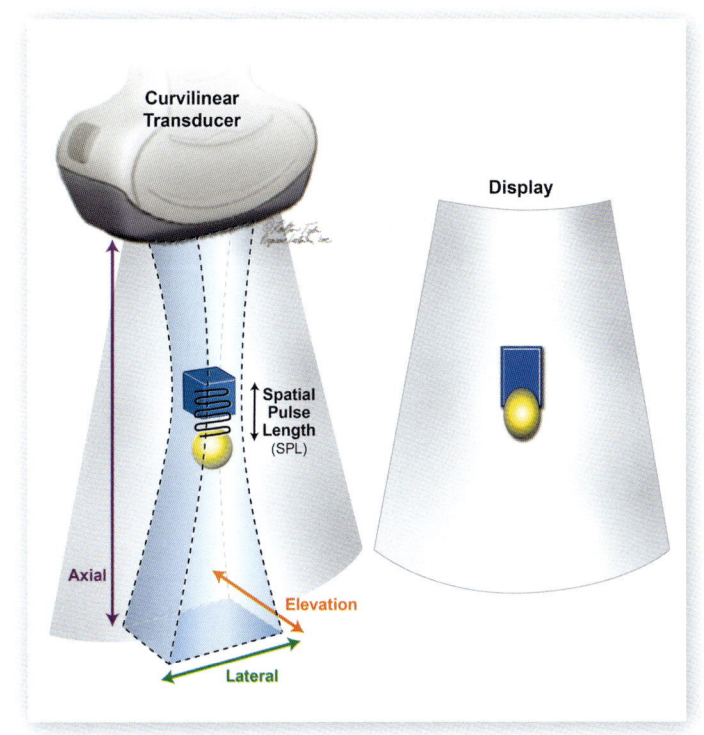

Fig. 2 **Axial resolution is determined by the spatial pulse length (Axial Res = SPL/2)**

For lateral resolution, we learned that the resolution was determined primarily by the effective beamwidth, such that narrower beams yield better resolution. Note that understanding the beamwidth limitation is much simpler when considering sequential imaging (focused line-by-line) than when considering multi-line approaches which use parallel processing to generate multiple lines from a single transmit event. In these cases, it is helpful to consider the fact that the "effective beamwidth" is the result of using beamforming techniques such as retrospective focusing, signal averaging, and any signal processing technique used to improve the ability to differentiate laterally located structures.

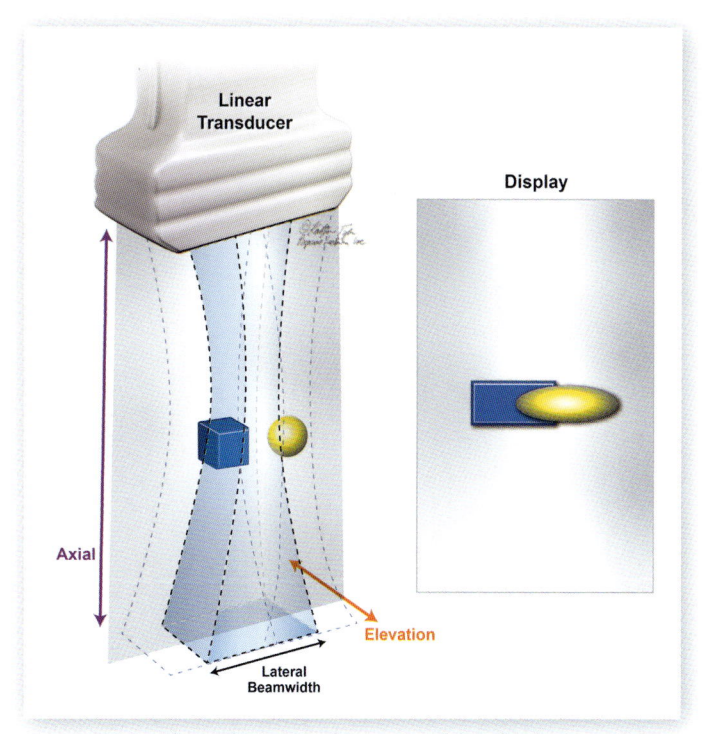

Fig. 3 **Lateral resolution is determined by the beamwidth in the lateral dimension**

The following test phantom image (*Figure 4*) demonstrates limited axial and lateral resolution.

- The "V" shaped group of pins near label 1 is used for testing axial resolution. Notice how the two pins indicated by the arrow tip have converged into nearly one object in the image.

- The pin group identified by the white arrow labeled number 2 is used to demonstrate lateral resolution. In this pin group there are actually six pins spaced laterally at varying intervals. On the right side of the arrow, it is possible to distinguish each pin distinctly. To the left of the arrow tip, the limited lateral resolution causes the pins to appear as one "blurred" object.

- The pin indicated by the white arrow labeled number 3 has the same physical dimension as the entire row of pins linearly located directly above. Notice that the pin dimension is "smeared" laterally so as to appear approximately five times wider than the second and third pin down from the top. The reason for this lateral distortion is twofold. First as the depth increases, the beamwidth is increasing, decreasing lateral resolution. Also, for a curved linear transducer, since the beams angle away from the transducer face, the beam density in the near field is higher than the beam density in the far field. Therefore, the received beam must be drawn wider in the far field. In Chapter 6, this point was discussed relative to the non-linear transformation needed for the scan conversion to create non-rectangular image shapes.

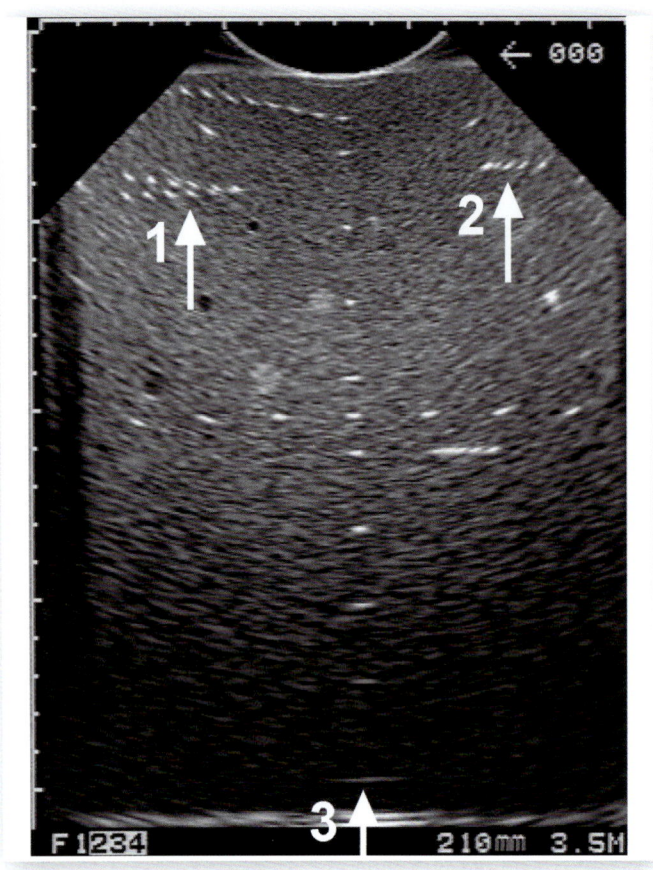

Fig. 4 Phantom image demonstrating limits of detail resolution

3.2 Elevation Resolution
A 2D image presentation does not have a means of indicating the slice thickness of the image. This limitation implies that structures which overlap a portion of the beam in the elevation plane will appear at the same location in the image, as shown in *Figure 5*.

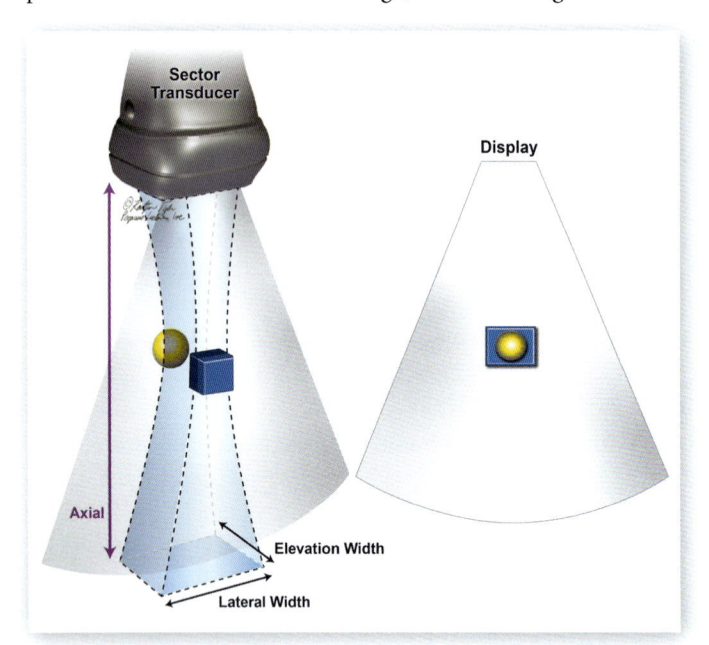

Fig. 5 Elevation resolution is determined by the beamwidth in the elevation direction

The following image, *Figure 6*, demonstrates how the elevation resolution (discussed in Chapter 5) can impact an image, and potentially lead to an incorrect conclusion.

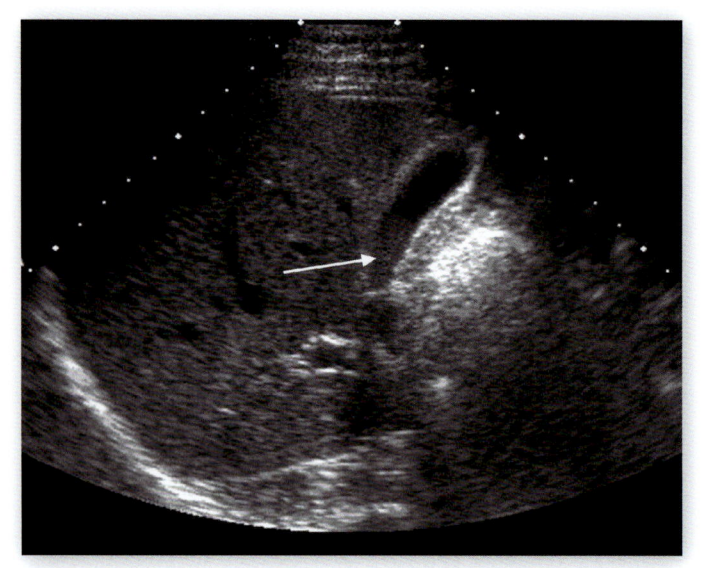

Fig. 6 "Noise" in the gallbladder from "slice thickness"

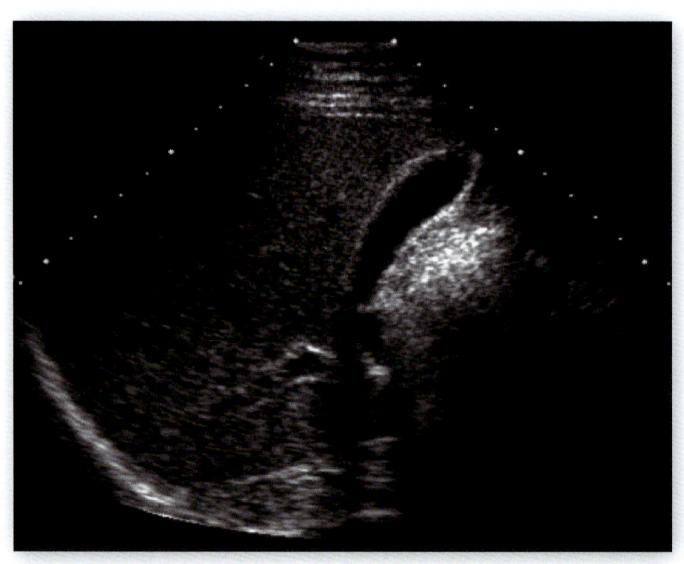

Fig. 7 Elimination of "noise" related to slice thickness

The image of *Figure 6* demonstrates lower level signals within the gallbladder that are the result of the beam elevation thickness. The image in *Figure 7* is from the same patient using harmonic imaging (discussed in Chapter 10). The use of harmonics makes the beamwidth narrower both laterally and elevationally. Because of the improved elevation resolution, the low-level echoes of *Figure 6* are no longer present in the gallbladder in *Figure 7*.

4. "Locational" Artifacts

4.1 Refraction

As discussed in Chapter 3, refraction can result in a lateral displacement of an object. The line drawing of *Figure 8* represents the basic refractive mechanism that results in lateral displacement. Notice that the beam is directed away from the correct path (refracted). The redirected beam insonifies a structure ("strong reflector real") and the echo is refracted back to the transducer. Since the system always assumes echoes are received from the straight ahead direction (indicated by the dotted line) the structure is artificially drawn in the image, laterally displaced. In other words, the structure is artifactually drawn along the presumed straight ahead dotted path even though the real structure causing the reflection is from the bent path indicated by the solid line.

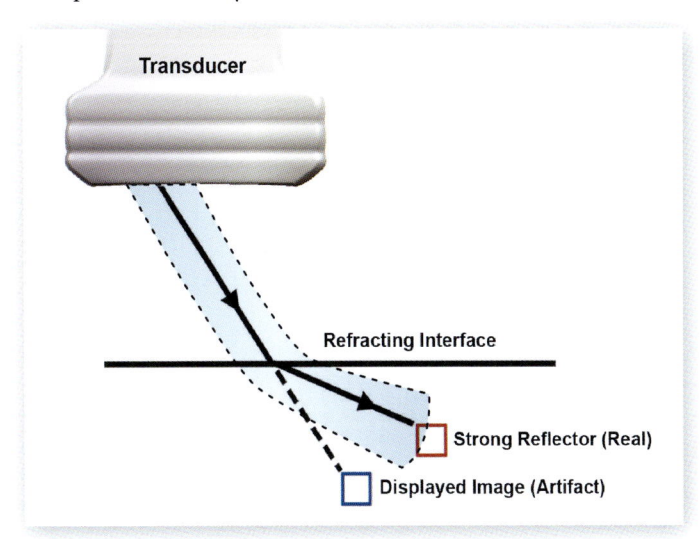

Fig. 8 Lateral displacement caused by refraction

Recall that the amount of refraction can be determined by employing Snell's law. As the incident angle increases (the further from perpendicular – equivalent to 0° incidence), the amount of refraction increases (given that there is a change in propagation velocity across an interface between two media).

In *Figure 9* there is an artifactual, laterally displaced second abdominal aorta. The mechanism which produces this artifact is refraction from the rectus sheath. At approximately 2 cm, there is a bright curved "line" which represents the liver capsule. Since the beam is perpendicular to this interface, there is no associated refraction. However, just above the liver capsule are the rectus sheath and the rectus muscles. As indicated by the dotted line, when transmitting in the direction of the artifactual aorta, the beam is refracted and insonifies the true aorta. On the return path, the beam is refracted back toward the transducer. The system always assumes that the signals arrive from the steered direction. Therefore, a second (artifactual) aorta is drawn laterally displaced from the true abdominal aorta. The refraction indicated in this figure would also occur for color Doppler and spectral Doppler. Therefore, this artifact will not be "identified" by turning on color Doppler or by performing spectral Doppler in the artifactual abdominal aorta.

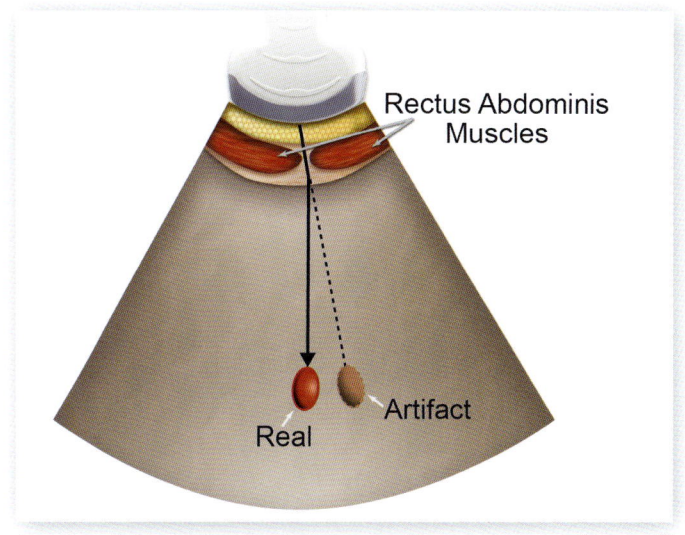

Fig. 9a Schematic of refraction artifact creating a "second" abdominal aorta

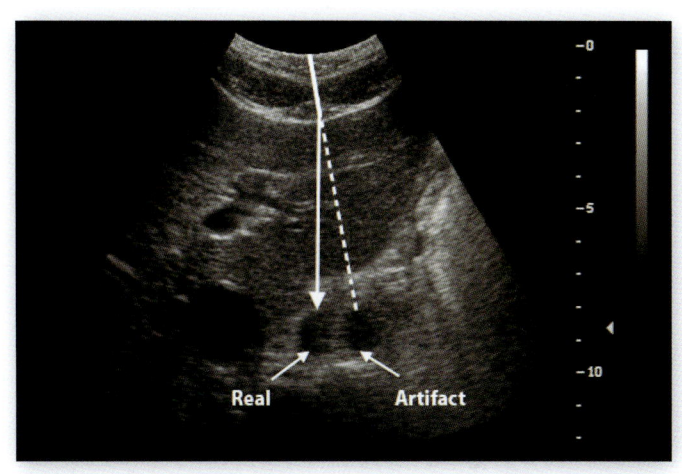

Fig. 9b Ultrasound image of refraction artifact creating a "second" abdominal aorta

The color Doppler and the spectral Doppler will both produce artifactual signals from the region where the 2D artifactual aorta is drawn. The image of *Figure 10* demonstrates how the artifactual abdominal aorta has color filling similar to the color filling of the actual abdominal aorta.

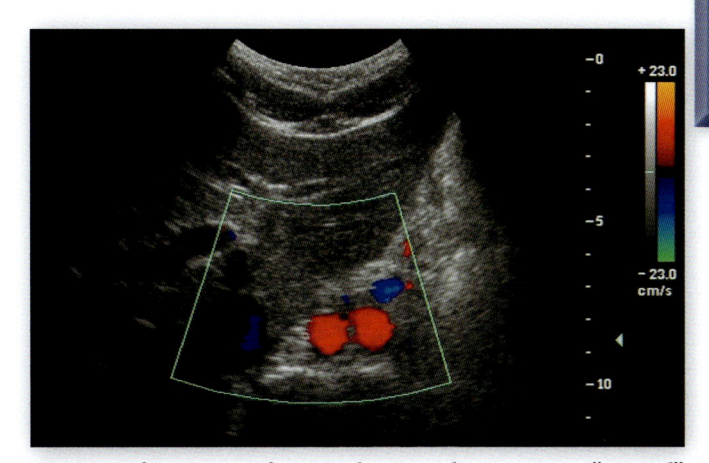

Fig. 10 Refraction artifact in color Doppler creating a "second" abdominal aorta

View ONLINE Animation and Image Library

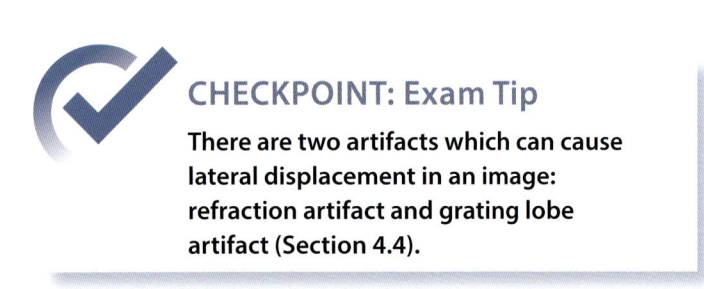

CHECKPOINT: Exam Tip

There are two artifacts which can cause lateral displacement in an image: refraction artifact and grating lobe artifact (Section 4.4).

4.2 Reverberation

As the name suggests, reverberation is an artifact caused by sound bouncing between multiple structures. Reverberation can occur between any two, or more, strong specular reflectors. In general, reverberation artifacts occur more commonly from relatively superficial reflectors since the reverberation paths for deep structures result in greater attenuation. The mechanisms of reverberation and how the artifact presents can be very complex. Unfortunately, many texts give such an oversimplified and rudimentary treatment of reverberation that the artifact is often misunderstood and misinterpreted. You must realize that when reverberation occurs, all "tissues" between the reverberating structures can be replicated, not just the specular reverberating structures. This fact implies that it is possible for reverberated tissue signals to be superimposed over a blood pool or other issue, giving the impression of a thrombus or a mass which does not truly exist.

4.2.1 A Simple Case: Between a Specular Reflector and the Transducer Face

In Chapter 3 we learned that sound reflects based on the acoustic impedance mismatch and the geometric aspect of the reflecting surface relative to the wavelength. As the sound returns to the transducer, some of that sound gets reflected back into the body since there is a large acoustic impedance mismatch between the body and the transducer. This reflected sound acts as a second "undesired" transmit. Again, some of the sound reflects back towards the transducer, of which some is received and some is reflected. In general, this "second" reflection does not cause too much degradation to the image since the second reflections are generally relatively weak. However, when there is a strong specular reflector in the relative near field, the "second" signal can be quite strong and result in a second appearance of the reflecting structure. This second appearance is called reverberation artifact since the sound is "reverberated" between two structures. Depending on signal strength, this process can occur multiple times. In this simple case, the result is the appearance of the strongly reflecting structure multiple times at constant depth increments with diminishing intensity.

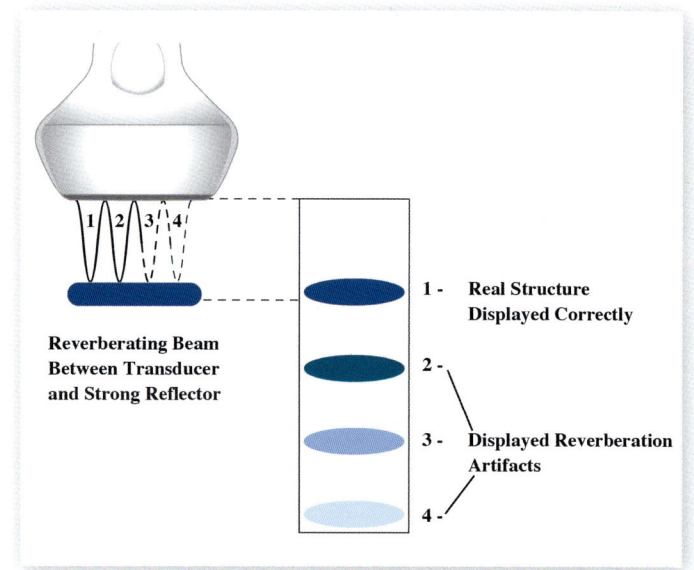

Fig. 11a **Schematic of reverberation artifact**

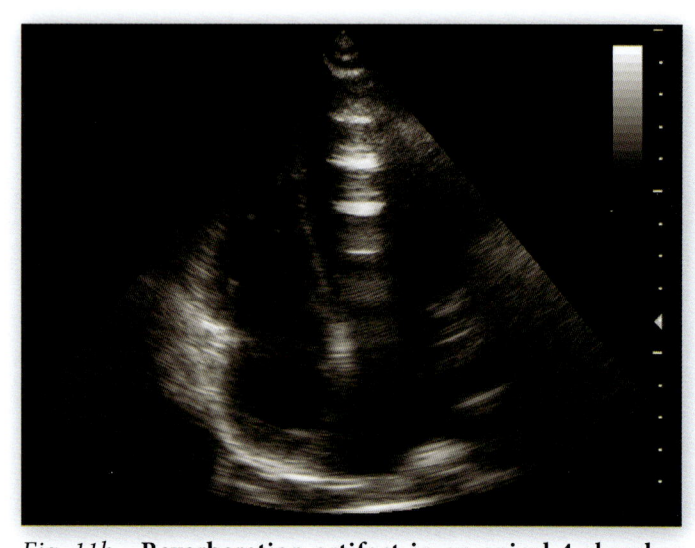

Fig. 11b **Reverberation artifact in an apical 4-chamber cardiac view**

View ONLINE Animation and Image Library

The same type of reverberation apparent in the cardiac image takes place between the transducer-to-skin interface and the visceral pleura of the lungs. The visceral pleura-lung air boundary, because of the large acoustic impedance mismatch, results in nearly 100% reflection and an inferior acoustic shadow. The large resulting echo returns back toward the transducer where, again, a large percentage is reflected back into the patient. The reverberating echoes result in multiple, artifactual representations of the "pleural line" at uniform depths within the ultrasound image. The reverberating echoes, of course, re-image all of the intervening skin, subcutaneous fat, muscle, and soft tissues between the transducer face and visceral pleura resulting in a "hazy" appearance overlaid over the acoustic shadow between the brighter reverberation representations of the pleural line. This hazy appearance within the acoustic shadow is often referred to as a "dirty shadow." The reverberations of the pleural line are referred to as "A-lines" in lung ultrasound and expected with a normal lung. Changes in and the absence of A-lines can occur in the presence of pleural effusion, pneumonia, pulmonary fibrosis, and a series of other lung related conditions.

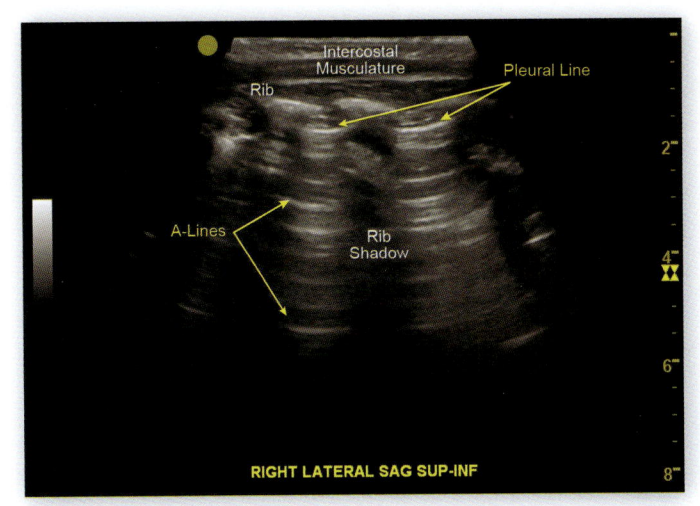

Fig. 12 **Ultrasound image showing A-lines (reverberation artifact) from the pleural line in the lung**

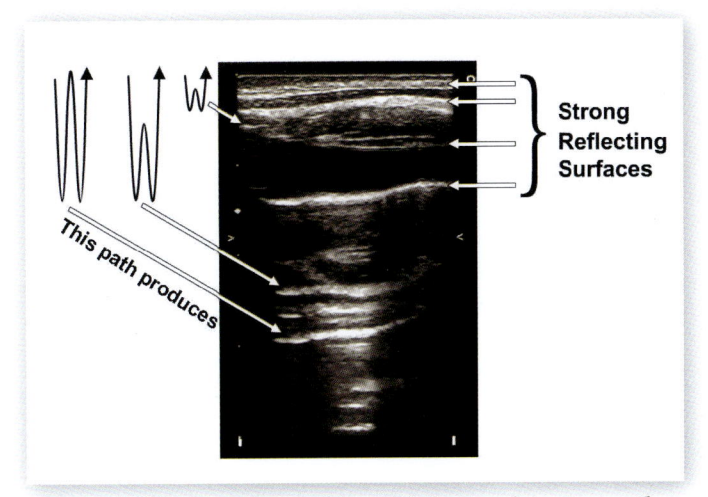

Fig. 13 **Subclavian artery with multiple reverberation paths**

The following image exhibits a reverberation artifact commonly seen when imaging the uterus through a full bladder. Fluid within the bladder should appear anechoic. In this case, reverberation occurs multiple times between the interface of the subcutaneous layer of fat and the lower fascia of the abdominal muscle (as indicated by the arrows). As shown by the colored lines, sound is reverberating between the anterior surface of the bladder, and the interface between the abdominal muscles and the subcutaneous fat layer. Notice the brighter lines which represent the bladder interface represented three times (at the tips of each of the arrows) while the intervening tissue appears as a lighter echo superimposed over the dark representation of the fluid.

4.2.2 More Complex Cases: Between Multiple Specular Reflectors

Reverberation can become significantly more complex when the reverberation occurs between multiple strong specular reflectors within the body. The mechanism for the artifact is the same as explained previously, except now the reverberation artifacts are not necessarily equidistantly spaced. Additionally, when there is reverberation between specular reflectors within the body, there is often also reverberation between these same structures and the transducer face. The result can be a very confusing compounding of image and artifacts. *Figure 13*, an image of the subclavian artery, demonstrates reverberation caused from both the surface of the transducer and between multiple reflectors within the body.

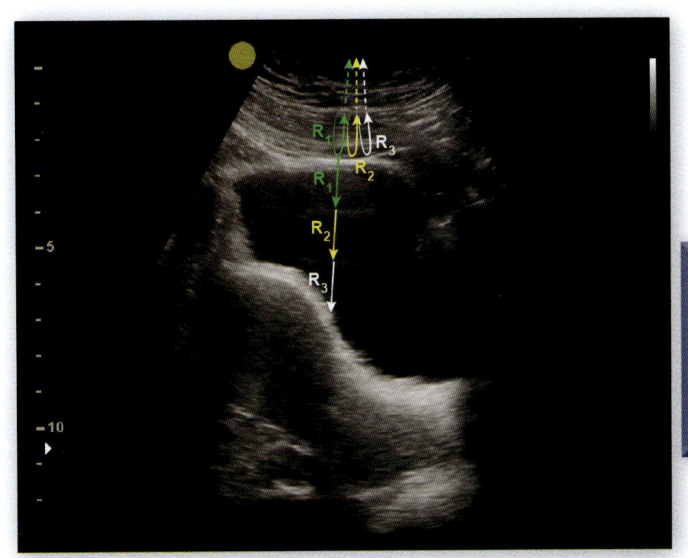

Fig. 14 **Ultrasound image of uterus with a superior, fluid-filled bladder showing echo (reverberation artifact) within the bladder**

Reverberation artifacts are quite common. The following figure shows another example of reverberation artifact in the jugular vein. *Figure 15a* calls out the major anatomical landmarks with *Figure 15b* highlighting the reverberation effect. In this case, the fascial sheathing of the sternocleidomastoid muscle appears reverberated into the lumen of the jugular vein (as indicated by the arrows).

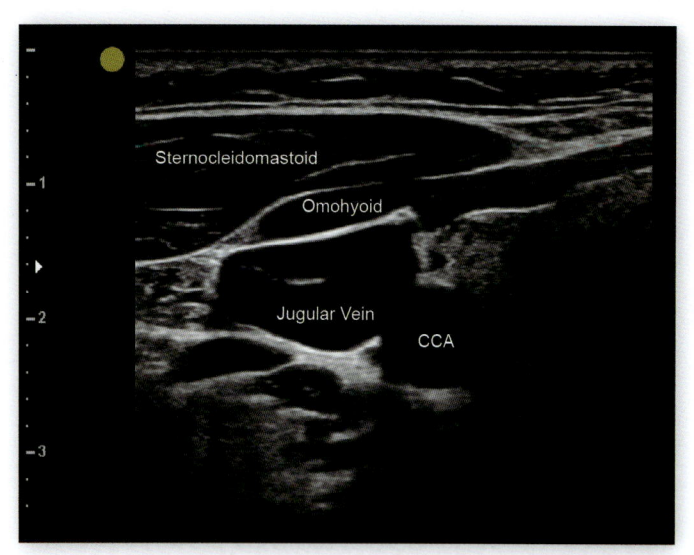

Fig. 15a **Mirroring artifact in jugular vein with anatomical landmarks**

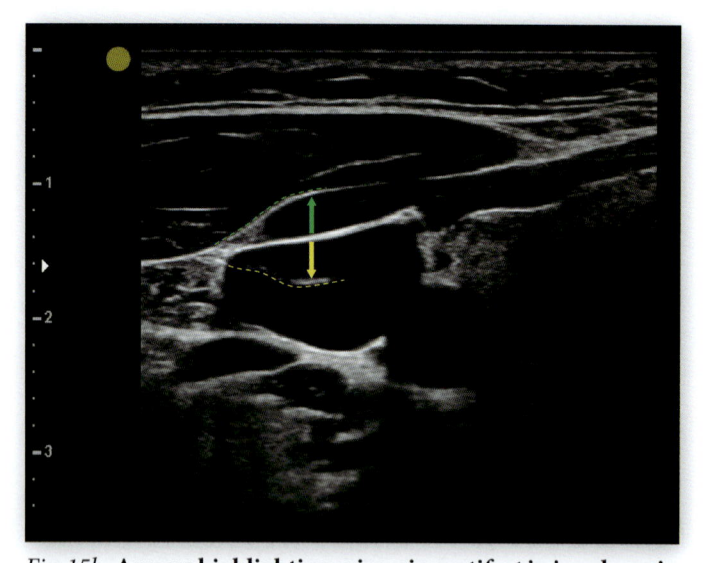

Fig. 15b **Arrows highlighting mirroring artifact in jugular vein**

A Very Complex Case: "Ghosting" or "Mirrored" Arteries
As already mentioned, reverberation artifacts can become complex and can occur much more frequently than most people recognize. Another way in which reverberation can manifest is when there is a scattering from another structure which then reverberates between two strong specular reflectors. This situation occurs frequently with signals from blood, causing the signals to then reverberate between the vessel's walls.

The color image in *Figure 16* demonstrates what many texts call mirror artifact due to the almost perfect "mirror" of the subclavian artery about the pleura. In reality this artifact is caused by reverberation. True mirror artifact occurs with a strong specular reflector acting as a mirror and an object which also yields a relatively specular reflection. The reflection from blood cells is Rayleigh scattering and will not produce the multiple reflections necessary to create the mirror artifact. The reverberation path which creates the spurious subclavian artery is demonstrated in the image. In essence, the reverberation is between the anterior wall and the pleura, as shown by the extended path length (the solid path line). Note that the color in the actual artery appears at the correct location as indicated by the normal reflection path (the dashed line).

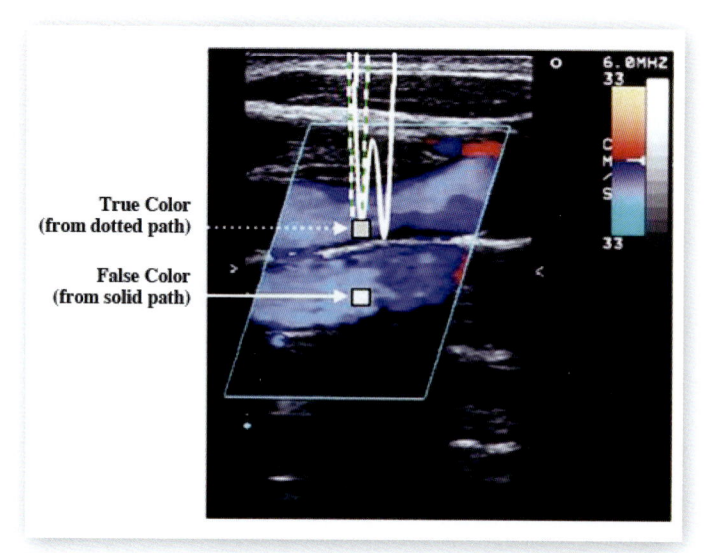

Fig. 16 **Subclavian artery with false color from reverberation**

So how do you answer questions on mirror versus reverberation artifact? It is unfortunate that most textbooks refer to the dual artery in this example as a "mirror artifact," since in reality it is caused by reverberation. With reverberation artifact, when movement exists, the movement of the artifact will be in the same direction as the movement of the actual involved structures. As you will see later, with mirroring, the movement is in opposing directions as the movement is reflected about the mirroring surface. Whenever you see a "false image" relatively symmetric about a strong specular reflector, the artifact will most likely be deemed as mirror artifact on an exam. Most texts assume that reverberation artifacts are uniformly spaced multiple reflections only.

View ONLINE Animation and Image Library

CHECKPOINT: Exam Tip

If there is motion with reverberation artifact, the motion of the artifact will be in the same direction as the motion of the actual structure.

Be Vigilant Not to Confuse a Reverberation Artifact with a Thrombus

You should always be vigilant for reverberation-related artifacts. The simple cases of reverberation present as exact replications of the reverberating structure at equidistant depths of the true depth. As shown, reverberation can have very complex paths creating spurious images at many different depths, and sometimes create an area of haze which could be misinterpreted as thrombus. The best way not to miss this artifact is to always watch for imaging situations in which there are strong specular reflectors in the relative near field. Recall that specular reflection is highly dependent on angular incidence. Changing the imaging or steering angle will often change the reflection path and hence, change the image. An additional technique often helpful to identify reverberation artifact is to slightly increase and decrease probe pressure on the patient. With increasing pressure, real structures from all depths should get closer to the surface at the same rate, commensurate with the tissue compression. However, since reverberation is the result of multiple reflections, reverberation echoes will move up in the image faster than actual structures. Your job is to prove what is real and what is artifact.

The images of *Figures 17* and *18* show examples in which reverberation can easily be confused with the presence of a thrombus or mass.

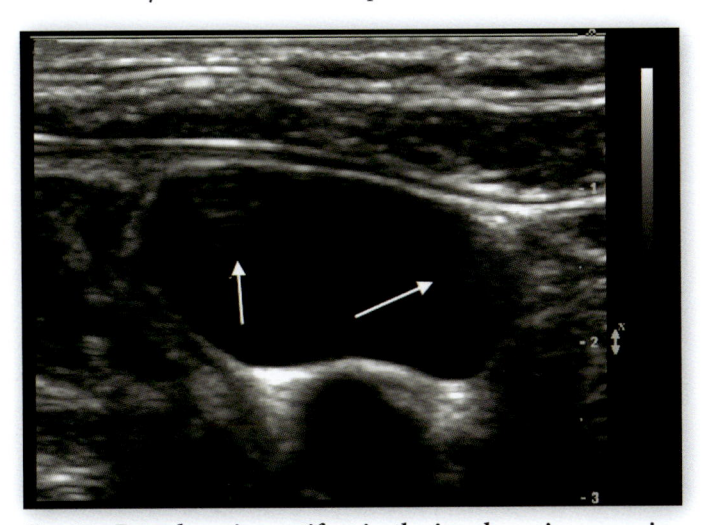

Fig. 17 **Reverberation artifact in the jugular vein appearing like thrombus**

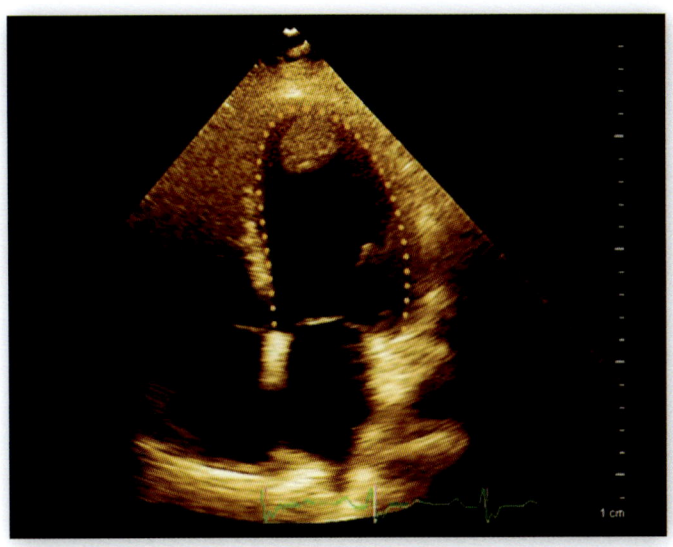

Fig. 18a **Apparent pedunculated mass in the apex of the ventricle caused by reverberation artifact**

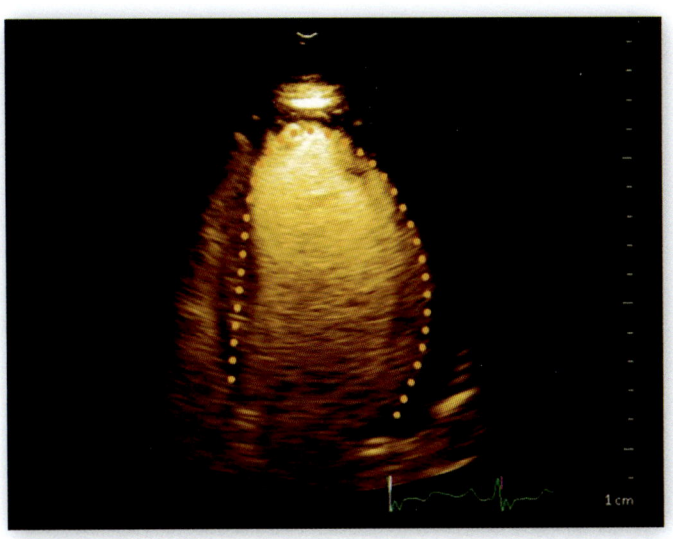

Fig. 18b **The ultrasound enhancement agent study rules out the presence of a mass as evidenced by apical opacification**

In the apical view, reverberations in the apex of the ventricle often appear as a mass or thrombus (as seen near the top of the dotted curve in *Figure 18a*). Correct identification as artifact or actual thrombus can be difficult, since the artifact can move with ventricular contraction just as an actual thrombus would. In some cases, color flow imaging can help in the identification of the artifact, as flow will not pass through actual thrombus or a mass. In these cases it is important to increase the color priority, decreasing the tissue amplitude threshold at which color is presented. It is important to note that if the reverberation signal is high enough amplitude, it may not be possible to display the color. In these cases, the use of contrast can be very useful to rule out mass or thrombus (as seen in *Figure 18b*).

Reverberation artifacts sometimes create a haze or "clutter" within an image. Recognizing this clutter can be challenging in a still image and is usually facilitated by viewing the motion in a cine clip. In

Figure 19, echoes from relatively stationary structures, such as the ribs and the chest wall result in a persistent speckle pattern which seems to overlay the dynamic echoes from the moving structures.

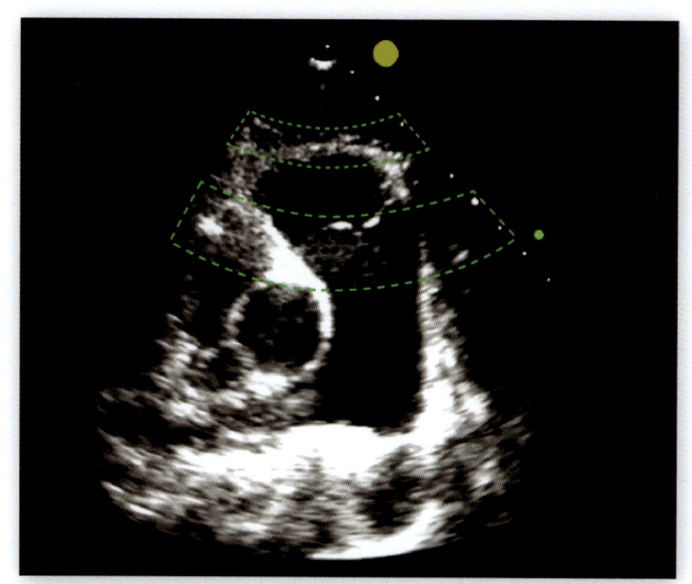

Fig. 19 Clutter artifact (as outlined by the green dotted regions) in a parasternal short axis view of the pulmonary valve and artery

Note that the clutter artifact is more easily differentiated by the movement in the corresponding cine clip (online).

View ONLINE Animation and Image Library

Ring Down and Comet Tail (Specific Forms of Reverberation)

When sound reverberates within an air sac, the boundaries of the air sac are redrawn repeatedly creating a bright "tail-like" image below the air sac. This artifact has been given the name of ring down. *Figure 20* is a transverse image of a patient with a biliary stent causing pneumobilia (air in the biliary system). The bright white echoes (indicated by the white arrows) represent the strong reflection from the large acoustic impedance mismatch with the air. Below the bright reflectors are white "flashlights" caused by the sound reverberating within the air bubbles.

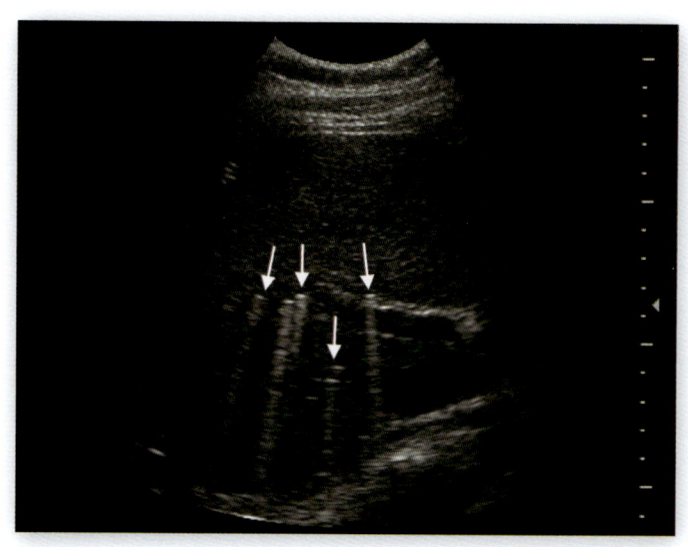

Fig. 20 Ring down artifact caused by air in the biliary system

Figure 21 provides another example of ring down artifact (indicated by the yellow arrows), occurring from air at the diaphragm (bright, white, echogenic structure) below the lung and above the liver.

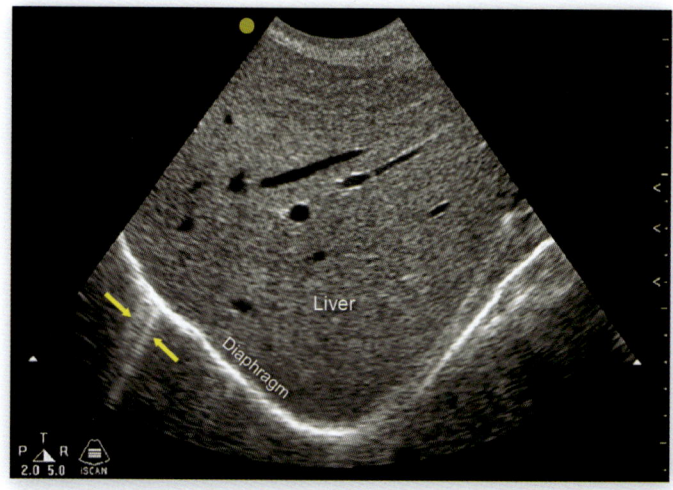

Fig. 21 Image of a liver, diaphragm, and lung with ring down artifact caused by air at the boundary of the diaphragm and lung

As mentioned previously, artifacts are often very helpful. For example, the artifact of ring down is very helpful in detecting interstitial lung disease[2]. When imaging the lung, ring down artifacts that emanate from the pleural line and are present to the bottom of the image are referred to as B-lines or B-line artifact (BLA). Three or more B-lines in the same interstitial space are referred to as "lung rockets" and imply interstitial lung disease (interstitial syndrome). You will also see the B-lines referred to sometimes as "comet tail" artifact as a holdover from some early publications.

Figure 22 is an emergency department ultrasound of the left lung and shows diffuse B-lines consistent with acute pulmonary edema. This ultrasound also shows no A-lines consistent with B-lines obliterating the A-lines. Note that the presence of multiple B-lines per interstitial spacing is more readily appreciated in the corresponding video (online).

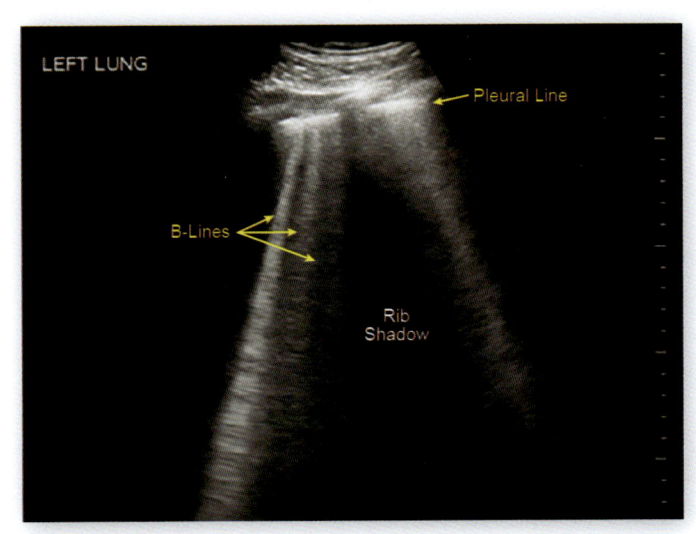

Fig. 22 **Emergency ultrasound of a lung showing diffuse B-lines consistent with acute pulmonary edema**

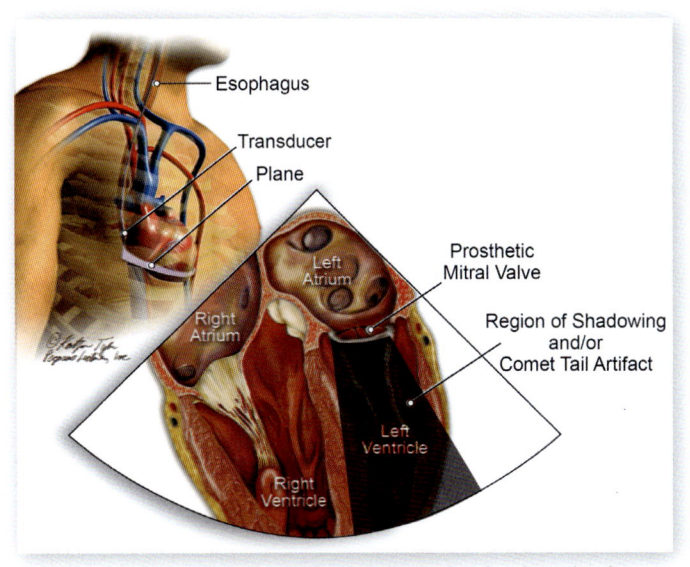

Fig. 23b **Schematic of a transesophageal echo (TEE) of prosthetic mitral valve showing the area of shadowing / comet tail artifact**

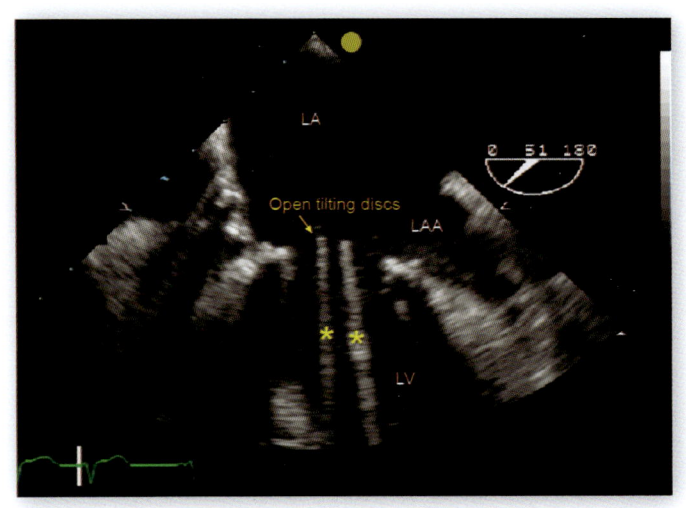

A similar phenomenon called comet tail occurs when the sound reverberates within a calcific structure or a metallic structure such as a surgical clip, catheter, or needle tip. In these cases, there is usually a striated tail of bright reflection below the structure, representing the front and back impedance mismatch of the structure. Sometimes these striations are even more obvious than in *Figure 23c*. In this case, the metal discs of the St. Jude valve (*Figure 23a*) are causing reverberation which is seen well below the extent of the disc. You should also notice the dark regions on either side which are caused by acoustic shadowing from the valve struts.

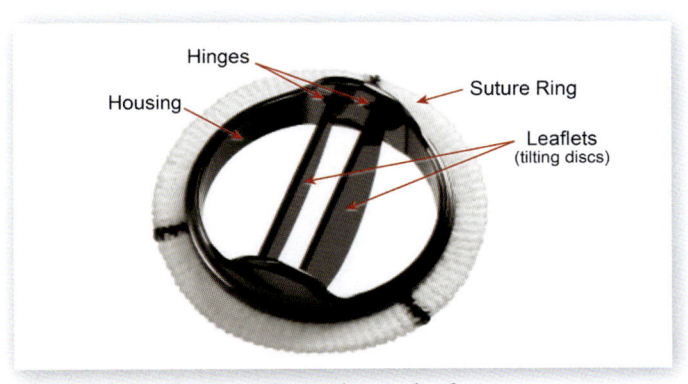

Fig. 23c **TEE image of comet tail artifacts (asterisks) created by the two discs from a bileaflet St. Jude mechanical prosthetic mitral valve**

This same valve, but in the closed position, is displayed in the upcoming section on shadowing.

Fig. 23a **Bileaflet St. Jude mechanical valve**

Figure 24a shows an Amplatzer septal occluder used for percutaneous closure of septal defects. This mesh device can be seen causing a reverberation (comet tail) artifact immediately below the catheter and throughout the entire depth of the image in *Figure 24b*.

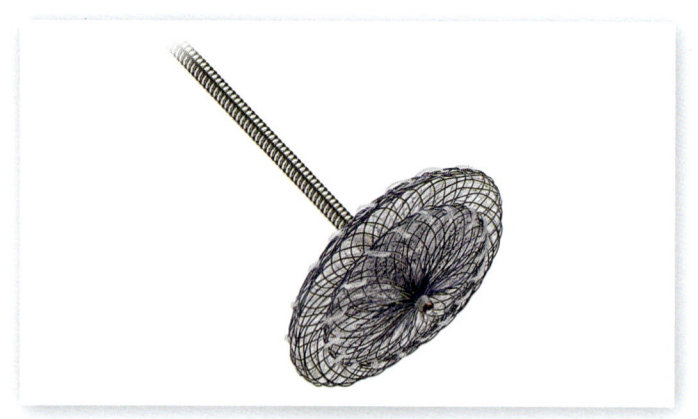

Fig. 24a Amplatzer septal occluder device attached to the catheter used for closure of an atrial septal defect

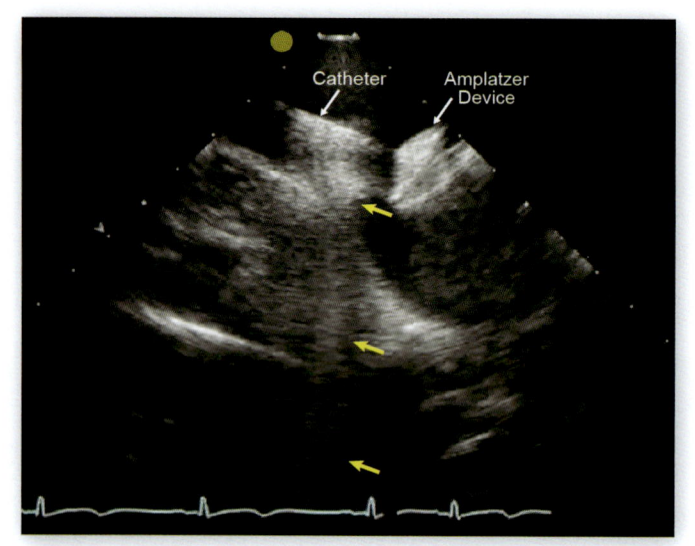

Fig. 24b Intracardiac echocardiography image taken during surgery to place an Amplatzer septal occluder device showing reverberation (comet tail) artifact emanating from the catheter (as indicated by arrows)

As already mentioned, reverberation from calcific and other mineral structures are also referred to as comet tail artifact. These artifacts are usually apparent below the hyperechoic reflection of the stone or structure itself, as seen in *Figure 25*.

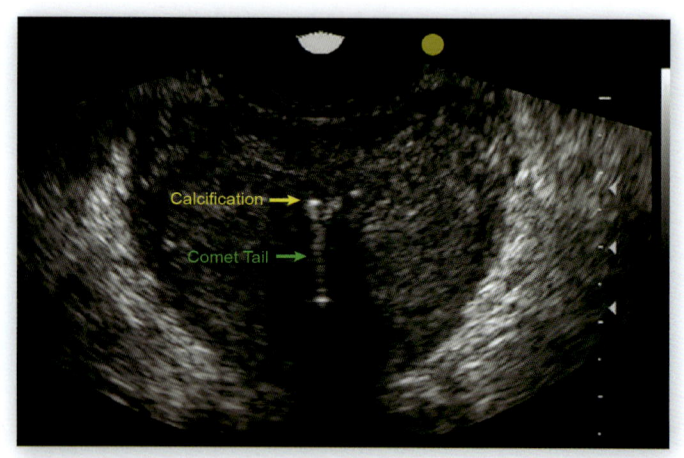

Fig. 25 Endorectal image of a prostate gland with a comet tail artifact emanating from a calcification

When comet tail occurs within color Doppler, it is often referred to as "twinkle" artifact. The color manifestation is similar to that of 2D in that there is a color "tail" that begins at the point of reverberation and extends inferiorly as seen in the next two figures.

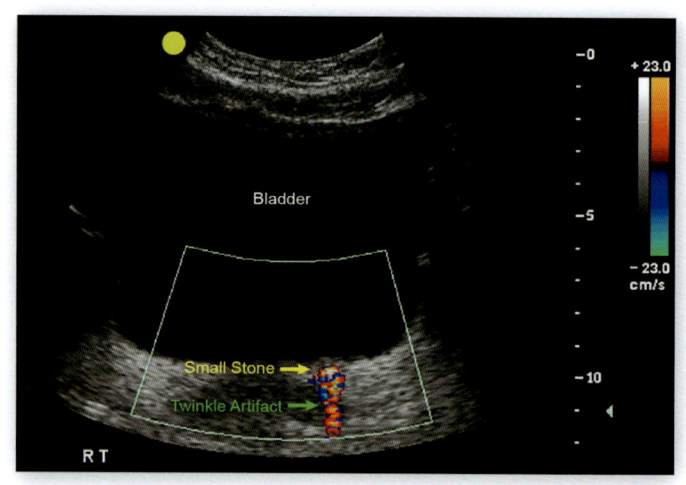

Fig. 26 Transverse scan through bladder illustrating comet tail artifact in color Doppler, also known as twinkle artifact; the artifact emanates from a small stone in the distal ureter

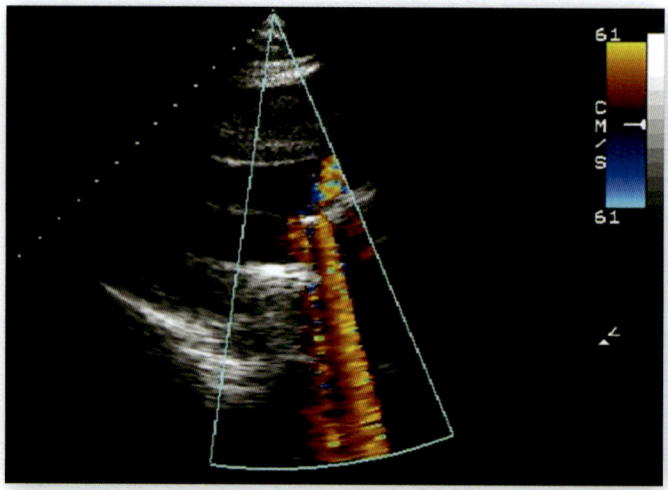

Fig. 27 Prosthetic aortic valve with evident color Doppler twinkle artifact (comet tail) emanating from the metal of the valve

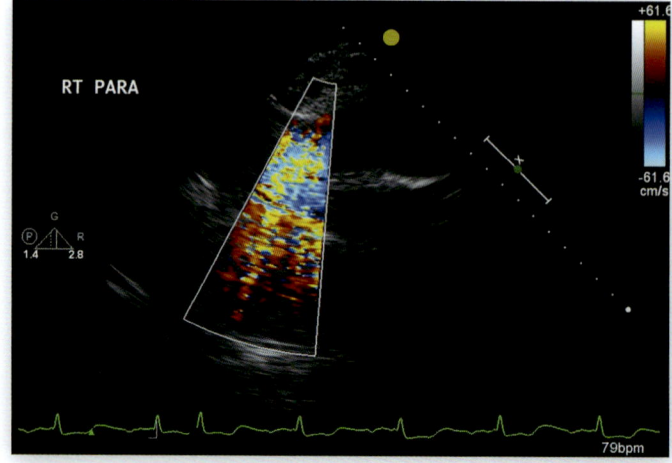

Fig. 28 Twinkle artifact from mitral annulus calcification

View ONLINE Animation and Image Library

4.3 Multi-Path Artifact

Multi-path artifact incorrectly displays the depth of a structure. This artifact is generally the result of insonification of a specular reflector at an oblique angle (not perpendicular). Since specular reflection is very directional and the reflection angle equals the incident angle, the reflection is not directed toward the transducer.

If the reflection encounters another strong reflector off-axis (which redirects the beam toward the transducer), the path lengthens and therefore, acoustic transit (travel) time is longer than expected, and the structure is represented deeper than reality.

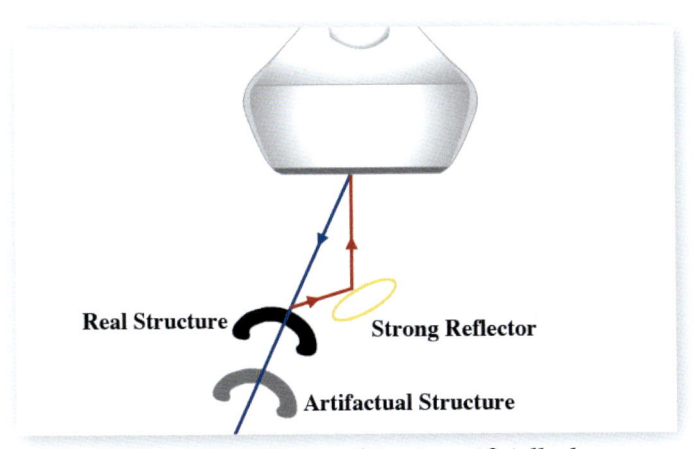

Fig. 29 Multi-path artifact resulting in artificially deeper appearance of a structure

View ONLINE Animation and Image Library

4.4 Side Lobe (Single Element) and Grating Lobe (Arrays) Artifacts

Actual beam patterns are extremely complex (especially in the Fresnel zone). The beam profiles drawn to teach about beams and resolution in ultrasound are highly simplified. One known complexity to the beam shape is the existence of weaker beams pointing off-axis. These weaker beam artifacts are called side lobes for single element transducers and grating lobes for multi-element transducers.

These grating lobe beams exist, in part, because of partial constructive interference. Ideally, we would be able to create beams that added completely constructively in the desired direction, and completely destructively in all other directions. In reality, the waves created from each of the elements are never completely out-of-phase off-axis of the main beam. The result is that energy propagates in undesired directions, returning echoes from undesired locations. Generally the energy in these lobes is much less than the main beam and therefore goes unnoticed. However, if these lobes encounter a strong specular reflector, the reflected energy will be added to the reflected energy of the main beam either creating a spurious structure or "clouding" over the image. When a spurious structure is created, it is displayed laterally displaced from the real structure which also appears in the image in the correct location. Caution must be taken since this artifact is sometimes misinterpreted as a thrombus or mass.

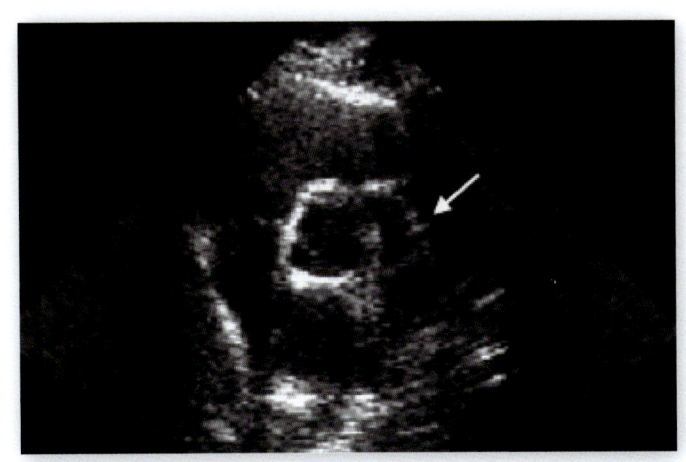

Fig. 30 Spurious second aortic valve root caused by grating lobe artifact

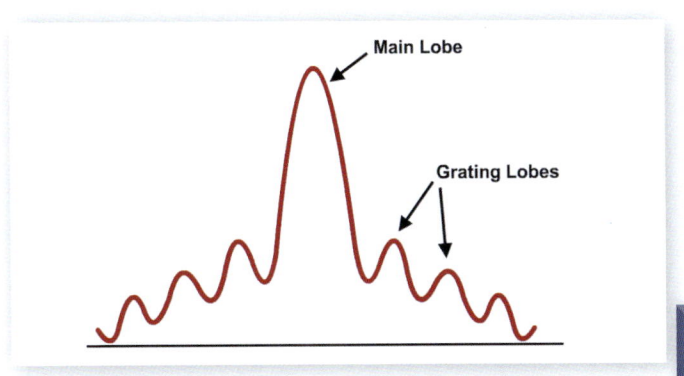

Fig. 31 Beam directivity and grating lobe artifact

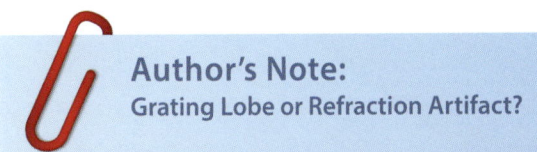

> **Author's Note:**
> **Grating Lobe or Refraction Artifact?**
>
> The other principal mechanism that results in an artifactual lateral translation of a structure is refraction. Depending on the refractive path length, refraction usually causes the spurious structure to be slightly deeper, as well as lateral, to the true structure. From the still image in *Figure 30* alone, it is not possible to determine if the artifact is caused by grating lobes or by refraction from the rib. However, analyzing the appearance and disappearance with angle changes in real time demonstrates this artifact to be a grating lobe artifact.

The distribution and size of grating lobes depends on the spacing of the elements relative to the wavelength. As the spacing becomes, larger, the grating lobes become higher amplitude, resulting in more frequent and more evident artifacts in the image. The following beamplot shows a main beam with significant grating lobes at angles nearly ± 30° relative to the main beam.

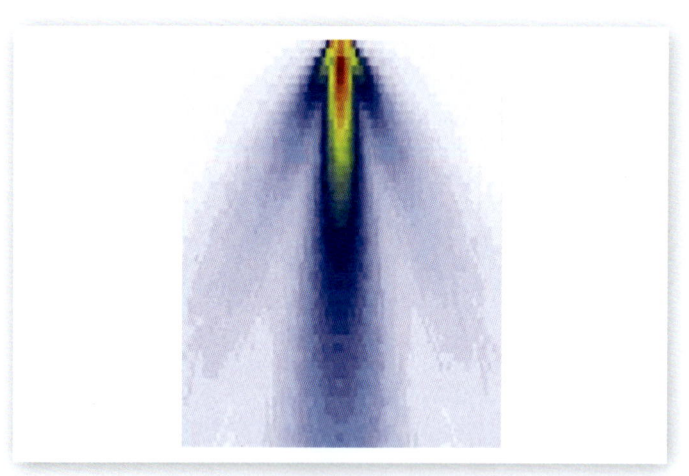

Fig. 32 **Beamplot of a sparse phased array with high amplitude grating lobes approximately 30° relative to the main beam** *(Courtesy Olympus Corporation)*

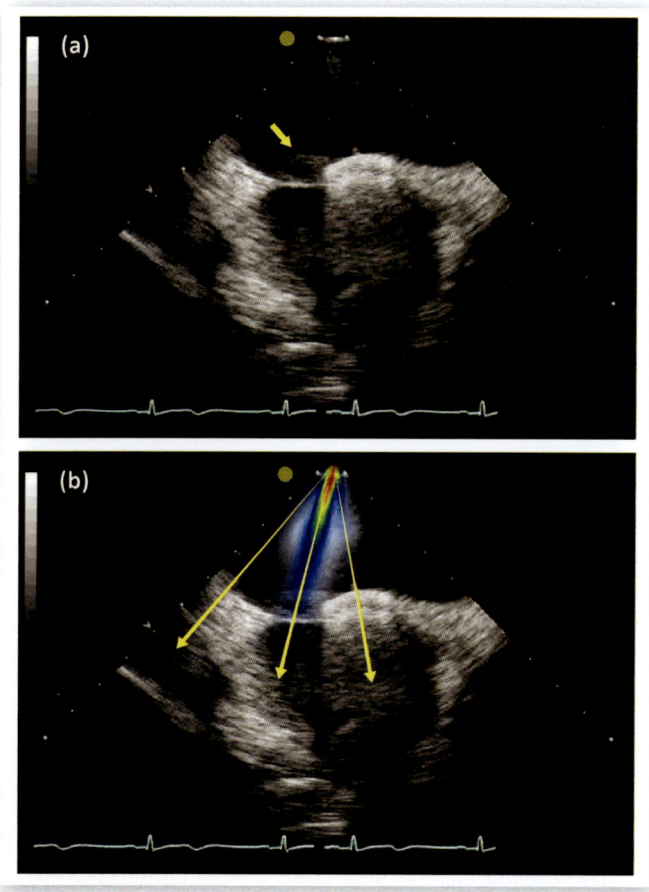

Fig. 33 **(a) Grating lobe artifact (arrow) using a catheter-based intracardiac phased array transducer (ICE) imaging an Amplatzer closure device; (b) depiction of transmitted and grating lobe beam causing artifact**

View ONLINE Animation and Image Library

KEY CONCEPT

Reverberation artifact results in replication of structures or tissues because of reverberating sound beams. Many artifact names such as comet tail, ring down, and twinkle artifact are really just specialized cases of reverberation artifact.

4.5 Speed Error Artifact

In diagnostic ultrasound, a propagation velocity of 1540 m/sec is assumed. By the distance equation, an ultrasound system calculates the depth based on this assumed propagation velocity and the time from the transmit until receiving the echo. If the propagation velocity anywhere within the path varies from the assumed 1540, the system will display the structures deeper than that location at an incorrect depth as shown in *Figure 34*.

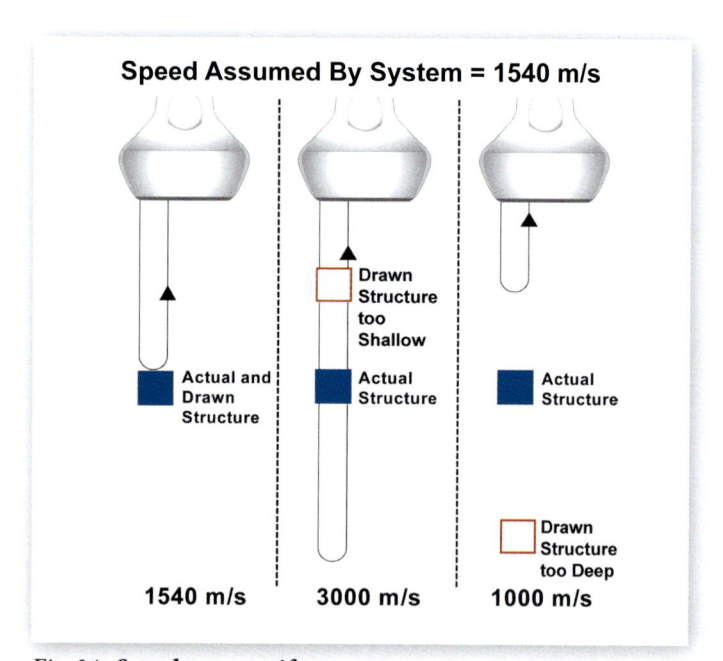

Fig. 34 **Speed error artifact**

Notice how the ultrasound beam travels different distances in the same duration of time (based on the propagation speed) resulting in structures appearing at different depths in the image.

If the propagation speed is higher than 1540 m/sec, the echoes will return sooner, and the structures will be drawn artificially shallow. Conversely, if the propagation speed is slower than 1540 m/

sec, echoes will arrive later in time and hence be displayed deeper than reality.

You should expect speed error anytime the sound propagates through a medium that has a different density than the surrounding tissue and, hence, a different propagation velocity than the presumed 1540 m/sec of soft tissue. Besides the obvious candidates of air and bone, just about everything man-made which is put into the body should be suspected (the silastic rubber of a ball and cage valve, metal discs, wires, clips, needles, etc.).

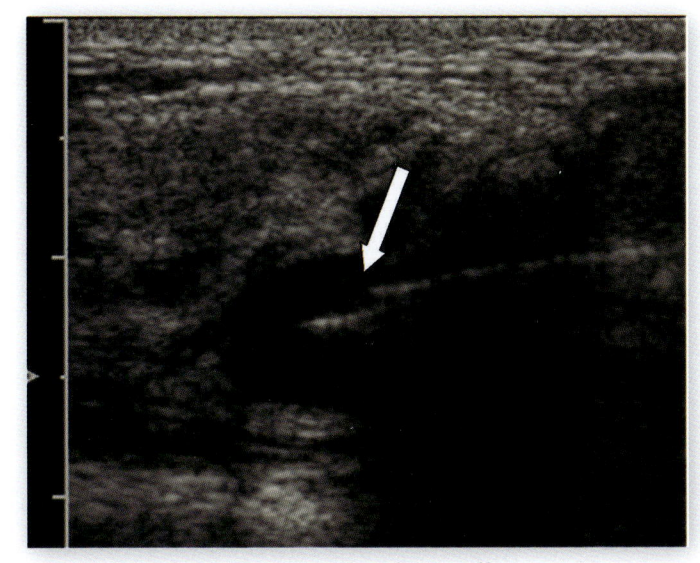

Fig. 35 **Speed error associated with a needle**

In the image of *Figure 35*, the needle appears as if broken as a result of speed error. Since the propagation velocity is faster in the tissue than in the fluid of the cyst, the echo from the needle returning through the cyst takes more time than the echo returning from the needle through the tissue. As a result, the tip of the needle is displayed deeper in the image, given the appearance of a bend or break at the point of entry into the cyst. This artifact is sometimes referred to as a "bayonet sign" and is useful in that it confirms that the needle is within the cyst/mass. If the propagation velocity of a mass is close to the propagation velocity of the surrounding tissue, the bayonet sign may not be evident.

It is important to realize that all structures inferior to a structure with a speed of sound different from the assumed 1540 m/sec will appear either shallower or deeper than reality.

The following figure outlines the effects of speed error. In *Figure 36a*, no artifact occurs since the speed of sound is the assumed 1540 m/sec. *Figure 36b* shows the effect of a higher than assumed speed of sound. Notice that the structure with the higher speed of sound appears thinner than reality, and the inferior structure appears shallower than reality (and distorted because of the non-uniform thickness of the superior structure). Conversely, *Figure 36c* shows the effect of a lower than assumed speed of sound. Notice that the structure with the lower speed of sound appears thicker than reality, and the inferior structure appears deeper than reality (and distorted because of the non-uniform thickness of the superior structure).

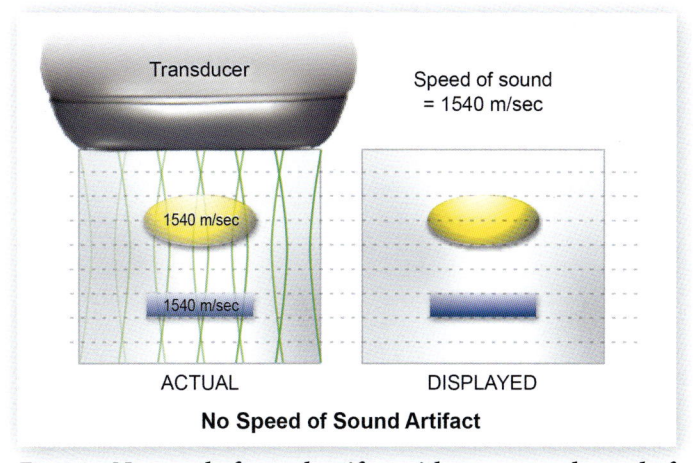

Fig. 36a **No speed of sound artifact with an assumed speed of sound equal to 1540 m/sec**

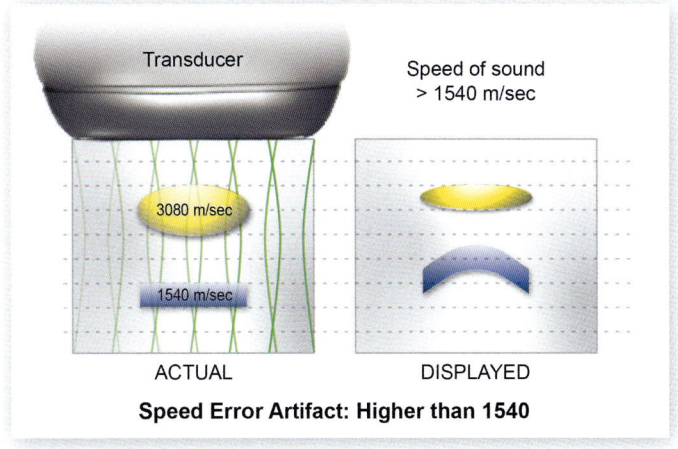

Fig. 36b **Speed error artifact with speed of sound > 1540 m/sec**

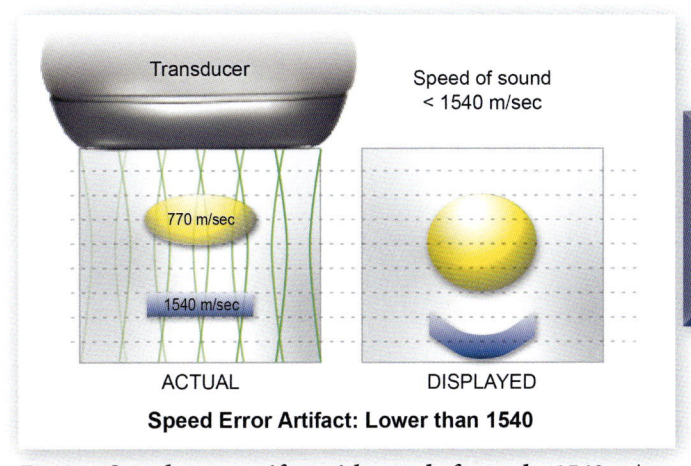

Fig. 36c **Speed error artifact with speed of sound < 1540 m/sec**

View ONLINE Animation and Image Library

In Chapter 6, Part II, we discussed a retrospective, adaptive processing technique which performs sound speed compensation. This process generally improves image quality, penetration, and detail resolution. Although lessons on artifacts usually include warnings about incorrect depth registration resulting from speed error, the lessons rarely include the deleterious effects on image quality as demonstrated in the following image.

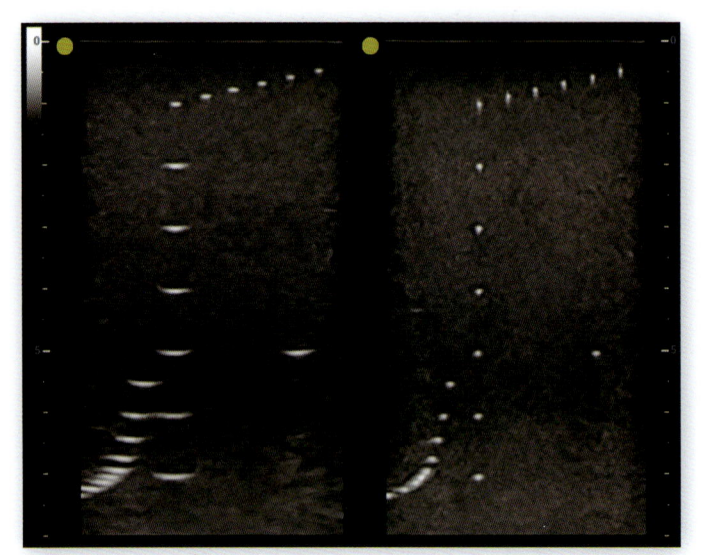

Fig. 37 **Side-by-side images of a phantom without (left) and with (right) sound speed compensation** *(Courtesy of Mindray)*

Notice the improved lateral (detail) resolution and the more uniform speckle pattern using sound speed compensation.

KEY CONCEPT

By the distance equation, depth is directly proportional to time. The assumption is that sound travels at 1540 m/sec in tissue. When the actual speed of sound is higher than 1540 m/sec, the sound reaches and returns from a structure faster, resulting in structures being drawn artifactually shallow. Conversely, when the sound is slower than the assumed 1540 m/sec, the sound takes longer than if the speed were the assumed value, resulting in structure being drawn deeper than reality.

4.6 Range Ambiguity Artifact

Range ambiguity can exist with both sequential and plane wave imaging, but is more likely with sequential imaging. Range ambiguity artifact is usually only significant at shallow depth settings. (The same artifact occurs in PW Doppler and was described in detail in Chapter 7.) A pulse will travel in a medium until all the energy is scattered or absorbed. At shallow depth settings, the required acoustic transit time for a pulse is very short, which means transmit pulses can be fired rapidly. If an echo from a previous pulse (prior acoustic line or plane wave) arrives after the transmit of a new pulse (a new acoustic line or plane wave), the system cannot discriminate between the echo of the prior transmit pulse and the echo from the new pulse. The result is that echoes from two locations are superimposed. This artifact often results in a grayish haze and/or scintillations in the relative near field of an image, sometimes referred to as "herbies," (commonly seen in the apical views of the left ventricle or in superficial views like an image of the thyroid).

Since the frame rates are so high with plane wave imaging, the solution is to simply add some dead time between transmitted plane waves. The dead time allows the echoes from the previous transmitted pulse to decay before the next transmitted pulse, decreasing the likelihood of this artifact. Similarly, for sequential imaging, some dead time is included between each successive transmitted pulse, increasing the PRP and decreasing the PRF. The extra time between successive lines allows for increased attenuation, decreasing the likelihood of this artifact.

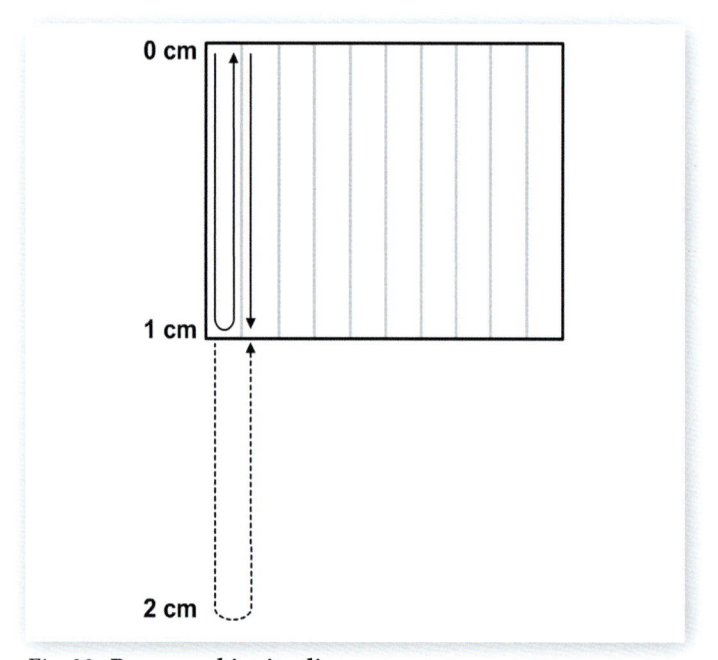

Fig. 38 **Range ambiguity diagram**

4.7 Mirror Artifact

The mechanism for a mirrored image is an oblique incidence on a specular reflector. The specular reflection directs the reflected beam toward a structure. The reflection from the structure is then reflected by the specular reflector back to the transducer. The result is a spurious structure "mirrored" through the specular reflector.

When there is motion with mirror artifact, the motion in the artifact is opposite to that of the actual structure. This is similar to how you will appear deeper in the mirror if you take a step back from the mirror, as you move away from the mirror, your reflection moves away from you. The diaphragm is a good example of a structure which often acts as an acoustic mirror.

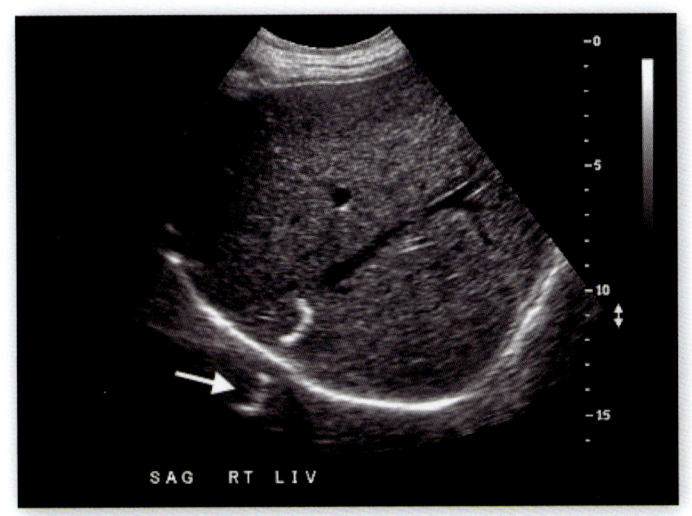

Fig. 39a **Image showing mirror of a calcification in liver from the diaphragm**

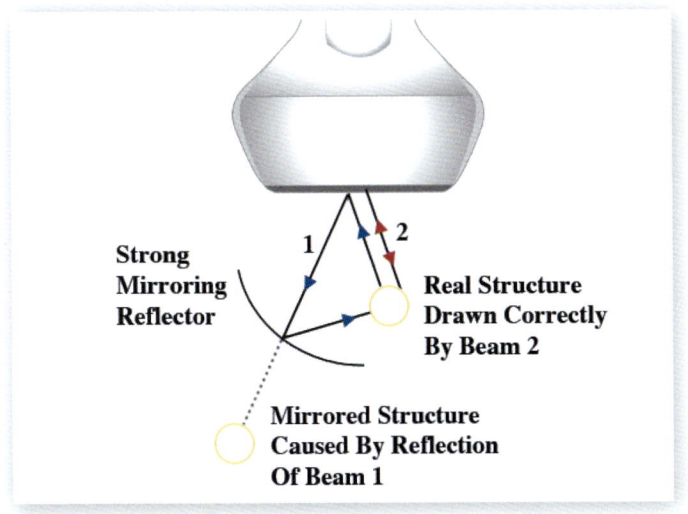

Fig. 39b **Schematic demonstrating the same mirror effect**

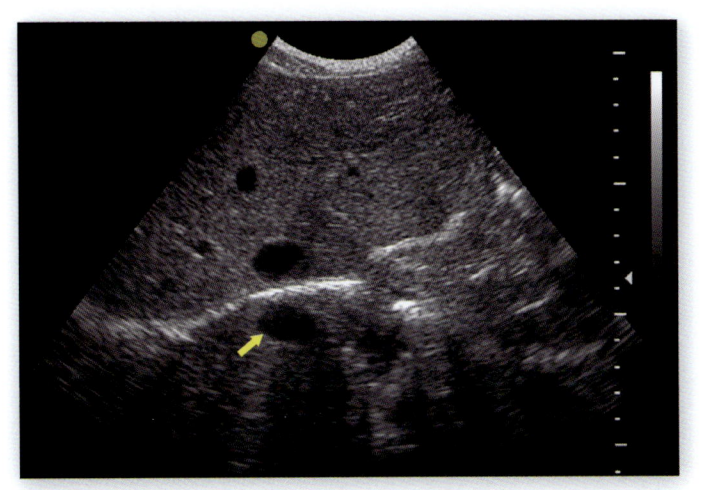

Fig. 40 **Transverse image of normal liver demonstrating mirroring artifact (arrow) of the inferior vena cava (IVC) across the diaphragm (bright, echogenic structure)**

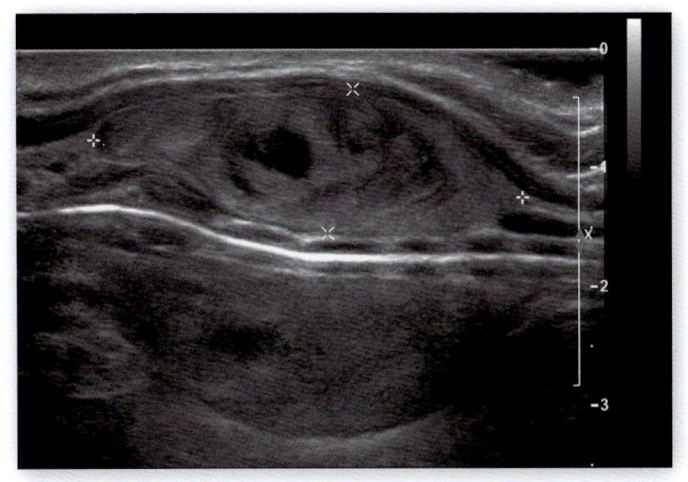

Fig. 41 **Large mirror artifact reflected across the trachea**

The image of *Figure 41* is a large heterogeneous thyroid isthmus between calipers compatible with a multi-nodular goiter. The bright white specular reflection running horizontally through the image is the trachea. Below the strong reflection of the trachea you will note a remarkable mirror image of the multi-nodular goiter.

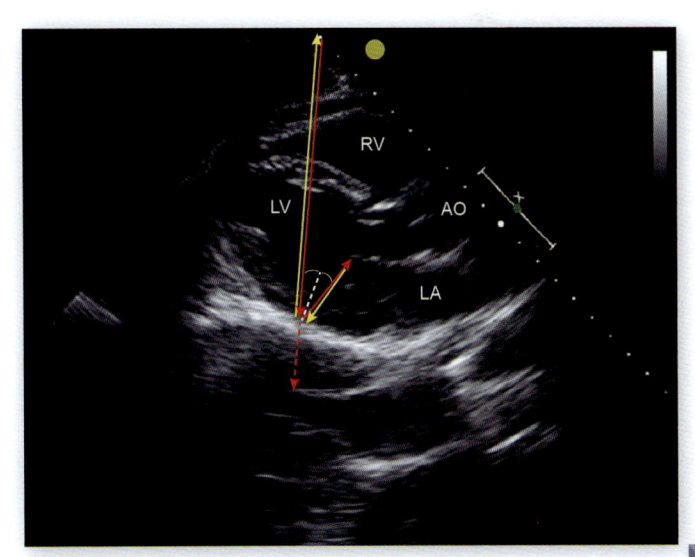

Fig. 42 **Mirror artifact with lines indicating ultrasound path which creates the mirror of the anterior mitral valve leaflet**

Note that the mirroring artifact in *Figure 42* is easier to see in the accompanying online video.

View ONLINE Animation and Image Library

It is important to note that the same mechanisms which result in artifacts in 2D imaging can also result in artifacts in 3D imaging.

Figure 43 shows a mirror artifact occurring during the implantation of an Amplatzer occluder device. This 3D image was captured during a transesophageal echo as the device was being pushed through the septal defect and deployed (but not yet anchored).

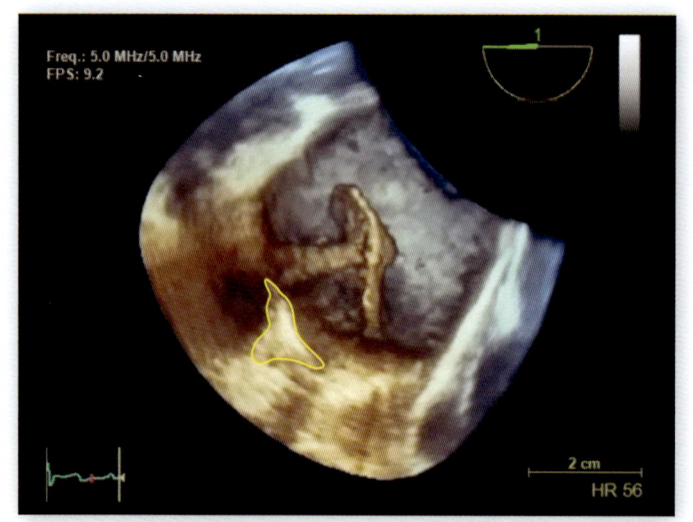

Fig. 43 **3D TEE image during implantation of an Amplatzer occluder with a mirror image artifact (outlined in yellow) about the interatrial septum**

The mirroring artifact can also occur with color and spectral Doppler. This artifact should not be confused with "spectral mirroring" which is based on a completely different mechanism and is discussed later in this chapter. Mirroring for color and spectral Doppler is based on the same sound interactions as for 2D/3D images. An oblique sound beam is redirected by a specular reflector toward a region of flow, which is then scattered back to the mirror and reflected back to the transducer. Since color and spectral Doppler rely on the weaker reflective mechanism of scattering, this artifact is much more likely to occur when there is a highly specular mirror such as a metallic structure.

In the following case (*Figure 44*), the mirroring surface is the strut of a prosthetic mitral valve. The result is artifactual presentation of the LVOT color flow below the mitral valve giving the appearance of mitral regurgitation that does not exist ("pseudo MR"). Since the spectral Doppler beam takes the same path as the color Doppler beam, placing a sample volume in the pseudo MR results in a Doppler spectrum with the same characteristics as the LVOT flow. Note that the color appearance of the pseudo MR does not match the color of the LVOT flow in (a) of *Figure 44* because the mirroring beam path (green lines) encounters the LVOT flow at a different angle than the beams which generate the actual LVOT flow (yellow lines).

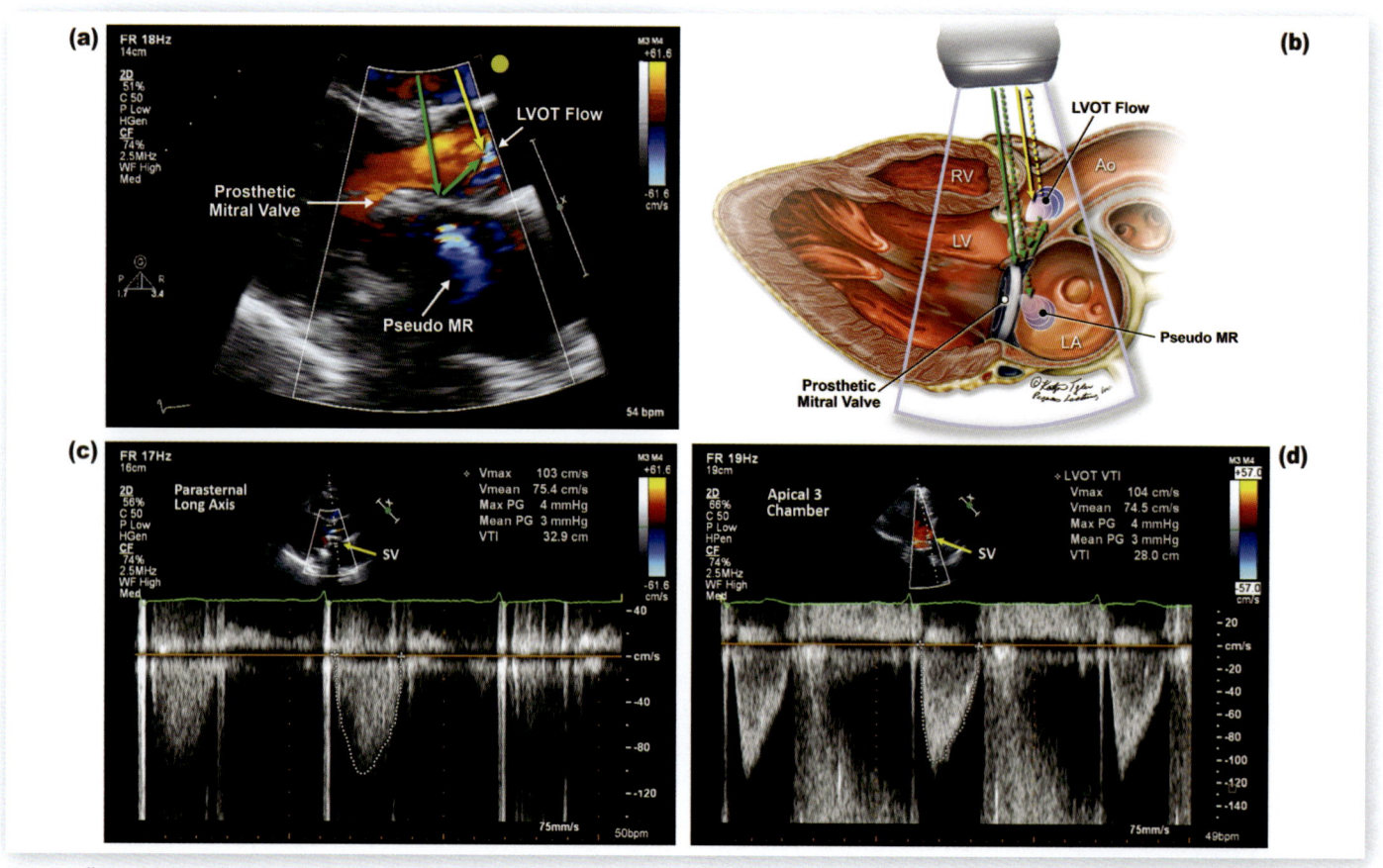

Fig. 44 **"Pseudo MR" as a result of mirror artifact; (a) color Doppler image illustrating mirror artifact from a mechanical prosthetic mitral valve resulting in LVOT flow presenting as "pseudo mitral regurgitation (MR)" flow in the left atrium (LA); (b) schematic illustrating the ultrasound beam path resulting in the mirrored flow (pseudo MR); (c) PW Doppler sample volume (SV) placed at the site of the "pseudo" MR (arrow) in a parasternal long-axis view; (d) PW Doppler sample volume (SV) placed at the site of the LVOT flow (arrow) in the apical 3-chamber view; note that the Doppler profile timing, velocity, pressure gradient, and distance of the pseudo MR matches the measurements made for the LVOT** (*Case images courtesy of Jeffrey Hill, ACS, FASE*)

You must be careful before assuming that an image represents an artifact. The image of *Figure 45* is an example for which many students would see the seemingly duplicated vessels and automatically assume a mirror artifact. In reality, these two vessels represent actual anatomy, showing both the aorta and the inferior vena cava (IVC) simultaneously. This image is significant as it emphasizes the importance of knowing the patient anatomy, understanding the physics of the underlying mechanisms that cause artifacts, and recognizing that multiple ultrasound modalities should corroborate the clinical conclusion. In this case, we do not see any clear reflecting structure which could serve as a mirror. Also, by activating color Doppler, you will very quickly see that the flow directions are opposite and with different velocity profiles, indicating that these are different, not mirrored vessels.

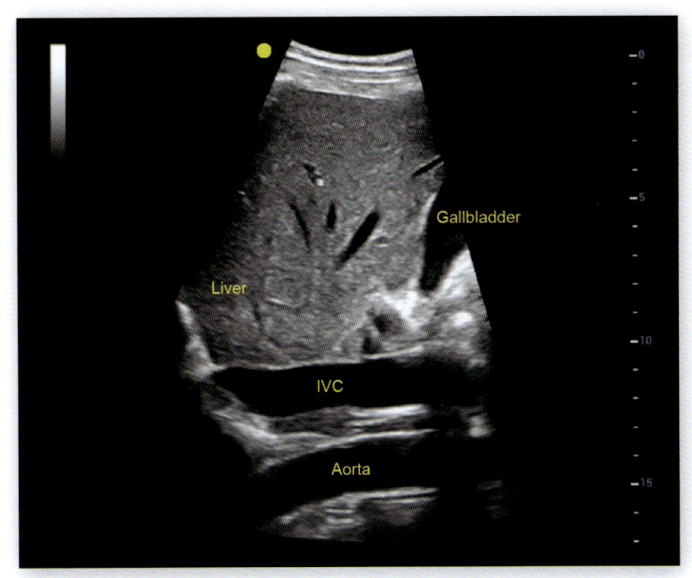

Fig. 45 **Curvilinear image easily confused with mirroring artifact exhibiting the aorta and IVC simultaneously** (Courtesy of Michelle Carter, Mindray)

> **KEY CONCEPT**
>
> When motion exists with a mirror artifact, the motion of the artifact is opposite the motion of the actual structure (the motion is mirrored). This is the opposite behavior of what happens with motion and the reverberation artifact.

5. Attenuation Artifacts

5.1 Shadowing

As suggested by the name, a "shadow" is a darker than normal appearance below a structure in an image. Shadowing is caused by any form of attenuation stronger than the attenuation of the surrounding area. A shadow can be cast on the image below by a strong reflector or absorber. Both strong reflection and absorption decrease the beam intensity thereby attenuating the echoes from deeper structures more than usual. Additionally, a shadow can be cast by beam refraction.

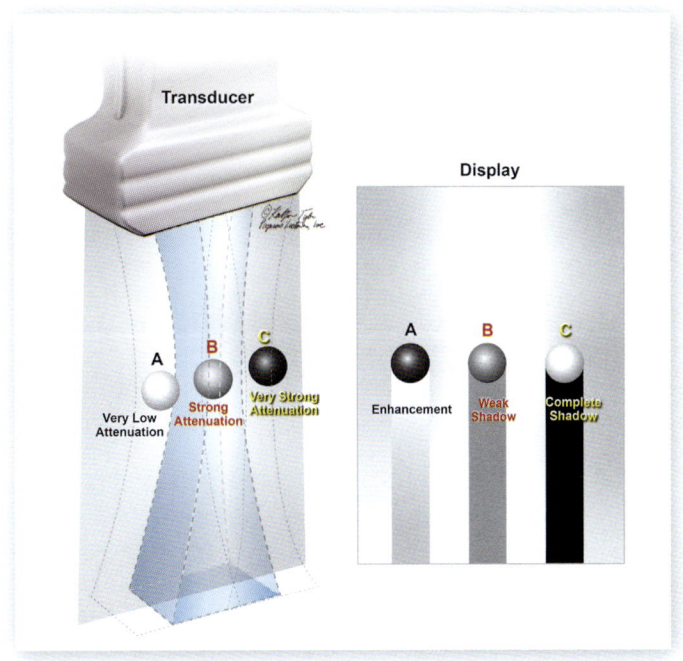

Fig. 46 **Demonstration of differing levels of attenuation-related artifacts**

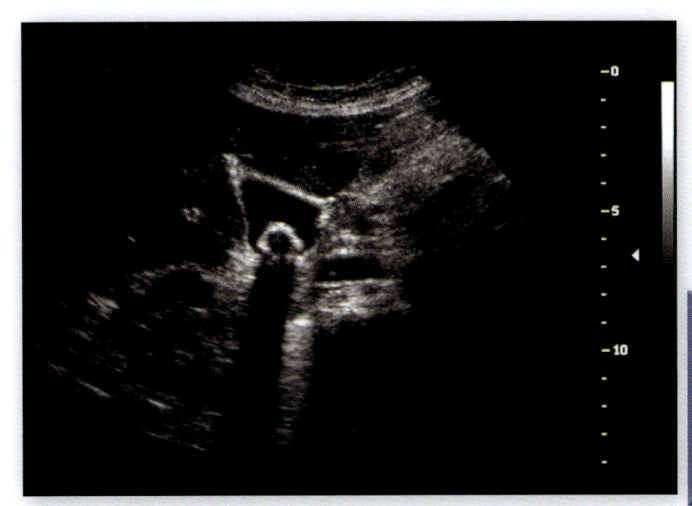

Fig. 47 **Transverse image of a gallbladder with acoustic shadowing from a gallstone**

The following figure shows the same transesophageal image of a St. Jude bileaflet prosthetic mitral valve as was depicted in *Figure 23c* (Section 4.2.2, Comet Tail Artifacts), but in *Figure 48* the valve is in the closed position. Notice the dark shadowing from the metal valve housing and the filled-in shadow below the metal leaflets from reverberation and clutter signals.

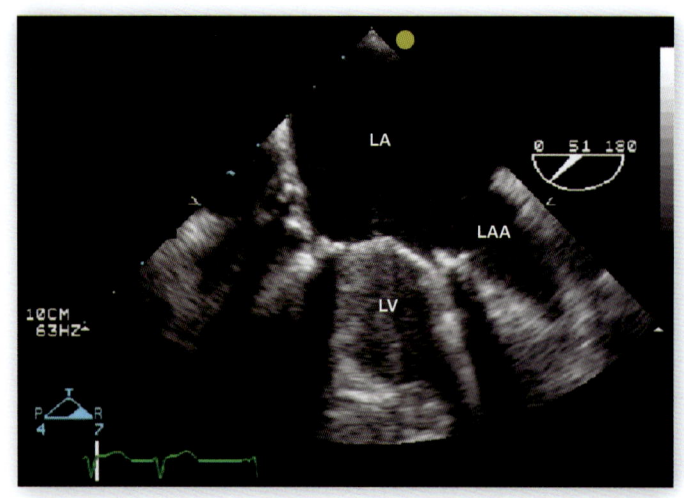

Fig. 48 **TEE image of a St. Jude bileaflet prosthetic mitral valve in the closed position with dark shadowing from the metal housing and filled in shadow below the metal leaflets from reverberation and clutter signals**

View ONLINE Animation and Image Library

In Chapter 3 we discussed the fact that the reflection percentage increases with an increasing acoustic impedance mismatch. Bones relative to surrounding tissue almost always create a large percentage of reflection, significantly reducing the transmission percentage into the bone. In Chapter 3, we also learned that bones are significantly more absorptive than most other tissues. This fact implies that much of the sound that does transmit into bone is converted into heat, with little through transmission to the inferior tissue. As a result, acoustic shadows are very common inferior to bones. The following liver image demonstrates the shadowing artifacts from ribs obscuring parts of the liver and the kidney.

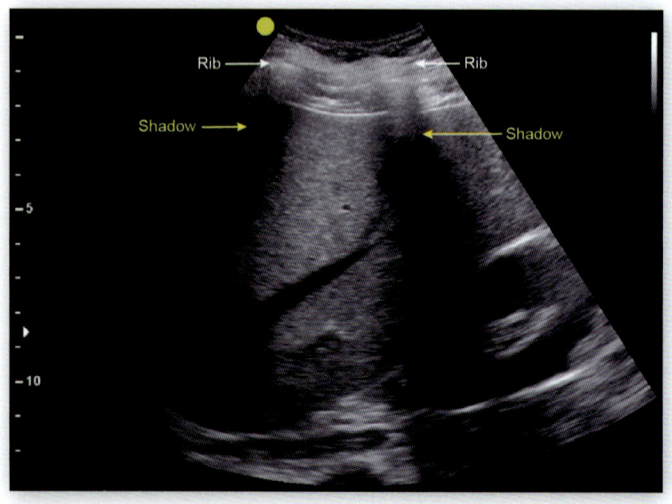

Fig. 49 **Image of the liver and right kidney with acoustic shadowing caused by the ribs; note how the shadow widens with depth as beams fan out in curvilinear image**

As we have just seen, shadowing can result from increased reflection or absorption, but shadowing can also occur from refraction. In Chapter 3, we learned about refraction as governed by Snell's law. Recall that refraction occurs when there is a change in propagation velocity and non-zero degree incidence (when the beam direction is not perpendicular to the interface). With round structures, the incident angle often becomes very large as the beam becomes more tangential to the circle, increasing the amount of refraction that occurs. Refractive edge shadow results when the acoustic beam is either totally internally reflected (critical angle reached) or bent so much that little or no echo returns back to the transducer. A refractive edge shadow occurs both when transitioning from a higher to lower propagation velocity (*Figure 50a*) and when transitioning from a lower to higher propagation velocity (*Figure 50b*). The refractive edge shadow appearance changes based on how much the propagation velocity varies and based on the curvature and size of the refracting structure. When the propagation velocity varies more significantly, the shadowed region becomes broader.

As sound propagates from a higher to lower propagation velocity and is incident at non-zero degree angles (*Figure 50a*), refraction results in total internal reflection for beams closest to the edge (beams most tangential). Beams that are slightly less tangential (farther from the edge) undergo significant refraction, bending so far that little energy returns back to the transducer. The area below these critically and highly refracted beams is shadowed. As the beams become incident at smaller angles (moving more toward the center of the structure), there is less refraction and the shadowing disappears. The effect is of course symmetric, on both sides of the structure.

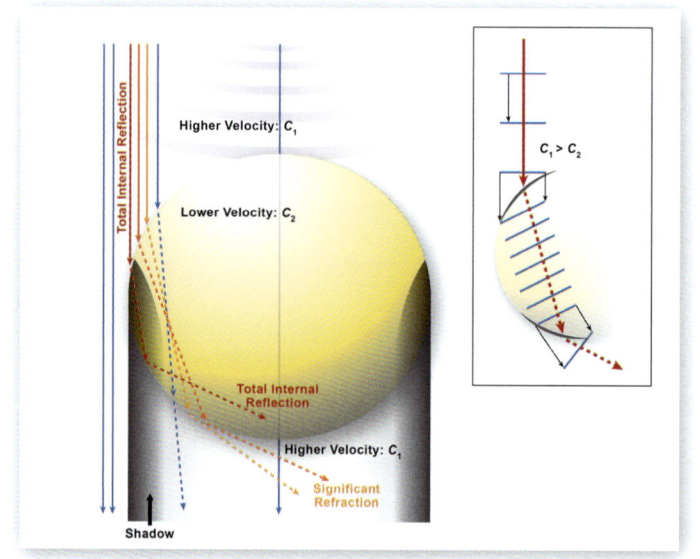

Fig. 50a **Refractive edge shadowing with sound propagating from higher to lower propagation velocity resulting in total internal reflection for most tangential beams**

Conversely, as sound propagates from a lower to higher propagation velocity and is incident at non-zero degree angles (*Figure 50b*), refraction results in the beams bending in the opposite direction. Again, for the beams closest to the structure's edge, total internal reflection occurs. Slightly over from these beams, there is significant refraction. As in *Figure 50a*, there is an acoustic shadow below these beams. Moving toward the center of the structure, the incident angle becomes smaller, and the refraction is reduced such that there is no longer acoustic shadowing.

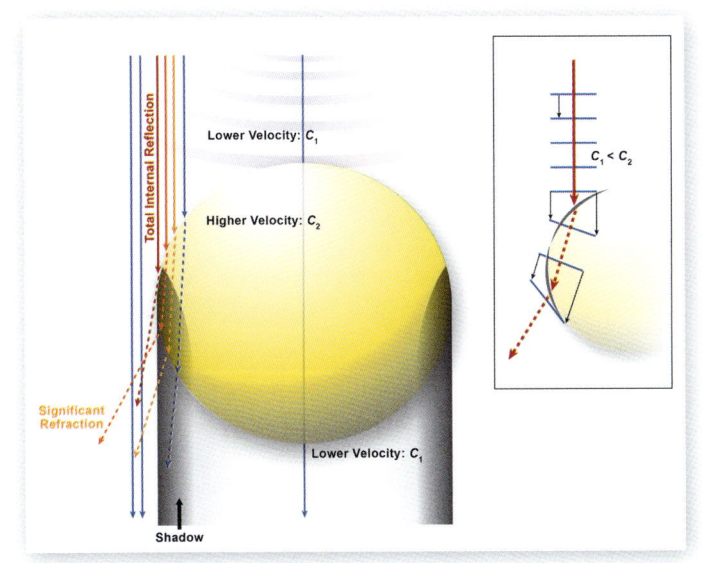

Fig. 50b **Refractive edge shadowing with sound propagating from lower to higher propagation velocity resulting in beams bending in the opposite direction**

In the following fetal cranial image, the shadowing is caused by refraction. The calculation showing that the critical angle has been reached is performed below.

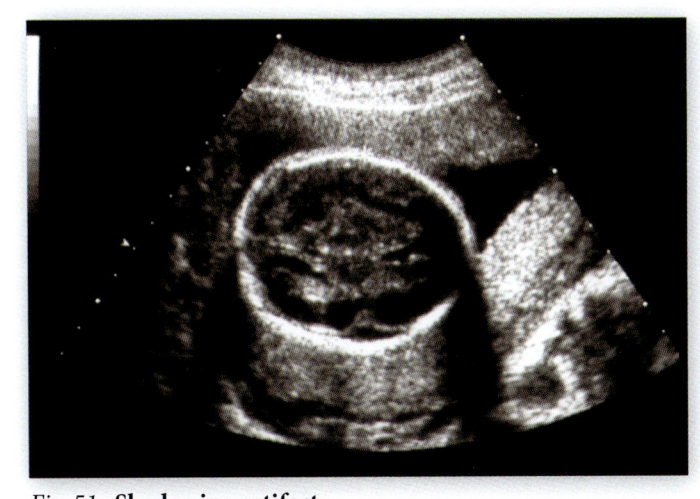

Fig. 51 **Shadowing artifact**

Applying Snell's law, the critical angle is determined as approximately 25°. The incident angle in this image appears to be slightly greater than 25° implying total internal reflection.

Therefore, shadowing which occurs is the result of total internal reflection.

$$c_i = 1540 \text{ m/sec}$$
$$c_t = 4080 \text{ m/sec}$$
$$\theta_t = 90° \text{ (for total internal reflection)}$$

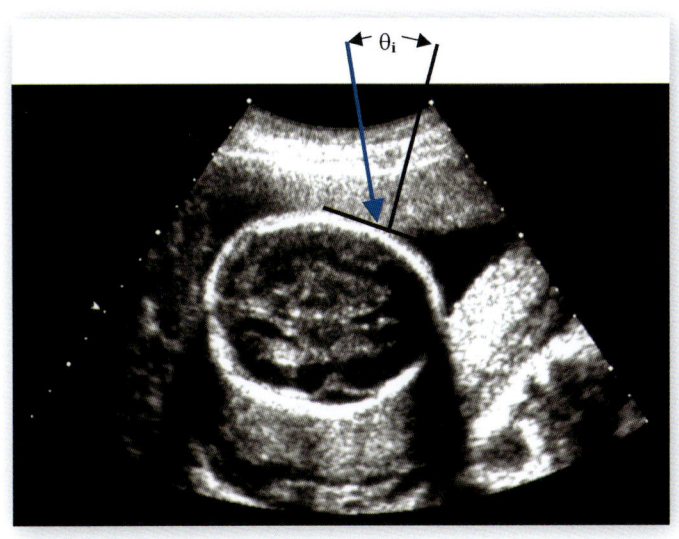

Fig. 52 **Measuring the critical angle**

Recall from Chapter 6, Part II, that one of the consequences of compound imaging is the reduction of angle-related artifacts. Since the composite (displayed) image results from compounding multiple images generated at varying angles, and since refraction is angle dependent, compound imaging often reduces the artifact of refractive edge shadowing (as seen in *Figure 53b*).

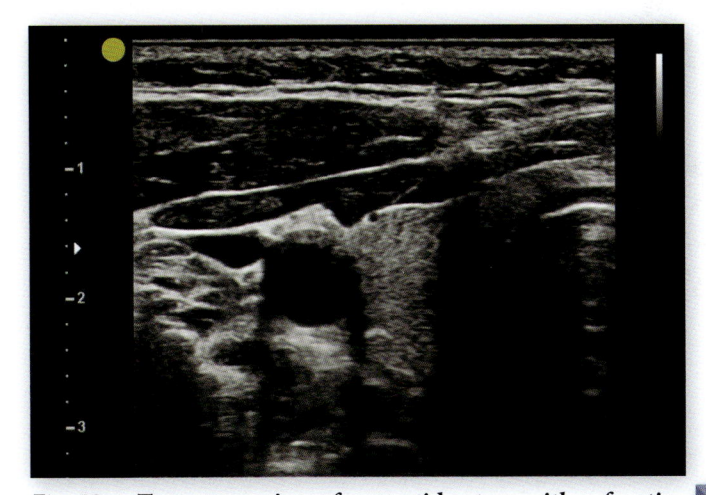

Fig. 53a **Transverse view of a carotid artery with refractive edge shadowing without compound imaging**

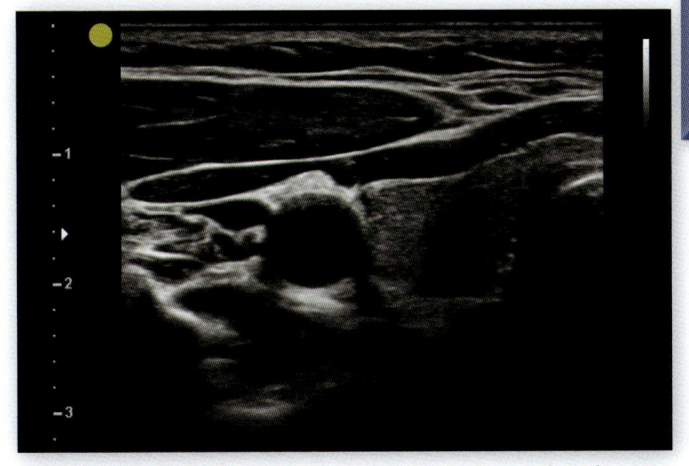

Fig. 53b **Transverse view of a carotid artery with refractive edge shadowing with compound imaging**

Notice in *Figure 53b* that the decrease in the refractive shadowing results from the angles between the frames being averaged to create each image.

5.2 Figure-of-Eight Artifact

A relatively new artifact is the "figure-of-eight" artifact which occurs when imaging the coronal view of the Amplatzer septal closure device (Amplatzer PFO Occluder)[1]. This device (previously pictured in *Figure 24a*) is constructed as two discs connected together by a short metal waist. Each disc consists of a series of interconnected Nitinol wire mesh loops connected by thin polyester fabric and sewn in place with polyester thread. The mesh discs have shape memory so that the device can be stretched to pass through a catheter and still return to its original shape. From the coronal view, the device can create a very interesting artifact based on the angle dependence of specular reflection. When the incident angle is close to 0°, the Nitinol wire is visualized. When the angle becomes oblique, the reflection is not directed back toward the transducer, and the wire is not visualized.

The result is that a very interesting figure-of-eight pattern is generated as shown in the following figures. Note that the figure-of-eight changes shape based on the rate of "fan out" of the beams. If the beams are parallel, or close to parallel, then the top and bottom loop will be close to the same size and symmetric. The more the beams are fanning out, the greater the difference between the top and bottom loop of the figure-of-eight artifact. This fact implies that the shape of the artifact will generally be different for a TEE and TTE image. For the TEE image, the device is nearer to the apex where the beams are fanning out rapidly, resulting in a more lopsided figure-of-eight. For TTE, the device is captured deeper in the image at which point the beams do not spread at such a rapid rate, making the figure-of-eight more symmetric on top and bottom.

The schematic of *Figure 54* shows a figure-of-eight artifact being created by an Amplatzer septal occluder device from a coronal perspective. The pullout shows a single metal loop of the device and the corresponding reflections where the ultrasound beam intersects perpendicularly. Notice that, since the beams from the TEE transducer are fanning outward in this depiction, the top loop of the "8" is narrower than the bottom loop.

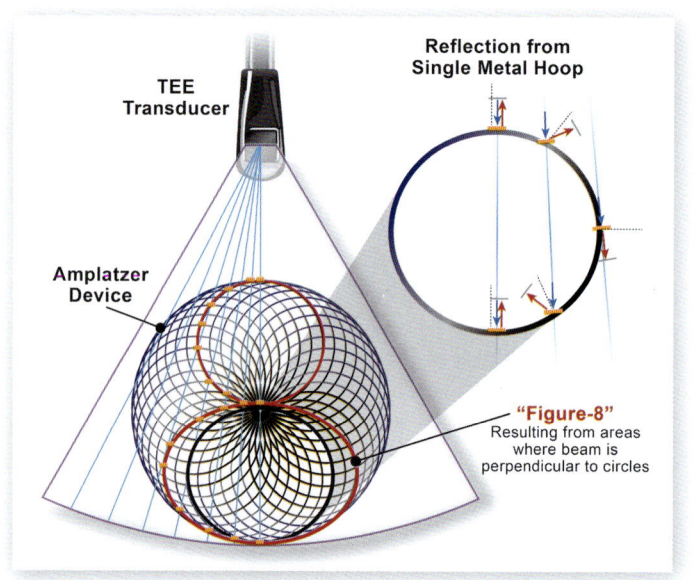

Fig. 54 **Creation of figure-of-eight artifact from Amplatzer septal occluder device from a coronal perspective**

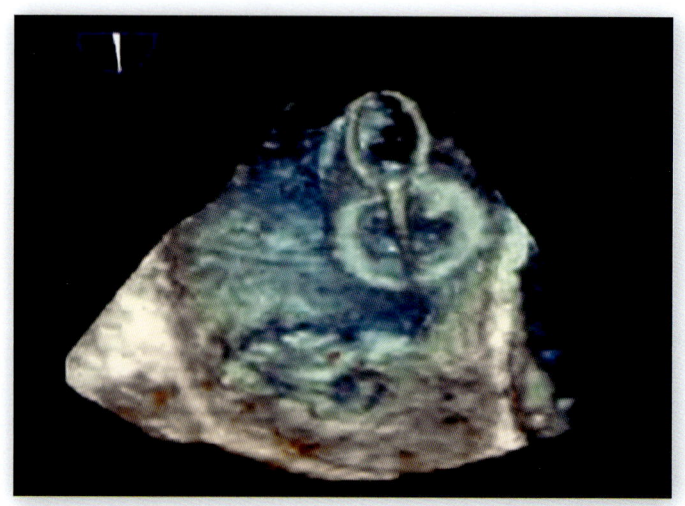

Fig. 55 **3D TEE image of a figure-of-eight artifact resulting from the presence of an Amplatzer septal occluder device**

5.3 Enhancement Artifact

Enhancement is the "reciprocal" of shadowing. If a structure is a weaker reflector than normal or less absorbing than normal, the beam is attenuated less than normal "enhancing" the amplitude of echoes below the weak reflector or poor absorber. The term "increased through transmission" is also sometimes used to refer to the same effect as enhancement.

Typically fluids are relatively homogeneous and less absorbing than tissues. As a result, enhancement often occurs when sound propagates through a fluid-filled region. The most common examples are cystic structures, the bladder, and a blood pool.

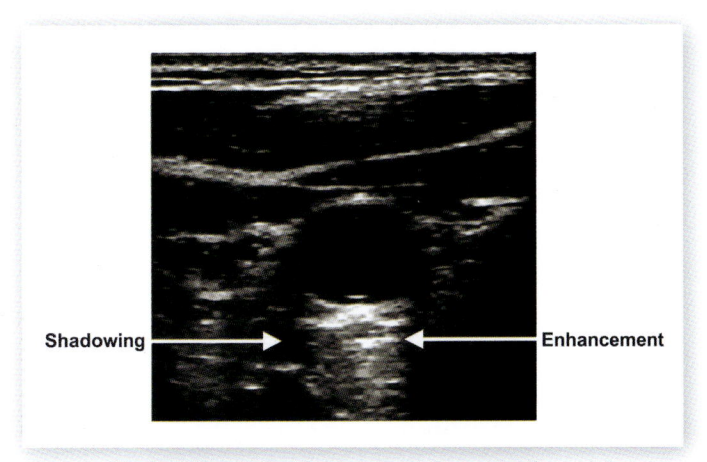

Fig. 56 **Shadowing and enhancement from the femoral artery**

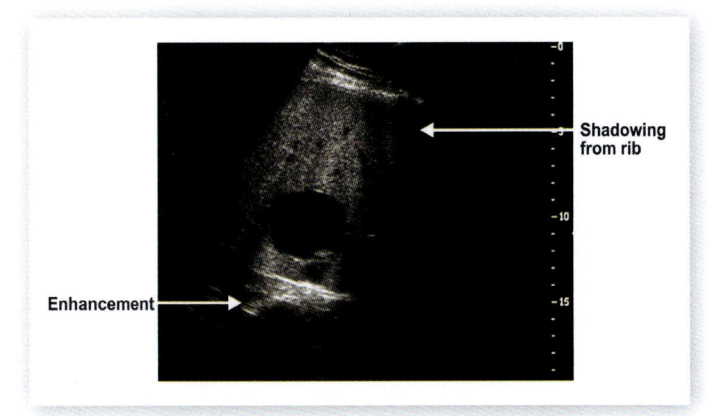

Fig. 57 **Enhancement from an anechoic cyst in the liver**

It is important to note that the signal does not become "stronger" because the sound beam travels through a less attenuative medium like a fluid. What actually occurs is that the signal is less attenuated than the signal which traveled through the normally attenuative tissue, making the signal appear stronger relative to the signals on either side. Since the compensation is set for the standard amount of attenuation, in essence, the signal below a less attenuative structure is actually overgained, resulting in the characteristic bright appearance.

View ONLINE Animation and Image Library

6. Phase-Related Artifacts

As we have learned throughout the book, the wavelength and phase control are very important in ultrasound image acquisition. In this section we will discuss the results of variations of the phase and the corresponding effects on the generated ultrasound image. Discussing these limitations will also lead to observations relating to more recent advances designed specifically to improve image quality by better controlling the phase during image generation.

6.1 Speckle Basics

In Chapter 3: Section 9.2, there was a brief discussion regarding speckle. Although speckle gives the appearance of tissue texture, the speckle pattern is not representative of true tissue characteristics. As noted, speckle occurs when there are reflecting structures smaller than the resolution of the ultrasound being used. Since the speckle pattern is not directly indicative of true tissue characteristics, speckle quite often obscures smaller structures or degrades resolution. Therefore, myriad techniques to reduce speckle have been implemented in ultrasound in order to improve signal-to-noise in the image.

In order to understand the concept of speckle we will begin by considering an imaging situation in which a very small region of tissue is perfectly homogeneous. Let's imagine that the acoustic properties of this region would result in a uniform light gray region (as shown in *Figure 58a*). *Note the region is being drawn extremely wide to make color variations more easily visualized.*

Fig. 58a **Uniform appearance of uniform tissue if speckle did not exist**

Speckle results in a variation of intensity (as shown in *Figure 58b*) from the ideal uniform appearance.

Fig. 58b **Non-uniform appearance of uniform tissue which results from speckle artifact**

Understanding Speckle

Understanding both the mechanism that causes speckle and the approaches employed to reduce it within an image requires a review of the concept of constructive and destructive interference (first discussed in Chapter 2: Waves. Recall that when two signals are purely out of phase (180° apart) wave cancellation occurs (destructive interference). When two waves are purely in phase (0° apart) constructive interference occurs. Of course any phase shift between 0° and 180° results in partial constructive (also called partial destructive) interference. From within a small region of tissue, the distance to elements of the transducer will vary slightly, resulting in a phase difference relative to the wavelength. The resulting variation in amplitude is shown in *Figure 59*. Notice that the bar below is intended to represent a region of uniform tissue, but where there is better constructive interference (red and blue waves in phase), the amplitude increases (black resultant wave) and the intensity is displayed as brighter white. Similarly, in the region where the phase has varied enough so that waves are further out of phase (red and blue waves at or close to 180° out of phase), the resultant wave amplitude drops (black wave) and the intensity of the region is displayed as weaker, or dark black.

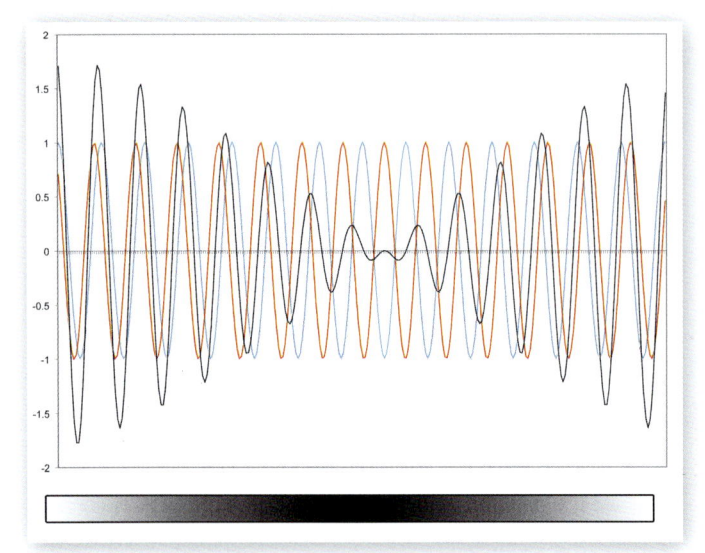

Fig. 59 **Lower frequency – notice how slowly the waves move from constructive to destructive and back to constructive interference; the result is a larger speckle pattern size (as demonstrated in the grayscale bar at the bottom of the figure)**

The Effects of Frequency on Speckle Pattern

The use of a higher frequency has two advantages relative to speckle production. First, higher frequencies result in shorter wavelengths, narrower beams, and generally weaker grating lobes, all promoting improved resolution. Second, since higher frequencies produce shorter wavelengths, high frequency beams transition from in to out of phase over shorter distances within the medium. The result is a smaller speckle pattern as demonstrated by comparing *Figure 59* above with *Figure 60* below.

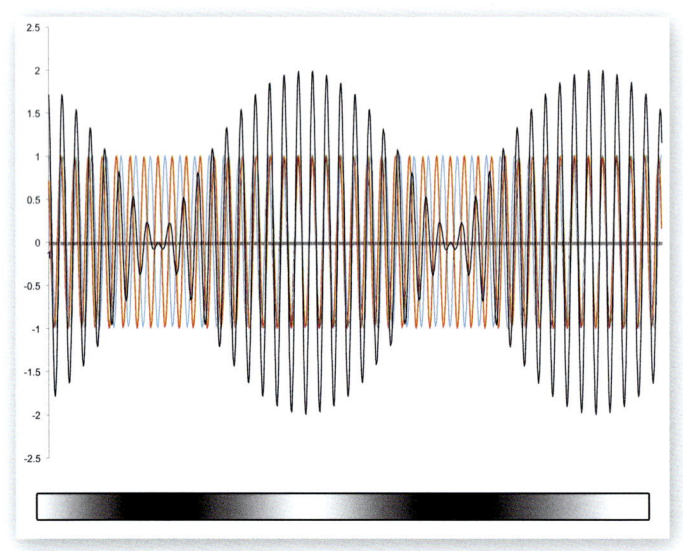

Fig. 60 **Higher frequency – notice how the waves more quickly transition from constructive to destructive and back to constructive interference; the result is a smaller speckle pattern size (as demonstrated in the grayscale bar at the bottom of the figure)**

Improvements in Speckle

Improved Resolution and Sensitivity

Given that speckle occurs when reflecting structures are smaller than the system resolution, one of the most obvious approaches to reducing speckle degradation of the image is to improve system resolution. Improving resolution has been a primary goal of system engineers since diagnostic ultrasound first started. Of late, there have been many improvements, which have also reduced speckle noise. Specifically, tissue harmonic imaging has allowed for use of higher frequencies than conventional imaging. Further advantages were realized with the introduction of pulse inversion harmonics and coded harmonics (discussed in Chapter 10). Since both pulse inversion and coded harmonics have improved penetration relative to conventional harmonic imaging, it can be used more frequently than when only conventional harmonic imaging existed. Transducer technology advancements have also played a role in allowing for higher frequency imaging. Specifically, newer composite materials, better impedance matching, PMN-PT single crystals, and CMUT have all promoted increased sensitivity, allowing for the use of higher imaging frequencies.

Averaging Techniques

The second approach taken to reduce speckle in order to improve image quality is based on averaging and the concepts of constructive interference. Recall from Chapter 6, Part II, the concept of signal-to-noise was extensively discussed, including the explanation of how image averaging results in an improvement in the signal-to-noise by the square root of the number of images (so if 16 images are averaged, the signal-to-noise improves by the square root of 16, or a factor of 4). In order for averaging to result in an improvement, the detected signal of each of the images being averaged must remain in phase and the noise must be random (no fixed relationship within the noise from image to image). When these conditions hold true, the signal from sample to sample averages fully constructively and the noise adds up partially constructively. The net result (when averaging multiple frames together) is that the signal adds faster than the noise, reducing the amount of speckle (as can be seen by comparing (a) and (b) in *Figure 61* below).

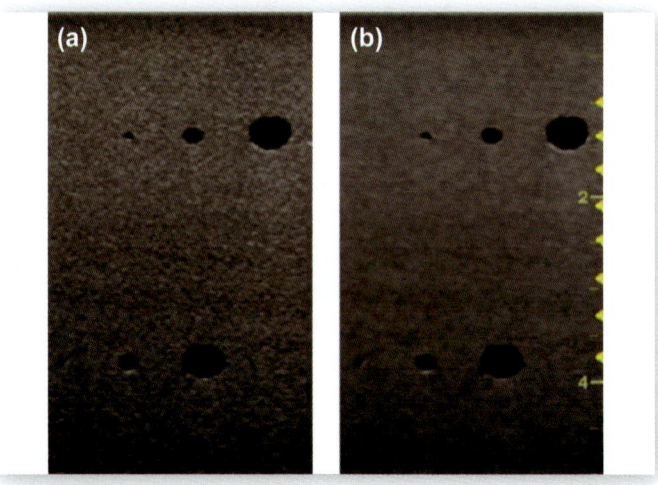

Fig. 61 **Phantom image from conventional imaging (a) compared to image with speckle reduction and improved SNR as the result of constructive and destructive interference (b)**

Given that speckle pattern must be random for averaging approaches to improve SNR, the question is: "what are the imaging situations which can result in random speckle?" There are currently two basic approaches to gathering multiple images of the same structure(s) by which random speckle will exist from image to image:
- Spatial compounding
- Frequency compounding

Spatial Compounding (Compound Imaging)

Canon: ApliPure™
GE: CrossXBeam™
Generic (used most commonly on exam): Compound Imaging
Mindray: iBeam™
Philips: SonoCT
Samsung: MultiVision™
Siemens: Spatial Compounding

A more basic discussion of compound imaging is included in Chapter 6, Part II. Recall that compound imaging is typically performed by averaging multiple frames, each created by steering the image at a slightly different angle. The frame rate in compound imaging is maintained by essentially "buffering" the data. As a new frame is acquired, the oldest frame in the average is removed. Therefore, for each new frame of data acquired, there is a new average displayed to the user. As discussed is Chapter 6, by using different angles between each frame, specular-based artifacts within the resulting compounded image are generally reduced. But there is another advantage that occurs by using different steering angles for frame acquisition which has not yet been discussed. By changing the steering angle from frame to frame, the ultrasound beam takes a different path in each frame. Since the wave has encountered different scattering structures, the speckle pattern is random from frame to frame. Therefore, when the frames are added together, the signal remains relatively coherent (in phase) and the speckle is random. The net result when averaging is a reduction in speckle, improving structure visualization.

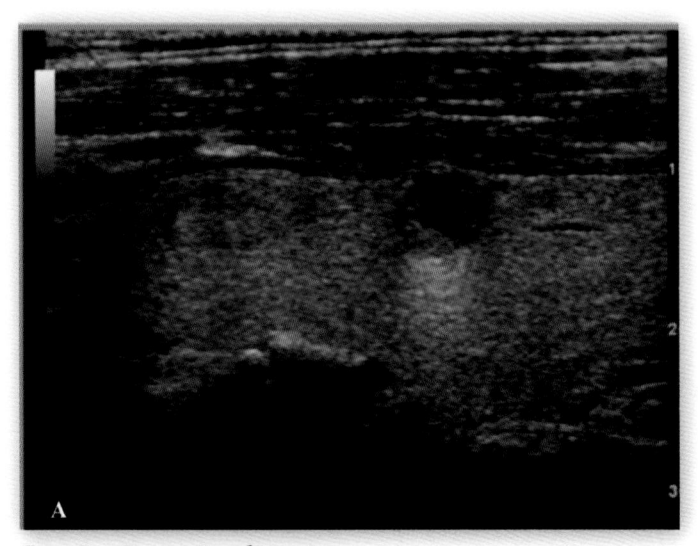

Fig. 62a **Conventional imaging**

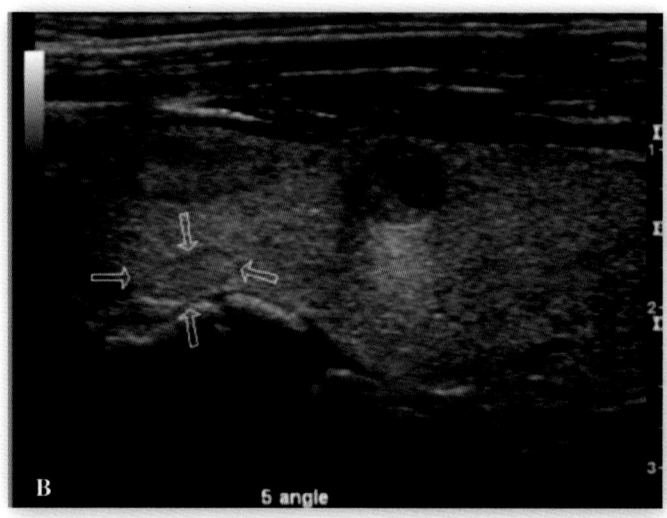

Fig. 62b **Compound imaging (note identification of nodule not seen with conventional ultrasound as indicated by yellow arrows)**

Whereas significant improvement in SNR through speckle reduction can be achieved with compound imaging, there are some potential drawbacks to the technique. The most obvious issue is that this approach can only be used in relatively static situations. If the structures to be imaged are moving fast enough relative to the time needed to acquire each frame used in the average, then the signal from the structures will not be in phase from frame to frame. In essence, even though the displayed frame rate remains high (since for each new frame of data acquired a new frame of data is displayed), the temporal resolution is compromised by averaging frames acquired at different times. For sequentially generated images that have relative low frame rates, it is more likely that there is movement between frames. For this reason, compound imaging is not commonly used in sequentially generated cardiac imaging, or other situations in which temporal resolution is critical. For ultrafast imaging (using plane or diverging waves), since the frame rate is significantly faster than for sequential imaging, the movement between successive frames becomes much less, making compounding significantly more practical in the presence of motion.

Frequency Compounding (Frequency Fusion)

Besides compound imaging, the other averaging-based technique commonly used to reduce speckle is frequency compounding (fusion). Again, for speckle to be reduced by frame averaging, the speckle must be random from frame to frame within the set of images to be averaged. Changing the transmit frequency results in a change in wavelength. As we have already seen, changing the wavelength results in a change in the speckle pattern for the same tissue. Therefore, if multiple images are acquired using different transmit frequencies, the signals from the structures will be highly correlated (in phase), while the speckle will be random.

With the advent of broadband transducers and computationally powerful digital systems, the ability to transmit and receive images at more than one frequency simultaneously became possible. Perhaps the easiest way to grasp how multiple images can be acquired simultaneously is to consider a transducer bandwidth plot (as shown in *Figure 63*). Notice that the full bandwidth of the transducer is used when transmitting. For the transducer bandwidth depicted in *Figure 63*, the transmit frequencies range from about 2 MHz to about 6 MHz. On receive, the system performs parallel processing. The received signals are filtered into two smaller receive frequency bands and then processed as if two imaging systems were imaging the same tissue simultaneously. In this example the receive bandwidth is divided into a 3 MHz and a 5 MHz image. The speckle pattern from the 3 MHz received image is completely independent of the speckle pattern acquired in the 5 MHz image. By averaging (or fusing) these two images together, speckle reduction and improved SNR are achieved. Of course, other than the bandwidth requirement and computational power, there is nothing which restricts a system from using more than two receive bandwidths simultaneously.

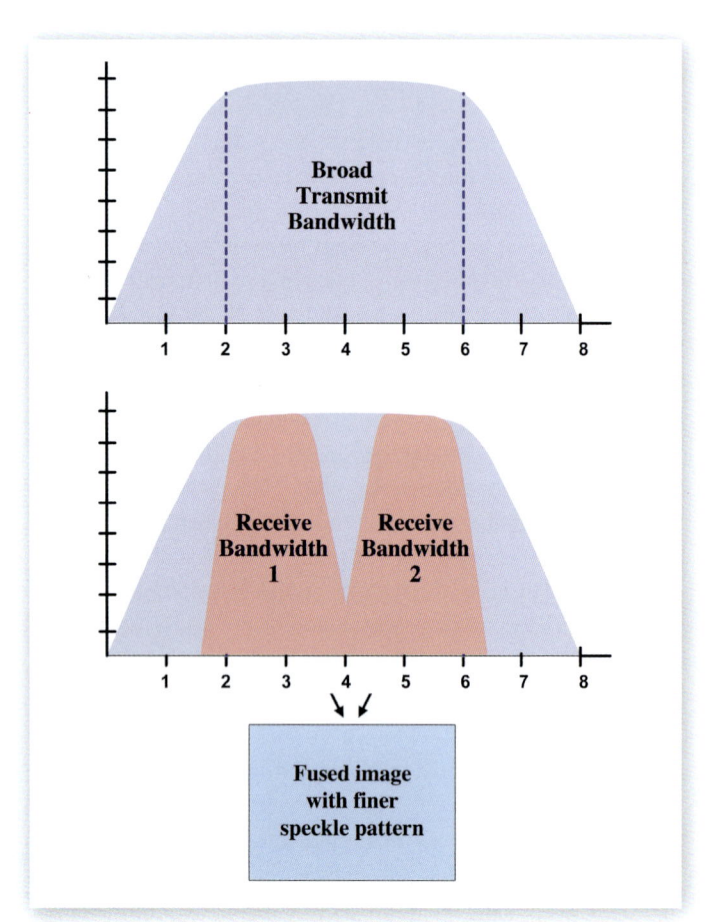

Fig. 63 **Frequency compounding (fusion)**

Since the images used in averaging are generated simultaneously, frequency compounding does not suffer the same degradation that occurs with spatial compound imaging. However, the improvement in the signal-to-noise and speckle reduction is generally greater with compound imaging than with frequency fusion since more frames are used in the production of the compound image. Of course, it is possible for an ultrasound system to actually employ both techniques simultaneously, to further reduce speckle and improve sensitivity.

With the advent of CMUT technology, there is potentially another method to simultaneously generate multiple images at different frequencies for compounding. Transducers can conceivably be designed with interspersed cells designed specifically to transmit at different frequencies simultaneously. This potentially could allow for two or more wideband transmits such that multiple frequencies are simultaneously received for compounding. With the further development of CMUT, there are considerable advancements possible for ultrasound.

Statistics-Based Adaptive Processing

In the latter part of the 1990s, the first real-time, adaptive process improving signal-to-noise ratio of signals was patented in an application called adaptive Doppler processing (ADP) by Miele and Mucci. This technique was based on a statistical treatment of the signal and noise characteristics so as to make intelligent, pixel by pixel decisions of how to reduce noise and enhance signal. The ability to perform real-time, adaptive signal enhancement became possible as computational power had increased dramatically in the prior 10 to 15 years. The same fundamentals of this adaptive processing are now being applied to achieve many different advantages in imaging. Speckle reduction can now be achieved adaptively, in real time, by algorithmically considering the amplitude of each pixel in the image relative to all of the neighboring pixels. In this manner, when a pixel's intensity has a high probability of being related to speckle, the intensity can be adjusted to a closer uniformity with surrounding pixels, reducing the apparent speckle. When pixels show strong correlation with neighboring pixels, these signals are most likely related to actual structure and can be adjusted to make the image of the structure more uniform.

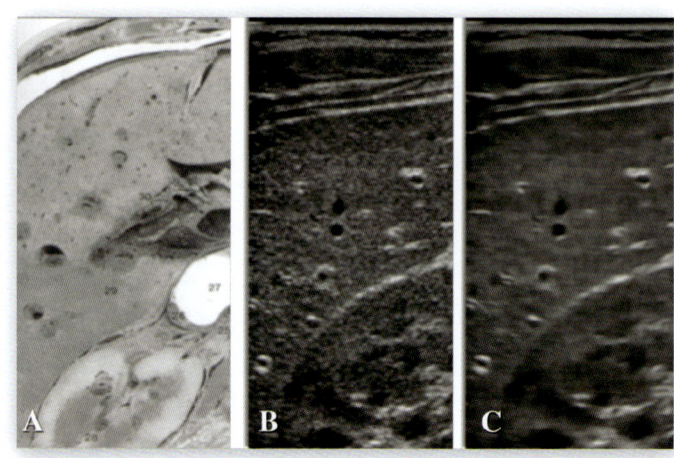

Fig. 64a **Liver and kidney images (A) optical, (B) standard ultrasound with speckle (C) with speckle reduction**

Chapter 8: Artifacts **407**

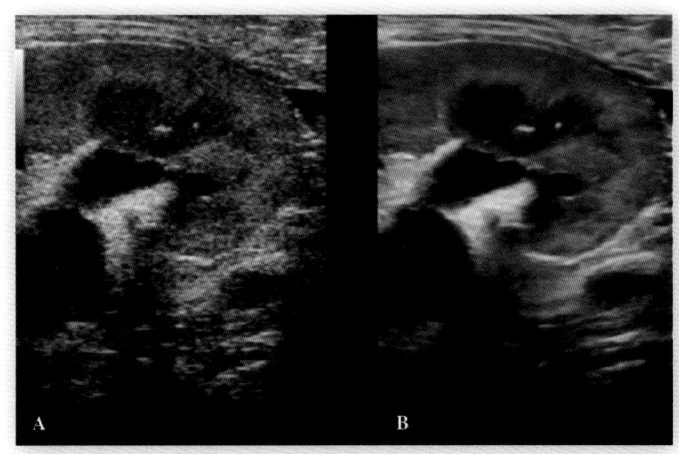

Fig. 64b **Adult kidney with conventional imaging (A) and adult kidney with speckle reduction (B)**

Combinations of Approaches

Each of the methodologies for improving image quality by speckle reduction discussed above is an independent approach. This fact implies that employing any of these techniques does not preclude the user from applying an additional approach simultaneously. In fact, you can imagine how benefits could be achieved by implementing harmonic imaging with compound imaging and adaptive processing to further enhance an image, as illustrated in *Figures 65a* and *65b* below.

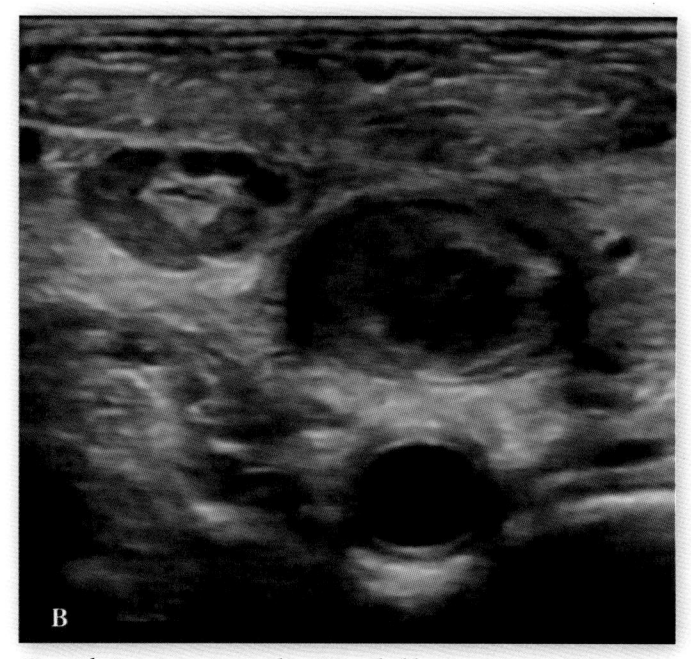

Fig. 65b **Image generated using coded harmonics, speckle reduction, and compound imaging**

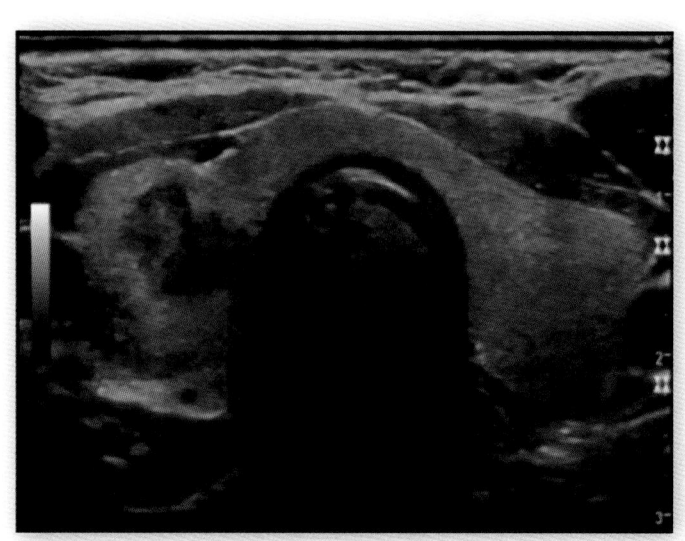

Fig. 66 **Thyroid lesion; image generated using coded harmonics, speckle reduction, and compound imaging**

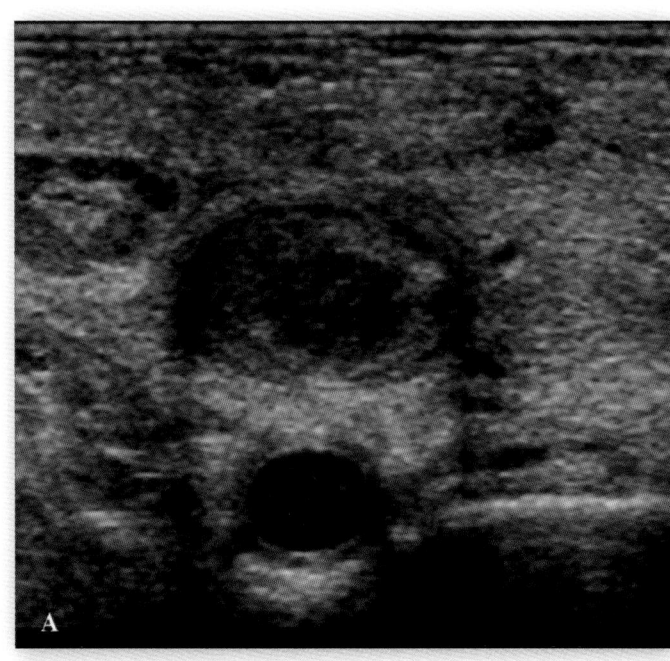

Fig. 65a **Conventional imaging**

KEY CONCEPT

Speckle appears as pseudo tissue texture. The scattering from multiple structures occurs simultaneously and adds to varying degrees constructively and destructively, creating brighter and darker spots within the image. Since higher frequencies have shorter wavelengths, the reflected waves go in and out of phase in a shorter distance than do lower frequency waves. The result is that higher frequencies produce finer speckle patterns, making tissue appear to be finer in texture.

CH 8

6.2 Beam Aberration

In Chapter 2, we learned that ultrasound systems begin with the assumption that the transmit speed of sound is 1540 m/sec. We also learned that transmit speeds vary with the properties of the medium, such that this assumption of 1540 m/sec does not always hold true. In this chapter, we have discussed the artifact of speed error which results directly from a violation of the assumed propagation speed. Clearly the greater the difference between the assumed propagation speed and the actual propagation speed, the greater the speed error in an image. However, there is another error which results from imaging tissues which have varying propagation velocities. This error is referred to as beam aberration. Beam aberration results in degradation in resolution (as relates to the image detail), an increase in grating lobes, a decrease in contrast resolution, and a reduction in the signal-to-noise ratio (resulting in decreased sensitivity).

Discussion of beam aberration, until recently, has been somewhat limited in the clinical ultrasound community. Whereas speed error is commonly discussed, beam aberration has been a virtually anonymous artifact. In part, speed error has been known, since as an artifact, it is relatively easy to quantify and to visualize. In contrast, limits to resolution are a complex composite of multiple effects including but not limited to the beamwidth, spatial pulse length, grating lobe artifacts, reverberation artifact, poor signal-to-noise, and beam aberration. Furthermore, understanding the cause of beam aberration is certainly more complex than understanding the cause of speed error. However, now that multiple ultrasound systems are employing techniques to reduce beam aberration (often with dramatic improvement in the quality of imaging) discussing beam aberration is now warranted.

What is Beam Aberration?

Beam aberration can be defined simply as a distortion of the beam as a result of differing propagation velocities. To understand the concept of how this distortion occurs, we will need to review some concepts discussed in Chapters 5 and 6 (transducer operation, phasing, focusing, and resolution). Recall that a phased array transducer improves resolution by focusing the beam through varying phase delay profiles.

For simplicity sake, let's start with an ideal situation which does not match reality but will help get across the point. We will then add complexity that more closely mimics reality so as to illustrate the effects of beam aberration.

Let's imagine that you want to resolve the structure labeled "A," imaging with a transducer with N elements as shown in *Figure 67*. Notice that the path lengths for the returning echoes from structure "A" to each of the transducer elements vary.

Clearly for the scenario depicted, the echo from structure A arrives at element 1 earliest, element 2 slightly later in time, element 3 later, etc, and element N last. (Pictorially, this fact is represented by the number of wavelengths required to get from structure A to each of the elements.)

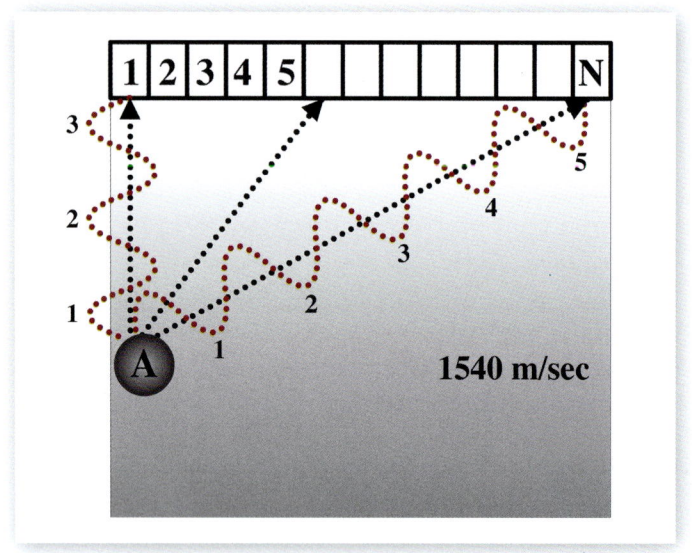

Fig. 67 **Varying path length from object A to each transducer element**

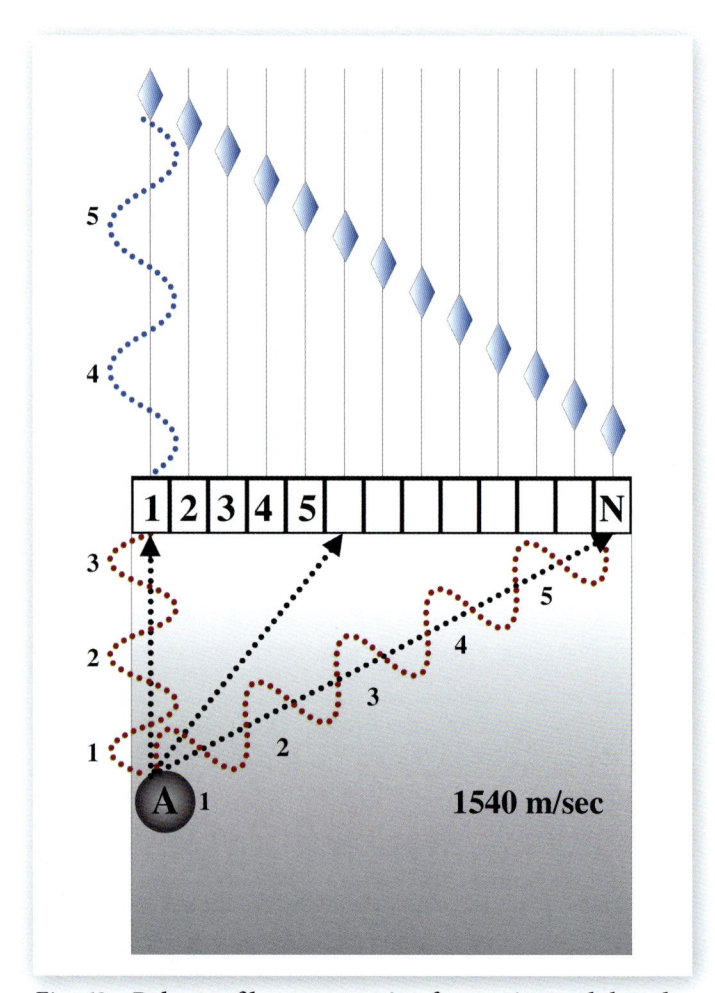

Fig. 68 **Delay profile compensating for varying path lengths; note the "wavelengths" superimposed on the pictorial delay for element 1 to illustrate timing and phase – there are now 5 "cycles" from structure A to both element 1 and from structure A to element N**

Since ultimately the signals from each element are added together, the ideal situation is to have the signal from structure A arrive at each element at the same time so that signals can add constructively. With the signals arriving at different times, a receive delay profile must be applied to compensate for the variances in the path lengths from the object to each of the elements. By delaying the echoes received from element 1 the most, element 2 a little less, etc. and element N the least, a focus for object A is essentially achieved. This delay profile is illustrated in *Figure 68*.

Notice that wavelengths have been superimposed on top of the delay to element 1 to illustrate that the echoes to element 1 and element N now arrive at the same time and with the same phase.

As illustrated in *Figure 68*, in a perfect world, applying the delay profile to the echoes received at each of the N elements from structure A would yield a well-focused image of structure A. However, the world is not "perfect." The path from structure A to element N is through tissue that may be different than the tissue in the path from structure A to element 1. As a result, the delay profile, which was based on the assumption that the propagation speed is uniformly 1540 m/sec, may not be correct.

Let's consider a slightly more complex case in which there are two discrete layers within the patient, specifically, a layer of fat superior to "soft tissue." We will begin by considering what happens to the echoes returning from structure A to each element, as we did in the idealized case with a uniform propagation velocity of 1540 m/sec. You should now notice that not only are the path lengths different to elements 1 and N, but also that an echo returning to element A spends a greater period of time traveling through the layer of fat than the echo returning to element 1. (Pictorially, this fact is illustrated by comparing the wavelengths returning to element N with the wavelengths for the echo returning to element 1 in *Figure 69*.)

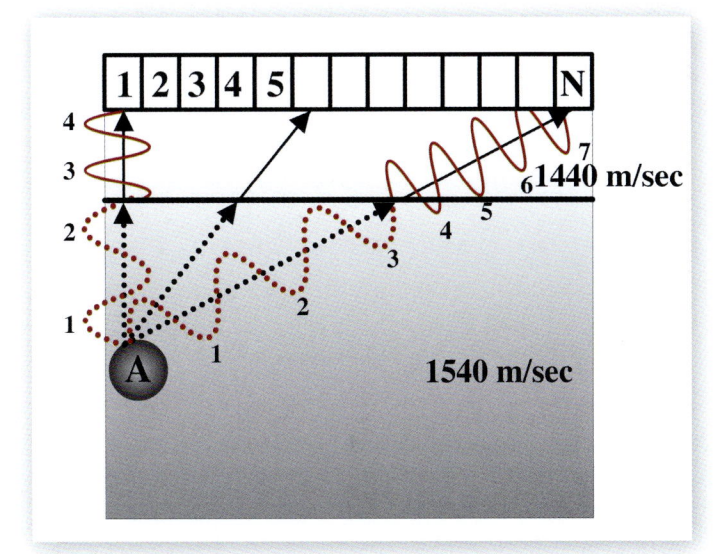

Fig. 69 **Wavelength changes with change in speed of sound; note that because of the angle, more time is spent traveling at 1440 m/sec returning to element N than returning to element 1**

Now consider how a standard system treats these signals returning at different times. The delay profile to compensate for the time discrepancy between elements, under standard system operation, is determined based on the assumption that the propagation velocity is uniformly 1540 m/sec. So when the standard delay profile is applied to signals that have traversed tissue with non-uniform propagation velocity, the signals arriving at each element are not correctly delayed, and the structure is not completely focused (pictorially illustrated in *Figure 70*).

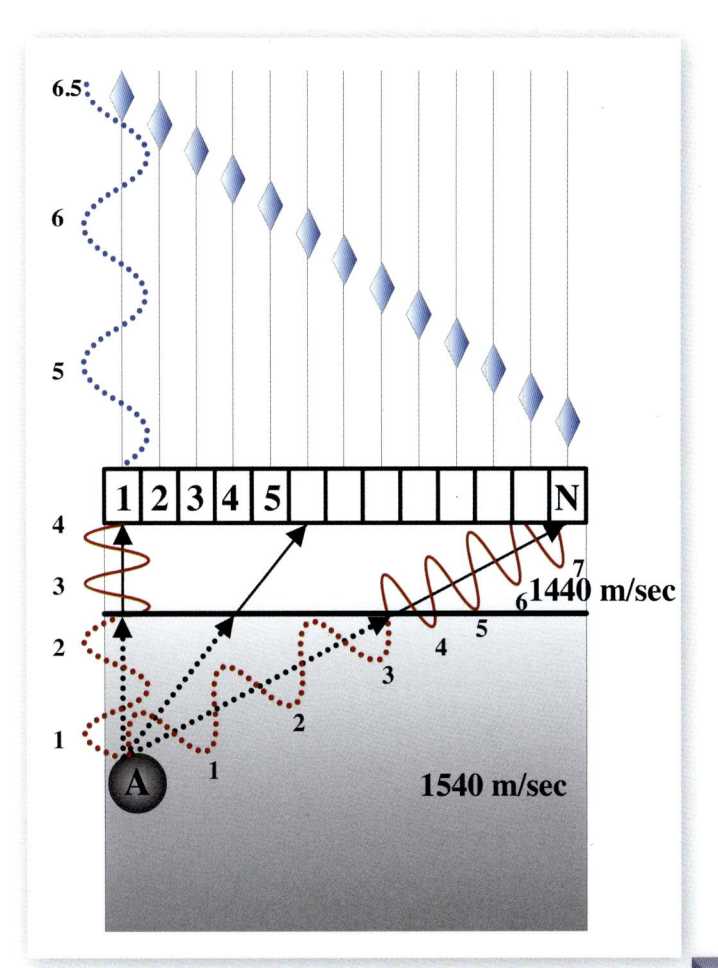

Fig. 70 **Standard delays are incorrect when the propagation velocity is not uniformly 1540 m/sec throughout the scan region (only 6.5 cycles from structure A to element 1 and 7 cycles from structure A to element N)**

Varying Tissue Types and Varying Propagation Velocities

The model just employed consisting of two distinct layers with different propagation velocities still overly simplifies what happens when imaging the body. The body wall is comprised of skin, fat, connective tissue, and muscle. The amount of fat, muscle and connective tissue can vary significantly from patient to patient. As discussed in Chapter 2, the speed of sound in fat is lower than in muscle, which is lower than in skin. Once the sound propagates through the body wall, the speed of sound also varies for different organs and from patient to patient. The result is that the assumed speed of 1540 m/sec is different enough from reality to cause beam aberration. Of course, imaging situations in which the actual speeds vary more significantly from the assumed 1540 m/sec result in the greatest amount of aberration, and hence the most blurring and degradation of the image.

What Factors Exacerbate Beam Aberration?

The result of incorrect delays is essentially a defocusing which results in increased grating lobes and degraded detail resolution. In the ideal situation, an ultrasound system is able to correct for time differences associated with imaging across an array of elements so that every point in the image has a relatively good focus. As a result of aberration, the smallest resolvable point will vary throughout the image, getting worse whenever greater changes in propagation velocities exist, and where differences in path lengths between structures and elements increase. The phase errors associated with varying propagation speeds tend to build up with depth, making the defocusing effects of aberration worse with increasing depth. Additionally, a higher transmit frequency results in a shorter wavelength, resulting in increased aberration. The impact that transmit frequency has on aberration should be evident from the fact that higher frequencies result in shorter wavelengths — and distance errors, which result from a change in propagation velocity, cause greater phase changes when the wavelength is shorter.

Decreasing Beam Aberration

Since beam aberration is the result of an incorrect assumption regarding a uniform propagation velocity of 1540 m/sec, any technique which more accurately reflects the true propagation velocities tends to decrease aberration, improving image quality. Fundamentally, there are two different approaches which can be employed: make assumptions that better model tissue changes that commonly exist or employ a technique that attempts to measure the actual propagation velocities existing within the scan region of interest.

Non-adaptive: Model-Based Correction

The simpler approach to beam aberration correction is to develop models based on what commonly occurs within typical patients. For example, for abdominal scanning, if most larger patients have at least 2 cm of fat below the skin layer, a model which assumes 2 cm of fat just below the skin level can be employed. Accounting for the difference between the propagation velocity in fat versus the propagation velocity in tissue, the delay profile used for beamforming the image is modified. By linking the model to imaging presets, the model can be adjusted so that as key parameters such as depth are changed, the model employed can also change, resulting in improved focusing, better resolution, and better sensitivity. Different models can be tied to presets so that the aberration correction for thin patients with very little adipose tissue is not the same correction as employed for patients with a larger body habitus. Of course, no model will be perfect for all patients and consequently some degree of aberration still exists.

Adaptive: Correlation-Based Correction

A more complicated approach is for the system to attempt to calculate correction factors based on calculations from returned data. There are many different potential adaptive approaches with complexity beyond the scope of this text. However, the basic idea used by many systems is to iteratively transmit with varying assumed propagation velocities. The returning data for each assumed propagation velocity is then assessed to determine which yielded the best image. The optimized value is now used to determine the phase delay correction profiles to reduce beam aberration, producing improved focusing and contrast in the image. Although more complex, adaptive approaches potentially result in better phase aberration correction, as the correction is "tailored" to the specific imaging situation based on the returning echoes. Even so, the approaches currently employed only make first order corrections, and do not completely remove the deleterious effects of phase aberration.

Clinical Applications of Beam Aberration Correction

Even though corrective approaches currently employed do not fully correct for beam aberration, the effects have been dramatic. Beam aberration correction has significantly improved abdominal imaging, especially with larger patients. Beam aberration correction is also very important for newer ultrasound treatment technologies such as HIFU (see Chapter 18). In these applications, achieving a well-controlled focus is critical to ablating diseased tissue while leaving undamaged surrounding healthy tissues. For conventional imaging, perhaps the greatest impact of beam aberration correction techniques has been on breast imaging. Because breast tissue is a complex combination of fat, muscle, connective tissues, and glandular tissues, there is generally a significant variance in propagation velocities within the breast. Furthermore, breast imaging is performed using high frequencies, resulting in shorter wavelengths. The widely varying velocities in conjunction with the shorter wavelengths result in more significant aberration. Since there is greater distortion from aberration, aberration correction has the potential to be more efficacious.

7. Doppler and Color Doppler Artifacts

7.1 Aliasing

Aliasing is the result of violating the Nyquist criterion (which states that to detect a given frequency, sampling must occur at greater than twice that frequency). For PW Doppler the sample rate is equivalent to the PRF, so the maximum detectable Doppler frequency shift is determined by one half the PRF. The maximum detectable frequency shift is converted through the Doppler equation into the maximum velocity displayed on the Doppler scales.

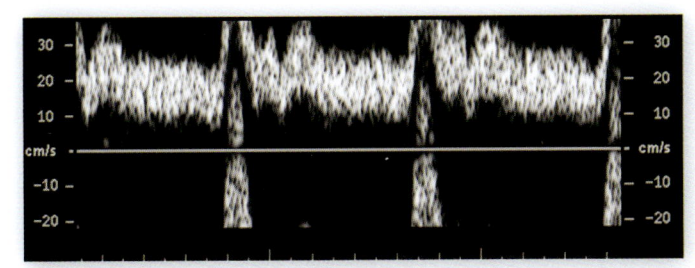

Fig. 71 **Aliased Doppler spectrum**

> **Author's Note:**
> **Aliased Doppler Spectrums**
>
> Although the signal in the above spectrum is "aliased," shifting the baseline down will almost "unwrap" the signal. When the aliasing gets worse, the signal wraps so far around that it is not possible to infer the true peak velocity. This, of course, presumes that the Doppler scales have already been increased to the maximum possible.

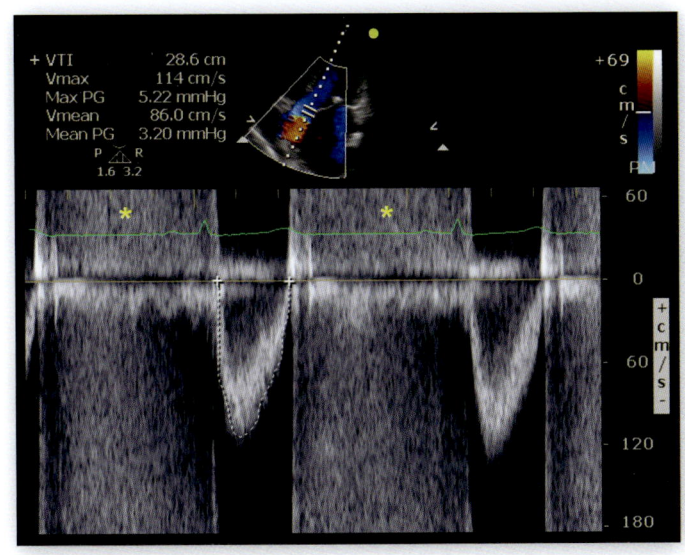

Fig. 72 **PW Doppler sample volume placed at the LVOT in a patient with aortic regurgitation; aliasing is observed (asterisks)**

In the spectrum of *Figure 72*, you will note that the peak velocity of the regurgitant jet wraps completely around the velocity range (scales) and cannot be determined by a baseline shift.

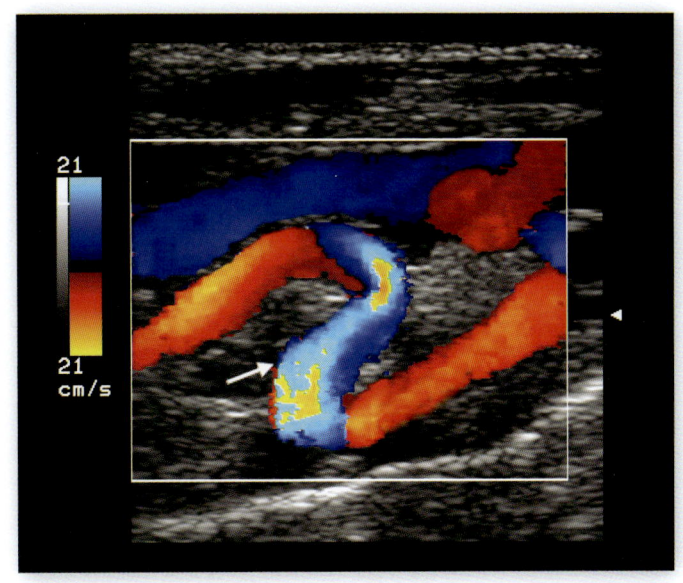

Fig. 73 **Color aliasing**

Notice that in the tortuous internal carotid artery (the lower vessel), the color changes with flow direction. In the middle region in which the flow is almost directly toward the transducer, the cosine becomes larger such that the recorded Doppler shifts increase, leading to color aliasing. Notice that the two specific regions where the aliasing occurs are near bends in the vessel where acceleration occurs, increasing the Doppler shift.

7.2 Range Ambiguity

As discussed earlier in this chapter, if a second transmit pulse is transmitted before all of the echoes from the first are received, the system might detect flow from deeper vessels. This artifact is particularly disturbing to sonographers when the sample volume is placed in tissue and blood flow is detected. Fortunately, registration of range ambiguous flow rarely happens since there is increased attenuation with increasing depth and because of the possibility that flow does not exist at the ambiguous depth. Range ambiguity is more likely to occur with shallow gate depths and also with a fixed focus transducer such as the pencil probes or the older-style mechanical transducers (now virtually extinct).

7.3 Spectral Mirroring

Bidirectional Doppler uses quadrature detection to determine flow toward and away from the transducer. If the signal amplitude is greater than the separation between the two channels of forward and reverse flow, a mirrored spectrum (which is weaker in amplitude) will appear in the opposite direction of the real flow.

View ONLINE Animation and Image Library

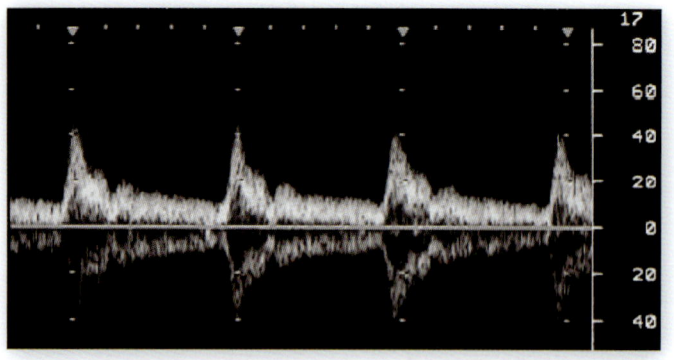

Fig. 74 **Spectral mirroring**

The primary cause for spectral mirroring is poor electronic design with inadequate "separation" between the forward and reverse channels (I and Q). Spectral mirroring can be exacerbated by very strong signals as the result of very superficial Doppler with high frequency transducers, high transmit power, and too high receive gain.

Additionally, the angle of insonation can increase the likelihood of spectral mirroring as demonstrated in *Figure 75*. Recall that a beam has physical width. When the beam is close to perpendicular to flow (90° insonification angle), part of the beam may be at an angle less than 90°, resulting in forward flow, and part of the beam may be at an angle greater than 90°, resulting in reverse flow.

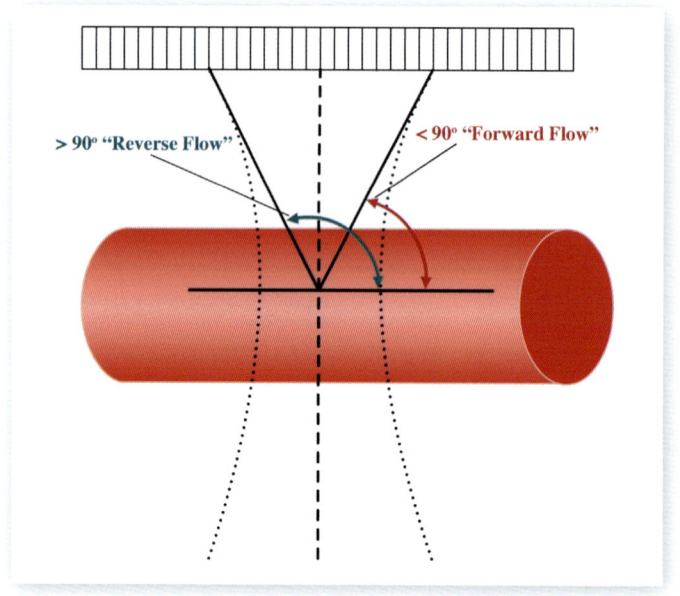

View ONLINE Animation and Image Library

Fig. 75 **Spectral mirroring caused by poor angle**

7.4 Harmonic Double Spectral Artifact

Recently, there has been a debate in cardiology regarding a specific TEE Doppler spectrum which has a double envelope[3-5]. Whereas some people are referring to this situation as "ghosting" artifact, others are arguing that the higher velocity envelope represents actual flow. Neither of these explanations makes sense. First, you must realize that a reverberating Doppler signal would not, by itself, create a different Doppler shift which is necessary to create the higher velocity envelope, dispelling the "ghosting" argument. Others are theorizing that this higher velocity envelope is not artifact but is the result of the vena contracta and complex flow acceleration that results from impingement of this flow on the septal wall. Although this type of acceleration is possible, it is difficult to believe that the envelope characteristics of the higher velocity envelope would exactly replicate the characteristics of the lower velocity envelope. Furthermore, it seems too coincidental that the second envelope is exactly twice the velocity of the lower velocity envelope.

Although not yet proven, my theory is that the second envelope results from non-linear sound wave propagation. When the Doppler signal reverberates, it goes through an area of increased and decreased density which results in a slight increase and then decrease in propagation velocity. This propagation velocity change distorts the normal sinusoid so that harmonic components are added to the signal (the same mechanism that is intentionally produced to create harmonic imaging as discussed in Chapter 10). The harmonic signals would then exist at multiples of the fundamental (Doppler shift) signal. Of course, each harmonic becomes successively weaker in amplitude such that there is only enough energy in the second harmonic to be visualized.

Normally, a Doppler signal from blood flow would not be strong enough to produce visible harmonics because Rayleigh scattering is such a weak reflective mode. However, when using a TEE transducer, there is no air-tissue interface, the flow is much closer to the transducer, there is very little interceding tissue, and the transmit frequency is higher (without significant attenuation). All of these facts taken together imply that the signal strength is stronger than what normally occurs in spectral Doppler. This higher amplitude signal is critical because harmonic generation is very non-linear with signal strength. Also, the reflecting mechanism that causes the reverberation must be very efficient (like a calcification or a prosthetic valve).

Figure 76 shows a calcified native mitral valve resulting in a harmonic double spectral envelope artifact. On the spectrum, the actual flow has been outlined in yellow with the reverberated and harmonic-generated artifact outlined in red. Note that the artifact has an envelope approximately twice the actual flow envelope.

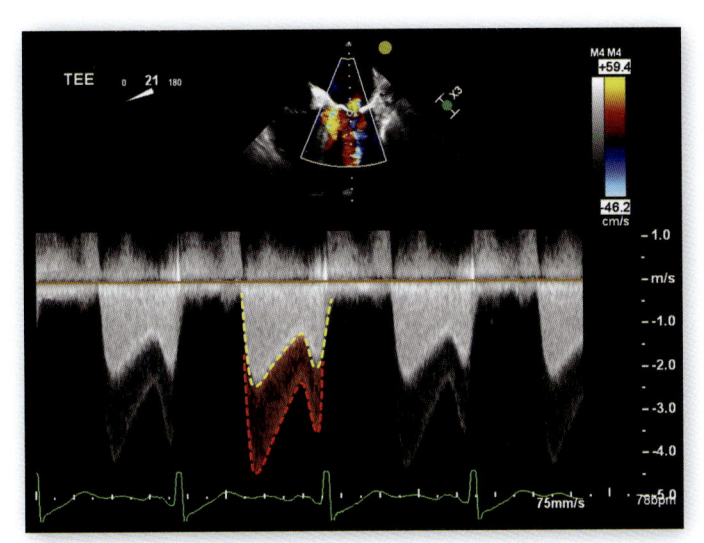

Fig. 76 TEE of calcified mitral valve resulting in harmonic double spectral envelope artifact (red)

7.5 Spectral Spread (Broadening) Artifact

In addition to normal spectral broadening which results from differing blood velocities within a sample volume, an artificial spectral broadening exists. Artificial spectral broadening (spectral spread) artificially smears out the spectrum, increasing the peak velocity. The principal cause for this artifact is the varying angle to flow that occurs from each element of the array. For small insonification angles and small transducer apertures this effect is negligible. For large linear arrays with insonification angles of 70° or greater and superficial imaging, this effect becomes very substantial. The result can be inaccurate measurements, leading to peak velocity overestimation and pressure gradient overestimation.

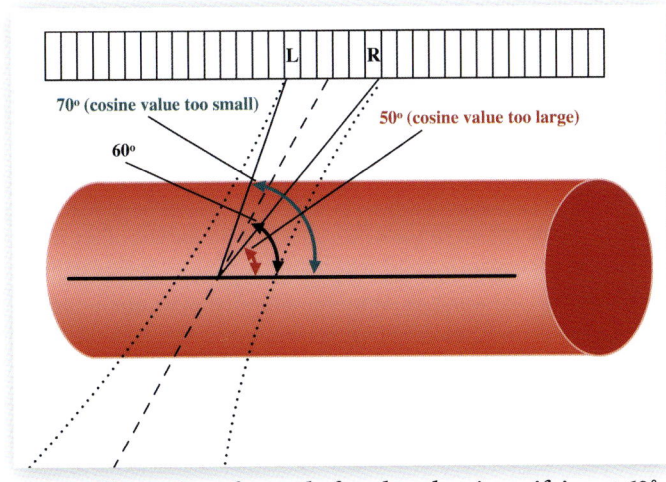

Fig. 77 Illustration of spread of angles when insonifying at 60°

Notice from *Figure 77* that the angle to flow from some elements is greater than the central angle of 60° and that the angle to flow to other elements is less than the central angle of 60°. However, the system assumes a 60° angle such that some signals are overcompensated and other signals are undercompensated. This over and undercompensation leads to a spreading of the Doppler spectrum as depicted in *Figure 78*.

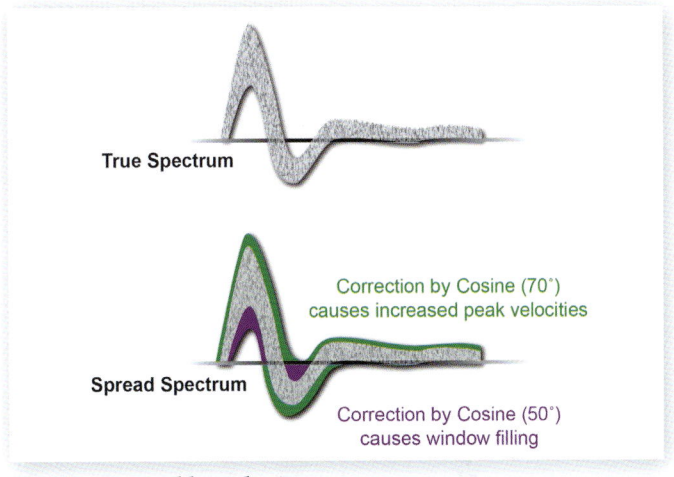

Fig. 78 **Spectral broadening**

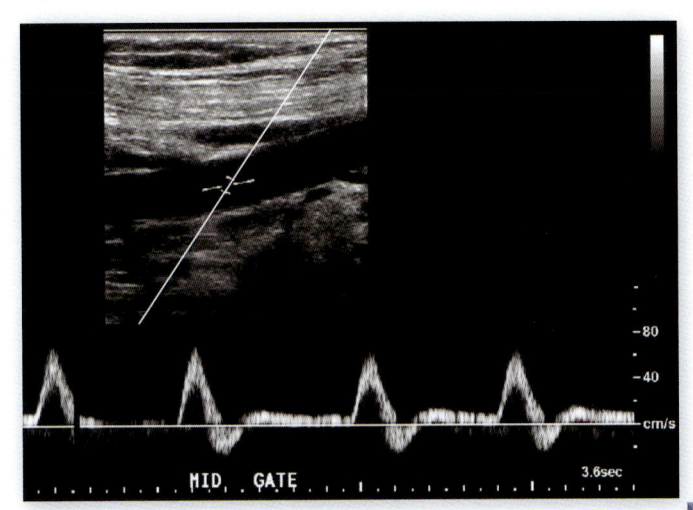

Fig. 79a **Insonification angle of 55°**

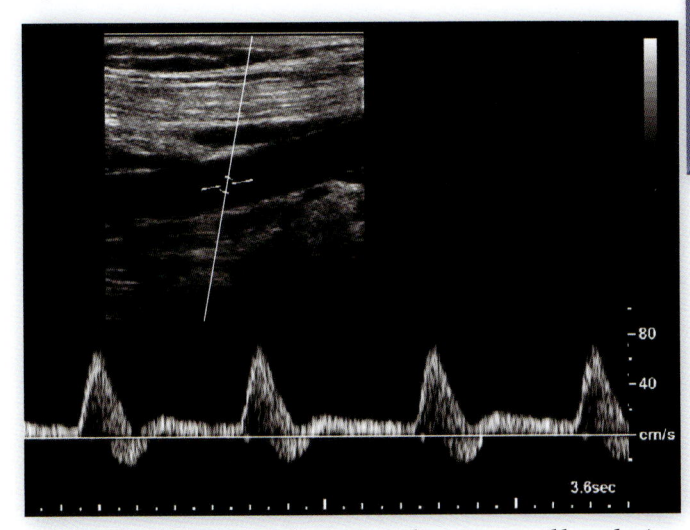

Fig. 79b **Insonification angle of 70° producing spectral broadening**

The spectrum in *Figure 79a* is the result of using a 55° insonification angle whereas the spectrum in *Figure 79b* is the result of approximately a 70° insonification angle. Notice how the peak is slightly overestimated and that the spectral window is diminished.

7.6 Blossoming

The term blossoming is used to refer to a signal that is essentially overgained such that the signal "bleeds" into neighboring regions of the spectrum. Overgaining can be the result of too high a transmit power generally for very superficial flow, or too much receiver gain, again usually for superficial flow. In the presence of blossoming artifact, the peak velocity is usually artificially high. Also, in PW Doppler, blossoming can cause the loss of a spectral window when a window should be present.

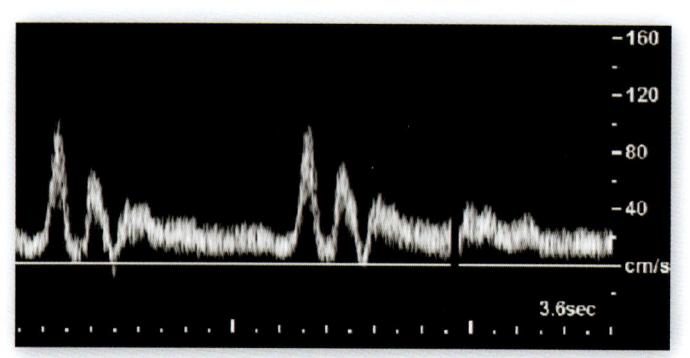

Fig. 80 **Appropriate Doppler gain**

The Doppler gain in *Figure 80* is appropriate. Notice that the peak velocity is slightly over 100 cm/sec with appropriate gain.

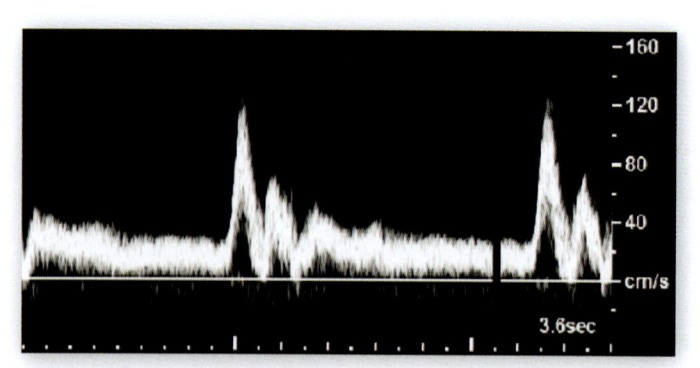

Fig. 81 **Blossoming artifact**

The Doppler gain in *Figure 81* is excessive, causing blossoming artifact. Notice that the peak velocity is over 120 cm/sec, a 20% increase from *Figure 80*, when using appropriate gain.

View ONLINE Animation and Image Library

7.7 Color Blossoming (Bleeding)

If the color Doppler signal is overgained, color signals can potentially overlap non-flow tissue regions leading to over-interpretation of vessel or flow region size *(Figure 82)*.

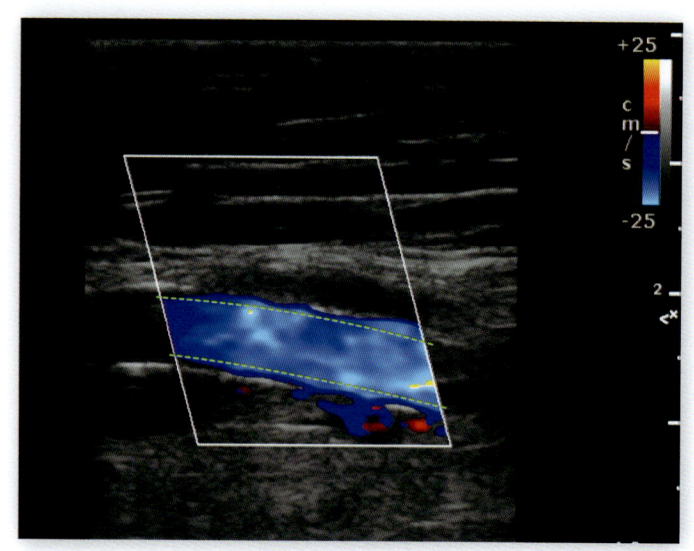

Fig. 82 **Color bleeding from overgaining**

Even with appropriate gain, the bleeding of color flow signals over tissue regions is possible. The problem is related to limited axial resolution related to the "tail" of the transmit pulse *(Figure 83)*.

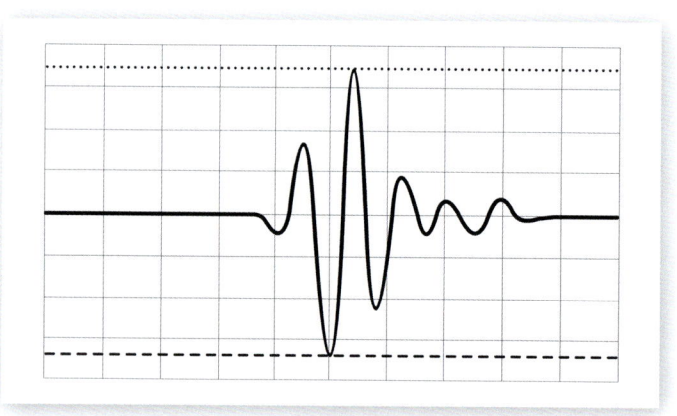

Fig. 83 **Pulse response for a 2 MHz transducer**

The effect of this tail is that the spatial pulse length is longer than ideal, resulting in reduced axial resolution. With color, this pulse tail results in color signals extending beyond the posterior aspect of the actual flow region *(Figure 84)*. Since the amplitude of the tail is weaker than the main cycle(s) within the pulse, the signal amplitude is weaker than the true flow signals acquired from within the actual flow region. If the receiver gain is turned up too high, these weaker signals from the pulse tails are mapped above the color threshold and presented as flow bleeding over the actual tissue. Therefore, when overgaining occurs for stronger color signals, the color signals tend to bleed into neighboring regions, making the color region appear larger than reality. The solution is to reduce the color receiver gain until the amplitude of these artifactual signals drop below the color threshold but keeping the gain high enough so as to preserve the amplitude of the true color signals above the color threshold. Of course, if the color gain is set too low, color dropout will occur, giving the artificial appearance of no or limited flow.

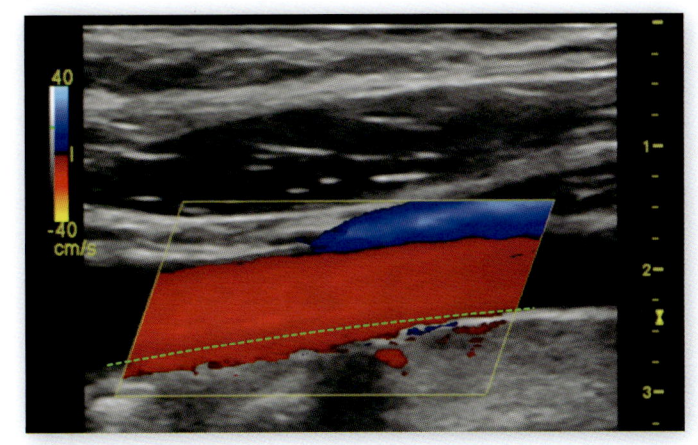

Fig. 84 **Color bleeding because of color tail**

7.8 Circuit Saturation

In Chapter 7, we reviewed the function of wall filters. We also discussed the fact that when the "clutter" signals are not adequately attenuated, the signal dynamic range becomes too large causing circuit saturation. The following example demonstrates saturation of the wall filters when using CW Doppler.

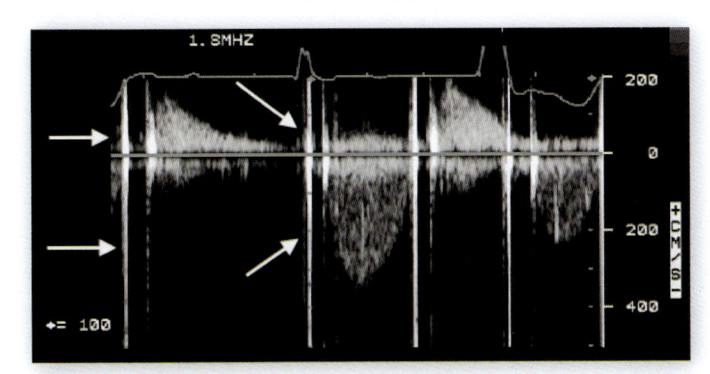

Fig. 85 **Saturation of Doppler wall filters**

In this case, the saturation occurs from the strong specular reflection from a mechanical valve. Notice that as the valve opens and closes, the Doppler insonification angle changes. When the incident angle is close to 0°, (the beam is close to perpendicular to the valve leaflets), the specular reflection returns to the transducer and drives the Doppler circuit to saturation. During this period of time, the electronics are ringing between the voltage supply rails resulting in the bright white spikes from top to bottom of the spectrum.

7.9 Wall Filter Saturation

The following image is an example of circuit saturation in PW Doppler while assessing mitral flow with a native valve. Because the baseline is shifted, a fair portion of the bright white spikes associated with the saturation appear to emanate from the top of the spectrum. Notice how these aliased bright white spikes taper, consistent with the ringing down of the circuit electronics.

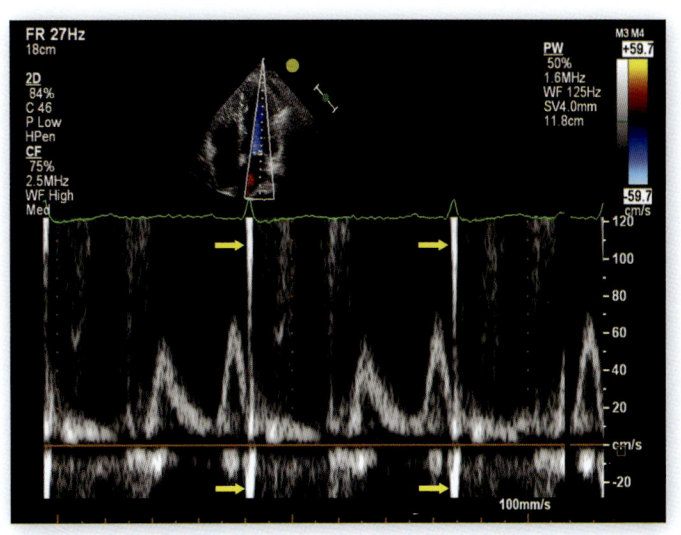

Fig. 86 **PW Doppler sample volume (gate) placement towards MV annulus with wall filter saturation (arrows)**

Observe the prominent valve closure artifact (arrows) in *Figure 86* along with aliasing of the MR jet. This indicates the SV was incorrectly placed above the mitral valve leaflet tips too far into the left atrium.

Besides motion associated with walls, valves, movement, and respiration, there are clinical situations which can result in circuit saturation. Because Rayleigh scattering from blood is generally a weak reflective mechanism, the receive gain needs to be set high. The high amplification implies that any unusually high amplitude reflection, such as occurs from air or fat embolism can result in circuit saturation. Generally, this saturation is not as extensive as occurs with cardiac valves as shown in the previous two images. Patients with long bone fractures or bone surgery often exhibit fat emboli. In color Doppler, this saturation may appear as "tails" of color posterior to the vessel wall. In power Doppler, the saturation generally appears as high amplitude (bright) spots within the more uniform, lower amplitude flow. In spectral Doppler, the embolism results in presence of thin white spikes with concomitant sounds sometimes referred to as "hits."

Figure 87 shows the circuit saturation resulting from mobile fat emboli about four to six hours after a total knee replacement. Note the differences between color Doppler (*a*), power Doppler (*b*), and spectral Doppler (*c*) images.

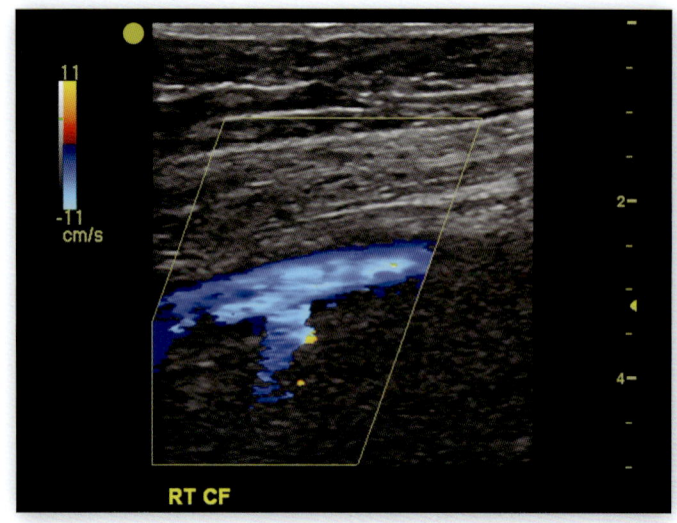

Fig. 87a **Posterior color Doppler tail resulting from circuit saturation from passing fat globules (emboli) in the right common femoral vein**

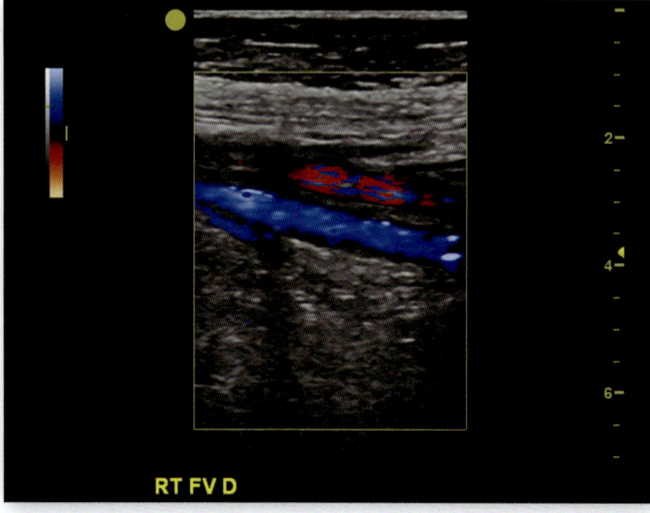

Fig. 87b **Power Doppler showing high amplitude propagating fat globules**

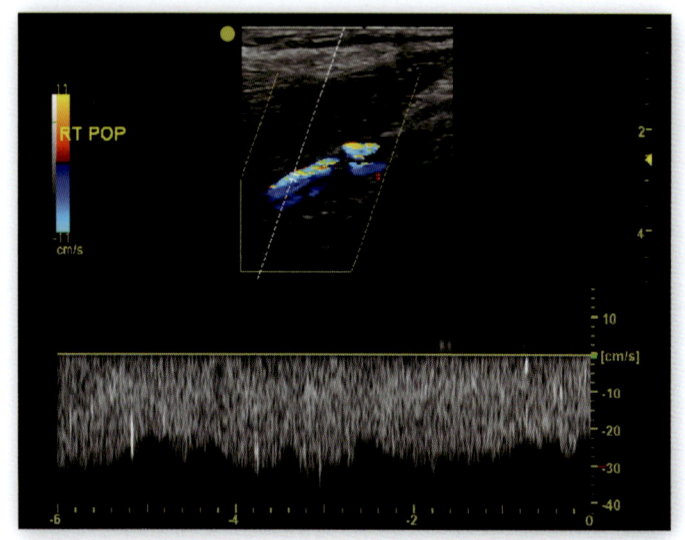

Fig. 87c **Spectral Doppler with "hits" (bright white spikes within the spectrum)**

7.10 Color and Power Doppler Flash Artifact

Flash artifact in color Doppler and color power Doppler appears as a short term flash of color within the color box related to relative motion between the patient and the transducer, and not actual flow. Flash is a relatively obvious artifact when viewing real-time or cine loop (video) imaging. With still images, if the capture happened contemporaneously with the flash artifact occurring, the image can be somewhat deceiving, as seen in the color power Doppler image of a hematoma *(Figure 88)* captured during flash artifact.

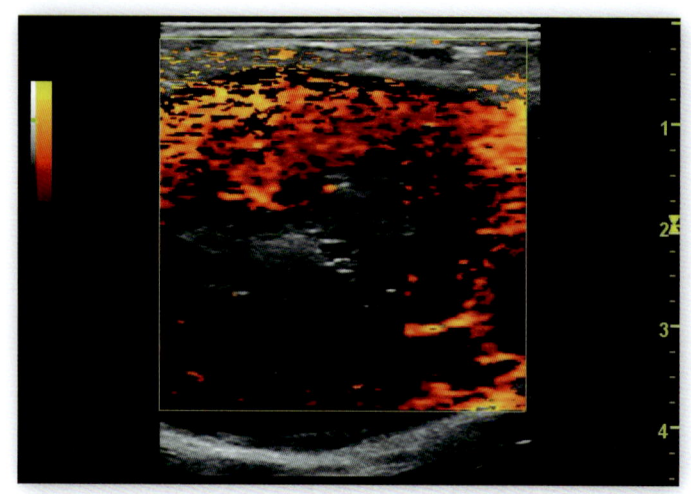

Fig. 88 **Flash artifact with color power Doppler**

View ONLINE Animation and Image Library

For sequentially generated color, ultrasound systems have implemented flash reduction algorithms which make flash artifact less common than in years past. However, flash artifact still occurs, especially when color wall filters and color scales are set low, and when power Doppler is being used.

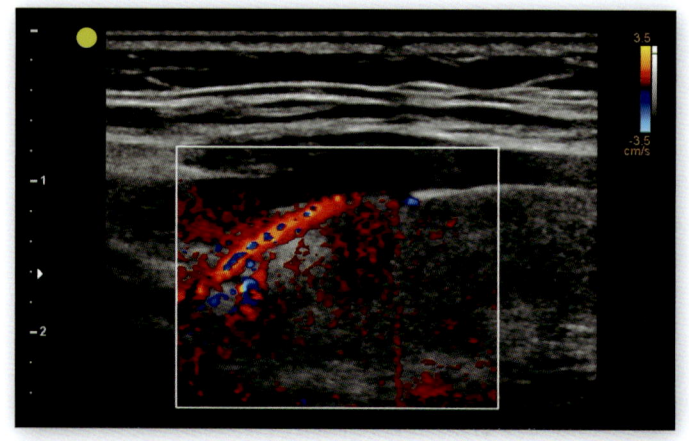

Fig. 89a **Linear image of thyroid with flash artifact associated with respiration and swallowing**

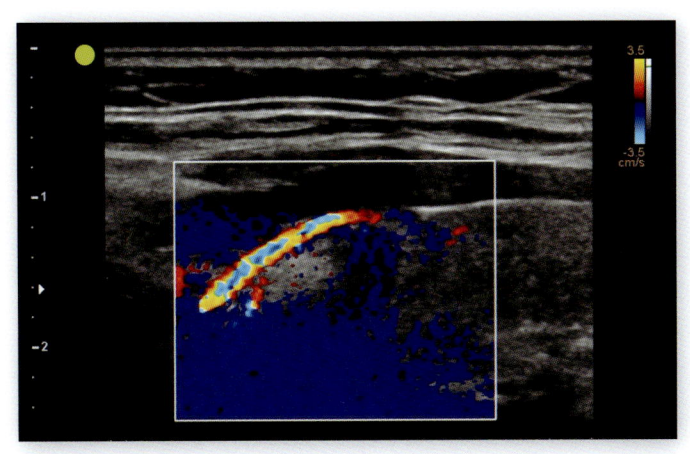

Fig. 89b **Linear image of thyroid with flash artifact associated with respiration and swallowing**

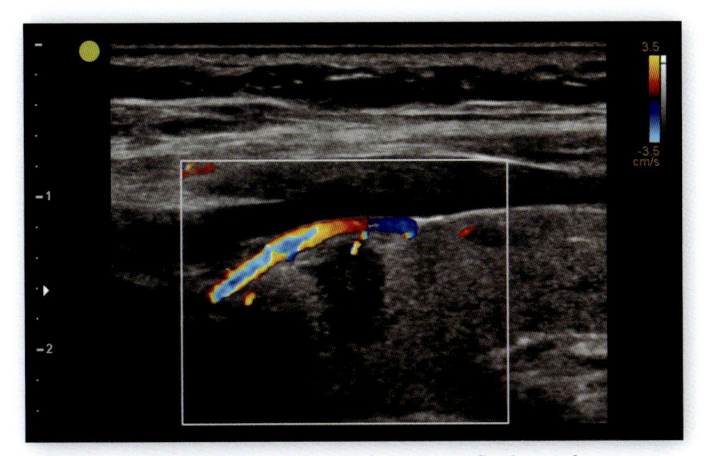

Fig. 89c **Linear image of thyroid without flash artifact**

Note that flash artifact is less common when performing ultrafast color Doppler. As discussed in Chapter 7: Doppler, the increased number of frames compounded to create a single color frame allow for much better control of the wall filters than with sequential imaging. Additionally, the new spatiotemporal filtering further improves the ability to reduce clutter signals from tissue, further reducing the incidence of color flash artifact.

7.11 Doppler Spectral Dropout

Spectral dropout can occur for many reasons including:
- poor Doppler angle (close to 90°)
- high wall filter setting relative to low-flow velocities
- inadequate sensitivity
  - transmit frequency too high (usually when depth set to deeper than 3 cm)
  - transmit power too low
  - weak signal from insignificant number of red blood cells (low flow)
- inappropriate settings such as low receiver gain or improper grayscale setting
- refraction artifact
- shadowing artifact (sample volume in acoustic shadow from superior attenuator)

With the exception of refraction artifact, each of these causes for Doppler spectral dropout has been discussed in prior sections. Refraction artifact as relates to imaging was discussed extensively in Chapter 2 and again within this chapter. With respect to spectral Doppler, refraction artifact can significantly weaken Doppler signals, and in extreme cases, make the signal completely disappear. Recall from Chapter 3 that when the incident angle reaches the critical angle, the beam is totally internally reflected, and no energy actually transmits across the interface between two structures. It should be clear that, with diving vessels, there is frequently the possibility of reaching the critical angle. Approaching the critical angle, the Doppler signal will weaken. Once the critical angle is reached, the Doppler signal will completely disappear.

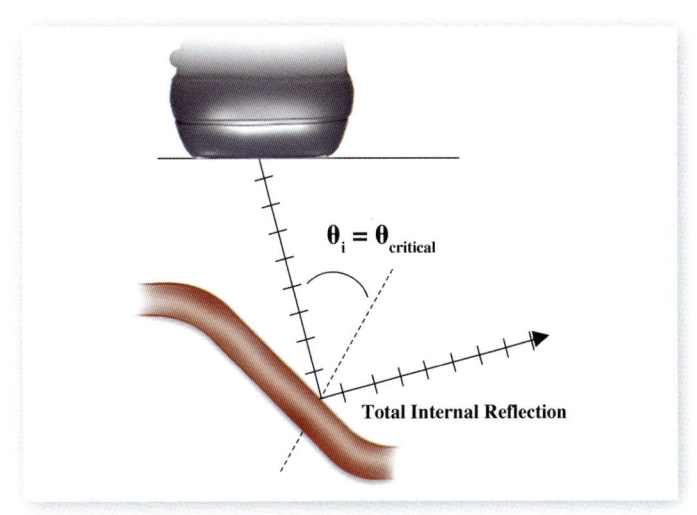

Fig. 90 **Critical angle and spectral dropout**

8. Color Doppler Dropout

8.1 Color Dropout

Like spectral Doppler, there are many factors which can contribute to color flow dropout, including:
- poor Doppler angle (close to 90°)
- inadequate sensitivity
  - transmit frequency too high (usually when depth set to deeper than 3 cm)
  - transmit power too low
  - weak signal from insignificant number of red blood cells (low flow)
  - packet size small when imaging low flow, small, deeper vessels
- high color scale settings (PRF) which results in high wall filter settings relative to low-flow velocities
- inappropriate settings such as low receiver gain
- low color priority setting (especially if 2D receiver gain is high)
- refraction artifact
- shadowing artifact (imaging in acoustic shadow from superior attenuator)

8.2 Flow Dropout Related to Occlusion

Flow dropout as a result of a critical stenosis or occlusion is not an artifact, but of course needs to be differentiated from cases of dropout which are the result of artifact. When no flow is appreciated, you must check to see if all of the ultrasound modalities (2D, color, spectral Doppler) confirm the absence of flow and are consistent with other tests and patient symptoms, realizing that the same artifact could be causing artifactual dropout in each modality (such as shadowing.) In these cases, it is helpful to try various system control changes such as lower scales, lowering wall filters, changing angle, trying power Doppler, assessing for collateralization or steal conditions, etc. *Figure 91b* is an example of an occlusion which results in the non-artifactual absence of a color flow signal.

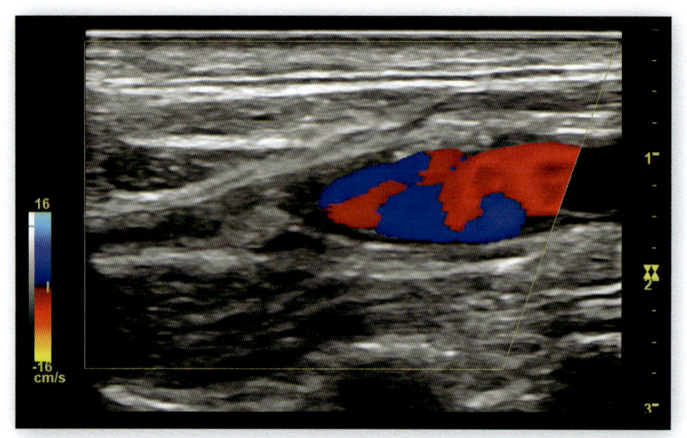

Fig. 91a **ICA image with absence of color signal (non-artifactual color dropout) from an occlusion**

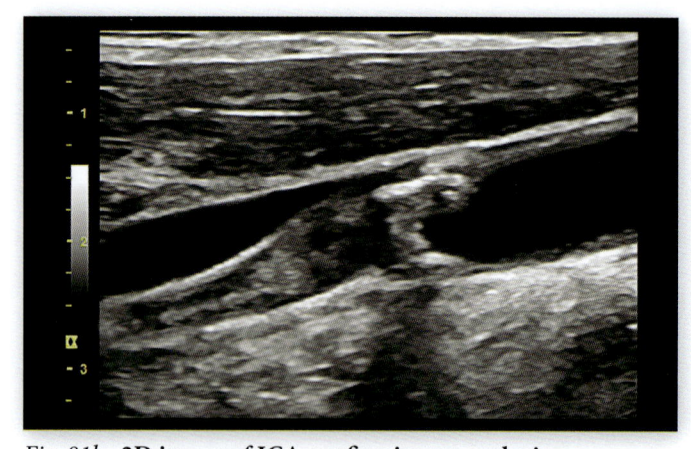

Fig. 91b **2D image of ICA confirming an occlusion**

8.3 Doppler Angle

As discussed in detail in Chapter 7, the Doppler shift is angle dependent. When the angle is at or close to 90 degrees there is no or little Doppler shift. When the Doppler shift is small, the resulting signal is usually below the wall filters and filtered out, resulting in color dropout. *Figure 92* demonstrates a carotid artery tortuous vessel where the angle is close to 90°. Notice that because of the tortuosity, there is an acceleration component toward the longer path such that there is less extensive dropout there than in the region of the shorter path. Also notice that because of the frictional and viscous effects near the walls, the velocities are lower there as well, resulting in lower shifts which are filtered out by the wall filters.

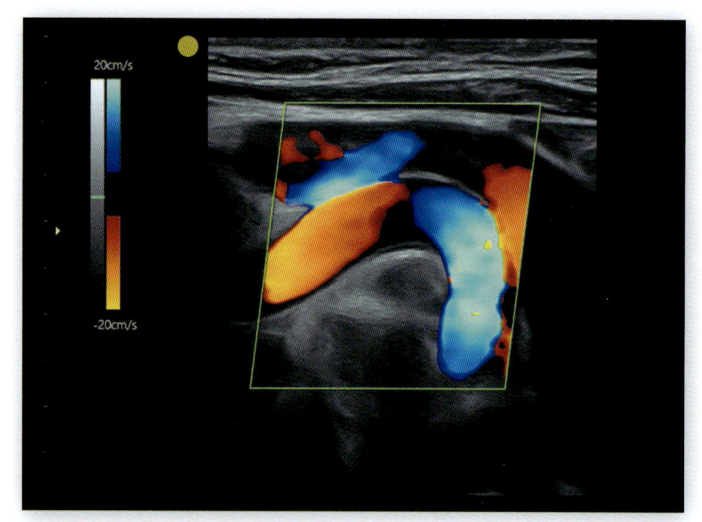

Fig. 92 **Color dropout related to Doppler angle; also note the effects of the vessel walls on dropout: there is more dropout along vessel wall where lower velocities exist, but less dropout along the walls where acceleration and smaller Doppler angles exist**

8.4 Inadequate Sensitivity

Since most Doppler applications are based on the very weak reflection mechanism of Rayleigh scattering, every effort must be made to make certain that there is adequate sensitivity. When there is inadequate sensitivity, poor color filling (color dropout) will occur. In Chapter 7 we discussed the many parameters which affect Doppler signal strength. The following images demonstrate the poor color Doppler signal that results from using an operating frequency that is too high, resulting in excessive attenuation.

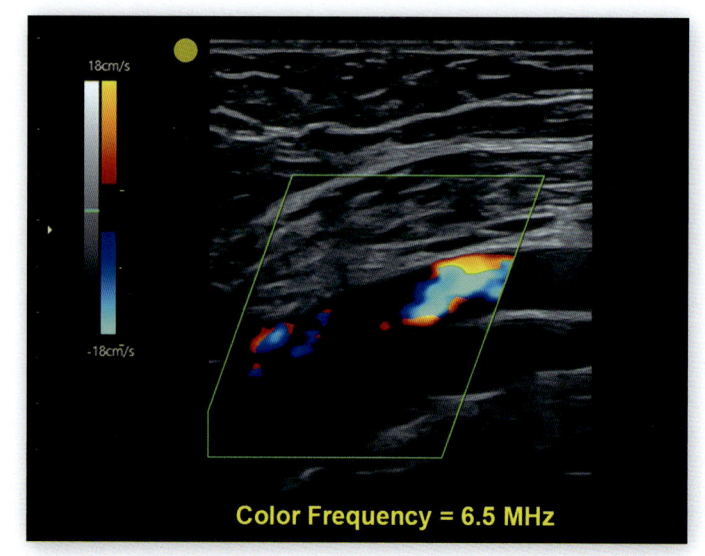

Fig. 93a **Linear image of a carotid artery with depth set to 5 cm and color transmit frequency set to 6.5 MHz resulting in inadequate sensitivity and color dropout**

Chapter 8: Artifacts 419

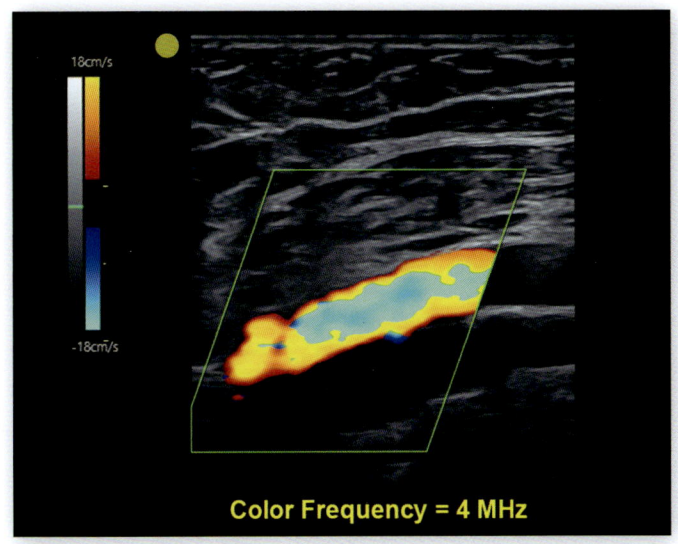

Fig. 93b Linear image of a carotid artery with depth set to 5 cm and color transmit frequency set to 4 MHz with adequate penetration for complete color filling

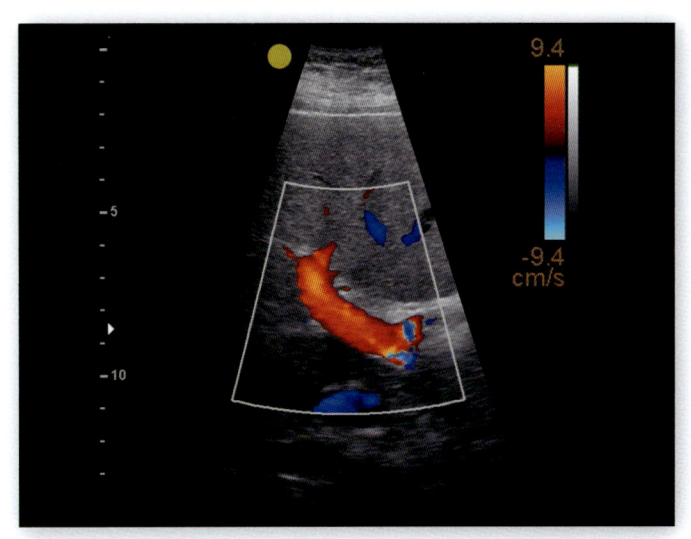

Fig. 94b Curvilinear image of main portal vein with appropriate color scales

8.5 Color Dropout Related to Scales and Wall Filtering

Dropout can also result from excessive color Doppler wall filtering. As discussed in Chapter 7, for sequentially generated color Doppler, the wall filters are directly affected by changing the color scales (PRF). As the color scales increase, the wall filters also increase. As a result, when imaging low-velocity flow, high color scales (which result in high wall filters) will cause color dropout to occur as seen with the following sequence of images.

Note that when higher frame rate color Doppler is performed, the color wall filters no longer have to be "tied" to the color scales. This fact means that the higher scale settings will not necessarily result in color dropout with ultrafast color Doppler.

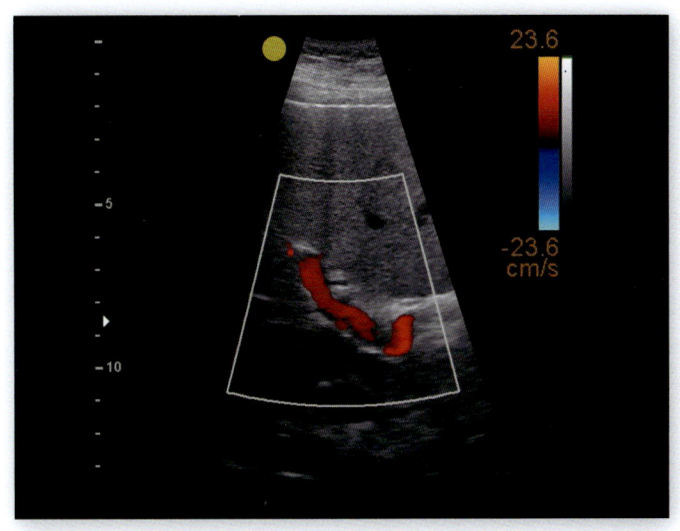

Fig. 94c Curvilinear image of main portal vein with higher color scales resulting in reduced color filling

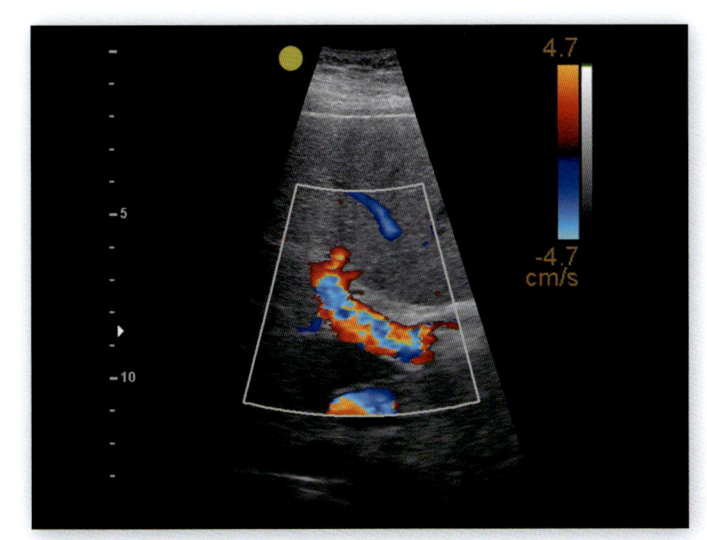

Fig. 94a Curvilinear image of main portal vein with low color scales (PRF) resulting in color aliasing

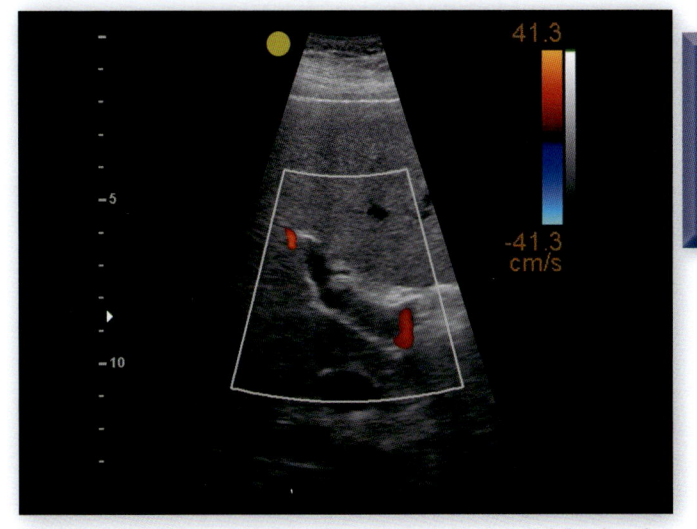

Fig. 94d Curvilinear image of main portal vein with high color scales resulting in color dropout as a result of higher wall filters (as discussed in Chapter 7)

You should realize that dropout related to wall filtering is more likely to occur wherever lower velocities exist or where Doppler angles (close to 90°) result in low Doppler shifts. Lower velocities can exist for many hemodynamic reasons such as low-volumetric flow through large flow areas, low pressure differentials such as late diastole, or high resistance such as near vessel walls or flow through critical stenoses (see Chapter 13). This fact implies that flow dropout may occur in only a portion of a vessel and/or only during a certain phase of the cardiac cycle, as occurs in the figure below. Note that in this case, the dropout exists in V Flow.

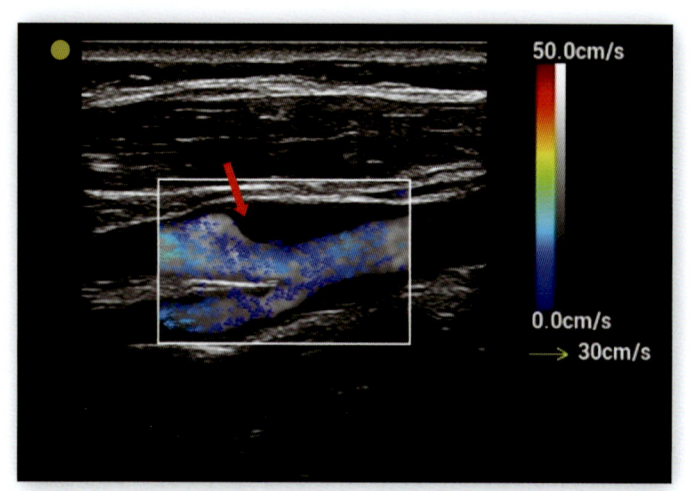

Fig. 95a V Flow image of the carotid bifurcation demonstrating flow dropout artifact in the carotid bulb during diastole as a result of wall filtering

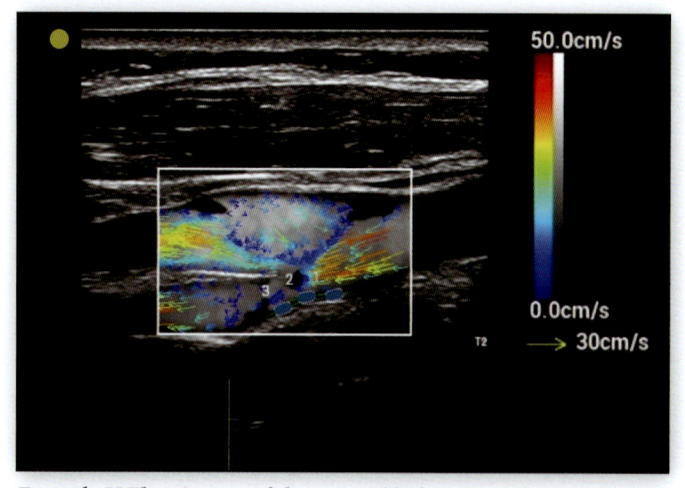

Fig. 95b V Flow image of the carotid bifurcation demonstrating low velocity "helical" flow separation when the velocities are high enough to overcome the wall filters during systole

8.6 Color Dropout and Speckle Noise Related to Gain

Recall from discussions in Chapter 7 that color Doppler is presented based on a threshold. When the color signal is above the set threshold, the color signal is presented. When the 2D signal is high amplitude and the color signal is below the threshold, the 2D is presented. Reducing the color gain reduces the color signal amplitude. If the signal amplitude is reduced below the threshold, the color signal will simply disappear, also known as color dropout. Because of this thresholding effect, sometimes a very slight change in gain will result in going from overgained to appropriately gained, or from appropriately gained to undergained. Adjusting the color gain between these "threshold points" seems to have little or no effect on the color Doppler image. The following two sets of images, an abdominal study and a vascular study, demonstrate the effects of color gain on color dropout.

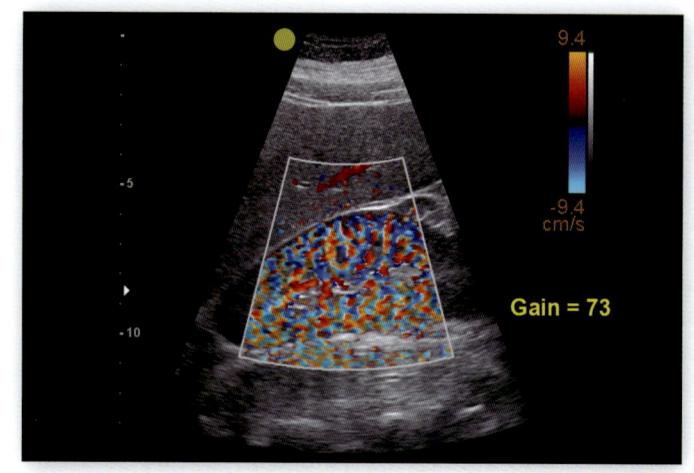

Fig. 96a Curvilinear renal image with excessive color gain resulting in color speckle noise

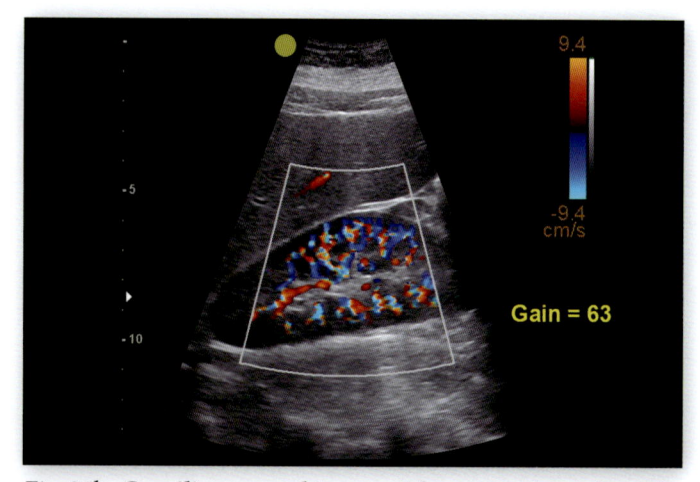

Fig. 96b Curvilinear renal image with appropriate color gain

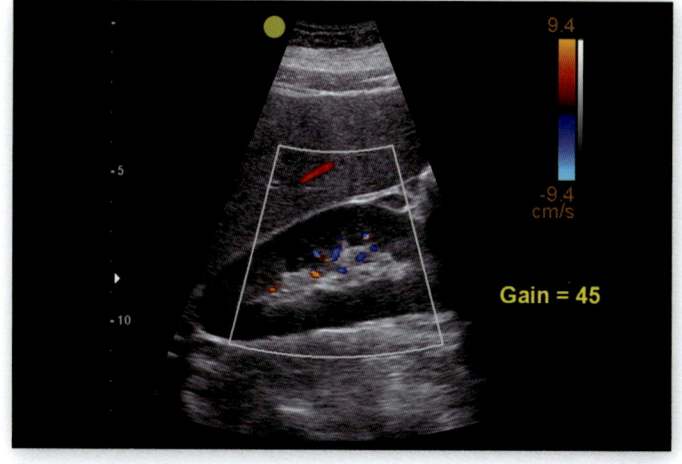

Fig. 96c Curvilinear renal image with color dropout from color receiver gain being set too low

Chapter 8: Artifacts   421

8.7 Color Dropout Related to Color Priority

The threshold level which determines whether color or grayscale is displayed at a particular pixel location is user-determined by setting the color priority (discussed in detail in Chapter 7). A lower color priority setting means that even lower level grayscale signals will be displayed instead of color. In other words, if the color priority is set too low, color dropout will occur. It is also important to note that increasing the 2D receiver gain will impact what color priority setting is necessary to have adequate color filling. As the 2D gain is increased, more of the 2D signal will have a high amplitude, resulting in less color being presented.

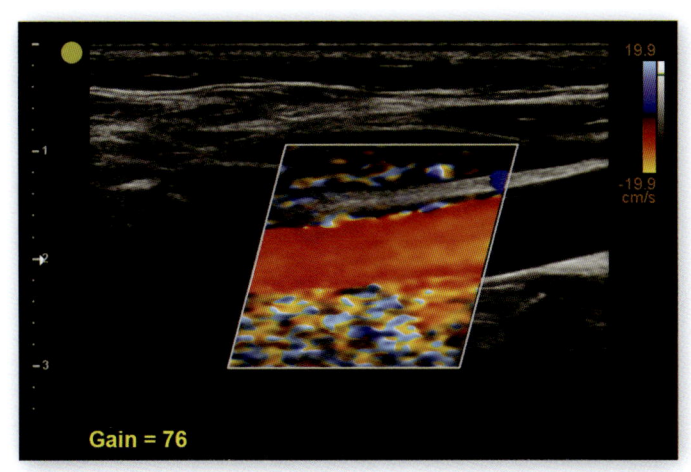

Fig. 97a **Linear image of a common carotid artery with excessive color gain resulting in color speckle noise**

Notice in *Figure 97a* how the noise is most evident outside the regions of flow. Also notice the evident color bleeding over the posterior wall. Comparing this image to *Figure 97b*, you can see how the threshold being even a little over makes a big difference. Decreasing the gain a very small amount (76 to 72) transitions from overgaining to appropriate gain.

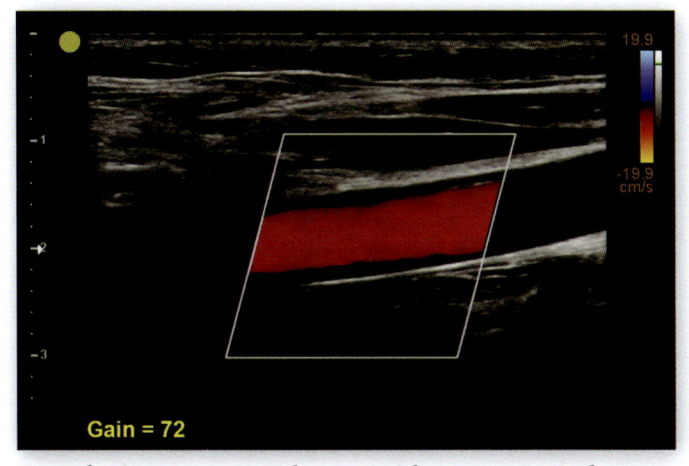

Fig. 97b **Common carotid artery with appropriate color gain**

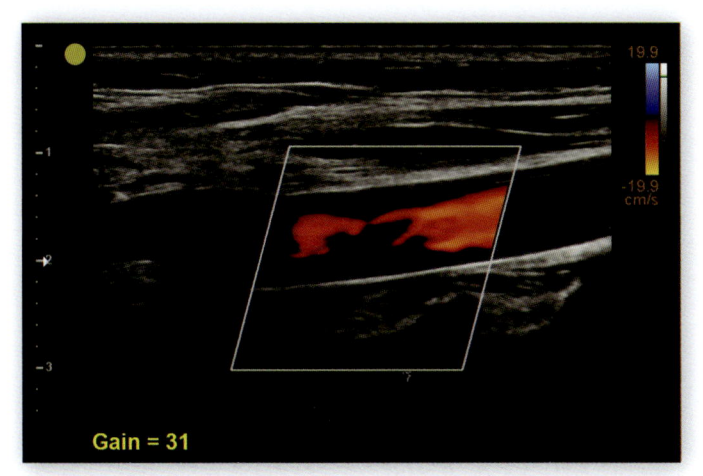

Fig. 97c **Common carotid artery with color dropout from color receiver gain set too low**

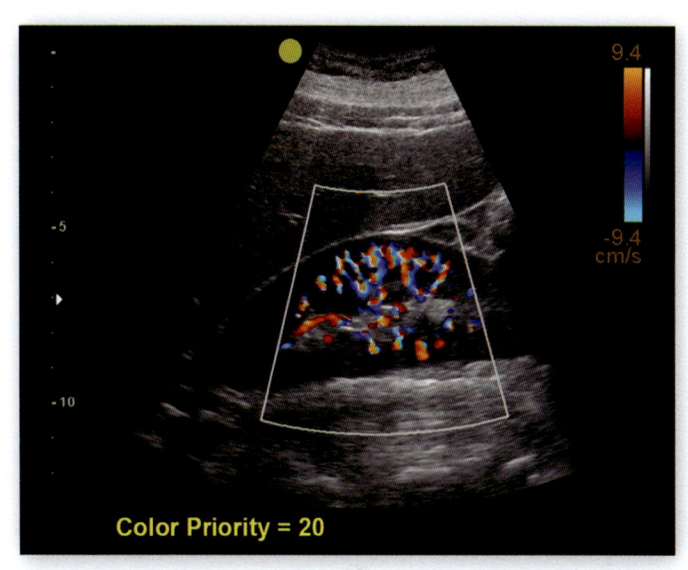

Fig. 98a **Curvilinear renal image at color priority level 20**

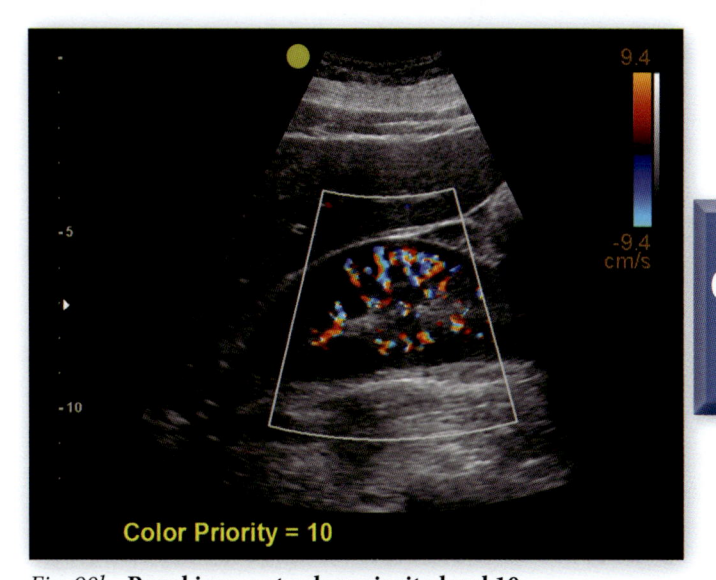

Fig. 98b **Renal image at color priority level 10**

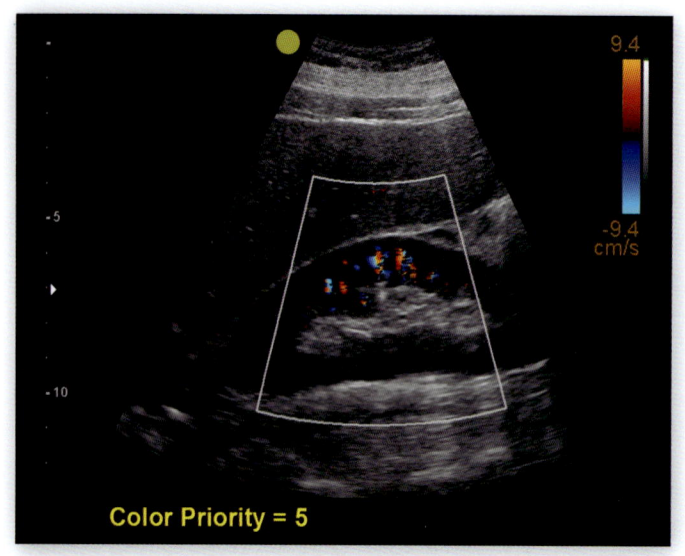

Fig. 98c **Renal image at color priority level 5**

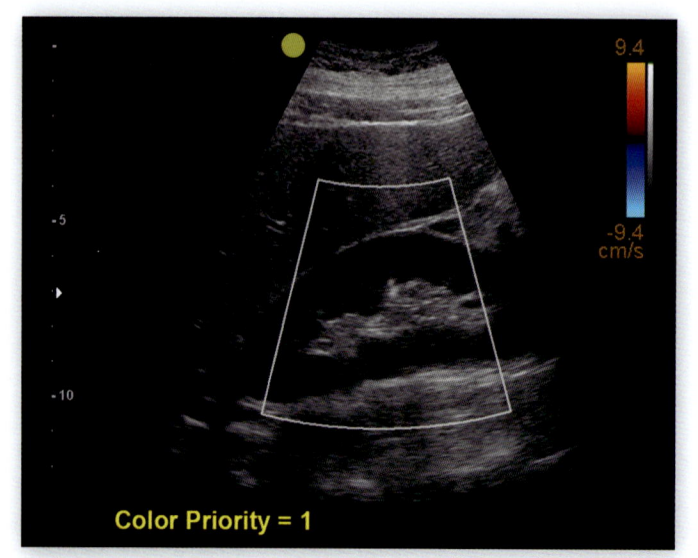

Fig. 98d **Renal image at color priority level 1; note that once the color priority is set too low, complete color dropout occurs**

8.8 Color Dropout from Acoustic Shadowing

Not surprisingly, acoustic shadowing affects spectral and color Doppler as it affects 2D imaging. Shadowing in Doppler occurs whenever the attenuation above the assessed flow region is greater than normal. Shadowing is common below air, stents, bones, calcifications, or any other material that results in a large acoustic impedance mismatch and corresponding large percentage of reflection.

Figure 99 shows color dropout in a vertebral artery as a result of excessive reflection and absorption in the superior bony transverse process of the spine. Note that the 2D shadow is at a different angle than the color Doppler shadow because of the color box steering.

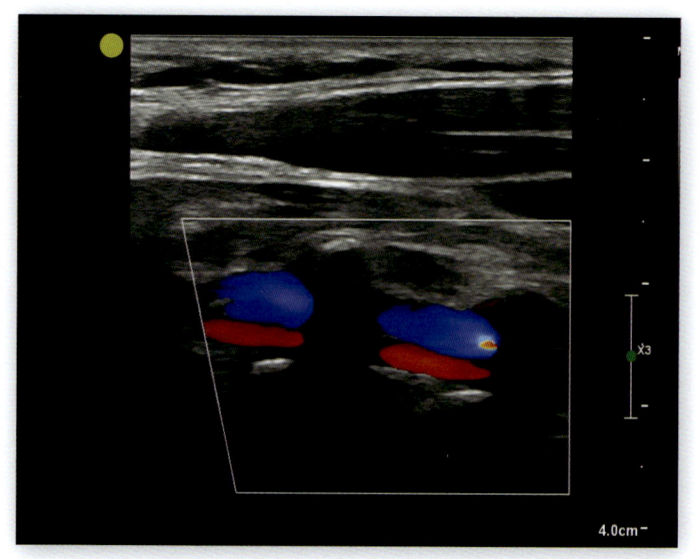

Fig. 99 **Vertebral artery with color dropout caused by shadowing from the bony transverse process of the spine**

9. Conceptual Questions

View ONLINE Conceptual Questions

COMMON MISCONCEPTION: Artifacts

MISCONCEPTION: *All artifacts are bad.*

Artifacts, are often very useful when interpreting ultrasound images. Frequently, information regarding properties of the tissues is revealed by considering the underlying mechanism responsible for the artifact generation. As an example, shadowing can help identify micro-calcifications, enhancement can help differentiate between cystic and non-cystic structures, speed error can help identify when a needle is appropriately introduced during a biopsy, etc. Of course, artifacts which occur as the result of outside interference such as RF pickup and power supply noise have completely no value.

✗ COMMON MISCONCEPTION: Artifacts

MISCONCEPTION: *Mirror artifact is just a type of reverberation artifact.*

Although sometimes challenging to differentiate the source of an artifactual duplicate structure, as with mirroring or reverberation, there is a fundamental difference in the mechanism. Mirroring results in symmetry about the specular reflector and hence motion of the artifactual and actual structure in opposite directions. Conversely, reverberation results in an "anti-symmetric" reflection with motion of the artifactual structure in the same direction as the actual structure.

✗ COMMON MISCONCEPTION: Artifacts

MISCONCEPTION: *Spectral mirroring is related to mirroring imaging artifact.*

Mirror imaging artifact is caused by sound reflecting from a strong specular reflector to another structure and back to the transducer, resulting in a symmetric, artifactual structure (a mirrored structure). In contrast, spectral mirroring is not based on an indirect sound path, but rather the inability to completely separate the forward (I) and reverse (Q) channels of the Doppler spectrum, allowing for some signal to "leak" into the opposite direction channel resulting in a mirrored component to the spectrum.

CHAPTER SUMMARY: Artifacts

- Artifacts can result from interactions within the body, processing within the equipment, incorrect imaging technique, or from external sources such as radio signals.
- Understanding artifacts originates with an understanding of all of the principles taught throughout the earlier chapters and from understanding the implicit assumptions made in ultrasound. Without the fundamentals, it is very difficult to recognize or identify artifacts.
- The presence of artifacts in an image is not always bad. For artifacts that result from interactions within the body, quite frequently the artifact reveals information about the tissue or imaging situation.
- Lateral displacement generally occurs as the result of either grating lobe artifact or refraction artifact.
- Incorrect location in depth can result from speed error artifact, multi-path artifact, reverberation artifact, range ambiguity artifact, and mirroring artifact.
- Most imaging artifacts result from sounds interaction with specular reflectors.
- Since most (but not all) imaging artifacts are caused by specular reflections, you should always assess the presence of specular reflectors as well as the angle of insonation of the reflectors so as to identify artifacts or the likelihood of artifacts.
- Since specular reflection is highly angle dependent, changing the angle (steering, rocking the transducer, using a different imaging plane, etc.) is one of the most effective techniques to differentiate artifact from reality.
- Reverberation artifact is often broken into many subcategories such as ring down, comet tail, and "twinkle" artifact.
- Attenuation-based artifacts include shadowing and enhancement.
- Doppler artifacts include:
  - Aliasing
  - Range ambiguity
  - Spectral broadening
  - Spectral mirroring
  - Blossoming
  - Wall filter saturation
  - Flash artifact
  - Signal dropout

ONLINE EXTRAS

For additional support material and to view your completion progress, visit:

www.pegasuslectures.com/6thEdExtras

Extras by Chapter include:
- Animations
- Videos
- Additional Images
- Clarifying Clips
- Supplemental Exercises
- Conceptual Questions

See page x of Preface for access instructions

References

[1] FDA. *AMPLATZER PFO Occluder Patient Information Guide.* https://www.fda.gov/media/97988/download#:~:text=The%20AMPLATZER%20PFO%20Occluder%20is,by%20a%20short%20connecting%20waist.

[2] Dietrich, C. F., Mathis, G., Blaivas, M., Volpicelli, G., Seibel, A., Wastl, D., ... & Yi, D. (2016). Lung B-line artefacts and their use. *Journal of thoracic disease, 8*(6), 1356.

[3] Ranjan, R. & Pressman, G. S. (2018, July 30). *Doppler Never Lies. Or Does It?*. American College of Cardiology. https://www.acc.org/education-and-meetings/image-and-slide-gallery/media-detail?id=f3572aaff37d4450a73f9081d281dfd1.

[4] Cobey, F. C., & Khoche, S. (2019). Double Envelope With Continuous Wave Doppler: Not an Artifact. *Journal of cardiothoracic and vascular anesthesia, 33*(11), 3223-3227.

[5] Couture, E. J., Kuo, A. S., Andrawes, M. N., & Fitzsimons, M. G. (2019). Double envelope on continuous wave mitral inflow Doppler profile. *Journal of cardiothoracic and vascular anesthesia, 33*(11), 3222-3223.

Bioeffects

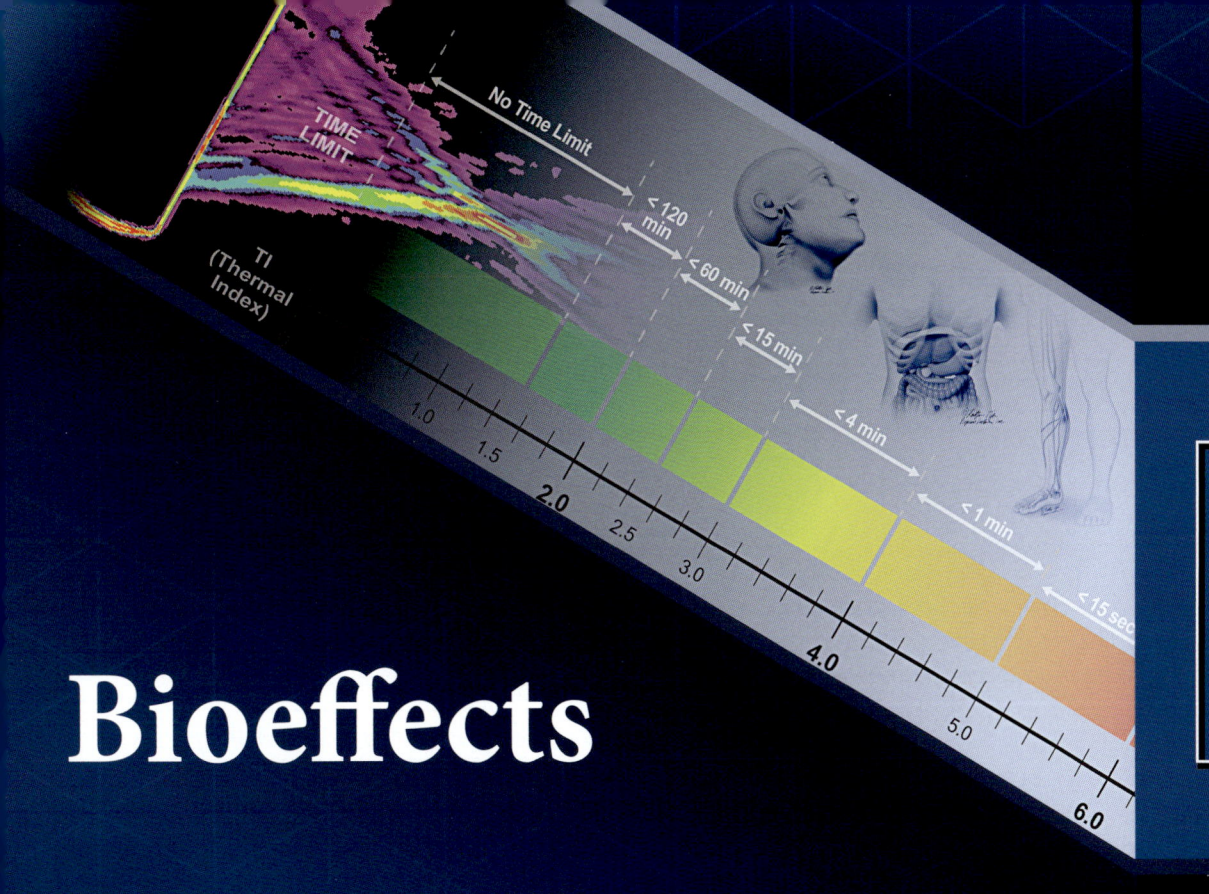

Chapter 9

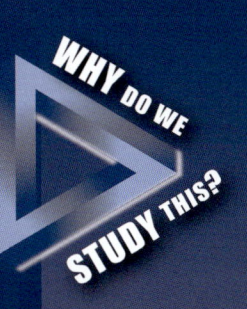

WHY DO WE STUDY THIS?

▷ Understanding bioeffects helps inform us of the potential risk of causing harm to a patient through the process of ultrasound scanning.

▷ Knowing the mechanisms of the risks of thermal and mechanical bioeffects and how to minimize them helps practitioners of sonography safeguard their patients.

▷ Specialized transducers, called hydrophones, offer power and intensity measurements which provide additional information on bioeffects.

WHAT'S IN THIS CHAPTER?

LEVEL 2 — BOARD LEVEL
Begins with a discussion of thermal and mechanical bioeffects including parameters and measurements of intensity and the limitations thereof. Thermal and mechanical indices are introduced along with AIUM guidelines and the ALARA principle with warnings intended to reduce patient risk.

Level 3 — ADVANCED TOPICS
The mathematical approach to converting between various intensities is presented along with more detailed information about hydrophones.

LEARNING OBJECTIVES

▷ Identify the principal bioeffect mechanisms

▷ List the parameters that increase the risk of mechanical and thermal bioeffects

▷ Describe the thermal (TI) and mechanical (MI) indices and the potential limitations to these models

▷ Recognize the official ultrasound safety statements, describe prudent use, and be able to paraphrase the ALARA principle

▷ Apply the absolute maximum recommended scan times for various TI values for specific types of scanning

Chapter 9
Bioeffects

Overview

The foundation for discussing bioeffects has been developed throughout the entire book. In Chapter 2: Waves, we learned that sound is a mechanical wave and that all waves are a cyclical transference of energy. We also learned that as the wave propagates, the wave physically interacts with the medium causing changes within the medium. These changes are measurable in four different quantities called the acoustic variables. Recall that the changes are related to pressure, temperature, particle displacement, and density. Chapter 2 also introduced the general concept of acoustic power and intensity.

In Chapter 3: Attenuation, we learned that the principal form of attenuation for soft tissue is absorption. Recall that absorption is the conversion of some of the mechanical wave energy into heat within the body. As we will learn, absorption and absorption rates are key indicators of the risk of inducing a thermal bioeffect. Additionally, the concept of non-linear frequency dependent absorption was introduced.

In Chapter 4: Pulsed Wave Operation, we learned different ways of timing the transmitted pulse so as to achieve some longitudinal resolution. Within Chapter 4, the foundation was laid for discussing temporal issues as relates to bioeffects. Specifically, the concepts of the duty factor, frame rates, and scanned versus non-scanned modalities, including sequential and plane wave imaging, were introduced and explained.

In Chapter 5: Transducers, we learned about transducers and beam shapes when sequentially generating (line-by-line) images. We learned that the beam is narrowest at the focus and hence, the highest intensity always exists at or shallower than the focus. Great effort was taken to consider how the intensity of the beam changes with convergence and divergence.

In Chapter 6, Part I: System Operation Fundamentals, we learned about signal-to-noise ratio and how the output power increases the beam intensity, thereby increasing the signal-to-noise ratio. We also learned about receiver gain, and improving "apparent" signal-to-noise. In Part II, we learned more about the different approaches to generating images which impact the beam focus and timing including sequential multi-line acquisition (MLA), multi-line transmission (MLT), and ultrafast (planar) imaging.

In Chapter 7: Doppler, we learned about the non-scanned modalities of spectral Doppler as well as the differences between PW and CW Doppler. We also learned the intricacies of how conventional (sequential) color is produced as a scan of non-scanned packets as well as introducing the concept of how ultrafast Doppler is performed. Clearly, the type of Doppler being performed and how the Doppler data is generated affects the timing and beam characteristics which, in turn, determine the risk of bioeffects.

As should be evident from summarizing most of the previous chapters, the content we have learned to this point is related to the risks and mechanisms of bioeffects. When all of these facts are considered together there is a very solid foundation for discussing bioeffects.

1. Mechanisms of Bioeffects

The term "bioeffect" refers to a biological change to tissues as a result of interaction with the insonating beam. The fact that the potential for bioeffects exists should have been evident with the very description of sound as a transport of energy. Since energy can perform work, the possibility that the work performed leads to adverse biological situations is well within the realm of reasonable speculation. Since there are myriad interactions and uses of ultrasound, we also expect that there is more than one mechanism by which damage could potentially result. Fortunately, the list of these effects can be categorized according to the mechanisms which create them. There are two principal mechanisms for creating bioeffects: thermal and mechanical.

1.1 Thermal Bioeffects

Although extremely complex in terms of identifying, measuring, and accurately predicting thermal bioeffects, understanding the basic mechanism of thermal bioeffects is relatively simple. Recall that absorption is a conversion of the sound energy into heat. If the temperature in a region rises too high, metabolic breakdown results, and cellular damage can occur.

Enzymes

Healthy cellular activity is based on chemical reactions. These chemical reactions are dependent on enzymatic activity and rates. An enzyme is a catalyst that controls the rate at which chemical reactions occur in living organisms. Enzymatic activity is sensitive to temperature such that below a threshold temperature, a 10°C increase in temperature can result in an increase in enzymatic activity of 50 to 100% as shown in the figure below.[1]

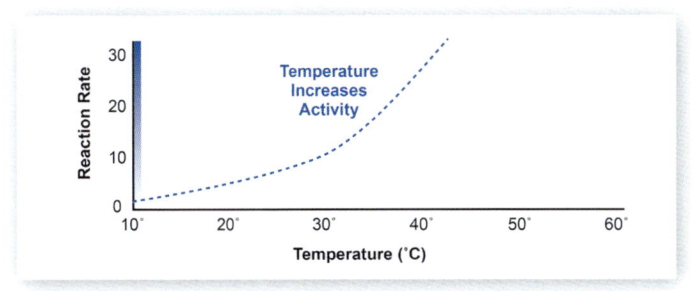

Fig. 1a **Temperature dependence of enzymatic activity**[1]

Denaturing is a process by which proteins lose their native structure leading to the disruption of cell function and potentially cell death. Denaturing can result because of changes in the pH, chemical interactions, exposure to radiation, or from increased temperature. Since enzymes are proteins that catalyze reactions, the denaturing of proteins results in a cessation of the function of enzymes. The temperature at which denaturing occurs varies for different proteins. For many proteins a temperature above 41°C (105.8°F) results in denaturing.[2] The following figure shows how sensitive proteins are to a threshold temperature just slightly above normal human body temperature (37°C).

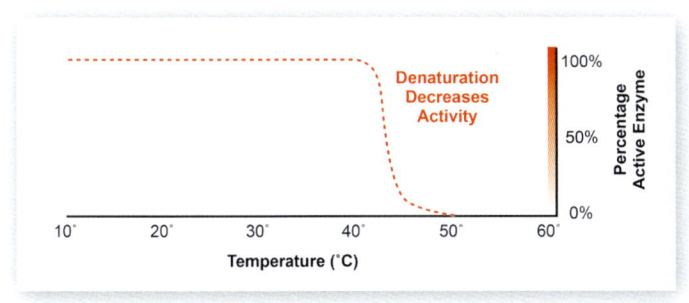

Fig. 1b **Temperature dependence of denaturing of proteins**[1]

By combining the two previous graphs, the overall temperature dependence can be displayed, showing the dramatic decrease in enzymatic activity that occurs with protein denaturation.

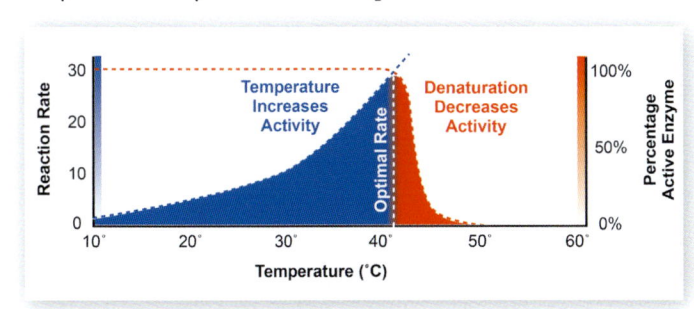

Fig. 1c **Temperature of optimal enzyme reaction rate**

1.2 Mechanical Bioeffects

In addition to thermal bioeffects, there is a risk of mechanical damage from interaction between the wave and tissues in the body. This fact should not be surprising since sound is a mechanical wave. Although there is more than one type of "mechanical" mechanism, the principal agency of bioeffects is called cavitation. The word cavitation has as its root the word cavity or "cavus" which means a hollow space. In the presence of surrounding fluids, a bubble represents a "cavity." Therefore, when a bubble is generated within a structure, there is a production of a cavity and hence the term cavitation. In the simplest definition, cavitation is essentially when bubbles are produced, vibrate or oscillate, and in extreme cases burst or implode. There are two types of cavitation described, one type is referred to as stable and the other type is referred to as inertial (sometimes referred to as transient).

Stable Cavitation

Stable cavitation occurs when the oscillation of the microbubbles does not lead to collapse. In general, when bubbles undergo stable cavitation, the bubbles oscillate with the varying acoustic pressure field in a "stable" manner. In the presence of stable cavitation, fluids surrounding the bubbles may begin to flow or stream. This flow is the result of eddy currents which develop as energy is imparted to the fluid through the oscillating bubbles. This effect of fluid streaming as a result of bubble oscillation is referred to as "micro-streaming." The momentum of the flow is potentially capable of inducing cellular wall stresses that can cause cellular harm.

View ONLINE Animation and Image Library

Inertial Transient Cavitation

Unlike stable cavitation, inertial cavitation results in implosion of the microbubbles. The microbubbles may completely fragment or their "destruction" may lead to a collection of smaller microbubbles. The likelihood of implosion is related to the peak rarefactional pressure. During the rarefactional phase, the pressure within the bubble relative to the lower decreasing pressure external to the bubble causes the bubble to expand. Clearly, during compression, the increasing external pressure causes the bubble to contract. With increasing "negative" pressure of rarefaction, the bubble expands more and more.

Eventually, the bubble expands to the extent that when the compression begins, there is so much inertia from the surrounding fluid, that the bubble collapses inwardly (implodes). This collapse can be extremely violent, generating high amplitude shock waves and producing extremely high temperatures (as high as 10,000 degrees Kelvin). These shock waves and localized high-temperature increases can cause damage to surrounding regions. In the case of metals such as propellers, turbine blades, regulator valves, and pressurized hydraulic pipes, this violent collapse results in pitting and eventually structural damage. In the case of surrounding tissue, this cavitation can cause localized cellular death. Fortunately, the affected region is very small, potentially damaging only a few cells. The term "transient" is also used synonymously with the term inertial cavitation. The term transient is indicative of the fact that there is a change in "state" of the bubble. The word inertial is indicative of the fact that the dramatic change in state is the result of inertia.

View ONLINE Animation and Image Library

1.3 The Concept of a Threshold Effect

In order to relate the principal bioeffect mechanisms to parameters of ultrasound, a fundamental understanding of the concept of a threshold effect is extremely helpful. A threshold is a limit or boundary. A threshold effect implies that there is a limit or boundary above which a specific outcome is achieved, and below which a different outcome occurs. As an example, a threshold effect could be that if you score above a certain number on a test you graduate and if you score below that threshold, you don't. With respect to bioeffects, threshold-related bioeffects will force different scanning behavior and protocols than non-threshold effects.

To date, the best science indicates that inertial cavitation is a threshold effect. Cavitation is stable up to a certain threshold, above which inertial cavitation occurs. In other words, long periods of time at lower rarefactional pressures will not produce inertial cavitation. On the other hand, even a very brief exposure at a pressure level exceeding the threshold rarefactional pressure will result in bubble collapse.

With respect to cellular damage, whether or not thermal bioeffects exhibit a threshold behavior depends on the reference point. On the one hand, there is no specific point at which a slight increase in power or scan duration will cause a dramatic increase in tissue temperature. Instead, the temperature change tends to be gradual over periods of time and, of course, are dependent on absorption rates and the movement of fluids in and out of the region to duct away heat. This behavior is in stark contrast to the threshold behavior of cavitation, for which stable cavitation will occur right up to a threshold and only a slight increase above this intensity will cause an abrupt change in bubble response. On the other hand, relative to a threshold temperature, temperatures below 40° Celsius seemingly produce no irreversible bioeffects. From this perspective, thermal bioeffects exhibit a threshold behavior. Regardless of "threshold" perspective, the most important aspect of this discussion is the fact that temperature-related bioeffects have a time-dependence and that cellular damage increases with increased exposure time and with increased intensities resulting in temperatures above 40° Celsius. In contrast, mechanical effects of cavitation are related to the short-term event during the transmit burst and are not related to longer time periods.

CHECKPOINT: Exam Tip

There are two primary bioeffect mechanisms of concern for ultrasound: thermal bioeffects related to temperature rise and mechanical bioeffects related to cavitation.

2. Safeguarding the Patient

The ultimate goal of studying ultrasound-related bioeffects is to assure that no harm is induced to the patient. Since the potential exists, studies must be performed to understand the mechanisms, identify the parameters of each mechanism which correlate best with bioeffects, create restriction guidelines, and create usage models so as to safeguard from inducing damage. In this endeavor, countless hours of research and work have been devoted.

2.1 Confirming Safe Levels

Confirming the existence of potential bioeffects is not the challenge that exists. If the acoustic power is set at levels beyond what is currently used in diagnostic ultrasound, the existence of bioeffects is easily confirmed. The true challenge is to determine guidelines and ultrasound use models that ensure patient safety.

The task of determining a verifiable standard which guarantees that ultrasound is always safe while preserving efficacy is daunting at best and intractable (unsolvable) at worst. The complexity of the interactions between the waves and tissue types, the various ways in which ultrasound is used, the wave parameters which are routinely varied, differences in patient body habitus, and physiology all enter into the equation. The following is a partial list of impediments to conclusive findings regarding bioeffects and definitive thresholds.

1. In vitro testing cannot adequately address the complexity of live mammalian tissues or the interactions that result. This is not to say that in vitro testing has no value, but that extrapolating the results as they apply to clinical situations is tenuous.
2. Differences in tissue composition, tissue thicknesses, fluid content, and regional blood volume all can have significant impact on bioeffect mechanisms.

3. Testing in a graduated manner on live human tissues until levels are reached at which bioeffects are observed is unacceptable and unethical.
4. Adverse effects of ultrasound may become evident only after a latency period.
5. Adverse effects can potentially be attributed to many interdependent parameters; isolation to just the use of ultrasound is very challenging.
6. Epidemiologic studies have a potential built-in bias since many of the patients being tested are already infirmed.
7. In vivo studies may not be predictive of effects for all patients.

And the list could go on indefinitely. The point of displaying this list is not to state that there is no good information on which to base safety standards. On the contrary, there is a wealth of information that has been gathered over many years through much diligence and effort. The point is to stress that:

1. Definitive results relating to bioeffects and safety limits do not exist and are not likely to ever exist.
2. Results of new tests should be constantly assessed and assimilated into the body of knowledge.
3. Changes in use models of diagnostic ultrasound (new modalities and techniques) may lead to situations which have not thoroughly been tested.

Taken together, these points should lead to an understanding of a need for a cautious but balanced approach to the use of ultrasound. As an analogy, consider how different your driving behavior would be given the following two scenarios. First imagine that every time you drive your car at exactly 43 miles per hour or faster, the wheels start to shake, you lose control, and you crash the car. In comparison, imagine if the potential for the tires to start shaking increases with higher speeds, but there are many other parameters that can affect this less than desired outcome such as the changing conditions of the road, the temperature of the air, and the atmospheric pressure. In the first case, there is a known threshold beyond which you will never drive your car, insuring safety. In the second scenario, you would need to exercise more caution in certain situations, and weigh the greater risk of crashing the car against the benefit of getting to a destination faster.

3. Research and Standards

Owing to the wide acceptance of ultrasound, there are many groups which have published guidelines, standards, or research regarding bioeffects. A few of the most notable are:

1. American Institute of Ultrasound in Medicine (AIUM)
2. National Council on Radiation Protection and Measurements (NCRP)
3. World Federation of Ultrasound in Medicine and Biology (WFUMB)
4. National Institutes of Health (NIH)
5. Food and Drug Administration (FDA)
6. The British Medical Ultrasound Society (BMUS)

A Congressional amendment was passed in 1976 requiring the FDA to regulate all medical devices including diagnostic ultrasound. The resulting restriction on power limits by the FDA was based on performance and power predating their regulatory period. In essence, the regulatory standard became the existing "performance" levels including maximum power levels prior to 1976. In the parlance of FDA approval for new designs and devices, comparisons are made to a predicate device. If data is in evidence supporting that a "new" system behaves similarly to an existing device, then FDA approval is granted through a process called a 510K submission. If a predicate device cannot be shown, a much more elaborate FDA approval process is required with full clinical trial testing for safety and efficacy. Interestingly, equipment power levels predating the FDA regulation charter were not necessarily determined strictly by rigorous science, but rather on historical experience and empirical results which indicated no serious existing bioeffects. Since no bioeffects had been confirmed at the existing power levels, it was believed that there was a margin of safety built into these power limits.

Since 1976, all of the organizations listed above have produced official statements regarding bioeffects and safety. Additionally, the FDA has allowed ultrasound equipment manufacturers the ability to increase transmit power levels beyond the pre-existing 1976 limits by presenting an output display standard (ODS) as a guideline for the user to interpret and weigh benefits versus increased risk. We will concentrate primarily on the conclusions of the AIUM. Specifically, the AIUM formed a bioeffects committee with the express purpose of monitoring and evaluating research reports related to biological effects. In 1987 and again in 1992, the committee held an AIUM sponsored conference. The meeting in 1992 reexamined the publication which resulted from the 1987 meeting. The amended guidelines with official statements in many ultrasound-related categories were published in printed form in 1993. Since then, these official statements have been either reconfirmed or updated with new official statements added as necessary through online publication on the AIUM website.

KEY CONCEPT

In order to safeguard the patient from possible harm associated with bioeffects, significant effort has been expended to determine safe levels below which bioeffects will not occur, or at least are very unlikely to occur. For many reasons, finding a definitive threshold below which "safe" can always be claimed is very challenging.

5.4 Putting the Concepts Together

From comparing the two figures above, it is obvious that both the temporal peak (TP) and the pulse peak (PP) refer to the exact same parameter of the wave. Therefore, there is no need to use both terms. The abbreviation TP is used and the abbreviation PP is dropped.

In Chapter 4, we also learned that the ratio of the PD to the PRP was called the duty factor. Do you see how the PA (pulse average) and the TA (temporal average) are related?

Since the PA is the energy of the pulse divided by the PD, and the TA is the energy in the pulse divided by the PRP, the ratio of the TA and the PA is also the duty factor.

$$\frac{TA}{PA} = \frac{\left(\frac{Energy}{PRP}\right)}{\left(\frac{Energy}{PD}\right)} = \left(\frac{Energy}{PRP}\right) \cdot \left(\frac{PD}{Energy}\right) = \left(\frac{PD}{PRP}\right) = \text{Duty Factor}$$

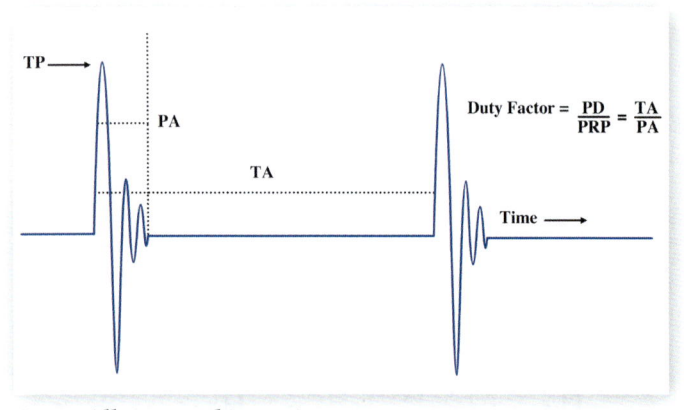

Fig. 6 **All temporal intensity measurements**

As measured, the greatest intensity is where the intensity is maximum both spatially and temporally, or:

$$I_{SPTP} \text{ (\underline{S}patial \underline{P}eak, \underline{T}emporal \underline{P}eak)}$$

Since a pulse average is less than a temporal peak, the measured spatial peak, pulse average must be less than the spatial peak, temporal peak, or:

I_{SPTP} (<u>S</u>patial <u>P</u>eak, <u>T</u>emporal <u>P</u>eak) > I_{SPPA} (<u>S</u>patial <u>P</u>eak, <u>P</u>ulse <u>A</u>verage)

The smallest measured intensity is where the intensity is minimum, both spatially and temporally, or:

$$I_{SATA} \text{ (\underline{S}patial \underline{A}verage, \underline{T}emporal \underline{A}verage)}$$

> **CHECKPOINT: Exam Tip**
>
> **Understanding common intensities is facilitated by some basic principles. The first two subscripted letters refer to the spatial distribution of the power (Spatial Peak (SP) or Spatial Average (SA)). The second two letters refer to the temporal distribution of the power (Temporal Peak (TP), Pulse Average (PA), or Temporal Average (TA)). Additionally, a peak is always greater than (or in extreme cases equal to) a mean.**

6. The Significance of the Common Intensities

6.1 Common Intensity Analogy

Knowing that there are multiple ways in which to measure an intensity, and knowing that there are multiple mechanisms for bioeffects is not the same as intuitively understanding the differences between the common intensities, why each exists, and which bioeffect mechanism is associated with which intensity. The following analogy should help develop some insight.

Imagine that you have a bathtub that you would like to fill. However, whatever you do, you must make certain not to overfill the tub, allowing the water to spill over and ruin the bathroom floor. In this analogy, the tub is the equivalent to the patient, the water is equivalent to the energy in the transmitted waveforms, and an overflow is the equivalent to bioeffects.

There are two extreme cases that can cause the tub to overflow. One extreme is to turn the faucet on full so that in a short time there is an overflow. The other extreme is to allow the faucet to trickle flow into the tub, but allow the trickle to continue for a long period of time. Either case results in an overflow and a bioeffect. Of course, there is an inverse relationship between the flow rate and time. As the flow increases, the time until overflow decreases.

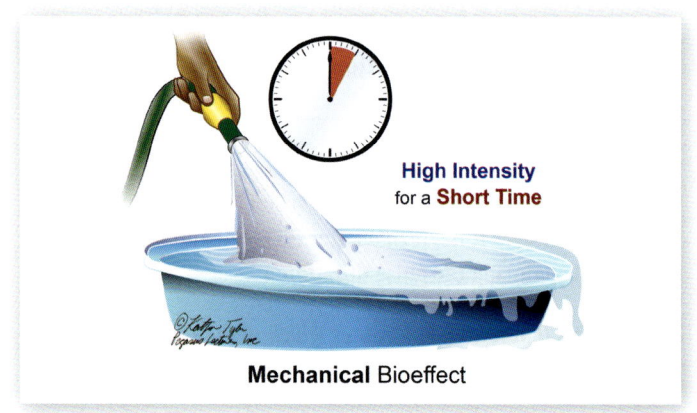

Fig. 7a **High intensity over a short time represents a mechanical bioeffect**

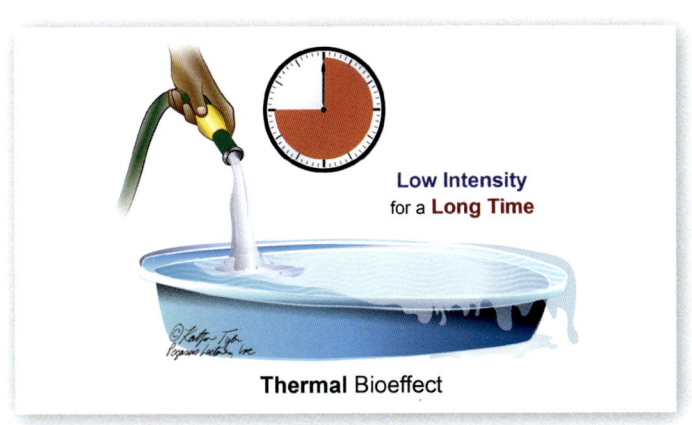

Fig. 7b **Low intensity over a long time represents a thermal bioeffect**

6.2 Mechanical Bioeffects and the I_{SPPA}

This first extreme overflow scenario is analogous to the mechanical bioeffect of cavitation. If there is enough energy in the short duration pulse, cavitation occurs. Therefore to predict cavitation, the intensity measurement is made over the short duration of the transmit pulse, referred to as the pulse average. Since the common intensities measure intensity with respect to space and time, we must also consider the spatial component more likely to predict cavitation. Clearly, where the beam reaches the highest intensity in physical space would have a greater likelihood of cavitation than where the beam is at average intensity. Therefore, in terms of common intensities, the best indicator for cavitation is the spatial peak, pulse average, or the I_{SPPA}. Common I_{SPPA} values are below 190 W/cm².

> **Author's Note:**
> **Indicator of Cavitation**
>
> Frequent confusion arises from the fact that cavitation is related to the pulse average and not the temporal peak. In terms of the analogy, the overflow of the bathtub is associated with too much volume over a short time, not the instantaneous peak volume. In terms of the cavitation of bubbles, because of inertia, it takes time to mechanically oscillate the bubble. Therefore, it is the average energy of the pulse that is the "better" indicator of cavitation, not the instantaneous peak.

6.3 Thermal Bioeffects and the I_{SPTA}

The second overflow scenario is analogous to the risk of thermal bioeffects. Heating occurs over time. The intensity parameter that would best relate to a thermal bioeffect must measure the intensity with respect to longer time intervals. Therefore, the temporal average is the best indicator to predict thermal conditions and hence thermal-related bioeffects. Since the common intensities reference the beam intensity both over space and distance, we must consider the spatial distribution and the likelihood of increased heating. Again, we would expect that where the beam reaches the highest intensity in physical space would have a greater likelihood of generating heat than where the beam is at average intensity. Therefore, in terms of common intensities, the best indicator for thermal bioeffects is the spatial peak, temporal average, or the I_{SPTA}. Common I_{SPTA} values are below 720 mW/cm².

> **KEY CONCEPT**
>
> The mechanisms which result in thermal versus mechanical bioeffects can be represented by a bathtub analogy, in which overfilling the tub is equivalent to causing tissue damage. Thermal bioeffects are modeled by the case where the tub is filled slowly over a long time period. Cavitation is represented by a high volume filling over a short duration.

6.4 Conversion Between a PA and a TA Intensity: (Duty Factor)

In Section 5.4, we learned that the ratio of a temporal average intensity to a pulse average intensity is the same as the ratio of the PD to the PRP, referred to as the duty factor. Therefore, the duty factor can be thought of as the constant of conversion between a temporal average and a pulse average.

$$Duty\ Factor = \frac{PD}{PRP} = \frac{TA}{PA}$$

To convert from a pulse average to a temporal average (PA ⇒ TA), you multiply the pulse average by the duty factor, or:

$$PA \cdot DF = TA$$

And similarly, to convert the (TA ⇒ PA), you divide the TA by the duty factor as follows:

$$PA = TA/DF$$

CHECKPOINT: Exam Tip

Recall that the duty factor represents the percentage of time the transducer is producing energy that will interact with the patient. The highest possible duty factor is 1, or 100%, which occurs in continuous wave. All pulsed wave modalities must have a duty factor less than 1. A higher duty factor implies a greater potential for heat to build up within the patient, increasing the likelihood of thermal bioeffects.

6.5 Conversion Between SP and SA Intensity: (BUF)

The Beam Uniformity Factor (BUF)

The beam uniformity factor or coefficient is defined as the spatial peak divided by the spatial average. The BUF is a measure of how uniform a beam is distributed spatially.

$$BUF = \frac{SP}{SA}$$

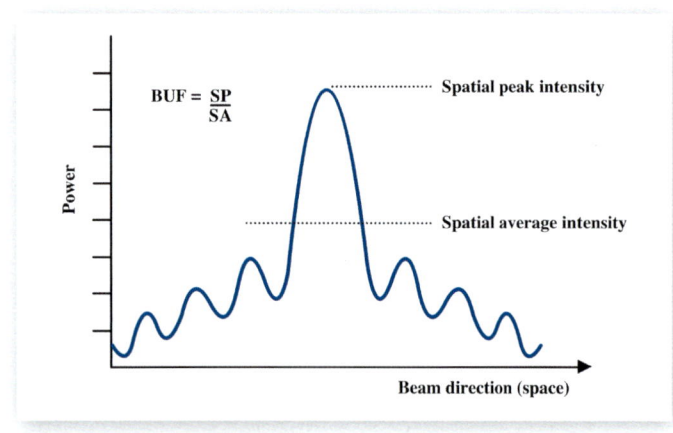

Fig. 8 **Beam uniformity**

◊ **Example:**
What is the BUF if the spatial peak intensity is 700 mW/cm² and the spatial average intensity is 400 mW/cm²?

$$\text{Beam Uniformity Coefficient} = \frac{700}{400} = \frac{7}{4} = 1.75$$

As noted above, the beam uniformity factor is defined as the spatial peak divided by the spatial average. Since a peak is always greater than or equal to an average, the BUF is always greater than or equal to 1, and in reality always greater than 1. A perfectly uniform beam would have a BUF equal to 1.

Converting between the SA and the SP

To convert a spatial average to spatial peak, you multiply the spatial average by the BUF as follows:

$$SA \cdot BUF = SA \cdot \frac{SP}{SA} = SP$$

KEY CONCEPT

The pulse average (PA) refers to the energy divided by the pulse duration (PD). The temporal average (TA) refers to the same energy but divided by the pulse repetition period (PRP). Therefore, the ratio of the TA to the PA is the same as the PD/PRP which is the definition of the duty factor.

7. Exercises

View ONLINE Exercises

8. Relating Risks of Bioeffects to Ultrasound Modes

8.1 Scanned Versus Non-scanned Modalities

In Chapter 4, we began the discussion about scanned versus non-scanned modalities. Recall that non-scanned modalities such as PW Doppler, CW Doppler, A-mode, and M-mode, repeatedly transmit in the same direction whereas scanned modalities (such as 2D and color Doppler) transmit in differing directions over time. With respect to thermal bioeffects, the risk is worse for non-scanned modalities.

For a scanned modality the energy is distributed line-by-line over a wide area, allowing time for heat generated through absorption to dissipate. In comparison, a non-scanned modality repeatedly transmits energy in the same direction leaving little time between transmit pulses for heat to dissipate. Therefore, the propensity for localized heating is greater in modes like CW Doppler and PW Doppler than in modes like sequentially generated color Doppler and 2D imaging. How much heating occurs depends on the beam intensity (power and spatial distribution), the pulse duration and pulse repetition period (the duty cycle), the absorption rate of the tissues, and the ability of that region of the body to duct away heat.

> **Author's Note:**
> **Bioeffects and Newer Imaging Techniques**
>
> Although the introduction of newer image generation techniques such as plane wave/ultrafast, MLT, MLA, and shear wave imaging have added complexity to what is considered a scanned and non-scanned modality, the underlying principles can still be applied to determine the associated bioeffect risks.

8.2 Ultrasound Modalities in Order of Thermal Risks

If we consider the effect of duty cycle in conjunction with non-scanned modalities, it becomes clear that the ultrasound mode with the greatest potential risk of thermal bioeffects is CW Doppler. As a non-scanned modality with a duty factor of 1, CW is the mode which usually generates the highest I_{SPTA} values. The next modality on the thermal list is PW Doppler. PW Doppler is also a non-scanned modality but generally has a considerably lower duty factor than 1. The modality with the lowest risk of thermal bioeffects is generally sequentially generated 2D imaging. The reason is not only because this type of 2D image is a purely scanned modality, but also because the transmit pulses are designed to be as short as possible for optimal axial resolution, producing a very low duty factor.

Of the conventional modes still in use, we have not yet specified the ranking of thermal effects for sequential color Doppler and M-mode. For many reasons there is no easy means by which to determine which of these two modalities will have potentially worse thermal effects. Although M-mode is a non-scanned modality, M-mode usually has a very low duty factor like 2D imaging, so as to achieve high axial resolution. Color is a partially scanned, partially non-scanned modality and generally has a higher duty factor than M-mode. The imaging situations which make color more likely to produce higher temporal average intensities are when there are narrower color sectors, shallower imaging depths, larger color packet sizes, and of course, higher transmit power. The most that can be said about the relative heating from M-mode and color Doppler is that these two modalities are generally not the most likely to be restricted by thermal issues, and they are also not the least likely to be restricted by thermal issues.

8.3 Transmit Voltages for Various Modalities

As a result of the thermal restriction imposed by the high I_{SPTA} values for CW Doppler, the maximum allowed transmit voltage is relatively low. Typical peak transmit voltages for CW Doppler are on the order of 8 Volts (peak-to-peak). For the same transmit voltage, PW has a lower I_{SPTA} value. As a result, the maximum transmit voltage is higher for PW Doppler than CW Doppler. How high the transmit voltage can go depends on the Doppler gate depth, Doppler gate size, and the PRF, but in general, the maximum voltage is approximately 30 Volts (peak-to-peak). For 2D imaging, a transmit voltage of 35 Volts would produce a very low I_{SPTA} value. As a result, the maximum allowed transmit voltage is as high as 150 or even 200 Volts peak-to-peak. Understanding this relationship is facilitated by the bathtub analogy. When the faucet is left running for a long duration, the flow is only allowed to trickle (CW transmit voltage). As the duration is shorter, the flow is allowed to increase. In the extreme, if you want to fill a bathtub in one short burst of water, the flow is allowed to be extremely high during that short duration (2D imaging). *Figure 9* demonstrates the relative relations of the transmit voltage between CW Doppler, PW Doppler, and 2D imaging. Note that these voltages cannot be drawn to scale because of the significant differences in amplitude.

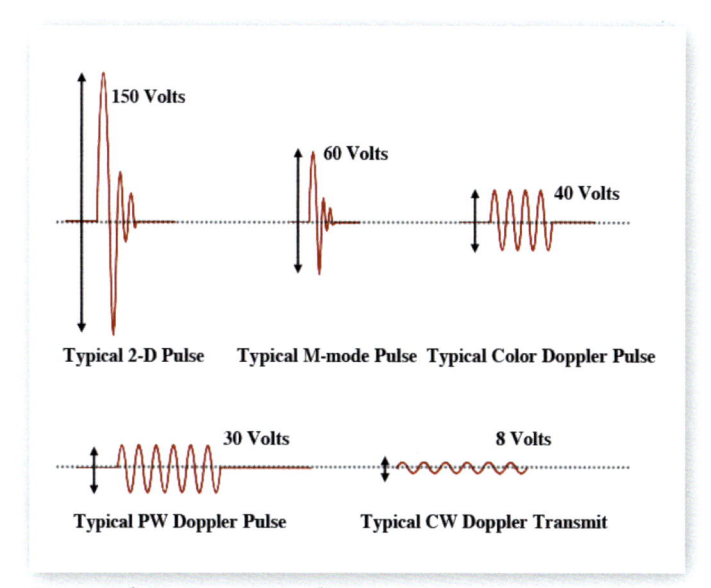

Fig. 9 **Relative transmit voltages**

> **KEY CONCEPT**
>
> Non-scanned modalities such as PW Doppler, CW Doppler, and M-mode generally have a greater risk of thermal bioeffects since the power is repeatedly transmitted in the same direction. Sequentially generated 2D (a scanned modality) generally has the greatest risk of cavitation.

8.4 Ultrasound Modalities in Terms of Cavitation

As already discussed, the likelihood of inertial cavitation is a threshold effect which does not, for the most part, depend on the duration of the imaging. As a result, first order determination of which modalities have the greatest risk of cavitation is a simple process of looking at the "maximum allowed" transmit voltages in *Figure 9*. Clearly, 2D imaging presents the greatest "potential" risk whereas CW offers relatively little, if any, risk of cavitation. In essence there is an inverse relationship between the modalities with the highest risk of thermal damage and the corresponding risk of mechanical damage.

8.5 Theory of FDA Limits

In theory, if all testing and predictive models are correct, no modality would have any real risk of producing bioeffects. By measuring the various beam intensities and guaranteeing the system never goes above threshold limits, bioeffects should not exist. Therefore, in a perfect world, even though CW Doppler runs closer to the I_{SPTA} limit than 2D, no real thermal risk should exist. This is precisely the reason why CW transmit voltages are so low in comparison to 2D transmit voltages. Similarly, in a perfect world, the risk of bioeffects with 2D imaging would also be zero for allowed imaging situations. The difficulty, as discussed in Section 2.1, is that no mathematical models are perfect and not all imaging situations can be anticipated and factored in. As a result, relatively conservative intensity limits have been set to try to safeguard the patient. As you will see from the AIUM statements regarding the safety of ultrasound, this approach has been relatively successful. On the other hand, you must appreciate that there are still potential risks, and that these risks must be minimized while simultaneously producing the best diagnostic quality data possible. This "trade-off" will be covered by the AIUM's ALARA principle regarding prudent use of ultrasound.

> **KEY CONCEPT**
>
> Higher duty factors generally result in a need to reduce the transmit voltage to decrease the risks of bioeffects. For example, since CW has a duty factor of 1, the maximum allowed transmit voltage is much lower than in 2D, for which the duty factor is much less than 1. This fact also helps to explain why 2D has a much greater risk of mechanical damage than CW.

9. Acoustic Power Measurements

9.1 Overview of Acoustic Power Measurements

Equipment manufacturers use power models and acoustic power testing to determine an acceptable range for the acoustic intensity parameters. The models are used to help limit the tests required by predicting the worst-case (highest intensity) scenarios. Specifically, the computer models predict the "worst case" ultrasound analyzing

Modality	Exacerbating Factors	Mitigating Factors	Predominant Risk
Ultrafast Doppler	• Non-scanned • Entire field of view scanned at once • Relatively high duty factor (multiple cycles per pulse)	• Transmit power set low • Scan duration limited to only a few seconds (at a time) • Beam not focused	Thermal
CW Doppler (single line)	• Non-scanned • Duty factor = 100% • Focused beam	Transmit power set very low	Thermal
PW Doppler (single line)	• Non-scanned • Very high duty factor • Focused beam	Transmit power set low	Thermal
M-Mode (single line)	• Non-scanned • High duty factor • Focused beam	Transmit lower than for 2D	Thermal
Color Doppler (sequential)	• Color packets are non-scanned • High duty factor • Focused beam	• Transmit lower than for 2D • Packets are scanned (sequential image generation)	Thermal / Mechanical
2D (sequential)	Very high transmit power	• Low duty factor • Scanned (allows time for heat dissipation)	Mechanical
ARFI/Shearwave (sequential)	• Transmit power (MI) similar to 2D imaging • Extremely long PD (up to 25 times as many cycles per pulse as for PW)	ARFI push pulse generally only once per image	Mechanical* (MI: 1.0-1.9)

* In general, although the ARFI push pulses have a very high duty factor (approximately 200 cycles whereas PW is typically between 4 and 16 (sometimes as high as 32)), the thermal risk is low since a single ARFI push pulse is usually necessary to create a single image (dependent on image format and manufacturer). However, Hermon et al showed that at or near the focus, in bone, the temperature rise could be as high as 8° Celsius[3].

Table 1 **Bioeffect risk factors by modality**

modes by each of the imaging modalities at various power levels, focal configurations, depth settings and PRF's. The "worst case" modes are the imaging situations which are predicted to generate the highest temporal and pulse average intensities.

From this data, a system is tested by attaching a transducer and placing the face of the transducer in a water tank. The system is configured so as to be in one of the expected "worst case" modes. A special ultrasound sensitive transducer (called a hydrophone) in the water tank is then used to measure the acoustic pressure and calculate the various intensity measurements. The system configuration is then changed to another "worst case" predicted mode, and the measurement process repeated. Multiple transducers are put through the same testing procedure and the resulting power data is analyzed. If the computer modeling was correct, then all of the transducers tested, for all of the various system configurations will have intensities which fall within the accepted power limits. If any specific system configurations, or any transducers result in measurements above the power limits, the maximum allowed power is "dialed back" in the system software and the tests repeated. For new products, the data collected is then submitted to the FDA for verification of meeting predicated device standards. In this way, a system is tested to "assure" safe power levels.

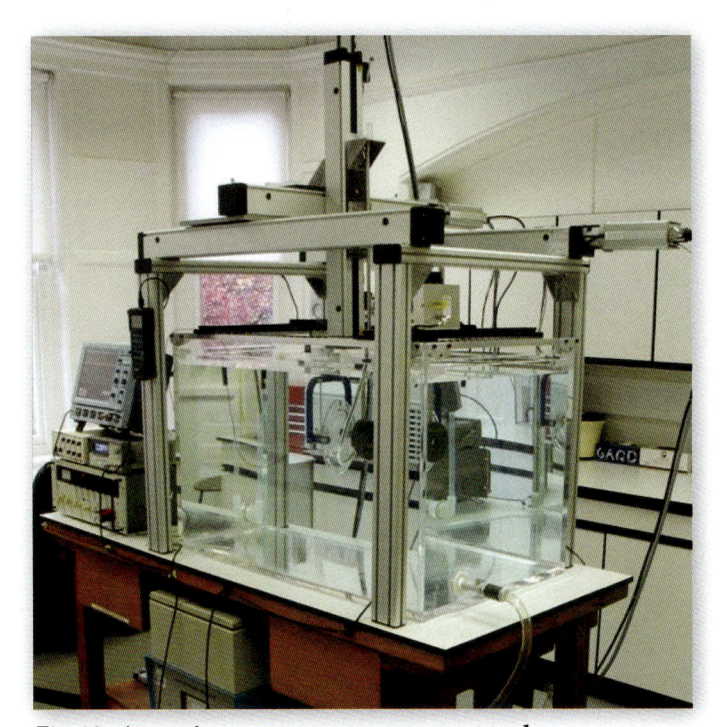

Fig. 10 **Acoustic power measurement test tank**

9.2 The Hydrophone

A hydrophone is a specialized ultrasound transducer, designed to measure acoustic pressure fields. Since hydrophones are used in water baths, the sensitivity requirements are not nearly as rigorous as for imaging transducers. On the other hand, to be useful, a hydrophone must be very stable over time, with a near flat response (or correctable response) over a wide frequency range. If the hydrophone sensitivity were to vary significantly, the acoustic power testing data would be completely unreliable. As a result, hydrophones used for acoustic power measurement testing are routinely tested and calibrated. This calibration must also take into account the temperature of the water.

There are a few different types of hydrophones which can be used for acoustic power testing. The two most commonly used hydrophones for diagnostic ultrasound transducer testing are the needle hydrophone and the membrane hydrophone. Parameters of importance are bandwidth, sensitivity, directivity, and flatness of response.

Fig. 11a **Membrane hydrophone**

Fig. 11b **Needle hydrophone**

9.3 Six Degrees of Freedom

As simple as the principle of acoustic testing sounds, reality is in sharp juxtaposition. For accurate power measurements there are actually six different degrees of freedom. The hydrophone must be aligned to the beam laterally, elevationally, and axially. In addition to the normal scan plane dimensions, since the surface of the hydrophone represents a specular reflector, the hydrophone must be aligned in the three angles referred to as pitch, yaw, and roll. As a result, the process of testing a transducer and the associated power field is complicated. Very large, semi-automated tanks have been designed to help reduce the complexity, but the fact remains that power testing using a hydrophone in an acoustic tank is still very time consuming.

> **KEY CONCEPT**
>
> A hydrophone is a specialized ultrasound transducer used to measure acoustic pressure fields in a water bath. Through the use of computer modeling and testing multiple transducers, the hydrophone data can be used to statistically determine that the power levels are set "safely."

9.4 Beamplots

While scanning the acoustic field over the imaging scan planes (power testing), the measurement system actually digitizes and stores the power registered by the hydrophone. This data can then be plotted and analyzed. Analysis can include maximum sensitivity, bandwidth, sensitivity over bandwidth, lateral beam dimensions, elevation beam dimensions, beam shape over depth, variations with changes to the focus, and grating lobes to name a few. In addition to testing for safety (relative to the guidelines and power restriction to minimize risk of bioeffects), and for quality assurance (to ensure adequate performance), these results are used in the design process. For engineers, the output results of the acoustic testing frequently become what drives iterations of design and system implementation. Computer models are the beginning, but given the complexities of ultrasound beams, ultimately, the models do not always accurately predict what happens in real life.

Another approach to testing has been developed called a pulse Schlieren system. A Schlieren system uses an intense focused light source to illuminate a transparent medium. The light source is strobed in time, very accurately synchronized with the transmit pulse driving the transducer. Since the sound wave interacts with the medium as it propagates, the medium is "perturbed" from its normal state. The perturbations in the medium cause phase disturbances in the reflected light. Optics are used to create an image from the very weak phase perturbed scattered light. The phase disturbances are on the order of a few wavelengths of the light. These phase disturbances are converted into an intensity and displayed. This new approach holds the promise of significantly faster beam assessment and power measurements.

The following images are of beam patterns produced using Schlieren imaging.

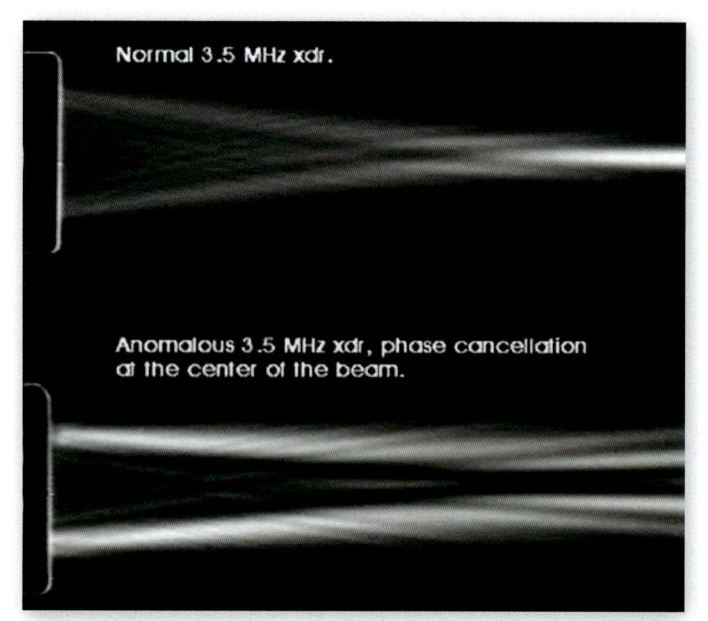

Fig. 12 **Schlieren image of a normal and abnormal 3.5 MHz beam** *(Courtesy of Onda Corporation)*

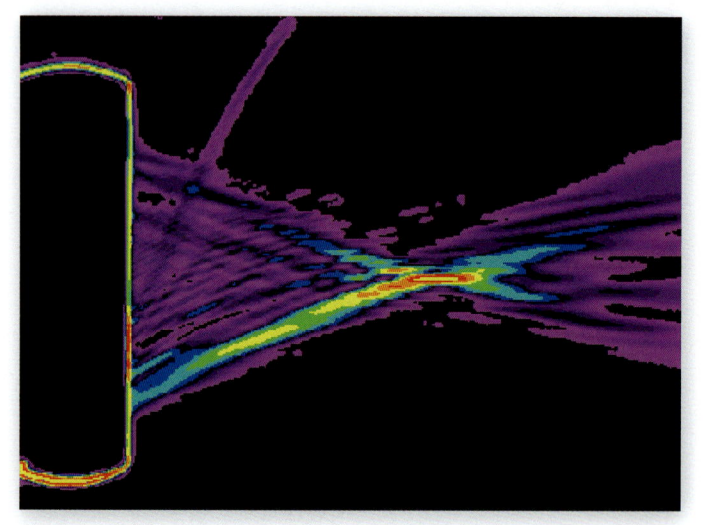

Fig. 13 **Schlieren image of a focused beam from a transducer with a bad element** *(Courtesy of Onda Corporation)*

As already mentioned, the temporal distribution affects the risk of thermal bioeffects. Schlieren images provide an incredible ability to visualize the temporal aspects of sound propagation. The following image represents a 5-cycle pulsed wave signal a short while after being generated by the transducer. The black regions represent areas not currently being insonified by the transmitted pulse. You can imagine that if a second pulse were transmitted some time later, you would see two pulses, one very close to the transducer and one farther away as determined by the time between transmitting events (PRP). The result would then be a representation of the duty factor, representing the percentage of time energy is performing work on the tissue (PD/PRP).

Fig. 14 **Screen capture of actual pulsed wave beam traveling over time using Schlieren imaging**

Notice the bright regions in *Figure 14* which correspond to areas of compression. The dark regions between the compressions correspond to regions of rarefaction. In this case, there are five cycles in the pulse of approximately equal amplitude and a sixth cycle that is either weaker or ring down of the crystal.

Figure 15 represents a Schlieren image of a continuous wave (CW) signal. On the left, the image represents a time average signal showing that the energy from the CW transmit exists at all depths simultaneously. On the right, the image represents the same beam captured by a very short light burst synchronized with the pulse so as to capture the series of compressions and rarefactions associated with the longitudinal sound wave. Notice that, unlike *Figure 14*, there is no "black region" representing the absence of signal along the beam path, consistent with the concept of a duty factor of 100%.

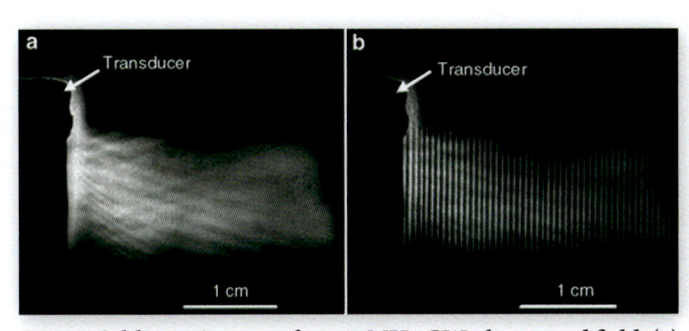

Fig. 15 **Schlieren images of a 1.62 MHz CW ultrasound field; (a) time-averaged image acquired using a continuous light source; (b) the same field visualized using short light pulses synchronized with the ultrasound phase**[4] *(Courtesy of Onda Corporation)*

View ONLINE Animation and Image Library

10. Output Display Standards

In 1985, a joint committee formed by the AIUM, the FDA, and NEMA (National Electrical Manufacturers Association) developed an alternative to the existing paradigm for FDA approval of ultrasound devices. The previous standard was based on the I_{SPTA} maximums as follows:

Trans-ophthalmic	17 mW/cm²
Fetal imaging	94 mW/cm²
Small parts	94 mW/cm²
Pediatric echo	94 mW/cm²
Adult echo	430 mW/cm²
Vascular	720 mW/cm²

Table 2 I_{SPTA} **limits prior to 1985**

The new output standard removed the individual limits, opting for one overriding limit that the maximum I_{SPTA} allowed never exceed 720 mW/cm². As part of the new paradigm, ultrasound equipment was required to post one of two indices, the mechanical index (MI) or the thermal index (TI). The user is then expected to make a decision based on the posted index as to whether presumed increased risk was outweighed by the expected improvement in diagnostic quality. Equipment manufacturers were now given an option of following the old track for FDA approval or the new track. All systems today follow the new paradigm.

> **KEY CONCEPT**
>
> After 1985, a new paradigm was created which removed individual limits, leaving one overriding limit in conjunction with displaying "output standards." The output standards include a mechanical index (MI) and a thermal index (TI).

11. Mechanical Index (MI)

Before the mechanical index, the restriction on acoustic output power levels most closely associated with the risk of cavitation was the spatial peak pulse average. The pulse average intensity measurement refers only to the distribution of the power temporally and spatially, but does not take into account the fact that the risk of cavitation also has a frequency relationship. The MI is now considered the index which best correlates with the likelihood of cavitation. A higher MI implies a greater likelihood of cavitation, but does not actually specify when cavitation occurs.

The mechanical index is defined as the peak rarefactional pressure divided by the square root of the operating frequency, or:

$$MI = \frac{\text{peak rarefactional pressure}}{\sqrt{\text{operating frequency}}}.$$

The mechanical index mathematically expresses the fact that the risk of inertial cavitation has been found to increase proportionally with increasing rarefactional pressure and decrease by a square root relationship with increasing frequency.

As a result of the new standard, ultrasound systems present mechanical indices instead of following the old acoustic output standards. The standard only specifies that one index be displayed per application, although there are times when displaying both makes more sense. The MI is always present when performing sequential 2D imaging, since this modality generally presents the greatest potential for mechanical bioeffects. Since thermal effects are highly improbable, there is less of a need to post a thermal index as well. As we will see, Doppler modes are likely to present a thermal index and less likely to display an MI.

> **KEY CONCEPT**
>
> The MI is dimensionless. The MI is related to the peak rarefactional pressure. A higher MI indicates a potentially higher risk of cavitation occurring, but does not specify a specific limit at which cavitation will occur.

12. Thermal Indices

12.1 Absorption Rates of Various Mediums
Absorption in the body tends to increase with an increase in collagen content. Therefore, the highest rate of absorption is expected in tissue types such as bone, cartilage, tendons, scar tissue, and fascia. At the opposite end of the absorption spectrum are fluids. The absorption rate in water is 0.0022 dB per cm at 1 MHz of operation. In comparison, the absorption rate in bone varies from around 14 dB per cm to 25 dB per cm at 1 MHz. This is a ratio of approximately 10,000 to 1. Since absorption rates differ so dramatically, clearly the risk of thermal bioeffects will vary significantly with the tissue types within the ultrasound path. A table including absorption rates for some biological tissues is given in Chapter 3: Advanced Topics, Section 13.

12.2 Thermal Indices Defined
The thermal index actually represents the collective title for three different indices:
- Thermal Index in Soft Tissue (TIS)
- Thermal Index in Bone (TIB)
- Thermal Index in Cranial Bone (TIC)

The thermal index is a predictive value which estimates the "maximum" temperature rise expected for the current imaging situation. Therefore, a TI of 1 indicates that the maximum temperature rise expected over time would be 1 degree Celsius. A TI of 1 does not imply a temperature increase of 1 degree, but rather what the model predicts as the "worst case." How accurately the worst-case model predicts the actual temperature rise depends on many parameters including:
- How and where the beam is focused
- What tissues and absorption rates occur in the path
- Blood flow and fluids in the region which can dissipate heat
- How well the attenuation rates match the values assumed in the model

12.3 The Three Thermal Indices
The reason that three different thermal indices exist is the fact that absorption rates vary significantly depending on the medium. The TIS predicts the temperature rise presuming the predominant presence of relatively homogeneous soft tissue. The TIC indicates the likely worst-case temperature rise for a bone at the surface such as cranial bone when performing transcranial imaging. The TIB is the predictive value for bone presuming that the surface of the bone is near the focus of the beam, as occurs commonly with fetal imaging.

12.4 Underestimation of Worst Case
In general, it is presumed that a thermal index gives the maximum possible temperature rise, but this is not always the case. As with all algorithmic-based models, the conclusions are only accurate when the situation modeled is covered by parameters within the model. In other words, clinical situations can occur which could potentially produce higher temperature increases than predicted by the models. One such example would be the TIS in the presence of a large cystic structure. Since absorption within fluids is very low, less attenuation occurs in the beam path than expected. As a result, there is an "enhancement" effect where more power reaches greater depths. Accordingly, a higher temperature rise than predicted might occur deeper than the cystic structure. There are other possible parameters which potentially could affect the accuracy such as dehydration and severe fever. Although these possibilities exist, for the most part, the TI is a pretty fair estimate of the "worst-case" temperature rise.

> **KEY CONCEPT**
>
> The thermal index indicates the calculated, worst-case temperature rise (in Celsius) based on predictive models. Since different tissues have different absorption rates, different models are required for different imaging scenarios, leading to three different thermal indices: TIS = thermal index soft tissue, TIB = thermal index bone, and TIC = thermal index cranial bone. A TIS of 2 implies that the expected worse case temperature rise of the current imaging scenario would be 2 degrees Celsius.

13. AIUM Statements Regarding Ultrasound and Bioeffects

13.1 Acknowledging the AIUM
Special thanks to the American Institute of Ultrasound in Medicine (AIUM) for granting permission to include excerpts from their official guidelines published online at: https://www.aium.org/resources/statements.aspx. (Note that additional AIUM statements can be found on this site.)

In addition, the AIUM has produced many subsequent documents to further promulgate the dissemination of information pertaining to bioeffects. Some of these documents are referenced at the end of the chapter as well, with a brief description.

13.2 How Best to Use the Following Pages
The most critical information in the following pages has been set in bold type, but all of the information is valuable, especially to provide contextual understanding. To facilitate recognition of direct quoting, all excerpts from the AIUM guidelines are presented in shaded areas.

It is strongly suggested that when you read the excerpted official statements, you relate the information to the fundamental concepts discussed about the mechanisms for bioeffects. It should make sense that some of the statements are related to the risk of mechanical damage, some statements are related to the risk of thermal bioeffects, some statements are related to how to minimize the risks, and some statements describe how this information was developed and tested. If you attempt to categorize each statement and distill the information to its core purpose for being included, learning and comprehending this complex but important topic should become significantly easier.

13.3 Conclusions Regarding the Safety of Ultrasound
Although up to this point we have focused on the risks associated with bioeffects, it must be stressed that conservative use has proven ultrasound to be a very safe modality. To date there have been no confirmed bioeffects resulting from diagnostic ultrasound at accepted power levels. However, you must realize that the statement "no confirmed bioeffects" does not necessarily mean that there have been no bioeffects. The potential for bioeffects assuredly exists, and the possibility that some bioeffects have occurred and do still occur is very real. This possibility of bioeffects mandates that caution be exercised so as to minimize risk while maximizing clinical utility (prudent use).

The use of ultrasound for non-medical purposes is discouraged. Remember that although ultrasound has proven to be a safe modality there is still a potential risk. The AIUM statement regarding prudent use defines responsible use for fetal imaging by specifying that non-medical scans, including obtaining images of a fetus to determine fetal gender without a specific medical need, is inappropriate.

> American Institute of Ultrasound in Medicine Official Statement
> ***Prudent Clinical Use and Safety of Diagnostic Ultrasound***
> *Approved: 03/19/2007; Reapproved: 04/01/2012, 05/20/2019*
>
> *Diagnostic ultrasound has been in use since the late 1950s. Given its known benefits and recognized efficacy for medical diagnosis, including use during human pregnancy, the American Institute of Ultrasound in Medicine herein addresses the clinical safety of such use:* **No independently confirmed adverse effects caused by exposure from present diagnostic ultrasound instruments have been reported in human patients in the absence of contrast agents.** *Biological effects (such as localized pulmonary bleeding) have been reported in experimental mammalian systems at diagnostically relevant exposures, but the clinical relevance of such effects is either not significant or is not yet known. Increased outputs and time of exposure can increase the likelihood of bioeffects.* **Ultrasound should be used only by qualified health professionals to provide medical benefit to the patient.** *Ultrasound exposures during examinations should be as low as reasonably achievable (ALARA).*[1,2]

13.4 ALARA Principle
The ALARA Principle is a simple acronym which stands for "as low as reasonably achievable." In essence, the ALARA principle is a guideline to define "prudent" use. The word "low" refers to exposure to acoustic energy. As we have learned, there are a two principal components to exposure: the intensity (related to the output power) and the scan duration (time). ALARA mandates that the lowest possible power be used with the shortest scan time while still maintaining a clinical study. The term "achievable" is a balancing word which expresses the recognition of a potential trade-off between the quality of a scan and exposure parameters. In

other words, using higher transmit powers and increasing scanning time may be perfectly appropriate when the trade-off is improved diagnostic information. The goal of diagnostic testing is to "achieve" accurate clinical results. Therefore, the lowest exposure that yields good clinical results is the appropriate condition. In a paraphrased form of the safety statement, remember that although the possibility of biological effects exists, the benefits to the patient of diagnostic ultrasound, to date, have outweighed those risks.

The ramifications of the ALARA principle to you the sonographer include:

- identifying the mechanisms which cause bioeffects
- defining the parameters which increase the risk of bioeffects
- recognizing the system controls and functions that directly control these parameters
- understanding the control of post-processing controls that can secondarily affect where the power-related controls are set
- defining the differences in modalities (applications)
- performing clinical studies only when there are potential benefits which outweigh the risks

---

American Institute of Ultrasound in Medicine Official Statement
As Low As Reasonable Achievable (ALARA Principle)
Approved: 03/16/2008; Reapproved: 04/02/2014, 05/19/2020

The potential benefits and risks of each examination should be considered. The as low as reasonably achievable (ALARA) principle should be observed when adjusting controls that affect the acoustic output and by considering both the transducer dwell time and overall scanning time. Practicing ALARA requires that users do all of the following:

1. **Apply correct examination presets if built into the diagnostic ultrasound device.** *The review of manufacturer default presets for appropriateness is encouraged.*
2. **Adjust the power to the lowest available setting that provides diagnostic-quality images.** *If appropriate, reduce power at the end of each examination so the next user will start with the lowest acoustic output setting.*
3. **Monitor the mechanical index (MI) and thermal index (TI).** *Know the recommended upper limit of the MI, TI, and related duration limitations for the type of examination being performed.* [1,2]
4. **Move/lift the transducer when stationary imaging is not necessary to reduce the dwell time on a particular anatomic structure. When possible, avoid fields of view that include sensitive tissues such as the eye, gas-filled tissues (lung and intestines), and fetal calcified structures (skull and spine).**
5. **Minimize the overall scanning time** *to that needed to obtain the required diagnostic information.*

13.5 Safety Concerns Regarding the Use of Ultrasound in Training and Research

In academic environments, the question frequently arises as to what constitutes prudent use when using ultrasound in educational and research settings. In these cases, the person being scanned generally does not present with a medical need for imaging. For these cases in which the intended purpose may result in an indirect instead of a direct medical benefit, the AIUM has made a specific recommendation as included in the AIUM's official statement regarding Live Scanning for Educational Purposes.

American Institute of Ultrasound in Medicine Official Statement
Live Scanning for Educational Purposes
Approved: 03/29/2017

Live scanning of human subjects should be permitted only under controlled conditions and only when there is a medical or public health benefit. *The education of health care specialists in what are the latest ultrasound technologies, their capabilities, and how best used in these individuals' own hands is a critical exercise for evaluation and for skill development. At the present time, this benefit is very difficult to obtain in any other way, and ultimately benefits future patients.*

The specifics of how this scanning is to be performed is further elucidated by two additional statements, one regarding nonpregnant subjects (a portion of which is included below) and one for pregnant subjects, included in the section on fetal safety.

American Institute of Ultrasound in Medicine Official Statement
[Excerpted from] *Safety in Diagnostic Ultrasound Educational Activities Using Nonpregnant Participants*
Approved: 05/19/2020

Statement. *Ultrasound examinations conducted for the purpose of education and training require adherence to prudent and conservative use guidelines. Specifically, the guidelines below should be followed:*

1. **Demonstration scans on live, nonpregnant participants should be performed in a manner consistent with the ALARA principle**, *including limiting the thermal index (TI; (≤ 0.7 for neonatal transcranial and neonatal spinal examinations, ≤ 1.0 for ophthalmic examinations, or ≤ 1.5 for all other examinations)*[3,6] *and mechanical index (MI; ≤ 0.23 for ophthalmic examinations, <0.4 specifically for contrast-aided and lung examinations, ≤ 1.4 for intestine examinations, and ≤ 1.9 for other examinations such as liver ultrasound).*[4,6-8]
2. **If higher exposure conditions or contrast agents are needed for the training, then either (a) a tissue-mimicking phantom should be used, or (b) the live participant should only be scanned once per day similar to the exposures**

experienced during clinical practice. The use of contrast agents should be in accordance with the product label and recommendations of relevant professional organizations, and dosage should be the minimum required to produce diagnostic-quality images.[9-12] In some cases, this might be considerably less than the dose specified in the product label.

3. *All participants should provide appropriate informed consent for the ultrasound study after a discussion of the risks and benefits, including safety and potential biological effects. If an injectable contrast agent is used, the discussion and consent should also include details about vascular access, possible adverse reactions such as cardiopulmonary reactions consistent with labeling, and possible bioeffects of contrast imaging.[6] Female participants should provide a statement to the best of their knowledge that they are not pregnant.*

4. *All equipment must be used in a manner consistent with its US Food and Drug Administration (FDA)-cleared indications for use. In particular, only equipment that has been FDA-cleared for ophthalmic indications should be used to scan the eye during training due to the sensitivity of the eye to heating, as reflected by lower FDA-recommended maximum output levels (MI ≤0.23 and TI ≤1.0).[4]*

13.6 Mammalian In Vivo Biological Effects

The term "in vivo" literally means "in the living." As mentioned, direct testing to threshold levels on living human patients is ethically not an option. As a result, acquiring data which relates directly to the application of ultrasound in common practice is difficult. The use of non-human "in vivo" testing is a means by which to provide recommendations for appropriate use models of ultrasound. Of course, results from "in vivo" tests on non-human subjects may not translate precisely to risks in human tissue but nonetheless are useful for cause and effect limits by which to conservatively set limits (well below the threshold levels indicated by these studies).

American Institute of Ultrasound in Medicine Official Statement
Statement on Mammalian Biological Effects of Ultrasound In Vivo
Approved: 08/04/1976; Reapproved: 10/20/1992, 11/08/2008, 03/25/2015

Information from experiments using laboratory mammals has contributed significantly to our understanding of ultrasonically induced biological effects and the mechanisms that are most likely responsible. Adverse biological effects have been observed in some animal studies under conditions that may be achieved by using diagnostic scanners (see associated specific statements). The following statement summarizes observations relative to minimal diagnostic ultrasound parameters and indices.

In the low-megahertz frequency range, there have been no independently confirmed adverse biological effects in mammalian tissues exposed in vivo under experimental ultrasound conditions, as follows:

I. Thermal Mechanisms

1. *No effects have been observed for an unfocused beam having free-field spatial-peak temporal-average (SPTA) intensities* below 100 mW/cm², a focused** beam having intensities below 1 W/cm², or temperature increases of less than 1.5 °C.*

2. *For fetal exposures, no effects have been reported for a temperature increase above the normal physiologic temperature, ΔT, when $\Delta T < 4.5 - (\log_{10} t)/0.6$, where t is exposure time ranging from 1 to 250 minutes, including off time for pulsed exposure.*

3. *For postnatal exposures producing temperature increases of 6 °C or less, no effects have been reported when $\Delta T < 6 - (\log_{10} t)/0.6$, including off time for pulsed exposure. For example, for temperature increases of 6.0 °C and 2.0 °C, the corresponding limits for the exposure durations t are 1 and 250 minutes.*

4. *For postnatal exposures producing temperature increases of 6 °C or higher, no effects have been reported when $\Delta T < 6 - (\log_{10} t)/0.3$, including off time for pulsed exposure. For example, for a temperature increase of 9.6 °C, the corresponding limit for the exposure duration is 5 seconds (= 0.083 minutes) (see AIUM "Statement on Mammalian Biological Effects of Heat").*

II. Nonthermal Mechanisms

1. *For diagnostic ultrasound exposure by actual medical devices or laboratory equipment, no adverse effects have been observed in tissues containing naturally occurring gas bodies for in situ peak rarefactional pressures below approximately 0.4 MPa (estimated mechanical index [MI] values less than ≈0.4) (see AIUM "Statement Regarding Mammalian Biological Effects in Tissues With Naturally Occurring Gas Bodies").*

2. *For contrast-enhanced diagnostic ultrasound, no adverse effects in mammalian tissue in vivo have been reported and independently confirmed for an MI below about 0.4 (see AIUM "Statement on Mammalian Biological Effects in Tissues With Gas Body Contrast Agents").*

3. *In tissues that do not contain well-defined gas bodies, no adverse nonthermal bioeffects have been observed for MI values below 1.9: the upper limit for diagnostic ultrasound (see AIUM "Statement on Mammalian Biological Effects in Tissues Without Gas Bodies").*

*   *Free-field SPTA intensity for continuous wave and pulsed exposures.*
** *Quarter-power (−6 dB) beam width smaller than 4 wavelengths or 4 mm, whichever is less at the exposure frequency.*

13.7 The Mechanical Index and Gas Bodies

The adoption of the MI as an acceptable standard for users to base risk/benefit determination is based on the many advantages of the MI relative to the shortcomings of the I_{SPPA}. As stated in AIUM's *Statement on Mammalian Biological Effects in Tissues Without Gas Bodies* (not included here) – no bioeffects have been observed in mammalian tissue with MI's lower than 1.9 in tissues without gas bodies. For tissues with naturally occurring gas bodies, the in vivo studies indicate a lower threshold as indicated by the following AIUM statement.

American Institute of Ultrasound in Medicine Official Statement
**Statement on Mammalian Biological Effects
in Tissues with Naturally Occurring Gas Bodies**
*Approved: 10/07/1987; Reapproved: 03/18/1993,
11/08/2008, 03/25/2015*

Biologically significant adverse nonthermal effects have been identified in tissues containing stable bodies of gas for diagnostically relevant exposure conditions. Gas bodies occur naturally in postnatal lungs and in the folds of the intestinal mucosa. This statement concerns naturally occurring gas bodies encountered in pulmonary and abdominal ultrasound, whereas a separate statement deals with the use of gas body contrast agents.

1. **The outputs of some currently available diagnostic ultrasound devices can generate levels that produce capillary hemorrhage in the lungs[1] and intestines[2] of laboratory animals.**
2. **Thresholds for adverse nonthermal effects associated with naturally occurring gas bodies depend on tissue characteristics and the physiologic status, including anesthesia,[3]** *and on physical ultrasound parameters, including attenuation by intervening tissue, exposure duration, ultrasonic output, frequency, pulse duration, and pulse repetition frequency.*[2]
3. **A mechanical index (MI)* has been formulated to assist users in evaluating the likelihood of mechanical (nonthermal) adverse biological effects for diagnostically relevant exposures**, *and its value is displayed on screen in accordance with output display specifications.*
4. **The minimum threshold value of the experimental MI** *(the in situ value of the peak rarefactional pressure amplitude divided by the square root of the frequency)* **for pulmonary capillary hemorrhage in laboratory mammals is approximately 0.4. The corresponding threshold for the intestine is MI = 1.4.**
5. *The implications of these observations for human exposure during thoracic or abdominal ultrasound examinations are yet to be determined.*

* *The MI is equal to the derated peak rarefactional pressure (in megapascals) at the point of the maximum derated pulse intensity integral divided by the square root of the ultrasonic center frequency (in megahertz).*[4]

The AIUM also produced a statement regarding the Mechanical Index for scanning with the use of contrast agents. The MI has been beneficial to the use of contrast agents as a means of standardizing performance across manufacturers' platforms as well as allowing for more predictable and controllable use.

American Institute of Ultrasound in Medicine Official Statement
[Excerpted from] **Statement on Mammalian Biological Effects of Diagnostic Ultrasound with Gas Body Contrast Agents**
Approved: 03/13/2002; Reapproved: 11/08/2008, 03/25/2015

Induction of premature ventricular contractions, microvascular leakage with petechiae, glomerular capillary hemorrhage, local cell killing, and other effects in mammalian tissue in vivo have been reported and independently confirmed for diagnostic ultrasound exposure with a mechanical index (MI) above about 0.4 and a gas body contrast agent present in the circulation.

Although the medical significance of such microscale bioeffects is uncertain, minimizing the potential for such effects represents prudent use of diagnostic ultrasound. **In general, for imaging with contrast agents at an MI above 0.4, practitioners should use the minimal agent dose**, *MI, and examination time consistent with efficacious acquisition of diagnostic information.* **In addition, the echocardiogram should be monitored during high-MI contrast cardiac-gated perfusion echocardiography, particularly in patients with a history of myocardial infarction or unstable cardiovascular disease.** *Furthermore, physicians and sonographers should follow all guidance provided in the package inserts of these drugs, including precautions, warnings, and contraindications.*

13.8 Conclusion Regarding Heat and the Thermal Indices (TIS, TIB, TIC)

The absorption rates for tissue types vary significantly. As presented earlier in this chapter, tendons and bones absorb acoustic energy at a much greater rate than soft tissue, which absorbs at a much greater rate than fluids. A spatial average intensity is a measure of how acoustic energy is distributed over time. A limitation to using a spatial average metric is that it does not reflect the fact that heat generation is a function not only of the beam distribution, but also of the absorption coefficient. The thermal indices, although not perfect, reflect the impact of both of these parameters. To make an informed decision so as to perform prudent ultrasound, the thermal indices must be heeded.

American Institute of Ultrasound in Medicine Official Statement
Statement on Mammalian Biological Effects of Heat
Approved: 10/07/1987; Reapproved: 03/26/1997, 04/06/2009, 03/25/2015, 10/30/2016

1. An excessive temperature increase can result in toxic effects in mammalian systems. **The biological effects observed depend on many factors, such as the exposure duration, the type of tissue exposed, its cellular proliferation rate, and its potential for regeneration.** Age and stage of development are important factors when considering fetal and neonatal safety. Temperature increases of several degrees Celsius above the normal core range can occur naturally. **The probability of an adverse biological effect increases with both the duration and the magnitude of the temperature rise.**

2. **In general, adult tissues are more tolerant of temperature increases than fetal and neonatal tissues.** Therefore, higher temperatures and/or longer exposure durations would be required for thermal damage. The considerable data available on the thermal sensitivity of adult tissues support the following inferences[1]:

   a. For exposure durations up to 50 hours, there have been no significant adverse biological effects observed due to temperature increases less than or equal to 1.5°C above normal.[2]

   b. For temperature increases between 1.5°C and 6°C above normal, there have been no significant adverse biological effects observed due to temperature increases less than or equal to 6 – [log10(t/60)]/0.6 where t is the exposure duration in seconds. For example, for temperature increases of 4°C and 6°C, the corresponding limits for the exposure durations t are 16 minutes and 1 minute, respectively.

   c. For temperature increases greater than 6°C above normal, there have been no significant adverse biological effects observed due to temperature increases less than or equal to 6 – [log10(t/60)]/0.3 where t is the exposure duration in seconds. For example, for temperature increases of 9.6°C and 6.0°C, the corresponding limits for the exposure durations t are 5 and 60 seconds, respectively.

   d. For exposure durations less than 5 seconds, there have been no significant, adverse biological effects observed due to temperature increases less than or equal to 9 – [log10(t/60)]/0.3 where t is the exposure duration in seconds. For example, for temperature increases of 18.3°C, 14.9°C, and 12.6°C, the corresponding limits for the exposure durations t are 0.1, 1, and 5 seconds, respectively.

3. Acoustic-output from diagnostic ultrasound devices is sufficient to cause temperature elevations in fetal tissue. Although fewer data are available for fetal tissues, the following conclusions are justified[1,3]:

   e. In general, temperature elevations become progressively greater from B-mode to color Doppler to spectral Doppler applications.

   f. For identical exposure conditions, the potential for thermal bioeffects increases with the dwell time during examination.

   g. **For identical exposure conditions, the temperature rise near bone is significantly greater than in soft tissues, and it increases with ossification development throughout gestation.** For this reason, conditions in which an acoustic beam impinges on ossifying fetal bone deserve special attention due to its close proximity to other developing tissues.

   h. The current US Food and Drug Administration regulatory limit for the derated spatial-peak temporal-average intensity (ISPTA.3) is 720 mW/cm². For this exposure, the theoretical estimate of the maximum temperature increase in the conceptus may exceed 1.5°C.

   i. **Although an adverse fetal outcome is possible at any time during gestation, most severe and detectable effects of thermal exposure in animals have been observed during the period of organogenesis. For this reason, exposures during the first trimester should be restricted to the lowest outputs consistent with obtaining the necessary diagnostic information.**

   j. **Ultrasound exposures that elevate fetal temperature by 4°C above normal for 5 minutes or more have the potential to induce severe developmental defects.** Thermally induced congenital anomalies have been observed in a large variety of animal species. In current clinical practice, using commercially available equipment, **it is unlikely that such thermal exposure would occur at a specific fetal anatomic site provided that the thermal index (TI) is at or below 2.5 and the dwell time on that site does not exceed 4 minutes.**

   k. Transducer self-heating is a significant component of the temperature rise of tissues close to the transducer. This may be of significance in transvaginal scanning, but no data for the fetal temperature rise are available.

4. The temperature increase during exposure of tissues to diagnostic ultrasound fields is dependent on: (1) output characteristics of the acoustic source, such as frequency, source dimensions, scan rate, output power, pulse repetition frequency, pulse duration, transducer self-heating, exposure time, and wave shape; and (2) tissue properties, such as attenuation, absorption, speed of sound, acoustic impedance, perfusion, thermal conductivity, thermal diffusivity, anatomic structure, and the non linearity parameter.

5. Calculations of the maximum temperature increase resulting from ultrasound exposure in vivo are not exact because of the uncertainties and approximations associated with the thermal, acoustic, and structural characteristics of the tissues involved. **However, experimental evidence shows that calculations are generally capable of predicting measured values within a factor of 2.** Thus, such calculations are used to obtain safety guidelines for clinical exposures in which direct temperature measurements are not feasible. **These guidelines, called ther-**

mal indices,* provide a real-time display of the relative probability that a diagnostic system could induce thermal injury in the exposed subject. Under most clinically relevant conditions, the soft tissue thermal index (TIS) and the bone thermal index (TIB) either overestimate or closely approximate the best available estimate of the maximum temperature increase ($\Delta Tmax$). For example, if TIS = 2, then $\Delta Tmax = 2\,°C$; actual temperature increases are also dependent on dwell time.

However, in some applications, such as fetal examinations in which the ultrasound beam passes through a layer of relatively unattenuating liquid, such as urine or amniotic fluid, the TI can underestimate $\Delta Tmax$ by up to a factor of 2.[4,5]

* *The thermal indices are the non-dimensional ratios of attenuated acoustic power at a specific point to the attenuated acoustic power required to raise the temperature at that point in a specific tissue model by 1\,°C.[6]*

13.9 Fetal Safety

For numerous reasons, many of the greatest concerns with respect to thermal bioeffects are related to the use of ultrasound for fetal scanning. One of the reasons for concern is simply the sheer number of studies performed. It is now estimated that more than 10 million fetal studies are performed each year in the US alone. The concern is based on the fact that fetal scans generally involve scanning through bones, which have much higher absorption rates than other tissue types. This issue is exacerbated by the fact that the fluid surrounding the fetus is primarily water and hence, not very absorptive. As a result, the potential for a significant temperature rise exists. Furthermore, there is certainly reason to be concerned with cellular damage in the presence of rapid fetal growth and specialization. For adults, the damage to a "few cells" is less problematic than damage to a similar number of cells for a fetus.

As relates to fetal safety, the AIUM guidelines primarily reflect the desire to decrease the risk of thermal bioeffects. As such, guidelines are offered for how fetal heart rate evaluation should be performed, limiting the use of Doppler, and stating that "keepsake" image generation occur only as the result of a medically indicated ultrasound exam or from imaging performed on volunteers for ultrasound training purposes.

Figure 16, created from information in an AIUM statement, represents the recommended maximum scans times at varying thermal indices for adult transcranial, general abdominal, vascular, neonatal (except head and spine), and other ultrasound scanning with the exception of fetal and scanning through the eye. You will notice that the recommended max times are less than the values listed for which no bioeffects have been confirmed.

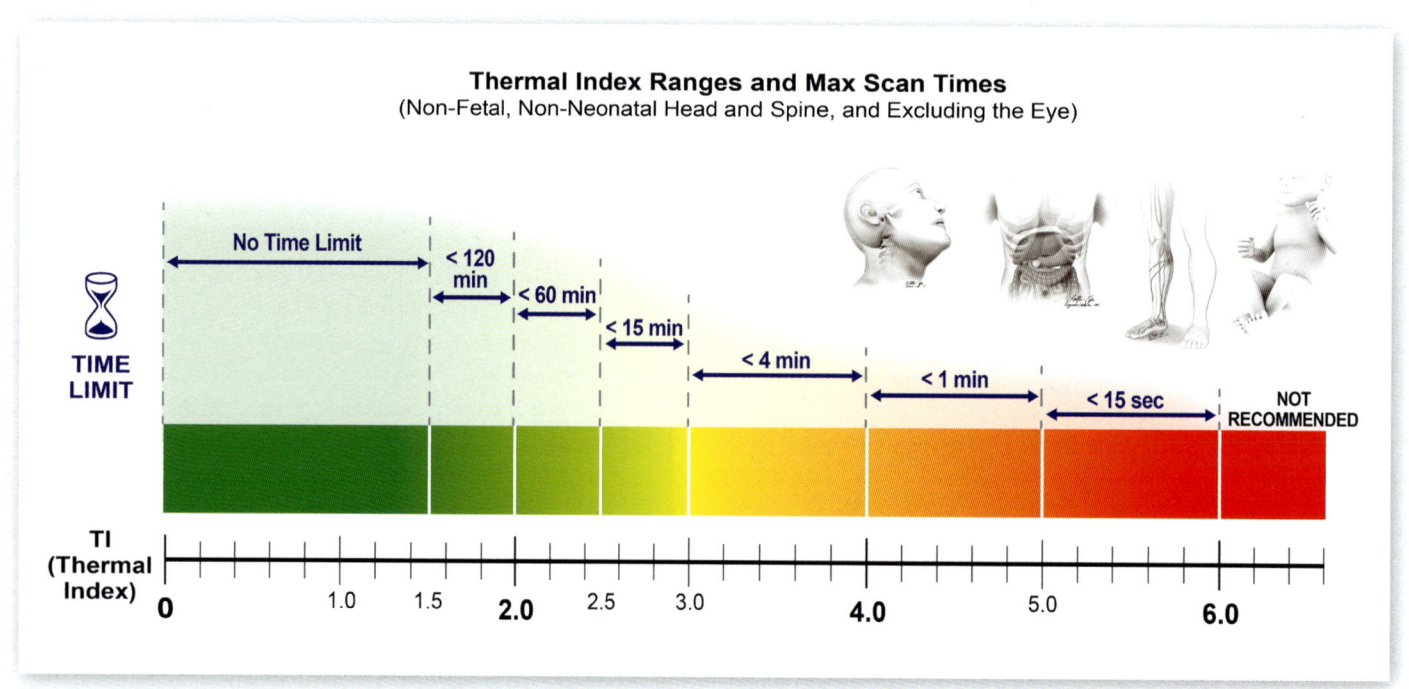

Fig. 16 Recommended maximum scanning time and TI ranges for adult transcranial, general abdominal, peripheral vascular, neonatal (except head and spine), and other scanning examinations (excluding the eye) *(Based on AIUM Official Statement regarding Maximum Scan Times for Displayed Thermal Index Values)*

American Institute of Ultrasound in Medicine Official Statement
[Excerpted from] **Prudent Use and Safety of Diagnostic Ultrasound in Pregnancy**
Approved: 05/19/2020

Fetal Heart Rate Evaluation
Although Doppler instruments without imaging capability are permissible to be used, spectral Doppler **imaging should not be used to document the fetal heart rate unless clinically indicated.** When attempting to document the fetal cardiac activity or obtain the heart rate with a diagnostic ultrasound system, the AIUM recommends using either an M-mode or a B-mode scan, keeping the TI as low as possible, preferably less than or equal to 0.7, and not prolonging the procedure beyond what is necessary to obtain the measurement.[1] Use the TI for soft tissues for the TI if pregnancy is less than 10 weeks; use the TI for bone if 10 or more weeks.

If an M-mode scan cannot be obtained at an embryonic size (crown-rump length) of 2 mm to 1 cm (approximately 5+ to 7 weeks), the heartbeat may be visualized by B-mode imaging and retained for documentation. Pulsed Doppler (spectral, power, and color flow imaging) ultrasound should not be used routinely due to increased acoustic output.

Doppler Ultrasound During 11- to 14-Week Scans (or Earlier in Pregnancy)
The use of Doppler ultrasound during the first trimester is currently being promoted as an aid for screening and diagnosis of some congenital abnormalities. The procedure requires considerable skill and subjects the fetus to extended periods of relatively high ultrasound exposure levels. Due to the increased acoustic output of spectral Doppler ultrasound, its use in the first trimester should be viewed with caution. **Spectral Doppler imaging should only be used when there is a clear benefit/risk advantage and both the TI and examination duration are kept low. Protocols that typically involve TI values lower than 1.0 reflect minimal risk.** Comparable to the World Federation for Ultrasound in Medicine and Biology/International Society of Ultrasound in Obstetrics and Gynecology statement, we recommend that[2]:

1. **All scans should begin at a displayed TI of 0.7 because the total duration of an ultrasound examination during pregnancy cannot be known in advance.** Higher outputs should be used only if needed to obtain adequate images and in accordance with the as low as reasonably achievable (ALARA) principle.[3]
2. **Pulsed Doppler (spectral, power, and color flow imaging) ultrasound should not be used routinely.**
3. **Spectral Doppler ultrasound may be used for specific clinical indications**, such as to refine risks for trisomies, and color Doppler imaging may be useful in an early anatomic evaluation of the fetus or placenta.
4. When performing a Doppler ultrasound examination, the displayed TI should be less than or equal to 0.7, provided adequate images can be obtained, and the exposure time should be kept as short as possible, consistent with acquisition of needed clinical information.
5. When using Doppler ultrasound for research, teaching, and training purposes, the displayed TI should be less than or equal to 0.7, and the exposure time should be kept as short as possible, consistent with the purposes of the scan. Informed consent should be obtained.
6. In educational settings, a discussion of first-trimester pulsed or color Doppler ultrasound should be accompanied by information on safety and bioeffects (eg, TI, exposure times, and how to reduce the output power).
7. **When scanning maternal uterine arteries in the first trimester, there are unlikely to be any fetal safety implications as long as the embryo/fetus lies outside the Doppler ultrasound beam.**

Keepsake Fetal Imaging
The AIUM encourages patients to make sure that practitioners using ultrasound have received formal education and training in fetal imaging to ensure the best possible results.

The AIUM recognizes the growing pressures from patients for the performance of ultrasound examinations for bonding and reassurance purposes largely driven by advances in image quality of 3-dimensional (3D) sonography and by more widely available information about these advances. Although there is only some scientific evidence that 3D sonography has a positive impact on parental-fetal bonding, the AIUM recognizes that many parents may pursue scanning for this purpose. Such "keepsake imaging" currently occurs in a variety of settings, including the following:

1. Images or video clips given to parents during the course of a medically indicated ultrasound examination.
2. Images or clips given to volunteers who are scanned as part of diagnostic ultrasound education programs or demonstrations, provided that images are not used as an enticement to participate.
3. Freestanding commercial fetal imaging sites, usually without any physician review of acquired images and with no regulation of the training of the individuals obtaining the images; these sites are sometimes called "baby video studios," and these videos are sometimes called "entertainment videos."
4. As added-cost visits to a medical facility (office or hospital) outside the coverage of contractual arrangements between the provider and the patient's insurance carrier. The AIUM believes that added-cost arrangements other than those for providing patients images or copies of their medical records at cost may violate the principles of medical ethics of the American Medical Association (AMA)[4-6] and the American College of Obstetricians and Gynecologists (ACOG).[7]

The AIUM, therefore, recommends that only scenarios 1 and 2 above are consistent with the ethical principles of the AIUM and those of the AMA and ACOG.

The market for keepsake images is driven in part by past medical approaches that have used medicolegal concerns as a reason not to provide images to patients. Sharing images with patients is unlikely to have a detrimental medicolegal impact. The AIUM encourages sharing images with patients as appropriate when medically indicated obstetric ultrasound examinations are performed.

Thermal Index Ranges and Max Scan Times
(Fetal and Neonatal Transcranial / Spinal Scanning)

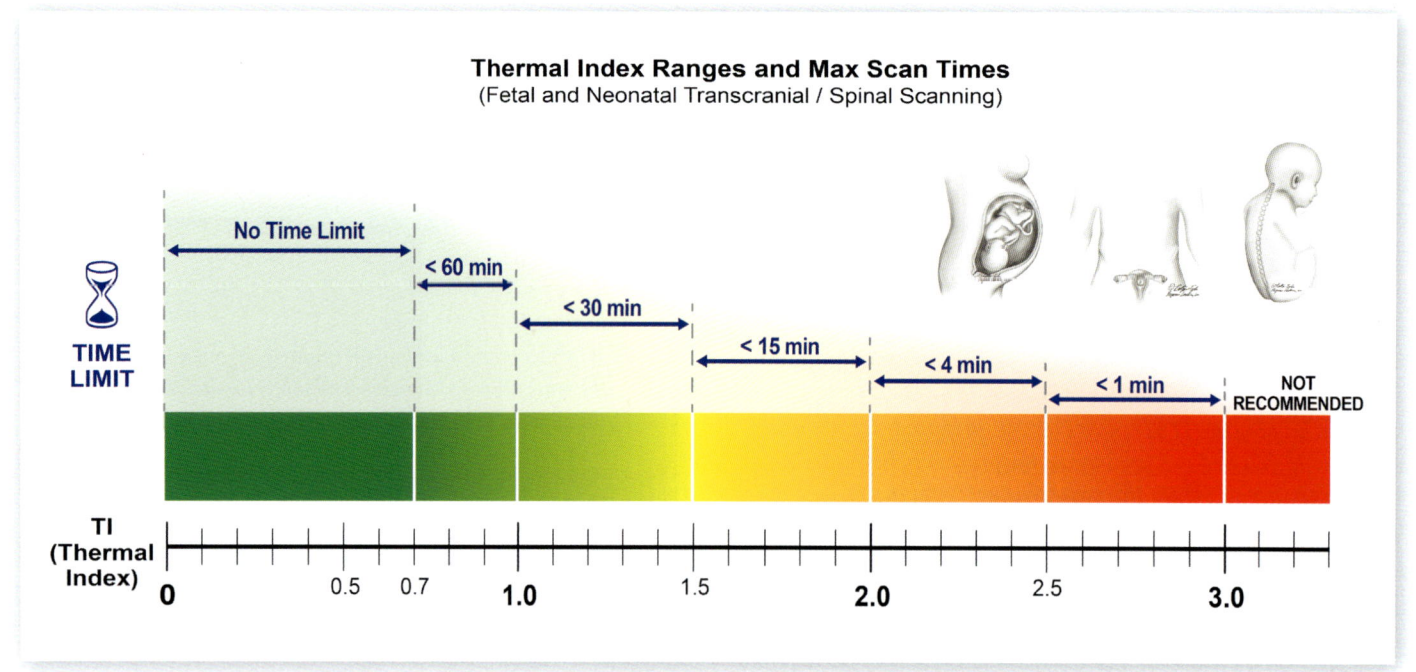

Fig. 17 **Recommended maximum scanning time and TI ranges for OB, GYN (when pregnancy is possible), neonatal transcranial, and neonatal spinal examinations; for OB, monitoring the TIS is recommended up to 10 weeks from last menstrual period (LMP) and TIB thereafter** *(Based on AIUM Official Statement regarding Maximum Scan Times for Displayed Thermal Index Values)*

Figure 17, created from information in an AIUM statement, illustrates the maximum scan times suggested per thermal index (TI) for OB, GYN (when possibly pregnant), and neonatal transcranial or spinal examinations.

> **CHECKPOINT: Exam Tip**
>
> The AIUM recommends a thermal index (TI) range under 6.0 for most adult scans and under 3.0 for most fetal scans. Time limits apply for adult scans with a TI > 1.5 and for fetal scans with a TI > 0.7.

13.10 "In Vitro" Biological Effects

The term "in vitro" literally means "in glass" and refers to testing that is performed or modeled outside of living tissues. Included in this classification of tests is algorithm-based computer modeling. These models may use parameters derived from in vivo testing as part of the algorithmic basis. With respect to studying, identifying, and classifying bioeffects, much testing is performed in vitro. The value of in vitro testing is not that the results necessarily predict bioeffects with great specificity or accuracy, but rather that the results serve as a means by which to limit testing on live tissue (in vivo studies) as well as to serve as a guideline to design more specific testing.

> American Institute of Ultrasound in Medicine Official Statement
> **Statement on In Vitro Biological Effects**
> *Approved: 03/09/2007; Reapproved: 04/01/2012, 04/07/2019*
>
> *It is often difficult to evaluate reports of ultrasonically induced in vitro biological effects with respect to their clinical significance. An in vitro effect can be regarded as a real biological effect. However, acoustic exposures[1,2] and predominant physical and biological interactions and mechanisms involved in an in vitro effect may not pertain to the in vivo situation.* **Results from in vitro experiments suggest new end points and serve as a basis for design of in vivo experiments. In vitro studies provide the capability to control experimental variables that may not be controllable in vivo and thus offer a means to explore and evaluate specific mechanisms and test hypotheses.** *Although they may have limited applicability to in vivo biological effects, such studies can disclose fundamental cellular or extracellular effects of ultrasound. Although it is valid for authors to place their results in context and to suggest further relevant investigations, extrapolations to clinical practice should be viewed with caution.*

13.11 AIUM Conclusions Regarding Epidemiology for Obstetric Ultrasound

Epidemiologic studies in ultrasound involve analyzing populations of which some individuals have been exposed to ultrasound and of which some have not been exposed so as to determine if there is a statistical prevalence of an adverse outcome. Epidemiologic studies can be extremely useful, but can also lead to incorrect conclusions.

For example, if 47 of 100 patients who come into a hospital to be tested for the flu test positive, the assumption that 47% of the population at large has the flu may be completely erroneous. Quite simply, people experiencing severe flu symptoms are more likely to go for flu testing than people who are not sick with the flu. The value of an epidemiologic study with respect to ultrasound is that a very large number of patients is included so that regional biases become statistically smaller or insignificant. The problem with an epidemiologic study is the only "adverse" outcomes recognized are those that are presumed as possible outcomes by the test. In other words, if ultrasound makes hair become thin and turn prematurely gray, but the study uses as metrics fetal weight, height, and hearing loss, the "adverse effect" of premature hair changes will not be identified.

> **American Institute of Ultrasound in Medicine Official Statement**
> **Conclusions Regarding Epidemiology for Obstetric Ultrasound**
> Approved: 03/29/1995; Reapproved: 06/22/2005, 03/27/201, 10/30/2016
>
> Based on the epidemiologic data available and on current knowledge of interactive mechanisms, there is insufficient justification to warrant conclusion of a causal relationship between diagnostic ultrasound and recognized adverse effects in humans. Some studies have reported effects of exposure to diagnostic ultrasound during pregnancy, such as low birth weight, delayed speech, dyslexia, and non-right-handedness. Other studies have not demonstrated such effects. The epidemiologic evidence is based primarily on exposure conditions prior to 1992, the year in which acoustic limits of ultrasound machines were substantially increased for fetal/obstetric applications.

KEY CONCEPT

Although ultrasound is considered to be very safe, there is still a small risk of bioeffects, thus requiring prudent use of ultrasound. Prudence implies that no needless scans should be performed, scan times should not be extended needlessly, and that the lowest power necessary be used to achieve good clinical results (ALARA principle).

14. Conceptual Questions

View ONLINE Conceptual Questions

LEVEL 3: Advanced Topics

15. Review Sheet for Converting Intensities

15.1 Conversion Between Spatial Peak and Spatial Average
Recall that:
$$\frac{SP}{SA} = BUF\,(\geq 1)$$

To convert between a Spatial Peak (SP) and a Spatial Average (SA), you must use the BUF.

(Think about the fact that the SP should be greater than the SA and the BUF ≥ 1.)

So:
The SP divided by the BUF yields the SA.
The SA multiplied by the BUF yields the SP.

15.2 Converting Between the Pulse Average and the Temporal Average
Recall that:
$$\frac{PD}{PRP} = Duty\ Factor\,(\leq 1)$$

(Think about the fact that the PRP should be greater than the PD and the DF ≤ 1.)

So:
The PD divided by the duty factor yields the PRP.
The PRP multiplied by the duty factor yields the PD.

15.3 Steps for Converting Between Intensities
The following is a step-by-step recipe for converting between one intensity measurement and another intensity measurement.

- Step 1: Break the four-letter cluster into two-letter clusters (SP, SA, TP, PA, TA).
- Step 2: Analyze which letter cluster or clusters is changed.
- Step 3: Determine what factor(s) are needed to perform conversion.
- Step 4: Determine if the value should become larger or smaller.*
- Step 5: Multiply or divide accordingly by conversion factor(s).
- Step 6: Sanity check (make sure that the answer makes sense).

*Note:
a) Multiplying a number by a number greater than one makes the number bigger.
b) Multiplying a number by a number less than one makes the number smaller.

Since division is the inverse operation of multiplication:
c) Dividing a number by a number greater than 1 makes the number smaller.
d) Dividing a number by a number less than 1 makes the number larger.

◊ *Example:*
Convert the I_{SPPA} into an I_{SAPA}, given that the I_{SPPA} = 200 mW/cm² and the BUF = 2.

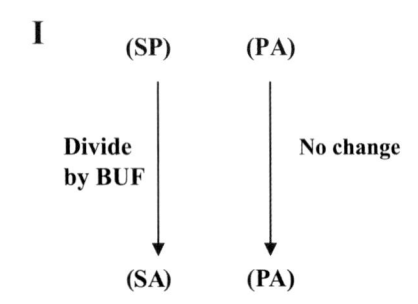

```
        I
   (SP)     (PA)
    |        |
  Divide   No change
  by BUF     |
    ↓        ↓
   (SA)     (PA)
```

So the $I_{SAPA} = \dfrac{I_{SPPA}}{BUF} = \dfrac{\left(200\dfrac{mW}{cm^2}\right)}{2} = 100\dfrac{mW}{cm^2}$.

◊ *Example:*
Convert the I_{SPPA} into an I_{SPTA}, given the I_{SPPA} = 700 mW/cm² and the DF = 10%.

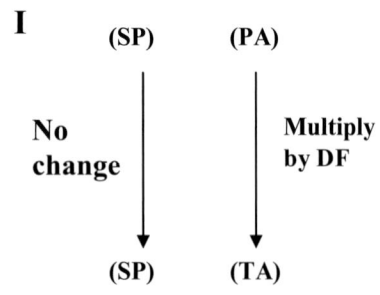

```
        I
   (SP)     (PA)
    |        |
   No      Multiply
  change   by DF
    ↓        ↓
   (SP)     (TA)
```

So the $I_{SPTA} = I_{SPPA} \cdot DF = \left(700\dfrac{mW}{cm^2}\right)\cdot 0.10 = 70\dfrac{mW}{cm^2}$.

◊ *Example:*
Convert the I_{SATA} into an I_{SPPA}, given the I_{SATA} = 100 mW/cm², the DF = 10%, and the BUF = 3.

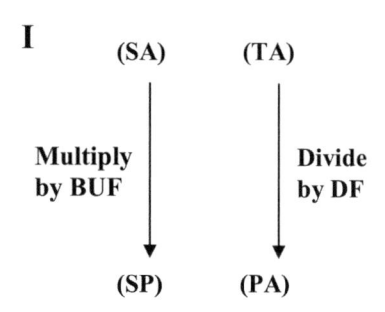

```
        I
   (SA)     (TA)
    |        |
 Multiply  Divide
 by BUF    by DF
    ↓        ↓
   (SP)     (PA)
```

So the $I_{SPPA} = \dfrac{I_{SATA} \cdot BUF}{DF} = \dfrac{\left(100\dfrac{mW}{cm^2}\right)\cdot 3}{0.1} = 3{,}000\dfrac{mW}{cm^2} = 3\dfrac{W}{cm^2}$.

16. Hydrophones

The following data regarding types of hydrophones and performance characteristics was provided by the ONDA Corporation. The purpose for inclusion is to demonstrate some of the parameters that matter relative to accurate acoustic testing.

16.1 Hydrophone Performance Comparison
Table 3 offers a quick visual and technical comparison of several industry-standard hydrophones. Specific differences between these models is discussing in the following sections. Content provided in the following sections (16.2 through 16.6) is based on information provided by Onda Corporation, as noted by the asterisk (*).

16.2 Membrane Hydrophones*
For most pulsed wave applications that require a flat response over a broad bandwidth, membrane hydrophones are the gold standard.

16.3 Capsule "Golden Lipstick" Hydrophones*
This unique design, created by Alan Selfridge, bridges the gap between membrane and needle hydrophones. It has an extremely flat sensitivity similar to membrane devices, yet it does not have a frame that affects the acoustic field and is very convenient for moving around a tank.

16.4 Needle Hydrophones*
These hydrophones tend to be less sensitive and have a less-flat frequency response than membrane hydrophones. Note that these

	HM Series (Membrane)	HGL Series (Capsule)	HNP Series (Needle)	HNC Series (Needle)	HNR Series (Needle)	HNR Series (Needle)	HFO Series (Fiber Optic)
Aperture Size (μm)	200/500	85, 200, 400, 1000	200, 400, 1000, 1500	200, 400, 1000, 1500	400	400	100
Frequency Response (MHz)	0.5 – 45 (±3 dB)	0.25 – 40 (±3 dB)	1 – 20 (±6 dB)	1 – 10 (±6 dB)	1 – 10 (±6 dB)	1 – 10 (±6 dB)	0.0001 – 100 (±3 dB)
Normal Sensitivity	Medium	Medium	Medium	High	Low	Low	Low
Ruggedness	Low	Medium	Low	Low	High	High	High
Field Disturbance	High	Low	Low	Low	Low	Low	High
Typical Application	Pulse Standard/ Reference Regulatory	Pulse + CW General Regulatory	CW General Purpose Doppler	CW General Purpose Photoacoustics	HIFU	HIFU	HIFU Lithotripsy
Cost	$$$	$$	$$	$$	$$$	$$$	$$$$

Table 3 **Hydrophone Comparison Chart**

hydrophones have advantages based on their shape. Because of their needle shape, these hydrophones can be inserted inside objects like foams or gels which makes them very convenient for many experiments. The small size also makes them easier to use in acoustic measuring tanks, and their small surface area reduces the amount of reflection that occurs relative to the large, specular surface of the membrane hydrophones (see *Figure 18*).

16.5 Needle Reflecting Hydrophones*
In general shape, these hydrophones are still needle-like, however they have flat tips, about 2.4 mm in diameter. The main advantage these devices have is that they are very rugged and able to withstand pressures and cavitation that would ruin a needle-type device.

16.6 Fiber Optic Hydrophones*
Fiber optic hydrophones are designed specifically to support very high intensity fields for applications such as HIFU and lithotripsy. These hydrophones provide both acoustic pressure and temperature measurements simultaneously. These devices can withstand acoustic pressures up to 500 MPa over a wide bandwidth.

* Based on information provided by Onda Corporation

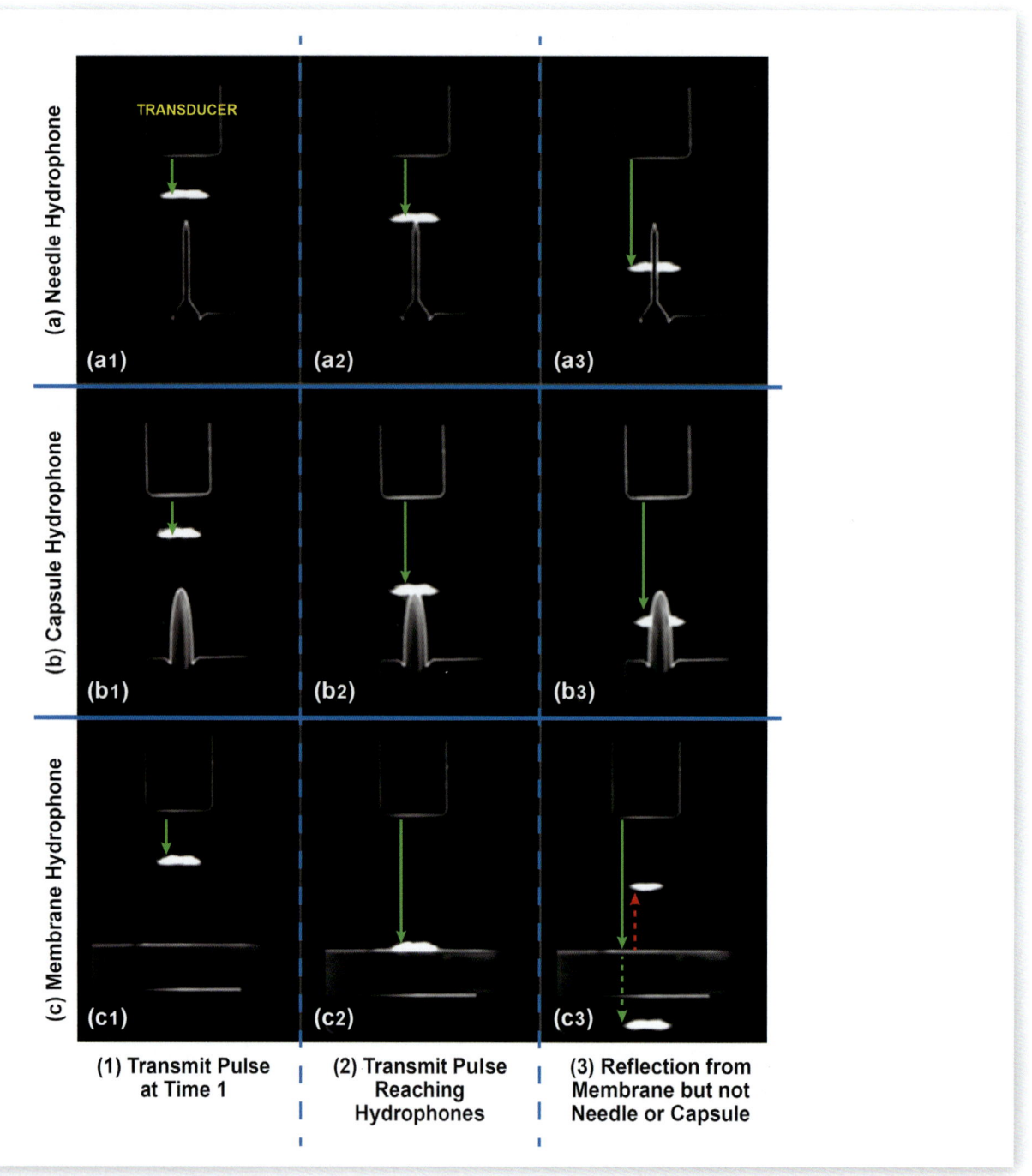

Fig. 18 Schlieren images of a single cycle pulse with three different types of hydrophones: (a) needle (note there is no reflection as shown in a3), (b) capsule (like the needle hydrophone, the shape prevents the production of a reflected wave), and (c) membrane (note the reflection from the specular surface of the membrane hydrophone as indicated by the red dotted line in c3) *(Courtesy of Onda Corporation)*

COMMON MISCONCEPTION: Bioeffects

MISCONCEPTION: *Cavitation occurs during compression.*

During compression, the pressure outside the bubbles increases, causing the bubbles to shrink. During rarefaction, the pressure external to the bubble decreases causing the bubble to expand. Just like when blowing a bubble with bubble gum, the bubble is more likely to "pop" as the bubble gets larger and the walls are stretched. Therefore, cavitation occurs typically when there is the highest rarefactional pressure (peak rarefaction) causing the bubble to implode.

ONLINE EXTRAS

For additional support material and to view your completion progress, visit:

www.pegasuslectures.com/6thEdExtras

Extras by Chapter include:
- Animations
- Videos
- Additional Images
- Clarifying Clips
- Supplemental Exercises
- Conceptual Questions

See page x of Preface for access instructions

CHAPTER SUMMARY: Bioeffects

- There are two principal mechanisms of bioeffects: mechanical and thermal.
- Mechanical bioeffects are primarily related to cavitation.
- Cavitation is the production, oscillation, or destruction of bubbles.
- Cavitation is believed to be a threshold mechanism: below certain power levels cavitation tends to be stable, above certain power levels cavitation tends to be transient (inertial).
- Stable cavitation occurs when the oscillations do not lead to bubble collapse.
- Inertial (transient) cavitation results in bubble destruction (implosion).
- Although the potential for bioeffects exists, ultrasound is considered a very safe modality.
- Thermal bioeffects are related to the beam intensity, the duration of the scan, the absorption rate of the medium, the ability to duct away heat from the region being scanned, and whether the technique being performed is a scanned or non-scanned modality.
- According to the AIUM, no confirmed bioeffects have occurred using accepted power levels.
- You should know the ALARA (as low as reasonably achievable) principle and its meaning. In essence, the lowest power necessary to achieve good clinical results should be used, constituting prudent use of ultrasound.
- Furthermore, you should be aware that scan times should not be extended needlessly, nor should needless scans be performed.
- The common intensities are a way of assessing the potential risk of bioeffects.
- Spatial measurements refer to the power distribution over physical dimensions.
- Temporal and pulse measurements refer to the distribution of power over time.
- The largest intensity measurement is the spatial peak, temporal peak. The smallest is the spatial average, temporal average.
- CW Doppler has the highest potential risk of thermal bioeffects since the duty factor is 1 (always transmitting) and CW is a "non-scanned" modality.
- In terms of the common intensities, the best indicator for the risk of thermal bioeffects is the spatial peak temporal average (intensity over the long period of time).
- The mechanical index (MI) has become the standard for indication of risk of bioeffects.
- The MI is the indicator for the risk of mechanical damage.

- There are three thermal indices to indicate the potential risk of thermal-related bioeffects:
  - TIS: thermal index in soft tissue
  - TIC: thermal index in cranial bone
  - TIB: thermal index in bone
- The thermal index indicates the model based prediction of the highest expected temperature rise for the current imaging situation. A thermal index of 1 implies the maximum temperature rise expected is 1° Celsius.
- It is possible that the models underestimate the worst case situations, and that the temperature could rise above the value predicted.
- The TI value above which fetal imaging (along with neonatal transcranial and spinal scanning) is not recommended is 3.0.
- Fetal scanning should always start with the TI at 0.7 or below.
- The TI value above which non-fetal imaging, neonatal transcranial, neonatal spinal scanning, and transorbital imaging is not recommended is 6.0.
- The maximum beam intensity allowed is 100 mW/cm^2 for an unfocused beam and 1 W/cm^2 for a focused beam.
- Acoustic power measurements are made to assure transducer performance both in terms of adequate sensitivity as well as safety.
- Hydrophones are routinely used to make power measurements in a water bath.
- Power measurements are difficult to make and very time consuming.
- There are hopes of newer technologies to make power measurements simpler, faster, and better.

References

[1] Worthington Biochemical Corporation. (2021). *Introduction to Enzymes*. http://www.worthington-biochem.com/introBiochem/tempEffects.html.

[2] Holme, T. A. (2017). *Denaturation*. Chemistry Explained. http://www.chemistryexplained.com/Co-Di/Denaturation.html#ixzz6a6KPA700.

[3] Herman, B. A., & Harris, G. R. (2002). Models and regulatory considerations for transient temperature rise during diagnostic ultrasound pulses. *Ultrasound in medicine & biology, 28*(9), 1217-1224.

American Institute of Ultrasound in Medicine. *Official Statements*. https://www.aium.org/resources/statements.aspx.

Wikipedia. (2021, March 11). *Denaturation (Biochemistry)*. https://en.wikipedia.org/wiki/Denaturation_(biochemistry).

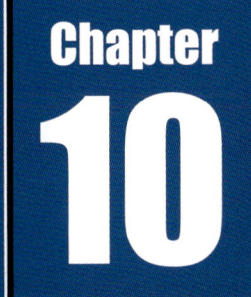

Contrast and Harmonics

Chapter 10

WHY DO WE STUDY THIS?

▷ Harmonic imaging has revolutionized ultrasound imaging by reducing near field clutter with improved penetration and lateral resolution.

▷ Contrast provides a very important tool for increasing signal strength and assessing tissue perfusion.

▷ Current approved uses of contrast imaging includes cardiac and liver-specific applications with hopes for additional applications in the future.

WHAT'S IN THIS CHAPTER?

LEVEL 2 — BOARD LEVEL
A discussion of the fundamentals of contrast imaging including the underlying physics principles. Foundational as well as specific principles of harmonic imaging, including benefits and drawbacks, are introduced.

LEVEL 3 — ADVANCED TOPICS
In-depth information on the applications of contrast and the specific modes of operation. For harmonic imaging, more advanced modes such as harmonic power Doppler and coded excitation are explained. The section concludes with a discussion of some future anticipated applications.

LEARNING OBJECTIVES

▷ Explain the fundamental principles of both harmonic and contrast imaging

▷ Recognize the non-linear aspects of harmonic signal generation

▷ Identify the non-linear response to contrast agents

▷ Describe the advantages and disadvantages of harmonic imaging

▷ Define the different modes of contrast imaging

▷ Recognize the relationship between the bioeffect of cavitation and the cavitation of contrast agent

Chapter 10
Contrast and Harmonics
Co-authored by Patrick Rafter, MS

1. Motivation for Contrast Imaging

1.1 Overcoming Too Much Attenuation
One of the motivating factors for creating contrast imaging is how incredibly low the signals are when imaging red blood cells. As we have already discussed, reflections from blood can be very weak due to the nature of Rayleigh scattering and the minimal acoustic impedance mismatch within blood itself. The weak reflection often causes very poor signal-to-noise, sometimes poor enough so that the signal is either non-diagnostic or even not detected.

Recall the equation which relates operating frequency, propagation speed, and wavelength: $\lambda = \dfrac{c}{f}$.

Substituting 1540 m/sec for c and using the range of 2 MHz to 20 MHz as the normal range for diagnostic ultrasound, the typical range for the wavelength is calculated as 770 μm to 77 μm. A typical red blood cell has a diameter of approximately 6 - 7 μm. Clearly, red blood cells look small in comparison to the wavelength, and therefore yield weak Rayleigh scattering.

1.2 Conventional Approaches
The approaches usually taken to overcome poor signal-to-noise are to use a lower frequency transducer, a different imaging approach, a higher transmit power, or even to use a more invasive approach such as transesophageal (TEE). All of these approaches rely on trying to create a better interrogating signal. So, the question arises: "Is there anything which can be done to enhance the strength or mechanism of reflection?"

1.3 Increasing the Acoustic Impedance Mismatch
There are clearly two ways to increase the amount of backscatter: increase the surface of the reflector, or increase the acoustic impedance mismatch. Consider if an agent was added to the blood to enhance the signal. It is obviously a very poor idea to try to add an agent with a large backscattering surface, since the diameter of the agent must be able to pass through capillaries without causing obstruction. Therefore, the idea of contrast imaging is not to increase the backscattering surface, but rather to use a contrast agent which increases the acoustic impedance mismatch within the blood.

Given that the contrast agent will reside in the blood pool, the agent needs to have an acoustic impedance which varies significantly relative to the plasma and red blood cells. The most obvious choice is to use a gas.

Recall that the acoustic impedance is given by the equation: $Z = \rho * c$. Since gases tend to have relatively low densities and high compressibility, it is expected that they will also have a low propagation velocity. Therefore, since the density and propagation speed in a gas are low, the acoustic impedance of a gas is extremely low. In comparison, the density and propagation speed of the blood are both significantly higher, resulting in a significantly higher acoustic impedance. Also recall that the amount of reflection is dependent on the acoustic impedance mismatch, given by the equation:

$$Reflection\% = \left[\dfrac{Z_2 - Z_1}{Z_2 + Z_1}\right]^2$$

1.4 Increase in Signal Amplitude with Contrast
Since with a contrast agent there is a significant mismatch within the blood, there will be significantly more backscattered energy, and hence significantly better signal-to-noise. In fact, the increase in signal strength using a contrast agent, in comparison to the signal strength of normal blood, is typically on the order of 30 dB, as shown in *Figure 1*.

The specifics of contrast imaging are further discussed in Level 3 of this chapter.

KEY CONCEPT

Reflection from blood is very weak. By increasing the acoustic impedance mismatch within blood, contrast significantly increases reflectivity from blood (by about 30 dB).

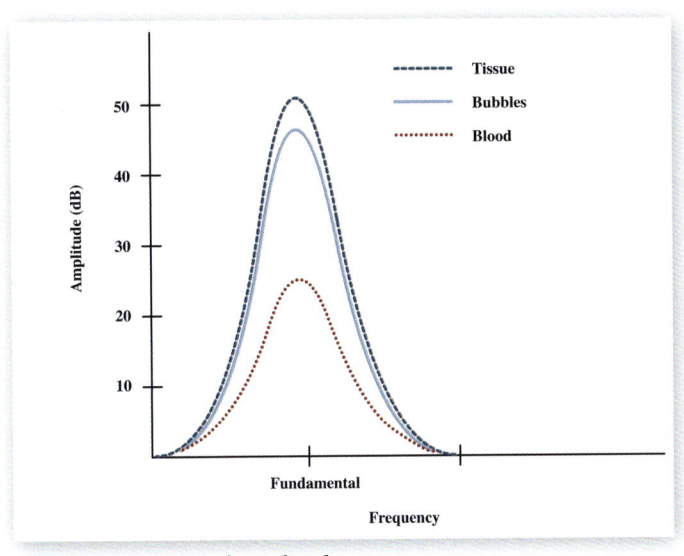

Fig. 1 **Relative signal amplitudes**

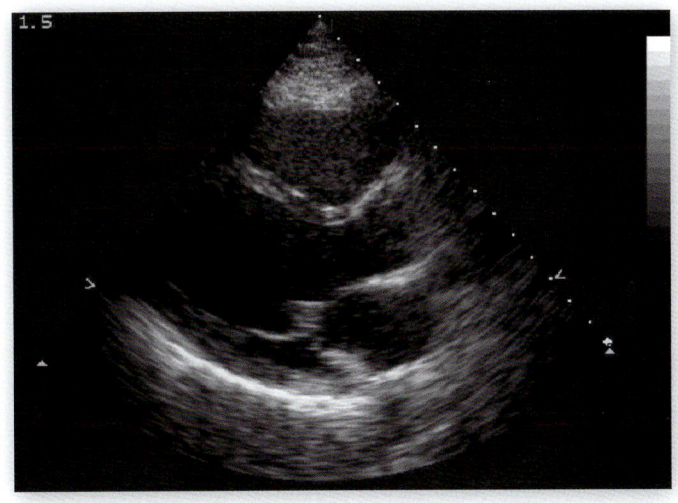

Fig. 2b **Low frequency with poor resolution**

2. Fundamentals of Harmonics

2.1 Motivation for Harmonic Imaging

The clear advantage of using a higher transmit frequency for imaging is better detail resolution (resolution is discussed in Chapters 4, 5, 6, and 8). One of the clear disadvantages of using a higher transmit frequency is significantly greater attenuation (recall that the amount of absorption increases exponentially with increasing frequency). Therefore, we ask: "Is there a way to get better resolution while still preserving the ability to visualize deeper structures without having to use more invasive techniques?"

Figure 2a depicts how using a high frequency is inappropriate when penetration is necessary. *Figure 2b* shows how using a lower frequency provides the penetration required, but does not yield optimal resolution.

The concept of harmonic imaging is to transmit at a lower frequency and receive at a higher frequency. Specifically, the word harmonics refers to a multiple of the operating frequency. For example, the first harmonic refers to the fundamental frequency or operating frequency, the second harmonic refers to the frequency that is twice the fundamental frequency, while the third harmonic refers to the frequency that is three times the fundamental frequency. There is sometimes confusion between the naming convention of overtones and harmonics. The first overtone is the same as the second harmonic, whereas the second overtone is the same as the third harmonic.

Transmitting at the lower frequency (the fundamental frequency) allows for better penetration, while receiving at the higher frequency (the harmonic frequency), generally yields better resolution. Compare the image of *Figure 3* with *Figure 2a* and *Figure 2b*. Notice the significant improvement in resolution and reduction in reverberation. The question is, "How does this work?"

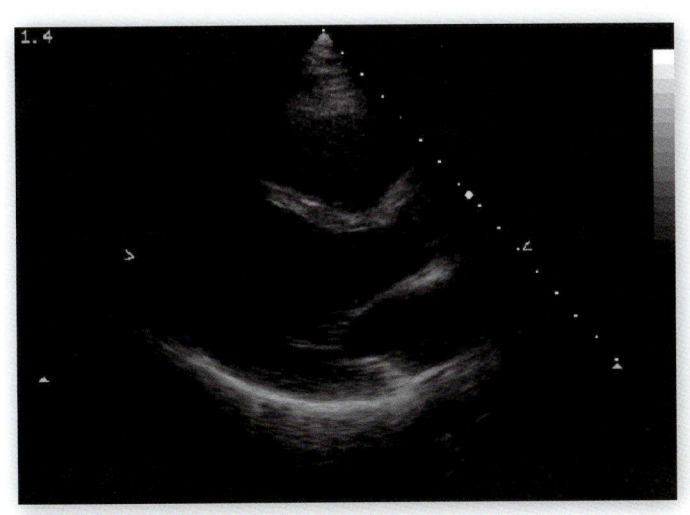

Fig. 2a **High frequency with inadequate penetration**

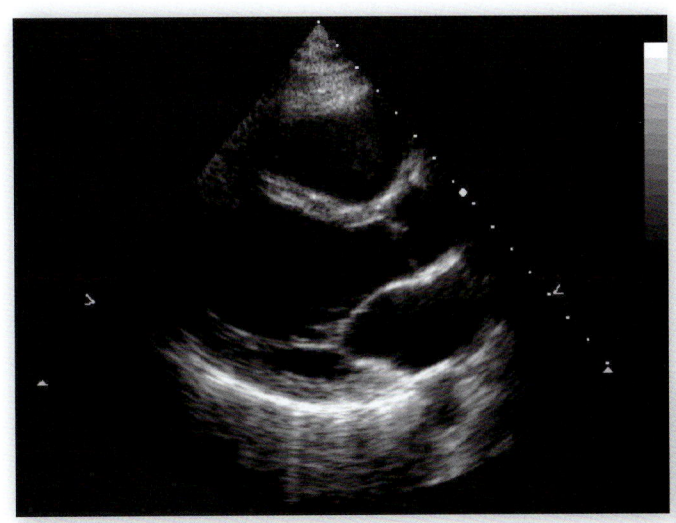

Fig. 3 **Harmonic imaging (fundamental at 1.8 MHz and harmonic at 3.6 MHz)**

2.2 Mechanisms that Produce Harmonic Signals

There are two different mechanisms for producing harmonic signals used in diagnostic ultrasound:

- Non-linear propagation through tissue producing "native" or "tissue harmonic imaging"
- Resonance of contrast agents producing "contrast harmonic imaging"

> **KEY CONCEPT**
>
> Harmonic imaging is based on transmitting at a lower frequency, called the fundamental frequency, and receiving at twice the fundamental frequency, called the second harmonic. There are two primary mechanisms that produce harmonic signals, resonance of contrast agents and non-linear propagation of sound through tissue.

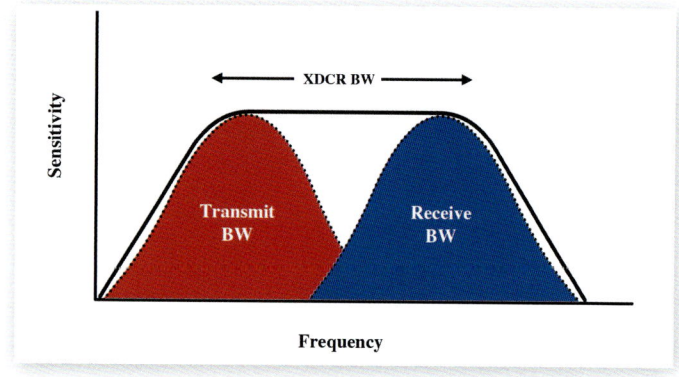

Fig. 4 **Broadband transducer capable of harmonic imaging**

Somewhat surprisingly, the reflected signal was not purely comprised of harmonic energy from the contrast agent. Instead, the reflected signal also was comprised of harmonic content generated by the tissue as well as the contrast agent. Although, the harmonic contrast signal was of higher amplitude than the signal from the surrounding blood, the harmonic tissue signals were quite strong and often masked the desired contrast signal. Therefore, even without the use of contrast agents, harmonic energy is generated by the propagation of sound waves through the body as depicted in *Figure 5*.

3. Technology Advances

The first attempt to develop techniques to image ultrasound contrast agents led to the development of harmonic imaging. Initial uses of contrast agents were somewhat limited by some of the same general types of problems which plague conventional imaging, and a few new problems. Specifically, reflection from near field specular structures still generated many imaging artifacts. New problems arose such as shadowing from the increased reflectivity due to the large acoustic impedance mismatch of the bubbles, and the too rapid destruction of the contrast agent. As a result, a new approach was desired. It was well known that bubbles could reach resonant frequencies where non-linear excitation would produce harmonic energy. The "new approach," called harmonic contrast imaging, was to change the system operation so as to enhance the non-linear resonance effects and then process the resulting harmonic signals.

While improving the system operation for contrast harmonic imaging, a few technological advancements in the mid 1990s made harmonic imaging a possibility. Specifically, the combination of broadband transducers capable of transmitting at one frequency and receiving at twice that frequency (as depicted in *Figure 4* and discussed in Chapter 4) and broadband digital beamformers (discussed in Chapter 6) with programmable digital filtering, made harmonic imaging feasible. At the time, to improve harmonic contrast imaging, it was hoped, and even expected, that the harmonic signal would be purely generated by the contrast agents. Therefore, by processing only the frequency range of signals in the harmonic band, the source of many imaging artifacts would be completely eliminated.

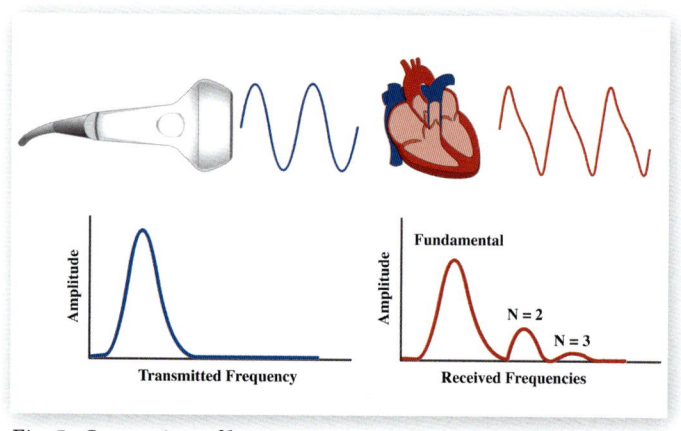

Fig. 5 **Generation of harmonic energy from propagation through tissue**

4. Relative Amplitudes

Figure 6 demonstrates the relative amplitudes of tissue, blood, contrast bubbles, and tissue harmonic signals.

Notice that at the harmonic frequency, the amplitude of the contrast signal has enhanced the normal blood signal by approximately 30 dB to 40 dB. Also notice that in general, the contrast signal has a higher amplitude than the harmonic tissue signal and that the difference in amplitude is not that large.

Fig. 6 Relative amplitudes

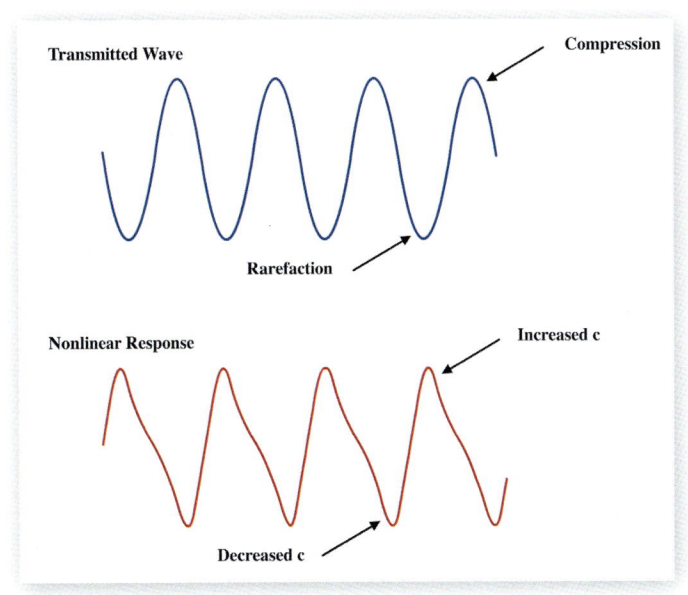

Fig. 7 Generation of harmonics from non-linear wave propagation through body

> **KEY CONCEPT**
>
> The use of contrast agent results in higher reflectivity from blood, but results in less differentiation between blood pool and tissue signal amplitudes.

5. Generation of Harmonics

5.1 Non-linear Wave Propagation

To understand how tissue harmonic energy is generated, you must reconsider the mechanism by which a mechanical wave propagates. Recall that a mechanical wave propagates through a series of compressions and rarefactions. Also recall that propagation speed changes with the density and stiffness of the medium. During the compression phase of the wave the material becomes denser. As a result, the propagation speed increases slightly. During the rarefactional phase, the medium becomes a little less stiff and is a little more elastic. As a result, the propagation speed decreases slightly. These changes in propagation speeds are noted in *Figure 7*.

Notice that the wave propagating through the body has a characteristically different shape than the transmitted wave. Notice how there are sharp edges to the wave propagating through the body due to the changes from lower to higher and higher to lower propagation speeds. These "quick" changes represent higher frequency energy. In reality, there is energy at many different harmonics of the fundamental frequency. If the signal is decomposed into individual frequency bands (much like the FFT process described in Chapter 7 on Doppler processing), energy will exist not just at the second harmonic, but also at the third harmonic, fourth harmonic, etc. The amplitude of each successive higher harmonic reduces non-linearly, so that the third harmonic is much weaker than the second, and the fourth harmonic much weaker than the third. The following diagram, *Figure 8*, demonstrates the relative amplitudes of the various harmonics generated by non-linear propagation.

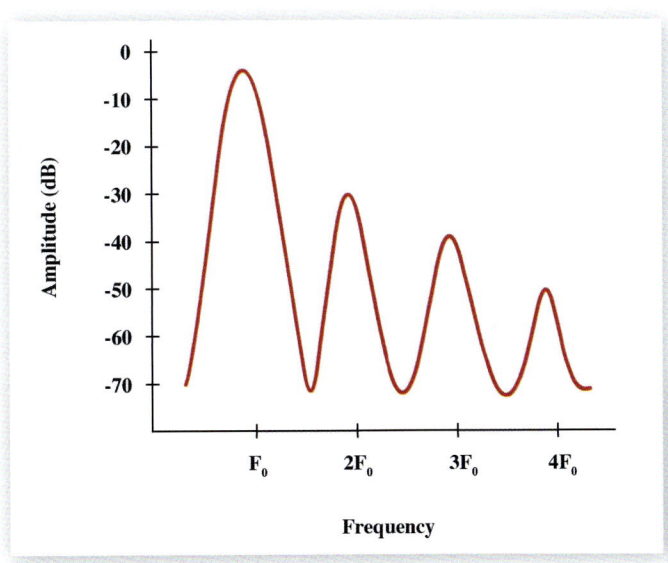

Fig. 8 Relative amplitudes of harmonic series

5.2 Harmonics and Depth Dependence

As illustrated in *Figure 7*, as the sound wave propagates through the body, the characteristic shape of the wave changes. In general, this "distortion" of the transmitted signal accumulates as the waveform propagates through tissue, leading to an increasing level of second harmonic signal with depth. Where the wave starts out at the face of the transducer there are no harmonic components. As the wave propagates into the body, distortion resulting in harmonic energy begins to occur. The rate at which harmonic energy builds up is dependent on multiple factors such as the acoustic transmit pressure, the transmit frequency, and the attenuation rate. As the beam converges towards the focus, the acoustic pressure increases (higher beam intensities) leading to a higher level of distortion. The increase in harmonic energy with higher intensities is the result of greater variation in propagation velocity resulting from higher amplitude compressions and rarefactions.

With increasing depth, there is increased beam attenuation, decreasing the pressure intensity. As we learned in Chapter 5, past the focus, the beam diverges rapidly reducing the acoustic pressure field. As a result of the increased attenuation, eventually the rate of increase in harmonic energy will decrease, and the harmonic generation rate will drop well below the rate of attenuation at the fundamental frequency. In other words, the rate of decreasing harmonic energy will be faster than the already high rate of attenuation at the fundamental frequency. Recall that the harmonic signal is weaker than the fundamental signal. Furthermore, since the harmonic signal is at a higher frequency, the attenuation rate on return to the transducer is higher than the attenuation rate of the fundamental signal. The combined effect (weaker harmonics, higher attenuation rates, and decreased harmonic production because of decreasing beam intensity) leads to significantly lower levels of harmonic signal in the far field. Therefore, in the very near field and in the far field, there are times when fundamental imaging will outperform harmonic imaging in terms of signal-to-noise ratio. The loss of harmonic signal in the far field is most noticeable at higher transmit frequencies (e.g., > 2.5 MHz for adult echo and greater than 4.0 MHz for most vascular applications) due to the greater rate of absorption at these frequencies. The following diagram, *Figure 9*, illustrates the gradual "build up" and decrease of harmonic energy as a function of depth.

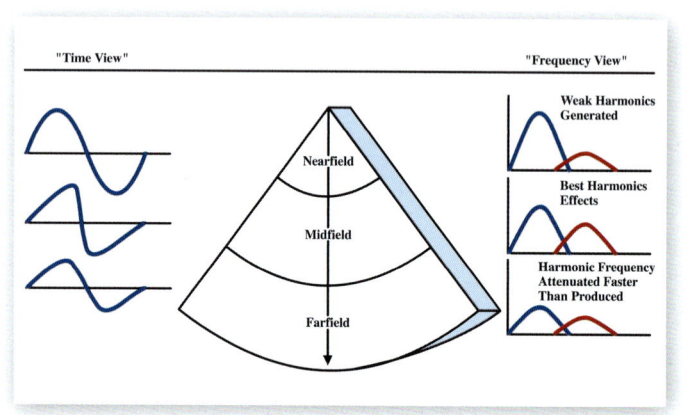

Fig. 9 **Harmonic generation versus depth**

5.3 Effective Harmonic Beam Shape

As a result of the increasing harmonic generation with depth, the effective harmonic beam shape differs greatly from the transmitted fundamental beam shape. *Figure 10* demonstrates these differences.

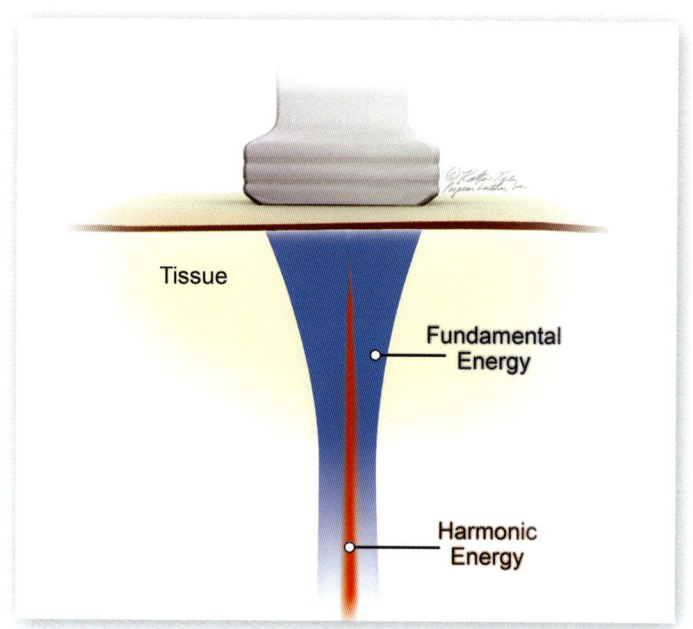

Fig. 10 **Comparison of harmonic beamwidth and fundamental beamwidth**

> **KEY CONCEPT**
>
> Harmonic generation is non-linear with the acoustic pressure field. As a result, harmonics tend to be best near the focus, and then drop off precipitously with increasing depth (as the pressure decreases rapidly with the diverging beam and the increased attenuation with depth). As a result, when performing harmonic imaging, focus placement is very important.

6. Advantages and Disadvantages of Conventional Harmonics

6.1 Improved Lateral Resolution

When there is adequate signal-to-noise, there are many possible improvements in image quality from tissue harmonic imaging (THI) relative to fundamental imaging such as improved lateral resolution. This improvement leads to the question: "To improve lateral resolution, why not just use a higher transmit frequency?" The answer is, there are other benefits to tissue harmonic imaging such as improved penetration relative to fundamental imaging at higher frequencies and more importantly, dramatic reduction in imaging artifacts.

6.2 Reduction in Grating Lobes

One source of noise and artifact in an ultrasound image is from off-axis objects mapping energy into the main beam (grating lobe artifact as discussed in Chapter 8). Since grating lobes result in lateral translation of signal in an image, real anatomical structures may be obscured, or artificial structures "manufactured." The use of harmonics significantly reduces the deleterious effects of grating lobes. As already discussed, higher harmonic energy generation is very dependent on incident pressure. Higher pressure fields result in much greater harmonic energy. Recall that the energy in the grating lobe is significantly less than the energy in the main lobe (usually 30 dB to 60 dB less). As a result, the harmonic energy produced by the undesired grating lobe of the beam is much lower in amplitude than the harmonic energy produced by the main lobe of the beam. Consequently, there is significantly less noise and artifact associated with grating lobes. The following illustration in *Figure 11* depicts the decrease in grating lobes with harmonic production.

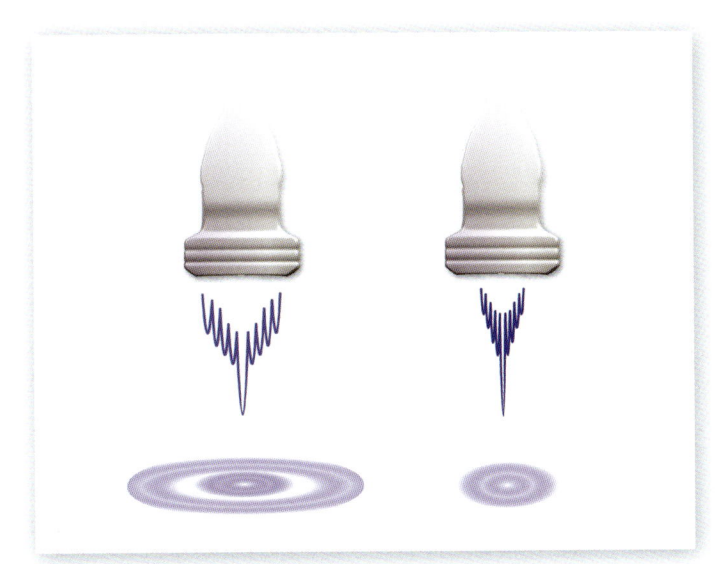

Fig. 11 Decreased grating lobes with harmonic imaging

6.3 Reduction in Reverberation and Clutter Artifacts

Another important source of artifact and noise is multi-path reverberations. As discussed in many chapters including Chapter 8, reverberation is caused by large acoustic impedance mismatches usually from specular reflectors, which results in the sound beam being redirected back and forth between structures or between structures and the transducer face. For example, in cardiac imaging sound will reverberate between the skin, the chest wall, the ribs, and the transducer. Since multiple reflections have occurred, the actual path the ultrasound wave has traveled when reflected back to the transducer is longer than the distance from the transducer to the original structures that redirected the energy. To the ultrasound scanner, this energy appears to come from deeper in the body, often appearing as a haze in the image that obscures structures, or worse, appearing as an artifactual thrombus. There are two effects that work in tandem to reduce reverberation with harmonic imaging. First, the intensity of each reverberation is lower than the intensity of the actual reflection. Lower intensity waves produce less distortion and hence less harmonic energy. Second, most imaging artifacts are caused by specular reflectors in the relative near field where the beam is still converging and hence producing relatively weak harmonic energy.

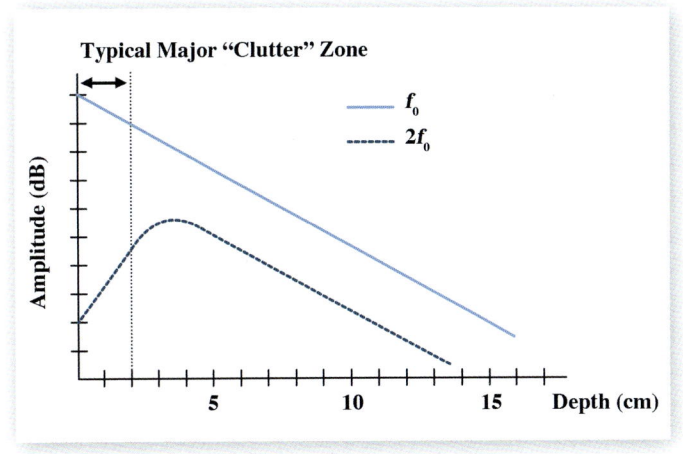

Fig. 12 Reduction in "clutter" from harmonics

Referring to *Figure 12*, notice that in the near field, the source of most imaging artifacts, the harmonic signal is significantly weaker than the fundamental signal. The result is that the strong "clutter" signals responsible for the majority of artifacts are reduced, and artifacts are either diminished or eliminated entirely. This is perhaps one of the biggest benefits of harmonic imaging.

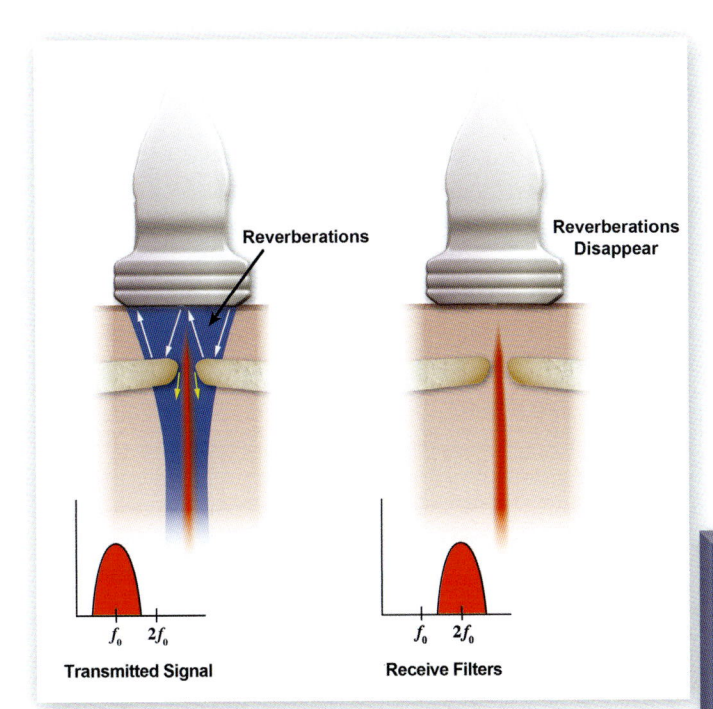

Fig. 13 Reduction in reverberation artifact

Figure 13 demonstrates how reverberation from ribs in a cardiac setting is significantly reduced by harmonic imaging. Note that there is very little attenuation of the fundamental frequency in the near field such that the system is very sensitive to these reverberating signals when using conventional imaging (at the fundamental). In contrast, since the harmonic effect increases as the beam intensifies while converging, the harmonic system is less sensitive to these reverberating signals.

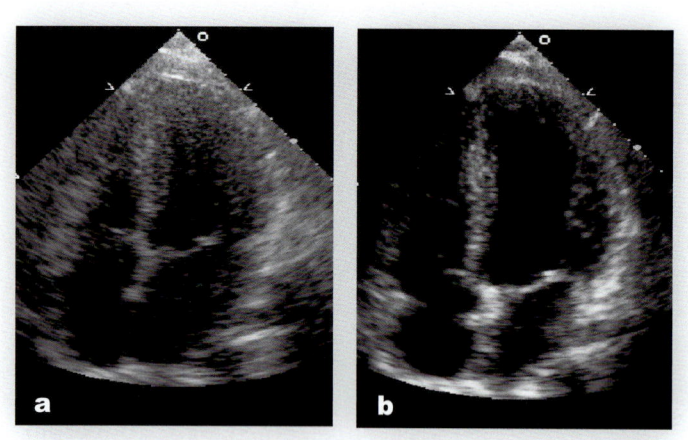

Fig. 14 Conventional imaging (a) vs. harmonic imaging (b)(apical 4-chamber)

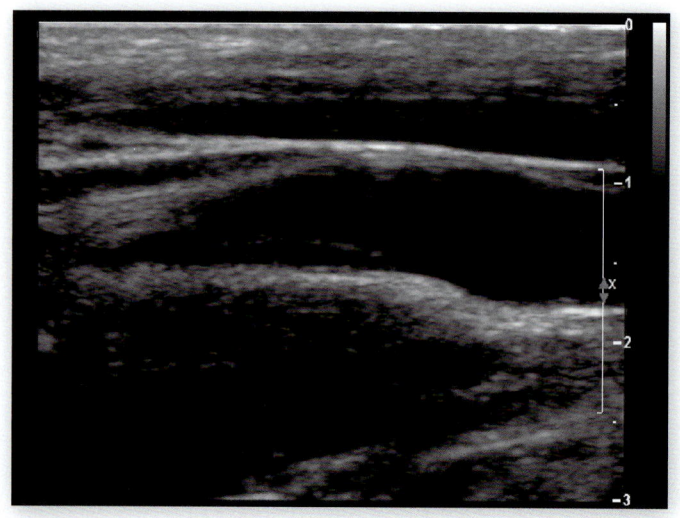

View ONLINE Animation and Image Library

Fig. 15a Conventional imaging of right ICA with reverberation artifact

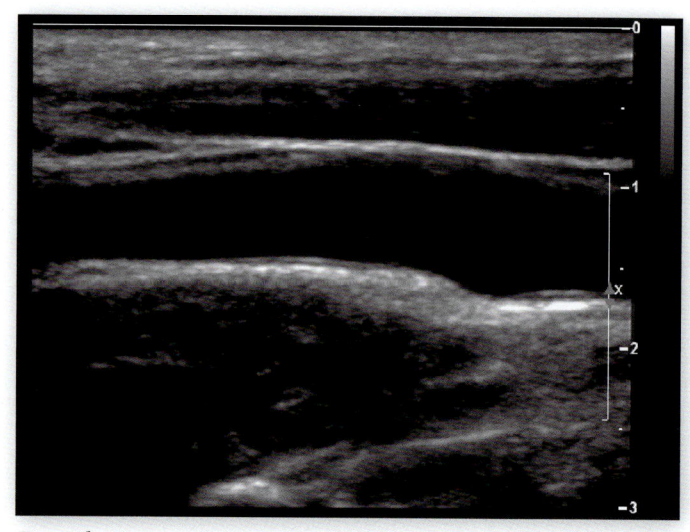

Fig. 15b **Harmonic imaging of right ICA**

6.4 Reduction in Phase Aberration

Another benefit of harmonic imaging relative to transmitting at a higher frequency is the reduction in effects from phase aberration. Phase aberration is a distortion of the ultrasound beam caused by differences in the speed of sound due to inhomogeneity in tissue. For example, fat has a lower speed of sound (1440 m/sec) than muscle (1560 m/sec). As the spherical waves from each of the transducer elements propagates through different distances of tissues with varying propagation speeds they arrive at a point along the beam at different times. In other words, the differences in the acoustic path of each spherical wave have caused a phase delay. In essence, this phase delay counteracts the phase delays produced by the system to steer and focus the beam. The result is a less directed and less focused beam, referred to as "aberration." The result of this aberration is a decrease in the "main lobe" energy and an increase in the grating lobe energy. This effect is reduced by harmonic imaging since the focusing of lower frequencies is less affected by changes in the speed of sound than higher frequencies. Recall that higher frequencies produce shorter wavelengths. For shorter wavelengths, less of a time delay results in more destructive interference. Therefore transmitting at a lower frequency, as done with harmonic imaging, reduces phase aberration effects.

KEY CONCEPT

The non-linear generation of harmonics results in a reduction in grating lobes and an effectively narrower beam than conventional imaging. The result is improved lateral resolution and a decrease in grating lobes artifacts. Additionally, multi-path travel reduces beam intensity and hence reduces harmonic generation. The result is fewer clutter-related artifacts (such as reverberation), especially in the near field of the image.

6.5 Degradation in Axial Resolution

A drawback of basic harmonic imaging relative to higher frequency conventional imaging is a degradation of axial resolution. In order to gain the full benefit of THI, separation of the fundamental and harmonic bandwidths is required. Any overlap of the fundamental and receive bandwidth can cause noise and haze in the image. The overlap of the bandwidths can be reduced by transmitting a narrower bandwidth of frequencies. As we learned in Chapter 4, the bandwidth is inversely related to the pulse duration. Therefore, to create a narrower bandwidth, the transducer is allowed to ring for more cycles. This relationship is depicted in *Figure 16*. Since the number of cycles also affects the spatial pulse length, an increase in the number of cycles increases the spatial pulse length, decreasing axial resolution. In the cardiac world, this decrease in axial resolution often results in an apparent "thickening" of the valve leaflets. Therefore when axial resolution is critical, conventional (basic) harmonics should be turned off.

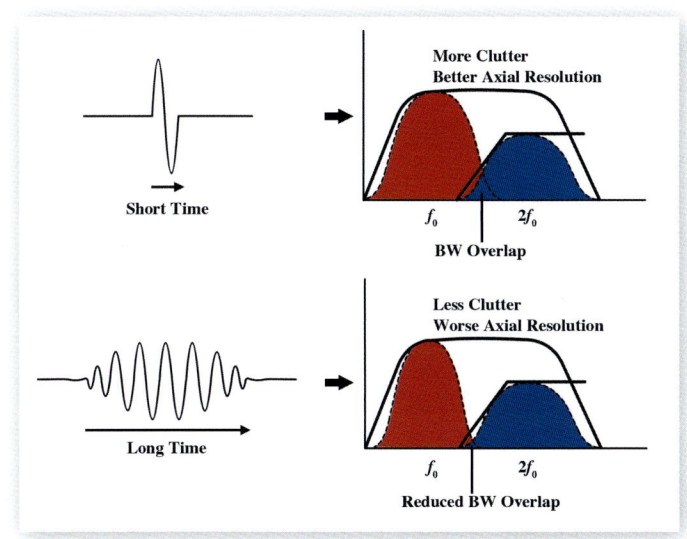

Fig. 16 **Narrow banding reduces clutter but also decreases axial resolution**

KEY CONCEPT

In an attempt to reduce the overlap between the transmitted fundamental bandwidth and the second harmonic receive bandwidth, conventional harmonic imaging uses a narrowband transmit approach. A narrower bandwidth is generated by using a longer spatial pulse length, thereby degrading axial resolution.

7. Pulse or Phase Inversion

Pulse inversion has proven very beneficial in reversing the degradation in axial resolution that occurs with conventional harmonic imaging. To understand how pulse inversion works, we will first need to demonstrate a very interesting phenomenon. A fundamental pulse 180 degrees out of phase with another fundamental pulse, will generate the same phase harmonic signal. In the following figure (*Figure 17*) notice that the fundamental frequency at both 0 degrees and at 180 degrees corresponds to the same phase for the harmonic signal. This result is fortuitous, since it becomes the basis for how pulse inversion works.

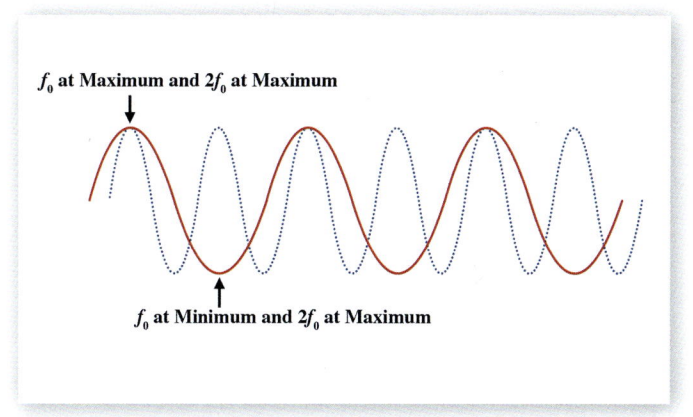

Fig. 17 **The phase of 2nd harmonic is the same for the maxima and for the minima of the fundamental frequency**

Unlike conventional harmonics, pulse inversion harmonics requires multiple acoustic lines to produce a single display line. A transmit pulse is generated creating the first acoustic line. A second transmit pulse is then transmitted in the same scan direction, but this time with the phase inverted (180 degrees out of phase). The received response from the first pulse is then summed with the response from the second pulse. Any energy that reflects linearly (at the fundamental frequency) will be 180 degrees out of phase between the first and second transmit pulses. When added together destructive interference occurs (as discussed in Chapter 2: Waves), and the fundamental energy is cancelled out. In comparison, any energy that reflects non-linearly (harmonics) will be in phase (0 degrees out of phase) between the first and second pulses. When added together, two signals in phase add constructively, producing a larger signal. There are therefore two major advantages to pulse inversion: since the fundamental energy is cancelled out, no narrowbanding is needed to preserve axial resolution, and the averaging effect improves the signal-to-noise ratio by a factor of 1.4 (the square root of 2). *Figure 18* demonstrates the basic principle of pulse inversion harmonics. The one disadvantage is that since two acoustic lines are transmitted per display line, the frame rate, and hence the temporal resolution, is degraded by a factor of 2.

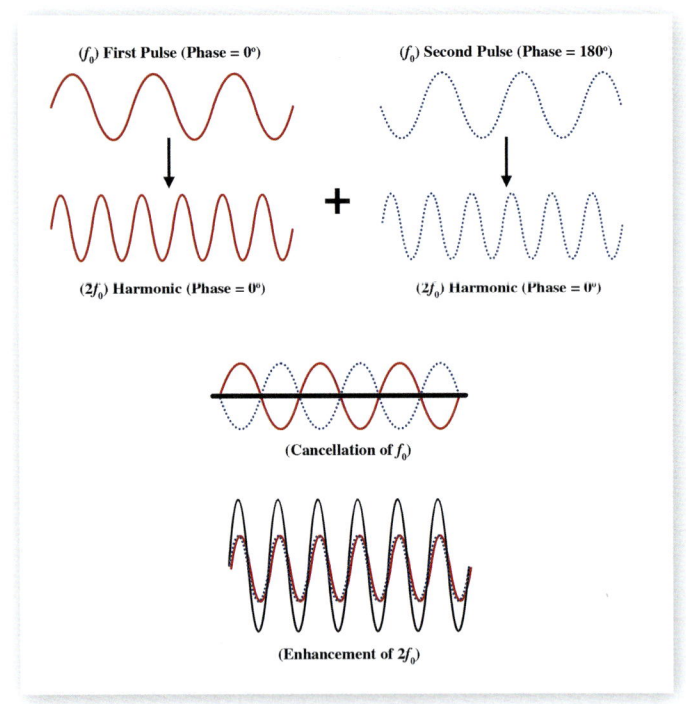

Fig. 18 **Pulse inversion: fundamental frequency destructively adds while harmonic energy constructively adds**

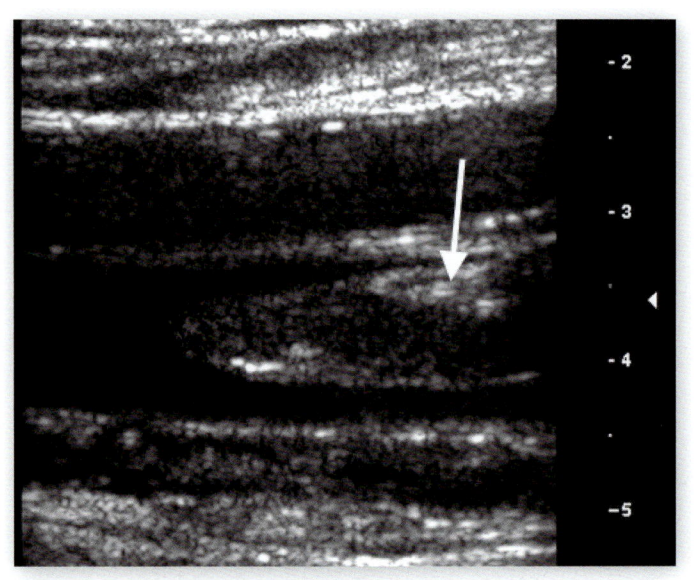

Fig. 19b **Pulse inversion harmonics**

Figure 19b shows how dramatic the improvement from pulse inversion harmonics can be relative to fundamental imaging (*Figure 19a*). In this case a large thrombus becomes evident using pulse inversion harmonics which is not visualized with conventional imaging.

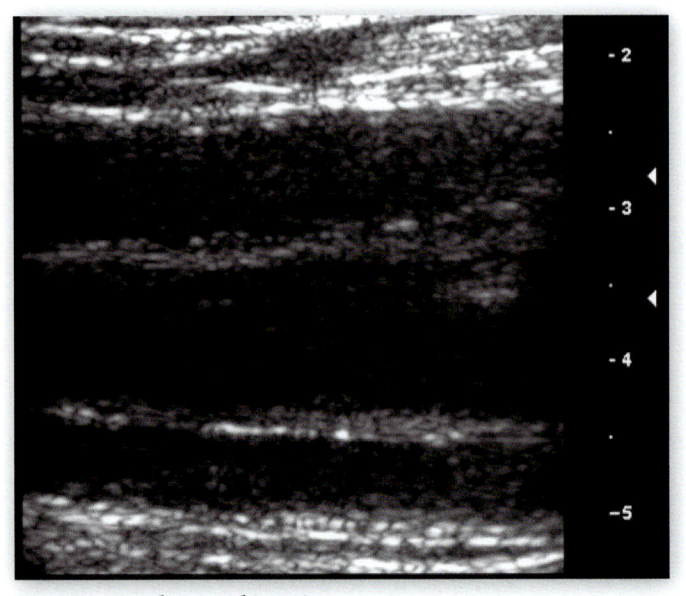

Fig. 19a **Fundamental imaging**

KEY CONCEPT

Pulse inversion harmonics reduces the axial resolution degradation and improves the signal-to-noise ratio relative to standard harmonic imaging. By transmitting two beams with inverted phases, the fundamental reflections add destructively, eliminating the need to use a longer spatial pulse length. Since the harmonic signals add constructively, the harmonic signal increases in amplitude by the square root of two. However, temporal resolution is degraded by a factor of two since it takes twice as long to create an image.

LEVEL 3: Advanced Topics

8. Current Uses of Contrast Imaging

Ultrasound contrast agents have been commercially available in the US since 1994. Up until 2016, the only approved indication by the FDA was for left ventricular opacification (LVO) to aid in the delineation of endocardial borders (see *Figure 20a*). In April 2016, the FDA approved the first agent in the United States for use in a non-cardiac application when Lumason was approved for the characterization of focal liver lesions in both adult and pediatric patients. In Europe and in Asia, use of contrast for detection and characterization of focal liver lesions has been routine clinical practice for well over a decade and is still on the rise.

In the coming years a myocardial perfusion indication is hoped for as well as further indications (see *Figure 20b*). Today's ultrasound contrast agents consist of microbubbles that act as intravascular tracers – moving at the same velocities as red blood cells and going everywhere red blood cells go. A typical contrast agent is less than 6 microns diameter and is designed with the goal of passing through the pulmonary microcirculation when administered with an intravenous injection. After reaching the arterial side of the heart, they are pumped everywhere red blood cells go and are therefore ideal for imaging and studying microcirculation.

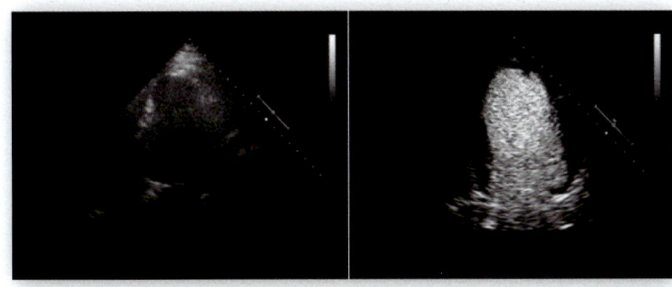

Fig. 20a **Left: a baseline non-contrast image demonstrating lack of endocardial border definition; Right: following an intravenous injection of contrast endocardial borders are now clearly delineated even in this difficult-to-image patient** *(Reproduced with permission from Medicamundi)*

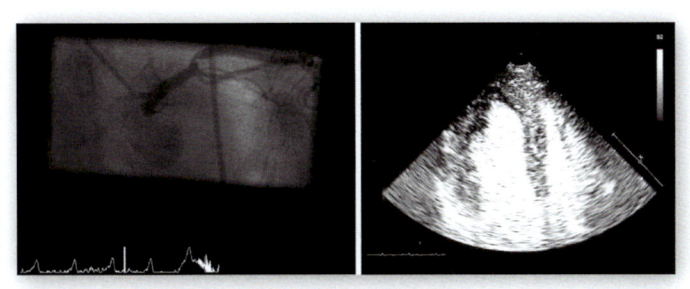

Fig. 20b **An example of myocardial perfusion echo in acute coronary syndrome; left image shows angiogram with proximal LAD stenosis; right image shows the resulting large subendocardial resting defect** *(Reproduced with permission from Medicamundi)*

View ONLINE Animation and Image Library

9. Properties of Contrast

9.1 Composition of Bubbles

Today's contrast agents consist of bubbles encapsulated by a stabilizing shell. In order to be effective, it is necessary for the contrast agent to last several minutes in the blood stream to allow for ample imaging time. Since the bubbles are micron sized, a shell is necessary to keep them from dissolving quickly in the blood stream. Typical shells consist of sonicated albumin, phospholipids, or more recently, synthetic polymers. Since the shell used in a particular agent can cause it to be either stiff or pliable, "the shell" plays an extremely important role in determining acoustic properties. The gas plays an important part as well – especially in determining the longevity of the contrast effect. Early contrast agents were air-based but due to the high diffusibility of air, they would dissolve rather rapidly in the blood stream. More recently higher density gases such as sulfur hexafluoride and perfluorocarbons have been introduced which allow for higher longevity. However, pharmaceutical companies have also shown that with the right shell composition it is possible to construct a stable air-filled microbubble.

9.2 Microbubble Interaction with Ultrasound and Resonance

Microbubbles, around the size of contrast agent bubbles, generally have a strong acoustic response when excited by waveforms with frequencies in the low MHz range, corresponding nicely with the typical range of diagnostic ultrasound frequencies. This natural response frequency is referred to as a "resonance". *Figure 21* demonstrates the increase in signal amplitude which results from insonating a bubble at its resonant frequency.

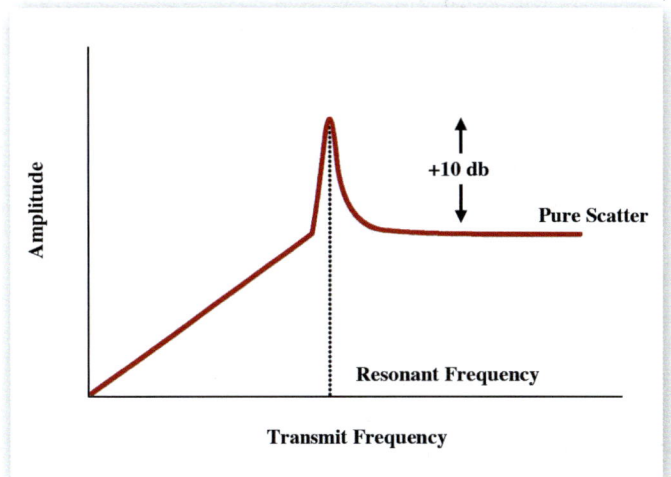

Fig. 21 **Microbubble resonance**

To understand resonance, we will need to consider the bubble response to the mechanical wave.

During the compressional phase of the mechanical wave, there is increased pressure on the microbubble and it becomes smaller or contracts. During the rarefaction phase of the ultrasound wave, the pressure surrounding the microbubble decreases and it becomes larger or expands. As the microbubble oscillates in the varying acoustic field, it reradiates an ultrasound wave back towards the transducer. The amplitude, frequency, and duration of the driving pulse all play very important roles in determining the acoustic response from microbubbles. However, the actual dynamics of the microbubble oscillation is altered by the microbubble's "desire" to resonate at its natural frequency.

This resonance effect is very similar to a string of a guitar. The length of the string and its tension help define the tone or frequency that results when the string is plucked. In a similar manner, a microbubble's natural resonance frequency is strongly influenced by its radius as well as its shell properties. For an unencapsulated "free" air bubble the resonance is given by:

$$Frequency(MHz) = \frac{330}{Resting\ Radius(\mu m)}$$

For example, a 2 micron bubble will resonate at 1.65 MHz. A typical contrast agent is comprised of a wide range of bubble sizes with varying shell thickness and therefore has a corresponding wide range of responses. The combination of these factors has made it extremely challenging to mathematically predict microbubble behavior under various ultrasound conditions. To date, most of the understanding of interaction for ultrasound with microbubbles has come from observed acoustic behavior when imaging microbubbles in vitro and in vivo. Recently, a great deal of understanding has come from high-speed cameras capable of taking pictures of single microbubbles under ultrasound excitation at very fast frame rates.

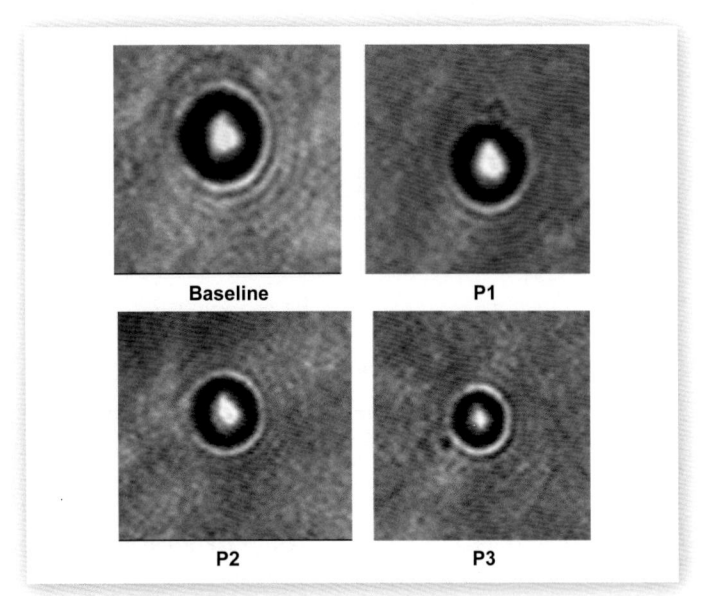

Fig. 22 **Stable oscillation of a lipid bubble**

Referring to *Figure 22*, the first frame labeled "baseline" is a light microscopy image of a lipid bubble prior to excitation. The frame labeled "P1" is the bubble after one pulse with a mechanical index (MI) of 0.4. Note that the bubble has been compressed. The frames labeled "P2" and "P3" are the bubble after the second and third pulse.

> **KEY CONCEPT**
>
> Contrast microbubbles grow and shrink with rarefaction and compression of sound waves, re-radiating sound waves. When a bubble is excited near its resonant frequency, there is a significant increase in signal amplitude.

10. The Mechanical Index (MI)

10.1 Understanding the MI
One of the keys to optimizing ultrasound images with contrast agents is to understand more about the interaction between output power and the contrast effect. Not only does output power have a dramatic influence on contrast enhancement level, it has also been observed in vivo that diagnostic levels of ultrasound output power can cause microbubble disruption. The MI was introduced several years ago as an indicator of the likelihood of cavitation in tissue. (The MI is discussed in Chapter 9: Bioeffects) The MI is currently displayed on all newer ultrasound systems since its adoption as a standard. The MI is the primary indicator of output power on ultrasound equipment and is the most critical parameter in determining microbubble response. For a given transmit frequency, the MI is directly related to the peak rarefactional, or negative, pressure. The equation is:

$$MI = \frac{Peak\ Negative\ Pressure\ (MPa)}{\sqrt{frequency(MHz)}}$$

Since the actual acoustic pressure that tissue is exposed to can vary a great deal depending on the patient and the acoustic window, the displayed MI is only an estimate. A constant level of attenuation (0.3 dB/MHz/cm) is assumed when equipment manufacturers determine the MI. Due to the complexities of making these measurements, there are also slight variations between manufacturers. Therefore, machines reporting the same MI may in fact be somewhat different in terms of their actual output.

10.2 Non-uniformity of the MI
It is important to understand that the reported MI is for only one location throughout the entire image. Often, the point of peak MI is

much closer to the face of the transducer than the actual placement of the transmit focus. Due to directivity of the elements of transducers, the scan lines at angles will also tend to have lower MIs than the centerline — the one fired "straight ahead" or perpendicular to the transducer face (as indicated in *Figure 23*). This variation in signal strength with angular direction is very similar to the effect of sound being louder when you are standing right in front of a speaker rather than off to the side. Also, it is important to realize that the movement of the transmit focus will alter the distribution of power in the image, even if the reported MI remains the same. For example, when the focus is in the far field the transmit beam will tend to be more uniform and less variable with depth.

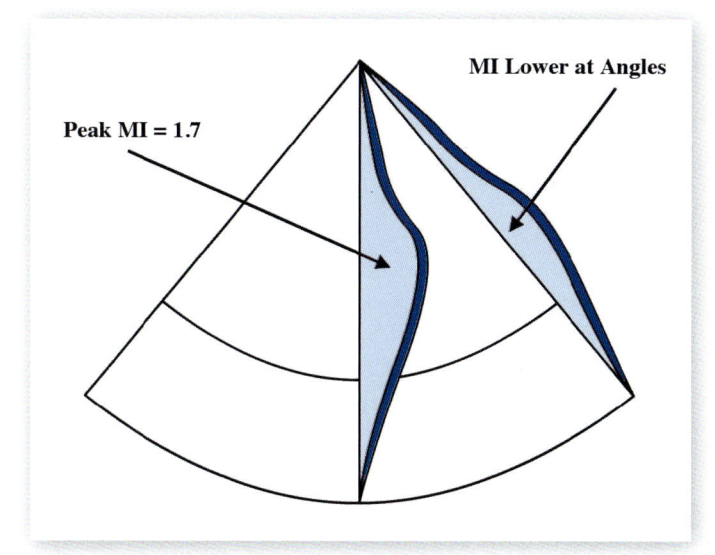

Fig. 23 Dependence of MI on steer angle

KEY CONCEPT

The mechanical index (MI) is the primary indicator of output power and is critical to determining microbubble response. The MI indicates the likelihood of cavitation. MI is directly related to the peak rarefactional pressure which tends to be highest near the beam focus and also generally toward the center of an image when created with varying electronic steering (phasing).

10.3 Effect of MI on Microbubbles

2018 American Society of Echocardiography (ASE) Terminology for MI

In 2018, the ASE published recommendations that includes new terminology for ultrasound contrast agents. One of these recommendations includes referring to ultrasound contrast agents as Ultrasonic Enhancing Agents (UEA). There was also new ranges of mechanical indices defined to try to standardize the reference to the mechanical indices for contrast agents. The range of MIs less than 0.2 is referred to in the document as very low MI. The range between 0.2 and 0.3 is called low MI. The range between 0.3 and 0.5 is called medium MI and any MI above 0.5 is called high MI.

Linear Response for Extremely Low MIs

The mechanism for microbubble destruction is highly dependent on the MI as well as the properties of the contrast agent. For simplification purposes, it is possible to break up the realm of responses into different ranges of MIs. At extremely low MIs (typically < 0.1) there is essentially a "linear" response from the microbubbles. This means that during a transmit pulse the signal reflected from the microbubble looks similar to the excitation pulse. With extremely low MIs, the variations in radius of a microbubble are very small and the bubble grows the same amount as it shrinks, or it undergoes symmetric oscillation. Since the reradiated returning signal looks very much like the transmitted signal, the frequency response will be composed of primarily the fundamental frequencies. The linear response of contrast bubbles at extremely low MIs is demonstrated in *Figure 24*.

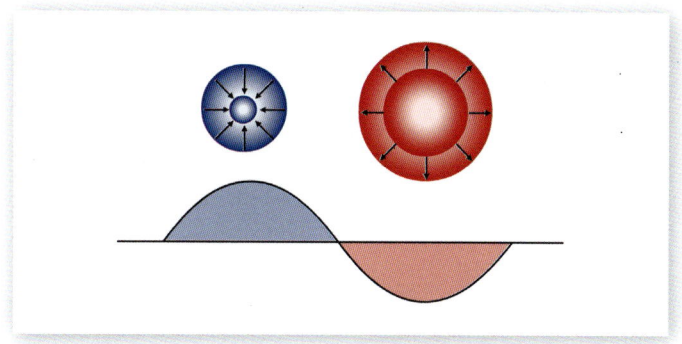

Fig. 24 Linear response to compression and rarefaction of wave: symmetric oscillation

Non-linear Response for Higher MIs

For slightly higher MIs (typically > 0.1) there are certain microbubbles within the population of a contrast agent that begin to respond in a "non-linear" fashion. If the transmit frequency is close to the resonant frequency of a particular size bubble, the bubble will undergo larger excursions. Because there are high internal pressures as the microbubble contracts, it is easier for the bubble to expand than it is for it to contract. As a result, the bubble radius increases more during the rarefactional phase of the wave than it contracts during the compressional phase. This non-symmetric oscillation implies that the reradiated response from these resonating bubbles is no longer symmetric and the reflected wave is distorted. The frequency content of the acoustic response is now comprised of higher order harmonics as well as the fundamental frequency. The strongest harmonic signal is usually located at twice the transmit frequency, referred to as the "second harmonic." It is this second harmonic signal that plays a very important part in helping to discriminate contrast signal from tissue signal at these very low MIs.

The distorted waveform from non-linear resonance is illustrated in *Figure 25*.

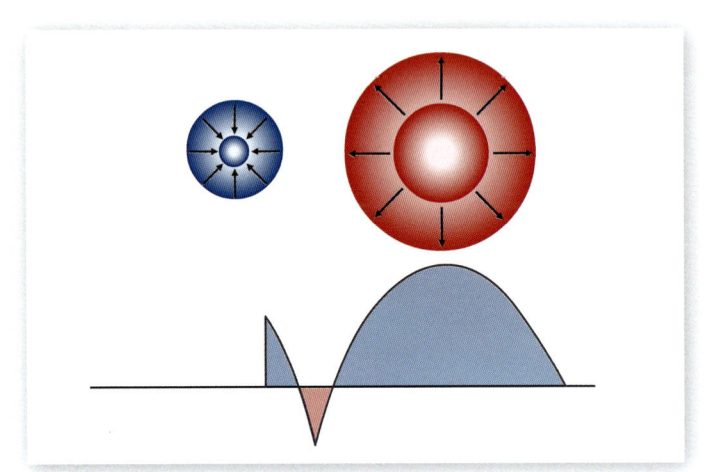

Fig. 25 **Non-linear response to compression and rarefaction of wave : non-symmetric oscillation**

The result of the non-linear resonance of the bubbles to insonification is a harmonic reflected wave as illustrated in *Figure 26*. In this example, a 2 MHz fundamental frequency results not only in a reflected signal at 2 MHz (linear response) but also a reflected signal at 4 MHz (the harmonic or non-linear response).

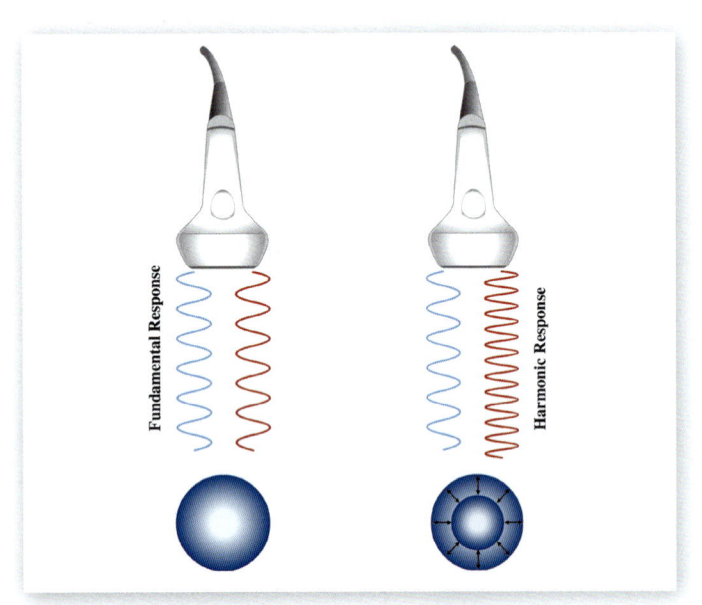

Fig. 26 **Comparison of fundamental response and harmonic response in non-linear resonance of bubbles**

The following frames of *Figure 27* were captured from stable non-linear oscillations of a lipid microbubble using a high speed camera. A video is included in the online image library so that time variance can be appreciated.

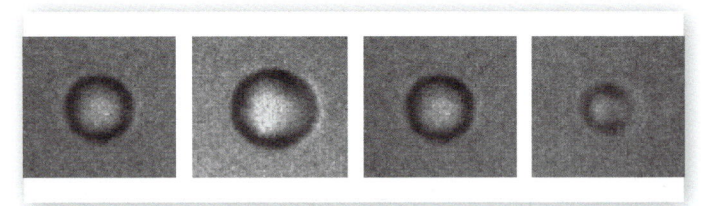

Fig. 27 **Non-linear bubble oscillation**

View ONLINE Animation and Image Library

10.4 Bubble Disruption

Even at these very low MIs, where bubbles can exhibit stable non-linear behavior, some microbubbles begin to be disrupted or "destroyed." Since a given contrast agent is comprised of a wide range of microbubbles with varying sizes and shell thicknesses, the disruption occurs over a continuum of MIs rather than at a certain threshold. A typical range where this may occur would be between an MI of 0.1 and 0.4. However, if the MI is kept below 0.2, most contrast agents will "survive" and continue to work effectively.

The composition of the shell of a particular contrast agent can lead to differences in the mechanism for disruption. Lipid encapsulated microbubbles tend to be more pliable than albumin-shelled microbubbles and thus tend to be more acoustically responsive at lower MIs. At these very low MIs, microbubble disruption can be caused by the forced outward diffusion of gas, often referred to as acoustically driven diffusion. The oscillation of the microbubble will cause some gas to be "squeezed" out with each transmit pulse. This effect has been seen more in lipid-encapsulated microbubbles than in albumin-shelled microbubbles. It has been proposed that this is due to the increased flexibility of the lipid shell coupled with the high concentration gradient of the gas. Larger excursions about the resting radius cause a larger pressure gradient to be created during maximal compression which leads to an increase in outward diffusion. At very low MIs even small changes in resting microbubble size can have a significant effect in terms of the acoustic response. For bubbles close to resonance size, there will be a significant decrease in response before the microbubble has completely dissolved.

With stiffer-shelled microbubbles, such as those that are albumin-based, there is often the creation of a shell defect caused by the ultrasound pulse. This is followed by subsequent diffusion through the "crack" and dissolution of the free gas into the surrounding blood. This dissolution can occur quickly if the gas is nitrogen based (e.g., 10 ms) or much slower if it contains a higher density, less diffusible gas such as a perfluorocarbon. The signal from a free perfluorocarbon bubble can last for hundreds of milliseconds before it dissolves. As in the forced-diffusion case, there will be significant decrease in received signal intensity even before the microbubble is completely dissolved.

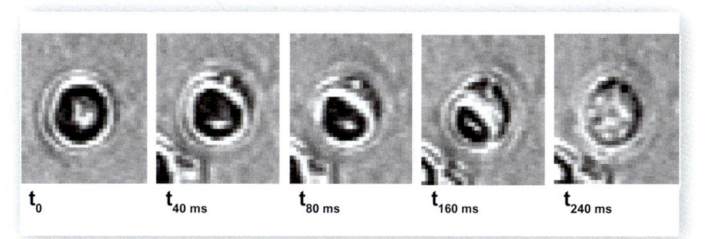

Fig. 28 **Shell defect produced by ultrasound pulse**

Figure 28 demonstrates diffusion of gas from the microbubble followed by dissolution. The first frame labeled "t_o" represents the bubble prior to excitation. The subsequent frames indicate the time transpired from excitation and make apparent the diffusion of gas from a shell defect produced by the ultrasound pulse.

View ONLINE Animation and Image Library

As the MI continues to increase single pulse destruction can occur. Under the appropriate conditions, large excursions of a microbubble radius can lead to fragmentation or can break up a single microbubble into multiple microbubbles. In this case, one ultrasound pulse can cause a microbubble to be "pinched off" or to be split into multiple smaller microbubbles that then dissolve very quickly. The decrease in intensity from the microbubble will happen almost instantaneously, over microseconds. This effect can happen to either nitrogen-based bubbles or perfluorocarbonbased-bubbles. High-speed cameras confirm that the conditions under which fragmentation will occur are when the maximum-to-minimum variation of microbubble radius during excitation from the ultrasound pulse approaches a factor of 10. Transmit waveform properties such as frequency and duration, as well as microbubble properties such as size and shell thickness, lead to a continuum of MIs over which fragmentation will occur.

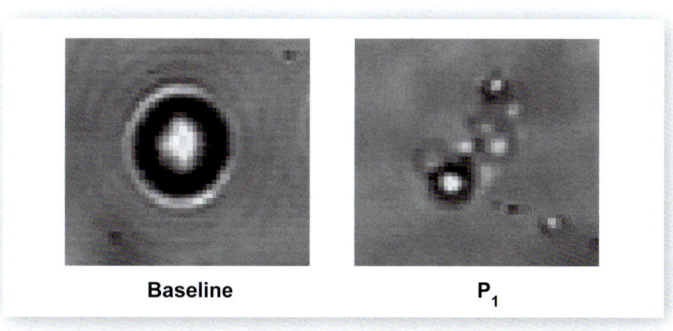

Fig. 29 **Rapid destruction of a lipid bubble from a pulse with a high MI of 1.6**

As illustrated in *Figure 30*, during fragmentation, strong, transient broadband signals are radiated from the microbubble with significant energy not only at the harmonics but also *between* the harmonics. This specific signature can be used to distinguish microbubbles from tissue. Compared to tissue signal that only appears at harmonics, microbubble destruction leads to broadband response. Improvement in contrast-to-tissue ratio can be obtained when filters are applied that remove the tissue harmonic signals. The lines in the figure demonstrate the frequency band at which RF filters could be applied to remove tissue signal.

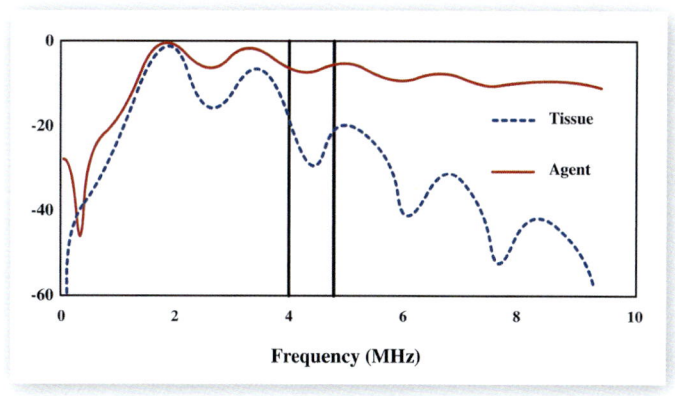

Fig. 30 **Broadband signals from bubble defragmentation and RF filtering**

KEY CONCEPT

At low MI, there is a relatively linear response of the microbubbles, reflecting primarily fundamental echoes. With an intermediate MI, the bubble expands more than it contracts, resulting in harmonic signal generation. Even at lower MIs, bubble disruption can occur.

Generally, below an MI of 0.2, most contrast agents will "survive" and continue to work effectively.

11. Transmit Focus

Besides the MI, there are other imaging parameters under control of the user that play an important role in the interaction of ultrasound and contrast. As mentioned earlier, moving the transmit focus changes the distribution of MI in the image. This is not only important along the direction of the transmit pulse (i.e., in the axial direction), but also in areas where the transmit beams overlap (laterally) enough to cause some microbubble disruption. For sector images, this area of "transmit beam" overlap often occurs very close to the face of the transducer. As an example, consider how the transmit beam changes when the focal depth is increased. To create a deeper focus, a wider beam is produced in the near field. Since a sector image "fans out" the result of laterally wider beams is greater beam overlap in the near field. This increase in overlap can cause an artifact in some patients such as decreased concentration of contrast agent resulting in a decreased acoustic response in the near field. Moving the focus closer to the transducer will cause a tightening of the beam and will generally reduce the overlap. The shallower focus will often entirely eliminate this artifact, of course at the expense of signal-to-noise in the far field. While equipment manufacturers strive to find a solution to this trade-off, it is important to be aware of the effect of transmit focus on contrast detection.

11.1 Bubble Concentration and Signal Amplitude

When the first commercial agents, Albunex and Levovist, became approved in various countries, it was hoped that the signal enhancement in standard fundamental imaging would allow visualization of microbubbles in the myocardium. Since higher concentrations of contrast leads to an increase in scattering and therefore increased received signal intensity, it seems plausible that adding more agent would allow visualization of microbubbles in the myocardium. However, there is in fact a limit to how much contrast can be successfully administered. Within a certain range of microbubble concentrations, scattered intensity is directly related to the local concentration of microbubbles. Above this linear range, interference from scattering from multiple microbubbles leads to a loss of linearity with contrast dose. This means a higher concentration will no longer give a proportional enhancement. At even higher dosages, bubble concentration is so high that an "acoustic shield" is created, actually decreasing the signal dramatically, particularly when "looking" through large pools of blood such as the left ventricular cavity (as illustrated in *Figure 31*). Essentially, so much ultrasound energy is scattered back that very little is available at deeper depths (shadowing artifact). Therefore, there is a need for contrast-specific imaging modalities to enhance bubble detection.

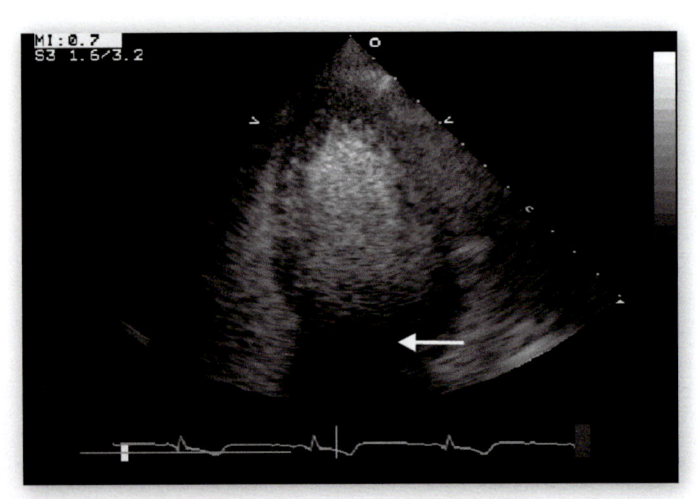

Fig. 31 **Attenuation from excessive contrast in LV**

View ONLINE Animation and Image Library

KEY CONCEPT

Harmonics is very dependent on the transmit focus. For sector images with contrast, the dependency is not just a function of the MI, but also the result of transmit beam overlap that occurs near the transducer face. With more beam overlap, there is greater annihilation of the contrast agent. Using a shallower focus reduces the problem of contrast reduction, but at the expense of significant penetration loss.

12. Contrast-Specific Detection Techniques

Over the last several years there has been an increase in the understanding of the interaction between ultrasound and ultrasound contrast agents. This knowledge has fueled equipment manufacturer's progress and has resulted in the invention and introduction of new contrast-specific detection techniques and image acquisition methods and tools. The goal of these newer modalities has been to improve the visualization of ultrasound contrast agents within tissue.

12.1 Contrast Harmonic Imaging

Figure 32 illustrates typical relative amplitudes of tissue versus contrast at a mid level MI (around a value of 0.5). The graph compares the received frequency components from tissue to the signal from a typical contrast agent in a large blood pool such as the left ventricular (LV) cavity. At the fundamental or transmitted frequency the tissue signal is greater than the signal from the contrast agent. Therefore, if the ultrasound system filters are set up to remove the harmonic signal and process the fundamental frequency, the tissue signal will be brighter than the contrast signal in the LV cavity. This was the result that motivated harmonic imaging techniques. By removing the fundamental frequencies and processing the harmonic frequencies, the contrast-to-tissue ratio is dramatically improved. However, in many cases this increase in contrast-to-tissue ratio is not enough to image microbubbles inside the tissue which is necessary to obtain information regarding tissue perfusion. The blood volume in tissue is often < 5% and therefore the concentration of microbubbles inside the tissue is a small fraction of that inside a large vessel or large cavity which is 100% blood. Due to the low concentration of microbubbles in the tissue, the signals from the tissue will often dominate the contrast signals, leading to difficulty in bubble detection and discrimination.

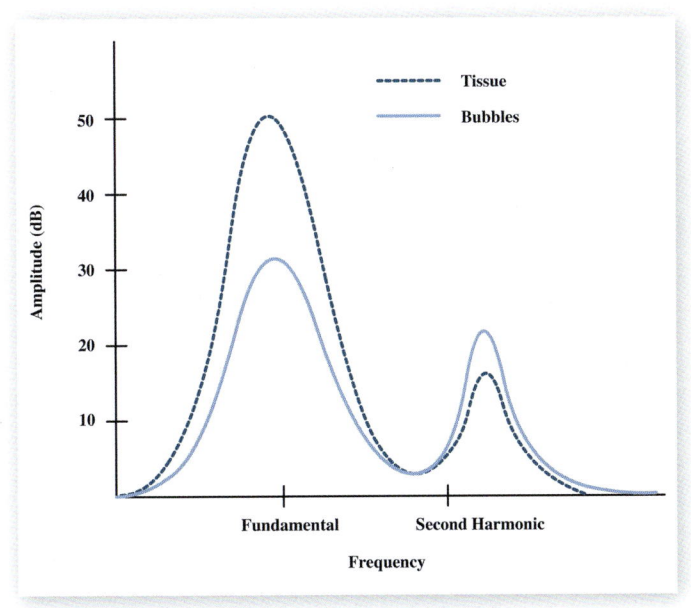

Fig. 32 **Relative amplitudes of tissue and bubbles**

As we have already discussed, higher MIs produce much larger tissue harmonic signals. Therefore, when using higher MIs with contrast agents, the increased tissue harmonics will further dominate the harmonics produced by the contrast agent in the tissue. Therefore there will be a reduction in contrast-to-tissue ratio at the high MIs. However, the signal returning from the microbubbles is still very large and well above the noise floor of the system. High MI imaging, although destructive in nature, offers the possibility for extremely sensitive contrast detection given a method or technique for suppressing the tissue harmonic signals. On the other hand, lowering the MI will have the benefit of preserving microbubbles and will also reduce the tissue harmonic signal resulting in better contrast-to-tissue ratios. However, lowering the MI will also result in lowering the amplitudes of the returning signals. Since the goal of any contrast-specific imaging technique is to reduce the tissue signal while maximizing the signal from the contrast agent, it is important that the techniques maintain an excellent "contrast-to-tissue" ratio *and* "contrast-to-noise floor" ratio. In other words, not only does the technique need to do a great job of suppressing tissue but it also has to have excellent signal-to-noise, such that the contrast signal is well above the noise floor of the system. Effective techniques have been developed to improve contrast-to-tissue ratio at high MIs. Also, extremely sensitive techniques have been developed to improve signal-to-noise at very low MIs.

12.2 High MI Techniques

Triggered Imaging

Imaging contrast agents with MIs that are high enough to cause disruption of the majority of microbubbles, to be effective, require much slower frame rates than with non-destructive MIs. The velocity in a typical capillary is on the order of 1 mm/s and each scan plane of ultrasound will destroy a slice of microbubbles of several millimeters in width. With standard frame rates, bubbles are subjected to continuous exposure and thus don't have the opportunity to flow back into the scan plane in time for the next image acquisition. It is therefore necessary to pause scanning and to wait several seconds for contrast agents to replenish the capillary bed after destruction. For cardiac imaging this can correspond to five or more cardiac cycles between images. For musculoskeletal imaging, this may be 20 seconds or more. To deal with this reality, equipment manufacturers have developed triggered or intermittent imaging techniques. With triggered imaging geared towards imaging myocardial perfusion, the transmission of ultrasound frames is synchronized to the ECG such that the frames are always acquired during the same phase of the cardiac cycle. The displayed image is no longer updated at a frame rate of 30 frames per second but instead potentially only one frame acquired every five cardiac cycles. Precisely because of the lack of a real-time display, it is crucial to maintain the same transducer position, making it possible to see the refilling of microbubbles into the exact same scan plane in which they were disrupted. If the acquisition were not synchronized to the cardiac cycle, cardiac rotation and translation would cause different scan planes to be visualized yielding inaccurate contrast replenishment information.

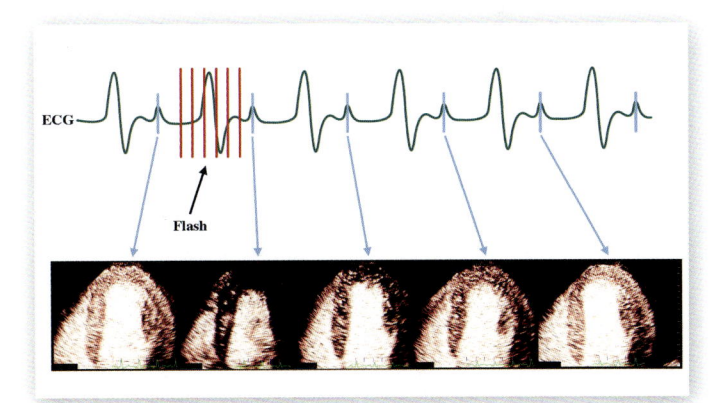

Fig. 33a **Flash replenishment sequence obtained in an ECG triggered mode demonstrating replenishment of microbubbles post-destruction; short blue lines indicate very low MI frames; large red lines indicate flash frames at higher MI; note initial very low MI image post-flash is black followed by subsequent increase in intensity indicating an increase in microbubble concentration**

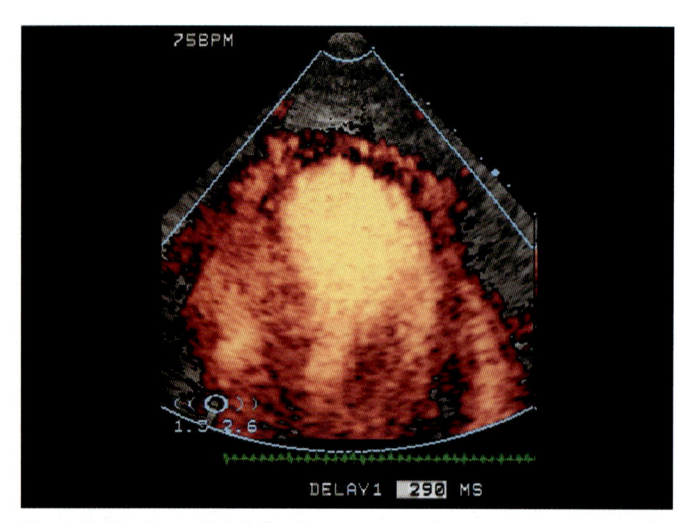

Fig. 33b Endocardial defect in apex using harmonic power Doppler

Harmonic Power Doppler

Contrast harmonic power Doppler using high MIs results in a contrast-to-tissue ratio improvement over standard high MI B-mode harmonic imaging. In order to understand the source of this improvement, it is important to first review how power Doppler works.

Power Doppler has been available for many years in vascular and abdominal imaging, where it is used primarily to look at slow flow in smaller vessels. Power Doppler (as discussed in Chapter 7) is similar to color Doppler since both are "multi-pulse" correlation techniques. Like color Doppler, power Doppler is created by transmitting a packet of acoustic lines (usually between 4 and 12) to form a single display line. The returning echoes from each acoustic line are "compared" or correlated to the echoes of the previous acoustic line: the 2nd pulse is compared to the 1st; the 3rd is compared to the 2nd and so on. Power Doppler is also similar to B-mode in that intensity is displayed rather than velocity. In short, power Doppler displays the intensity of particles that are moving or changing, whereas color Doppler displays the velocity of particles moving.

With imaging contrast agents there are potential sources of "change" other than movement. The pulse of the first acoustic line fragments some of the microbubbles, breaking them into several smaller bubbles. This change in bubble structure is detected as a change by power Doppler. Other mechanisms of destruction can occur as well, such as the shell can become damaged allowing the gas inside to "leak out." These free bubbles then dissolve over time, at a rate that depends on the density of the gas and its diffusivity in blood. Furthermore, it is also possible that the pulse doesn't destroy a particular microbubble but instead alters its size or shape—such as in the case of acoustically forced diffusion. Within a population of microbubbles, it is likely that more than one of these change mechanisms occurs. Throughout the length of the packet, each successive acoustic line detects changes from the previous acoustic line while simultaneously acting as the source of change in the microbubbles for the subsequent acoustic line. Free bubbles have vastly different resonance and backscatter characteristics than encapsulated microbubbles. The system detects these bubbles due to differences in backscattered intensity as well as changes in frequency or phase shifts between pulses. These changes produce a power Doppler signal. The greater the change observed between pulses, the larger the power Doppler signal.

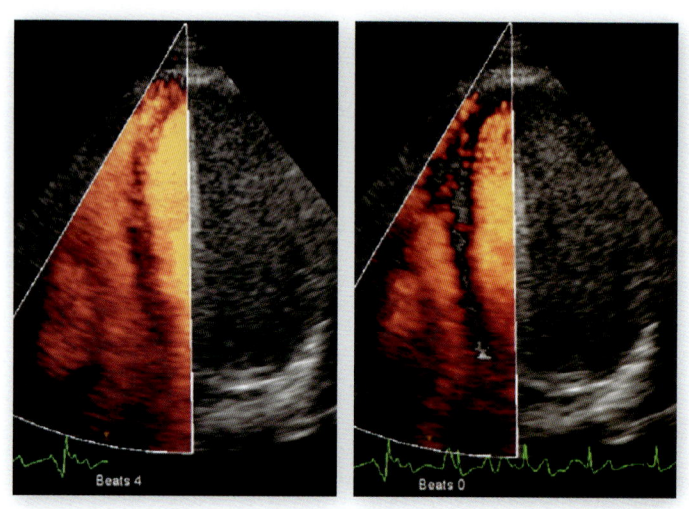

Fig. 34 Harmonic power Doppler showing bubble destruction through triggering

Benefits of Lower-than-Conventional Fundamental Frequencies

There are many more benefits of using transmit frequencies lower than frequencies conventionally used for diagnostic B-mode imaging (less than 2 MHz). Since many of the contrast detection techniques used receive frequencies that are much higher than the transmit frequency, such as with harmonic modes, even though very low transmit frequencies are used, resolution can still be maintained.

One such benefit to using lower transmit frequencies for harmonic contrast is the reduction in the undesirable tissue harmonic signal. The amount of harmonic distortion that builds up in a propagating wave depends on the distance traveled in wavelengths of the transmit frequency. Lower frequencies have longer wavelengths, and therefore for the same distance traveled in the patient, there will be less harmonic generation than for a higher frequency. In other words, higher frequencies tend to produce more harmonic distortion than lower frequencies. Therefore, using a lower transmit can increase contrast-to-tissue ratio.

Lower frequencies have additional benefits in terms of homogeneous contrast detection and disruption. For the same output power or

MI, lower frequencies are more effective at destruction of contrast agent. This increased destruction is primarily due to the longer intervals of compression and rarefaction with lower frequency waves. These longer periods give the bubble a longer duration of time to expand and contract, leading to increased destruction. Therefore, lower frequencies will destroy and image a larger portion of the microbubble population. Additionally, since attenuation in the body is strongly frequency dependent, a lower transmit frequency will also have reduced attenuation and a more homogeneous MI. Since the MI is extremely important in terms of microbubble detection, a more uniform MI results in a more uniform response from the contrast agent throughout the scan plane. The combination of these factors makes a lower transmit frequency attractive for detection of ultrasound contrast agents.

> **KEY CONCEPT**
>
> Bubble destructive, high MI techniques require a pause between image acquisitions to allow for contrast replenishment, resulting in "triggered" or intermittent imaging modes. For cardiac muscle this is generally five or more cardiac cycles. For skeletomuscular muscle, this may be 20 seconds or more.

13. Challenges at High MI: Triggered Acquisition

High MI techniques are extremely sensitive but have some drawbacks in terms of image acquisition. Since each high MI frame of ultrasound both detects the agent and destroys the agent, it is necessary to pause scanning for long periods of time. In fact, the time between frames can be greater than 10 seconds. This time period requires the sonographer to maintain the same scan plane for long durations without the availability of a reference image. Any motion by the patient or sonographer will make it extremely challenging to obtain high quality images. To facilitate acquisition of high MI imaging, manufacturers have provided a very low MI non-destructive monitoring mode or "scout" image in real time that allows the user to more easily maintain the scan plane in between the high MI triggered images.

14. Very Low MI Techniques

14.1 Fundamentals of Low MI Imaging

The creation of very low MI techniques allows contrast detection techniques to work at higher frame rates, much closer to normal imaging frame rates. Since at very low MIs there is very little microbubble disruption, it is no longer necessary to trigger image acquisition. Similar to high MI detection techniques, very low MI techniques need to be effective at suppressing tissue signal while maintaining contrast signal. However, the manner by which tissue suppression is accomplished is very different than with the high MI techniques. For many contrast agents there is a range of MIs where microbubbles behave non-linearly, and therefore have harmonic energy, yet remain stable such that they are not disrupted. The MIs in these cases are typically quite low (e.g., MI of 0.1) such that there is insignificant harmonic distortion from propagation in tissue. Therefore, the received signal from tissue will have very little harmonic content and is essentially linear. This means that multi-pulse techniques based on the assumption of linearity can be designed to subtract out the undesirable linear or fundamental tissue signal leaving only the non-linear signal from contrast. Such multi-pulse linear cancellation techniques include schemes that vary amplitude, phase, or a combination of both from pulse-to-pulse. The received echoes from these pulses are then combined in such a manner as to remove the linear signals. As was discussed in Chapter 6, these "averaging" based techniques have the advantage of improved signal-to-noise through coherent (constructive interference) of desired signals and incoherent (destructive interference) of noise and undesired signals.

Since there is no microbubble disruption with these techniques, a different approach has to be used to assess myocardial perfusion. With very low MI imaging, the use of high MI "flashes" or frames that have high enough power to destroy the agent are used. Contrast agent replenishment is then observed allowing for determination of microbubble velocity in different regions of the myocardium. This enables the clinician to assess information about relative blood flow in different myocardial segments.

In general, these techniques are easier to use than triggered high MI imaging modalities, not requiring "motionless" behavior on the part of the sonographer and patient over long periods of time. These techniques also have very good contrast-to-tissue ratios. However, even with the summing gain from signal coherence, due to the low transmit power, the resultant echoes received with these techniques typically come with a reduction in signal-to-noise compared to high MI (destructive) techniques.

View ONLINE Animation and Image Library

14.2 Pulse or Phase Inversion

Recall the use of pulse inversion to enhance tissue harmonic imaging. This technique can also be applied to contrast imaging. With pulse inversion, the scattered echoes from the non-linear microbubbles will no longer be mirror images of each other and will not subtract. This is the case when imaging a microbubble close to resonance size at very low MIs. Due to the ability of the microbubble to expand more than it can contract, the response during the compression portion of the pulse will not exactly cancel the response to the rarefaction portion of the pulse. When adding the mirror image responses from the linear scatterers, such as tissue signal at very low MIs, cancellation occurs. However, addition of the acoustic responses from microbubbles will not cancel due to this asymmetrical response. The non-linear components from the microbubble will actually add, improving signal-to-noise over harmonic imaging.

14.3 Amplitude or Power Modulation

Figure 35 shows how amplitude or power modulation works. This is another multi-pulse imaging technique geared at eliminating tissue signal at very low MIs and allowing the system to "see" only bubbles. In its simplest form, this technique works by transmitting two consecutive identically shaped pulses, one with half amplitude (e.g., MI of 0.05) and one with full amplitude (e.g., MI of 0.1). The lower amplitude pulse is received and amplified to match the projected signal expected from a higher power pulse. In this case, the lower amplitude received signal would be multiplied by a factor of two. Subsequent subtraction of the scaled response from the actual response obtained from the higher amplitude pulse leaves a result that consists of non-linear signals with the linear signals canceling.

As in the case of pulse inversion, at these low power levels, tissue responds relatively linearly to changes in transmit pressure and doesn't have sufficient harmonic energy. Therefore, doubling the MI will give the same shape waveform from tissue signal, undistorted and at twice the amplitude. However, microbubbles don't respond linearly to these very low MIs and therefore are not removed. A simplistic way to look at this technique is that the half amplitude pulse (typically MI < 0.1) generates a linear response from the microbubbles, whereas the full amplitude pulse (MI > 0.1) generates a non-linear response. In comparison with pulse inversion which generates signals at the even harmonics (2nd, 4th, etc.), changing the amplitude or power of the pulses gives a significant non-linear response from bubbles at the fundamental frequency as well as all other harmonics. Therefore, it is possible to image with amplitude modulation at the fundamental frequency. Due to the lower level of attenuation at the fundamental frequency, contrast energy at that frequency can provide an important improvement in signal-to-noise over harmonic-based techniques.

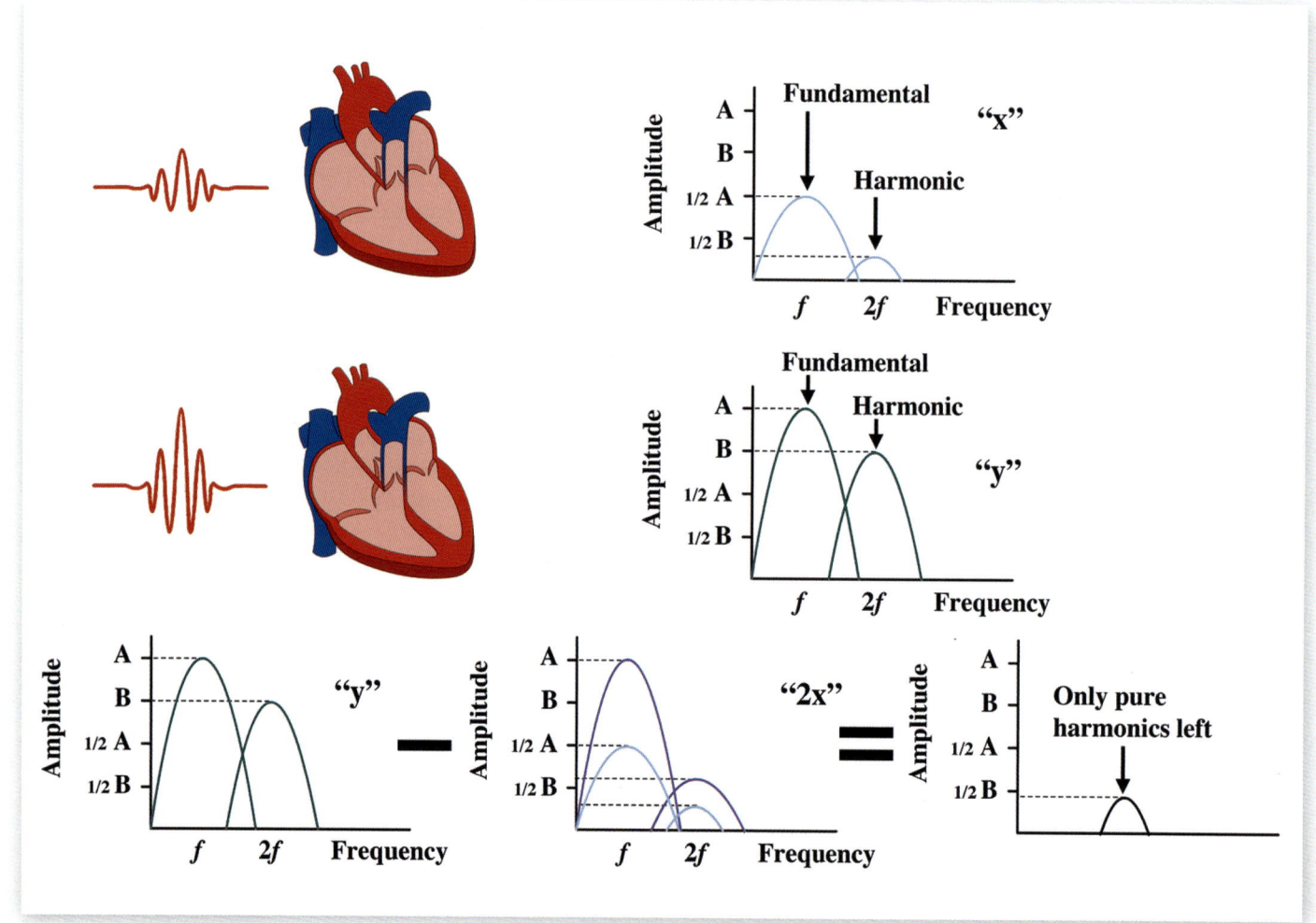

Fig. 35 **Power modulation**

14.4 Importance of Low Frequencies

Just as with high MI techniques, the use of low frequencies plays an important role in very low MI techniques. As previously discussed, low frequencies provide lower levels of tissue distortion and a more homogeneous MI throughout the scan plane. These advantages apply to very low MI techniques as well.

At high MIs, lower frequencies destroy (and therefore detect) a larger portion of the contrast agent population. Although greater "destruction" with lower transmit frequencies does not necessarily occur with non-destructive very low MI techniques, there is still a benefit to using lower than conventional frequencies with very low MIs. Larger bubbles have lower resonant frequencies. Therefore, lower frequencies will resonate larger microbubbles, producing higher amplitude signals. Also, at very low MIs, there is a significant response from bubbles whose resonance frequency is at integer multiples of the transmit frequency. For example, a 1 MHz transmit will get a strong non-linear response from microbubbles that resonate close to 1 MHz, 2 MHz, 3 MHz, etc. Therefore when imaging non-destructively, low frequencies will potentially induce a greater acoustic response from a larger portion of the contrast agent population than will higher frequencies. The combination of these factors, as well as a reduction in attenuation, leads to enhanced non-destructive detection at low transmit frequencies.

> **KEY CONCEPT**
>
> Low MI techniques do not require long periods of time between image acquisition since there is significantly less bubble destruction. However, low MI techniques tend to have lower signal-to-noise than high MI techniques.

15. Challenges at Very Low MIs: Signal-to-Noise

As mentioned above, the major drawback for very low MI imaging modalities is the reduction in signal-to-noise relative to high MI approaches. For very low MI techniques, the amplitude of the transmitted signals are up to 20 dB (10 times) smaller than those for high MI techniques. Additionally, the amount of energy scattered from a free or destroyed microbubble is much higher than that of an encapsulated microbubble undergoing stable resonance. Therefore, as discussed throughout, increasing the MI improves microbubble response but increases tissue non-linearity faster. Also, as was discussed earlier, an increase in MI increases microbubble destruction and may actually *decrease* the contrast signal due to the lower contrast bubble concentration. The range over which contrast-to-tissue ratio and signal-to-noise ratio are optimized is both patient and contrast agent dependent. To optimize real-time very low MI techniques, it is usually necessary to maintain MIs in the 0.1-0.2 range. In order to increase signal-to-noise of very low MI techniques, the best method is to increase the dosage or infusion rate of the contrast agent. Therefore, very low MI techniques may use considerably more contrast agent to get sufficient signal-to-noise. The extra contrast used is usually offset by the increase in speed of the acquisition that very low MI real time offers. Although optimizing the contrast concentration is crucial with all techniques, it can be more challenging with very low MI techniques.

15.1 Coded Pulses (Coded Excitation)

Recent research and development has focused on further improvement of the signal-to-noise ratio (SNR) for very low MI contrast detection techniques. Lower dosages of contrast leads to lower levels of attenuation and therefore better visualization of deeper structures. To improve SNR, either the system noise level can be decreased or the contrast signal energy level can be increased. The noise level is mainly fixed by system front-end electronics. Furthermore, increasing the contrast signal energy level by raising the transmission amplitude (transmit power or MI) is limited by bubble destruction. Therefore, the two most obvious approaches cannot be employed. However, another way in which the contrast signal can be enhanced, increasing SNR, is to use a longer transmitting pulse (spatial pulse length). By using a longer spatial pulse length without increasing the amplitude, there is more energy in the transmit pulse, increasing the signal-to-noise without a significant increase in bubble cavitation (recall that cavitation is directly related to the square root of the peak rarefactional power). However, using a longer spatial pulse length results in a degradation of axial resolution causing inadequate image resolution. So the question is, "How can longer pulses be used to achieve better SNR without degrading the axial resolution?"

Recently, equipment manufacturers have had success improving SNR noise for very low MI techniques by using coded pulses. Coded pulses involve transmitting very long pulses encoded in a certain pattern and then decoding the received echoes. This is done by trying to "look" for, or match, the original transmitted signal with the returning signal. As a result of "matching" the coded transmitted and receive signals, it is as if multiple shorter pulses were used instead of one long pulse (see *Figure 36*).

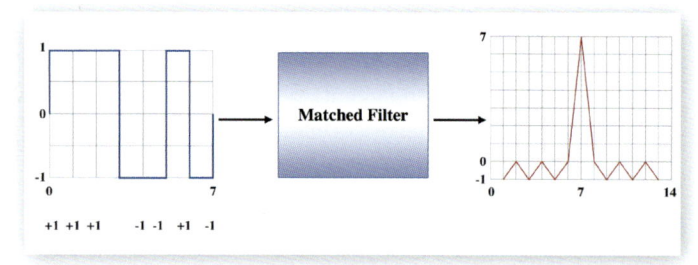

Fig. 36 **Method for coded excitation**

As discussed in Chapter 6, by adding together multiple signals, there is an improvement in SNR by the square root of the number of signals being averaged. Additionally, since a longer pulse results in degraded resolution, the matched "shorter" pulses result in adequate resolution. One example of coding that has proven to be effective is frequency coding, where the frequency changes during the transmit pulse, referred to as CHIRP frequencies (see *Figure 37*). CHIRPs have the additional benefit of resonating a wider population of bubbles, further improving SNR.

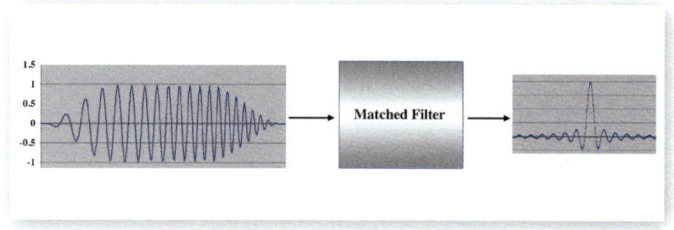

Fig. 37 **Method for CHIRP excitation**

KEY CONCEPT

The issues of poor signal-to-noise associated with low MI techniques are reduced by using coded excitation, including coded pulses and chirp transforms.

15.2 New Indication for the US: Liver Contrast

In April 2016, the FDA approved Lumason for the characterization of focal liver lesions in both adults and children, making it the first non-cardiac indication for ultrasound contrast agents in the United States. Use of ultrasound contrast agents in the liver is not new to the rest of the world, as it has been used extensively in Europe and Asia for well over a decade. Intravenous bolus injections of ultrasound contrast agents take advantage of the dual blood supply of the liver in determining the type of liver lesion. The liver receives about 25-30% of its blood flow from the hepatic artery and 70-75% of its blood flow from the portal vein. The portal vein carries venous blood from the gastrointestinal tract, gallbladder, pancreas, and spleen to be detoxified by the liver. By examining the relative arrival and washout times of these two blood supplies, it is possible to characterize different types of liver lesions.

A bolus injection of an ultrasound contrast agent generally has three phases in the liver:
1. Arterial phase
2. Portal venous phase
3. Late phase

The arterial phase starts about 10 seconds after an IV injection with a typical duration of 10-15 seconds. The portal venous phase typically starts about 30 seconds after the IV injection of contrast, since the bolus has to first travel through the gastrointestinal tract before entering the portal vein, and can last up to 2 minutes. The late phase starts after the portal venous phase and lasts until the microbubbles are cleared from the liver parenchyma, which can be 5 minutes or longer for Lumason.

The arterial phase can be used to determine the vascularity patterns of a lesion to help discriminate between malignant and benign. A malignant lesion, such as an HCC (hepatocellular carcinoma), demonstrates enhanced vascularity during the arterial phase. The portal venous phase and the late phase provide information about the patterns of wash out of the liver lesions relative to the rest of the normal liver parenchyma. For example, enhancement of the lesion sustained in the portal venous and late phase compared to the rest of the liver is characteristic of a benign lesion such as a hemangioma or a focal nodular hyperplasia (FNH). This is in contrast to most malignant lesions, which are hypo-intense compared to the rest of the liver during the portal and late phases.

The enhancement patterns of liver lesions in the three phases are the key to characterization and have been published as guidelines by organizations such as European Federation of Societies for Ultrasound and Medicine in Biology (EFSUMB).

One feature that has proven to be extremely useful in liver scanning is Contrast Side-by-Side. This feature displays both a contrast image and tissue image simultaneously by interleaving a contrast specific image, such as power modulation, with a fundamental image. Several imaging parameters can be optimized independently to improve the visualization of each side. For example, the mechanical index on the tissue image must be kept very low to minimize destruction of the contrast agent while the MI on the contrast side should be set for optimal contrast performance. One of the advantages of this technique is that it allows the user to visualize some tissue landmarks and help them to maintain the image plane during acquisition. A second advantage is Contrast Side-by-Side aids in the detection of lesions in B-mode and allows the user to more easily locate them on the contrast image.

The following figures demonstrate the comparison between contrast images (left) and fundamental, non-contrast images (right) for various pathologies.

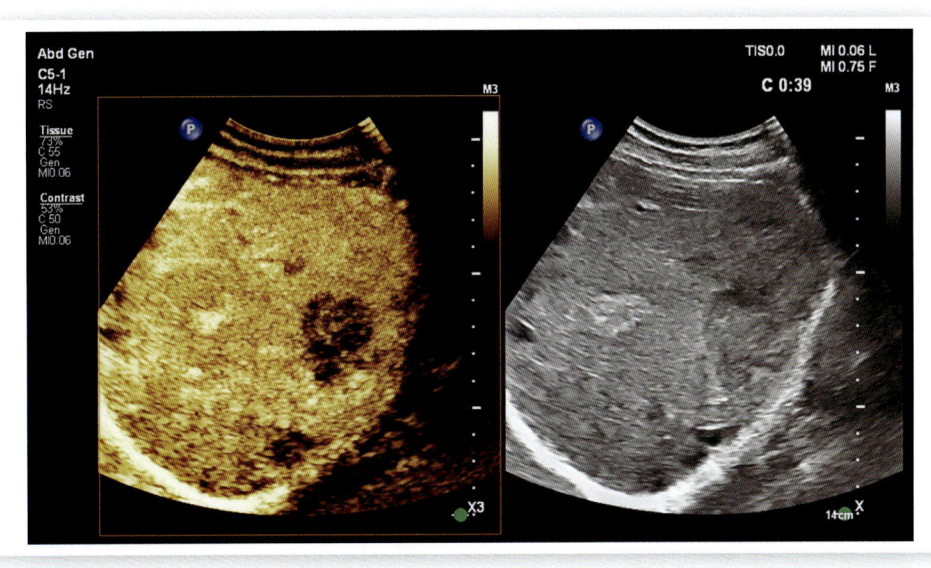

Fig. 38 Contrast side-by-side display demonstrating the contrast wash in pattern of a metastasis in the liver; the image on the left is the contrast image and the image on the right is the fundamental, non-contrast image

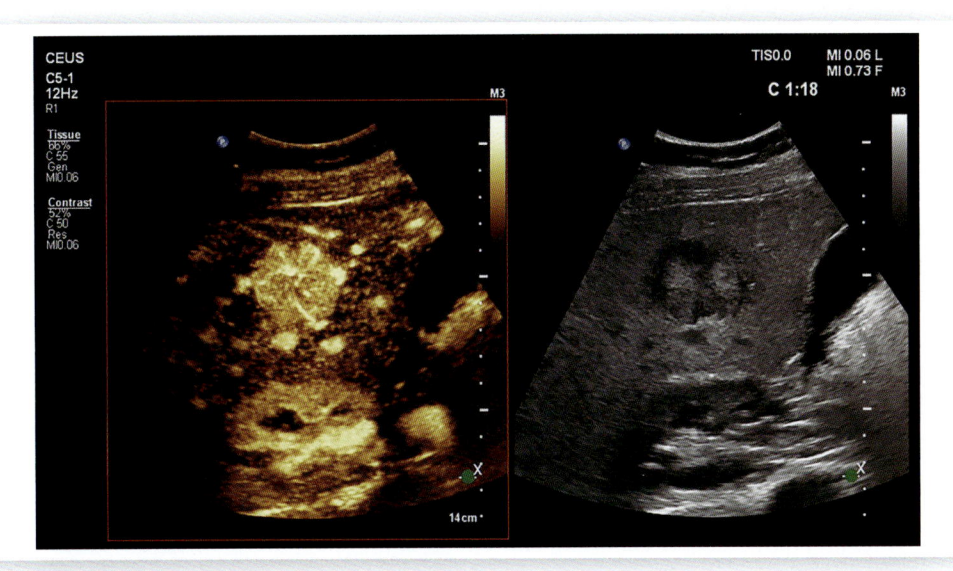

Fig. 39 Side-by-side image demonstrating a benign focal nodular hyperplasia (FNH) portal inflow pattern using contrast

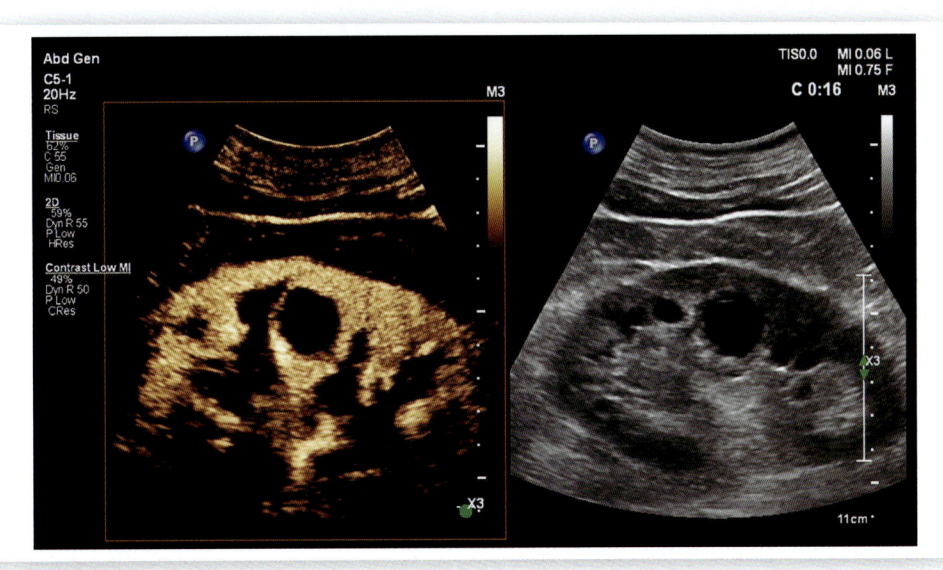

Fig. 40 Side-by-side image of a kidney lesion as seen using contrast, demonstrating no blood flow to the small septation in the lesion

16. The Future

16.1 3D Contrast

Over the last several years 2D array transducer technology has been developed that enables live 3D imaging (as discussed in Chapter 5). With this technology, transducers can be diced into a matrix containing approximately 3000 or more acoustic elements. Having a grid or matrix of transducer elements allows three-dimensional (3D) images to be acquired. That is, the matrix of transducer elements (elements in two dimensions) makes possible the steering and electronic focusing of ultrasound energy in any arbitrary direction so that full volumes can be interrogated. Standard phased array transducers allow steering and electronic focusing in only one plane (the lateral direction). In earlier iterations of 2D arrays, only some elements could be used at one time, referred to as a "sparse matrix design." Being able to use only a small fraction of the elements in the array, sparse matrix 2D arrays suffered from significant grating lobe artifacts as well as low acoustic output power. With newer matrix arrays, electronics inside the matrix transducer perform micro-beamforming, utilizing all of the available elements. The micro-beamformer contains circuitry which controls the signals applied to groups of elements ("patches") for the array transducer and does some processing of the echo signals received by the elements of each group. Micro-beamforming in the probe advantageously reduces the number of conductors in the cable between the probe and the ultrasound system mainframe.

This new 3D technology has many clinical possibilities; one of the most exciting is the combination with contrast. The ability to quickly acquire a full 3D volume, or two or more planes simultaneously, has great potential for quicker and more accurate stress echoes as well as for better LV volume calculations with echocardiography. Early results with harmonic imaging and contrast have shown that just like in 2D imaging, contrast can help immensely in the discrimination of a border in 3D.

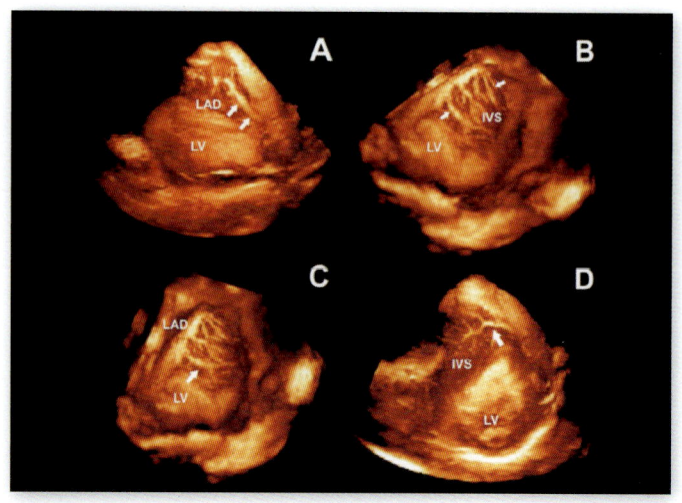

Fig. 41 **Visualization of coronary arteries by contrast-enhanced real-time 3D echocardiography** (*Reprinted with permission of Blackwell publishing*)

Figure 42 is an example of 3D left ventricular opacification image using a power modulation technique. Manufacturers have features to allow high quality 2D slices to be generated from the 3D dataset. In this case, acquired from the apical window, three long-axis images are displayed as well as nine short-axis images.

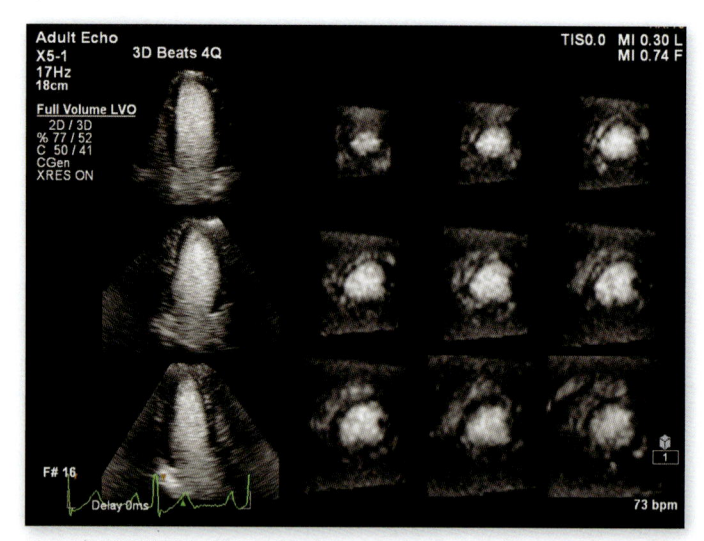

Fig. 42 **3D LVO with multiplanar reconstruction acquired with power modulation**

Most recently, researchers have begun to look at perfusion imaging with real-time 3D. 3D technology can potentially lead to shorter studies while improving diagnostic accuracy through acquisition of the entire LV myocardium rather than select planes as is done today. Not everything is known and understood in terms of the best way to use Matrix transducers and 3D technology for perfusion imaging. There are questions to be answered regarding the replenishment kinetics when going from a plane of bubble destruction to a volume of bubble destruction. It is likely that use of this technology will allow more robust detection of small defects that 2D imaging may miss. Although there are challenges to overcome in maintaining a high enough frame rate with multi-pulse techniques and large volumes, the ultimate goal of measurement of myocardial mass at risk is closer to becoming a reality.

View ONLINE Animation and Image Library

In oncology, 3D with contrast holds promise for more accurate serial assessment of tumor volume and vascularity. This can potentially be used to assess early response to chemotherapy and radiation treatments. Also, use of 3D and contrast can help in minimally invasive procedures such as radiofrequency ablation. Radiofrequency ablation, sometimes referred to as RFA, is a treatment for cancer. It is an image-guided technique that heats and destroys cancer cells.

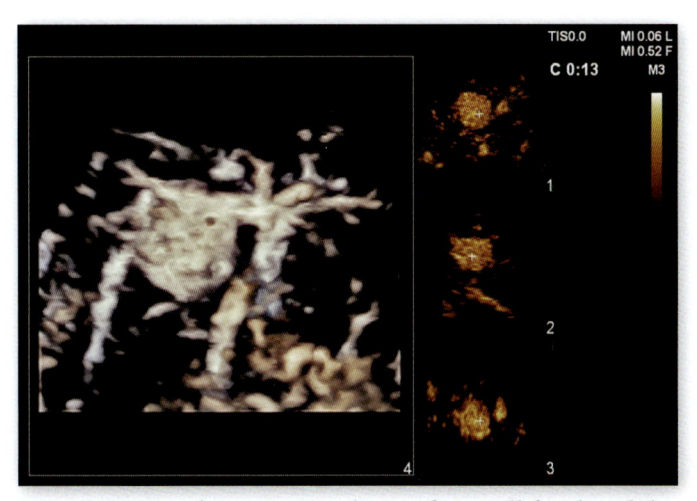

Fig. 43 **Image of a contrast volume of a small focal nodular hyperplasia (FNH) using the X6-1 matrix transducer; images on the right are multi-planar reconstructions generated from the 3D volume**

Another useful mode enabled by matrix technology is biplane or xPlane imaging. In this case, two 2D imaging planes are acquired simultaneously in a side-by-side format. The user has the ability to tilt or rotate one of the imaging planes relative to the other in order to obtain a cross-sectional cut of the lesion during a contrast exam.

Figure 44 shows an example of xPlane contrast with the X6-1 transducer.

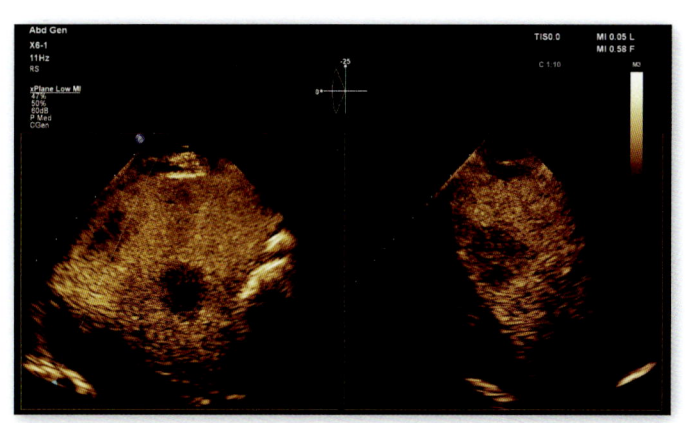

Fig. 44 **xPlane imaging technology allows 2 planes to be visualized simultaneously; image on the right is orthogonal to the image on the left and tilted 25° through the lesion**

View ONLINE Animation and Image Library

16.2 Development of Fast Frame Rates for 3D Contrast

Maintaining a clinically useful frame rate has been a technical challenge in the development of 3D imaging and this has been especially true of contrast imaging. Since contrast detection techniques such as power modulation and pulse inversion require multiple transmit pulses per image line, the achievable frame rates are between ½ and ¼ the typical frame rates. Since the number of transmit beams that can be used to cover a volume determines the achievable volume rate, the only way to increase the frame rate is to use fewer transmit beams. This can be done simply by decreasing the transmit line density but this alone will ultimately lead to reduced spatial resolution. In order to maintain adequate image quality in 3D contrast, the transmit spacing cannot be further decreased. This has led to a further reliance on the use of multi-beat triggered acquisitions in order to maintain volume rates.

Recently, the development of faster frame rates using wider transmit beams, either plane waves or divergent beams, in combination with very high parallel receive beamforming has allowed for an increase in volume rates, without significant degradation in image quality. The beams are retrospectively focused from multiple transmit beams to improve the lateral resolution that is lost by using a wider transmit beam. These techniques will allow an improvement in volume rate and combining these techniques with power modulation and pulse inversion will be critical to achieving the goals of real-time 3D contrast imaging.

View ONLINE Animation and Image Library

16.3 Direction

Ultrasound contrast agents have now been approved for the first non-cardiac indications by the FDA. Investigations have demonstrated that the use of contrast ultrasound for detecting and characterizing liver masses is at least equal to, if not better than, contrast enhanced CT.

Excellent contrast agents are FDA approved for left ventricular opacification (LVO) and are available in the United States. Equipment manufacturers provide excellent contrast detection techniques with high sensitivity and contrast-to-tissue ratio. Techniques operating at very low MIs offer real-time acquisition capabilities and lead to faster examinations while high MI techniques offer the highest sensitivity. All techniques remain viable alternatives for imaging contrast agents.

In 2007, the FDA had issued a black box warning with regard to the use of contrast agents after reports of rare (incidence rate 1:10,000) anaphylactic reactions, including several deaths in high-risk patients within 30 minutes of contrast agent administration. The jury is still out on whether these deaths were due to pseudo-complications or due to a reaction to the contrast agent. The labels for Definity and Optison were modified in October 2007 to contain several contraindications including use in patients with pulmonary hypertension, worsening or unstable heart failure, and recent or suspected acute myocardial infarction. Following a detailed review of the risk-benefits the FDA has subsequently removed these contraindications but the black box warning remains. In the coming years, based on the demographics of an aging global population and the potentially imminent epidemic of cardiovascular disease and diabetes on a worldwide scale, as well as the high incidence of liver disease in many parts of the world, there will be a growing need for cost-effective diagnosis. Contrast ultrasound is likely to play an increasingly important role.

16.4 Molecular Imaging Field

Ultrasound contrast agents are also playing a key role in the developing molecular imaging field. Research is ongoing to detect disease states earlier by identifying and targeting molecular signatures that occur in the early stages of disease. Contrast agents can then be modified by the addition of ligands to bind to or target those molecular signatures and imaging techniques such as those described previously can be used to image these disease states. The hope is that early identification of disease as well as the optimization of treatment strategies will lead to improvement in patient outcome. Angiogenesis (the growth of new blood vessels), and inflammation both play an important role in many disease states such as vulnerable plaques and cancer, and are therefore the focus of much of this work.

16.5 Sonothrombolysis and Other Therapeutic Applications

In recent years, ultrasound has moved beyond diagnostics and is now being used in therapeutic applications, such as in high intensity focused ultrasound (HIFU) now more commonly referred to simply as "focused ultrasound" (see Chapter 18). With focused ultrasound, output levels exceed the FDA diagnostic limits in order to aid in the ablation of cancerous tissue. When combined with contrast microbubbles, the power levels at which ultrasound can generate these effects has been shown to be dramatically reduced, primarily due to the shear stresses caused by the cavitation of microbubbles in an ultrasound field. In fact, therapeutic effects have been demonstrated within the diagnostic ranges of ultrasound output powers. This has caused an increase in research in applications where contrast and ultrasound are combined in a "theranostic" type approach, where the procedures consist of both therapeutic treatment and diagnostics. Areas of active research include enhancing drug delivery and in the lysis of thrombus.

Sonothrombolysis, by which microbubbles, combined with the use of ultrasound, have been shown to aid in the lysis of clots, has been an area of research for some time. This technique has recently been used in a study published in the Journal of American College of Cardiology in June 2019. In this study, 100 patients suffering from ST elevation myocardial infarction (STEMI) were randomized into two categories; one with the standard of care of percutaneous coronary intervention (PCI) and the other with PCI plus the addition of contrast and ultrasound. Sonothrombolysis was performed prior to the PCI upon arrival to the emergency department as well as post-PCI. The procedure consisted of imaging of three apical views (apical 4-chamber, apical 2-chamber and apical 3-chamber) with a continuous infusion of contrast agent. The physicians waited until the appearance of the microbubbles in the myocardium and then used flash to destroy the contrast agent. The therapeutic effect has been attributed to the shear stresses of the cavitating microbubbles causing dissolution of the thrombus.

It has also been demonstrated in animal studies that the high mechanical indices of the flash pulses in the presence of microbubbles can cause the endothelial and red blood cells to release ATP, which will lead to microvascular vasodilation, and a corresponding improvement of myocardial blood flow. The patients receiving the treatment not only had a higher recanalization rate where the coronaries are opened prior to the PCI procedure than the group of PCI only, but also had smaller infarct sizes and improved ejection fractions. Further studies are being planned, attempting to bring the treatment into the ambulance, in patient populations with non-ST segment elevation myocardial infarction (NSTEMI), as well as to underserved areas that do not have access to PCI.

Another area of research in the therapeutic use of contrast agents is the method by which to aid in the delivery of drugs though sonoporation. Similar to the mechanical shear stresses in sonothrombolysis helping to dissolve thrombi, sonoporation is the temporary improvement in cell membrane permeability due to transient openings allowing larger molecules to more easily pass through. Treatment of cancers with chemotherapeutic drugs can possibly be improved with sonoporation. Ultrasound energy can be targeted to different areas of the body, and then drug delivery can be improved selectively in those areas. Research is also ongoing to target a contrast agent to a disease state, making it possible to optimize drug delivery or to research gene delivery. Higher dosages of a drug may be possible while minimizing systemic side effects by targeting the actual delivery sites and delivering the drug through ultrasound activated microbubble destruction. Delivery of genes is also an area of ongoing research including the promotion of angiogenesis by delivery of genetic growth factors.

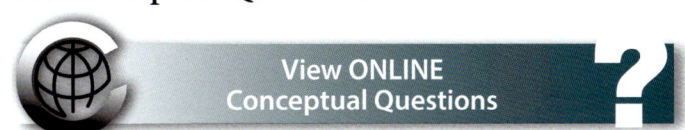

> **COMMON MISCONCEPTION: Contrast and Harmonics**
>
> **MISCONCEPTION:** *The first harmonic is the same as the first overtone.*
>
> Confusion sometimes occurs with terminology relating to harmonics. The second harmonic is the frequency which is twice the fundamental (or transmit) frequency. The third harmonic is the frequency which is three times the fundamental frequency. The first overtone is the same as the second harmonic.
>
> Note: The terms harmonics and overtones are used commonly in music. The first overtone is the note that is an octave above the fundamental (or first harmonic), hence the term "overtone."

17. Conceptual Questions

View ONLINE Conceptual Questions

CHAPTER SUMMARY: Contrast and Harmonics

- Harmonic imaging currently implies that the received frequency is at the second harmonic frequency (twice the fundamental (transmit) frequency).

Harmonic Naming Conventions	
First Harmonic	Fundamental frequency or operating frequency
Second Harmonic	Frequency that is twice the fundamental frequency
Third Harmonic	Frequency that is three times the fundamental frequency

- Harmonic imaging currently processes harmonic energy produced through two different mechanisms: contrast agents and non-linear tissue propagation.
- The premise for using tissue produced harmonic imaging is basically a trade-off between conventional imaging at the fundamental frequency and conventional imaging at the harmonic frequency. With harmonic imaging, the fundamental frequency produces good penetration and the harmonic response generates relatively good resolution.
- One of the greatest benefits of harmonic imaging is the reduction of "clutter" related artifacts in the near field.

- Harmonic energy is weaker than the energy at the fundamental frequency, so the use of harmonics is not always optimal when significant penetration is required.
- The strongest harmonic response is generated in the midfield.
- The harmonic response is non-linear relative to the intensity of sound (MI). Higher MIs produce much more harmonic energy than lower MIs.
- In order to perform harmonic imaging, transducers must have enough bandwidth to support transmitting at the lower frequency and receiving at the higher frequency.
- In order to reduce the overlap between the transmit and receive bandwidth, conventional harmonic imaging usually narrowbands the transmit pulse by increasing the pulse duration (recall that bandwidth and pulse duration are inversely related). Increasing the pulse duration also results in an increase in the spatial pulse length, reducing axial resolution.
- New approaches to relieve the need to narrowband the transmit pulse have resulted in powerful techniques such as power modulated harmonic imaging, pulse inversion harmonic imaging, and coded harmonics.

- The primary advantage of coded harmonics relative to conventional harmonic imaging is improved signal-to-noise (SNR) without significant degradation in axial resolution.

- Contrast imaging can be performed at the fundamental frequency (conventional contrast imaging) or at the harmonic frequency (harmonic contrast imaging).

- The harmonic response from a microbubble is the result of non-linear expansion and contraction of a bubble.

- In the presence of high intensity fields (high MIs) the bubble can expand much more than it can contract.

- The contrast agent is designed to significantly increase the reflectivity of the blood by a dramatic increase in the acoustic impedance mismatch (highly compressible and low density gas in contrast to much higher density and much less compressible red blood cells and plasma).

- High MI techniques can result in a rapid destruction of bubbles as well as difficulty distinguishing bubble harmonic response from tissue harmonic response.

- As a result of the trade-offs with high MI techniques, many very low MI techniques have been created such as pulse inversion and power modulation (the same fundamental approaches as used for harmonic imaging to improve signal-to-noise).

- The use of 3D and contrast holds promise for both cardiac and non-cardiac applications. Cardiac applications include improved endocardial definition as well as myocardial perfusion. Radiology applications include assessment of tumor volume and vascularity.

- The future of contrast and harmonics is very promising, including more therapeutic and treatment-related ultrasound.

ONLINE EXTRAS

For additional support material and to view your completion progress, visit:

www.pegasuslectures.com/6thEdExtras

Extras by Chapter include:
- Animations
- Videos
- Additional Images
- Clarifying Clips
- Supplemental Exercises
- Conceptual Questions

See page x of Preface for access instructions

Quality Assurance

Chapter 11

WHY DO WE STUDY THIS?

▷ Quality assurance (QA) helps ensure patient care is as accurate and effective as possible through lab accreditation, personal certification, equipment maintenance, equipment testing, statistical validation, and more.

▷ QA programs establish and/or maintain processes and procedures to verify equipment used on patients is functioning correctly and personnel can optimally perform patient tests.

▷ Statistical validation mathematically compares patient results with a reference "gold standard" exam to ensure quality studies and interpretations.

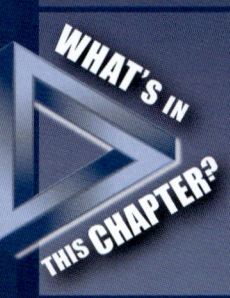

WHAT'S IN THIS CHAPTER?

LEVEL 2

BOARD LEVEL
Begins by briefly discussing laboratory accreditation and personal certification followed by a discussion regarding transducer care, equipment testing, and the various phantoms and test objects which exist to facilitate this testing. The chapter concludes with statistical validation, including the meaning and significance of parameters such as sensitivity, specificity, negative/positive predictive values, and overall accuracy.

LEARNING OBJECTIVES

▷ Describe the necessity for a quality program

▷ Explain the basic role of various phantoms in equipment testing

▷ Recognize the procedures used for testing various resolutions including lateral, axial, and contrast

▷ Identify the underlying principle of statistical validation

▷ Apply the calculations for sensitivity, specificity, negative predictive and positive predictive values, and the overall accuracy

▷ Define the true meaning and potential over-interpretation of statistical calculations relative to the quality of the "gold standard"

Chapter 11
Quality Assurance

Introduction

There are many facets of quality assurance. Quality assurance can include everything from routine maintenance of the ultrasound and laboratory equipment through record keeping, patient tracking, cleaning of transducers, and making certain that the correct exams are performed on the correct patient. Quality assurance can also include statistical processing to compare a testing procedure against a "gold standard" testing procedure, peer review, QA meetings, and how to ascertain the overall accuracy of the laboratory studies. Intricately tied to quality assurance is the process of lab accreditation and individual certification.

We will not go into extensive detail regarding patient tracking and appropriate clinical testing, however we will briefly discuss the role and importance of lab accreditation and a good quality assurance program. In general, good practice is dictated by lab protocols. Your lab should develop consistent, methodical protocols to minimize the number and severity of oversights and errors. The more rigorous the process and process controls prescribed by the protocol, the less likely there will be major errors within your lab.

The two aspects of quality control we will discuss in greater detail are related to statistical indices and equipment performance testing. As you will see, both of these topics present challenges to providing quality in day-to-day ultrasound.

1. Laboratory Accreditation

1.1 Accreditation Providers
The laboratory accreditation process is designed to recognize laboratories that provide quality services. An accredited laboratory requires that their interpreting physicians and practicing sonographers be adequately trained and experienced to perform and/or interpret sonography. Currently, there are several organizations that provide ultrasound lab accreditation including the Intersocietal Accreditation Commission (IAC), the American College of Radiology (ACR), and the American Institute of Ultrasound in Medicine (AIUM).

1.2 Commitment to Quality
Beyond the financial reasons, lab accreditation demonstrates a full commitment to quality patient care and self-assessment. The accreditation process requires the lab to weigh every aspect of daily operation and its impact on the quality of health care provided to patients. While validating their quality assurance programs for the accreditation process, labs often identify and correct potential problems before they occur, thereby saving time and money and reducing stress. Once a lab has gained accreditation, they must continue their commitment to quality and self-assessment by renewing their accreditation every few years.

The natural tendency of anyone with too many demands on their time is to claim that there is inadequate time to develop and review a quality assurance program. "Recent data collected by ICAVL accredited vascular laboratories has shown that repeat carotid duplex examination of patients referred for surgical evaluation for carotid endarterectomy have documented clinically significant differences in as high as 61% of the reexamined patients. It was found that the common thread amongst these outside (unaccredited) laboratories was the lack of a quality assurance program which would have identified the reason for these errors and provided the laboratories with the data necessary to adjust their criteria, or refine technical errors that may have contributed to the erroneous results." *Brown OW, Bendick PJ, Bove PG, Long GW, Cornelius P, Zelenock GB. Shanley CJ " Reliability of Extracranial Carotid Artery Duplex Ultrasound Scanning: Value of Laboratory Accreditation." Journal of Vascular Surgery 2004; 39: 366-371.* As mentioned earlier, taking the time required to create a quality program ultimately saves time and reduces the number of errors.

A 2019 study, *Accreditation, Credentialing, and Quality Improvement in Diagnostic Medical Sonography: A Literature Review*, summarized the findings of 19 research studies on accreditation, credentialing, and quality improvement. Although the review revealed differences in facility accreditation status based on geographical area and sonographer specialty, positive correlations between accreditation and credentialing were documented. Many articles found correlations between quality and lab accreditation and/or individual credentialing, and many articles raised concerns regarding the unknown quality of ultrasound studies performed in nonaccredited facilities or by personnel without individual sonography credentials.

> **Author's Note:**
> **Credentialed Personnel**
>
> It is always good to put information into perspective. Imagine if you were the patient, would you prefer that your study was performed by credentialed or non-credentialed personnel? Would you prefer that the facility had undergone the accreditation process to ensure quality measures were in place?

1.3 Individual Personnel Credentialing / Certification

Individual certification goes hand in hand with laboratory accreditation and is increasingly important. Most lab accreditation standards require that one or more sonographers be registered, and many employers hire only credentialed staff. Additionally some states now require licensure in order to perform ultrasound, and these states recognize the major ultrasound credentials as acceptable prerequisites for obtaining licensure. Several organizations provide credentialing in ultrasound including The American Registry for Diagnostic Medical Sonography (ARDMS), Cardiovascular Credentialing International (CCI), and the American Registry of Radiologic Technologists (ARRT).

The field of sonography is ever changing with an increasingly rapid pace of advancement in technology and applications. As a result, it is extremely important that ultrasound professionals keep up to date with the latest innovations, new procedures and the "best practices" in patient care. Once an individual has achieved registry status in their specialty area(s) of ultrasound, they are required to complete continuing medical education credit hours (CME) every few years. The rules regarding the number of CME to maintain credentials varies with the credentialing organization. This requirement represents a commitment to lifelong learning and the best in quality patient care.

1.4 Personnel Qualifications

Accreditation specifies roles that must be fulfilled in each laboratory to meet quality standards. Specifics on all of the various roles may vary between accrediting bodies, and not all specific roles are addressed in this text. For details on the specific roles of the physician directors, interpreting physician, nursing, clerical, and administrative support, documentation is easily found on the websites from any of the accrediting organizations. The following information describes, in general terms, the role of the clinical staff related to the accreditation process.

Medical Director

The medical director must be a legally licensed physician with a thorough understanding of indications for ultrasound examinations as well as familiarity with the basic physical principles and limitations of the technologies that are performed in the laboratory. Additional criteria may include completion of a formal training program, demonstration of interpretation of ultrasound examinations and/or successful completion of board certification examinations. Pathways for meeting the medical director qualifications vary depending on the accreditation organization and the area of specialty.

The medical director is responsible for the entire operation of the laboratory, clinical services provided, quality and appropriateness of services offered as well as adherence of the clinical staff to accreditation standards. Specific operations may be delegated to the technical director and/or associated directors.

Technical Director

Ideally, the technical director should hold appropriate credentialing in all areas of accreditation application. Each of the accrediting bodies specifies certification, training and experience qualifications in their standards. Responsibilities of the technical director may include general supervision of technical and ancillary staff, daily technical operation of the laboratory, technical training, operation and maintenance of laboratory equipment, compliance of the technical and ancillary staff to accreditation standards, and coordination with medical staff to ensure quality patient care.

Medical Staff

All medical staff must be legally qualified physicians and demonstrate competency in interpretation of ultrasound. Requirements generally include demonstration of a formal or informal training program with further documentation of experience interpreting under the supervision of physicians who have already met the standards of accreditation.

Technical Staff

Again, ideally all technical staff should strive to be credentialed in all areas in which they are performing examinations. All technical staff should demonstrate an appropriate level of training, technical certification or documented experience. With respect to certification, during the initial accreditation application phase, accrediting bodies may offer a "grace" period for technical staff who are eligible for certification by the American Registry of Diagnostic Medical Sonographers (ARDMS), Cardiovascular Credentialing International (CCI) or American Registry of Radiologic Technologists (ARRT), Sonography. Most accrediting bodies require proper technical certification upon reapplication.

Continuing Education Requirements

All medical and technical staff must meet the specific continuing medical education requirements of the accreditation standards. Continuing education should be relevant to the areas of accreditation.

Examination Protocols / Documentation of Examinations

Two of the principal focuses of the accreditation application process are evaluation of exam protocols and documentation of examinations. Laboratory protocols are carefully evaluated to ensure that comprehensive examinations are performed with sufficient documentation for interpretation. Representative clinical images and video clips, including spectral Doppler and/or color Doppler are submitted for review. Diagnostic criteria are evaluated for appropriateness and consistent application by all technical and medical staff. Final reports should follow a standardized format and include a description of the examination performed, the clinical indication(s) for the test, exam finding, and pertinent positive and negative conclusions relevant to the diagnostic criteria. Final reports should be signed by the interpreting physician and available in a timely fashion to the referring physician.

1.5 Document Storage and Record Keeping

Accreditation requirements generally have specific standards regarding record keeping and storage of documentation. These requirements may vary between credentialing organizations, but usually require specifications for access and retrieval and the file format in which studies are saved. Lab reports and records must be maintained according to applicable federal, state, and local or facility policy and/or medical records law.

A comprehensive, written Quality Improvement Policy is required and should include a description of objectives of the program and the responsibilities of lab personnel in participating in and maintaining aspects of the program. In addition to instrument and equipment maintenance records and safety checks, the lab should compile annual volumes statistics. Regular, ongoing comparison of test results and correlation with gold standard tests is critical for determining accuracy of testing, appropriateness of exam protocols, and diagnostic criteria, and for maintaining and improving overall quality in the lab.

2. Transducer Care

2.1 Inspection and General Care

Proper transducer care ranges from obvious basic handling precautions to complex sterilization procedures. Since transducers come in direct contact with the patient, the transducer represents the greatest potential risk to the patient, although this risk is small if common sense rules are followed. Transducers should of course be handled with care. Cables should not be kinked or crimped, and care should be exercised to not apply excessive force to the cabling, to the connector, or to the strain relief (the thicker material around the area where the cable connects to the transducer head), or to the transducer head itself. Transducers should be inspected for mechanical signs of damage before each use. If there are any signs of exposed wires, cable housing cracks, cracks within the transducer housing, damage to the lens or transducer surface, etc., the transducer should not be used until inspected by a service representative or qualified personnel.

2.2 Current Leakage Tests

The International Electrotechnical Commission (IEC) has produced general requirements for basic safety and essential performance of electrical medical devices. According to the standard IEC 60601-1, transducers should periodically be tested for electrical current leakage. The purpose of the current leakage test is to check the mechanical integrity of the transducer to ensure patient safety. The current leakage test can be used to detect minute flaws within the transducer housing, lens, cable-to-housing connection, transesophageal (TEE) probe jacket, etc. This test is important for two reasons. First, mechanical discontinuities and fissures represent a potential electrical safety hazard to the patient. Second, small mechanical deformities can reduce the efficacy of cleaning and disinfecting procedures, with microbial forms sheltered within the mechanical breaches.

There are now many commercially and readily available devices sold for current leakage testing. As shown in *Figure 1*, the basic test is performed by connecting a transducer to a testing platform which creates transmit signals. The transducer is placed into a water bath which contains sensors which connect to the testing device. The testing device presents the current sensed in the water bath, indicating whether or not an electrical current leak exists.

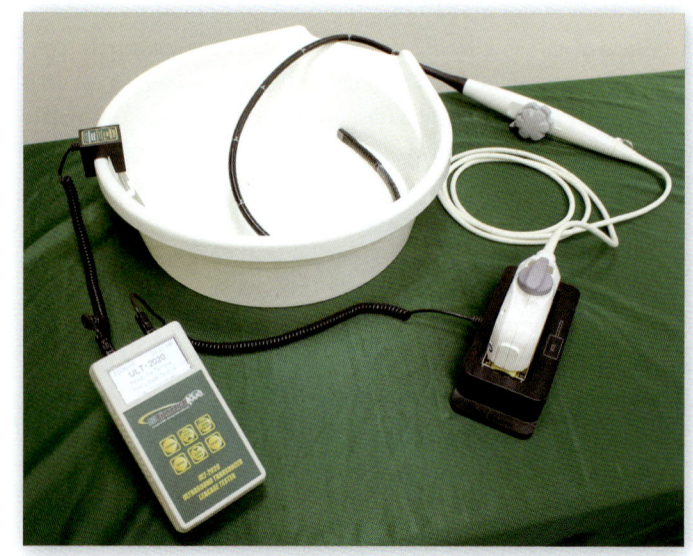

Fig. 1 **Example of a current leakage test setup for a TEE transducer** *(Used with permission from BC Group International, Inc.)*

The frequency appropriate for current leakage testing is generally specified in the safety guidelines and transducer specifications provided with transducer purchase. Transducers which present a greater risk are of course suggested to be tested more frequently. For example, the TEE probes have a greater potential risk for two reasons. First, because of contact with the patient, small holes can be created by the bite of the patient. These small bite holes can potentially interrupt the integrity of the TEE probe jacket. Second, since the transducer is inserted into the patient and is within close proximity to the heart when in use, current leakage represents a potentially more lethal risk. As such, current leakage tests are generally recommended to be performed more frequently on TEE probes than on standard transcutaneous transducers.

2.3 Disinfection and Sterilization
There are four levels of disinfection and sterilization:*
- **Sterilization:** Complete elimination of all forms of microbial life including spores and viruses.
- **High-level disinfection:** Destruction/removal of all micro-organisms except bacterial spores.
- **Intermediate-level disinfection:** Inactivation of Mycobacterium Tuberculosis, bacteria, most viruses and most fungi, and some bacterial spores.
- **Low-level disinfection:** Destruction of most bacteria, some viruses, and some fungi. Low-level disinfection will not necessarily inactivate Mycobacterium Tuberculosis or bacterial spores.

Health Canada Infection Control Guidelines – Hand Washing, Cleaning, Disinfection and Sterilization in Health Care

The following graphic is adapted from the Center for Disease Control (CDC) website and illustrates the levels of disinfection.

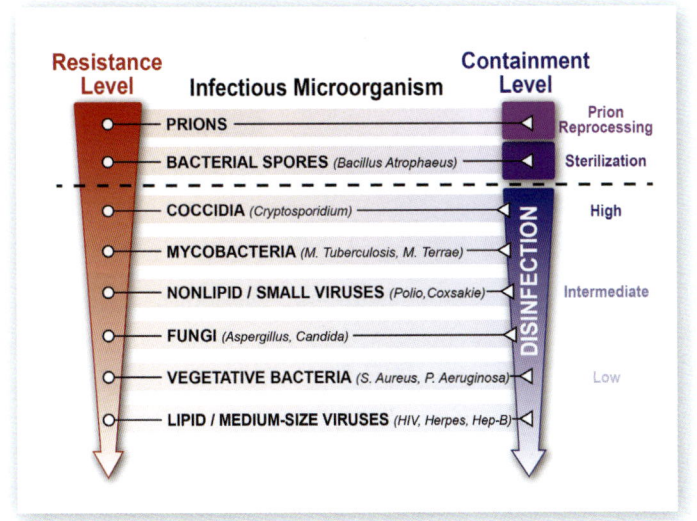

Fig. 2 Levels of resistance and corresponding required levels of sterilization and disinfection *(Modified from CDC.gov)*

2.4 General Cleaning
Cleaning of a transducer is generally a simple process of using soap and water with a soft cloth to remove any residual gel and biological-related residues from the transducer. In general, using a brush on the transducer housing is not recommended unless specifically stated in the manufacturer's directions for care. Using a brush on the transducer surface is never a good idea as surface damage can easily occur. Once the transducer has been cleaned, it can then either be allowed to air dry or dried using a soft cloth or gauze pad.

2.5 Low-Level Disinfection
Low-level disinfecting requires the use of germicide. The transducer is either sprayed or immersed in the germicide and then rinsed with sterile water. The transducer can then be air dried or dried with a soft cloth or gauze pad. Before disinfection, a general cleaning should always be performed to remove as much material as possible, improving the efficiency of the disinfection.

2.6 High-Level Disinfecting
High-level disinfection is intended for transducers the use of which makes the spread of disease more likely because of contact with blood, other bodily fluids, or mucous membranes (semi-critical devices which come in contact with, but which do not penetrate, the skin or mucous membranes). For these transducers (such as the transesophageal (TEE) and endocavity transducers such as transvaginal (TV) and transrectal (TR)) the transducers are immersed in a disinfecting solution. Additionally, when performing semi-critical tests, the health care provider should be wearing gloves for both the safety of the health care provider and for the safety of the patient.

The basic process is as follows: (Of course, procedures may vary according to disinfecting agent and transducer type, and should be referenced from the specific manufacturer and followed explicitly.)
- Perform a general cleaning using soap and water first.
- Make sure to use disinfecting solution compatible with the transducer to be disinfected. (The appropriate disinfectants are specified by the transducer manufacturer. *Be careful not to assume that all transducer types from the same manufacturers can be disinfected using the same disinfecting solutions. Differences in materials and manufacturing processes may render a solution safe for one type of transducer, destructive to another type of transducer.*)
- Immerse transducers following specific disinfecting guidelines.
- Rinse the transducer (usually using sterile water) to remove residual disinfectant from transducer (following guidelines specifically).
- Allow transducer to air dry or dry using a sterile soft cloth or gauze pads.
- Examine transducer to be sure that there is no structural damage such as cracks, cuts, exposed wires, etc.

2.7 Sterilization
Sterilization is required when using a device considered "critical." A device is considered critical when the device penetrates the skin or

a mucous membrane and is used without a protective covering or if protective covering is compromised during a study. For ultrasound transducers, sterilization does not imply autoclaving as heating the transducer will likely ruin the transducer principally because of delamination of materials bonded by epoxies and other glues.

2.8 Potential Risks of Not Following Sterilization/Disinfection Guidelines

Not precisely following the guidelines can have a range of consequences. Some consequences are minor, such as transducer discoloration or a temporary staining of the patient's skin with contact of the transducer. Other consequences can be much more severe, including skin irritation, chemical burns, and infectious disease transmission. When performing disinfections and sterilizations, care should be taken to soak transducers for the specified time period (not under or over the time specified) as well as making certain that the rinses are thorough (often requiring multiple water immersions). Additional precautions should be taken to ensure the safety of the people performing the disinfecting process.

2.9 Precautions to Take When Performing High-level Disinfection or Sterilization

Although the chemicals used to disinfect are not considered carcinogens, they are generally classified as toxic. As such, caution should always be observed when handling and utilizing these disinfecting chemicals. The following is a list of considerations for anyone performing the disinfection or sterilization process *(as always, you should carefully read and follow the specific warnings given with each disinfecting chemical)*.

- Wear gloves
- Wear protective eye wear
- Pay attention to expiration dates of solutions
- Pay attention to appropriate solution concentrations
- Pay attention to specified conditions such as ideal temperature of solution
- Pay attention to immersion times
- Pay close attention to prescribed immersion depths
- Of course, never immerse the electrical connector
- Be certain that there is proper ventilation (hooded or closed ventilation systems are best)
- Make certain to follow all guidelines when disposing of used solution

Figure 3 is reproduced with permission from the AIUM guidelines and summarizes transducer preparation and cleaning.

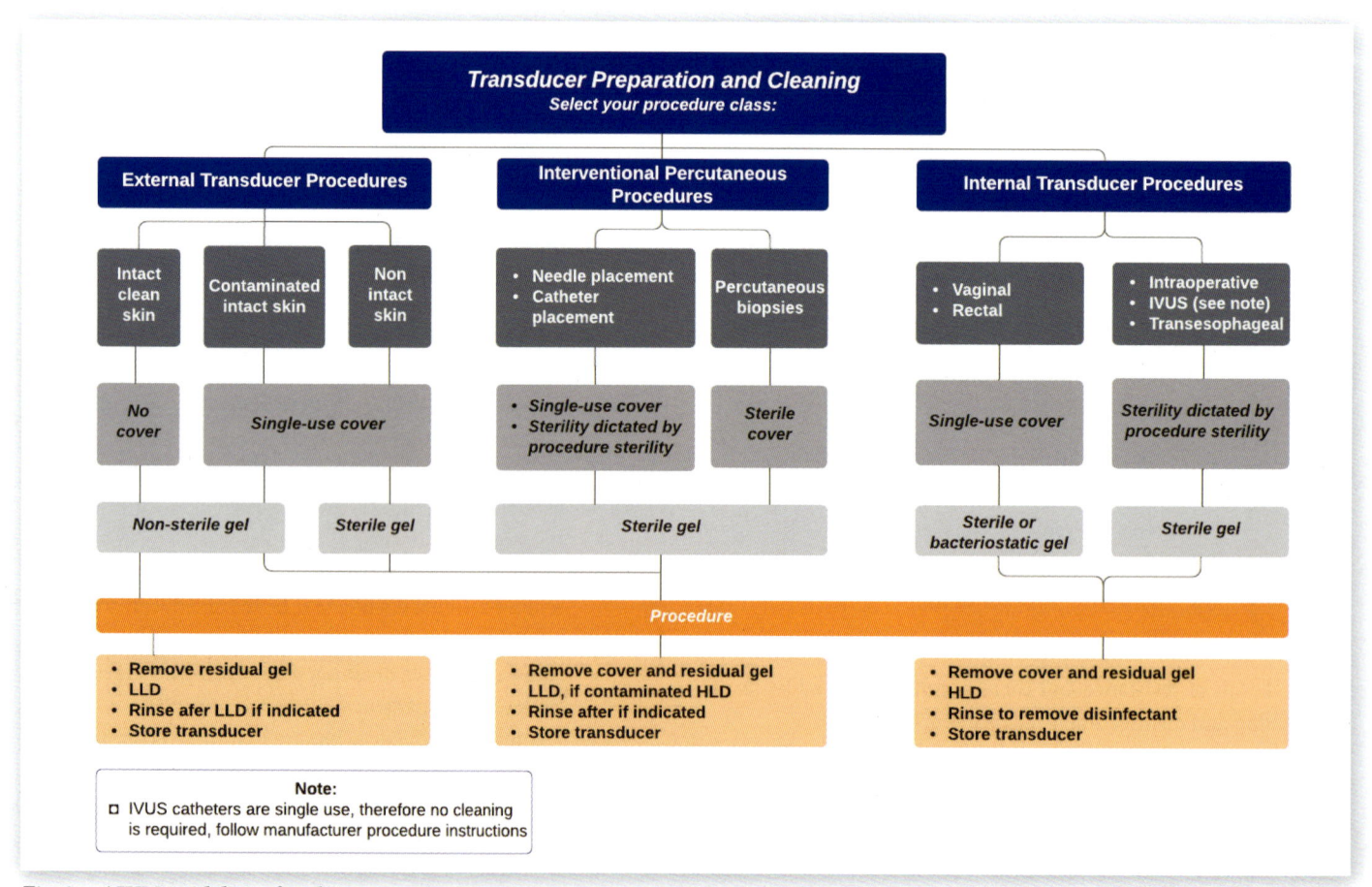

Fig. 3 **AIUM guidelines for cleaning and preparing external- and internal-use ultrasound transducers and equipment between patients as well as safe handling and use of ultrasound coupling gel** *(Reprinted with permission)*

2.10 Instrumentation and Quality Assurance

System testing for performance and degradation is naturally part of every quality assurance program. Again, there is no national "standard" policy that must be adopted. Instead many organizations have created guidelines, recommendations, and standards that are adopted by various accrediting organizations. Almost all quality testing programs include the basic categories of having up-to-date equipment, making sure the system and transducers are in proper operating condition and regularly serviced, and that no degradation in performance has occurred. We will later devote considerable effort to discussing the concept of testing for performance and degradation, the mechanisms for testing, and the related issues. Some recommendations go further in stressing which test should be performed daily, which monthly, and which semi-annually or annually.

3. Equipment Testing

3.1 The Need for Tight Testing Controls

Testing and maintenance of ultrasound equipment is an interesting, complex topic. On the one hand, there is a desire for equipment testing to make certain that system performance is adequate. On the other hand, the testing procedures and methodologies are often very complex requiring extensive system knowledge and extremely well controlled testing procedures. Given the ever-increasing complexity of ultrasound equipment and the intricacies of accurate equipment testing, quite frequently an important component to a quality program is the purchase of a system and transducer service contract.

With that said, there have been a series of tests designed to verify continuing performance of the ultrasound equipment. To implement these "performance" tests, equipment such as test objects and test phantoms are often necessary. The use of test objects and phantoms is an attempt to provide a constant reference frame so that a standard can be developed, and so that changes over time can be identified. It is important to note that although most test phantoms offer a stable means by which to "calibrate" and compare performance over time, the ability to accurately mimic the characteristics and complexities of tissues is limited. As a result, there is no way of guaranteeing that a specific result or metric with a test phantom necessarily corresponds to a measure of accuracy in a system on live patients.

3.2 Purpose of Testing

Test objects and phantoms are used for ultrasound system validation and performance testing. The testing can be performed by the ultrasound manufacturer, regulatory bodies, or within ultrasound laboratories. The purpose of these tests is:

- To assess performance differences between different ultrasound system designs
- To assess a system's performance and/or manufacturing
- To monitor system degradation over time
- To minimize artifacts

4. 2D and Doppler Testing

4.1 Tested Parameters

It is helpful to dichotomize the testing equipment into two principal categories: 2D imaging and Doppler-based techniques. Recalling the Doppler effect, this distinction should be intuitive. For 2D testing, static structures are adequate, but to test Doppler performance, the test equipment must provide or simulate movement. The following list includes the parameters generally assessed using test objects for 2D and Doppler techniques:

2D Imaging:
1) Detail resolution
   - axial resolution
   - lateral resolution
   - elevation resolution

2) Contrast resolution

3) Penetration (sensitivity)

4) Range accuracy

5) Measurement accuracy

Doppler:
1) Penetration (sensitivity)
   - PW spectral
   - CW spectral
   - Color Doppler

2) Range accuracy
   - PW spectral
   - Color Doppler

3) Velocity accuracy
   - PW spectral (peak velocity)
   - CW spectral (peak velocity)
   - Color Doppler (mean velocity)

4) Spectral Broadening
   - PW spectral

5) Lateral Resolution
   - Color Doppler

5. Doppler Testing and Phantoms

5.1 Types of Doppler Phantoms

Testing Doppler provides greater challenges than testing 2D parameters. Since repeatable, calibratable, and accurate movement must be generated to make a useful phantom, there are a myriad of problems to overcome. There are two families of Doppler testing equipment: flow-based phantoms and non-flow-based phantoms. Both types have advantages and disadvantages. We will begin by considering flow-based phantoms.

> **Author's Note:**
> **Test and Design Engineer Testing**
>
> There is actually a third type of testing used principally by test and design engineers which bypasses the transducer and involves pure electronic signals. This technique involves the use of a special input device that plugs in as if it were a transducer and electronically couples the system receive channels to an external electronic device, such as a waveform generator, to generate phase varying signals.

5.2 Flow Phantoms

Basic Design

In its simplest form, a flow phantom consists of a pump and fluid reservoir, a fluid constraining tube or conduit, a fluid, and a surrounding medium.

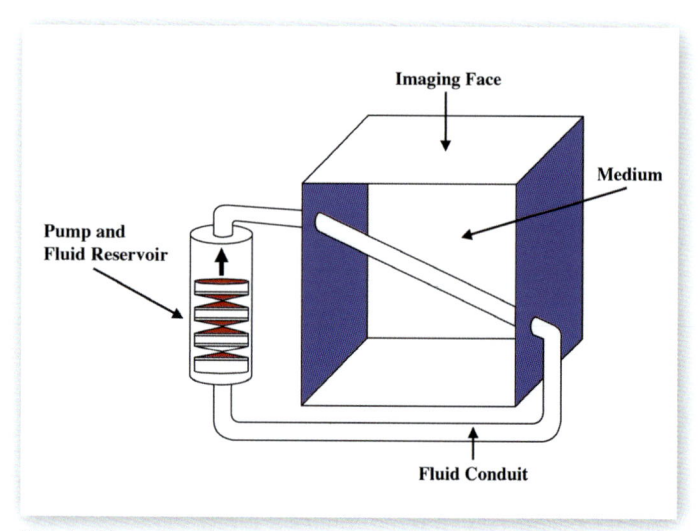

Fig. 4 **Flow phantoms**

Blood Mimicking Fluids

Depending on the pumping mechanism, flow phantoms can provide either continuous or pulsatile flow. In either case, there are some real world difficulties to overcome to make Doppler flow phantoms work well. The first problem is how to create a fluid which mimics blood. Water cannot be used since ultrasound requires an acoustic impedance mismatch to cause reflections. Since water is homogeneous, it creates virtually no reflection.

For research, there are times where human or animal blood is used. You can imagine the issues associated with using real blood. There are obvious issues of contamination, cleanliness, consistency over time (changes in blood viscosity), variations in blood lots (variation in hematocrit), accessibility, etc. Given the difficulties of using real blood, other fluids are much more commonly used. Since water cannot be used, quite frequently a suspension is created to increase the scattering properties. Problems still exist since over time the particles tend to precipitate out of solution, making the scattering property of the fluid variable over time. Additionally, air bubbles tend to develop in the fluid causing specular reflections which tend to saturate the Doppler circuitry and wall filters.

Other Potential Issues

Depending on the flow phantom design, other problems can exist such as: unwieldy size, weight, collapsing flow tubes (conduits), in-adherence of tubes to medium walls, and leaks. For all of these reasons, it is very difficult to develop a flow phantom which is consistent enough over time to develop a stable sensitivity reference.

Examples of Flow Phantoms

The following pages contain examples of various types of flow phantoms and related products from multiple vendors. An attempt was made to include a variety of phantoms from multiple vendors so as to demonstrate the range of testing approaches.

Note: Text in the color blue indicates wording excerpted from equipment manufactures' product descriptions.

Fig. 5 **ATS Model 527: Doppler Flow Directional Discrimination Phantom**

Chapter 11: Quality Assurance

Key Tests with Model ATS 527:
- Directional Discrimination
- Flow Velocity
- Flow Location
- Sensitivity at varying depths
- Maximum Penetration

Product Description

The Model 527 rubber-based tissue mimicking phantom is designed to test the ability of color Doppler flow imaging systems to discriminate the direction of flow in small, closely spaced vessels at varying depths. This phantom contains four pairs of 2 mm flow-channels. The edge-to-edge spacing between each pair of flow- channels progressively increases from 1 mm to 4 mm. If greater distances are desired, a combination of two flow-channel pairs can be used. Two fixed-angle scan surfaces of 18° and 56° maintain the sound beam and the Doppler Test Fluid flowing through the phantom. These angles permit continuous scanning at depths ranging from 3 to 17 cm.

peripheral flow and deeper abdominal vessels. The phantom is filled with Zerdine® tissue mimicking gel with a speed of sound of 1540 m/s, an attenuation of 0.7 dB/cm/MHz and a backscatter contrast designed to match that of the liver

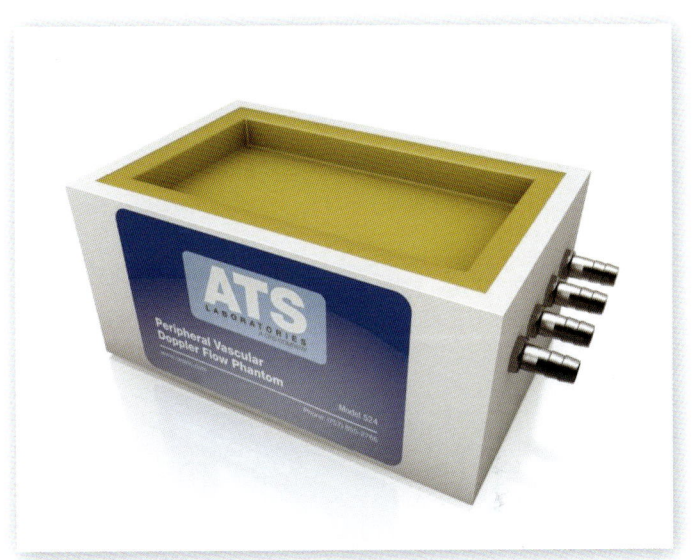

Fig. 7 **ATS Model 524 & 525: Peripheral Vascular Doppler Flow Phantom**

Key Tests with Models 524 and 525:
- Sensitivity
- Flow Velocity
- Maximum Penetration
- Flow Location
- Demonstration of the effects of stenosis (Model 525)

Product Description

The Models 524 and 525 tissue mimicking Doppler flow phantoms contain four flow channels simulating superficial vasculature. The simulated vessels are located 15 mm below the scan surface. Built-in scanning wells are provided to permit the use of water or a low viscosity gel as acoustic coupling agents.

The two models are distinguished by different structures. The Model 524 has four constant diameter channels, 2, 4, 6 and 8 mm. The Model 525 mimics a vascular stenosis by narrowing at the middle from an entrance diameter of 8 mm to varying stenosis levels (0, 50, 75 and 90%).

Fig. 6 **ATS Model 069A: Doppler Ultrasound Flow Phantom**

Key Tests with Model ATS 069A:
- Doppler Sensitivity
- Velocity Accuracy

Product Description

The Doppler Ultrasound Flow Phantom, when used with the model 769 Doppler Flow Pump, provides a complete solution for QA testing of Doppler ultrasound devices. The two most common tests are sensitivity and velocity accuracy, but many other useful tests are also described in the literature. The phantom is a tissue-mimicking flow phantom with a blood-vessel-simulating, ultrasound-compatible tube that enters the phantom at an angle. The phantom has both a top and bottom scanning surface that allows testing at varying depths and angles of orientation. This makes the phantom suitable for testing both

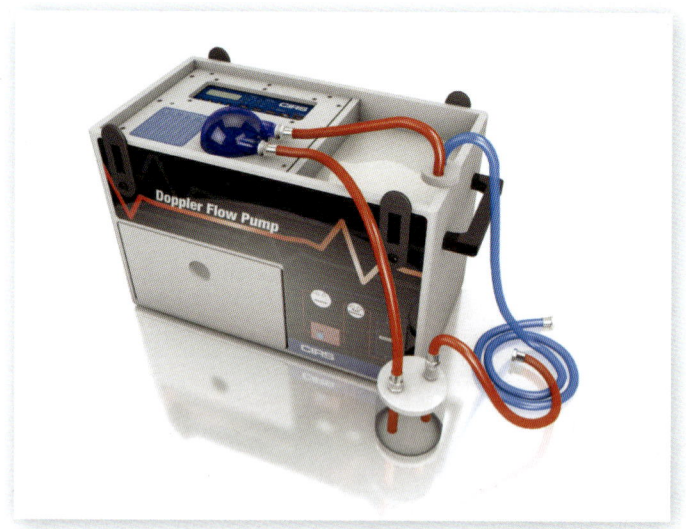

Fig. 8a ATS Model 769: Flow Pump

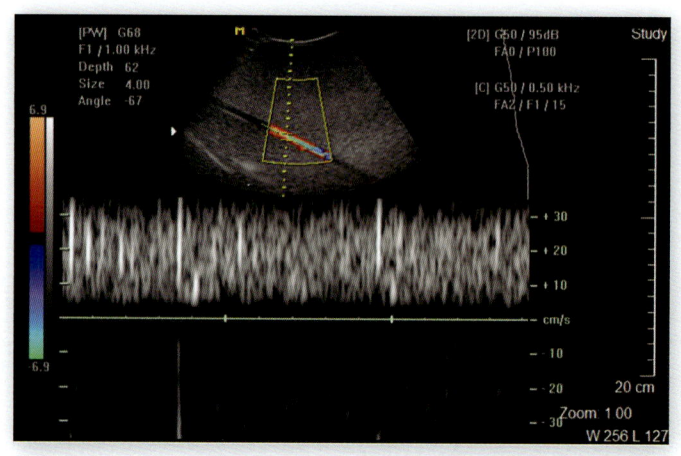

Fig. 8b Constant velocity flow created by flow pump

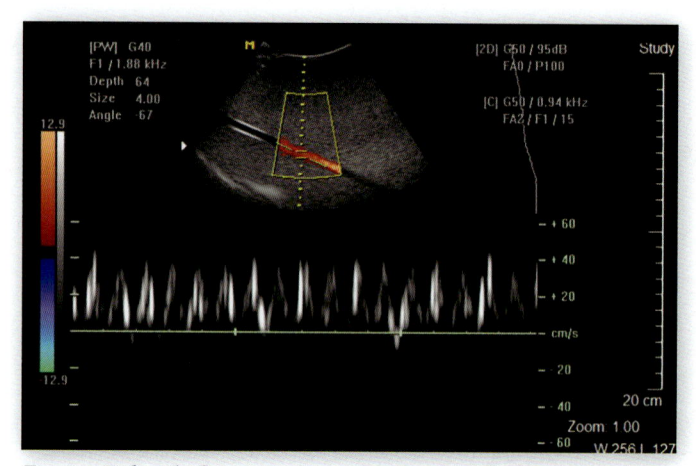

Fig. 8c Pulsatile flow waveform generated by flow pump

Features:
- Used in conjunction with ATS Urethane or CIRS Zerdine Phantoms
- Max Flow Rate is 750 mL/min
- Min Flow Rate can be as low as 0.004 mL/min
- Pulsatile or Constant Velocity configurations available
- Varying tube depths for peripheral and abdominal vessel simulation
- Doppler Fluid simulates acoustic and physical characteristics of blood
- All components stored in compact case for easy transport

Product Description

The Doppler Flow Pump is used to simulate blood flow when testing Doppler ultrasound devices. When used in conjunction with a tissue mimicking phantom (sold separately), the flow pump supports routine Doppler quality assurance measurements of velocity accuracy, directional accuracy, sample volume accuracy and sensitivity. The configurable design also supports advanced research and engineering tests. For instance, test circuit may be modified to support either constant velocity flow or pulsatile flow. When in pulsatile flow mode, the peristaltic pump may be programmed to produce physiologic waveforms. In addition, the external tubing circuit ensures laminar flow rates over a wide range of flow rates, and it allows users to easily inject contrast agents for testing contrast enhanced ultrasound (CEUS).

Fig. 9a ATS Model 769: Doppler Pump Fluid

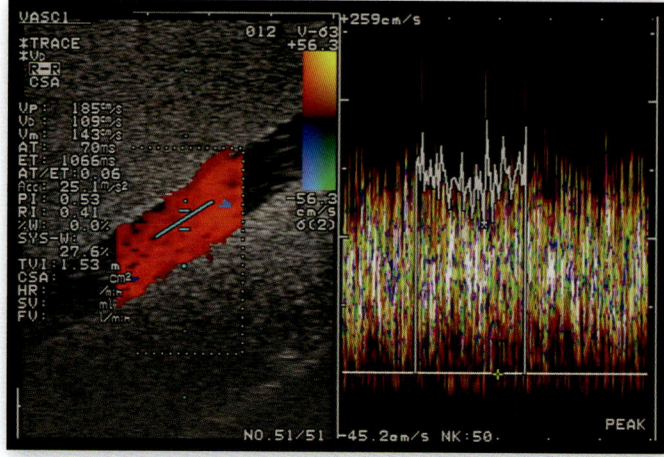

Fig. 9b Constant velocity flow (left) and pulsatile flow waveform (right) generated by flow pump

Property	Human Blood (37°C)	IEC 61685:201 BMF Specifications	Blood Mimicking Fluid (769DF)
Viscosity (cP)	3 - 4	4 ± 0.4	4 ± 0.5
Density (g/cc)	1.0565	1.05 ± 0.04	1.05 ± 0.04
Velocity (m s^{-1})	1578	1570 ± 30	1570 ± 15
Attenuation (dB cm^{-1} MHz)	0.15	< 0.10	0.1 ± 0.02
Backscatter (f^{-4} m^{-1} sr^{-1})	4 × 10^{-31}	1 × 10^{-31} – 1 × 10^{-30}	≈ 10^{-30}
Fluid Properties	Non Newtonian	Non Newtonian	Newtonian

Table 1 **Properties of Human Blood vs. Doppler Pump Fluid**

Product Description
CIRS Doppler Fluid, model 769DF, is a reliable, stable and non-hazardous fluid formulated to mimic the acoustic and physical properties of human blood. The fluid, when used in conjunction with ultrasound Doppler flow phantoms and pumping systems, can be used to evaluate the system performance of a Doppler imaging system. The 769DF formulation is based on published standards. It is fully degassed prior to packaging to minimize noise from air bubbles. The fluid is tested for speed of sound, attenuation, density and viscosity using test equipment traceable to NIST.

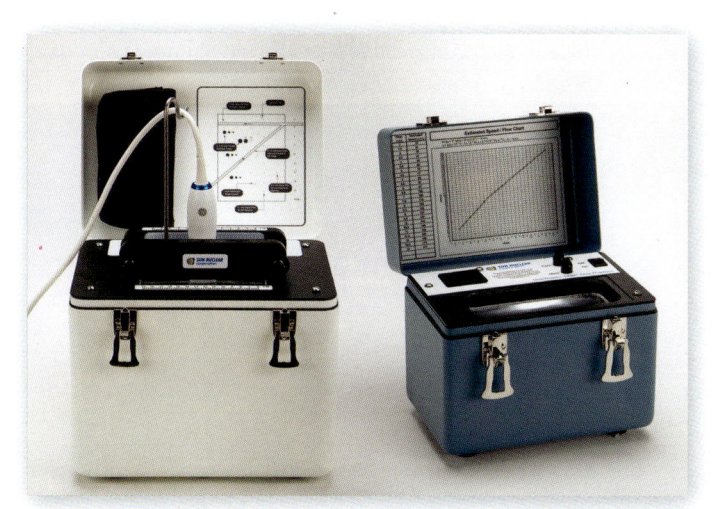

Fig. 10 **1430™ Flow Phantom with Transducer Holder (left) and Gammex Doppler 403™ and Mini-Doppler Flow Phantom (right)**

Key Tests with 403 & 1430 Models:
Doppler Related:
- Sensitivity
- Flow Velocity
- Maximum Penetration
- Flow Location

2D Related:
- Depth Accuracy
- Lateral Resolution
- Axial Resolution
- Contrast Resolution
- Sensitivity

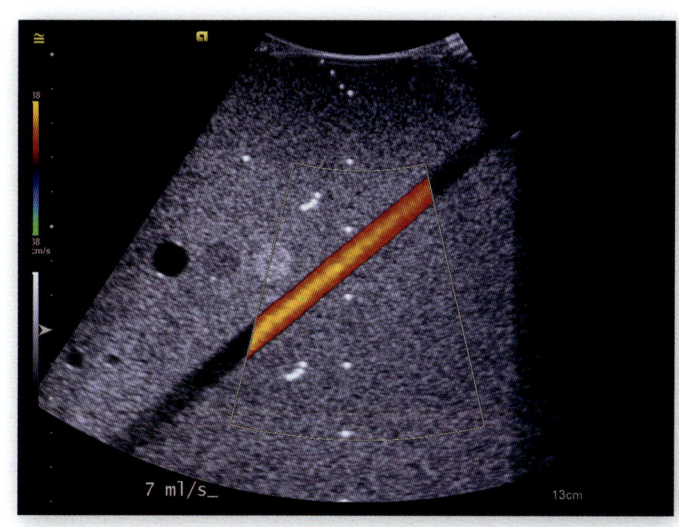

Fig. 11a **Gammex Doppler 403™ color Doppler imaging; note the various pin groups, masses, and cystic structures also included within the phantom**

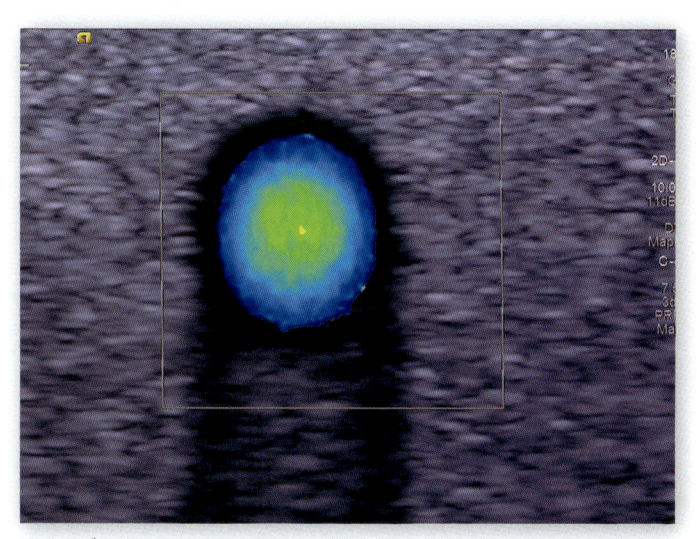

Fig. 11b **Gammex Doppler 403™ transverse color image showing the laminar profile of the flow**

Product Description
These phantoms contain blood-mimicking fluid ultrasonically similar to human tissue, with an electronic flow of 1550 m/s. Patented High Equivalency Gel (HE Gel™) offers tissue mimicking for evaluating image uniformity, detecting dead transducer elements, and assessing maximum penetration depth. Both phantoms are self-contained Doppler flow and B-Mode QA test systems, with streamlined fluid flow at variable rates in a continuous or pulsed mode.

Fig. 12 True Phantom Doppler Phantom; each of the three windows represents a different simulated bone thickness

Features of DP-C01 Model (customizable):
- Partial skull phantom with a customized thickness
- Filling the phantom with the acoustically correct brain-mimicking material
- Custom blood vessels
- Standard tubes and connectors connected to the custom vessels
- Incorporating the phantom within a standard compact box
- Implementing a thin film on top of the phantom
- Custom target wires

Product Description
True Phantom Solutions offers novel technology to fabricate unique materials with realistic physical and mechanical properties similar to the properties of real human tissue and bones. The unique proprietary composition of our material allows for imitating healthy and unhealthy human bones with the adjustable features to suit your research or teaching needs.

Our highly realistic anthropomorphic phantoms are powerful tools for the testing and calibration of new medical devices, training students, and treatment planning and targeting before applying the new non-invasive surgical HIFU procedures.

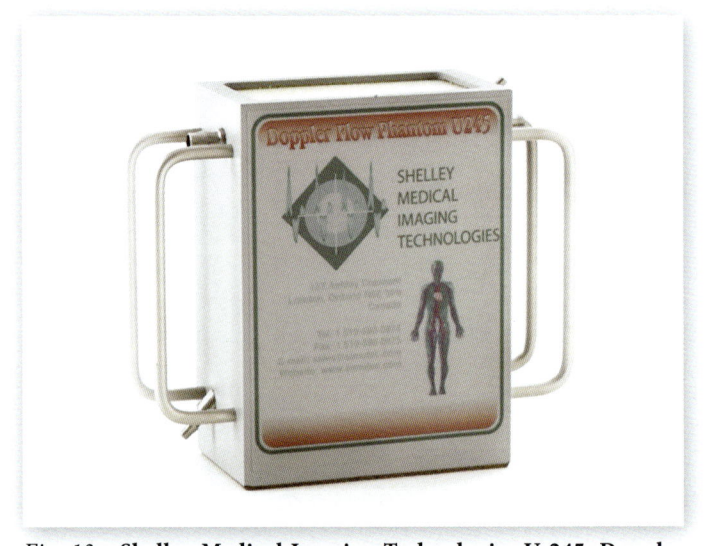

Fig. 13 Shelley Medical Imaging Technologies U-245: Doppler Flow Phantom

Key Tests with Model U-245:
- Sensitivity
- Volume Flow
- Flow Velocity
- Flow Location
- Penetration
- Image Uniformity
- Directional Discrimination
- Flow Visualization

Product Description
The Model U-245 contains a long-lasting tissue equivalent urethane and incorporates two wall-less vessels. An 8 mm diameter vessel,

which is positioned horizontally 2 cm below the scanning surface simulating the common carotid artery and a 4 mm vessel angled 45° from the scanning surface.

Fig. 14a **Shelley Medical Imaging Technologies AccuFlow-Q: Physiologic Flow System (flow controller)**

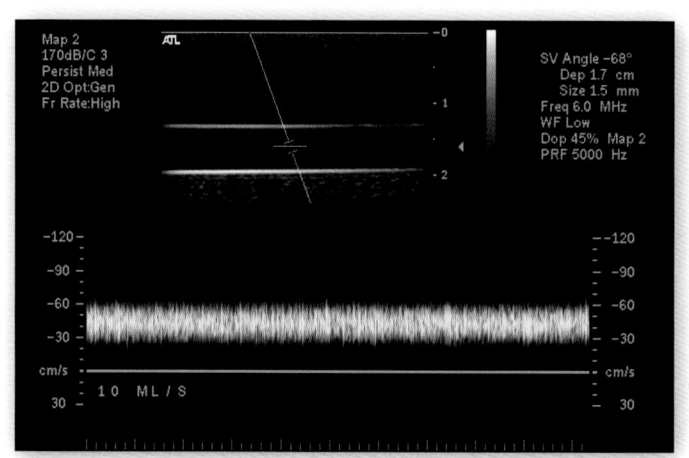

Fig. 14b **PW of constant flow generated by AccuFlow-Q controller at a programmed flow rate of 10 mL/s**

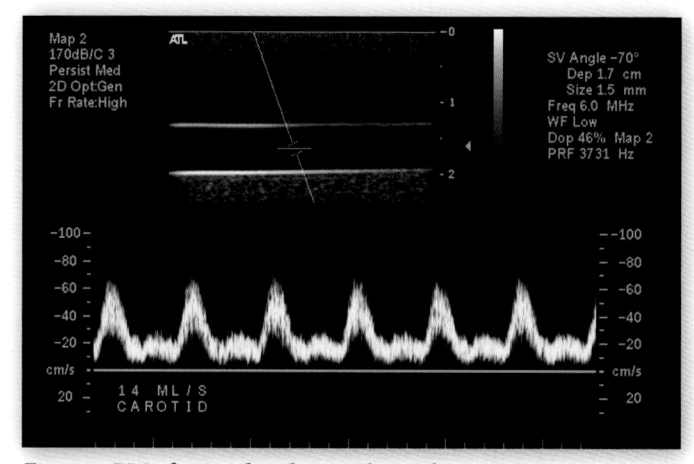

Fig. 14c **PW of a simulated carotid waveform with a programmed flow rate of 14 mL/s**

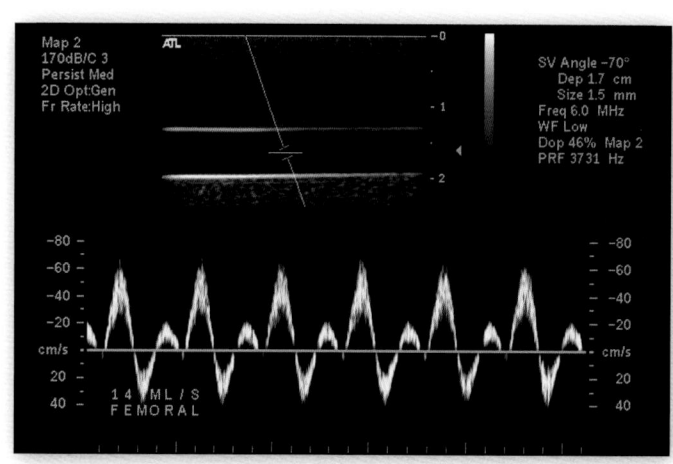

Fig. 14d **PW of a simulated femoral artery waveform with a programmed flow rate of 14 mL/s**

Features (used in conjunction with U-245 Doppler Flow Phantom):

- Offers pre-programmed carotid, femoral, constant flow, triangle, and sine waveforms
- Produces accurate physiologic waveforms including those with reverse flow such as the femoral waveform
- Peak flow rate is easily selected in 0.1 mL/s increments
- Internal volumetric calibration enables verification of constant and pulsatile flow rates during a measurement
- For automated and more advanced studies, the AccuFlow-Q can be controlled by a serial (RS-232) interface
- A trigger output allows the user to check gated acquisition such as ECG-gated color flow
- Incorporates a high-visibility front panel vacuum fluorescent display and backlit panel
- Quick disconnect leak-free fluid input and output fittings

Product Description

AccuFlow-Q is a robust and portable flow pump system designed to generate realistic, accurate and repeatable physiological volume flow waveforms, including carotid, femoral, sine, triangle and constant flow waveforms. Combine the AccuFlow-Q with an appropriate tissue phantom and blood mimicking fluid, and the resulting flow system ensures easy, accurate, repeatable evaluation and validation of diagnostic ultrasound systems. The pump system is designed for evaluation of most common ultrasound techniques: fluid velocity measurements, volume flow measurements, sensitivity measurements at varying depths, maximum penetration, location and directional discrimination, as well as flow visualization. AccuFlow-Q is a novel design that features a built-in reservoir and volumetric calibration device to ensure highly accurate measurements.

Model BMF-US: Blood Mimicking Fluid

Properties:
- *Speed of sound: 1548 ± 5 m/s*
- *Density of fluid: 1037 ± 2 kg/m³*
- *Scattering particle diameter: 5 µm*
- *Scattering particle density: 1.03 g/cm³*
- *Particle concentration: 1.82%*
- *Acoustic attenuation: 0.05 ± 0.01 (dB/(cm MHz))*
- *Viscosity: 4.1 ± 0.1 (mPa s)*

Product Description
Model BMF-US is a validated, stable, non-hazardous fluid that mimics the acoustic and physical properties of human blood for the evaluation of Doppler ultrasound techniques. The fluid is strained through a micro-filter to remove any clumps and fully degassed prior to packaging to eliminate artifacts from air bubbles. The scatterers are neutrally buoyant thus preventing clumping and settling scattering particles. The BMF-US is formulated to meet the requirements for recommended blood-mimicking fluids as described in the IEC 1685 draft specifications.

5.3 Doppler String Phantoms

Eliminating Variable Reflectivity
Given the challenges of flow phantoms, non-flow type Doppler phantoms were created. To create the necessary Doppler shifts, moving targets such as vibrating plates, moving belts, and moving strings have been used. These phantoms eliminate some of the issues associated with stabilizing reflection variability over time but often introduce new challenges related to signal strength. Whereas there used to be many different types of these phantoms, most are no longer offered on the market, with the exception of the Doppler string phantom.

String Phantoms (Moving Targets)
A string phantom is created using a motor, a motor controller, a pulley or series of pulleys, a string stretched across the pulley, and a water tank. The motor controller is programmed to move the pulleys in a specific manner. Since the string is attached to the pulleys, moving the pulleys causes the string to move. The Doppler sample volume is placed over the string so that the motion of the string causes a corresponding Doppler frequency shift. Since sound will not couple well through air, the string is immersed in a water bath, and the transducer surface placed in the water. Since the string velocity can be controlled very precisely, these phantoms are intended for peak velocity calibration primarily, as well as Doppler gate registration accuracy and spectral broadening. A variation of the string phantom is a moving or vibrating plate phantom. With a vibrating plate, the Doppler shift is created by insonating the moving plate or target.

Blossoming
Whereas repeatability is less of an issue with moving target phantoms, there is a significant problem introduced by using a reflector which varies so much from blood. Obviously, in comparison with blood, string and plate targets are extremely specular as reflectors. The result is that the reflections from the targets are much stronger than the normal signals processed by the Doppler circuit, often causing saturation of the electronics. When the electronics saturate, the signals often "bleed' into adjacent FFT bins during the signal processing phase. When signals artificially spread into adjacent bins, the resulting spectrum is spread, creating an artificially high peak velocity. This artifact is called "blossoming."

Need to Use Much Lower Gains and Transmit Power
As a result of blossoming, moving target Doppler phantoms often cause an overestimation in peak velocity. Additionally, since the signal is so strong, sensitivity is not well tested using a target phantom. To mitigate these problems the Doppler transmit and receiver gain must be turned down significantly below the normal use range. If standard transmit and receive levels are used, the peak velocity registered will be well beyond the expected velocity as determined by the true string velocity.

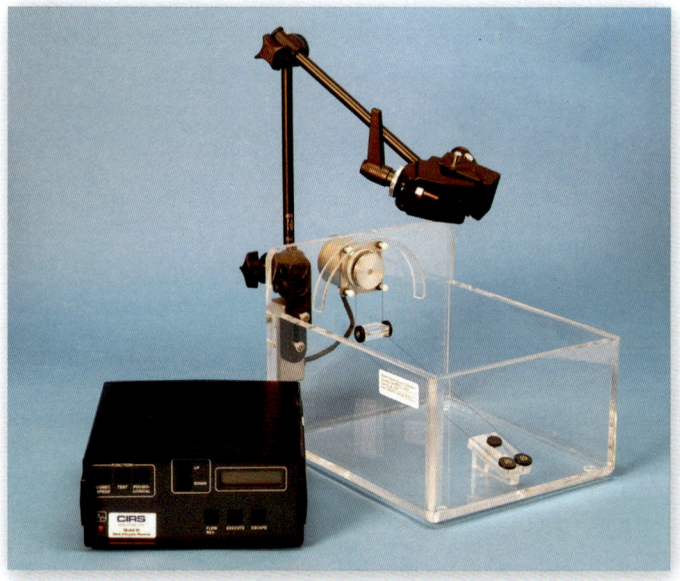

Fig. 15 **CIRS Model 043 Doppler String Phantom**

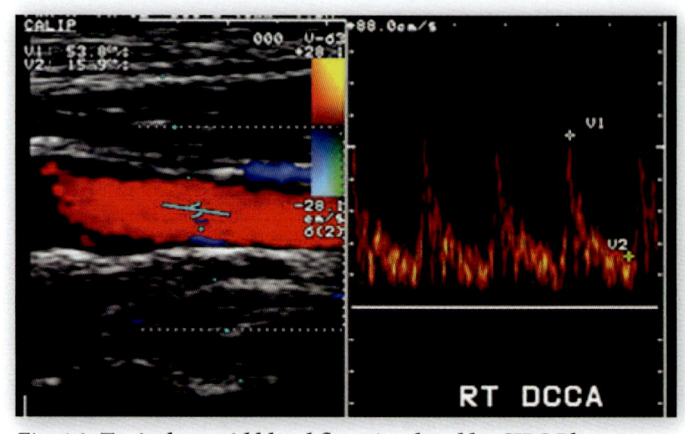

Fig. 16 **Typical carotid blood flow simulated by CIRS Phantom**

Features:

- *Digital Display: Waveform readout, string speed, help statements and instructions, and computer host information*
- *Flow Simulation Speeds: 10 to 200 cm/sec and bidirectional*
- *Speed Drift: Crystal-locked to 20 parts per million (0.002%)*
- *Accuracy: ± 1% of stated speed*
- *Pulsatile Waveforms: 16 pre-programmed and optional customer specified*
- *Waveforms Included: Adult common carotid, stenotic carotid, femoral, aortic; Fetal middle cerebral artery, renal artery, umbilical artery; Pediatric descending thoracic artery, patent ductus arteriosus; Test waveforms: sine waves with peak speeds of 100, 150, and 200 cm/second; Triangle waves with peak speeds of 100, 150, and 200 cm/second; Stepped ramp wave with stops at 0, 20, 40, 60, 80, and 100 cm/sec*
- *Waveform Resolution: Each waveform simulation contains 1000 points of resolution, or speed adjustments, enabling extremely complex simulation*
- *Computer Interface: Industry standard RS-232 interface built-in for future enhancements and remote control; very useful for automated quality control in a manufacturing environment*
- *Fluids Used in Tank: Plain tap water (velocity 1480 m/sec at 20 °C) or velocity corrected water/glycol solution giving 1540 m/sec at 20 °C; phantom adjusts itself for either fluid*
- *Physical Specifications: 120 V AC, 50 W*
  – *Total weight in travel case: 10 kg (22 lb)*
  – *Travel case dimensions: 25x19.5x14 cm (17x17x10 in)*

Product Description

The CIRS Model 043 Doppler String Phantom is an essential tool for people who work with Doppler Ultrasound. The crystal controlled motor accurately generates sixteen pre-programmed waveforms using advanced string target technology. Since the speed is adjusted 1000 times every second, you know it's precise and repeatable.

The Model 043 can be set for use with water or velocity-corrected fluid. If you're using water, it adjusts the string speed accordingly so the different speed of sound in water won't affect your tests. And unlike fluid-flow phantoms, the target never changes; you know what your test results should be every time.

6. Imaging Phantoms and Test Objects

6.1 Detecting Performance Degradation

In addition to Doppler testing, there is a desire to test a system's imaging capability. The central concept is that testing should be performed periodically to ensure that system performance has not degraded over time.

6.2 Test Repeatability

Imaging phantoms have been designed to test many imaging parameters. In terms of true quality assurance and equipment testing for imaging, the difficulties arise in the repeatability of the test. Let's presume that a system is to be tested bimonthly to ensure that there is no loss of sensitivity. The perceived sensitivity will depend on many system controls, including but not limited to the:

- Transducer
- Positioning of transducer on phantom
- Transmit power
- Receiver gain
- Focus depth
- Post-processing curves (compression/dynamic range)
- Ambient light (lighting of the room)
- Monitor contrast setting

From test to test, if any of these controls is set differently, the perceived sensitivity will change, leading to the incorrect conclusion that the system performance has degraded. Therefore, for these quality tests to have merit, careful documentation of the testing procedure and strict adherence to it is paramount. Care must be taken when testing equipment to make certain that the derived conclusion is based on actual system variation and not a change in procedure.

6.3 Varying Pin Separation and Testing Detail Resolution

Most of the imaging tests are easily understood from the descriptions of test objects included. However, there are a few tests which require some explanation. For example, assume that you are imaging the pins in the configuration shown in *Figure 17*. What type of resolution would be tested?

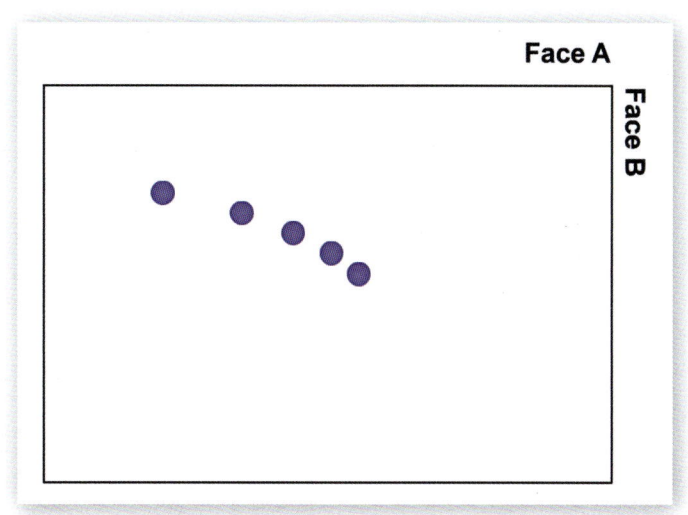

Fig. 17 **Phantom pin groups for resolution testing**

The correct answer is that you cannot determine what resolution you are testing unless you know on which face of the phantom the transducer is being placed. If the transducer were placed on face A, for the pin configuration given, lateral resolution would be tested. If the transducer were placed on face B, then axial resolution would be tested. Notice that with the transducer on face A, the pins are uniformly spaced axially, but have varying separations laterally.

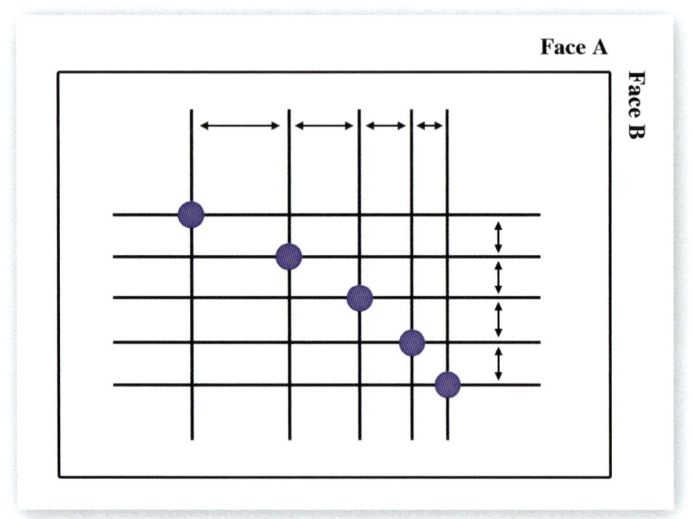

Fig. 18 **Determining "tested" resolution**

By placing the same transducer on face B, the pins would be uniformly spaced laterally, but vary in separation in the axial direction. In order to test detail resolution, there must be a variation in separation distance. If all the pins are the same distance apart, the system can either detect all of the pins or none of the pins. With varying separation distances, the resolution is determined as the smallest separation the system still detects between two structures.

KEY CONCEPT

In order to test detail resolution, pins must be separated by varying distances in the dimension to be tested. When two pins "converge" into one within the image, the resolution limit has been reached.

6.4 Uniformly Spaced Pins and Testing Depth Accuracy and Sensitivity

When pins are uniformly spaced, as shown in *Figure 19*, there are two different tests possible: depth accuracy, and sensitivity. Since the pins are at known depths in the phantom, measuring depth accuracy is a simple matter of placing a caliper at the top of the phantom image (with the transducer imaging from face A), and then a second caliper at the depth of a specific pin. The distance between the calipers can be compared with the specified pin depth to determine depth calibration accuracy. This test is only valid when the phantom is constituted with tissue mimicking material, so that the speed of sound matches the system's assumed speed of sound (1540 m/sec). Testing sensitivity requires that the medium be attenuative. This concept is relatively simple. With each transducer, you image the phantom and record the deepest pin that can be visualized. If degradation occurs over time, the deepest visualized pin will be a shallower pin, indicating a loss in sensitivity. Performing this test well is challenging as you must make certain that every single parameter is set identically from test to test, including transducer position, transmit power, transmit focus, receiver gain, compression, monitor setting, ambient light, etc.

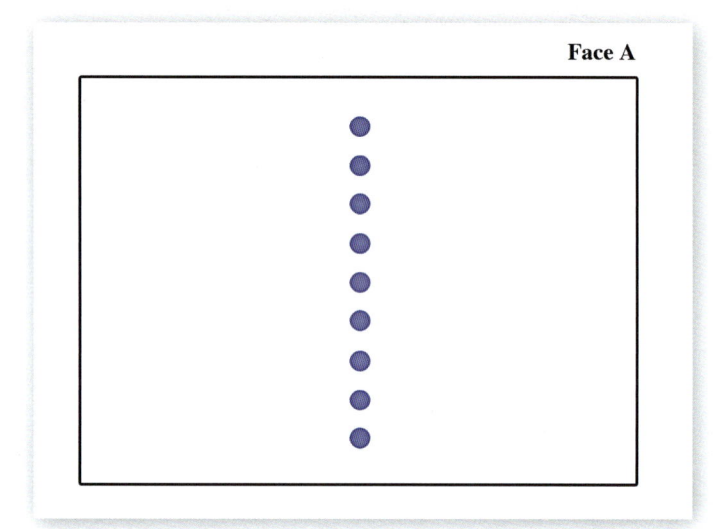

Fig. 19 **Phantom pin groups for testing depth accuracy and sensitivity (when tissue mimicking medium is in phantom)**

6.5 Area and Volume Measurement Accuracy

Some phantoms are designed for testing measurement accuracy. Depending on the phantom and the purpose for the phantom, the objects may be two or three dimensional.

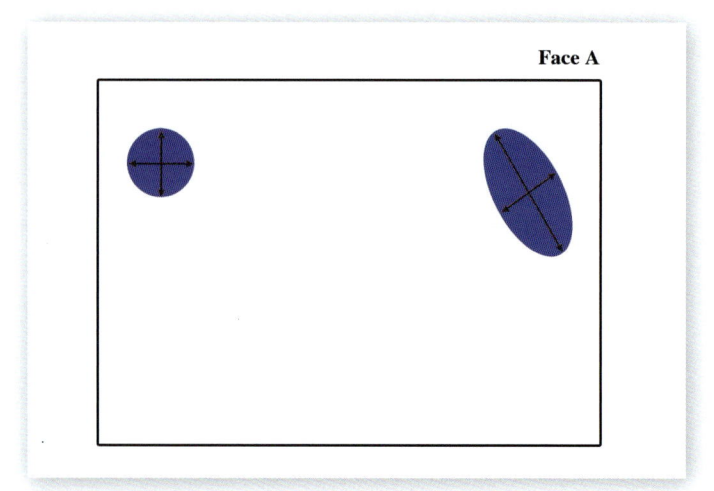

Fig. 20 **Phantom with objects designed for measurement accuracy testing**

6.6 Contrast Resolution Testing

The ability to differentiate structures based on contrast (signal brightness) is critical for recognition of masses and thrombus. Phantoms designed for contrast resolution testing have a structure or structures with varying reflectivity relative to the surrounding background medium as indicated by *Figure 21*.

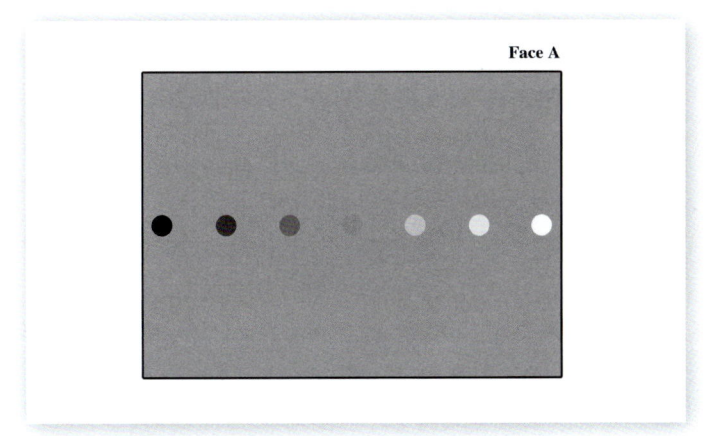

Fig. 21 **Phantoms with objects of varying contrast**

7. Commercially Available Imaging Phantoms

The following is a partial list of commercially available imaging phantoms along with associated features, descriptions, and target drawings.

Note: Text in the color blue indicates wording excerpted from equipment manufactures' product descriptions.

Fig. 22a **CIRS ATS Model 539 Multi-Purpose Phantom**

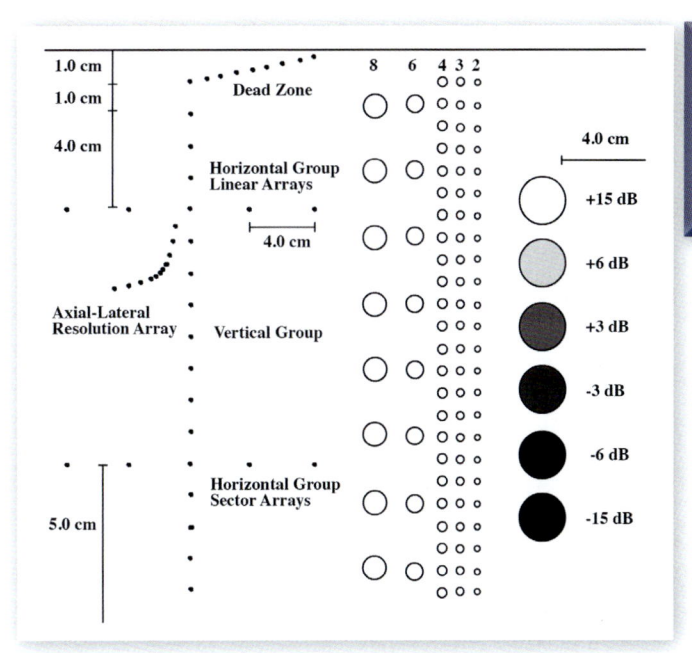

Fig. 22b **Target drawing of ATS Model 539 Multipurpose Phantom**

Key Tests with Model ATS 539:
- Uniformity
- Depth of Penetration
- Beam Profile / Focal Zone / Lateral Response Width
- Vertical Distance Measurement
- Horizontal Distance Measurement
- Axial and Lateral Resolution
- Elevational Resolution
- Contrast Resolution
- Grayscale Contrast Sensitivity
- Dead Zone Assessment

Product Description

The Model 539 Multipurpose phantom is an easy, comprehensive means of evaluating imaging systems over the full range of clinical imaging frequencies (2 MHz to 18 MHz).

Our phantom is designed with a combination of monofilament line targets for distance measurements and tissue mimicking target structures of varying sizes and contrasts. Cystic-like target structures are positioned in-line vertically, thereby permitting an entire target group to be displayed in one view. Due to the acoustic similarity of the background material and the target structures, artifacts caused by distortion, shadowing or enhancement have been eliminated. Six grayscale targets ranging in contrast from +15 to -15 dB are provided to evaluate the system's displayed dynamic range and grayscale processing performance.

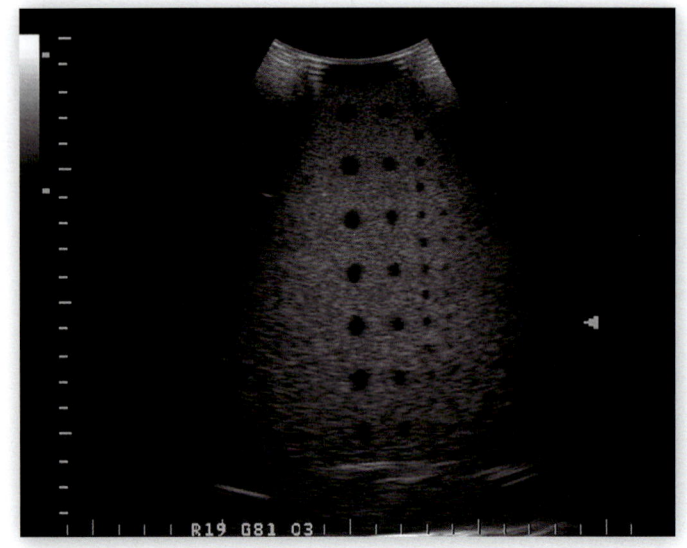

Fig. 23 **Curved linear image of ATS Multipurpose Phantom**

Notice that *Figure 23* was created using a curved linear transducer. Because of the curve of the surface, there is no contact with the phantom on the left and right edge of the transducer. Within these two regions there is image dropout. Within these two regions there is significant reverberation within the gel causing acoustic shadowing below. You should also notice that the first 7 cysts of 8 mm diameter are detected, the very bottom cyst is not. For the 4 mm cysts, the very top cyst is not detected because of insufficient lateral resolution. Furthermore, deeper than 12 cm, the ability to detect the 4 mm cysts deteriorates. For the top 5 cm, the 3 mm cysts are in the region of dropout caused by lack of contact. By 10 cm, the ability to detect the 3 mm cysts is pretty difficult, and the cyst certainly appears smaller than 3 mm. Only 1 of the 2 mm cysts is visible at the depth of about 8 cm.

Features of the Fluke Model 84-317:
- Complies with the AIUM standard for quality assurance
- The best-performing phantom in the industry, for evaluating system and transducer performance
- Includes cyst-like and solid structures in various sizes
- Simulates liver tissue scattering and attenuation
- Now available with 0.5 dB/cm/MHz or 0.7 dB/cm/MHz attenuation coefficients
- Provides resolution targets at several depths
- Compatible with all types of imaging equipment, including small parts scanners
- Withstands extreme temperatures, making it ideal for service and quality control use
- Three large scanning surfaces

Product Description
The 84-317 Multipurpose Tissue/Cyst Ultrasound Phantom helps provide both quantitative and qualitative information on the performance of all diagnostic ultrasound-imaging systems. When used on a regular basis, it promotes uniform system performance, better patient data, and more productive work schedules. Imaging equipment can be evaluated for axial and lateral resolution, vertical and horizontal distance calibration and linearity, and ring down. This updated and improved phantom is filled with Zerdine®, a solid-elastic, water-based polymer that exhibits echogenic patterns similar to those encountered in human liver parenchyma. Unlike other phantom materials, Zerdine® is elastic and is not damaged by heavier scanning pressures. It is also highly resistant to damage by extreme temperatures.

Fig. 24 **Fluke 84-317 Multi-Purpose Tissue/Cyst Ultrasound Phantom**

Fig. 25a **CIRS Model 040GSE Multi-Purpose Multi-Tissue Ultrasound Phantom (including structures of varying elasticity)**

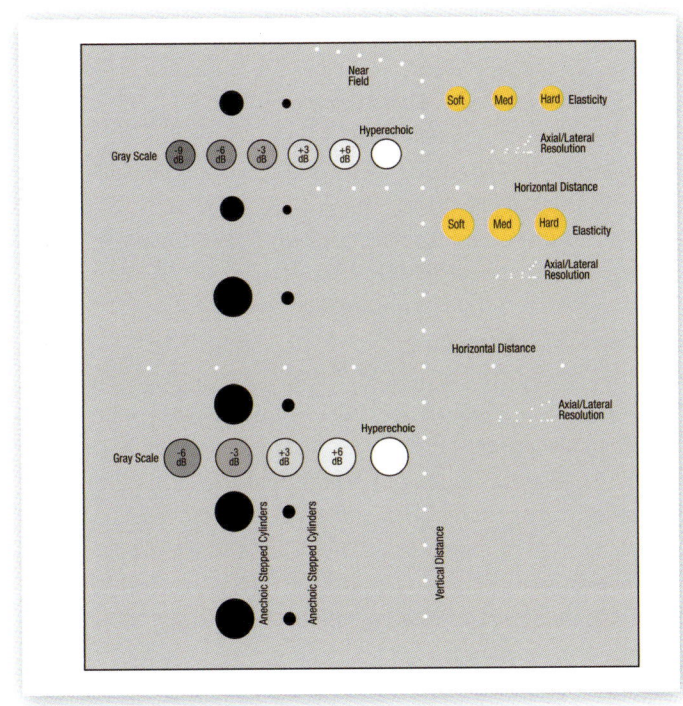

Fig. 25b **Target drawing of CIRS Model 040GSE**

Key Tests with Model 040GSE:
- Uniformity
- Depth of Penetration
- Beam Profile / Focal Zone / Lateral Response Width
- Vertical Distance Measurement
- Horizontal Distance Measurement
- Axial and Lateral Resolution
- Elevational Resolution
- Contrast Resolution
- Grayscale Contrast Sensitivity
- Elasticity Sensitivity
- Dead Zone Assessment

Features:
- Test the full range of standard diagnostic ultrasound probes (2 MHz to 18 MHz)
- Dual attenuation design provides challenging testing environment for high sensitivity probes
- Detachable water wells allow for testing curvilinear and endocavity probes
- Only general purpose QA phantom on market with elasticity targets
- Ensure over ten years of reliable use through reinspection and repair services

Product Description
The CIRS Model 040GSE Multi-Purpose, Multi-Tissue Ultrasound Phantom is the most complete solution available for performance and quality assurance testing. Its dual frequency design and detachable water wells allows testing of most transducer shapes – including curvilinear and endocavity – and frequencies. It is also the only QA phantom on the market that provides both elasticity targets and all the standard B-mode imaging test objects. The phantom is made of CIRS' proprietary Zerdine® hydrogel polymer, which has been formulated to provide tissue mimicking properties including compatibility with harmonic imaging. To maximize phantom lifetime, this gel is contained in a rugged ABS plastic housing with a Saran-based laminate membrane.

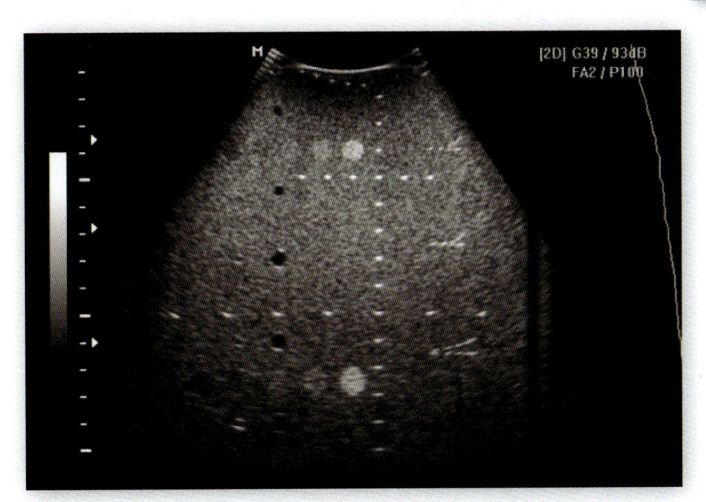

Fig. 26 **Curved linear image of CIRS Model 040GSE Phantom**

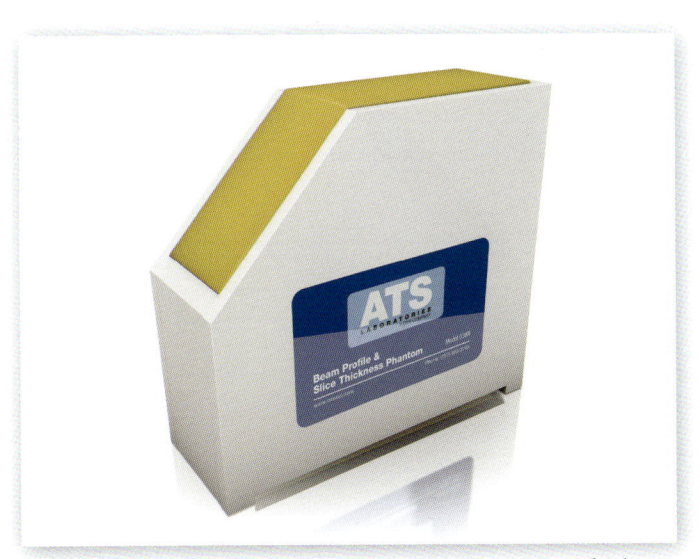

Fig. 27 **CIRS Model ATS 538NH Beam Profile & Slice Thickness Phantom**

Key Tests with Model ATS 538H:
- Tissue Harmonic Imaging Compatibility
- Beam Profile / Focal Zone / Lateral Response Width

Product Description
The Model 538NH can measure the beam profile and slice thickness of ultrasound imaging systems by evaluating the appearance of a thin plane of echogenic material against an anechoic background. Scanning the scattering plane from one surface, perpendicular to the thin plane, obtains an image of the beam profile at varying depths

of the 538NH. This image contains a great deal of information about the sound beam as it propagates through the tissue-mimicking media such as the focal length, focal zone, beam width, side and grating lobes, and far-field beam divergence. In addition, the near field region of the beam can be easily distinguished from the far field as varying degrees of brightness close to the scan surface versus the homogeneous amplitude further down.

Scanning the scattering plane from a second surface, 45° from the scattering plane, allows users to evaluate the slice thickness of an imaging system at varying depths. Slice thickness or elevational resolution, the third component of spatial resolution, displays reflections produced by structures in front of or behind the beam's main axis. The effect of changes in the slice thickness is identical to those seen with axial and lateral resolution. The thinner the slice thickness, the better the resolution: as the slice thickness increases, the degree of spatial resolution decreases. All ATS urethane phantoms are guaranteed for the useful life of the phantom, defined as 10 years.

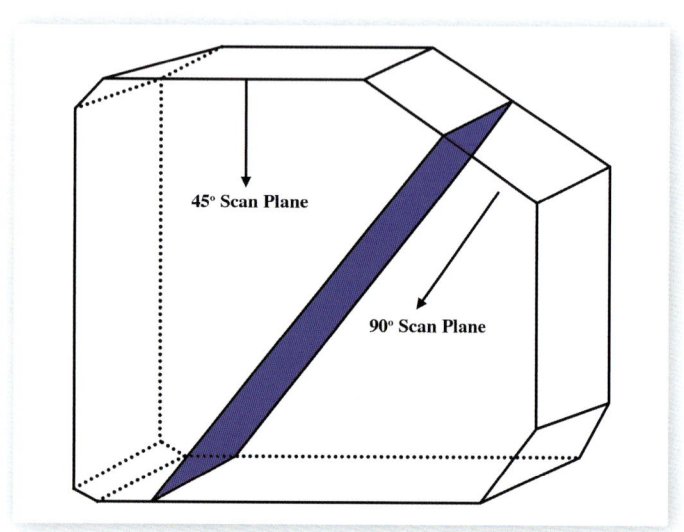

Fig. 28 **Geometry ATS Model 538N**

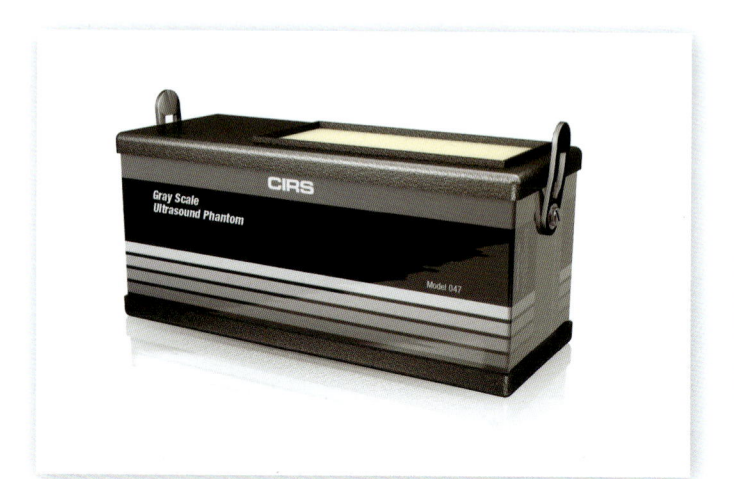

Fig. 29 **CIRS Model 047 Gray Scale Ultrasound Phantom**

Features:
- 21 testing objects
- Diameters: 2.4, 4, and 6.4 mm
- Contrast: anechoic, -9, -6, -3, +3, +6, +9 dB
- Depth of test object varies continuously as phantom is scanned laterally
- Scatter controlled independently from attenuation
- Carry case included

Product Description

The CIRS Gray Scale Ultrasound Phantom is a single, simple tool to assess resolution of masses varying in size, depth and contrast. The phantom's unique design allows for rapid visualization of grayscale resolution power at continuous depths from 1 to 12 cm. Due to the controlled scatter characteristics of the targets, the Model 047 may be used to evaluate grayscale sensitivity on all diagnostic ultrasound machines with a wide range of transducer frequencies. This phantom is an ideal training tool for learning optimum system setup and evaluating system performance.

Masses may be viewed with either a circular or elliptical cross-section. The mass diameters were selected so the volume imaged would double as the diameter increased. The grayscale levels were selected to achieve a doubling in signal intensity as you move from mass to mass. The anechoic masses comply with the ACR accreditation program.

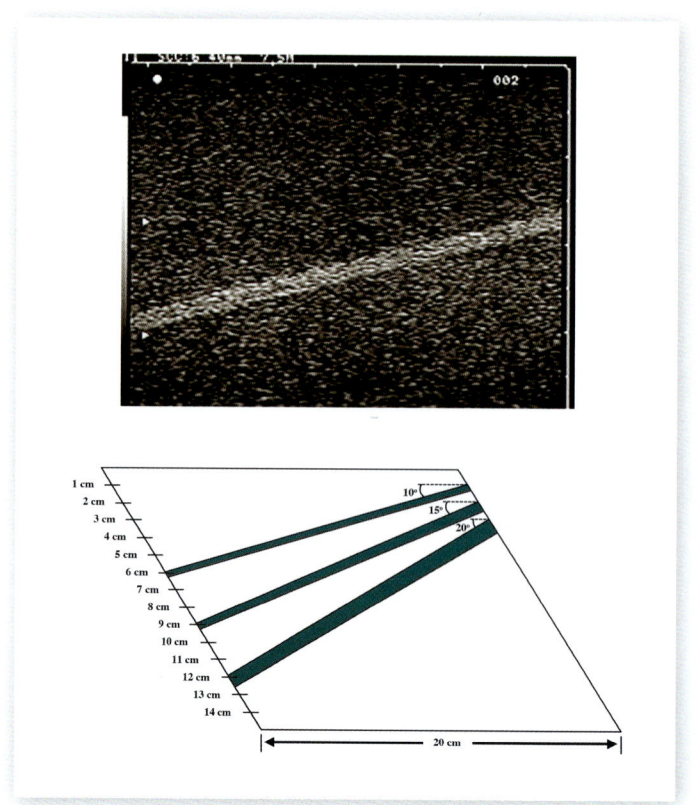

Fig. 30a **Longitudinal view and target drawing**

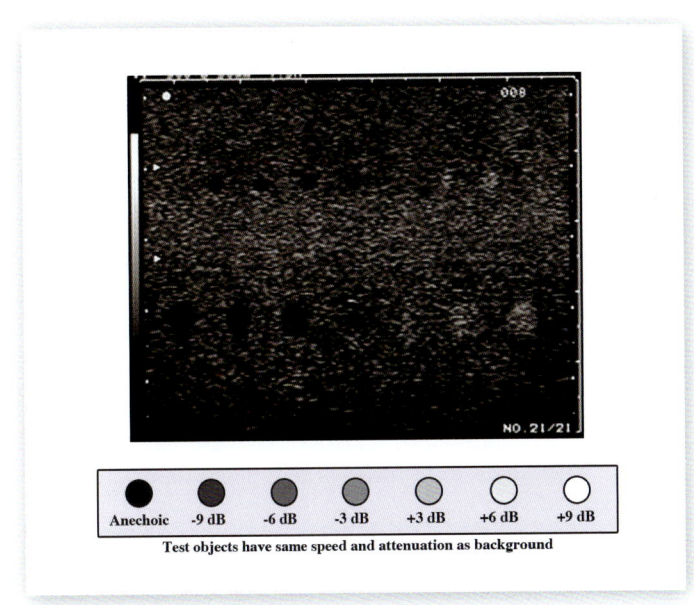

Fig. 30b **Transverse view and target drawing**

In *Figure 30b*, notice that the -3 dB cyst and +3 dB mass are virtually indistinguishable from the surrounding tissue mimicking material. This image gives a relatively good idea of what a 3 dB noise figure looks like. Also notice that an increase from 3 dB to 6 dB makes the signal easier to appreciate but still does not represent very good signal-to-noise. By 9 dB, the signal, although not pristine is at least immediately detectable with some degree of confidence.

Fig. 31 **CIRS Model 055 & 055A Ultrasound Phantoms for 2D and 3D Evaluation**

Key Tests with Models 055 and 055A:
- *Linear Distance*
- *Perimeter*
- *Area*
- *Surface Area*
- *Volume*

Product Description
The CIRS Model 055 3D Ultrasound Calibration Phantom and 055A 3D Wire Test Object, may be used to perform the following tests of the accuracy of spatial measurements, which is especially for 3D and 4D ultrasound systems equipped with spatial encoding algorithms. In the Model 055, these tests are performed with the aid of three volumetric targets, while in the Model 055A they are performed using wire targets. The phantoms can also be used to perform Image uniformity and depth of penetration tests.

Both phantoms are made of CIRS, proprietary Zerdine® hydrogel polymer, which has been formulated to provide tissue mimicking properties including compatibility with harmonic imaging. To maximize phantom lifetime, this gel is contained in a rugged ABS plastic housing with a Saran- based laminate membrane.

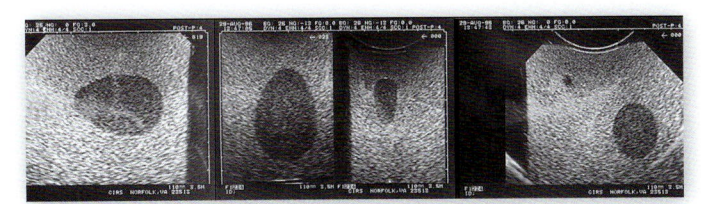

Fig. 32a **Images of 3D eggs within 055 3D Phantom**

The Model 055A 3D Wire Test Object is a wire-target phantom. In 2D, the wires can be used to trace imaginary elliptical or rectangular shapes while, in 3D-mode, the same wire targets can trace out elliptical and/or rectangular rods. These are used to measure perimeters, volumes and surface areas. The phantom also can be used to determine image uniformity and depth of penetration.

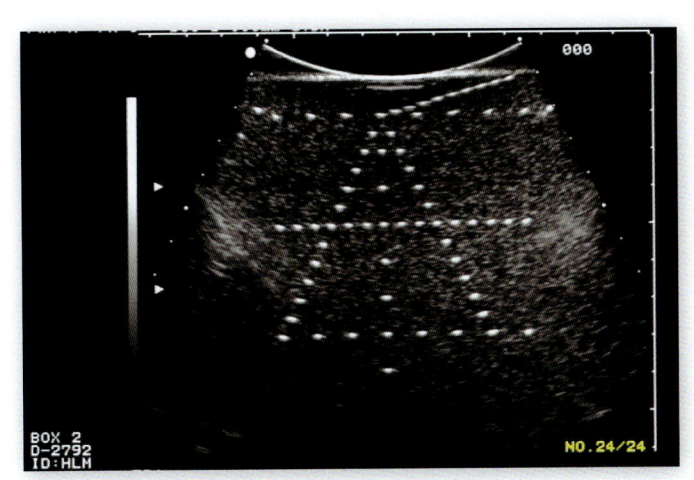

Fig. 32b **Image of the 055A 3D Wire Test Object**

8. Commercially Available Specialty Phantoms

With the ever expanding role of ultrasound, a significant number of specialty phantoms have been created. Phantoms existed for practicing ultrasound guided needle biopsies, focused ultrasound treatment, beating heart models, brain models, fetal image models, and many more. Following are a few examples of some of the specialty phantoms which exist.

Note: Text in the color blue indicates wording excerpted from equipment manufactures' product descriptions.

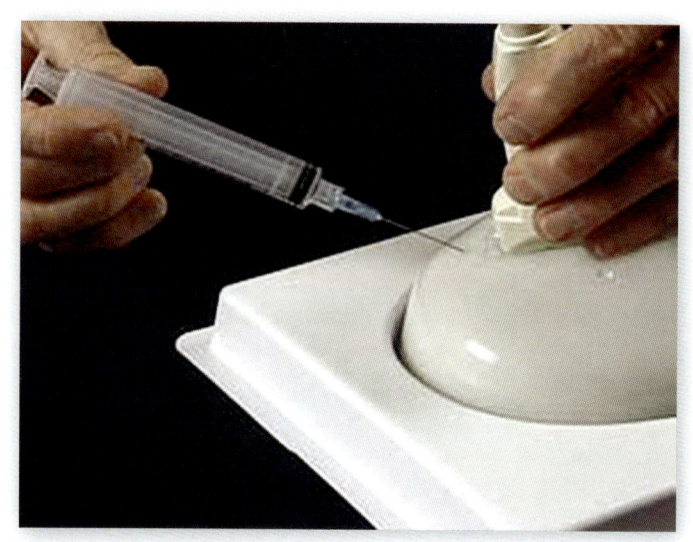

Fig. 33 **CIRS Model 052A Needle Biopsy (Breast) Phantom with Amorphous Lesions**

Benefits of Model 052A:
- *Improve hand-eye coordination*
- *Build confidence and reduce patient anxiety*
- *Test new equipment*
- *Experiment with new techniques*
- *Instruct others*
- *Contains cysts which can be aspirated*
- *Contains solids which can be biopsied*

Product Description
The Model 052A, Ultrasound Needle Breast Biopsy Phantom with Amorphous Lesions, was designed specifically for ultrasound-guided needle biopsy training and experimentation. The non-spherical shape of the embedded targets enable practice with 2D, 3D and 4D image acquisition. The Model 052A accurately mimics the ultrasonic characteristics of tissues found in the average human breast. The size and shape of the phantom simulates that of an average patient in the supine position. Within each phantom, there are six cystic masses and six dense masses which are randomly positioned.

Because it is constructed of a self-healing formulation of Zerdine®, the phantom will allow multiple biopsy insertions with minimal needling tracking. Needle tracks will usually disappear within minutes (sometimes seconds) of needle removal. Each cystic mass may be aspirated once and each dense mass may be biopsied multiple times.

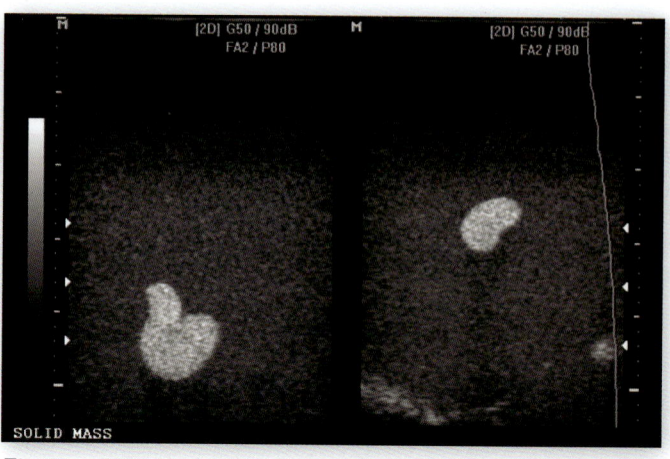

Fig. 34a **CIRS Model 052A image of amorphous solid masses**

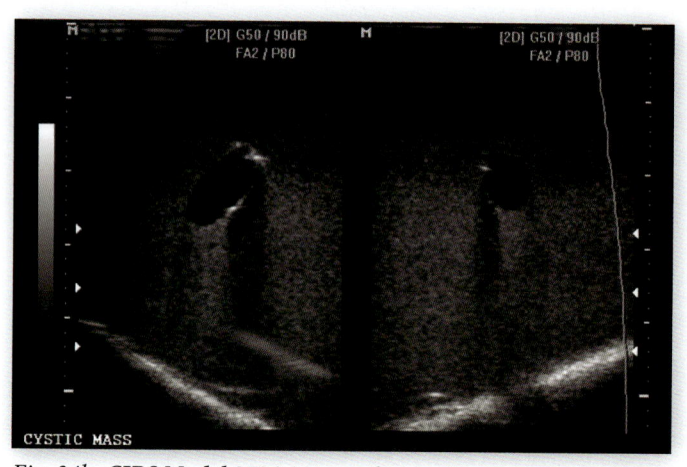

Fig. 34b **CIRS Model 052A image of amorphous cystic structures**

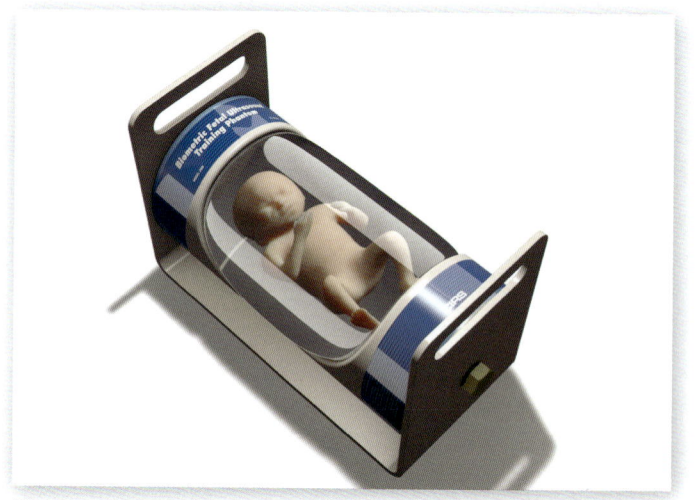

Fig. 35 **CIRS Model 068 Fetal Ultrasound Biometrics Phantom**

Features:
- *Demonstrates system capabilities*
- *Teach imaging protocols to estimate gestational age*
- *Practice 2D, 3D, and 4D fetal scan techniques*
- *Measure CRL, BPD, FL and AC*
- *Gain competency in performing prenatal ultrasound*

Product Description

The mid-term ultrasound exam is used to estimate gestational age and to diagnose fetal malformation so students can gain competency with hands-on practice. Unfortunately, access to patients can be limited. The CIRS Model 068 Fetal Ultrasound Biometrics Phantom facilitates teaching and demonstration of fetal ultrasound techniques in a non-stressful situation. A tissue equivalent full fetal model is suspended in a non- echoic, amniotic fluid-like environment. The model is housed in a rotatable cylinder with 2 fields of view. A variety of fetal/ transducer orientations can be achieved.

The Model 068 contains an asymmetric head with upper portion of the skull, right and left brain lobes and lateral and third ventricles. These anatomical references are used to measure the biparietal diameter (BPD) and anterior/posterior diameter (APD). Right and left femoral shafts with distal epiphysis are provided for femur length (FL) measurements. An umbilical marker indicates proper position for taking abdominal circumference (AC). Crown-Rump length (CRL) can also be taken. In addition, the model has full facial details making it suitable for demonstrating multi-dimensional systems and assessment of fetal anomalies.

All anatomies are based on published biometric data for normal fetal growth rates for a gestational age of 21 weeks. This enables assessment of composite measurement techniques and biometric analysis programs common to most ultrasound scanners.

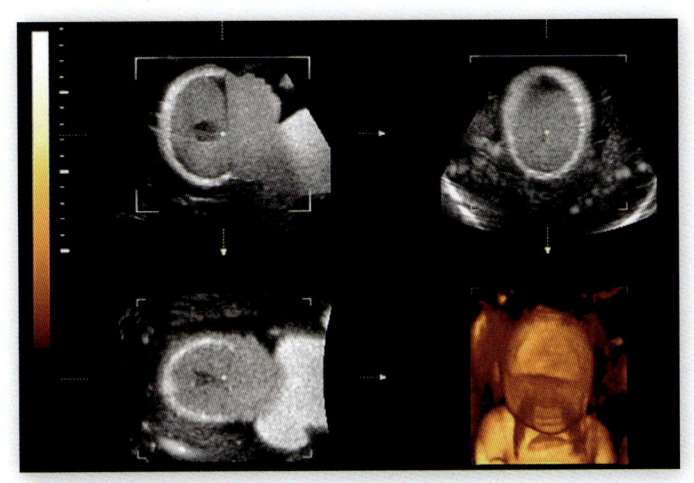

Fig. 36a **CIRS Model 068 images of fetal head and face**

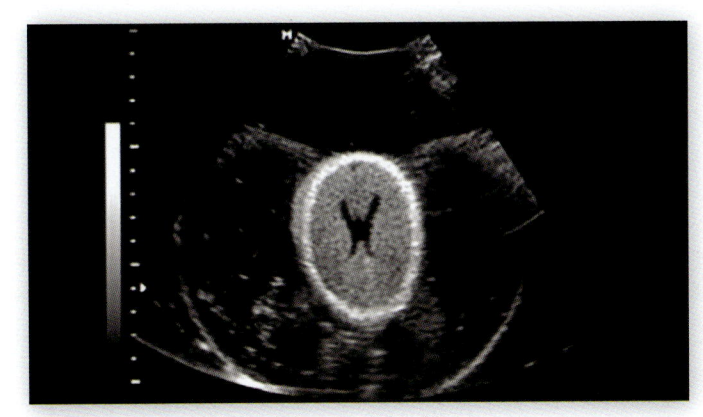

Fig. 36b **CIRS Model 068 image of fetal brain**

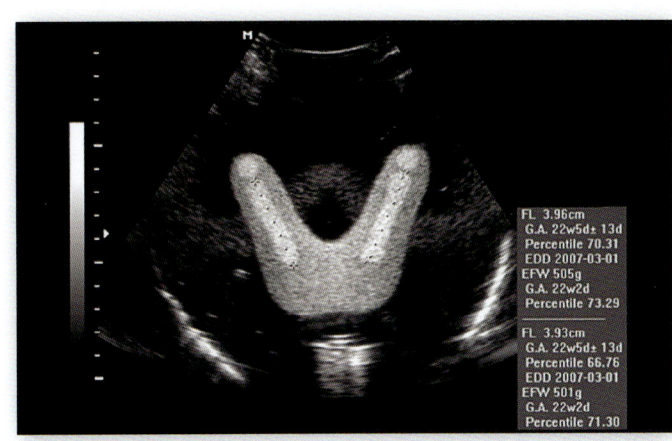

Fig. 36c **CIRS Model 068 image and measurements of fetal femur**

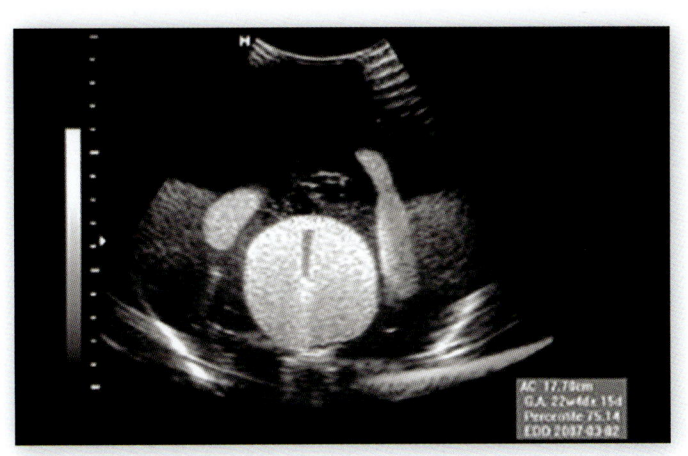

Fig. 36d **CIRS Model 068 image and measurements of fetal arm**

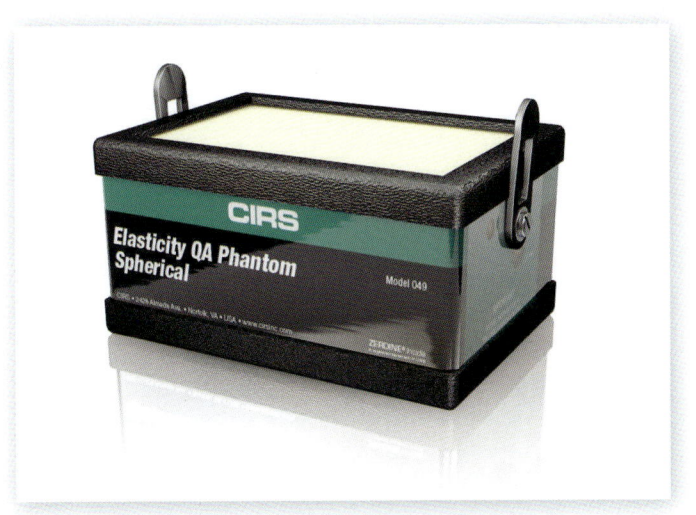

Fig. 37 **CIRS Model 049 && 049A Elasticity QA Phantom**

Features:
- Four types of lesions with discrete elastic moduli (contact CIRS for custom moduli)
- Compatible with both shear wave and compression elastography
- Customized versions available for magnetic resonance elastography

- *Ensure over ten years of reliable use through reinspection and repair services*

Models 049 and 049A are Suitable for:
- Determining dynamic range
- Checking system performance over time
- Training and demonstrating of system features
- Research and development

Product Description
The Model 049 and 049A Elasticity QA Phantoms are tools developed for both shear wave and compression elastography. These are the only phantoms commercially available for sonoelastography quality assurance. The phantoms contain targets of known stiffness relative to the background material and range in stiffness, diameter and depth.

The Model 049 is a basic QA phantom as it contains two sizes of spheres positioned at two different depths. At each depth there are two spheres that are softer than the background and two that are harder than the background. For a broader range of target sizes, the Model 049A phantom has stepped mass targets instead of spheres. Each stepped mass consists of six diameters so that you can evaluate the ability to visualize targets that are located at the same depth and have the same relative stiffness but vary in diameter. The Model 049A is housed in the same size container as the original Model 049.

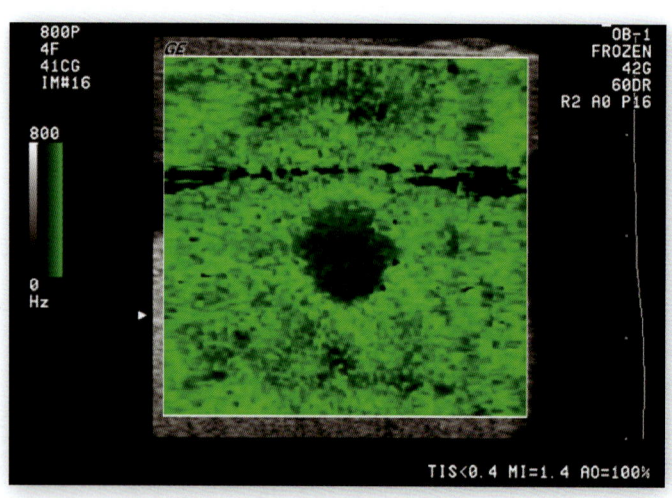

Fig. 38a **CIRS 049 Elastography Phantom image**

Fig. 38b **Schematic of stepped cylinders of the 049A Phantom**

Fig. 39a **Onda HIFU Phantom Gel**

Fig. 39b **Lesions generated in phantom gel using focused ultrasound**

For (High Intensity Focused Ultrasound) HIFU imaging, the idea is to generate high enough intensities so as to cause bioeffects to lesions. These ultrasound images clearly demonstrate that high intensities can produce dramatic effects.

Key Features and Benefits of Onda HIFU Phantom Gel:
- *Record the progression of the lesion growth to characterize the shape and size*
- *Identify defects in HIFU systems such as beam shape variations and alignment problems*
- *Enhance operating training by providing real-time visualization feedback*

Product Description
The complexity of testing HIFU devices in animal tissue is significantly reduced by using our proprietary recording gels. Phantom gels are crystal clear synthetic gels that produce lesions of the same position, size and shape as those produced in real tissue when ultrasonic power is applied to the gel. The lesions appear as white three-dimensional solid profiles inside the clear gel and are stable for many weeks. The gels are shipped in clear plastic boxes with lids. The product is stable for several weeks at room temperature, and longer if refrigerated.

Applications for HIFU phantoms:

R&D
Many ultrasonic transducer parameters such as transducer geometry, frequency, and power profiles can be evaluated in a short amount of time without the problems caused by tissue variability. The progression of lesion growth, position, size and shape versus time can be recorded and evaluated.

Manufacturing Quality Control
Phantom gels can detect many defects in HIFU systems such as beam shape variations and alignment problems.

Transducer Performance Evaluation and Protocol development
For any medical procedure it is critical to detect even subtle changes in HIFU and other ultrasonic system performance before and after the procedure. One can use phantom gels to confirm ultrasonic systems, system protocol, and detector feedback loop performance.

Training
The use of these clear phantom gels in training can dramatically improve system operator performance by providing immediate visual feedback. Watching the lesion grow as power is applied is not possible using living tissue.

HIFU Phantom Material Properties

Density:	1060 kg / m³
Phase Velocity:	1600 m/s
Attenuation Coefficient:	0.6 dB/(cm-MHz)
Specific Heat:	3850 J/(kg-°K)
Thermal Conductivity:	0.55 W/(cm-°K)
Optical:	Turns permanently opaque when temperature reaches a threshold of 70°C (this phenomenon results in the formation of tissue mimicking lesions when the phantom is exposed to high intensity ultrasound)

Figure 40 shows a balloon-surrounded radially firing catheter delivering ultrasound to a tissue-mimicking phantom. The areas that turn opaque indicate the treatment regions where temperatures exceed 70°C. The clinical application relies on heat to decrease over-activity of the nerve leading to the kidney.

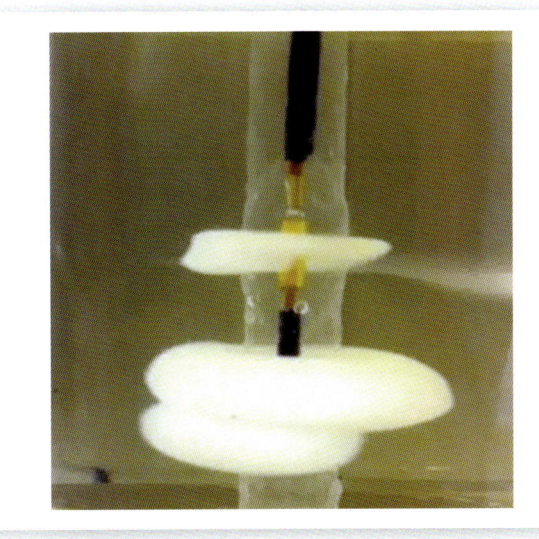

Fig. 40 **Balloon-surrounded radially firing catheter delivering ultrasound to a tissue-mimicking phantom** *(Courtesy Recor Medical, 2013)*

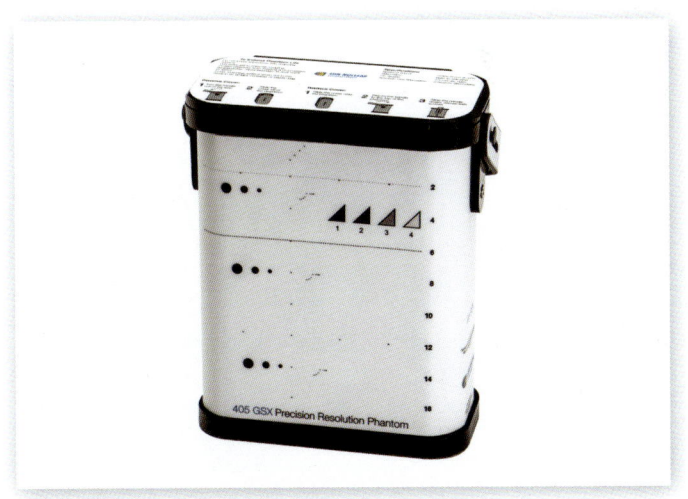

Fig. 41 **405 GSX LE: Troubleshooting Phantom**

Features:
- *Supports Biomeds who need to troubleshoot ultrasound systems*
- *Two horizontal cross fibers in the middle of the phantom can be used for aligning the transducer and as reference markers to ensure consistent setup over time*
- *Triangular grayscale targets support resolution testing of high-performance ultrasound scanner*

Product Description

Advanced tissue mimicking gel and grey scale targets are designed for the exacting standards of today's high-resolution ultrasound systems. The Precision Resolution Grey Scale Phantom 405GSX LE incorporates our new Tissue Mimicking (TM) gel which provides a smoother background texture than conventional tissue mimicking gels. Gammex TM gels are fully compatible with the latest in tissue harmonics equipment and technology. The phantom can be scanned using normal control settings and ensures that the performance measured closely approximates the scanner's performance in a clinical examination.

In addition, the phantom has a new composite film scanning surface that has improved transmission properties so more of the ultrasound beam can be transmitted and received. The 405GSX LE contains all of the quality indicators for performing evaluations of axial resolution, lateral resolution, dead zone cyst imaging, vertical and horizontal distance accuracy and image uniformity. The Precision Resolution Grey Scale Phantom also contains triangular grey scale targets which test the resolution of today's high-performance ultrasound scanners. Unique to the 405GSX LE are two horizontal cross fibers located in the middle of the phantom. These fibers help the user align the transducer and can be used as a reference "marker" to ensure that QA tests are consistently performed on the same scan slice. When both fibers are illuminated, the user can be certain the transducer is exactly perpendicular to the scanning surface.

Fig. 42 True Phantom Adult Skull with Brain

Product Description

Adult Human Skull with brain Phantom is similar to our Head Phantom without the skin mimicking tissue. It can serve multiple purpose(s) such as medical imaging research and treatment planning of non-invasive HIFU brain surgeries. True Phantom Solutions are pioneers in developing these phantoms and hold strength in customizing them to suit the needs of researchers and medical practitioners. The design of the skull phantom is based on an average human male skull and it is made out of realistic patented bone material that is suitable for Ultrasound, MRI and CT applications (any other part of the skull can be fabricated based on the customer order). The brain inside this phantom is similar to our standard brain phantom with an addition of brain blood vessels and bifurcation feature.

The skull phantom has a realistic three-layered structure and the inner porosity can be adjusted according to the requirement of the particular project.

As mentioned above, the phantom is visible on Ultrasound, MR and CT scans. The brain parenchyma inside of the skull phantom is made of an ultra-soft polyurethane-based material that mimics soft tissue and its anatomical shape was created based on the optical scan of an average human brain model used in the anatomy class for medical students. The materials used to build the phantom are stable over time and they do not dry out.

The phantom comprises the entire ventricular system (lateral, third and fourth ventricles) which can be used to generate pressure inside the brain, and more closely approximate real cerebral anatomy. The ventricles are inflatable and can be filled with any liquid.

Prior to imaging the phantom please fill the ventricles completely with water (or chosen contrast agent) using the tube on the back of the brain. After the ventricles are filled, plug the tube with a removable blue silicone plug

Technical Properties of Adult Skull Phantom

Type of Tissue	Sound Velocity (m/s)	Density (g/cm^3)	Hardness (Shore 00)	T2 (ms)	Speckles	Attenuation measured at 2.25 MHz (dB/cm)
Cortical bone material used to fabricate the skull bone phantom	3000 ± 30	2.31	N/A	N/A	N/A	6.4 ± 0.3
Trabecular bone material used to fabricate the trabecular layer within the bone phantom	2800 ± 50	2.03	N/A	N/A	N/A	21 ± 2

Table 2 Technical Properties of Adult Skull Phantom

Technical Properties of Brain Material Phantom

Type of Tissue	Sound Velocity (m/s)	Density (g/cm^3)	Hardness (Shore 00)	T2 (ms)	Speckles	Attenuation measured at 2.25 MHz (dB/cm)
Brain tissue	1400 ± 10	0.99	20	70	Variable	1.0 ± 0.2
Falx cerebri	1400 ± 10	1.01	60	50	Yes	1.7 ± 0.2
Tumor feature	1400 ± 10	1.00	30	65	Yes	1.2 ± 0.2

Table 3 Technical Properties of Adult Brain Phantom

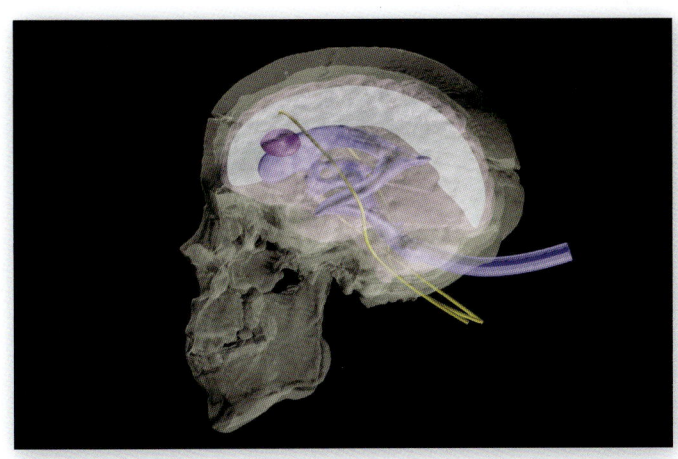

Fig. 43a **Lateral view of True Phantom Adult Skull with Brain**

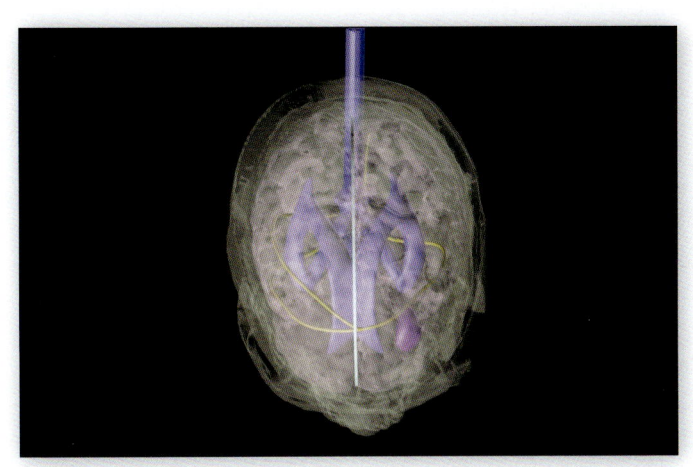

Fig. 43b **Top view of True Phantom Adult Skull with Brain**

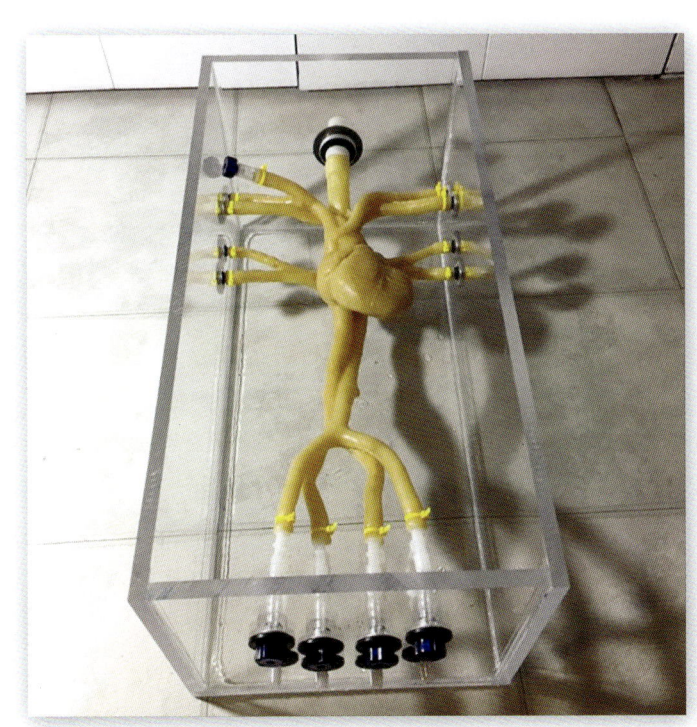

Fig. 44a **True Phantom Adult Heart Phantom**

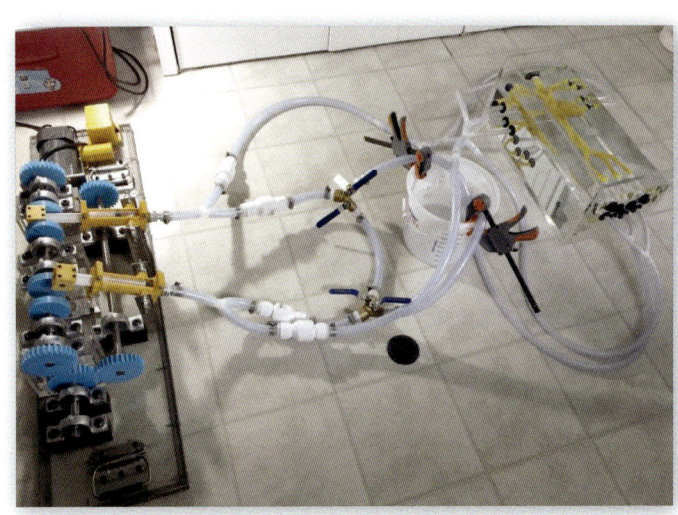

Fig. 44b **True Phantom Adult Heart Phantom Pump attached for Adult Heart Phantom**

Technical Properties of Adult Heart Phantom					
Type of Tissue	Sound Velocity (m/s)	Density (g/cm³)	Hardness (Shore 00)	T2 (ms)	Speckles	Attenuation measured at 2.25 MHz (dB/cm)
Heart tissue	1400 ± 10	1.02	60	50	Yes	1.7 ± 0.2

Table 4 **Technical Properties of Adult Heart Phantom**

Features:
- 2 Atria, 2 Ventricles
- 4 valves
- Appendage feature
- Partial SVC
- Aorta
- Vena cava
- Pulmonic and pulmonary veins attached to LA
- Flexible valvular structures
- Right ventricle:
  – Moderator band that runs from the anterior wall to the septum (bridge)
- Left ventricle:
  – Papillary muscles to the anterior and posterior walls
- Right atrium:
  – Right atrial appendage with distinct muscle structures
- Left atrium:
  – Unique muscle structure to the appendage of the left atrium

Implementing motion to the heart (optional):
- Beating heart model with cyclic motion of the heart walls based on a mechanical pump
- System installed on a plex glass
- Chambers fillable with water without air pockets
- Adjustable heart rate (0-140 BPM)
- Hysteresis in motion (diastole and systole of the cardiac cycle)
- Asymmetrical displacement of the heart chambers
- Complete system installed on a plex glass

Implementing additional features of the heart (optional):
- *Controlled pressure wave in the left atrium heart chamber*
- *Realistic pressure pulses in left atrium*
- *Pressure wave simplified to sinus wave*
- *Control to change the pressure*
- *Heating chamber to achieve realistic temperatures*
- *Pressurized heating chamber*
- *Regulator unit*
- *Major Accommodating Tube*

Product Description

Adult Heart Phantom is a realistic simulator of human heart that is anatomically correct and compatible with ultrasound, X-RAT CT, and MRI. This product has wide range of applications as it has potential to support beating functionality. Ultrasound navigated endoscopy, catheter insertion under ultrasound probe and other research and development based applications.

True Phantom Solutions designs and creates biomedical phantoms that are ultrasound, MRI and CT compatible. We use patented synthetic material to create life-like phantoms that mimic the acoustical, physical and mechanical properties of real biological tissues. Using 3D printing technology and synthetic material, the phantoms are made to be an exact model of anatomical structures. The phantoms are fully customizable and able to suit any biomedical project. Upon special request, the geometry and dimensions of feature and its properties can be customized based on the requirements of any particular project. The picture represents the phantom/model without a water tank. An optional water tank helps researchers in obtaining an enhanced view of the internal structure of the heart.

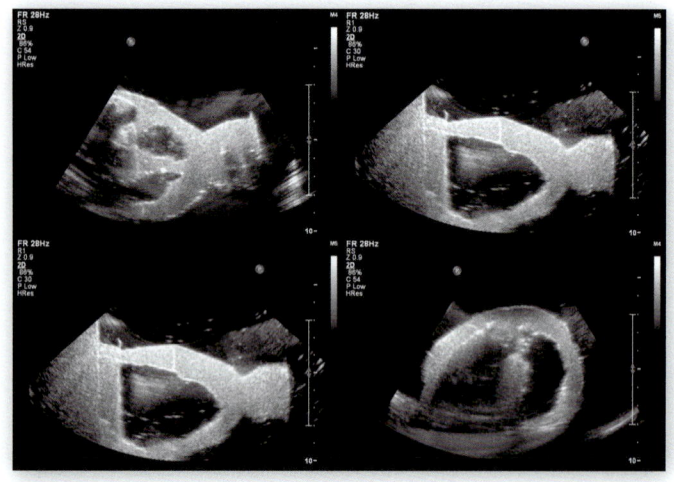

Fig. 45 **Various imaging views of the True Phantom Adult Heart Phantom**

9. Conceptual Questions

View ONLINE Conceptual Questions

10. Quality Assurance Statistics

10.1 As Part of the Quality Program

A part of every quality program is comparing lab test results against a metric to assess lab performance. Ultimately, a laboratory must ensure that the results of their clinical testing correlate well with results from other diagnostic exams. The starting point for this assessment is tracking the data through tables or patient logs. The information documented in these logs then becomes the data for statistical calculations which compare the laboratory "comparison test" against the metric test generally referred to as the "gold standard". There are many different statistical indices which can be used to assess the correlation of lab tests with other modalities such as the accuracy, sensitivity, specificity, and positive and negative predictive values. Throughout the next section, the specifics of these statistical indices, as well as the practical issues of how to calculate these parameters is discussed.

11. Q&A Statistics

11.1 The Value of Statistics

It is often said that one can reach any desired conclusion through manipulation of statistics. If you know how to "spin" the numbers, you can support any claim and reach any conclusion that serves your purpose. Merely by changing the reference point, statistics can lead to very different conclusions. Therefore, for statistics to have any real meaning, it is critical to clearly express the reference point and/or any assumptions. When this simple, common-sense approach is followed, statistics regarding clinical testing can be very valuable.

11.2 What is Statistical Testing?

Statistical testing in medicine involves two different tests: a reference test and a comparison test. The reference test is referred to as the "gold standard". The comparison test is the procedure you desire to validate. A test becomes the gold standard when it is recognized as the most consistent and accurate test for a particular disease. A comparison test is any other testing procedure, competing technology, or variation from the "gold standard" test.

To begin, statistical testing assumes that there is a relatively meaningful gold standard against which to compare. If a test is compared

View ONLINE Animation and Image Library

with a "gold standard" with some degree of error, then the results of that statistical test will reflect that error. For example, imagine that you have to correct an exam to see how many times a student answered correctly and how many times that student answered incorrectly for a given number of questions. The answer key for the exam is like the "gold standard." In essence, if there are errors in the answer key, then there will be errors in the "corrected exam." In other words, the resulting score will not be a true or accurate representation of the student's knowledge. Similarly, if the gold standard is not 100% accurate, then the statistical indices that specify the quality of the testing procedure will also not be completely accurate. We will further discuss the implications of an inaccurate gold standard later in this chapter.

12. Making Statistical Indices More Intuitive

There are three things you must do if you want to develop an intuitive and practical understanding of statistical indices:

1. Realize that all indices start with a presumption that the gold standard is perfect.

2. Pay particular attention to the English of the statistical terminology.

3. Pay close attention to the labels and layout of any table of data.

As we learn about statistical indices, each of these three points will be further detailed and discussed.

12.1 Presume that the Gold Standard is Perfect, Adhering to the "Golden" Rule

The term "gold standard" sometimes misleads people. As already mentioned, there is no guarantee that any test that has been deemed the "gold standard" is perfect, or even very good. This fact seems inconsistent with the term "gold" for some people. However, you must understand that the term "gold" does not refer to a test being perfect, but rather the term refers to a test being "the best" at a given moment in time. In medicine, in reality, the gold standard may better be termed "the test that has had the most repeatable results to date which will be used as a reference for all new tests or competing technologies". Clearly, this terminology is cumbersome at best and the term "gold standard" is much easier to port around. Again you must realize that the gold standard test for a specific procedure today will eventually likely be replaced with a better "gold standard."

> **Author's Note:**
> **Assumption of the Golden Rule**
>
> For statistical indices to make sense, you will need to presume that the gold standard is perfect even if it is not. Since the "gold standard" is the best information we have to use as a reference, we will need to assume that this reference is perfect. Since this presumption will be referred to many times, this starting point assumption will be referred to as the "golden rule."

The Golden Rule

> For the purposes of statistical indices, the assumption is that the gold standard is perfect.

As you will see, all statistical indices are relative to this assumption. Let's look at the first application of this rule.

The Meaning of the Words "True" and "False" with Respect to the Golden Rule

If the results of a test match the results of the gold standard (which by the golden rule we trust implicitly) then the test is said to be "true." In other words, truth is when you match the gold standard since we presume that the gold standard is perfect. To reiterate, when the test matches the gold standard it is presumed to be correct, or "true."

> "True" is when the test result matches the gold standard result

Similarly, if the results of a test do not match those of a gold standard (which again by the golden rule we implicitly trust) then the test is said to be "false."

> "False" is when the test result does not match the gold standard result

You will see further applications of the "golden rule" as we discuss the testing data in detail.

> **KEY CONCEPT**
>
> Statistical test validation is a method for assessing the quality of a test relative to the performance of a reference test referred to as the "gold standard."

12.2 Pay Particular Attention to the English of the Statistical Terminology

The second key to understanding statistical indices is to pay close attention to the language and English meanings. Trying to memorize the definition of each calculation is difficult and the definitions tend to evaporate from your memory over time. Quite frequently, you will see the calculations taught as a series of arrows overlapping a graph with no reference made to the true meaning or significance of the calculation. By really thinking about the connotation of each word, and using a little logic, you can learn how to calculate and interpret these indices much more easily without the pain of pure memorization.

> **Author's Note:**
> **Understanding Statistical Indices**
>
> The approach usually taught for calculating statistical indices involves memorizing a series of circles and arrows overlaid on a 2 x 2 table of data. There is no guarantee that the data will always be presented in the "conventional" format as is displayed in *Figures 46-50*. If the data is presented in any format other than the "conventional format," the arrow approach becomes invalid unless you transpose the arrows with the data. In other words, the arrow approach is particularly troublesome when the data in the table is not presented in standard format, as may be the case on an exam. When you really understand statistical indices, and do not just memorize calculation technique, transposition of the data will not present a problem.

The Meaning of the Words "Positive" and "Negative"

Remember that both the comparison test and the gold standard test are attempting to predict the presence of disease. Therefore, if the result of a test is positive, it means that the test predicted the presence of disease. Similarly, if the test is negative, it means that the test predicted the absence of disease. Now if we take this simple English interpretation and combine it with our application of the golden rule, we get the following terms:

Remember all tests are referenced to the gold standard.

True Positive (**TP**):	The test is correct (T) because it matches the gold standard and the test is positive for disease (P).
True Negative (**TN**):	The test is correct (T) because it matches the gold standard and the test is negative for disease (N).
False Positive (**FP**):	The test is incorrect (F) because it does not match the gold standard and the test is positive for disease (P).
False Negative (**FN**):	The test is incorrect (F) because it does not match the gold standard and the test is negative for disease (N).

12.3 Pay Close Attention to the Labels and Layout of any Table of Data

When calculating statistical indices, it is common to format the data in a 2 x 2 table. Conventionally, the gold standard data is displayed in columns below the title "Gold Standard" and the comparison test data is displayed in rows next to the title of the comparison test. It is important to realize that the data can be presented in any format, forcing you to pay strict attention to the labels on the axes of the table. We will start by building up the table of data in the "conventional format."

> **KEY CONCEPT**
>
> For the purposes of statistical validation, the gold standard is assumed to be perfect, and hence, the definition of "truth."

13. Building the Table of Data

Let's begin by building up the table one piece at a time, as demonstrated in the graphs below. Notice that next to the title "Comparison Test" there is a plus sign (+). As you would anticipate, the plus sign stands for the word positive. Therefore, every positive test for disease by the comparison test will be contained in this row.

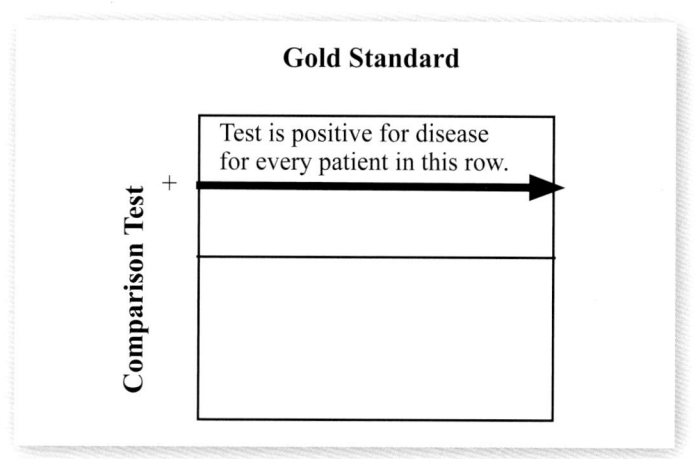

Fig. 46 **When the test predicts disease**

In the table below notice that a minus sign has been added next to the comparison test. As you would anticipate, the negative sign stands for the test being negative for disease. Therefore, every negative test for disease by the comparison test will be contained in this row.

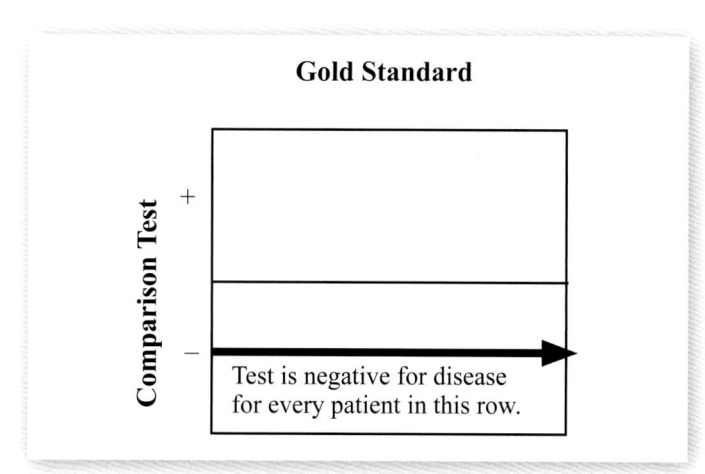

Fig. 47 **When the test predicts no disease**

So far, these two partial tables (above) only represent the results of the test, but do not indicate how well the test matches the gold standard. We will now add symbols below the "gold standard" to create columns to use as a reference for the test results.

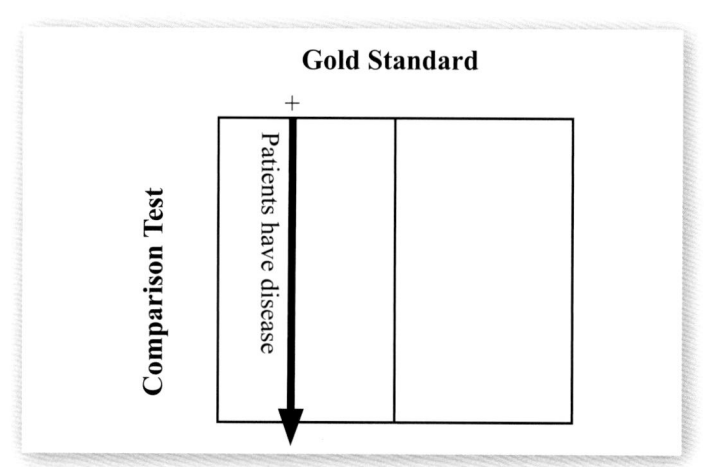

Fig. 48 **When the gold standard predicts disease**

Referring to *Figure 48*, since the plus sign indicates positive for disease, any entry in the column below the plus sign of the gold standard indicates that the gold standard was positive for disease. Since by the golden rule we always presume the gold standard is correct, we presume everyone in this column really does have disease.

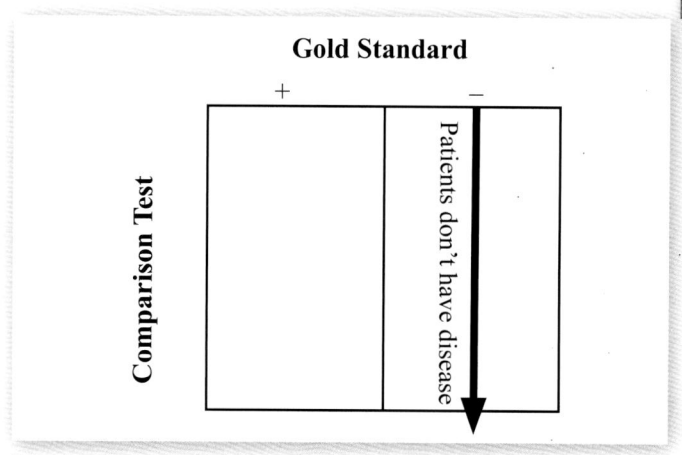

Fig. 49 **When the gold standard predicts no disease**

Similarly, any entry displayed in the column below the negative sign implies that the gold standard was negative for disease. Since we believe the gold standard, this means that anyone below the minus sign really does not have disease.

Now if we combine all four of these partial tables together, the "conventional" format is achieved (*Figure 50*). When combining these four partial tables, whenever the comparison test matches the gold standard, since we trust the gold standard, the test is called "true." In contrast, whenever the test results do not agree with the gold standard, the test is called "false." For example, notice that in the upper left quadrant, both the test and the gold standard predicted disease, thereby making the test a true positive (TP).

	Gold Standard +	Gold Standard −
Comparison Test +	(TP) test correctly predicted disease	(FP) test incorrectly predicted disease
Comparison Test −	(FN) test incorrectly predicted no disease	(TN) test correctly predicted no disease

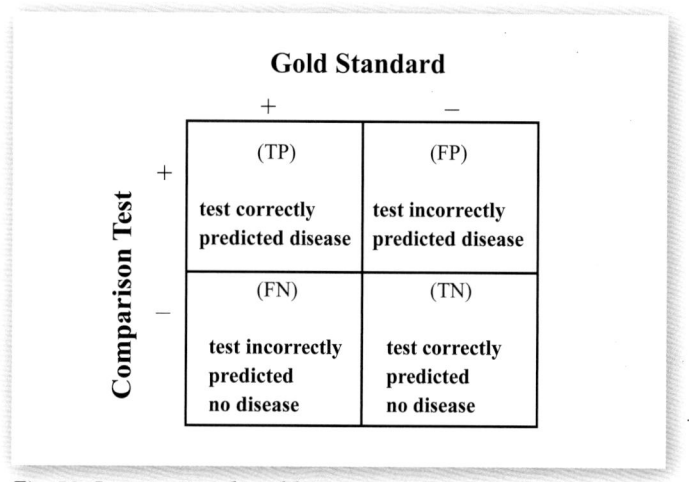

Fig. 50 **Interpreting the table**

14. Exercises: Interpreting the Statistical Table

View ONLINE Exercises

15. Statistical Parameters

Once data has been classified according to true or false and positive or negative, there are a series of calculations which can be made. Each of these statistical parameters tells us something different about the quality of the testing procedure (relative to the gold standard).

Again, paying close attention to the true meaning of the names for each calculation can make life infinitely simpler. For example, you should learn the distinction between the words specificity, sensitivity, and accuracy. Let's look at the meaning of each of these words so as to determine how each of these parameters can be calculated mathematically.

15.1 Sensitivity

The word "sensitive" implies the ability to detect small parameters. Since the prevalence of disease should be less than the absence of disease (i.e., should be a small number) sensitivity refers to the ability of a test to detect disease. Now recalling that the quality of the test is made in reference to the gold standard (the golden rule) we can easily state that the sensitivity is the times the test correctly predicted disease divided by all of the times the disease really does exist, or

$$\text{Sensitivity} = \frac{TP}{TP + FN} \times 100\%$$

15.2 Specificity

The word "specific" refers to the ability to "not paint everything with the same broad brush." Imagine that only one patient has disease but your test claims that every patient tested has disease. For the one patient who has disease, the test was certainly correct; however, the test was not very specific. In other words, the test did not do a good job of detecting how many people do not have disease. The specificity refers to the ability of a test to detect the absence of disease relative to the number of people who in reality do not have disease, or

$$\text{Specificity} = \frac{TN}{TN + FP} \times 100\%$$

15.3 Accuracy

The word accurate refers to how often something is correct overall. So the accuracy of a test is the percentage of times the test is correct, of course relative to the gold standard. Therefore the accuracy is all of the times the test is correct divided by all of the tests, or

$$\text{Accuracy} = \frac{TP + TN}{TP + FN + TN + FP} \times 100\%$$

15.4 Positive Predictive Value

As the name suggests, the positive predictive value is a measure of how often the test is correct when positive for disease as a percentage of the total times the test is positive for disease, or

$$\text{Positive Predictive Value} = \frac{TP}{TP + FP} \times 100\%$$

(Notice how the calculation involves only "positive" terms.)

15.5 Negative Predictive Value

As the names suggests, the negative predictive value is a measure of how often the test is correct when negative for disease as a percentage of the total times the test is negative for disease, or

$$\text{Negative Predictive Value} = \frac{TN}{TN + FN} \times 100\%$$

(Notice how the calculation involves only "negative" terms.)

> **KEY CONCEPT**
>
> The accuracy is an overall measure which includes both a calculation of when the test was correct when positive for disease and when the test was correct when negative for disease. As a result, the accuracy must be between the sensitivity and the specificity. Also, the accuracy must be between the negative predictive value and the positive predictive value.

Note that neither of the statements in the Key Concept is the same as saying that the accuracy is the average of the sensitivity and specificity or that accuracy is the average of the negative and positive predictive values. This point will become clear in the next set of exercises.

16. Numerical Example

Let's use an example to demonstrate how to perform these calculations.

◊ **Example:**
A series of tests was performed and compared with a gold standard test. The test under question resulted in:

- 120 predictions of no disease which agreed with the gold standard
- 20 predictions of no disease which did not agree with the gold standard
- 70 predictions of disease which agreed with the gold standard
- 10 predictions of disease which did not agree with the gold standard

What are the sensitivity, specificity, accuracy, positive predictive value, and negative predictive value?
(Again, use the standard English definitions to help.)

- Predictions of no disease when there is no disease is called a true negative, so: TN = 120
- Predictions of no disease when there is disease is called a false negative, so: FN = 20
- Predictions of disease when there is disease is called a true positive, so: TP = 70
- Predictions of disease when there is not disease is called a false positive, so: FP = 10

Putting the data into the "standard" table format, the table becomes:

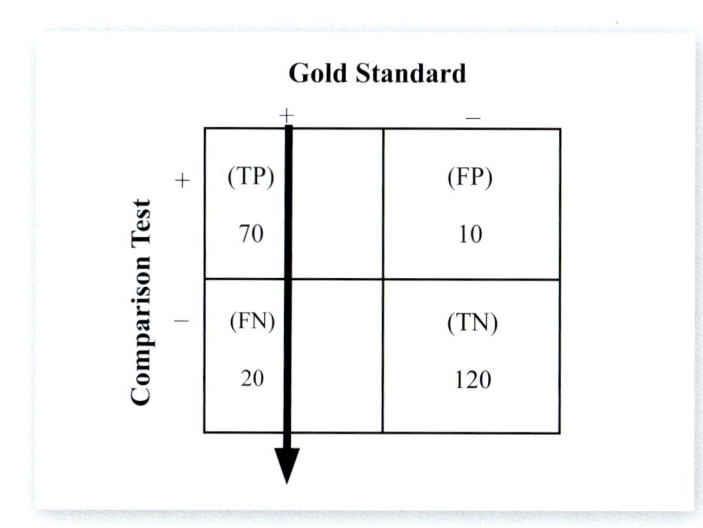

	Gold Standard +	Gold Standard −
Comparison Test +	(TP) 70	(FP) 10
Comparison Test −	(FN) 20	(TN) 120

Now recall that the sensitivity refers to how many times the test correctly predicted disease divided by all the times there truly is disease, so

$$\text{Sensitivity} = \frac{TP}{TP+FN} = \frac{70}{70+20} = \frac{70}{90} = \frac{7}{9} = 77.8\%$$

Now recall that specificity refers to how many times the test correctly predicted the absence of disease divided by the total number of times there was no disease, so

$$\text{Specificity} = \frac{TN}{TN+FP} = \frac{120}{120+10} = \frac{120}{130} = \frac{12}{13} = 92.3\%$$

Now recall that the accuracy is the total number of times the test was correct divided by the total number of tests, so

$$\text{Accuracy} = \frac{TP+TN}{TP+FN+TN+FP} = \frac{70+120}{70+20+120+10} = \frac{190}{220} = 86.4\%$$

Now recall that the positive predictive value is the number of times the test correctly predicted disease divided by the total number of positive predictions, so

$$\text{Positive Predictive Value} = \frac{TP}{TP+FP} = \frac{70}{70+10} = \frac{70}{80} = \frac{7}{8} = 87.5\%$$

Now recall that the negative predictive value is the number of times the test correctly predicted no disease divided by the total number of negative predictions:

$$\text{Negative Predictive Value} = \frac{TN}{TN+FN} = \frac{120}{120+20} = \frac{120}{140} = \frac{12}{14} = \frac{6}{7} = 85.7\%$$

> **CHECKPOINT: Exam Tip**
>
> From this example, notice that the accuracy is numerically between the sensitivity and the specificity, but it is not the average of the sensitivity and the specificity. Similarly, the accuracy is numerically between the positive predictive value and the negative predictive value, but is not the average of the two.

17. Real World Understanding

To develop a more intuitive understanding of these statistical indices, a real world analogy is usually helpful. Let's say that you go for a series of tests because you are experiencing symptoms that might be caused by an ailment called "X-disease." Let's consider some different possible scenarios based on the resulting data for X-disease testing relative to a gold standard.

Gold Standard for X-disease

	+	−
Test for X-disease +	7	10
Test for X-disease −	3	180

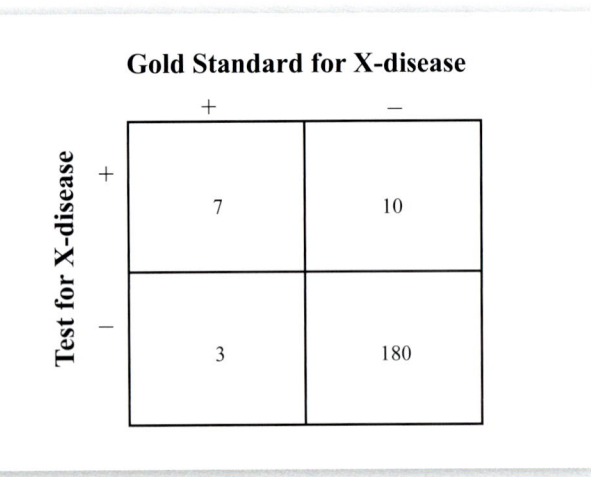

Fig. 51 **Sample data for X-disease testing scenarios**

Scenario 1:
The test for X-disease is negative. How confident should you be that you do not have X-disease?

Answer: Pretty confident

$$\text{The Negative Predictive Value} = \frac{TN}{TN + FN} = \frac{180}{180 + 3} = \frac{180}{183} = 98\%$$

$$\text{The Specificity} = \frac{TN}{TN + FP} = \frac{180}{180 + 10} = \frac{18}{19} = 95\%$$

Therefore, most of the time that the test is negative, the test is correct. Also, most of the time that X-disease is not present, the test results are correct.

Scenario 2:
The test for X-disease is positive. How worried should you be that you really have X-disease?

Answer: Somewhat worried but not convinced

$$\text{The Positive Predictive Value} = \frac{TP}{TP + FP} = \frac{7}{7 + 10} = \frac{7}{17} = 41\%.$$

$$\text{The Sensitivity} = \frac{TP}{TP + FN} = \frac{7}{7 + 3} = \frac{7}{10} = 70\%.$$

From the sensitivity we know that the test is fair at detecting the presence of disease (70% of the time). However, when positive, the test is only correct 41% of the time. Therefore, a positive result has a fairly good probability of being incorrect.

Scenario 3:
What can be said about the sensitivity and positive predictive value of this test for X-disease if the gold standard is poor?

Answer: Nothing

It is possible that the test is correct more times or fewer times relative to "truth." Therefore, the true sensitivity and positive predictive value could be very good, very bad, or change very little.

18. Exercises: Statistical Indices

View ONLINE Exercises

ONLINE EXTRAS

For additional support material and to view your completion progress, visit:

www.pegasuslectures.com/6thEdExtras

Extras by Chapter include:
- Animations
- Videos
- Additional Images
- Clarifying Clips
- Supplemental Exercises
- Conceptual Questions

See page x of Preface for access instructions

✗ COMMON MISCONCEPTION: Quality Assurance

MISCONCEPTION: *The accuracy is the average of the sensitivity and specificity.*

The overall accuracy, as a percentage, must be somewhere between the sensitivity and the specificity. However, the accuracy is not necessarily the average of the sensitivity and the specificity, In fact, the accuracy is more often closer to the specificity than the sensitivity, since there tend to be more negative than positive outcomes when testing a patient population.

The same reasoning implies that accuracy must be between the negative (NPV) and positive predictive values (PPV), but that the accuracy is not necessarily the mean of the PPV and NPV.

✗ COMMON MISCONCEPTION: Quality Assurance

MISCONCEPTION: *High statistical measures necessarily imply a good test.*

When we compare a test against a gold standard, we start with the assumption that the gold standard is a perfect test. So when a test matches a gold standard well, the sensitivity, specificity, accuracy, etc. are high values. The reality is that gold standards are rarely perfect tests. As such, if a comparison test statistically matches closely to a gold standard test that has errors, then the comparison test also has errors. With all statistics, it is critical to understand the reference for the statistical measure. Without knowledge about the reference, statistical measures are often misinterpreted and even potentially meaningless.

CHAPTER SUMMARY: Quality Assurance

- Quality assurance has many components including lab protocols, record keeping, laboratory accreditation, individual certification, equipment testing, and statistical analysis of laboratory results for efficacy.
- There are many phantoms and test objects designed to test various system performance parameters.
- Ideally tests are performed routinely by qualified personnel, with results compared to past results, when possible, for identification of changes.
- Doppler testing is very challenging. There are two different fundamental approaches to Doppler testing:
  – Flow phantoms
  – String phantoms
- Imaging phantoms can include string targets, pins, cystic structures, and masses as well as tissue mimicking material.
- Tissue mimicking material is designed to create attenuation as well as yield the approximate propagation velocity of 1540 m/sec as expected in tissue.
- You should be aware of how different geometries of pin layouts can be used to test various system performance parameters such as lateral, axial, and elevation resolution.
- Specialized phantoms exist from multiple companies to test performance aspects of 3D imaging, elastography, intravascular imaging, interventional techniques like needle biopsies, and therapeutic ultrasound techniques such as high intensity focused ultrasound (HIFU).
- Statistics play a vital role in assuring quality patient testing.
- The reference for the quality of a test is the recognized "gold standard" procedure.
- Gold standards are not always correct; however, for statistical comparison, the assumption is that the gold standard is perfect.
- When a test matches the gold standard, the test is considered to be correct or "True".
- When a test does not match the gold standard, the test is considered to be incorrect, or "False".
- The terms "Positive" and "Negative" refer to whether the test indicated disease (positive) or the absence of disease (negative).
- The overall accuracy is the measure of the times the test was considered to be correct (all the "Trues") divided by all the tests performed:

$$\text{Accuracy} = \left(\frac{TP + TN}{TP + FN + TN + FP}\right)$$

- The sensitivity of a test is a measure of the test's ability to detect the presence of disease when disease exists:

$$\text{Sensitivity} = \left(\frac{TP}{TP + FN}\right)$$

- The specificity of a test is a measure of the test's ability to detect the absence of disease when no disease exists:

$$\text{Specificity} = \left(\frac{TN}{TN + FP}\right)$$

- The accuracy must be between the sensitivity and the specificity.

- The positive predictive value (PPV) is a measure of how many times the test is correct of all the times the test predicts disease:

$$PPV = \left(\frac{TP}{TP + FP}\right)$$

- The negative predictive value (NPV) is a measure of how many times the test is correct of all the times the test predicts no disease:

$$NPV = \left(\frac{TN}{TN + FN}\right)$$

- The accuracy must also be between the negative and positive predictive values.

References

American Institute of Ultrasound in Medicine. *Official Statements*. https://www.aium.org/resources/statements.aspx.

BC Group. (1998) *Welcome to BC Group*. http://www.bcgroupintl.com/.

Centers for Disease Control and Prevention. (2008). *Decreasing order of resistance of microorganisms to disinfection and sterilization and the level of disinfection or sterilization*. https://www.cdc.gov/infectioncontrol/guidelines/disinfection/tables/figure1.html. (*Figure 2*)

Centers for Disease Control and Prevention. (2008). *Guideline for Disinfection and Sterilization in Healthcare Facilities*. https://www.cdc.gov/infectioncontrol/guidelines/disinfection/index.html.

CIRS Tissue Stimulation & Phantom Technology. *MRgRT Motion Management QA Phantom*. https://www.cirsinc.com/products/.

Fluke Biomedical. (2021). *Phantoms and Test Tools*. https://www.flukebiomedical.com/products/radiation-measurement/phantoms-and-test-tools.

ONDA Corporation. (2020). *Products*. https://www.ondacorp.com/products/ http://www.simutec.com/index.html.

Sorrentino, K. (2019). Accreditation, credentialing, and quality improvement in diagnostic medical sonography: a literature review. *Journal of Diagnostic Medical Sonography*, 35(5), 401-411.

Trapotsis, Arthur. (2021). *The Challenge of Prion Sterilization*. Consolidated Sterilizer Systems. https://consteril.com/prion-sterilization-guide/.

True Phantom Solutions. *Doppler Phantom*. https://www.truephantom.com/product/doppler-phantom/.

ONLINE CHAPTERS

Chapters 12-20 are online chapters which can be accessed through your 'My Pegasus' account at **www.pegasuslectures.com**

Please see page **x** of **Preface** for access instructions.

Appendix A
Glossary

1-D array transducers A transducer which consists of multiple elements in one dimension (the lateral direction). 1-D (or 1D) arrays can be steered and focused electronically in only one plane (laterally).

1.5-D array transducers A transducer which has a multiple elements in the lateral dimension and a few (usually) three elements in the elevation dimension. In addition to the ability to steer laterally like the 1-D arrays, a 1.5-D (or 1.5D) array is capable of producing two different foci in the elevation plane.

2D array transducers A transducer that has multiple elements in both the lateral and elevation direction. 2D (or 2-D) arrays can be both steered and focused in two planes (lateral and elevation) such that 3D scans can be produced.

2nd harmonic Twice the fundamental (transmit) frequency.

3D imaging Any imaging technique which results in a three dimensional representation of structures and images. 3D (or 3-D) imaging can be produced by manually moving a 1-D array across the patient, by using a motor and mechanically steering a 1-D array, or completely electronically with a 2D array.

60 degrees For vascular imaging, the angle originally chosen as the standard. Whenever possible Doppler should be performed at angles less than or equal to 60 degrees.

60 Hz An approximate limit in the rate at which humans can perceive changes. Many monitors refresh at a 60 Hz rate.

Aberration (beam) A distortion of the beam that results from non-uniform sound propagation through varying tissues. Beam aberration results in degraded detail resolution as well as decreased sensitivity.

Ablate (ablation) To remove or destroy tissue.

Absolute refractory period The period immediately following the activation of a nerve fiber when it cannot be stimulated no matter how great the action potential applied.

Absorption The conversion of energy from the sound wave into heat within the medium. Absorption depends on properties of the medium as well as the frequency of operation.

Absorption coefficient An acoustic parameter which specifies the rate of absorption of sound within a medium.

Acceleration The rate of change of velocity per unit of time.

Accuracy The overall percentage of times a comparison test is correct when compared with a gold standard test. The accuracy is calculated as the total number of times the test agrees with the gold standard divided by the total number of tests performed.

Acoustic Relating to, involving, or typical of sound, hearing, or the study of sound.

Acoustic impedance (Z) A measure of the resistance to sound traveling within a medium. The acoustic impedance (units of Rayls) is calculated by multiplying the density of the medium by the propagation speed of the medium ($Z = \rho \times c$). Greater differences in acoustic impedances at an acoustic interface (acoustic impedance mismatch) produce stronger reflections.

Acoustic intensity A measure of the distribution of acoustic power over area. Higher acoustic intensities produce stronger echoes but also increase risk of bioeffects.

Acoustic line A single transmitted sound beam in a specific direction and the associated echoes.

Acoustic power A measure of the rate at which acoustic energy is produced from a transducer or is transferred within a medium.

Acoustic radiation force impulse (ARFI) A method of producing transverse (shear waves) for elastography imaging.

Acoustic variable The name given to the changes that occur to a medium as a result of mechanical interaction with an acoustic wave. The word variable refers to a changing quantity, and acoustic refers to sound. The four acoustic variables are pressure, density, temperature, and particle motion.

Acoustic window The location on the body used to create an ultrasound image, assessment, or treatment

Acoustic window (CMUT) A membrane placed over the capacitive cells to act as a barrier between the patient and the CMUT cells.

Acoustic zoom (write zoom or write magnification) A method of producing a larger specified region of a reference image by transmitting new acoustic lines so as to improve resolution. Since new data is written to the scan converter memory, this technique is often referred to as a "write zoom".

A/D converter (analog to digital converter) An electronic device which converts an analog input signal into a digital output signal.

Adaptive processing Any process which changes how the image (data) is presented based on the characteristics of the data itself. Adaptive processes usually involve complex statistical algorithms to acquire information about how best to present the data for optimal visualization. There are many different names used by the various vendors to refer to this function including terms such as "Auto-Optimize," "iScan," "NTEQ," etc.

Afterload The force against which the ventricle must pump related primarily to the vascular resistance.

ALARA principle Stands for "as low as reasonably achievable" and is a guideline to define "prudent use" of diagnostic ultrasound instruments.

Aliasing The effect which occurs when a signal is sampled too slowly to accurately detect the true frequency of the signal (a violation of the Nyquist criterion). Specifically, aliasing occurs if the sample rate is less than twice the frequency of the signal to be detected. For Doppler, aliasing occurs when the PRF is less than twice the Doppler shift.

Alternating current (AC) An electric current that reverses its direction at regularly recurring intervals. In the US, the phase reversal occurs at 60 Hz.

Ambient light The background light existing within a room. Ambient light affects the ability to visualize low-level signals on a display monitor.

A-mode (amplitude mode) An early mode of ultrasound which displays the amplitude of the returning echo with respect to the depth along a single line. The amplitude is related to the signal strength (reflected signal). The amplitude was generally displayed on the vertical axis and depth on the horizontal axis. This modality is rarely used except is a few ophthalmic cases.

Amplatzer septal occluder A percutaneous, transcatheter, atrial septal defect closure device consisting of double-disc occluders made of nitinol mesh and polyester material.

Amplification Making something larger, greater, or stronger. The term amplification is used synonymously with the term "gain".

Amplitude The amplitude (Amp) of a physical quantity is defined as the strength, volume, or size of that physical quantity. In more formal terms, the amplitude is defined as the maximum variation of a variable from its mean value. The units for the four acoustic variables represent amplitude measurements. For electrical variables, the unit of amplitude measure is volts.

Amplitude (power) modulation A multi-pulse contrast imaging technique geared at eliminating tissue signal at very low MIs and allowing the system to "see" only bubbles.

Analog Refers to any mechanism in which data is represented by continuously variable physical quantities.

Analog to digital conversion (*See A/D converter*)

Anechoic No echogenicity; the absence of an echo or reflection which results in the image appearing black.

Angio (color power Doppler) A color imaging technique, more sensitive to low flow than color Doppler, that encodes flow based on the signal amplitude (power) instead of the Doppler shift.

Angiogenesis The generation and growth of new blood vessels.

Angle correction (Doppler) The mathematical correction by the cosine of the Doppler angle to compensate the Doppler shift when the Doppler angle is not 0° or 180°.

Angle of incidence The angle formed between a wavefront and the acoustic interface between two structures. The angle of incidence can also be measured as the angle between the wave direction and the line perpendicular (normal) to the acoustic interface.

Angle of reflection The angle formed between a reflected wavefront and the acoustic interface between two structures. The angle of reflection can also be measured as the angle between the reflected wave direction and the line perpendicular (normal) to the acoustic interface. For specular reflection, the angle of incidence equals the angle of reflection.

Angle of transmission The angle formed between the transmitted wavefront and the acoustic interface between two structures. The angle of transmission can also be measured as the angle between the transmitted wave direction and the line perpendicular (normal) to the acoustic interface. If the transmission angle does not equal the angle of incidence, refraction has occurred.

Angle of steering (Doppler) The angle formed between the transmit beam direction and the line normal (perpendicular) to the transducer face.

Anisotropic (anisotropy) The property of varying appearance (brightness) with varying incident angle as occurs with specular reflectors such as tendons.

Annular array A transducer type in which the elements are concentric rings (annuli). These transducers are no longer common since the advent of phased array transducers. Annular arrays are steered mechanically and have a variable focus both laterally and elevationally.

Antegrade (flow) Flow in the forward direction (generally implies flow in the appropriate direction).

Anterograde (flow) (*See Antegrade; synonyms when describing flow*)

Aortic stenosis A narrowing or obstruction of the heart's aortic valve or aorta which restricts the flow of blood from the left ventricle to the aorta.

Aperture The portion or "window" of the transducer elements being utilized to transmit (transmit aperture) or receive (receive aperture).

Apodization Refers to a process of varying the sensitivity of some elements relative to other elements so as to affect beam characteristics. For ultrasound, apodization is commonly used with array transducers to decrease the amplitude of the grating lobes. To reduce grating lobe energy, the center elements of the aperture are excited with higher amplitude voltages than the elements near the edge of the aperture. Apodization can also be applied to the receive beam by varying the amplification applied to varying elements of the receive aperture.

Apparent resolution The appearance of improved resolution related to displaying an image larger or smaller than the original image. An image with very good resolution but displayed in a small image format will give the appearance of improved resolution than when depicted in a larger format. If an image has poor resolution and the image is displayed in a large format, reducing the image display format often yields the appearance of improved resolution.

Apparent signal-to-noise (*See Signal-to-noise ratio*)

Apparent viscosity (See Viscosity)

Area A two-dimensional physical measurement calculated by multiplying a length and a width. Area can also be determined using the fundamental concept of integration (from calculus) as a summation of small regions bounded by a curve.

Array A collection of transducer elements.

Arterial hemodynamics A branch of physiology that deals with the circulation of the blood in the arteries.

Arteries The branching muscular and elastic-walled vessels that carry blood from the heart through the body.

Arterioles The small, muscularly banded regulating branch of the arterial system before the capillaries. The arterioles are referred to as the resistive component of the cardiovascular system, and are the principal compensatory control mechanism for regulation of blood volume through vasodilation and vasoconstriction.

Arteriovenous fistula An abnormal communication between the arterial and venous systems.

Artifact A broad category which includes an image feature or characteristic which is not representative of the true anatomical location or characteristic. There are two very distinct sources of artifacts in ultrasound images, physical interaction of the sound beam within the body, and external sources such as radio frequencies and power supply noise. Artifacts related to physical interactions are often instructive in that the artifact mechanism reveals a characteristic of the medium.

Attenuation A decrease in intensity and amplitude due to wave interactions with the medium including absorption, refraction, and reflection. Caution: some texts use the word attenuation synonymously with the term absorption.

Attenuation artifacts Artifacts that result from attenuation such as shadowing, enhancement or refraction.

Audible sound (See Human audible range)

Auto-optimize Any signal processing technique which attempts to improve the image display without user interaction, usually based on signal statistics and adaptive algorithms.

Autoclave A type of machine that uses steam under pressure to sterilize items that are placed inside.

Autocorrelation A mathematical process that analyzes the similarity between signals taken in a time sequence (used to generate color Doppler images).

Auxetic The description of a material that has a negative Poisson's ratio. When stretched, auxetic materials become thicker in the direction perpendicular to the applied force.

Average (mean) The mean value of a set of numbers computed as the sum of the values divided by the number of values within the set. (Example: the average of 3, 7, and 23 is 33/3 = 11)

Averaging (See also Spatial averaging, Signal-to-noise ratio and Compound imaging) Refers to any technique which adds together the data from multiple samples and then divides by the number of samples. Averaging can be done over time (adding together data captured sequentially in time) or over space (adding together data that comes from nearby locations). The advantages of averaging can be smoothing out data and improving the signal amplitude relative to the noise amplitude (SNR ratio).

Axial (longitudinal/radial/depth/range) resolution The ability to distinguish between two objects in depth and/or the ability to accurately determine the dimension of a structure along the pulse length of the beam (depth). The axial resolution approximately equals the spatial pulse length (SPL) divided by 2.

Azimuthal resolution (See Lateral resolution)

Back scattering A type of reflection which results in energy being redirected back toward the source. This type of reflection occurs from surfaces which are rough with respect to the wavelength. Backscattering is relatively angle independent. (The term scattering is commonly used synonymously.)

Backend (ultrasound system) Refers to the collection of electronics and functions of an ultrasound system that converts the detected and receiver processed signals into an interpretable, measurable, and storable scan.

Backing material The material used in transducer construction to decrease the number of cycles a sound source rings. By decreasing the number of cycles in the pulse, the spatial pulse length is shortened improving longitudinal resolution. Additionally, fewer cycles implies that the pulse duration is decreased, increasing the transducer bandwidth. The backing material is also referred to as the damping material.

Banding noise An artifact related to the change in system parameters that occurs at boundaries between focal zones when using multiple transmit foci.

Bandwidth The useful range of frequencies over which a device can operate. The bandwidth is typically defined as the difference between the upper frequency corner and lower frequency corner of the device's frequency response.

Baseband The lower frequency signals which remain after removing (demodulating) a signal. In Doppler, the baseband signal is the remaining Doppler shifts (kHz) after removing the radio frequency (RF) transmit frequency (MHz).

Baseline (Doppler) The Doppler display line in the Doppler spectrum which represents no Doppler shift. Signal on either side of the baseline represents flow in opposite directions.

Basic angle (trig.) Angles in quadrant I (between 0° and 90° inclusively) which are easily visualized on the unit circle (0°, 30°, 45°, 60°, 90°). You should know the sines and cosines of the basic angles and the corresponding angles in quadrant II (180°, 150°, 135°, 120°).

Bayonet sign An artifact associated with speed error which results in straight structures appearing bent like the bayonet of a rifle.

Beam (sound) Similar to the concept of a light beam, the path that focused sound takes as it propagates through a medium.

Beam aberration Distortion of the sound beam through non-uniform transmission which results in a defocusing effect.

Beam shape The physical dimensions (shape) formed over time as the sound wave passes through the medium.

Beam steering Any technique which results in a change in primary direction of the ultrasound wave over time.

Beam uniformity factor (coefficient) A measure of beam intensity uniformity over space, defined as the spatial peak intensity divided by the spatial average intensity. (Always greater than or equal to 1.)

Beamformer The collection of electronics and software which control delays, apertures, transmit amplitudes, and phase to focus and steer the transmit and receive waves.

Beamplots Data taken while scanning the acoustic field over the imaging scan planes (power testing) that is plotted to help determine power distribution and focusing characteristics of a transducer.

Beamwidth The physical width of the effective wave in the lateral direction (lateral beamwidth) or elevation direction (elevational beamwidth). The beamwidth determines the lateral resolution and the elevation resolution.

Bernoulli's equation A restatement of the conservation of energy theorem which can be applied to express changes in pressure with fluid flow related to energy conversion between kinetic and potential energy. The equation is simplified to a form which relates the pressure drop (mmHg) across a flow narrowing to $4v^2$.

B-flow An ultrasound imaging technique that allows directionless visualization of blood flow by detecting and enhancing the moving blood cell signals relative to the tissue signal.

BGR (blue, green, red) artifact An artifact on some ultrasound systems when performing elastography which presents as blue, green, and red bands when imaging cystic structures.

Binary/Base 2 Digits are restricted to 0 and 1. Each column represents a power of 2, just as each column in base 10 represents a power of 10. Binary is the basis for virtually all electronic devices. Historically, the digit 0 is represented by 0 volts and the digit 1 is represented by +5 volts.

Bioeffects An undesired biological change to tissues as a result of interaction with the ultrasound beam.

Bit The smallest division of a binary number or the smallest division of the digital output from an A/D converter.

Blind Doppler probe (*See also Pedof or Pencil*) A simple round crystal used only to generate spectral Doppler.

Blossoming artifact Refers to a transducer signal that is essentially overgained such that the signal "bleeds" into neighboring regions of the spectrum.

B-mode Brightness mode. B-mode is a means of converting signal amplitudes into grayscaled pixels so that a readily interpretable image can be created. The standard convention of B-mode is to present higher amplitude signals as brighter shades of white.

Brightness mode (*See B-mode*)

Broad bandwidth (broadband) Refers to the ability of a device (such as an ultrasound transducer) to operate over a wide range of frequencies.

Bruit An audible sound generally caused by vibration such as occurs with a stenosis or high degree of stenosis.

B-scan An obsolete ultrasound technique in which the sonographer physically moved the transducer over the patient to create a scan over time.

Bubbles (*See Contrast*)

Bubble disruption The destruction of contrast bubbles primarily during the peak rarefactional phase of the transmit pulse (*see Cavitation*).

Bulk modulus (K) A physical parameter of a material defined by the percent change in pressure (stress) divided by the fractional change in volume (strain). The bulk modulus is inversely related to the compressibility of a material. The propagation velocity of sound in a medium is directly proportional to the square root of the bulk modulus.

Bull's-eye sign (artifact) An artifact that occurs when performing an elastography scan that occurs on certain manufacturer's ultrasound systems which is useful in classifying a lesion as a benign cystic lesion. The artifact appears similar to a bull's eye with a black outer ring, a white central signal, and a distal white area.

Byte 8 bits comprise one byte. A byte is a natural grouping of bits since 8 is a power of 2.

Calf muscle pump Sometimes referred to as a "second heart," the calf muscle pump aids in venous return from the lower extremities toward the heart when the calf muscles contract.

Capacitance (electrical) The ratio of the amount of electric charge (q) stored on a conductor to a difference in electric potential (V). Varying capacitance is the driving mechanism for CMUT transducers.

Capacitance (fluid) A measure of the ability to hold a change in volume per time. The capacitance is critical in the arterial system as a means of storing energy to drive blood flow in diastole as well as part of a system which dampens the pulsatility into more continuous flow. The venous system is referred to as the capacitive component of the cardiovascular system since at rest approximately 65% of the volume resides in the venous system.

Capacitor micromachined ultrasound transducers (CMUT) CMUT refers to a new transducer technology which serves as an alternative to using piezoelectric materials. CMUT technology utilizes capacitance as the means of generating sound waves and, unlike piezoelectric crystals, is machined directly onto a silicone substrate, making it possible to build in direct electrical connections.

Capillaries The smallest blood vessels connecting arterioles with venules and forming networks throughout the body. Metabolic exchange occurs through diffusion at the level of the capillaries.

Cardiac index A method for normalizing the cardiac output relative to the size of the patient.

Cardiac output A measure of the volumetric flow, or volume of blood per time that the heart pumps usually expressed in liters per minute.

Cardiac reserve The difference between the cardiac output or volume at rest and the maximum cardiac output or volume the heart is capable of pumping during stress (exercise).

Cardiac rotation The movement of the heart through angular displacement (one of the cardiac motions that makes assessing wall motion more difficult).

Cardiac torsion Cardiac motion in which there are different rates of rotation about the rotational axis creating a twisting phenomenon.

Cardiac translation Linear displacement of the heart throughout the cardiac cycle (one of the cardiac motions that makes assessing wall motion more difficult).

Cathode ray tube (CRT) The standard monitor technology for many years in which beams of electrons are scanned across a phosphorescent screen to display an image. For color monitors, three CRTs are used to produce red, green, and blue (RGB).

Cavitation Formally refers to the formation of bubbles within a medium. For ultrasound, the term has also come to refer to the interaction of bubbles with wave energy. The rapid phase transition from liquid to gaseous as a result of the rarefactional ultrasound pressure. Stable cavitation implies that the created bubbles expand and contract with the varying pressure field without violent collapse. Transient cavitation implies that the peak rarefactional pressure is significant enough to cause violent collapse (implosion).

Cell (CMUT) The smallest active component of a CMUT transducer capable of producing sound waves. Each cell is a variable capacitor.

Cephalad Toward the head or anterior end of the body.

Cine loop A bank of digital memory which stores imaging data for replay. The replay can either be in real time, or played back in "slow time" frame-by-frame. It is referred to as a loop since the oldest data is overwritten when the memory is full so that the data forms a "loop" in time.

Circuit saturation When a circuit becomes unstable because the signal becomes larger than the circuit can handle. In Doppler, wall filter saturation results in bright white spikes in the spectrum corresponding to loud pops in the audio.

Claudication Pain in the calf or thigh muscle that occurs after increased metabolic demand as a result of ischemia.

Clutter signals Large returning echoes from structures, which dominate weaker signals.

C-mode (constant depth mode) Any ultrasound mode which listens to echoes returning only from a specific depth such as PW Doppler.

Coded excitation (harmonics) A method to produce harmonic imaging with improved signal-to-noise ratio (SNR). Coded excitation approaches are based on the concept of improving the SNR by increasing the spatial pulse length of the transmit pulse. However, a longer spatial pulse length generally results in worse axial resolution. By encoding the pulses with a specific pattern and then decoding the received echoes, longer pulses can be used without degrading the axial resolution. In essence the returning echoes are "matched" with the transmitting pulse making it seem as if multiple shorter pulses were used instead of one long pulse.

Coded harmonics (See Coded excitation)

Collapse mode In collapse mode (with CMUT cells), a bias (DC) voltage is applied so that the center of the flexible plate is attracted to the bottom electrode and comes in actual contact with the top of the insulating material. Collapse mode makes the cell more efficient and can be used to tune the transmit frequency.

Collateral flow Circulation of blood through dilated (usually smaller) vessels when a more significant vein or artery is functionally impaired (as by obstruction).

Color angio (see Color power Doppler)

Color bar (See Color scales)

Color bleeding (See Color blossoming)

Color blossoming An artifact in which color flow is presented in non-flow regions. This artifact is often the result of excessive color signal strength, but can also occur from degraded axial resolution that results from the "tail" of the transmitted color pulse.

Color Doppler An imaging technique based on Doppler principles which allows for flow assessment over a two-dimensional region of the body. The flow information is encoded using a color scale. The color representation is an estimate of the mean velocity at each location for that instant in time. (Also referred to as color imaging, color Doppler imaging, and color flow.)

Color Doppler dropout An area of no color flow within a region where flow is expected. Color dropout can be the result of actual flow restricting disease such as occlusion, or as the result of artifact. Some of the many artifacts which can cause color dropout include, inadequate sensitivity, acoustic shadowing, inappropriate color wall filters (color scales too high), poor Doppler, angle, etc.

Color ensemble (See Color packet)

Color flash artifact A bright, short duration flash of color which generally covers a large or entire region within the color box. Flash artifact results from relative motion between the transducer and regions in the body such as tissue motion from breathing or hand movement while scanning.

Color gain Amplification (multiplication) of the received color signal. Setting appropriate color gain is different when the color signal is strong (usually more superficially) than when the color signal is weak. For strong color signal, the color gain must be turned down until there is no visible overlap of the color flow with the known tissue. For weak color signal, the color gain should be decreased until the color noise speckle in non-flow regions just disappears.

Color line density A control which allows the user to change the number of color display lines per color box width. A higher line density potentially results in improved lateral resolution but at the expense of frame rate and temporal resolution.

Color noise (floor) The level at which color noise (speckle) becomes apparent in a color image.

Color packet The number of acoustic lines used to create a single color display line. Multiple acoustic lines (a packet or ensemble of lines) are used to produce an estimate of the mean velocity through correlation. A larger color packet size produces a better estimate, reducing noise within the color, but at the expense of time to create a color line and hence, a the time to produce a color frame. Therefore, a large packet size reduces the frame rate, decreasing the temporal resolution.

Color persistence A processing technique which averages frames over time so as to improve the signal-to-noise ratio by constructive interference of the signal (signal coherence) and partially destructive interference of the noise. Caution must be used with too much persistence since short duration events can be "persisted" out, while longer duration events may be persisted artificially in time.

Color power Doppler A technique that presents flow based on the amplitude of the flow signal (power related), not the velocity of the flow as presented in standard color Doppler. Conventional color power Doppler does not present flow direction. Since color power Doppler encodes flow based on signal strength and not the Doppler shift, power Doppler is less angle sensitive. Power Doppler is often useful for detection of flow in low flow states.

Color priority A threshold technique allowing the user to maximize color filling while minimizing color bleed overlaying tissue. Color priority sets a threshold level to determine whether the 2D signal or the color signal is displayed when both signals exist for the same pixel at the same time.

Color scales (PRF/bar) In color Doppler, the legend which indicates how the mean velocity is color encoded. The color bar indicates the color(s) which indicate forward flow, reverse flow, and the mean velocity at which aliasing exists. Some color bars also indicate the color wall filter setting around the baseline.

Color speckle (noise) Pixels of random color that represent noise in the color image. When color speckle exists, it is generally first visible in non-flow regions, and presents as all colors depicted in the color bar.

Comet tail (artifact) A specific form of reverberation named for the appearance of a flashlight or "tail" produced when sound reverberates within a metallic structure such as surgical clips, needles, and prosthetic valve apparatus.

Common intensities The various methods by which intensity is measured for ultrasound based on spatial and temporal distributions (sometimes referred to as alphabet soup).

Compensation The name given for varying amplification with depth to compensate for increased attenuation with depth. Controlled on the system by the TGCs (time gain compensation).

Complex plaque A term used to describe complicated plaque characteristics implying a non-uniform pattern which may include hemorrhage, calcifications, and lipid deposits.

Compliance A measure of the change in volume per pressure. The compliance is tightly coupled with the capacitance. Although technically not the same parameter, the two terms are often used interchangeably since a high compliance usually implies high capacitance in the cardiovascular system.

Composite (effective) beam The results of adding two or more individual beams to create an effective beam with improved characteristics.

Compound imaging A technique to improve signal-to-noise and reduce artifacts by transmitting multiple frames at slightly varying steer angles and then averaging together to create one image. This technique is referred by different terminology by each of the vendors. ATL (now part of Philips) released this technology first under the name Sono CT. GE calls this technique "crossbeam" imaging and Siemens refers to it as "spatial compound" imaging. The generic terminology commonly used on exams is simply "compound" imaging.

Compressibility The inverse of stiffness and proportional to elasticity. As the compressibility of a material increases, the propagation velocity decreases.

Compression (acoustic wave) The state during wave propagation when the particles occupy a smaller region in the medium than normal (higher density).

Compression (signal processing) A technique to reduce dynamic range by mapping the larger range into a smaller range. Because of the extraordinary dynamic range of ultrasound signals from the body, compression occurs in many places in the ultrasound system including the receiver and the scan converter. Compression techniques almost always result in a loss of data.

Conservation of energy One of the fundamental tenets of physics. This theorem states that energy cannot be created or destroyed but is only changed from one form to another form.

Constructive interference When two signals or waves interact so as to produce one larger signal or wave. Constructive interference occurs when the two or more signals have similar phases. The principles of constructive interference are the foundation for phased array operation as well as many averaging based processing techniques.

Continuity equation A conservation of energy expression that states that in a closed fluid flow system, all of the flow through one region must equal all of the flow through another region. The continuity equation states the volumetric flow equals the spatial average velocity times the cross-sectional flow area.

Continuous mode (See CW Doppler)

Continuous wave (CW) Refers to the fact that the transmit wave is continuous – in contrast with pulsed wave operation which intermittently turns the transmit wave on and off.

Contrast agents Microbubbles usually consisting of a shell filled with a dense gas used to enhance the reflectivity of blood. The increased reflectivity is the result of an increase in the acoustic impedance mismatch as a result of the low density and high compressibility of the contrast agent. The ASE now recommends the more patient friendly term of "ultrasound enhancing agents."

Contrast imaging Any imaging technique which utilizes contrast agent for signal enhancement.

Contrast resolution Ability to distinguish structures based on variations of brightness.

Converge To narrow such as occurs at the beam focus.

Corner (cutoff) frequency For Doppler wall filters, the frequency above which signals are passed and below which signals are attenuated.

Cosine A trigonometric function that for an acute angle is the ratio between the leg adjacent to the angle and the hypotenuse. On the unit circle, the cosine of an angle is determined by plotting the angle and projecting the intersection of the angle with the unit circle to the x-axis.

Critical angle The incident angle at which total internal reflection occurs.

Critical stenosis A narrowing of an artery that results in a significant reduction in volumetric flow.

Crossbeam imaging *(See Compound imaging)*

Crosstalk Undesired communication of signals between transducer elements or channels in the ultrasound system.

Cross-section A cut at right angles to an axis.

Curie point The temperature at which a piezoelectric material loses its piezoelectric properties. (300° Celsius for PZT)

Current (electrical) A stream of electrons which move along a conductor from a high potential to a low potential. Electrical current is measured in amperes (Amps).

Current leakage test An electrical test performed to determine the safety of electrical equipment so as to not cause patient electrocution. When the touch (TC) current (current that flows when a human body touches an electrical device) is below the value hazardous to humans, the device is considered safe from causing electrocution.

Curved linear phased array transducers A family of phased array transducers that have a convex surface so as to produce relatively broad near field images and even broader far field images.

Cutoff frequency *(See Corner frequency)*

CW Doppler A technique which measures the Doppler shifted frequencies by transmitting and receiving waves continuously and simultaneously. CW has the advantage of virtually unlimited maximum detectable frequency shifts (no aliasing) but suffers from no range specificity.

Cyanosis A dusky bluish discoloration of the skin.

Cyclical Periodic or repetitive.

Damping material *(See Backing material)*

Decibels (dB) A logarithmic power ratio. Decibels express the relative relationship between two powers or intensities. An amplitude form exists which converts the amplitude ratio into a power ratio. Since decibels are based on logarithms, decibels exhibit the same non-linear benefits and drawbacks of compression as logarithms.

Decimal The counting system based on using ten digits (0 through 9). Each column in a decimal (base 10) number represents a power of 10. Base 10 is the standard counting system used primarily because we are born with 10 fingers and 10 toes.

Delay (phase) Time difference between signals used to compensate for difference in path lengths so as to electronically steer and/or focus. Delays can be used both on transmit and on receive.

Delta (Δ) An abbreviation for the word "change" or gradient.

Demodulation The process of recovering a signal from a modulated (varied frequency) carrier wave. Also sometimes referred to as signal detection.

Denominator The part of a fraction below the division line.

Density A measure of how tightly "packed" a material is – calculated as the mass per unit volume.

Dependent rubor A deep red color that occurs on the skin due to blood pooling in the arterioles.

Depth of field (focal region) Refers to the general region above and below the focus where the beam is approximately the same width.

Destructive interference The reduction in overall amplitude when two or more waves or signals interfere with different phases. Complete destructive interference occurs when two waves are completely out of phase (180° apart). Destructive interference is critical to produce narrow beams from phased array transducers.

Detail resolution Ability to distinguish between two objects in any of the three dimensions: axial, lateral, or elevation.

Diagnostic range Refers to the range of frequencies commonly used for conventional, non-invasive ultrasound. (Currently considered to be approximately 2-12 MHz.)

Diastole The low pressure phase of the cardiac cycle in which ventricular filling occurs.

Diastolic pressure The force of blood in the arteries during the diastolic phase.

Dicing The method of creating transducer elements in a block of piezoelectric material by slicing parallel cuts part way through the block.

Dicrotic notch The corresponding bump up in pressure (producing a second peaking in the pressure waveform) that occurs as a result of inertia as the aortic valve closes.

Dielectric (layer) A material that does not conduct electricity commonly used in capacitors to increase the capacitance. Also used in CMUT transducer capacitive cells to keep electrodes from shorting in collapse mode.

Digital filtering Any signal processing technique which removes signal components mathematically in contrast to analog filtering.

Digital scan converter The name given to the part of the system in which individual scan lines are processed and converted into a format for visualization as an image. The digital scan converter is often referred to as a large block of digital memory and the processing unit responsible for grayscale mapping and scan formatting. In actuality, the scan converter is one functional block of the system referred to as the backend which includes the scan converter, the cine loop memory, storage devices, measurement and analysis software, and video display drivers.

Digital signals Any signal which exists as discrete levels at discrete time intervals (a time series of numbers). Analog signals are often converted into discrete digital signals through electronics called an analog to digital converter (A/D converter).

Direct current (DC) Electrical current that does not change direction or amplitude and so maintains constant voltage. DC is produced by batteries.

Direct (non-linear) proportionality A mathematical relationship whereby two physical quantities (expressed as variables) are related such that as one quantity increases, the other quantity also increases but at a faster rate. Similarly, if one quantity decreases, the other related quantity also decreases at a faster rate.

Disinfection The process of eliminating or reducing harmful microorganisms. Note that although both disinfection and sterilization are both decontamination processes, sterilization is the complete elimination of all forms of microbial life including spores and viruses.

Display alias When a Doppler signal appears aliased on the screen but can be "unwrapped" by shifting the baseline or increasing the scales.

Display dynamic range The ratio of the biggest to the smallest signal that can be displayed on a monitor or other display device.

Display line The data displayed on the screen that corresponds to a single direction within the patient.

Disruption (bubble) *(See Bubble disruption)*

Distal flow Flow that occurs downstream.

Distal resistance The resistance associated with the extremity farther down the flow path.

Distance equation The equation which specifies that distance is calculated as the velocity (rate) multiplied by time.

Disturbed flow Any deviation from laminar flow.

Diverge To widen as occurs deeper than the focus of a beam.

Doppler A broad category of techniques based on the Doppler effect which includes spectral Doppler, audio Doppler and color flow imaging. See Doppler effect.

Doppler angle The angle that is formed between the observer's line of sight and the direction of the target object. The Doppler angle is also referred to as the insonification angle.

Doppler artifacts Artifacts that affect any Doppler based modality. Some examples of Doppler artifacts include aliasing, range ambiguity, spectral broadening, and spectral mirroring.

Doppler effect An apparent shift in frequency of any interrogating wave caused by a change in wavelength from relative motion between the observer and the target. A shorter wavelength implies a higher frequency and indicates relative movement toward the observer. Conversely, a longer wavelength implies a lower frequency and relative movement away from the observer.

Doppler gain Amplification of the Doppler received signal.

Doppler gate (sample volume) The indicator placed by the user along the PW Doppler line which determines the time between the transmit pulse and receiving. The Doppler gate also determines the listening time and the number of cycles in the transmit pulse.

Doppler scales (PRF) The setting which determines the maximum displayable velocity in the forward and in the reverse direction before aliasing will begin. When not operating at the maximum PRF, the Doppler scales inform the system of how much "dead time" to include after the sample volume to increase the PRP (decreasing the PRF) and thereby decreasing the maximum displayable velocity.

Doppler shift The difference in frequency between the transmitted and reflected wave caused by the Doppler effect. A higher reflected signal frequency implies a positive frequency shift (motion towards the observer).

Doppler spectral window A region of no or little signal between the peak velocity and the baseline which indicates that the flow is accelerating and decelerating together indicating laminar flow. Note that a spectral window will generally not exist if using a sample volume which includes flow near the vessel wall, if using CW, if the signal is overgained, or artifactual spectral broadening exists.

Doppler spectrum The graphical display of the range of Doppler frequency shifts (or velocities) over time.

Duplex Simultaneous display of both B-mode (2D image) and spectral Doppler.

Duty cycle/Duty factor Refers to the percentage of time energy is actively being transmitted into the body. The duty factor is calculated as the pulse duration divided by the pulse repetition period. In CW, the duty factor is 1. In PW the duty factor is always less than 1.

Dynamic frequency tuning (sliding receive filters) An imaging approach which uses a broadband transmit and then changes the receive frequency to optimize the image, using the highest frequency receive in the near field and lowest frequency receive at the maximum imaging depth.

Dynamic range The ratio of the maximum to the minimum of any quantity.

Dynamic receive focus A receiver based technique which automatically changes the phase delays to provide optimal focusing for the data being received. Dynamic receive focusing became relatively standard with the introduction of digital beamformers.

Echo A sound wave which has been reflected off a surface and is heard after the original sound. The term "echo" is often used to refer to a cardiac scan.

Echogenicity Refers to the strength and/or type of the signal reflection.

Echopalpation *(See also Palpation)* The technique of applying pressure with a finger while simultaneously imaging with ultrasound to detect differences in elasticity by viewing differences in compression.

Edema An abnormal excess accumulation of serous fluid in connective tissue or in a serous cavity.

Effective beam *(See Composite beam)*

Effective resistance The total resistance of a network which can consist of any combination of parallel and series combinations of individual resistances.

Ejection fraction The percentage of blood ventricular volume ejected per beat.

EKG *(See Electrocardiogram)*

Elasticity The capability of a strained body to recover its size and shape after deformation.

Elastic limit The maximum stress (force per unit area) that can exist within a material before permanent deformation occurs. At stresses below the elastic limit, materials return to their original form when the stress is removed.

Elastography A technique that detects tumors based on their stiffness (elasticity) compared to normal tissue.

Electrical interference Caused when transducers or ultrasound machines receive energy emanating from other electrical devices or electromagnetic waves.

Electrocardiogram (ECG) The time display of electrical signals which stimulate myocardial contraction.

Electrode An electrical conductor which carries electrical current into non-metallic materials. Electrodes are used to carry an electrical current into and out of CMUT cells to produce and capture sound vibrations.

Electromagnetic (EM) wave An electromagnetic wave is a transfer of energy through a varying electrical and magnetic field.

Electronic noise Random signals added to a signal during amplification from random excitation of electrons.

Electronic (phasing) focusing The use of small time or phase delays between the excitation pulses to each of the transducer elements within an array to cause a beam to focus (on transmit or receive).

Electronic (phasing) steering The use of small time or phase delays between the excitation pulses to each of the transducer elements within an array to cause a beam to steer (on transmit or receive).

Elevation resolution The ability to resolve structure in the elevation plane (slice thickness for 2D imaging).

Energy The ability to perform work. Energy is power integrated over time.

Energy gradient A difference in energy levels.

Enhancement artifact A brighter than normal echo below a structure which is either a weaker reflector or less absorbing than normal.

Ensemble length *(See Color packet)*

Envelope detection Part of the receiver function of signal detection which traces the signal peaks and valleys while simultaneously applying some averaging or smoothing.

Ergonomics According to OSHA, ergonomics is defined as: "the science of fitting workplace conditions and job demands to the capabilities of the working population."

Exponential notation A way of expressing numbers in terms of a number raised to a power.

Extended field of view *(See Panoramic imaging)*

Factor A number that divides into another number exactly. The word factor implies the mathematical operation of multiplication (or its inverse: division).

False negative (FN) Implies that the test incorrectly predicts there is no disease (the test predicts no disease when the gold standard predicts disease).

False positive (FP) Implies that the test incorrectly predicts there is disease (the test predicts disease when the gold standard does not).

Far field or Fraunhofer zone The region deeper than the natural focus.

Fast Fourier transform (FFT) A mathematical technique for separating a spectrum into its individual frequency components.

Field of view (FOV) The physical extent of the image (width and depth).

Figure-of-eight artifact An artifact which occurs when imaging an Amplatzer septal occluder in a coronal view as a result of differing angles to each mesh hoop.

Flash artifact *(See Color flash artifact)*

Fluid dynamics The study of fluid flow through a flow system.

Fluid viscosity *(See Viscosity)*

Focal region (depth of field) Region over which the transducer beam is most tightly focused.

Focus Where the beam reaches its minimum diameter.

Focused ultrasound (FUS) A non-invasive ultrasound technique being used to destroy lesions through the intentional development of (localized) bioeffects. The ultrasound beam is very tightly focused and then used to heat or ablate the target tissue without causing damage to surrounding healthy tissues.

Force Any interaction that, when unopposed, will change the motion of an object.

Fraction A numerical representation (as 1/7, 2/9, 7/15) indicating the quotient of two numbers.

Fractional bandwidth A figure of merit for transducers which indicates information about the bandwidth relative to the center frequency. The fractional bandwidth is determined by dividing the operating or center frequency by the bandwidth.

Frame averaging The combination of more than one frame to create a single frame of data, improving the signal-to-noise ratio (SNR).

Frame frequency *(See Frame rate)*

Frame rate The frequency at which frames of data are produced or presented. The acoustic frame rate represents how many frames of data per second are produced during imaging. The display frame rate represents the number of frames per second that appear on the monitor. The frame rate (also referred to as the frame frequency) is the reciprocal of the frame time.

Frame time The amount of time it takes to acquire a frame.

Frank-Starling's Law Describes the relationship between cardiac filling (preload) and force of contraction.

Fraunhofer zone *(See Far field)*

Frequency The number of cycles of a particular event in one second (per time).

Frequency bins Divisions of the frequency spectrum that result from performing a Fast Fourier Transform (FFT). Each bin represents a narrow range of frequencies which can be related to velocity through the Doppler equation.

Frequency compounding (fusion) *(See Frequency fusion)*

Frequency fusion (compounding) Frequency fusion entails averaging two or more images created at different transmit frequencies. The benefits are based on the concept that the lower frequency image(s) can provide better penetration whereas the higher frequency image(s) can provide better resolution. By fusing the images together, better texture results than would be produced by using only a lower frequency, and better penetration is achieved than would result from using a only a higher frequency.

Fresnel zone (See Near field)

Friction The force that resists relative motion between two bodies in contact. Friction results in a conversion of kinetic energy into heat.

Front-end The collection of electronics and functions on ultrasound equipment where all of the processing takes place before the signal is sent to the "back-end" for conversion into an interpretable, measurable, and storable scan.

Fundamental frequency The term used to refer to the transmit frequency when performing harmonic imaging.

FUS (See Focused ultrasound)

Gain An increase in signal power, voltage, or current expressed as the ratio of the output to the input. The gain ratio in ultrasound and most electronics is often expressed in decibels.

Gain dynamic range The range over which a signal can be amplified. The ratio of the maximum to the minimum amplification possible.

General processing unit (GPU) A programmable device designed specifically to rapidly process data and present images.

Global longitudinal strain (GLS) A measure of LV longitudinal deformation in the apical views. The GLS typically includes six segments (base, mid, apex) from the apical 2, 3, and 4-chamber views totaling 18 segments. The strains are averaged to report the GLS.

Gold standard The diagnostic test considered the best and therefore used as a reference for statistical analysis of other diagnostic tests.

Grating lobe artifact Energy that is produced in undesired directions other than the main beam direction. Grating lobes are exacerbated by using larger elements relative to the wavelength of the frequency being transmitted. Grating lobes generally produce laterally displaced structures or a "haze" that may be misconstrued as thrombus.

Grayscale The range of shades of black through white used to present ultrasound data based on signal intensity (strength).

Hanafy lens A type of transducer design that achieves more uniform beams at greater depths by using crystals which are thinner in the middle and thicker near the edges. The varying thickness varies the frequency response so that the higher frequency of the center produces a narrow beam in the near field whereas the lower frequency of the outside edge produces a narrower effective beam in the far field.

Harmonic contrast imaging Uses harmonic imaging in conjunction with a contrast agent. The system transmits at the fundamental frequency and then receives at the second harmonic frequency.

Harmonic imaging The technique of transmitting at a lower frequency (the fundamental frequency) and receiving at a harmonic frequency (currently only second harmonic). The technique yields better penetration than conventional imaging operating purely at the higher frequency and better resolution than conventional imaging operating purely at the lower frequency. One of the biggest advantages to harmonic imaging is the reduction in clutter related artifacts in the relative near field.

Haze A gray appearance in the image (usually in the relative near field) usually caused by grating lobe artifact or reverberation artifact.

Hematocrit The ratio of the volume of red blood cells to the total volume of blood.

Hemodynamics The laws of fluid dynamics as applied to blood flow and the cardiovascular system.

Hertz The unit for frequency (cycles/second).

Heterogeneous Implies that there is variation within the signal.

High intensity focused ultrasound (HIFU) (See Focused ultrasound)

High-level disinfection The treatment of medical devices to destroy most viable microorganisms, with the exception of a small number of bacterial spores.

High pass filter An electronic circuit which allows signals with a frequency higher than the specified corner frequency to pass through while reducing the amplitude of signals with frequencies below the corner frequency. Wall filters in Doppler are high pass filters.

Homogeneous Implies that the signal is relatively uniform.

Hooke's law of elasticity States that, for relatively small deformations of an object, the displacement is directly proportional to the deforming force or load.

HPRF Doppler High pulse repetition frequency Doppler intentionally utilizes the artifact of range ambiguity to increase the maximum detectable velocity without aliasing, at the expense of some range resolution.

Human audible range Sound within the range of human hearing (purported to be 20 Hz to 20 kHz – although usually lower than 17 kHz for most adults).

Huygens' principle States that all points on a wavefront can be treated as point sources producing spherical secondary wavelets, whose tangential surface predicts the new position of the wavefront over time.

Hydrophone A specialized ultrasound transducer that is designed to measure acoustic pressure fields. Hydrophones are used to make power measurements to verify transducer performance as well as make certain that maximum power levels are not exceeded.

Hydrostatic pressure The pressure which results from the weight of the fluid from above in a column. The hydrostatic pressure is related to the height of the column, the density of the fluid, and gravity.

Hyperechoic Moderate-to-high echogenicity.

Hyperostosis An increase in skull density and thickness.

Hypertension A situation where blood pressure is persistently higher than normal.

Hypoechoic The area of an ultrasound image in which echoes are weaker than normal or in surrounding regions.

Image persistence A processing technique designed to reduce noise in the image through an "averaging" technique of images over time. Most persistence techniques do not use standard averages, but rather weighted averages so that newer frames are more heavily weighted than older frames.

Imaging depth The setting on the ultrasound system that allows the user to determine the maximum depth of interest to display. The imaging depth basically determines the time required between transmitting the next line of data (the PRP).

Impedance (acoustic) (*See Acoustic impedance*)

Impedance (electrical) The resistance to current flow down a pathway. The unit for impedance is Ohms.

Impedance (fluid or hydraulic) The resistance to fluid flow down a pathway. The impedance (also referred to as the resistance) is directly related to the length of the flow path and the viscosity of the fluid. The resistance is inversely related to the radius of the flow path raised to the fourth power.

Implied consent In cases of emergency when the patient is incapable of consenting and, when the patient's family, or a legal representative are not available to give consent, there is a state of implied consent under which the healthcare provider performs treatment.

Impulse response The response of a transducer crystal to a single, short duration pulse. The impulse response demonstrates the bandwidth of a transducer.

Incident angle (θ_i) The angle formed between the beam direction and the normal at the point of incidence. The incident angle can also be measured as the angle formed between the wavefront and the reflecting interface at the point of reflection.

Informed consent A legal form signed by a patient in which the patient voluntarily gives the right for a medical procedure to be performed. For the consent to be considered legal, the patient must first be informed of the procedure risks, benefits, and alternatives.

Inertia Property of matter by which it continues in it's existing state unless changed by external force.

Infrasound Sound below human hearing (below 20 Hz).

In phase Phase refers to the timing relationships between waves. When two waves are purely in phase (0°), there is no separation between the maximum peak (compression) or minimum peak (rarefaction).

Input dynamic range The range of signal amplitudes a system can receive and process without causing harmonic distortion.

Insonification (Doppler) angle The Doppler angle is measured between the beam steering direction and the direction (head) of the flow.

Intensity Equals the concentration of energy or power per unit area. The unit for intensity is Watts per square cm. The intensity is a useful parameter to help predict signal strength as well as the risk of bioeffects.

Interlaced (monitor or display) Interlacing is a technique for presenting data as two different fields that are interwoven to produce the complete frame. The technique involves presenting the lines of one field (the odd field or odd lines) and then interlacing the even field (or even lines) between the odd lines. A clear disadvantage of interlacing the fields of data is a reduction in the monitor frame rate and potential blurring of dynamic structures. Newer monitors are now "non-interlaced" or progressive displays.

Intima media thickness (IMT) A measurement of the thickness of the innermost two layers of the arterial wall (the tunica intima and tunica media). The IMT measurement is used to detect the presence of atherosclerotic disease as a predictive indicator of the likelihood of future cardiovascular events.

Inverse proportionality Implies an "opposite" relationship between two variables. If one variable increases, the related variable decreases.

In vitro Studies done in a test tube.

In vivo Studies done within living tissue.

Isoechoic Having similar echogenicity (brightness) as neighboring tissue. The prefix "iso" means "the same" so isoechoic literally means having the same level of echo.

Isotropy (isotropic) Having the same physical properties when measured from any direction such as acoustic appearance, propagation velocities, etc.

Isovolumic Unchanging volume. (*See also Isovolumic contraction*)

Isovolumic contraction During ventricular contraction when both the mitral and aortic valves (for the left side) and the tricuspid and pulmonic valves (for the right side) are closed, the volumes remain unchanged while the pressures increase dramatically.

Isovolumic systolic pressure curve Displays the pressure curve, which results for various volumes of blood under ventricular contraction, with the restriction that no blood is allowed to be ejected.

Joule The unit for work/energy.

JPEG A process for compressing image files. The degree of compression can be adjusted which allows for a trade-off between file size and image quality.

Kerf The gaps between the elements which are created when dicing the piezoelectric block.

Kinetic energy Energy related to motion, proportional to the velocity squared of movement.

Korotokov sounds Circulatory sounds heard through the stethoscope in auscultation of blood pressure with cuff inflation. The Korotokov (heart) sounds are produced when releasing the pressure in the cuff such that the intravascular pressure exceeds the cuff pressure and a volume of blood rams into a static column of blood distal to the cuff location.

Laminar flow When fluid flows smoothly without vortices or other turbulence.

Lateral displacement (artifact) The artifactual lateral translation of a structure in an image. Lateral displacement occurs from either grating lobe or refraction artifact.

Lateral (azimuthal/transverse/angular/side-by-side) resolution The ability to distinguish between two side-by-side objects and/or the ability to accurately determine the dimension of a structure along the width of the beam (depth). The lateral resolution is approximately equal to the beamwidth.

Leakage current The electrical current that flows through the protective ground conductor to ground or system chassis. If there is improper grounding, this current can take a different path such as through the human body.

Left ventricular opacification (LVO) Opacification is the filling of an echo free region with echoes from contrast microbubbles. Therefore LVO is the filling of the left ventricular chamber with echoes from an injected contrast agent.

Length Distance or extent in space.

Lens A material used to help to focus the beam. (For 1-D arrays, a lens is used to help focus in the elevation plane.)

Lift A net upward force created when there is greater pressure pushing up on the wing than pressure pushing down on the wing as predicted by Bernoulli's equation.

Line averaging A technique to improve signal-to-noise by adding together the data from more than one acoustic line to create a single display line.

Line density (color) *(See Color line density)*

Linear phased array transducer A family of phased array transducers that have multiple elements in the lateral dimension. These transducer are frequently physically large and consist of as many as 200 to 300 elements or more and were produced for vascular applications where contact must be maintained with a relatively flat surface. For unsteered imaging, the image is produced by sequencing. For steered imaging the image is produced by both sequencing and phasing.

Linear proportionality (relationships) A specific proportionality in which the rate of change between two variables is the same (i.e. a 10% increase in one variable results in a corresponding 10% increase in the related variable). This relationship between two variables is such that their graph results in a straight line, implying a constant rate of change.

Linear switched array transducer An obsolete transducer design that used a large group of elements in the linear dimension that could be turned either on or off through electronic switches. The linear switched array is the grandfather to current phased linear array transducers.

Liquid crystal display (LCD) One of the monitor technologies that has significantly replaced the older CRT technology. The basic premise of an LCD display is simple: there is a light source and a control mechanism that either blocks or allows transmission of the light to the screen on a pixel by pixel basis. The light gating is performed by liquid crystals.

Locational artifacts Artifacts that result in structures appearing either displaced in an image from the true location or the presence of a structure or signal which does not even exist.

Logarithms The power to which a base must be raised to get the desired number. Logarithms inherently serve as a non-linear compression scheme.

Longitudinal (beam dimension) The dimension along the axis of the beam corresponding to depth into the patient. Other terms commonly used are axial, radial, depth, and range.

Longitudinal resolution *(See Axial resolution)*

Longitudinal wave A wave which propagates through a series of compressions and rarefactions along (in the same direction) as the wave direction. Conventional ultrasound imaging is based on longitudinal sound waves.

Longitudinal wave speed Determined by the square root of the bulk modulus divided by the density of the medium.

Lossless compression Any scheme which reduces dynamic range without loss of data.

Low echogenicity Low-level reflected signals.

Low-level disinfection Used for non-critical medical devices which come in contact with intact skin. Low-level disinfectants are able to kill fungi, amoebas, mold, many types of microbes, and most viruses.

Low MI techniques Approaches for ultrasound-enhanced assessment (contrast) which uses transmit MIs between 0.2 and 0.3. At low MI, there is a relatively linear response of the microbubbles, reflecting primarily fundamental echoes.

Lung rockets artifact When imaging the lung, ring down artifacts that emanate from the pleural line and are present to the bottom of the image are referred to as B-lines or B-line artifact (BLA) and sometimes "comet tail." Three or more B-lines in the same interstitial space are referred to as "lung rockets" and imply interstitial lung disease (interstitial syndrome).

Manual steering Physically moving a transducer over the scan region of interest.

Matching layer A thin layer of material attached to the crystal of the transducer to reduce the acoustic impedance mismatch between the high impedance of the crystal and the low impedance of the tissue. The ideal thickness for a matching layer is quarter wavelength.

Maximum venous capacitance (MVC) The ability of the veins to fill with blood during a period in which the venous outflow is halted.

Maximum venous outflow (MVO) The amount of venous emptying that occurs when the occluding cuff is deflated.

Mean velocity The average velocity. The mean velocity can be calculated relative to time, relative to space (cross-sectional area) or both.

Mechanical annular array transducer A nearly obsolete transducer design which uses multiple rings (annuli) to allow for a varying focus both laterally and elevationally. By turning on or off rings, the transducer aperture is changed, changing the focus. These transducers were usually steered by a motor (mechanical steering).

Mechanical bioeffects Bioeffects that are caused by the physical interaction between the wave and the tissues in the body related to cavitation. Mechanical bioeffects generally occur during the peak rarefactional phase of the wave cycle.

Mechanical index (MI) A parameter that indicates the likelihood of mechanical bioeffects (cavitation) occurring. The MI is calculated by dividing the peak rarefactional pressure by the square root of the operating frequency.

Mechanical steering Refers to changing the ultrasound beam direction through a mechanical means (such as attaching a crystal to a motor) which physically points the crystal in different directions.

Mechanical wave A wave which requires a medium.

Medium The material through which a mechanical wave propagates. During imaging, the medium is the part of the patient being scanned.

Membrane (CMUT) The component of a CMUT cell which vibrates resulting in transmitting and receiving sound waves.

Metric system Measurement system based on the decimal form (multiples of 10).

Microbubbles Bubbles defined as being larger than 1 micrometer but smaller than 10 mm. Ultrasound enhancing agents (contrast) utilize microbubbles.

Microflow imaging (MFI) Ultrasound imaging technique which portrays low flow and low-velocity flow enabled by techniques such as power Doppler and spatiotemporal filtering.

Mirror image artifact An artifact produced when a structure is located in front of a specular reflector which results in the structure being displayed twice: once in the correct location, and one distal to and symmetric about the specular reflecting surface.

Mismatch Difference or having disparate properties. *(See also Acoustic impedance)*

Mitral regurgitant fraction The difference in the left ventricular inflow and outflow volume normalized by the inflow volume.

M-mode (motion mode) An ultrasound mode commonly used for cardiac and fetal cardiac studies. A single acoustic line is repeatedly transmitted in the same direction such that depth is displayed on the vertical axis and time is displayed on the horizontal axis. The signal amplitude is represented using grayscale (shades of gray). Since time is plotted on the horizontal axis, motion is detected by changes in depth along the horizontal axis.

Modal velocity The most commonly occurring velocity.

Modulation To change or modify. As a mechanical wave propagates through the body, the interaction modulates the wave. Demodulation is therefore the process of removing the modulation from the initial wave.

Momentum The mass of an object multiplied by its velocity.

Moore's law Expresses the rate of growth of technology.

Motion mode *(See M-mode)*

MPEG (Moving Pictures Expert Group) A standard for encoding and compressing video images.

Multi-line acquisition (MLA) Any technique (such as parallel processing, zone imaging, plane wave, and diverging wave imaging) which generates multiple received lines from a single transmit.

Multi-line transmit (MLT) Creating multiple receive lines simultaneously by transmitting multiple pulses simultaneously in different directions.

Multipath artifact An artifact that results in a structure being displayed artificially deeper than reality because the beam does not propagate in a straight line to and from the object. Like most imaging artifacts, multipath artifact occurs generally in the presence of specular reflectors.

Multiple transmit foci A technique to improve lateral resolution by sequentially transmitting multiple beams with varying focal depths and then combining the narrowest regions of each received beam to create one composite display beam. The improved lateral resolution is achieved at the expense of temporal resolution.

Native or "Tissue" harmonics The production of harmonic energy from non-linear wave propagation through tissue. The harmonic energy results from changes in the propagation velocity which occur with compression and rarefaction. The general term of "harmonic imaging" is now commonly used to refer to "native" or "tissue" harmonics. The terms native harmonics was created to distinguish between harmonics produced from tissue as opposed to harmonics produced by contrast agent.

Natural focus The depth at which a transducer will naturally focus without any application of any focusing techniques.

Natural rate of the cell The rate at which a cell depolarizes without an "external" stimulus.

Near field or Fresnel zone The area between the face of the transducer and the beam focus (also referred to as the near zone).

Near zone length (NZL) The distance from the surface of the transducer to the natural focus (also referred to as the focal depth).

Negative predictive value (NPV) The percentage of times a test is correct when negative for disease (where correct is defined as results which match the gold standard). The NPV is calculated as the true negatives (TN) divided by the TN plus the false negatives (FN).

Newtonian fluid A fluid whose viscosity is variable only with changes in temperature.

Noise Any unwanted signal or signals which mask or obscure desired signals.

Noise floor The signal level below which no signals are visible because of the presence of noise.

Non-acoustic zoom (read zoom) A magnification of a specified region into a larger display region. Non-acoustic zooms do not change the true resolution but may improve the apparent resolution.

Non-Interlaced (monitor or display) *(See Progressive)*

Non-linear proportionality (relationships) A proportional relationship in which the rate of change between two variables is not the same, or not "linear." (e. g. a doubling of one variable results in a quadrupling in the related variable).

Non-scanned modality Any modality which repeatedly transmits in the same direction (such as PW Doppler, CW Doppler, A-mode, and M-mode). Non-scanned modalities generally have greater risks of thermal bioeffects.

Normal incidence Implies that the wave propagation direction is perpendicular to the interface (or that the wavefront is parallel to the interface). For normal incidence there is no refraction.

Numerator The part of a fraction that is above the division line.

Nyquist criterion States that the sampling frequency must be at least twice the highest frequency in the signal to be detected. Violation of the Nyquist criterion results in incorrect frequency estimation (aliasing).

Nyquist limit Related to the Nyquist criterion. The Nyquist limit refers to the highest detectable Doppler frequency shift without aliasing. The Nyquist limit is determined by the PRF divided by two. If the Doppler shift is less than half of the PRF, then there is no aliasing. If the Doppler shift is greater than half the PRF, aliasing will occur.

Oblique Non-perpendicular and non-parallel.

Oculoplethysmography (OPG) Indirect method used to measure the systolic pressure in the ophthalmic artery by obtaining an indirect measurement of the pulse delay within the ophthalmic artery.

OHM's law The analogous law to the simplified law of hemodynamics for electrical current. Ohm's law dictates that the change in voltage equals the electrical current multiplied by the electrical resistance.

OLED monitor (organic light-emitting diodes) A display technology based on a series of organic thin films between two conductors which emit light when stimulated with an electrical signal (electroluminescence). Since OLED displays do not require backlights like LCD displays, OLED monitors can be thinner, lighter, and more efficient than LCD displays.

Opacification (left ventricular) The process by which the dark blood pool becomes bright by the injection of contrast, used to better delineate the borders of the left ventricle.

Operating frequency The center frequency of the transmit bandwidth for transducers.

Orthogonal (See Perpendicular)

Out of phase Phase refers to the timing relationships between waves. When two waves are out of phase, there is a separation between the maximum peaks (compression) of the waves. When two waves are purely out of phase (180°), the maximum peak (compression) of one wave is aligned with the minimum peak (rarefaction) of the other wave.

Palpation (See also Echopalpation) Using light pressure exerted by the fingers or the hand to sense differences in underlying tissues.

Panoramic imaging Any of a group of techniques that result in displaying a much larger anatomic field of view. This technique is generally very helpful for imaging superficial structures such as a thyroid by displaying both lobes of the thyroid gland in a single image. Panoramic images are usually generated by sweeping the transducer over a region of the patient. Using statistical correlation techniques, the system determines which lines of data are unique and should be displayed and which are repeats of lines already captured.

Parabolic flow A special type of laminar flow in which the velocity profile is shaped like a parabola across the vessel. The flow in the center of the vessel has a higher velocity than flow along the vessel walls which lose more energy through friction and viscous effects.

Parallel processing A processing technique generally used to improve temporal resolution. Parallel processing is performed by transmitting a wider beam than normal and then dividing the transducer elements and receiver channels into two or more parallel groups. Each receiver group processes a receive beam allowing for twice as many (or more) receive beams to be generated in the time required to transmit a single acoustic beam. Almost all digital systems now use parallel processing for color and 2D. Most systems now perform quad parallel processing (or more).

Parasympathetic nervous system Plays a minor role in regulation of circulation and can affect the heart rate via the parasympathetic fibers carried to the heart in the vagus nerve.

Partially constructive interference When two waves add so that the new wave is not as "big" as when the two waves were in phase and not as small as when the two waves were completely out of phase.

Particle motion One of the four acoustic variables. Occurs when particles oscillate back and forth about their original location, allowing the concentration of energy to propagate along the wave path.

Pedof (See Pencil probe)

Pencil probe A simple transducer designed to perform only Doppler and no imaging. The pencil probe consists of a single round crystal for PW and a split round crystal for CW Doppler. These transducers are often the most sensitive for Doppler since no trade-offs are made to accommodate imaging. Since no image is possible these transducers are commonly referred to as a "blind" or "Doppler blind" transducer. Another name for this transducer type is a "pedof".

Pennate Having a structure like that of a feather such as muscle in which fibers extend obliquely from either side of a central tendon.

Percentage A part of a whole expressed in hundredths. A specific way of expressing the ratio of two numbers in terms of hundredths.

Pericardium The thin sac (membrane) that surrounds the heart and the roots of the great blood vessels.

Perimeter The distance around a structure or shape. A perimeter is a one-dimensional measure and has units of distance such as meters or centimeters.

Period The reciprocal of the frequency, representing the amount of time it takes for one full cycle to occur.

Peripheral resistance A measure of the resistance of the entire vascular system to flow.

Perpendicular Meeting at a right angle (90°).

Persistence (See Image persistence or Color persistence)

Phantom An object used to perform equipment quality assurance testing. These objects usually use materials which mimic properties of tissue in terms of propagation velocity, absorption, and reflection.

Phase A term used to determine a time reference. For cyclical phenomena such as waves, phase is often specified in degrees instead of time.

Phase delay A time delay which results in a waves reaching maxima at different times. Phase delays are used with multiple elements to produce electronic steering and focusing.

Phase difference (See Phase delay)

Phase inversion (See Pulse inversion)

Phased array sector transducer A family of phase array transducers that produce a sector formatted image. The sector image format is produced by phasing. The sector transducer type was designed with rib access in mind.

Photoplethysmography Light produced from an infrared light-emitting diode and a photosensor to detect changes in blood volume.

Piezoelectric crystals A material which converts electropotential (voltage) into acoustic waves and acoustic waves back into voltage.

Piezoelectric effect The phenomenon of mechanical deformation, which results when an electric field (voltage) is applied to certain crystal materials.

Pixel The smallest division of a display.

Plane wave An approach to transmitting without using focusing so that the entire field of view is imaged with a single transmit resulting in very high frame rate imaging. Multiple frames (angles) are averaged to increase the signal-to-noise ratio since the SNR of a single frame from a plane wave is generally low.

Plethysmography A category of methods which records changes in volume.

Plug flow A special type of laminar flow in which the velocity profile is relatively constant across the entire vessel. Plug flow occurs as an entrance effect as the result of acceleration.

PMN-PT crystal *(See Single crystal)*

Poiseuille's (equation) law Expresses the relationship between volumetric flow and the pressure gradient, the radius of the flow conduit, the length of the flow conduit, and the viscosity of the fluid. Poiseuille's law assumes that there is no energy lost to friction and a Newtonian fluid. Poiseuille's law was derived empirically.

Poisson's ratio The negative of the ratio of transverse contraction strain to longitudinal extension strain in the direction of stretching force.

Polarization The process of displacing electrical charges such that positive charges exist on one side and negative charges exist on the other side.

Poling A process used to polarize a crystal material so as to enhance the piezoelectric properties. Poling involves heating a crystal to high temperatures and then applying a powerful electromagnetic field.

Popliteal fossa An anatomical region behind the knee.

Poroelastic A poroelastic material is a material consisting of fluid that flows relative to a deforming solid matrix. When a sustained strain is applied to a poroelastic tissue, the lateral-to-axial strain ratio decreases with time as the fluid flows out of the solid matrix.

Positive predictive value (PPV) The percentage of times a test is correct when positive for disease (where correct is defined as results which match the gold standard). The PPV is calculated as the true positives (TP) divided by the TP plus the false positives (FP).

Post-processing Any processing which can be changed post data acquisition such as data compression, colorization, and reject. Post-processing techniques are applied in the backend (scan converter) of the ultrasound system.

Potential energy Stored energy which can be converted to other forms of energy such as kinetic. Pressure across vessel walls represents potential energy.

Power The rate at which work is being performed. The unit for power is Watts.

Power Doppler *(See Color power Doppler)*

Power ratio The same as the power gain factor. The power ratio is the final power divided by the initial power, where the final represents the power after a change (such as increasing the transmit power) and the initial power represents the power before the change. The power ratio is used to convert the relative change into decibels.

Pre-compensated TGC A feature of many ultrasound systems that internally applies a predetermined TGC profile usually based on a few system settings such as the transducer, depth, and preset. When pre-compensated TGC is applied, the TGC controls are generally set to approximately the center position, with small variations about the center to adjust the depths where the predetermined profile was not ideal.

Preload The stretched condition of the heart muscle related to the volume within the ventricle at the end of diastolic filling just before contraction.

Pre-processing Signal conditioning that occurs in real time and cannot be removed from an image once acquired. Pre-processing occurs before the signal is stored in the backend (scan converter).

Pressure A measure of force per area.

Pressure gradient The change in pressure that occurs as a result of energy conversion with flow. Measuring the pressure at the site of a stenosis, the pressure is decreased relative to the pressure proximal to the stenosis since some of the potential energy is converted to kinetic energy within the narrowed region. The difference between the proximal pressure and the lower pressure within the stenosis is referred to as a pressure gradient.

Processing Any conditioning of a signal in an attempt to interpret or improve the display of that signal.

Progressive (monitor or display) Unlike interlaced displays which present a frame of data as two interleaved fields (an odd and an even field), progressive displays update all of the lines in order (progressively). A clear advantage of "non-interlaced" progressive displays is improved frame rates with less blurring of dynamic structures.

Propagation A means of transmission from one location to another location through interaction. Sound propagates through a medium by interacting with particles within the medium.

Propagation velocity The rate at which a wave travels through a medium. The propagation velocity is related to the bulk modulus and density of a material. As the bulk modulus increases (assuming no change in density), the propagation velocity increases. As the density increases (assuming no change in bulk modulus), the propagation velocity decreases. In biological materials, an increase in density usually indicates a significant increase in the bulk modulus such that more dense materials have higher propagation velocities than lower density materials.

Proportionality A mathematical relationship between variables which indicates that an increase in the value of one variable results in an increase in the value of the related variable. (See also Linear proportionality, Direct non-linear proportionality, Inverse proportionality, and Direct proportionality)

PRF (See Pulse repetition frequency)

PRP (See Pulse repetition period)

Pseudoaneurysm A false aneurysm created by the perforation of the intima and media, it is contained by a thin layer of adventitia or thrombus.

Pulmonic stenosis An abnormal narrowing of the orifice between the right ventricle and the pulmonary artery which leads to an increase in resistance to blood flow into the pulmonary artery. (Also referred to as pulmonary stenosis.)

Pulsatile flow Flow that dynamically varies cyclically with time. The variation of flow that occurs from the peak of systole to the end of diastole.

Pulse duration The amount of time for which a pulse lasts. The pulse duration equals the period multiplied by the number of cycles within the pulse.

Pulse inversion A technique used with harmonic imaging to remove the fundamental signal leaving only the harmonic signal by transmitting two pulses with inverted phase (180° apart) and then adding the resultant signals together. This technique was created to overcome the fundamental degradation in axial resolution which comes from narrowbanding the transmit in an attempt to reduce the fundamental signal overlapping with the harmonic signal. Another advantage of pulse inversion is signal gain which results from using more than one sample.

Pulse length (See Spatial pulse length)

Pulse pressure The difference between the peak systolic and end diastolic pressures.

Pulse Repetition Frequency (PRF) The number of pulses that occur in one second and equal to the reciprocal of the PRP.

Pulse Repetition Period (PRP) The time between the start of one transmit pulse until the start of the next transmit pulse. Primarily determined by the imaging depth.

Pulsed mode (See Pulsed wave)

Pulsed wave (PW) To transmit and receive intermittently, alternatively.

Pulsed wave (PW) Doppler A Doppler technique which uses pulses to achieve range specificity. The Doppler gate size and depth is set by the user. The system produces a pulse which matches the gate size, and waits the appropriate time for the sound wave to travel to the desired gate depth and return. Unlike continuous wave operation, by restricting the pulse length, signals are primarily received from the depth of interest.

Pulsed wave range ambiguity (See Range ambiguity artifact)

Pulser The part of the front end of the system responsible for creating the transmit pulses to drive the transducer elements.

Purewave (See Single crystal)

PZT (lead zirconate titanate) An inorganic material used for the creation of ultrasound transducer, speakers, microphones, etc., because of its piezoelectric properties.

Quadrant One quarter of the circumference of a circle equivalent to 90 degrees.

Quadrature detection Signifies that the information is detected at two different phases, 90° apart. Quadrature detection is used in Doppler so as to distinguish forward flow from reverse flow.

Quality assurance The combination of steps taken by a lab to guarantee accuracy in testing. Some aspects of quality assurance include routine testing of equipment, having well defined lab protocols, holding regular review meetings, lab accreditation, and individual certification.

Quality factor The reciprocal of the fractional bandwidth.

Radial resolution (See Axial resolution)

Radiantflow (See Surface rendered color Doppler)

Radius (r) A line segment extending from the center of a circle or sphere to the circumference or bounding surface.

Range ambiguity artifact An undesirable result of the fact that sound continues to travel and reflect back from depths deeper than the Doppler gate depth. As a result, signals from multiples of the PRP return and are added with signals from the desired gate depth. All pulsed modes suffer from range ambiguity. This phenomenon is generally not a major problem unless the Doppler sample volume (gate) is shallow.

Range resolution (See Axial resolution)

Rarefaction The state of wave propagation in which the particles of the medium are stretched farther apart than normal (lower density).

Rayleigh scattering Frequency-dependent scattering. This type of reflection occurs from structures which are small relative to the wavelength.

Rayls The unit for acoustic impedance (kg/m²sec).

Reactive hyperemia A condition of temporary ischemia which results in increased blood flow.

Read zoom (See Non-acoustic zoom)

Real-time imaging Implies that all the ultrasound lines are being transmitted, recorded, processed, and displayed so as to appear instant and continuous in time.

Receive line The returning echoes registered by the system from a single direction over the time between the transmit event and the time until the next transmit occurs as dictated by the imaging depth.

Receiver The front end of the system which registers and processes the echoes that are detected by the transducer elements.

Receiver gain Amplification of the signal after it has already returned from the patient.

Reciprocal The absolute inverse of a quantity. The product of reciprocals is 1.

Rectification The process of inverting the negative component of a signal. To make (an alternating current) unidirectional. The process of rectification is applied in signal detection.

Reflection The phenomenon of causing a propagating wave to change direction such that some of the wave does not continue to propagate forward.

Reflective mode One form of medical imaging (like diagnostic ultrasound) where a form of energy is transmitted into the patient and the reflected component is used to create the image. (In contrast with transmission modes such as X-ray which process the transmitted energy.)

Refraction The bending of a beam at an interface of two media. For refraction to occur, there must be a change in propagation speed and an incident angle other than 0° (other than normal).

Refraction artifacts Artifacts that result from refraction, which results in lateral displacement of a structure in the image.

Refractive (edge) shadowing A drop out or decrease in intensity which results from refraction. Refractive shadowing generally occurs from the edges of specular reflections, hence, refractive shadowing is often commonly referred to as edge shadowing.

Regurgitation The backward flow of blood through a valve.

Reject A means by which to ignore any signal or noise below a certain amplitude.

Relative refractory period The period shortly after the activation of a nerve fiber when partial repolarization has occurred and only a greater than normal stimulus can stimulate a second response.

Resistance (*See Impedance*)

Resolution The ability to discern a difference between structures spatially separated, temporally separated, or separated by contrast level. (*See Longitudinal resolution, Lateral resolution, Elevation resolution, Temporal resolution, and Contrast resolution*)

Retrospective transmit focusing A dynamic focusing technique which is performed after data is received to improve focusing relative to the static transmit approach, which results in a single focal point with wider beams at all other depths. Retrospective transmit focusing is based on storing massive amounts of data received element by element over time, and then, based on a geometric model, retrospectively, adding the signals with varying time delays basically reversing time.

Reverberation artifact An artifact caused by sound bouncing between multiple structures.

Reynolds number A dimensionless index which indicates the likelihood of turbulence occurring for a particular flow situation. When the Reynolds number exceeds 2,000, turbulence usually (but not always) develops. Reynolds number is defined as the ratio between the inertial forces and the viscous forces.

Right to refuse Patients can rescind informed consent and always have the right to refuse treatment.

Ring down artifact When sound reverberates within an air sac so that the boundaries of the air sac are redrawn repeatedly, creating a bright tail or "ring down." The term ring down also refers to the reverberation which commonly occurs at the surface of a transducer.

Ring time Another term for the pulse duration – the time for which the transducer rings.

Rouleaux formation The word "rouleaux" refers to a small row or coil of coins, or anything which forms a similar coiled shape. In low-shear flow states, red blood cells tend to change their shape, aggregate, and form a connected chain that resembles a coil, hence called rouleaux flow. Because of the larger cross-sectional area relative to individual blood cells, rouleaux formations generally have greater scattering properties than individual red blood cells, making it more likely to visualize the blood (often described as smoke or spontaneous contrast) within the 2D image.

Roundtrip effect The fact that sound travels twice as far as the distance to the structure (down and back).

Sagittal plane An anatomical plane which divides the body into left and right parts.

Sampling rate The frequency at which signals are "viewed". From the Nyquist criterion, the highest frequency detectable equals half the sample rate.

Saturation The non-linear state of electronics when the signals being processed become larger than the voltage rails of the electronics.

Scan conversion The process of taking data from the receiver and converting into data which can be displayed as an image. Essentially, the data from the receivers is in A-mode format. The scan converter converts the amplitudes into grayscale levels and then formats each successive line to create an image.

Scanned modality Modalities which transmit acoustic lines in different directions over time so as to present a scan (such as 2D and color Doppler). Scanned modalities have lower risks of thermal bioeffects but are more likely to suffer mechanical bioeffects.

Scattering Refers to a disorganized redirection of sound wave energy away from the transmitted direction.

Sector The pie-shaped image produced from a sector transducer, used primarily for cardiac imaging.

Sensitivity A measure of the ability to detect small signals. Sensitivity improves with better transducer designs, better electronic design, and using higher transmit power.

Sensitivity (statistical) The ability of a test to detect the presence of disease. Calculated as the true positives (TP) divided by the (TP) plus the false negatives (FN).

Sequencing Exciting groups of elements in a specific pattern to create a desired scan "pattern" or "shape."

Sequential imaging The temporally-limited imaging approach that has been used in 2D (B-mode) and color Doppler for many years by which the image is built up line-by-line, with each line having a transmit focus. This approach is in contrast with ultrafast imaging which creates an entire image all at once, and then uses frame averaging to improve the signal-to-noise ratio.

Shadowing artifact Caused by any form of attenuation stronger than the attenuation of the surrounding area.

Shear modulus (G) The shear modulus of a material is defined as the ratio of shear stress to the shear strain, which indicates the tendency of that material to deform (shear) when acted upon by opposing forces.

Shear wave speed (SWS) The speed of a transverse or secondary wave (S-wave), which is determined by the square root of the shear elasticity modulus divided by the density. The shear wave speed is generally much slower than the longitudinal wave speed.

Side lobe artifact The existence of lower pressure or weaker beams pointing off-axis that occur with single element transducers.

SieScape *(See Panoramic imaging)*

Signal Any phenomenon desired to be measured.

Signal-to-noise ratio (SNR) The amplitude of the signal divided by the amplitude of the noise. A poor signal-to-noise ratio indicates that the image may not be of adequate quality for diagnosis. Methods of improving the signal-to-noise ratio include, using a lower transducer frequency, increasing the transmit power, appropriate setting of the transmit focus, averaging techniques, use of different imaging planes, etc.

Simplified law of hemodynamics Expresses the fact that the pressure gradient is proportional to the volumetric flow and the resistance to flow.

Sine The trigonometric function that, for an acute angle, is the ratio between the leg opposite the angle and the hypotenuse. On the unit circle, the sine is determined by drawing the angle and projecting the intersection of the angle and the unit circle onto the y-axis.

Single crystal (PMN-PT) Lead magnesium niobate-lead titanate. This material is slowly extruded to create a "single crystal" without the random grain boundaries of PZT (and other composites) which result in a decrease in piezoelectric response. Transducers made with PMN-PT are generally much more sensitive and have greater bandwidth than transducers made with other piezoelectric materials.

Sliding receive filters *(See Dynamic frequency tuning)*

Slow flow detection *(See Microflow imaging)*

Sonoelastography Ultrasound-based techniques which create displays and/or measurements based on the elastic properties of the tissues being assessed.

Snell's law The rule which predicts how much refraction occurs. When the incident angle does not equal the transmitted angle, refraction has occurred. The greater the difference between the incident angle and the transmit angle, the more refraction has occurred.

Sono CT *(See Compound imaging)*

Sound A mechanical, longitudinal wave which propagates through a series of compressions and rarefactions. A physical phenomenon that stimulates the sense of hearing.

Sound speed compensation Any technique which attempts to correct for the aberration and defocusing which results from using time delays based on an assumed but incorrect 1540 m/s speed of sound.

Sparse matrix A method used in early 2-dimensional arrays to limit the number of electrical connections required within transducers with large numbers of elements (e. g. more than 2,000). Since only some of the elements were used, bad grating lobes generally existed as well as poor harmonic signal generation. These limitations became the motivation for creating fully active 2D matrix transducers using a new technology called micro-beamforming.

Spatial Used as a modifier to refer to physical dimensions such as the spatial pulse length or the spatial average intensity.

Spatial average Determining the mean value over a cross-sectional area (in contrast with a temporal average which determines a mean over time).

Spatial averaging (processing) A processing technique which attempts to reduce random noise by subdividing an image into small local regions and averaging.

Spatial compounding *(See Compound imaging)*

Spatial pulse length (SPL) The physical length a pulse occupies in a medium. The spatial pulse length equals the wavelength multiplied by the number of cycles in the pulse. Since the wavelength is medium dependent, the SPL is medium dependent.

Spatiotemporal filter The foundational approach used for filtering to allow for microflow detection. Spatiotemporal refers to using information based on both spatial distribution and time. Spatiotemporal coherence refers to how similar the speckle pattern is from a moving reflector (or reflective region) over time. This technique allows for a better separation of signals derived from flow versus signals derived from moving tissue.

Specificity The ability of a test to detect the absence of disease. The specificity is calculated as the true negatives (TN) divided by the TN plus the false positives (FP).

Speckle The appearance as tissue texture of random variations of signal strength from constructive and destructive interference. Note that although speckle gives the appearance of tissue texture, the speckle pattern is not representative of true tissue characteristics.

Speckle reduction (techniques) The improvement in signal-to-noise by reducing the artifactual appearance of tissue texture referred to as speckle. There are a series of techniques used to reduce speckle including: improved resolution and sensitivity, compound imaging (spatial), compound imaging (frequency fusion), and statistics-based adaptive processes.

Speckle tracking A method to track the motion of tissue over time. Much like radar which looks for a specific signature and then follows that signatures motion through space over time, the speckle characteristics of the tissue are analyzed from frame to frame to determine if any regions of the tissue have moved and by how much. The tissue speckle movement is usually determined by performing cross correlations of consecutive B-mode (2D) images (frames). Speckle tracking is a useful technique to measure strain.

Spectral broadening The term generally used to refer to the broadened appearance of a spectrum. A spectrum may appear "broadened" because of varying velocities within the Doppler sample volume (also referred to as "spectral spread"), or as an artifact associated with varying angles between the flow and each of the transducer elements. As an artifact, spectral broadening can also be caused by excessive Doppler gain (sometimes referred to as blossoming artifact).

Spectral Doppler A subcategory of Doppler techniques which includes PW Doppler, CW Doppler, and HPRF Doppler which displays a range of frequency shifts (related to a range of velocities through the Doppler equation) on the vertical axis and time on the horizontal axis. Unlike waveform Doppler systems, variations of flow characteristics are visualized such as spectral broadening, turbulence, and laminar flow.

Spectral Doppler dropout When little or no spectral flow is presented from Doppler in a region in which flow is expected. Spectral Doppler dropout can be the result of actual flow restricting disease such as occlusion, or as the result of artifact. Some of the many artifacts which can cause spectral dropout include, inadequate sensitivity, acoustic shadowing, excessively high wall filters, poor Doppler, angle, etc.

Spectral mirroring artifact A Doppler artifact which results from one of two sources: imperfect separation between the forward and reverse flow channels (In phase (I) and quadrature (Q) channels), or from an insonification angle close to 90° such that the elements on one side of the center of the aperture are seeing flow at an angle less than 90° while elements on the other side of the center line of the aperture are seeing flow at angles greater than 90°. Since performing Doppler at 90° is highly discouraged, most spectral mirroring is the results of signal bleeding across channels. This bleeding is the result of either poorly designed electronics or extraordinarily strong signals. The former cannot be compensated whereas the latter can be ameliorated by decreasing the transmit power.

Spectral window The open area between the spectrum and the baseline which indicates the presence of laminar flow at the location of the Doppler sample volume. The absence of a spectral window may or may not be an indication of turbulence.

Specular reflection Strong angularly dependent reflection in which the angle of incidence equals the angle of reflection. Mirror-like reflection.

Speed error artifact The presentation of structures at incorrect depths as a result of a propagation velocity other than the presumed propagation velocity of 1540 m/sec.

Spontaneous contrast (See Rouleaux)

Sphygmomanometer An instrument used to measure blood pressure.

Stable cavitation (See Cavitation)

Standard Precautions (previously known as Universal Precautions) Standard precautions are a method of infection control to prevent the transmission of blood borne diseases. In 1996, the CDC expanded the concept and changed the term to Standard Precautions. The expansion included adding the protocols to maintain an aseptic field and to prevent contamination and cross-contamination between health providers, between patients, and between healthcare providers and patients.

Standoff pad A structure with low absorption and an acoustic impedance close to that of tissue used to increase the imaging depth for superficial structures so as to improve focus, decrease clutter, and achieve better imaging angles.

Static (strain) elastography Elastography performed by applying compression, usually by pressing downward on the ultrasound transducer, while holding the transducer over a single spot on the patient. The pre- and post-compression images are compared to produce strain images.

Steady flow Constant volumetric flow.

Stenosis A narrowing of a vessel or flow path that results in increased resistance to flow.

Sterilization The complete elimination of all forms of microbial life including spores and viruses.

Stiffness A property of a material which indicates a lack of compressibility. As the stiffness of a material increases, the propagation velocity through the material increases.

Strain (ε) A dimensionless measure of the percentage change in length. When the length of a structure decreases, the change is negative and hence the strain is considered negative. When the length of a structure increases, the change is positive, and hence the strain is considered positive. Since longitudinally oriented fibers shorten, normal strain is negative as is circumferential strain. However, the normal myocardium thickens during systole so radial strain is typically positive.

Stress (σ) Defined as the pressure or tension on an object or the deforming force per unit area.

Stroke volume (SV) The stroke volume is the amount of blood ejected from the heart on a beat-by-beat basis.

Subcritical stenosis A narrowing in a flow path the causes an increase in velocity but does not result in enough energy loss to result in a decrease in volumetric flow. A subcritical stenosis can be "unmasked" by stressing the system through increasing volumetric flow demand.

Superposition When two or more waves arrive at the same point, the disturbances of each add together. This is the fundamental principle behind constructive and destructive interference which is used for focusing and steering as the signal gain achieved with averaging.

Supine Lying on ones back.

Surface rendered color Doppler An image rendering technique based on Phong shading (originally created by Bui Tuong Phong) which adds together an ambient, diffuse, and specular rendering of an image to create a three-dimensional appearance of the image.

Sympathetic nervous system The part of the autonomic nervous system that exerts influence over the heart through catecholamines, adrenaline, and noradrenaline circulating in the blood.

Synthetic aperture Uses the concept of linear superposition to create an effectively larger or different aperture retrospectively by adding together the signals received at differing times from two or more individual elements or apertures.

Systole The phase of the cardiac cycle during which myocardial contraction occurs increasing circulatory pressure.

Systolic flow Blood flow that occurs during the systolic phase of the cardiac cycle.

TAMV (time average mean velocity) A Doppler technique used to determine volumetric flow by multiplying the 2D estimated cross-sectional area with the mean velocity averaged over time. (Some systems refer to this as TAMEAN.)

Tamponade A condition involving compression of the heart caused by blood or fluid accumulation in the sac around the heart (pericardium).

Tangent The (trigonometric) ratio between the adjacent side and the opposite side of a right triangle containing that angle. The tangent of an angle is also equal to the sine of the angle divided by the cosine of the angle.

Temperature Degree of hot and coldness measured on a definite scale such as Celsius, Fahrenheit, or Kelvin.

Temporal distortion Any process which results in a change in the temporal accuracy of a signal such as time-based "averaging" techniques to improve the signal-to-noise ratio. Temporal distortion also occurs naturally when the frame rate is inadequate relative to the dynamics of the structures or hemodynamics.

Temporal resolution The ability to distinguish dynamics, or changes, over time. Inadequate temporal resolution results in temporal distortion. The temporal resolution is commonly limited by the frame rate.

Thermal bioeffects Bioeffects caused by high temperature in a region causing metabolic breakdown and cellular damage.

Thermal index (TI, TIS, TIB, TIC) A model produced parameter that indicates the calculated worst case temperature rise in degrees Celsius. The TI is further classified into the TIS (thermal index in soft tissue), the TIB (thermal index in bone), and the TIC (thermal index in cranial bone). A TIS of 1.4 implies that, for the given imaging situation, it is expected that the greatest temperature increase that will over time occur within the patient is 1.4 degrees Celsius.

Thermal indices Collective title for three different indices: Thermal Index in Soft Tissue (TIS,) Thermal Index in Bone (TIB,) and Thermal Index in Cranial Bone (TIC). The thermal indices are produced by mathematical models which take into account imaging and system parameters such as the transmit power, the focal depth, the imaging depth, the region of the body being scanned, etc. A thermal index of 1 implies that the model predicts a highest temperature rise expected to be 1 degree Celsius. It is possible for the thermal indices to underestimate the true temperature rise.

Threshold effect Implies that there is a limit or boundary above which a specific outcome is achieved, and below which a different outcome occurs.

TI (TIS/TIB/TIC) *(See Thermal indices)*

Time The measured or measurable period during which an action, process, or condition exists or continues. (An ineffable parameter that we squander frequently and never have enough of.)

Time gain compensation (TGC) *(See also Compensation and Pre-compensated TGC)* The system control that allows the user to adjust amplification based on depth. The compensation is necessary to adjust for the higher attenuation that results from traveling through greater tissue thickness. Typically there are eight sliding controls that range from 0 dB at the far left position to about 50 or 60 dB at the far right. The sliders divide up the image into "depth" zones such that the top slider adjusts the gain at the skin surface, the bottom slider at the maximum imaging depth, and the intermediate sliders adjusting for the depth zones in between.

Tissue colorization (tint) The use of colorization maps to improve visualization when significant dynamic range must be preserved.

Tissue Doppler A Doppler-based method for measuring the velocity of tissue over time. Processing tissue Doppler is very similar to processing PW spectral Doppler except that low pass filters are employed to eliminate the higher Doppler frequency shifts that occur from the blood velocity. Because of its angle dependence, spectral tissue Doppler measures motion only "toward or away" from the transducer. Therefore, spectral tissue Doppler can be used to determine strain (tissue deformation) in one direction.

Tortuosity When vessels have multiple bends or twists which results in flow disturbance.

Total internal reflection The result of dramatic refraction at an interface between two structures such that no energy is transmitted across the interface, and all of the energy is reflected internally. The incident angle at which total internal reflection occurs is called the critical angle.

Transcranial Doppler A non-invasive Doppler technique to assess the major cerebral arteries through natural cranial windows.

Transcutaneous oxygen tension measurements (toPo2) These are used to measure the metabolic demand of the tissue. The values are a function of cutaneous blood flow, metabolic activity, oxyhemoglobin and oxygen diffusion of the tissue.

Transducer Any device which converts one form of energy to another form of energy. Many ultrasound transducers use the piezoelectric effect to convert electropotential energy to mechanical energy and mechanical energy back to electropotential energy. Some ultrasound transducers now use CMUT technology based on varying capacitance.

Transient cavitation *(See Cavitation)*

Transmission mode One form of medical imaging (like x-ray) where the x-rays are transmitted through a patient and the change in transmission properties is used to produce an image. (In contrast to reflective modes like ultrasound which utilize the reflected energy instead of the transmitted energy.)

Transmit Refers to the process of driving a transducer with an electropotential (voltage) to produce energy to propagate into the patient. The transmit is the active phase of imaging which has the most direct consequence on signal strength as well as a significant impact on the risk of bioeffects.

Transmit frequency The frequency of operation. The transmit frequency is the frequency of the wave that is being produced to travel into the patient.

Transmit gain One of many terms which refers to the transmit power.

Transmit power On the electrical side of the transducer, the transmit power refers to the rate of delivering electrical energy to excite the transducer crystals (related to the voltage squared). On the acoustic side of the transducer the transmit power refers to rate of delivering acoustic energy to the patient.

Transmitter The part of the ultrasound system responsible for creating the transmit voltage and communicating the transmit energy to the transducer elements. The transmitter is also sometimes referred to as the pulser.

Transmural pressure The difference between the intravascular pressure and the surrounding tissue pressure. The transmural pressure is always referenced from the inside of the vessel to the outside of the vessel. Therefore, when the intravascular pressure is higher than the surrounding tissue pressure, the vessel dilates and the transmural pressure is said to be high. Conversely, when the intravascular pressure is lower than the surrounding tissue pressure, the vessel tends to collapse and the transmural pressure is referred to as low.

Transorbital Through the eye.

Transtemporal Through the temporal bone. One of the "windows" used for transcranial Doppler and transcranial imaging.

Transverse wave A wave which propagates by particle motion perpendicular to the wave propagation direction. A sine wave is a depiction of a transverse wave. Although sound is a longitudinal wave, in drawings sound is often depicted as a transverse wave because of the ease of drawing in contrast to a longitudinal wave. Elastography makes use of transverse waves to determine tissue elasticity and stiffness properties.

Trapezoidal format An image format created with a linear phased array transducer used to extend the field of view by adding half sector images on either side of an unsteered linear image, resulting in an image with a trapezoidal shape.

Trigonometry A mathematical discipline that deals with the physical relationship between angles and dimensions of triangles.

Trophic Relating to nutrition.

True negative (TN) Implies that the test correctly predicts that there is no disease (the test predicts no disease when the gold standard predicts no disease).

True positive (TP) Implies that the test correctly predicts that there is disease (the test predicts disease when the gold standard predicts disease).

Tunable frequency The ability to vary the transmit frequency of a CMUT cell by changing the DC bias voltage.

Turbulence A disturbed state of flow in which flow is virtually random in all directions. Turbulence occurs when the flow conditions result in a high Reynolds number. Turbulence occurs primarily as an exit effect transitioning from a narrowed region of high kinetic energy to a broader region.

Turbulent flow When a fluid does not move in a "well behaved" manner nor in a uniform direction. When turbulence exists, the velocity of the fluid at any specific location experiences variation in both speed and direction. The variations in velocity result in a broadening of the Doppler spectrum.

Twinkle artifact An artifact in color Doppler which appears below metallic, calcified, or other structures; similar to comet tail.

Ultrafast Doppler A method for producing color images at extremely high frame rates by creating color images from averaged angled frames instead of sequential line transmission. The color image is viewable in a cine loop-type review after the capture period. Current ultrafast Doppler systems allow for retrospective placement of a Doppler sample volume (or volumes) anywhere within the color image to generate a spectral Doppler waveform (or waveforms).

Ultrafast Imaging Any image generation methodology which results in significantly faster frame rates than conventional, sequential image generation. Whereas sequentially-generated 2D frame rates are generally below 100 Hz (frames per second), ultrafast image techniques result in frame rates frequently in the kHz range. The faster image generation can be achieved through multi-line acquisition (MLA), multi-line transmit (MLT), plane wave, or diverging wave techniques (and any combination of approaches as well).

Ultrasound Any sound with frequencies above human hearing. (Typically referred to as above 20 kHz.)

Ultrasound transducer Converts electropotential energy (voltage) into mechanical vibration and mechanical vibrations into voltages. Ultrasound transducers act as both a transmitter and a receiver for sound waves.

Unit Reference for how a measurement of a physical quantity is made.

Unit circle A circle where the radius has a length of one or one unit.

Universal Precautions *(See Standard precautions)*

Vacuum The absence of a medium.

Variable Mathematical or physical quantity that does not have a fixed numerical value. A physical parameter that can have a varying value.

Variable gain The ability to change the amount of amplification. User controllable gain as opposed to a fixed gain.

Vasoconstrict The decrease in diameter of a blood vessel, such as an arteriole, resulting in an increase in resistance and restricted blood flow to an organ or portion of the body.

Vasodilate The increase in diameter of a blood vessel, such as an arteriole, resulting in a decrease in resistance and an increase in blood flow to an organ or portion of the body.

Vector A quantity determined by magnitude and direction such as velocity.

Veins Any of the tubular branching vessels that carry blood from the capillaries toward the heart. Veins generally have valves to help prevent reflux of blood in the presence of gravity as well as thinner walls than the arteries.

Velocity A vector quantity which implies both the rate and direction of movement. For ultrasound, we generally presume straight travel such that the scalar quantity of speed can be used. As a result, the term velocity is commonly used to refer to speed. However, with respect to Doppler, since the flow direction is known, the value measured is truly velocity when direction is stated.

Velocity time integral (VTI) The VTI is calculated as the area under the spectral Doppler velocity curve relative to time resulting in a measurement of distance per time (commonly meters per heartbeat). By multiplying the VTI by the vessel cross-sectional area, a volumetric flow measurement results (such as the stroke volume, or m³/beat).

Venous capacitance A measure of the ability of the venous system to hold a change in volume per time. The venous system is highly capacitive, and is referred to as the capacitive component of the cardiovascular system.

Venous outflow (See *Maximum venous outflow*)

Venous refill time (VRT) Method using photoplethysmography to evaluate the presence and severity of venous insufficiency. Dorsiflexion maneuvers empty the cutaneous circulation and the recovery time is measured. Periods below 20 seconds indicate venous reflux.

Venous reflux testing Evaluates the presence and severity of venous insufficiency.

Venous resistance A measure of the resistivity to flow in the venous system.

Vertebral artery A large branch of the subclavian artery that ascends through the foramen in the transverse processes of each of the cervical vertebrae. The right and left vertebral arteries enter the cranium through the foramen magnum, and unite to form the basilar artery.

V Flow An approach to illustrate flow as vectors created by autocorrelating the data from a series of transmitted plane waves.

Viscosity The ratio of the shear stress to the shear rate of a fluid, or more simply stated: a measure of the resistance of a fluid to flow due to attraction of the molecules.

Voltage The difference in electrical potential that drives an electric current to flow from a high potential to a low potential.

Volume The amount of space occupied by a three-dimensional object as measured in cubic units.

Volumetric flow (Q) The amount or quantity of fluid which moves past a point per unit time. Volumetric flow is a volume of flow per time such as liters per minute. The simplified law of hemodynamics and Poiseuille's law express the volumetric flow in terms of the pressure gradient and the resistance to flow. The continuity equation expresses the volumetric flow in terms of the average spatial velocity and the flow cross-sectional area.

Wall filter artifacts Artifacts that result from when the "clutter" signals are not adequately attenuated and the signal dynamic range becomes too large, causing circuit saturation.

Wall filters A circuit or mathematical process that eliminates signals based on their frequency. For Doppler based techniques, wall filters are high pass filters which "pass" higher frequency signals and reduce the amplitude of lower frequency signals. Wall filters are critical to reduce the enormous dynamic range that exists with Doppler signals. Setting a wall filter too low results in circuit saturation. Setting wall filters too high can result in elimination of actual low-velocity signals leading to incorrect hemodynamic conclusions.

Watts The unit for power.

Wavefront The front surface of the wave.

Wavelength The physical distance between cyclical wave peaks within a medium. The wavelength is determined by the propagation velocity divided by the operating frequency. The wavelength is one of the most critical parameters in ultrasound since the wavelength partially determines the axially resolution as well as affects the type of reflection that occurs.

Wavelength equation ($\lambda = c / f$)

Waves Mechanism by which energy is conveyed from one place to another. For electromagnetically propagated waves this energy transfer occurs without the transference of matter. For mechanical sound waves, the energy transfer process results in variations of the acoustic variables.

Write zoom (See *Acoustic zoom*)

Young's modulus (Elastic modulus) (E) The Young's modulus of a material is defined as the ratio of tensile stress to tensile strain which indicates the tendency of an object to deform along an axis when opposing forces are applied along that axis.

Zone imaging An image generation technique which transmits unfocused wide beams, or zones, and then utilizes multi-line acquisition (MLA) and parallel processing, resulting in significantly higher frame rates.

Zoom (See *Acoustic and Non-acoustic zoom*)

Appendix B

Index

Symbols

1.5-D array 151, 156, 169, 224, 739
1-D array 151, 161, 163, 166-169, 172, 177, 180, 185-186, 703, 706-707, 739
2-D array 150-151, 156, 162-164, 167, 169, 170, 177-180, 187, 224, 482, 641, 644-645, 706, 739
2nd harmonic 125, 412, 461-464, 467, 471, 478, 485, 681-682, 739
3D imaging 111-112, 115, 146, 149, 166, 168-170, 187, 214, 231, 251-252, 281-285, 294-295, 360, 397-398, 402, 449, 482-483, 486, 509, 523, 655, 658, 666, 711, 713, 739
4D imaging 169, 282-284
60° (and Doppler angle) 80-81, 331, 333, 413, 581, 718-722, 739
60 Hz (and frame rate) 233, 237, 246-247, 739

A

Abbreviations (combining) 12-13
Aberration (beam) 60, 199, 279, 281, 295, 408, 410, 466, 664, 666, 702, 705, 708, 739-741
Ablate (ablation) 410, 483-484, 661, 663-665, 668, 670, 739
Abscess 685
Absorption
 and attenuation 72, 83-85, 91, 96, 100, 399, 422, 428, 447, 530, 664, 702, 704
 and fluids 72, 85, 402, 442, 446, 560
 and frequency 72, 84-85, 92, 216, 310
 coefficient 739
 in ultrasound 111, 148, 184, 204, 402, 664-667, 687, 694, 739
Absorption rate 96, 184-185, 428-430, 436, 442-448, 464, 618, 664, 706
 bone 400, 442, 446, 448, 687
 water 442, 448, 706
Acceleration 80, 300, 349-350, 411-412, 418, 532, 543-548, 552, 564-565, 575-580, 586, 590, 728, 739

Accuracy
 of statistical measures 244, 516-517, 520-524, 739
 transducer testing 495, 504
Acoustic
 aspects of reflection 76, 88, 184, 642
 beam 111, 216
 energy 38, 62, 133-134, 204, 428, 530, 663-668, 712
 gain 195
 impedance 76-83, 88-100, 134-135, 144-145, 148-150, 154, 170, 176-177, 183-187, 191, 447, 608, 612-613, 629, 667, 679, 687-688, 739
  and density 88, 144, 486, 612, 642, 687, 708
  definition of 739
  equation 100, 144, 460
  examples of 88
  units (Rayls) 13, 754
 impedance mismatch
  See Impedance: mismatch
 intensity 63-64, 96, 207, 432, 438, 465, 664-665, 739
 line 111-119, 128, 221-222, 240, 254, 256, 263, 265, 271, 335-336, 396, 467, 476, 734-735, 739
 power 62, 169, 195, 205-206, 216-217, 428, 430, 438-448, 644, 664, 739
  and focus 143, 217, 248, 662, 664
  measurements 432, 438-440, 455-456
 pressure 62, 66, 186, 253, 274, 429, 432, 439-440, 453, 464, 470, 664-665, 681, 711-712
 variables 42-43, 50, 61, 66, 68-69, 428, 663, 739
 zoom 237-239, 280, 739
  See also Write zoom
Acoustic radiation force impulse (ARFI) 438, 607, 617-619, 621-625, 630, 635-636, 644, 710, 739
Acoustic window (CMUT) 184-185, 191, 739
Adaptive processing 251, 279-281, 295, 396, 406-407, 410, 736, 739
  See also Auto-optimize

A/D converter 199-206, 210, 220-224, 234, 319, 324, 328, 739-740, 745
Adipose tissue 702, 705; See also Fat
Afterload 652, 740
Air 89-90, 154, 181, 184, 191, 379, 386, 390, 395, 412, 415, 422, 469, 496, 502, 542, 564, 622, 629, 663, 667, 679, 706, 708
 propagation velocity in 59, 90, 708
ALARA principle 427, 438, 443-444, 449-451, 455, 594, 740
Albumin 469, 472
Aliasing 349, 351-354, 419
 by the Nyquist criterion 111, 204, 322, 410, 721, 724
 definition of 204, 380-381, 716, 740
 display 324, 724-725
 in a Doppler spectrum 323, 342, 382, 410-411, 708, 721-727
 in PW Doppler 110, 322-326, 329, 374, 378, 410, 714-716, 724-727
 of the display 746
A-lines artifact 387, 390, 696
Alternating current (AC) 187, 740
Alzheimer's 666
Ambient light 229, 235-236, 246-247, 249, 359, 503-504, 740
A-Mode (amplitude mode) 151, 213-214, 221-223, 239, 248, 282, 436, 636, 740
 interpretation 213
 uses of 111, 214, 636
Amplatzer device 284-285, 391-392, 394, 398, 402, 740
 See also Septal: occluder
Amplification 196-199, 206-209, 211, 213, 217, 220, 225, 247-248, 314, 318-319, 340, 365, 415, 720
 See also Receiver: gain
 definition of 206, 740
Amplitude
 calculating 50-51, 65-68, 208, 215, 463, 565
 control of 62, 110, 134, 195, 204-213, 340, 389, 415, 460, 706
 definition of 50, 61-62, 316, 740
 form 65-66, 69, 221, 320-321

power modulation 62, 195, 216, 478, 480-486, 712-713, 740
 ratio / factor 65-66, 195, 197, 210, 308, 475
 units of 13, 50
 wave parameter 42, 44, 66-69, 113, 182, 214, 294, 403, 644, 664
Analog 263
 definition of 199, 740
 signals 199-203, 220, 223-224, 319
Analog Doppler 312, 319
Analog to digital
 conversion (A/D) 199-202, 206, 210, 220, 223-224, 234, 319, 324, 328, 739-740
 the motivation for conversion 220
Anechoic 82, 91, 387, 403, 688, 690-692, 740
Angio 356, 367, 371, 707, 729-734, 740
 See also Color Doppler: power Doppler
Angiogenesis 361, 371, 484-485, 740
Angle
 basic 28-31, 35, 311, 741
 correction 307, 330-333, 339-340, 364, 371-372, 381, 579, 717-722, 727, 740
 critical 71, 81-82, 93-95, 100, 381, 400-401, 417, 745
 Doppler 158, 307-311, 331-333, 336, 348-349, 352-357, 372-374, 381, 417-420, 581, 584, 685, 698, 707, 716-722, 727, 731, 734, 746, 749
  See also Angle: of insonation
 incident 71-100, 160, 163, 257-258, 372, 381, 385, 389, 393, 400-402, 415-417, 665, 685, 692-693, 706-707, 740, 749
 of insonation 310, 412, 423, 574, 579, 693; See also Insonification
 of reflection 74, 85, 654, 687, 692-693, 740
 of transmission 71, 74-75, 79, 81, 94-95, 163, 257, 275, 321, 716, 740
 refraction 81, 92, 381, 693, 716
 steering 165, 177, 331, 335, 345, 389, 405, 423, 471, 693, 698, 731, 740
Angular resolution 149, 223; See also Lateral, Transverse, Azimuthal, and Side-by-Side resolution entries
Anisotropic 615-616, 630, 636, 640, 644-645
Anisotropy artifact 675, 679-680, 685-686, 692-694, 698
 definition of 692, 740
Annular array 156, 740
 mechanical (transducer) 155-156, 750
Antegrade 352-354, 579, 740

Aorta 260, 300, 330, 360, 368, 385, 393, 399, 539, 543, 551-553, 560-567, 578, 589, 703
 aneurysm of 260
 compliance 552, 561, 565
 insufficiency 411, 530, 578
 stenosis of 665, 668, 740
Aperture 215-216, 252-254, 263-270, 277, 293-296, 413, 453, 664-666, 704
 and NZL 141-142, 176-177, 664
 definition of 142, 159, 177, 740
 synthetic 267-270, 277, 293-296, 757
Apex 652-654, 656
Apodization 215-216, 267, 274, 740
Apparent
 SNR See Signal-to-noise ratio
 viscosity See Viscosity
Area measurements 8, 13, 25, 181, 191, 204, 230-231, 249, 504, 536-537, 556, 564, 572, 579, 581, 588, 741
Array 131, 143, 148-172, 177-180, 185-188, 204-205, 243-244, 252, 265, 269-270, 393, 410, 413, 641, 741
 See also 1.5-D, 1-D, and 2-D array entries
Arterioles 541, 553, 562-563, 565-567, 572-573, 578, 589-590
 definition of 561, 741
 resistive component 553, 562-563, 565, 572
Arteriovenous fistula 584
 definition of 741
 imaging 300, 582
Artery / Arterial 551-554, 560-563, 565-567, 570, 572-573, 578-580, 584-585, 587, 590, 710, 716, 719, 723, 726, 728, 730, 733-734
 brachial 567
 brachiocephalic 578
 carotid 83, 166, 197-198, 222, 259-260, 301, 338-340, 352, 367, 369, 401, 411, 418-421, 466, 490, 501-502, 576, 587, 599, 635, 716, 730
 coronary 55, 469, 482, 484, 652
 definition of 741
 elasticity 553, 570, 589
 femoral 315, 368, 403, 501, 576, 734
 pulmonary 563-564
 radial 213
 spectrum 575
 subclavian 387-388, 578
 vertebral 90-91, 353-354, 422, 578
Artifact 377-426
 A-lines 387, 390, 696
 anisotropy 675, 679-680, 685-686, 692-694, 698

 attenuation-based 257, 382, 399, 403, 423, 711, 741
 banding noise 267, 741
 bayonet sign 379, 395, 741
 BGR sign 638, 742
 B-line (BLA) 390-391
 blossoming 340, 368, 371, 381-382, 414, 423, 720-722, 742-743
 bull's-eye 638, 742
 comet tail 87, 379, 382, 390-392, 394, 399, 423, 692, 696-697, 744
 definition of 378, 741
 Doppler 199, 204, 322, 381-382, 392, 410, 423, 746
 double spectral (harmonic) 412-413
 dropout 679-680, 693, 698
  See also Shadowing artifact
 enhancement 85, 378-379, 382, 402-403, 422, 692, 695-696, 698, 747
 figure-of-eight 402, 747
 flash 357, 360, 371, 380, 416, 423, 707
  color 416-417, 743
 grating lobes 51, 156, 169, 259, 274, 277, 294, 378-382, 386, 393-394, 404-410, 423, 465-466, 482, 682, 707, 748
 grouping 272-273, 277
  See also Corduroy artifact
 image detail resolution-related 378, 382, 384, 396, 408
 lateral displacement 92, 156, 385-386, 423, 709, 749
 locational 382, 385, 750
 lung rocket 390, 750
 mirror image 87, 379, 382, 388, 396-399, 423, 751
  See also Reverberation artifact
 motion of 246, 388-389, 396, 399, 423, 655, 663
 multipath 87, 379, 382, 393, 423, 465, 751
 phase-related 382, 403
 pseudo MR 398
 range ambiguity 115, 322, 328-330, 373-374, 378, 381-382, 396, 411, 423, 707, 754
 reduction of 257-260, 280, 293-294, 401, 417, 461, 465, 474, 485, 495, 644, 679, 682, 706-707
 refraction 378-386, 393, 400-401, 417, 423, 692, 755
 reverberation 184-185, 191, 257, 279, 379, 382, 386-391, 394, 399, 408, 423, 461, 465-466, 506, 655, 682, 692, 696-698, 755
 ring down 87, 379, 382, 390, 394, 415, 423, 441, 692, 706, 755

shadowing 95, 257, 378-379, 391-403, 417, 422, 462, 474, 506, 655, 687, 692-698, 710-716, 722, 731, 755
side lobes 199, 382, 393, 655, 682, 756
sources of 86-87, 92, 95, 100, 162, 199, 254-267, 378, 462-467, 474, 635-638, 692, 719
spectral Doppler 199, 204, 398, 719-720
spectral mirroring 381-382, 398, 411-412, 423, 757
spectral spread (broadening) 413, 577, 579, 719, 722
specular reflection-related 257-259, 378, 386-389, 393, 402, 405, 423, 465, 692-693, 707
speed error 47, 60, 378-379, 382, 394-396, 408, 422-423, 710, 757
swirling 711-712
twinkle 379, 382, 392, 394, 423, 692, 696-697, 759; See also Comet tail
wall filter 760
Artificial intelligence (AI) 251-252, 287-289, 295-296
  definition of 287
  history of 288
  types of 289
  ultrasound applications 290-292
ASIC 169, 187, 214, 224
Atherosclerotic 370, 608, 668
Atrial 658-659
Attenuation 71-102
  and absorption 72, 84, 399, 447, 461, 664, 702-706
  and compensation 208-210, 218
  and reflection 72, 91, 99, 124, 214, 308-309, 316, 386, 399, 460
  artifacts 379, 382, 386, 403, 423, 474, 695-696, 711, 741
  calculating 66, 84
  cause of shadowing 257, 399, 474, 711
  definition of 64, 72, 96, 741
  rates 83, 85, 96, 99, 143, 257, 365, 442, 464, 640, 646
Audible range 53, 748
Audio 241-242, 319
  Doppler 300, 317-319, 371, 381, 586, 708
Auto-calculation 291, 657
Autoclave 135, 494, 741
Autocorrelation 741
Auto-optimize 279, 736, 741
  See also Adaptive processing
Auxetic 614-615, 741
Averaging 251, 253-259, 261-263, 275, 287, 292-294
  and brightness 254, 635, 729
  definition of 293, 327, 741

frame 253, 256-259, 262, 287, 292-294, 355-357, 402, 404-405, 707, 733, 747
line 256, 467, 734, 750
mean 327, 433-434, 579, 635, 741
  See also Mean
signal-to-noise ratio 254-257, 293, 339, 355, 366, 404-406, 705
spatial 262-263, 293-294, 433
AVI 241-242
Avulsion 684, 691
Axial (dimension) 132, 137, 139, 142, 144, 146-147, 149-150, 172, 383, 440, 473, 504, 664, 678
Axial resolution 103, 108, 110, 115-116, 122, 126-128, 146, 150, 252, 293, 340, 355, 367-368, 380-383, 414, 437, 467-468, 479, 485-486, 495, 504, 514, 523, 618
  definition of 108, 110, 741
  degradation of 467-468, 479, 486
  equation 115, 127, 147, 383
  limit (artifact) 379-383, 414, 732
  See also Depth, Longitudinal, Radial, and Range resolution entries
Azimuthal resolution 139, 142, 149, 223
  See also Lateral, Transverse, Azimuthal, and Side-by-Side resolution entries

B

Backing material 150, 184, 191
  and axial resolution 115, 147
  and ring time 126, 147
  definition of 116, 127, 177, 185, 741
  See also Damping material
Backscatter 75, 91, 199, 314, 460, 476, 640, 644-645, 687, 741
Banding noise 267, 741
Bandwidth
  and acoustic window 184
  and operating frequency 124-128, 136, 168, 187-189, 261, 406, 467, 706
  broad (broadband) 123, 125-128, 171, 176, 188, 191, 406, 452, 462, 473, 702-705, 708, 714, 742
  calculation of 123
  definition of 122, 124, 128, 741
  flexibility 123-124
  fractional 123, 128, 184, 186, 747
  pictorial representation 123, 406
  transducer 123, 125-126, 136-137, 163, 170-171, 180, 191, 439-440
Base (counting system) 7, 31-32
  Base 10 system 26, 31, 33
Baseband 741

Baseline (Doppler) 312-318, 323-328, 336, 342, 354, 724-725, 741
Basic angle 28, 31, 35, 311, 741
Bayonet sign 379, 395, 741
Beam
  aberration 199, 279-281, 295, 382, 408-410, 466, 664-666, 702, 705, 708, 739-741
  acoustic 111
  bending (refraction) 79, 82, 92-94, 161, 385, 399-401, 665, 695, 716
  characteristics (single disc transducer) 138-139
  dimensions 138-139, 146, 440
  divergence and intensity 142-144, 161, 168, 176, 254, 272, 464-466
  energy 80, 662, 665
  focusing 55, 140, 143, 148, 150, 160-161, 168, 176, 216, 264-273, 294, 330, 408, 466, 662-666, 704, 715
  parameters: depth 139-140, 716
  receive 111-112, 159, 161, 222, 263-266, 271, 294, 715-716
  shape 138, 177, 215, 263, 273, 440
    and continuous wave 138, 715-717
    and harmonics 464, 474, 707
    and pulsed wave 138-139, 143, 666, 715, 717
    definition of 138, 142, 741
  sound 111, 386, 679, 686-687, 719, 741
  steering 144, 151, 159-165, 223, 270, 310, 313, 344, 466, 685-686, 741
  uniformity factor (BUF) 436, 451-452, 742
  width 142, 252-253, 266, 270-273, 412
    lateral 149, 273
Beamformer 169, 205, 215-216, 220-224, 263, 267, 270-277, 282, 288, 295-296, 314, 338, 462, 482, 716, 742
Beamplot 264-268, 274, 277, 394, 440, 621-623, 742
Beamwidth 138-139, 144, 147-149, 157, 168-169, 177, 217, 271, 273, 379, 383-384, 408, 464, 641, 664, 742
Bernoulli's
  equation 332, 527, 539-542, 548, 557, 560, 565-567, 573, 576, 579, 590, 717-718, 742
  principle 541
B-flow 366-368, 371, 375, 742
BGR artifact 638, 742
Bias voltage 182-187, 191
Binary 31, 234
  and brightness levels 235
  base counting system 31-33, 235
  base decimal 31-32
  definition of 32, 742
  numbers to digital conversion 200

Bioeffects 43, 427-458, 664-670
    and scanned modalities 128, 216, 436-437, 455, 512
    and non-scanned modalities 128, 436-437, 455
    definition of 38, 110, 428, 742
    duty factor 122, 127, 435, 438, 451
    mechanical 216, 429, 434-438, 443, 446, 455, 666-667, 750
        cavitation 429, 455, 470, 665
    risks 37, 38, 44, 62-64, 68-69, 99, 107, 110, 124, 128, 132, 195, 206, 216, 248, 366, 428, 432, 436-438, 440, 444, 451, 455, 594, 717
    thermal 71, 84, 103, 107, 111, 127, 216, 427-448, 455-456, 665-667, 715, 758
        intensity parameter 430-435, 455
    See also In vitro and In vivo entries
Biplane 483
Bistable 235
Bit 200, 234-235, 742
Bladder 387, 392, 402
Blind transducer 151, 742
B-line artifact (BLA) 390-391
    See also Comet tail artifact
Blood 82, 88, 199, 462-463, 469, 472, 474, 496, 502, 554-560, 564, 568-569, 595, 652, 664-665, 688, 691, 711, 715, 717, 722, 734
    attenuation rate 83, 499
    cells, red (RBC) 75, 88, 92, 204, 307-310, 314, 320, 356, 361-362, 388, 417, 460, 469, 484, 486, 559-560, 587-588, 717, 732
    pressure 567, 571, 590
    propagation velocity in 59, 300, 460, 499, 612
    vessel 207, 209, 229-230, 314, 326, 360-361, 369, 388, 411, 417, 484, 543, 552, 558-560, 563, 565, 666, 684, 703, 707, 715-720, 722, 729-730, 732-734
    volume 554, 560-561, 567, 570, 588-589
Blood-mimicking fluid 496, 499, 502
Blossoming artifact 340, 368, 371, 414, 720-722
    and PW doppler 414
    definition of 381, 414, 742
    Doppler phantoms 502
    effects on peak velocity 414, 720-721
B-Mode (brightness mode) 92, 95, 112, 123, 126, 214, 221-223, 239-240, 248, 279, 282, 319-320, 366, 374, 447, 449, 476, 480, 608, 634-637, 640-641, 667, 712, 742
Body Mass Index (BMI) 702-705, 713, 728

Bone 86, 90-91, 100, 154, 214, 400, 422, 447, 449, 615, 619, 663, 668, 678-679, 687-691, 696, 722
    absorption rate 442, 446, 448, 687
    fracture 415
    propagation velocity in 59, 95, 395, 612, 665, 716
Brain 246-247, 352, 562
    imaging 285-286, 358, 363, 662-670, 733
    phantom 514-515
    propagation velocity in 59, 612, 716
Breast
    cancer 291, 613, 624-625, 633-646, 709
    imaging 185, 208, 212, 258, 266, 285, 410, 613, 617, 625, 637-642, 646, 663, 709
    phantom 510
Brightness
    and contrast resolution 226, 232, 234, 252, 293, 505, 712
    levels 197, 207-211, 221-229, 234-235, 247-248, 272, 320, 341, 403, 415, 635-636, 688, 721
    mode (B-mode) See B-Mode
Broadband 123-124, 128, 260-261, 405, 462, 676, 702-705, 708, 714
    definition of 123, 742
Bruit 585-586, 742
B-scan 151-153, 278, 742
Bubble 154, 429, 435, 455, 462, 545, 665, 667, 711
    concentration 474-479, 711
    contrast 469-486, 665, 711, 734
    disruption 92, 430, 472-477, 711-713, 742
Bulb (carotid) 340, 367, 420
Bulk modulus (K) 59, 88, 608-619, 625-630
    definition of 56-58, 629, 742
    propagation and density 59, 612, 629
Bull's-eye
    display (global longitudinal strain) 656-657
    sign (artifact) 638, 742
Bursa 680, 688, 690, 695
Bursitis 55, 278, 680-681, 683, 695
Byte 742

C

Calcified / Calcification 83, 85, 378, 391-392, 397, 412-413, 422, 444, 637, 665, 694-697
    and echogenicity 83, 690
Calcium 690-692, 697
Calculating
    automatic 291, 657

pressure gradients 332, 538-541, 557, 572-573, 576, 579, 717-719
Calf muscle pump 566-569, 584, 589, 742
Calibrate 236, 249, 285, 439, 495, 500-506, 571, 640
Cancer
    breast See Breast: cancer
    detection of 55, 361-362, 483-484, 608, 613, 619, 624, 634-637, 642-646, 710
    liver 480-481
    pancreatic 260, 668
    prostate 363-634, 639-640, 663, 668
    skin 189
Candela 234
Capacitance 533
    electrical 180-185, 191, 742
    equation 181
    fluid 529, 533, 548, 589, 742
    maximum venous (MVC) 750
    of aorta 553, 561, 565-567, 578
    venous 554, 561, 564-569, 588-589
Capacitive micromachined ultrasound (CMUT) 195, 404-406, 706
    definition of 180, 742
    transducer 151, 180, 184-189
    See also CMUT
Capacitor 179-182, 185, 191
Capillaries 446, 460, 475, 553, 561-567, 571, 573, 588-589, 742
Capsule hydrophone 452-454
Cardiac
    imaging 153, 161, 170, 215, 227-231, 240, 256, 266, 270, 277, 280, 284, 291, 307, 330, 345, 353, 359, 374, 386, 389-390, 393, 405, 446, 465-469, 475-477, 484-486, 599, 609, 640, 652-657, 711-712, 716-723, 726, 734
    index 742
    output 300, 552, 560-567, 571, 580-581, 584, 742
    reserve 742
    rotation 475, 652-653, 742
    torsion 652-653, 658, 743
    translation (motion) 284, 475, 607, 617-618, 652-655, 743
Cardiovascular system 530-533, 551-554, 560-567, 571, 584, 588-589, 668
    fundamental purpose of 560
    resistive component 563
Carotid artery 83, 166, 197-198, 222, 259-260, 301, 338-340, 352, 367, 369, 401, 411, 418-421, 466, 490, 501-502, 576, 587, 599, 635, 716, 730
Cartilage 689

Cathode ray tube (CRT) 231-233, 743
Caudal 678
Cavitation 429-430, 435-442, 453-455, 459, 470-471, 479, 484, 661-667, 708, 711, 743
Cell
 CMUT 179-188, 191, 406, 743
 damage to 428-430, 446-450, 483, 665, 668
 membrane 485, 566, 665-666
 natural rate of 751
 red blood (RBC) 75, 88, 92, 100, 173, 204, 307-310, 314, 320, 356, 361-362, 388, 417, 460, 469, 484, 486, 559, 566, 571, 575, 614, 667, 717, 732
Celsius 43
Center frequency 123, 128, 172, 186, 189
 and bandwidth 123, 126, 168, 189
Cephalad 568, 570, 678, 743
CEUS (contrast enhanced ultrasound) 285, 295, 361-362, 375, 389, 445, 470, 643, 701, 711-713, 734
Channel 223, 271-273, 314, 412, 423
Charge (electrical) 173-174, 180-181, 185, 191
CHIRP frequency 480
 See also Frequency: coding
Cine loop (cine) 233, 236-237, 248, 338-339, 369, 389-390, 416, 634, 686, 708-710, 743
Circle 223, 622
 cross-sectional area 8, 230, 532, 536-537, 553-566, 572-575, 580-581, 588-589
 in trigonometry 30-31, 314
 of Willis 286, 358, 733
Circuit 196, 200, 202, 214, 220, 223-224
 Doppler 312-322, 502, 586, 721
 saturation 318, 357, 374, 378, 381-382, 415-416, 423, 723
  See also Valve: click
 cause of 318, 381, 415, 502, 723
 definition of 196, 743
 example of in CW Doppler 415
Circular
 area equation 8
 dimensions 13
Circulation 567, 604, 712
Circumference (and radius) 580
Claudication 573-574, 743
Clot 484, 587, 668, 688
Clutter
 artifact 389-390, 465-466, 485, 655, 706-707
 signal 199, 315-320, 36-365, 374-375, 380, 399-400, 415-417, 465, 722-723, 731, 743

C-Mode (constant depth mode) 239-240, 743
CMUT 179-192, 195, 404, 406, 706
 arrays 185, 187
  1-D 185-186
  matrix (2-D) 187
 definition of 180
Coagulation 666
CODEC 193, 241-245
Coded excitation (pulses) 367, 459, 479-480, 705, 713
 harmonics 485-486, 743
Coefficient 4, 7
Coherence 254-255, 258, 281, 296, 361-362, 375, 405, 477
Collagen 442, 645, 688, 694
Collapse mode 181-187, 191, 743
Collateralization 418, 574, 743
Color bar 236, 264, 336, 340-345, 348, 350, 352, 358, 365, 374, 744
 relative to Nyquist limit 343
 relative to spectral Doppler 342
 relative to wall filters 336, 342-343
Color bleed (artifact) 340-341, 355, 380, 414-415, 421
 See also Blossoming artifact
 See also Color blossoming
Color blossoming (artifact) 340, 368, 371, 414, 743
Color box 120, 166, 334-337, 340, 345, 349, 351, 357, 371, 380, 416, 422, 732-736
Color Doppler 51, 111, 188, 199, 204, 216-229, 240-241, 277, 322, 334, 355-356, 375, 727
 absence of color/dropout 341-344, 357, 368, 379-381, 415-423, 727, 731, 743
 and flow direction 51, 165, 311, 332, 335, 337, 342, 344, 347, 350-356, 399, 411, 569, 718-719
 and frame rate 118, 272, 277, 336, 731, 734, 736
 and temporal resolution 118-119, 128, 271-272, 334-336, 729-734
 and timing 336-337, 432
 definition of 743
 ensemble 118, 335; See also Color packet
 flow imaging 262, 286, 300, 322, 326, 332-335, 389, 398, 414, 449, 476, 716-719, 726, 730-734
 frame rate 119, 734
 gain See Color gain
 imaging 111, 165, 188, 256, 262, 272, 279, 286, 334-335, 378, 385, 392, 398, 436, 447, 684, 705-707, 727, 740

mean velocity 118, 300, 334, 337, 368, 495
 noise/speckle 199, 340-341, 355-356, 374, 380, 420-421, 729-731
 packet See Color packet
 packet size 256, 337, 437, 729-731, 735-736; See also Ensemble length
 persistence See Color persistence
 power Doppler 356-358, 362, 416, 685, 707, 729-734, 744
  See also Power Doppler and Angio
 priority See Color priority
 processing 118-119, 335
 scales (PRF) 313, 342-344, 349-354, 361, 372, 380, 417-419, 732-734
 sequentially generated 334-343, 368-374, 416, 436, 729-736
 ultrafast 334-342, 371, 380, 417-419, 729-736
 vs. spectral Doppler 118, 334, 337, 447, 727, 731
Color flash (artifact) 416-417, 743
Color gain 218, 337-341, 356, 366, 415, 420-421, 729, 743
Colorization 199, 220-225, 230, 698
 of tissue (tint) 230, 684-685, 758
Color line density 735, 743
Color mapping 230, 241, 336-368
Color noise 120, 218, 336, 340-341, 355-356, 380, 743-744
Color packet 118-120, 256, 335-338, 361, 364, 437, 729-736, 743
Color persistence 292, 355, 373-375, 729-731, 744
Color priority 355-356, 375, 389, 417, 421-422, 729-734, 744
Color scales 366, 372, 375, 380, 416, 417, 419, 732, 734
 PRF bar 336-337, 342-344, 349, 351, 354, 361, 744
Color wall filters 336, 342-344, 360-361, 364-366, 372, 375, 419-420, 732, 734
 compared to spectral Doppler 731, 734
Comet tail (artifact) 87, 379-382, 390-394, 399, 423, 692, 696-697, 744
Compensation 206, 208-210, 214, 217-220, 248, 413
 definition of 744
 hemodynamic 570-573
 sound speed 281, 295, 396
 TGCs 208-210, 217-220, 225, 247-248
Complex echogenicity 83
Compliance 529, 708
 and hemodynamics 533, 552-554, 565, 570, 578, 587, 744
 aortic 552, 561, 565
 equation 534

Composite
    beam (effective) 263-273, 294, 744
    materials in transducer 135, 145, 148, 170, 176, 404
    time 266
Compound imaging 225, 257-262, 271, 275-276, 292-294, 337-339, 401, 405-407; See also Crossbeam imaging *and* Sono CT *entries*
    benefits 168, 257-258, 275-276, 337, 339, 401
    definition of 257, 405, 744
    spatial 257-261, 275, 405-406, 707
Compressibility 56-58, 68, 744
Compression
    and dynamic range 69, 92, 198, 210-211, 225-227, 279, 319, 327, 503, 687, 712
    and information loss 211, 227, 243-245
    and sound travel 40-43, 53, 68, 301-303, 429, 455, 470, 612, 622-623
    controls 227-229, 247, 328
    data 199, 211, 226-227, 236, 241-244, 248
    in backend of ultrasound system 195, 206, 211, 225-226, 248
    lossless 211, 236, 241-243, 248, 750
    manual (or cuff) 569, 571, 589, 617, 634-635, 641, 644, 709, 710
    mapping 211-212, 227-230, 320, 367
    mathematical 26-27, 226, 244-245
    of materials 610-614, 645-646, 711
    ratio 211, 236, 241-245
    signal processing 204-210, 225, 320, 366, 744
    tissue 389, 635, 639-641, 645, 658, 708-710
    waves 57, 463, 471-472, 623-624, 635-636, 711, 744
Compressions 40, 441
    and frequency 45, 136
    and wavelength 47, 301-303
Concave 168, 663
Conduction 180-181, 191, 447, 656
Consent
    implied 595, 749
    informed 445, 449, 593-597, 605, 749
Constant
    depth mode (C-mode) 239-240, 743
    mathematical 4, 7
Constructive interference
    See Interference: constructive
Contamination 496, 595
Continuity equation (volumetric flow) 527, 533, 536-537, 544, 548, 564-565, 572, 580, 589, 744
Continuous wave (CW) mode 127, 172, 176, 322, 666, 715-716

and beam shape 138-139, 441, 716
and Doppler *See* CW Doppler
and range ambiguity 104, 727
and ultrasound 188, 191, 438
operating frequency 136
vs. pulsed wave (PW) 106-114, 125-126, 136-139, 215, 321, 328, 337, 374, 436, 714-716, 722, 727
Contractility 640, 652, 659
Contraction 560, 563, 568-569, 580, 604, 645, 651-658, 711
    isovolumic 560, 563, 749
Contrast
    agent 443-446, 459-463, 468-486, 665, 711-712, 734, 744
    enhanced ultrasound (CEUS) 285, 295, 361-362, 375, 389, 445, 470, 643, 701, 711-713, 734
    grayscale 227, 275, 279, 505, 684, 687, 712
    harmonics 309, 462, 474, 476, 486, 711-712, 748
        low and high MI 711-713
    imaging 445, 459-462, 468-469, 477, 480-486, 613, 665-666, 744
    ratio 232-235, 254, 259, 275, 473-479, 484
    resolution 226-227, 234, 249, 252-254, 267, 270, 275-277, 281, 293-294, 495, 499, 505, 507, 712, 744
    inadequate (artifact) 379, 408
Converging 138, 143, 160-161
    beam 160, 168, 263-265, 464-466, 662, 704, 744
Conversion
    between units 11, 14, 43
    binary to base 10 32
    decimal to binary 33
    of digital scans 745, 755
    of signals 199-206, 220, 225, 272-273
Converter (A/D) *See* A/D converter
Corduroy artifact 272
Coronal 284, 402, 678
Coronary artery 55, 469, 482, 484, 652
Correlated 285, 617
    image processing 729-731, 735
Cortex 687-689
Cosecant 29
Cosine (cos) 28-30, 35, 308-311, 314, 320, 330-333, 345, 364, 372-373, 381, 411, 716-718, 744
    determining 28
Cotangent 29
Coupling coefficient 135, 174-175, 706
CPU 221
Credentialing 3, 68, 110, 121-122, 219, 234-235, 312, 344, 490-491, 593-594

Critical
    angle 71, 81-82, 93-95, 100, 381, 400-401, 417, 745
    device 493
    frequency 246, 249
    stenosis 418, 420, 559, 745
Crossbeam imaging *See* Compound imaging *and* Sono CT *entries*
Cross-section 230-231, 483, 532, 536-537, 542-548, 553-559, 562, 564-566, 572, 574-575, 580-581, 588-589, 692
    definition of 745
Crosstalk 158, 274, 277, 294, 296, 745
CRT monitors 231-233, 743
Crystal 88-90, 97, 100, 322
    and focus 138, 141, 144, 148, 155
    and frequency of operation 136, 168, 172
    and propagation velocity 136, 144
    distortion of 133, 195
    impulse response 137
    piezoelectric 133-138, 145, 150-151, 158, 163, 171-176, 184-188, 753
    round 138-139, 143, 155
    simple
        acoustic impedance 144
        fixed focus 144, 152, 155
        limitations of 144, 151
    structure of 131, 171-176, 180
    transducer 53, 62, 116, 145, 151-154, 170, 176, 321
Curie point 135, 173, 745
    and poling 135
Current
    definition of 180, 745
    direct (DC) 182, 185-187, 191, 745
    leakage test 492-493, 745, 749
Curved linear phased array 157-158, 167-168, 171, 177, 278, 347, 676, 678, 698, 745
Cutoff frequency 316, 318, 361, 744
CW Doppler 103, 111-114, 125-128, 204, 216, 313-315, 321-330, 334, 337, 371, 374, 415, 428, 433-438, 455, 708, 714-717, 721-727, 745
    practical limits 324, 328, 577
    thermal bioeffects 433, 437-438
Cyanosis 745
Cyclical wave 38, 42, 745
Cyst 82, 85, 94, 281, 379, 395, 402-403, 422, 442, 499, 506, 509-510, 514, 523, 638, 681

D

Damping material 115-116, 127, 147
    See also Backing material
Data
    CODEC 193, 241-245

compression/decompression 199, 226-227, 236, 241-244, 248
processing 194, 199, 204, 206, 221-222, 277, 641, 644
storage 194, 199-205, 211, 225, 230, 236-237, 248, 268, 274, 288, 291, 320, 598
Deceleration 543-544, 548, 564, 577-578
Doppler measurement 300, 575-579
Decibels (dB) 13, 64-69, 84, 99, 226, 745
Decimal
system 31, 745
to binary: conversion 33
Decompression 241, 244, 302-303, 665
See also Rarefaction
Decubitus 570, 679
Defocusing 382, 410, 665
Deformation 609-610, 615, 617, 625, 629, 652-659
Degassed 666
Delamination 135, 494
Delay
definition of 159, 745
phase 52, 159-168, 204-205, 214, 216, 223, 254, 265, 270, 281, 314, 408, 410, 466, 666, 752
receive 159-163, 263, 270, 409
transmit 160-161, 270
Delta (definition of) 745
Demodulation 206, 212-213, 248, 314
See also Envelope: detection
definition of 212, 745
signal 213
Denature 429
Denominator 4, 23, 653, 745
Density 59, 68
and absorption 85, 664
and acoustic impedance 76, 88, 96, 144, 486, 612, 642, 687, 708
and propagation velocity 60, 67, 395, 412, 463, 612, 624-636, 687
as an acoustic variable 42-43, 68, 96, 428, 469
definition of 745
equation 13, 42, 540, 636
of pixels 234
particle / medium 40, 57-58, 88, 231, 395, 476, 486, 532, 546-548, 567, 612, 687, 711
Dependent rubor 745
Depth
and harmonics 464, 474, 682, 705, 707, 711
and TGC zones 208-209, 217-220, 247-248
determining 60, 93, 99, 394, 504, 665, 706, 716

focal 139-144, 151, 161, 168, 176, 185, 217, 253-254, 263-270, 277, 294, 473, 503, 623, 664-665, 681, 705, 707, 714
gain compensation 208-210
imaging 21, 35, 84, 99, 103-127, 141-153, 165, 205-218, 266, 275, 322-326, 374, 393-394, 461, 474, 634-644, 676, 681-682, 704-716, 728, 749
resolution 108, 115, 127, 139, 150, 177
See also Axial, Longitudinal, Radial, and Range resolution entries
Depth of field 142, 177
and lateral resolution 142-144, 252, 263
definition of 142, 172, 745, 747
See also Focal region
Depth resolution 108
Destructive interference
See Interference: destructive
Detail resolution 115, 120, 142-149, 171-172, 232-249, 252-254, 275, 281, 293, 378-384, 396, 408-410, 461, 495, 503-504, 677, 702-705, 745
Detected signal 204, 212-213, 715
envelope 212, 327, 412, 708, 747
Diagnostic range 54-55, 69, 745
See also Ultrasound: diagnostic
Diameter 13, 138-155, 168, 172-177, 185, 308, 326, 460, 469, 539, 543-548, 554-561, 570, 581-582, 590, 614-615, 662, 714-716
Diaphragm 85, 92, 390, 397, 569-570, 710
propagation velocity of 59
Diastole / Diastolic 240, 369, 381, 420, 552-553, 578-584, 658
flow 355, 575-584, 654
phase 561
pressure 578, 745-760
Dicing 170
transducer elements 158, 715, 745
DICOM 234-236, 248
Dicrotic notch 552, 745
Dielectric 181, 185-187, 191, 745
Diffraction 148-149, 161, 177, 640, 654, 664
Diffusion 232, 447, 472-476, 564-566, 588, 654, 664
Digital
conversion 220, 245
from analog 200, 220, 319
scan lines 745
filtering 364, 745
formats (video) 236, 241-245
signal 200-201, 220, 745
storage 598
Digital converter See A/D converter
Dimensional 10

Dipole 133-135, 173-174
Direct current (DC) 182-187, 191, 745
Direction 337, 342-347, 352
and force 612-615, 626-630, 635, 641-645
and velocity 311, 336, 342, 344, 350, 411, 544, 718
Directional power Doppler 357-360, 368, 371
Direct proportionality 16-18, 22, 745
Dirty shadow 387, 692, 695
Disinfection 492-494, 524, 746
high-level vs. low-level 493-494, 748, 750; See also Sterilization
Displacement 617, 622, 630, 634-638, 641, 645, 655
lateral 92-93, 156-157, 165, 379, 385-386, 393, 423, 709
particle 428, 496, 608
Display 320, 713
aliasing 724-725
dynamic range 195-196, 210, 230
liquid crystal (LCD) 231-234, 237, 245-246, 249, 750
Display alias 323-324, 746
Display line 111, 118-120, 128, 223, 232-234, 336-338, 374, 467, 476, 729, 734-735, 746
Disruption (bubble) 472, 477, 711, 713
Distal
blood flow 565, 572-573, 590, 746
resistance 532, 544, 556-557, 573, 578, 584, 746
Distance
equation 18-22, 35, 109, 114-115, 213, 240, 337, 394, 396, 746
measurements 204, 230, 435, 533, 542
units of 6, 13
Distortion 31, 56, 62, 78-80, 92, 199, 207, 222-223, 241, 245, 395, 410, 613, 624, 642, 710
harmonic 464-465, 471, 476-477
lateral 383
mechanical 133-135
temporal 245, 256, 355, 373, 758
Disturbance (in flow) 344, 527, 543-547, 560, 577, 585, 746
See also Turbulent flow
Diverge
beam 138-139, 142, 161, 168, 254, 263-267, 277, 464, 483, 704
definition of 746
wave 111, 269-277, 293-294, 337-338, 368, 374
Doppler 299-376
aliasing 322-328, 342, 349, 368, 374, 382, 411, 419, 714, 724-727
analog 319

angle 31, 158, 307-311, 321, 331-333, 348-357, 372-374, 381, 417-420, 581, 685, 698, 707, 716-722, 727, 731, 734, 746
artifacts 199, 381-382, 410, 746
audio 300, 317-319, 371, 586
block diagram 312-313
color *See* Color Doppler
continuous wave (CW) *See* CW Doppler
definition of 746
display 320
dropout 95, 341, 380, 417-423, 727-731
effect 47, 299-314, 330, 334, 373, 622, 746
equation 299, 304-308, 311, 314-320, 323, 325, 331, 336, 342, 372, 374, 410, 575, 717-718, 723, 725
FFT 319, 320, 335, 366, 381, 502, 720
frequency vs. depth 54, 88, 100, 161, 30-310, 323, 713-714
gain 314-319, 327-328, 339-340, 366, 412, 414, 420, 502, 717, 720-721, 729, 746
gate 113, 240, 313, 321-330, 334-340, 371-374, 411, 415, 437, 502, 577, 618, 714-716, 722-727, 746; *See also* Sampling: volume (Doppler)
high pulse repetition frequency 748
indices 300, 551, 583-584
probe 151-156
pulsed wave (PW) *See* PW Doppler
risetime 575-576
sample volume *See* Sampling: volume (Doppler)
scales (PRF) 115, 323-330, 342-343, 361, 373-374, 381, 410-411, 717, 721-732, 746
shift *See* Shift (Doppler frequency)
spectral *See* Spectral: Doppler
spectrum 196, 199, 300, 311-330, 339-342, 354, 371, 378, 381, 398, 411-413, 423, 569, 575-576, 580-581, 585-586, 708, 719-724, 746
tissue signals 357, 360-362, 367-368, 375, 734
tissue (TDI) *See* Tissue: Doppler imaging
transcranial 716-717, 730, 758
ultrafast *See* Ultrafast: Doppler
velocity 307, 311, 532-533, 552, 717-723
mean 118, 300, 315, 326, 334-344, 356-357, 371, 374, 579
peak 300, 322-324, 328, 332, 337, 371, 381, 495, 717-726
versus M-mode 240
wall filters 315-320, 332, 336, 342-344, 360-366, 370-375, 415, 420, 496, 582-583, 722-724, 731-734
Doppler string phantom 502

Dual screen 683-684, 713
Duplex 335, 746
Duty factor 106, 188, 216, 428, 434-438, 441, 451, 455, 705, 715
and PRP 106, 109, 122, 127, 435-436, 441, 451
and wave parameters 109, 121
definition of 106, 127, 435, 746
Dynamic frequency tuning 124, 128, 187, 191, 705
and bandwidth 124-125
definition of 124, 746
Dynamic range (DNR) 194-198, 202, 210-213, 217-218, 225-230, 235, 247-248, 315-320, 327, 344, 367, 374, 381, 415, 684, 712, 722, 731, 746-749
definition of 194-195, 746
display 195-196, 210, 746
gain 195, 687, 748
human eye 26, 92, 196, 225, 315-316, 319, 367, 684, 698, 712
input 195, 749
of Doppler 315-320, 327, 344, 367, 374, 415, 712, 722
output 195, 503
Dynamic receive focusing 164-168, 263, 266-273, 293, 746

E

Echocardiography 318, 392, 441, 446, 464, 471, 482, 651-655, 658-659, 711, 723-724
Echogenicity 71, 82-83, 91, 280, 608, 634-638, 642, 667, 683, 686, 688, 691, 693, 705, 746
low 366, 750
Echopalpation 746
Edema 390, 391, 568, 571, 640, 645, 685, 690, 746
Edge shadowing 92-93, 379, 400-401, 692, 695, 755
See also Refractive shadowing
Effective
beam (composite) 263-268, 272-273, 294, 744
resistance 555-557, 561-563, 572, 746
Ejection fraction (EF) 291, 484, 565, 652-658, 746
Elastic / Elasticity 56, 463, 746
arteries 552-553, 570, 589
characteristics 608-617, 624, 642-646, 687, 708
law of 748
limit 553, 609-610, 629, 746
modulus (Young's) (E) 608-630, 635-636, 639-640, 644-646, 760

veins 554, 570-571, 589
Elastogram 624-625, 630, 633-638, 641-642, 708-710
Elastography 40, 252, 633-650, 747
imaging 512, 523, 607-609, 617-619, 624, 630, 634, 640, 670, 708
shear wave 619, 624, 634-635, 639-645, 710-711
static /strain 618, 624, 634-646, 708-709, 757
Electrical
and crystal "distortion" 232
current *See* Current
field 133-135, 179-185, 191, 285, 563
impedance 749
interference 199, 747
Electrocardiogram (ECG/EKG) 199, 475, 552, 658, 747
Electrode 133, 170, 174, 182, 185, 191, 195, 232-233, 747
Electromagnetic waves 39, 68, 199, 285, 747
Electronic
components 196, 199, 206, 213, 221-224, 233, 240, 254, 316-318, 367, 415
and the binary system 32-33
focusing 131, 148-149, 158, 161, 172, 265, 482, 747
for receive 161
for transmit 160
noise 171, 180, 196, 199, 254, 747
steering (phasing) 151, 158-164, 176, 215, 270, 685, 707, 719-722, 747
for receive 159
for transmit 159
Electropotential 133, 176, 204, 530-531
Element (transducer) 151, 156-177, 185-187, 191, 215-216, 222-223, 252-254, 263-270, 272, 281, 294, 314, 321-322, 338, 393, 403, 408-413, 440, 471, 482, 499, 641, 645, 662, 666, 703-704, 714-715
Elevation
direction (dimension) 139, 146, 149, 151, 156, 162-164, 167-169, 172, 177, 187, 281-282, 333, 364, 384, 440, 577, 703, 706, 709
focus 144, 149, 151, 156, 162, 164, 167-169, 187, 703, 706-707
resolution 144, 149-150, 168, 177, 252, 293, 384, 495, 523, 747
limit (artifact) 379, 382, 384
See also Slice thickness
Emboli 83, 309, 415-416, 585
Encode 241-245, 730, 733
Endocardial 468, 469, 476, 486, 652, 655-656

Endocavity transducer 493, 507
Endovaginal transducer 280
Energy 529-530, 537, 539
   conservation of 77, 529-532, 539-542, 548, 557, 565, 579, 744
   converted to heat 72, 77, 84, 100, 428, 435, 531, 557-559, 664, 687
   definition of 529-530, 747
   frictional loss 541, 544, 557-560, 572-576, 588-589, 717
   gradient 747
   kinetic 529-532, 540-542, 546-548, 557-558, 565-566, 572-573, 590, 749
   potential 180, 529, 531-532, 540-542, 548, 557, 561, 572-573, 753
   reflected 77, 80, 393, 708
   thermal 216, 428, 434, 530, 663-668
   transfer of 38-41, 72, 76, 96, 100, 124, 199, 428, 434, 529, 539, 612, 662-667, 708
Enhancement artifact 85, 378-379, 382, 402-403, 422, 692, 695-698, 747
Ensemble length 119, 128, 256, 743
   See also Packet: size
Entrance effects 543-545, 586-587
Envelope
   detection 212-213, 708, 747
      signal processing 327
      smoothing 212-213
   spectral 327-328, 412
Enzymes 429, 456
Epicardial 652-653
Epidemiology 450-451, 595
Equation (assessing) 23
Equipment testing 489-490, 495, 503, 523, 594
Ergonomics 593, 600-601, 605, 747
Error
   in dimensional measurements 410
   in Doppler measurements 330, 381-382, 413, 580-584, 655, 717-722, 727
   in speckle tracking 655
Exercise 552-554, 571, 573, 588
Exit effects 543-544, 586-587
Expiration 566-570, 584, 589, 710
   See also Respiration
Exponent
   definition of 7, 747
   negative 8, 10
   notation / rules of 9, 10, 84
   positive 10
Extended field of view 166, 251, 278, 683; See also Panoramic imaging
Eye 26, 196-198, 210-211, 214, 225-238, 246-248, 293, 316-319, 338-339, 367, 444-445, 494, 667, 684, 712

F

Factor 9-10, 19-20, 26, 108, 747
Fahrenheit 43
False
   negative (FN) 291, 518-523, 642, 747
   positive (FP) 287, 291, 518-523, 747
Farads 181
Far field (Fraunhofer) 139-143, 149, 154, 168, 172, 176-177, 217, 222-223, 247, 253, 267, 270, 273, 279, 383, 464, 471, 474, 665, 704, 712, 747
Fascia 387-388, 568, 679, 690, 722
Fascicles 684, 688-689, 693
Fast Fourier Transform (FFT) 381, 463, 502, 720, 731, 747
Fat 387, 415-416, 640-641, 663, 676, 704
   fatty liver 640-643, 676
   propagation velocity in 59, 409-410, 466, 612, 702, 705
   See also Adipose tissue and Body mass index (BMI) entries
FDA (Food and Drug Administration) 431-432, 438-441, 445, 447, 468, 480, 484, 642, 644, 668, 670, 711
Ferroelectric material 174
Fetal
   imaging 85-86, 261, 282-284, 290, 359-360, 363, 401, 441-443, 449, 456, 635, 728, 733
   phantom 510-511
   safety 443-451, 456
FFT (Fast Fourier Transform) 463, 502, 720, 731, 747
Fiber optic hydrophone 453
Fibers / Fibrous 83, 652-655, 689, 693
Fibrillar 678, 685-689, 691-694, 698
Fibroadenoma 208, 210, 212, 637-638
Fibrocartilage 684, 689
Fibroid 662, 665, 667-668
Fibroscan 625, 639, 642, 644
Fibrosis 571, 608, 634, 639-640, 644, 646
Field of view (FOV) 157, 166-168, 176, 251-253, 270-271, 278, 286, 293-294, 444, 636, 676-678, 681, 683, 698, 707, 747
FIFO buffering 258, 294
Figure-of-eight artifact 402, 747
Filter
   digital 364, 745
   high pass 316-317, 344, 360, 374, 723, 731, 748
   RF 473-474
   sliding receive 124, 705, 746
   spatiotemporal 361-363, 368-371, 375, 417, 707, 734, 756
   wall See Wall filters

Flash
   artifact 357, 360, 371, 380, 416-417, 423, 707, 743
   pulses 475, 477, 484
Flicker fusion 246, 249
Flow direction 307, 310-311, 315, 331, 336, 342-358, 368-374, 399, 411, 531, 544, 718-722
   determining in Color Doppler 165, 331-336, 344-354, 374, 718-719
   distal 544-547, 573, 746
   forward 314, 319, 339, 381, 411-412, 423, 561, 569, 578-579
   reversal 315, 319, 339, 381, 411-412, 423, 561, 564, 569, 577-579, 589
Flow phantom 496-501, 523
Flow (Q)
   analogy 434, 528, 535
   blood flow 528, 531, 551-570, 575-580, 587, 589, 640, 643, 652, 710, 715-719, 723, 729-730
   constant velocity 498, 501
   definition of 533
   disturbed 344, 527, 543-544, 560, 577, 585, 746
   dropout 417-420
   equation 533, 538, 541, 552, 556, 575, 578, 580-581
   laminar See Laminar flow
   modal 327, 337
   parabolic See Parabolic flow
   plug See Plug flow
   principles of 332, 531, 545, 558, 563, 707
   pulsatile 496-498, 501, 539, 543, 551-553, 565-566, 575, 584-587, 710, 754
   turbulent 527, 543-548, 560, 573, 759
   velocity 531-537, 541-546, 552, 558-559, 576-582, 589, 717-734
   See also Volumetric flow (Q)
Fluid 82-83, 85, 91, 100, 690
   and absorption 429, 442, 446, 560
   dynamics 528-529, 547-548, 747
   imaging 278-279, 378, 387, 395, 402-403, 448, 645, 682-688, 691-695
   impedance 688, 749
   propagation velocity 58, 395, 402
   properties of 557, 638, 645, 688, 691
   viscosity 496, 529-531, 538-542, 546-548, 552, 557-560, 573, 587, 589, 646, 708
Fluttering 586
Focal depth (depth of focus) 140, 148, 155, 168, 177, 185, 217, 253-254, 263-267, 270, 277, 294, 473, 623, 664, 681, 705, 707, 713-714, 717
   equation 140

Focal region (depth of field) 142, 172, 176-177, 270, 662-666, 745, 747
Focus
  active single 264, 270, 275-276, 294
  and acoustic power 143, 217, 248, 662, 664
  and harmonics 464, 466, 473-474, 682, 707, 712
  change of 148-150, 159, 216-217, 254, 263-267, 330, 409, 440, 666, 704-706, 712-713
  definition of 139, 176, 747
  dynamic (continuous) 166, 263-264, 266, 271
  dynamic (receive) 164, 166-168, 263, 268-270, 273, 746
  elevation 144, 149, 151, 156, 162-169, 187, 703, 706-707
  fixed 329, 411
  multiple transmit foci 264-271, 276, 294, 623, 630, 751
    banding noise 267
  natural 139-144, 148-150, 161, 168, 172, 177, 263, 714, 751
Focused ultrasound (FUS) 55, 509, 512, 523, 618, 661-674, 747
  See also HIFU
Focusing 55, 148, 184, 216, 264, 267, 410, 640, 664
  and steering 144, 151, 155-156, 161, 164, 169, 187, 215, 223, 270, 281, 314, 321, 466, 482
  electronic 131, 148-149, 158, 160-161, 172, 265, 747
  receive 263, 296, 338, 715
  retrospective transmit 267-277, 293-294, 338, 383, 483, 755
Follicle 283
Footprint (transducer) 152, 154, 162, 278, 676-677, 703
Force 56, 174, 747
  acoustic radiation See Acoustic radiation force impulse (ARFI)
  and pressure 529-532, 541-542, 548, 567, 618, 636
  and stress / strain 608-618, 626, 629, 634-635, 645
  compressional 613-620, 623, 627, 634-635, 639, 641, 645, 708-710
  tensile 611-616, 626-627, 645
Foreign body 692, 695-696
Format
  data 236
  imaging 86, 169, 204, 222, 236, 278, 367, 676, 683-686
  trapezoidal 164, 166, 278, 676-678, 698, 707, 759
FOV (field of view) See Field of view (FOV)

Fractions 4
  and patterns 5
  decimals and percentages 4-5
  definition of 747
  simplest form of 5
Fractional bandwidth 123, 128, 184, 186, 747
Fragmentation 473
Frame
  angulation 257
  averaging 253, 256-258, 262, 287, 292-294, 355, 357, 402-405, 707, 733, 747
  generation 152, 165, 222, 338
  rate 117-118, 204, 216, 224, 233, 237-238, 246-253, 258, 266, 271-277, 284, 292-294, 428, 644, 655, 658, 701, 705, 712-713, 731-736
    and color Doppler 119, 271, 335-340, 731-736
    and monitors 233, 237, 246, 271, 338-339
    and speckle tracking 655
    definition of 13, 53, 111, 116-118, 121, 128, 747
    equation 117, 119, 121, 128
    optimizing 120, 170, 339
  time 13, 111, 116-121, 128, 238, 252-256, 266, 270-274, 293, 335-340, 732-735, 747
Frank-Starling's Law 747
Fraunhofer zone (far field) See Far field
Frequency 44, 51, 87
  and absorption 72, 83-84
  and NZL 140, 142, 176
  and penetration 84, 113, 140, 142, 187, 381, 461, 664, 676, 682, 702-703, 713
  and pulse length 106, 115, 125
  and resolution 111, 124, 336, 404, 676-677, 702
  and sensitivity 125, 171, 309, 702-703, 714, 717, 722-727, 731
    See also Bandwidth
  and signal sampling 201-204, 323
  and transmit power 216, 676
  and wavelength 48, 75, 92, 301-308, 404-405, 410, 460, 476, 665
  bins 320, 747
  coding See Coded excitation (pulses)
  compared with amplitude 66, 123, 204, 308, 316-321, 462-463, 469, 475
  cutoff (corner) 123, 316-318, 342-343, 361, 364-365, 723, 731, 744
  definition of 53, 68, 747
  frame See Frame: rate
  fundamental See Fundamental frequency

harmonic 54, 125, 128, 461-464, 472, 474, 485-486, 586, 682, 711
  of a sound wave 45, 216
  operating (transmit)
    See Operating frequency
  ranges 53, 122-128, 161, 176, 439, 445, 676-677, 698, 711, 713
  receive 261, 474, 485
  resonant 462, 469-471, 479
    See also Resonance
  tuning (dynamic) 124-125, 183, 187, 191, 705, 746, 759
  wave parameter 44-45, 67, 642-646
Frequency compounding (fusion) 125, 128, 260-261, 287, 293-294, 405-406, 713, 747
Frequency shift
  in Doppler 300-325, 334-337, 342, 344, 349, 356-357, 360-365, 374, 476, 574-576, 585, 725, 729, 734
  maximum detectable 323, 325, 410
  range of 320, 381
Fresnel zone (near field)
  See Near field (Fresnel)
Friction 327, 370, 418, 531, 539-541, 557-559, 573, 576-577, 588-590, 690, 717, 748
Front-end 748
Fundamental frequency 125, 461-478, 485-486, 681-682, 705, 711, 748
FUS See Focused ultrasound (FUS)
Fusion (modalities) 251, 261, 285-287, 293, 295-296

G

Gain 207, 318
  and TGC 208-210, 217-220, 225, 247-248, 337, 706
  definition of 65, 196, 748
  Doppler See Doppler: gain
  dynamic range 195, 197, 687, 748
  factor 64-66
  receiver 66, 195-199, 206-209, 220, 247, 337-341, 380-381, 412-421, 502-504, 706-707, 712, 717, 720-722, 729, 731, 754
  transmit 502, 759
Gate (Doppler) See Doppler: gate
    See also Sampling: volume (Doppler)
Gating 240
  retrospective 148-149, 267
Gel
  phantom 507, 509, 512, 514
  ultrasound coupling 90-91, 453, 493-494, 497, 506, 679-681, 698, 706-709
Germicide 493

Ghosting 412
  mirror artifact 388
  monitor display 233-234
Global longitudinal strain (GLS) 651-658, 748
Gloves (and safety) 493-494, 595
Golden rule
  and statistical indices 517-518, 522
  false negative *See* False: negative (FN)
  false positive *See* False: positive (FP)
  true negative *See* True: negative (TN)
  true positive *See* True: positive (TP)
  See also Gold standard
Gold standard 452, 489-490, 516-523, 639, 748
  and accuracy 492, 517, 521-524
  and sensitivity 520-524
  and specificity 520-523
  See also Golden rule
GPU 221, 224, 274, 288, 748
Gradient
  energy 747
  pressure *See* Pressure: gradient
Grating lobe artifact 51, 156, 169, 215, 223, 259, 274, 277, 294, 378-379, 382, 386, 393-394, 404, 408, 410, 423, 440, 465-466, 482, 682, 707, 748
Gravitational 548, 567-568, 641, 709
  potential energy 529, 532, 541
Grayscale 226, 229-230, 235, 247-248, 252, 320, 687, 712, 717, 732
  definition of 748
  mapping 220-223, 229, 335-341
Guidelines 492-495, 524

H

Hanafy lens 168-169, 187, 748
Harmonic
  coded 404, 407, 743
  distortion 464-465, 471, 476-477, 681
  double spectrum artifact 382, 412-413
  frequencies 54, 461-462, 474, 485-486, 586, 681-682, 711
  imaging 43, 125, 128, 170, 261, 277, 309, 384, 404, 407, 412, 459-468, 474-478, 482, 485-486, 586, 681-682, 698, 702, 705, 707, 711, 748
    and artifacts 465
    and depth 464
    contrast 309, 462, 473-474, 486, 711-712, 748
    pulse inversion 404, 467-468, 477-478, 483-486, 712-713
    reducing reverberation 384, 461, 465-466, 682
  power Doppler 459, 476
  signal generation 412, 459, 462, 464, 473, 681-682, 711
  tissue (THI) 462-467, 473-477, 486, 681-682, 751
Hazard (electrical safety) 492
Haze artifact 199, 387, 389, 396, 465, 467, 748; *See also* Dirty shadow
Hearing 53, 210
Heart phantom 515-516
Heat 43, 72, 84, 110-111, 171, 223, 231, 234, 400, 428, 430, 435-438, 445-447, 455, 529-534, 539-543, 548, 557-559, 572, 589, 661-667, 687
Hematocrit 309, 496, 539, 558-559, 748
  definition of 558-559
Hematoma 691
Hemodynamics 300, 309, 327, 334, 337, 365, 371, 374, 420, 551-592
  and Doppler 574, 579
  and equations 24, 531, 534, 556, 575
  arterial 741
  cardiovascular 530-531
  definition of 589, 748
  example of 556
  simplified law of 534-539, 548, 553-554, 560, 565, 572-575, 590, 756
  units of 13
Hemorrhage 83, 446, 554, 639, 691
Hepatitis 639, 643, 646
Hepatocellular 640
Herbies artifact 396
Hertz (Hz) (definition of) 13, 44, 748
Heterodyning (mixing to baseband) 314
Heterogeneous 83, 397, 635, 637, 666, 687, 690, 710, 748
Hexafluoride 469, 711
HIFU (high intensity focused ultrasound) 55, 183, 410, 453, 484, 500, 512-514, 523, 662, 666, 747
  See also Focused ultrasound (FUS)
High-level *See* Disinfection: high-level
High pass filter 316-317, 344, 360, 374, 723, 731, 748
Histotripsy 665, 668, 670
Homogeneous 76, 83, 91, 174-175, 213-214, 402-403, 442, 476-479, 496, 508, 540-543, 559, 624, 635-636, 640, 642, 666, 687-689, 748
Hooke's law 607-611, 626-629, 635, 748
Horizontal lines (into pixels) 234
HPRF Doppler (High PRF) 313, 322, 325, 329-330, 334, 371, 373, 721, 725-727, 748
Humerus 85, 696
Huygens' principle 159-161, 269, 748
Hydraulic (impedance) 749
Hydrophone 439-440, 452-456, 748
Hydrostatic pressure 532, 539-541, 548, 551, 566-570, 584, 589, 748
Hyperechoic 82-83, 392, 684, 688-692, 748; *See also* Echogenicity
Hyperemia 685, 754
Hyperkinetic 663
Hyperostosis 748
Hypertension 484, 568, 571, 748
Hyperthermia 663, 666
Hypertonic 663
Hypertrophy 657, 726
Hypoechoic 82-83, 634, 637, 685, 688-690, 748; *See also* Echogenicity
Hypotenuse 29

I

Identification band (ID) 595
Image persistence 262, 294, 748
Image planes 112, 146, 230-231, 285, 287, 293, 475, 483, 641, 655, 683, 691, 705, 709, 713, 731
Image size
  and temporal resolution 252, 732
  and thermal bioeffects 216
  and transmit power 216
  in scanning 681, 735
Imaging
  cardiac 153, 161, 170, 215, 227-231, 240, 256, 266, 270, 277, 280, 284, 291, 307, 330, 345, 353, 374, 386, 389-390, 393, 405, 446, 465-469, 475-477, 484, 486, 599, 609, 652-657, 711-726, 734
  compound *See* Compound imaging
  contrast 469, 480-482, 666, 711
  depth *See* Depth: imaging
  dimensions *See* Imaging dimensions
  dynamic evaluation 686, 692
  harmonic *See* Harmonic: imaging
  microflow (MFI) 751
  molecular 484
  panoramic 278, 294, 683, 698, 707, 752
  phantoms 258, 266-268, 275-276, 281, 384, 396, 404, 444, 489, 495-505, 508-516, 523-524, 594, 623-624, 642-644, 703; *See also* Phantoms
  plane wave 111-112, 118, 160, 215, 225, 269, 274-276, 293-294, 334, 483, 623, 644, 705
    See also Plane wave
  real-time *See* Real-time imaging
  resolution 189, 403, 408, 655, 676-677, 712; *See also* Detail resolution
  sequential *See* Sequential: imaging
  shear wave elastography (SWE)
    See Shear: wave: elastography
  triggered 475-477, 483

ultrafast *See* Ultrafast: imaging
zone *See* Zone imaging
Imaging dimensions 139, 146, 440, 653
  axial 139, 383, 473, 504, 664
  elevation 139, 149, 151, 156, 162-172, 177, 187, 384, 577, 703, 706
  lateral 139, 147-153, 157, 162, 164, 167-168, 172, 187, 383, 482, 706
Immersion 494
Impedance
  acoustic *See* Acoustic: impedance
  electrical 749
  fluid/hydraulic 565, 749
  mismatch 76-83, 88-100, 134-135, 144-145, 148, 150, 154, 176-177, 183-184, 213-214, 225-226, 386, 390-391, 400, 422, 708, 711, 751
    minimizing 144, 184, 404, 465, 679, 706, 708
Implants 614
Implied consent 595, 749
Impulse response 125, 128, 137, 144, 364, 749
Inadequate sensitivity 196, 380-381, 417-418, 504, 579, 714, 717, 722, 729, 731; *See also* Sensitivity
Incidence 385, 389, 396, 400, 417
  angle of *See* Incident angle
Incident angle 257-258, 381, 385, 393, 400-402, 415-417, 685, 692-693, 698, 706-707, 740
  definition of 73-74, 749
  normal 74, 77-81, 88-97, 163, 165, 225, 692-693, 698, 751
  oblique 79, 88, 97, 100, 160, 393, 396, 402, 665, 693, 695
Incompliant 554
Incompressible 540-543, 615-617, 628, 630, 645, 652
Index
  Doppler 551, 583-584
    pulsatility / Gosling 583
    resistive / Pourcelot 583
    S/D ratio (A/B ratio) 583
  lookup table 243
  mechanical 277, 441-446, 455, 470-471, 480, 484, 711-713
  quality 291
  statistical 490, 516-518, 521
  thermal 441-450, 456, 758
Inelastic 56, 611
Inertia 429-430, 435, 543-547, 749
Inertial cavitation 429-430, 438, 442, 455, 665, 711; *See also* Transient: cavitation
Infarction 657
Inferior Vena Cava (IVC) 397, 399, 563-564, 569-570, 584-585, 589, 703

Informed consent 445, 449, 593, 595, 597, 749
Infrasound 53, 69, 749
In phase 51, 158, 254-257, 275, 281, 294, 361, 403-407, 467, 749
Input (dynamic range) 195, 749
Insonation angle *See* Insonification angle
Insonification angle 308, 310-311, 323, 328-336, 344-349, 357, 372-373, 385, 393, 412-415, 440, 579, 749
  See also Doppler: angle
Inspiration 566, 569-570, 584, 589, 710
  See also Respiration
Integers 3
  and exponents 8
Intensity 83
  acoustic 207, 432, 438, 446, 465, 618, 664, 665
  and beam convergence 143, 464-466, 662
  and beam divergence 92, 143-144, 254, 272, 464, 466
  definition of 13, 63, 69, 744, 749
  equation 64, 69, 176, 432
  measurements (common) 427, 432-435, 439, 441, 451, 455
  PA and TA 433-435, 451, 618
  relationship to power 63, 69, 84, 143-144, 176, 195, 206, 216, 255, 267, 432, 704
  spatial distribution 270, 335, 403-404, 433-441, 455
  units of 63, 234
Interface 73-74, 77-85, 88-100
Interference 254, 474
  constructive 51-52, 87, 145, 156-159, 163-165, 254-258, 268, 292-294, 309, 393, 403-404, 467, 468, 477, 622-623, 654, 665, 744
  destructive 52, 87, 145, 156-158, 254, 258, 268, 292-294, 379, 403-404, 466-468, 477, 642, 654, 745
  electrical 199, 747
  partially constructive 52, 87, 255, 294, 361, 393, 403-404, 752
Interlaced 749
Interpolation 233, 244
Intimal 83
  intima media thickness (IMT) 146, 749
Intravascular 523
  pressure 568-571, 590
  ultrasound (IVUS) 55
Intravenous 469, 480, 665-666, 712
Inverse proportionality 6, 16-17, 23, 35, 749
Invert / Inversion 312, 323, 336, 342, 345, 346, 354, 467, 468, 712, 713
  of flow (reverse flow) 315, 319, 577

In vitro 470, 616
  biological effects 430, 450
  definition of 749
In vivo 85, 470, 646
  biological effects 431, 445-447, 450
  definition of 749
Irrational numbers 3
I_{SAPA} 432, 452
I_{SATA} 432, 434, 452
I_{SATP} 432
iScan 279
iScape 278
Ischemia 573-574, 640, 652
Isoechoic 688, 749
Isotropic 615, 626-630, 636, 640, 642, 645, 693, 749
Isovolumic 652, 749
  contraction 560, 563, 653, 749
  relaxation 578, 653
  systolic pressure curve 749
I_{SPPA} 432, 434-435, 446, 452, 618, 666
I_{SPTA} 432, 435, 437-438, 441, 445, 447, 452, 618
I_{SPTP} 432, 434
iTouch 279
IVUS *See* Intravascular: ultrasound

J

Joint 678-679, 682, 686, 688-689
Joint Commission on Accreditation of Healthcare Organizations (JCAHO) 595
  See also TJC (The Joint Commission)
Joules 529-530, 749
JPEG 236, 749
  JPEG 2000 236

K

Kelvin 43, 430
Kerf 158, 749
Kidney 88-91
  imaging 273, 285-287, 400, 406-407, 420-422, 481, 704
  propagation velocity in 59, 612
Kinetic energy 529-532, 540-542, 546-548, 557-558, 565-566, 572-573, 590, 749
Korotokov sounds 749

L

Laboratory accreditation 489-491, 523
Laminar flow 309, 326-328, 352, 370, 499, 527, 538-539, 543-548, 558-560, 576-577, 584, 716-717, 722, 734, 749; *See also* Parabolic flow

Lateral
  dimension 139, 142-149, 151, 153, 156, 157, 162-164, 167-168, 172, 177, 187, 281-282, 333-334, 364, 383, 440, 482, 614, 706, 749
  distortion 92, 93, 95, 222-223, 383
  resolution *See* Lateral resolution
Lateral displacement artifact 92-93, 156, 379, 385-386, 393, 423, 709, 749
Lateral resolution 92, 147-149, 177, 223, 238, 252-254, 263-281, 293-294, 374, 383, 495, 504-508, 514, 523, 658, 735
  and depth of field 142, 144, 254, 263
  improved 253-254, 263-264, 266-272, 277, 280-281, 294, 396, 464, 466, 483, 681, 735
  limit (artifact) 379, 382-383
  See also Angular, Azimuthal, Side-by-side, *and* Transverse resolution *entries*
LCD (liquid crystal display) 231-234, 237, 245-246, 249, 750
Leaflet 240, 285, 391, 397, 399-400, 415, 467, 578
Leakage (current) 492-493, 745, 749
LED (light emitting diode) 231-234, 245-246
Left ventricular opacification (LVO) 468, 482, 484, 750
Length 535-538, 542, 548, 554-555, 614-615, 618, 627, 653, 750
Lens 150
  Hanafy 187, 748
  of transducer 148, 161-162, 168, 172, 177, 184, 492, 750
Lesion 237, 239, 287, 291, 407, 468-469, 480-481, 483, 510, 512, 607-608, 613, 634, 636-642, 644-646, 663, 681, 708, 713
Lift 541-542, 750
Ligaments 676, 686, 688-693, 698
Linear
  imaging 222-223, 238
  phased array 157-158, 163, 167, 278, 413, 676-677, 698, 707, 719-720, 750
  proportionality 16-18, 35, 750
  relationships 16-17, 23, 35
  response 459, 471-473, 478-479
  scale 26
  switched array 156-158, 163-164, 750
Line averaging 256, 734, 750
Line density 223, 238, 252-253, 271, 280, 483, 658, 712, 735-736
  color 735, 743
Liquid crystal displays *See* LCD
Lithotripsy 453

Liver 82-83, 88, 91, 120, 554, 640
  imaging 237, 239, 266, 273, 279, 281, 285-286, 359, 367, 379, 384-385, 390, 397-406, 444, 468-469, 480-481, 484, 634, 636, 639, 642-643, 646, 663, 670, 702-704, 710-713
  propagation velocity of 59, 612
Lobe (beam) 393
Locational artifacts 382, 385, 750
Logarithm (log)
  decibels (dB) 54, 84, 226
  definition of 26-27, 35, 750
  properties of 27, 35
  scale 27
  ultrasound function 26, 211, 227
Long axis (LAX) 652-653, 656, 678, 684, 686, 689, 693, 696, 707, 709, 719-720
Longitudinal
  beam dimension 750
  mode 39, 68
  resolution 108, 115, 127, 150, 177, 185, 428, 741; *See also* Axial, Depth, Radial, *and* Range resolution *entries*
  wave (P-wave)
    definition of 40-41, 750
    depiction of 49, 441, 613, 620
    propagation of 42, 57, 139, 612-613, 617-623, 629
    speed 612-613, 622-623, 629-630, 750
Loop (cine) *See* Cine loop
Lossless (compression) 211, 236, 241, 243, 248, 750
Lossy (compression) 211, 241
Low-level *See* Disinfection: low-level
Lumason 468, 480
Lumen (of vessel) 198, 207, 213, 222, 335, 366, 388, 559, 581-582, 716, 732
Luminance 234, 236
Lung 199, 386-387, 390-391
  function of 560, 564
  imaging 387, 444, 446, 663, 696
  propagation velocity of 59, 612
Lung rockets artifact 390, 750
  See also B-line artifact (BLA)
Lymphatic 571, 639, 645
Lysis 484, 668

M

Mach cone 621-623, 629
Machine learning 289, 291, 295
Magnetic resonance imaging (MRI) 236, 285-287, 295-296, 370, 635, 644, 662-663, 666-670, 686
Manual steering 750

Map
  color 230, 241, 336, 345, 367-368
  compression 211, 227, 229, 320, 367
Mass
  abnormal tissue 82, 90-91, 208, 212, 226, 247, 254, 260, 280, 283-284, 286-287, 291, 294, 386, 389, 393, 395, 484, 505, 508-510, 523, 608, 624-625, 635-642, 695, 710
  amount of matter 42, 57, 529, 532, 546, 652
Matching layer 89-90, 97-100, 135, 145, 148-152, 170, 174, 177, 184-185, 191, 750
Mathematical 1-36
  definitions 3, 4, 19
  notations 4
  terminology 19
Matrix (array) 169-170, 187, 482-483
Maxima 204, 294, 467
Maximum 115, 704
  detectable frequency shift 323, 325, 725
  detectable velocity 204, 325-329, 342, 365, 371, 410, 716-718, 724-727
  intensity (IM) 432, 664
  venous capacitance (MVC) 750
  venous outflow (MVO) 750
Mean
  average 327, 433-434, 635, 741
    See also Averaging
  velocity 118-119, 281, 300, 315, 326, 334-344, 356-357, 368, 371, 374, 380, 495, 537, 540, 546, 572-573, 579, 581, 590, 750
Measurement 13, 194, 201-205, 221, 230-231, 237, 241, 246, 249, 252, 283, 290-291, 300, 305, 310-311, 319, 330-340, 366, 370, 372, 398, 401, 413, 432, 438-440, 453-456, 483, 495, 551-557, 565-589, 624, 637-642, 652-657, 663, 717-728
Mechanical
  bioeffects 216, 429, 434-435, 438, 443, 666-667, 750
  distortion 134
  index *See* MI (Mechanical index)
  steering 131, 151-155, 159, 162, 164, 167, 176, 750
  transducers 151-159, 162, 164, 167, 169, 329, 373, 411, 750
  waves 39, 72, 212-213, 248, 301, 428-429, 469
    compressional phase 463, 470
    definition of 39, 750
    propagation of 39, 42, 68, 301, 463
Mechanical index
  See MI (Mechanical index)

Medical director 491, 594
Medium
 material types 39, 40, 68, 212, 306-308, 440, 496, 609-610, 750
 properties of 56, 72, 77, 83, 140, 181, 213-214, 395, 403, 408, 463, 469, 504, 608, 612-617, 687
 variations in 42, 76, 80, 93, 134, 428, 442
Membrane
 CMUT 182-185, 191, 751
 hydrophone 439, 452-454
 of a cell *See* Cell: membrane
Metal 399-400, 430, 615
 acoustic properties of 59, 395
 and reflection artifacts 379, 391-392, 398, 402, 696-697
Metastatic 82, 639, 713
Metric
 abbreviations 11, 35
 converting between units 13-16
 system 11, 35, 751
Microbubble 429, 469-486, 665, 712-713, 744, 751; *See also* Bubble
Microcirculation 665-666
Microflow 362
 imaging (MFI) 751
Micro-streaming 429
Microvascular 360-363, 371, 375, 446
 flow detection 734
MI (mechanical index) 277, 441-446, 455, 470-480, 484-486, 618, 711-713, 750
 definition of 441, 750
 techniques 712
  high 475-479, 484, 486
  low 713, 750
  very low 472, 475, 477-479, 484-486
Minima 204, 294, 467
Minimum 115
Mirror 73
 acoustic 397
 artifact 87, 379-382, 388, 396-399, 423, 751; *See also* Reverberation artifact
 focusing 148, 172, 177
Mismatch *See* Impedance: mismatch
Mitral regurgitant fraction 721, 751
Mitral valve 86, 240, 285, 290, 310, 352, 391-392, 397-400, 412-415, 564
Mixers (Doppler) 314, 319
 See also Baseband
M-Mode (motion mode) 111, 116, 154, 156, 162, 216, 239-241, 256, 322, 374, 436-437, 449, 734, 736, 751
Modal flow 326-327, 337
Modalities 216, 256, 271-272, 285, 287, 439, 444
 non-scanned 111-112, 116-119, 128, 216, 240, 334-335, 428, 436-437, 751

 scanned vs. non-scanned 111-113, 116-118, 128, 216, 221, 334, 436, 437, 455
Modal velocity 327, 337, 751
Mode
 definition of (Doppler) 327
 transmission 182, 191, 204, 758
 ultrasound type 239, 436
Modulate (and signal processing) 212, 478, 751
Modulus
 Bulk (K) 56-60, 67-68, 608, 612-613, 616, 619, 625, 628-630, 742
 shear (G) 607-610, 616-619, 625-626, 629-630, 756
 Young's elastic (E) 608, 611, 615-619, 624-630, 636, 760
Molecular imaging 484
Molecules 57, 133-135, 173-174, 529
 and energy 40-41, 133, 173, 485, 711
 and force 534, 610-613, 692
 density 40, 486, 612, 630
Momentum 40, 74-77, 134, 751
Monitors 210, 231, 245-249
 and ambient light 235
 calibration 503-504
 CRT 231-233
 frame rate 233, 237, 246, 271
 height 602-603
 interlaced 749
 LCD 231-237, 245-246, 249, 750
 LED 231-246, 752
 progressive 753
 See also Display
Moore's law 170, 324, 751
Motion detection 244-247, 256, 285, 303, 307, 311, 617-618, 635-636, 641, 644, 652, 655, 658, 686, 707-710, 713, 716
Motion mode (M-mode) *See* M-Mode
MP4 241
MPEG (video format) 241-242, 751
Multi-Hertz operation 123-124
Multi-line acquisition (MLA) 215-216, 271-274, 277, 293-294, 428, 437, 751
Multi-line transmit (MLT) 215-216, 274, 277, 293-296, 428, 437, 734, 751
Multipath artifact 87, 379, 382, 423, 465, 751
Multiple transmit foci 264-271, 276, 294, 623, 630, 751
Murmur (cardiac) 585
Muscle 615, 636, 640, 644-645, 663, 679, 683, 698
 and speed of sound 409, 466, 687
 attenuation rate 83-84, 100

 heart *See* Myocardial
 propagation velocity of 59, 409, 466, 612
 ultrasound appearance 88, 278, 387-388, 677, 682-688, 690-694, 704
Musculoskeletal 172, 278, 285, 475, 574, 597, 605, 668, 675-700
Myocardial 446, 469, 474-477, 483-486, 640, 651-659

N

Natural
 constant 4
 focus 139-144, 148-150, 161, 168, 172, 177, 185, 263, 714, 751
 numbers 3, 8
 rate of the cell 751
Near field (Fresnel) 139-143, 149, 154, 172, 176-177, 208, 216-223, 247, 252-254, 266, 273, 383, 386, 389, 396, 459, 462-466, 474, 485, 662, 665, 682, 701-707, 751
 and interference 143
 definition of 86, 139-140, 751
Near zone length (NZL)
 and aperture 141, 177, 664
 and frequency 140, 142, 185
 definition of 13, 139-140, 176, 664, 751
Necrosis 300, 574, 652, 665-666
Needle 595
 hydrophone 439, 452-454
 visualization of 285, 287, 379, 391, 395, 422, 509-510, 686, 697
Negative predictive value (NPV) 516, 520-524, 751
Nerve 676, 679, 684, 686, 689, 693, 698
 propagation velocity in 59
 visualization of 684, 689
Nervous system
 parasympathetic 560, 752
 sympathetic 560, 757
Neural network 289, 295
Neuroma 696
Neuromodulation 668
Neurotherapeutic 668
Newtonian
 and blood viscosity 559
 fluid 538-539, 542, 559, 587, 589, 751
Nit 234
Noise 195; *See also* Speckle
 and spatial averaging 262, 294
 color speckle 120, 340-341, 355-356, 420-421, 729, 731, 744
 definition of 194, 196, 751
 electronic 171, 180, 199, 254, 380, 747
 floor 194-198, 213, 340-341, 367, 475, 721-722, 743, 751

reduction 254-257, 260-263, 294, 355-356, 374, 384, 404, 406, 708, 710
  See also Speckle: reduction of
sources of 199, 213, 247, 465-467, 636, 641, 708, 713
thermal 99, 199, 254, 380
threshold 420, 721, 729
Non-acoustic zoom 237, 239, 751
  See also Read zoom
Non-collapse mode 181-183
Non-linear
  imaging 43, 462-466, 681
  proportionality 22, 35, 745, 751
  relationships 22-26, 31, 35, 229, 245, 412, 717-718
  response 459, 471-472, 478-479, 485, 711
Non-Scanned modalities 216, 240, 334-335, 428, 436-437, 455
  and temporal resolution 116, 118
  definition of 111-112, 751
Normal incidence 225, 692, 698
  definition of 74, 751
  varying propagation velocity 80, 94
Normal line 73-74, 79
Notation (mathematical) 4, 10
Notch
  dicrotic *See* Dicrotic notch
  of transducer 352-353, 678-679
NTEQ 279 *See also* Adaptive processing
Numbers
  negative powers 8
  positive powers 7
  zero power 9
Numerator 4, 23, 653, 751
Nyquist
  criterion 111, 201-204, 248-249, 322-325, 354, 374, 410, 721, 724, 751
  limit 320-323, 337, 342-343, 365, 724, 751

O

Oblique
  angles (definition of) 752
  incidence *See* Incident angle: oblique
Oculoplethysmography (OPG) 752
ODS (output display standard) 431, 441
  See also Power: limits (bioeffects)
OHM's law 752
OLED (monitor) 245-246, 752
Opacification
  left ventricular 750, 752
Operating (transmit) frequency 13, 44, 53, 60, 85, 100, 108-115, 121-128, 136-150, 161, 168, 172, 176, 179, 183-191, 205, 216, 225, 304-318, 323-326, 342, 371-374, 404-405, 410-419, 442, 461, 464, 470-479, 485, 618, 664-665, 676-678, 698, 702-706, 711-714, 721-727, 752, 759
  and bandwidth 122-123, 126, 128, 168, 189, 467, 706
  and wavelength 304, 306, 373, 410, 460, 476, 665
  definition of 53, 60, 172, 752
  determining 61, 100, 121, 183, 187, 713-714
  effect on wall filter setting 318, 418, 723-724
  in PW: equation 110, 121, 136, 138
  resolution vs. penetration 142, 189, 461, 676, 682, 702, 713-714
Ophthalmic 214, 249, 441, 444-445
Optimize 196, 253, 271, 279-280, 291-293, 410, 675-676, 681, 701-738
  automatic 279, 736, 741
  See also Adaptive processing
Optison 484
Orthogonal 80, 282, 483, 613, 626-627, 652, 683
Oscillate 40, 43, 134, 195, 429, 435, 455, 470-472, 546-547, 665
Osteoporosis 687
Outflow 557, 561, 576, 726
  maximum venous (MVO) 750
Out of phase 52, 145, 158, 255, 257, 294, 361, 393, 403-404, 407, 467, 752
Output
  acoustic 169, 206, 441-442, 444, 447, 449, 644
  cardiac 300, 552, 560-564, 567, 571, 580-581, 584
  display standard (ODS) 431, 441
  dynamic range 195
  intensity 195, 227, 255
  power 169, 195, 206, 428, 441, 443, 447, 449, 470-471, 476, 482, 712
    See also Transmit: power
    See also Transmit: voltage
  pressure 186, 206
Overamplified 207; *See also* Overgained
Overestimation (of Doppler velocity) 382, 719, 722
Overgained 196, 207-210, 327, 340-341, 356, 381, 403, 414, 420-421, 577-579, 720; *See also* Overamplified

P

PA and TA intensity 435, 618
  duty factor 451
  See also Intensity
Packet
  color packet 118-120, 128, 336, 729, 734-736, 743
  size 118-120, 256, 337-338, 361, 364, 366, 374, 437, 476, 729, 731, 735-736
PACS 211, 236, 248, 604
Palpation 634, 746, 752
Pancreas 120, 260, 480, 668
Panoramic imaging 278, 294, 683, 698, 707, 752
  See also Extended field of view
Parabolic flow 352, 543-544, 548, 558-559, 578, 581-582, 752
  See also Laminar flow
Parallel 80, 402
  plate capacitor 181, 191
  processing 159, 162, 164, 168, 215, 221, 224, 260-261, 271-273, 288, 293-294, 338, 383, 406, 735-736, 752
    multiple receive beams 111-113, 271-273
  resistance 551, 555-557, 561-563, 588-589
Parasympathetic nervous system 560, 752
Paratenon 688-689
Parkinson's 668
Partially-constructive interference
  See Interference: partially constructive
Particle motion 40-43, 68, 72, 76, 496, 608, 752
Patient
  communication 596, 603, 605, 710
  identification 594-595, 605
  positioning 597-600, 604, 636, 679, 709, 713
  safety 216, 430-431, 438, 443-444, 448, 492-493, 594-595, 597, 605, 667, 704
Peak
  strain 656
  velocity 300, 322-324, 328, 332, 335, 337, 371, 381-382, 411, 413-414, 495, 502, 565, 574, 576, 579, 584, 717-726
Pedof transducer 151-152, 312, 714, 752
  See also Blind transducer
  See also Pencil probe transducer
Pencil probe transducer 312, 411, 752
Penetration 44, 55, 61-62, 69, 84-85, 89-96, 115, 124-127, 142-144, 171, 176, 187, 189, 206, 252-253, 261, 267, 281, 294, 380-381, 396, 404, 419, 459-464, 474, 485, 495, 664, 676, 682, 687, 701-705, 713, 728
Pennate 752
Perceived resolution 237
Perceived sensitivity 503
Percentage
  change in 24-26, 78, 332, 343, 460, 520, 523, 562, 581, 653
  definition of 19, 752

Perfluorocarbon 469, 472-473, 711
Perfusion 299-300, 446-447, 459, 469, 474-477, 482-486, 551, 560, 566, 571-574, 664, 712
  definition of 560
Pericardium 752
Perimeter 752
Period (P) 13, 108, 752
  and frequency 45, 68, 106, 113, 116, 136, 301
  as a wave parameter 44-48, 109, 121
  characteristics in ultrasound 41
Peripheral
  blood flow 553, 558, 561, 565, 568, 569-570, 733
    See also Distal: blood flow
  edema 568, 571
  resistance 552, 557, 560-566, 570, 752
Permeability 571, 661, 666
Permittivity 181
Perpendicular 80, 95, 230, 257, 282, 385, 393, 400, 402, 412, 415, 581, 608, 613, 615, 621, 626, 679, 686, 693-695, 698, 709, 752
Persistence
  color 292, 355, 373, 375, 729, 731, 744
  image 262, 294, 748
  important points 355
Phantoms 85
  definition of 495, 752
  Doppler 496-502, 524
  specialty 509, 642-644
  See also Imaging: phantoms
Phase 51-52, 666
  aberration 410, 466; *See also* Aberration
  arterial 480
  definition of 158, 752
  delay 52, 159-168, 204-205, 214, 216, 223, 254, 265, 270, 281, 314, 408, 410, 466, 666, 745, 752
  difference, sine 29, 35, 52, 158, 654
  disturbances 440
  in phase *See* In phase
  inversion (pulse inversion) 467-468, 477-478, 483, 485-486, 712-713
  late 480
  out of phase *See* Out of phase
  portal venous 480, 584
Phased array 394
  sector 161-162, 177, 753
  transducers 51, 151, 156, 159-164, 167-169, 172, 177, 204, 223-224, 252, 265, 312-313, 329, 394, 408, 482, 663, 716, 750
Phasicity 575, 578-579, 584
  and respiration 584
Phasing 131, 151, 156-169, 177, 205, 214-215, 270

electronic 747
Phong 358-359, 375
Phospholipids 469, 711
Photoplethysmography 753
Physiotherapy 55
Piezoceramic 144, 170-171, 174
  and high impedance 144
Piezocomposite materials 152, 170
Piezocrystal 171, 174
Piezoelectric 131-178
  crystals 136, 138, 145, 150-151, 158, 163, 171, 173, 184-188, 753
  effect
    and crystal molecules 133-134, 173
    and ultrasound transducers 133, 135, 173, 180
    definition of 173, 753
  material 135, 174
    and propagation velocity 136
    manufactured 135, 170, 185
    quartz, etc. 135
    usage 148, 173-174, 180, 183, 191
Piston mode 135, 170
Pitch 67, 69, 156, 170, 223, 301-302, 440, 641
Pixel 199, 221-223, 232-237, 242-248, 262-263, 268-269, 293-294, 334-337, 340-341, 355, 368, 375, 406, 421, 663, 729
  and averaging 262
  definition of 753
Planar 160, 275, 276, 294
Plane wave 111-112, 116-119, 160, 215-216, 225, 269, 274-277, 293-296, 334-337, 368-369, 374, 379, 396, 483, 623, 644, 705, 753
Plaque 55, 71, 82-83, 259, 368-370, 484, 559, 668
  complex 744
Plasma 88, 92, 460, 486, 557-560, 571
Plethysmography 753
Plug flow 543-544, 548, 580-581, 753
  See also Laminar flow
PMN-PT crystal 171, 174-175, 756
Pneumobilia 390
Poiseuille's law 527, 534, 538-539, 548, 553-554, 560, 753
Poisson's ratio 607, 613-616, 625-630, 645, 753
Polarity 133, 174, 712
Polarization 171-175, 232, 753
Poling 135, 170-176, 753
Polybutadiene 184
Polydimethylsiloxane 184
Polymer 145, 170, 173, 469, 711
Popliteal fossa 753
Poroelastic 645, 753

Positive predictive value (PPV) 516, 520-524, 753
Post-processing 195, 199, 202, 205, 211, 220, 225-229, 237, 239, 247, 319-320, 337
  curves 320
  definition of 199, 753
Potential energy 180, 529-532, 540-542, 548, 557, 561, 572-573, 753
Power 529
  amplitude vs. pulse inversion 478
  (amplitude) modulation 195, 280, 478-486, 712-713
  definition of 62, 529, 753
  gain 195
  limits (bioeffects) 431, 438-441, 445, 451, 714
  numbers raised to (exponent) 7-9, 33
  ratio 64-69, 84, 753
  relationship to amplitude 62, 68, 77, 195, 206, 664
  relationship to intensity 63, 143, 176, 195, 206, 216, 267, 432, 438, 704
  relationship to work 529-530
  transmit *See* Transmit: power
  units of 13, 62, 529, 760
Power Doppler 356-363, 368, 415-418, 449, 476, 685, 698, 707, 731, 744
  directional 357-360, 368
  harmonic 459, 476
  See also Angio
Precautions (standard) 595, 757
Pre-compensated (TGCs) 218-220, 753
Preload 753
Pre-processing 195, 199, 205, 211, 225, 239, 753
Presets 704-705, 714, 736
Pressure
  acoustic 42, 62, 253, 274, 428-432, 439-440, 445, 453, 464, 470, 664, 665, 681, 711-712
  and compressibility 56, 429-430, 442, 612, 617-618, 636, 702
  and respiration 568-570, 584, 589, 617
  and volume 534, 548, 553-554, 561, 564-567, 575
  characteristics of waveform 552, 565, 572-575, 577, 579, 584-587
  definition of 13, 42, 529, 753
  dynamic 529, 543, 566, 570, 584
  gradient 332, 398, 413, 537-548, 551, 554, 557, 560-566, 569, 572-573, 576-580, 590, 717-719
    and peak velocity 332-333, 565, 717
    definition of 13, 753
  hydrostatic 532, 539-541, 548, 551, 566-570, 584, 589, 748
  isovolumic systolic 560, 578, 749

of the probe 389, 617, 618, 634, 639, 678-681, 702, 708-710 *See also* Tissue: compression of
output 186, 206, 565, 575
pulse 361, 552, 565-566, 582, 754
transmural 566, 570-571, 590, 759
units of 13, 42
Probe 169, 188, 677, 703
pencil (Pedof) 151, 312, 411, 714, 752
See also Transducer
Processing 111, 251-252, 260-263, 271-282, 287, 288, 293-295, 753
of data 193-195, 199-206, 211-215, 218-229, 236-239, 245-247, 277, 635, 641, 644-646
parallel (scanned modality) 111-113, 118-120, 125, 159, 162, 164, 168, 215, 221, 224, 260-261, 271-273, 288, 293-294, 383, 735-736, 752
Processor 221, 224, 244, 635
Progressive (monitor / display) 753
Prone 679
Propagation 39-42, 46, 301, 321, 607-613, 617-625, 636, 666, 753
Propagation velocity (speed)
analogy 55-56
and axial resolution 110
and density 60, 67, 76, 88, 90, 96, 100, 395, 412, 460, 463, 612, 624, 629-630, 636, 687
and frequency of operation 110, 136, 176, 323, 665
and incident angle 79-81, 93-95, 100, 323, 385, 665, 716
and ultrasound 21-22, 35, 46, 55, 60, 109, 281, 394, 408, 612, 665
and wavelength 305-306, 373, 460, 642, 665
definition of 46, 753
in the body 21, 59, 93-96, 281, 409, 463, 612, 618, 624, 665, 702
of longitudinal wave
See Longitudinal: wave: propagation
of transverse/shear wave
See Transverse: waves: speed
in various materials 58, 68, 78-80, 96, 136, 184, 409, 612, 665
units of 13, 46, 76
wave parameter 44-48, 110, 121, 303
Proportionality 24, 35
definition of 16-17, 754
direct (non-linear)
See Direct proportionality
inverse *See* Inverse proportionality
linear *See* Linear: proportionality
Prosthetic 94
valve 59, 85-86, 285, 391-392, 395, 398-400, 412, 415, 723

Prudent use 427, 432, 438, 443-446, 449, 451, 455
Pseudoaneurysm 367, 754
Pseudo MR 398
Pulmonic stenosis 754
Pulsatile flow 539, 543, 551-553, 565-566, 575, 584-587, 710, 754
Pulse
and modality 105, 110, 113-114, 205, 215-216
duration (PD) 109, 121, 205, 263, 432-433, 446-447, 451, 473, 618
and duty factor 106-109, 216, 428, 435-436, 451, 715
definition of 13, 105, 107, 113, 127, 754
vs. bandwidth 125-128, 137, 147, 467, 485
inversion (phase inversion) 712-713, 754
length 105-110, 115-116, 126-128, 139, 366, 367
and frequency 110, 115
pressure 361, 552, 565-566, 582, 754
Pulse average and temporal average (PA, TA) 433-439, 451, 455, 618
See also Intensity: PA and TA
Pulsed mode 172, 176, 374
Pulsed wave (PW) mode 108, 110, 126
advantages of 104, 110, 328, 666
and beam shape 138-139, 715
and Doppler *See* PW Doppler
and frequency of operation 136, 172
and piezoelectric material 136
and timing 110, 321, 378, 432
and ultrasound 111-114, 188, 191, 666
definition of 105, 107, 111, 754
duration 105, 114, 715
foundational diagram 110, 122, 432
parameters 111, 113, 121, 127, 139
distance related 107, 109
time related 105, 108
repetition period 115
spatial pulse length 107-110, 115-116, 126-128, 137
Pulser 204, 214, 754
transmit beamformer 205, 215, 313
Pulse repetition frequency (PRF) 13, 116, 126, 205, 344, 361-365, 380-381, 396, 410, 417-419, 437, 446-447, 746, 754
and imaging depth 109, 114, 329, 439, 724-725
definition of 106, 121, 127, 313, 322
equation 106, 115, 121, 127, 322-323, 343, 374, 724-725
Pulse repetition period (PRP) 396, 432-433, 451, 707, 724, 735

and imaging depth 109, 114, 126, 324-329, 441, 707, 724
and propagation velocity 323
definition of 13, 106, 121, 127, 313, 754
equation 106-107, 114, 117, 121, 127, 322, 433, 436
Pulse Schlieren system 440
Purewave *See* PMN-PT crystal
PW Doppler 111-115, 121, 126, 204, 216, 240, 313, 315, 321-330, 334, 337, 339, 370-374, 396, 398, 410-415, 432, 436-438, 577, 618, 714, 717, 722-727, 754
scales 324, 724, 727
PZT (lead zirconate titanate) 88-89, 131, 135, 144-145, 170-171, 174-176, 184-188, 754

Q

QIBA (Quantitative Imaging Biomarker Alliance) 642-644
QLED (monitor) 245-246
See also Monitors
Quadrant 311, 314
of a circle 30, 35, 754
Quadrature detection 314-315, 319, 411, 754
Quality
assurance 440, 489-526, 754
factor 123, 128, 147, 152, 176, 754
image 396, 403-404, 407, 410, 641, 655, 663, 703-713
index 291
Quartz 135

R

Radial resolution 741
See also Axial, Longitudinal, Depth *and* Range resolution *entries*
Radius
and bubbles 471-473
and calculations 8, 13, 25, 230-231, 249, 535-538, 544, 548, 556, 561, 580
and resistance 535-538, 548, 556, 559, 563, 565, 572, 588
definition of 754
Range
accuracy 495
ambiguity 104-105, 111, 115, 126, 322, 328-330, 371-374, 378, 381-382, 396, 411, 423, 707, 725-727, 754
audible 53
diagnostic 54-55, 69, 745
display 746
dynamic *See* Dynamic range (DNR)
of sound 54

resolution 104-108, 127, 146, 150, 322, 328-329, 741
    See also Axial, Depth, Longitudinal, *and* Radial resolution *entries*
  specificity 104, 107, 110, 126, 322-323, 328-329, 371-374, 714, 716, 726-727
Rarefaction 40, 430, 442-446, 455, 665
  and compression 40, 43, 46-47, 68, 301, 429, 441, 455, 463-464, 470-472, 477-478, 608, 612, 617, 620, 622, 711
  definition of 41, 754
Rational numbers 3
Rayleigh scattering 75-76, 88, 91-92, 96, 100, 124, 308, 315, 388, 412, 415, 418, 460, 654, 713, 722, 727, 729, 754; *See also* Scattering
Rayls 13, 76-77, 96, 754
Reactive hyperemia 754
Read zoom 237-239, 751
    See also Non-acoustic zoom
Real-time imaging 194, 237, 241, 248, 271, 280, 282, 287, 366, 477, 641, 663, 667, 686
  basic processes 194, 241
  definition of 241, 754
Receive
  beam 111-112, 161-163, 222, 263-266, 271, 294, 715-716
  focus 158, 161-168, 263, 268, 272, 277, 296, 746
  gain 66, 195-199, 206-209, 220, 247, 337, 340-341, 502-504, 706, 712, 717, 720-722, 729, 731, 754
    and TGCs 208-210, 217-220, 225, 247-248, 706
  line 111, 163, 754
Receiver 195-199, 204-214, 220-225, 240, 247-248, 263, 272, 279, 322, 754
Reciprocal 6-7, 9, 12-13, 19, 25, 35, 45, 125, 754
Reconstructed signal 200-203
Rectification 212-213, 754
Red blood cells (RBCs) *See* Cell: red blood
Reflection
  acoustic 76-78, 88, 96, 104, 177, 184, 204, 225, 665
  and diagnostic ultrasound 72-73, 91, 144, 213-214, 308, 310, 460, 642, 684, 687, 711
  angle 71-75, 79, 654, 687, 692-693, 740
  definition of 72, 755
  equation 77-78, 88, 97, 100, 460
  geometric aspects 73, 85, 100
  mode 20, 755

percentage 77-78, 88-90, 96-100, 309, 400, 422, 460, 575
specular 74-75, 83-88, 92, 96, 100, 225, 308, 359, 378-379, 386-389, 393, 396-398, 402, 415, 423, 465, 654, 685, 687, 692-693, 707, 722, 757
    See also Specular reflection
total internal 81-82, 94-95, 100, 381, 400-401, 417, 693, 716, 758
Refraction
  and incident angle 79-83, 94-95, 385, 401, 665, 693
  and transmission angle 81, 93, 693, 716
  artifact 378-386, 393, 400-401, 417, 423, 692, 755
  definition of 78-79, 100, 755
  effects of 92, 184, 545, 695
  in the body 92, 204, 530, 665, 693, 716
    See also Snell's law
Refractive shadowing 93-94, 402, 755
  edge shadowing 258, 379, 400-401, 692, 695
Refractory period 739, 755
Regurgitation 310, 327, 352, 355, 366, 578-580, 708
  aortic 578; *See also* Aorta: insufficiency
  definition of 755
  mitral regurgitant fraction 721, 751
  pulmonary valve 327
Reject 199, 206, 213, 248, 317, 320, 332, 362, 755
  and signal processing 723, 731
Relative
  motion 301-308, 357, 373, 405, 416, 655
    and Doppler effect 301, 305, 308
  near field 86
  permittivity 181
  relationship 2, 23, 35, 562
  shift 303
Renal 357, 368, 577, 640, 704-705, 726, 728
Replenishment (contrast) 475, 477, 483
Resistance 13, 529, 534-535
  distal 532, 544, 556-557, 573, 578-579, 584, 746
  effective 555-557, 561-563, 572, 746
  equation 534-538, 548, 555-556, 572, 589
  level (infection) 493
  peripheral 552, 557, 560-566, 570, 752
  to flow 530-538, 544, 548, 555-562, 566, 570-579, 584, 588-589, 652
Res mode (zoom) 237
Resolution 96, 252-253, 287-288
  apparent 740
  axial/depth/longitudinal/radial/range
    See Axial, Depth, Longitudinal, Radial, *and* Range resolution *entries*

angular/azimuthal/lateral/side-by-side/transverse
    See Angular, Azimuthal, Lateral, Side-by-side, *and* Transverse resolution *entries*
  contrast *See* Contrast resolution
  detail *See* Detail resolution
  elevation *See* Elevation resolution
  improving 261, 264-266, 271-272, 276, 280, 294, 404-410, 461, 464, 466, 623, 705-706, 713, 734-736
  perceived 54, 237
  spatial 483, 667
  temporal *See* Temporal resolution
  testing 503-505, 513
Resonance 134-137, 168, 462, 469-480, 662-663
Respiration 554, 568-570, 584, 589
  and imaging 287, 415-417, 617-618, 641, 710, 713
  effects on venous flow 307, 316, 361, 554, 568-570, 584, 589
Retinaculum 684, 689, 694
Retrograde 352, 354, 568
Retrospective
  focusing 267-277, 293-294, 338, 383, 483, 755
  gating 148-149, 267
Reverberation 86, 185, 222, 257, 260, 279, 379, 386-400, 408, 412, 423
  artifact 145, 184, 191, 257, 279, 379, 382-394, 399, 408, 423, 461, 465-466, 506, 655, 682, 692-698, 755
  complex cause of 387
  definition of 184, 386
  simple cause of 145, 386
Reynolds number 527, 546-547, 560, 755
    See also Turbulent flow
RF signal 207-212, 225, 248, 378, 422-423, 617
Rib 152-154, 161-163, 177, 390, 393, 400, 465-466, 635, 670, 696, 710
Right
  of refusal 597, 755
  side of heart 554, 557, 560-570, 584-585, 589, 658
Ring down artifact 87, 379, 382, 390, 394, 415, 423, 441, 692, 706, 755
Ring time 147, 755
Rotation (cardiac) 475, 652
Rouleaux formation 309-310, 366, 755
Roundtrip effect 18, 20, 35, 60, 108, 115, 127, 147, 150, 305, 321, 755
Rubber 184, 395, 613, 615
Rubor 745
Run Length Encoding (RLE) 243

S

Sagittal plane 254, 284, 678, 755
Sampling 322-324
  of signal 200-202
  rate 111, 201-204, 248, 322-324, 755
  volume (Doppler) 113-114, 126, 277, 314, 326-331, 339-340, 371, 398, 411-417, 502, 576-577, 581-582, 715-717, 722, 746
Saturation
  circuit 723
  definition of 502, 755
  of wall filters 318, 382, 423, 496
Scalar 46
Scales (Doppler) 324, 330, 381, 410-411, 717, 721-727, 732, 746
Scan
  converter 202, 204, 220-225, 236-238, 248, 272, 745, 755
  region 111, 116, 120, 152-153, 157, 165, 216, 238, 269-274, 280, 336-337, 368, 374, 409-410, 636, 656, 658, 681, 707, 713-717, 722, 736
Scanned modalities 216, 221, 240, 428, 436-437
  and temporal resolution 116-118, 334-335
  color and temporal resolution 119, 734
  definition of 111-113, 128, 755
  vs. non-scanned 334, 428, 436-437, 455
Scattering 83, 91, 96, 100, 308-309, 315, 320, 359, 398, 440, 496
  and strain 645
  definition of 75, 654, 741, 755
  in the body 85-88, 92, 388, 474, 613, 687
  Rayleigh 75-76, 88, 91-92, 96, 100, 124, 308, 315, 388, 412-418, 460, 654, 713, 722, 727, 729, 754
Schlieren image 440-441, 454, 622, 662
Secant 29
Sector 154, 755
  image creation 163, 166, 177, 188, 222-223, 473-474, 713
  transducer, mechanical 153-154
  transducer, phased array 161-162, 177, 276, 278, 344-348, 753
Seizure 668
Sensitivity 99, 120-127, 135-136, 143-144, 150, 152, 163, 168-171, 176, 180-185, 196, 213, 223, 229-231, 247, 252-256, 267, 272-277, 291, 294, 309, 321, 328-330, 337-340, 355-358, 366, 371, 374-375, 404-410, 439-440, 452, 456, 475, 502, 504, 657, 702-717, 721-735, 755
  equation 521-524

inadequate (color dropout) 380-381, 417-418, 717, 722, 727, 731
  statistical 520-524, 755
Sensor 285, 644
Sepia 286, 367
Septal
  defect 392, 398
  occluder 284-285, 391-392, 398, 402
    See also Amplatzer device
  structure 284, 398, 412, 656
Sequencing 156-158, 164-168, 177, 270, 755
Sequential
  B-mode 112
  color Doppler 112, 334-343, 372, 416, 436, 729-736
  imaging 112-119, 152, 170, 215-217, 221, 225, 251-253, 256, 259, 261, 264, 270-272, 276, 293-294, 334-337, 383, 396, 405, 416-417, 436-437, 442, 729-736, 755
Shades of gray 212, 225-227, 235, 247, 315, 366; See also Grayscale
Shadowing 400, 462, 634, 637, 655, 688-689, 716
  artifact 83, 91, 378-379, 391, 399-403, 417, 474, 692-698, 711-713, 722, 731
  cause of 91-93, 153-154, 257, 386, 391, 400, 422, 506, 687, 710, 755
  dirty 387, 695
Shear
  modulus (G) 607-608, 616-619, 625-626, 629-630, 756
  strain imaging 271, 637, 645-646, 658
  stress 484, 529, 534, 560, 608-610, 627
  wave 607, 612-630, 710
    depiction of 613, 620-624
    elastography (SWE) 40, 160, 224, 277, 294, 437, 619, 624, 634-645, 710-711
    equation 613
    generation 619-629, 635, 639, 644
    imaging 224, 277, 624-625
    speed (SWS) 613-630, 636-646, 710-711, 756
Sheath 688-689
Shift (Doppler frequency) 118, 151, 204, 299-336, 342, 344, 349, 354-357, 360, 362, 372-374, 381, 411-412, 418, 420, 476, 502, 574-576, 585, 716-717, 721-734, 746
Shockwave 38, 429-430, 621-622
Short axis (SAX) 678-679, 683-684, 689, 693, 696, 707, 719-720
Short duration pulse 618
Shunt 300
  and flow 120, 562, 573, 584

Side-by-side resolution 139, 149
  See also Angular, Azimuthal, Lateral, and Transverse resolution entries
Side lobes artifact 199, 382, 393, 655, 682, 756
Siescape 278
Signal
  amplitudes 26, 62, 92, 110, 197-198, 205-208, 211-214, 221, 320, 337, 340-341, 356, 365, 381, 411, 414, 420, 460-463, 469-470, 474-475, 479, 575, 711
  conversion 200, 204-206, 212, 220-225, 272
  definition of 150, 194-196, 756
  detection 182, 185, 204, 206, 212-213, 279, 314, 386, 460, 715-716
    See also Demodulation
  digital 200-201, 745
  reflection (echogenicity) 82-85, 91-93, 99, 460, 684, 687-688
  RF (radio frequency) See RF signal
  strength and color wall filtering 342, 365, 731, 734
Signal-to-noise ratio (SNR) 252-259, 267, 275, 280, 293
  apparent 196-198, 340, 740
  calculating improvements 254-256, 404
  definition of 195, 756
  determining good SNR 143, 195-196, 254, 366, 720-721
  gain 196-197, 293, 720-721
  improving 62, 171, 196-197, 253-259, 262, 267, 269, 275, 293-294, 337, 339, 355, 403-406, 460, 467-468, 475-480, 486, 676, 682, 705, 707, 721-722, 730, 734
  true vs. apparent 196, 247, 340
Silicon 184, 187, 191
Simplified law of hemodynamics 553-554, 560, 565, 572-575, 590, 756
Sine (sin) 28-29, 35, 80, 95, 202, 314, 570, 756
Single
  crystal (PMN-PT) 154, 171, 174, 185, 187, 223, 703, 756
  focus 252, 263-270, 275-277, 294
Skin 493-494, 514, 554, 571, 595, 614, 618, 645, 666, 670, 679, 690, 706-710, 717
  and speed of sound 409, 465, 687
  dry 708
  propagation velocity of 59, 409
Skull 500, 511, 514-515, 662-666, 716
Slice thickness 284, 382, 384, 507
  and elevation 168
  artifacts 169
  See also Elevation: resolution

Slider *See* Time gain compensation (TGC)
Sliding receive filters 124
　and bandwidth 124
　dynamic frequency tuning 705, 746
Slope 311, 316, 332, 608, 610, 617, 629, 717
Slow flow
　detection of 360, 723-724, 731-734
　　See also Microvascular
　imaging 476
Smoothing 262-263
　and envelope detection 212-213
Snell's law 80, 385, 400-401, 756
　application of 81, 94, 385
　equation 80
　refraction 94, 100, 385
Soap 493
Soft tissue 83-85, 95-96, 100, 442-449, 612-620, 630, 667, 704
　density of 612, 624, 629-630, 636, 664, 687
　propagation velocity in 59, 271, 281, 395, 409-410, 612, 665
Sono CT 405; *See also* Crossbeam imaging
Sonoelastography 756
Sonographer 490-491
　and safety 594, 597-598, 604-605
　neutral posture 598, 600-603, 710
Sonoporation 484-485
Sonothrombolysis 484
Sound
　audible range 53, 748
　beam 111, 386, 679, 686-687, 719, 741
　classification 39-41, 53-54, 69
　definition of 756
　infrasound 53, 69, 749
　Korotokov 749
　propagation velocity 42, 46, 163, 281, 305
　ranges 54
　speed compensation 281, 295, 396, 756
　speed of *See* Speed: of sound
　ultrasound 53, 133, 759
　　See also Ultrasound
　waves 41, 44-47, 53, 68, 195, 213, 301, 462, 470, 608-609, 617, 621-623, 629
Sparse matrix 169, 482, 756
Spatial
　averaging (processing) 262-263, 293-294, 741, 756
　compound imaging 257-262, 271, 275-276, 292-294, 405-406, 707
　definition of 107, 756
　filtering / smoothing 262
　intensity 455
　　average (SA) 433-436, 446, 451, 581
　　conversion (SP and SA) 436, 451

　　peak (SP) 433-436, 441, 451
　　interpolation 243-244
　　pulse length *See* Spatial pulse length (SPL)
Spatial compounding
　　See Crossbeam imaging
Spatial pulse length (SPL) 13, 115, 252, 340, 383, 408, 414, 756
　and axial resolution 467-468, 485
　and contrast signals 479
　and range resolution 107-108, 137, 144, 146-147, 150, 408
　and wavelength 109
　definition of 107, 121
　equation 109, 121, 177
Spatiotemporal filters 361-363, 368-369, 371, 375, 417, 658, 707, 734, 756
Speakers (audio) 319
Specificity 104-105, 322, 489, 516, 520-524, 714, 716, 726-727, 756
　equation 520-524
Speckle 379, 382, 390, 396, 403-406, 420-421, 617, 624, 630, 707, 721, 731; *See also* Noise
　and strain 654-658, 709
　definition of 87, 196, 254, 403, 407, 654, 744, 756
　pattern 655
　reduction of 254-257, 261, 293, 361-362, 404-407, 421, 655, 707, 721, 756
　tracking 361, 442-443, 446, 448, 450, 456, 652-658, 756
Spectral
　broadening 310, 333-337, 381-382, 413, 423, 495, 502, 577-579, 719, 722, 756; *See also* Artifact: spectral spread (broadening)
　Doppler 118, 196, 199, 204, 256, 277, 279, 299-300, 312-322, 327, 334-344, 354-355, 361-366, 371, 374, 378-385, 398, 412-418, 449, 495, 551-552, 565, 569, 574-580, 585, 589-590, 701-702, 713, 717-722, 727-736
　　and flow direction 51, 574
　　bidirectional 315
　　definition of 757
　　display 319, 746
　　dropout 95, 381-382, 417-418, 423, 714, 757
　　processes 196, 320
　　vs. color Doppler 118, 334, 337, 447, 727, 731
　　wall filters 317-319, 582-583, 722-724
　mirroring (artifact) 398, 411, 757
　window 326-328, 381, 576-577, 716-719, 722, 746, 757

Spectroscopy 663
Specular reflection 75, 83, 91, 225, 359, 685, 687, 707, 722
　and artifacts 96, 259, 316, 378-379, 386-389, 393, 396-405, 423, 465, 692-693, 707
　definition of 74, 85, 654, 757
Speed
　error (artifact) 22, 47, 60, 378-382, 394-396, 408, 422-423, 710, 757
　longitudinal (compression) wave 612-613, 619, 622-623
　longitudinal (transverse) wave 46, 750
　of sound 13, 21-22, 44-47, 57-58, 104, 108, 115, 126, 137, 152, 172, 251, 271, 281, 295, 382, 395-396, 408-409, 447, 466, 497, 499, 503-504, 612, 621-622, 629, 640, 667, 687, 705
　shear wave (SWS) *See* Shear: wave: speed
Sphygmomanometer 757
Spine 278, 284, 422, 444, 450, 456, 598, 601
SPL *See* Spatial pulse length
Spontaneous contrast 309
　　See also Rouleaux
Spores 493
Stable cavitation 429, 455, 665
Standard precautions 595, 757
Standoff (acoustic) 91, 719
Standoff pad 91, 698, 706-707, 720, 757
Static
　B-Scan 151, 153
　pressure 529, 553
　strain elastography 618, 624, 630, 634-646, 708-709, 757
Statistical 516
　indices 490, 516-518, 521-522
　parameters 520
　testing 451, 516-517, 523
Steady-state flow 537-544, 552-553, 565, 757
Steering
　and focusing 151, 158, 161, 164, 187, 215, 223, 270, 281, 314, 321, 466, 482
　angle of 87, 158, 165, 331, 335, 389, 405, 423, 471, 698, 731, 740
　beam 92, 163, 310, 313, 344, 346, 685-686, 741
　electronic 158-164, 176, 685, 707, 719-722, 747
　image 165, 169, 405, 693, 698
　lines 310, 314, 321, 331, 335, 344-352, 372
　manual 151, 158, 750
　mechanical 131, 151-155, 159, 162, 164, 167, 176, 750

Stenosis
  aortic 580, 665, 668, 740
  critical 418, 420, 559, 745
  definition of 300, 757
  general 259, 322, 327, 469, 541, 543, 547, 551, 557, 571-580, 585, 590, 652, 717
  pulmonary 754
  subcritical 559, 571, 573-574, 757
Stent 59, 259, 390, 586-587, 615
Sterilization 492-494, 524, 757
Stiffness 56-60, 68, 463, 565, 610-612, 616-617, 624-625, 630, 633-646, 667, 687, 708-710, 757
St. Jude prosthetic mitral valve 391, 399-400
Storage (data) See Data: storage
Strain (ε)
  definition of 56, 609, 613-616, 629, 652, 757
  equation 626-629, 653-654
  imaging 271, 609, 617, 634-645, 651-660, 708-709
  inducing 617-619, 653
  of muscle 691
  rate 640, 654, 657
  static elastography
    See Static: strain elastography
Stress (σ)
  definition of 56, 608, 617, 629, 635, 757
  equation 608, 611, 626-629
  shear 484, 529, 534, 560, 608-610, 627
String flow 559, 574
String phantom 523
Stroke volume (SV) 565, 573, 578-581, 590, 757
Subcritical stenosis See Stenosis: subcritical
Subcutaneous 571
Subluxation 686
Subpixel 232
Substrate 184
Superposition 268, 294, 623, 757
  See also Interference: constructive
Supersonic 622-624, 629-630
Supine 567-568, 637, 641, 679, 757
Suprasternal 152, 717
Surface rendering 282, 358-363
  and color Doppler 757
Swept gain compensation (TGC) 208
Sympathetic nervous system 560, 757
Synovitis 682, 685
Synthetic
  aperture 267-270, 277, 293-296, 757
  polymers 469, 711; See also Polymer
Systole / Systolic 240, 350-351, 369-370, 381, 420, 543, 575-584, 652, 655, 658, 758
  flow 350, 566, 575, 577-578, 583, 654, 758

T

Tamponade 758
TAMV (time average mean velocity) 300, 580-583, 590, 758
Tangent 29, 160, 400, 758
Technical director 491, 594
TEE (transesophageal echo) 162, 310, 346-348, 391, 398-402, 412-413, 460, 492-493
Temperature 234, 758
  and propagation velocity 58
  as an acoustic variable 42-43, 68, 428
  Curie 135, 173, 176; See also Curie point
  measuring 43, 430, 438, 442-443, 447-448, 456, 663-664, 667
  threshold 429-430, 445, 447-448
  See also Denature
Temporal
  artifacts 204
  distortion 245, 256, 355, 373, 656, 758
  interpolation 243-245
  resolution 103, 110-111, 116-122, 128, 155-156, 170, 233, 237, 241, 249-258, 261-277, 281, 284, 292-294, 334-340, 355, 357, 367-368, 371, 374, 405, 658, 701, 729-736, 758
    and color Doppler 118-119, 271, 334-336, 729-735
    and monitor display 233, 237
    and sequential image generation 170, 271, 336-337, 729, 733-736
    and ultrafast image generation 337, 340, 736
    definition of 110, 111, 758
    degraded 258, 261, 266, 270, 292-293, 405, 467-468, 729, 735
    for non-scanned modalities 116, 118
    for scanned modalities 118
    improving / optimizing 120, 271, 274, 294, 337, 658, 734-736
Tendinosis 690, 693
Tendon 636-645, 676-693, 698, 722
  acoustic appearance of 214, 691-692, 694, 697
  properties of 678, 690, 692
Tendonitis 55
Thalamus 662
Therapeutic 55, 188, 191, 484, 486, 661-664, 667
Thermal
  bioeffects 85, 103, 107, 111, 127-128, 216, 427-443, 447-448, 455, 665-667, 715, 758
  energy 216, 530, 663-668
  indices 441-448, 456, 758
    TI 427, 441-450, 456, 758
    TIB See TIB (thermal index bone)
    TIC See TIC (thermal index cranial bone)
    TIS See TIS (thermal index soft tissue)
  noise 199, 254
Thermometry 663, 667-668, 670
Threshold effect 420, 430, 438, 729, 758
Thrombosis 357
Thrombus 83, 92, 226-229, 247, 259, 294, 309, 386, 389, 393, 465, 468, 484, 505, 571
Through plane motion 655, 658
Thyroid 87, 260, 279-280, 291, 362-363, 396-397, 407, 416-417, 599, 607, 617, 635, 639, 663, 734
TIB (thermal index bone) 442-443, 446, 448, 450, 456, 758
TIC (thermal index cranial bone) 442-443, 446, 456, 758
Time 159-160, 758
  and frequency 45, 271, 320, 335
  and PW 107, 110-111, 122, 724
  and volume 533-534, 548, 561, 575, 580; See also Capacitance
  frame See Frame: time
  interval 200, 202, 477, 654, 663
  of exposure 430, 434-435, 443-451, 455, 712, 714
Time gain compensation (TGC) 279
  and imaging situations 219
  and receiver gain 209, 706
  definition of 208, 758
  zones and depth 209, 247-248
Tint (colorization) 367, 684-685, 698, 758
Tissue 570-571, 663
  aberration correction 705
  adipose 702; See also Fat
  and waves 39, 53, 429-430, 619-620
  appearance (signature) 83, 87, 386, 608, 687-688, 690, 697
  colorization (grayscale) 221-222, 230, 252
  colorization (tint) See Tint
  compression of 389, 617, 634-636, 639, 641, 645-646, 708-710
  Doppler imaging (TDI) 199, 640, 652, 654, 758
  harmonic imaging (THI) 462-464, 467, 473-477, 486, 681-682, 751
  mismatch 91, 135
  signals (Doppler) 357, 360-362, 367-368, 375, 734
  See also Soft tissue
TIS (thermal index soft tissue) 442-443, 446, 448, 450, 456, 758
TJC (The Joint Commission) 595
Tomography 285
  computed (CT) 251, 285-287, 293, 295-296, 484, 635, 666

positron emission (PET) 251, 285, 287, 293, 295
Torsion 652-653, 658
Tortuosity 344, 349, 418, 728, 758
Total internal reflection 81-82, 95, 100, 381, 400-401, 417, 693, 716, 758
Tracing 291
Tracking *See* Speckle: tracking
Transcranial 442, 444, 448, 450, 456, 662
　Doppler 357, 716-717, 730, 758
Transcutaneous oxygen tension measurements (toPo2) 758
Transducer
　1.5D array *See* 1.5-D array
　1D array *See* 1-D array
　2D array *See* 2-D array
　beam characteristics 138
　block diagram 150, 184-185
　cardiac 711
　care of 489, 492, 594
　CMUT 151, 179-192, 195, 404, 645
　crystal 53, 62, 89-90, 136, 145, 151-155, 170
　curved linear 154, 157-158, 167-168, 171, 177, 278, 346-348, 383, 506, 676, 678, 698, 745
　deep abdominal (DAX) 703-704, 728
　definition of 132-133, 176, 758
　endovaginal 447, 493
　evolution of 144, 151-155, 179-180, 224
　helmet 662, 666
　"hockey stick" 676-678, 698
　impulse response 137
　linear 278, 346-351, 645, 676-678, 685, 698, 707, 719-720
　　switched array 156-158, 163-164, 750
　maneuver 707, 709-710, 716, 719-720, 722
　　heel-toe 693, 719-720
　　toggle 693, 719-720
　mechanical 151-155, 329, 373, 411
　　annular array 156, 750
　　sector *See* Sector
　　steering *See* Steering: mechanical
　notch 678-679
　orientation 291, 353, 678-679, 698, 710
　Pedof *See* Pedof transducer
　　See also Blind transducer
　　See also Pencil probe transducer
　phased array 51, 151, 156-158, 161, 163-169, 172, 177, 252, 265, 312-313, 329, 394, 408, 413, 482, 645, 663, 716, 750
　　sector 161-162, 177, 276, 278, 344, 346, 347, 348, 753
　PZT (lead zirconate titanate) *See* PZT
　single crystal (PMN-PT) *See* PMN-PT
　single disc 138-139

transcatheter 55, 284, 392
transrectal *See* Transrectal
　ultrasound 133, 600, 676, 702, 705, 711, 717, 722, 728, 759
wireless 171-172
Transesophageal echo (TEE) *See* TEE
Transient
　cavitation *See* Inertial cavitation
　elastography 639
Translation 278, 652
　cardiac motion 284, 652, 655
　language 596
Transmission
　angle 71-81, 94-95, 257, 321, 716, 740
　equation 77
　mode 20, 204, 442, 758
　percentage 74, 77-78, 89-91, 96-100, 144, 400
Transmit 204, 208
　aperture 215-216, 252-254, 265, 268
　beamformer *See* Beamformer
　definition of 263, 758
　foci 143, 158, 161-162, 168, 217, 225, 254, 263-264, 268-270-277, 294, 471, 704, 751
　frequency *See* Operating frequency
　gain 62, 195, 759
　power 62, 63, 66, 111, 124, 143, 194-198, 206, 216-217, 225, 247-248, 267, 269, 280, 313, 365-366, 380-381, 412-417, 431-432, 437-438, 460, 477, 479, 503-504, 662, 676, 704-717, 728, 731, 759
　　See also Output: power
　and frequency 216, 676
　voltage 62-65, 133, 171-172, 195, 432, 437-438, 705, 715
Transmitter 205-206, 322, 759
Transmural pressure 566, 570-571, 590, 759
Transorbital 759
Transrectal 392, 493
Transtemporal 759
Transverse
　mode 39, 68
　resolution 149; *See also* Angular, Azimuthal, Lateral, *and* Side-by-side resolution *entries*
　view 83, 284, 635, 678
　waves 40-41, 68, 608-613, 620-621, 630, 759; *See also* Shear: wave
　speed *See* Shear: wave: speed
Trapezoidal format 164, 166, 278, 676-678, 698, 707, 759
Tricuspid valve 563, 579-580, 708
Triggered imaging 475-477, 483
Trigonometry 575, 627, 759
　definition of 27-31

in ultrasound 31, 35, 311
Trophic 759
True
　negative (TN) 518-523, 759
　positive (TP) 518-523, 759
　SNR 196
Truncation 243
TTE (transthoracic echo) 402
Tumor 357, 361-362, 645
　assessment of 483, 486, 637, 646
　　See also Lesion
　　See also Mass: abnormal tissue
Tunable frequency 191, 759
Turbulence 309, 326-327, 337, 560, 573, 576-577, 585-586, 759
Turbulent flow 527, 543-548, 759
Twinkle artifact 379, 382, 392-394, 423, 692, 696-697, 759
　See also Comet tail artifact
Twist 653, 658-659

U

Ultrafast
　Doppler 299, 334-342, 361, 368, 371, 374, 417, 729-736, 759
　imaging 112, 119, 160, 216, 224, 271, 274, 277, 294, 296, 334-342, 362, 368, 371, 379, 405, 417, 437, 623-624, 729-736, 759
Ultrasonic 663-667, 670
Ultrasound
　contrast agents *See* Contrast: agent
　coupling gel *See* Gel
　definition of 53, 69, 759
　diagnostic 20-22, 49, 53-54, 69, 105, 110-113, 185-191, 211, 243, 264, 291, 300, 307-308, 319, 377, 394, 404, 430-431, 439, 443-451, 456, 460, 462, 469, 484, 608, 612, 646, 664, 686, 697, 734
　equipment testing 495
　focused (FUS) *See* Focused ultrasound; *See also* HIFU
　functional (fUltrasound) 361, 375
　guidance 662-663, 667-670
　system 22, 194, 201, 206-208, 214, 218-225, 231, 598-603, 642, 676, 681, 702, 709, 732
　　backend 226, 248, 272, 741
　　basic functions 194, 214
　　block diagram 205, 214-215, 312
　　presets *See* Presets
　therapeutic (physiotherapy) 55, 188, 191, 484, 486, 662-663, 667
Unfocused 139, 143, 160, 176, 272-273, 445, 456
Unidirectional Doppler 312, 315

Unit circle 27-31, 95, 759
Units (definition of) 6, 14, 759
Universal precautions
　　See Standard precautions
Unsteered 112, 160-166, 256, 346-348, 676, 683; See also Steering

V

Vacuum 39, 181, 759
Validation 495
Valsalva 569, 589
Valve 316, 568-569, 589, 722
　cardiac 85-86, 229, 241, 290, 327-328, 393, 467, 530, 552, 560-563, 578, 581, 584, 652, 668
　click 378, 381
　prosthetic 59, 85-86, 285, 391-392, 395, 398, 399-400, 412, 415, 723
　reflux 568-571, 589
Variable 4, 6, 17, 22, 80, 96, 306
　acoustic 42-43, 50, 61, 66-69, 428
　definition of 759
　determining dominance 23
　gain 318, 759
　relationship between 35
Vascular 153, 156-158, 163, 172, 227, 256, 278, 285, 307, 312, 330, 333, 363, 374-375, 420, 424, 441, 445, 448, 464, 476, 490, 551, 554, 562, 571-572, 574, 578-579, 584, 641, 667-668, 710, 717-723
Vasoconstrict 759
Vasodilate 572-573, 578-579, 590, 759
Vector 46, 368-369, 759
　flow (V Flow) imaging See V Flow
Vein / Venous 553-554, 563-571, 588-589, 710
　calf muscle pump See Calf muscle pump
　capacitance 554, 561, 566-569, 588-589, 750, 760
　definition of 759
　edema 568, 571
　elasticity 554, 570-571, 589
　femoral 368, 416, 584, 734
　hepatic 367, 585
　hypertension 571
　imaging 309, 569, 732
　insufficiency 568, 571
　jugular 260, 387-389, 585
　portal 343, 419, 480, 584, 710, 732
　pressure 554, 563-571, 584, 589
　　hydrostatic 566-568
　pulmonary 564
　refill time (VRT) 760
　reflux testing 569-570, 760
　resistance 562-563, 566, 570-571, 760

　spectrum 569, 584
　splenic 357
　valvular reflux See Valve: reflux
Velocity 529, 542
　and color Doppler 204, 334-339, 342, 351-352, 361, 417, 532-533, 552, 577, 722, 726, 734
　and Doppler shift 196, 204, 301-303, 311-324, 333, 575, 717, 722-723
　and volumetric flow 420, 531-548, 552, 558-559, 564-566, 572-579, 589, 652, 717-734
　definition of 46, 533, 543, 760
　maximum detectable 204, 325-329, 342, 365, 371, 410, 716-718, 724-727
　mean See Mean: velocity
　modal See Modal velocity
　peak See Peak: velocity
　time integral (VTI) See VTI
　units of 13, 46, 543, 579
Ventilation 494
Ventricular 652, 656, 658
　function 654
　opacification 752
Venule 562-563, 566-567, 571, 589
Vertebral artery 353-354, 422, 578, 760
Vertebral steal 578
Vessel
　blood 207, 209, 213, 229-230, 311, 326, 331-335, 339, 344, 349-356, 360-361, 369, 388, 411, 417, 475, 484, 543, 554, 558, 560, 563, 566, 571, 666, 684, 703, 707, 715-722, 729-734
　capacitance 529, 561, 589
　parallel connection 555-557, 561-563, 588-589
　resistance 529, 538, 556, 560, 573
　series connection 555, 557, 560, 562, 589
　walls 55, 85, 91, 165, 214, 222, 230, 241, 314, 326, 339, 349-352, 368, 370, 380, 388, 415, 418, 420, 531, 537, 540, 542, 548, 553, 557-561, 565-566, 570, 576-589, 722, 732
V Flow 368-370, 375, 420, 760
Video
　compression 211, 226, 241-245, 279, 320; See also Dynamic range (DNR)
　display 231, 236 See also Monitor
Virtual reality (VR) 246-249
Virtual source (focus) 269, 270, 295
Virus 493
Viscoelastic 642, 644-646
Viscosity 72, 534, 536, 642
　apparent 560, 741
　definition of 529, 534, 536, 558, 760

　effects 327, 418, 534-541, 547, 557-560, 572, 576-577, 588-590, 717
　of fluid 85, 370, 496, 529, 531, 536-548, 552, 557-560, 573, 587, 589, 646, 708
Voltage (Volts) (V) 13, 32-33, 50, 61-62, 68, 133-136, 150, 159, 171-187, 191, 195-196, 204-206, 210, 215-220, 248, 318, 415, 432, 437-438, 705, 715, 760
Volume
　and density 42
　calculating 8, 13, 204, 283-284, 533, 662
　change in 56, 529, 533-534, 548, 553-554, 561, 564, 570, 612, 628
　definition of 760
　imaging 282-291, 295, 482-486, 504
　of blood 554, 560-561, 564-567, 570, 573, 580-581, 588-589
　of sound 50
　sample (Doppler) See Sampling: volume
　stroke (SV) See Stroke volume
Volumetric flow (Q) 13, 300, 309, 372, 420, 527-548, 551-590, 652, 731, 734, 760; See also Flow (Q)
Voxel 663
VTI (velocity time integral) 580-581, 590, 760

W

Wall filter 299, 316-320, 332, 336-337, 342-344, 357, 360-366, 370-375, 380-381, 415-420, 582-584, 722-724, 731-734
　artifacts 380-381, 415, 419-420, 760
　color 336, 342-344, 360-361, 364-366, 372, 375, 419-420, 731-734
　definition of 316-317, 760
　effect of 316-317, 360-361, 365, 582-583, 723-724
　graphic depiction 316-319, 361, 364-365
　in spectral Doppler 364-365, 582-583, 722-724
　saturation See Circuit: saturation
　settings 318, 360, 366, 372-375, 419, 582-583, 723-724, 732
　spatiotemporal 361-363, 368-371
Wall Shear Stress (WSS) 299, 370-371, 375
Water 539, 615-616, 630, 663, 666
　absorption rates 85, 442, 448, 706
　and speed of sound 687
　bath 706-707
　boiling/freezing point of 43
　path scanners 91
　propagation velocitiy in 59, 184, 612
　tanks / hydrophones 439-440, 452-453, 502

Watts (W) 62-63, 530, 662
  definition of 13, 760
Wave
  amplitude 72, 294, 404, 565, 644
  characteristics in ultrasound 38, 41, 44, 53
  compression 57, 302, 613, 623-624, 635, 636; See also Wave: longitudinal (P-wave)
  definition of 38, 760
  direction and wavefront 72-74, 78, 86, 159-160, 612, 622
  energy 41, 68, 72, 74, 84, 87, 91, 96, 106, 204, 434
  longitudinal (P-wave) 608, 612-613, 619-622, 629-630
  parameters 44, 108-109, 121, 136
    time-related 53, 108
  propagation 39-41, 68, 76, 138-139, 301, 607-629, 636, 666
  speed
    longitudinal 612-613, 622-623, 629-630, 750
    shear (SWS) 613-630, 636-646, 710-711, 756
  types 38-40
    electromagnetic 39, 68, 199, 747
    longitudinal (P-wave) 40-41, 750
    mechanical 39, 42, 68, 212-213, 248, 428-429, 463, 469, 750
    shear / transverse (S-wave) 40, 68, 607-630, 710, 759
Waveform 204, 213, 216
  and unidirectional Doppler 300, 312
  characteristics of pressure 199, 552, 565, 572-579, 584-587
Wavefront 73-74, 77-80, 92-93, 104, 159-160, 268, 270, 301-304, 622, 760
Wavelength 87
  and frequency 54, 75, 92, 145, 301-304, 404-405, 410, 476, 665
  and period 41, 48, 304, 305
  and resolution 61, 87, 115, 403, 408-409, 654
  and spatial pulse length 109, 147, 383
  and the Doppler effect 301-308, 622
  and velocity 281, 304-305, 408-409, 622, 642
  definition of 13, 47, 760
  determining 48, 60-61, 68, 88, 121, 281
  equation 49, 60-61, 68, 121, 281, 303-305, 460, 664, 760
Whole blood 559-560; See also Blood
Window
  acoustic (CMUT) 184-185, 191

  cardiac / vascular 656-657, 716-722, 731
  spectral (Doppler)
    See Spectral: Doppler: window
Wireless transducers 171-172
Work 529-530
Write zoom 238-239, 280
  See also Acoustic: zoom
WRMSD (work-related musculoskeletal disorders) 593, 597, 605

X

X-ray 20, 31, 72, 236, 667
Xres 279-280

Y

Young's modulus (E) 608, 611, 615-619, 624-630, 636, 760

Z

Zone imaging 112, 224, 273, 276, 736, 760
Zoom 237-239, 707
  See also Non-acoustic zoom
  See also Read zoom

Appendix C
Abbreviations

Physical Units

Related to time:
- **P or T** — Period (seconds)
- **PD** — Pulse duration (the time for which the transmit pulse lasts)
- **PRP** — Pulse repetition period (the time to transmit and receive an acoustic line of data)
- **Frame time** — The time required to build up a frame = the time per acoustic line multiplied the total number of lines in the frame.

Related to frequency:
- f — Frequency (Hz)
- f_o — Operating or transmit frequency of a transducer (for diagnostic ultrasound 2-12 MHz common)
- **PRF** — Pulse repetition frequency = 1/PRP (typically less than 10 kHz)
- **Frame rate** — The reciprocal of the frame time (typically less than 100 Hz)
- **Hz** — Hertz = 1 cycle/second

Various parameters that have units of amplitude:
- **V** — Volts: unit of electromotive force
- **m** — Meters: unit of distance (metric system)
- **Z** — Rayls: unit of acoustic impedance
- **R** — Resistance, either electrical or to fluid flow
- **P** — Pressure: mmHg, atm, dynes/cm^2, kg/m^2, etc...,: unit of pressure (*not to be confused with P for period or P for power)

Related to power:
- **P** — Power: units of Watts (*not to be confused with P for period or P for pressure)
- **W** — Watts
- **I** — Intensity = power/area = W/m^2
- **dB** — Decibels: a logarithmic power ratio

Related to distance:
- **d** — distance (*not to be confused with D or d for diameter)
- **λ** — Lambda: wavelength which has units of distance
- **SPL** — Spatial Pulse Length
- **NZL** — The distance from the transducer face to the focus of the transducer

Related to measure or circular dimensions:
- **ρ** — Density = mass/volume = kg/m^3
- **r** — Radius of a circle: units of distance
- **d** — Diameter of a circle = 2*radius: units of distance
- **A** — Area: units of m^2
- **Vol** — Volume: units of m^3
- **Q** — Volumetric flow: volume per time, or m^3/sec

Related to motion:

r	the general term usually used in the distance equation for the velocity. (*not to be confused with r for radius)
v	velocity of blood: units of m/sec
c	propagation speed of sound: units of m/sec

Related to hemodynamics:

P	Pressure: mmHg, atm, dynes/cm^2, kg/m^2, etc…,: units of pressure (*not to be confused with P for period or P for power)
ΔP	Pressure gradient (change in pressure = $P_2 - P_1$ where P_2 is the distal pressure and P_1 is the proximal pressure): units as above
Q	Volumetric flow: volume per time, or m^3/sec
R	Resistance, either electrical or to fluid flow

Related to stress and strain:

ε	Strain
σ	Stress
G	Shear modulus
K	Bulk modulus
E	Young's elastic modulus

Note: Caution must be used since many letters can stand for more than one physical quantity. Also pay attention as to whether the letter is uppercase or lower case, since in some cases a capitalized letter indicates a different parameter than a lower case letter.

Common Ultrasound-Related Terms

AC	Alternating current	M-mode	Motion mode
A/D	Analog to digital (converter)	MRgFUS	Magnetic resonance guided focused ultrasound
ALARA	As low as reasonably achievable (principle)	MRgHIFU	Magnetic resonance guided high intensity focused ultrasound
A-mode	Amplitude mode		
ARFI	Acoustic radiation force impulse		
BBB	Blood-brain barrier	NPV	Negative predictive value
B-flow	Blood flow (visualization technique)	NZL	Near zone length
BGR	Blue, green, red (artifact)	OLED	Organic light-emitting diodes (monitor)
C-mode	Constant depth mode	OPG	Oculoplethysmography
CMUT	Capacitor micromachined ultrasound transducers	PPV	Positive predictive value
CRT	Cathode ray tube	PRF	Pulse repetition frequency
CW	Continuous wave	PRP	Pulse repetition period
DC	Direct current	PW	Pulsed wave
ECG/EKG	Electrocardiogram	PZT	Lead zirconate titanate
FFT	Fast Fourier transform	SNR	Signal-to-noise ratio
FN	False negative	SPL	Spatial pulse length
FOV	Field of view	SV	Stroke volume
FP	False positive	S-wave	Secondary wave
FUS	Focused ultrasound	SWS	Shear wave speed
GLS	Global longitudinal strain	TAMEAN	Time average mean (velocity)
GPU	General processing unit	TAMV	Time average mean velocity
HIFU	High intensity focused ultrasound	TDI	Tissue Doppler imaging
HPRF	High pulse repetition frequency (Doppler)	TGC	Time gain compensation
IMT	Intima media thickness	TI	Thermal index
LCD	Liquid crystal display	TIB	Thermal index in bone
LED	Light-emitting diodes	TIC	Thermal index in cranial bone
LVO	Left ventricular opacification	TIS	Thermal index in soft tissue
MFI	Microflow imaging	TN	True negative
MI	Mechanical index	VRT	Venous refill time
MLT	Multi-line transmit	VTI	Velocity time integral

Appendix D
Equations

Related to Time and Frequency

1) $Period\ (P) = \dfrac{1}{frequency\ (f)}$

2) $PD = P * (\#\ of\ cycles\ in\ pulse)$

3) $PRP = \dfrac{13\ \mu sec}{cm} * imaging\ depth\ (cm) = \dfrac{1}{PRF}$

4) $Frame\ time = \dfrac{time}{line} \times \dfrac{\#lines}{frame} = PRP \times \dfrac{\#lines}{frame} = \dfrac{1}{Frame\ rate}$

5) $Duty\ Factor = \dfrac{PD}{PRP} * 100\% = \dfrac{Temporal\ Average\ Intensity\ (TA)}{Pulse\ Average\ Intensity\ (PA)} * 100\%$

Related to Frame Time and Frame Rate

A) Sequentially Generated

1) $Frame\ rate\ (frequency) = \dfrac{1}{Frame\ time}$

2) $PRP = \dfrac{time}{line} = \dfrac{13\ \mu sec}{cm} \times \dfrac{cm}{line}$

3) $Frame\ time = \dfrac{time}{line} \times \dfrac{lines}{frame}$

4) $Color\ frame\ time = \dfrac{time}{packet\ line} \times \dfrac{packet\ lines}{display\ line} \times \dfrac{display\ lines}{frame}$

B) Plane Wave Generated

5) $Planar\ frame\ time = \dfrac{13\ \mu sec}{cm} \times \dfrac{cm}{angle} \times \dfrac{angles}{frame}$

Related to Amplitude and Power

1) $Amplitude = max - mean = mean - min = \dfrac{max - min}{2}$

2) $Power \propto (Amplitude)^2$

3) $Intensity = \dfrac{Power}{Beam\ Area}$

4) a) $dB \triangleq 10 * \log\left(\dfrac{P_f}{P_i}\right)$ where $\left(\dfrac{P_f}{P_i}\right)$ is the power ratio (power gain factor)

   b) $dB \triangleq 20 * \log\left(\dfrac{A_f}{A_i}\right)$ where $\left(\dfrac{A_f}{A_i}\right)$ is the amplitude ratio (amplitude gain factor)

Related to Signal-to-Noise Ratio

1) $Improvement\ in\ SNR = \dfrac{n}{\sqrt{n}} = \sqrt{n}$

Related to Distance (Physical Dimension)

1) $d = r * t$

2) $\lambda = \dfrac{c}{f}$

3) $SPL = \lambda * (\#\ cycles\ in\ pulse)$

Related to Circular Dimensional Measurement

1) $Circle\ circumference = 2\pi r = \pi d$

2) $Circle\ area = \pi r^2$

3) $Circle\ volume\ (sphere) = \dfrac{4\pi r^3}{3}$

Related to Resolution

1) $Axial\ Resolution = \dfrac{SPL}{2}$

2) $Lateral\ Resolution = lateral\ beamwidth$

3) $Elevation\ Resolution = elevation\ beamwidth$

4) Temporal Resolution is determined by the acoustic frame rate and the monitor frame rate

5) Nyquist Limit (Maximum detectable frequency) = $\dfrac{\text{Sample frequency}}{2}$

6) Contrast resolution of a monitor = 2^n :
   Where n = number of bits assigned to greyscale of monitor

Related to Transducers

1) $NZL = \dfrac{D^2}{4\lambda} \approx \dfrac{D^2 f}{6}$ (D must be in mm and f must be in MHz to use the approximate form)

2) Beamwidth $\approx \dfrac{D}{2}$ (at the focal depth, the beam is approximately half the crystal diameter)

3) Beamwidth $\approx D$ (at twice the focal depth, or $2 * NZL$)

4) a) $f_0 = $ frequency of the drive Voltage (for CW)

   b) $f_0 = \dfrac{C_{crystal}}{2 * thickness_{crystal}}$ (for PW)

5) Bandwidth (BW) = upper frequency corner - lower frequency corner

6) $FBW\% = \dfrac{BW}{f_O} * 100\%$

7) Quality (Q) factor = $\dfrac{1}{FBW}$

8) BUF (beam uniformity factor) = $\dfrac{\text{Spatial Peak Intensity (SP)}}{\text{Spatial Average Intensity (SA)}}$

9) CMUT Related

   a) $C = \dfrac{q}{V}$

   b) $C = \dfrac{\kappa \varepsilon_0 A}{d}$

Related to Properties of Material and Attenuation

1) $\rho = \dfrac{mass}{volume}$

2) $Z = \rho * c$

3) % reflection + % transmission = 100%

4) % reflection = $\left[\dfrac{Z_2 - Z_1}{Z_2 + Z_1}\right]^2$

5) $R = \dfrac{8\ell\eta}{\pi r^4}$

6) $c_i * \sin(\theta_t) = c_t * \sin(\theta_i)$

7) Attenuation rate: $\approx \dfrac{0.5\ dB}{cm \times MHz}$ soft tissue

$\approx \dfrac{1\ dB}{cm \times MHz}$ muscle

Related to Hemodynamics and Doppler

1) $f_{Dop} = \dfrac{2 f_o v * \cos(\theta)}{c}$

2) $f_{Dop}(max) = \dfrac{PRF}{2}$ (without aliasing by Nyquist)

3) Resistive index $= \dfrac{A-B}{A} = \dfrac{Systolic - Diastolic}{Systolic}$

4) Pulsatility index $= \dfrac{A-B}{\bar{v}} = \dfrac{Systolic - Diastolic}{mean\ velocity}$

5) Systolic / Diastolic ratio $= \dfrac{Systolic}{Diastolic}$

6) $\Delta P = Q * R$ (simplified law of hemodynamics)

7) $Q = \bar{v} * area$ (continuity equation)

8) $R = \dfrac{8 \ell h}{\pi r^4}$

9) $Q = \dfrac{\Delta P \pi r^4}{8 \ell \eta}$ (Poiseiulle's Law)

10) $K.E. = \dfrac{1}{2}\rho v^2 \Rightarrow \Delta P \approx 4\left(v_2^2 - v_1^2\right) \approx 4\left(v_2^2\right)$ if $v_2 \gg v_1$

11) Hydrostatic pressure $= mgh \approx 2\dfrac{mmHg}{inch}$

Related to Stress and Strain

1) $\sigma(stress) = \dfrac{Force}{Area}$

2) $\varepsilon(strain) = \dfrac{\Delta size}{size}$

3) $\varepsilon_L = \dfrac{\Delta L}{L}$

4)

Type of Stress	Elastic Modulus	Hooke's Law
Normal (longitudinal)	E (Young's)	$\sigma_n = E \times \varepsilon_n$
Shear	G (Shear)	$\sigma_s = G \times \varepsilon_s$
Bulk (volume)	K (Bulk)	$\sigma_v = K \times \varepsilon_v$

5) $c_L = \sqrt{\dfrac{k}{\rho}}$

6) $c_S = \sqrt{\dfrac{G}{\rho}}$

7) $\upsilon = \dfrac{-\text{Lateral Strain}}{\text{Linear Strain}} = \dfrac{-\varepsilon_{lateral}}{\varepsilon_{linear}} = \dfrac{-\left(\dfrac{D_1 - D}{D}\right)}{\left(\dfrac{L_1 - L}{L}\right)}$

8) $E = 2G(1+\upsilon) \approx 3G = 3\rho \times c_s^2$

9) $E = 3K(1-2\upsilon)$

10) $E = \dfrac{9KG}{(G+3K)}$